T0134684

Lecture Notes in Computer Science 11218

Commenced Publication in 1973
Founding and Former Series Editors:
Gerhard Goos, Juris Hartmanis, and Jan van Leeuwen

More information about this series at http://www.springer.com/series/7412

Vittorio Ferrari · Martial Hebert
Cristian Sminchisescu · Yair Weiss (Eds.)

Computer Vision – ECCV 2018

15th European Conference
Munich, Germany, September 8–14, 2018
Proceedings, Part XIV

Springer

Editors
Vittorio Ferrari
Google Research
Zurich
Switzerland

Cristian Sminchisescu
Google Research
Zurich
Switzerland

Martial Hebert
Carnegie Mellon University
Pittsburgh, PA
USA

Yair Weiss
Hebrew University of Jerusalem
Jerusalem
Israel

ISSN 0302-9743   ISSN 1611-3349   (electronic)
Lecture Notes in Computer Science
ISBN 978-3-030-01263-2   ISBN 978-3-030-01264-9   (eBook)
https://doi.org/10.1007/978-3-030-01264-9

Library of Congress Control Number: 2018955489

LNCS Sublibrary: SL6 – Image Processing, Computer Vision, Pattern Recognition, and Graphics

This Springer imprint is published by the registered company Springer Nature Switzerland AG
The registered company address is: Gewerbestrasse 11, 6330 Cham, Switzerland

Foreword

It was our great pleasure to host the European Conference on Computer Vision 2018 in Munich, Germany. This constituted by far the largest ECCV event ever. With close to 2,900 registered participants and another 600 on the waiting list one month before the conference, participation more than doubled since the last ECCV in Amsterdam. We believe that this is due to a dramatic growth of the computer vision community combined with the popularity of Munich as a major European hub of culture, science, and industry. The conference took place in the heart of Munich in the concert hall Gasteig with workshops and tutorials held at the downtown campus of the Technical University of Munich.

One of the major innovations for ECCV 2018 was the free perpetual availability of all conference and workshop papers, which is often referred to as open access. We note that this is not precisely the same use of the term as in the Budapest declaration. Since 2013, CVPR and ICCV have had their papers hosted by the Computer Vision Foundation (CVF), in parallel with the IEEE Xplore version. This has proved highly beneficial to the computer vision community.

We are delighted to announce that for ECCV 2018 a very similar arrangement was put in place with the cooperation of Springer. In particular, the author's final version will be freely available in perpetuity on a CVF page, while SpringerLink will continue to host a version with further improvements, such as activating reference links and including video. We believe that this will give readers the best of both worlds; researchers who are focused on the technical content will have a freely available version in an easily accessible place, while subscribers to SpringerLink will continue to have the additional benefits that this provides. We thank Alfred Hofmann from Springer for helping to negotiate this agreement, which we expect will continue for future versions of ECCV.

September 2018

Horst Bischof
Daniel Cremers
Bernt Schiele
Ramin Zabih

Preface

Welcome to the proceedings of the 2018 European Conference on Computer Vision (ECCV 2018) held in Munich, Germany. We are delighted to present this volume reflecting a strong and exciting program, the result of an extensive review process. In total, we received 2,439 valid paper submissions. Of these, 776 were accepted (31.8%): 717 as posters (29.4%) and 59 as oral presentations (2.4%). All oral presentations were presented as posters as well. The program selection process was complicated this year by the large increase in the number of submitted papers, +65% over ECCV 2016, and the use of CMT3 for the first time for a computer vision conference. The program selection process was supported by four program co-chairs (PCs), 126 area chairs (ACs), and 1,199 reviewers with reviews assigned.

We were primarily responsible for the design and execution of the review process. Beyond administrative rejections, we were involved in acceptance decisions only in the very few cases where the ACs were not able to agree on a decision. As PCs, and as is customary in the field, we were not allowed to co-author a submission. General co-chairs and other co-organizers who played no role in the review process were permitted to submit papers, and were treated as any other author is.

Acceptance decisions were made by two independent ACs. The ACs also made a joint recommendation for promoting papers to oral status. We decided on the final selection of oral presentations based on the ACs' recommendations. There were 126 ACs, selected according to their technical expertise, experience, and geographical diversity (63 from European, nine from Asian/Australian, and 54 from North American institutions). Indeed, 126 ACs is a substantial increase in the number of ACs due to the natural increase in the number of papers and to our desire to maintain the number of papers assigned to each AC to a manageable number so as to ensure quality. The ACs were aided by the 1,199 reviewers to whom papers were assigned for reviewing. The Program Committee was selected from committees of previous ECCV, ICCV, and CVPR conferences and was extended on the basis of suggestions from the ACs. Having a large pool of Program Committee members for reviewing allowed us to match expertise while reducing reviewer loads. No more than eight papers were assigned to a reviewer, maintaining the reviewers' load at the same level as ECCV 2016 despite the increase in the number of submitted papers.

Conflicts of interest between ACs, Program Committee members, and papers were identified based on the home institutions, and on previous collaborations of all researchers involved. To find institutional conflicts, all authors, Program Committee members, and ACs were asked to list the Internet domains of their current institutions. We assigned on average approximately 18 papers to each AC. The papers were assigned using the affinity scores from the Toronto Paper Matching System (TPMS) and additional data from the OpenReview system, managed by a UMass group. OpenReview used additional information from ACs' and authors' records to identify collaborations and to generate matches. OpenReview was invaluable in refining conflict definitions and in generating quality matches. The only glitch is that, once the matches were generated, a small percentage of papers were unassigned because of discrepancies between the OpenReview conflicts and the conflicts entered in CMT3. We manually assigned these papers. This glitch is revealing of the challenge of using multiple systems at once (CMT3 and OpenReview in this case), which needs to be addressed in future.

After assignment of papers to ACs, the ACs suggested seven reviewers per paper from the Program Committee pool. The selection and rank ordering were facilitated by the TPMS affinity scores visible to the ACs for each paper/reviewer pair. The final assignment of papers to reviewers was generated again through OpenReview in order to account for refined conflict definitions. This required new features in the OpenReview matching system to accommodate the ECCV workflow, in particular to incorporate selection ranking, and maximum reviewer load. Very few papers received fewer than three reviewers after matching and were handled through manual assignment. Reviewers were then asked to comment on the merit of each paper and to make an initial recommendation ranging from definitely reject to definitely accept, including a borderline rating. The reviewers were also asked to suggest explicit questions they wanted to see answered in the authors' rebuttal. The initial review period was five weeks. Because of the delay in getting all the reviews in, we had to delay the final release of the reviews by four days. However, because of the slack included at the tail end of the schedule, we were able to maintain the decision target date with sufficient time for all the phases. We reassigned over 100 reviews from 40 reviewers during the review period. Unfortunately, the main reason for these reassignments was reviewers declining to review, after having accepted to do so. Other reasons included technical relevance and occasional unidentified conflicts. We express our thanks to the emergency reviewers who generously accepted to perform these reviews under short notice. In addition, a substantial number of manual corrections had to do with reviewers using a different email address than the one that was used at the time of the reviewer invitation. This is revealing of a broader issue with identifying users by email addresses that change frequently enough to cause significant problems during the timespan of the conference process.

The authors were then given the opportunity to rebut the reviews, to identify factual errors, and to address the specific questions raised by the reviewers over a seven-day rebuttal period. The exact format of the rebuttal was the object of considerable debate among the organizers, as well as with prior organizers. At issue is to balance giving the author the opportunity to respond completely and precisely to the reviewers, e.g., by including graphs of experiments, while avoiding requests for completely new material or experimental results not included in the original paper. In the end, we decided on the two-page PDF document in conference format. Following this rebuttal period, reviewers and ACs discussed papers at length, after which reviewers finalized their evaluation and gave a final recommendation to the ACs. A significant percentage of the reviewers did enter their final recommendation if it did not differ from their initial recommendation. Given the tight schedule, we did not wait until all were entered.

After this discussion period, each paper was assigned to a second AC. The AC/paper matching was again run through OpenReview. Again, the OpenReview team worked quickly to implement the features specific to this process, in this case accounting for the existing AC assignment, as well as minimizing the fragmentation across ACs, so that each AC had on average only 5.5 buddy ACs to communicate with. The largest number was 11. Given the complexity of the conflicts, this was a very efficient set of assignments from OpenReview. Each paper was then evaluated by its assigned pair of ACs. For each paper, we required each of the two ACs assigned to certify both the final recommendation and the metareview (aka consolidation report). In all cases, after extensive discussions, the two ACs arrived at a common acceptance decision. We maintained these decisions, with the caveat that we did evaluate, sometimes going back to the ACs, a few papers for which the final acceptance decision substantially deviated from the consensus from the reviewers, amending three decisions in the process.

We want to thank everyone involved in making ECCV 2018 possible. The success of ECCV 2018 depended on the quality of papers submitted by the authors, and on the very hard work of the ACs and the Program Committee members. We are particularly grateful to the OpenReview team (Melisa Bok, Ari Kobren, Andrew McCallum, Michael Spector) for their support, in particular their willingness to implement new features, often on a tight schedule, to Laurent Charlin for the use of the Toronto Paper Matching System, to the CMT3 team, in particular in dealing with all the issues that arise when using a new system, to Friedrich Fraundorfer and Quirin Lohr for maintaining the online version of the program, and to the CMU staff (Keyla Cook, Lynnetta Miller, Ashley Song, Nora Kazour) for assisting with data entry/editing in CMT3. Finally, the preparation of these proceedings would not have been possible without the diligent effort of the publication chairs, Albert Ali Salah and Hamdi Dibeklioğlu, and of Anna Kramer and Alfred Hofmann from Springer.

September 2018

Vittorio Ferrari
Martial Hebert
Cristian Sminchisescu
Yair Weiss

Organization

General Chairs

Horst Bischof   Graz University of Technology, Austria
Daniel Cremers   Technical University of Munich, Germany
Bernt Schiele   Saarland University, Max Planck Institute for Informatics, Germany
Ramin Zabih   CornellNYCTech, USA

Program Committee Co-chairs

Vittorio Ferrari   University of Edinburgh, UK
Martial Hebert   Carnegie Mellon University, USA
Cristian Sminchisescu   Lund University, Sweden
Yair Weiss   Hebrew University, Israel

Local Arrangements Chairs

Björn Menze   Technical University of Munich, Germany
Matthias Niessner   Technical University of Munich, Germany

Workshop Chairs

Stefan Roth   TU Darmstadt, Germany
Laura Leal-Taixé   Technical University of Munich, Germany

Tutorial Chairs

Michael Bronstein   Università della Svizzera Italiana, Switzerland
Laura Leal-Taixé   Technical University of Munich, Germany

Website Chair

Friedrich Fraundorfer   Graz University of Technology, Austria

Demo Chairs

Federico Tombari   Technical University of Munich, Germany
Joerg Stueckler   Technical University of Munich, Germany

Publicity Chair

Giovanni Maria   University of Catania, Italy
  Farinella

Industrial Liaison Chairs

Florent Perronnin   Naver Labs, France
Yunchao Gong   Snap, USA
Helmut Grabner   Logitech, Switzerland

Finance Chair

Gerard Medioni   Amazon, University of Southern California, USA

Publication Chairs

Albert Ali Salah   Boğaziçi University, Turkey
Hamdi Dibeklioğlu   Bilkent University, Turkey

Area Chairs

Kalle Åström   Lund University, Sweden
Zeynep Akata   University of Amsterdam, The Netherlands
Joao Barreto   University of Coimbra, Portugal
Ronen Basri   Weizmann Institute of Science, Israel
Dhruv Batra   Georgia Tech and Facebook AI Research, USA
Serge Belongie   Cornell University, USA
Rodrigo Benenson   Google, Switzerland
Hakan Bilen   University of Edinburgh, UK
Matthew Blaschko   KU Leuven, Belgium
Edmond Boyer   Inria, France
Gabriel Brostow   University College London, UK
Thomas Brox   University of Freiburg, Germany
Marcus Brubaker   York University, Canada
Barbara Caputo   Politecnico di Torino and the Italian Institute
                          of Technology, Italy
Tim Cootes   University of Manchester, UK
Trevor Darrell   University of California, Berkeley, USA
Larry Davis   University of Maryland at College Park, USA
Andrew Davison   Imperial College London, UK
Fernando de la Torre   Carnegie Mellon University, USA
Irfan Essa   GeorgiaTech, USA
Ali Farhadi   University of Washington, USA
Paolo Favaro   University of Bern, Switzerland
Michael Felsberg   Linköping University, Sweden

Sanja Fidler   University of Toronto, Canada
Andrew Fitzgibbon   Microsoft, Cambridge, UK
David Forsyth   University of Illinois at Urbana-Champaign, USA
Charless Fowlkes   University of California, Irvine, USA
Bill Freeman   MIT, USA
Mario Fritz   MPII, Germany
Jürgen Gall   University of Bonn, Germany
Dariu Gavrila   TU Delft, The Netherlands
Andreas Geiger   MPI-IS and University of Tübingen, Germany
Theo Gevers   University of Amsterdam, The Netherlands
Ross Girshick   Facebook AI Research, USA
Kristen Grauman   Facebook AI Research and UT Austin, USA
Abhinav Gupta   Carnegie Mellon University, USA
Kaiming He   Facebook AI Research, USA
Martial Hebert   Carnegie Mellon University, USA
Anders Heyden   Lund University, Sweden
Timothy Hospedales   University of Edinburgh, UK
Michal Irani   Weizmann Institute of Science, Israel
Phillip Isola   University of California, Berkeley, USA
Hervé Jégou   Facebook AI Research, France
David Jacobs   University of Maryland, College Park, USA
Allan Jepson   University of Toronto, Canada
Jiaya Jia   Chinese University of Hong Kong, SAR China
Fredrik Kahl   Chalmers University, USA
Hedvig Kjellström   KTH Royal Institute of Technology, Sweden
Iasonas Kokkinos   University College London and Facebook, UK
Vladlen Koltun   Intel Labs, USA
Philipp Krähenbühl   UT Austin, USA
M. Pawan Kumar   University of Oxford, UK
Kyros Kutulakos   University of Toronto, Canada
In Kweon   KAIST, South Korea
Ivan Laptev   Inria, France
Svetlana Lazebnik   University of Illinois at Urbana-Champaign, USA
Laura Leal-Taixé   Technical University of Munich, Germany
Erik Learned-Miller   University of Massachusetts, Amherst, USA
Kyoung Mu Lee   Seoul National University, South Korea
Bastian Leibe   RWTH Aachen University, Germany
Aleš Leonardis   University of Birmingham, UK
Vincent Lepetit   University of Bordeaux, France and Graz University
                            of Technology, Austria
Fuxin Li   Oregon State University, USA
Dahua Lin   Chinese University of Hong Kong, SAR China
Jim Little   University of British Columbia, Canada
Ce Liu   Google, USA
Chen Change Loy   Nanyang Technological University, Singapore
Jiri Matas   Czech Technical University in Prague, Czechia

Yasuyuki Matsushita	Osaka University, Japan
Dimitris Metaxas	Rutgers University, USA
Greg Mori	Simon Fraser University, Canada
Vittorio Murino	Istituto Italiano di Tecnologia, Italy
Richard Newcombe	Oculus Research, USA
Minh Hoai Nguyen	Stony Brook University, USA
Sebastian Nowozin	Microsoft Research Cambridge, UK
Aude Oliva	MIT, USA
Bjorn Ommer	Heidelberg University, Germany
Tomas Pajdla	Czech Technical University in Prague, Czechia
Maja Pantic	Imperial College London and Samsung AI Research Centre Cambridge, UK
Caroline Pantofaru	Google, USA
Devi Parikh	Georgia Tech and Facebook AI Research, USA
Sylvain Paris	Adobe Research, USA
Vladimir Pavlovic	Rutgers University, USA
Marcello Pelillo	University of Venice, Italy
Patrick Pérez	Valeo, France
Robert Pless	George Washington University, USA
Thomas Pock	Graz University of Technology, Austria
Jean Ponce	Inria, France
Gerard Pons-Moll	MPII, Saarland Informatics Campus, Germany
Long Quan	Hong Kong University of Science and Technology, SAR China
Stefan Roth	TU Darmstadt, Germany
Carsten Rother	University of Heidelberg, Germany
Bryan Russell	Adobe Research, USA
Kate Saenko	Boston University, USA
Mathieu Salzmann	EPFL, Switzerland
Dimitris Samaras	Stony Brook University, USA
Yoichi Sato	University of Tokyo, Japan
Silvio Savarese	Stanford University, USA
Konrad Schindler	ETH Zurich, Switzerland
Cordelia Schmid	Inria, France and Google, France
Nicu Sebe	University of Trento, Italy
Fei Sha	University of Southern California, USA
Greg Shakhnarovich	TTI Chicago, USA
Jianbo Shi	University of Pennsylvania, USA
Abhinav Shrivastava	UMD and Google, USA
Yan Shuicheng	National University of Singapore, Singapore
Leonid Sigal	University of British Columbia, Canada
Josef Sivic	Czech Technical University in Prague, Czechia
Arnold Smeulders	University of Amsterdam, The Netherlands
Deqing Sun	NVIDIA, USA
Antonio Torralba	MIT, USA
Zhuowen Tu	University of California, San Diego, USA

Tinne Tuytelaars   KU Leuven, Belgium
Jasper Uijlings   Google, Switzerland
Joost van de Weijer   Computer Vision Center, Spain
Nuno Vasconcelos   University of California, San Diego, USA
Andrea Vedaldi   University of Oxford, UK
Olga Veksler   University of Western Ontario, Canada
Jakob Verbeek   Inria, France
Rene Vidal   Johns Hopkins University, USA
Daphna Weinshall   Hebrew University, Israel
Chris Williams   University of Edinburgh, UK
Lior Wolf   Tel Aviv University, Israel
Ming-Hsuan Yang   University of California at Merced, USA
Todd Zickler   Harvard University, USA
Andrew Zisserman   University of Oxford, UK

Technical Program Committee

Hassan Abu Alhaija	Peter Anderson	Arunava Banerjee
Radhakrishna Achanta	Juan Andrade-Cetto	Atsuhiko Banno
Hanno Ackermann	Mykhaylo Andriluka	Aayush Bansal
Ehsan Adeli	Anelia Angelova	Yingze Bao
Lourdes Agapito	Michel Antunes	Md Jawadul Bappy
Aishwarya Agrawal	Pablo Arbelaez	Pierre Baqué
Antonio Agudo	Vasileios Argyriou	Dániel Baráth
Eirikur Agustsson	Chetan Arora	Adrian Barbu
Karim Ahmed	Federica Arrigoni	Kobus Barnard
Byeongjoo Ahn	Vassilis Athitsos	Nick Barnes
Unaiza Ahsan	Mathieu Aubry	Francisco Barranco
Emre Akbaş	Shai Avidan	Adrien Bartoli
Eren Aksoy	Yannis Avrithis	E. Bayro-Corrochano
Yağız Aksoy	Samaneh Azadi	Paul Beardlsey
Alexandre Alahi	Hossein Azizpour	Vasileios Belagiannis
Jean-Baptiste Alayrac	Artem Babenko	Sean Bell
Samuel Albanie	Timur Bagautdinov	Ismail Ben
Cenek Albl	Andrew Bagdanov	Boulbaba Ben Amor
Saad Ali	Hessam Bagherinezhad	Gil Ben-Artzi
Rahaf Aljundi	Yuval Bahat	Ohad Ben-Shahar
Jose M. Alvarez	Min Bai	Abhijit Bendale
Humam Alwassel	Qinxun Bai	Rodrigo Benenson
Toshiyuki Amano	Song Bai	Fabian Benitez-Quiroz
Mitsuru Ambai	Xiang Bai	Fethallah Benmansour
Mohamed Amer	Peter Bajcsy	Ryad Benosman
Senjian An	Amr Bakry	Filippo Bergamasco
Cosmin Ancuti	Kavita Bala	David Bermudez

Jesus Bermudez-Cameo
Leonard Berrada
Gedas Bertasius
Ross Beveridge
Lucas Beyer
Bir Bhanu
S. Bhattacharya
Binod Bhattarai
Arnav Bhavsar
Simone Bianco
Adel Bibi
Pia Bideau
Josef Bigun
Arijit Biswas
Soma Biswas
Marten Bjoerkman
Volker Blanz
Vishnu Boddeti
Piotr Bojanowski
Terrance Boult
Yuri Boykov
Hakan Boyraz
Eric Brachmann
Samarth Brahmbhatt
Mathieu Bredif
Francois Bremond
Michael Brown
Luc Brun
Shyamal Buch
Pradeep Buddharaju
Aurelie Bugeau
Rudy Bunel
Xavier Burgos Artizzu
Darius Burschka
Andrei Bursuc
Zoya Bylinskii
Fabian Caba
Daniel Cabrini Hauagge
Cesar Cadena Lerma
Holger Caesar
Jianfei Cai
Junjie Cai
Zhaowei Cai
Simone Calderara
Neill Campbell
Octavia Camps

Xun Cao
Yanshuai Cao
Joao Carreira
Dan Casas
Daniel Castro
Jan Cech
M. Emre Celebi
Duygu Ceylan
Menglei Chai
Ayan Chakrabarti
Rudrasis Chakraborty
Shayok Chakraborty
Tat-Jen Cham
Antonin Chambolle
Antoni Chan
Sharat Chandran
Hyun Sung Chang
Ju Yong Chang
Xiaojun Chang
Soravit Changpinyo
Wei-Lun Chao
Yu-Wei Chao
Visesh Chari
Rizwan Chaudhry
Siddhartha Chaudhuri
Rama Chellappa
Chao Chen
Chen Chen
Cheng Chen
Chu-Song Chen
Guang Chen
Hsin-I Chen
Hwann-Tzong Chen
Kai Chen
Kan Chen
Kevin Chen
Liang-Chieh Chen
Lin Chen
Qifeng Chen
Ting Chen
Wei Chen
Xi Chen
Xilin Chen
Xinlei Chen
Yingcong Chen
Yixin Chen

Erkang Cheng
Jingchun Cheng
Ming-Ming Cheng
Wen-Huang Cheng
Yuan Cheng
Anoop Cherian
Liang-Tien Chia
Naoki Chiba
Shao-Yi Chien
Han-Pang Chiu
Wei-Chen Chiu
Nam Ik Cho
Sunghyun Cho
TaeEun Choe
Jongmoo Choi
Christopher Choy
Wen-Sheng Chu
Yung-Yu Chuang
Ondrej Chum
Joon Son Chung
Gökberk Cinbis
James Clark
Andrea Cohen
Forrester Cole
Toby Collins
John Collomosse
Camille Couprie
David Crandall
Marco Cristani
Canton Cristian
James Crowley
Yin Cui
Zhaopeng Cui
Bo Dai
Jifeng Dai
Qieyun Dai
Shengyang Dai
Yuchao Dai
Carlo Dal Mutto
Dima Damen
Zachary Daniels
Kostas Daniilidis
Donald Dansereau
Mohamed Daoudi
Abhishek Das
Samyak Datta

Achal Dave
Shalini De Mello
Teofilo deCampos
Joseph DeGol
Koichiro Deguchi
Alessio Del Bue
Stefanie Demirci
Jia Deng
Zhiwei Deng
Joachim Denzler
Konstantinos Derpanis
Aditya Deshpande
Alban Desmaison
Frédéric Devernay
Abhinav Dhall
Michel Dhome
Hamdi Dibeklioğlu
Mert Dikmen
Cosimo Distante
Ajay Divakaran
Mandar Dixit
Carl Doersch
Piotr Dollar
Bo Dong
Chao Dong
Huang Dong
Jian Dong
Jiangxin Dong
Weisheng Dong
Simon Donné
Gianfranco Doretto
Alexey Dosovitskiy
Matthijs Douze
Bruce Draper
Bertram Drost
Liang Du
Shichuan Du
Gregory Dudek
Zoran Duric
Pınar Duygulu
Hazım Ekenel
Tarek El-Gaaly
Ehsan Elhamifar
Mohamed Elhoseiny
Sabu Emmanuel
Ian Endres

Aykut Erdem
Erkut Erdem
Hugo Jair Escalante
Sergio Escalera
Victor Escorcia
Francisco Estrada
Davide Eynard
Bin Fan
Jialue Fan
Quanfu Fan
Chen Fang
Tian Fang
Yi Fang
Hany Farid
Giovanni Farinella
Ryan Farrell
Alireza Fathi
Christoph Feichtenhofer
Wenxin Feng
Martin Fergie
Cornelia Fermuller
Basura Fernando
Michael Firman
Bob Fisher
John Fisher
Mathew Fisher
Boris Flach
Matt Flagg
Francois Fleuret
David Fofi
Ruth Fong
Gian Luca Foresti
Per-Erik Forssén
David Fouhey
Katerina Fragkiadaki
Victor Fragoso
Jan-Michael Frahm
Jean-Sebastien Franco
Ohad Fried
Simone Frintrop
Huazhu Fu
Yun Fu
Olac Fuentes
Christopher Funk
Thomas Funkhouser
Brian Funt

Ryo Furukawa
Yasutaka Furukawa
Andrea Fusiello
Fatma Güney
Raghudeep Gadde
Silvano Galliani
Orazio Gallo
Chuang Gan
Bin-Bin Gao
Jin Gao
Junbin Gao
Ruohan Gao
Shenghua Gao
Animesh Garg
Ravi Garg
Erik Gartner
Simone Gasparin
Jochen Gast
Leon A. Gatys
Stratis Gavves
Liuhao Ge
Timnit Gebru
James Gee
Peter Gehler
Xin Geng
Guido Gerig
David Geronimo
Bernard Ghanem
Michael Gharbi
Golnaz Ghiasi
Spyros Gidaris
Andrew Gilbert
Rohit Girdhar
Ioannis Gkioulekas
Georgia Gkioxari
Guy Godin
Roland Goecke
Michael Goesele
Nuno Goncalves
Boqing Gong
Minglun Gong
Yunchao Gong
Abel Gonzalez-Garcia
Daniel Gordon
Paulo Gotardo
Stephen Gould

Venu Govindu
Helmut Grabner
Petr Gronat
Steve Gu
Josechu Guerrero
Anupam Guha
Jean-Yves Guillemaut
Alp Güler
Erhan Gündoğdu
Guodong Guo
Xinqing Guo
Ankush Gupta
Mohit Gupta
Saurabh Gupta
Tanmay Gupta
Abner Guzman Rivera
Timo Hackel
Sunil Hadap
Christian Haene
Ralf Haeusler
Levente Hajder
David Hall
Peter Hall
Stefan Haller
Ghassan Hamarneh
Fred Hamprecht
Onur Hamsici
Bohyung Han
Junwei Han
Xufeng Han
Yahong Han
Ankur Handa
Albert Haque
Tatsuya Harada
Mehrtash Harandi
Bharath Hariharan
Mahmudul Hasan
Tal Hassner
Kenji Hata
Soren Hauberg
Michal Havlena
Zeeshan Hayder
Junfeng He
Lei He
Varsha Hedau
Felix Heide

Wolfgang Heidrich
Janne Heikkila
Jared Heinly
Mattias Heinrich
Lisa Anne Hendricks
Dan Hendrycks
Stephane Herbin
Alexander Hermans
Luis Herranz
Aaron Hertzmann
Adrian Hilton
Michael Hirsch
Steven Hoi
Seunghoon Hong
Wei Hong
Anthony Hoogs
Radu Horaud
Yedid Hoshen
Omid Hosseini Jafari
Kuang-Jui Hsu
Winston Hsu
Yinlin Hu
Zhe Hu
Gang Hua
Chen Huang
De-An Huang
Dong Huang
Gary Huang
Heng Huang
Jia-Bin Huang
Qixing Huang
Rui Huang
Sheng Huang
Weilin Huang
Xiaolei Huang
Xinyu Huang
Zhiwu Huang
Tak-Wai Hui
Wei-Chih Hung
Junhwa Hur
Mohamed Hussein
Wonjun Hwang
Anders Hyden
Satoshi Ikehata
Nazlı Ikizler-Cinbis
Viorela Ila

Evren Imre
Eldar Insafutdinov
Go Irie
Hossam Isack
Ahmet Işcen
Daisuke Iwai
Hamid Izadinia
Nathan Jacobs
Suyog Jain
Varun Jampani
C. V. Jawahar
Dinesh Jayaraman
Sadeep Jayasumana
Laszlo Jeni
Hueihan Jhuang
Dinghuang Ji
Hui Ji
Qiang Ji
Fan Jia
Kui Jia
Xu Jia
Huaizu Jiang
Jiayan Jiang
Nianjuan Jiang
Tingting Jiang
Xiaoyi Jiang
Yu-Gang Jiang
Long Jin
Suo Jinli
Justin Johnson
Nebojsa Jojic
Michael Jones
Hanbyul Joo
Jungseock Joo
Ajjen Joshi
Amin Jourabloo
Frederic Jurie
Achuta Kadambi
Samuel Kadoury
Ioannis Kakadiaris
Zdenek Kalal
Yannis Kalantidis
Sinan Kalkan
Vicky Kalogeiton
Sunkavalli Kalyan
J.-K. Kamarainen

Shih-Yao Lin
Tsung-Yi Lin
Weiyao Lin
Yen-Yu Lin
Haibin Ling
Or Litany
Roee Litman
Anan Liu
Changsong Liu
Chen Liu
Ding Liu
Dong Liu
Feng Liu
Guangcan Liu
Luoqi Liu
Miaomiao Liu
Nian Liu
Risheng Liu
Shu Liu
Shuaicheng Liu
Sifei Liu
Tyng-Luh Liu
Wanquan Liu
Weiwei Liu
Xialei Liu
Xiaoming Liu
Yebin Liu
Yiming Liu
Ziwei Liu
Zongyi Liu
Liliana Lo Presti
Edgar Lobaton
Chengjiang Long
Mingsheng Long
Roberto Lopez-Sastre
Amy Loufti
Brian Lovell
Canyi Lu
Cewu Lu
Feng Lu
Huchuan Lu
Jiajun Lu
Jiasen Lu
Jiwen Lu
Yang Lu
Yujuan Lu

Simon Lucey
Jian-Hao Luo
Jiebo Luo
Pablo Márquez-Neila
Matthias Müller
Chao Ma
Chih-Yao Ma
Lin Ma
Shugao Ma
Wei-Chiu Ma
Zhanyu Ma
Oisin Mac Aodha
Will Maddern
Ludovic Magerand
Marcus Magnor
Vijay Mahadevan
Mohammad Mahoor
Michael Maire
Subhransu Maji
Ameesh Makadia
Atsuto Maki
Yasushi Makihara
Mateusz Malinowski
Tomasz Malisiewicz
Arun Mallya
Roberto Manduchi
Junhua Mao
Dmitrii Marin
Joe Marino
Kenneth Marino
Elisabeta Marinoiu
Ricardo Martin
Aleix Martinez
Julieta Martinez
Aaron Maschinot
Jonathan Masci
Bogdan Matei
Diana Mateus
Stefan Mathe
Kevin Matzen
Bruce Maxwell
Steve Maybank
Walterio Mayol-Cuevas
Mason McGill
Stephen Mckenna
Roey Mechrez

Christopher Mei
Heydi Mendez-Vazquez
Deyu Meng
Thomas Mensink
Bjoern Menze
Domingo Mery
Qiguang Miao
Tomer Michaeli
Antoine Miech
Ondrej Miksik
Anton Milan
Gregor Miller
Cai Minjie
Majid Mirmehdi
Ishan Misra
Niloy Mitra
Anurag Mittal
Nirbhay Modhe
Davide Modolo
Pritish Mohapatra
Pascal Monasse
Mathew Monfort
Taesup Moon
Sandino Morales
Vlad Morariu
Philippos Mordohai
Francesc Moreno
Henrique Morimitsu
Yael Moses
Ben-Ezra Moshe
Roozbeh Mottaghi
Yadong Mu
Lopamudra Mukherjee
Mario Munich
Ana Murillo
Damien Muselet
Armin Mustafa
Siva Karthik Mustikovela
Moin Nabi
Sobhan Naderi
Hajime Nagahara
Varun Nagaraja
Tushar Nagarajan
Arsha Nagrani
Nikhil Naik
Atsushi Nakazawa

Gernot Riegler
Hayko Riemenschneider
Tammy Riklin Raviv
Ergys Ristani
Tobias Ritschel
Mariano Rivera
Samuel Rivera
Antonio Robles-Kelly
Ignacio Rocco
Jason Rock
Emanuele Rodola
Mikel Rodriguez
Gregory Rogez
Marcus Rohrbach
Gemma Roig
Javier Romero
Olaf Ronneberger
Amir Rosenfeld
Bodo Rosenhahn
Guy Rosman
Arun Ross
Samuel Rota Bulò
Peter Roth
Constantin Rothkopf
Sebastien Roy
Amit Roy-Chowdhury
Ognjen Rudovic
Adria Ruiz
Javier Ruiz-del-Solar
Christian Rupprecht
Olga Russakovsky
Chris Russell
Alexandre Sablayrolles
Fereshteh Sadeghi
Ryusuke Sagawa
Hideo Saito
Elham Sakhaee
Albert Ali Salah
Conrad Sanderson
Koppal Sanjeev
Aswin Sankaranarayanan
Elham Saraee
Jason Saragih
Sudeep Sarkar
Imari Sato
Shin'ichi Satoh

Torsten Sattler
Bogdan Savchynskyy
Johannes Schönberger
Hanno Scharr
Walter Scheirer
Bernt Schiele
Frank Schmidt
Tanner Schmidt
Dirk Schnieders
Samuel Schulter
William Schwartz
Alexander Schwing
Ozan Sener
Soumyadip Sengupta
Laura Sevilla-Lara
Mubarak Shah
Shishir Shah
Fahad Shahbaz Khan
Amir Shahroudy
Jing Shao
Xiaowei Shao
Roman Shapovalov
Nataliya Shapovalova
Ali Sharif Razavian
Gaurav Sharma
Mohit Sharma
Pramod Sharma
Viktoriia Sharmanska
Eli Shechtman
Mark Sheinin
Evan Shelhamer
Chunhua Shen
Li Shen
Wei Shen
Xiaohui Shen
Xiaoyong Shen
Ziyi Shen
Lu Sheng
Baoguang Shi
Boxin Shi
Kevin Shih
Hyunjung Shim
Ilan Shimshoni
Young Min Shin
Koichi Shinoda
Matthew Shreve

Tianmin Shu
Zhixin Shu
Kaleem Siddiqi
Gunnar Sigurdsson
Nathan Silberman
Tomas Simon
Abhishek Singh
Gautam Singh
Maneesh Singh
Praveer Singh
Richa Singh
Saurabh Singh
Sudipta Sinha
Vladimir Smutny
Noah Snavely
Cees Snoek
Kihyuk Sohn
Eric Sommerlade
Sanghyun Son
Bi Song
Shiyu Song
Shuran Song
Xuan Song
Yale Song
Yang Song
Yibing Song
Lorenzo Sorgi
Humberto Sossa
Pratul Srinivasan
Michael Stark
Bjorn Stenger
Rainer Stiefelhagen
Joerg Stueckler
Jan Stuehmer
Hang Su
Hao Su
Shuochen Su
R. Subramanian
Yusuke Sugano
Akihiro Sugimoto
Baochen Sun
Chen Sun
Jian Sun
Jin Sun
Lin Sun
Min Sun

Qing Sun
Zhaohui Sun
David Suter
Eran Swears
Raza Syed Hussain
T. Syeda-Mahmood
Christian Szegedy
Duy-Nguyen Ta
Tolga Taşdizen
Hemant Tagare
Yuichi Taguchi
Ying Tai
Yu-Wing Tai
Jun Takamatsu
Hugues Talbot
Toru Tamak
Robert Tamburo
Chaowei Tan
Meng Tang
Peng Tang
Siyu Tang
Wei Tang
Junli Tao
Ran Tao
Xin Tao
Makarand Tapaswi
Jean-Philippe Tarel
Maxim Tatarchenko
Bugra Tekin
Demetri Terzopoulos
Christian Theobalt
Diego Thomas
Rajat Thomas
Qi Tian
Xinmei Tian
YingLi Tian
Yonghong Tian
Yonglong Tian
Joseph Tighe
Radu Timofte
Massimo Tistarelli
Sinisa Todorovic
Pavel Tokmakov
Giorgos Tolias
Federico Tombari
Tatiana Tommasi

Chetan Tonde
Xin Tong
Akihiko Torii
Andrea Torsello
Florian Trammer
Du Tran
Quoc-Huy Tran
Rudolph Triebel
Alejandro Troccoli
Leonardo Trujillo
Tomasz Trzcinski
Sam Tsai
Yi-Hsuan Tsai
Hung-Yu Tseng
Vagia Tsiminaki
Aggeliki Tsoli
Wei-Chih Tu
Shubham Tulsiani
Fred Tung
Tony Tung
Matt Turek
Oncel Tuzel
Georgios Tzimiropoulos
Ilkay Ulusoy
Osman Ulusoy
Dmitry Ulyanov
Paul Upchurch
Ben Usman
Evgeniya Ustinova
Himanshu Vajaria
Alexander Vakhitov
Jack Valmadre
Ernest Valveny
Jan van Gemert
Grant Van Horn
Jagannadan Varadarajan
Gul Varol
Sebastiano Vascon
Francisco Vasconcelos
Mayank Vatsa
Javier Vazquez-Corral
Ramakrishna Vedantam
Ashok Veeraraghavan
Andreas Veit
Raviteja Vemulapalli
Jonathan Ventura

Matthias Vestner
Minh Vo
Christoph Vogel
Michele Volpi
Carl Vondrick
Sven Wachsmuth
Toshikazu Wada
Michael Waechter
Catherine Wah
Jacob Walker
Jun Wan
Boyu Wang
Chen Wang
Chunyu Wang
De Wang
Fang Wang
Hongxing Wang
Hua Wang
Jiang Wang
Jingdong Wang
Jinglu Wang
Jue Wang
Le Wang
Lei Wang
Lezi Wang
Liang Wang
Lichao Wang
Lijun Wang
Limin Wang
Liwei Wang
Naiyan Wang
Oliver Wang
Qi Wang
Ruiping Wang
Shenlong Wang
Shu Wang
Song Wang
Tao Wang
Xiaofang Wang
Xiaolong Wang
Xinchao Wang
Xinggang Wang
Xintao Wang
Yang Wang
Yu-Chiang Frank Wang
Yu-Xiong Wang

Zhaowen Wang
Zhe Wang
Anne Wannenwetsch
Simon Warfield
Scott Wehrwein
Donglai Wei
Ping Wei
Shih-En Wei
Xiu-Shen Wei
Yichen Wei
Xie Weidi
Philippe Weinzaepfel
Longyin Wen
Eric Wengrowski
Tomas Werner
Michael Wilber
Rick Wildes
Olivia Wiles
Kyle Wilson
David Wipf
Kwan-Yee Wong
Daniel Worrall
John Wright
Baoyuan Wu
Chao-Yuan Wu
Jiajun Wu
Jianxin Wu
Tianfu Wu
Xiaodong Wu
Xiaohe Wu
Xinxiao Wu
Yang Wu
Yi Wu
Ying Wu
Yuxin Wu
Zheng Wu
Stefanie Wuhrer
Yin Xia
Tao Xiang
Yu Xiang
Lei Xiao
Tong Xiao
Yang Xiao
Cihang Xie
Dan Xie
Jianwen Xie

Jin Xie
Lingxi Xie
Pengtao Xie
Saining Xie
Wenxuan Xie
Yuchen Xie
Bo Xin
Junliang Xing
Peng Xingchao
Bo Xiong
Fei Xiong
Xuehan Xiong
Yuanjun Xiong
Chenliang Xu
Danfei Xu
Huijuan Xu
Jia Xu
Weipeng Xu
Xiangyu Xu
Yan Xu
Yuanlu Xu
Jia Xue
Tianfan Xue
Erdem Yörük
Abhay Yadav
Deshraj Yadav
Payman Yadollahpour
Yasushi Yagi
Toshihiko Yamasaki
Fei Yan
Hang Yan
Junchi Yan
Junjie Yan
Sijie Yan
Keiji Yanai
Bin Yang
Chih-Yuan Yang
Dong Yang
Herb Yang
Jianchao Yang
Jianwei Yang
Jiaolong Yang
Jie Yang
Jimei Yang
Jufeng Yang
Linjie Yang

Michael Ying Yang
Ming Yang
Ruiduo Yang
Ruigang Yang
Shuo Yang
Wei Yang
Xiaodong Yang
Yanchao Yang
Yi Yang
Angela Yao
Bangpeng Yao
Cong Yao
Jian Yao
Ting Yao
Julian Yarkony
Mark Yatskar
Jinwei Ye
Mao Ye
Mei-Chen Yeh
Raymond Yeh
Serena Yeung
Kwang Moo Yi
Shuai Yi
Alper Yılmaz
Lijun Yin
Xi Yin
Zhaozheng Yin
Xianghua Ying
Ryo Yonetani
Donghyun Yoo
Ju Hong Yoon
Kuk-Jin Yoon
Chong You
Shaodi You
Aron Yu
Fisher Yu
Gang Yu
Jingyi Yu
Ke Yu
Licheng Yu
Pei Yu
Qian Yu
Rong Yu
Shoou-I Yu
Stella Yu
Xiang Yu

Yang Yu
Zhiding Yu
Ganzhao Yuan
Jing Yuan
Junsong Yuan
Lu Yuan
Stefanos Zafeiriou
Sergey Zagoruyko
Amir Zamir
K. Zampogiannis
Andrei Zanfir
Mihai Zanfir
Pablo Zegers
Eyasu Zemene
Andy Zeng
Xingyu Zeng
Yun Zeng
De-Chuan Zhan
Cheng Zhang
Dong Zhang
Guofeng Zhang
Han Zhang
Hang Zhang
Hanwang Zhang
Jian Zhang
Jianguo Zhang
Jianming Zhang
Jiawei Zhang
Junping Zhang
Lei Zhang
Linguang Zhang
Ning Zhang
Qing Zhang

Quanshi Zhang
Richard Zhang
Runze Zhang
Shanshan Zhang
Shiliang Zhang
Shu Zhang
Ting Zhang
Xiangyu Zhang
Xiaofan Zhang
Xu Zhang
Yimin Zhang
Yinda Zhang
Yongqiang Zhang
Yuting Zhang
Zhanpeng Zhang
Ziyu Zhang
Bin Zhao
Chen Zhao
Hang Zhao
Hengshuang Zhao
Qijun Zhao
Rui Zhao
Yue Zhao
Enliang Zheng
Liang Zheng
Stephan Zheng
Wei-Shi Zheng
Wenming Zheng
Yin Zheng
Yinqiang Zheng
Yuanjie Zheng
Guangyu Zhong
Bolei Zhou

Guang-Tong Zhou
Huiyu Zhou
Jiahuan Zhou
S. Kevin Zhou
Tinghui Zhou
Wengang Zhou
Xiaowei Zhou
Xingyi Zhou
Yin Zhou
Zihan Zhou
Fan Zhu
Guangming Zhu
Ji Zhu
Jiejie Zhu
Jun-Yan Zhu
Shizhan Zhu
Siyu Zhu
Xiangxin Zhu
Xiatian Zhu
Yan Zhu
Yingying Zhu
Yixin Zhu
Yuke Zhu
Zhenyao Zhu
Liansheng Zhuang
Zeeshan Zia
Karel Zimmermann
Daniel Zoran
Danping Zou
Qi Zou
Silvia Zuffi
Wangmeng Zuo
Xinxin Zuo

Contents – Part XIV

Poster Session

Matching and Recognition

Poster Session

Shift-Net: Image Inpainting via Deep Feature Rearrangement

Zhaoyi Yan[1] , Xiaoming Li[1] , Mu Li[2] , Wangmeng Zuo[1(✉)] ,
and Shiguang Shan[3]

[1] School of Computer Science and Technology, Harbin Institute of Technology,
Harbin, China
yanzhaoyi@outlook.com, csxmli@hit.edu.cn, wmzuo@hit.edu.cn
[2] Department of Computing, The Hong Kong Polytechnic University,
Hung Hom, Hong Kong
csmuli@comp.polyu.edu.hk
[3] Institute of Computing Technology, CAS, Beijing 100049, China
sgshan@ict.ac.cn

Abstract. Deep convolutional networks (CNNs) have exhibited their
potential in image inpainting for producing plausible results. However,
in most existing methods, e.g., context encoder, the missing parts are
predicted by propagating the surrounding convolutional features through
a fully connected layer, which intends to produce semantically plausible
but blurry result. In this paper, we introduce a special shift-connection
layer to the U-Net architecture, namely Shift-Net, for filling in missing
regions of any shape with sharp structures and fine-detailed textures.
To this end, the encoder feature of the known region is shifted to serve
as an estimation of the missing parts. A guidance loss is introduced on
decoder feature to minimize the distance between the decoder feature
after fully connected layer and the ground-truth encoder feature of the
missing parts. With such constraint, the decoder feature in missing region
can be used to guide the shift of encoder feature in known region. An
end-to-end learning algorithm is further developed to train the Shift-Net.
Experiments on the Paris StreetView and Places datasets demonstrate
the efficiency and effectiveness of our Shift-Net in producing sharper,
fine-detailed, and visually plausible results. The codes and pre-trained
models are available at https://github.com/Zhaoyi-Yan/Shift-Net.

Keywords: Inpainting · Feature rearrangement · Deep learning

1 Introduction

Image inpainting is the process of filling in missing regions with plausible hypothesis, and can be used in many real world applications such as removing distracting objects, repairing corrupted or damaged parts, and completing occluded

Electronic supplementary material The online version of this chapter (https://
doi.org/10.1007/978-3-030-01264-9_1) contains supplementary material, which is
available to authorized users.

regions. For example, when taking a photo, rare is the case that you are satisfied with what you get directly. Distracting scene elements, such as irrelevant people or disturbing objects, generally are inevitable but unwanted by the users. In these cases, image inpainting can serve as a remedy to remove these elements and fill in with plausible content.

(a)   (b)   (c)   (d)

Fig. 1. Qualitative comparison of inpainting methods. Given (a) an image with a missing region, we present the inpainting results by (b) Content-Aware Fill [11], (c) context encoder [28], and (d) our Shift-Net.

Despite decades of studies, image inpainting remains a very challenging problem in computer vision and graphics. In general, there are two requirements for the image inpainting result: (i) global semantic structure and (ii) fine detailed textures. Classical exemplar-based inpainting methods, e.g., PatchMatch [1], gradually synthesize the content of missing parts by searching similar patches from known region. Even such methods are promising in filling high-frequency texture details, they fail in capturing the global structure of the image (See Fig. 1(b)). In contrast, deep convolutional networks (CNNs) have also been suggested to predict the missing parts conditioned on their surroundings [28,41]. Benefited from large scale training data, they can produce semantically plausible inpainting result. However, the existing CNN-based methods usually complete the missing parts by propagating the surrounding convolutional features through a fully connected layer (i.e., bottleneck), making the inpainting results sometimes lack of fine texture details and blurry. The introduction of adversarial loss is helpful in improving the sharpness of the result, but cannot address this issue essentially (see Fig. 1(c)).

In this paper, we present a novel CNN, namely Shift-Net, to take into account the advantages of both exemplar-based and CNN-based methods for image inpainting. Our Shift-Net adopts the U-Net architecture by adding a special shift-connection layer. In exemplar-based inpainting [4], the patch-based replication and filling process are iteratively performed to grow the texture and structure from the known region to the missing parts. And the patch processing order plays a key role in yielding plausible inpainting result [22,40]. We note that CNN is effective in predicting the image structure and semantics of the missing parts. Guided by the salient structure produced by CNN, the filling process in our Shift-Net can be finished concurrently by introducing a shift-connection layer to connect the encoder feature of known region and the decoder feature of missing parts. Thus, our Shift-Net inherits the advantages of exemplar-based and CNN-based methods, and can produce inpainting result with both plausible semantics and fine detailed textures (See Fig. 1(d)).

Guidance loss, reconstruction loss, and adversarial learning are incorporated to guide the shift operation and to learn the model parameters of Shift-Net. To ensure that the decoder feature can serve as a good guidance, a guidance loss is introduced to enforce the decoder feature be close to the ground-truth encoder feature. Moreover, ℓ_1 and adversarial losses are also considered to reconstruct the missing parts and restore more detailed textures. By minimizing the model objective, our Shift-Net can be end-to-end learned with a training set. Experiments are conducted on the Paris StreetView dataset [5], the Places dataset [43], and real world images. The results show that our Shift-Net can handle missing regions with any shape, and is effective in producing sharper, fine-detailed, and visually plausible results (See Fig. 1(d)).

Besides, Yang et al. [41] also suggest a multi-scale neural patch synthesis (MNPS) approach to incorporating CNN-based with exemplar-based methods. Their method includes two stages, where an encoder-decoder network is used to generate an initial estimation in the first stage. By considering both global content and texture losses, a joint optimization model on VGG-19 [34] is minimized to generate the fine-detailed result in the second stage. Even Yang et al. [41] yields encouraging result, it is very time-consuming and takes about $40,000$ millisecond (ms) to process an image with size of 256×256. In contrast, our Shift-Net can achieve comparable or better results (See Figs. 4 and 5 for several examples) and only takes about 80 ms. Taking both effectiveness and efficiency into account, our Shift-Net can provide a favorable solution to combine exemplar-based and CNN-based inpainting for improving performance.

To sum up, the main contribution of this work is three-fold:

1. By introducing the shift-connection layer to U-Net, a novel Shift-Net architecture is developed to efficiently combine CNN-based and exemplar-based inpainting.
2. The guidance, reconstruction, and adversarial losses are introduced to train our Shift-Net. Even with the deployment of shift operation, all the network parameters can be learned in an end-to-end manner.
3. Our Shift-Net achieves state-of-the-art results in comparison with [1,28,41] and performs favorably in generating fine-detailed textures and visually plausible results.

2   Related Work

In this section, we briefly review the work on each of the three sub-fields, i.e., exemplar-based inpainting, CNN-based inpainting, and style transfer, and specially focus on those relevant to this work.

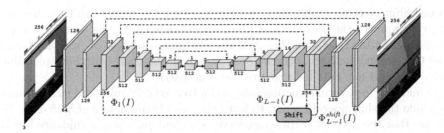

Fig. 2. The architecture of our model. We add the shift-connection layer at the resolution of 32×32.

2.1 Exemplar-Based Inpainting

In exemplar-based inpainting [1,2,4,6,8,15,16,20–22,29,33,35,37,38,40], the completion is conducted from the exterior to the interior of the missing part by searching and copying best matching patches from the known region. For fast patch search, Barnes *et al.* suggest a PatchMatch algorithm [1] to exploit the image coherency, and generalize it for finding k-nearest neighbors [2]. Generally, exemplar-based inpainting is superior in synthesizing textures, but is not well suited for preserving edges and structures. For better recovery of image structure, several patch priority measures have been proposed to fill in structural patches first [4,22,40]. Global image coherence has also been introduced to the Markov random field (MRF) framework for improving visual quality [20,29,37]. However, these methods only work well on images with simple structures, and may fail in handling images with complex objects and scenes. Besides, in most exemplar-based inpainting methods [20,21,29], the missing part is recovered as the shift representation of the known region in pixel/region level, which also motivates our shift operation on convolution feature representation.

2.2 CNN-Based Inpainting

Recently, deep CNNs have achieved great success in image inpainting. Originally, CNN-based inpainting is confined to small and thin masks [19,31,39]. Phatak *et al.* [28] present an encoder-decoder (i.e., context encoder) network to predict the missing parts, where an adversarial loss is adopted in training to improve the visual quality of the inpainted image. Even context encoder is effective in capturing image semantics and global structure, it completes the input image with only one forward-pass and performs poorly in generating fine-detailed textures. Semantic image inpainting is introduced to fill in the missing part conditioned on the known region for images from a specific semantic class [42]. In order to obtain globally consistent result with locally realistic details, global and local discriminators have been proposed in image inpainting [13] and face completion [25]. For better recovery of fine details, MNPS is presented to combine exemplar-based and CNN-based inpainting [41].

2.3 Style Transfer

Image inpainting can be treated as an extension of style transfer, where both the content and style (texture) of missing part are estimated and transferred from the known region. In the recent few years, style transfer [3,7,9,10,12,17,24,26,36] has been an active research topic. Gatys *et al.* [9] show that one can transfer style and texture of the style image to the content image by solving an optimization objective defined on an existing CNN. Instead of the Gram matrix, Li *et al.* [24] apply the MRF regularizer to style transfer to suppress distortions and smears. In [3], local matching is performed on the convolution layer of the pre-trained network to combine content and style, and an inverse network is then deployed to generate the image from feature representation.

3 Method

Given an input image I, image inpainting aims to restore the ground-truth image I^{gt} by filling in the missing part. To this end, we adopt U-Net [32] as the baseline network. By incorporating with guidance loss and shift operation, we develop a novel Shift-Net for better recovery of semantic structure and fine-detailed textures. In the following, we first introduce the guidance loss and Shift-Net, and then describe the model objective and learning algorithm.

3.1 Guidance Loss on Decoder Feature

The U-Net consists of an encoder and a symmetric decoder, where skip connection is introduced to concatenate the features from each layer of encoder and those of the corresponding layer of decoder. Such skip connection makes it convenient to utilize the information before and after bottleneck, which is valuable for image inpainting and other low level vision tasks in capturing localized visual details [14,44]. The architecture of the U-Net adopted in this work is shown in Fig. 2. Please refer to the supplementary material for more details on network parameters.

Let Ω be the missing region and $\overline{\Omega}$ be the known region. Given a U-Net of L layers, $\Phi_l(I)$ is used to denote the encoder feature of the l-th layer, and $\Phi_{L-l}(I)$ the decoder feature of the $(L-l)$-th layer. For the end of recovering I^{gt}, we expect that $\Phi_l(I)$ and $\Phi_{L-l}(I)$ convey almost all the information in $\Phi_l(I^{gt})$. For any location $\mathbf{y} \in \Omega$, we have $(\Phi_l(I))_{\mathbf{y}} \approx 0$. Thus, $(\Phi_{L-l}(I))_{\mathbf{y}}$ should convey equivalent information of $(\Phi_l(I^{gt}))_{\mathbf{y}}$.

In this work, we suggest to explicitly model the relationship between $(\Phi_{L-l}(I))_{\mathbf{y}}$ and $(\Phi_l(I^{gt}))_{\mathbf{y}}$ by introducing the following guidance loss,

$$\mathcal{L}_g = \sum_{\mathbf{y} \in \Omega} \left\| (\Phi_{L-l}(I))_{\mathbf{y}} - (\Phi_l(I^{gt}))_{\mathbf{y}} \right\|_2^2. \tag{1}$$

We note that $(\Phi_l(I))_{\mathbf{x}} \approx (\Phi_l(I^{gt}))_{\mathbf{x}}$ for any $\mathbf{x} \in \overline{\Omega}$. Thus the guidance loss is only defined on $\mathbf{y} \in \Omega$ to make $(\Phi_{L-l}(I))_{\mathbf{y}} \approx (\Phi_l(I^{gt}))_{\mathbf{y}}$. By concatenating $\Phi_l(I)$ and $\Phi_{L-l}(I)$, all information in $\Phi_l(I^{gt})$ can be approximately obtained.

Experiment on deep feature visualization is further conducted to illustrate the relation between $(\Phi_{L-l}(I))_{\mathbf{y}}$ and $(\Phi_l(I^{gt}))_{\mathbf{y}}$. For visualizing $\{(\Phi_l(I^{gt}))_{\mathbf{y}} \,|\, \mathbf{y} \in \Omega\}$, we adopt the method [27] by solving an optimization problem

$$H^{gt} = \arg\min_H \sum_{\mathbf{y} \in \Omega} \left\| (\Phi_l(H))_{\mathbf{y}} - (\Phi_l(I^{gt}))_{\mathbf{y}} \right\|_2^2. \tag{2}$$

Analogously, $\{(\Phi_{L-l}(I))_{\mathbf{y}} \,|\, \mathbf{y} \in \Omega\}$ is visualized by

$$H^{de} = \arg\min_H \sum_{\mathbf{y} \in \Omega} \left\| (\Phi_l(H))_{\mathbf{y}} - (\Phi_{L-l}(I))_{\mathbf{y}} \right\|_2^2. \tag{3}$$

Figures 3(b) and (c) show the visualization results of H^{gt} and H^{de}. With the introduction of guidance loss, obviously H^{de} can serve as a reasonable estimation of H^{gt}, and U-Net works well in recovering image semantics and structures. However, in compared with H^{gt} and I^{gt}, the result H^{de} is blurry, which is consistent with the poor performance of CNN-based inpainting in recovering fine textures [41]. Finally, we note that the guidance loss is helpful in constructing an explicit relation between $(\Phi_{L-l}(I))_{\mathbf{y}}$ and $(\Phi_l(I^{gt}))_{\mathbf{y}}$. In the next section, we will explain how to utilize such property for better estimation to $(\Phi_l(I^{gt}))_{\mathbf{y}}$ and enhancing inpainting result.

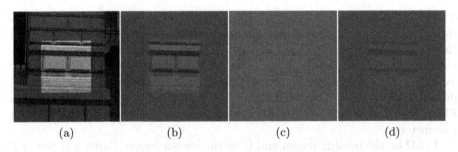

| (a) | (b) | (c) | (d) |

Fig. 3. Visualization of features learned by our model. Given (a) an input image, (b) is the visualization of $\left(\Phi_l(I^{gt})\right)_{\mathbf{y}}$ (i.e., H^{gt}), (c) shows the result of $(\Phi_{L-l}(I))_{\mathbf{y}}$ (i.e., H^{de}) and (d) demonstrates the effect of $\left(\Phi_{L-l}^{shift}(I)\right)_{\mathbf{y}}$.

3.2   Shift Operation and Shift-Net

In exemplar-based inpainting, it is generally assumed that the missing part is the spatial rearrangement of the pixels/patches in the known region. For each pixel/patch localized at $\mathbf{y}$ in missing part, exemplar-based inpainting explicitly or implicitly find a shift vector $\mathbf{u_y}$, and recover $(I)_{\mathbf{y}}$ with $(I)_{\mathbf{y}+\mathbf{u_y}}$, where $\mathbf{y} + \mathbf{u_y} \in \overline{\Omega}$ is in the known region. The pixel value $(I)_{\mathbf{y}}$ is unknown before inpainting. Thus, the shift vectors usually are obtained progressively from the exterior to the interior of the missing part, or by solving a MRF model by considering global image coherence. However, these methods may fail in recovering complex image semantics and structures.

We introduce a special shift-connection layer in U-Net, which takes $\Phi_l(I)$ and $\Phi_{L-l}(I)$ to obtain an updated estimation on $\Phi_l(I^{gt})$. For each $(\Phi_{L-l}(I))_{\mathbf{y}}$ with $\mathbf{y} \in \Omega$, its nearest neighbor (NN) searching based on cross-correlation in $(\Phi_l(I))_{\mathbf{x}}$ ($\mathbf{x} \in \overline{\Omega}$) can be independently obtained by,

$$\mathbf{x}^*(\mathbf{y}) = \arg\max_{\mathbf{x} \in \overline{\Omega}} \frac{\left\langle (\Phi_{L-l}(I))_{\mathbf{y}}, (\Phi_l(I))_{\mathbf{x}} \right\rangle}{\|(\Phi_{L-l}(I))_{\mathbf{y}}\|_2 \|(\Phi_l(I))_{\mathbf{x}}\|_2}, \tag{4}$$

and the shift vector is defined as $\mathbf{u}_{\mathbf{y}} = \mathbf{x}^*(\mathbf{y}) - \mathbf{y}$. We also empirically find that cross-correlation is more effective than ℓ_1 and ℓ_2 norms in our Shift-Net. Similar to [24], the NN searching can be computed as a convolutional layer. Then, we update the estimation of $(\Phi_l(I^{gt}))_{\mathbf{y}}$ as the spatial rearrangement of the encoder feature $(\Phi_l(I))_{\mathbf{x}}$,

$$\left(\Phi_{L-l}^{shift}(I)\right)_{\mathbf{y}} = (\Phi_l(I))_{\mathbf{y}+\mathbf{u}_{\mathbf{y}}}. \tag{5}$$

See Fig. 3(d) for visualization. Finally, as shown in Fig. 2, the convolution features $\Phi_{L-l}(I)$, $\Phi_l(I)$ and $\Phi_{L-l}^{shift}(I)$ are concatenated and taken as inputs to the $(L - l + 1)$-th layer, resulting in our Shift-Net.

The shift operation is different with exemplar-based inpainting from several aspects. (i) While exemplar-based inpainting is operated on pixels/patches, shift operation is performed on deep encoder feature domain which is end-to-end learned from training data. (ii) In exemplar-based inpainting, the shift vectors are obtained either by solving an optimization problem or in particular order. As for shift operation, with the guidance of $\Phi_{L-l}(I)$, all the shift vectors can be computed in parallel. (iii) For exemplar-based inpainting, both patch processing orders and global image coherence are not sufficient for preserving complex structures and semantics. In contrast, in shift operation $\Phi_{L-l}(I)$ is learned from large scale data and is more powerful in capturing global semantics. (iv) In exemplar-based inpainting, after obtaining the shift vectors, the completion result can be directly obtained as the shift representation of the known region. As for shift operation, we take the shift representation $\Phi_{L-l}^{shift}(I)$ together with $\Phi_{L-l}(I)$ and $\Phi_l(I)$ as inputs to $(L - l + 1)$-th layer of U-Net, and adopt a data-driven manner to learn an appropriate model for image inpainting. Moreover, even with the introduction of shift-connection layer, all the model parameters in our Shift-Net can be end-to-end learned from training data. Thus, our Shift-Net naturally inherits the advantages of exemplar-based and CNN-based inpainting.

3.3   Model Objective and Learning

Objective. Denote by $\Phi(I; \mathbf{W})$ the output of Shift-Net, where $\mathbf{W}$ is the model parameters to be learned. Besides the guidance loss, the ℓ_1 loss and the adversarial loss are also included to train our Shift-Net. The ℓ_1 loss is defined as,

$$\mathcal{L}_{\ell_1} = \|\Phi(I; \mathbf{W}) - I^{gt}\|_1, \tag{6}$$

which is suggested to constrain that the inpainting result should approximate the ground-truth image.

Moreover, adversarial learning has been adopted in low level vision [23] and image generation [14,30], and exhibits its superiority in restoring fine details and photo-realistic textures. Thus, we use $p_{data}(I^{gt})$ to denote the distribution of ground-truth images, and $p_{miss}(I)$ to denote the distribution of input image. Then the adversarial loss is defined as,

$$\mathcal{L}_{adv} = \min_{\mathbf{W}} \max_{D} \mathbb{E}_{I^{gt} \sim p_{data}(I^{gt})} [\log D(I^{gt})] \tag{7}$$

$$+ \mathbb{E}_{I \sim p_{miss}(I)} [\log(1 - D(\Phi(I; \mathbf{W})))], \tag{8}$$

where $D(\cdot)$ denotes the discriminator to predict the probability that an image is from the distribution $p_{data}(I^{gt})$.

Taking guidance, ℓ_1, and adversarial losses into account, the overall objective of our Shift-Net is defined as,

$$\mathcal{L} = \mathcal{L}_{\ell_1} + \lambda_g \mathcal{L}_g + \lambda_{adv} \mathcal{L}_{adv}, \tag{9}$$

where λ_g and λ_{adv} are two tradeoff parameters.

Learning. Given a training set $\{(I, I^{gt})\}$, the Shift-Net is trained by minimizing the objective in Eq. (9) via back-propagation. We note that the Shift-Net and the discriminator are trained in an adversarial manner. The Shift-Net $\Phi(I; \mathbf{W})$ is updated by minimizing the adversarial loss $\mathcal{L}_{adv}$, while the discriminator D is updated by maximizing $\mathcal{L}_{adv}$.

Due to the introduction of shift-connection, we should modify the gradient w.r.t. the l-th layer of feature $F_l = \Phi_l(I)$. To avoid confusion, we use F_l^{skip} to denote the feature F_l after skip connection, and of course we have $F_l^{skip} = F_l$. According to Eq. (5), the relation between $\Phi_{L-l}^{shift}(I)$ and $\Phi_l(I)$ can be written as,

$$\Phi_{L-l}^{shift}(I) = \mathbf{P}\Phi_l(I), \tag{10}$$

where $\mathbf{P}$ denotes the shift matrix of $\{0, 1\}$, and there is only one element of 1 in each row of $\mathbf{P}$. Thus, the gradient with respect to $\Phi_l(I)$ consists of three terms: (i) that from $(l+1)$-th layer, (ii) that from skip connection, and (iii) that from shift-connection, and can be written as,

$$\frac{\partial \mathcal{L}}{\partial F_l} = \frac{\partial \mathcal{L}}{\partial F_l^{skip}} + \frac{\partial \mathcal{L}}{\partial F_{l+1}} \frac{\partial F_{l+1}}{\partial F_l} + \mathbf{P}^T \frac{\partial \mathcal{L}}{\partial \Phi_{L-l}^{shift}(I)}, \tag{11}$$

where the computation of the first two terms are the same with U-Net, and the gradient with respect to $\Phi_{L-l}^{shift}(I)$ can also be directly computed. Thus, our Shift-Net can also be end-to-end trained to learn the model parameters $\mathbf{W}$.

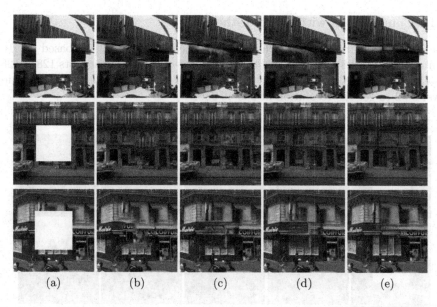

Fig. 4. Qualitative comparisons on the Paris StreetView dataset. From the left to the right are: (a) input, (b) Content-Aware Fill [11], (c) context encoder [28], (d) MNPS [41] and (e) Ours. All images are scaled to 256 × 256.

4   Experiments

We evaluate our method on two datasets: Paris StreetView [5] and six scenes from Places365-Standard dataset [43]. The Paris StreetView contains 14,900 training images and 100 test images. We randomly choose 20 out of the 100 test images in Paris StreetView to form the validation set, and use the remaining as the test set. There are 1.6 million training images from 365 scene categories in the Places365-Standard. The scene categories selected from Places365-Standard are *butte, canyon, field, synagogue, tundra* and *valley*. Each category has 5,000 training images, 900 test images and 100 validation images. The details of model selection are given in the supplementary materials. For both Paris StreetView and Places, we resize each training image to let its minimal length/width be 350, and randomly crop a subimage of size 256 × 256 as input to our model. Moreover, our method is also tested on real world images for removing objects and distractors. Our Shift-Net is optimized using the Adam algorithm [18] with a learning rate of 2×10^{-4} and $\beta_1 = 0.5$. The batch size is 1 and the training is stopped after 30 epochs. Data augmentation such as flipping is also adopted during training. The tradeoff parameters are set as $\lambda_g = 0.01$ and $\lambda_{adv} = 0.002$. It takes about one day to train our Shift-Net on an Nvidia Titan X Pascal GPU.

4.1   Comparisons with State-of-the-Arts

We compare our results with Photoshop Content-Aware Fill [11] based on [1], context encoder [28], and MNPS [41]. As context encoder only accepts 128×128 images, we upsample the results to 256×256. For MNPS [41], we set the pyramid level be 2 to get the resolution of 256×256.

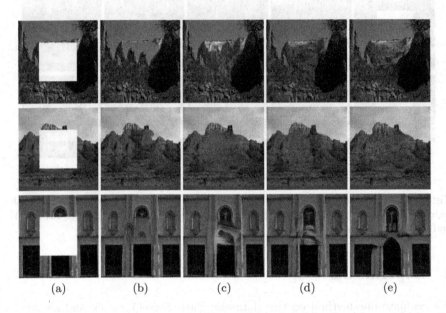

(a)   (b)   (c)   (d)   (e)

Fig. 5. Qualitative comparisons on the Places. From the left to the right are: (a) input, (b) Content-Aware Fill [11], (c) context encoder [28], (d) MNPS [41] and (e) Ours. All images are scaled to 256×256.

Evaluation on Paris StreetView and Places. Figure 4 shows the comparisons of our method with the three state-of-the-art approaches on Paris StreetView. Content-Aware Fill [11] is effective in recovering low level textures, but performs slightly worse in handling occlusions with complex structures. Context encoder [28] is effective in semantic inpainting, but the results seem blurry and detail-missing due to the effect of bottleneck. MNPS [41] adopts a multi-stage scheme to combine CNN and examplar-based inpainting, and generally works better than Content-Aware Fill [11] and context encoder [28]. However, the multi-scales in MNPS [41] are not jointly trained, where some adverse effects produced in the first stage may not be eliminated by the subsequent stages. In comparison to the competing methods, our Shift-Net combines CNN and examplar-based inpainting in an end-to-end manner, and generally is able to generate visual-pleasing results. Moreover, we also note that our Shift-Net is much more efficient than MNPS [41]. Our method consumes only about 80 ms for a 256×256 image, which is about $500\times$ faster than MNPS [41] (about 40 s). In addition, we also evaluate our method on the Places dataset (see Fig. 5).

Again our Shift-Net performs favorably in generating fine-detailed, semantically plausible, and realistic images.

Quantitative Evaluation. We also compare our model quantitatively with the competing methods on the Paris StreetView dataset. Table 1 lists the PSNR, SSIM and mean ℓ_2 loss of different methods. Our Shift-Net achieves the best numerical performance. We attribute it to the combination of CNN-based with examplar-based inpainting as well as the end-to-end training. In comparison, MNPS [41] adopts a two-stage scheme and cannot be jointly trained.

Table 1. Comparison of PSNR, SSIM and mean ℓ_2 loss on Paris StreetView dataset.

Method	PSNR	SSIM	Mean ℓ_2 Loss
Content-Aware Fill [11]	23.71	0.74	0.0617
Context encoder [28] (ℓ_2 + adversarial loss)	24.16	0.87	0.0313
MNPS [41]	25.98	0.89	0.0258
Ours	**26.51**	**0.90**	**0.0208**

Fig. 6. Random region completion. From top to bottom are: input, Content-Aware Fill [11], and Ours.

Random Mask Completion. Our model can also be trained for arbitrary region completion. Figure 6 shows the results by Content-Aware Fill [11] and our Shift-Net. For textured and smooth regions, both Content-Aware Fill [11] and our Shift-Net perform favorably. While for structural region, our Shift-Net is more effective in filling the cropped regions with context coherent with global content and structures.

4.2   Inpainting of Real World Images

We also evaluate our Shift-Net trained on Paris StreetView for the inpainting of real world images by considering two types of missing regions: (i) central region, (ii) object removal. From the first row of Fig. 7, one can see that our Shift-Net trained with central mask can be generalized to handle real world images. From the second row of Fig. 7, we show the feasibility of using our Shift-Net trained with random mask to remove unwanted objects from the images.

Fig. 7. Results on real images. From the top to bottom are: central region inpainting, and object removal.

5   Ablation Studies

The main differences between our Shift-Net and the other methods are the introduction of guidance loss and shift-connection layer. Thus, experiments are first conducted to analyze the effect of guidance loss and shift operation. Then we respectively zero out the corresponding weight of $(L - l + 1)$-th layer to verify the effectiveness of the shift feature Φ_{L-l}^{shift} in generating fine-detailed results. Moreover, the benefit of shift-connection does not owe to the increase of feature map size. So we also compare Shift-Net with a baseline model by substituting the NN searching with random shift-connection in the supplementary materials.

5.1   Effect of Guidance Loss

Two groups of experiments are conducted to evaluate the effect of guidance loss. In the first group, we add and remove the guidance loss $\mathcal{L}_g$ for U-Net and our Shift-Net to train the models. Figure 8 shows the inpainting results by these four

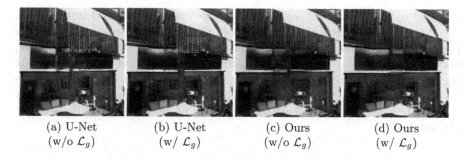

(a) U-Net   (b) U-Net   (c) Ours   (d) Ours
(w/o $\mathcal{L}_g$)   (w/ $\mathcal{L}_g$)   (w/o $\mathcal{L}_g$)   (w/ $\mathcal{L}_g$)

Fig. 8. The effect of guidance loss $\mathcal{L}_g$ in U-Net and our Shift-Net.

(a) $\lambda_g = 1$ (b) $\lambda_g = 0.1$ (c) $\lambda_g = 0.01$ (d) $\lambda_g = 0.001$

Fig. 9. The effect of the tradeoff parameter λ_g of guidance loss.

methods. It can be observed that, for both U-Net and Shift-Net the guidance loss is helpful in suppressing artifacts and preserving salient structure.

In the second group, we evaluate the effect of tradeoff parameter λ_g. Note that the guidance loss is introduced for both recovering the semantic structure of missing region and guiding the shift of encoder feature. Thus, proper tradeoff parameter λ_g should be chosen. Figure 9 shows the results by setting different λ_g values. When λ_g is small (e.g., $= 0.001$), the decoder feature may not serve as a suitable guidance to guarantee the correct shift of the encoder feature. From Fig. 9(d), some artifacts can still be observed. When λ_g becomes too large (e.g., ≥ 0.1), the constraint will be too excessive, and artifacts may also be introduced (see Fig. 9(a) and (b)). Thus, we empirically set $\lambda_g = 0.01$ in our experiments.

5.2 Effect of Shift Operation at Different Layers

The shift operation can be deployed to different layer, e.g., $(L - l)$-th, of the decoder. When l is smaller, the feature map size goes larger, and more computation time is required to perform the shift operation. When l is larger, the feature map size becomes smaller, but more detailed information may lost in the corresponding encoder layer. Thus, proper l should be chosen for better trade-off between computation time and inpainting performance. Figure 10 shows the results of Shift-Net by adding the shift-connection layer to each of the $(L-4)$-th, $(L-3)$-th, and $(L-2)$-th layers, respectively. When the shift-connection layer is added to the $(L-2)$-th layer, Shift-Net generally works well in producing visually pleasing results, but it takes more time, i.e., ~400 ms per image (See Fig. 10(d)). When the shift-connection layer is added to the $(L-4)$-th layer, Shift-Net becomes very efficient (i.e., ~40 ms per image) but tends to generate the result with less textures and coarse details (See Fig. 10(b)). By performing the shift operation in $(L-3)$-th layer, better tradeoff between efficiency (i.e., ~80 ms per image) and performance can be obtained by Shift-Net (See Fig. 10(c)).

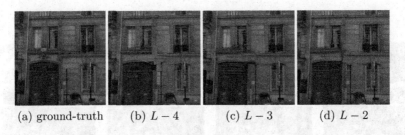

(a) ground-truth   (b) $L-4$ (c) $L-3$ (d) $L-2$

Fig. 10. The effect of performing shift operation on different layers $L-l$.

5.3   Effect of the Shifted Feature

The $(L-l+1)$-th layer of Shift-Net takes $\Phi_{L-l}(I)$, $\Phi_l(I)$ and Φ_{L-l}^{shift} as inputs. To analyze their effect, Fig. 11 shows the results of Shift-Net by zeroing out the weight of each slice in $(L-l+1)$-th layer. When we abandon $\Phi_{L-l}(I)$, the central part fails to restore any structures (See Fig. 11(b)). When we ignore $\Phi_l(I)$, the general structure can be restored (See (Fig. 11(c)) but its quality is inferior to the final result in Fig. 11(e). Finally, when we discard the shift feature Φ_{L-l}^{shift}, the result becomes totally a mixture of structures (See Fig. 11(d)). Thus, we conclude that Φ_{L-l}^{shift} acts as a refinement and enhancement role in recovering clear and fine details in our Shift-Net.

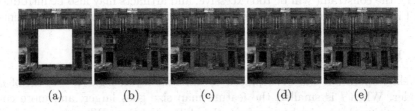

(a)   (b)   (c)   (d)   (e)

Fig. 11. Given (a) the input, (b), (c) and (d) are respectively the results when the 1st, 2nd, 3rd parts of weights in $(L-l+1)$-th layer are zeroed. (e) is the result of Ours.

6   Conclusion

This paper proposes a novel Shift-Net for image completion that exhibits fast speed with promising fine details via deep feature rearrangement. The guidance loss is introduced to enhance the explicit relation between the encoded feature in known region and decoded feature in missing region. By exploiting such relation, the shift operation can be efficiently performed and is effective in improving inpainting performance. Experiments show that our Shift-Net performs favorably in comparison to the state-of-the-art methods, and is effective in generating sharp, fine-detailed and photo-realistic images. In future, more studies will be given to extend the shift-connection to other low level vision tasks.

Acknowledgements. This work was supported in part by the National Natural Science Foundation of China under grant Nos. 61671182 and 61471146.

References

1. Barnes, C., Shechtman, E., Finkelstein, A., Goldman, D.B.: Patchmatch: a randomized correspondence algorithm for structural image editing. ACM Trans. Graph. (TOG) **28**, 24 (2009)
2. Barnes, C., Shechtman, E., Goldman, D.B., Finkelstein, A.: The generalized Patch-Match correspondence algorithm. In: Daniilidis, K., Maragos, P., Paragios, N. (eds.) ECCV 2010. LNCS, vol. 6313, pp. 29–43. Springer, Heidelberg (2010). https://doi.org/10.1007/978-3-642-15558-1_3
3. Chen, T.Q., Schmidt, M.: Fast patch-based style transfer of arbitrary style. arXiv preprint arXiv:1612.04337 (2016)
4. Criminisi, A., Perez, P., Toyama, K.: Object removal by exemplar-based inpainting. In: 2003 IEEE Computer Society Conference on Computer Vision and Pattern Recognition, Proceedings, vol. 2, p. II. IEEE (2003)
5. Doersch, C., Singh, S., Gupta, A., Sivic, J., Efros, A.: What makes paris look like paris? ACM Trans. Graph. **31**(4), 101 (2012)
6. Drori, I., Cohen-Or, D., Yeshurun, H.: Fragment-based image completion. ACM Trans. Graph. (TOG) **22**, 303–312 (2003)
7. Dumoulin, V., Shlens, J., Kudlur, M.: A learned representation for artistic style. arXiv preprint arXiv:1610.07629 (2016)
8. Efros, A.A., Leung, T.K.: Texture synthesis by non-parametric sampling. In: The Proceedings of the Seventh IEEE International Conference on Computer Vision, vol. 2, pp. 1033–1038. IEEE (1999)
9. Gatys, L.A., Ecker, A.S., Bethge, M.: A neural algorithm of artistic style. arXiv preprint arXiv:1508.06576 (2015)
10. Gatys, L.A., Ecker, A.S., Bethge, M., Hertzmann, A., Shechtman, E.: Controlling perceptual factors in neural style transfer. arXiv preprint arXiv:1611.07865 (2016)
11. Goldman, D., Shechtman, E., Barnes, C., Belaunde, I., Chien, J.: Content-aware fill. https://research.adobe.com/project/content-aware-fill
12. Huang, X., Belongie, S.: Arbitrary style transfer in real-time with adaptive instance normalization. arXiv preprint arXiv:1703.06868 (2017)
13. Iizuka, S., Simo-Serra, E., Ishikawa, H.: Globally and locally consistent image completion. ACM Trans. Graph. (Proc. SIGGRAPH 2017) **36**(4), 107:1–107:14 (2017)

14. Isola, P., Zhu, J.Y., Zhou, T., Efros, A.A.: Image-to-image translation with conditional adversarial networks. arXiv preprint arXiv:1611.07004 (2016)
15. Jia, J., Tang, C.K.: Image repairing: Robust image synthesis by adaptive ND tensor voting. In: 2003 IEEE Computer Society Conference on Computer Vision and Pattern Recognition, Proceedings, vol. 1, pp. 643–650. IEEE (2003)
16. Jia, J., Tang, C.K.: Inference of segmented color and texture description by tensor voting. IEEE Trans. Pattern Anal. Mach. Intell. **26**(6), 771–786 (2004)
17. Johnson, J., Alahi, A., Fei-Fei, L.: Perceptual losses for real-time style transfer and super-resolution. In: Leibe, B., Matas, J., Sebe, N., Welling, M. (eds.) ECCV 2016. LNCS, vol. 9906, pp. 694–711. Springer, Cham (2016). https://doi.org/10.1007/978-3-319-46475-6_43
18. Kingma, D.P., Ba, J.L.: Adam: a method for stochastic optimization. In: International Conference on Learning Representations (2015)
19. Köhler, R., Schuler, C., Schölkopf, B., Harmeling, S.: Mask-specific inpainting with deep neural networks. In: Jiang, X., Hornegger, J., Koch, R. (eds.) GCPR 2014. LNCS, vol. 8753, pp. 523–534. Springer, Cham (2014). https://doi.org/10.1007/978-3-319-11752-2_43
20. Komodakis, N.: Image completion using global optimization. In: 2006 IEEE Computer Society Conference on Computer Vision and Pattern Recognition, vol. 1, pp. 442–452. IEEE (2006)
21. Komodakis, N., Tziritas, G.: Image completion using efficient belief propagation via priority scheduling and dynamic pruning. IEEE Trans. Image Process. **16**(11), 2649–2661 (2007)
22. Le Meur, O., Gautier, J., Guillemot, C.: Examplar-based inpainting based on local geometry. In: 2011 18th IEEE International Conference on Image Processing (ICIP), pp. 3401–3404. IEEE (2011)
23. Ledig, C., et al.: Photo-realistic single image super-resolution using a generative adversarial network. arXiv preprint arXiv:1609.04802 (2016)
24. Li, C., Wand, M.: Combining Markov random fields and convolutional neural networks for image synthesis. In: Proceedings of the IEEE Conference on Computer Vision and Pattern Recognition, pp. 2479–2486 (2016)
25. Li, Y., Liu, S., Yang, J., Yang, M.H.: Generative face completion. arXiv preprint arXiv:1704.05838 (2017)
26. Luan, F., Paris, S., Shechtman, E., Bala, K.: Deep photo style transfer. arXiv preprint arXiv:1703.07511 (2017)
27. Mahendran, A., Vedaldi, A.: Understanding deep image representations by inverting them. In: Proceedings of the IEEE Conference on Computer Vision and Pattern Recognition, pp. 5188–5196 (2015)
28. Pathak, D., Krahenbuhl, P., Donahue, J., Darrell, T., Efros, A.A.: Context encoders: feature learning by inpainting. In: Proceedings of the IEEE Conference on Computer Vision and Pattern Recognition, pp. 2536–2544 (2016)
29. Pritch, Y., Kav-Venaki, E., Peleg, S.: Shift-map image editing. In: 2009 IEEE 12th International Conference on Computer Vision, pp. 151–158. IEEE (2009)
30. Radford, A., Metz, L., Chintala, S.: Unsupervised representation learning with deep convolutional generative adversarial networks. arXiv preprint arXiv:1511.06434 (2015)
31. Ren, J.S., Xu, L., Yan, Q., Sun, W.: Shepard convolutional neural networks. In: Advances in Neural Information Processing Systems, pp. 901–909 (2015)
32. Ronneberger, O., Fischer, P., Brox, T.: U-Net: convolutional networks for biomedical image segmentation. In: Medical Image Computing and Computer-Assisted Intervention (MICCAI) (2015)

33. Simakov, D., Caspi, Y., Shechtman, E., Irani, M.: Summarizing visual data using bidirectional similarity. In: IEEE Conference on Computer Vision and Pattern Recognition, CVPR 2008, pp. 1–8. IEEE (2008)
34. Simonyan, K., Zisserman, A.: Very deep convolutional networks for large-scale image recognition. arXiv preprint arXiv:1409.1556 (2014)
35. Sun, J., Yuan, L., Jia, J., Shum, H.Y.: Image completion with structure propagation. ACM Trans. Graph. (ToG) **24**(3), 861–868 (2005)
36. Ulyanov, D., Lebedev, V., Vedaldi, A., Lempitsky, V.S.: Texture networks: feedforward synthesis of textures and stylized images. In: ICML, pp. 1349–1357 (2016)
37. Wexler, Y., Shechtman, E., Irani, M.: Space-time video completion. In: Proceedings of the 2004 IEEE Computer Society Conference on Computer Vision and Pattern Recognition, CVPR 2004, vol. 1, pp. 120–127. IEEE (2004)
38. Wexler, Y., Shechtman, E., Irani, M.: Space-time completion of video. IEEE Trans. Pattern Anal. Mach. Intell. **29**(3), 463–476 (2007)
39. Xie, J., Xu, L., Chen, E.: Image denoising and inpainting with deep neural networks. In: Advances in Neural Information Processing Systems, pp. 341–349 (2012)
40. Xu, Z., Sun, J.: Image inpainting by patch propagation using patch sparsity. IEEE Trans. Image Process. **19**(5), 1153–1165 (2010)
41. Yang, C., Lu, X., Lin, Z., Shechtman, E., Wang, O., Li, H.: High-resolution image inpainting using multi-scale neural patch synthesis. In: The IEEE Conference on Computer Vision and Pattern Recognition (CVPR), July 2017
42. Yeh, R.A., Chen, C., Lim, T.Y., Schwing, A.G., Hasegawa-Johnson, M., Do, M.N.: Semantic image inpainting with deep generative models. In: Proceedings of the IEEE Conference on Computer Vision and Pattern Recognition, pp. 5485–5493 (2017)
43. Zhou, B., Lapedriza, A., Khosla, A., Oliva, A., Torralba, A.: Places: a 10 million image database for scene recognition. IEEE Trans. Pattern Anal. Mach. Intell. **40**(6), 1452–1464 (2017)
44. Zhu, J.Y., Park, T., Isola, P., Efros, A.A.: Unpaired image-to-image translation using cycle-consistent adversarial networks. arXiv preprint arXiv:1703.10593 (2017)

Interactive Boundary Prediction
for Object Selection

Hoang Le[1]([⊠]), Long Mai[2], Brian Price[2], Scott Cohen[2], Hailin Jin[2],
and Feng Liu[1]

[1] Portland State University, Portland, OR, USA
hoanl@cs.pdx.edu
[2] Adobe Research, San Jose, CA, USA

Abstract. Interactive image segmentation is critical for many image
editing tasks. While recent advanced methods on interactive segmentation focus on the region-based paradigm, more traditional boundary-
based methods such as Intelligent Scissor are still popular in practice as
they allow users to have active control of the object boundaries. Existing
methods for boundary-based segmentation solely rely on low-level image
features, such as edges for boundary extraction, which limits their ability
to adapt to high-level image content and user intention. In this paper,
we introduce an interaction-aware method for boundary-based image segmentation. Instead of relying on pre-defined low-level image features, our
method adaptively predicts object boundaries according to image content
and user interactions. Therein, we develop a fully convolutional encoder-
decoder network that takes both the image and user interactions (e.g.
clicks on boundary points) as input and predicts semantically meaningful boundaries that match user intentions. Our method explicitly models
the dependency of boundary extraction results on image content and user
interactions. Experiments on two public interactive segmentation benchmarks show that our method significantly improves the boundary quality of segmentation results compared to state-of-the-art methods while
requiring fewer user interactions.

1 Introduction

Separating objects from their backgrounds (the process often known as interactive object selection or interactive segmentation) is commonly required in many
image editing and visual effect workflows [6,25,33]. Over the past decades, many
efforts have been dedicated to interactive image segmentation. The main goal of
interactive segmentation methods is to harness user input as guidance to infer
the segmentation results from image information [11,18,22,30,36]. Many existing interactive segmentation methods follow the region-based paradigm in which
users roughly indicate foreground and/or background regions and the algorithm
infers the object segment. While the performance of region-based methods has
improved significantly in recent years, it is still often difficult to accurately trace

© Springer Nature Switzerland AG 2018
V. Ferrari et al. (Eds.): ECCV 2018, LNCS 11218, pp. 20–36, 2018.
https://doi.org/10.1007/978-3-030-01264-9_2

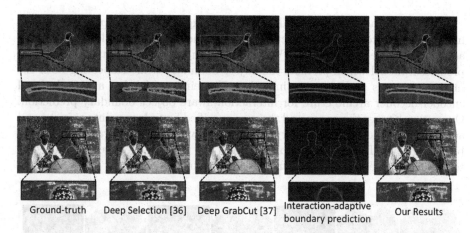

Ground-truth   Deep Selection [36]   Deep GrabCut [37]   Interaction-adaptive boundary prediction   Our Results

Fig. 1. Boundary-based segmentation with interactive boundary prediction. Our method adaptively predicts appropriate boundary maps for boundary-based segmentation, which enables segmentation results with better boundary quality compared to region-based approaches [36,37] in challenging cases such as thin, elongated objects (1st row), highly textured regions (2nd row).

the object boundary, especially for complex cases such as textures with large patterns or low-contrast boundaries (Fig. 1).

To segment objects with high-quality boundaries, more traditional boundary-based interactive segmentation tools [11,16,28] are still popular in practice [6, 33]. These methods allow users to explicitly interact with boundary pixels and have a fine-grained control which leads to high-quality segmentation results. The main limitation faced by existing boundary-based segmentation methods, however, is that they often demand much more user input. One major reason is that those methods rely solely on low-level image features such as gradients or edge maps which are often noisy and lack high-level semantic information. Therefore, a significant amount of user input is needed to keep the boundary prediction from getting distracted by irrelevant image features.

In this paper, we introduce a new approach that enables a user to obtain accurate object boundaries with relatively few interactions. Our work is motivated by two key insights. First, a good image feature map for boundary-based segmentation should not only encode high-level semantic image information but also adapt to the user intention. Without high-level semantic information, the boundary extraction process would be affected by irrelevant high-signal background regions as shown in Fig. 1. Second, we note that a unique property of interactive segmentation is that it is inherently ambiguous without knowledge of the user intentions. The boundary of interest varies across different users and different specific tasks. Using more advanced semantic deep feature maps, which can partially address the problem, may risk missing less salient boundary parts that users want (Fig. 2). In other words, a good boundary prediction model should be made adaptively throughout segmentation process.

Our key idea is that instead of using a single feature map pre-computed independently from user interactions, the boundary map should be predicted adaptively as the user interacts. We introduce an interaction-adaptive boundary prediction model which predicts the object boundary while respecting both the image semantics and the user intention. Therein, we develop a convolutional encoder-decoder architecture for interaction-aware object boundary prediction. Our network takes the image and the user-specified boundary points as input and adaptively predicts the boundary map, which we call the interaction-adaptive boundary map. The resulted boundary map can then be effectively leveraged to segment the object using standard geodesic path solvers [11].

Input Image   Our Result   Our Boundary   Result Using Low-   Low-level Edge   Result Using   Semantic Edge
                             Map   level Edge Map   Map [7]   Semantic Edge Map   Map [38]

Fig. 2. Adaptive boundary map vs. pre-computed feature maps. Low-level image features (e.g. image gradient maps or edge maps) often lack high-level semantic information, which distracts the boundary extraction with irrelevant image details. Using more advanced semantic deep feature maps [38], while partially addressing the problem, may risk missing parts of the desired boundary as the user intention is unknown prior to interaction.

Our main contribution in this paper is the novel boundary-based segmentation framework based on interactive boundary prediction. Our method adaptively predicts the boundary map according to both the input image and the user provided control points. Our predicted boundary map can not only predict the high-level boundaries in the image but also adapt the prediction to respect the user intention. Evaluations on two interactive segmentation benchmarks show that our method significantly improves the segmentation boundary quality compared to state-of-the-art methods while requiring fewer user interactions.

2   Related Work

Many interactive object selection methods have been developed over the past decades. Existing methods can be categorized into two main paradigms: region-based and boundary-based algorithms [16,22,24]. Region-based methods let users roughly indicate the foreground and background regions using bounding boxes [21,30,34,37], strokes [2,3,5,13,15,19,22,36], or multi-label strokes [31]. The underlying algorithms infer the actual object segments based on this user feedback. Recent work in region-based segmentation has been able to achieve impressive object segmentation accuracy [36,37], thanks to advanced deep learning frameworks. However, since no boundary constraints have been encoded, these methods often have difficulties generating high-quality segment boundaries, even with graph-cut based optimization procedures for post-processing.

Our research focuses on boundary-based interactive segmentation. This frameworks allow users to directly interact with object boundaries instead of image regions. Typically, users place a number of control points along the object boundary and the system optimizes the curves connecting those points in a piecewise manner [9,10,26,28,32]. It has been shown that the optimal curves can be formulated as a minimal-cost path finding problem on grid-based graphs [11,12]. Boundary segments are extracted as geodesic paths (i.e. minimal paths) between the user provided control points where the path cost is defined by underlying feature maps extracted from the image [9,10,17,26–28]. One fundamental limitation is that existing methods solely rely on low-level image features such as image gradient or edge maps, which prevents leveraging high-level image semantics. As a result, users must control the curve carefully which demands significant user feedback for difficult cases. In this paper, we introduce an alternative approach which predicts the boundary map adaptively as users interacts. In our method, the appropriate boundary related feature map is generated from a boundary map prediction model, leveraging the image and user interaction points as inputs.

Significant research has been conducted to better handle noisy low-level feature maps for boundary extraction [9,10,26,27,32]. The key principle is to leverage advanced energy models and minimal path finding methods that enable the incorporation of high-level priors and regularization such as curvature penalization [9,10,27], boundary simplicity [26], and high-order regularization [32]. Our work in this paper follows an orthogonal direction and can potentially benefit from the advances in this line of research. While those methods focus on developing new path solvers that work better with traditional image feature maps, we focus on obtaining better feature maps from which high-quality object boundaries can be computed using standard path solvers.

Our research is in part inspired by recent successes of deep neural networks in semantic edge detection [23,35,38]. It has been shown that high-level semantic edge and object contours can be predicted using convolutional neural networks trained end-to-end on segmentation data. While semantic edge maps can address the aforementioned lack of semantics in low-level feature maps, our work demonstrates that it is possible and more beneficial to go beyond pre-computed semantic edge maps. This paper is different from semantic edge detection in that we aim to predict the interaction-adaptive boundary with respect to not only the image information but also the user intention.

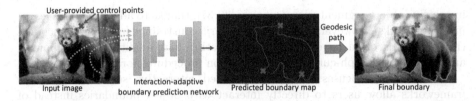

Fig. 3. Boundary extraction with interactive boundary map prediction. Given an image and a set of user provided control points, the boundary prediction network is used to predict a boundary map that reflects both high-level semantics in the image and user intention encoded in the control points to enable effective boundary extraction.

Our method determines the object boundary segments by connecting pairs of control points placed along the object boundary. In that regard, our system shares some similarities with the PolygonRNN framework proposed by Castrejon et al. [8]. There are two important differences between our method and PolygonRNN. First, our method takes arbitrary set of control points provided by the users while PolygonRNN predicts a set of optimal control points from an initial bounding box. More importantly, PolygonRNN mainly focuses on predicting the control points. They form the final segmentation simply by connecting those points with straight lines, which does not lead to highly accurate boundaries. Our method, on the other hand, focuses on predicting a boundary map from the user provided control points. The predicted boundary map can then be used to extract high-quality object boundaries with a minimal path solver.

3   Interactive Boundary Prediction for Object Selection

We follow the user interaction paradigm proposed by recent works in boundary-based segmentation [9,10,26] to support boundary segmentation with sparse user inputs: given an image and a set of user provided control points along the desired object boundary, the boundary segments connecting each pair of consecutive points are computed as minimal-cost paths in which the path cost is accumulated based on an underlying image feature map. Different from existing works in which the feature maps are low-level and pre-computed before any user interaction, our method adapts the feature map to user interaction: the appropriate feature map (boundary map) is predicted on-the-fly during the user interaction process using our boundary prediction network. The resulting boundary prediction map is used as the input feature map for a minimal path solver [12] to extract the object boundary. Figure 3 illustrates our overall framework.

3.1   Interaction-Adaptive Boundary Prediction Network

The core of our framework is the interaction-adaptive boundary map prediction network. Given an image and an ordered set of user provided control points as input, our network outputs a predicted boundary map.

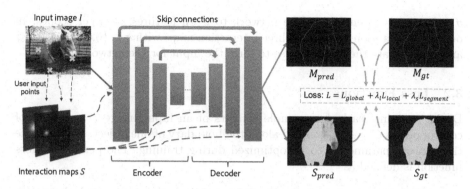

Fig. 4. Interactive boundary prediction network. The user-provided input points are converted to interaction maps S to use along with the image I as input channels for an encoder-decoder network. The predicted boundary map M_{pred} and segment map S_{pred} are used along with the corresponding ground-truth maps M_{gt}, S_{gt} to define the loss function during training.

Our interactive boundary prediction network follows a convolutional encoder-decoder architecture. The encoder consists of five convolutional blocks, each contains a convolution-ReLU layer and a 2×2 Max-Pooling layer. All convolutional blocks use 3×3 kernels. The decoder consists of five up-convolutional blocks, with each up-convolutional layer followed by a ReLU activation. We use 3×3 kernels for the first two up-convolutional blocks, 5×5 kernels for the next two blocks, and 7×7 kernels for the last blocks. To avoid blurry boundary prediction results, we include three skip-connections from the output of the encoder's first three convolutional blocks to the decoder's last three deconvolutional blocks. The network outputs are passed through a sigmoid activation function to transform their values to the range $[0, 1]$. Figure 4 illustrates our network model. It takes the concatenation of the RGB input image I and interaction maps as input. Its main output is the desired predicted boundary map. Additionally, the network also outputs a rough segmentation mask used for computing the loss function during training as described below.

Input Representation: To serve as the prediction network's input channels, we represent the user control points as 2-D maps which we call *interaction maps*. Formally, let $C = \{c_i | i = 1..N\}$ be spatial coordinates of the N user control points along the boundary. We compute a two-dimensional spatial map $S_{c_i}^{\sigma}$ for each point c_i as $S_{c_i}^{\sigma}(p) = \exp\left(\frac{-d(p,c_i)^2}{2(\sigma \cdot L)^2}\right)$ where $d(p, c_i)$ represents the Euclidean distance between pixel p and a control point c_i. L denotes the length of the smaller side of the image. Combining the interaction maps $S_{c_i}^{\sigma}$ from all individual control points c_i's with the pixel-wise max operator, the overall interaction map S for the control point set C is obtained.

The parameter σ controls the spatial extent of the control point in the interaction map. We observe that different values of σ offer different advantages. While a small σ value provides exact information about the location of selection, a larger

σ value tends to encourage the network to learn features at larger scopes. In our implementation, we create three interaction maps with $\sigma \in \{0.02, 0.04, 0.08\}$ and concatenate them depth-wise to form the input for the network.

3.2 Loss Functions

During training, each data sample consists of an input image I and a set of control points $C = \{c_i\}$ sampled along the boundary of one object. Let θ denote the network parameters to be optimized during training. The per-sample loss function is defined as

$$L(I, \{c_i\}; \theta) = L_{global}(I, \{c_i\}; \theta) + \lambda_l L_{local}(I, \{c_i\}; \theta) + \lambda_s L_{seg}(I, \{c_i\}; \theta) \quad (1)$$

where L_{local}, L_{global}, and $L_{segment}$ are the three dedicated loss functions designed specifically to encourage the network to leverage the global image semantic and the local boundary patterns into the boundary prediction process. λ_l and λ_s are the weights to balance the contribution of the loss terms. In our experiment, λ_l and λ_s are chosen to be 0.25 and 1.0 respectively using cross validation.

Global Boundary Loss: This loss encourages the network to learn useful features to detect the pixels belonging to the appropriate boundary. We treat the boundary detection problem as pixel-wise binary classification. The boundary pixel detection loss is defined using the binary cross entropy loss [4,14]

$$L_{global}(I, \{c_i\}; \theta) = \frac{-M_{gt} \cdot \log(M_{pred})^\top - (1 - M_{gt}) \cdot \log(1 - M_{pred})^\top}{|M_{gt}|} \quad (2)$$

where $M_{pred} = F_B(I, \{c_i\}; \theta)$ denotes the predicted boundary map straightened into a row vector. $|M_{gt}|$ denotes the total number of pixels in the ground-truth boundary mask M_{gt} (which has value 1 at pixels on the desired object boundary, and 0 otherwise). Minimizing this loss function encourages the network to be able to differentiate boundary and non-boundary pixels.

Local Selection-Sensitive Loss: We observe that a network trained with only L_{global} may perform poorly at difficult local boundary regions such as those with weak edges or complex patterns. Therefore, we design the local loss term L_{local} which penalizes low-quality boundary prediction near the user selection points.

Let G_i denote a spatial mask surrounding the control point c_i. Let $M_i = F_B(I, C_i; \theta)$ be the predicted boundary map generated with only one control point c_i. The local loss L_{local} is defined as a weighted cross entropy loss

$$L_{local}(I, \{c_i\}; \theta) = \frac{1}{|C|} \sum_{c_i \in C} \frac{-M_{gt} \odot G_i \cdot \log(M_i \odot G_i)^\top - (1 - M_{gt} \odot G_i) \cdot \log(1 - M_i \odot G_i)^\top}{|M_{gt}|}$$

$$(3)$$

where $\odot$ denotes the element-wise multiplication operation. This loss function is designed to explicitly encourage the network to leverage local information under the user selected area to make good localized predictions. To serve as the local mask, we use the interaction map component with $\sigma = 0.08$ at the corresponding location. Instead of aggregating individual interaction maps, we form a batch of inputs, each with the interaction map corresponding to one input control point. The network then produces a batch of corresponding predicted maps which are used to compute the loss value.

Segmentation-Aware Loss: While the boundary losses defined above encourage learning boundary-related features, it tends to lack the knowledge of what distinguishes foreground and background regions. Having some knowledge about whether neighboring pixels are likely foreground or background can provide useful information to complement the boundary detection process. We incorporate a segmentation prediction loss to encourage the network to encode knowledge of foreground and background. We augment our network with an additional decision layer to predict the segmentation map in addition to the boundary map.

Let $S_{pred} = F_S(I, \{c_i\}; \theta)$ denote the segmentation map predicted by the network. The loss function is defined in the form of binary cross entropy loss on the ground-truth binary segmentation map S_{gt} whose pixels have value 1 inside the object region, and 0 otherwise.

$$L_{segment}(I, \{c_i\}; \theta) = \frac{-S_{gt} \cdot \log(S_{pred})^\top - (1 - S_{gt}) \cdot \log(1 - S_{pred})^\top}{|S_{gt}|} \tag{4}$$

We note that all three loss terms are defined as differentiable functions over the network's output. The network parameters θ can hence be updated via back-propagation during training with standard gradient based methods [14].

3.3   Implementation Details

Our boundary prediction model is implemented in TensorFlow [1]. We train our network using the ADAM optimizer [20] with initial learning rate $\eta = 10^{-5}$. The network is trained for one million iterations, which takes roughly one day on an NVIDIA GTX 1080 Ti GPU.

Network Training with Synthetic User Inputs. To train our adaptive boundary prediction model, we collect samples from an image segmentation dataset [38] which consists of 2908 images from the PASCAL VOC dataset, post-processed for high-quality boundaries. Each training image is associated with multiple object masks. To create each data sample, we randomly select a subset of them to create the ground-truth boundary mask. We then randomly select k points along the ground-truth boundary to simulate user provided control points. Our training set includes data samples with k randomly selected in the range of 2 and 100 to simulate the effect of varying difficulty. We also use cropping, scaling, and blending for data augmentation.

Training with Multi-scale Prediction. To encourage the network to learn useful features to predict boundary at different scales, we incorporate multi-scale prediction into our method. Specifically, after encoding the input, each of the last three deconvolutional blocks of the decoder is trained to predict the boundary represented at the corresponding scale. The lower layers are encouraged to learn useful information to capture the large-scale boundary structure, while higher layers are trained to reconstruct the more fine-grained details. To encourage the network to take the user selection points into account, we also concatenate each decoder layer with the user selection map S described in Sect. 3.1.

Running Time. Our system consists of two steps. The boundary map prediction step, running a single feed-forward pass, takes about 70 ms. The shortest-path-finding step takes about 0.17 s to connect a pair of control points of length 300 pixels along the boundary.

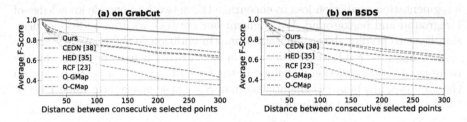

Fig. 5. Boundary quality at different boundary segment lengths. As expected, for all methods, the F-score quality decreases as l increases. Our adaptively predicted map consistently obtains higher F-score than non-adaptive feature maps. More importantly, our method performs significantly better with long boundary segments.

4   Experiments

We evaluate our method on two public interactive image segmentation benchmarks **GrabCut** [30] and **BSDS** [24] which consist of 50 and 96 images, respectively. Images in both datasets are associated with human annotated high-quality ground-truth object masks. For evaluation, we make use of two segmentation metrics proposed in [29]:

Intersection Over Union (IU): This is a region-based metric which measures the intersection over the union between a predicted segmentation mask S_{pred} and the corresponding ground-truth mask S_{gt}.

Boundary-Based F-score: This metric is designed to specifically evaluate the boundary quality of the segmentation result [29]. Given the ground-truth boundary map B_{gt} and the predicted boundary map B_{pred} connecting the same two control points, the F-score quality of B_{pred} is measured as:

$$F(B_{pred}; B_{gt}) = \frac{2 \times P(B_{pred}; B_{gt}) \times R(B_{pred}; B_{gt})}{P(B_{pred}; B_{gt}) + R(B_{pred}; B_{gt})} \qquad (5)$$

The P and R denote the precision and recall values, respectively computed as:

$$P(B_{pred}; B_{gt}) = \frac{|B_{pred} \odot dil(B_{gt}, w)|}{|B_{pred}|}; R(B_{pred}; B_{gt}) = \frac{|B_{gt} \odot dil(B_{pred}, w)|}{|B_{gt}|} \qquad (6)$$

where $\odot$ represents the pixel-wise multiplication between maps. $dil(B, w)$ denotes the dilation operator expanding the map B by w pixels. In our evaluation, we use $w = 2$ to emphasize accurate boundary prediction.

4.1 Effectiveness of Adaptive Boundary Prediction

This paper proposes the idea of adaptively generating the boundary map along with the user interaction instead of using pre-computed low-level feature maps. Therefore, we test the effectiveness of our adaptively predicted boundary map compared to non-adaptive feature maps in the context of path-based boundary extraction. To evaluate that quantitatively, we randomly sample the control points along the ground-truth boundary of each test image such that each pair of consecutive points are l pixels apart. We create multiple control point sets for each test image using different values of l ($l \in \{5, 10, 25, 50, 100, 150, 200, 250, 300\}$). We then evaluate each feature map by applying the same geodesic path solver [12] to extract the boundary-based segmentation results from the feature map and measure the quality of the result. We compare our predicted boundary map with two classes of non-adaptive feature maps:

Low-Level Image Features. Low-level feature maps based on image gradient are widely used in existing boundary-based segmentation works [11,18,26,28]. In this experiment, we consider two types of low-level feature maps: continuous image gradient maps and binary Canny edge maps [7]. We generate multiple of these maps from each test image using different edge sensitivity parameters ($\sigma \in 0.4, 0.6, 0.8, 1.0$). We evaluate results from all the gradient maps and edge maps and report the oracle best results among them which we named as **O-GMap** (for gradient maps) and **O-CMap** (for Canny edge maps).

Semantic Contour Maps. We also investigate replacing the low-level feature maps with semantic maps. In particular, we consider the semantic edge map produced by three state-of-the-art semantic edge detection methods [23,35,38], denoted as **CEDN**, **HED**, and **RCF** in our experiments.

Table 1 compares the overall segmentation result quality of our feature maps as well as the non-adaptive feature maps. The reported IU and F-score values are averaged over all testing data samples. This result indicates that in general the boundary extracted from our adaptive boundary map better matches the ground-truth boundary compared to those extracted from non-adaptive feature maps, especially in terms of the boundary-based quality metric F-score.

Table 1. Average segmentation quality from different feature maps.

		CEDN [38]	HED [35]	RCF [23]	O-GMap	O-CMap	Ours
GrabCut	F-score	0.7649	0.7718	0.8027	0.5770	0.6628	*0.9134*
	IU	0.8866	0.8976	0.9084	0.8285	0.8458	*0.9158*
BSDS	F-score	0.6825	0.7199	0.7315	0.5210	0.6060	*0.7514*
	IU	0.7056	0.7241	0.7310	0.6439	0.7230	*0.7411*

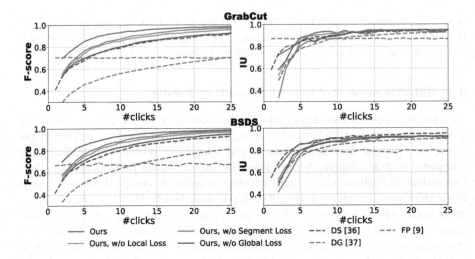

Fig. 6. Interactive segmentation quality. In terms of region-based metric IU, our method performs comparably with the state-of-the-art region-based method DS. Notably, our method significantly outperforms DS in terms of boundary F-score.

We further inspect the average F-score separately for different boundary segment lengths l. Intuitively, the larger the value of l the further the controls points are apart, making it more challenging to extract an accurate boundary. Figure 5 shows how the F-scores quality varies for boundary segments with different lengths l. As expected, for all methods, the F-score quality decreases as l increases. Despite that, we can observe the quality of our adaptively predicted map is consistently higher than that of non-adaptive feature map. More importantly, our method performs significantly better with long boundary segments, which demonstrates the potential of our method to extract the full object boundary with far fewer user clicks.

4.2 Interactive Segmentation Quality

The previous experiment evaluates the segmentation results generated when the set of control points are provided all at once. In this section, we evaluate our method in a more realistic interactive setting in which control points are provided sequentially during the segmentation process.

Evaluation with Synthetic User Inputs. Inspired by previous works on interactive segmentation [15,36], we quantitatively evaluate the segmentation performance by simulating the way a real user sequentially adds control points to improve the segmentation result. In particular, each time a new control point is added, we update the interaction map (Sect. 3.1) and use our boundary prediction network to re-generate the boundary map which in turn is used to update the segmentation result. We mimic the way a real user often behaves when using our system: a boundary segment (between two existing consecutive control points) with lowest F-score values is selected. From the corresponding ground-truth boundary segment, the simulator selects the point farthest from the currently predicted segment to serve as the new control point. The process starts with two randomly selected control points and continues until the maximum number of iterations (chosen to be 25 in our experiment) is reached.

We compare our method with three state-of-the-art interactive segmentation algorithms, including two region-based methods Deep Object Selection (DS) [36], Deep GrabCut (DG) [37] and one advanced boundary-based method Finsler-based Path Solver (FP) [9]. Note that FP uses the same user interaction mode as ours. Therefore, we evaluate those methods using the same simulation process as ours. For DS, we follow the simulation procedure described in [36] using the author provided implementation. For DG, we use the following simulation strategy: at the kth simulation step, k bounding boxes surrounding the ground-truth mask are randomly sampled. We always additionally include the tightest bounding box. From those bounding boxes, we use DG to generate k segmentation results and the highest-score one is selected as the result for that iteration.

| Ground-truth | Interaction adaptive boundary prediction | Our result | Deep Selection[36] | Deep Grabcut[37] | Finsler-based[9] |

Fig. 7. Visual comparison of segmentation results. We compare the segmentation results of our method to three state-of-the-art interaction segmentation methods.

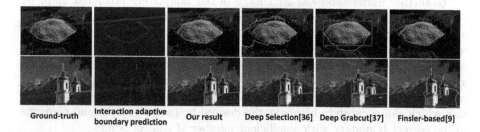

Fig. 8. Adaptivity analysis. By learning to predict the object boundary using both image content and user input, the boundary map produced by our network can evolve adaptively to reflect user intention as more input points are provided.

Figure 6 shows the average F-score and IU of each method for differing numbers of simulation steps on the GrabCut and the BSDS datasets. In terms of the region-based metric IU, our method performs as well as the state-of-the-art region-based method DS. Notably, our method significantly outperforms DS in terms of boundary F-score, which confirms the advantage of our method as a boundary-based method. This result demonstrates that our method can achieve superior boundary prediction even with fewer user interactions. We also perform an ablation study, evaluating the quality of the results generated with different variants of our boundary prediction network trained with different combinations of the loss functions. Removing each loss term during the network training tends to decrease the boundary-based quality of the resulting predicted map.

Figure 7 shows a visual comparison of our segmentation results and other methods after 15 iterations. These examples consist of objects with highly textured and low-contrast regions which are challenging for region-based segmentation as they rely on boundary optimization process such as graph-cut [36] or dense-CRF [37]. Our model, in contrast, learns to predict the boundary directly from both the input image and the user inputs to better handle these cases.

To further understand the advantage of our adaptively predicted map, we visually inspect the boundary maps predicted by our network as input points are added (Fig. 8). We observe that initially when the number of input points are too few to depict the boundary, the predicted boundary map tends to focus its confidence value at the local boundary regions surrounding the selected points and may generate some fuzzy regions. As more input points are provided, our model leverages the information from the additional points to update its prediction which can accurately highlight the desired boundary regions and converge to the correct boundary with a sufficient number of control points.

4.3 Evaluation with Human Users

We examine our méthod when used by human users with a preliminary user study. In this study, we compare our method with Intelligent Scissors (IS) [28] which is one of the most popular object selection tool in practice [25,33]. We utilize a publicly available implementation of IS[1]. In addition, we also experiment with a commercial version of IS known as Adobe Photoshop Magnetic Lasso (ML) which has been well optimized for efficiency and user interaction. Finally, we also include the state-of-the-art region-based system Deep Selection (DS) [36] in this study.

We recruit 12 participants for the user study. Given an input image and the expected segmentation result, each participant is asked to sequentially use each of the four tools to segment the object in the image to reproduce the expected result. Participants are instructed to use each tool as best as they can to obtain the best results possible. Prior to the study, each participant is provided a comprehensive training session to help them familiarize with the tasks and the segmentation tools. To represent challenging examples encountered in real-world

---

[1] github.com/AzureViolin.

tasks, we select eight real-world examples from the online image editing forum Reddit Photoshop Requests[2] by browsing with the keywords "isolate", "crop", and "silhouette" and picked the images that have a valid result accepted by the requester. Each image is randomly assigned to the participants. To reduce the order effect, we counter-balance the order of the tools used among participants.

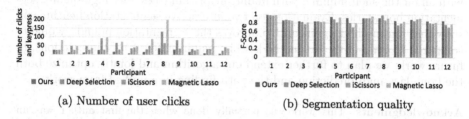

(a) Number of user clicks   (b) Segmentation quality

Fig. 9. Evaluation with real user inputs. In general, our method enables users to obtain segmentation results with better or comparable quality to state-of-the-art methods while using fewer interactions.

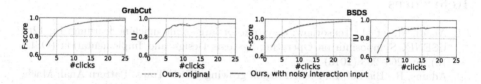

Fig. 10. Our method is robust against noisy interaction inputs

Figure 9 shows the amount of interaction (represented as number of mouse clicks) that each participant used with each methods and the corresponding segmentation quality. We observe that in most cases, the results obtained from our method are visually better or comparable with competing methods while needing much fewer user interactions.

Robustness Against Imperfect User Inputs. To examine our method's robustness with respect to noisy user inputs, we re-run the experiment in Sect. 4.2 with randomly perturbed simulated input points. Each simulated control point $c_i = (x_i, y_i)$ is now replaced by its noisy version $c'_i = (x_i + \delta_x, y_i + \delta_y)$. δ_x and δ_y are sampled from the real noise distribution gathered from our user study data (Sect. 4.3). For each user input point obtained in the user study, we identify the closest boundary point from it and measure the corresponding δ_x and δ_y. We collect the user input noise over all user study sessions to obtain the empirical noise distribution and use it to sample δ_x, δ_y. Figure 10 shows that our method is robust against the noise added to the input control points.

---

[2] www.reddit.com/r/PhotoshopRequest.

5   Conclusion

In this paper, we introduce a novel boundary-based segmentation method based on interaction-aware boundary prediction. We develop an adaptive boundary prediction model predicting a boundary map that is not only semantically meaningful but also relevant to the user intention. The predicted boundary can be used with an off-the-shelf minimal path finding algorithm to extract high-quality segmentation boundaries. Evaluations on two interactive segmentation benchmarks show that our method significantly improves the segmentation boundary quality compared to state-of-the-art methods while requiring fewer user interactions. In future work, we plan to further extend our algorithm and jointly optimize both the boundary map prediction and the path finding in a unified framework.

Acknowledgments. This work was partially done when the first author was an intern at Adobe Research. Figure 2 uses images from Flickr user Liz West and Laura Wolf, Fig. 3 uses an image from Flickr user Mathias Appel, and Fig. 8 uses an image from Flickr user GlobalHort Image Library/ Imagetheque under a Creative Commons license.

References

1. Abadi, M., et al.: Tensorflow: a system for large-scale machine learning. In: 12th USENIX Symposium on Operating Systems Design and Implementation (OSDI 16), pp. 265–283 (2016)
2. Adams, R., Bischof, L.: Seeded region growing. IEEE Trans. Pattern Anal. Mach. Intell. **16**(6), 641–647 (1994)
3. Bai, X., Sapiro, G.: A geodesic framework for fast interactive image and video segmentation and matting. In: IEEE International Conference on Computer Vision, pp. 1–8 (2007)
4. Bishop, C.M.: Pattern Recognition and Machine Learning. Springer, New York (2006)
5. Boykov, Y., Funka-Lea, G.: Graph cuts and efficient N-D image segmentation. Int. J. Comput. Vis. **70**(2), 109–131 (2006)
6. Brinkmann, R.: The Art and Science of Digital Compositing, 2nd edn. Morgan Kaufmann Publishers Inc., San Francisco (2008)
7. Canny, J.: A computational approach to edge detection. IEEE Trans. Pattern Anal. Mach. Intell. PAMI **8**(6), 679–698 (1986)
8. Castrejon, L., Kundu, K., Urtasun, R., Fidler, S.: Annotating object instances with a polygon-RNN. In: IEEE Conference on Computer Vision and Pattern Recognition, pp. 4485–4493 (2017)
9. Chen, D., Mirebeau, J.M., Cohen, L.D.: A new Finsler minimal path model with curvature penalization for image segmentation and closed contour detection. In: IEEE Conference on Computer Vision and Pattern Recognition, pp. 355–363 (2016)
10. Chen, D., Mirebeau, J.M., Cohen, L.D.: Global minimum for a finsler elastica minimal path approach. Int. J. Comput. Vis. **122**(3), 458–483 (2017)
11. Cohen, L.: Minimal paths and fast marching methods for image analysis. In: Paragios, N., Chen, Y., Faugeras, O. (eds.) Handbook of Mathematical Models in Computer Vision, pp. 97–111. Springer, Boston (2006). https://doi.org/10.1007/0-387-28831-7_6

12. Cohen, L.D., Kimmel, R.: Global minimum for active contour models: a minimal path approach. In: IEEE Conference on Computer Vision and Pattern Recognition, pp. 666–673 (1996)

13. Criminisi, A., Sharp, T., Blake, A.: GeoS: Geodesic Image Segmentation. In: Forsyth, D., Torr, P., Zisserman, A. (eds.) ECCV 2008. LNCS, vol. 5302, pp. 99–112. Springer, Heidelberg (2008). https://doi.org/10.1007/978-3-540-88682-2_9

14. Goodfellow, I., Bengio, Y., Courville, A.: Deep Learning. MIT Press (2016). http://www.deeplearningbook.org

15. Gulshan, V., Rother, C., Criminisi, A., Blake, A., Zisserman, A.: Geodesic star convexity for interactive image segmentation. In: IEEE Conference on Computer Vision and Pattern Recognition, pp. 3129–3136 (2010)

16. He, J., Kim, C.S., Kuo, C.C.J.: Interactive image segmentation techniques. Interactive Segmentation Techniques. SpringerBriefs in Electrical and Computer Engineering, pp. 17–62. Springer, Singapore (2014). https://doi.org/10.1007/978-981-4451-60-4_3

17. Jung, M., Peyré, G., Cohen, L.D.: Non-local active contours. In: Bruckstein, A.M., ter Haar Romeny, B.M., Bronstein, A.M., Bronstein, M.M. (eds.) SSVM 2011. LNCS, vol. 6667, pp. 255–266. Springer, Heidelberg (2012). https://doi.org/10.1007/978-3-642-24785-9_22

18. Kass, M., Witkin, A., Terzopoulos, D.: Snakes: active contour models. Int. J. Comput. Vis. 1(4), 321–331 (1988)

19. Kim, T.H., Lee, K.M., Lee, S.U.: Generative image segmentation using random walks with restart. In: Forsyth, D., Torr, P., Zisserman, A. (eds.) ECCV 2008. LNCS, vol. 5304, pp. 264–275. Springer, Heidelberg (2008). https://doi.org/10.1007/978-3-540-88690-7_20

20. Kingma, D.P., Ba, J.: Adam: a method for stochastic optimization. CoRR abs/1412.6980 (2014)

21. Lempitsky, V., Kohli, P., Rother, C., Sharp, T.: Image segmentation with a bounding box prior. In: IEEE International Conference on Computer Vision, pp. 277–284 (2009)

22. Li, Y., Sun, J., Tang, C.K., Shum, H.Y.: Lazy snapping. ACM Trans. Graph. 23(3), 303–308 (2004)

23. Liu, Y., Cheng, M.M., Hu, X., Wang, K., Bai, X.: Richer convolutional features for edge detection. In: IEEE Conference on Computer Vision and Pattern Recognition, pp. 5872–5881 (2017)

24. McGuinness, K., O'connor, N.E.: A comparative evaluation of interactive segmentation algorithms. Pattern Recognit. 43(2), 434–444 (2010)

25. McIntyre, C.: Visual Alchemy: The Fine Art of Digital Montage. Taylor & Francis, New York (2014)

26. Mille, J., Bougleux, S., Cohen, L.D.: Combination of piecewise-geodesic paths for interactive segmentation. Int. J. Comput. Vis. 112(1), 1–22 (2015)

27. Mirebeau, J.M.: Fast-marching methods for curvature penalized shortest paths. J. Math. Imaging Vis. 60(6), 784–815 (2017)

28. Mortensen, E.N., Barrett, W.A.: Intelligent scissors for image composition. In: Annual Conference on Computer Graphics and Interactive Techniques, SIGGRAPH 1995, pp. 191–198. ACM, New York (1995)

29. Perazzi, F., Pont-Tuset, J., McWilliams, B., Van Gool, L., Gross, M., Sorkine-Hornung, A.: A benchmark dataset and evaluation methodology for video object segmentation. In: IEEE Conference on Computer Vision and Pattern Recognition, pp. 724–732 (2016)

30. Rother, C., Kolmogorov, V., Blake, A.: GrabCut: interactive foreground extraction using iterated graph cuts. ACM Trans. Graph. **23**(3), 309–314 (2004)

31. Santner, J., Pock, T., Bischof, H.: Interactive multi-label segmentation. In: Kimmel, R., Klette, R., Sugimoto, A. (eds.) ACCV 2010. LNCS, vol. 6492, pp. 397–410. Springer, Heidelberg (2011). https://doi.org/10.1007/978-3-642-19315-6_31

32. Ulen, J., Strandmark, P., Kahl, F.: Shortest paths with higher-order regularization. IEEE Trans. Pattern Anal. Mach. Intell. **37**(12), 2588–2600 (2015)

33. Whalley, R.: Photoshop Layers: Professional Strength Image Editing: Lenscraft Photography (2015)

34. Wu, J., Zhao, Y., Zhu, J., Luo, S., Tu, Z.: MILCut: a sweeping line multiple instance learning paradigm for interactive image segmentation. In: IEEE Conference on Computer Vision and Pattern Recognition, pp. 256–263 (2014)

35. Xie, S., Tu, Z.: Holistically-nested edge detection. In: IEEE International Conference on Computer Vision, pp. 1395–1403 (2015)

36. Xu, N., Price, B., Cohen, S., Yang, J., Huang, T.S.: Deep interactive object selection. In: IEEE Conference on Computer Vision and Pattern Recognition, pp. 373–381 (2016)

37. Xu, N., Price, B.L., Cohen, S., Yang, J., Huang, T.S.: Deep grabcut for object selection. In: British Machine Vision Conference (2017)

38. Yang, J., Price, B., Cohen, S., Lee, H., Yang, M.H.: Object contour detection with a fully convolutional encoder-decoder network. In: IEEE Conference on Computer Vision and Pattern Recognition, pp. 193–202 (2016)

X-Ray Computed Tomography Through Scatter

Adam Geva[1], Yoav Y. Schechner[1(✉)], Yonatan Chernyak[1], and Rajiv Gupta[2]

[1] Viterbi Faculty of Electrical Engineering, Technion - Israel Institute of Technology, Haifa, Israel
{adamgeva,yonatanch}@campus.technion.ac.il, yoav@ee.technion.ac.il
[2] Massachusetts General Hospital, Harvard Medical School, Boston, USA
rgupta1@mgh.harvard.edu

Abstract. In current Xray CT scanners, tomographic reconstruction relies only on directly transmitted photons. The models used for reconstruction have regarded photons scattered by the body as noise or disturbance to be disposed of, either by acquisition hardware (an anti-scatter grid) or by the reconstruction software. This increases the radiation dose delivered to the patient. Treating these scattered photons as a source of information, we solve an inverse problem based on a 3D radiative transfer model that includes both elastic (Rayleigh) and inelastic (Compton) scattering. We further present ways to make the solution numerically efficient. The resulting tomographic reconstruction is more accurate than traditional CT, while enabling significant dose reduction and chemical decomposition. Demonstrations include both simulations based on a standard medical phantom and a real scattering tomography experiment.

Keywords: CT · Xray · Inverse problem · Elastic/inelastic scattering

1 Introduction

Xray computed tomography (CT) is a common diagnostic imaging modality with millions of scans performed each year. Depending on the Xray energy and the imaged anatomy, 30–60% of the incident Xray radiation is scattered by the body [15,51,52]. Currently, this large fraction, being regarded as noise, is either blocked from reaching the detectors or discarded algorithmically [10,15,20,27, 33,34,38,51,52]. An *anti-scatter grid* (ASG) is typically used to block photons scattered by the body (Fig. 1), letting only a filtered version pass to the detectors. Scatter statistics are sometimes modeled and measured in order to counter this "noise" algorithmically [20,27,32,44]. Unfortunately, scatter rejection techniques also discard a sizable portion of non-scattered photons.

Electronic supplementary material The online version of this chapter (https://doi.org/10.1007/978-3-030-01264-9_3) contains supplementary material, which is available to authorized users.

V. Ferrari et al. (Eds.): ECCV 2018, LNCS 11218, pp. 37–54, 2018.
https://doi.org/10.1007/978-3-030-01264-9_3

Scatter rejection has been necessitated by reconstruction algorithms used in conventional CT. These algorithms assume that radiation travels in a straight line through the body, from the Xray source to any detector, according to a linear, attenuation-based transfer model. This simplistic model, which assigns a linear attenuation coefficient to each reconstructed voxel in the body, simplifies the mathematics of Xray radiative transfer at the expense of accuracy and radiation dose to the patient. For example, the Bucky factor [7], i.e. the dose amplification necessitated by an ASG, ranges from 2× to 6×. Motivated by the availability of fast, inexpensive computational power, we reconsider the tradeoff between computational complexity and model accuracy.

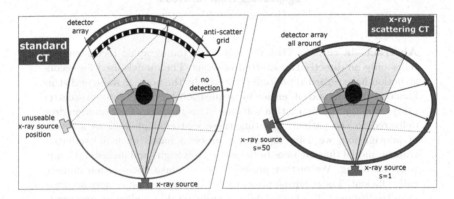

Fig. 1. In standard CT [left panel], an anti-scatter grid (ASG) near the detectors blocks the majority of photons scattered by the body (red), and many non-scattered photons. An ASG suits only one projection, necessitating rigid rotation of the ASG with the source. Removing the ASG [right panel] enables simultaneous multi-source irradiation and allows all photons passing through the body to reach the detector. Novel analysis is required to enable Xray scattering CT. (Color figure online)

In this work, we remove the ASG in order to tap scattered Xray photons for the image reconstruction process. We are motivated by the following potential advantages of this new source of information about tissue: (i) Scattering, being sensitive to individual elements comprising the tissue [5,11,35,38], may help deduce the chemical composition of each reconstructed voxel; (ii) Analogous to natural vision which relies on reflected/scattered light, back-scatted Xray photons may enable tomography when 360° access to the patient is not viable [22]; (iii) Removal of ASG will simplify CT scanners (Fig. 1) and enable 4th generation (a static detector ring) [9] and 5th generation (static detectors and distributed sources) [15,51] CT scanners; (iv) By using all the photons delivered to the patient, the new design can minimize radiation dose while avoiding related reconstruction artifacts [40,46] related to ASGs.

High energy scatter was previously suggested [5,10,22,31,38] as a source of information. Using a traditional γ-ray scan, Ref. [38] estimated the extinction field of the body. This field was used in a second γ-ray scan to extract a field of Compton scattering. Refs. [5,38] use nuclear γ-rays ($\mathscr{O}(100)$ keV) with an energy-sensitive photon detector and assume dominance of Compton *single* scattering events. Medical Xrays ($\mathscr{O}(10)$ keV) significantly undergo both Rayleigh and Compton scattering. Multiple scattering events are common and there is significant angular spread of scattering angles. Unlike visible light scatter [13,14,17–19,29,30,36,42,45,48,49], Xray Compton scattering is *inelastic* because the photon energy changes during interaction; this, in turn, changes the interaction cross sections. To accommodate these effects, our model does not limit the scattering model, angle and order and is more general than that in [13,14,19,29]. To handle the richness of Xrays interactions, we use first-principles for model-based image recovery.

2   Theoretical Background

2.1   Xray Interaction with an Atom

An Xray photon may undergo one of several interactions with an atom. Here are the major interactions relevant[1] to our work.

Rayleigh Scattering: An incident photon interacts with a *strongly bounded* atomic electron. Here the photon energy E_b does not suffice to free an electron from its bound state. No energy is transferred to or from the electron. Similarly to Rayleigh scattering in visible light, the photon changes direction by an angle θ_b while maintaining its energy. The photon is scattered effectively by the atom as a whole, considering the wave function of all Z_k electrons in the atom. Here Z_k is the atomic number of element k. This consideration is expressed by a *form factor*, denoted $F^2(E_b, \theta_b, Z_k)$, given by [21]. Denote solid angle by $d\Omega$. Then, the Rayleigh differential cross section for scattering to angle θ_b is

$$\frac{d\sigma_k^{\text{Rayleigh}}(E_b, \theta_b)}{d\Omega} = \frac{r_e^2}{2}\left[1 + \cos^2(\theta_b)\right] F^2(E_b, \theta_b, Z_k), \tag{1}$$

where r_e is the classical electron radius.

Compton Scattering: In this major Xray effect, which is inelastic and different from typical visible light scattering, the *photon changes its wavelength as it changes direction*. An incident Xray photon of energy E_b interacts with a *loosely bound* valence electron. The electron is ionized. The scattered photon now has a lower energy, E_{b+1}, given by a wavelength shift:

$$\Delta\lambda = hc\left(\frac{1}{E_{b+1}} - \frac{1}{E_b}\right) = \frac{h}{m_e c}(1 - \cos\theta_b). \tag{2}$$

---

[1] Some interactions require energies beyond medical Xrays. In *pair production*, a photon of at least 1.022 MeV transforms into an electron-positron pair. Other Xray processes with negligible cross sections in the medical context are detailed in [12].

Here h is Planck constant, c is the speed of light, and m_e is electron mass. Using $\epsilon = \frac{E_{b+1}}{E_b}$, the scattering cross section [26] satisfies

$$\frac{d\sigma_k^{\text{compton}}}{d\epsilon} = \pi r_e^2 \frac{m_e c^2}{E_b} Z_k \left[\frac{1}{\epsilon} + \epsilon\right] \left[1 - \frac{\epsilon \sin^2(\theta_b)}{1 + \epsilon^2}\right] . \tag{3}$$

Photo-Electric Absorption: In this case, an Xray photon transfers its entire energy to an atomic electron, resulting in a free photoelectron and a termination of the photon. The absorption cross-section of element k is $\sigma_k^{\text{absorb}}(E_b)$.

The scattering interaction is either *process* $\in \{\text{Rayleigh}, \text{Compton}\}$. Integrating over all scattering angles, the scattering cross sections are

$$\sigma_k^{\text{process}}(E_b) = \int_{4\pi} \frac{d\sigma_k^{\text{process}}(E_b, \theta_b)}{d\Omega} d\Omega , \tag{4}$$

$$\sigma_k^{\text{scatter}}(E_b) = \sigma_k^{\text{Rayleigh}}(E_b) + \sigma_k^{\text{Compton}}(E_b) . \tag{5}$$

The extinction cross section is

$$\sigma_k^{\text{extinct}}(E_b) = \sigma_k^{\text{scatter}}(E_b) + \sigma_k^{\text{absorb}}(E_b) . \tag{6}$$

Several models of photon cross sections exist in the literature, trading complexity and accuracy. Some parameterize the cross sections using experimental data [6, 21,47]. Others interpolate data from publicly evaluated libraries [37]. Ref. [8] suggests analytical expressions. Section 3 describes our chosen model.

2.2   Xray Macroscopic Interactions

In this section we move from atomic effects to macroscopic effects in voxels that have chemical compounds and mixtures. Let N^a denote Avogadro's number and A_k the molar mass of element k. Consider a voxel around 3D location $\mathbf{x}$. Atoms of element k reside there, in mass concentration $c_k(\mathbf{x})$ [grams/cm^3]. The number of atoms of element k per unit volume is then $N^a c_k(\mathbf{x})/A_k$. The *macroscopic differential cross sections* for scattering are then

$$\frac{d\Sigma^{\text{process}}(\mathbf{x}, \theta_b, E_b)}{d\Omega} = \sum_{k \in \text{elements}} \frac{N^a}{A_k} c_k(\mathbf{x}) \frac{d\sigma_k^{\text{process}}(E_b, \theta_b)}{d\Omega}. \tag{7}$$

The Xray *attenuation coefficient* is given by

$$\mu(\mathbf{x}, E_b) = \sum_{k \in \text{elements}} \frac{N^a}{A_k} c_k(\mathbf{x}) \sigma_k^{\text{extinct}}(E_b). \tag{8}$$

2.3   Linear Xray Computed Tomography

Let $I_0(\psi, E_b)$ be the Xray source radiance emitted towards direction ψ, at photon energy E_b. Let $S(\psi)$ be a straight path from the source to a detector. In traditional CT, the imaging model is a simplified version of the radiative transfer equation (see [12]). The simplification is expressed by the Beer-Lambert law,

$$I(\psi, E_b) = I_0(\psi, E_b) \exp \left[- \int_{S(\psi)} \mu(\mathbf{x}, E_b) d\mathbf{x} \right] . \qquad (9)$$

Here $I(\psi, E_b)$ is the intensity arriving to the detector in direction ψ. This model assumes that the photons scattered into $S(\psi)$ have no contribution to the detector signals. To help meet this assumption, traditional CT machines use an ASG between the object and the detector array. This model and the presence of the ASG necessarily mean that:

1. Scattered Xray photons, which constitute a large fraction of the total irradiation, are eliminated by the ASG.
2. Scattered Xray photons that reach the detector despite the ASG are treated as noise in the simplified model (9).
3. CT scanning is sequential because an ASG set for one projection angle cannot accommodate a source at another angle. Projections are obtained by rotating a large gantry with the detector, ASG, and the Xray source bolted on it.
4. The rotational process required by the ASG imposes a circular form to CT machines, which is generally not optimized for human form.

Medical Xray sources are polychromatic while detectors are usually energy-integrating. Thus, the attenuation coefficient μ is modeled for an effective energy E^*, yielding the linear expression

$$\ln \frac{I(\psi)}{I_0(\psi)} \approx - \int_{S(\psi)} \mu(\mathbf{x}, E^*) d\mathbf{x}. \qquad (10)$$

Measurements I are acquired for a large set of projections, while the source location and direction vary by rotation around the object. This yields a set of linear equations as Eq. (10). Tomographic reconstruction is obtained by solving this set of equations. Some solutions use filtered back-projection [50], while others use iterative optimization such as algebraic reconstruction techniques [16].

3   Xray Imaging Without an Anti-Scatter Grid

In this section we describe our forward model. It explicitly accounts for both elastic and inelastic scattering.

A photon path, denoted $\mathscr{L} = \mathbf{x}_0 \to \mathbf{x}_1 \to \dots \to \mathbf{x}_B$ is a sequence of B interaction points (Fig. 2). The line segment between $\mathbf{x}_{b-1}$ and $\mathbf{x}_b$ is denoted

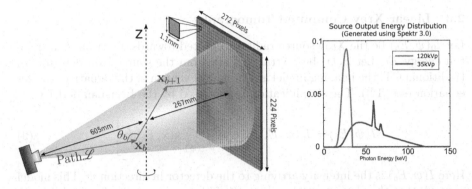

Fig. 2. [Left] `Cone to screen` setup. [Right] Energy distribution of emitted photons for 120 kVP (simulations), and 35 kVp (the voltage in the experiment), generated by [39].

$\overline{\mathbf{x}_{b-1}\mathbf{x}_b}$. Following Eqs. (8 and 9), the transmittance of the medium on the line segment is

$$a(\overline{\mathbf{x}_{b-1}\mathbf{x}_b}, E_b) = \exp\left[-\int_{\mathbf{x}_{b-1}}^{\mathbf{x}_b} \mu(\mathbf{x}, E_b)dx\right] . \tag{11}$$

At each scattering node b, a photon arrives with energy E_b and emerges with energy E_{b+1} toward $\mathbf{x}_{b+1}$. The unit vector between $\mathbf{x}_b$ and $\mathbf{x}_{b+1}$ is denoted $\widehat{\mathbf{x}_b\mathbf{x}_{b+1}}$. The angle between $\overline{\mathbf{x}_{b-1}\mathbf{x}_b}$ and $\widehat{\mathbf{x}_b\mathbf{x}_{b+1}}$ is θ_b. Following Eqs. (7 and 11), for either *process*, associate a probability for a scattering event at $\mathbf{x}_b$, which results in photon energy E_{b+1}

$$p(\overline{\mathbf{x}_{b-1}\mathbf{x}_b}\ \widehat{\mathbf{x}_b\mathbf{x}_{b+1}}, E_{b+1}) = a(\overline{\mathbf{x}_{b-1}\mathbf{x}_b}, E_b)\frac{d\Sigma^{process}(\mathbf{x}_b, \theta_b, E_b)}{d\Omega} . \tag{12}$$

If the process is Compton, then the energy shift $(E_b - E_{b+1})$, and angle θ_b are constrained by Eq. (2). Following [13], the probability P of a general path $\mathscr{L}$ is:

$$P(\mathscr{L}) = \prod_{b=1}^{B-1} p(\overline{\mathbf{x}_{b-1}\mathbf{x}_b}\ \widehat{\mathbf{x}_b\mathbf{x}_{b+1}}, E_{b+1}) . \tag{13}$$

The set of all paths which start at source s and terminate at detector d is denoted $\{s \to d\}$. The source generates N_p photons. When a photon reaches a detector, its energy is $E_B = E_{B-1}$. This energy is determined by Compton scattering along $\mathscr{L}$ and the initial source energy. The signal measured by the detector is modeled by the expectation of a photon to reach the detector, multiplied by the number of photons generated by the source, N_p.

$$i_{s,d} = N_p \int_{\mathscr{L}} \mathbb{1}_{s\to d}P(\mathscr{L})E_B(\mathscr{L})d\mathscr{L} \quad \text{where } \mathbb{1}_{s\to d} = \begin{cases} 1 \text{ if } \mathscr{L} \in \{s \to d\} \\ 0 \text{ else} \end{cases} \tag{14}$$

In Monte-Carlo, we sample this result empirically by generating virtual photons and aggregating their contribution to the sensors:

$$i_{s,d} = \sum_{\mathscr{L} \in \{s \to d\}} E_B(\mathscr{L}) \,. \tag{15}$$

Note that the signal integrates energy, rather than photons. This is in consistency with common *energy integrator* Xray detectors (Cesium Iodine), which are used both in our experiment and simulations.

For physical accuracy of Xray propagation, the Monte-Carlo model needs to account for many subtleties. For the highest physical accuracy, we selected the Geant4 Low Energy Livermore model [4], out of several publicly available Monte-Carlo codes [1,23,41]. Geant4 uses cross section data from [37], modified by atomic shell structures. We modified Geant4 to log every photon path. We use a voxelized representation of the object. A voxel is indexed v, and it occupies a domain $\mathscr{V}_v$. Rendering assumes that each voxel is internally uniform, i.e., the mass density of element k has a spatially uniform value $c_k(\mathbf{x}) = c_{k,v}, \forall \mathbf{x} \in \mathscr{V}_v$.

We dispose of the traditional ASG. The radiation sources and detectors can be anywhere around the object. To get insights, we describe two setups. Simulations in these setups reveal the contributions of different interactions:

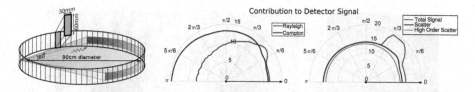

Fig. 3. [Left] **Fan to ring** setup. [Middle] Log-polar plots of signals due to Rayleigh and Compton single scattering. The source is irradiating from left to right. [Right] Log-polar plots of signals due to single scattering, all scattering, and all photons (red). The latter include direct transmission. The strong direct transmission side lobes are due to rays that do not pass through the object. (Color figure online)

Fan to ring; monochromatic rendering (Fig. 3): A ring is divided to 94 detectors. 100 fan beam sources are spread uniformly around the ring. The Xray sources in this example are monochromatic (60 keV photons), and generate 10^8 photons. Consequently, pixels between -60 deg and $+60$ deg opposite the source record direct transmission and scatter. Detectors in angles higher than 60 deg record only scatter. Sources are turned on sequentially.

The phantom is a water cube, 25 cm wide, in the middle of the rig. Figure 3 plots detected components under single source projection. About 25% of the total signal is scatter, almost half of which is of high order. From Fig. 3, Rayleigh dominates at forward angles, while Compton has significant backscatter.

Cone to screen; wide band rendering (Fig. 2): This simulation uses an Xray tube source. In it, electrons are accelerated towards a Tungsten target at 35 kVp.

As the electrons are stopped, Bremsstrahlung Xrays are emitted in a cone beam shape. Figure 2 shows the distribution of emitted photons, truncated to the limits of the detector. Radiation is detected by a wide, flat 2D screen (pixel array). This source-detector rig rotates relative to the object, capturing 180 projections.

The phantom is a discretized version of XCAT [43], a highly detailed phantom of the human body, used for medical simulations. The 3D object is composed of $100 \times 100 \times 80$ voxels. Figure 4 shows a projection and its scattering component. As seen in Fig. 4[Left] and [40], the scattering component varies spatially and cannot be treated as a DC term.

4 Inverse Problem

We now deal with the inverse problem. When the object is in the rig, the set of measurements is $\{i_{s,d}^{\mathrm{measured}}\}_{s,d}$ for $d = 1..N_{\mathrm{detectors}}$ and $s = 1..N_{\mathrm{sources}}$. A corresponding set of baseline images $\{j_{s,d}^{\mathrm{measured}}\}_{s,d}$ is taken when the object is absent. The unit-less ratio $i_{s,d}^{\mathrm{measured}}/j_{s,d}^{\mathrm{measured}}$ is invariant to the intensity of source s and the gain of detector d. Simulations of a rig empty of an object yield baseline model images $\{j_{s,d}\}_{s,d}$.

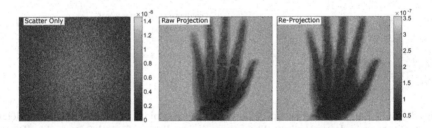

Fig. 4. [Left,Middle] Scatter only and total signal of one projection (1 out of 180) of a hand XCAT phantom. [Right] Re-projection of the reconstructed volume after 45 iterations of our Xray Scattering CT (further explained in the next sections).

To model the object, per voxel v, we seek the concentration $c_{k,v}$ of each element k, i.e., the voxel unknowns are $\boldsymbol{\nu}(v) = [c_{1,v}, c_{2,v}, ..., c_{N_{\mathrm{elements}},v}]$. Across all N_{voxels} voxels, the vector of unknowns is $\boldsymbol{\Gamma} = [\boldsymbol{\nu}(1), \boldsymbol{\nu}(2), ..., \boldsymbol{\nu}(N_{\mathrm{voxels}})]$. Essentially, we estimate the unknowns by optimization of a cost function $\mathscr{E}(\boldsymbol{\Gamma})$,

$$\hat{\boldsymbol{\Gamma}} = \arg\min_{\Gamma > 0} \mathscr{E}(\boldsymbol{\Gamma}) \ . \tag{16}$$

The cost function compares the measurements $\{i_{s,d}^{\mathrm{measured}}\}_{s,d}$ to a corresponding model image set $\{i_{s,d}(\boldsymbol{\Gamma})\}_{s,d}$, using

$$\mathscr{E}(\boldsymbol{\Gamma}) = \frac{1}{2} \sum_{d=1}^{N_{\mathrm{detectors}}} \sum_{s=1}^{N_{\mathrm{sources}}} m_{s,d} \left[i_{s,d}(\boldsymbol{\Gamma}) - j_{s,d} \frac{i_{s,d}^{\mathrm{measured}}}{j_{s,d}^{\mathrm{measured}}} \right]^2 \ . \tag{17}$$

Here $m_{s,d}$ is a mask which we describe in Sect. 4.2. The problem (16,17) is solved iteratively using stochastic gradient descent. The gradient of $\mathscr{E}(\boldsymbol{\Gamma})$ is

$$\frac{\partial \mathscr{E}(\boldsymbol{\Gamma})}{\partial c_{k,v}} = \sum_{d=1}^{N_{\text{detectors}}} \sum_{s=1}^{N_{\text{sources}}} m_{s,d} \left[i_{s,d}(\boldsymbol{\Gamma}) - j_{s,d} \frac{i_{s,d}^{\text{measured}}}{j_{s,d}^{\text{measured}}} \right] \frac{\partial i_{s,d}(\boldsymbol{\Gamma})}{\partial c_{k,v}} . \tag{18}$$

We now express $\partial i_{s,d}(\boldsymbol{\Gamma})/\partial c_{k,v}$. Inspired by [13], define a *score* of variable z

$$V_{k,v}\{z\} \equiv \frac{\partial \log(z)}{\partial c_{k,v}} = \frac{1}{z} \frac{\partial z}{\partial c_{k,v}} . \tag{19}$$

From Eq. (14),

$$\frac{\partial i_{s,d}}{\partial c_{k,v}} = \sum_{\mathscr{L} \in \text{paths}} \mathbb{1}\{s \to d\} \frac{\partial P(\mathscr{L})}{\partial c_{k,v}} E_B(\mathscr{L}) d\mathscr{L} =$$

$$N_{\text{p}} \int_{\mathscr{L} \in \text{paths}} \mathbb{1}\{s \to d\} P(\mathscr{L}) V_{k,v}\{P(\mathscr{L})\} E_B(\mathscr{L}) d\mathscr{L} . \tag{20}$$

Similarly to Monte-Carlo process of Eq. (15), the derivative (20) is stochastically estimated by generating virtual photons and aggregating their contribution:

$$\frac{\partial i_{s,d}}{\partial c_{k,v}} = \sum_{\mathscr{L} \in \{s \to d\}} V_{k,v}\{P(\mathscr{L})\} E_B(\mathscr{L}) . \tag{21}$$

Using Eqs. (12 and 13),

$$V_{k,v}\{P(\mathscr{L})\} = \sum_{b=1}^{B-1} V_{k,v}\{p(\overline{\mathbf{x}_{b-1}\mathbf{x}_b} \ \widehat{\mathbf{x}_b\mathbf{x}_{b+1}}, E_{b+1})\} =$$

$$\sum_{b=1}^{B-1} \left[V_{k,v}\{a(\overline{\mathbf{x}_{b-1}\mathbf{x}_b}, E_b)\} + V_{k,v}\left\{ \frac{d\Sigma^{\text{process}}(\mathbf{x}_b, \theta_b, E_b)}{d\Omega} \right\} \right] . \tag{22}$$

Generally, the line segment $\overline{\mathbf{x}_{b-1}\mathbf{x}_b}$ traverses several voxels, denoted $v' \in \overline{\mathbf{x}_{b-1}\mathbf{x}_b}$. Attenuation on this line segment satisfies

$$a(\overline{\mathbf{x}_{b-1}\mathbf{x}_b}, E_b) = \prod_{v' \in \overline{\mathbf{x}_{b-1}\mathbf{x}_b}} a_{v'}(E_b) , \tag{23}$$

where $a_{v'}$ is the transmittance by voxel v' of a ray along this line segment. Hence,

$$V_{k,v}\{a(\overline{\mathbf{x}_{b-1}\mathbf{x}_b}, E_b)\} = \sum_{v' \in \overline{\mathbf{x}_{b-1}\mathbf{x}_b}} V_{k,v}\{a_{v'}(E_b)\} . \tag{24}$$

Relying on Eqs. (6 and 8),

$$V_{k,v}\{a(\overline{\mathbf{x}_{b-1}\mathbf{x}_b}, E_b)\} = \begin{cases} \frac{N^{\text{a}}}{A_k} \sigma_{k,v}^{\text{extinct}}(E_b) l_v & \text{if } v \in \overline{\mathbf{x}_{b-1}\mathbf{x}_b} \\ 0 & \text{else} \end{cases} , \tag{25}$$

where l_v is the length of the intersection of line $\overline{\mathbf{x}_{b-1}\mathbf{x}_b}$ with the voxel domain $\mathscr{V}_v$. A similar derivation yields

$$V_{k,v}\left\{\frac{d\Sigma^{\text{process}}(\mathbf{x}_b,\theta_b,E_b)}{d\Omega}\right\}=$$

$$\begin{cases} \frac{N}{A_k}\left[\frac{d\Sigma^{\text{process}}(\mathbf{x}_b,\theta_b,E_b)}{d\Omega}\right]^{-1}\frac{d\sigma_k^{\text{process}}(E_b,\theta_b)}{d\Omega} & \text{if } \mathbf{x}_b \in \mathscr{V}_v \\ 0 & \text{else} \end{cases}. \tag{26}$$

A Geant4 Monte-Carlo code renders photon paths, thus deriving $i_{s,d}$ using Eq. (15). Each photon path log then yields $\partial i_{s,d}(\boldsymbol{\Gamma})/\partial c_{k,v}$, using Eqs. (21, 22, 25 and 26). The modeled values $i_{s,d}$ and $\partial i_{s,d}(\boldsymbol{\Gamma})/\partial c_{k,v}$ then derive the cost function gradient by Eq. (18). Given the gradient (18), we solve the problem (16, 17) stochastically using adaptive moment estimation (ADAM) [25].

4.1   Approximations

Solving an inverse problem requires the gradient to be repeatedly estimated during optimization iterations. Each gradient estimation relies on Monte-Carlo runs, which are either very noisy or very slow, depending on the number of simulated photons. To reduce runtime, we incorporated several approximations.

Fewer Photons. During iterations, only 10^7 photons are generated per source when rendering $i_{s,d}(\boldsymbol{\Gamma})$. For deriving $\partial i_{s,d}(\boldsymbol{\Gamma})/\partial c_{k,v}$, only 10^5 photons are tracked. **A reduced subset of chemical elements.** Let us focus only on elements that are most relevant to Xray interaction in tissue. Elements whose contribution to the macroscopic *scattering* coefficient is highest, cause the largest deviation from the linear CT model (Sect. 2.3). From (5), the macroscopic scattering coefficient due to element k is $\Sigma_k^{\text{scatter}}(\mathbf{x},E_b)=(N^{\text{a}}/A_k)c_k(\mathbf{x})\sigma_k^{\text{scatter}}(E_b)$. Using the typical concentrations c_k of all elements k in different tissues [43], we derive $\Sigma_k^{\text{scatter}}$, $\forall k$. The elements leading to most scatter are listed in Table 1. Optimization of $\boldsymbol{\Gamma}$ focuses only on the top six.

Table 1. Elemental macroscopic scatter coefficient $\Sigma_k^{\text{scatter}}$ in human tissue $[m^{-1}]$ for photon energy 60keV. Note that for a typical human torso of $\approx 0.5\,\text{m}$, the optical depth of Oxygen in blood is ≈ 9, hence high order scattering is significant.

Element	Muscle	Lung	Bone	Adipose	Blood
O	17.1	5.0	19.2	6.1	18.2
C	3.2	0.6	6.2	11.9	2.4
H	3.9	1.1	2.4	3.9	3.9
Ca	0.0	0.0	18.2	0.0	0.0
P	0.1	0.0	6.4	0.0	0.0
N	0.8	0.2	1.8	0.1	0.8
K	0.2	0.0	0.0	0.0	0.1

Furthermore, we cluster these elements into *three* arch-materials. As seen in Fig. 5, Carbon (C), Nitrogen (N) and Oxygen (O) form a cluster having similar absorption and scattering characteristics. Hence, for Xray imaging purposes, we treat them as a single arch-material, denoted $\widetilde{O}$. We set the atomic cross section of $\widetilde{O}$ as that of Oxygen, due to the latter's dominance in Table 1. The second arch-material is simply hydrogen (H), as it stands distinct in Fig. 5. Finally, note that in bone, Calcium (Ca) and Phosphor (P) have scattering significance. We thus set an arch-material mixing these elements by a fixed ratio $c_{P,v}/c_{Ca,v} = 0.5$, which is naturally occurring across most human tissues. We denote this arch-material $\widetilde{Ca}$. Following these physical considerations, the optimization thus seeks the vector $\boldsymbol{\nu}(v) = [c_{\widetilde{O},v}, c_{H,v}, c_{\widetilde{Ca},v}]$ for each voxel v.

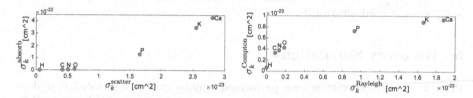

Fig. 5. [Left] Absorption vs. scattering cross sections (σ_k^{absorb} vs. $\sigma_k^{\text{scatter}}$) of elements which dominate scattering by human tissue. Oxygen (O), Carbon (C) and Nitrogen (N) form a tight cluster, distinct from Hydrogen (H). They are all distinct from bone-dominating elements Calcium (Ca) and Phosphor (P). [Right] Compton vs. Rayleigh cross sections ($\sigma_k^{\text{Compton}}$ vs. $\sigma_k^{\text{Rayleigh}}$). Obtained for 60keV photon energy.

No Tracking of Electrons. We modified Geant4, so that object electrons affected by Xray photons are not tracked. This way, we lose later interactions of these electrons, which potentially contribute to real detector signals.

Ideal Detectors. A photon deposits its entire energy at the detector and terminates immediately upon hitting the detector, rather than undergoing a stochastic set of interactions in the detector.

4.2 Conditioning and Initialization

Poissonian photon noise means that $i_{s,d}^{\text{measured}}$ has uncertainty of $(i_{d,s}^{\text{measured}})^{1/2}$. Mismatch between model and measured signals is thus more tolerable in high-intensity signals. Thus, Eq. (18) includes a mask $m_{s,d} \sim (i_{d,s}^{\text{measured}})^{-1/2}$. Moreover, $m_{s,d}$ is null if $\{s \to d\}$ is a straight ray having no intervening object. Photon noise there is too high, which completely overwhelms subtle off-axis scattering from the object. These s, d pairs are detected by thresholding $i_{s,d}^{\text{measured}}/j_{s,d}^{\text{measured}}$.

Due to extinction, a voxel v deeper in the object experiences less passing photons P_v than peripheral object areas. Hence, $\partial i_{s,d}(\boldsymbol{\Gamma})/\partial c_{k,v}$ is often much lower for voxels near the object core. This effect may inhibit conditioning of the inverse problem, jeopardizing its convergence rate. We found that weighting $\partial i_{s,d}(\boldsymbol{\Gamma})/\partial c_{k,v}$ by $(P_v + 1)^{-1}$ helps to condition the approach.

Optimization is initialized by the output of linear analysis (Sect. 2.3), which is obtained by a simultaneous algebraic reconstruction technique (SART) [3]. That is, the significant scattering is ignored in this initial calculation. Though it erroneously assumes we have an ASG, SART is by far faster than scattering-based analysis. It yields an initial extinction coefficient $\mu_v^{(0)}$, which provides a crude indicator to the tissue type at v.

Beyond extinction coefficient, we need initialization on the relative proportions of $[c_{\widetilde{O},v}, c_{H,v}, c_{\widetilde{Ca},v}]$. This is achieved using a rough preliminary classification of the tissue type per v, based on $\mu_v^{(0)}$, through the DICOM toolbox [24]. For this assignment, DICOM uses data from the International Commission on Radiation Units and Measurements (ICRU). After this initial setting, the concentrations $[c_{\widetilde{O},v}, c_{H,v}, c_{\widetilde{Ca},v}]$ are free to change. The initial extinction and concentration fields are not used afterwards.

5   Recovery Simulations

Prior to a real experiment, we performed simulations of increasing complexity. Simulations using a `Fan to ring; box phantom` setup are shown in [12]. We now present the `Cone to screen; XCAT phantom` example. We initialized the reconstruction with linear reconstruction using an implementation of the FDK [50] algorithm. We ran several tests:

(i) We used the XCAT hand materials and densities. We set the source tube voltage to 120kVp, typical to many clinical CT scanners (Fig. 2). Our scattering CT algorithm ran for 45 iterations. In every iteration, the cost gradient was calculated based on random three (out or 180) projections. To create a realistic response during data rendering, 5×10^7 photons were generated in every projection. A re-projection after recovery is shown in Fig. 4. Results of a reconstructed slice are shown in Fig. 6[Top]. Table 2 compares linear tomography to our Xray Scattering CT using the error terms ϵ, δ_{mass} [2,12,19,29,30]. Examples of other reconstructed slices are given in [12]. Figure 6[Bottom] shows the recovered concentrations $c_k(\mathbf{x})$ of the three arch-materials described in Sect. 4. Xray scattering CT yields information that is difficult to obtain using traditional linear panchromatic tomography.

Table 2. Reconstruction errors. Linear tomography vs. Xray Scattering CT recovery

		Z Slice #40	Y Slice #50	Total volume
Linear Tomography	ϵ, δ_{mass}	76%, 72%	24%, 15%	80%, 70%
Xray Scattering CT	ϵ, δ_{mass}	28%, 3%	18%, −11%	30%, 1%

(ii) *Quality vs. dose analysis*, XCAT human thigh. To assess the benefit of our method in reducing dose to the patient, we compared linear tomography with/without ASG to our scattering CT (with no ASG). Following [9,28], the ASG was simulated with fill factor 0.7, and cutoff incident scatter angle $\pm 6°$. We measured the reconstruction error for different numbers of incident photons (proportional to dose). Figure 7 shows the reconstructions ϵ error, and the contrast to noise ratio (CNR) [40].

(iii) *Single-Scatter Approximation* [17] was tested as a means to advance initialization. In our thigh test (using 9×10^9 photons), post linear model initialization, single-scatter analysis yields CNR = 0.76. Using single-scatter to initialize multi-scatter analysis yields eventual CNR = 1.02. Histograms of scattering events in the objects we tested are in [12].

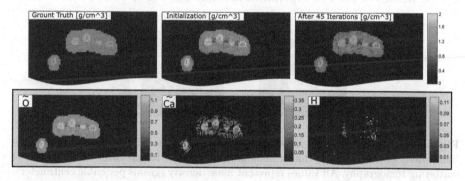

Fig. 6. [Top] Results of density recovery of slice # 40 (Z-axis, defined in Fig. 2) of the XCAT hand phantom. [Bottom] concentration of our three arch-materials. Material $\widetilde{O}$ appear in all tissues and in the surrounding air. Material $\widetilde{Ca}$ is dominant in the bones. Material H appears sparsely in the soft tissue surrounding the bones.

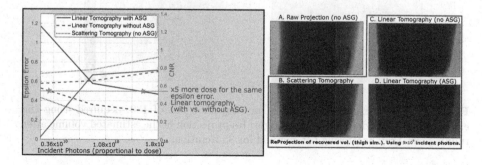

Fig. 7. Simulated imaging and different recovery methods of a human thigh.

6   Experimental Demonstration

The experimental setup was identical to the Cone to screen simulation of the XCAT hand. We mounted a Varian flat panel detector having resolution of 1088×896 pixels. The source was part of a custom built 7-element Xray source, which is meant for future experiments with several sources turned on together. In this experiment, only one source was operating at 35kVp, producing a cone beam. This is contrary to the simulation (Sect. 5) where the Xray tube tube voltage is 120 kVp. We imaged a swine lung, and collected projections from 180 angles. The raw images were then down-sampled by 0.25. Reconstruction was done for a $100 \times 100 \times 80$ 3D grid. Here too, linear tomography provided initialization. Afterward the scattering CT algorithm ran for 35 iterations. Runtime was ≈ 6 min/iteration using 35 cores of Intel(R) Xeon(R) E5-2670 v2 @ 2.50 GHz CPU's. Results of the real experiment are shown in Figs. 8 and 9.

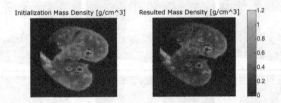

Fig. 8. Real data experiment. Slice (#36) of the reconstructed 3D volume of the swine lung. [Left] Initialization by linear tomography. [Right]: Result after 35 iterations of scattering tomography. All values represent mass density (grams per cubic centimeter).

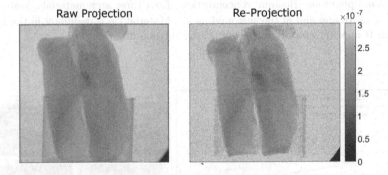

Fig. 9. Real data experiment. [Left] One projection out of 180, acquired using the experimental setup detailed in [12]. [Right] Re-projection of the estimated volume after running our Xray Scattering CT method for 35 iterations.

7 Discussion

This work generalized Xray CT to multi-scattering, all-angle imaging, without an ASG. Our work, which exploits scattering as part of the signal rather than rejecting it as noise, generalizes prior art on scattering tomography by incorporating inelastic radiative transfer. Physical considerations about chemicals in the human body are exploited to simplify the solution.

We demonstrate feasibility using small body parts (e.g., thigh, hand, swine lung) that can fit in our experimental setup. These small-sized objects yield little scatter (scatter/ballistic ≈ 0.2 for small animal CT [33]). As a result, improvement in the estimated extinction field (e.g., that in Fig. 6 [Top]) is modest. Large objects have much more scattering (see caption of Table 1). For large body parts (e.g., human pelvis), scatter/ballistic >1 has been reported [46]. Being large, a human body will require larger experimental scanners than ours.

Total variation can improve the solution. A multi-resolution procedure can be used, where the spatial resolution of the materials progressively increases [13]. Runtime is measured in hours on our local computer server. This time is comparable to some current routine clinical practices (e.g. vessel extraction). Runtime will be reduced significantly using variance reduction techniques and Monte-Carlo GPU implementation. Hence, we believe that scattering CT can be developed for clinical practice. An interesting question to follow is how multiple sources in a 5th generation CT scanner can be multiplexed, while taking advantage of the ability to process scattered photons.

Acknowledgments. We thank V. Holodovsky, A. Levis, M. Sheinin, A. Kadambi, O. Amit, Y. Weissler for fruitful discussions, A. Cramer, W. Krull, D. Wu, J. Hecla, T. Moulton, and K. Gendreau for engineering the static CT scanner prototype, and I. Talmon and J. Erez for technical support. YYS is a Landau Fellow - supported by the Taub Foundation. His work is conducted in the Ollendorff Minerva Center. Minerva is funded by the BMBF. This research was supported by the Israeli Ministry of Science, Technology and Space (Grant 3-12478). RG research was partially supported by the following grants: Air Force Contract Number FA8650-17-C-9113; US Army USAMRAA Joint Warfighter Medical Research Program, Contract No. W81XWH-15-C-0052; Congressionally Directed Medical Research Program W81XWH-13-2-0067.

References

1. Agostinelli, S., et al.: Geant4-a simulation toolkit. Nucl. Instrum. Methods Phys. Res. Sect. A: Accel., Spectrometers, Detect. Assoc. Equip. **506**(3), 250–303 (2003)
2. Aides, A., Schechner, Y.Y., Holodovsky, V., Garay, M.J., Davis, A.B.: Multi sky-view 3D aerosol distribution recovery. Opt. Express **21**(22), 25820–25833 (2013)
3. Andersen, A., Kak, A.: Simultaneous algebraic reconstruction technique (SART): a superior implementation of the art algorithm. Ultrason. Imaging **6**(1), 81–94 (1984)
4. Apostolakis, J., Giani, S., Maire, M., Nieminen, P., Pia, M.G., Urbàn, L.: Geant4 low energy electromagnetic models for electrons and photons. CERN-OPEN-99-034, August 1999

5. Arendtsz, N.V., Hussein, E.M.A.: Energy-spectral compton scatter imaging - part 1: theory and mathematics. IEEE Trans. Nucl. Sci. **42**, 2155–2165 (1995)
6. Biggs, F., Lighthill, R.: Analytical approximations for X-ray cross sections. Preprint Sandia Laboratory, SAND 87–0070 (1990)
7. Bor, D., Birgul, O., Onal, U., Olgar, T.: Investigation of grid performance using simple image quality tests. J. Med. Phys. **41**, 21–28 (2016)
8. Brusa, D., Stutz, G., Riveros, J., Salvat, F., Fernández-Varea, J.: Fast sampling algorithm for the simulation of photon compton scattering. Nucl. Instrum. Methods Phys. Res., Sect. A: Accel., Spectrometers, Detect. Assoc. Equip. **379**(1), 167–175 (1996)
9. Buzug, T.M.: Computed Tomography: From Photon Statistics to Modern Cone-Beam CT. Springer, Heidelberg (2008). https://doi.org/10.1007/978-3-540-39408-2
10. Cong, W., Wang, G.: X-ray scattering tomography for biological applications. J. X-Ray Sci. Technol. **19**(2), 219–227 (2011)
11. Cook, E., Fong, R., Horrocks, J., Wilkinson, D., Speller, R.: Energy dispersive X-ray diffraction as a means to identify illicit materials: a preliminary optimisation study. Appl. Radiat. Isot. **65**(8), 959–967 (2007)
12. Geva, A., Schechner, Y., Chernyak, Y., Gupta, R.: X-ray computed tomography through scatter: Supplementary material. In: Ferrari, V. (ed.) ECCV 2018, Part XII. LNCS, vol. 11218, pp. 37–54. Springer, Cham (2018)
13. Gkioulekas, I., Levin, A., Zickler, T.: An evaluation of computational imaging techniques for heterogeneous inverse scattering. In: European Conference on Computer Vision (ECCV) (2016)
14. Gkioulekas, I., Zhao, S., Bala, K., Zickler, T., Levin, A.: Inverse volume rendering with material dictionaries. ACM Trans. Graph. **32**, 162 (2013)
15. Gong, H., Yan, H., Jia, X., Li, B., Wang, G., Cao, G.: X-ray scatter correction for multi-source interior computed tomography. Med. Phys. **44**, 71–83 (2017)
16. Gordon, R., Bender, R., Herman, G.: Algebraic reconstruction techniques (ART) for three-dimensional electron microscopy and X-ray photography. J. Theor. Biol. **29**(3), 471–476 (1970)
17. Gu, J., Nayar, S.K., Grinspun, E., Belhumeur, P.N., Ramamoorthi, R.: Compressive structured light for recovering inhomogeneous participating media. IEEE Trans. Pattern Anal. Mach. Intell. **35**(3), 1–1 (2013)
18. Heide, F., Xiao, L., Kolb, A., Hullin, M.B., Heidrich, W.: Imaging in scattering media using correlation image sensors and sparse convolutional coding. Opt. Express **22**(21), 26338–26350 (2014)
19. Holodovsky, V., Schechner, Y.Y., Levin, A., Levis, A., Aides, A.: In-situ multi-view multi-scattering stochastic tomography. In: IEEE International Conference on Computational Photography (ICCP) (2016)
20. Honda, M., Kikuchi, K., Komatsu, K.I.: Method for estimating the intensity of scattered radiation using a scatter generation model. Med. Phys. **18**(2), 219–226 (1991)
21. Hubbell, J.H., Gimm, H.A., Øverbø, I.: Pair, triplet, and total atomic cross sections (and mass attenuation coefficients) for 1 MeV to 100 GeV photons in elements Z = 1 to 100. J. Phys. Chem. Ref. Data **9**(4), 1023–1148 (1980)
22. Hussein, E.M.A.: On the intricacy of imaging with incoherently-scattered radiation. Nucl. Inst. Methods Phys. Res. B **263**, 27–31 (2007)
23. Kawrakow, I., Rogers, D.W.O.: The EGSnrc code system: Monte carlo simulation of electron and photon transport. NRC Publications Archive (2000)

24. Kimura, A., Tanaka, S., Aso, T., Yoshida, H., Kanematsu, N., Asai, M., Sasaki, T.: DICOM interface and visualization tool for Geant4-based dose calculation. IEEE Nucl. Sci. Symp. Conf. Rec. **2**, 981–984 (2005)

25. Kingma, D.P., Ba, J.: Adam: a method for stochastic optimization. In: 3rd International Conference for Learning Representations (ICLR) (2015)

26. Klein, O., Nishina, Y.: Über die streuung von strahlung durch freie elektronen nach der neuen relativistischen quantendynamik von dirac. Zeitschrift für Physik **52**(11), 853–868 (1929)

27. Kyriakou, Y., Riedel, T., Kalender, W.A.: Combining deterministic and Monte Carlo calculations for fast estimation of scatter intensities in CT. Phys. Med. Biol. **51**(18), 4567 (2006)

28. Kyriakou, Y., Kalender, W.A.: Efficiency of antiscatter grids for flat-detector CT. Phys. Med. Biol. **52**(20), 6275 (2007)

29. Levis, A., Schechner, Y.Y., Aides, A., Davis, A.B.: Airborne three-dimensional cloud tomography. In: IEEE International Conference on Computer Vision (ICCV) (2015)

30. Levis, A., Schechner, Y.Y., Davis, A.B.: Multiple-scattering microphysics tomography. In: IEEE Computer Vision and Pattern Recognition (CVPR) (2017)

31. Lionheart, W.R.B., Hjertaker, B.T., Maad, R., Meric, I., Coban, S.B., Johansen, G.A.: Non-linearity in monochromatic transmission tomography. arXiv: 1705.05160 (2017)

32. Lo, J.Y., Floyd Jr., C.E., Baker, J.A., Ravin, C.E.: Scatter compensation in digital chest radiography using the posterior beam stop technique. Med. Phys. **21**(3), 435–443 (1994)

33. Mainegra-Hing, E., Kawrakow, I.: Fast Monte Carlo calculation of scatter corrections for CBCT images. J. Phys.: Conf. Ser. **102**(1), 012017 (2008)

34. Mainegra-Hing, E., Kawrakow, I.: Variance reduction techniques for fast monte carlo CBCT scatter correction calculations. Phys. Med. Biol. **55**(16), 4495–4507 (2010)

35. Malden, C.H., Speller, R.D.: A CdZnTe array for the detection of explosives in baggage by energy-dispersive X-ray diffraction signatures at multiple scatter angles. Nucl. Instrum. Methods Phys. Res. Sect. A: Accel., Spectrometers, Detect. Assoc. Equip. **449**(1), 408–415 (2000)

36. Narasimhan, S.G., Gupta, M., Donner, C., Ramamoorthi, R., Nayar, S.K., Jensen, H.W.: Acquiring scattering properties of participating media by dilution. ACM Trans. Graph. **25**(3), 1003–1012 (2006)

37. Perkins, S.T., Cullen, D.E., Seltzer, S.M.: Tables and graphs of electron-interaction cross sections from 10 eV to 100 Gev derived from the LLNL evaluated electron data library (EEDL), Z = 1 to 100. Lawrence Livermore National Lab, UCRL-50400 31 (1991)

38. Prettyman, T.H., Gardner, R.P., Russ, J.C., Verghese, K.: A combined transmission and scattering tomographic approach to composition and density imaging. Appl. Radiat. Isot. **44**(10–11), 1327–1341 (1993)

39. Punnoose, J., Xu, J., Sisniega, A., Zbijewski, W., Siewerdsen, J.H.: Technical note: spektr 3.0-a computational tool for X-ray spectrum modeling and analysis. Med. Phys. **43**(8), 4711–4717 (2016)

40. Rana, R., Akhilesh, A.S., Jain, Y.S., Shankar, A., Bednarek, D.R., Rudin, S.: Scatter estimation and removal of anti-scatter grid-line artifacts from anthropomorphic head phantom images taken with a high resolution image detector. In: Proceedings of SPIE 9783 (2016)

41. Salvat, F., Fernández-Varea, J., Sempau, J.: Penelope 2008: a code system for Monte Carlo simulation of electron and photon transport. In: Nuclear energy agency OECD, Workshop proceedings (2008)

42. Satat, G., Heshmat, B., Raviv, D., Raskar, R.: All photons imaging through volumetric scattering. Sci. Rep. **6**, 33946 (2016)

43. Segars, W., Sturgeon, G., Mendonca, S., Grimes, J., Tsui, B.M.W.: 4D XCAT phantom for multimodality imaging research. Med. Phys. **37**, 4902–4915 (2010)

44. Seibert, J.A., Boone, J.M.: X ray scatter removal by deconvolution. Med. Phys. **15**(4), 567–575 (1988)

45. Sheinin, M., Schechner, Y.Y.: The next best underwater view. In: IEEE Computer Vision and Pattern Recognition (CVPR) (2016)

46. Siewerdsen, J.H., Jaffray, D.A.: Cone-beam computed tomography with a flat-panel imager: magnitude and effects of X-ray scatter. Med. Phys. **28**(2), 220–231 (2001)

47. Storm, L., Israel, H.I.: Photon cross sections from 1 keV to 100 MeV for elements $Z = 1$ to $Z = 100$. At.Ic Data Nucl. Data Tables **7**(6), 565–681 (1970)

48. Swirski, Y., Schechner, Y.Y., Herzberg, B., Negahdaripour, S.: Caustereo: range from light in nature. Appl. Opt. **50**(28), F89–F101 (2011)

49. Treibitz, T., Schechner, Y.Y.: Recovery limits in pointwise degradation. In: IEEE International Conference on Computational Photography (ICCP) (2009)

50. Turbell, H.: Cone-beam reconstruction using filtered backprojection. Thesis (doctoral) - Linköping Universitet. (2001)

51. Wadeson, N., Morton, E., Lionheart, W.: Scatter in an uncollimated X-ray CT machine based on a Geant4 Monte Carlo simulation. In: Proceedings of SPIE 7622 (2010)

52. Watson, P.G.F., Tomic, N., Seuntjens, J., Mainegra-Hing, E.: Implementation of an efficient Monte Carlo calculation for CBCT scatter correction: phantom study. J. Appl. Clin. Med. Phys. **16**(4), 216–227 (2015)

Video Re-localization

Yang Feng[2]([⊠]), Lin Ma[1], Wei Liu[1], Tong Zhang[1], and Jiebo Luo[2]

[1] Tencent AI Lab, Shenzhen, China
forest.linma@gmail.com, wl2223@columbia.edu, tongzhang@tongzhang-ml.org
[2] University of Rochester, Rochester, USA
{yfeng23,jluo}@cs.rochester.edu

Abstract. Many methods have been developed to help people find the video content they want efficiently. However, there are still some unsolved problems in this area. For example, given a query video and a reference video, how to accurately localize a segment in the reference video such that the segment semantically corresponds to the query video? We define a distinctively new task, namely **video re-localization**, to address this need. Video re-localization is an important enabling technology with many applications, such as fast seeking in videos, video copy detection, as well as video surveillance. Meanwhile, it is also a challenging research task because the visual appearance of a semantic concept in videos can have large variations. The first hurdle to clear for the video re-localization task is the lack of existing datasets. It is labor expensive to collect pairs of videos with semantic coherence or correspondence, and label the corresponding segments. We first exploit and reorganize the videos in ActivityNet to form a new dataset for video re-localization research, which consists of about 10,000 videos of diverse visual appearances associated with the localized boundary information. Subsequently, we propose an innovative cross gated bilinear matching model such that every time-step in the reference video is matched against the attentively weighted query video. Consequently, the prediction of the starting and ending time is formulated as a classification problem based on the matching results. Extensive experimental results show that the proposed method outperforms the baseline methods. Our code is available at: https://github.com/fengyang0317/video_reloc.

Keywords: Video re-localization · Cross gating · Bilinear matching

1 Introduction

A massive amount of videos is generated every day. To effectively access the videos, several kinds of methods have been developed. The most common and mature one is searching by keywords. However, keyword-based search largely depends on user tagging. The tags of a video are user specified and it is unlikely

---

Y. Feng—This work was done while Yang Feng was a Research Intern with Tencent AI Lab.

© Springer Nature Switzerland AG 2018
V. Ferrari et al. (Eds.): ECCV 2018, LNCS 11218, pp. 55–70, 2018.
https://doi.org/10.1007/978-3-030-01264-9_4

for a user to tag all the content in a complex video. Content-based video retrieval (CBVR) [3,11,22] emerges to address these shortcomings. Given a query video, CBVR systems analyze the content in it and retrieve videos with relevant content to the query video. After retrieving videos, the user will have many videos in hand. It is time-consuming to watch all the videos from the beginning to the end to determine the relevance. Thus video summarization methods [21,30] are proposed to create a brief synopsis of a long video. Users are able to get the general idea of a long video quickly with the help of video summarization. Similar to video summarization, video captioning aims to summarize a video using one or more sentences. Researchers have also developed localization methods to help users quickly seek some video clips in a long video. The localization methods mainly focus on localizing video clips belonging to a list of pre-defined classes, for example, actions [13,26]. Recently, localization methods with natural language queries have been developed [1,7].

Fig. 1. The top video is a clip of an action performed by two characters. The middle video is a whole episode which contains the same action happening in a different environment (marked by the green rectangle). The bottom is a video containing the same action but performed by two real persons. Given the top query video, video re-localization aims to accurately detect the starting and ending points of the green segment in the middle video and the bottom video, which semantically corresponds to the given query video. (Color figure online)

Although existing video retrieval techniques are powerful, there still remain some unsolved problems. Consider the following scenario: when a user is watching YouTube, he finds a very interesting video clip as shown in the top row of Fig. 1. This clip shows an action performed by two boy characters in a cartoon named "Dragon Ball Z". What should the user do if he wants to find when such action also happens in that cartoon? Simply finding exactly the same content with copy detection methods [12] would fail for most cases, as the content variations between videos are of great difference. As shown in the middle video of

Fig. 1, the action takes place in a different environment. Copy detection methods cannot handle such complicated scenarios. An alternative approach is relying on the action localization methods. However, action localization methods usually localize pre-defined actions. When the action within the video clip, as shown in Fig. 1, has not been pre-defined or seen in the training dataset, action localization methods will not work. Therefore, an intuitive way to solve this problem is to crop the segment of interest as the query video and design a new model to localize the semantically matched segments in full episodes.

Motivated by this example, we define a distinctively new task called video re-localization, which aims at localizing a segment in a reference video such that the segment semantically corresponds to a query video. Specifically, the inputs to the task are one query video and one reference video. The query video is a short clip which users are interested in. The reference video contains at least one segment semantically corresponding to the content in the query video. Video re-localization aims at accurately detecting the starting and ending points of the segment, which semantically corresponds to the query video.

Video re-localization has many real applications. With a query clip, a user can quickly find the content he is interested in by video re-localization, thus avoiding seeking in a long video manually. Video re-localization can also be applied to video surveillance or video-based person re-identification [19,20].

Video re-localization is a very challenging task. First, the appearance of the query and reference videos may be quite different due to environment, subject, and viewpoint variances, even though they express the same visual concept. Second, determining the accurate starting and ending points is very challenging. There may be no obvious boundaries at the starting and ending points. Another key obstacle to video re-localization is the lack of video datasets that contain pairs of query and reference videos as well as the associated localization information.

In order to address the video re-localization problem, we create a new dataset by reorganizing the videos in ActivityNet [6]. When building the dataset, we assume that the action segments belonging to the same class semantically correspond to each other. The query video is the segment that contains one action. The paired reference video contains both one segment of the same type of action and the background information before and after the segment. We randomly split the 200 action classes into three parts. 160 action classes are used for training and 20 action classes are used for validation. The remaining 20 action classes are used for testing. Such a split guarantees that the action class of a video used for testing is unseen during training. Therefore, if the performance of a video re-localization model is good on the testing set, it should be able to generalize to other unseen actions as well.

To address the technical challenges of video re-localization, we propose a cross gated bilinear matching model with three recurrent layers. First, local video features are extracted from both the query and reference videos. The feature extraction is performed considering only a short period of video frames. The first recurrent layer is used to aggregate the extracted features and generate a new video feature considering the context information. Based on the aggregated representations, we perform matching of the query and reference videos. The feature of every reference video is matched with the attentively weighted query video. In each matching step, the reference video feature and the query video feature are processed by factorized bilinear matching to generate their interaction results. Since not all the parts in the reference video are equally relevant to the query video, a cross gating strategy is stacked before bilinear matching to preserve the most relevant information while gating out the irrelevant information. The computed interaction results are fed into the second recurrent layer to generate a query-aware reference video representation. The third recurrent layer is used to perform localization, where prediction of the starting and ending positions is formulated as a classification problem. For each time step, the recurrent unit outputs the probability that the time step belongs to one of the four classes: starting point, ending point, inside the segment, and outside the segment. The final prediction result is the segment with the highest joint probability in the reference video.

In summary, our contributions lie in four-fold:

1. We introduce a novel task, namely video re-localization, which aims at localizing a segment in the reference video such that the segment semantically corresponds to the given query video.
2. We reorganize the videos in ActivityNet [6] to form a new dataset to facilitate the research on video re-localization.
3. We propose a cross gated bilinear matching model with the localization task formulated as a classification problem for video re-localization, which can comprehensively capture the interactions between the query and reference videos.
4. We validate the effectiveness of our model on the new dataset and achieve favorable results better than the baseline methods.

2   Related Work

CBVR systems [3,11,22] have evolved for over two decades. Modern CBVR systems support various types of queries such as query by example, query by objects, query by keywords and query by natural language. Given a query, CBVR systems can retrieve a list of entire videos related to the query. Some of the retrieved videos will inevitably contain content irrelevant to the query. Users may still need to manually seek the part of interest in a retrieved video, which is time-consuming. Video re-localization proposed in this paper is different from CBVR in that it can locate the exact starting and ending points of the semantically coherent segment in a long reference video.

Action localization [16,17] is related to our video re-localization in that both are intended to find the starting and ending points of a segment in a long video. The difference is that action localization methods only focus on certain pre-defined action classes. Some attempts were made to go beyond pre-defined classes. Seo et al. [25] proposed a one-shot action recognition method that does not require prior knowledge about actions. Soomro and Shah [27] moved one step further by introducing unsupervised action discovery and localization. In contrast, video re-localization is more general than one-shot or unsupervised action localization in that video re-localization can be applied to many other concepts besides actions or involving multiple actions.

Recently, Hendricks et al. [1] proposed to retrieve a specific temporal segment from a video by a natural language query. Gao et al. [7] focused on temporal localization of actions in untrimmed videos using natural language queries. Compared to existing action localization methods, it has the advantage of localizing more complex actions than the actions in a pre-defined list. Our method is different in that we directly match the query and reference video segments in a single video modality.

3   Methodology

Given a query video clip and a reference video, we design one model to address the video re-localization task by exploiting their complicated interactions and predicting the starting and ending points of the matched segment. As shown in Fig. 2, our model consists of three components, specifically they are aggregation, matching, and localization.

3.1   Video Feature Aggregation

In order to effectively represent the video content, we need to choose one or several kind of video features depending on what kind of semantics we intend to capture. For our video re-localization task, the global video features are not considered, as we need to rely on the local information to perform segment localization.

After performing feature extraction, two lists of local features with a temporal order are obtained for the query and reference videos, respectively. The query video features are denoted by a matrix $Q \in \mathbb{R}^{d \times q}$, where d is the feature dimension and q is the number of features in the query video, which is related to the video length. Similarly, the reference video is denoted by a matrix $R \in \mathbb{R}^{d \times r}$, where r is the number of features in the reference video. As aforementioned, feature extraction only considers the video characteristics within a short range. In order to incorporate the contextual information within a longer range, we employ the long short-term memory (LSTM) [10] to aggregate the extracted features:

$$h_i^q = \text{LSTM}(q_i, h_{i-1}^q)$$
$$h_i^r = \text{LSTM}(r_i, h_{i-1}^r), \tag{1}$$

where q_i and r_i are the i-th column in Q and R, respectively. h_i^q, $h_i^r \in \mathbb{R}^{l \times 1}$ are the hidden states at the i-th time step of the two LSTMs, with l denoting the dimensionality of the hidden state. Note that the parameters of the two LSTM are shared to reduce the model size. The yielded hidden state of the LSTM is

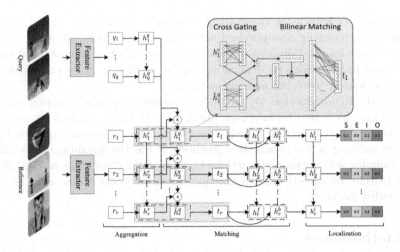

Fig. 2. The architecture of our proposed model for video re-localization. Local video features are first extracted for both query and reference videos and then aggregated by LSTMs. The proposed cross gated bilinear matching scheme exploits the complicated interactions between the aggregated query and reference video features. The localization layer, relying on the matching results, detects the starting and ending points of a segment in the reference video by performing classification on the hidden state of each time step. The four possible classes are **S**tarting, **E**nding, **I**nside and **O**utside. (A) denotes the attention mechanism described in Sect. 3. $\odot$ and $\otimes$ are inner and outer products, respectively.

regarded as the new video representation. Due to the natural characteristics and behaviors of LSTM, the hidden states can encode and aggregate the previous contextual information.

3.2 Cross Gated Bilinear Matching

At each time step, we perform matching of the query and reference videos, based on the aggregated video representations h_i^q and h_i^r. Our proposed cross gated bilinear matching scheme consists of four modules, specifically the generation of attention weighted query, cross gating, bilinear matching, and matching aggregation.

Attention Weighted Query. For video re-localization, the segment corresponding to the query clip can potentially be anywhere in the reference video. Therefore, every feature from the reference video needs to be matched against the query video to capture their semantic correspondence. Meanwhile, the query video may be quite long, thus only some parts in the query video actually correspond to one feature in the reference video. Motivated by the machine comprehension method in [29], an attention mechanism is used to select which part in the query video is to be matched with the feature in the reference video.

At the i-th time step of the reference video, the query video is weighted by an attention mechanism:

$$e_{i,j} = \tanh(W^q h_j^q + W^r h_i^r + W^m h_{i-1}^f + b^m),$$

$$\alpha_{i,j} = \frac{\exp(w^\top e_{i,j} + b)}{\sum_k \exp(w^\top e_{i,k} + b)}, \tag{2}$$

$$\bar{h}_i^q = \sum_j \alpha_{i,j} h_j^q,$$

where $W^q, W^r, W^m \in \mathbb{R}^{l \times l}$, $w \in \mathbb{R}^{l \times 1}$ are the weight parameters in our attention model with $b^m \in \mathbb{R}^{l \times 1}$ and $b \in \mathbb{R}$ denoting the bias terms. It can be observed that the attention weight $\alpha_{i,j}$ relies on not only the current representation h_i^r of the reference video but also the matching result $h_{i-1}^f \in \mathbb{R}^{l \times 1}$ in the previous stage, which can be obtained by Eq. (7) and will be introduced later. The attention mechanism tries to find the most relevant h_j^q to h_i^r and use the relevant h_j^q to generate the query representation $\bar{h}_i^q$, which is believed to better match h_i^r for the video re-localization task.

Cross Gating. Based on the attention weighted query representation $\bar{h}_i^q$ and reference representation h_i^r, we propose a cross gating mechanism to gate out the irrelevant reference parts and emphasize the relevant parts. In cross gating, the gate for the reference video feature depends on the query video. Meanwhile, the query video features are also gated by the current reference video feature. The cross gating mechanism can be expressed by the following equation:

$$\begin{aligned} g_i^r = \sigma(W_r^g h_i^r + b_r^g), &\qquad \tilde{h}_i^q = \bar{h}_i^q \odot g_i^r, \\ g_i^q = \sigma(W_q^g \bar{h}_i^q + b_q^g), &\qquad \tilde{h}_i^r = h_i^r \odot g_i^q, \end{aligned} \tag{3}$$

where $W_r^g, W_q^g \in \mathbb{R}^{l \times l}$, and $b_r^g, b_q^g \in \mathbb{R}^{l \times 1}$ denote the learnable parameters. σ denotes the non-linear sigmoid function. If the reference feature h_i^r is irrelevant to the query video, both the reference feature h_i^r and query representation $\bar{h}_i^q$ are filtered to reduce their effect on the subsequent layers. If h_i^r closely relates to $\bar{h}_i^q$, the cross gating strategy is expected to further enhance their interactions.

Bilinear Matching. Motivated by bilinear CNN [18], we propose a bilinear matching method to further exploit the interactions between $\tilde{h}_i^q$ and $\tilde{h}_i^r$, which can be written as:

$$t_{ij} = \tilde{h}_i^{q\top} W_j^b \tilde{h}_i^r + b_j^b, \tag{4}$$

where t_{ij} is the j-th dimension of the bilinear matching result, given by $t_i = [t_{i1}, t_{i2}, \ldots, t_{il}]^\top$. $W_j^b \in \mathbb{R}^{l \times l}$ and $b_j^b \in \mathbb{R}$ are the learnable parameters used to calculate t_{ij}.

The bilinear matching model in Eq. (4) introduces too many parameters, thus making the model difficult to learn. Normally, to generate an l-dimension bilinear output, the number of parameters introduced would be $l^3 + l$. In order to reduce the number of parameters, we factorize the bilinear matching model as:

$$\hat{h}_i^q = F_j \tilde{h}_i^q + b_j^f,$$
$$\hat{h}_i^r = F_j \tilde{h}_i^r + b_j^f, \tag{5}$$
$$t_{ij} = \hat{h}_i^{q\top} \hat{h}_i^r,$$

where $F_j \in \mathbb{R}^{k \times l}$ and $b_j^f \in \mathbb{R}^{k \times 1}$ are the parameters to be learned. k is a hyperparameter much smaller than l. Therefore, only $k \times l \times (l + 1)$ parameters are introduced by the factorized bilinear matching model.

The factorized bilinear matching scheme captures the relationships between the query and reference representations. By expanding Eq. (5), we have the following equation:

$$t_{ij} = \underbrace{\tilde{h}_i^{q\top} F_j^\top F_j \tilde{h}_i^r}_{\text{quadratic term}} + \underbrace{b_j^{f\top} F_j (\tilde{h}_i^q + \tilde{h}_i^r)}_{\text{linear term}} + \underbrace{b_i^{f\top} b_i^f}_{\text{bias term}} . \tag{6}$$

Each t_{ij} consists of a quadratic term, a linear term, and a bias term, with the quadratic term capable of capturing the complex dynamics between $\tilde{h}_i^q$ and $\tilde{h}_i^r$.

Matching Aggregation. Our obtained matching result t_i captures the complicated interactions between the query and reference videos from the local view point. Therefore, an LSTM is used to further aggregate the matching context:

$$h_i^f = \text{LSTM}(t_i, h_{i-1}^f). \tag{7}$$

Following the idea in bidirectional RNN [24], we also use another LSTM to aggregate the matching results in the reverse direction. Let h_i^b denote the hidden state of the LSTM in the reverse direction. By concatenating h_i^f together with h_i^b, the aggregated hidden state h_i^m is generated.

3.3   Localization

The output of the matching layer h_i^m indicates whether the content in the i-th time step in the reference video matches well with the query clip. We rely on h_i^m to predict the starting and ending points of the matching segment. We formulate the localization task as a classification problem. As illustrated in Fig. 2, at each time step in the reference video, the localization layer predicts the probability that this time step belongs to one of the four classes: starting point, ending point, inside point, and outside point. The localization layer is given by:

$$h_i^l = \text{LSTM}(h_i^m, h_{i-1}^l),$$
$$p_i = \text{softmax}(W^l h_i^l + b^l), \tag{8}$$

where $W^l \in \mathbb{R}^{4 \times l}$ and $b^l \in \mathbb{R}^{4 \times 1}$ are the parameters in the softmax layer. p_i is the predicted probability for time step i. It has four dimensions p_i^1, p_i^2, p_i^3, and p_i^4, denoting the probability of starting, ending, inside and outside, respectively.

3.4 Training

We train our model using the weighted cross entropy loss. We generate a label vector for the reference video at each time step. For a reference video with a ground-truth segment $[s, e]$, we assume $1 \leq s \leq e \leq r$. The time steps belonging to $[1, s)$ and $(e, r]$ are outside the ground-truth segment, the generated label probabilities for them are $g_i = [0, 0, 0, 1]$. The s-th time step is the starting time step, which is assigned with label probability $g_i = [\frac{1}{2}, 0, \frac{1}{2}, 0]$. Similarly, the label probability at the e-th time step is $g_i = [0, \frac{1}{2}, \frac{1}{2}, 0]$. The time steps in the segment (s, e) are labeled as $g_i = [0, 0, 0, 1]$. When the segment is very short and falls in only one time step, s will be equal to e. In that case, the label probability for that time step would be $[\frac{1}{3}, \frac{1}{3}, \frac{1}{3}, 0]$. The cross entropy loss for one sample pair is given by:

$$loss = -\frac{1}{r} \sum_{i=1}^{r} \sum_{n=1}^{4} g_i^n \log(p_i^n),$$ (9)

where g_i^n is the n-th dimension of g_i.

One problem of using the above loss for training is that the predicted probabilities of the starting point and ending point would be orders smaller than the probabilities of the other two classes. The reason is that the positive samples for the starting and ending points are much fewer than those of the other two classes. For one reference video, there is only one starting point and one ending point. In contrast, all the other positions are either inside or outside of the segment. So we decide to pay more attention to losses at the starting and ending positions, with a dynamic weighting strategy:

$$w_i = \begin{cases} c_w, & \text{if } g_i^1 + g_i^2 > 0 \\ 1, & \text{otherwise} \end{cases}$$ (10)

where c_w is a constant. Thus, the weighted loss used for training can be further formulated as:

$$loss^w = -\frac{1}{r} \sum_{i=1}^{r} w_i \sum_{n=1}^{4} g_i^n \log(p_i^n).$$ (11)

3.5 Inference

After the model is properly trained, we can perform video re-localization on a pair of query and reference videos. We localize the segment with the largest joint probability in the reference video, which is given by:

$$s, e = \arg\max_{s,e} p_s^1 p_e^2 \left(\prod_{i=s}^{e} p_i^3 \right)^{\frac{1}{e-s+1}},$$ (12)

where s and e are the predicted time steps of the starting and ending points, respectively. As shown in Eq. (12), the geometric mean of all the probabilities inside the segment is used such that the joint probability will not be affected by the length of the segment.

4   The Video Re-localization Dataset

Existing video datasets are usually created for classification [8,14], temporal localization [6], captioning [4] or video summarization [9]. None of them can be directly used for the video re-localization task. To train our video re-localization model, we need pairs of query videos and reference videos, where the segment in the reference video semantically corresponding to the query video should be annotated with its localization information, specifically the starting and ending points. It would be labor expensive to manually collect query and reference videos and localize the segments having the same semantics with the query video.

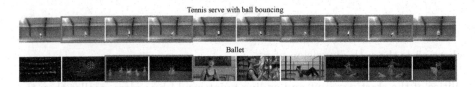

Fig. 3. Several video samples in our dataset. The segments containing different actions are marked by the green rectangles. (Color figure online)

Therefore, in this study, we create a new dataset based on ActivityNet [6] for video re-localization. ActivityNet is a large-scale action localization dataset with segment-level action annotations. We reorganize the video sequences in ActivityNet aiming to relocalize the actions in one video sequence given another video segment of the same action. There are 200 classes in ActivityNet and the videos of each class are split into training, validation and testing subsets. This split is not suitable for our video re-localization problem because we hope a video re-localization method should be able to relocalize more actions than the actions defined in ActivityNet. Therefore, we split the dataset by action classes. Specifically, we randomly select 160 classes for training, 20 classes for validation, and the remaining 20 classes for testing. This split guarantees that the action classes used for validation and testing will not be seen during training. The video re-localization model is required to relocalize unknown actions during testing. If it works well on the testing set, it should be able to generalize well to other unseen actions.

Many videos in ActivityNet are untrimmed and contain several action segments. First, we filter the videos with two overlapped segments, which are annotated with different action classes. Second, we merge the overlapped segments of the same action class. Third, we also remove the segments that are longer than

512 frames. After such processes, we obtain 9, 530 video segments. Figure 3 illustrates several video samples in the dataset. It can be observed that some video sequences contain more than one segment. One video segment can be regarded as a query video clip, while its paired reference video can be selected or cropped from the video sequence to contain only one segment with the same action label as the query video clip. During our training process, the query video and reference video are randomly paired, while the pairs are fixed for validation and testing. In the future, we will release the constructed dataset to the public and continuously enhance the dataset.

5   Experiments

In this section, we conduct several experiments to verify our proposed model. First, three baseline methods are designed and introduced. Then we will introduce our experimental settings including evaluation criteria and implementation details. Finally, we demonstrate the effectiveness of our proposed model through performance comparisons and ablation studies.

5.1   Baseline Models

Currently, there is no model specifically designed for video re-localization. We design three baseline models, performing frame-level and video-level comparisons, and action proposal generation, respectively.

Frame-Level Baseline. We design a frame-level baseline motivated by the backtracking table and diagonal blocks described in [5]. We first normalize the features of query and reference videos. Then we calculate a distance table $D \in \mathbb{R}^{q \times r}$ by $D_{ij} = \|h_i^q - h_j^r\|_2$. The diagonal block with the smallest average distances is searched by dynamic programming. The output of this method is the segment in which the diagonal block lies. Similar to [5], we also allow horizontal and vertical movements to allow the length of the output segment to be flexible. Please note that no training is needed for this baseline.

Video-Level Baseline. In this baseline, each video segment is encoded as a vector by an LSTM. The L2-normalized last hidden state in the LSTM is selected as the video representation. To train this model, we use the triplet loss in [23], which enforces anchor positive distance to be smaller than anchor negative distance by a margin. The query video is regarded as the anchor. Positive samples are generated by sampling a segment in the reference video having temporal overlap (tIoU) over 0.8 with the ground-truth segment while negative samples are obtained by sampling a segment with tIoU less than 0.2. When testing, we perform exhaustively search to select the most similar segment with the query video.

Action Proposal Baseline. We train the SST [2] model on our training set and perform the evaluation on the testing set. The output of the model is the proposal with the largest confidence score.

5.2 Experimental Settings

We use C3D [28] features released by ActivityNet Challenge 2016[1]. The features are extracted by publicly available pre-trained C3D model having a temporal resolution of 16 frames. The values in the second fully-connected layer (fc7) are projected to 500 dimensions by PCA. We temporally downsample the provided features by a factor of two so they do not have overlap with each other. Adam [15] is used as the optimization method. The parameters for the Adam optimization method are left at defaults: $\beta_1 = 0.9$ and $\beta_2 = 0.999$. The learning rate, dimension of the hidden state l, loss weight c_w and factorized matrix rank k are set to 0.001, 128, 10, and 8, respectively. We manually limit the maximum allowed length of the predicted segment to 1024 frames.

Following the action localization task, we report the average top-1 mAP computed with tIoU thresholds between 0.5 and 0.9 with the step size of 0.1.

5.3 Performance Comparisons

Table 1 shows the results of our method and baseline methods. According to the results, we have several observations. The frame-level baseline performs better than randomly guesses, which suggests that the C3D features preserve the similarity between videos. The result of the frame-level baseline is significantly inferior to our model. The reasons may be attributed to the fact that no training process is involved in the frame-level baseline.

The performance of the video-level baseline is slightly better than the frame-level baseline, which suggests that the LSTM used in the video-level baseline learns to project corresponding videos to similar representations. However, the LSTM encodes the two video segments independently without considering their complicated interactions. Therefore, it cannot accurately predict the starting and ending points. Additionally, this video-level baseline is very inefficient during the

Table 1. Performance comparisons on our constructed dataset. The top entry is highlighted in boldface.

mAP @1	0.5	0.6	0.7	0.8	0.9	Average
Chance	16.2	11.0	5.4	2.9	1.2	7.3
Frame-level baseline	18.8	13.9	9.6	5.0	2.3	9.9
Video-level baseline	24.3	17.4	12.0	5.9	2.2	12.4
SST [2]	33.2	24.7	17.2	7.8	2.7	17.1
Ours	**43.5**	**35.1**	**27.3**	**16.2**	**6.5**	**25.7**

---

[1] http://activity-net.org/challenges/2016/download.html.

inference process because the reference video needs to be encoded multiple times for an exhaustive search.

Our method is substantially better than the three baseline methods. The good results of our method indicate that the cross gated bilinear matching scheme indeed helps to capture the interactions between the query and the reference videos. The starting and ending points can be accurately detected, demonstrating its effectiveness for the video re-localization task.

Some qualitative results from the testing set are shown in Fig. 4. It can be observed that the query and reference videos are of great visual difference, even though they express the same semantic meaning. Although our model has not seen these actions during the training process, it can effectively measure their semantic similarities, and consequently localizes the segments correctly in the reference videos.

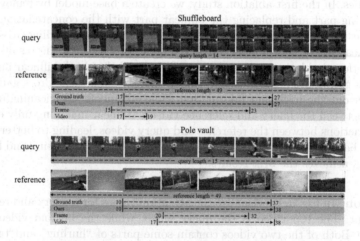

Fig. 4. Qualitative results. The segment corresponding to the query is marked by green rectangles. Our model can accurately localize the segment semantically corresponding to the query video in the reference video. (Color figure online)

Fig. 5. Visualization of the attention mechanism. The top video is the query, while the bottom video is the reference. The color intensity of the blue lines indicates the attention strength. The darker the colors are, the higher the attention weights are. Note that only the connections with high attention weights are shown. (Color figure online)

Table 2. Performance comparisons of the ablation study. The top entry is highlighted in boldface.

mAP @1	0.5	0.6	0.7	0.8	0.9	Average
Base	40.8	32.4	22.8	15.9	6.4	23.7
Base + cross gating	40.5	33.5	25.1	16.2	6.1	24.3
Base + bilinear	42.3	34.9	25.7	15.4	**6.5**	25.0
Ours	**43.5**	**35.1**	**27.3**	**16.2**	**6.5**	**25.7**

5.4 Ablation Study

Contributions of Different Components. To verify the contribution of each part of our proposed cross gated bilinear matching model, we perform three ablation studies. In the first ablation study, we create a base model by removing the cross gating part and replacing the bilinear part with the concatenation of two feature vectors. The second and third studies are designed by adding cross gating and bilinear to the base model, respectively. Table 2 lists all the results of the aforementioned ablation studies. It can be observed that both bilinear matching and cross gating are helpful for the video re-localization task. Cross gating can help filter out the irrelevant information while enhancing the meaningful interactions between the query and reference videos. Bilinear matching fully exploits the interactions between the reference and query videos, leading to better results than the base model. Our full model, consisting of both cross gating and bilinear matching, achieves the best results.

Attention. In Fig. 5, we visualize the attention values for a query and reference video pair. The top video is the query video, while the bottom video is the reference. Both of the two videos contain some parts of "hurling" and "talking". It is clear that the "hurling" parts in the reference video highly interact with the "hurling" parts in the query with larger attention weights.

6 Conclusions

In this paper, we first define a distinctively new task called video re-localization, which aims at localizing a segment in the reference video such that the segment semantically corresponds to the query video. Video re-localization has many real-world applications, such as finding interesting moments in videos, video surveillance, and person re-id. To facilitate the new video re-localization task, we create a new dataset by reorganizing the videos in ActivityNet [6]. Furthermore, we propose a novel cross gated bilinear matching network, which effectively performs the matching between the query and reference videos. Based on the matching results, an LSTM is applied to localize the query video in the reference video. Extensive experimental results show that our model is effective and outperforms several baseline methods.

Acknowledgement. We would like to thank the support of New York State through the Goergen Institute for Data Science and NSF Award #1722847.

References

1. Hendricks, L.A., Wang, O., Shechtman, E., Sivic, J., Darrell, T., Russell, B.: Localizing moments in video with natural language. In: ICCV (2017)
2. Buch, S., Escorcia, V., Shen, C., Ghanem, B., Niebles, J.C.: SST: single-stream temporal action proposals. In: CVPR (2017)
3. Chang, S.F., Chen, W., Meng, H.J., Sundaram, H., Zhong, D.: A fully automated content-based video search engine supporting spatiotemporal queries. IEEE CSVT **8**(5), 602–615 (1998)
4. Chen, D.L., Dolan, W.B.: Collecting highly parallel data for paraphrase evaluation. In: ACL (2011)
5. Chou, C.L., Chen, H.T., Lee, S.Y.: Pattern-based near-duplicate video retrieval and localization on web-scale videos. TMM **17**(3), 382–395 (2015)
6. Caba Heilbron, F., Escorcia, V., Ghanem, B., Carlos Niebles, J.: Activitynet: A large-scale video benchmark for human activity understanding. In: CVPR (2015)
7. Gao, J., Sun, C., Yang, Z., Nevatia, R.: TALL: temporal activity localization via language query. In: ICCV (2017)
8. Gorban, A., et al.: THUMOS challenge: action recognition with a large number of classes (2015). http://www.thumos.info/
9. Gygli, M., Grabner, H., Riemenschneider, H., Van Gool, L.: Creating summaries from user videos. In: Fleet, D., Pajdla, T., Schiele, B., Tuytelaars, T. (eds.) ECCV 2014. LNCS, vol. 8695, pp. 505–520. Springer, Cham (2014). https://doi.org/10.1007/978-3-319-10584-0_33
10. Hochreiter, S., Schmidhuber, J.: Long short-term memory. Neural Comput. **9**(8), 1735–1780 (1997)
11. Hu, W., Xie, N., Li, L., Zeng, X., Maybank, S.: A survey on visual content-based video indexing and retrieval. IEEE Trans. Syst. Man Cybern. **41**(6), 797–819 (2011)
12. Jiang, Y.G., Wang, J.: Partial copy detection in videos: a benchmark and an evaluation of popular methods. IEEE Trans. Big Data **2**(1), 32–42 (2016)
13. Kalogeiton, V., Weinzaepfel, P., Ferrari, V., Schmid, C.: Action tubelet detector for spatio-temporal action localization. In: ICCV (2017)
14. Kay, W., et al.: The kinetics human action video dataset. arXiv preprint arXiv:1705.06950 (2017)
15. Kingma, D., Ba, J.: Adam: a method for stochastic optimization. arXiv preprint arXiv:1412.6980 (2014)
16. Kläser, A., Marszałek, M., Schmid, C., Zisserman, A.: Human focused action localization in video. In: Kutulakos, K.N. (ed.) ECCV 2010. LNCS, vol. 6553, pp. 219–233. Springer, Heidelberg (2012). https://doi.org/10.1007/978-3-642-35749-7_17
17. Lan, T., Wang, Y., Mori, G.: Discriminative figure-centric models for joint action localization and recognition. In: ICCV (2011)
18. Lin, T.Y., RoyChowdhury, A., Maji, S.: Bilinear CNN models for fine-grained visual recognition. In: ICCV (2015)
19. Liu, H., et al.: Neural person search machines. In: ICCV (2017)
20. Liu, H., et al.: Video-based person re-identification with accumulative motion context. In: CSVT (2017)
21. Plummer, B.A., Brown, M., Lazebnik, S.: Enhancing video summarization via vision-language embedding. In: CVPR (2017)

22. Ren, W., Singh, S., Singh, M., Zhu, Y.S.: State-of-the-art on spatio-temporal information-based video retrieval. Pattern Recognit. **42**(2), 267–282 (2009)
23. Schroff, F., Kalenichenko, D., Philbin, J.: FaceNet: a unified embedding for face recognition and clustering. In: CVPR (2015)
24. Schuster, M., Paliwal, K.K.: Bidirectional recurrent neural networks. IEEE Trans. Sig. Process. **45**(11), 2673–2681 (1997)
25. Seo, H.J., Milanfar, P.: Action recognition from one example. PAMI **33**(5), 867–882 (2011)
26. Shou, Z., Chan, J., Zareian, A., Miyazawa, K., Chang, S.F.: CDC: convolutional-de-convolutional networks for precise temporal action localization in untrimmed videos. In: CVPR (2017)
27. Soomro, K., Shah, M.: Unsupervised action discovery and localization in videos. In: CVPR (2017)
28. Tran, D., Bourdev, L., Fergus, R., Torresani, L., Paluri, M.: Learning spatiotemporal features with 3D convolutional networks. In: ICCV (2015)
29. Wang, S., Jiang, J.: Machine comprehension using match-LSTM and answer pointer. arXiv preprint arXiv:1608.07905 (2016)
30. Zhang, K., Chao, W.L., Sha, F., Grauman, K.: Video summarization with long short-term memory. In: ECCV (2016)

Mask TextSpotter: An End-to-End Trainable Neural Network for Spotting Text with Arbitrary Shapes

Pengyuan Lyu[1] , Minghui Liao[1] , Cong Yao[2] , Wenhao Wu[2],
and Xiang Bai[1]($\boxtimes$)

[1] Huazhong University of Science and Technology, Wuhan, China
lvpyuan@gmail.com, {mhliao,xbai}@hust.edu.cn
[2] Megvii (Face++) Technology Inc., Beijing, China
yaocong2010@gmail.com, wwh@megvii.com

Abstract. Recently, models based on deep neural networks have dominated the fields of scene text detection and recognition. In this paper, we investigate the problem of scene text spotting, which aims at simultaneous text detection and recognition in natural images. An end-to-end trainable neural network model for scene text spotting is proposed. The proposed model, named as Mask TextSpotter, is inspired by the newly published work Mask R-CNN. Different from previous methods that also accomplish text spotting with end-to-end trainable deep neural networks, Mask TextSpotter takes advantage of simple and smooth end-to-end learning procedure, in which precise text detection and recognition are acquired via semantic segmentation. Moreover, it is superior to previous methods in handling text instances of irregular shapes, for example, curved text. Experiments on ICDAR2013, ICDAR2015 and Total-Text demonstrate that the proposed method achieves state-of-the-art results in both scene text detection and end-to-end text recognition tasks.

Keywords: Scene text spotting · Neural network · Arbitrary shapes

1 Introduction

In recent years, scene text detection and recognition have attracted growing research interests from the computer vision community, especially after the revival of neural networks and growth of image datasets. Scene text detection and recognition provide an automatic, rapid approach to access the textual information embodied in natural scenes, benefiting a variety of real-world applications, such as geo-location [58], instant translation, and assistance for the blind.

P. Lyu and M. Liao—Contribute equally.

Electronic supplementary material The online version of this chapter (https://doi.org/10.1007/978-3-030-01264-9_5) contains supplementary material, which is available to authorized users.

© Springer Nature Switzerland AG 2018
V. Ferrari et al. (Eds.): ECCV 2018, LNCS 11218, pp. 71–88, 2018.
https://doi.org/10.1007/978-3-030-01264-9_5

Scene text spotting, which aims at concurrently localizing and recognizing text from natural scenes, have been previously studied in numerous works [21, 49]. However, in most works, except [3, 27], text detection and subsequent recognition are handled separately. Text regions are first hunted from the original image by a trained detector and then fed into a recognition module. This procedure seems simple and natural, but might lead to sub-optimal performances for both detection and recognition, since these two tasks are highly correlated and complementary. On one hand, the quality of detections larges determines the accuracy of recognition; on the other hand, the results of recognition can provide feedback to help reject false positives in the phase of detection.

Recently, two methods [3, 27] that devise end-to-end trainable frameworks for scene text spotting have been proposed. Benefiting from the complementarity between detection and recognition, these unified models significantly outperform previous competitors. However, there are two major drawbacks in [3, 27]. First, both of them can not be completely trained in an end-to-end manner. [27] applied a curriculum learning paradigm [1] in the training period, where the sub-network for text recognition is locked at the early iterations and the training data for each period is carefully selected. Busta *et al.* [3] at first pre-train the networks for detection and recognition separately and then jointly train them until convergence. There are mainly two reasons that stop [3, 27] from training the models in a smooth, end-to-end fashion. One is that the text recognition part requires accurate locations for training while the locations in the early iterations are usually inaccurate. The other is that the adopted LSTM [17] or CTC loss [11] are difficult to optimize than general CNNs. The second limitation of [3, 27] lies in that these methods only focus on reading horizontal or oriented text. However, the shapes of text instances in real-world scenarios may vary significantly, from horizontal or oriented, to curved forms.

Fig. 1. Illustrations of different text spotting methods. The left presents horizontal text spotting methods [27, 30]; The middle indicates oriented text spotting methods [3]; The right is our proposed method. Green bounding box: detection result; Red text in green background: recognition result. (Color figure online)

In this paper, we propose a text spotter named as *Mask TextSpotter*, which can detect and recognize text instances of arbitrary shapes. Here, *arbitrary shapes* mean various forms text instances in real world. Inspired by Mask R-CNN [13], which can generate shape masks of objects, we detect text by segment the instance text regions. Thus our detector is able to detect text of arbitrary shapes. Besides, different from the previous sequence-based recognition methods [26,44,45] which are designed for 1-D sequence, we recognize text via semantic segmentation in 2-D space, to solve the issues in reading irregular text instances. Another advantage is that it does not require accurate locations for recognition. Therefore, the detection task and recognition task can be completely trained end-to-end, and benefited from feature sharing and joint optimization.

We validate the effectiveness of our model on the datasets that include horizontal, oriented and curved text. The results demonstrate the advantages of the proposed algorithm in both text detection and end-to-end text recognition tasks. Specially, on ICDAR2015, evaluated at a single scale, our method achieves an F-Measure of 0.86 on the detection task and outperforms the previous top performers by 13.2%–25.3% on the end-to-end recognition task.

The main contributions of this paper are four-fold. (1) We propose an end-to-end trainable model for text spotting, which enjoys a simple, smooth training scheme. (2) The proposed method can detect and recognize text of various shapes, including horizontal, oriented, and curved text. (3) In contrast to previous methods, precise text detection and recognition in our method are accomplished via semantic segmentation. (4) Our method achieves state-of-the-art performances in both text detection and text spotting on various benchmarks.

2 Related Work

2.1 Scene Text Detection

In scene text recognition systems, text detection plays an important role [59]. A large number of methods have been proposed to detect scene text [7,15,16,19, 21,23,30,31,34–37,43,47,48,50,52,54,54–57]. In [21], Jaderberg et al. use Edge Boxes [60] to generate proposals and refine candidate boxes by regression. Zhang et al. [54] detect scene text by exploiting the symmetry property of text. Adapted from Faster R-CNN [40] and SSD [33] with well-designed modifications, [30,56] are proposed to detect horizontal words.

Multi-oriented scene text detection has become a hot topic recently. Yao et al. [52] and Zhang et al. [55] detect multi-oriented scene text by semantic segmentation. Tian et al. [48] and Shi et al. [43] propose methods which first detect text segments and then link them into text instances by spatial relationship or link predictions. Zhou et al. [57] and He et al. [16] regress text boxes directly from dense segmentation maps. Lyu et al. [35] propose to detect and group the corner points of the text to generate text boxes. Rotation-sensitive regression for oriented scene text detection is proposed by Liao et al. [31].

Compared to the popularity of horizontal or multi-oriented scene text detection, there are few works focusing on text instances of arbitrary shapes. Recently, detection of text with arbitrary shapes has gradually drawn the attention of researchers due to the application requirements in the real-life scenario. In [41], Risnumawan et al. propose a system for arbitrary text detection based on text symmetry properties. In [4], a dataset which focuses on curve orientation text detection is proposed. Different from most of the above-mentioned methods, we propose to detect scene text by instance segmentation which can detect text with arbitrary shapes.

2.2 Scene Text Recognition

Scene text recognition [46,53] aims at decoding the detected or cropped image regions into character sequences. The previous scene text recognition approaches can be roughly split into three branches: character-based methods, word-based methods, and sequence-based methods. The character-based recognition methods [2,22] mostly first localize individual characters and then recognize and group them into words. In [20], Jaderberg *et al.* propose a word-based method which treats text recognition as a common English words (90k) classification problem. Sequence-based methods solve text recognition as a sequence labeling problem. In [44], Shi *et al.* use CNN and RNN to model image features and output the recognized sequences with CTC [11]. In [26,45], Lee *et al.* and Shi *et al.* recognize scene text via attention based sequence-to-sequence model.

The proposed text recognition component in our framework can be classified as a character-based method. However, in contrast to previous character-based approaches, we use an FCN [42] to localize and classify characters simultaneously. Besides, compared with sequence-based methods which are designed for a 1-D sequence, our method is more suitable to handle irregular text (multi-oriented text, curved text *et al.*).

2.3 Scene Text Spotting

Most of the previous text spotting methods [12,21,29,30] split the spotting process into two stages. They first use a scene text detector [21,29,30] to localize text instances and then use a text recognizer [20,44] to obtain the recognized text. In [3,27], Li *et al.* and Busta *et al.* propose end-to-end methods to localize and recognize text in a unified network, but require relatively complex training procedures. Compared with these methods, our proposed text spotter can not only be trained end-to-end completely, but also has the ability to detect and recognize arbitrary-shape (horizontal, oriented, and curved) scene text.

2.4 General Object Detection and Semantic Segmentation

With the rise of deep learning, general object detection and semantic segmentation have achieved great development. A large number of object detection and segmentation methods [5,6,8,9,13,28,32,33,39,40,42] have been proposed. Benefited from those methods, scene text detection and recognition have achieved obvious progress in the past few years. Our method is also inspired by those methods. Specifically, our method is adapted from a general object instance segmentation model Mask R-CNN [13]. However, there are key differences between the mask branch of our method and that in Mask R-CNN. Our mask branch can not only segment text regions but also predict character probability maps, which means that our method can be used to recognize the instance sequence inside character maps rather than predicting an object mask only.

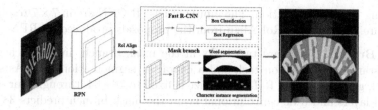

Fig. 2. Illustration of the architecture of the our method.

3 Methodology

The proposed method is an end-to-end trainable text spotter, which can handle various shapes of text. It consists of an instance-segmentation based text detector and a character-segmentation based text recognizer.

3.1 Framework

The overall architecture of our proposed method is presented in Fig. 2. Functionally, the framework consists of four components: a feature pyramid network (FPN) [32] as backbone, a region proposal network (RPN) [40] for generating text proposals, a Fast R-CNN [40] for bounding boxes regression, a mask branch for text instance segmentation and character segmentation. In the training phase, a lot of text proposals are first generated by RPN, and then the RoI features of the proposals are fed into the Fast R-CNN branch and the mask branch to generate the accurate text candidate boxes, the text instance segmentation maps, and the character segmentation maps.

Backbone. Text in nature images are various in sizes. In order to build high-level semantic feature maps at all scales, we apply a feature pyramid structure [32] backbone with ResNet [14] of depth 50. FPN uses a top-down architecture to fuse the feature of different resolutions from a single-scale input, which improves accuracy with marginal cost.

RPN. RPN is used to generate text proposals for the subsequent Fast R-CNN and mask branch. Following [32], we assign anchors on different stages depending on the anchor size. Specifically, the area of the anchors are set to $\{32^2, 64^2, 128^2, 256^2, 512^2\}$ pixels on five stages $\{P_2, P_3, P_4, P_5, P_6\}$ respectively. Different aspect ratios $\{0.5, 1, 2\}$ are also adopted in each stages as in [40]. In this way, the RPN can handle text of various sizes and aspect ratios. RoI Align [13] is adapted to extract the region features of the proposals. Compared to RoI Pooling [8], RoI Align preserves more accurate location information, which is quite beneficial to the segmentation task in the mask branch. Note that no special design for text is adopted, such as the special aspect ratios or orientations of anchors for text, as in previous works [15,30,34].

Fast R-CNN. The Fast R-CNN branch includes a classification task and a regression task. The main function of this branch is to provide more accurate bounding boxes for detection. The inputs of Fast R-CNN are in 7×7 resolution, which are generated by RoI Align from the proposals produced by RPN.

Mask Branch. There are two tasks in the mask branch, including a global text instance segmentation task and a character segmentation task. As shown in Fig. 3, giving an input RoI, whose size is fixed to $16 * 64$, through four convolutional layers and a de-convolutional layer, the mask branch predicts 38 maps (with $32 * 128$ size), including a global text instance map, 36 character maps, and a background map of characters. The global text instance map can give accurate localization of a text region, regardless of the shape of the text instance. The character maps are maps of 36 characters, including 26 letters and 10 Arabic numerals. The background map of characters, which excludes the character regions, is also needed for post-processing.

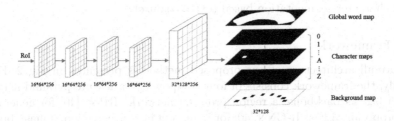

Fig. 3. Illustration of the mask branch. Subsequently, there are four convolutional layers, one de-convolutional layer, and a final convolutional layer which predicts maps of 38 channels (1 for global text instance map; 36 for character maps; 1 for background map of characters).

3.2 Label Generation

For a training sample with the input image I and the corresponding ground truth, we generate targets for RPN, Fast R-CNN and mask branch. Generally, the ground truth contains $P = \{p_1, p_2...p_m\}$ and $C = \{c_1 = (cc_1, cl_1), c_2 = (cc_2, cl_2), ..., c_n = (cc_n, cl_n)\}$, where p_i is a polygon which represents the localization of a text region, cc_j and cl_j are the category and location of a character respectively. Note that, in our method C is not necessary for all training samples.

We first transform the polygons into horizontal rectangles which cover the polygons with minimal areas. And then we generate targets for RPN and Fast R-CNN following [8,32,40]. There are two types of target maps to be generated for the mask branch with the ground truth P, C (may not exist) as well as the proposals yielded by RPN: a global map for text instance segmentation and a character map for character semantic segmentation. Given a positive proposal r, we first use the matching mechanism of [8,32,40] to obtain the best matched horizontal rectangle. The corresponding polygon as well as characters (if any) can be obtained further. Next, the matched polygon and character boxes are

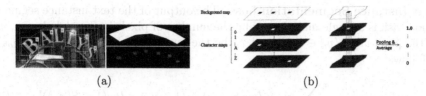

(a)   (b)

Fig. 4. (a) Label generation of mask branch. Left: the blue box is a proposal yielded by RPN, the red polygon and yellow boxes are ground truth polygon and character boxes, the green box is the horizontal rectangle which covers the polygon with minimal area. Right: the global map (top) and the character map (bottom). (b) Overview of the pixel voting algorithm. Left: the predicted character maps; right: for each connected regions, we calculate the scores for each character by averaging the probability values in the corresponding region. (Color figure online)

shifted and resized to align the proposal and the target map of $H \times W$ as the following formulas:

$$B_x = (B_{x_0} - min(r_x)) \times W/(max(r_x) - min(r_x)) \tag{1}$$

$$B_y = (B_{y_0} - min(r_y)) \times H/(max(r_y) - min(r_y)) \tag{2}$$

where (B_x, B_y) and (B_{x_0}, B_{y_0}) are the updated and original vertexes of the polygon and all character boxes; (r_x, r_y) are the vertexes of the proposal r.

After that, the target global map can be generated by just drawing the normalized polygon on a zero-initialized mask and filling the polygon region with the value 1. The character map generation is visualized in Fig. 4a. We first shrink all character bounding boxes by fixing their center point and shortening the sides to the fourth of the original sides. Then, the values of the pixels in the shrunk character bounding boxes are set to their corresponding category indices and those outside the shrunk character bounding boxes are set to 0. If there are no character bounding boxes annotations, all values are set to -1.

3.3 Optimization

As discussed in Sect. 3.1, our model includes multiple tasks. We naturally define a multi-task loss function:

$$L = L_{rpn} + \alpha_1 L_{rcnn} + \alpha_2 L_{mask}, \tag{3}$$

where L_{rpn} and L_{rcnn} are the loss functions of RPN and Fast R-CNN, which are identical as these in [8,40]. The mask loss L_{mask} consists of a global text instance segmentation loss L_{global} and a character segmentation loss L_{char}:

$$L_{mask} = L_{global} + \beta L_{char}, \tag{4}$$

where L_{global} is an average binary cross-entropy loss and L_{char} is a weighted spatial soft-max loss. In this work, the α_1, α_2, β, are empirically set to 1.0.

Text Instance Segmentation Loss. The output of the text instance segmentation task is a single map. Let N be the number of pixels in the global map, y_n be the pixel label ($y_n \in 0, 1$), and x_n be the output pixel, we define the L_{global} as follows:

$$L_{global} = -\frac{1}{N} \sum_{n=1}^{N} [y_n \times log(S(x_n)) + (1 - y_n) \times log(1 - S(x_n))] \qquad (5)$$

where $S(x)$ is a sigmoid function.

Character Segmentation Loss. The output of the character segmentation consists of 37 maps, which correspond to 37 classes (36 classes of characters and the background class). Let T be the number of classes, N be the number of pixels in each map. The output maps X can be viewed as an $N \times T$ matrix. In this way, the weighted spatial soft-max loss can be defined as follows:

$$L_{char} = -\frac{1}{N} \sum_{n=1}^{N} W_n \sum_{t=0}^{T-1} Y_{n,t} log(\frac{e^{X_{n,t}}}{\sum_{k=0}^{T-1} e^{X_{n,k}}}), \qquad (6)$$

where Y is the corresponding ground truth of X. The weight W is used to balance the loss value of the positives (character classes) and the background class. Let the number of the background pixels be N_{neg}, and the background class index be 0, the weights can be calculated as:

$$W_i = \begin{cases} 1 & \text{if } Y_{i,0} = 1, \\ N_{neg}/(N - N_{neg}) & \text{otherwise} \end{cases} \qquad (7)$$

Note that in inference, a sigmoid function and a soft-max function are applied to generate the global map and the character segmentation maps respectively.

3.4   Inference

Different from the training process where the input RoIs of mask branch come from RPN, in the inference phase, we use the outputs of Fast R-CNN as proposals to generate the predicted global maps and character maps, since the Fast R-CNN outputs are more accurate.

Specially, the processes of inference are as follows: first, inputting a test image, we obtain the outputs of Fast R-CNN as [40] and filter out the redundant candidate boxes by NMS; and then, the kept proposals are fed into the mask branch to generate the global maps and the character maps; finally the predicted polygons can be obtained directly by calculating the contours of text regions on global maps, the character sequences can be generated by our proposed *pixel voting* algorithm on character maps.

Pixel Voting. We decode the predicted character maps into character sequences by our proposed pixel voting algorithm. We first binarize the background map, where the values are from 0 to 255, with a threshold of 192. Then we obtain all character regions according to connected regions in the binarized map. We calculate the mean values of each region for all character maps. The values can be seen as the character classes probability of the region. The character class with the largest mean value will be assigned to the region. After that, we group all the characters from left to right according to the writing habit of English.

Weighted Edit Distance. Edit distance can be used to find the best-matched word of a predicted sequence with a given lexicon. However, there may be multiple words matched with the minimal edit distance at the same time, and the algorithm can not decide which one is the best. The main reason for the above-mentioned issue is that all operations (delete, insert, replace) in the original edit distance algorithm have the same costs, which does not make sense actually.

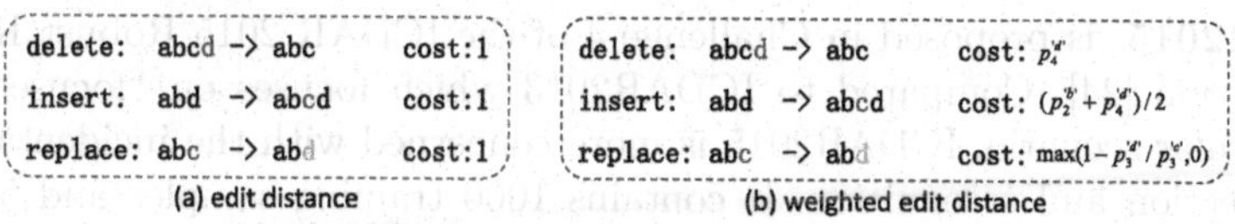

delete:	abcd -> abc	cost:1
insert:	abd -> abcd	cost:1
replace:	abc -> abd	cost:1

(a) edit distance

delete:	abcd -> abc	cost: p_i^c
insert:	abd -> abcd	cost: $(p_i^{a_i} + p_i^c)/2$
replace:	abc -> abd	cost: $\max(1 - p_i^{a_i}/p_i^c, 0)$

(b) weighted edit distance

Fig. 5. Illustration of the edit distance and our proposed weighted edit distance. The red characters are the characters will be deleted, inserted and replaced. Green characters mean the candidate characters. p_{index}^c is the character probability, $index$ is the character index and c is the current character. (Color figure online)

Inspired by [51], we propose a weighted edit distance algorithm. As shown in Fig. 5, different from edit distance, which assign the same cost for different operations, the costs of our proposed weighted edit distance depend on the character probability p_{index}^c which yielded by the pixel voting. Mathematically, the weighted edit distance between two strings a and b, whose length are $|a|$ and $|b|$ respectively, can be described as $D_{a,b}(|a|, |b|)$, where

$$D_{a,b}(i,j) = \begin{cases} \max(i,j) & \text{if } \min(i,j) = 0, \\ \min \begin{cases} D_{a,b}(i-1,j) + C_d \\ D_{a,b}(i,j-1) + C_i \\ D_{a,b}(i-1,j-1) + C_r \times 1_{(a_i \neq b_j)} \end{cases} & \text{otherwise.} \end{cases}$$

(8)

where $1_{(a_i \neq b_j)}$ is the indicator function equal to 0 when $a_i = b_j$ and equal to 1 otherwise; $D_{a,b}(i,j)$ is the distance between the first i characters of a and the first j characters of b; C_d, C_i, and C_r are the deletion, insert, and replace cost respectively. In contrast, these costs are set to 1 in the standard edit distance.

4   Experiments

To validate the effectiveness of the proposed method, we conduct experiments and compare with other state-of-the-art methods on three public datasets: a horizontal text set ICDAR2013 [25], an oriented text set ICDAR2015 [24] and a curved text set Total-Text [4].

4.1 Datasets

SynthText. is a synthetic dataset proposed by [12], including about 800000 images. Most of the text instances in this dataset are multi-oriented and annotated with word and character-level rotated bounding boxes, as well as text sequences.

ICDAR2013. is a dataset proposed in Challenge 2 of the ICDAR 2013 Robust Reading Competition [25] which focuses on the horizontal text detection and recognition in natural images. There are 229 images in the training set and 233 images in the test set. Besides, the bounding box and the transcription are also provided for each word-level and character-level text instance.

ICDAR2015. is proposed in Challenge 4 of the ICDAR 2015 Robust Reading Competition [24]. Compared to ICDAR2013 which focuses on "focused text" in particular scenario, ICDAR2015 is more concerned with the incidental scene text detection and recognition. It contains 1000 training samples and 500 test images. All training images are annotated with word-level quadrangles as well as corresponding transcriptions. Note that, only localization annotations of words are used in our training stage.

Total-Text. is a comprehensive scene text dataset proposed by [4]. Except for the horizontal text and oriented text, Total-Text also consists of a lot of curved text. Total-Text contains 1255 training images and 300 test images. All images are annotated with polygons and transcriptions in word-level. Note that, we only use the localization annotations in the training phase.

4.2 Implementation Details

Training. Different from previous text spotting methods which use two independent models [22,30] (the detector and the recognizer) or alternating training strategy [27], all subnets of our model can be trained synchronously and end-to-end. The whole training process contains two stages: pre-trained on SynthText and fine-tuned on the real-world data.

In the pre-training stage, we set the mini-batch to 8, and all the shorter edge of the input images are resized to 800 pixels while keeping the aspect ratio of the images. The batch sizes of RPN and Fast R-CNN are set to 256 and 512 per image with a 1 : 3 sample ratio of positives to negatives. The batch size of the mask branch is 16. In the fine-tuning stage, data augmentation and multi-scale training technology are applied due to the lack of real samples. Specifically, for data augmentation, we randomly rotate the input pictures in a certain angle range of $[-15°, 15°]$. Some other augmentation tricks, such as modifying the hue, brightness, contrast randomly, are also used following [33]. For multi-scale training, the shorter sides of the input images are randomly resized to three scales (600, 800, 1000). Besides, following [27], extra 1162 images for character detection from [56] are also used as training samples. The mini-batch of images is kept to 8, and in each mini-batch, the sample ratio of different datasets is set to 4:1:1:1:1 for SynthText, ICDAR2013, ICDAR2015, Total-Text and the extra images respectively. The batch sizes of RPN and Fast R-CNN are kept as the pre-training stage, and that of the mask branch is set to 64 when fine-tuning.

We optimize our model using SGD with a weight decay of 0.0001 and momentum of 0.9. In the pre-training stage, we train our model for 170k iterations, with an initial learning rate of 0.005. Then the learning rate is decayed to a tenth at the 120k iteration. In the fine-tuning stage, the initial learning rate is set to 0.001, and then be decreased to 0.0001 at the 40k iteration. The fine-tuning process is terminated at the 80k iteration.

Inference. In the inference stage, the scales of the input images depend on different datasets. After NMS, 1000 proposals are fed into Fast R-CNN. False alarms and redundant candidate boxes are filtered out by Fast R-CNN and NMS respectively. The kept candidate boxes are input to the mask branch to generate the global text instance maps and the character maps. Finally, the text instance bounding boxes and sequences are generated from the predicted maps.

We implement our method in Caffe2 and conduct all experiments on a regular workstation with Nvidia Titan Xp GPUs. The model is trained in parallel and evaluated on a single GPU.

4.3   Horizontal Text

We evaluate our model on ICDAR2013 dataset to verify its effectiveness in detecting and recognizing horizontal text. We resize the shorter sides of all input images to 1000 and evaluate the results on-line.

The results of our model are listed and compared with other state-of-the-art methods in Tables 1 and 3. As shown, our method achieves state-of-the-art results among detection, word spotting and end-to-end recognition. Specifically, for detection, though evaluated at a single scale, our method outperforms some previous methods which are evaluated at multi-scale setting [16,18] (F-Measure: 91.7% *v.s.* 90.3%); for word spotting, our method is comparable to the previous best method; for end-to-end recognition, despite amazing results have been achieved by [27,30], our method is still beyond them by 1.1%–1.9%.

4.4   Oriented Text

We verify the superiority of our method in detecting and recognizing oriented text by conducting experiments on ICDAR2015. We input the images with three different scales: the original scale (720×1280) and two larger scales where shorter sides of the input images are 1000 and 1600 due to a lot of small text instance in ICDAR2015. We evaluate our method on-line and compare it with other methods in Tables 2 and 3. Our method outperforms the previous methods by a large margin both in detection and recognition. For detection, when evaluated at the original scale, our method achieves the F-Measure of 84%, higher than the current best one [16] by 3.0%, which evaluated at multiple scales. When evaluated at a larger scale, a more impressive result can be achieved (F-Measure: 86.0%), outperforming the competitors by at least 5.0%. Besides, our method also achieves remarkable results on word spotting and end-to-end recognition. Compared with the state of the art, the performance of our method has significant improvements by 13.2%–25.3%, for all evaluation situations.

Table 1. Results on ICDAR2013. "S", "W" and "G" mean recognition with strong, weak and generic lexicon respectively.

Method	Word spotting			End-to-End			FPS
	S	W	G	S	W	G	
Jaderberg et al. [21]	90.5	-	76	86.4	-	-	-
FCRNall+multi-filt [12]	-	-	84.7	-	-	-	-
Textboxes [30]	93.9	92.0	85.9	91.6	89.7	83.9	-
Deep text spotter [3]	92	89	81	89	86	77	**9**
Li et al. [27]	**94.2**	**92.4**	**88.2**	91.1	89.8	84.6	1.1
Ours	92.5	92.0	**88.2**	**92.2**	**91.1**	**86.5**	4.8

Table 2. Results on ICDAR2015. "S", "W" and "G" mean recognition with strong, weak and generic lexicon respectively.

Method	Word Spotting			End-to-End			FPS
	S	W	G	S	W	G	
Baseline OpenCV3.0 + Tesseract [24]	14.7	12.6	8.4	13.8	12.0	8.0	-
TextSpotter [38]	37.0	21.0	16.0	35.0	20.0	16.0	1
Stradvision [24]	45.9	-	-	43.7	-	-	-
TextProposals + DictNet [10,20]	56.0	52.3	49.7	53.3	49.6	47.2	0.2
HUST_MCLAB [43,44]	70.6	-	-	67.9	-	-	-
Deep text spotter [3]	58.0	53.0	51.0	54.0	51.0	47.0	**9.0**
Ours (720)	71.6	63.9	51.6	71.3	62.5	50.0	6.9
Ours (1000)	77.7	71.3	58.6	77.3	69.9	60.3	4.8
Ours (1600)	**79.3**	**74.5**	**64.2**	**79.3**	**73.0**	**62.4**	2.6

4.5   Curved Text

Detecting and recognizing arbitrary text (e.g. curved text) is a huge superiority of our method beyond other methods. We conduct experiments on Total-Text to verify the robustness of our method in detecting and recognizing curved text.

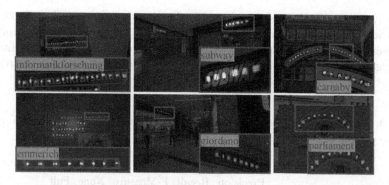

Fig. 6. Visualization results of ICDAR 2013 (the left), ICDAR 2015 (the middle) and Total-Text (the right).

Table 3. The detection results on ICDAR2013 and ICDAR2015. For ICDAR2013, all methods are evaluated under the "DetEval" evaluation protocol. The short sides of the input image in "Ours (det only)" and "Ours" are set to 1000.

Method	ICDAR2013			FPS	ICDAR2015			FPS
	Precision	Recall	F-Measure		Precision	Recall	F-Measure	
Zhang et al. [55]	88.0	78.0	83.0	0.5	71.0	43.0	54.0	0.5
Yao et al. [52]	88.9	80.2	84.3	1.6	72.3	58.7	64.8	1.6
CTPN [48]	93.0	83.0	88.0	7.1	74.0	52.0	61.0	-
Seglink [43]	87.7	83.0	85.3	**20.6**	73.1	76.8	75.0	-
EAST [57]	-	-	-	-	83.3	78.3	80.7	-
SSTD [15]	89.0	86.0	88.0	7.7	80.0	73.0	77.0	**7.7**
Wordsup [18]	93.3	87.5	90.3	2	79.3	77.0	78.2	2
He et al. [16]	92.0	81.0	86.0	1.1	82.0	80.0	81.0	1.1
Ours (det only)	94.1	88.1	91.0	4.6	85.8	**81.2**	83.4	4.8
Ours	**95.0**	**88.6**	**91.7**	4.6	**91.6**	81.0	**86.0**	4.8

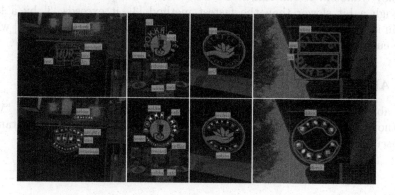

Fig. 7. Qualitative comparisons on Total-Text without lexicon. Top: results of TextBoxes [30]; Bottom: results of ours.

Similarly, we input the test images with the short edges resized to 1000. The evaluation protocol of detection is provided by [4]. The evaluation protocol of end-to-end recognition follows ICDAR 2015 while changing the representation of polygons from four vertexes to an arbitrary number of vertexes in order to handle the polygons of arbitrary shapes.

Table 4. Results on Total-Text. "None" means recognition without any lexicon. "Full" lexicon contains all words in test set.

Method	Detection			End-to-End	
	Precision	Recall	F-Measure	None	Full
Ch'ng *et al.* [4]	40.0	33.0	36.0	-	-
Liao *et al.* [30]	62.1	45.5	52.5	36.3	48.9
Ours	**69.0**	**55.0**	**61.3**	**52.9**	**71.8**

To compare with other methods, we also trained a model [30] using the code in [30][1] with the same training data. As shown in Fig. 7, our method has a large superiority on both detection and recognition for curved text. The results in Table 4 show that our method exceeds [30] by 8.8 points in detection and at least 16.6% in end-to-end recognition. The significant improvements of detection mainly come from the more accurate localization outputs which encircle the text regions with polygons rather than the horizontal rectangles. Besides, our method is more suitable to handle sequences in 2-D space (such as curves), while the sequence recognition network used in [3,27,30] are designed for 1-D sequences.

4.6   Speed

Compared to previous methods, our proposed method exhibits a good speed-accuracy trade-off. It can run at 6.9 FPS with the input scale of 720×1280. Although a bit slower than the fastest method [3], it exceeds [3] by a large margin in accuracy. Moreover, the speed of ours is about 4.4 times of [27] which is the current state-of-the-art on ICDAR2013.

4.7   Ablation Experiments

Some ablation experiments, including "With or without character maps", "With or without character annotation", and "With or without weighted edit distance", are discussed in the Supplementary.

---

[1] https://github.com/MhLiao/TextBoxes.

5   Conclusion

In this paper, we propose a text spotter, which detects and recognizes scene text in a unified network and can be trained end-to-end completely. Comparing with previous methods, our proposed network is very easy to train and has the ability to detect and recognize irregular text (e.g. curved text). The impressive performances on all the datasets which includes horizontal text, oriented text and curved text, demonstrate the effectiveness and robustness of our method for text detection and end-to-end text recognition.

Acknowledgements. This work was supported by National Key R&D Program of China No. 2018YFB1 004600, NSFC 61733007, and NSFC 61573160, to Dr. Xiang Bai by the National Program for Support of Top-notch Young Professionals and the Program for HUST Academic Frontier Youth Team.

References

1. Bengio, Y., Louradour, J., Collobert, R., Weston, J.: Curriculum learning. In: Proceeding of ICML, pp. 41–48 (2009)
2. Bissacco, A., Cummins, M., Netzer, Y., Neven, H.: PhotoOCR: reading text in uncontrolled conditions. In: Proceedings of ICCV, pp. 785–792 (2013)
3. Busta, M., Neumann, L., Matas, J.: Deep TextSpotter: an end-to-end trainable scene text localization and recognition framework. In: Proceedings of ICCV, pp. 2223–2231 (2017)
4. Chng, C.K., Chan, C.S.: Total-Text: a comprehensive dataset for scene text detection and recognition. In: Proceedings of ICDAR, pp. 935–942 (2017)
5. Dai, J., He, K., Li, Y., Ren, S., Sun, J.: Instance-sensitive fully convolutional networks. In: Proceedings of ECCV, pp. 534–549 (2016)
6. Dai, J., Li, Y., He, K., Sun, J.: R-FCN: object detection via region-based fully convolutional networks. In: Proceedings of NIPS, pp. 379–387 (2016)
7. Epshtein, B., Ofek, E., Wexler, Y.: Detecting text in natural scenes with stroke width transform. In: Proceedings of CVPR, pp. 2963–2970 (2010)
8. Girshick, R.B.: Fast R-CNN. In: Proceedings of ICCV, pp. 1440–1448 (2015)
9. Girshick, R.B., Donahue, J., Darrell, T., Malik, J.: Rich feature hierarchies for accurate object detection and semantic segmentation. In: Proceedings of CVPR, pp. 580–587 (2014)
10. Gómez, L., Karatzas, D.: TextProposals: a text-specific selective search algorithm for word spotting in the wild. Pattern Recognit. **70**, 60–74 (2017)
11. Graves, A., Fernández, S., Gomez, F.J., Schmidhuber, J.: Connectionist temporal classification: labelling unsegmented sequence data with recurrent neural networks. In: Proceedings of ICML, pp. 369–376 (2006)
12. Gupta, A., Vedaldi, A., Zisserman, A.: Synthetic data for text localisation in natural images. In: Proceedings of CVPR, pp. 2315–2324 (2016)
13. He, K., Gkioxari, G., Dollár, P., Girshick, R.B.: Mask R-CNN. In: Proceedings of ICCV, pp. 2980–2988 (2017)
14. He, K., Zhang, X., Ren, S., Sun, J.: Deep residual learning for image recognition. In: Proceedings of CVPR, pp. 770–778 (2016)
15. He, P., Huang, W., He, T., Zhu, Q., Qiao, Y., Li, X.: Single shot text detector with regional attention. In: Proceedings of ICCV, pp. 3066–3074 (2017)

16. He, W., Zhang, X., Yin, F., Liu, C.: Deep direct regression for multi-oriented scene text detection. In: Proceedings ICCV, pp. 745–753 (2017)
17. Hochreiter, S., Schmidhuber, J.: Long short-term memory. Neural Comput. **9**(8), 1735–1780 (1997)
18. Hu, H., Zhang, C., Luo, Y., Wang, Y., Han, J., Ding, E.: WordSup: exploiting word annotations for character based text detection. In: Proceedings of ICCV, pp. 4950–4959 (2017)
19. Huang, W., Qiao, Y., Tang, X.: Robust scene text detection with convolution neural network induced MSER trees. In: Proceedings of ECCV, pp. 497–511 (2014)
20. Jaderberg, M., Simonyan, K., Vedaldi, A., Zisserman, A.: Synthetic data and artificial neural networks for natural scene text recognition. CoRR abs/1406.2227 (2014)
21. Jaderberg, M., Simonyan, K., Vedaldi, A., Zisserman, A.: Reading text in the wild with convolutional neural networks. Int. J. Comput. Vis. **116**(1), 1–20 (2016)
22. Jaderberg, M., Vedaldi, A., Zisserman, A.: Deep features for text spotting. In: Fleet, D., Pajdla, T., Schiele, B., Tuytelaars, T. (eds.) ECCV 2014. LNCS, vol. 8692, pp. 512–528. Springer, Cham (2014). https://doi.org/10.1007/978-3-319-10593-2_34
23. Kang, L., Li, Y., Doermann, D.S.: Orientation robust text line detection in natural images. In: Proceedings of CVPR, pp. 4034–4041 (2014)
24. Karatzas, D., et al.: ICDAR 2015 competition on robust reading. In: Proceedings of ICDAR, pp. 1156–1160 (2015)
25. Karatzas, D., et al.: ICDAR 2013 robust reading competition. In: Proceedings of ICDAR, pp. 1484–1493 (2013)
26. Lee, C., Osindero, S.: Recursive recurrent nets with attention modeling for OCR in the wild. In: Proceedings of CVPR, pp. 2231–2239 (2016)
27. Li, H., Wang, P., Shen, C.: Towards end-to-end text spotting with convolutional recurrent neural networks. In: Proceedings of ICCV, pp. 5248–5256 (2017)
28. Li, Y., Qi, H., Dai, J., Ji, X., Wei, Y.: Fully convolutional instance-aware semantic segmentation. In: Proceedings of CVPR, pp. 4438–4446 (2017)
29. Liao, M., Shi, B., Bai, X.: TextBoxes++: a single-shot oriented scene text detector. IEEE Trans. Image Process. **27**(8), 3676–3690 (2018)
30. Liao, M., Shi, B., Bai, X., Wang, X., Liu, W.: TextBoxes: a fast text detector with a single deep neural network. In: Proceedings of AAAI, pp. 4161–4167 (2017)
31. Liao, M., Zhu, Z., Shi, B., Xia, G.s., Bai, X.: Rotation-sensitive regression for oriented scene text detection. In: Proceedings of CVPR, pp. 5909–5918 (2018)
32. Lin, T., Dollár, P., Girshick, R.B., He, K., Hariharan, B., Belongie, S.J.: Feature pyramid networks for object detection. In: Proceedings of CVPR, pp. 936–944 (2017)
33. Liu, W., et al.: SSD: single shot multibox detector. In: Leibe, B., Matas, J., Sebe, N., Welling, M. (eds.) ECCV 2016. LNCS, vol. 9905, pp. 21–37. Springer, Cham (2016). https://doi.org/10.1007/978-3-319-46448-0_2
34. Liu, Y., Jin, L.: Deep matching prior network: toward tighter multi-oriented text detection. In: Proceedings of CVPR, pp. 3454–3461 (2017)
35. Lyu, P., Yao, C., Wu, W., Yan, S., Bai, X.: Multi-oriented scene text detection via corner localization and region segmentation. In: Proceedings of CVPR, pp. 7553–7563 (2018)
36. Neumann, L., Matas, J.: A method for text localization and recognition in real-world images. In: Proceedings of ACCV, pp. 770–783 (2010)
37. Neumann, L., Matas, J.: Real-time scene text localization and recognition. In: Proceedings of CVPR, pp. 3538–3545 (2012)

38. Neumann, L., Matas, J.: Real-time lexicon-free scene text localization and recognition. IEEE Trans. Pattern Anal. Mach. Intell. **38**(9), 1872–1885 (2016)
39. Redmon, J., Divvala, S.K., Girshick, R.B., Farhadi, A.: You only look once: unified, real-time object detection. In: Proceedings of CVPR, pp. 779–788 (2016)
40. Ren, S., He, K., Girshick, R.B., Sun, J.: Faster R-CNN: towards real-time object detection with region proposal networks. IEEE Trans. Pattern Anal. Mach. Intell. **39**(6), 1137–1149 (2017)
41. Risnumawan, A., Shivakumara, P., Chan, C.S., Tan, C.L.: A robust arbitrary text detection system for natural scene images. Expert Syst. Appl. **41**(18), 8027–8048 (2014)
42. Shelhamer, E., Long, J., Darrell, T.: Fully convolutional networks for semantic segmentation. IEEE Trans. Pattern Anal. Mach. Intell. **39**(4), 640–651 (2017)
43. Shi, B., Bai, X., Belongie, S.J.: Detecting oriented text in natural images by linking segments. In: Proceedings of CVPR, pp. 3482–3490 (2017)
44. Shi, B., Bai, X., Yao, C.: An end-to-end trainable neural network for image-based sequence recognition and its application to scene text recognition. IEEE Trans. Pattern Anal. Mach. Intell. **39**(11), 2298–2304 (2017)
45. Shi, B., Wang, X., Lyu, P., Yao, C., Bai, X.: Robust scene text recognition with automatic rectification. In: Proceedings of CVPR, pp. 4168–4176 (2016)
46. Shi, B., Yang, M., Wang, X., Lyu, P., Yao, C., Bai, X.: ASTER: an attentional scene text recognizer with flexible rectification. IEEE Trans. Pattern Anal. Mach. Intell. (2018)
47. Tian, S., Pan, Y., Huang, C., Lu, S., Yu, K., Tan, C.L.: Text flow: a unified text detection system in natural scene images. In: Proceedings of ICCV, pp. 4651–4659 (2015)
48. Tian, Z., Huang, W., He, T., He, P., Qiao, Y.: Detecting text in natural image with connectionist text proposal network. In: Leibe, B., Matas, J., Sebe, N., Welling, M. (eds.) ECCV 2016. LNCS, vol. 9912, pp. 56–72. Springer, Cham (2016). https://doi.org/10.1007/978-3-319-46484-8_4
49. Wang, K., Babenko, B., Belongie, S.: End-to-end scene text recognition. In: Proceedings of ICCV, pp. 1457–1464 (2011)
50. Yao, C., Bai, X., Liu, Wenyu and, M.Y., Tu, Z.: Detecting texts of arbitrary orientations in natural images. In: 2012 IEEE Conference on Computer Vision and Pattern Recognition, pp. 1083–1090. IEEE (2012)
51. Yao, C., Bai, X., Liu, W.: A unified framework for multioriented text detection and recognition. IEEE Trans. Image Process. **23**(11), 4737–4749 (2014)
52. Yao, C., Bai, X., Sang, N., Zhou, X., Zhou, S., Cao, Z.: Scene text detection via holistic, multi-channel prediction. CoRR abs/1606.09002 (2016)
53. Yao, C., Bai, X., Shi, B., Liu, W.: Strokelets: a learned multi-scale representation for scene text recognition. In: Proceedings of the IEEE Conference on Computer Vision and Pattern Recognition, pp. 4042–4049 (2014)
54. Zhang, Z., Shen, W., Yao, C., Bai, X.: Symmetry-based text line detection in natural scenes. In: Proceedings of CVPR, pp. 2558–2567 (2015)
55. Zhang, Z., Zhang, C., Shen, W., Yao, C., Liu, W., Bai, X.: Multi-oriented text detection with fully convolutional networks. In: Proceeding of CVPR, pp. 4159–4167 (2016)
56. Zhong, Z., Jin, L., Zhang, S., Feng, Z.: DeepText: a unified framework for text proposal generation and text detection in natural images. CoRR abs/1605.07314 (2016)

57. Zhou, X., Yao, C., Wen, H., Wang, Y., Zhou, S., He, W., Liang, J.: EAST: an efficient and accurate scene text detector. In: Proceedings of CVPR, pp. 2642–2651 (2017)
58. Zhu, Y., Liao, M., Yang, M., Liu, W.: Cascaded segmentation-detection networks for text-based traffic sign detection. IEEE Trans. Intell. Transport. Syst. **19**(1), 209–219 (2018)
59. Zhu, Y., Yao, C., Bai, X.: Scene text detection and recognition: recent advances and future trends. Front. Comput. Sci. **10**(1), 19–36 (2016)
60. Zitnick, C.L., Dollár, P.: Edge boxes: locating object proposals from edges. In: Fleet, D., Pajdla, T., Schiele, B., Tuytelaars, T. (eds.) ECCV 2014. LNCS, vol. 8693, pp. 391–405. Springer, Cham (2014). https://doi.org/10.1007/978-3-319-10602-1_26

DFT-based Transformation Invariant Pooling Layer for Visual Classification

Jongbin Ryu[1], Ming-Hsuan Yang[2], and Jongwoo Lim[1($\boxtimes$)]

[1] Hanyang University, Seoul, South Korea
jlim@hanyang.ac.kr
[2] University of California, Merced, USA

Abstract. We propose a novel discrete Fourier transform-based pooling layer for convolutional neural networks. The DFT magnitude pooling replaces the traditional max/average pooling layer between the convolution and fully-connected layers to retain translation invariance and shape preserving (aware of shape difference) properties based on the shift theorem of the Fourier transform. Thanks to the ability to handle image misalignment while keeping important structural information in the pooling stage, the DFT magnitude pooling improves the classification accuracy significantly. In addition, we propose the DFT$^+$ method for ensemble networks using the middle convolution layer outputs. The proposed methods are extensively evaluated on various classification tasks using the ImageNet, CUB 2010-2011, MIT Indoors, Caltech 101, FMD and DTD datasets. The AlexNet, VGG-VD 16, Inception-v3, and ResNet are used as the base networks, upon which DFT and DFT$^+$ methods are implemented. Experimental results show that the proposed methods improve the classification performance in all networks and datasets.

1 Introduction

Convolutional neural networks (CNNs) have been widely used in numerous vision tasks. In these networks, the input image is first filtered with multiple convolution layers sequentially, which give high responses at distinguished and salient patterns. Numerous CNNs, e.g., AlexNet [1] and VGG-VD [2], feed the convolution results directly to the fully-connected (FC) layers for classification with the soft-max layer. These fully-connected layers do not discard any information and encode shape/spatial information of the input activation feature map. However, the convolution responses are not only determined by the image content, but also affected by the location, size, and orientation of the target object in the image.

To address this misalignment problem, recently several CNN models, e.g., GoogleNet [3], ResNet [4], and Inception [5], use an average pooling layer.

Electronic supplementary material The online version of this chapter (https://doi.org/10.1007/978-3-030-01264-9_6) contains supplementary material, which is available to authorized users.

V. Ferrari et al. (Eds.): ECCV 2018, LNCS 11218, pp. 89–104, 2018.
https://doi.org/10.1007/978-3-030-01264-9_6

The structure of these models is shown in the top two rows of Fig. 1. It is placed between the convolution and fully-connected layers to convert the multi-channel 2D response maps into a 1D feature vector by averaging the convolution outputs in each channel. The channel-wise averaging disregard the location of activated neurons in the input feature map. While the model becomes less sensitive to misalignment, the shapes and spatial distributions of the convolution outputs are not passed to the fully-connected layers.

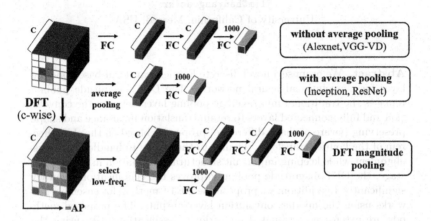

Fig. 1. Feature maps at the last layers of CNNs. Top two rows: conventional layouts, without and with average pooling. Bottom two rows: the proposed DFT magnitude pooling. The DFT applies the channel-wise transformation to the input feature map and uses the magnitudes for next fully-connected layer. Note that the top-left cell in the DFT magnitude is the same as the average value since the first element in DFT is the average magnitude of signals. Here C denotes the number of channels of the feature map.

Figure 2 shows an example of the translation invariance and shape preserving and properties in CNNs. For CNNs without average pooling, the FC layers give all different outputs for the different shaped and the translated input with same number of activations (topmost row). When an average pooling layer is used, the translation in the input is ignored, but it cannot distinguish different patterns with the same amount of activations (second row). Either without or with average pooling, the translation invariance and shape preserving properties are not simultaneously preserved.

Ideally, the pooling layer should be able to handle such image misalignments and retain the prominent signal distribution from the convolution layers. Although it may seem that these two properties are incompatible, we show that the proposed novel DFT magnitude pooling retains both properties and consequently improves classification performance significantly. The shift theorem of Fourier transform [6] shows that the magnitude of Fourier coefficients of two signals are identical if their amplitude and frequency (shape) are identical,

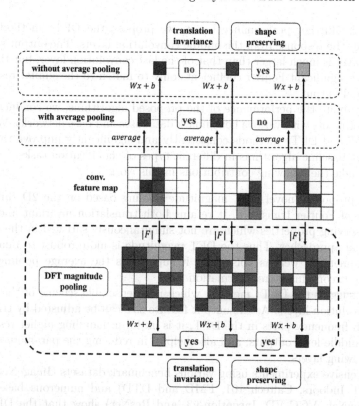

Fig. 2. Comparison of DFT magnitude with and without average pooling. The middle row shows the feature maps of the convolution layers, where all three have the same amount of activations, and the first two are same shape but in different positions. The output of the fully-connected layer directly connected to this input will output different values for all three inputs, failing to catch the first two have the same shape. Adding an average pooling in-between makes all three outputs same, and thus it achieves translation invariance but fails to distinguish the last from the first two. On the other hand, the proposed pooling outputs the magnitudes of DFT, and thus the translation in the input patterns is effectively ignored and the output varies according to the input shapes.

regardless of the phase shift (translation). In DFT magnitude pooling, 2D-DFT (discrete Fourier transform) is applied to each channel of the input feature map, and the magnitudes are used as the input to the fully-connected layer (bottom rows of Fig. 1). Further by discarding the high-frequency coefficients, it is possible to maintain the crucial shape information, minimize the effect of noise, and reduce the number of parameters in the following fully-connected layer. It is worth noting that the average pooling response is same as the first coefficient of DFT (DC part). Thus the DFT magnitude is a superset of the average pooling response, and it can be as expressive as direct linking to FC layers if all coefficients are used.

For the further performance boost, we propose the DFT⁺ method which ensembles the response from the middle convolution layers. The output size of a middle layer is much larger than that of the last convolution layer, but the DFT can select significant Fourier coefficients only to match to the similar resolution of the final output.

To evaluate the performance of the proposed algorithms, we conduct extensive experiments with various benchmark databases and base networks. We show that DFT and DFT⁺ methods consistently and significantly improve the state-of-the-art baseline algorithms in different types of classification tasks.

We make the following contributions in this work:

(i) We propose a novel DFT magnitude pooling based on the 2D shift theorem of Fourier transform. It retains both translation invariant and shape preserving properties which are not simultaneously satisfied in the conventional approaches. Thus the DFT magnitude is more robust to image misalignment as well as noise, and it supersedes the average pooling as its output contains more information.

(ii) We suggest the DFT⁺ method, which is an ensemble scheme of the middle convolution layers. As the output feature size can be adjusted by trimming high-frequency parts in the DFT, it is useful in handling higher resolution of middle-level outputs, and also helpful in reducing the parameters in the following layers.

(iii) Extensive experiments using various benchmark datasets (ImageNet, CUB, MIT Indoors, Caltech 101, FMD and DTD) and numerous base CNNs (AlexNet, VGG-VD, Inception-v3, and ResNet) show that the DFT and DFT⁺ methods significantly improve classification accuracy in all settings.

2   Related Work

One of the most widely used applications of CNNs is the object recognition task [1–5] on the ImageNet dataset. Inspired by the success, CNNs have been applied to other recognition tasks such as scene [7,8] and fine-grained object recognition [9–11], as well as other tasks like object detection [12–14], and image segmentation [15–17]. We discuss the important operations of these CNNs and put this work in proper context.

2.1   Transformation Invariant Pooling

In addition to rich hierarchical feature representations, one of the reasons for the success of CNN is the robustness to certain object deformations. For further robustness over misalignment and deformations, one may choose to first find the target location in an image and focus on those regions only. For example, in the faster R-CNN [13] model, the region proposal network evaluates sliding windows in the activation map to compute the probability of the target location. While it is able to deal with uncertain object positions and outlier background regions, this approach entails high computational load. Furthermore, even with good object proposals, it is difficult to handle the misalignment in real images effectively by pre-processing steps such as image warping. Instead, numerous methods have been developed to account for spatial variations within the networks.

The max or average pooling layers are developed for such purpose [4,5,18]. Both pooling layers reduce a 2D input feature map in each channel into a scalar value by taking the average or max value.

Another approach to achieve translation invariance is orderless pooling, which generates a feature vector insensitive to activation positions in the input feature map. Gong *et al.* [19] propose the multi-scale orderless pooling method for image classification. Cimpoi *et al.* [20] develop an orderless pooling method by applying the Fisher vector [21] to the last convolution layer output. Bilinear pooling [9] is proposed to encode orderless features by outer-product operation on a feature map. The α-pooling method for fine-grained object recognition by Simon *et al.* [22] combines average and bi-linear pooling schemes to form orderless features. Matrix backpropagation [23] is proposed to train entire layers of a neural network based on higher order pooling. Gao *et al.* [24] suggest compact bilinear pooling that reduce dimensionality of conventional bilinear pooling. Kernel pooling [25] is proposed to encode higher order information by fast Fourier transform method. While the above methods have been demonstrated to be effective, the shape information preserving and translation invariant properties are not satisfied simultaneously in the pooling.

The spectral pooling method, which uses DFT algorithm, is proposed by [26]. It transforms the input feature map, crop coefficients of the low frequency of transformed feature map, and then the inverse transform is applied to get the output pooled feature map on the original signal domain. They use DFT to reduce the feature map size, so they can preserve shape information but do not consider the translation property. However, proposed approach in this work outputs the feature map satisfying both properties by the shift theorem of DFT.

2.2   Ensemble Using Multi-convolution Layers

Many methods have been developed to use the intermediate features from multi-convolution layers for performance gain [27]. The hypercolumn [28] features ensemble outputs of multi-convolution layers via the upsampling method upon which the decision is made. For image segmentation, the fully convolutional network (FCN) [15] combines outputs of multiple convolution layers via the upsampling method. In this work, we present DFT$^+$ method by ensembling middle layer features using DFT and achieve further performance improvement.

3   Proposed Algorithm

In this section, we discuss the 2D shift theorem of the Fourier transform and present DFT magnitude pooling method.

3.1 2D Shift Theorem of DFT

The shift theorem [6] from the Fourier transform describes the shift invariance property in the one-dimensional space. For two signals with same amplitude and frequency but different phases, the magnitudes of their Fourier coefficients are identical. Suppose that the input signal f_n is converted to F_k by the Fourier transform,

$$F_k = \sum_{n=0}^{N-1} f_n \cdot e^{-j2\pi kn/N},$$

a same-shaped input signal but phase-shifted by θ can be denoted as $f_{n-\theta}$, and its Fourier transformed output as $F_{k-\theta}$. Here, the key feature of the shift theorem is that the magnitude of $F_{k-\theta}$ is same as the magnitude of F_k, which means the magnitude is invariant to phase differences. For the phase-shifted signal, we have

$$F_{k-\theta} = \sum_{n=0}^{N-1} f_{n-\theta} \cdot e^{-j2\pi kn/N} = \sum_{m=-\theta}^{N-1-\theta} f_m \cdot e^{-j2\pi k(m+\theta)/N}$$

$$= e^{-j2\pi\theta k/N} \sum_{m=0}^{N-1} f_m \cdot e^{-j2\pi km/N} = e^{-j2\pi\theta k/N} \cdot F_k.$$

Since $e^{-j2\pi\theta k/N} \cdot e^{j2\pi\theta k/N} = 1$, we have

$$|F_{k-\theta}| = |F_k|. \tag{1}$$

The shift theorem can be easily extended to 2D signals. The shifted phase θ of Eq. 1 in 1D is replaced with (θ_1, θ_2) in 2D. These two phase parameters represent the 2D translation in the image space and we can show the following equality extending the 1D shift theorem, i.e.,

$$F_{k_1-\theta_1, k_2-\theta_2} = e^{-j2\pi(\theta_1 k_1/N_1 + \theta_2 k_2/N_2)} \cdot F_{k_1, k_2}.$$

Since $e^{-j2\pi(\theta_1 k_1/N_1 + \theta_2 k_2/N_2)} \cdot e^{j2\pi(\theta_1 k_1/N_1 + \theta_2 k_2/N_2)} = 1$, we have

$$|F_{k_1-\theta_1, k_2-\theta_2}| = |F_{k_1, k_2}|. \tag{2}$$

The property of Eq. 2 is of critical importance in that the DFT outputs the same magnitude values for the translated versions of a 2D signal.

3.2 DFT Magnitude Pooling Layer

The main stages in the DFT magnitude pooling are illustrated in the bottom row of Fig. 1. The convolution layers generate an $M \times M \times C$ feature map, where M is determined by the spatial resolution of the input image and convolution filter size. The $M \times M$ feature map represents the neuron activations in each channel, and it encodes the visual properties including shape and location, which can be used in distinguishing among different object classes. The average or max pooling removes location dependency, but at the same time, it discards valuable shape information.

In the DFT magnitude pooling, 2D-DFT is applied to each channel of the input feature map, and the resulting Fourier coefficients are cropped to $N \times N$ by cutting off high frequency components, where N is a user-specified parameter used to control the size. The remaining low-frequency coefficients is then fed into the next fully-connected layer. As shown in Sect. 3.1, the magnitude of DFT polled coefficients is translation invariant, and by using more pooled coefficients of DFT, the proposed method can propagate more shape information in the input signal to the next fully-connected layer. Hence the DFT magnitude pooling can achieve both translation invariance and shape preserving properties, which are seemingly incompatible. In fact, the DFT supersedes the average pooling since the average of the signal is included in the DFT pooled magnitudes.

As mentioned earlier, we can reduce the pooled feature size of the DFT magnitude by only selecting the low frequency parts of the Fourier coefficients. This is one of the merits of our method as we can reduce the parameters in the fully-connected layer without losing much spatial information. In practice, the additional computational overhead of DFT magnitude pooling is negligible considering the performance gain (Tables 1 and 2). The details of the computational overhead and number of parameters are explained in the supplementary material.

Table 1. Classification error of the networks trained from scratch on the ImageNet (top1/top5 error). Both DFT and DFT$^+$ methods significantly improve the baseline networks, while average$^+$ does not improve the accuracy meaningfully.

Method	AlexNet (no-AP)	VGG-VD16 (no-AP)	ResNet-50 (with-AP)
Baseline	41.12/9.08	29.09/9.97	25.15/ 7.78
DFT	40.23/18.12	27.28/9.10	24.37/7.45
	$-0.89/-0.96$	$-1.81/-0.87$	$-0.78/-0.33$
DFT$^+$	39.80/18.32	27.07/9.02	24.10/7.31
	$-1.32/-0.76$	$-2.02/-0.95$	$-1.05/-0.47$
average$^+$	41.09/19.53	28.97/9.91	25.13/7.77
	$-0.03/+0.45$	$-0.12/-0.06$	$-0.02/-0.01$

3.3   Late Fusion in DFT+

In typical CNNs, only the output of the final convolution layer is used for classification. However, the middle convolution layers contain rich visual information that can be utilized together with the final layer's output. In [29], the SVM

Table 2. Classification accuracy of transferring performance to different domains. DFT magnitude pooling results and the best results of DFT$^+$ method are marked as bold. The accuracy of DFT method is improved in all cases except Caltech101-AlexNet, and DFT$^+$ always outperforms average$^+$, as well as the baseline and DFT. See Section 4.2 for more details.

Data	Network	Base	DFT	DFT$^+_1$	average$^+_1$	DFT$^+_2$	average$^+_2$	DFT$^+_3$	average$^+_3$
CUB	AlexNet	64.9	**68.1**	**68.7**	64.9	68.5	64.7	68.6	64.9
	VGG-VD16	75.0	**79.6**	79.7	75.0	79.9	74.8	**80.1**	75.0
	Inception-v3	80.1	**80.9**	82.2	80.4	**82.4**	80.2	82.0	80.2
	ResNet-50	77.5	**81.0**	81.8	77.7	82.0	77.9	**82.7**	77.8
	ResNet-101	80.4	**82.1**	82.7	81.0	**83.1**	81.0	82.9	80.8
	ResNet-152	81.4	**83.7**	83.6	81.5	83.8	81.6	**83.8**	81.5
MIT Indoor	AlexNet	59.2	**59.4**	**59.9**	59.3	59.6	58.9	**59.9**	59.0
	VGG-VD16	72.2	**72.6**	74.2	73.1	74.6	72.8	**75.2**	73.1
	Inception-v3	73.2	**73.4**	76.9	74.5	**77.3**	74.5	74.3	73.9
	ResNet-50	73.0	**74.8**	**76.9**	75.0	76.3	75.2	75.9	75.0
	ResNet-101	73.3	**76.0**	76.1	75.1	**76.9**	75.2	76.6	74.9
	ResNet-152	73.5	**75.3**	76.4	75.5	**76.5**	75.3	76.3	74.9
Caltech 101	AlexNet	88.1	**87.4**	88.1	88.0	88.2	88.1	**88.3**	88.1
	VGG-VD16	93.2	**93.2**	93.4	93.3	93.4	93.2	**93.6**	93.2
	Inception-v3	94.0	**94.1**	**95.2**	94.2	95.1	94.2	94.5	94.0
	ResNet-50	93.2	**93.9**	94.6	93.5	**94.8**	93.3	94.7	93.5
	ResNet-101	93.1	**94.2**	94.0	93.4	94.2	93.3	**94.4**	93.2
	ResNet-152	93.2	**94.0**	94.3	93.7	**94.7**	93.7	94.4	93.3

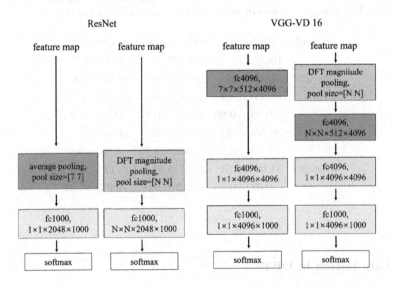

Fig. 3. Examples of DFT magnitude pooling usage. It replaces the average pooling layer of ResNet [4] and it is inserted between the last convolution layer and first fc4096 layer of VGG-VD 16 [2].

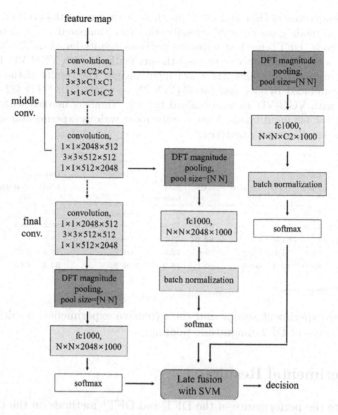

Fig. 4. Example of DFT$^+$ usage for ResNet. The DFT magnitude pooling, fully-connected and softmax layers together with batch-normalization are added to the middle convolution layers. The SVM is used for the late fusion.

classifier output is combined with the responses of spatial and temporal networks where these two networks are trained separately. Similar to [29], we adopt the late fusion approach to combine the outputs of multiple middle layers. The mid-layer convolution feature map is separately processed through a DFT, a fully-connected, a batch normalization, and a softmax layers to generate the mid-layer probabilistic classification estimates. In the fusion layer, all probabilistic estimates from the middle layers and the final layer are vectorized and concatenated, and SVM on the vector determines the final decision.

Furthermore, we use a group of middle layers to incorporate more and richer visual information. The middle convolution layers in the network are grouped according to their spatial resolutions ($M \times M$) of output feature maps. Each layer group consists of more than one convolution layers of the same size, and depending on the level of fusion, different numbers of groups are used in training and testing. The implementation of this work is available at http://cvlab.hanyang.ac.kr/project/eccv_2018_DFT.html. In the following section we present

Table 3. Comparison of DFT and DFT$^+$ methods with state-of-the-art methods. DFT and DFT$^+$ methods gives favorable classification rate compared to previous state-of-the-art methods. DFT$^+$ method improves previous results based on ResNet-50 and also enhances the performance of state-of-the-art methods with VGG-VD 16 in most cases, while we use only single 224×224 input image. The results of the FV on all cases are reproduced by [30] and the B-CNN [9] on FMD [31], DTD [32] and MIT Indoor [33] with VGG-VD 16 are obtained by [34]. Numbers marked with $*$ are the results by 448×448 input image. More results under various experimental settings are shown in the supplementary material.

VGG-VD 16						ResNet-50			
Method	Dataset					Method	Dataset		
	FMD	DTD	Caltech 101	CUB	MIT Indoor		FMD	Caltech 101	MIT Indoor
FV	75.0	-	83.0	-	67.8	FV$_{multi}$	78.2	-	76.1
B-CNN	77.8	69.6	-	84.0*	72.8	Deep-TEN	80.2	85.3	71.3
B-CNN$_{compact}$	-	64.5*	-	84.0*	72.7*	Deep-TEN$_{multi}$	78.8	-	76.2
DFT	78.8	72.4	93.2	79.6	72.6	DFT	79.2	93.9	74.8
DFT$^+$	**80.0**	**73.2**	**93.6**	80.1	**75.2**	DFT$^+$	**81.2**	**94.8**	**76.9**

the detailed experiment setups and the extensive experimental results showing the effectiveness of DFT magnitude pooling.

4   Experimental Results

We evaluate the performance of the DFT and DFT$^+$ methods on the large scale ImageNet [35] dataset, and CUB [36], MIT67 [33], as well as Caltech 101 [37] datasets. The AlexNet [1], VGG-VD16 [2], Inception-v3 [5], ResNet-50, ResNet-101, and ResNet-152 [4] are used as the baseline algorithm. To show the effectiveness of the proposed approaches, we replace only the pooling layer in each baseline algorithm with the DFT magnitude pooling and compare the classification accuracy. When the network does not have an average pooling layer, e.g., AlexNet and VGG, the DFT magnitude pooling is inserted between the final convolution and first fully-connected layers.

The DFT$^+$ uses the mid layer outputs, which are fed into a separate DFT magnitude pooling and fully-connected layers to generate the probabilistic class label estimates. The estimates by the mid and final DFT magnitude pooling are then combined using a linear SVM for the final classification. In the DFT$^+$ method, batch normalization layers are added to the mid DFT method for stability in back-propagation. In this work, three settings with the different number of middle layers are used. The DFT$^+{}_1$ method uses only one group of middle layers located close to the final layer. The DFT$^+{}_2$ method uses two middle layer groups, and the DFT$^+{}_3$ method uses three. Figures 3 and 4 show network structures and settings of DFT and DFT$^+$ methods.

For performance evaluation, DFT and DFT$^+$ methods are compared to the corresponding baseline network. For DFT$^+$, we also build and evaluate the average$^+$, which is an ensemble of the same structure but using average pooling.

Unless noted otherwise, N is set to the size of the last convolution layer of the base network (6, 7, or 8).

4.1 Visual Classification on the ImageNet

We use the AlexNet, VGG-VD16, and ResNet-50 as the baseline algorithm and four variants (baseline with no change, DFT, DFT$^+$, and average$^+$) are trained from scratch using the ImageNet database with the same training settings and standard protocol for fair comparisons. In this experiment, DFT$^+$ only fuses the second last convolution layer with the final layer, and we use a weighted sum of the two softmax responses instead of using an SVM.

Table 1 shows that the DFT magnitude pooling reduces classification error by 0.78 to 1.81%. In addition, the DFT$^+$ method further reduces the error by 1.05 to 2.02% in all three networks. On the other hand, the A-pooling+ method hardly reduce the classification error rate.

The experimental results demonstrate that the DFT method performs favorably against the average pooling (with-AP) or direct connection to the fully-connected layer (no-AP). Furthermore, the DFT$^+$ is effective in improving classification performance by exploiting features from the mid layer.

4.2 Transferring to Other Domains

The transferred CNN models have been applied to numerous domain-specific classification tasks such as scene classification and fine-grained object recognition. In the following experiments, we evaluate the generalization capability, i.e., how well a network can be transferred to other domains, with respect to the pooling layer. The baseline, DFT and DFT$^+$ methods are fine-tuned using the CUB (fine-grained), MIT Indoor (scene), and Caltech 101 (object) datasets using the standard protocol to divide training and test samples. As the pre-trained models, we use the AlexNet, VGG-VD16, and ResNet-50 networks trained from scratch using the ImageNet in Sect. 4.1. For the Inception-v3, ResNet-101, and ResNet-152, the pre-trained models in the original work are used. Also, the soft-max and the final convolution layers in the original networks are modified for the transferred domain. Table 2 shows that DFT magnitude pooling outperforms the baseline algorithms in all networks except one case of the AlexNet on the Caltech101 dataset. In contrast the A-pool+ model does not improve the results.

4.3 Comparison with State-of-the-Art Methods

We also compare proposed DFT based method with state-of-the-art methods such as the Fisher Vector(FV) [21] with CNN feature [20], the bilinear pooling [9,34], the compact bilinear pooling [24] and the texture feature descriptor e.g.Deep-TEN [30]. The results of the single image scale are reported for the fair comparison except that the results of Deep-TEN$_{multi}$ and FV$_{multi}$ of ResNet-50 are acquired on the multiscale setting. The input image resolution is 224×224 for all methods except some results of Bilinear(B-CNN) and compact bilinear(B-CNN$_{compact}$) pooling methods, which uses 448×448 images. The results of Table 3 shows that DFT and DFT$^+$ methods improves classification accuracy of state-of-the-art methods in most cases. DFT and DFT$^+$ methods does not enhance the classification accuracy with only one case: B-CNN and B-CNN$_{compact}$ of CUB dataset with VGG-VD 16, which use larger input image compared to our implementation. In the other cases, DFT$^+$ method performs favorably compared to previous transformation invariant pooling methods. Especially, DFT$^+$ method improves classification accuracy about 10% for Caltech 101. This is because the previous pooling methods are designed to consider the orderless property of images. While considering the orderless property gives fine results to fine-grained recognition dataset (CUB 2000-2201), it is not effective for object image dataset (Caltech 101). Since, shape information, that is the order of object parts, is very informative to recognize object images, so orderless pooling does not improve performance for Caltech 101 dataset. However, DFT and DFT$^+$ methods acquire favorable performance by also preserving the shape information

Table 4. Experimental result of the DFT and DFT$^+$ methods with respect to the pooling size. Performance tends to get better as pooling size increases, but it can be seen that $N = 4$ is enough to improve the baseline method significantly.

Dataset	Network	Base	DFT			DFT$^+{}_3$		
			$N=2$	$N=4$	full	$N=2$	$N=4$	full
CUB	Alexnet	64.9	67.9	67.9	68.1	68.2	68.4	68.6
	VGG-VD 16	75.0	79.0	78.9	79.6	78.9	79.0	80.1
	Inception v3	80.1	78.3	79.1	80.9	80.3	80.7	82.0
	ResNet-50	77.5	76.2	78.2	81.0	78.7	81.1	82.7
	ResNet-101	80.4	81.7	82.4	82.1	82.1	83.1	82.9
	ResNet-152	81.4	82.6	83.1	83.7	82.7	83.3	83.8
MIT Indoor	Alexnet	59.2	59.4	59.3	59.4	61.2	61.6	59.9
	VGG-VD 16	72.2	75.2	74.1	72.6	75.5	75.4	75.2
	Inception v3	73.3	72.8	72.0	73.4	74.8	74.1	74.3
	ResNet-50	73.0	73.5	73.8	74.8	76.0	75.6	75.9
	ResNet-101	73.3	74.0	75.4	76.0	74.5	76.2	76.6
	ResNet-152	73.5	73.4	75.6	75.3	74.0	76.3	76.3
Caltech 101	Alexnet	88.1	87.4	87.3	87.4	88.0	87.9	88.3
	VGG-VD 16	93.2	92.5	92.9	93.2	92.6	93.6	93.6
	Inception v3	94.0	93.1	93.0	94.1	94.0	93.8	94.5
	ResNet-50	93.2	92.8	92.8	93.9	93.2	93.3	94.7
	ResNet-101	93.1	93.4	94.0	94.2	93.5	93.7	94.3
	ResNet-152	93.2	93.8	94.2	94.0	93.9	94.0	94.4

for object images. Therefore, this result also validates the generalization ability of the proposed method for the deep neural network architecture.

5   Discussion

To further evaluate the DFT magnitude pooling, the experiment with regard to the pooling sizes are performed in Table 4. It shows that the small pooling size also improves the performance of the baseline method. Figure 5 shows the classification accuracy of the individual middle layers by the DFT magnitude and average pooling layers before the late fusion. The DFT method outperforms the average pooling, and the performance gap is much larger in the lower layers than the higher ones. It is known that higher level outputs contain more abstract and robust information, but middle convolution layers also encode more detailed and discriminant features that higher levels cannot capture. The results are consistent with the findings in the supplementary material that the DFT method is robust to spatial deformation and misalignment, which are more apparent in the lower layers in the network (i.e., spatial deformation and misalignment are related to low level features than semantic ones). Since the class estimated by the DFT method from the lower layers is much more informative than those by the average pooling scheme, the DFT^+ achieves more performance gain compared to the baseline or the $average^+$ scheme. These results show that the performance of ensemble using the middle layer outputs can be enhanced by using the DFT as in the DFT^+ method.

The DFT^+ method can also be used to facilitate training CNNs by supplying additional gradient to the middle layers in back-propagation. One of such examples is the auxiliary softmax layers of the GoogleNet [3], which helps back-propagation stable in training. In GoogleNet, the auxiliary softmax with average pooling layers are added to the middle convolution layers during training. As such, the proposed DFT^+ method can be used to help training deep networks.

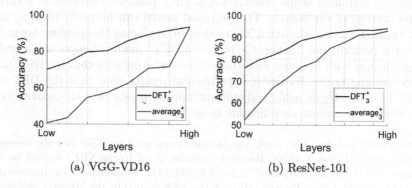

(a) VGG-VD16   (b) ResNet-101

Fig. 5. Performance comparison of average with DFT magnitude pooling in $average^+{}_3$ and $DFT^+{}_3$ methods on Caltech 101. The reported classification accuracy values are obtained from the middle softmax layers independently.

Another question of interest is whether a deep network can learn translation invariance property without adding the DFT function. The DFT magnitude pooling explicitly performs the 2D-DFT operation, but since DFT function itself can be expressed as a series of convolutions for real and imaginary parts (referred to as a DFT-learnable), it may be possible to learn such a network to achieve the same goal. To address this issue, we design two DFT-learnable instead of explicit DFT function, where one is initialized with the correct parameters of 2D-DFT, and the other with random values. AlexNet is used for this experiment to train DFT-learnable using the ImageNet. The results are presented in Table 5. While both DFT-learnable networks achieve lower classification error than the baseline method, their performance is worse than that by the proposed DFT magnitude pooling. These results show that while DFT-learnable may be learned from data, such approaches do not perform as well as the proposed model in which both translation invariance and shape preserving factors are explicitly considered.

Table 5. Comparison of learnable DFT with the baseline DFT (top1/top5 error). The classification error is measured on the AlexNet with learning from scratch using the ImageNet.

Baseline	DFT	DFT-learnable	
		2D DFT-init	Random-init
41.12/19.08	40.23/18.12	40.64/18.76	40.71/18.87

6   Conclusions

In this paper, we propose a novel DFT magnitude pooling for retaining transformation invariant and shape preserving properties, as well as an ensemble approach utilizing it. The DFT magnitude pooling extends the conventional average pooling by including shape information of DFT pooled coefficients in addition to the average of the signals. The proposed model can be easily incorporated with existing state-of-the-art CNN models by replacing the pooling layer. To boost the performance further, the proposed DFT$^+$ method adopts an ensemble scheme to use both mid and final convolution layer outputs through DFT magnitude pooling layers. Extensive experimental results show that the DFT and DFT$^+$ based methods achieve significant improvements over the conventional algorithms in numerous classification tasks.

Acknowledgements. This work was partially supported by Basic Science Research Program through the National Research Foundation of Korea(NRF) funded by the Ministry of Education (NRF-2017R1A6A3A11031193), Next-Generation Information Computing Development Program through the NRF funded by the Ministry of Science, ICT (NRF-2017M3C4A7069366) and the NSF CAREER Grant #1149783.

References

1. Krizhevsky, A., Sutskever, I., Hinton, G.E.: Imagenet classification with deep convolutional neural networks. In: Neural Information Processing Systems (2012)
2. Simonyan, K., Zisserman, A.: Very deep convolutional networks for large-scale image recognition. Arxiv (2014)
3. Szegedy, C., et al.: Going deeper with convolutions. In: IEEE Conference on Computer Vision and Pattern Recognition (2015)
4. He, K., Zhang, X., Ren, S., Sun, J.: Deep residual learning for image recognition. In: IEEE Conference on Computer Vision and Pattern Recognition (2016)
5. Szegedy, C., Vanhoucke, V., Ioffe, S., Shlens, J., Wojna, Z.: Rethinking the inception architecture for computer vision. In: IEEE Conference on Computer Vision and Pattern Recognition, pp. 2818–2826 (2016)
6. Bracewell, R.N.: The Fourier Transform and its Applications, vol. 31999. McGraw-Hill, New York (1986)
7. Zhou, B., Lapedriza, A., Xiao, J., Torralba, A., Oliva, A.: Learning deep features for scene recognition using places database. In: Neural Information Processing Systems, pp. 487–495 (2014)
8. Herranz, L., Jiang, S., Li, X.: Scene recognition with CNNs: objects, scales and dataset bias. In: IEEE Conference on Computer Vision and Pattern Recognition, pp. 571–579 (2016)
9. Lin, T.Y., RoyChowdhury, A., Maji, S.: Bilinear CNN models for fine-grained visual recognition. In: IEEE International Conference on Computer Vision (2015)
10. Krause, J., Jin, H., Yang, J., Fei-Fei, L.: Fine-grained recognition without part annotations. In: IEEE Conference on Computer Vision and Pattern Recognition, pp. 5546–5555 (2015)
11. Zhang, X., Xiong, H., Zhou, W., Lin, W., Tian, Q.: Picking deep filter responses for fine-grained image recognition. In: IEEE Conference on Computer Vision and Pattern Recognition (2016)
12. Girshick, R., Donahue, J., Darrell, T., Malik, J.: Rich feature hierarchies for accurate object detection and semantic segmentation. In: IEEE Conference on Computer Vision and Pattern Recognition, pp. 580–587 (2014)
13. Girshick, R.: Fast R-CNN. In: IEEE International Conference on Computer Vision, pp. 1440–1448 (2015)
14. Redmon, J., Divvala, S., Girshick, R., Farhadi, A.: You only look once: Unified, real-time object detection. In: IEEE Conference on Computer Vision and Pattern Recognition, pp. 779–788 (2016)
15. Long, J., Shelhamer, E., Darrell, T.: Fully convolutional networks for semantic segmentation. In: IEEE Conference on Computer Vision and Pattern Recognition, pp. 3431–3440 (2015)
16. Chen, L.C., Papandreou, G., Kokkinos, I., Murphy, K., Yuille, A.L.: Deeplab: Semantic image segmentation with deep convolutional nets, atrous convolution, and fully connected CRFs. Arxiv (2016)
17. Liu, Z., Li, X., Luo, P., Loy, C.C., Tang, X.: Semantic image segmentation via deep parsing network. In: IEEE International Conference on Computer Vision (2015)
18. Tolias, G., Sicre, R., Jégou, H.: Particular object retrieval with integral max-pooling of CNN activations. Arxiv (2015)
19. Gong, Y., Wang, L., Guo, R., Lazebnik, S.: Multi-scale orderless pooling of deep convolutional activation features. In: Fleet, D., Pajdla, T., Schiele, B., Tuytelaars, T. (eds.) ECCV 2014. LNCS, vol. 8695, pp. 392–407. Springer, Cham (2014). https://doi.org/10.1007/978-3-319-10584-0_26

20. Cimpoi, M., Maji, S., Vedaldi, A.: Deep filter banks for texture recognition and segmentation. In: IEEE Conference on Computer Vision and Pattern Recognition, pp. 3828–3836 (2015)
21. Perronnin, F., Dance, C.: Fisher kernels on visual vocabularies for image categorization. In: IEEE Conference on Computer Vision and Pattern Recognition (2007)
22. Simon, M., Rodner, E., Gao, Y., Darrell, T., Denzler, J.: Generalized orderless pooling performs implicit salient matching. Arxiv (2017)
23. Ionescu, C., Vantzos, O., Sminchisescu, C.: Matrix backpropagation for deep networks with structured layers. In: IEEE International Conference on Computer Vision, pp. 2965–2973 (2015)
24. Gao, Y., Beijbom, O., Zhang, N., Darrell, T.: Compact bilinear pooling. In: IEEE Conference on Computer Vision and Pattern Recognition, pp. 317–326 (2016)
25. Cui, Y., Zhou, F., Wang, J., Liu, X., Lin, Y., Belongie, S.J.: Kernel pooling for convolutional neural networks. In: IEEE Conference on Computer Vision and Pattern Recognition (2017)
26. Rippel, O., Snoek, J., Adams, R.P.: Spectral representations for convolutional neural networks. In: Neural Information Processing Systems, pp. 2449–2457 (2015)
27. Zheng, L., Zhao, Y., Wang, S., Wang, J., Tian, Q.: Good practice in CNN feature transfer. Arxiv (2016)
28. Hariharan, B., Arbeláez, P., Girshick, R., Malik, J.: Hypercolumns for object segmentation and fine-grained localization. In: IEEE Conference on Computer Vision and Pattern Recognition (2015)
29. Simonyan, K., Zisserman, A.: Two-stream convolutional networks for action recognition in videos. In: Neural Information Processing Systems, pp. 568–576 (2014)
30. Zhang, H., Xue, J., Dana, K.: Deep ten: texture encoding network. In: IEEE Conference on Computer Vision and Pattern Recognition (2017)
31. Sharan, L., Rosenholtz, R., Adelson, E.: Material perception: what can you see in a brief glance? J. Vis. $9(8)$, 784–784 (2009)
32. Cimpoi, M., Maji, S., Kokkinos, I., Mohamed, S., Vedaldi, A.: Describing textures in the wild. In: IEEE Conference on Computer Vision and Pattern Recognition, pp. 3606–3613 (2014)
33. Quattoni, A., Torralba, A.: Recognizing indoor scenes. In: IEEE Conference on Computer Vision and Pattern Recognition (2009)
34. Lin, T.Y., Maji, S.: Visualizing and understanding deep texture representations. In: IEEE Conference on Computer Vision and Pattern Recognition, pp. 2791–2799 (2016)
35. Russakovsky, O., Deng, J., Su, H., Krause, J., Satheesh, S., Ma, S., Huang, Z., Karpathy, A., Khosla, A., Bernstein, M.: Imagenet large scale visual recognition challenge. Int. J. Comput. Vis. $115(3)$, 211–252 (2015)
36. Wah, C., Branson, S., Welinder, P., Perona, P., Belongie, S.: The caltech-ucsd birds-200-2011 dataset. Technical report (2011)
37. Fei-Fei, L., Fergus, R., Perona, P.: Learning generative visual models from few training examples: An incremental bayesian approach tested on 101 object categories. Comput. Vis. Image Underst. $106(1)$, 59–70 (2007)

Appearance-Based Gaze Estimation via Evaluation-Guided Asymmetric Regression

Yihua Cheng[1], Feng Lu[1,2($\boxtimes$)], and Xucong Zhang[3]

[1] State Key Laboratory of Virtual Reality Technology and Systems,
School of Computer Science and Engineering, Beihang University, Beijing, China
{yihua_c,lufeng}@buaa.edu.cn
[2] Beijing Advanced Innovation Center for Big Data-Based Precision Medicine,
Beihang University, Beijing, China
[3] Max Planck Institute for Informatics, Saarland Informatics Campus, Saarbrücken,
Germany
xczhang@mpi-inf.mpg.de

Abstract. Eye gaze estimation has been increasingly demanded by recent intelligent systems to accomplish a range of interaction-related tasks, by using simple eye images as input. However, learning the highly complex regression between eye images and gaze directions is nontrivial, and thus the problem is yet to be solved efficiently. In this paper, we propose the Asymmetric Regression-Evaluation Network (ARE-Net), and try to improve the gaze estimation performance to its full extent. At the core of our method is the notion of "two eye asymmetry" observed during gaze estimation for the left and right eyes. Inspired by this, we design the multi-stream ARE-Net; one asymmetric regression network (AR-Net) predicts 3D gaze directions for both eyes with a novel asymmetric strategy, and the evaluation network (E-Net) adaptively adjusts the strategy by evaluating the two eyes in terms of their performance during optimization. By training the whole network, our method achieves promising results and surpasses the state-of-the-art methods on multiple public datasets.

Keywords: Gaze estimation · Eye appearance
Asymmetric regression

1 Introduction

The eyes and their movements carry important information that conveys human visual attention, purpose, intention, feeling and so on. Therefore, the ability to automatically track human eye gaze has been increasingly demanded by many recent intelligent systems, with direct applications ranging from human-computer interaction [1,2], saliency detection [3] to video surveillance [4].

This work was supported by NSFC under Grant U1533129, 61602020 and 61732016.

V. Ferrari et al. (Eds.): ECCV 2018, LNCS 11218, pp. 105–121, 2018.
https://doi.org/10.1007/978-3-030-01264-9_7

As surveyed in [5], gaze estimation methods can be divided into two categories: model-based and appearance-based. Model-based methods are usually designed to extract small eye features, e.g., infrared reflection points on the corneal surface, to compute the gaze direction. However, they share common limitations such as (1) requirement on specific hardware for illumination and capture, (2) high failure rate when used in the uncontrolled environment, and (3) limited working distance (typically within 60 cm).

Different with model-based methods, appearance-based methods do not rely on small eye feature extraction under special illumination. Instead, they can work with just a single ordinary camera to capture the eye appearance, then learn a mapping function to predict the gaze direction from the eye appearance directly. Whereas this greatly enlarges the applicability, the challenge part is that human eye appearance can be heavily affected by various factors, such as the head pose, the illumination, and the individual difference, making the mapping function difficult to learn. In recent years, the Convolutional Neural Network (CNN) has shown to be able to learn very complex functions given sufficient training data. Consequently, the CNN-based methods have been reported to outperform the conventional methods [6].

The goal of this work is to further exploit the power of CNNs and improve the performance of appearance-based gaze estimation to a higher level. At the core of our method is the notion of asymmetric regression for the left and the right eyes. It is based on our key observation that (1) the gaze directions of two eyes should be consistent physically, however, (2) even if we apply the same regression method, the gaze estimation performance on two eyes can be very different. Such "two eye asymmetry" implys a new gaze regression strategy that no longer treats both eyes equally but tends to rely on the "high quality eye" to train a more efficient and robust regression model.

In order to do so, we consider the following technical issues, i.e., how to design a network that processes both eyes simultaneously and asymmetrically, and how to control the asymmetry to optimize the network by using the high quality data. Our idea is to **guide the asymmetric gaze regression by evaluating the performance of the regression strategy w.r.t. different eyes**. In particular, by analyzing the "two eye asymmetry" (Sect. 3), we propose the asymmetric regression network (AR-Net) to predict 3D gaze directions of two eyes (Sect. 4.2), and the evaluation networks (E-Net) to adaptively evaluate and adjust the regression strategy (Sect. 4.3). By integrating the AR-Net and the E-Net (Sect. 4.4), the proposed Asymmetric Regression-Evaluation Network (ARE-Net) learns to maximize the overall performance for the gaze estimator.

Our method makes the following assumptions. First, as commonly assumed by previous methods along this direction [6,7], the user head pose can be obtained by using existing head trackers [8]. Second, the user should roughly fixate on the same targets with both eyes, which is usually the case in practice.

With these assumptions, our method is capable of estimating gaze directions of the two eyes from their images.

In summary, the contributions of this work are threefold:

- We propose the multi-stream AR-Net for asymmetric two-eye regression. We also propose the E-Net to evaluate and help adjust the regression.
- We observe the "two eye asymmetry", based on which we propose the mechanism of evaluation-guided asymmetric regression. This leads to asymmetric gaze estimation for two eyes which is new.
- Based on the proposed mechanism and networks, we design the final ARE-Net and it shows promising performance in gaze estimation for both eyes.

2   Related Work

There have been an increasing number of recent researches proposed for the task of remote human gaze estimation, which can be roughly divided into two major categories: model-based and appearance-based [5,9].

The Model-Based Methods estimate gaze directions using certain geometric eye models [10]. They typically extract and use near infrared (IR) corneal reflections [10–12], pupil center [13,14] and iris contours [15,16] from eye images as the input features to fit the corresponding models [17]. Whereas this type of methods can predict gaze directions with a good accuracy, the extraction of eye features may require hardware that may be composed of infrared lights, stereo/high-definition cameras and RBG-D cameras [15,16]. These devices may not be available when using many common devices, and they usually have limited working distances. As a result, the model-based methods are more suitable for being used in the controlled environments, e.g., in the laboratory, rather than in outdoor scenes or with large user-camera distances, e.g., for advertisement analysis [18].

The Appearance-Based Methods have relatively lower demand compared with the model-based methods. They typically need a single camera to capture the user eye images [19]. Certain non-geometric image features are produced from the eye images, and then used to learn a gaze mapping function that maps eye images to gaze directions. Up to now, various mapping functions have been explored, such as neural networks [20,21], local linear interpolation [19], adaptive linear regression [22], Gaussian process regression [23], and dimension reduction [24,25]. Some other methods use additional information such as saliency maps [22,26] to guide the learning process. These methods all aim at reducing the number of required training samples while maintaining the regression accuracy. However, since the gaze mapping is highly non-linear, the problem still remains challenging to date.

The CNNs-Based Methods have already shown their ability to handle complex regression tasks, and thus they have outperformed traditional appearance-based methods. Some recent works introduce large appearance-based gaze datasets [27] and propose effective CNN-based gaze estimators [6,28]. More recently, Krafka *et al.* implement the CNN-based gaze tracker in the mobile devices [29]. Zhang *et al.* take into consideration the full face as input to the CNNs [30]. Deng *et al.* propose a CNN-based method with geometry constraints [7]. In general, these methods can achieve better performance than traditional ones. Note that they all treat the left and the right eyes indifferently, while in this paper we try to make further improvement by introducing and utilizing the two eye asymmetry.

Besides the eye images, recent appearance-based methods may also take the face images as input. The face image can be used to compute the head pose [6,31] or input to the CNN for gaze regression [29,30]. In our method, we only assume available head poses that can be obtained by using any existing head tracker, and we do not require high resolution face images as input for gaze estimation.

3   Two Eye Asymmetry in Gaze Regression

Before getting into the technical details, we first review the problem of 3D gaze direction estimation, and introduce the "two eye asymmetry" that inspires our method.

3.1   3D Gaze Estimation via Regression

Any human gaze direction can be denoted by a 3D unit vector $\mathbf{g}$, which represents the eyeball orientation in the 3D space. Meanwhile, the eyeball orientation also determines the eye appearance in the eye image, e.g., the location of the iris contour and the shape of the eyelids. Therefore, there is a strong relation between the eye gaze direction and the eye appearance in the image. As a result, the problem of estimating the 3D gaze direction $\mathbf{g} \in \mathbb{R}^3$ from a given eye image $I \in \mathbb{R}^{H \times W}$ can be formulated as a regression problem $\mathbf{g} = f(I)$.

The regression is usually highly non-linear because the eye appearance is complex. Besides, there are other factors that will affect I, and the head motion is a major one. In order to handle head motion, it is necessary to also consider the head pose $\mathbf{h} \in \mathbb{R}^3$ in the regression, which results in

$$\mathbf{g} = f(I, \mathbf{h}), \tag{1}$$

where f is the regression function.

In the literature, various regression models have been used, such as the Neural Network [20], the Gaussian Process regression model [32], and the Adaptive Linear Regression model [22]. However, the problem is still challenging. In recent years, with the fast development of the deep neural networks, solving such a highly complex regression problem is becoming possible with the existence of large training dataset, while designing an efficient network architecture is the most important work to do.

3.2 Two Eye Asymmetry

Existing gaze regression methods handles the two eyes indifferently. However, in practice, we observe the two eye asymmetry regarding the regression accuracy.

> **Observation.** *At any moment, we cannot expect the same accuracy for two eyes, and either eye has a chance to be more accurate.*

The above "two eye asymmetry" can be due to various factors, e.g., head pose, image quality and individuality. It's a hint that the two eyes' images may have different 'qualities' in gaze estimation. Therefore, when training a gaze regression model, it is better to identify and rely on the high quality eye image from the input to train a more efficient and robust model.

4 Asymmetric Regression-Evaluation Network

Inspired by the "two eye asymmetry", in this section, we deliver the Asymmetric Regression-Evaluation Network (ARE-Net) for appearance-based gaze estimation of two eyes.

4.1 Network Overview

The proposed networks use two eye images $\{I_l^{(i)}\}$, $\{I_r^{(i)}\}$ and the head pose vector $\{h^{(i)}\}$ as input, to learn a regression that predicts the ground truth $\{g_l^{(i)}\}$ and $\{g_r^{(i)}\}$, where $\{g_l^{(i)}\}$ and $\{g_r^{(i)}\}$ are 3D gaze directions and i is the sample index. For this purpose, we first introduce the Asymmetric Regression Network (AR-Net), and then propose the Evaluation Network (E-Net) to guide the regression. The overall structure is shown in Fig. 1.

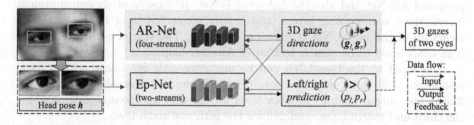

Fig. 1. Overview of the proposed Asymmetric Regression-Evaluation Network (ARE-Net). It consists of two major sub-networks, namely, the AR-Net and the E-Net. The AR-Net performs asymmetric regression for the two eyes, while the E-Net predicts and adjust the asymmetry to improve the gaze estimation accuracy.

Asymmetric Regression Network (AR-Net). It is a four-stream convolutional network and it performs 3D gaze direction regression for both the left and the right eyes (detailed in Sect. 4.2). Most importantly, it is designed to be able to optimize the two eyes in an asymmetric way.

Evaluation Network (E-Net). It is a two stream convolutional network that learns to predict the current asymmetry state, i.e., which eye the AR-Net tends to optimize at that time, and accordingly it adjusts the degree of asymmetry (detailed in Sect. 4.3).

Network training. During training, parameters of both the AR-Net and the E-Net are updated simultaneously. The loss functions and other details will be given in the corresponding sections.

Testing stage. During test, the output of the AR-Net are the 3D gaze directions of both eyes.

4.2 Asymmetric Regression Network (AR-Net)

The AR-Net processes two eye images in a joint and asymmetric way, and estimates their 3D gaze directions.

Architecture. The AR-Net is a four-stream convolutional neural network, using the "base-CNN" as the basic component followed by some fully connected layers, as shown in Fig. 2(a). Follow the idea that both the separate features and joint feature of the two eyes should be extracted and utilized, we design the first two streams to extract a 500D deep features from each eye independently, and the last two streams to produce a joint 500D feature in the end.

Note that the head pose is also an important factor to affect gaze directions, and thus we input the head pose vector (3D for each eye) before the final regression. The final 1506D feature vector is produced by concatenating all the outputs from the previous networks, as shown in Fig. 2(a).

The Base-CNN. The so called "base-CNN" is the basic component of the proposed AR-Net and also the following E-Net. It consists of six convolutional layers, three max-pooling layers, and a fully connected layer in the end. The structure of the base-CNN is shown in Fig. 2(c). The size of each layer in the base-CNN is set to be similar to that of AlexNet [33].

The input to the base-CNN can be any gray-scale eye image with a fixed resolution of 36×60. For the convolutional layers, the learnable filters size is 3×3. The output channel number is 64 for the first and second layer, 128 for the third and fourth layer, and 256 for the fifth and sixth layer.

Loss Function. We measure the angular error of the currently predicted 3D gaze directions for the two eyes by

$$e_l = \arccos \left(\frac{\mathbf{g}_l \cdot f(\mathbf{I}_l)}{\|\mathbf{g}_l\|\|f(\mathbf{I}_l)\|} \right), \tag{2}$$

and

$$e_r = \arccos \left(\frac{\mathbf{g}_r \cdot f(\mathbf{I}_r)}{\|\mathbf{g}_r\|\|f(\mathbf{I}_r)\|} \right), \tag{3}$$

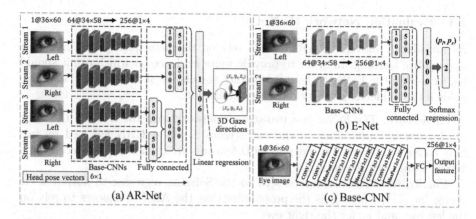

Fig. 2. Architecture of the proposed networks. (a) The AR-Net is a four-stream network to produce features from both the eye images. A linear regression is used to estimate the 3D gaze directions of the two eyes. (b) The E-Net is a two-stream network for two eye evaluation. The output is a two-dimensional probability vector. (c) The base-CNN is the basic component to build up the AR-Net and the E-Net. It uses an eye image as input. The output is a 1000D feature after six convolutional layers.

where $f(\cdot)$ indicates the gaze regression. Then, we compute the weighted average of the two eye errors

$$e = \lambda_l \cdot e_l + \lambda_r \cdot e_r \qquad (4)$$

to represent the loss in terms of gaze prediction accuracy of both eyes.

Asymmetric Loss. The weights λ_l and λ_r determine whether the accuracy of the left or the right eye should be considered more important. In the case that $\lambda_l \neq \lambda_r$, the loss function becomes asymmetric. According to the "two eye asymmetry" discussed in Sect. 3.2, if one of the two eyes is more likely to achieve a smaller error, we should enlarge its weight in optimizing the network. Following this idea, we propose to set the weights according to the following:

$$\begin{cases} \lambda_l/\lambda_r = \dfrac{1/e_l}{1/e_r}, \\ \lambda_l + \lambda_r = 1, \end{cases} \qquad (5)$$

whose solution is

$$\lambda_l = \frac{1/e_l}{1/e_l + 1/e_r}, \quad \lambda_r = \frac{1/e_r}{1/e_l + 1/e_r}. \qquad (6)$$

By substituting the λ_l and λ_r in Eq. (4), the final asymmetric loss becomes

$$\mathcal{L}_{AR} = 2 \cdot \frac{e_l \cdot e_r}{e_l + e_r}, \qquad (7)$$

which encourages to rely on the high quality eye in training.

4.3   Evaluation Network (E-Net)

As introduced above, the AR-Net can rely on the high quality eye image for asymmetric learning. In order to provide more evidence on which eye it should be, we design the E-Net to learn to predict the choice of the AR-Net, and also guide its asymmetric strategy during optimization.

Architecture. The E-Net is a two-stream network with the left and the right eye images as input. Each of the two stream is a base-CNN followed by two fully connected layers. The output 500D features are then concatenated to be a 1000D feature, as shown in Fig. 2(b).

Finally, the 1000D feature is sent to the Softmax regressor to output a 2D vector $[p_l, p_r]^{\mathrm{T}}$, where p_l is the probability that the AR-Net chooses to rely on the left eye, and p_r for the right eye.

During training, the ground truth for p is set to be 1 if $e_l < e_r$ from the AR-Net, otherwise p is set to be 0. In other words, the evaluation network is trained to predict the probability of the left/right eye image being more efficient in gaze estimation.

Loss Function: In order to train the E-Net to predict the AR-Net's choice, we set its loss function as below:

$$\mathcal{L}_E = -\{\eta \cdot \arccos(f(\boldsymbol{I}_l) \cdot f(\boldsymbol{I}_r)) \cdot \log(p_l) + \\ (1-\eta) \cdot \arccos(f(\boldsymbol{I}_l) \cdot f(\boldsymbol{I}_r)) \cdot \log(p_r)\}, \tag{8}$$

where $\eta = 1$ if $e_l \leq e_r$, and $\eta = 0$ if $e_l > e_r$. Besides, $\arccos(f(\boldsymbol{I}_l) \cdot f(\boldsymbol{I}_r))$ computes the angular difference of the two eye gaze directions estimated by the AR-Net, which measures the inconsistency of $\mathbf{g}_l$ and $\mathbf{g}_r$.

This loss function can be intuitively understood as follows: if the left eye has smaller error in the AR-Net, i.e., $e_l < e_r$, the E-Net should choose to maximize p_l to learn this fact in order to adjust the regression strategy of the AR-Net, especially in the case when $\mathbf{g}_l$ and $\mathbf{g}_r$ are inconsistent. In this way, the E-Net is trained to predict the high quality eye that can help optimize the AR-Net.

Modifying the Loss Function of AR-Net. An important task of the E-Net is to adjust the asymmetry of the AR-Net, with the aim to improve the gaze estimation accuracy, as explained before. In order to do so, by integrating the E-Net, the loss function of the AR-Net in Eq. (7) can be modified as

$$\mathcal{L}_{AR}^* = \omega \cdot \mathcal{L}_{AR} + (1-\omega) \cdot \beta \cdot \left(\frac{e_l + e_r}{2}\right), \tag{9}$$

where ω balances the weight between asymmetric learning (the first term) and symmetric learning (the second term). β scales the weight of symmetric learning, and was set to 0.1 in our experiments. In particular, given the output (p_l, p_r) of the E-Net, we compute

$$\omega = \frac{1 + (2\eta - 1) \cdot p_l + (1 - 2\eta) \cdot p_r}{2}. \tag{10}$$

Again, $\eta = 1$ if $e_l \leq e_r$, and $\eta = 0$ if $e_l > e_r$. Here we omit the derivation of ω, while it is easy to see that $\omega = 1$ when both the AR-Net and E-Net have a strong agreement on the high quality eye, meaning that a heavily asymmetric learning strategy can be recommended; $\omega = 0$ when they completely disagree, meaning that it is better to just use a symmetric learning strategy as a compromise. In practice, ω is a decimal number between 0 and 1.

4.4 Guiding Gaze Regression by Evaluation

Following the explanations above, we summarize again how the AR-Net and the E-Net are integrated together (Fig. 1), and how the E-Net can guide the AR-Net.

- **AR-Net**: takes both eye images as input; loss function modified by the E-Net's output (p_l, p_r) to adjust the asymmetry adaptively (Eq. (9)).
- **E-Net**: takes both eye images as input; loss function modified by the AR-Net's output $(f(\boldsymbol{I}_l), f(\boldsymbol{I}_r))$ and the errors (e_l, e_r) to predict the high quality eye image for optimization (Eq. (8)).
- **ARE-Net**: as shown in Fig. 1, the AR-Net and the E-Net are integrated and trained together. The final gaze estimation results are the output $(f(\boldsymbol{I}_l), f(\boldsymbol{I}_r))$ from the AR-Net.

5 Experimental Evaluation

In this section, we evaluate the proposed Asymmetric Regression-Evaluation Network by conducting multiple experiments.

5.1 Dataset

The proposed is a typical appearance-based gaze estimation method. Therefore, we use the following datasets in our experiments as previous methods do. Necessary modification have been done as described.

Modified MPIIGaze Dataset: the MPIIGaze dataset [6] is composed of 213659 images of 15 participants, which contains a large variety of different illuminations, eye appearances and head poses. It is among the largest datasets for appearance-based gaze estimation and thus is commonly used. All the images and data in the MPIIGaze dataset have already been normalized to eliminate the effect due to face misalignment.

The MPIIGaze dataset provides a standard subset for evaluation, which contains 1500 left eye images and 1500 right eye images independently selected from each participants. However, our method requires paired eye images captured at the same time. Therefore, we modify the evaluation set by finding out the missing image of every left-right eye image pair from the original dataset. This doubles the image number in the evaluation set. In our experiments, we use such a modified dataset instead of the original MPIIGaze dataset.

Besides, we also conduct experiments to compare with methods using full face images as input. As a result, we use the same full face subset from the MPIIGaze dataset as described in [30].

UT Multiview Dataset [34]: it contains dense gaze data of 50 participants. Both the left and right eye images are provided directly for use. The data normalization is done as for the MPIIGaze dataset.

EyeDiap Dataset [27]: it contains a set of video clips of 16 participants with free head motion under various lighting conditions. We randomly select 100 frames from each video clip, resulting in 18200 frames in total. Both eyes can be obtained from each video frame. Note that we need to apply normalization for all the eye images and data in the same way as the MPIIGaze dataset.

5.2   Baseline Methods

For comparison, we use the following methods as baselines. Results of the baseline methods are obtained from our implementation or the published paper.

- **Single Eye** [6]: One of the typical appearance-based gaze estimation method based on deep neural networks. The input is the image of a single eye. We use the original Caffe codes provided by the authors of [6] to obtain all the results in our experiments. Note that another method [28] also uses the same network for gaze estimation and thus we regard [6,28] to be the same baseline.
- **RF:** One of the most commonly used regression method. It is shown to be effective for a variety of applications. Similar to [34], multiple RF regressors are trained for each head pose cluster.
- **iTracker** [29]: A multi-streams method that takes the full face image, two individual eye images, and a face grid as input. The performance of iTracker has already been reported in [30] on the MPIIGaze dataset and thus we use the reported numbers.
- **Full Face** [30]: A deep neuroal network-based method that takes the full face image as input with a spatial weighting strategy. Its performance has also been tested and reported on the same MPIIGaze dataset.

5.3   Within Dataset Evaluation

We first conduct experiments with training data and test data from the same dataset. In particular, we use the modified MPIIGaze dataset as described in Sect. 5.1 since it contains both eye images and the full face images of a large amount. Note that because the training data and test data are from the same dataset, we use the leave-one-person-out strategy to ensure that the experiments are done in a fully person-independent manner.

Eye image-Based Methods. We first consider the scenario where only eye images are used as the input. The accuracy is measured by the average gaze error of all the test samples including both the left and right images. The results

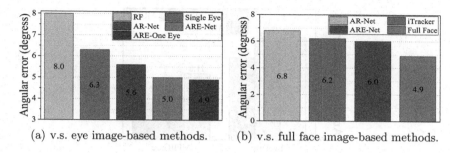

(a) v.s. eye image-based methods.   (b) v.s. full face image-based methods.

Fig. 3. Experimental results of the within-dataset evaluation and comparison.

of all the methods are obtained by running the corresponding codes on our modified MPIIGaze dataset with the same protocol. The comparison is shown in Fig. 3(a). The proposed method clearly achieves the best accuracy. As for the AR-Net, the average error is 5.6°, which is more than 11% improved compared to the Single Eye method, and also 30% improved compared to the RF method. This is benefited from both our new network architecture and loss fuction design. In addition, by introducing the E-Net, the final ARE-Net further improves the accuracy by a large margin. This demonstrates the effectiveness of the proposed E-Net as well as the idea of evaluation-guided regression. The final accuracy of 5.0° achieves the state-of-the-art for eye image-based gaze estimation.

Full Face Image-Based Methods. Recent methods such as [30] propose to use the full face image as input. Although our method only requires eye images as input, we still make a comparison with them. As for the dataset, we use the face image dataset introduced previously, and extract the two eye images as our input. Note that following [30], the gaze origin is defined at the face center for both the iTracker and Full Face methods. Therefore, in order to make a fair comparison, we also convert our estimated two eye gaze vectors to have the same origin geometrically, and then take their average as the final output.

As shown in Fig. 3(b), the Full Face method achieves the lowest error, while the proposed AR-Net and ARE-Net also show good performance which is comparable with the iTracker. Note the fact that our method is the only one that does not need full face image as input, its performance is quite satisfactory considering the save of computational cost (face image resolution 448 × 448 v.s. eye image resolution 36 × 60).

5.4   Cross-Dataset Evaluation

We then present our evaluation results in a cross-dataset setting. For the training dataset, we choose the UT Multiview dataset since it covers the largest variation of gaze directions and head poses. Consequently, we use data from the other two datasets, namely the MPIIGaze and EyeDiap datasets, as test data. As for the test data from the Eyediap dataset, we extract 100 images from each video clip, resulting in 18200 face images for test.

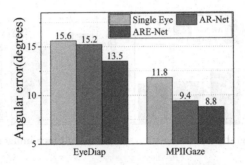

Fig. 4. Experimental results of the cross-dataset evaluation. The proposed methods outperform the Single Eye method on the EyeDiap and MPIIGaze datasets.

We first compare our method with the Single Eye method, which is a typical CNN-based method. As shown in Fig. 4, the proposed ARE-Net outperforms the Single Eye method on both the MPIIGaze and the EyeDiap datasets. In particular, compared with the Single Eye method, the performance improvement is 13.5% on the EyeDiap dataset, and 25.4% on the MPIIGaze dataset. This demonstrates the superior of the proposed ARE-Net. Note that our basic AR-Net also achieves a better accuracy than the Single Eye method. This shows the effectiveness of the proposed four-stream network with both eyes as input.

5.5 Evaluation on Each Individual

Previous experiments show the advantage of the proposed method in terms of the average performance. In this section, we further analyse its performance for each subject. As shown in Table 1, results for all the 15 subjects in the MPI-IGaze dataset are illustrated, with a comparison to the Single Eye method. The proposed ARE-Net and AR-Net outperform the Single Eye method for almost every subject (with only one exception), and the ARE-Net is also consistently better than the AR-Net. This validates our key idea and confirms the robustness of the proposed methods.

Table 1. Comparison of the Single Eye, AR and ARE methods regarding their accuracy on each subject.

Method	Subject															Avg.
	1	2	3	4	5	6	7	8	9	10	11	12	13	14	15	
Single Eye	4.9	7.1	5.8	6.5	5.9	6.4	5.6	7.6	6.6	7.7	6.0	6.0	6.1	6.9	5.5	6.3
AR-Net	4.0	4.4	5.9	6.8	3.7	6.1	4.3	5.8	6.0	7.1	6.5	5.5	5.6	6.8	6.2	5.7
ARE-Net	3.8	3.4	5.1	5.0	3.2	6.2	3.9	5.6	5.5	5.7	6.7	5.1	4.0	5.7	6.3	**5.0**

5.6   Analysis on E-Net

The proposed E-Net is the key component of our method and thus it is important to know how it benefits the method. To this end, we make further analysis based on the initial results obtained in Sect. 5.3. According to the comparisons shown in Table 2, we have the following conclusions:

- Regarding the overall gaze error, the existence of the E-Net improves the accuracy greatly in all cases compared to other methods.
- The E-Net can still select the relatively better eye to some extent from the already very ballanced output of the ARE-Net, while those other strategies cannot make more efficient selection.
- With the E-net, the difference between the better/worse eyes reduces greatly (to only 0.4°). Therefore, the major advantage of the E-Net is that it can optimize both the left and the right eyes simultaneously and effectively.
- Even if compared with other methods with correctly selected better eyes, the ARE-Net still achieves the best result without selection.

Table 2. Analysis on average gaze errors of: (left to right) average error of two eyes/E-Net's selection/the better eye/the worse eye/difference between the better and worse eyes/the eye near the camera/the more frontal eye.

Methods	Two eyes	E-Net select	Better eye	Worse eye	Δ	Near	Frontal
RF	8.0	–	6.7	9.4	2.7	8.1	8.1
Single Eye	6.3	–	5.0	7.6	2.6	6.2	6.4
AR-Net	5.7	–	5.3	6.0	0.7	5.6	5.7
ARE-Net	**5.0**	**4.9**	**4.8**	**5.2**	**0.4**	5.0	5.0

5.7   Additional Anaysis

Additional analyses and discussions on the proposed method are presented in this section.

Convergency. Figure 5 shows the convergency analysis of the proposed ARE-Net tested on the MPIIGaze dataset. During iteration, the estimation error tends to decrease guadually, and achieves the minimum after around 100 epochs. In general, during our experiments, the proposed network is shown to be able to converge quickly and robustly.

Case Study. We show some representative cases that explain why the proposed method is superior to the previous one, as shown in Fig. 6. In these cases, using only a single eye image, e.g., as the Single Eye method, may perform well for one eye but badly for the other eye, and the bad one will affect the final accuracy

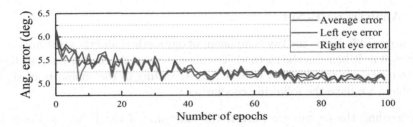

Fig. 5. Validation on the convergency of the ARE-Net.

greatly. On the other hand, the ARE-Net performs asymmetric optimization and helps improve both the better eye and the worse eye via the designed evaluation and feedback strategy. Therefore, the output gaze errors tend to be small for both eyes and this results in a much better overall accuracy. This is also demonstrated in Table 2.

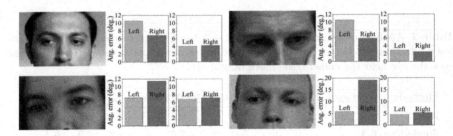

Fig. 6. Comparison of two eyes' gaze errors. The Single Eye method (left plot of each case) usually produces large errors in one eye while the proposed ARE-Net (right plot of each case) reduces gaze errors for both eyes.

Only One Eye Image as Input. Our method requires both the left and the right eye images as input. In the case that only one of the eye images is available, we can still test our network as follows.

Without loss of generality, assume we only have a left eye image. In order to run our method, we need to feed the network with something as the substitute for the right eye. In our experiment, we use (1) **0** matrix, i.e., a black image, (2) a copy of the left eye, (3) a randomly selected right eye image from a different person in the dataset, and (4) a fixed right eye image (typical shape, frontal gaze) from a different person in the dataset.

We test the trained models in Sect. 5.3 in the same leave-one-person-out manner. The average results of all the 15 subjects on the modified MPIIGaze dataset are shown in Table 3. It is interesting that if we use a black image or a copy of the input image to serve as the other eye image, the estimation errors are quite good ($\sim$6°). This confirms that our network is quite robust even if there is a very low quality eye image.

Table 3. Gaze estimation errors using only one eye image as input to the ARE-Net.

Input image	Substitute for the missing eye image			
	0 matrix	Copy input	Random eye	Fixed eye
Left eye	6.3° (left)	6.1° (left)	8.5° (left)	10.7° (left)
Right eye	6.2° (right)	6.1° (right)	7.9° (right)	9.3° (right)

6   Conclusion and Discussion

We present a deep learning-based method for remote gaze estimation. This problem is challenging because learning the highly complex regression between eye images and gaze directions is nontrivial. In this paper, we propose the Asymmetric Regression-Evaluation Network (ARE-Net), and try to improve the gaze estimation performance to its full extent. At the core of our method is the notion of "two eye asymmetry", which can be observed on the performance of the left and the right eyes during gaze estimation. Accordingly, we design the multistream ARE-Net. It contains one asymmetric regression network (AR-Net) to predict 3D gaze directions for both eyes with an asymmetric strategy, and one evaluation networks (E-Net) to adaptively adjust the strategy by evaluating the two eyes in terms of their quality in optimization. By training the whole network, our method achieves good performances on public datasets.

There are still future works to do along this line. First, we consider extending our current framework to also exploit the full face information. Second, since our current base-CNN is simple, it is possible to further enhance its performance if we use more advanced network structures.

References

1. Zhang, X., Sugano, Y., Bulling, A.: Everyday eye contact detection using unsupervised gaze target discovery. In: Proceedings of the ACM Symposium on User Interface Software and Technology (UIST), pp. 193–203 (2017)
2. Sugano, Y., Zhang, X., Bulling, A.: Aggregaze: collective estimation of audience attention on public displays. In: Proceedings of the ACM Symposium on User Interface Software and Technology (UIST), pp. 821–831 (2016)
3. Sun, X., Yao, H., Ji, R., Liu, X.M.: Toward statistical modeling of saccadic eye-movement and visual saliency. IEEE Trans. Image Process. **23**(11), 4649 (2014)
4. Cheng, Q., Agrafiotis, D., Achim, A., Bull, D.: Gaze location prediction for broadcast football video. IEEE Trans. Image Process. **22**(12), 4918–4929 (2013)
5. Hansen, D., Ji, Q.: In the eye of the beholder: A survey of models for eyes and gaze. IEEE Trans. PAMI **32**(3), 478–500 (2010)
6. Zhang, X., Sugano, Y., Fritz, M., Bulling, A.: Appearance-based gaze estimation in the wild. In: IEEE Conference on Computer Vision and Pattern Recognition, pp. 4511–4520 (2015)
7. Zhu, W., Deng, H.: Monocular free-head 3D gaze tracking with deep learning and geometry constraints. In: The IEEE International Conference on Computer Vision (ICCV) (2017)

8. Lepetit, V., Moreno-Noguer, F., Fua, P.: EPNP: an accurate o(n) solution to the pnp problem. Int. J. Comput. Vis. **81**(2), 155 (2008)
9. Morimoto, C., Mimica, M.: Eye gaze tracking techniques for interactive applications. CVIU **98**(1), 4–24 (2005)
10. Guestrin, E., Eizenman, M.: General theory of remote gaze estimation using the pupil center and corneal reflections. IEEE Trans. Biomed. Eng. **53**(6), 1124–1133 (2006)
11. Zhu, Z., Ji, Q.: Novel eye gaze tracking techniques under natural head movement. IEEE Trans. Biomed. Eng. J. **54**(12), 2246–2260 (2007)
12. Nakazawa, A., Nitschke, C.: Point of gaze estimation through corneal surface reflection in an active illumination environment. In: Fitzgibbon, A., Lazebnik, S., Perona, P., Sato, Y., Schmid, C. (eds.) ECCV 2012. LNCS, pp. 159–172. Springer, Heidelberg (2012). https://doi.org/10.1007/978-3-642-33709-3_12
13. Valenti, R., Sebe, N., Gevers, T.: Combining head pose and eye location information for gaze estimation. IEEE Trans. Image Process. Publ. IEEE Signal Process. Soc. **21**(2), 802–815 (2012)
14. Jeni, L.A., Cohn, J.F.: Person-independent 3d gaze estimation using face frontalization. In: Computer Vision and Pattern Recognition Workshops, pp. 792–800 (2016)
15. Funes Mora, K.A., Odobez, J.M.: Geometric generative gaze estimation (g3e) for remote RGB-D cameras. In: IEEE Computer Vision and Pattern Recognition Conference, pp. 1773–1780 (2014)
16. Xiong, X., Liu, Z., Cai, Q., Zhang, Z.: Eye gaze tracking using an RGBD camera: a comparison with a RGB solution. The 4th International Workshop on Pervasive Eye Tracking and Mobile Eye-Based Interaction (PETMEI 2014), pp. 1113–1121 (2014)
17. Wang, K., Ji, Q.: Real time eye gaze tracking with 3d deformable eye-face model. In: The IEEE International Conference on Computer Vision (ICCV) (2017)
18. Duchowski, A.T.: A breadth-first survey of eye-tracking applications. Behav. Res. Methods Instrum. Comput. **34**(4), 455–470 (2002)
19. Tan, K., Kriegman, D., Ahuja, N.: Appearance-based eye gaze estimation. In: WACV, pp. 191–195 (2002)
20. Baluja, S., Pomerleau, D.: Non-Intrusive Gaze Tracking Using Artificial Neural Networks. Carnegie Mellon University (1994)
21. Xu, L.Q., Machin, D., Sheppard, P.: A novel approach to real-time non-intrusive gaze finding. In: BMVC, pp. 428–437 (1998)
22. Lu, F., Sugano, Y., Okabe, T., Sato, Y.: Adaptive linear regression for appearance-based gaze estimation. IEEE Trans. Pattern Anal. Mach. Intell. **36**(10), 2033–2046 (2014)
23. Williams, O., Blake, A., Cipolla, R.: Sparse and semi-supervised visual mapping with the S^3GP. In: CVPR, pp. 230–237(2006)
24. Schneider, T., Schauerte, B., Stiefelhagen, R.: Manifold alignment for person independent appearance-based gaze estimation. In: International Conference on Pattern Recognition (ICPR), pp. 1167–1172 (2014)
25. Lu, F., Chen, X., Sato, Y.: Appearance-based gaze estimation via uncalibrated gaze pattern recovery. IEEE Trans. Image Process. **26**(4), 1543–1553 (2017)
26. Sugano, Y., Matsushita, Y., Sato, Y., Koike, H.: Appearance-based gaze estimation with online calibration from mouse operations. IEEE Trans. Hum. Mach. Syst. **45**(6), 750–760 (2015)

27. Mora, K.A.F., Monay, F., Odobez, J.M.: Eyediap:a database for the development and evaluation of gaze estimation algorithms from RGB and RGB-D cameras. In: Symposium on Eye Tracking Research and Applications, pp. 255–258 (2014)
28. Wood, E., Morency, L.P., Robinson, P., Bulling, A.: Learning an appearance-based gaze estimator from one million synthesised images. In: Biennial ACM Symposium on Eye Tracking Research & Applications, pp. 131–138 (2016)
29. Krafka, K., et al.: Eye tracking for everyone. In: Computer Vision and Pattern Recognition, pp. 2176–2184 (2016)
30. Zhang, X., Sugano, Y., Fritz, M., Bulling, A.: It's written all over your face: Full-face appearance-based gaze estimation. In: Proceedings of the IEEE Conference on Computer Vision and Pattern Recognition Workshops (CVPRW) (2017)
31. Lu, F., Sugano, Y., Okabe, T., Sato, Y.: Head pose-free appearance-based gaze sensing via eye image synthesis. In: International Conference on Pattern Recognition, pp. 1008–1011 (2012)
32. Sugano, Y., Matsushita, Y., Sato, Y.: Appearance-based gaze estimation using visual saliency. IEEE Trans. Pattern Anal. Mach. Intell. **35**(2), 329 (2013)
33. Krizhevsky, A., Sutskever, I., Hinton, G.E.: Imagenet classification with deep convolutional neural networks. In: Advances in Neural Information Processing Systems (2012)
34. Sugano, Y., Matsushita, Y., Sato, Y.: Learning-by-synthesis for appearance-based 3D gaze estimation. In: Computer Vision and Pattern Recognition, pp. 1821–1828 (2014)

ShuffleNet V2: Practical Guidelines
for Efficient CNN Architecture Design

Ningning Ma[1,2](✉) [iD], Xiangyu Zhang[1](✉) [iD], Hai-Tao Zheng[2] [iD],
and Jian Sun[1] [iD]

[1] Megvii Inc (Face++), Beijing, China
{maningning,zhangxiangyu,sunjian}@megvii.com
[2] Tsinghua University, Beijing, China
zheng.haitao@sz.tsinghua.edu.cn

Abstract. Currently, the neural network architecture design is mostly guided by the *indirect* metric of computation complexity, i.e., FLOPs. However, the *direct* metric, e.g., speed, also depends on the other factors such as memory access cost and platform characterics. Thus, this work proposes to evaluate the direct metric on the target platform, beyond only considering FLOPs. Based on a series of controlled experiments, this work derives several practical *guidelines* for efficient network design. Accordingly, a new architecture is presented, called *ShuffleNet V2*. Comprehensive ablation experiments verify that our model is the state-of-the-art in terms of speed and accuracy tradeoff.

Keywords: CNN architecture design · Efficiency · Practical

1 Introduction

The architecture of deep convolutional neutral networks (CNNs) has evolved for years, becoming more accurate and faster. Since the milestone work of AlexNet [15], the ImageNet classification accuracy has been significantly improved by novel structures, including VGG [25], GoogLeNet [28], ResNet [5,6], DenseNet [11], ResNeXt [33], SE-Net [9], and automatic neutral architecture search [18,21,39], to name a few.

Besides accuracy, computation complexity is another important consideration. Real world tasks often aim at obtaining best accuracy under a limited computational budget, given by target platform (e.g., hardware) and application scenarios (e.g., auto driving requires low latency). This motivates a series of works towards light-weight architecture design and better speed-accuracy tradeoff, including Xception [2], MobileNet [8], MobileNet V2 [24], ShuffleNet [35], and

---

N. Ma and X. Zhang—Equal contribution.

Electronic supplementary material The online version of this chapter (https://doi.org/10.1007/978-3-030-01264-9_8) contains supplementary material, which is available to authorized users.

V. Ferrari et al. (Eds.): ECCV 2018, LNCS 11218, pp. 122–138, 2018.
https://doi.org/10.1007/978-3-030-01264-9_8

CondenseNet [10], to name a few. Group convolution and depth-wise convolution are crucial in these works.

To measure the computation complexity, a widely used metric is the number of float-point operations, or $FLOPs^1$. However, FLOPs is an *indirect* metric. It is an approximation of, but usually not equivalent to the *direct* metric that we really care about, such as speed or latency. Such discrepancy has been noticed in previous works [7,19,24,30]. For example, *MobileNet v2* [24] is much faster than *NASNET-A* [39] but they have comparable FLOPs. This phenomenon is further exmplified in Fig. 1(c) and (d), which show that networks with similar FLOPs have different speeds. Therefore, using FLOPs as the only metric for computation complexity is insufficient and could lead to sub-optimal design.

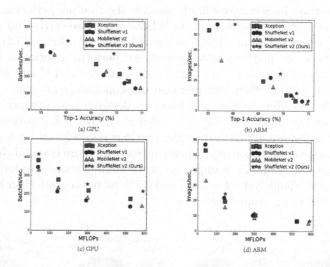

Fig. 1. Measurement of accuracy (ImageNet classification on validation set), speed and FLOPs of four network architectures on two hardware platforms with four different level of computation complexities (see text for details). (a, c) GPU results, *batchsize* = 8. (b, d) ARM results, *batchsize* = 1. The best performing algorithm, our proposed ShuffleNet v2, is on the top right region, under all cases.

The discrepancy between the indirect (FLOPs) and direct (speed) metrics can be attributed to two main reasons. First, several important factors that have considerable affection on speed are not taken into account by FLOPs. One such factor is *memory access cost* (MAC). Such cost constitutes a large portion of runtime in certain operations like group convolution. It could be bottleneck on devices with strong computing power, e.g., GPUs. This cost should not be simply ignored during network architecture design. Another one is *degree of parallelism*. A model with high degree of parallelism could be much faster than another one with low degree of parallelism, under the same FLOPs.

---

[1] In this paper, the definition of *FLOPs* follows [35], i.e. the number of multiply-adds.

Second, operations with the same FLOPs could have different running time, depending on the platform. For example, tensor decomposition is widely used in early works [14,36,37] to accelerate the matrix multiplication. However, the recent work [7] finds that the decomposition in [36] is even slower on GPU although it reduces FLOPs by 75%. We investigated this issue and found that this is because the latest CUDNN [1] library is specially optimized for 3×3 conv. We cannot certainly think that 3×3 conv is 9 times slower than 1×1 conv.

With these observations, we propose that two principles should be considered for effective network architecture design. First, the direct metric (e.g., speed) should be used instead of the indirect ones (e.g., FLOPs). Second, such metric should be evaluated on the target platform.

In this work, we follow the two principles and propose a more effective network architecture. In Sect. 2, we firstly analyze the runtime performance of two representative state-of-the-art networks [24,35]. Then, we derive four guidelines for efficient network design, which are beyond only considering FLOPs. While these guidelines are platform independent, we perform a series of controlled experiments to validate them on two different platforms (GPU and ARM) with dedicated code optimization, ensuring that our conclusions are state-of-the-art.

In Sect. 3, according to the guidelines, we design a new network structure. As it is inspired by ShuffleNet [35], it is called *ShuffleNet V2*. It is demonstrated much faster and more accurate than the previous networks on both platforms, via comprehensive validation experiments in Sect. 4. Figure 1(a) and (b) gives an overview of comparison. For example, given the computation complexity budget of 40M FLOPs, ShuffleNet v2 is 3.5% and 3.7% more accurate than ShuffleNet v1 and MobileNet v2, respectively.

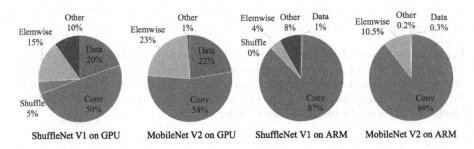

Fig. 2. Run time decomposition on two representative state-of-the-art network architectures, *ShuffeNet v1* [35] ($1\times$, $g = 3$) and *MobileNet v2* [24] ($1\times$).

2   Practical Guidelines for Efficient Network Design

Our study is performed on two widely adopted hardwares with industry-level optimization of CNN library. We note that our CNN library is more efficient than most open source libraries. Thus, we ensure that our observations and conclusions are solid and of significance for practice in industry.

- *GPU.* A single NVIDIA GeForce GTX 1080Ti is used. The convolution library is CUDNN 7.0 [1]. We also activate the benchmarking function of CUDNN to select the fastest algorithms for different convolutions respectively.
- *ARM.* A Qualcomm Snapdragon 810. We use a highly-optimized Neon-based implementation. A single thread is used for evaluation.

Other settings include: full optimization options (e.g. tensor fusion, which is used to reduce the overhead of small operations) are switched on. The input image size is 224×224. Each network is randomly initialized and evaluated for 100 times. The average runtime is used.

To initiate our study, we analyze the runtime performance of two state-of-the-art networks, *ShuffleNet v1* [35] and *MobileNet v2* [24]. They are both highly efficient and accurate on ImageNet classification task. They are both widely used on low end devices such as mobiles. Although we only analyze these two networks, we note that they are representative for the current trend. At their core are group convolution and depth-wise convolution, which are also crucial components for other state-of-the-art networks, such as ResNeXt [33], Xception [2], MobileNet [8], and CondenseNet [10].

The overall runtime is decomposed for different operations, as shown in Fig. 2. We note that the FLOPs metric only account for the convolution part. Although this part consumes most time, the other operations including data I/O, data shuffle and element-wise operations (AddTensor, ReLU, etc) also occupy considerable amount of time. Therefore, FLOPs is not an accurate enough estimation of actual runtime.

Based on this observation, we perform a detailed analysis of runtime (or speed) from several different aspects and derive several practical guidelines for efficient network architecture design.

Table 1. Validation experiment for **Guideline 1**. Four different ratios of number of input/output channels ($c1$ and $c2$) are tested, while the total FLOPs under the four ratios is fixed by varying the number of channels. Input image size is 56×56.

$c1{:}c2$	($c1$,$c2$ for $\times 1$)	GPU (Batches/sec.)			($c1$,$c2$) for $\times 1$	ARM (Images/sec.)		
		$\times 1$	$\times 2$	$\times 4$		$\times 1$	$\times 2$	$\times 4$
1:1	(128,128)	1480	723	232	(32,32)	76.2	21.7	5.3
1:2	(90,180)	1296	586	206	(22,44)	72.9	20.5	5.1
1:6	(52,312)	876	489	189	(13,78)	69.1	17.9	4.6
1:12	(36,432)	748	392	163	(9,108)	57.6	15.1	4.4

(G1) Equal Channel width Minimizes Memory Access Cost (MAC). The modern networks usually adopt *depthwise separable convolutions* [2,8,24, 35], where the pointwise convolution (i.e., 1×1 convolution) accounts for most of the complexity [35]. We study the kernel shape of the 1×1 convolution. The shape is specified by two parameters: the number of input channels c_1 and output channels c_2. Let h and w be the spatial size of the feature map, the FLOPs of the 1×1 convolution is $B = hwc_1c_2$.

For simplicity, we assume the cache in the computing device is large enough to store the entire feature maps and parameters. Thus, the memory access cost (MAC), or the number of memory access operations, is $\text{MAC} = hw(c_1+c_2)+c_1c_2$. Note that the two terms correspond to the memory access for input/output feature maps and kernel weights, respectively.

From mean value inequality, we have

$$\text{MAC} \geq 2\sqrt{hwB} + \frac{B}{hw}. \tag{1}$$

Therefore, *MAC has a lower bound given by FLOPs. It reaches the lower bound when the numbers of input and output channels are equal.*

The conclusion is theoretical. In practice, the cache on many devices is not large enough. Also, modern computation libraries usually adopt complex blocking strategies to make full use of the cache mechanism [3]. Therefore, the real MAC may deviate from the theoretical one. To validate the above conclusion, an experiment is performed as follows. A benchmark network is built by stacking 10 building blocks repeatedly. Each block contains two convolution layers. The first contains c_1 input channels and c_2 output channels, and the second otherwise.

Table 1 reports the running speed by varying the ratio $c_1 : c_2$ while fixing the total FLOPs. It is clear that when $c_1 : c_2$ is approaching $1 : 1$, the MAC becomes smaller and the network evaluation speed is faster.

Table 2. Validation experiment for **Guideline 2**. Four values of group number g are tested, while the total FLOPs under the four values is fixed by varying the total channel number c. Input image size is 56×56.

g	c for ×1	GPU (Batches/sec.)			c for ×1	CPU (Images/sec.)		
		×1	×2	×4		×1	×2	×4
1	128	2451	1289	437	64	40.0	10.2	2.3
2	180	1725	873	341	90	35.0	9.5	2.2
4	256	1026	644	338	128	32.9	8.7	2.1
8	360	634	445	230	180	27.8	7.5	1.8

(G2) Excessive Group Convolution Increases MAC. Group convolution is at the core of modern network architectures [12,26,31,33–35]. It reduces the computational complexity (FLOPs) by changing the dense convolution between all channels to be sparse (only within groups of channels). On one hand, it allows usage of more channels given a fixed FLOPs and increases the network capacity (thus better accuracy). On the other hand, however, the increased number of channels results in more MAC.

Formally, following the notations in **G1** and Eq. 1, the relation between MAC and FLOPs for 1×1 group convolution is

$$
\begin{aligned}
\text{MAC} &= hw(c_1 + c_2) + \frac{c_1 c_2}{g} \\
&= hwc_1 + \frac{Bg}{c_1} + \frac{B}{hw},
\end{aligned}
\tag{2}
$$

where g is the number of groups and $B = hwc_1c_2/g$ is the FLOPs. It is easy to see that, given the fixed input shape $c_1 \times h \times w$ and the computational cost B, MAC increases with the growth of g.

To study the affection in practice, a benchmark network is built by stacking 10 pointwise group convolution layers. Table 2 reports the running speed of using different group numbers while fixing the total FLOPs. It is clear that using a large group number decreases running speed significantly. For example, using 8 groups is more than two times slower than using 1 group (standard dense convolution) on GPU and up to 30% slower on ARM. This is mostly due to increased MAC. We note that our implementation has been specially optimized and is much faster than trivially computing convolutions group by group.

Therefore, we suggest that *the group number should be carefully chosen based on the target platform and task. It is unwise to use a large group number simply because this may enable using more channels, because the benefit of accuracy increase can easily be outweighed by the rapidly increasing computational cost.*

Table 3. Validation experiment for **Guideline 3**. c denotes the number of channels for *1-fragment*. The channel number in other fragmented structures is adjusted so that the FLOPs is the same as *1-fragment*. Input image size is 56×56.

	GPU (Batches/sec.)			CPU (Images/sec.)		
	$c = 128$	$c = 256$	$c = 512$	$c = 64$	$c = 128$	$c = 256$
1-fragment	2446	1274	434	40.2	10.1	2.3
2-fragment-series	1790	909	336	38.6	10.1	2.2
4-fragment-series	752	745	349	38.4	10.1	2.3
2-fragment-parallel	1537	803	320	33.4	9.1	2.2
4-fragment-parallel	691	572	292	35.0	8.4	2.1

(G3) Network Fragmentation Reduces Degree of Parallelism. In the GoogLeNet series [13,27–29] and auto-generated architectures [18,21,39]), a "multi-path" structure is widely adopted in each network block. A lot of small operators (called "fragmented operators" here) are used instead of a few large ones. For example, in *NASNET-A* [39] the number of fragmented operators (i.e. the number of individual convolution or pooling operations in one building block) is 13. In contrast, in regular structures like ResNet [5], this number is 2 or 3.

Table 4. Validation experiment for **Guideline 4**. The ReLU and shortcut operations are removed from the "bottleneck" unit [5], separately. c is the number of channels in unit. The unit is stacked repeatedly for 10 times to benchmark the speed.

ReLU	Short-cut	GPU (Batches/sec.)			CPU (Images/sec.)		
		$c = 32$	$c = 64$	$c = 128$	$c = 32$	$c = 64$	$c = 128$
yes	yes	2427	2066	1436	56.7	16.9	5.0
yes	no	2647	2256	1735	61.9	18.8	5.2
no	yes	2672	2121	1458	57.3	18.2	5.1
no	no	2842	2376	1782	66.3	20.2	5.4

Though such fragmented structure has been shown beneficial for accuracy, it could decrease efficiency because it is unfriendly for devices with strong parallel computing powers like GPU. It also introduces extra overheads such as kernel launching and synchronization.

To quantify how network fragmentation affects efficiency, we evaluate a series of network blocks with different degrees of fragmentation. Specifically, each building block consists of from 1 to 4 1 × 1 convolutions, which are arranged in sequence or in parallel. The block structures are illustrated in appendix. Each block is repeatedly stacked for 10 times. Results in Table 3 show that fragmentation reduces the speed significantly on GPU, e.g. 4-fragment structure is 3× slower than 1-fragment. On ARM, the speed reduction is relatively small.

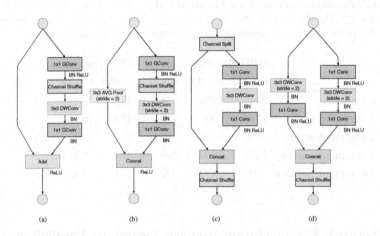

(a)   (b)   (c)   (d)

Fig. 3. Building blocks of ShuffleNet v1 [35] and this work. (a): the basic ShuffleNet unit; (b) the ShuffleNet unit for spatial down sampling (2×); (c) our basic unit; (d) our unit for spatial down sampling (2×). **DWConv**: depthwise convolution. **GConv**: group convolution.

(G4) Element-wise Operations are Non-negligible. As shown in Fig. 2, in light-weight models like [24,35], element-wise operations occupy considerable amount of time, especially on GPU. Here, the element-wise operators include ReLU, AddTensor, AddBias, etc. They have small FLOPs but relatively heavy MAC. Specially, we also consider *depthwise convolution* [2,8,24,35] as an element-wise operator as it also has a high MAC/FLOPs ratio.

For validation, we experimented with the "bottleneck" unit (1×1 conv followed by 3×3 conv followed by 1×1 conv, with ReLU and shortcut connection) in ResNet [5]. The ReLU and shortcut operations are removed, separately. Runtime of different variants is reported in Table 4. We observe around 20% speedup is obtained on both GPU and ARM, after ReLU and shortcut are removed.

Conclusion and Discussions. Based on the above guidelines and empirical studies, we conclude that an efficient network architecture should (1) use"balanced"convolutions (equal channel width); (2) be aware of the cost of using group convolution; (3) reduce the degree of fragmentation; and (4) reduce element-wise operations. These desirable properties depend on platform characterics (such as memory manipulation and code optimization) that are beyond theoretical FLOPs. They should be taken into accout for practical network design.

Recent advances in light-weight neural network architectures [2,8,18,21,24, 35,39] are mostly based on the metric of FLOPs and do not consider these properties above. For example, *ShuffleNet v1* [35] heavily depends group convolutions (against **G2**) and bottleneck-like building blocks (against **G1**). *MobileNet v2* [24] uses an inverted bottleneck structure that violates **G1**. It uses depthwise convolutions and ReLUs on "thick" feature maps. This violates **G4**. The auto-generated structures [18,21,39] are highly fragmented and violate **G3**.

3 ShuffleNet V2: An Efficient Architecture

Review of ShuffleNet v1 [35]. ShuffleNet is a state-of-the-art network architecture. It is widely adopted in low end devices such as mobiles. It inspires our work. Thus, it is reviewed and analyzed at first.

According to [35], the main challenge for light-weight networks is that only a limited number of feature channels is affordable under a given computation budget (FLOPs). To increase the number of channels without significantly increasing FLOPs, two techniques are adopted in [35]: pointwise group convolutions and bottleneck-like structures. A "channel shuffle" operation is then introduced to enable information communication between different groups of channels and improve accuracy. The building blocks are illustrated in Fig. 3(a) and (b).

As discussed in Sect. 2, both pointwise group convolutions and bottleneck structures increase MAC (**G1** and **G2**). This cost is non-negligible, especially for light-weight models. Also, using too many groups violates **G3**. The element-wise "Add" operation in the shortcut connection is also undesirable (**G4**). Therefore, in order to achieve high model capacity and efficiency, the key issue is how to

Table 5. Overall architecture of ShuffleNet v2, for four different levels of complexities.

Layer	Output size	KSize	Stride	Repeat	Output channels			
					0.5×	1×	1.5×	2×
Image	224×224				3	3	3	3
Conv1	112×112	3×3	2	1	24	24	24	24
MaxPool	56×56	3×3	2					
Stage2	28×28		2	1	48	116	176	244
	28×28		1	3				
Stage3	14×14		2	1	96	232	352	488
	14×14		1	7				
Stage4	7×7		2	1	192	464	704	976
	7×7		1	3				
Conv5	7×7	1×1	1	1	1024	1024	1024	2048
GlobalPool	1×1	7×7						
FC					1000	1000	1000	1000
FLOPs					41M	146M	299M	591M
# of Weights					1.4M	2.3M	3.5M	7.4M

maintain a large number and equally wide channels with neither dense convolution nor too many groups.

Channel Split and ShuffleNet V2. Towards above purpose, we introduce a simple operator called *channel split*. It is illustrated in Fig. 3(c). At the beginning of each unit, the input of c feature channels are split into two branches with $c - c'$ and c' channels, respectively. Following **G3**, one branch remains as identity. The other branch consists of three convolutions with the same input and output channels to satisfy **G1**. The two 1×1 convolutions are no longer group-wise, unlike [35]. This is partially to follow **G2**, and partially because the split operation already produces two groups.

After convolution, the two branches are concatenated. So, the number of channels keeps the same (**G1**). The same "channel shuffle" operation as in [35] is then used to enable information communication between the two branches.

After the shuffling, the next unit begins. Note that the "Add" operation in ShuffleNet v1 [35] no longer exists. Element-wise operations like ReLU and *depthwise convolutions* exist only in one branch. Also, the three successive element-wise operations, "Concat", "Channel Shuffle" and "Channel Split", are merged into a single element-wise operation. These changes are beneficial according to **G4**.

For spatial down sampling, the unit is slightly modified and illustrated in Fig. 3(d). The channel split operator is removed. Thus, the number of output channels is doubled.

The proposed building blocks (c)(d), as well as the resulting networks, are called *ShuffleNet V2*. Based the above analysis, we conclude that this architecture design is highly efficient as it follows all the guidelines.

The building blocks are repeatedly stacked to construct the whole network. For simplicity, we set $c' = c/2$. The overall network structure is similar to ShuffleNet v1 [35] and summarized in Table 5. There is only one difference: an additional 1×1 convolution layer is added right before *global averaged pooling* to mix up features, which is absent in ShuffleNet v1. Similar to [35], the number of channels in each block is scaled to generate networks of different complexities, marked as $0.5\times$, $1\times$, etc.

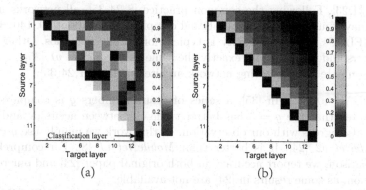

(a)   (b)

Fig. 4. Illustration of the patterns in feature reuse for *DenseNet* [11] and ShuffleNet V2. (a) (courtesy of [11]) the average absolute filter weight of convolutional layers in a model. The color of pixel (s, l) encodes the average $l1$-norm of weights connecting layer s to l. (b) The color of pixel (s, l) means the number of channels *directly* connecting block s to block l in ShuffleNet v2. All pixel values are normalized to $[0, 1]$. (Color figure online)

Analysis of Network Accuracy. ShuffleNet v2 is not only efficient, but also accurate. There are two main reasons. First, the high efficiency in each building block enables using more feature channels and larger network capacity.

Second, in each block, half of feature channels (when $c' = c/2$) directly go through the block and join the next block. This can be regarded as a kind of *feature reuse*, in a similar spirit as in *DenseNet* [11] and *CondenseNet* [10].

In *DenseNet*[11], to analyze the feature reuse pattern, the $l1$-norm of the weights between layers are plotted, as in Fig. 4(a). It is clear that the connections between the adjacent layers are stronger than the others. This implies that the dense connection between all layers could introduce redundancy. The recent *CondenseNet* [10] also supports the viewpoint.

In ShuffleNet V2, it is easy to prove that the number of "directly-connected" channels between i-th and $(i+j)$-th building block is $r^j c$, where $r = (1-c')/c$. In other words, the amount of feature reuse decays exponentially with the distance between two blocks. Between distant blocks, the feature reuse becomes much weaker. Figure 4(b) plots the similar visualization as in (a), for $r = 0.5$. Note that the pattern in (b) is similar to (a).

Thus, the structure of ShuffleNet V2 realizes this type of feature re-use pattern *by design*. It shares the similar benefit of feature re-use for high accuracy as in *DenseNet* [11], but it is much more efficient as analyzed earlier. This is verified in experiments, Table 8.

4   Experiment

Our ablation experiments are performed on ImageNet 2012 classification dataset [4,23]. Following the common practice [8,24,35], all networks in comparison have four levels of computational complexity, i.e. about 40, 140, 300 and 500+ MFLOPs. Such complexity is typical for mobile scenarios. Other hyperparameters and protocols are exactly the same as *ShuffleNet v1* [35].

We compare with following network architectures [2,11,24,35]:

- *ShuffleNet v1* [35]. In [35], a series of group numbers g is compared. It is suggested that the $g = 3$ has better trade-off between accuracy and speed. This also agrees with our observation. In this work we mainly use $g = 3$.
- *MobileNet v2* [24]. It is better than *MobileNet v1* [8]. For comprehensive comparison, we report accuracy in both original paper [24] and our reimplemention, as some results in [24] are not available.
- *Xception* [2]. The original *Xception* model [2] is very large (FLOPs >2G), which is out of our range of comparison. The recent work [16] proposes a modified light weight Xception structure that shows better trade-offs between accuracy and efficiency. So, we compare with this variant.
- *DenseNet* [11]. The original work [11] only reports results of large models (FLOPs >2G). For direct comparison, we reimplement it following the architecture settings in Table 5, where the building blocks in Stage 2–4 consist of *DenseNet* blocks. We adjust the number of channels to meet different target complexities.

Table 8 summarizes all the results. We analyze these results from different aspects.

Accuracy vs. FLOPs. It is clear that the proposed ShuffleNet v2 models outperform all other networks by a large margin[2], especially under smaller computational budgets. Also, we note that MobileNet v2 performs pooly at 40 MFLOPs level with 224×224 image size. This is probably caused by too few channels. In contrast, our model do not suffer from this drawback as our efficient design allows using more channels. Also, while both of our model and DenseNet [11] reuse features, our model is much more efficient, as discussed in Sect. 3.

---

[2] As reported in [24], MobileNet v2 of 500+ MFLOPs has comparable accuracy with the counterpart ShuffleNet v2 (25.3% vs. 25.1% top-1 error); however, our reimplemented version is not as good (26.7% error, see Table 8).

Table 8 also compares our model with other state-of-the-art networks including *CondenseNet* [10], *IGCV2* [31], and *IGCV3* [26] where appropriate. Our model performs better consistently at various complexity levels.

Inference Speed vs. FLOPs/Accuracy. For four architectures with good accuracy, ShuffleNet v2, MobileNet v2, ShuffleNet v1 and Xception, we compare their actual speed vs. FLOPs, as shown in Fig. 1(c) and (d). More results on different resolutions are provided in Appendix Table 1.

ShuffleNet v2 is clearly faster than the other three networks, especially on GPU. For example, at 500MFLOPs ShuffleNet v2 is 58% faster than MobileNet v2, 63% faster than ShuffleNet v1 and 25% faster than Xception. On ARM, the speeds of ShuffleNet v1, Xception and ShuffleNet v2 are comparable; however, MobileNet v2 is much slower, especially on smaller FLOPs. We believe this is because MobileNet v2 has higher MAC (see **G1** and **G4** in Sect. 2), which is significant on mobile devices.

Compared with *MobileNet v1* [8], *IGCV2* [31], and *IGCV3* [26], we have two observations. First, although the accuracy of MobileNet v1 is not as good, its speed on GPU is faster than all the counterparts, including ShuffleNet v2. We believe this is because its structure satisfies most of proposed guidelines (e.g. for **G3**, the fragments of MobileNet v1 are even fewer than ShuffleNet v2). Second, IGCV2 and IGCV3 are slow. This is due to usage of too many convolution groups (4 or 8 in [26,31]). Both observations are consistent with our proposed guidelines.

Recently, automatic model search [18,21,22,32,38,39] has become a promising trend for CNN architecture design. The bottom section in Table 8 evaluates some auto-generated models. We find that their speeds are relatively slow. We believe this is mainly due to the usage of too many fragments (see **G3**). Nevertheless, this research direction is still promising. Better models may be obtained, for example, if model search algorithms are combined with our proposed guidelines, and the direct metric (speed) is evaluated on the target platform.

Finally, Fig. 1(a) and (b) summarizes the results of accuracy vs. speed, the direct metric. We conclude that ShuffleNet v2 is best on both GPU and ARM.

Compatibility with Other Methods. ShuffleNet v2 can be combined with other techniques to further advance the performance. When equipped with *Squeeze-and-excitation* (SE) module [9], the classification accuracy of ShuffleNet v2 is improved by 0.5% at the cost of certain loss in speed. The block structure is illustrated in Appendix Fig. 2(b). Results are shown in Table 8 (bottom section).

Generalization to Large Models. Although our main ablation is performed for light weight scenarios, ShuffleNet v2 can be used for large models (e.g, FLOPs ≥ 2G). Table 6 compares a 50-layer ShuffleNet v2 (details in Appendix) with the counterpart of ShuffleNet v1 [35] and *ResNet-50* [5]. ShuffleNet v2 still outperforms ShuffleNet v1 at 2.3GFLOPs and surpasses ResNet-50 with 40% fewer FLOPs.

Table 6. Results of large models. See text for details.

Model	FLOPs	Top-1 err. (%)
ShuffleNet v2-50 (ours)	**2.3G**	**22.8**
ShuffleNet v1-50 [35] (our impl.)	**2.3G**	25.2
ResNet-50 [5]	3.8G	24.0
SE-ShuffleNet v2-164 (ours, with residual)	**12.7G**	**18.56**
SENet [9]	20.7G	18.68

For very deep ShuffleNet v2 (e.g. over 100 layers), for the training to converge faster, we slightly modify the basic ShuffleNet v2 unit by adding a residual path (details in Appendix). Table 6 presents a ShuffleNet v2 model of 164 layers equipped with *SE* [9] components (details in Appendix). It obtains superior accuracy over the previous state-of-the-art models [9] with much fewer FLOPs.

Object Detection. To evaluate the generalization ability, we also tested COCO object detection [17] task. We use the state-of-the-art light-weight detector – *Light-Head RCNN* [16] – as our framework and follow the same training and test protocols. Only backbone networks are replaced with ours. Models are pretrained on ImageNet and then finetuned on detection task. For training we use *train+val* set in COCO except for 5000 images from *minival* set, and use the *minival* set to test. The accuracy metric is COCO standard *mmAP*, i.e. the averaged mAPs at the box IoU thresholds from 0.5 to 0.95.

ShuffleNet v2 is compared with other three light-weight models: *Xception* [2,16], *ShuffleNet v1* [35] and *MobileNet v2* [24] on four levels of complexities. Results in Table 7 show that ShuffleNet v2 performs the best.

Table 7. Performance on COCO object detection. The input image size is 800 × 1200. *FLOPs* row lists the complexity levels at 224 × 224 input size. For GPU speed evaluation, the batch size is 4. We do not test ARM because the *PSRoI Pooling* operation needed in [16] is unavailable on ARM currently.

Model	mmAP(%)				GPU Speed (Images/sec.)			
FLOPs	40 M	140 M	300 M	500 M	40 M	140 M	300 M	500 M
Xception	21.9	29.0	31.3	32.9	178	131	101	83
ShuffleNet v1	20.9	27.0	29.9	32.9	152	85	76	60
MobileNet v2	20.7	24.4	30.0	30.6	146	111	94	72
ShuffleNet v2 (ours)	22.5	29.0	31.8	33.3	**188**	**146**	**109**	**87**
ShuffleNet v2* (ours)	**23.7**	**29.6**	**32.2**	**34.2**	183	138	105	83

Compared the detection result (Table 7) with classification result (Table 8), it is interesting that, on classification the accuracy rank is ShuffleNet v2 $\geq$ MobileNet v2 > ShuffeNet v1 > Xception, while on detection the rank becomes

Table 8. Comparison of several network architectures over classification error (on validation set, single center crop) and speed, on two platforms and four levels of computation complexity. Results are grouped by complexity levels for better comparison. The batch size is 8 for GPU and 1 for ARM. The image size is 224 × 224 except: [*] 160 × 160 and [**] 192 × 192. We do not provide speed measurements for *CondenseNets* [10] due to lack of efficient implementation currently.

Model	Complexity (MFLOPs)	Top-1 err. (%)	GPU Speed (Batches/sec.)	ARM Speed (Images/sec.)
ShuffleNet v2 0.5× (ours)	41	**39.7**	417	**57.0**
0.25 MobileNet v1 [8]	41	49.4	**502**	36.4
0.4 MobileNet v2 [24] (our impl.)*	43	43.4	333	33.2
0.15 MobileNet v2 [24] (our impl.)	39	55.1	351	33.6
ShuffleNet v1 0.5× (g=3) [35]	38	43.2	347	56.8
DenseNet 0.5× [11] (our impl.)	42	58.6	366	39.7
Xception 0.5× [2] (our impl.)	40	44.9	384	52.9
IGCV2-0.25 [31]	46	45.1	183	31.5
ShuffleNet v2 1× (ours)	146	**30.6**	341	**24.4**
0.5 MobileNet v1 [8]	149	36.3	**382**	16.5
0.75 MobileNet v2 [24] (our impl.)**	145	32.1	235	15.9
0.6 MobileNet v2 [24] (our impl.)	141	33.3	249	14.9
ShuffleNet v1 1× (g=3) [35]	140	32.6	213	21.8
DenseNet 1× [11] (our impl.)	142	45.2	279	15.8
Xception 1× [2] (our impl.)	145	34.1	278	19.5
IGCV2-0.5 [31]	156	34.5	132	15.5
IGCV3-D (0.7) [26]	210	31.5	143	11.7
ShuffleNet v2 1.5× (ours)	299	**27.4**	255	**11.8**
0.75 MobileNet v1 [8]	325	31.6	**314**	10.6
1.0 MobileNet v2 [24]	300	28.0	180	8.9
1.0 MobileNet v2 [24] (our impl.)	301	28.3	180	8.9
ShuffleNet v1 1.5× (g=3) [35]	292	28.5	164	10.3
DenseNet 1.5× [11] (our impl.)	295	39.9	274	9.7
CondenseNet (G=C=8) [10]	274	29.0	-	-
Xception 1.5× [2] (our impl.)	305	29.4	219	10.5
IGCV3-D [26]	318	27.8	102	6.3
ShuffleNet v2 2× (ours)	591	**25.1**	217	**6.7**
1.0 MobileNet v1 [8]	569	29.4	**247**	6.5
1.4 MobileNet v2 [24]	585	25.3	137	5.4
1.4 MobileNet v2 [24] (our impl.)	587	26.7	137	5.4
ShuffleNet v1 2× (g=3) [35]	524	26.3	133	6.4
DenseNet 2× [11] (our impl.)	519	34.6	197	6.1
CondenseNet (G=C=4) [10]	529	26.2	-	-
Xception 2× [2] (our impl.)	525	27.6	174	**6.7**
IGCV2-1.0 [31]	564	29.3	81	4.9
IGCV3-D (1.4) [26]	610	25.5	82	4.5
ShuffleNet v2 2x (ours, with SE [9])	597	**24.6**	**161**	**5.6**
NASNet-A [39] (4 @ 1056, our impl.)	564	26.0	130	4.6
PNASNet-5 [18] (our impl.)	588	25.8	115	4.1

ShuffleNet v2 > Xception $\geq$ ShuffleNet v1 $\geq$ MobileNet v2. This reveals that Xception is good on detection task. This is probably due to the larger receptive field of Xception building blocks than the other counterparts (7 *vs.* 3). Inspired by this, we also enlarge the receptive field of ShuffleNet v2 by introducing an additional 3 × 3 depthwise convolution before the first pointwise convolution in each building block. This variant is denoted as *ShuffleNet v2**. With only a few additional FLOPs, it further improves accuracy.

We also benchmark the runtime time on GPU. For fair comparison the batch size is set to 4 to ensure full GPU utilization. Due to the overheads of data copying (the resolution is as high as 800 × 1200) and other detection-specific operations (like *PSRoI Pooling* [16]), the speed gap between different models is smaller than that of classification. Still, ShuffleNet v2 outperforms others, e.g. around 40% faster than ShuffleNet v1 and 16% faster than MobileNet v2.

Furthermore, the variant ShuffleNet v2* has best accuracy and is still faster than other methods. This motivates a practical question: how to increase the size of receptive field? This is critical for object detection in high-resolution images [20]. We will study the topic in the future.

5   Conclusion

We propose that network architecture design should consider the direct metric such as speed, instead of the indirect metric like FLOPs. We present practical guidelines and a novel architecture, ShuffleNet v2. Comprehensive experiments verify the effectiveness of our new model. We hope this work could inspire future work of network architecture design that is platform aware and more practical.

Acknowledgements. Thanks Yichen Wei for his help on paper writing. This research is partially supported by National Natural Science Foundation of China (Grant No. 61773229).

References

1. Chetlur, S., et al.: CUDNN: efficient primitives for deep learning. arXiv preprint arXiv:1410.0759 (2014)
2. Chollet, F.: Xception: deep learning with depthwise separable convolutions. arXiv preprint (2016)
3. Das, D., et al.: Distributed deep learning using synchronous stochastic gradient descent. arXiv preprint arXiv:1602.06709 (2016)
4. Deng, J., et al.: Imagenet: a large-scale hierarchical image database. In: IEEE Conference on Computer Vision and Pattern Recognition, 2009. CVPR 2009, pp. 248–255. IEEE (2009)
5. He, K., Zhang, X., Ren, S., Sun, J.: Deep residual learning for image recognition. In: Proceedings of the IEEE Conference on Computer Vision and Pattern Recognition, pp. 770–778 (2016)
6. He, K., Zhang, X., Ren, S., Sun, J.: Identity mappings in deep residual networks. In: Leibe, B., Matas, J., Sebe, N., Welling, M. (eds.) ECCV 2016. LNCS, vol. 9908, pp. 630–645. Springer, Cham (2016). https://doi.org/10.1007/978-3-319-46493-0_38

7. He, Y., Zhang, X., Sun, J.: Channel pruning for accelerating very deep neural networks. In: International Conference on Computer Vision (ICCV), vol. 2, p. 6 (2017)
8. Howard, A.G., et al.: Mobilenets: efficient convolutional neural networks for mobile vision applications. arXiv preprint arXiv:1704.04861 (2017)
9. Hu, J., Shen, L., Sun, G.: Squeeze-and-excitation networks. arXiv preprint arXiv:1709.01507 (2017)
10. Huang, G., Liu, S., van der Maaten, L., Weinberger, K.Q.: Condensenet: an efficient densenet using learned group convolutions. arXiv preprint arXiv:1711.09224 (2017)
11. Huang, G., Liu, Z., Weinberger, K.Q., van der Maaten, L.: Densely connected convolutional networks. In: Proceedings of the IEEE Conference on Computer Vision and Pattern Recognition, vol. 1, p. 3 (2017)
12. Ioannou, Y., Robertson, D., Cipolla, R., Criminisi, A.: Deep roots: improving CNN efficiency with hierarchical filter groups. arXiv preprint arXiv:1605.06489 (2016)
13. Ioffe, S., Szegedy, C.: Batch normalization: accelerating deep network training by reducing internal covariate shift. In: International Conference on Machine Learning, pp. 448–456 (2015)
14. Jaderberg, M., Vedaldi, A., Zisserman, A.: Speeding up convolutional neural networks with low rank expansions. arXiv preprint arXiv:1405.3866 (2014)
15. Krizhevsky, A., Sutskever, I., Hinton, G.E.: Imagenet classification with deep convolutional neural networks. In: Advances in Neural Information Processing Systems, pp. 1097–1105 (2012)
16. Li, Z., Peng, C., Yu, G., Zhang, X., Deng, Y., Sun, J.: Light-head R-CNN: In defense of two-stage object detector. arXiv preprint arXiv:1711.07264 (2017)
17. Lin, T.-Y., et al.: Microsoft COCO: common objects in context. In: Fleet, D., Pajdla, T., Schiele, B., Tuytelaars, T. (eds.) ECCV 2014. LNCS, vol. 8693, pp. 740–755. Springer, Cham (2014). https://doi.org/10.1007/978-3-319-10602-1_48
18. Liu, C., et al.: Progressive neural architecture search. arXiv preprint arXiv:1712.00559 (2017)
19. Liu, Z., Li, J., Shen, Z., Huang, G., Yan, S., Zhang, C.: Learning efficient convolutional networks through network slimming. In: 2017 IEEE International Conference on Computer Vision (ICCV), pp. 2755–2763. IEEE (2017)
20. Peng, C., Zhang, X., Yu, G., Luo, G., Sun, J.: Large kernel matters-improve semantic segmentation by global convolutional network. arXiv preprint arXiv:1703.02719 (2017)
21. Real, E., Aggarwal, A., Huang, Y., Le, Q.V.: Regularized evolution for image classifier architecture search. arXiv preprint arXiv:1802.01548 (2018)
22. Real, E., et al.: Large-scale evolution of image classifiers. arXiv preprint arXiv:1703.01041 (2017)
23. Russakovsky, O., Deng, J., Su, H., Krause, J., Satheesh, S., Ma, S., Huang, Z., Karpathy, A., Khosla, A., Bernstein, M.: Imagenet large scale visual recognition challenge. Int. J. Comput. Vis. **115**(3), 211–252 (2015)
24. Sandler, M., Howard, A., Zhu, M., Zhmoginov, A., Chen, L.C.: Inverted residuals and linear bottlenecks: mobile networks for classification, detection and segmentation. arXiv preprint arXiv:1801.04381 (2018)
25. Simonyan, K., Zisserman, A.: Very deep convolutional networks for large-scale image recognition. arXiv preprint arXiv:1409.1556 (2014)
26. Sun, K., Li, M., Liu, D., Wang, J.: Igcv 3: Interleaved low-rank group convolutions for efficient deep neural networks. arXiv preprint arXiv:1806.00178 (2018)
27. Szegedy, C., Ioffe, S., Vanhoucke, V., Alemi, A.A.: Inception-v4, inception-resnet and the impact of residual connections on learning. In: AAAI, vol. 4, p. 12 (2017)

28. Szegedy, C., et al.: Going deeper with convolutions. In: CVPR (2015)
29. Szegedy, C., Vanhoucke, V., Ioffe, S., Shlens, J., Wojna, Z.: Rethinking the inception architecture for computer vision. In: Proceedings of the IEEE Conference on Computer Vision and Pattern Recognition, pp. 2818–2826 (2016)
30. Wen, W., Wu, C., Wang, Y., Chen, Y., Li, H.: Learning structured sparsity in deep neural networks. In: Advances in Neural Information Processing Systems, pp. 2074–2082 (2016)
31. Xie, G., Wang, J., Zhang, T., Lai, J., Hong, R., Qi, G.J.: IGCV 2: Interleaved structured sparse convolutional neural networks. arXiv preprint arXiv:1804.06202 (2018)
32. Xie, L., Yuille, A.: Genetic CNN. arXiv preprint arXiv:1703.01513 (2017)
33. Xie, S., Girshick, R., Dollár, P., Tu, Z., He, K.: Aggregated residual transformations for deep neural networks. In: 2017 IEEE Conference on Computer Vision and Pattern Recognition (CVPR), pp. 5987–5995. IEEE (2017)
34. Zhang, T., Qi, G.J., Xiao, B., Wang, J.: Interleaved group convolutions for deep neural networks. In: International Conference on Computer Vision (2017)
35. Zhang, X., Zhou, X., Lin, M., Sun, J.: Shufflenet: an extremely efficient convolutional neural network for mobile devices. arXiv preprint arXiv:1707.01083 (2017)
36. Zhang, X., Zou, J., He, K., Sun, J.: Accelerating very deep convolutional networks for classification and detection. IEEE Trans. Pattern Anal. Mach. Intell. 38(10), 1943–1955 (2016)
37. Zhang, X., Zou, J., Ming, X., He, K., Sun, J.: Efficient and accurate approximations of nonlinear convolutional networks. In: Proceedings of the IEEE Conference on Computer Vision and Pattern Recognition, pp. 1984–1992 (2015)
38. Zoph, B., Le, Q.V.: Neural architecture search with reinforcement learning. arXiv preprint arXiv:1611.01578 (2016)
39. Zoph, B., Vasudevan, V., Shlens, J., Le, Q.V.: Learning transferable architectures for scalable image recognition. arXiv preprint arXiv:1707.07012 (2017)

Deep Clustering for Unsupervised Learning of Visual Features

Mathilde Caron$^{(\boxtimes)}$, Piotr Bojanowski, Armand Joulin, and Matthijs Douze

Facebook AI Research, Paris, France
{mathilde,bojanowski,ajoulin,matthijs}@fb.com

Abstract. Clustering is a class of unsupervised learning methods that has been extensively applied and studied in computer vision. Little work has been done to adapt it to the end-to-end training of visual features on large-scale datasets. In this work, we present DeepCluster, a clustering method that jointly learns the parameters of a neural network and the cluster assignments of the resulting features. DeepCluster iteratively groups the features with a standard clustering algorithm, k-means, and uses the subsequent assignments as supervision to update the weights of the network. We apply DeepCluster to the unsupervised training of convolutional neural networks on large datasets like ImageNet and YFCC100M. The resulting model outperforms the current state of the art by a significant margin on all the standard benchmarks.

Keywords: Unsupervised learning · Clustering

1 Introduction

Pre-trained convolutional neural networks, or convnets, have become the building blocks in most computer vision applications [8,9,50,65]. They produce excellent general-purpose features that can be used to improve the generalization of models learned on a limited amount of data [53]. The existence of ImageNet [12], a large fully-supervised dataset, has been fueling advances in pre-training of convnets. However, Stock and Cisse [57] have recently presented empirical evidence that the performance of state-of-the-art classifiers on ImageNet is largely underestimated, and little error is left unresolved. This explains in part why the performance has been saturating despite the numerous novel architectures proposed in recent years [9,21,23]. As a matter of fact, ImageNet is relatively small by today's standards; it "only" contains a million images that cover the specific domain of object classification. A natural way to move forward is to build a bigger and more diverse dataset, potentially consisting of billions of images. This, in turn, would require a tremendous amount of manual annotations, despite

Electronic supplementary material The online version of this chapter (https://doi.org/10.1007/978-3-030-01264-9_9) contains supplementary material, which is available to authorized users.

© Springer Nature Switzerland AG 2018
V. Ferrari et al. (Eds.): ECCV 2018, LNCS 11218, pp. 139–156, 2018.
https://doi.org/10.1007/978-3-030-01264-9_9

the expert knowledge in crowdsourcing accumulated by the community over the years [30]. Replacing labels by raw metadata leads to biases in the visual representations with unpredictable consequences [41]. This calls for methods that can be trained on internet-scale datasets with no supervision.

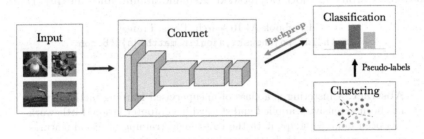

Fig. 1. Illustration of the proposed method: we iteratively cluster deep features and use the cluster assignments as pseudo-labels to learn the parameters of the convnet

Unsupervised learning has been widely studied in the Machine Learning community [19], and algorithms for clustering, dimensionality reduction or density estimation are regularly used in computer vision applications [27,54,60]. For example, the "bag of features" model uses clustering on handcrafted local descriptors to produce good image-level features [11]. A key reason for their success is that they can be applied on any specific domain or dataset, like satellite or medical images, or on images captured with a new modality, like depth, where annotations are not always available in quantity. Several works have shown that it was possible to adapt unsupervised methods based on density estimation or dimensionality reduction to deep models [20,29], leading to promising all-purpose visual features [5,15]. Despite the primeval success of clustering approaches in image classification, very few works [3,66,68] have been proposed to adapt them to the end-to-end training of convnets, and never at scale. An issue is that clustering methods have been primarily designed for linear models on top of fixed features, and they scarcely work if the features have to be learned simultaneously. For example, learning a convnet with k-means would lead to a trivial solution where the features are zeroed, and the clusters are collapsed into a single entity.

In this work, we propose a novel clustering approach for the large scale end-to-end training of convnets. We show that it is possible to obtain useful general-purpose visual features with a clustering framework. Our approach, summarized in Fig. 1, consists in alternating between clustering of the image descriptors and updating the weights of the convnet by predicting the cluster assignments. For simplicity, we focus our study on k-means, but other clustering approaches can be used, like Power Iteration Clustering (PIC) [36]. The overall pipeline is sufficiently close to the standard supervised training of a convnet to reuse many common tricks [24]. Unlike self-supervised methods [13,42,45], clustering has the advantage of requiring little domain knowledge and no specific signal from the inputs [63,71]. Despite its simplicity, our approach achieves significantly higher performance than previously published unsupervised methods on both ImageNet classification and transfer tasks.

Finally, we probe the robustness of our framework by modifying the experimental protocol, in particular the training set and the convnet architecture. The resulting set of experiments extends the discussion initiated by Doersch *et al.* [13] on the impact of these choices on the performance of unsupervised methods. We demonstrate that our approach is robust to a change of architecture. Replacing an AlexNet by a VGG [55] significantly improves the quality of the features and their subsequent transfer performance. More importantly, we discuss the use of ImageNet as a training set for unsupervised models. While it helps understanding the impact of the labels on the performance of a network, ImageNet has a particular image distribution inherited from its use for a fine-grained image classification challenge: it is composed of well-balanced classes and contains a wide variety of dog breeds for example. We consider, as an alternative, random Flickr images from the YFCC100M dataset of Thomee *et al.* [58]. We show that our approach maintains state-of-the-art performance when trained on this uncured data distribution. Finally, current benchmarks focus on the capability of unsupervised convnets to capture class-level information. We propose to also evaluate them on image retrieval benchmarks to measure their capability to capture instance-level information.

In this paper, we make the following contributions: (i) a novel unsupervised method for the end-to-end learning of convnets that works with any standard clustering algorithm, like k-means, and requires minimal additional steps; (ii) state-of-the-art performance on many standard transfer tasks used in unsupervised learning; (iii) performance above the previous state of the art when trained on an uncured image distribution; (iv) a discussion about the current evaluation protocol in unsupervised feature learning.

2   Related Work

Unsupervised Learning of Features. Several approaches related to our work learn deep models with no supervision. Coates and Ng [10] also use k-means to pre-train convnets, but learn each layer sequentially in a bottom-up fashion, while we do it in an end-to-end fashion. Other clustering losses [3,16,35,66,68] have been considered to jointly learn convnet features and image clusters but they have never been tested on a scale to allow a thorough study on modern convnet architectures. Of particular interest, Yang *et al.* [68] iteratively learn convnet features and clusters with a recurrent framework. Their model offers promising performance on small datasets but may be challenging to scale to the number of images required for convnets to be competitive. Closer to our work, Bojanowski and Joulin [5] learn visual features on a large dataset with a loss that attempts to preserve the information flowing through the network [37]. Their approach discriminates between images in a similar way as examplar SVM [39], while we are simply clustering them.

Self-supervised Learning. A popular form of unsupervised learning, called "self-supervised learning" [52], uses pretext tasks to replace the labels annotated by humans by "pseudo-labels" directly computed from the raw input data. For example, Doersch *et al.* [13] use the prediction of the relative position of patches in an image as a pretext task, while Noroozi and Favaro [42] train a network to spatially rearrange shuffled patches. Another use of spatial cues is the work of Pathak *et al.* [46] where missing pixels are guessed based on their surrounding. Paulin *et al.* [47] learn patch level Convolutional Kernel Network [38] using an image retrieval setting. Others leverage the temporal signal available in videos by predicting the camera transformation between consecutive frames [1], exploiting the temporal coherence of tracked patches [63] or segmenting video based on motion [45]. Appart from spatial and temporal coherence, many other signals have been explored: image colorization [33,71], cross-channel prediction [72], sound [44] or instance counting [43]. More recently, several strategies for combining multiple cues have been proposed [14,64]. Contrary to our work, these approaches are domain dependent, requiring expert knowledge to carefully design a pretext task that may lead to transferable features.

Generative Models. Recently, unsupervised learning has been making a lot of progress on image generation. Typically, a parametrized mapping is learned between a predefined random noise and the images, with either an autoencoder [4,22,29,40,62], a generative adversarial network (GAN) [20] or more directly with a reconstruction loss [6]. Of particular interest, the discriminator of a GAN can produce visual features, but their performance are relatively disappointing [15]. Donahue *et al.* [15] and Dumoulin *et al.* [17] have shown that adding an encoder to a GAN produces visual features that are much more competitive.

3   Method

After a short introduction to the supervised learning of convnets, we describe our unsupervised approach as well as the specificities of its optimization.

3.1   Preliminaries

Modern approaches to computer vision, based on statistical learning, require good image featurization. In this context, convnets are a popular choice for mapping raw images to a vector space of fixed dimensionality. When trained on enough data, they constantly achieve the best performance on standard classification benchmarks [21,32]. We denote by f_θ the convnet mapping, where θ is the set of corresponding parameters. We refer to the vector obtained by applying this mapping to an image as feature or representation. Given a training set $X = \{x_1, x_2, \ldots, x_N\}$ of N images, we want to find a parameter θ^* such that the mapping f_{θ^*} produces good general-purpose features.

These parameters are traditionally learned with supervision, *i.e.* each image x_n is associated with a label y_n in $\{0,1\}^k$. This label represents the image's membership to one of k possible predefined classes. A parametrized classifier g_W predicts the correct labels on top of the features $f_\theta(x_n)$. The parameters W of the classifier and the parameter θ of the mapping are then jointly learned by optimizing the following problem:

$$\min_{\theta, W} \frac{1}{N} \sum_{n=1}^{N} \ell\left(g_W\left(f_\theta(x_n)\right), y_n\right), \tag{1}$$

where ℓ is the multinomial logistic loss, also known as the negative log-softmax function. This cost function is minimized using mini-batch stochastic gradient descent [7] and backpropagation to compute the gradient [34].

3.2 Unsupervised Learning by Clustering

When θ is sampled from a Gaussian distribution, without any learning, f_θ does not produce good features. However the performance of such random features on standard transfer tasks, is far above the chance level. For example, a multilayer perceptron classifier on top of the last convolutional layer of a random AlexNet achieves 12% in accuracy on ImageNet while the chance is at 0.1% [42]. The good performance of random convnets is intimately tied to their convolutional structure which gives a strong prior on the input signal. The idea of this work is to exploit this weak signal to bootstrap the discriminative power of a convnet. We cluster the output of the convnet and use the subsequent cluster assignments as "pseudo-labels" to optimize Eq. (1). This deep clustering (DeepCluster) approach iteratively learns the features and groups them.

Clustering has been widely studied and many approaches have been developed for a variety of circumstances. In the absence of points of comparisons, we focus on a standard clustering algorithm, k-means. Preliminary results with other clustering algorithms indicates that this choice is not crucial. k-means takes a set of vectors as input, in our case the features $f_\theta(x_n)$ produced by the convnet, and clusters them into k distinct groups based on a geometric criterion. More precisely, it jointly learns a $d \times k$ centroid matrix C and the cluster assignments y_n of each image n by solving the following problem:

$$\min_{C \in \mathbb{R}^{d \times k}} \frac{1}{N} \sum_{n=1}^{N} \min_{y_n \in \{0,1\}^k} \|f_\theta(x_n) - C y_n\|_2^2 \quad \text{such that} \quad y_n^\top 1_k = 1. \tag{2}$$

Solving this problem provides a set of optimal assignments $(y_n^*)_{n \leq N}$ and a centroid matrix C^*. These assignments are then used as pseudo-labels; we make no use of the centroid matrix.

Overall, DeepCluster alternates between clustering the features to produce pseudo-labels using Eq. (2) and updating the parameters of the convnet by predicting these pseudo-labels using Eq. (1). This type of alternating procedure is prone to trivial solutions; we describe how to avoid such degenerate solutions in the next section.

3.3   Avoiding Trivial Solutions

The existence of trivial solutions is not specific to the unsupervised training of neural networks, but to any method that jointly learns a discriminative classifier and the labels. Discriminative clustering suffers from this issue even when applied to linear models [67]. Solutions are typically based on constraining or penalizing the minimal number of points per cluster [2, 26]. These terms are computed over the whole dataset, which is not applicable to the training of convnets on large scale datasets. In this section, we briefly describe the causes of these trivial solutions and give simple and scalable workarounds.

Empty Clusters. A discriminative model learns decision boundaries between classes. An optimal decision boundary is to assign all of the inputs to a single cluster [67]. This issue is caused by the absence of mechanisms to prevent from empty clusters and arises in linear models as much as in convnets. A common trick used in feature quantization [25] consists in automatically reassigning empty clusters during the k-means optimization. More precisely, when a cluster becomes empty, we randomly select a non-empty cluster and use its centroid with a small random perturbation as the new centroid for the empty cluster. We then reassign the points belonging to the non-empty cluster to the two resulting clusters.

Trivial Parametrization. If the vast majority of images is assigned to a few clusters, the parameters θ will exclusively discriminate between them. In the most dramatic scenario where all but one cluster are singleton, minimizing Eq. (1) leads to a trivial parametrization where the convnet will predict the same output regardless of the input. This issue also arises in supervised classification when the number of images per class is highly unbalanced. For example, metadata, like hashtags, exhibits a Zipf distribution, with a few labels dominating the whole distribution [28]. A strategy to circumvent this issue is to sample images based on a uniform distribution over the classes, or pseudo-labels. This is equivalent to weight the contribution of an input to the loss function in Eq. (1) by the inverse of the size of its assigned cluster.

3.4   Implementation Details

Training data and convnet architectures. We train DeepCluster on the training set of ImageNet [12] (1, 281, 167 images distributed uniformly into 1, 000 classes). We discard the labels. For comparison with previous works, we use a standard AlexNet [32] architecture. It consists of five convolutional layers with 96, 256, 384, 384 and 256 filters; and of three fully connected layers. We remove the Local Response Normalization layers and use batch normalization [24]. We also consider a VGG-16 [55] architecture with batch normalization. Unsupervised methods often do not work directly on color and different strategies have been considered as alternatives [13, 42]. We apply a fixed linear transformation based on Sobel filters to remove color and increase local contrast [5, 47].

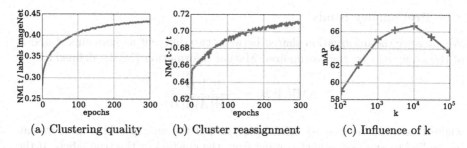

(a) Clustering quality   (b) Cluster reassignment   (c) Influence of k

Fig. 2. Preliminary studies. (a): evolution of the clustering quality along training epochs; (b): evolution of cluster reassignments at each clustering step; (c): validation mAP classification performance for various choices of k

Optimization. We cluster the features of the central cropped images and train the convnet with data augmentation (random horizontal flips and crops of random sizes and aspect ratios). This enforces invariance to data augmentation which is useful for feature learning [16]. The network is trained with dropout [56], a constant step size, an ℓ_2 penalization of the weights θ and a momentum of 0.9. Each mini-batch contains 256 images. For the clustering, features are PCA-reduced to 256 dimensions, whitened and ℓ_2-normalized. We use the k-means implementation of Johnson *et al.* [25]. Note that running k-means takes a third of the time because a forward pass on the full dataset is needed. One could reassign the clusters every n epochs, but we found out that our setup on ImageNet (updating the clustering every epoch) was nearly optimal. On Flickr, the concept of epoch disappears: choosing the tradeoff between the parameter updates and the cluster reassignments is more subtle. We thus kept almost the same setup as in ImageNet. We train the models for 500 epochs, which takes 12 days on a Pascal P100 GPU for AlexNet.

Hyperparameter Selection. We select hyperparameters on a down-stream task, *i.e.*, object classification on the validation set of PASCAL VOC with no fine-tuning. We use the publicly available code of Krähenbühl[1].

4 Experiments

In a preliminary set of experiments, we study the behavior of DeepCluster during training. We then qualitatively assess the filters learned with DeepCluster before comparing our approach to previous state-of-the-art models on standard benchmarks.

---

[1] https://github.com/philkr/voc-classification.

4.1   Preliminary Study

We measure the information shared between two different assignments A and B of the same data by the Normalized Mutual Information (NMI), defined as:

$$\text{NMI}(A;B) = \frac{\text{I}(A;B)}{\sqrt{\text{H}(A)\text{H}(B)}}$$

where I denotes the mutual information and H the entropy. This measure can be applied to any assignment coming from the clusters or the true labels. If the two assignments A and B are independent, the NMI is equal to 0. If one of them is deterministically predictable from the other, the NMI is equal to 1.

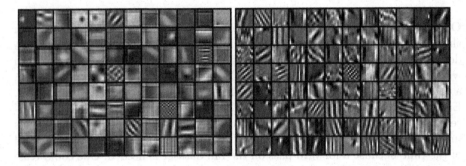

Fig. 3. Filters from the first layer of an AlexNet trained on unsupervised ImageNet on raw RGB input (left) or after a Sobel filtering (right) (Color figure online)

Relation Between Clusters and Labels. Fig. 2(a) shows the evolution of the NMI between the cluster assignments and the ImageNet labels during training. It measures the capability of the model to predict class level information. Note that we only use this measure for this analysis and not in any model selection process. The dependence between the clusters and the labels increases over time, showing that our features progressively capture information related to object classes.

Number of Reassignments Between Epochs. At each epoch, we reassign the images to a new set of clusters, with no guarantee of stability. Measuring the NMI between the clusters at epoch $t-1$ and t gives an insight on the actual stability of our model. Figure 2(b) shows the evolution of this measure during training. The NMI is increasing, meaning that there are less and less reassignments and the clusters are stabilizing over time. However, NMI saturates below 0.8, meaning that a significant fraction of images are regularly reassigned between epochs. In practice, this has no impact on the training and the models do not diverge.

Choosing the Number of Clusters. We measure the impact of the number k of clusters used in k-means on the quality of the model. We report the same down-stream task as in the hyperparameter selection process, *i.e.* mAP on the

PASCAL VOC 2007 classification validation set. We vary k on a logarithmic scale, and report results after 300 epochs in Fig. 2(c). The performance after the same number of epochs for every k may not be directly comparable, but it reflects the hyper-parameter selection process used in this work. The best performance is obtained with $k = 10,000$. Given that we train our model on ImageNet, one would expect $k = 1000$ to yield the best results, but apparently some amount of over-segmentation is beneficial.

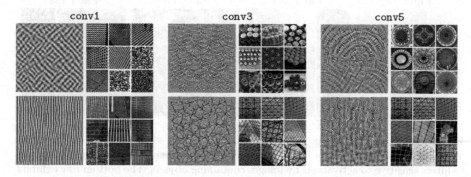

Fig. 4. Filter visualization and top 9 activated images from a subset of 1 million images from YFCC100M for target filters in the layers conv1, conv3 and conv5 of an AlexNet trained with DeepCluster on ImageNet. The filter visualization is obtained by learning an input image that maximizes the response to a target filter [69]

4.2 Visualizations

First Layer Filters. Figure 3 shows the filters from the first layer of an AlexNet trained with DeepCluster on raw RGB images and images preprocessed with a Sobel filtering. The difficulty of learning convnets on raw images has been noted before [5,13,42,47]. As shown in the left panel of Fig. 3, most filters capture only color information that typically plays a little role for object classification [61]. Filters obtained with Sobel preprocessing act like edge detectors.

Probing Deeper Layers. We assess the quality of a target filter by learning an input image that maximizes its activation [18,70]. We follow the process described by Yosinki et al. [69] with a cross entropy function between the target filter and the other filters of the same layer. Figure 4 shows these synthetic images as well as the 9 top activated images from a subset of 1 million images from YFCC100M. As expected, deeper layers in the network seem to capture larger textural structures. However, some filters in the last convolutional layers seem to be simply replicating the texture already captured in previous layers, as shown on the second row of Fig. 5. This result corroborates the observation by Zhang et al. [72] that features from conv3 or conv4 are more discriminative than those from conv5.

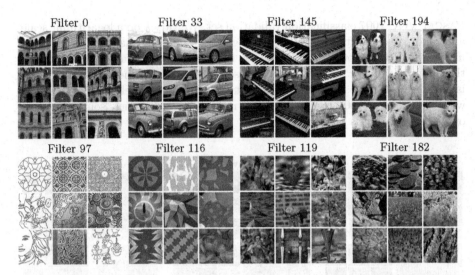

Fig. 5. Top 9 activated images from a random subset of 10 millions images from YFCC100M for target filters in the last convolutional layer. The top row corresponds to filters sensitive to activations by images containing objects. The bottom row exhibits filters more sensitive to stylistic effects. For instance, the filters 119 and 182 seem to be respectively excited by background blur and depth of field effects

Finally, Fig. 5 shows the top 9 activated images of some conv5 filters that seem to be semantically coherent. The filters on the top row contain information about structures that highly corrolate with object classes. The filters on the bottom row seem to trigger on style, like drawings or abstract shapes.

4.3   Linear Classification on Activations

Following Zhang *et al.* [72], we train a linear classifier on top of different frozen convolutional layers. This layer by layer comparison with supervised features exhibits where a convnet starts to be task specific, *i.e.* specialized in object classification. We report the results of this experiment on ImageNet and the Places dataset [73] in Table 1. We choose the hyperparameters by cross-validation on the training. On ImageNet, DeepCluster outperforms the state of the art from conv2 to conv5 layers by $1-6\%$. The largest improvement is observed in the conv3 layer, while the conv1 layer performs poorly, probably because the Sobel filtering discards color. Consistently with the filter visualizations of Sect. 4.2, conv3 works better than conv5. Finally, the difference of performance between DeepCluster and a supervised AlexNet grows significantly on higher layers: at layers conv2-conv3 the difference is only around 4%, But this difference rises to 12.3% at conv5, marking where the AlexNet probably stores most of the class level information. In the supplementary material, we also report the accuracy if a MLP is trained on the last layer; DeepCluster outperforms the state of the art by 8%.

Table 1. Linear classification on ImageNet and Places using activations from the convolutional layers of an AlexNet as features. We report classification accuracy averaged over 10 crops. Numbers for other methods are from Zhang *et al.* [72]

Method	ImageNet					Places				
	conv1	conv2	conv3	conv4	conv5	conv1	conv2	conv3	conv4	conv5
Places labels	–	–	–	–	–	22.1	35.1	40.2	43.3	44.6
ImageNet labels	19.3	36.3	44.2	48.3	50.5	22.7	34.8	38.4	39.4	38.7
Random	11.6	17.1	16.9	16.3	14.1	15.7	20.3	19.8	19.1	17.5
Pathak *et al.* [46]	14.1	20.7	21.0	19.8	15.5	18.2	23.2	23.4	21.9	18.4
Doersch *et al.* [13]	16.2	23.3	30.2	31.7	29.6	19.7	26.7	31.9	32.7	30.9
Zhang *et al.* [71]	12.5	24.5	30.4	31.5	30.3	16.0	25.7	29.6	30.3	29.7
Donahue *et al.* [15]	17.7	24.5	31.0	29.9	28.0	21.4	26.2	27.1	26.1	24.0
Noroozi and Favaro [42]	**18.2**	28.8	34.0	33.9	27.1	23.0	32.1	35.5	34.8	31.3
Noroozi *et al.* [43]	18.0	30.6	34.3	32.5	25.7	**23.3**	**33.9**	36.3	34.7	29.6
Zhang *et al.* [72]	17.7	29.3	35.4	35.2	32.8	21.3	30.7	34.0	34.1	32.5
DeepCluster	13.4	**32.3**	**41.0**	**39.6**	**38.2**	19.6	33.2	**39.2**	**39.8**	**34.7**

The same experiment on the Places dataset provides some interesting insights: like DeepCluster, a supervised model trained on ImageNet suffers from a decrease of performance for higher layers (conv4 versus conv5). Moreover, DeepCluster yields conv3-4 features that are comparable to those trained with ImageNet labels. This suggests that when the target task is sufficently far from the domain covered by ImageNet, labels are less important.

4.4 Pascal VOC 2007

Finally, we do a quantitative evaluation of DeepCluster on image classification, object detection and semantic segmentation on PASCAL VOC. The relatively small size of the training sets on PASCAL VOC (2, 500 images) makes this setup closer to a "real-world" application, where a model trained with heavy computational resources, is adapted to a task or a dataset with a small number of instances. Detection results are obtained using fast-rcnn[2]; segmentation results are obtained using the code of Shelhamer *et al.*[3]. For classification and detection, we report the performance on the test set of PASCAL VOC 2007 and choose our hyperparameters on the validation set. For semantic segmentation, following the related work, we report the performance on the validation set of PASCAL VOC 2012.

Table 2 summarized the comparisons of DeepCluster with other feature-learning approaches on the three tasks. As for the previous experiments, we outperform previous unsupervised methods on all three tasks, in every setting. The improvement with fine-tuning over the state of the art is the largest on semantic segmentation (7.5%). On detection, DeepCluster performs only slightly better than previously published methods. Interestingly, a fine-tuned random network

---

[2] https://github.com/rbgirshick/py-faster-rcnn.
[3] https://github.com/shelhamer/fcn.berkeleyvision.org.

performs comparatively to many unsupervised methods, but performs poorly if only FC6-8 are learned. For this reason, we also report detection and segmentation with FC6-8 for DeepCluster and a few baselines. These tasks are closer to a real application where fine-tuning is not possible. It is in this setting that the gap between our approach and the state of the art is the greater (up to 9% on classification).

Table 2. Comparison of the proposed approach to state-of-the-art unsupervised feature learning on classification, detection and segmentation on PASCAL VOC. * indicates the use of the data-dependent initialization of Krähenbühl *et al.* [31]. Numbers for other methods produced by us are marked with a †

Method	Classification		Detection		Segmentation	
	FC6-8	ALL	FC6-8	ALL	FC6-8	ALL
ImageNet labels	78.9	79.9	–	56.8	–	48.0
Random-rgb	33.2	57.0	22.2	44.5	15.2	30.1
Random-sobel	29.0	61.9	18.9	47.9	13.0	32.0
Pathak *et al.* [46]	34.6	56.5	–	44.5	–	29.7
Donahue *et al.* [15]*	52.3	60.1	–	46.9	–	35.2
Pathak *et al.* [45]	–	61.0	–	52.2	–	–
Owens *et al.* [44]*	52.3	61.3	–	–	–	–
Wang and Gupta [63]*	55.6	63.1	32.8†	47.2	26.0†	35.4†
Doersch *et al.* [13]*	55.1	65.3	–	51.1	–	–
Bojanowski and Joulin [5]*	56.7	65.3	33.7†	49.4	26.7†	37.1†
Zhang *et al.* [71]*	61.5	65.9	43.4†	46.9	35.8†	35.6
Zhang *et al.* [72]*	63.0	67.1	–	46.7	–	36.0
Noroozi and Favaro [42]	–	67.6	–	53.2	–	37.6
Noroozi *et al.* [43]	–	67.7	–	51.4	–	36.6
DeepCluster	**72.0**	**73.7**	**51.4**	**55.4**	**43.2**	**45.1**

5 Discussion

The current standard for the evaluation of an unsupervised method involves the use of an AlexNet architecture trained on ImageNet and tested on class-level tasks. To understand and measure the various biases introduced by this pipeline on DeepCluster, we consider a different training set, a different architecture and an instance-level recognition task.

5.1   ImageNet Versus YFCC100M

ImageNet is a dataset designed for a fine-grained object classification challenge [51]. It is object oriented, manually annotated and organised into well balanced object categories. By design, DeepCluster favors balanced clusters and, as
discussed above, our number of cluster k is somewhat comparable with the number
of labels in ImageNet. This may have given an unfair advantage to DeepCluster
over other unsupervised approaches when trained on ImageNet. To measure the
impact of this effect, we consider a subset of randomly-selected 1M images from
the YFCC100M dataset [58] for the pre-training. Statistics on the hashtags used
in YFCC100M suggests that the underlying "object classes" are severly unbalanced [28], leading to a data distribution less favorable to DeepCluster.

Table 3. Impact of the training set on the performance of DeepCluster measured on
the PASCAL VOC transfer tasks as described in Sect. 4.4. We compare ImageNet with a
subset of 1M images from YFCC100M [58]. Regardless of the training set, DeepCluster
outperforms the best published numbers on most tasks. Numbers for other methods
produced by us are marked with a †

Method	Training set	Classification		Detection		Segmentation	
		FC6-8	ALL	FC6-8	ALL	FC6-8	ALL
Best competitor	ImageNet	63.0	67.7	$43.4^\dagger$	53.2	$35.8^\dagger$	37.7
DeepCluster	ImageNet	72.0	73.7	51.4	55.4	43.2	45.1
DeepCluster	YFCC100M	67.3	69.3	45.6	53.0	39.2	42.2

Table 3 shows the difference in performance on PASCAL VOC of DeepCluster pre-trained on YFCC100M compared to ImageNet. As noted by Doersch
et al. [13], this dataset is not object oriented, hence the performance are expected
to drop by a few percents. However, even when trained on uncured Flickr images,
DeepCluster outperforms the current state of the art by a significant margin on
most tasks (up to +4.3% on classification and +4.5% on semantic segmentation).
We report the rest of the results in the supplementary material with similar conclusions. This experiment validates that DeepCluster is robust to a change of
image distribution, leading to state-of-the-art general-purpose visual features
even if this distribution is not favorable to its design.

5.2   AlexNet Versus VGG

In the supervised setting, deeper architectures like VGG or ResNet [21] have
a much higher accuracy on ImageNet than AlexNet. We should expect the
same improvement if these architectures are used with an unsupervised approach. Table 4 compares a VGG-16 and an AlexNet trained with DeepCluster on ImageNet and tested on the PASCAL VOC 2007 object detection task
with fine-tuning. We also report the numbers obtained with other unsupervised

approaches [13,64]. Regardless of the approach, a deeper architecture leads to a significant improvement in performance on the target task. Training the VGG-16 with DeepCluster gives a performance above the state of the art, bringing us to only 1.4 percents below the supervised topline. Note that the difference between unsupervised and supervised approaches remains in the same ballpark for both architectures (*i.e.* 1.4%). Finally, the gap with a random baseline grows for larger architectures, justifying the relevance of unsupervised pre-training for complex architectures when little supervised data is available.

Table 4. PASCAL VOC 2007 object detection with AlexNet and VGG-16. Numbers are taken from Wang *et al.* [64]

Method	AlexNet	VGG-16
ImageNet labels	56.8	67.3
Random	47.8	39.7
Doersch *et al.* [13]	51.1	61.5
Wang and Gupta [63]	47.2	60.2
Wang *et al.* [64]	–	63.2
DeepCluster	**55.4**	**65.9**

Table 5. mAP on instance-level image retrieval on Oxford and Paris dataset with a VGG-16. We apply R-MAC with a resolution of 1024 pixels and 3 grid levels [59]

Method	Oxford5K	Paris6K
ImageNet labels	72.4	81.5
Random	6.9	22.0
Doersch *et al.* [13]	35.4	53.1
Wang *et al.* [64]	42.3	58.0
DeepCluster	**61.0**	**72.0**

5.3   Evaluation on Instance Retrieval

The previous benchmarks measure the capability of an unsupervised network to capture class level information. They do not evaluate if it can differentiate images at the instance level. To that end, we propose image retrieval as a down-stream task. We follow the experimental protocol of Tolias *et al.* [59] on two datasets, *i.e.*, Oxford Buildings [48] and Paris [49]. Table 5 reports the performance of a VGG-16 trained with different approaches obtained with Sobel filtering, except for Doersch *et al.* [13] and Wang *et al.* [64]. This preprocessing improves by 5.5 points the mAP of a supervised VGG-16 on the Oxford dataset, but not on Paris. This may translate in a similar advantage for DeepCluster, but it does not account for the average differences of 19 points. Interestingly, random convnets perform particularly poorly on this task compared to pre-trained models. This suggests that image retrieval is a task where the pre-training is essential and studying it as a down-stream task could give further insights about the quality of the features produced by unsupervised approaches.

6 Conclusion

In this paper, we propose a scalable clustering approach for the unsupervised learning of convnets. It iterates between clustering with k-means the features produced by the convnet and updating its weights by predicting the cluster assignments as pseudo-labels in a discriminative loss. If trained on large dataset like ImageNet or YFCC100M, it achieves performance that are better than the previous state-of-the-art on every standard transfer task. Our approach makes little assumption about the inputs, and does not require much domain specific knowledge, making it a good candidate to learn deep representations specific to domains where annotations are scarce.

References

1. Agrawal, P., Carreira, J., Malik, J.: Learning to see by moving. In: ICCV (2015)
2. Bach, F.R., Harchaoui, Z.: Diffrac: a discriminative and flexible framework for clustering. In: NIPS (2008)
3. Bautista, M.A., Sanakoyeu, A., Tikhoncheva, E., Ommer, B.: Cliquecnn: deep unsupervised exemplar learning. In: Advances in Neural Information Processing Systems, pp. 3846–3854 (2016)
4. Bengio, Y., Lamblin, P., Popovici, D., Larochelle, H.: Greedy layer-wise training of deep networks. In: NIPS (2007)
5. Bojanowski, P., Joulin, A.: Unsupervised learning by predicting noise. In: ICML (2017)
6. Bojanowski, P., Joulin, A., Lopez-Paz, D., Szlam, A.: Optimizing the latent space of generative networks. arXiv preprint arXiv:1707.05776 (2017)
7. Bottou, L.: Stochastic Gradient Descent Tricks. In: Montavon, G., Orr, G.B., Müller, K.-R. (eds.) Neural Networks: Tricks of the Trade. LNCS, vol. 7700, pp. 421–436. Springer, Heidelberg (2012). https://doi.org/10.1007/978-3-642-35289-8_25
8. Carreira, J., Agrawal, P., Fragkiadaki, K., Malik, J.: Human pose estimation with iterative error feedback. In: CVPR (2016)
9. Chen, L.C., Papandreou, G., Kokkinos, I., Murphy, K., Yuille, A.L.: Deeplab: semantic image segmentation with deep convolutional nets, atrous convolution, and fully connected CRFs. arXiv preprint arXiv:1606.00915 (2016)
10. Coates, A., Ng, A.Y.: Learning feature representations with k-means. In: Montavon, G., Orr, G.B., Müller, K.R. (eds.) NN: Tricks of the Trade. LNCS, vol. 7700, pp. 561–580. Springer, Heidelberg (2012). https://doi.org/10.1007/978-3-642-35289-8_30
11. Csurka, G., Dance, C., Fan, L., Willamowski, J., Bray, C.: Visual categorization with bags of keypoints. In: Workshop on Satistical Learning in Computer Vision ECCV, vol. 1, pp. 1–2. Prague (2004)
12. Deng, J., Dong, W., Socher, R., Li, L.J., Li, K., Fei-Fei, L.: Imagenet: a large-scale hierarchical image database. In: CVPR (2009)
13. Doersch, C., Gupta, A., Efros, A.A.: Unsupervised visual representation learning by context prediction. In: ICCV (2015)
14. Doersch, C., Zisserman, A.: Multi-task self-supervised visual learning (2017)
15. Donahue, J., Krähenbühl, P., Darrell, T.: Adversarial feature learning. arXiv preprint arXiv:1605.09782 (2016)

16. Dosovitskiy, A., Springenberg, J.T., Riedmiller, M., Brox, T.: Discriminative unsupervised feature learning with convolutional neural networks. In: NIPS (2014)
17. Dumoulin, V., et al.: Adversarially learned inference. arXiv preprint arXiv:1606.00704 (2016)
18. Erhan, D., Bengio, Y., Courville, A., Vincent, P.: Visualizing higher-layer features of a deep network. Univ. Montr. **1341**, 3 (2009)
19. Friedman, J., Hastie, T., Tibshirani, R.: The Elements of Statistical Learning, vol. 1. Springer, New York (2001). https://doi.org/10.1007/978-0-387-21606-5
20. Goodfellow, I., et al.: Generative adversarial nets. In: NIPS (2014)
21. He, K., Zhang, X., Ren, S., Sun, J.: Delving deep into rectifiers: surpassing human-level performance on imagenet classification. In: ICCV (2015)
22. Huang, F.J., Boureau, Y.L., LeCun, Y., et al.: Unsupervised learning of invariant feature hierarchies with applications to object recognition. In: CVPR (2007)
23. Huang, G., Liu, Z., Weinberger, K.Q., van der Maaten, L.: Densely connected convolutional networks. arXiv preprint arXiv:1608.06993 (2016)
24. Ioffe, S., Szegedy, C.: Batch normalization: accelerating deep network training by reducing internal covariate shift. In: ICML (2015)
25. Johnson, J., Douze, M., Jégou, H.: Billion-scale similarity search with GPUs. arXiv preprint arXiv:1702.08734 (2017)
26. Joulin, A., Bach, F.: A convex relaxation for weakly supervised classifiers. arXiv preprint arXiv:1206.6413 (2012)
27. Joulin, A., Bach, F., Ponce, J.: Discriminative clustering for image co-segmentation. In: CVPR (2010)
28. Joulin, A., van der Maaten, L., Jabri, A., Vasilache, N.: Learning visual features from large weakly supervised data. In: Leibe, B., Matas, J., Sebe, N., Welling, M. (eds.) ECCV 2016. LNCS, vol. 9911, pp. 67–84. Springer, Cham (2016). https://doi.org/10.1007/978-3-319-46478-7_5
29. Kingma, D.P., Welling, M.: Auto-encoding variational bayes. arXiv preprint arXiv:1312.6114 (2013)
30. Kovashka, A., Russakovsky, O., Fei-Fei, L., Grauman, K.: Crowdsourcing in computer vision. Found. Trends® Comput. Graph. Vis. **10**(3), 177–243 (2016)
31. Krähenbühl, P., Doersch, C., Donahue, J., Darrell, T.: Data-dependent initializations of convolutional neural networks. arXiv preprint arXiv:1511.06856 (2015)
32. Krizhevsky, A., Sutskever, I., Hinton, G.E.: Imagenet classification with deep convolutional neural networks. In: NIPS (2012)
33. Larsson, G., Maire, M., Shakhnarovich, G.: Learning representations for automatic colorization. In: Leibe, B., Matas, J., Sebe, N., Welling, M. (eds.) ECCV 2016. LNCS, vol. 9908, pp. 577–593. Springer, Cham (2016). https://doi.org/10.1007/978-3-319-46493-0_35
34. LeCun, Y., Bottou, L., Bengio, Y., Haffner, P.: Gradient-based learning applied to document recognition. Proc. IEEE **86**(11), 2278–2324 (1998)
35. Liao, R., Schwing, A., Zemel, R., Urtasun, R.: Learning deep parsimonious representations. In: NIPS (2016)
36. Lin, F., Cohen, W.W.: Power iteration clustering. In: ICML (2010)
37. Linsker, R.: Towards an organizing principle for a layered perceptual network. In: NIPS (1988)
38. Mairal, J., Koniusz, P., Harchaoui, Z., Schmid, C.: Convolutional kernel networks. In: NIPS (2014)
39. Malisiewicz, T., Gupta, A., Efros, A.A.: Ensemble of exemplar-SVMS for object detection and beyond. In: ICCV (2011)

40. Masci, J., Meier, U., Cireşan, D., Schmidhuber, J.: Stacked convolutional auto-encoders for hierarchical feature extraction. In: Honkela, T., Duch, W., Girolami, M., Kaski, S. (eds.) ICANN 2011. LNCS, vol. 6791, pp. 52–59. Springer, Heidelberg (2011). https://doi.org/10.1007/978-3-642-21735-7_7

41. Misra, I., Zitnick, C.L., Mitchell, M., Girshick, R.: Seeing through the human reporting bias: visual classifiers from noisy human-centric labels. In: CVPR (2016)

42. Noroozi, M., Favaro, P.: Unsupervised learning of visual representations by Solving Jigsaw Puzzles. In: Leibe, B., Matas, J., Sebe, N., Welling, M. (eds.) ECCV 2016. LNCS, vol. 9910, pp. 69–84. Springer, Cham (2016). https://doi.org/10.1007/978-3-319-46466-4_5

43. Noroozi, M., Pirsiavash, H., Favaro, P.: Representation learning by learning to count. In: ICCV (2017)

44. Owens, A., Wu, J., McDermott, J.H., Freeman, W.T., Torralba, A.: Ambient sound provides supervision for visual learning. In: Leibe, B., Matas, J., Sebe, N., Welling, M. (eds.) ECCV 2016. LNCS, vol. 9905, pp. 801–816. Springer, Cham (2016). https://doi.org/10.1007/978-3-319-46448-0_48

45. Pathak, D., Girshick, R., Dollár, P., Darrell, T., Hariharan, B.: Learning features by watching objects move. In: CVPR (2017)

46. Pathak, D., Krahenbuhl, P., Donahue, J., Darrell, T., Efros, A.A.: Context encoders: feature learning by inpainting. In: CVPR (2016)

47. Paulin, M., Douze, M., Harchaoui, Z., Mairal, J., Perronin, F., Schmid, C.: Local convolutional features with unsupervised training for image retrieval. In: ICCV (2015)

48. Philbin, J., Chum, O., Isard, M., Sivic, J., Zisserman, A.: Object retrieval with large vocabularies and fast spatial matching. In: CVPR (2007)

49. Philbin, J., Chum, O., Isard, M., Sivic, J., Zisserman, A.: Lost in quantization: improving particular object retrieval in large scale image databases. In: CVPR (2008)

50. Ren, S., He, K., Girshick, R., Sun, J.: Faster R-CNN: Towards real-time object detection with region proposal networks. In: NIPS (2015)

51. Russakovsky, O., et al.: Imagenet large scale visual recognition challenge. IJCV 115(3), 211–252 (2015)

52. de Sa, V.R.: Learning classification with unlabeled data. In: NIPS (1994)

53. Sharif Razavian, A., Azizpour, H., Sullivan, J., Carlsson, S.: CNN features off-the-shelf: an astounding baseline for recognition. In: CVPR workshops (2014)

54. Shi, J., Malik, J.: Normalized cuts and image segmentation. TPAMI 22(8), 888–905 (2000)

55. Simonyan, K., Zisserman, A.: Very deep convolutional networks for large-scale image recognition. arXiv preprint arXiv:1409.1556 (2014)

56. Srivastava, N., Hinton, G.E., Krizhevsky, A., Sutskever, I., Salakhutdinov, R.: Dropout: a simple way to prevent neural networks from overfitting. JMLR 15(1), 1929–1958 (2014)

57. Stock, P., Cisse, M.: Convnets and imagenet beyond accuracy: explanations, bias detection, adversarial examples and model criticism. arXiv preprint arXiv:1711.11443 (2017)

58. Thomee, B., et al.: The new data and new challenges in multimedia research. arXiv preprint arXiv:1503.01817 (2015)

59. Tolias, G., Sicre, R., Jégou, H.: Particular object retrieval with integral max-pooling of CNN activations. arXiv preprint arXiv:1511.05879 (2015)

60. Turk, M.A., Pentland, A.P.: Face recognition using eigenfaces. In: CVPR (1991)

61. Van De Sande, K., Gevers, T., Snoek, C.: Evaluating color descriptors for object and scene recognition. TPAMI **32**(9), 1582–1596 (2010)
62. Vincent, P., Larochelle, H., Lajoie, I., Bengio, Y., Manzagol, P.A.: Stacked denoising autoencoders: learning useful representations in a deep network with a local denoising criterion. JMLR **11**(Dec), 3371–3408 (2010)
63. Wang, X., Gupta, A.: Unsupervised learning of visual representations using videos. In: ICCV (2015)
64. Wang, X., He, K., Gupta, A.: Transitive invariance for self-supervised visual representation learning. arXiv preprint arXiv:1708.02901 (2017)
65. Weinzaepfel, P., Revaud, J., Harchaoui, Z., Schmid, C.: Deepflow: Large displacement optical flow with deep matching. In: ICCV (2013)
66. Xie, J., Girshick, R., Farhadi, A.: Unsupervised deep embedding for clustering analysis. In: ICML (2016)
67. Xu, L., Neufeld, J., Larson, B., Schuurmans, D.: Maximum margin clustering. In: NIPS (2005)
68. Yang, J., Parikh, D., Batra, D.: Joint unsupervised learning of deep representations and image clusters. In: CVPR (2016)
69. Yosinski, J., Clune, J., Nguyen, A., Fuchs, T., Lipson, H.: Understanding neural networks through deep visualization. arXiv preprint arXiv:1506.06579 (2015)
70. Zeiler, M.D., Fergus, R.: Visualizing and understanding convolutional networks. In: Fleet, D., Pajdla, T., Schiele, B., Tuytelaars, T. (eds.) ECCV 2014. LNCS, vol. 8689, pp. 818–833. Springer, Cham (2014). https://doi.org/10.1007/978-3-319-10590-1_53
71. Zhang, R., Isola, P., Efros, A.A.: Colorful image colorization. In: Leibe, B., Matas, J., Sebe, N., Welling, M. (eds.) ECCV 2016. LNCS, vol. 9907, pp. 649–666. Springer, Cham (2016). https://doi.org/10.1007/978-3-319-46487-9_40
72. Zhang, R., Isola, P., Efros, A.A.: Split-brain autoencoders: unsupervised learning by cross-channel prediction. arXiv preprint arXiv:1611.09842 (2016)
73. Zhou, B., Lapedriza, A., Xiao, J., Torralba, A., Oliva, A.: Learning deep features for scene recognition using places database. In: NIPS (2014)

Modular Generative Adversarial Networks

Bo Zhao[1(✉)], Bo Chang[1], Zequn Jie[2], and Leonid Sigal[1]

[1] University of British Columbia, Vancouver, Canada
bchang@stat.ubc.ca, {bzhao03,lsigal}@cs.ubc.ca
[2] Tencent AI Lab, Bellevue, USA
zequn.nus@gmail.com

Abstract. Existing methods for multi-domain image-to-image translation (or generation) attempt to directly map an input image (or a random vector) to an image in one of the output domains. However, most existing methods have limited scalability and robustness, since they require building independent models for each pair of domains in question. This leads to two significant shortcomings: (1) the need to train exponential number of pairwise models, and (2) the inability to leverage data from other domains when training a particular pairwise mapping. Inspired by recent work on module networks, this paper proposes ModularGAN for multi-domain image generation and image-to-image translation. ModularGAN consists of several reusable and composable modules that carry on different functions (e.g., encoding, decoding, transformations). These modules can be trained simultaneously, leveraging data from all domains, and then combined to construct specific GAN networks at test time, according to the specific image translation task. This leads to ModularGAN's superior flexibility of generating (or translating to) an image in any desired domain. Experimental results demonstrate that our model not only presents compelling perceptual results but also outperforms state-of-the-art methods on multi-domain facial attribute transfer.

Keywords: Neural modular network
Generative adversarial network · Image generation · Image translation

1 Introduction

Image generation has gained popularity in recent years following the introduction of variational autoencoder (VAE) [15] and generative adversarial networks (GAN) [6]. A plethora of tasks, based on image generation, have been studied, including attribute-to-image generation [20,21,31], text-to-image generation [23, 24,30,32,33] or image-to-image translation [5,11,14,18,25,34]. These tasks can

Electronic supplementary material The online version of this chapter (https://doi.org/10.1007/978-3-030-01264-9_10) contains supplementary material, which is available to authorized users.

© Springer Nature Switzerland AG 2018
V. Ferrari et al. (Eds.): ECCV 2018, LNCS 11218, pp. 157–173, 2018.
https://doi.org/10.1007/978-3-030-01264-9_10

be broadly termed *conditional image generation*, which takes an attribute vector, text description or an image as the conditional input, respectively, and outputs an image. Most existing conditional image generation models learn a direct mapping from inputs, which can include an image or a random noise vector, and target condition to output an image containing target properties.

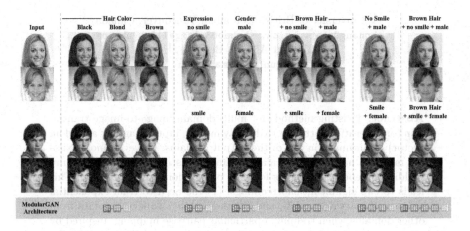

Fig. 1. ModularGAN: Results of proposed modular generative adversarial network illustrated on multi-domain image-to-image translation task on the CelebA [19] dataset.

Each condition, or condition type, effectively defines a generation or image-to-image output domain (*e.g.*, domain of *expression* (smiling) or *gender* (male / female) for facial images). For practical tasks, it is desirable to be able to control a large and variable number of conditions (*e.g.*, to generate images of person *smiling* or *brown haired smiling man*). Building a function that can deal with the exponential, in the number of conditions, domains is difficult. Most existing image translation methods [11, 14, 25, 34] can only translate images from one domain to another. For multi-domain setting this results in a number of shortcomings: (i) requirement to learn an exponential number of pairwise translation functions, which is computationally expensive and practically infeasible for more than a handful of conditions; (ii) it is impossible to leverage data from other domains when learning a particular pairwise mapping; and (iii) the pairwise translation function could potentially be arbitrarily complex in order to model the transformation between very different domains. To address (i) and (ii), multi-domain image (and language [13]) translation [5] models have been introduced very recently. A fixed vector representing the source/target domain information can be used as the condition for a single model to guide the translation process. However, the sharing of information among the domains is largely implicit and the functional mapping becomes even more excessively complex.

We posit that dividing the image generation process into multiple simpler generative steps can make the model easier and more robust to learn. In particular, we neither train pairwise mappings [11, 34] nor one complex model [5, 22];

instead we train a small number of simple generative modules that can compose to form complex generative processes. In particular, consider transforming an image from domain A (*man frowning*) to C (*woman smiling*): $\mathcal{D}_A \rightarrow \mathcal{D}_C$. It is conceivable, even likely, that first transforming the original image to depict a *female* and subsequently *smiling* ($\mathcal{D}_A \xrightarrow{female} \mathcal{D}_B \xrightarrow{smiling} \mathcal{D}_C$) would be more robust than directly going from domain A to C. The reason is two fold: (i) the individual transformations are simpler and spatially more local, and (ii) the amount of data in the intermediate *female* and *smile* domains are by definition larger than in the final domain of *woman smiling*. In other words, in this case, we are leveraging more data to learn simpler translation/transformation functions. This intuition is also consistent with recently introduced modular networks [1,2], which we here conceptually adopt and extend for generative image tasks.

To achieve and formalize this incremental image generation process, we propose the modular generative adversarial network (ModularGAN). ModularGAN consists of several different modules, including *generator, encoder, reconstructor, transformer* and *discriminator*, trained jointly. Each module performs specific functionality. The *generator* module, used in image generation tasks, generates a latent representation of the image from a random noise and an (optional) condition vector. The *encoder* module, used for image-to-image translation, encodes the input image into a latent representation. The latent representation, produced by either generator or encoder, is manipulated by the *transformer* module according to the provided condition. The *reconstructor* module then reconstructs the transformed latent representation to an image. The *discriminator* module is used to distinguish whether the generated or transformed image looks real or fake, and also to classify the attributes of the image. Importantly, different *transformer* modules can be composed dynamically at test time, in any order, to form generative networks that apply a sequence of feature transformations in order to obtain more complex mappings and generative processes.

Contributions: Our contributions are multi-fold,

- We propose ModularGAN – a novel modular multi-domain generative adversarial network architecture. ModularGAN consists of several reusable and composable modules. Different modules can be combined easily at test time, in order to generate/translate an image in/to different domains efficiently. To the best of our knowledge, this is the *first* modular GAN architecture.
- We provide an efficient way to train all the modules jointly end-to-end. New modules can be easily added to our proposed ModularGAN, and a subset of the existing modules can also be upgraded without affecting the others.
- We demonstrate how one can successfully combine different (transformer) modules in order to translate an image to different domains. We utilize mask prediction, in the transformer module, to ensure that only local regions of the feature map are transformed; leaving other regions unchanged.
- We empirically demonstrate the effectiveness of our approach on image generation (ColorMNIST dataset) and image-to-image translation (facial attribute transfer) tasks. Qualitative and quantitative comparisons with state-of-the-art GAN models illustrate improvements obtained by ModularGAN.

2 Related Work

2.1 Modular Networks

Visual question answering (VQA) is a fundamentally compositional task. By explicitly modeling its underling reasoning process, **Neural module networks** [2] are constructed to perform various operations, including attention, re-attention, combination, classification, and measurement. Those modules are assembled into all configurations necessary for different question tasks. A natural language parser decompose questions into logical expressions and dynamically lay out a deep network composed of reusable modules. **Dynamic neural module networks** [1] extend neural module networks by learning the network structure via reinforcement learning, instead of direct parsing of questions. Both work use predefined module operations with handcrafted module architectures. More recently, [12] proposes a model for visual reasoning that consists of a program generator and an execution engine. The program generator constructs an explicit representation of the reasoning process to be performed. It is a sequence-to-sequence model which inputs the question as a sequence of words and outputs a program as a sequence of functions. The execution engine executes the resulting program to produce an answer. It is implemented using a neural module network. In contrast to [1,2], the modules use a generic architecture. Similar to VQA, multi-domain image generation can also be regarded as a composition of several two domain image translations, which forms the bases of this paper.

2.2 Image Translation

Generative Adversarial Networks (GANs) [6] are powerful generative models which have achieved impressive results in many computer vision tasks such as image generation [9,21], image inpainting [10], super resolution [16] and image-to-image translation [4,11,17,22,27–29,34]. GANs formulate generative modeling as a game between two competing networks: a generator network produces synthetic data given some input noise and a discriminator network distinguishes between the generator's output and true data. The game between the generator G and the discriminator D has the minmax objective. Unlike GANs which learn a mapping from a random noise vector to an output image, **conditional GANs** (cGANs) [20] learn a mapping from a random noise vector to an output image conditioning on additional information. **Pix2pix**[11] is a generic image-to-image translation algorithm using cGANs [20]. It can produce reasonable results on a wide variety of problems. Given a training set which contains pairs of related images, pix2pix learns how to convert an image of one type into an image of another type, or vice versa. **Cycle-consistent GANs** (CycleGANs) [34] learn the image translation without paired examples. Instead, it trains two generative models cycle-wise between the input and output images. In addition to the adversarial losses, cycle consistency loss is used to prevent the two generative models from contradicting each other. Both Pix2Pix and CycleGANs are designed for two-domain image translation. By inverting the mapping of a cGAN [20], *i.e.*, mapping a real image into a latent space and a conditional representation, **IcGAN** [22] can reconstruct and modify an input image of a face conditioned on arbitrary attributes. More recently, **StarGAN** [5] is proposed to perform multi-domain image translation using a single network conditioned on the target domain label. It learns the mappings among multiple domains using only a single generator and a discriminator. Different from StarGAN, which learns all domain transformations within a single model, we train different simple composable translation networks for different attributes.

3 Modular Generative Adversarial Networks

3.1 Problem Formulation

We consider two types of multi-domain tasks: (i) *image generation* – which directly generates an image with certain attribute properties from a random vector (*e.g.*, an image of a digit written in a certain font or style); and (ii) *image translation* – which takes an existing image and minimally modifies it by changing certain attribute properties (*e.g.*, changing the hair color or facial expression in a portrait image). We pre-define an attribute set $\mathbf{A} = \{A_1, A_2, \cdots, A_n\}$, where n is the number of different attributes, and each attribute A_i is a meaningful semantic property inherent in an image. For example, attributes for facial images may include hair color, gender or facial expression. Each A_i has different attribute value(s), *e.g.*, black/blond/brown for hair color or male/female for gender.

For the *image generation* task, the goal is to learn a mapping $(z, \mathbf{a}) \mapsto y$. The input is a pair $(z, \mathbf{a})$, where z is a randomly sampled vector and $\mathbf{a}$ is a subset of attributes $\mathbf{A}$. Note that the number of elements in $\mathbf{a}$ is not fixed; more elements would provide finer control over generated image. The output y is the target image. For the *image translation* task, the goal is to learn a mapping $(x, \mathbf{a}) \mapsto y$. The input is a pair $(x, \mathbf{a})$, where x is an image and $\mathbf{a}$ are the target attributes to be present in the output image y. The number of elements in $\mathbf{a}$ indicates the number of attributes of the input image that need to be altered.

In the remainder of the section, we formulate the set of modules used for these two tasks and describe the process of composing them into networks.

3.2 Network Construction

Image Translation. We first introduce the ModularGAN that performs multi-domain image translation. Four types of modules are used in this task: the encoder module (**E**), which encodes an input image to an intermediate feature map; the transformer module (**T**), which modifies a certain attribute of the feature map; the reconstructor module (**R**), which reconstructs the image from an intermediate feature map; and the discriminator module (**D**), which determines whether an image is real or fake, and predicts the attributes of the input image. More details about the modules will be given in the following section.

Figure 2 demonstrates the overall architecture of the image translation model in the training and test phases. In the training phase (Fig. 2, left), the encoder module $\mathbf{E}$ is connected to multiple transformer modules $\mathbf{T}_i$, each of which is further connected to a reconstructor module $\mathbf{R}$ to generate the translated image. There are multiple discriminator modules $\mathbf{D}_i$ connected to the reconstructor to distinguish the generated images from real images, and to make predictions of corresponding attribute. All modules have the same interface, *i.e.*, the output of $\mathbf{E}$, the input of $\mathbf{R}$, and both the input and output of $\mathbf{T}_i$ have the same shape and dimensionality. This enables the modules to be assembled in order to build more complex architectures at test time, as illustrated in Fig. 2, right.

In the training phase, an input image x is first encoded by $\mathbf{E}$, which gives the intermediate representation $\mathbf{E}(x)$. Then different transformer modules $\mathbf{T}_i$ are applied to modify $\mathbf{E}(x)$ according to the pre-specified attributes a_i, resulting in $\mathbf{T}_i(\mathbf{E}(x), a_i)$. $\mathbf{T}_i$ is designed to transform a specific attribute $\mathbf{A}_i$ into a different attribute value[1], *e.g.*, changing the hair color from blond to brown, or changing the gender from female to male. The reconstructor module $\mathbf{R}$ reconstructs the transformed feature map into an output image $y = \mathbf{R}(\mathbf{T}_i(\mathbf{E}(x), a_i))$. The discriminator module $\mathbf{D}$ is designed to distinguish the generated image y and the real image x. It also predicts the attributes of the image x or y.

In the test phase (Fig. 2, right), different transformer modules can be dynamically combined to form a network that can sequentially manipulate any number of attributes in arbitrary order.

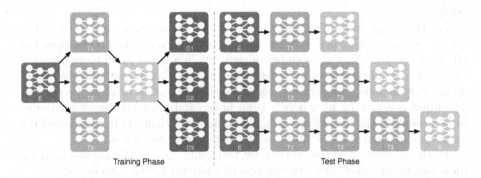

Training Phase   Test Phase

Fig. 2. ModularGAN Architecture: Multi-domain image translation architecture in training (left) and test (right) phases. ModularGAN consists of four different kinds of modules: the encoder module $\mathbf{E}$, transformer module $\mathbf{T}$, reconstructor module $\mathbf{R}$ and discriminator $\mathbf{D}$. These modules can be trained simultaneously and used to construct different generation networks according to the generation task in the test phase.

---

[1] This also means that, in general, the number of transformer modules is equal to the number of attributes.

Image Generation. The model architecture for the image generation task is mostly the same to the image translation task. The only difference is that the encoder module $\mathbf{E}$ is replaced with a generator module $\mathbf{G}$, which generates an intermediate feature map $\mathbf{G}(z, a_0)$ from a random noise z and a condition vector a_0 representing auxiliary information. The condition vector a_0 could determine the overall content of the image. For example, if the goal is to generate an image of a digit, a_0 could be used to control which digit to generate, say digit 7. A module $\mathbf{R}$ can similarly reconstruct an initial image $x = \mathbf{R}(\mathbf{G}(z, a_0))$, which is an image of digit 7 with any attributes. The remaining parts of the architecture are identical to the image translation task, which transform the initial image x using a sequence of transformer modules $\mathbf{T}_i$ to alter certain attributes, (e.g., color of the digit, stroke type or background).

3.3 Modules

Generator Module (G) generates a feature map of size $C \times H \times W$ using several transposed convolutional layers. Its input is the concatenation of a random variable z and a condition vector a_0. See supplementary materials for the network architecture.

Encoder Module (E) encodes an input image x into an intermediate feature representation of size $C \times H \times W$ using several convolutional layers. See supplementary materials for the network architecture.

Transformer Module (T) is the core module in our model. It transforms the input feature representation into a new one according to input condition a_i. A transformer module receives a feature map f of size $C \times H \times W$ and a condition vector a_i of length c_i. Its output is a feature map f_t of size $C \times H \times W$. Figure 3 illustrates the structure of a module $\mathbf{T}$. The condition vector a_i of length c_i is replicated to a tensor of size $c_i \times H \times W$, which is then concatenated with the input feature map f. Convolutional layers are first used to reduce the number of channels from $C + c_i$ to C. Afterwards, several residual blocks are sequentially applied, the output of which is denoted by f'. Using the transformed feature map f', additional convolution layers with the $Tanh$ activation function are used to generate a single-channel feature map g of size $H \times W$. This feature map g is further rescaled to the range $(0, 1)$ by $g' = (1 + g)/2$. The predicted g' acts like an alpha mask or an attention layer: it encourages the module $\mathbf{T}$ to transform only the regions of the feature map that are relevant to the specific attribute transformation. Finally, the transformed feature map f' and the input feature map f are combined using the mask g' to get the output $f_t = g' \times f' + (1 - g') \times f$.

Reconstructor Module (R) reconstructs the image from a $C \times H \times W$ feature map using several transposed convolutional layers. See supplementary materials for the network architecture.

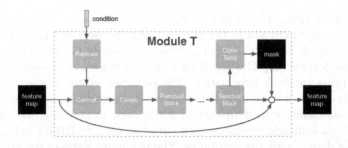

Fig. 3. Transformer Module

Discriminator Module (D) classifies an image as real or fake, and predicts one of the attributes of the image (*e.g.*, hair color, gender or facial image). See supplementary materials for the network architecture.

3.4   Loss Function

We adopt a combination of several loss functions to train our model.

Adversarial Loss. We apply the adversarial loss [6] to make the generated images look realistic. For the i-th transformer module $\mathbf{T}_i$ and its corresponding discriminator module $\mathbf{D}_i$, the adversarial loss can be written as:

$$\mathcal{L}_{\mathrm{adv}_i}(\mathbf{E}, \mathbf{T}_i, \mathbf{R}, \mathbf{D}_i) = \mathbb{E}_{y \sim p_{\mathrm{data}}(y)}[\log \mathbf{D}_i(y)] + \\ \mathbb{E}_{x \sim p_{\mathrm{data}}(x)}[\log(1 - \mathbf{D}_i(\mathbf{R}(\mathbf{T}_i(\mathbf{E}(x)))))], \qquad (1)$$

where $\mathbf{E}$, $\mathbf{T}_i$, $\mathbf{R}$, $\mathbf{D}_i$ are the encoder module, the i-th transformer module, the reconstructor module and the i-th discriminator module respectively. $\mathbf{D}_i$ aims to distinguish between transformed samples $\mathbf{R}(\mathbf{T}_i(\mathbf{E}(x)))$ and real samples y. All the modules $\mathbf{E}$, $\mathbf{T}_i$ and $\mathbf{R}$ try to minimize this objective against an adversary $\mathbf{D}_i$ that tries to maximize it, *i.e.* $\min_{\mathbf{E},\mathbf{T}_i,\mathbf{R}} \max_{\mathbf{D}_i} \mathcal{L}_{\mathrm{adv}_i}(\mathbf{E}, \mathbf{T}_i, \mathbf{R}, \mathbf{D}_i)$.

Auxiliary Classification Loss. Similar to [21] and [5], for each discriminator module $\mathbf{D}_i$, besides a classifier to distinguish the real and fake images, we define an auxiliary classifier to predict the i-th attribute of the image, *e.g.*, hair color or gender of the facial image. There are two components of the classification loss: real image loss $\mathcal{L}_{\mathrm{cls}_i}^r$ and fake image loss $\mathcal{L}_{\mathrm{cls}_i}^f$.

For real images x, the real image auxiliary classification loss $\mathcal{L}_{\mathrm{cls}_i}^r$ is defined as follows:

$$\mathcal{L}_{\mathrm{cls}_i}^r = \mathbb{E}_{x,c_i}[-\log \mathbf{D}_{\mathrm{cls}_i}(c_i|x)], \qquad (2)$$

where $\mathbf{D}_{\mathrm{cls}_i}(c|x)$ is the probability distribution over different attribute values predicted by $\mathbf{D}_i$, *e.g.*, black, blond or brown for hair color. The discriminator module $\mathbf{D}_i$ tries to minimize $\mathcal{L}_{\mathrm{cls}_i}^r$.

The fake image auxiliary classification loss $\mathcal{L}_{\text{cls}_i}^f$ is defined similarly, using generated images $\mathbf{R}(\mathbf{E}(\mathbf{T}_i(x)))$:

$$\mathcal{L}_{\text{cls}_i}^f = \mathbb{E}_{x,c_i}[-\log \mathbf{D}_{\text{cls}_i}(c_i|\mathbf{R}(\mathbf{E}(\mathbf{T}_i(x))))]. \tag{3}$$

The modules $\mathbf{R}$, $\mathbf{E}$ and $\mathbf{T}_i$ try to minimize $\mathcal{L}_{\text{cls}_i}^f$ to generate fake images that can be classified as the correct target attribute c_i.

Cyclic Loss. Conceptually, the encoder module $\mathbf{E}$ and the reconstructor module $\mathbf{R}$ are a pair of inverse operations. Therefore, for a real image x, $\mathbf{R}(\mathbf{E}(x))$ should resembles x. Based on this observation, the encoder-reconstructor cyclic loss $\mathcal{L}_{\text{cyc}}^{\mathbf{ER}}$ is defined as follows:

$$\mathcal{L}_{\text{cyc}}^{\mathbf{ER}} = \mathbb{E}_x[\|\mathbf{R}(\mathbf{E}(x)) - x\|_1]. \tag{4}$$

Cyclic losses can be defined not only on images, but also on intermediate feature maps. At training time, different transformer modules $\mathbf{T}_i$ are connected to the encoder module $\mathbf{E}$ in a parallel fashion. However, at test time $\mathbf{T}_i$ will be connected to each other sequentially, according to specific module composition for the test task. Therefore it is important to have the cyclic consistency of the feature maps so that a sequence of $\mathbf{T}_i$ modifies the feature map consistently. To enforce this, we define a cyclic loss on the transformed feature map and the encoded feature map of reconstructed output image. This cycle loss is defined as

$$\mathcal{L}_{\text{cyc}}^{\mathbf{T}_i} = \mathbb{E}_x[\|\mathbf{T}_i(\mathbf{E}(x)) - \mathbf{E}(\mathbf{R}(\mathbf{T}_i(\mathbf{E}(x))))\|_1], \tag{5}$$

where $\mathbf{E}(x)$ is the original feature map of the input image x, and $\mathbf{T}_i(\mathbf{E}(x))$ is the transformed feature map. The module $\mathbf{R}(\cdot)$ reconstructs the transformed feature map to a new image with the target attribute. The module $\mathbf{E}$ then encodes the generated image back to an intermediate feature map. This cyclic loss encourages the transformer module to output a feature map similar to the one produced by the encoder module. This allows different modules $\mathbf{T}_i$ to be concatenated at test time without loss in performance.

Full Loss. Finally, the full loss functions for $\mathbf{D}$ is

$$\mathcal{L}_D(\mathbf{D}) = -\sum_{i=1}^n \mathcal{L}_{\text{adv}_i} + \lambda_{\text{cls}} \sum_{i=1}^n \mathcal{L}_{\text{cls}_i}^r, \tag{6}$$

and the full loss functions for $\mathbf{E}$, $\mathbf{T}$, $\mathbf{R}$ is

$$\mathcal{L}_G(\mathbf{E}, \mathbf{T}, \mathbf{R}) = \sum_{i=1}^n \mathcal{L}_{\text{adv}_i} + \lambda_{\text{cls}} \sum_{i=1}^n \mathcal{L}_{\text{cls}_i}^f + \lambda_{\text{cyc}}(\mathcal{L}_{\text{cyc}}^{\mathbf{ER}} + \sum_{i=1}^n \mathcal{L}_{\text{cyc}}^{\mathbf{T}_i}), \tag{7}$$

where n is the total number of controllable attributes, and λ_{cls} and λ_{cyc} are hyper-parameters that control the importance of auxiliary classification and cyclic losses, respectively, relative to the adversarial loss.

4   Implementation

Network Architecture. In our ModularGAN, $\mathbf{E}$ has two convolution layers with stride size of two for down-sampling. $\mathbf{G}$ has four transposed convolution layers with stride size of two for up-sampling. $\mathbf{T}$ has two convolution layers with stride size of one and six residual block to transform the input feature map. Another convolution layer with stride size of one is added on top of the last residual block to predict a mask. $\mathbf{R}$ has two transposed convolution layers with stride size of two for up-sampling. Five convolution layers with stride size of two are used in $\mathbf{D}$, together with two additional convolution layers to classify an image as real or fake, and its attributes.

Training Details. To stabilize the training process and to generate images of high quality, we replace the adversarial loss in Eq. (1) with the Wasserstein GAN [3] objective function using gradient penalty [7] defined by

$$\mathcal{L}_{\mathrm{adv}_i}(\mathbf{E}, \mathbf{T}_i, \mathbf{R}, \mathbf{D}_i) = \mathbb{E}_x[\mathbf{D}_i(x)] - \mathbb{E}_x[\mathbf{D}_i(\mathbf{R}(\mathbf{T}_i(\mathbf{E}(x))))]$$
$$- \lambda_{\mathrm{gp}}\mathbb{E}_{\hat{x}}[(\|\nabla_{\hat{x}}\mathbf{D}_i(\hat{x})\|_2 - 1)^2], \qquad (8)$$

where $\hat{x}$ is sampled uniformly along a straight line between a pair of real and generated images. For all experiments, we set $\lambda_{\mathrm{gp}} = 10$ in Eq. 8, $\lambda_{\mathrm{cls}} = 1$ and $\lambda_{\mathrm{cyc}} = 10$ in Eqs. 6 and 7. We use the Adam optimizer [15] with a batch size of 16. All networks are trained from scratch with an initial learning rate of 0.0001. We keep the same learning rate for the first 10 epochs and linearly decay the learning rate to 0 over the next 10 epochs.

5   Experiments

We first conduct image generation experiments on a synthesized multi-attribute MNIST dataset. Next, we compare our method with recent work on image-to-image facial attributes transfer. Our method shows both qualitative and quantitative improvements as measured by user studies and attribute classification. Finally, we conduct an ablation study to examine the effect of mask prediction in module $\mathbf{T}$, the cyclic loss, and the order of multiple modules $\mathbf{T}$ on multi-domain image transfer.

5.1   Baselines

IcGAN first learns a mapping from a latent vector z to a real image y, $G : (z, c) \mapsto y$, then learns the inverse mapping from a real image x to a latent vector z and a condition representation c, $E : x \mapsto (z, c)$. Finally, it reconstructs a new image conditioned on z and a modified c', i.e. $G : (z, c') \mapsto y$.

CycleGAN learns two mappings $G : x \mapsto y$ and $F : y \mapsto x$ simultaneously, and uses a cycle consistency loss to enforce $F(G(x)) \approx x$ and $G(F(y)) \approx y$. We train different models of CycleGAN for each pair of domains in our experiments.

StarGAN trains a single G to translate an input image x into an output image y conditioned on the target domain label(s) c directly, i.e., $G : (x, c) \mapsto y$. Setting multiple entries in c allows StarGAN to perform multi-attribute transfer.

5.2 Datasets

ColorMNIST. We construct a synthetic dataset called the ColorMNIST, based on the MNIST Dialog Dataset [26]. Each image in ColorMNIST contains a digit with four randomly sampled attributes, i.e., number $= \{x \in \mathbb{Z} | 0 \leqslant x \leqslant 9\}$, color $= \{red, blue, green, purple, brown\}$, style $= \{flat, stroke\}$, and bgcolor $= \{cyan, yellow, white, silver, salmon\}$. We generate $50\,\mathrm{K}$ images of size 64×64.

CelebA. The CelebA dataset [19] contains 202,599 face images of celebrities, with 40 binary attributes such as young, smiling, pale skin and male. We randomly sampled 2,000 images as test set and use all remaining images as training data. All images are center cropped with size 178×178, and resized to 128×128. We choose three attributes with seven different attribute values for all the experiments: hair color $= \{black, blond, brown\}$, gender $= \{male, female\}$, and smile $= \{smile, nosmile\}$.

5.3 Evaluation

Classification Error. As a quantitative evaluation, we compute the classification error of each attribute on the synthesized images using a ResNet-18 network [8], which is trained to classify the attributes of an image. All methods use the same classification network for performance evaluation. Lower classification errors imply that the generated images have more accurate target attributes.

User Study. We also perform a user study using Amazon Mechanical Turk (AMT) to assess the image quality for image translation tasks. Given an input image, the Turkers were instructed to choose the best generated image based on perceptual realism, quality of transfer in attribute(s), and preservation of a figure's original identity.

5.4 Experimental Results on ColorMNIST

Qualitative Evaluation. Figure 4 shows the digit image generation results on ColorMNIST dataset. The generator module **G** and reconstructor module **R** first generate the correct digit according to the number attribute as shown in the first column. The generated digit has random color, stroke style and background color. By passing the feature representation produced by **G** through different $\mathbf{T}_i$, the digit color, stroke style and background of the initially generated image will change, as shown in the second to forth columns. The last four columns illustrate multi-attribute transformation by combining different $\mathbf{T}_i$. Each module $\mathbf{T}_i$ only changes a specific attribute and keeps other attributes untouched (at the previous attribute value). Note that there are scenarios where the initial image already has the target attribute value; in such cases the transformed image is identical to the previous one.

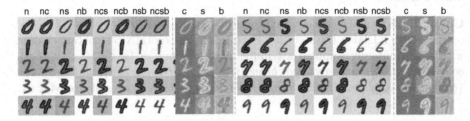

Fig. 4. Image Generation: Digits synthesis results on the ColorMNIST dataset. Note, that (n) implies conditioning on the digit number, (c) color, (s) stroke type, and (b) background. Columns denoted by more than one letter illustrate generation results conditioned on multiple attributes, *e.g.*, (ncs) – digit number, color, and stroke type. Greyscale images illustrate mask produced internally by $\mathbf{T}_i$ modules, $i \in \{c, s, b\}$. (Color figure online)

Visualization of Masks. In Fig. 4, we also visualize the predicted masks in each transformer module $\mathbf{T}_i$. It provides an interpretable way to understand where the modules apply the transformations. White pixels in the mask correspond to regions in the feature map that are modified by the current module; black pixels to regions that remain unchanged throughout the module. It can be observed that the color transformer module $\mathbf{T}_c$ mainly changes the interior of the digits, so only the digits are highlighted. The stroke style transformer module $\mathbf{T}_s$ correctly focuses on the borders of the digits. Finally, the masks corresponding to the background color transformer module $\mathbf{T}_b$ have larger values in the background regions.

5.5   Experimental Results on CelebA

Qualitative Evaluation. Figures 1 and 5 show the facial attribute transfer results on CelebA using the proposed method and the baseline methods, respectively. In Fig. 5, the transfer is between a female face image with neutral expression and black hair to a variety of combinations of attributes. The results show that IcGAN has the least satisfying performance. Although the generated images have the desired attributes, the facial identity is not well preserved. The generated images also do not have sharp details, caused by the information lost during the process of encoding the input image into a low-dimensional latent vector and decoding it back. The images generated by CycleGAN are better than IcGAN, but there are some visible artifacts. By using the cycle consistence loss, Cycle-GAN preserves the facial identity of the input image and only changes specific regions of the face. StarGAN generates better results than CycleGAN, since it is trained on the whole dataset and implicitly leverages images from all attribute domains. Our method generates better results than the baseline methods (*e.g.*, see Smile or multi-attribute transfer in the last column). It uses multiple transformer modules to change different attributes, and each transformer module learns a specific mapping from one domain to another. This is different from StarGAN, which learns all the transformations in one single model.

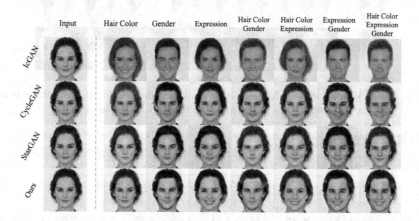

Fig. 5. Facial attribute transfer results on CelebA: See text for description.

Visualization of Masks. To better understand what happens when ModularGAN translates an image, we visualize the mask of each transformer module in Fig. 6. When multiple T_i are used, we add different predicted masks. It can be seen from the visualization that when changing the hair color, the transformer module only focuses on the hair region of the image. By modifying the mouth area of the feature maps, the facial expression can be changed from neutral to smile. To change the gender, regions around cheeks, chin and nose are used.

Table 1. AMT User Study: Higher values are better and indicating preference.

Method	H	S	G	HS	HG	SG	HSG
IcGAN	3.48	2.63	8.70	4.35	8.70	13.91	15.65
CycleGAN	17.39	16.67	29.57	18.26	20.00	17.39	9.57
StarGAN	30.43	36.84	**32.17**	31.30	27.83	27.83	27.83
Ours	**48.70**	**43.86**	29.57	**46.09**	**43.48**	**40.87**	**46.96**

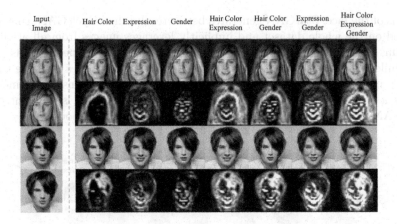

Fig. 6. Mask Visualization: Visualization of masks when performing attribute transfer. We sum the different masks when multiple modules **T** are used.

Table 2. Classification Error: Lower is better, indicating fewer attribute errors.

Method	H	S	G	HS	HG	SG	HSG
IcGAN	7.82	10.43	20.86	22.17	20.00	23.91	23.18
CycleGAN	4.34	10.43	13.26	13.67	10.43	17.82	21.01
StarGAN	**3.47**	4.56	4.21	4.65	6.95	5.52	7.63
Ours	3.86	**4.21**	**2.61**	**4.03**	**6.51**	**4.04**	**6.09**

Quantitative Evaluation. We train a model that classifies the hair color, facial expression and gender on the CelebA dataset using a ResNet-18 architecture [8]. The training/test set are the same as that in other experiments. The trained model classifies the hair color, gender and smile with accuracy of 96.5%, 97.9% and 98.3% respectively. We then apply this trained model on transformed images produced by different methods on the test set. As can be seen in Table 2, our model achieves a comparable classification error to StarGAN on the hair color task, and the lowest classification errors on all other tasks. This indicates that our model produces realistic facial images with desired attributes. Table 1 shows the results of the AMT experiments. Our model obtains the majority of votes for best transferring attributes in all the cases except gender. We observe that our gender transfer model better preserves original hair, which is desirable from the model's point of view, but sometimes perceived negatively by the Turkers.

5.6   Ablation Study

To analyze the effect of the mask prediction, the cyclic loss and the order of modules $\mathbf{T}_i$ when transferring multiple attributes, we conduct ablation experiments by removing the mask prediction, removing the cyclic loss and randomizing the order of $\mathbf{T}_i$.

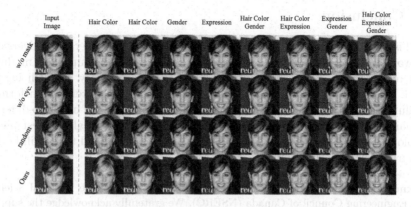

Fig. 7. Ablation: Images generated using different variants of our method. From top to bottom: ModularGAN w/o mask prediction in **T**, ModularGAN w/o cyclic loss, ModularGAN with random order of $\mathbf{T}_i$ when performing multi-attribute transfer.

Effect of Mask. Figure 7 shows that, without mask prediction, the model can still manipulate the images but tends to perform worse on gender, smile and multi-attribute transfer. Without the mask, **T** module not only needs to learn how to translate the feature map, but also needs to learn how to keep parts of the original feature map intact. As a result, without mask it becomes difficult to compose modules, as illustrated by higher classification errors in Table 3.

Effect of Cyclic Loss. Removing the cyclic loss does not affect the results of single-attribute manipulation, as shown in Fig. 7. However, when combining multiple transformer modules, the model can no loner generate images with desired attributes. This is also quantitatively verified in Table 3: the performance of multi-attribute transfer drops dramatically without the cyclic loss.

Effect of Module Order. We test our model by applying $\mathbf{T}_i$ modules in random order when performing multi-attribute transformations (as compared to fixed ordering - Ours). The results reported in Table 3 indicate that our model is unaffected by the order of transformer modules, which is a desired property.

Table 3. Ablation Results: Classification error for ModularGAN variants (see text).

Method	H	S	G	HS	HG	SG	HSG
Ours w/o mask	4.01	4.65	3.58	30.85	34.67	36.61	56.08
Ours w/o cyclic loss	3.93	4.48	2.87	25.34	28.82	30.96	52.87
Ours random order	**3.86**	**4.21**	**2.61**	4.37	**5.98**	4.13	6.23
Ours	**3.86**	**4.21**	**2.61**	**4.03**	6.51	**4.04**	**6.09**

6   Conclusion

In this paper, we proposed a novel modular multi-domain generative adversarial network architecture, which consists of several reusable and composable modules. Different modules can be jointly trained end-to-end efficiently. By utilizing the mask prediction within module **T** and the cyclic loss, different (transformer) modules can be combined in order to successfully translate the image to different domains. Currently, different modules are connected sequentially in test phase. Exploring different structure of modules for more complicated tasks will be one of our future work directions.

Acknowledgement. This research was supported in part by the National Sciences and Engineering Council of Canada (NSERC). We gratefully acknowledge the support of NVIDIA Corporation with the donation of the Titan Xp GPU used for this research.

References

1. Andreas, J., Rohrbach, M., Darrell, T., Klein, D.: Learning to compose neural networks for question answering. In: HLT-NAACL (2016)
2. Andreas, J., Rohrbach, M., Darrell, T., Klein, D.: Neural module networks. In: CVPR, pp. 39–48 (2016)
3. Arjovsky, M., Chintala, S., Bottou, L.: Wasserstein GAN. In: ICML (2017)
4. Chang, B., Zhang, Q., Pan, S., Meng, L.: Generating handwritten Chinese characters using Cyclegan. In: WACV (2018)
5. Choi, Y., Choi, M., Kim, M., Ha, J.W., Kim, S., Choo, J.: Stargan: unified generative adversarial networks for multi-domain image-to-image translation. In: CVPR (2018)
6. Goodfellow, I., et al.: Generative adversarial nets. In: NIPS (2014)
7. Gulrajani, I., Ahmed, F., Arjovsky, M., Dumoulin, V., Courville, A.: Improved Training of Wasserstein GANs. In: NIPS (2017)
8. He, K., Zhang, X., Ren, S., Sun, J.: Deep residual learning for image recognition. In: CVPR (2016)
9. Huang, X., Li, Y., Poursaeed, O., Hopcroft, J., Belongie, S.: Stacked generative adversarial networks. In: CVPR (2017)
10. Iizuka, S., Simo-Serra, E., Ishikawa, H.: Globally and locally consistent image completion. ACM Trans. Graph. (TOG) **36**, 107 (2017)
11. Isola, P., Zhu, J.Y., Zhou, T., Efros, A.A.: Image-to-image translation with conditional adversarial networks. In: CVPR (2016)
12. Johnson, J., et al.: Inferring and executing programs for visual reasoning. In: ICCV, pp. 3008–3017 (2017)
13. Johnson, M., et al.: Google's multilingual neural machine translation system: enabling zero-shot translation. In: TACL (2017)
14. Karacan, L., Akata, Z., Erdem, A., Erdem, E.: Learning to generate images of outdoor scenes from attributes and semantic layouts. arXiv.1612.00215 (2016)
15. Kingma, D.P., Welling, M.: Auto-encoding variational bayes. In: ICLR (2014)
16. Ledig, C., et al.: Photo-realistic single image super-resolution using a generative adversarial network. In: CVPR (2017)
17. Li, M., Zuo, W., Zhang, D.: Deep Identity-aware Transfer of Facial Attributes. arXiv.1610.05586 (2016)

18. Li, M., Huang, H., Ma, L., Liu, W., Zhang, T., Jiang, Y.G.: Unsupervised image-to-image translation with stacked cycle-consistent adversarial networks (2018)

19. Liu, Z., Luo, P., Wang, X., Tang, X.: Deep learning face attributes in the wild. In: ICCV (2015)

20. Mirza, M., Osindero, S.: Conditional generative adversarial nets. arXiv:1411.1784 (2014)

21. Odena, A., Olah, C., Shlens, J.: Conditional image synthesis with auxiliary classifier GANs. In: NIPS (2016)

22. Perarnau, G., van de Weijer, J., Raducanu, B., Álvarez, J.M.: Invertible conditional GANs for image editing. In: NIPS Workshop on Adversarial Training (2016)

23. Reed, S., Akata, Z., Mohan, S., Tenka, S., Schiele, B., Lee, H.: Learning what and where to draw. In: NIPS (2016)

24. Reed, S., Akata, Z., Yan, X., Logeswaran, L., Schiele, B., Lee, H.: Generative adversarial text to image synthesis. In: ICML (2016)

25. Sangkloy, P., Lu, J., Fang, C., Yu, F., Hays, J.: Scribbler: controlling deep image synthesis with sketch and color. In: CVPR (2016)

26. Seo, P.H., Lehrmann, A., Han, B., Sigal, L.: Visual reference resolution using attention memory for visual dialog. In: NIPS (2017)

27. Shen, W., Liu, R.: Learning residual images for face attribute manipulation. In: CVPR (2017)

28. Sun, Q., Tewari, A., Xu, W., Fritz, M., Theobalt, C., Schiele, B.: A hybrid model for identity obfuscation by face replacement. arXiv:1804.04779 (2018)

29. Xiao, T., Hong, J., Ma, J.: Elegant: exchanging latent encodings with GAN for transferring multiple face attributes. arXiv:1803.10562 (2018)

30. Xu, T., et al.: Attngan: fine-grained text to image generation with attentional generative adversarial networks. In: CVPR (2018)

31. Yan, X., Yang, J., Sohn, K., Lee, H.: Attribute2Image: conditional image generation from visual attributes. In: Leibe, B., Matas, J., Sebe, N., Welling, M. (eds.) ECCV 2016. LNCS, vol. 9908, pp. 776–791. Springer, Cham (2016). https://doi.org/10.1007/978-3-319-46493-0_47

32. Zhang, H., et al.: Stackgan: text to photo-realistic image synthesis with stacked generative adversarial networks. In: ICCV (2017)

33. Zhao, B., Wu, X., Cheng, Z.Q., Liu, H., Jie, Z., Feng, J.: Multi-view image generation from a single-view. In: MM (2018)

34. Zhu, J.Y., Park, T., Isola, P., Efros, A.A.: Unpaired image-to-image translation using cycle-consistent adversarial networks. In: ICCV (2017)

Graph Distillation for Action Detection with Privileged Modalities

Zelun Luo[1,2]([envelope]) [ORCID], Jun-Ting Hsieh[1], Lu Jiang[2], Juan Carlos Niebles[1,2], and Li Fei-Fei[1,2]

[1] Stanford University, Stanford, USA
alanzluo@stanford.edu
[2] Google Inc., Mountain View, USA

Abstract. We propose a technique that tackles action detection in multimodal videos under a realistic and challenging condition in which only limited training data and partially observed modalities are available. Common methods in transfer learning do not take advantage of the extra modalities potentially available in the source domain. On the other hand, previous work on multimodal learning only focuses on a single domain or task and does not handle the modality discrepancy between training and testing. In this work, we propose a method termed graph distillation that incorporates rich privileged information from a large-scale multimodal dataset in the source domain, and improves the learning in the target domain where training data and modalities are scarce. We evaluate our approach on action classification and detection tasks in multimodal videos, and show that our model outperforms the state-of-the-art by a large margin on the NTU RGB+D and PKU-MMD benchmarks. The code is released at http://alan.vision/eccv18_graph/.

1 Introduction

Recent advancements in deep convolutional neural networks (CNN) have been successful in various vision tasks such as image recognition [7,17,23] and object detection [13,43,44]. A notable bottleneck for deep learning, when applied to multimodal videos, is the lack of massive, clean, and task-specific annotations, as collecting annotations for videos is much more time-consuming and expensive. Furthermore, restrictions such as privacy or runtime may limit the access to only a subset of the video modalities during test time.

The scarcity of training data and modalities is encountered in many real-world applications including self-driving cars, surveillance, and health care. A representative example is activity understanding on health care data that contain

---

Z. Luo—Work done during an internship at Google Cloud AI.

Electronic supplementary material The online version of this chapter (https://doi.org/10.1007/978-3-030-01264-9_11) contains supplementary material, which is available to authorized users.

V. Ferrari et al. (Eds.): ECCV 2018, LNCS 11218, pp. 174–192, 2018.
https://doi.org/10.1007/978-3-030-01264-9_11

Personally Identifiable Information (PII) [16,34]. On the one hand, the number of labeled videos is usually limited because either important events such as falls [40, 63] are extremely rare or the annotation process requires a high level of medical expertise. On the other hand, RGB violates individual privacy and optical flow requires non-real-time computations, both of which are known to be important for activity understanding but are often unavailable at test time. Therefore, detection can only be performed on real-time and privacy-preserving modalities such as depth or thermal videos.

Fig. 1. Our problem statement. In the source domain, we have abundant data from multiple modalities. In the target domain, we have limited data and a subset of the modalities during training, and only one modality during testing. The curved connectors between modalities represent our proposed graph distillation.

Inspired by these problems, we study action detection in the setting of limited training data and partially observed modalities. To do so, we make use of a large action classification dataset that contains various *heterogeneous* modalities as the source domain to assist the training of the action detection model in the target domain, as illustrated in Fig. 1. Following the standard assumption in transfer learning [59], we assume that the source and target domain are similar to each other. We define a modality as a privileged modality if (1) it is available in the source domain but not in the target domain; (2) it is available during training but not during testing.

We identify two technical challenges in this problem. First of all, due to modality discrepancy in types and quantities, traditional domain adaption or transfer learning methods [12,41] cannot be directly applied. Recent work on knowledge and cross-modal distillation [18,26,33,48] provides a promising way of transferring knowledge between two models. Given two models, we can specify the distillation as the direction from the strong model to the weak model. With some adaptations, these methods can be used to distill knowledge between modalities. However, these adapted methods fail to address the second challenge: how to leverage the privileged modalities effectively. More specifically, given multiple privileged modalities, the distillation directions and weights are difficult to be pre-specified. Instead, the model should learn to dynamically adjust the distillation based on different actions or examples. For instance, some actions are easier to detect by optical flow whereas others are easier by skeleton features, and therefore the model should adjust its training accordingly. However, this dynamic distillation paradigm has not yet been explored by existing methods.

To this end, we propose the novel *graph distillation* method to learn a dynamic distillation across multiple modalities for action detection in multi-modal videos. The graph distillation is designed as a layer attachable to the original model and is end-to-end learnable with the rest of the network. The graph can dynamically learn the example-specific distillation to better utilize the complementary information in multimodal data. As illustrated in Fig. 1, by effectively leveraging the privileged modalities from both the source domain and the training stage of the target domain, graph distillation significantly improves the test-time performance on a single modality. Note that graph distillation can be applied to both single-domain (from training to testing) and cross-domain (from one task to another) tasks. For our cross-domain experiment (from action classification to detection), we utilized the most basic transfer learning approach, *i.e.* pre-train and fine-tune, as this is orthogonal to our contributions. We can potentially achieve even better results with advanced transfer learning and domain adaptation techniques and we leave it for future study.

We validate our method on two public multimodal video benchmarks: PKU-MMD [28] and NTU RGB+D [45]. The datasets represent one of the largest public multimodal video benchmarks for action detection and classification. The experimental results show that our method outperforms the state-of-the-art approaches. Notably, it improves the state-of-the-art by 9.0% on PKU-MMD [28] (at 0.5 tIoU threshold) and by 6.6% on NTU RGB+D [45]. The remarkable improvement on the two benchmarks is a convincing validation of our method.

To summarize, our contribution is threefold. (1) We study a realistic and challenging condition for multimodal action detection with limited training data and modalities. To the best of our knowledge, we are first to effectively transfer multimodal privileged information across domains for action detection and classification. (2) We propose the novel graph distillation layer that can dynamically learn to distill knowledge across multiple privileged modalities and can be attached to existing models and learned in an end-to-end manner. (3) Our method outperforms the state-of-the-art by a large margin on two popular benchmarks, including action classification task on the challenging NTU RGB+D [45] and action detection task on PKU-MMD [28].

2   Related Work

Multimodal Action Classification and Detection. The field of action classification [3,49,51] and action detection [2,11,14,64] in RGB videos has been studied by the computer vision community for decades. The success in RGB videos has given rise to a series of studies on action recognition in multimodal videos [10,20,22,25,50,54]. Specifically, with the availability of depth sensors and joint tracking algorithms, extensive research has been done on action classification and detection in RGB-D videos [39,46,47,60] as well as skeleton sequences [24,30–32,45,62]. Different from previous work, our model focuses on leveraging privileged modalities on a source dataset with abundant training examples. We show that it benefits action detection when the target training dataset is small in size, and when only one modality is available at test time.

Video Understanding Under Limited Data. Our work is largely motivated by real-world situations where data and modalities are limited. For example, surveillance systems for fall detection [40,63] often face the challenge that annotated videos of fall incidents are hard to obtain, and more importantly, yhr recording of RGB videos is prohibited due to privacy concerns. Existing approaches to tackling this challenge include using transfer learning [36,41] and leveraging noisy data from web queries [5,27,58]. Specifically to our problem, it is common to transfer models trained on action classification to action detection.

The transfer learning methods are proved to be effective. However, it requires the source and target domains to have the same modalities. In reality, the source domain often contains richer modalities. For instance, suppose the depth video is the only available modality in the target domain, it remains nontrivial to transfer the other modalities (*e.g.* RGB, optical flow) even though they are readily available in the source domain and could make the model more accurate. Our method provides a practical approach to leveraging the rich multimodal information in the source domain, benefiting the target domain of limited modalities.

Learning Using Privileged Information. Vapnik and Vashist [52] introduced a *Student-Teacher* analogy: in real-world human learning, the role of a teacher is crucial to the student's learning process since the teacher can provide explanations, comments, comparisons, metaphors, etc. They proposed a new learning paradigm called Learning Using Privileged Information (LUPI), where at training time, additional information about the training example is provided to the learning model. At test time, the privileged information is not available, and the student operates without the supervision of the teacher [52].

Several work employed privileged information (PI) on SVM classifiers [52,55]. Ding et al. [8] handled missing modality transfer learning using latent low-rank constraint. Recently, the use of privileged information has been combined with deep learning in various settings such as PI reconstruction [48,56], information bottleneck [38], and Multi-Instance Multi-Label (MIML) learning [57]. The idea more related to our work is the combination of distillation and privileged information, which will be discussed next.

Knowledge Distillation. Hinton et al. [18] introduced the idea of knowledge distillation, where knowledge from a large model is distilled to a small model, improving the performance of the small model at test time. This is done by adding a loss function that matches the outputs of the small network to the high-temperature soft outputs of the large network [18]. Lopez-Paz et al. [33] later proposed a generalized distillation that combined distillation and privileged information. This approach was adopted by [15,19] in cross-modality knowledge transfer. Our graph distillation method is different from prior work [18,26,33,48] in that the privileged information contains multiple modalities and that the distillation directions and weights are dynamically learned rather than being predefined by human experts.

3   Method

Our goal is to assist the training in the target domain with limited labeled data and modalities by leveraging the source domain dataset with abundant examples and multiple modalities. We address the problem by distilling the knowledge from the privileged modalities. Formally, we model action classification and detection as an L-way classification problem, where a "background class" is added in action detection.

Let $\mathcal{D}_t = \{(x_i, y_i)\}_{i=1}^{|\mathcal{D}_t|}$ denote the training set in the target domain, where $x_i \in \mathbb{R}^d$ is the input and $y_i \in \mathbb{R}$ is an integer denoting the class label. Since training data in the target domain is limited, we are interested in transferring knowledge from a source dataset $\mathcal{D}_s = \{(x_i, \mathcal{S}_i, y_i)\}_{i=1}^{|\mathcal{D}_s|}$, where $|\mathcal{D}_s| \gg |\mathcal{D}_t|$, and the source and target data may have different classes. The new element $\mathcal{S}_i = \{x_i^{(1)}, ..., x_i^{(|\mathcal{S}|)}\}$ is a set of privileged information about the i-th sample, where the superscript indexes the modality in $\mathcal{S}_i$. As an example, x_i could be the depth image of the i-th frame in a video and $x_i^{(1)}, x_i^{(2)}, x_i^{(3)} \in \mathcal{S}_i$ might be RGB, optical flow and skeleton features about the same frame, respectively. For action classification, we employ the standard softmax cross entropy loss:

$$\ell_c(f(x_i), y_i) = -\sum_{j=1}^{L} \mathbb{1}(y_i = j) \log \sigma(f(x_i)), \tag{1}$$

where $\mathbb{1}$ is the indicator function and σ is the softmax function. The class prediction function $f : \mathbb{R}^d \to [1, L]$ computes the probability for each action class.

In the rest of this section, Sect. 3.1 discusses the overall objective of privileged knowledge distillation. Section 3.2 details the proposed graph distillation over multiple modalities.

3.1   Knowledge Distillation with Privileged Modalities

To leverage the privileged information in the source domain data, we follow the standard transfer learning paradigm. We first train a model with graph distillation using all modalities in the source domain, and then transfer only the visual encoders (detailed in Sect. 4.1) of the target domain modalities. Finally, the visual encoder is finetuned with the rest of the target model on the target task. The visual feature encoding step is shared between the tasks in the source and target data and is therefore intuitive to use the same visual encoder architecture (as shown in Fig. 2) for both tasks.

To train a graph distillation model on the source data, we minimize:

$$\min \frac{1}{|\mathcal{D}_s|} \sum_{(x_i, y_i) \in \mathcal{D}_s} \ell_c(f(x_i), y_i) + \ell_m(x_i, \mathcal{S}_i). \tag{2}$$

The loss consists of two parts: the first term is the standard classification loss in Eq. (1) and the latter is the imitation loss [18]. The imitation loss is often defined as the cross-entropy loss on the *soft logits* [18]. In existing literatures, the imitation loss is computed using a pre-specified distillation direction. For example, Hinton et al. [18] computed the soft logits by $\sigma(f_\mathcal{S}(x_i)/T)$, where T is the temperature, and $f_\mathcal{S}$ is the class prediction function of the cumbersome model. Gupta et al. [15] employed the "soft logits" obtained from different layers of the labeled modality. In both cases, the distillation is pre-specified, *i.e.*, from a cumbersome model to a small model in [18] or from a labeled modality to an unlabeled modality in [15]. In our problem, the privileged information comes from multiple heterogeneous modalities and it is difficult to pre-specify the distillation directions and weights. To this end, our the imitation loss in Eq. (2) is derived from a dynamic distillation graph.

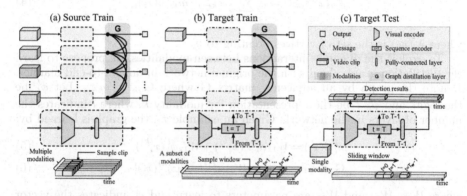

Fig. 2. An overview of our network architectures. (a) Action classification with graph distillation (attached as a layer) in the source domain. The visual encoders for each modality are trained. (b) Action detection with graph distillation in the target domain at training time. In our setting, the target training modalities is a subset of the source modalities (one or more). Note that the visual encoder trained in the source is transferred and finetuned in the target. (c) Action detection in the target domain at test time, with a single modality.

3.2 Graph Distillation

First, consider a special case of graph distillation where only two modalities are involved. We employ an imitation loss that combines the logits and feature representation. For notation convenience, we denote x_i as $x_i^{(0)}$ and fold it into $\mathcal{S}_i = \{x_i^{(0)}, \cdots, x_i^{(|\mathcal{S}|)}\}$. Given two modalities $a, b \in [0, |\mathcal{S}|]$ $(a \neq b)$, we use the network architectures discussed in Sect. 4 to obtain the logits and the output of the last convolution layer as the visual feature representation.

The proposed imitation loss between two modalities consists of the loss on the logits l_{logits} and the representation l_{rep}. The cosine distance is used on both logits and representations as we found the angle of the prediction to be more indicative and better than KL divergence or L1 distance for our problem.

The imitation loss ℓ_m from modality b to a is computed by the weighted sum of the logits loss and the representation loss. We encapsulate the loss between two modalities into a message $m_{a\leftarrow b}$ passing from b to a, calculated from:

$$m_{a\leftarrow b}(x_i) = \ell_m(x_i^{(a)}, x_i^{(b)}) = \lambda_1 l_{logits} + \lambda_2 l_{rep}, \tag{3}$$

where λ_1 and λ_2 are hyperparameters. Note that the message is directional, and $m_{a\leftarrow b}(x_i) \neq m_{b\leftarrow a}(x_i)$.

For multiple modalities, we introduce a directed graph of $|\mathcal{S}|$ vertices, named *distillation graph*, where each vertex v_k represents a modality and an edge $e_{k\leftarrow j} \geq 0$ is a real number indicating the strength of the connection from v_j to v_k. For a fixed graph, the total imitation loss for the modality k is:

$$\ell_m(x_i^{(k)}, \mathcal{S}_i) = \sum_{v_j \in \mathcal{N}(v_k)} e_{k\leftarrow j} \cdot m_{k\leftarrow j}(x_i), \tag{4}$$

where $\mathcal{N}(v_k)$ is the set of vertices pointing to v_k.

To exploit the dynamic interactions between modalities, we propose to learn the distillation graph along with the original network in an end-to-end manner. Denote the graph by an adjacency matrix $\mathbf{G}$ where $\mathbf{G}_{jk} = e_{k\leftarrow j}$. Let ϕ_k^l be the logits and ϕ_k^{l-1} be the representation for modality k, where l indicates the number of layers in the network. Given an example x_i, the graph is learned by:

$$z_i^{(k)}(x_i) = W_{11}\phi_k^{l-1}(x_i^{(k)}) + W_{12}\phi_k^l(x_i^{(k)}), \tag{5}$$

$$\mathbf{G}_{jk}(x_i) = e_{k\leftarrow j} = W_{21}[z_i^{(j)}(x_i)\|z_i^{(k)}(x_i)] \tag{6}$$

where W_{11}, W_{12} and W_{21} are parameters to learn and $\cdot\|\cdot$ indicates the vector concatenation. W_{21} maps a pair of inputs to an entry in $\mathbf{G}$. The entire graph is learned by repetitively applying Eq. (6) over all pairs of modalities in $\mathcal{S}$.

As a distillation graph is expected to be sparse, we normalize $\mathbf{G}$ such that the nonzero weights are dispersed over a small number of vertices. Let $\mathbf{G}_{j:} \in \mathbb{R}^{1\times|\mathcal{S}|}$ be the vector of its j-th row. The graph is normalized:

$$\mathbf{G}_{j:}(x_i) = \sigma(\alpha[\mathbf{G}_{j1}(x_i), ..., \mathbf{G}_{j|\mathcal{S}|}(x_i)]), \tag{7}$$

where α is used to scale the input to the softmax operator.

The message passing on distillation graph can be conveniently implemented by attaching a new layer to the original network. As shown in Fig. 2(a), each vertex represents a modality and the messages are propagated on the graph layer. In the forward pass, we learn a $\mathbf{G} \in \mathbb{R}^{|\mathcal{S}|\times|\mathcal{S}|}$ by Eqs. (6) and (7) and compute the message matrix $\mathbf{M} \in \mathbb{R}^{|\mathcal{S}|\times|\mathcal{S}|}$ by Eq. (3) such that $\mathbf{M}_{jk}(x_i) = m_{k\leftarrow j}(x_i)$. The imitation loss to all modalities is calculated by:

$$\ell_m = (\mathbf{G}(x_i) \odot \mathbf{M}(x_i))^T \mathbf{1}, \tag{8}$$

where $\mathbf{1} \in \mathbb{R}^{|\mathcal{S}|\times 1}$ is a column vector of ones; $\odot$ is the element-wise product between two matrices; $\ell_m \in \mathbb{R}^{|\mathcal{S}|\times 1}$ contains imitation loss for every modality in $\mathcal{S}$. In the backward propagation, the imitation loss ℓ_m is incorporated in Eq. (2)

to compute the gradient of the total training loss. This graph distillation layer is end-to-end trained with the rest of the network. As shown, the distillation graph is an important and essential structure which not only provides a base for learning dynamic message passing through modalities but also models the distillation as a few matrix operations which can be conveniently implemented as a new layer in the network.

For a modality, its performance on the cross-validation set often turns out to be a reasonable estimator to its contribution in distillation. Therefore, we add a constant bias term $\mathbf{c}$ in Eq. (7), where $\mathbf{c} \in \mathbb{R}^{|S| \times 1}$ and c_j is set w.r.t. the cross-validation performance of the modality j and $\sum_{k=1}^{|S|} c_k = 1$. Therefore, Eq. (8) can be rewritten as:

$$\ell_m = ((\mathbf{G}(x_i) + \mathbf{1c}^T) \odot \mathbf{M}(x_i))^T \mathbf{1} \tag{9}$$

$$= (\mathbf{G}(x_i) \odot \mathbf{M}(x_i))^T \mathbf{1} + (\mathbf{G}_{prior} \odot \mathbf{M}(x_i))^T \mathbf{1} \tag{10}$$

where $\mathbf{G}_{prior} = \mathbf{1c}^T$ is a constant matrix. Interestingly, by adding a bias term in Eq. (7), we decompose the distillation graph into two graphs: a learned example-specific graph $\mathbf{G}$ and a prior modality-specific graph $\mathbf{G}_{prior}$ that is independent to specific examples. The messages are propagated on both graphs and the sum of the message is used to compute the total imitation loss. There exists a physical interpretation of the learning process. Our model learns a graph based on the likelihood of observed examples to exploit complementary information in S. Meanwhile, it imposes a prior to encouraging accurate modalities to provide more contribution. By adding a constant bias, we use a more computationally efficient approach than actually performing message passing on two graphs.

So far, we have only discussed the distillation on the source domain. In practice, our method may also be applied to the target domain on which privileged modality is available. In this case, we apply the same method to minimize Eq. (2) on the target training data. As illustrated in Fig. 2(b), a graph distillation layer is added during the training of the target model. At the test time, as shown in Fig. 2(c), only a single modality is used.

4   Action Classification and Detection Models

In this section, we discuss our network architectures as well as the training and testing procedures for action classification and detection. The objective of action classification is to classify a trimmed video into one of the predefined categories. The objective of action detection is to predict the start time, the end time, and the class of an action in an untrimmed video.

4.1   Network Architecture

For action classification, we encode a short clip of video into a feature vector using the visual encoder. For action detection, we first encode all clips in a window of video (a window consists of multiple clips) into initial feature vectors using the visual encoder, then feed these initial feature vectors into a sequence encoder to generate the final feature vectors. For either task, each feature vector is fed into a task-specific linear layer and a softmax layer to get the probability distribution across classes for each clip. Note that a background class is added for action detection. Our action classification and detection models are inspired by [49] and [37], respectively. We design two types of visual encoders depending on the input modalities.

Visual Encoder for Images. Let $X = \{x_t\}_{t=1}^{T_c}$ denote a video clip of image modalities (*e.g.* RGB, depth, flow), where $x_t \in \mathbb{R}^{H \times W \times C}$, T_c is the number of frames in a clip, and $H \times W \times C$ is the image dimension. Similar to the temporal stream in [49], we stack the frames into a $H \times W \times (T_c \cdot C)$ tensor and encode the video clip with a modified ResNet-18 [17] with $T_c \cdot C$ input channels and without the last fully-connected layer. Note that we do not use the Convolutional 3D (C3D) network [3,51] because it is hard to train with limited amount of data [3].

Visual Encoder for Vectors. Let $X = \{x_t\}_{t=1}^{T_c}$ denote a video clip of vector modalities (*e.g.* skeleton), where $x_t \in \mathbb{R}^D$ and D is the vector dimension. Similar to [24], we encode the input with a 3-layer GRU network [6] with T_c timesteps. The encoded feature is computed as the average of the outputs of the highest layer across time. The hidden size of the GRU is chosen to be the same as the output dimension of the visual encoder for images.

Sequence Encoder. Let $X = \{x_t\}_{t=1}^{T_c \cdot T_w}$ denote a window of video with T_w clips, where each clip contains T_c frames. The visual encoder first encodes each clip individually into a single feature vector. These T_w feature vectors are then passed into the sequence encoder, which is a 1-layer GRU network, to obtain the class distributions of these T_w clips. Note that the sequence encoder is only used in action detection.

4.2   Training and Testing

Our proposed graph distillation can be applied to both action detection and classification. For action detection, we show that our method can optionally pre-train the action detection model on action classification tasks, and graph distillation can be applied in both pre-training and training stages. Both models are trained to minimize the loss in Eq. (2) on per-clip classification, and the imitation loss is calculated based on the representations and the logits.

Action Classification. Figure 2(a) shows how graph distillation is applied in training. During training, we randomly sample a video clip of T_c frames from the video, and the network outputs a single class distribution. During testing, we uniformly sample multiple clips spanning the entire video and average the outputs to obtain the final class distribution.

Action Detection. Figure 2(a) and (b) show how graph distillation is applied in training and testing, respectively. As discussed earlier, graph distillation can be applied to both the source domain and the target domain. During training, we randomly sample a window of T_w clips from the video, where each clip is of length

T_c and is sampled with step size s_c. As the data is imbalanced, we set a class-specific weight based on its inverse frequency in the training set. During testing, we uniformly sample multiple windows spanning the entire video with step size s_w, where each window is sampled in the same way as training. The outputs of the model are the class distributions on all clips in all windows (potentially with overlaps depending on s_w). These outputs are then post-processed using the method in [37] to generate the detection results, where the activity threshold γ is introduced as a hyperparameter.

5   Experiments

In this section, we evaluate our method on two large-scale multimodal video benchmarks. The results show that our method outperforms representative baseline methods and achieves the state-of-the-art performance on both benchmarks.

5.1   Datasets and Setups

We evaluate our method on two large-scale multimodal video benchmarks: NTU RGB+D [45] (classification) and PKU-MMD [28] (detection). These datasets are selected for the following reasons. (1) They are (one of the) largest RGB-D video benchmarks in each category. (2) The privileged information transfer is reasonable because the domains of the two datasets are similar. (3) They contain abundant modalities, which are required for graph distillation.

We use NTU RGB+D as our dataset in the source domain, and PKU-MMD in the target domain. In our experiments, unless stated otherwise, we apply graph distillation whenever applicable. Specifically, the visual encoders of all modalities are jointly trained on NTU RGB+D by graph distillation. On PKU-MMD, after initializing the visual encoder with the pre-trained weights obtained from NTU RGB+D, we also learn all available modalities by graph distillation on the target domain. By default, only a single modality is used at test time.

NTU RGB+D [45]. It contains 56,880 videos from 60 action classes. Each video has exactly one action class and comes with four modalities: RGB, depth, 3D joints, and infrared. The training and testing sets have 40,320 and 16,560 videos, respectively. All results are reported with cross-subject evaluation.

PKU-MMD [28]. It contains 1,076 long videos from 51 action classes. Each video contains approximately 20 action instances of various lengths and consists of four modalities: RGB, depth, 3D joints, and infrared. All results are evaluated based on the Average Precision (mAP) at different temporal Intersection over Union (tIoU) thresholds between the predicted and the ground truth intervals.

Modalities. We use a total of six modalities in our experiments: RGB, depth (D), optical flow (F), and three skeleton features (S) named Joint-Joint Distances (JJD), Joint-Joint Vector (JJV), and Joint-Line Distances (JLD) [9,24], respectively. The RGB and depth videos are provided in the datasets. The optical flow is calculated on the RGB videos using the dual TV-L1 method [61]. The three spatial skeleton features are extracted from 3D joints using the method in [9,24]. Note that we select a subset of the ten skeleton features in [9,24] to ensure the simplicity and reproducibility of our method, and our approach can potentially perform better with the complete set of features.

Baselines. In addition to comparing with the state-of-the-art, we implement three representative baselines that could be used to leverage multimodal privileged information: *multi-task learning* [4], *knowledge distillation* [18], and *cross-modal distillation* [15]. For the multi-task model, we predict the raw pixels of the other modalities from the representation of a single modality, and use the L_2 distance as the multi-task loss. For the distillation methods, the imitation loss is calculated as the high-temperature cross-entropy loss on the soft logits [18], and L_2 loss on both representations and soft logits in cross-modal distillation [15]. These distillation methods originally only support two modalities, and therefore we average the pairwise losses to get the final loss.

Table 1. Comparison with state-of-the-art on NTU RGB+D. Our models are trained on all modalities and tested on the single modality specified in the table. The available modalities are RGB, depth (D), optical flow (F), and skeleton (S).

Method	Test modality	mAP	Method	Test modality	mAP
Shahroudy [46]	RGB+D	0.749	Ours	RGB	**0.895**
Liu [29]	RGB+D	0.775	Ours	D	0.875
Liu [32]	S	0.800	Ours	F	0.857
Ding [9]	S	0.823	Ours	S	0.837
Li [24]	S	0.829			

Implementation Details. For action classification, we train the visual encoder from scratch for 200 epochs using SGD with momentum with learning rate 10^{-2} and decay to 10^{-1} at epoch 125 and 175. λ_1 and λ_2 are set to 10, 5 respectively in Eq. (3). At test time we sample 5 clips for inference. For action detection, the visual and sequence encoder are trained for 400 epochs. The visual encoder is trained using SGD with momentum with learning rate 10^{-3}, and the sequence encoder is trained with the Adam optimizer [21] with learning rate 10^{-3}. The activity threshold γ is set to 0.4. For both tasks, we down-sample the frame rates of the datasets by a factor of 3. The clip length and detection window T_c and T_w are both set to 10. For the graph distillation, α is set to 10 in Eq. (7). The output dimensions of the visual and sequence encoder are both set to 512. Since it is nontrivial to jointly train on multiple modalities from scratch, we employ curriculum learning [1] to train the distillation graph. To do so, we first fix the distillation graph as an identity matrix (uniform graph) in the first 200 epochs. In the second stage, we compute the constant vector **c** in Eq. (9) according to the cross-validation results, and then learn the graph in an end-to-end manner.

Table 2. Comparison of action detection methods on PKU-MMD with state-of-the-art models. Our models are trained with graph distillation using all privileged modalities and tested on the modalities specified in the table. "Transfer" refers to pre-training on NTU RGB+D on action classification. The available modalities are RGB, depth (D), optical flow (F), and skeleton (S).

Method	Test modality	mAP @ tIoU thresholds (θ)		
		0.1	0.3	0.5
Deep RGB (DR) [28]	RGB	0.507	0.323	0.147
Qin and Shelton [42]	RGB	0.650	0.510	0.294
Deep Optical Flow (DOF) [28]	F	0.626	0.402	0.168
Raw Skeleton (RS) [28]	S	0.479	0.325	0.130
Convolution Skeleton (CS) [28]	S	0.493	0.318	0.121
Wang and Wang [53]	S	0.842	-	0.743
RS+DR+DOF [28]	RGB+F+S	0.647	0.476	0.199
CS+DR+DOF [28]	RGB+F+S	0.649	0.471	0.199
Ours (w/o | w/ transfer)	RGB	0.824 | 0.880	0.813 | 0.868	0.743 | 0.801
Ours (w/o | w/ transfer)	D	0.823 | 0.872	0.817 | 0.860	0.752 | 0.792
Ours (w/o | w/ transfer)	F	0.790 | 0.826	0.783 | 0.814	0.708 | 0.747
Ours (w/o | w/ transfer)	S	0.836 | 0.857	0.823 | 0.846	0.764 | 0.784
Ours (w/ transfer)	RGB+D+F+S	**0.903**	**0.895**	**0.833**

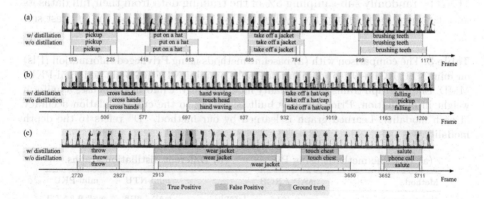

Fig. 3. A comparison of the prediction results on PKU-MMD. (a) Both models make correct predictions. (b) The model without distillation in the source makes errors. Our model learns motion and skeleton information from the privileged modalities in the source domain, which helps the prediction for classes such as "hand waving" and "falling". (c) Both models make reasonable errors.

5.2   Comparison with State-of-the-Art

Action Classification. Table 1 shows the comparison of action classification with state-of-the-art models on NTU RGB+D dataset. Our graph distillation models are trained and tested on the same dataset in the source domain. NTU RGB+D is a very challenging dataset and has been recently studied in numerous studies [24, 29, 32, 35, 46]. Nevertheless, as we see, our model achieves the state-of-the-art results on NTU RGB+D. It yields a 4.5% improvement, over the previous best result, using the depth video and a remarkable 6.6% using the RGB video. After inspecting the results, we found the improvement mainly attributes to the learned graph capturing complementary information across multiple modalities. Figure 4 shows example distillation graphs learned on NTU RGB+D. The results show that our method, without transfer learning, is effective for action classification in the source domain.

Action Detection. Table 2 compares our method on PKU-MMD with previous work. Our model outperforms existing methods across all modalities. The results substantiate that our method can effectively leverage the privileged knowledge from multiple modalities. Figure 3 illustrates detection results on the depth modality with and without the proposed distillation.

5.3   Ablation Studies on Limited Training Data

Section 5.2 has shown that our method achieves the state-of-the-art results on two public benchmarks. However, in practice, the training data are often limited in size. To systematically evaluate our method on limited training data, as proposed in the introduction, we construct mini-NTU RGB+D and mini-PKU-MMD by randomly sub-sampling 5% of the training data from their full datasets and use them for training. For evaluation, we test the model on the full test set.

Table 3. The comparison with (a) baseline methods using Privileged Information (PIs) on mini-NTU RGB+D, (b) distillation graphs on mini-NTU RGB+D and mini-PKU-MMD. Empty graph trains each modality independently. Uniform graph uses a uniform weight in distillation. Prior graph is built according to the cross-validation accuracy of each modality. Learned graph is learned by our method. "D" refers to the depth modality.

(a) Baseline methods using PIs.

Method	mAP / RGB
Empty graph	0.464
Multi-task [4]	0.456
Cross-distillation [15]	0.503
Knowledge distillation [18]	0.524
Learned graph	**0.619**

(b) Different distillation graphs.

Graph	mini-NTU	mini-PKU
	mAP / RGB	mAP @ 0.5 / D
Empty graph	0.464	0.501
Uniform graph	0.537	0.513
Prior graph	0.571	0.515
Learned graph	**0.619**	**0.559**

Table 4. The mAP comparison on mini-PKU-MMD at different tIoU threshold θ. The depth modality is chosen for testing. "src", "trg", and "PI" stand for source, target, and privileged information, respectively.

Method		mAP @ tIoU thresholds (θ)		
		0.1	0.3	0.5
1	trg only	0.248	0.235	0.200
2	src + trg	0.583	0.567	0.501
3	src w/ PIs + trg	0.625	0.610	0.533
4	src + trg w/ PIs	0.626	0.615	0.559
5	src w/ PIs + trg w/ PIs	0.642	0.629	0.562
6	src w/ PIs + trg	0.625	0.610	0.533
7	src w/ PIs + trg w/ 1 PI	0.632	0.615	0.549
8	src w/ PIs + trg w/ 2 PIs	0.636	0.624	0.557
9	src w/ PIs + trg w/ all PIs	0.642	0.629	0.562

Comparison with Baseline Methods. Table 3(a) shows the comparison with the baseline models that uses privileged information (see Sect. 5.1). The fact that our method outperforms the representative baseline methods validates the efficacy of the graph distillation method.

Efficacy of Distillation Graph. Table 3(b) compares the performance of pre-defined and learned distillation graphs. The proposed learned graph is compared with an empty graph (no distillation), a uniform graph of equal weights, and a prior graph computed using the cross-validation accuracy of each modality. Results show that the learned graph structure with modality-specific prior and example-specific information obtains the best results on both datasets.

Efficacy of Privileged Information. Table 4 compares our distillation and transfer under different training settings. The input at test time is a single depth modality. By comparing row 2 and 3 in Table 4, we see that when transferring the visual encoder to the target domain, the one pre-trained with privileged information in the source domain performs better than its counterpart. As discussed in Sect. 3.2, graph distillation can also be applied to the target domain. By comparing row 3 and 5 (or row 2 and 4) of Table 4, we see that performance gain is achieved by applying the graph distillation in the target domain. The results show that our graph distillation can capture useful information from multiple modalities in both the source and target domain.

Efficacy of Having More Modalities. The last three rows of Table 4 show that performance gain is achieved by increasing the number of modalities used as the privileged information. Note that the test modality is depth, the first privileged modality is RGB, and the second privileged modality is the skeleton feature JJD. The results also suggest that these modalities provide each other complementary information during the graph distillation.

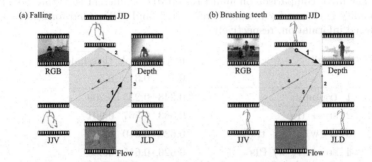

Fig. 4. The visualization of graph distillation on NTU RGB+D. The numbers indicate the ranks of the distillation weights, with 1 being the largest and 5 being the smallest. (a) Class "falling": Our graph assigns more weight to optical flow because optical flow captures the motion information. (b) Class "brushing teeth": In this case, motion is negligible, and our graph assigns the smallest weight to it. Instead, it assigns the largest weight to skeleton data.

6   Conclusion

This paper tackles the problem of action classification and detection in multi-modal video with limited training data and partially observed modalities. We propose the novel graph distillation method to assist the training of the model by leveraging privileged modalities dynamically. Our model outperforms representative baseline methods and achieves the state-of-the-art for action classification on NTU RGB+D dataset and action detection on the PKU-MMD. A direction for future work is to combine graph distillation with advanced transfer learning and domain adaptation techniques.

Acknowledgement. This work was supported in part by Stanford Computer Science Department and Clinical Excellence Research Center. We specially thank Li-Jia Li, De-An Huang, Yuliang Zou, and all the anonymous reviewers for their valuable comments.

References

1. Bengio, Y., Louradour, J., Collobert, R., Weston, J.: Curriculum learning. In: International Conference on Machine Learning (ICML) (2009)
2. Buch, S., Escorcia, V., Shen, C., Ghanem, B., Niebles, J.C.: SST: single-stream temporal action proposals. In: CVPR (2017)
3. Carreira, J., Zisserman, A.: Quo vadis, action recognition? A new model and the kinetics dataset. In: Computer Vision and Pattern Recognition (CVPR) (2017)
4. Caruana, R.: Multitask learning. In: Thrun, S., Pratt, L. (eds.) Learning to learn, pp. 95–133. Springer, Boston (1998). https://doi.org/10.1007/978-1-4615-5529-2_5
5. Chen, X., Gupta, A.: Webly supervised learning of convolutional networks. In: International Conference on Computer Vision (ICCV) (2015)

6. Chung, J., Gulcehre, C., Cho, K., Bengio, Y.: Empirical evaluation of gated recurrent neural networks on sequence modeling (2014)
7. Deng, J., Dong, W., Socher, R., Li, L.J., Li, K., Fei-Fei, L.: ImageNet: a large-scale hierarchical image database. In: Computer Vision and Pattern Recognition (CVPR) (2009)
8. Ding, Z., Shao, M., Fu, Y.: Missing modality transfer learning via latent low-rank constraint. IEEE Trans. Image Process. **24**(11), 4322–4334 (2015). https://doi.org/10.1109/TIP.2015.2462023
9. Ding, Z., Wang, P., Ogunbona, P.O., Li, W.: Investigation of different skeleton features for CNN-based 3D action recognition. arXiv preprint arXiv:1705.00835 (2017)
10. Du, Y., Wang, W., Wang, L.: Hierarchical recurrent neural network for skeleton based action recognition. In: Computer Vision and Pattern Recognition (CVPR) (2015)
11. Escorcia, V., Caba Heilbron, F., Niebles, J.C., Ghanem, B.: DAPs: deep action proposals for action understanding. In: Leibe, B., Matas, J., Sebe, N., Welling, M. (eds.) ECCV 2016. LNCS, vol. 9907, pp. 768–784. Springer, Cham (2016). https://doi.org/10.1007/978-3-319-46487-9_47
12. Fernando, B., Habrard, A., Sebban, M., Tuytelaars, T.: Unsupervised visual domain adaptation using subspace alignment. In: International Conference on Computer Vision (ICCV), pp. 2960–2967 (2013)
13. Girshick, R.: Fast R-CNN. In: International Conference on Computer Vision (ICCV) (2015)
14. Gorban, A., et al.: Thumos challenge: action recognition with a large number of classes. In: Computer Vision and Pattern Recognition (CVPR) Workshop (2015)
15. Gupta, S., Hoffman, J., Malik, J.: Cross modal distillation for supervision transfer. In: Computer Vision and Pattern Recognition (CVPR) (2016)
16. Haque, A., et al.: Towards vision-based smart hospitals: a system for tracking and monitoring hand hygiene compliance. In: Proceedings of Machine Learning for Healthcare 2017 (2017)
17. He, K., Zhang, X., Ren, S., Sun, J.: Deep residual learning for image recognition. In: Computer Vision and Pattern Recognition (CVPR) (2016)
18. Hinton, G., Vinyals, O., Dean, J.: Distilling the knowledge in a neural network. In: NIPS Workshop (2015)
19. Hoffman, J., Gupta, S., Darrell, T.: Learning with side information through modality hallucination. In: Computer Vision and Pattern Recognition (CVPR) (2016)
20. Jiang, L., Meng, D., Mitamura, T., Hauptmann, A.G.: Easy samples first: self-paced reranking for zero-example multimedia search. In: MM (2014)
21. Kingma, P.K., Ba, J.: Adam: a method for stochastic optimization (2015)
22. Koppula, H.S., Gupta, R., Saxena, A.: Learning human activities and object affordances from RGB-D videos. Int. J. Robot. Res. **32**(8), 951–970 (2013)
23. Krizhevsky, A., Sutskever, I., Hinton, G.E.: ImageNet classification with deep convolutional neural networks. In: Advances in Neural Information Processing Systems (NIPS) (2012)
24. Li, C., Zhong, Q., Xie, D., Pu, S.: Skeleton-based action recognition with convolutional neural networks. arXiv preprint arXiv:1704.07595 (2017)
25. Li, W., Chen, L., Xu, D., Gool, L.V.: Visual recognition in RGB images and videos by learning from RGB-D data. IEEE Trans. Pattern Anal. Mach. Intell. **40**(8), 2030–2036 (2018). https://doi.org/10.1109/TPAMI.2017.2734890
26. Li, Y., Yang, J., Song, Y., Cao, L., Luo, J., Li, J.: Learning from noisy labels with distillation. In: International Conference on Computer Vision (ICCV) (2017)

27. Liang, J., Jiang, L., Meng, D., Hauptmann, A.G.: Learning to detect concepts from webly-labeled video data. In: IJCAI (2016)
28. Liu, C., Hu, Y., Li, Y., Song, S., Liu, J.: PKU-MMD: a large scale benchmark for continuous multi-modal human action understanding. arXiv preprint arXiv:1703.07475 (2017)
29. Liu, J., Akhtar, N., Mian, A.: Viewpoint invariant action recognition using RGB-D videos. arXiv preprint arXiv:1709.05087 (2017)
30. Liu, J., Shahroudy, A., Xu, D., Wang, G.: Spatio-temporal LSTM with trust gates for 3D human action recognition. In: Leibe, B., Matas, J., Sebe, N., Welling, M. (eds.) ECCV 2016. LNCS, vol. 9907, pp. 816–833. Springer, Cham (2016). https://doi.org/10.1007/978-3-319-46487-9_50
31. Liu, J., Wang, G., Hu, P., Duan, L.Y., Kot, A.C.: Global context-aware attention LSTM networks for 3D action recognition. In: Computer Vision and Pattern Recognition (CVPR) (2017)
32. Liu, M., Liu, H., Chen, C.: Enhanced skeleton visualization for view invariant human action recognition. Pattern Recognit. 68, 346–362 (2017)
33. Lopez-Paz, D., Bottou, L., Schölkopf, B., Vapnik, V.: Unifying distillation and privileged information. In: International Conference on Learning Representations (ICLR) (2016)
34. Luo, Z., et al.: Computer vision-based descriptive analytics of seniors' daily activities for long-term health monitoring. In: Machine Learning for Healthcare (MLHC) (2018)
35. Luo, Z., Peng, B., Huang, D.A., Alahi, A., Fei-Fei, L.: Unsupervised learning of long-term motion dynamics for videos. In: Computer Vision and Pattern Recognition (CVPR) (2017)
36. Luo, Z., Zou, Y., Hoffman, J., Fei-Fei, L.: Label efficient learning of transferable representations across domains and tasks. In: Advances in Neural Information Processing Systems (NIPS) (2017)
37. Montes, A., Salvador, A., Giro-i Nieto, X.: Temporal activity detection in untrimmed videos with recurrent neural networks. arXiv preprint arXiv:1608.08128 (2016)
38. Motiian, S., Piccirilli, M., Adjeroh, D.A., Doretto, G.: Information bottleneck learning using privileged information for visual recognition. In: Computer Vision and Pattern Recognition (CVPR) (2016)
39. Ni, B., Wang, G., Moulin, P.: RGBD-HUDaACT: a color-depth video database for human daily activity recognition. In: Consumer Depth Cameras for Computer Vision (2013)
40. Noury, N., et al.: Fall detection-principles and methods. In: Engineering in Medicine and Biology Society (2007)
41. Pan, S.J., Yang, Q.: A survey on transfer learning. IEEE Trans. Knowl. Data Eng. 22(10), 1345–1359 (2010). https://doi.org/10.1109/TKDE.2009.191
42. Qin, Z., Shelton, C.R.: Event detection in continuous video: an inference in point process approach. IEEE Trans. Image Process. 26(12), 5680–5691 (2017)
43. Redmon, J., Divvala, S., Girshick, R., Farhadi, A.: You only look once: unified, real-time object detection. In: Computer Vision and Pattern Recognition (CVPR) (2016)
44. Ren, S., He, K., Girshick, R., Sun, J.: Faster R-CNN: towards real-time object detection with region proposal networks. In: Neural Information Processing Systems (NIPS) (2015)

45. Shahroudy, A., Liu, J., Ng, T.T., Wang, G.: NTU RGB+ D: a large scale dataset for 3D human activity analysis. In: Computer Vision and Pattern Recognition (CVPR) (2016)
46. Shahroudy, A., Ng, T.T., Gong, Y., Wang, G.: Deep multimodal feature analysis for action recognition in RGB+ D videos. IEEE Trans. Pattern Anal. Mach. Intell. (TPAMI) (2017)
47. Shao, L., Cai, Z., Liu, L., Lu, K.: Performance evaluation of deep feature learning for RGB-D image/video classification. Inf. Sci. **385**, 266–283 (2017)
48. Shi, Z., Kim, T.K.: Learning and refining of privileged information-based RNNS for action recognition from depth sequences. In: Computer Vision and Pattern Recognition (CVPR) (2017)
49. Simonyan, K., Zisserman, A.: Two-stream convolutional networks for action recognition in videos. In: Advances in Neural Information Processing Systems (NIPS) (2014)
50. Sung, J., Ponce, C., Selman, B., Saxena, A.: Human activity detection from RGBD images. In: AAAI Workshop on Pattern, Activity and Intent Recognition (2011)
51. Tran, D., Bourdev, L., Fergus, R., Torresani, L., Paluri, M.: Learning spatiotemporal features with 3D convolutional networks. In: International Conference on Computer Vision (ICCV) (2015)
52. Vapnik, V., Vashist, A.: A new learning paradigm: learning using privileged information. Neural Netw. **22**(5), 544–557 (2009)
53. Wang, H., Wang, L.: Learning robust representations using recurrent neural networks for skeleton based action classification and detection. In: International Conference on Multimedia & Expo Workshops (ICMEW) (2017)
54. Wang, J., Liu, Z., Wu, Y., Yuan, J.: Mining actionlet ensemble for action recognition with depth cameras. In: Computer Vision and Pattern Recognition (CVPR) (2012)
55. Wang, Z., Ji, Q.: Classifier learning with hidden information. In: Computer Vision and Pattern Recognition (CVPR) (2015)
56. Xu, D., Ouyang, W., Ricci, E., Wang, X., Sebe, N.: Learning cross-modal deep representations for robust pedestrian detection. In: Computer Vision and Pattern Recognition (CVPR) (2017)
57. Yang, H., Zhou, J.T., Cai, J., Ong, Y.S.: MIML-FCN+: multi-instance multi-label learning via fully convolutional networks with privileged information. In: Computer Vision and Pattern Recognition (CVPR) (2017)
58. Yeung, S., Ramanathan, V., Russakovsky, O., Shen, L., Mori, G., Fei-Fei, L.: Learning to learn from noisy web videos (2017)
59. Yosinski, J., Clune, J., Bengio, Y., Lipson, H.: How transferable are features in deep neural networks? In: Advances in Neural Information Processing Systems (NIPS) (2014)
60. Yu, M., Liu, L., Shao, L.: Structure-preserving binary representations for RGB-D action recognition. IEEE Trans. Pattern Anal. Mach. Intell. (TPAMI) **38**(8), 1651–1664 (2016)
61. Zach, C., Pock, T., Bischof, H.: A duality based approach for realtime TV-L^1 optical flow. In: Hamprecht, F.A., Schnörr, C., Jähne, B. (eds.) DAGM 2007. LNCS, vol. 4713, pp. 214–223. Springer, Heidelberg (2007). https://doi.org/10.1007/978-3-540-74936-3_22
62. Zhang, S., Liu, X., Xiao, J.: On geometric features for skeleton-based action recognition using multilayer LSTM networks. In: IEEE Winter Conference on Applications of Computer Vision (WACV) (2017)

63. Zhang, Z., Conly, C., Athitsos, V.: A survey on vision-based fall detection. In: Conference on PErvasive Technologies Related to Assistive Environments (PETRA) (2015)
64. Zhao, Y., Xiong, Y., Wang, L., Wu, Z., Tang, X., Lin, D.: Temporal action detection with structured segment networks. In: International Conference on Computer Vision (ICCV) (2017)

Weakly-Supervised Video Summarization Using Variational Encoder-Decoder and Web Prior

Sijia Cai[1,2], Wangmeng Zuo[3], Larry S. Davis[4], and Lei Zhang[1(✉)]

[1] Department of Computing, The Hong Kong Polytechnic University,
Kowloon, Hong Kong
{csscai,cslzhang}@comp.polyu.edu.hk
[2] DAMO Academy, Alibaba Group, Hangzhou, China
[3] School of Computer Science and Technology, Harbin Institute of Technology,
Harbin, China
cswmzuo@gmail.com
[4] Department of Computer Science, University of Maryland, College Park, USA
lsd@umiacs.umd.edu

Abstract. Video summarization is a challenging under-constrained problem because the underlying summary of a single video strongly depends on users' subjective understandings. Data-driven approaches, such as deep neural networks, can deal with the ambiguity inherent in this task to some extent, but it is extremely expensive to acquire the temporal annotations of a large-scale video dataset. To leverage the plentiful web-crawled videos to improve the performance of video summarization, we present a generative modelling framework to learn the latent semantic video representations to bridge the benchmark data and web data. Specifically, our framework couples two important components: a variational autoencoder for learning the latent semantics from web videos, and an encoder-attention-decoder for saliency estimation of raw video and summary generation. A loss term to learn the semantic matching between the generated summaries and web videos is presented, and the overall framework is further formulated into a unified conditional variational encoder-decoder, called variational encoder-summarizer-decoder (VESD). Experiments conducted on the challenging datasets CoSum and TVSum demonstrate the superior performance of the proposed VESD to existing state-of-the-art methods. The source code of this work can be found at https://github.com/cssjcai/vesd.

Keywords: Video summarization · Variational autoencoder

1 Introduction

Recently, it has been attracting much interest in extracting the representative visual elements from a video for sharing on social media, which aims to effectively

This research is supported by the Hong Kong RGC GRF grant (PolyU 152135/16E) and the City Brain project of DAMO Academy, Alibaba Group.

© Springer Nature Switzerland AG 2018
V. Ferrari et al. (Eds.): ECCV 2018, LNCS 11218, pp. 193–210, 2018.
https://doi.org/10.1007/978-3-030-01264-9_12

express the semantics of the original lengthy video. However, this task, often referred to as video summarization, is laborious, subjective and challenging since videos usually exhibit very complex semantic structures, including diverse scenes, objects, actions and their complex interactions.

A noticeable trend appeared in recent years is to use the deep neural networks (DNNs) [10,44] for video summarization since DNNs have made significant progress in various video understanding tasks [2,12,19]. However, annotations used in the video summarization task are in the form of frame-wise labels or importance scores, collecting a large number of annotated videos demands tremendous effort and cost. Consequently, the widely-used benchmark datasets [1,31] only cover dozens of well-annotated videos, which becomes a prominent stumbling block that hinders the further improvement of DNNs based summarization techniques. Meanwhile, annotations for summarization task are subjective and not consistent across different annotators, potentially leading to overfitting and biased models. Therefore, the advanced studies toward taking advantage of augmented data sources such as web images [13], GIFs [10] and texts [23], which are complimentary for the summarization purpose.

To drive the techniques along with this direction, we consider an efficient weakly-supervised setting of learning summarization models from a vast number of web videos. Compared with other types of auxiliary source domain data for video summarization, the temporal dynamics in these user-edited "templates" offer rich information to locate the diverse but semantic-consistent visual contents which can be used to alleviate the ambiguities in small-size summarization. These short-form videos are readily available from web repositories (*e.g.,* YouTube) and can be easily collected using a set of topic labels as search keywords. Additionally, these web videos have been edited by a large community of users, the risk of building a biased summarization model is significantly reduced. Several existing works [1,21] have explored different strategies to exploit the semantic relatedness between web videos and benchmark videos. So motivated, we aim to effectively utilize the large collection of weakly-labelled web videos in learning more accurate and informative video representations which: (i) preserve essential information within the raw videos; (ii) contain discriminative information regarding the semantic consistency with web videos. Therefore, the desired deep generative models are necessitated to capture the underlying latent variables and make practical use of web data and benchmark data to learn abstract and high-level representations.

To this end, we present a generative framework for summarizing videos in this paper, which is illustrated in Fig. 1. The basic architecture consists of two components: a variational autoencoder (VAE) [14] model for learning the latent semantics from web videos; and a sequence encoder-decoder with attention mechanism for summarization. The role of VAE is to map the videos into a continuous latent variable, via an inference network (encoder), and then use the generative network (decoder) to reconstruct the input videos conditioned on samples from the latent variable. For the summarization component, the association is temporally ambiguous since only a subset of fragments in the raw video is relevant to its summary semantics. To filter out the irrelevant fragments and identify informative temporal regions for the better summary generation, we exploit the soft attention mechanism where the attention vectors (*i.e.*, context representations) of raw videos are obtained by integrating the latent semantics trained from web videos. Furthermore, we provide a weakly-supervised semantic matching loss instead of reconstruction loss to learn the topic-associated summaries in our generative framework. In this sense, we take advantage of potentially accurate and flexible latent variable distribution from external data thus strengthen the expressiveness of generated summary in the encoder-decoder based summarization model. To evaluate the effectiveness of the proposed method, we comprehensively conduct experiments using different training settings and demonstrate that our method with web videos achieves significantly better performance than competitive video summarization approaches.

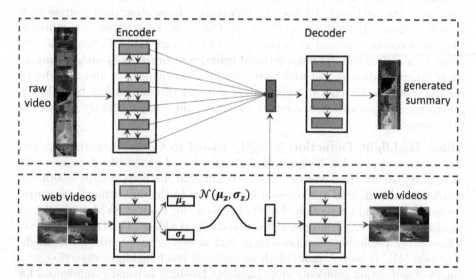

Fig. 1. An illustration of the proposed generative framework for video summarization. A VAE model is pre-trained on web videos (purple dashed rectangle area); And the summarization is implemented within an encoder-decoder paradigm by using both the attention vector and the sampled latent variable from VAE (red dashed rectangle area). (Color figure online)

2   Related Work

Video Summarization is a challenging task which has been explored for many years [18,37] and can be grouped into two broad categories: unsupervised and supervised learning methods. Unsupervised summarization methods focus on low-level visual cues to locate the important segments of a video. Various strategies have been investigated, including clustering [7,8], sparse optimizations [3,22], and energy minimization [4,25]. A majority of recent works mainly study the summarization solutions based on the supervised learning from human annotations. For instance, to make a large-margin structured prediction, submodular functions are trained with human-annotated summaries [9]. Gygli *et al.* [8] propose a linear regression model to estimate the interestingness score of shots. Gong *et al.* [5] and Sharghi *et al.* [28] learn from user-created summaries for selecting informative video subsets. Zhang *et al.* [43] show summary structures can be transferred between videos that are semantically consistent. More recently, DNNs based methods have been applied for video summarization with the help of pairwise deep ranking model [42] or recurrent neural networks (RNNs) [44]. However, these approaches assume the availability of a large number of human-created video-summary pairs or fine-grained temporal annotations, which are in practice difficult and expensive to acquire. Alternatively, there have been attempts to leverage information from other data sources such as web images, GIFs and texts [10,13,23]. Chu *et al.* [1] propose to summarize shots that co-occur among multiple videos of the same topic. Panda *et al.* [20] present an end-to-end 3D convolutional neural network (CNN) architecture to learn summarization model with web videos. In this paper, we also consider to use the topic-specific cues in web videos for better summarization, but adopt a generative summarization framework to exploit the complementary benefits in web videos.

Video Highlight Detection is highly related to video summarization and many earlier approaches have primarily been focused on specific data scenarios such as broadcast sport videos [27,35]. Traditional methods usually adopt the mid-level and high-level audio-visual features due to the well-defined structures. For general highlight detection, Sun *et al.* [32] employ a latent SVM model detect highlights by learning from pairs of raw and edited videos. The DNNs also have achieved big performance improvement and shown great promise in highlight detection [41]. However, most of these methods treat highlight detection as a binary classification problem, while highlight labelling is usually ambiguous for humans. This also imposes heavy burden for humans to collect a huge amount of labelled data for training DNN based models.

Deep Generative Models are very powerful in learning complex data distribution and low-dimensional latent representations. Besides, the generative modelling for video summarization might provide an effective way to bring scalability and stability in training a large amount of web data. Two of the most effective approaches are VAE [14] and generative adversarial network (GAN) [6]. VAE aims at maximizing the variational lower bound of the observation while encouraging the variational posterior distribution of the latent variables to be close to the prior distribution. A GAN is composed of a generative model and a discriminative model and trained in a min-max game framework. Both VAE and GAN have already shown promising results in image/frame generation tasks [17,26,38]. To embrace the temporal structures into generative modelling, we propose a new variational sequence-to-sequence encoder-decoder framework for video summarization by capturing both the video-level topics and web semantic prior. The attention mechanism embedded in our framework can be naturally used as key shots selection for summarization. Most related to our generative summarization is the work of Mahasseni *et al.* [16], who present an unsupervised summarization in the framework of GAN. However, the attention mechanism in their approach depends solely on the raw video itself thus has the limitation in delivering diverse contents in video-summary reconstruction.

3   The Proposed Framework

As an intermediate step to leverage abundant user-edited videos on the Web to assist the training of our generative video summarization framework, in this section, we first introduce the basic building blocks of the proposed framework, called variational encoder-summarizer-decoder (VESD). The VESD consists of three components: (i) an encoder RNN for raw video; (ii) an attention-based summarizer for raw video; (iii) a decoder RNN for summary video.

Following the video summarization pipelines in previous methods [24,44], we first perform temporal segmentation and shot-level feature extraction for raw videos using CNNs. Each video $\mathcal{X}$ is then treated as a sequential set of multiple non-uniform shots, where x_t is the feature vector of the t-th shot in video representation X. Most supervised summarization approaches aim to predict labels/scores which indicate whether the shots should be included in the summary, however, suffering from the drawbacks of selection of redundant visual contents. For this reason, we formulate video summarization as video generation task which allows the summary representation Y does not necessarily be restricted to a subset of X. In this manner, our method centres on the semantic essence of a video and can exhibit the high tolerance for summaries with visual differences. Following the encoder-decoder paradigm [33], our summarization framework is composed of two parts: the encoder-summarizer is an inference network $q_\phi(a|X, z)$ that takes both the video representation X and the latent variable z (sampled from the VAE module pre-trained on web videos) as inputs. Moreover, the encoder-summarizer is supposed to generate the video content representation a that captures all the information about Y. The summarizer-decoder is a generative network $p_\theta(Y|a, z)$ that outputs the summary representation Y based on the attention vector a and the latent representation z.

3.1   Encoder-Summarizer

To date, modelling sequence data with RNNs has been proven successful in video summarization [44]. Therefore, for the encoder-summarizer component, we employ a pointer RNN, *e.g.*, a bidirectional Long Short-Term Memory (LSTM), as an encoder that processes the raw videos, and a summarizer aims to select the shots of most probably containing salient information. The summarizer is exactly the attention-based model that generates the video context representation by attending to the encoded video features.

In time step t, we denote $\boldsymbol{x}_t$ as the feature vector for the t-th shot and $\boldsymbol{h}_t^e$ as the state output of the encoder. It is known that $\boldsymbol{h}_t^e$ is obtained by concatenating the hidden states from each direction:

$$\boldsymbol{h}_t^e = [\text{RNN}_{\overrightarrow{enc}}(\overrightarrow{\boldsymbol{h}_{t-1}}, \boldsymbol{x}_t); \text{RNN}_{\overleftarrow{enc}}(\overleftarrow{\boldsymbol{h}_{t+1}}, \boldsymbol{x}_t)]. \tag{1}$$

The attention mechanism is proposed to compute an attention vector $\boldsymbol{a}$ of input sequence by summing the sequence information $\{\boldsymbol{h}_t^e, t = 1, \ldots, |\boldsymbol{X}|\}$ with the location variable $\boldsymbol{\alpha}$ as follows:

$$\boldsymbol{a} = \sum_{t=1}^{|\boldsymbol{X}|} \alpha_t \boldsymbol{h}_t^e, \tag{2}$$

where α_t denotes the t-th value of $\boldsymbol{\alpha}$ and indicates whether the t-th shot is included in summary or not. As mentioned in [40], when using the generative modelling on the log-likelihood of the conditional distribution $p(\boldsymbol{Y}|\boldsymbol{X})$, one approach is to sample attention vector $\boldsymbol{a}$ by assigning the Bernoulli distribution to $\boldsymbol{\alpha}$. However, the resultant Monte Carlo gradient estimator of the variational lower-bound objective requires complicated variance reduction techniques and may lead to unstable training. Instead, we adopt a deterministic approximation to obtain $\boldsymbol{a}$. That is, we produce an attentive probability distribution based on $\boldsymbol{X}$ and $\boldsymbol{z}$, which is defined as $\alpha_t := p(\alpha_t|\boldsymbol{h}_t^e, \boldsymbol{z}) = \text{softmax}(\varphi_t([\boldsymbol{h}_t^e; \boldsymbol{z}]))$, where φ is a parameterized potential typically based on a neural network, $e.g.$, multilayer perceptron (MLP). Accordingly, the attention vector in Eq. (2) turns to:

$$\boldsymbol{a} = \sum_{t=1}^{N} p(\alpha_t|\boldsymbol{h}_t^e, \boldsymbol{z}) \boldsymbol{h}_t^e, \tag{3}$$

which is fed to the decoder RNN for summary generation. The attention mechanism extracts an attention vector $\boldsymbol{a}$ by iteratively attending to the raw video features based on the latent variable $\boldsymbol{z}$ learned from web data. In doing so the model is able to adapt to the ambiguity inherent in summaries and obtain salient information of raw video through attention. Intuitively, the attention scores α_ts are used to perform shot selection for summarization.

3.2 Summarizer-Decoder

We specify the summary generation process as $p_\theta(\boldsymbol{Y}|\boldsymbol{a}, \boldsymbol{z})$ which is the conditional likelihood of the summary given the attention vector $\boldsymbol{a}$ and the latent variable $\boldsymbol{z}$. Different with the standard Gaussian prior distribution adopted in VAE, $p(\boldsymbol{z})$ in our framework is pre-trained on web videos to regularize the latent semantic representations of summaries. Therefore, the summaries generated via $p_\theta(\boldsymbol{Y}|\boldsymbol{a}, \boldsymbol{z})$ are likely to possess diverse contents. In this manner, $p_\theta(\boldsymbol{Y}|\boldsymbol{a}, \boldsymbol{z})$ is then reconstructed via a RNN decoder at each time step t: $p_\theta(\boldsymbol{y}_t|\boldsymbol{a}, [\boldsymbol{\mu}_z, \boldsymbol{\sigma}_z^2])$, where $\boldsymbol{\mu}_z$ and $\boldsymbol{\sigma}_z$ are nonlinear functions of the latent variables specified by two learnable neural networks (detailed in Sect. 4).

3.3 Variational Inference

Given the proposed VESD model, the network parameters $\{\phi, \theta\}$ need to be updated during inference. We marginalize over the latent variables a and z by maximizing the following variational lower-bound $\mathcal{L}(\phi, \theta)$

$$\mathcal{L}(\phi, \theta) = \mathbb{E}_{q_\phi(a,z|X,Y)}[\log p_\theta(Y|a,z) - \mathrm{KL}(q_\phi(a,z|X,Y)|p(a,z))], \quad (4)$$

where $\mathrm{KL}(\cdot)$ is the Kullback-Leibler divergence. We assume the joint distribution of the latent variables a and z has a factorized form, $i.e.$, $q_\phi(a,z|X,Y) = q_{\phi^{(z)}}(z|X,Y)q_{\phi^{(a)}}(a|X,Y)$, and notice that $p(a) = q_{\phi^{(a)}}(a|X,Y)$ is defined with a deterministic manner in Sect. 3.1. Therefore the variational objective in Eq. (4) can be derived as:

$$\begin{aligned}
\mathcal{L}(\phi, \theta) &= \mathbb{E}_{q_{\phi^{(z)}}(z|X,Y)}[\mathbb{E}_{q_{\phi^{(a)}}(a|X,Y)}\log p_\theta(Y|a,z) \\
&\quad -\mathrm{KL}(q_{\phi^{(a)}}(a|X,Y)\|p(a))] + \mathrm{KL}(q_{\phi^{(z)}}(z|X,Y)\|p(z)) \\
&= \mathbb{E}_{q_\phi(z|X,Y)}[\log p_\theta(Y|a,z)] + \mathrm{KL}(q_\phi(z|X,Y)\|p(z)). \quad (5)
\end{aligned}$$

The above variational lower-bound offers a new perspective for exploiting the reciprocal nature of raw video and its summary. Maximizing Eq. (5) strikes a balance between minimizing generation error and minimizing the KL divergence between the approximated posterior $q_{\phi^{(z)}}(z|X,Y)$ and the prior $p(z)$.

4 Weakly-Supervised VESD

In practice, as only a few video-summary pairs are available, the latent variable z cannot characterize the inherent semantic in video and summary accurately. Motivated by the VAE/GAN model [15], we explore a weakly-supervised learning framework and endow our VESD the ability to make use of rich web videos for the latent semantic inference. The VAE/GAN model extends VAE with the discriminator network in GAN, which provides a method that constructs the latent space from inference network of data rather than random noises and implicitly learns a rich similarity metric for data. The similar idea has also been investigated in [16] for unsupervised video summarization. Recall that the discriminator in GAN tries to distinguish the generated examples from real examples; Following the same spirit, we apply the discriminator in the proposed VESD which naturally results in minimizing the following adversarial loss function:

$$\mathcal{L}(\phi, \theta, \psi) = -\mathbb{E}_{\hat{Y}}[\log D_\psi(\hat{Y})] - \mathbb{E}_{X,z}[\log(1 - D_\psi(Y))], \quad (6)$$

where $\hat{Y}$ refers to the representation of web video. Unfortunately, the above loss function suffers from the unstable training in standard GAN models and cannot be directly extended into supervised scenario. To address these problems, we propose to employ a semantic feature matching loss for the weakly-supervised setting of VESD framework. The objective requires the representation of generated summary to match the representation of web videos under a similarity function. For the prediction of the semantic similarity, we replace $p_\theta(Y|a, z)$ with the following sigmoid function:

$$p_\theta(c|a, h^d(\hat{Y})) = \sigma(a^T M h^d(\hat{Y})), \tag{7}$$

where $h^d(\hat{Y})$ is the last output state of $\hat{Y}$ in the decoder RNN and M is the sigmoid parameter. We randomly pick $\hat{Y}$ in web videos and c is the pair relatedness label, i.e., $c = 1$ if Y and $\hat{Y}$ are semantically matched. We can also generalize the above matching loss to multi-label case by replacing c with one-hot vector c whose nonzero position corresponds the matched label. Therefore, the objective (5) can be rewritten as:

$$\mathcal{L}(\phi, \theta, \psi) = \mathbb{E}_{q_\phi(z)}[\log p_\theta(c|a, h^d(\hat{Y}))] + \mathrm{KL}(q_\phi(z)\|p(z|\hat{Y})). \tag{8}$$

It is found that the above variational objective shares the similarity with conditional VAE (CVAE) [30] which is able to produce diverse outputs for a single input. For example, Walker et al. [39] use a fully convolutional CVAE for diverse motion prediction from a static image. Zhou and Berg [45] generate diverse time-lapse videos by incorporating conditional, twostack and recurrent architecture modifications to standard generative models. Therefore, our weakly-supervised VESD naturally embeds the diversity in video summary generation.

4.1   Learnable Prior and Posterior

In contrast to the standard VAE prior that assumes the latent variable z to be drawn from latent Gaussian (e.g., $p(z) = \mathcal{N}(0, I)$), we impose the prior distribution learned from web videos which infers the topic-specific semantics more accurately. Thus we impose z to be drawn from the Gaussian with $p(z|\hat{Y}) = \mathcal{N}(z|\mu(\hat{Y}), \sigma^2(\hat{Y})I)$ whose mean and variance are defined as:

$$\mu(\hat{Y}) = f_\mu(\hat{Y}), \log\sigma^2(\hat{Y}) = f_\sigma(\hat{Y}), \tag{9}$$

where $f_\mu(\cdot)$ and $f_\sigma(\cdot)$ denote any type of neural networks that are suitable for the observed data. We adopt two-layer MLPs with ReLU activation in our implementation.

Likewise, we model the posterior of $q_\phi(z|\cdot) := q_\phi(z|X, \hat{Y}, c)$ with the Gaussian distribution $\mathcal{N}(z|\mu(X, \hat{Y}, c), \sigma^2(X, \hat{Y}, c)$ whose mean and variance are also characterized by two-layer MLPs with ReLU activation:

$$\mu = f_\mu([a; h^d(\hat{Y}); c]), \log\sigma^2 = f_\sigma([a; h^d(\hat{Y}); c]). \tag{10}$$

4.2   Mixed Training Objective Function

One potential issue of purely weakly-supervised VESD training objective (8) is that the semantic matching loss usually results in summaries focusing on very few shots in raw video. To ensure the diversity and fidelity of the generated

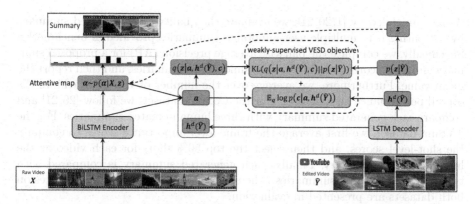

Fig. 2. The variational formulation of our weakly-supervised VESD framework.

summaries, we can also make use of the importance scores on partially finely-annotated benchmark datasets to consistently improves performance. For those detailed annotations in benchmark datasets, we adopt the same keyframe regularizer in [16] to measure the cross-entropy loss between the normalized ground-truth importance scores α_X^{gt} and the output attention scores α_X as below:

$$\mathcal{L}_{\text{score}} = \text{cross-entropy}(\alpha_X^{gt}, \alpha_X). \tag{11}$$

Accordingly, we train the regularized VESD using the following objective function to utilize different levels of annotations:

$$\mathcal{L}_{\text{mixed}} = \mathcal{L}(\phi, \theta, \psi, \omega) + \lambda \mathcal{L}_{\text{score}}. \tag{12}$$

The overall objective can be trained using back-propagation efficiently and is illustrated in Fig. 2. After training, we calculate the salience score α for each new video by forward passing the summarization model in VESD.

5   Experimental Results

Datasets and Evaluation. We test our VESD framework on two publicly available video summarization benchmark datasets CoSum [1] and TVSum [31]. The CoSum [1] dataset consists of 51 videos covering 10 topics including Base Jumping (BJ), Bike Polo (BP), Eiffel Tower (ET), Excavators River Cross (ERC), Kids Playing in leaves (KP), MLB, NFL, Notre Dame Cathedral (NDC), Statue of Liberty (SL) and SurFing (SF). The TVSum [31] dataset contains 50 videos organized into 10 topics from the TRECVid Multimedia Event Detection task [29], including changing Vehicle Tire (VT), getting Vehicle Unstuck (VU), Grooming an Animal (GA), Making Sandwich (MS), ParKour (PK), PaRade (PR), Flash Mob gathering (FM), BeeKeeping (BK), attempting Bike Tricks (BT), and Dog Show (DS). Following the literature [9,44], we randomly choose 80% of the videos for training and use the remaining 20% for testing on both datasets.

As recommended by [1,20,21], we evaluate the quality of a generated summary by comparing it to multiple user-annotated summaries provided in benchmarks. Specifically, we compute the pairwise average precision (AP) for a proposed summary and all its corresponding human-annotated summaries, and then report the mean value. Furthermore, we average over the number of videos to achieve the overall performance on a dataset. For the CoSum dataset, we follow [20,21] and compare each generated summary with three human-created summaries. For the TVSum dataset, we first average the frame-level importance scores to compute the shot-level scores, and then select the top 50% shots for each video as the human-created summary. Finally, each generated summary is compared with twenty human-created summaries. The top-5 and top-15 mAP performances on both datasets are presented in evaluation.

Web Video Collection. This section describes the details of web video collection for our approach. We treat the topic labels in both datasets as the query keywords and retrieve videos from YouTube for all the twenty topic categories. We limit the videos by time duration (less than 4 min) and rank by relevance to constructing a set of weakly-annotated videos. However, these downloaded videos are still very lengthy and noisy in general since they contain a proportion of frames that are irrelevant to search keywords. Therefore, we introduce a simple but efficient strategy to filter out the noisy parts of these web videos: (1) we first adopt the existing temporal segmentation technique KTS [24] to segment both the benchmark videos and web videos into non-overlapping shots, and utilize CNNs to extract feature within each shot; (2) the corresponding features in benchmark videos are then used to train a MLP with their topic labels (the shots do not belong to any topic label are set with background label) and perform prediction for the shots in web videos; (3) we further truncate web videos based on the relevant shots whose topic-related probability is larger than a threshold. In this way, we observe that the trimmed videos are sufficiently clean and informative for learning the latent semantics in our VAE module.

Architecture and Implementation Details. For the fair comparison with state-of-the-art methods [16,44], we choose to use the output of pool5 layer of the GoogLeNet [34] for the frame-level feature. The shot-level feature is then obtained by averaging all the frame features within a shot. We first use the features of segmented shots on web videos to pre-train a VAE module whose dimension of the latent variable is set to 256. To build encoder-summarizer-decoder, we use a two-layer bidirectional LSTM with 1024 hidden units, a two-layer MLP with [256, 256] hidden units and a two-layer LSTM with 1024 hidden units for the encoder RNN, attention MLP and decoder RNNs, respectively. For the parameter initialization, we train our framework from scratch using stochastic gradient descent with a minibatch size of 20, a momentum of 0.9, and a weight decay of 0.005. The learning rate is initialized to 0.01 and is reduced to its 1/10 after every 20 epochs (100 epochs in total). The trade-off parameter λ is set to 0.2 in the mixed training objective.

5.1 Quantitative Results

Exploration Study. To better understand the impact of using web videos and different types of annotations in our method, we analyzed the performances under the following six training settings: (1) benchmark datasets with weak supervision (topic labels); (2) benchmark datasets with weak supervision and extra 30 downloaded videos per topic; (3) benchmark datasets with weak supervision and extra 60 downloaded videos per topic; (4) benchmark datasets with strong supervision (topic labels and importance scores); (5) benchmark datasets with strong supervision and extra 30 downloaded videos per topic; and (6) benchmark datasets with strong supervision and extra 60 downloaded videos per topic. We have the following key observations from Table 1: (1) Training on the benchmark data with only weak topic labels in our VESD framework performs much worse than either that of training using extra web videos or that of training using detailed importance scores, which demonstrates our generative summarization model demands a larger amount of annotated data to perform well. (2) We notice that the more web videos give better results, which clearly demonstrates the benefits of using web videos and proves the scalability of our generative framework. (3) This big improvements with strong supervision illustrate the positive impact of incorporating available importance scores for mixed training of our VESD. That is not surprising since the attention scores should be imposed to focus on different fragments of raw videos in order to be consistent with ground-truths, resulting in the summarizer with the diverse property which is an important metric in generating good summaries. We use the training setting (5) in the following experimental comparisons.

Table 1. Exploration study on training settings. Numbers show top-5 mAP scores.

Training settings	CoSum	TVSum
Benchmark with weak supervision	0.616	0.352
Benchmark with weak supervision + 30 web videos/topic	0.684	0.407
Benchmark with weak supervision + 60 web videos/topic	0.701	0.423
Benchmark with strong supervision	0.712	0.437
Benchmark with strong supervision + 30 web videos/topic	0.755	0.481
Benchmark with strong supervision + 60 web videos/topic	0.764	0.498

Effect of Deep Feature. We also investigate the effect of using different types of deep features as shot representation in VESD framework, including 2D deep features extracted from GoogLeNet [34] and ResNet101 [11], and 3D deep features extracted from C3D [36]. In Table 2, we have following observations: (1) ResNet produces better results than GoogLeNet, with a top-5 mAP score improvement of 0.012 on the CoSum dataset, which indicates more powerful visual features still lead improvement for our method. We also compare

Table 2. Performance comparison using different types of features on CoSum dataset. Numbers show top-5 mAP scores averaged over all the videos of the same topic.

Feature	BJ	BP	ET	ERC	KP	MLB	NFL	NDC	SL	SF	Top-5
GoogLeNet	0.715	0.746	0.813	0.756	0.772	0.727	0.737	0.782	0.794	0.709	0.755
ResNet101	0.727	0.755	0.827	0.766	0.783	0.741	0.752	0.790	0.807	0.722	0.767
C3D		0.729	0.754	0.831	0.761	0.779	0.740	0.747	0.785	0.805	0.718	0.765

2D GoogLeNet features with C3D features. Results show that the C3D features achieve better performance over GoogLeNet features (0.765 vs 0.755) and comparable performance with ResNet101 features. We believe this is because C3D features exploit the temporal information of videos thus are also suitable for summarization.

Table 3. Experimental results on CoSum dataset. Numbers show top-5/15 mAP scores averaged over all the videos of the same topic.

Topic	Unsupervised methods					Supervised methods					VESD
	SMRS	Quasi	MBF	CVS	SG	KVS	DPP	sLstm	SM	DSN	
BJ	0.504	0.561	0.631	0.658	0.698	0.662	0.672	0.683	0.692	0.685	**0.715**
BP	0.492	0.625	0.592	0.675	0.713	0.674	0.682	0.701	0.722	0.714	**0.746**
ET	0.556	0.575	0.618	0.722	0.759	0.731	0.744	0.749	0.789	0.783	**0.813**
ERC	0.525	0.563	0.575	0.693	0.729	0.685	0.694	0.717	0.728	0.721	**0.756**
KP	0.521	0.557	0.594	0.707	0.729	0.701	0.705	0.714	0.745	0.742	**0.772**
MLB	0.543	0.563	0.624	0.679	0.721	0.668	0.677	0.714	0.693	0.687	**0.727**
NFL	0.558	0.587	0.603	0.674	0.693	0.671	0.681	0.681	0.727	0.724	**0.737**
NDC	0.496	0.617	0.595	0.702	0.738	0.698	0.704	0.722	0.759	0.751	**0.782**
SL	0.525	0.551	0.602	0.715	0.743	0.713	0.722	0.721	0.766	0.763	**0.794**
SF	0.533	0.562	0.594	0.647	0.681	0.642	0.648	0.653	0.683	0.674	**0.709**
Top-5	**0.525**	**0.576**	**0.602**	**0.687**	**0.720**	**0.684**	**0.692**	**0.705**	**0.735**	**0.721**	0.755
Top-15	**0.547**	**0.591**	**0.617**	**0.699**	**0.731**	**0.702**	**0.711**	**0.717**	**0.746**	**0.736**	0.764

Comparison with Unsupervised Methods. We first compare VESD with several unsupervised methods including SMRS [3], Quasi [13], MBF [1], CVS [21] and SG [16]. Table 3 shows the mean AP on both top 5 and 15 shots included in the summaries for the CoSum dataset, whereas Table 4 shows the results on TVSum dataset. We can observe that: (1) Our weakly supervised approach obtains the highest overall mAP and outperforms traditional non-DNN based methods SMRS, Quasi, MBF and CVS by large margins. (2) The most competing DNN based method, SG [16] gives top-5 mAP that is 3.5% and 1.9% less than

Table 4. Experimental results on TVSum dataset. Numbers show top-5/15 mAP scores averaged over all the videos of the same topic.

Topic	Unsupervised methods					Supervised methods					VESD
	SMRS	Quasi	MBF	CVS	SG	KVS	DPP	sLstm	SM	DSN	
VT	0.272	0.336	0.295	0.328	0.423	0.353	0.399	0.411	0.415	0.373	**0.447**
VU	0.324	0.369	0.357	0.413	0.472	0.441	0.453	0.462	0.467	0.441	**0.493**
GA	0.331	0.342	0.325	0.379	0.475	0.402	0.457	0.463	0.469	0.428	**0.496**
MS	0.362	0.375	0.412	0.398	0.489	0.417	0.462	0.477	0.478	0.436	**0.503**
PK	0.289	0.324	0.318	0.354	0.456	0.382	0.437	0.448	0.445	0.411	**0.478**
PR	0.276	0.301	0.334	0.381	0.473	0.403	0.446	0.461	0.458	0.417	**0.485**
FM	0.302	0.318	0.365	0.365	0.464	0.397	0.442	0.452	0.451	0.412	**0.487**
BK	0.297	0.295	0.313	0.326	0.417	0.342	0.395	0.406	0.407	0.368	**0.441**
BT	0.314	0.327	0.365	0.402	0.483	0.419	0.464	0.471	0.473	0.435	**0.492**
DS	0.295	0.309	0.357	0.378	0.466	0.394	0.449	0.455	0.453	0.416	**0.488**
Top-5	**0.306**	**0.329**	**0.345**	**0.372**	**0.462**	**0.398**	**0.447**	**0.451**	**0.461**	**0.424**	0.481
Top-15	**0.328**	**0.347**	**0.361**	**0.385**	**0.475**	**0.412**	**0.462**	**0.464**	**0.483**	**0.438**	0.503

ours on the CoSum and TVSum dataset, respectively. Note that with web videos only is better than training with multiple handcrafted regularizations proposed in SG. This confirms the effectiveness of incorporating a large number of web videos in our framework and learning the topic-specific semantics using a weakly-supervised matching loss function. (3) Since the CoSum dataset contains videos that have visual concepts shared with other videos from different topics, our approach using generative modelling naturally yields better results than that on the TVSum dataset. (4) It's worth noticing that TVSum is a quite challenging summarization dataset because topics on this dataset are very ambiguous and difficult to understand well with very few videos. By accessing the similar web videos to eliminate ambiguity for a specific topic, our approach works much better than all the unsupervised methods by achieving a top-5 mAP of 48.1%, showing that the accurate and user-interested video contents can be directly learned from more diverse data rather than complex summarization criteria.

Comparison with Supervised Methods. We then conduct comparison with some supervised alternatives including KVS [24], DPP [5], sLstm [44], SM [9] and DSN [20] (weakly-supervised), we have the following key observations from Tables 3 and 4: (1) VESD outperforms KVS on both datasets by a big margin (maximum improvement of 7.1% in top-5 mAP on CoSum), showing the advantage of our generative modelling and more powerful representation learning with web videos. (2) On the Cosum dataset, VESD outperforms SM [9] and DSN [20] by a margin of 2.0% and 3.4% in top-5 mAP, respectively. The results suggest that our method is still better than the fully-supervised methods and the weakly-supervised method. (3) On the TVSum dataset, a similar performance gain of 2.0% can be achieved compared with all other supervised methods.

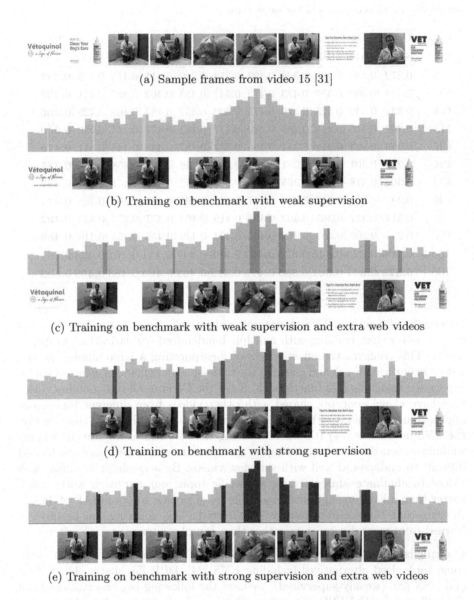

(a) Sample frames from video 15 [31]

(b) Training on benchmark with weak supervision

(c) Training on benchmark with weak supervision and extra web videos

(d) Training on benchmark with strong supervision

(e) Training on benchmark with strong supervision and extra web videos

Fig. 3. Qualitative comparison of video summaries using different training settings, along with the ground-truth importance scores (cyan background). In the last subfigure, we can easily see that weakly-supervised VESD with web videos and available importance scores produces more reliable summaries than training on benchmark videos with only weak labels. (Best viewed in colors) (Color figure online)

5.2 Qualitative Results

To get some intuition about the different training settings for VESD and their effects on the temporal selection pattern, we visualize some selected frames on an example video in Fig. 3. The cyan background shows the frame-level importance scores. The coloured regions are the selected subset of frames using the specific training setting. The visualized keyframes for different setting supports the results presented in Table 1. We notice that all four settings cover the temporal regions with the high frame-level score. By leveraging both the web videos and importance scores in datasets, VESD framework will shift towards the highly topic-specific temporal regions.

6 Conclusion

One key problem in video summarization is how to model the latent semantic representation, which has not been adequately resolved under the "single video understanding" framework in prior works. To address this issue, we introduced a generative summarization framework called VESD to leverage the web videos for better latent semantic modelling and to reduce the ambiguity of video summarization in a principled way. We incorporated flexible web prior distribution into a variational framework and presented a simple encoder-decoder with attention for summarization. The potentials of our VESD framework for large-scale video summarization were validated, and extensive experiments on benchmarks showed that VESD outperforms state-of-the-art video summarization methods significantly.

References

1. Chu, W.S., Song, Y., Jaimes, A.: Video co-summarization: video summarization by visual co-occurrence. In: Proceedings of the IEEE Conference on Computer Vision and Pattern Recognition, pp. 3584–3592 (2015)
2. Donahue, J., et al.: Long-term recurrent convolutional networks for visual recognition and description. In: Proceedings of the IEEE Conference on Computer Vision and Pattern Recognition, pp. 2625–2634 (2015)
3. Elhamifar, E., Sapiro, G., Vidal, R.: See all by looking at a few: sparse modeling for finding representative objects. In: 2012 IEEE Conference on Computer Vision and Pattern Recognition (CVPR), pp. 1600–1607. IEEE (2012)
4. Feng, S., Lei, Z., Yi, D., Li, S.Z.: Online content-aware video condensation. In: 2012 IEEE Conference on Computer Vision and Pattern Recognition (CVPR), pp. 2082–2087. IEEE (2012)
5. Gong, B., Chao, W.L., Grauman, K., Sha, F.: Diverse sequential subset selection for supervised video summarization. In: Advances in Neural Information Processing Systems, pp. 2069–2077 (2014)
6. Goodfellow, I., et al.: Generative adversarial nets. In: Advances in Neural Information Processing Systems, pp. 2672–2680 (2014)

7. Guan, G., Wang, Z., Mei, S., Ott, M., He, M., Feng, D.D.: A top-down approach for video summarization. ACM Trans. Multimed. Comput. Commun. Appl. (TOMM) **11**(1), 4 (2014)
8. Gygli, M., Grabner, H., Riemenschneider, H., Van Gool, L.: Creating summaries from user videos. In: Fleet, D., Pajdla, T., Schiele, B., Tuytelaars, T. (eds.) ECCV 2014. LNCS, vol. 8695, pp. 505–520. Springer, Cham (2014). https://doi.org/10.1007/978-3-319-10584-0_33
9. Gygli, M., Grabner, H., Van Gool, L.: Video summarization by learning submodular mixtures of objectives. Proc. CVPR **2015**, 3090–3098 (2015)
10. Gygli, M., Song, Y., Cao, L.: Video2gif: automatic generation of animated gifs from video. In: 2016 IEEE Conference on Computer Vision and Pattern Recognition (CVPR), pp. 1001–1009. IEEE (2016)
11. He, K., Zhang, X., Ren, S., Sun, J.: Deep residual learning for image recognition. In: Proceedings of the IEEE Conference on Computer Vision and Pattern Recognition, pp. 770–778 (2016)
12. Karpathy, A., Toderici, G., Shetty, S., Leung, T., Sukthankar, R., Fei-Fei, L.: Large-scale video classification with convolutional neural networks. In: Proceedings of the IEEE conference on Computer Vision and Pattern Recognition, pp. 1725–1732 (2014)
13. Kim, G., Sigal, L., Xing, E.P.: Joint summarization of large-scale collections of web images and videos for storyline reconstruction (2014)
14. Kingma, D.P., Welling, M.: Auto-encoding variational Bayes. arXiv preprint arXiv:1312.6114 (2013)
15. Larsen, A.B.L., Sønderby, S.K., Larochelle, H., Winther, O.: Autoencoding beyond pixels using a learned similarity metric. arXiv preprint arXiv:1512.09300 (2015)
16. Mahasseni, B., Lam, M., Todorovic, S.: Unsupervised video summarization with adversarial LSTM networks. In: Proceedings of the IEEE Conference on Computer Vision and Pattern Recognition (CVPR) (2017)
17. Mathieu, M., Couprie, C., LeCun, Y.: Deep multi-scale video prediction beyond mean square error. arXiv preprint arXiv:1511.05440 (2015)
18. Money, A.G., Agius, H.: Video summarisation: a conceptual framework and survey of the state of the art. J. Vis. Commun. Image Represent. **19**(2), 121–143 (2008)
19. Ng, J.Y.H., Hausknecht, M., Vijayanarasimhan, S., Vinyals, O., Monga, R., Toderici, G.: Beyond short snippets: deep networks for video classification. In: 2015 IEEE Conference on Computer Vision and Pattern Recognition (CVPR), pp. 4694–4702. IEEE (2015)
20. Panda, R., Das, A., Wu, Z., Ernst, J., Roy-Chowdhury, A.K.: Weakly supervised summarization of web videos. In: 2017 IEEE International Conference on Computer Vision (ICCV), pp. 3677–3686. IEEE (2017)
21. Panda, R., Roy-Chowdhury, A.K.: Collaborative summarization of topic-related videos. In: CVPR, vol. 2, p. 5 (2017)
22. Panda, R., Roy-Chowdhury, A.K.: Sparse modeling for topic-oriented video summarization. In: 2017 IEEE International Conference on Acoustics, Speech and Signal Processing (ICASSP), pp. 1388–1392. IEEE (2017)
23. Plummer, B.A., Brown, M., Lazebnik, S.: Enhancing video summarization via vision-language embedding. In: Computer Vision and Pattern Recognition (2017)
24. Potapov, D., Douze, M., Harchaoui, Z., Schmid, C.: Category-specific video summarization. In: Fleet, D., Pajdla, T., Schiele, B., Tuytelaars, T. (eds.) ECCV 2014. LNCS, vol. 8694, pp. 540–555. Springer, Cham (2014). https://doi.org/10.1007/978-3-319-10599-4_35

25. Pritch, Y., Rav-Acha, A., Gutman, A., Peleg, S.: Webcam synopsis: peeking around the world. In: IEEE 11th International Conference on Computer Vision, ICCV 2007, pp. 1–8. IEEE (2007)
26. Reed, S., Akata, Z., Yan, X., Logeswaran, L., Schiele, B., Lee, H.: Generative adversarial text to image synthesis. arXiv preprint arXiv:1605.05396 (2016)
27. Rui, Y., Gupta, A., Acero, A.: Automatically extracting highlights for TV baseball programs. In: Proceedings of the Eighth ACM International Conference on Multimedia, pp. 105–115. ACM (2000)
28. Sharghi, A., Gong, B., Shah, M.: Query-focused extractive video summarization. In: Leibe, B., Matas, J., Sebe, N., Welling, M. (eds.) ECCV 2016. LNCS, vol. 9912, pp. 3–19. Springer, Cham (2016). https://doi.org/10.1007/978-3-319-46484-8_1
29. Smeaton, A.F., Over, P., Kraaij, W.: Evaluation campaigns and TRECVid. In: Proceedings of the 8th ACM International Workshop on Multimedia Information Retrieval, pp. 321–330. ACM (2006)
30. Sohn, K., Lee, H., Yan, X.: Learning structured output representation using deep conditional generative models. In: Advances in Neural Information Processing Systems, pp. 3483–3491 (2015)
31. Song, Y., Vallmitjana, J., Stent, A., Jaimes, A.: TVSUM: summarizing web videos using titles. In: Proceedings of the IEEE Conference on Computer Vision and Pattern Recognition, pp. 5179–5187 (2015)
32. Sun, M., Farhadi, A., Seitz, S.: Ranking domain-specific highlights by analyzing edited videos. In: Fleet, D., Pajdla, T., Schiele, B., Tuytelaars, T. (eds.) ECCV 2014. LNCS, vol. 8689, pp. 787–802. Springer, Cham (2014). https://doi.org/10.1007/978-3-319-10590-1_51
33. Sutskever, I., Vinyals, O., Le, Q.V.: Sequence to sequence learning with neural networks. In: Advances in Neural Information Processing Systems, pp. 3104–3112 (2014)
34. Szegedy, C., et al.: Going deeper with convolutions. In: CVPR (2015)
35. Tang, H., Kwatra, V., Sargin, M.E., Gargi, U.: Detecting highlights in sports videos: cricket as a test case. In: 2011 IEEE International Conference on Multimedia and Expo (ICME), pp. 1–6. IEEE (2011)
36. Tran, D., Bourdev, L., Fergus, R., Torresani, L., Paluri, M.: Learning spatiotemporal features with 3d convolutional networks. In: 2015 IEEE International Conference on Computer Vision (ICCV), pp. 4489–4497. IEEE (2015)
37. Truong, B.T., Venkatesh, S.: Video abstraction: a systematic review and classification. ACM Trans. Multimed. Comput. Commun. Appl. (TOMM) **3**(1), 3 (2007)
38. Vondrick, C., Pirsiavash, H., Torralba, A.: Generating videos with scene dynamics. In: Advances in Neural Information Processing Systems, pp. 613–621 (2016)
39. Walker, J., Doersch, C., Gupta, A., Hebert, M.: An uncertain future: forecasting from static images using variational autoencoders. In: Leibe, B., Matas, J., Sebe, N., Welling, M. (eds.) ECCV 2016. LNCS, vol. 9911, pp. 835–851. Springer, Cham (2016). https://doi.org/10.1007/978-3-319-46478-7_51
40. Xu, K., et al.: Show, attend and tell: neural image caption generation with visual attention. In: International Conference on Machine Learning, pp. 2048–2057 (2015)
41. Yang, H., Wang, B., Lin, S., Wipf, D., Guo, M., Guo, B.: Unsupervised extraction of video highlights via robust recurrent auto-encoders. arXiv preprint arXiv:1510.01442 (2015)
42. Yao, T., Mei, T., Rui, Y.: Highlight detection with pairwise deep ranking for first-person video summarization (2016)

43. Zhang, K., Chao, W.L., Sha, F., Grauman, K.: Summary transfer: exemplar-based subset selection for video summarization. In: 2016 IEEE Conference on Computer Vision and Pattern Recognition (CVPR), pp. 1059–1067. IEEE (2016)

44. Zhang, K., Chao, W.-L., Sha, F., Grauman, K.: Video summarization with long short-term memory. In: Leibe, B., Matas, J., Sebe, N., Welling, M. (eds.) ECCV 2016. LNCS, vol. 9911, pp. 766–782. Springer, Cham (2016). https://doi.org/10. 1007/978-3-319-46478-7_47

45. Zhou, Y., Berg, T.L.: Learning temporal transformations from time-lapse videos. In: Leibe, B., Matas, J., Sebe, N., Welling, M. (eds.) ECCV 2016. LNCS, vol. 9912, pp. 262–277. Springer, Cham (2016). https://doi.org/10.1007/978-3-319-46484-8_16

Single Image Intrinsic Decomposition Without a Single Intrinsic Image

Wei-Chiu Ma[1,2](✉), Hang Chu[3], Bolei Zhou[1], Raquel Urtasun[2,3], and Antonio Torralba[1]

[1] Massachusetts Institute of Technology, Cambridge, USA
weichium@mit.edu
[2] Uber Advanced Technologies Group, Pittsburgh, USA
[3] University of Toronto, Toronto, Canada

Abstract. Intrinsic image decomposition—decomposing a natural image into a set of images corresponding to different physical causes—is one of the key and fundamental problems of computer vision. Previous intrinsic decomposition approaches either address the problem in a fully supervised manner, or require multiple images of the same scene as input. These approaches are less desirable in practice, as ground truth intrinsic images are extremely difficult to acquire, and requirement of multiple images pose severe limitation on applicable scenarios. In this paper, we propose to bring the best of both worlds. We present a two stream convolutional neural network framework that is capable of learning the decomposition effectively in the absence of any ground truth intrinsic images, and can be easily extended to a (semi-)supervised setup. At inference time, our model can be easily reduced to a single stream module that performs intrinsic decomposition on a single input image. We demonstrate the effectiveness of our framework through extensive experimental study on both synthetic and real-world datasets, showing superior performance over previous approaches in both single-image and multi-image settings. Notably, our approach outperforms previous state-of-the-art single image methods while using only 50% of ground truth supervision.

Keywords: Intrinsic decomposition · Unsupervised learning · Self-supervised learning

1 Introduction

In a scorching afternoon, you walk all the way through the sunshine and finally enter the shading. You notice that there is a sharp edge on the ground and the appearance of the sidewalk changes drastically. Without a second thought, you realize that the bricks are in fact identical and the color difference is due to the variation of scene illumination. Despite merely a quick glance, humans have the remarkable ability to decompose the intricate mess of confounds, which our visual

© Springer Nature Switzerland AG 2018
V. Ferrari et al. (Eds.): ECCV 2018, LNCS 11218, pp. 211–229, 2018.
https://doi.org/10.1007/978-3-030-01264-9_13

world is, into simple underlying factors. Even though most people have never seen a single intrinsic image in their lifetime, they can still estimate the intrinsic properties of the materials and reason about their relative albedo effectively [6]. This is because human visual systems have accumulated thousands hours of implicit observations which can serve as their priors during judgment. Such an ability not only plays a fundamental role in interpreting real-world imaging, but is also a key to truly understand the complex visual world. The goal of this work is to equip computational visual machines with similar capabilities by emulating humans' learning procedure. We believe by enabling perception systems to disentangle *intrinsic* properties (*e.g.* albedo) from *extrinsic* factors (*e.g.* shading), they will better understand the physical interactions of the world. In computer vision, such task of decomposing an image into a set of images each of which corresponds to a different physical cause is commonly referred to as *intrinsic decomposition* [4].

Despite the inverse problem being ill-posed [1], it has drawn extensive attention due to its potential utilities for algorithms and applications in computer vision. For instance, many low-level vision tasks such as shadow removal [14] and optical flow estimation [27] benefit substantially from reliable estimation of albedo images. Advanced image manipulation applications such as appearance editing [48], object insertions [24], and image relighting [49] also become much easier if an image is correctly decomposed into material properties and shading effects. Motivated by such great potentials, a variety of approaches have been proposed for intrinsic decomposition [6,17,28,62]. Most of them focus on monocular case, as it often arises in practice [13]. They either exploit manually designed priors [2,3,31,41], or capitalize on data-driven statistics [39,48,61] to address the ambiguities. The models are powerful, yet with a critical drawback—requiring ground truth for learning. The ground truth for intrinsic images, however, are extremely difficult and expensive to collect [16]. Current publicly available datasets are either small [16], synthetic [9,48], or sparsely annotated [6], which significantly restricts the scalability and generalizability of this task. To overcome the limitations, multi-image based approaches have been introduced [17,18,28,29,55]. They remove the need of ground truth and employ multiple observations to disambiguate the problem. While the unsupervised intrinsic decomposition paradigm is appealing, they require multi-image as input both during training and at inference, which largely limits their applications in real world.

In this work, we propose a novel approach to learning intrinsic decomposition that requires neither ground truth nor priors about scene geometry or lighting models. We draw connections between single image based methods and multi-image based approaches and explicitly show how one can benefit from the other. Following the derived formulation, we design an unified model whose *training* stage can be viewed as an approach to *multi-image intrinsic decomposition*. While at *test* time it is capable of decomposing arbitrary *single* image. To be more specific, we design a two stream deep architecture that observes a pair of images and aims to explain the variations of the scene by predicting the correct intrinsic decompositions. No ground truth is required for learning. The model reduces to a single stream network during inference and performs single image intrinsic decomposition. As the problem is under-constrained, we derive multiple objective functions based on image formation model to constrain the solution space and aid the learning process. We show that by regularizing the model carefully, the intrinsic images emerge automatically. The learned representations are not only comparable to those learned under full supervision, but can also serve as a better initialization for (semi-)supervised training. As a byproduct, our model also learns to predict whether a gradient belongs to albedo or shading without any labels. This provides an intuitive explanation for the model's behavior, and can be used for further diagnoses and improvements (Fig. 1).

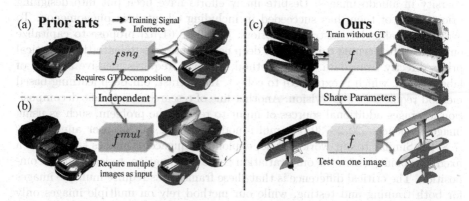

Fig. 1. Novelties and advantages of our approach: Previous works on intrinsic image decomposition can be classified into two categories, (a) single imaged based and (b) multi-image based. While single imaged based models are useful in practice, they require ground truth (GT) for training. Multi-image based approaches remove the need of GT, yet at the cost of flexibility (*i.e.*, always requires multiple images as input). (c) Our model takes the best of both world. We do not need GT during training (*i.e.*, training signal comes from input images), yet can be applied to arbitrary single image at test time.

We demonstrate the effectiveness of our model on one large-scale synthetic dataset and one real-world dataset. Our method achieves state-of-the-art performance on multi-image intrinsic decomposition, and significantly outperforms previous deep learning based single image intrinsic decomposition models using only 50% of ground truth data. To the best of our knowledge, we are the first attempt to bridge the gap between the two tasks and learn an intrinsic network without any ground truth intrinsic image.

2   Related Work

Intrinsic Decomposition. The work in intrinsic decomposition can be roughly classified into two groups: approaches that take as input only a single image [3,31,37,39,48,50,61,62], and algorithms that require addition sources of input [7,11,23,30,38,55]. For single image based methods, since the task is completely under constrained, they often rely on a variety of priors to help disambiguate the problem. [5,14,31,50] proposed to classify images edges into either albedo or shading and use [19] to reconstruct the intrinsic images. [34,41] exploited texture statistics to deal with the smoothly varying textures. While [3] explicitly modeled lighting conditions to better disentangle the shading effect, [42,46] assumed sparsity in albedo images. Despite many efforts have been put into designing priors, none of them has succeeded in including all intrinsic phenomenon. To avoid painstakingly constructing priors, [21,39,48,61,62] propose to capitalize on the feature learning capability of deep neural networks to learn the statistical priors directly from data. Their method, however, requires massive amount of labeled data, which is expensive to collect. In contrast, our deep learning based method requires no supervision. Another line of research in intrinsic decomposition leverages additional sources of input to resolve the problem, such as using image sequences [20,28–30,55], multi-modal input [2,11], or user annotations [7,8,47]. Similar to our work, [29,55] exploit a sequence of images taken from a fixed viewpoint, where the only variation is the illumination, to learn the decomposition. The critical difference is that these frameworks require multiple images for both training and testing, while our method rely on multiple images only during training. At test time, our network can perform intrinsic decomposition for an arbitrary single image.

Unsupervised/Self-supervised Learning from Image Sequences/ Videos. Leveraging videos or image sequences, together with physical constraints, to train a neural network has recently become an emerging topic of research [15,32,44,51,52,56–59]. Zhou et al. [60] proposed a self-supervised approach to learning monocular depth estimation from image sequences. Vijayanarasimhan et al. [53] extended the idea and introduced a more flexible structure from motion framework that can incorporate supervision. Our work is conceptually similar to [53,60], yet focusing on completely different tasks. Recently, Janner et al. [21] introduced a self-supervised framework for transferring intrinsics. They first trained their network with ground truth and then fine-tune with reconstruction loss. In this work, we take a step further and attempt to learn intrinsic decomposition in a fully unsupervised manner. Concurrently and independently, Li and Snavely [33] also developed an approach to learning intrinsic decomposition without any supervision. More generally speaking, our work is in spirit similar to visual representation learning whose goal is to learn generic features by solving certain pretext tasks [22,43,54].

3   Background and Problem Formulation

In this section, we first briefly review current works on single image and multi-image intrinsic decomposition. Then we show the connections between the two tasks and demonstrate that they can be solved with a single, unified model under certain parameterizations.

3.1   Single Image Intrinsic Decomposition

The single image intrinsic decomposition problem is generally formulated as:

$$\hat{A}, \hat{S} = f^{sng}(\mathcal{I}; \Theta^{sng}), \tag{1}$$

where the goal is to learn a function f that takes as input a natural image $\mathcal{I}$, and outputs an albedo image $\hat{A}$ and a shading image $\hat{S}$. The hat sign $\hat{\cdot}$ indicates that it is the output of the function rather than the ground truth. Ideally, the Hadamard product of the output images should be identical to the input image, i.e. $\mathcal{I} = \hat{A} \odot \hat{S}$. The parameter Θ and the function f can take different forms. For instance, in traditional Retinex algorithm [31], Θ is simply a threshold used to classify the gradients of the original image $\mathcal{I}$ and f^{sng} is the solver for Poisson equation. In recent deep learning based approaches [39,48], f^{sng} refers to a neural network and Θ represents the weights. Since these models require only a single image as input, they potentially can be applied to various scenarios and have a number of use cases [13]. The problem, however, is inherently ambiguous and technically ill-posed under monocular setting. Ground truths are required to train either the weights for manual designed priors [6] or the data-driven statistics [21]. They learn by minimizing the difference between the GT intrinsic images and the predictions.

3.2   Multi-image Intrinsic Decomposition

Another way to address the ambiguities in intrinsic decomposition is to exploit multiple images as input. The task is defined as:

$$\hat{\mathbf{A}}, \hat{\mathbf{S}} = f^{mul}(\mathbf{I}; \Theta^{mul}), \tag{2}$$

where $\mathbf{I} = \{\mathcal{I}_i\}_{i=1}^{N}$ is the set of input images of the same scene, and $\hat{\mathbf{A}} = \{\hat{A}_i\}_{i=1}^{N}$, $\hat{\mathbf{S}} = \{\hat{S}_i\}_{i=1}^{N}$ are the corresponding set of intrinsic predictions. The input images $\mathbf{I}$ can be collected with a moving camera [27], yet for simplicity they are often assumed being captured with a static camera pose under varying lighting conditions [29,36]. The extra constraint not only gives birth to some useful priors [55], but also open the door to solving the problem in an unsupervised manner [18]. For example, based on the observation that shadows tend to move and a pixel in a static scene is unlikely to contain shadow edges in multiple images,

Weiss [55] assumed that the median gradients across all images belong to albedo and solve the Poisson equation. The simple algorithm works well on shadow removal, and was further extend by [36] to combine with Retinex algorithm (W+Ret) to produce better results. More recently, Laffont and Bazin [29] derived several energy functions based on image formation model and formulate the task as an optimization problem. The goal simply becomes finding the intrinsic images that minimize the pre-defined energy. Ground truth data is not required under many circumstances [18,29,55]. This addresses one of the major difficulties in learning intrinsic decomposition. Unfortunately, as a trade off, these models rely on multi-image as input all the time, which largely limits their applicability in practice.

3.3   Connecting Single and Multi-image Based Approaches

The key insight is to use a same set of parameters Θ for both single image and multi-image intrinsic decomposition. Multi-image approaches have already achieved impressive results without the need of ground truth. If we can transfer the learned parameters from multi-image model to single image one, then we will be able to decompose arbitrary single image without any supervision. Unfortunately, previous works are incapable of doing this. The multi-image parameters Θ^{mul} or energy functions are often dependent on all input images $\mathbf{I}$, which makes them impossible to be reused under single image setting. With such motivation in mind, we design our model to have the following form:

$$f^{mul}(\mathbf{I}; \Theta) = g(f^{sng}(\mathcal{I}_1; \Theta), f^{sng}(\mathcal{I}_2; \Theta), ..., f^{sng}(\mathcal{I}_N; \Theta)), \qquad (3)$$

where g denotes some parameter-free, pre-defined constraints applied to the outputs of single image models. By formulating the multi-image model f^{mul} as a composition function of multiple single image model f^{sng}, we are able to share the same parameters Θ and further learn the single image model through multi-image training without any ground truth. The high-level idea of sharing parameters has been introduced in W+Ret [36]; however, our work exists three critical differences: first and foremost, their approach requires ground truth for learning, while ours does not. Second, they encode the information across several observations at the input level via some heuristics. In contrast, our aggregation function g is based on image formation model, and operates directly on the intrinsic predictions. Finally, rather than employing the relatively simple Retinex model, we parameterize f^{sng} as a neural network, with Θ being its weight, and g being a series of carefully designed, parameter-free, and differentiable operations. The details of our model are discussed in Sect. 4 and the differences between our method and several previous approaches are summarized in Table 1.

Table 1. Summary of different intrinsic decomposition approaches.

Methods	Supervision	Training input	Inference input	Learnable parameter Θ
Retinex [31]	✓	Single image	Single image	Gradient threshold
CNN [21,39,48]	✓	Single image	Single image	Network weights
CRF [6,61]	✓	Single image	Single image	Energy weights
Weiss [55]	✗	Multi-image	Multi-image	None
W+RET [36]	✓	Multi-image	Multi-image	Gradient threshold
Hauagge et al. [18]	✗	Multi-image	Multi-image	None
Laffont et al. [29]	✗	Multi-image	Multi-image	None
Our method	✗	Multi-image	Single image	Network weights

4   Unsupervised Intrinsic Learning

Our model consists of two main components: the *intrinsic network* f^{sng}, and the *aggregation function* g. The intrinsic network f^{sng} produces a set of intrinsic representations given an input image. The differentiable, parameter-free aggregation function g constrains the outputs of f^{sng}, so that they are plausible and comply to the image formation model. As all operations are differentiable, the errors can be backpropagated all the way through f^{sng} during training. Our model can be trained even no ground truth exists. The training stage is hence equivalent to performing multi-image intrinsic decomposition. At test time, the trained intrinsic network f^{sng} serves as an independent module, which enables decomposing an arbitrary single image. In this work, we assume the input images come in pairs during training. This works well in practice and an extension to more images is trivial. We explore three different setups of the aggregation function. An overview of our model is shown in Fig. 2.

4.1   Intrinsic Network f^{sng}

The goal of the intrinsic network is to produce a set of reliable intrinsic representations from the input image and then pass them to the aggregation function for further composition and evaluation. To be more formal, given a single image $\mathcal{I}_1$, we seek to learn a neural network f^{sng} such that $(\hat{\mathcal{A}}_1, \hat{\mathcal{S}}_1, \hat{\mathcal{M}}_1) = f^{sng}(\mathcal{I}_1; \Theta)$, where $\mathcal{A}$ denotes albedo, $\mathcal{S}$ refers to shading, and $\mathcal{M}$ represents a soft assignment mask (details in Sect. 4.2).

Following [12,45,48], we employ an encoder-decoder architecture with skip links for f^{sng}. The bottom-up top-down structure enables the network to effectively process and consolidate features across various scales [35], while the skip links from encoder to decoder help preserve spatial information at each resolution [40]. Since the intrinsic components (*e.g.* albedo, shading) are mutual dependent, they share the same encoder. In general, our network architecture is similar to the Mirror-link network [47]. We, however, note that this is not the only feasible choice. Other designs that disperse and aggregate information in different manners may also work well for our task. One can replace the current structure with arbitrary network as long as the output has the same resolution as the input. We refer the readers to supp. material for detailed architecture.

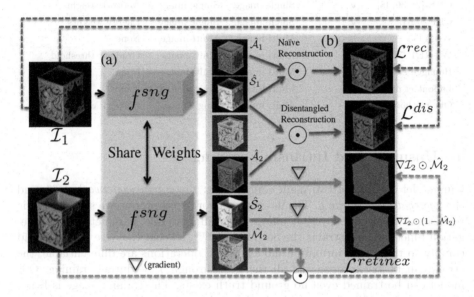

Fig. 2. Network architecture for training: Our model consists of *intrinsic networks* and *aggregation functions*. (a) The siamese intrinsic network takes as input a pair of images with varying illumination and generate a set of intrinsic estimations. (b) The aggregation functions compose the predictions into images whose ground truths are available via pre-defined operations (*i.e.* the orange, green, and blue lines). The objectives are then applied to the final outputs, and the errors are backpropagated all the way to the intrinsic network to refine the estimations. With this design, our model is able to learn intrinsic decomposition without a single ground truth image. Note that the model is symmetric and for clarity we omit similar lines. The full model is only employed during training. At test time, our model reduces to a single stream network f^{sng} (pink) and performs single image intrinsic decomposition. (Color figure online)

4.2   Aggregation Functions g and Objectives

Suppose now we have the intrinsic representations predicted by the intrinsic network. In order to evaluate the performance of these estimations, whose ground truths are unavailable, and learn accordingly, we exploit several differentiable aggregation functions. Through a series of fixed, pre-defined operations, the aggregation functions re-compose the estimated intrinsic images into images which we have ground truth for. We can then compute the objectives and use it to guide the network learning. Keeping such motivation in mind, we design the following three aggregation functions as well as the corresponding objectives.

Naive Reconstruction. The first aggregation function simply follows the definition of intrinsic decomposition: given the estimated intrinsic tensors $\hat{A}_1$ and $\hat{S}_1$, the Hadamard product $\hat{\mathcal{I}}_1^{rec} = \hat{A}_1 \odot \hat{S}_1$ should flawlessly reconstruct the original input image $\mathcal{I}_1$. Building upon this idea, we employ a pixel-wise regression loss $\mathcal{L}_1^{rec} = \|\hat{\mathcal{I}}_1^{rec} - \mathcal{I}_1\|_2$ on the reconstructed output, and constrain the network to learn only the representations that satisfy this rule. Despite such objective greatly reduce the solution space of intrinsic representations, the problem is still highly under-constrained—there exists infinite images that meet $\mathcal{I}_1 = \hat{A}_1 \odot \hat{S}_1$. We thus employ another aggregation operation to reconstruct the input images and further constrain the solution manifold.

Disentangled Reconstruction. According to the definition of intrinsic images, the albedo component should be invariant to illumination changes. Hence given a pair of images $\mathcal{I}_1, \mathcal{I}_2$ of the same scene, ideally we should be able to perfectly reconstruct $\mathcal{I}_1$ even with $\hat{A}_2$ and $\hat{S}_1$. Based on this idea, we define our second aggregation function to be $\hat{\mathcal{I}}_1^{dis} = \hat{A}_2 \odot \hat{S}_1$. By taking the albedo estimation from the other image yet still hoping for perfect reconstruction, we force the network to extract the illumination invariant component automatically. Since we aim to disentangle the illumination component through this reconstruction process, we name the output as disentangled reconstruction. Similar to naive reconstruction, we employ a pixel-wise regression loss $\mathcal{L}_1^{dis}$ for $\hat{\mathcal{I}}_1^{dis}$.

One obvious shortcut that the network might pick up is to collapse all information from input image into $\hat{S}_1$, and have the albedo decoder always output a white image regardless of input. In this case, the albedo is still invariant to illumination, yet the network fails. In order to avoid such degenerate cases, we follow Jayaraman and Grauman [22] and incorporate an additional embedding loss $\mathcal{L}_1^{ebd}$ for regularization. Specifically, we force the two albedo predictions $\hat{A}_1$ and $\hat{A}_2$ to be as similar as possible, while being different from the randomly sampled albedo predictions $\hat{A}_{neg}$.

Gradient. As natural images and intrinsic images exhibit stronger correlations in gradient domain [25], the third operation is to convert the intrinsic estimations to gradient domain, *i.e.* $\nabla \hat{A}_1$ and $\nabla \hat{S}_1$. However, unlike the outputs of the previous two aggregation function, we do not have ground truth to directly supervise the gradient images. We hence propose a self-supervised approach to address this issue.

Our method is inspired by the traditional Retinex algorithm [31] where each derivative in the image is assumed to be caused by either change in albedo or that of shading. Intuitively, if we can accurately classify all derivatives, we can then obtain ground truths for $\nabla \hat{A}_1$ and $\nabla \hat{S}_1$. We thus exploit deep neural network for edge classification. To be more specific, we let the intrinsic network predict a *soft* assignment mask $\mathcal{M}_1$ to determine to which intrinsic component each edge belongs. Unlike [31] where a image derivative can only belong to either albedo or shading, the assignment mask outputs the *probability* that a image derivative is caused by changes in albedo. One can think of it as a soft version of Retinex algorithm, yet completely data-driven without manual tuning. With the help of the soft assignment mask, we can then generate the "pseudo" ground truth

$\nabla \mathcal{I} \odot \hat{\mathcal{M}}_1$ and $\nabla \mathcal{I} \odot (1 - \hat{\mathcal{M}}_1)$ to supervise the gradient intrinsic estimations. The Retinex loss[1] is defined as follows:

$$\mathcal{L}_1^{retinex} = \|\nabla \hat{\mathcal{A}}_1 - \nabla \mathcal{I} \odot \hat{\mathcal{M}}_1\|_2 + \|\nabla \hat{\mathcal{S}}_1 - \nabla \mathcal{I} \odot (1 - \hat{\mathcal{M}}_1)\|_2 \qquad (4)$$

The final objective thus becomes:

$$\mathcal{L}_1^{final} = \mathcal{L}_1^{rec} + \lambda_d \mathcal{L}_1^{dis} + \lambda_r \mathcal{L}_1^{retinex} + \lambda_e \mathcal{L}_1^{ebd}, \qquad (5)$$

where λ's are the weightings. In practice, we set $\lambda_d = 1$, $\lambda_r = 0.1$, and $\lambda_e = 0.01$. We select them based on the stability of the training loss. $\mathcal{L}_2^{final}$ is completely identical as we use a siamese network structure.

Input	Janner	Shi	Ours-U	Ours-F	GT	Input	Janner	Shi	Ours-U	Ours-F	GT

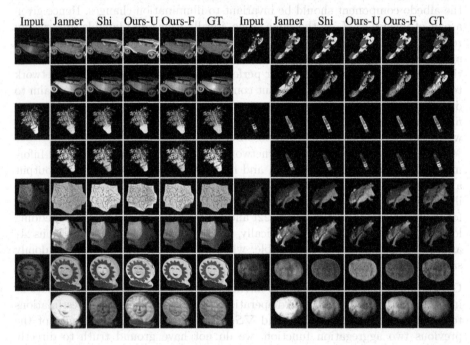

Fig. 3. Single image intrinsic decomposition: Our model (Ours-U) learns the intrinsic representations without any supervision and produces best results after fine-tuning (Ours-F).

4.3 Training and Testing

Since we only supervise the output of the aggregation functions, we do not enforce that each decoder in the intrinsic network solves its respective subproblem (*i.e.* albedo, shading, and mask). Rather, we expect that the proposed network structure encourages these roles to emerge automatically. Training the

---

[1] In practice, we need to transform all images into *logarithm* domain before computing the gradient and applying Retinex loss. We omit the log operator here for simplicity.

network from scratch without direction supervision, however, is a challenging problem. It often results in semantically meaningless intermediate representations [49]. We thus introduce additional constraints to carefully regularize the intrinsic estimations during training. Specifically, we penalize the L1 norm of the gradients for the albedo and minimize the L1 norm of the second-order gradients for the shading. While $\|\nabla\hat{\mathcal{A}}\|$ encourages the albedo to be piece-wise constant, $\|\nabla^2\hat{\mathcal{S}}\|$ favors smoothly changing illumination. To further encourage the emergence of the soft assignment mask, we compute the gradient of the input image and use it to supervise the mask for the first four epochs. The early supervision pushes the mask decoder towards learning a gradient-aware representation. The mask representations are later freed and fine-tuned during the joint self-supervised training process. We train our network with ADAM [26] and set the learning rate to 10^{-5}. We augment our training data with horizontal flips and random crops.

Extending to (Semi-)supervised Learning. Our model can be easily extended to (semi-)supervised settings whenever a ground truth is available. In the original model, the objectives are only applied to the final output of the aggregation functions and the output of the intrinsic network is left without explicit guidance. Hence, a straightforward way to incorporate supervision is to directly supervise the intermediate representation and guide the learning process. Specifically, we can employ a pixel-wise regression loss on both albedo and shading, *i.e.* $\mathcal{L}^A = \|\hat{\mathcal{A}} - \mathcal{A}\|_2$ and $\mathcal{L}^S = \|\hat{\mathcal{S}} - \mathcal{S}\|_2$.

5   Experiments

5.1   Setup

Data. To effectively evaluate our model, we consider two datasets: one larger-scale synthetic dataset [21,48], and one real world dataset [16]. For synthetic dataset, we use the 3D objects from ShapeNet [10] and perform rendering in Blender[2]. Specifically, we randomly sample 100 objects from each of the following 10 categories: airplane, boat, bottle, car, flowerpot, guitar, motorbike, piano, tower, and train. For each object, we randomly select 10 poses, and for each pose we use 10 different lightings. This leads to in total of $100 \times 10 \times 10 \times C_2^{10} = 450K$ pairs of images. We split the data by objects, in which 90% belong to training and validation and 10% belong to test split.

The MIT Intrinsics dataset [16] is a real-world image dataset with ground truths. The dataset consists of 20 objects. Each object was captured under 11 different illumination conditions, resulting in 220 images in total. We use the same data split as in [39,48], where the images are split into two folds by objects (10 for each split).

---

[2] We follow the same rendering process as [21]. Please refer to their paper for more details.

Metrics. We employ two standard error measures to quantitatively evaluate the performance of our model: the standard mean-squared error (MSE) and the local mean-squared error (LMSE) [16]. Comparing to MSE, LMSE provides a more fine-grained measure. It allows each local region to have a different scaling factor. We set the size of the sliding window in LSME to 12.5% of the image in each dimension.

5.2 Multi-image Intrinsic Decomposition

Since no ground truth data has been used during training, our training process can be viewed as an approach to multi-image intrinsic decomposition.

Baselines. For fair analysis, we compare with methods that also take as input a sequence of photographs of the same scene with varying illumination conditions. In particular, we consider three publicly available multi-image based approaches: Weiss [55], W+Ret [36], and Hauagge et al. [17].

Results. Following [16, 29], we use LMSE as the main metric to evaluate our multi-image based model. The results are shown in Table 2. As our model is able to effectively harness the optimization power of deep neural network, we outperform all previous methods that rely on hand-crafted priors or explicit lighting modelings.

Table 2. Comparison against multi-image based methods.

Methods	Average LMSE	
	MIT	ShapeNet
Weiss [55]	0.0215	0.0632
W+Ret [36]	0.0170	0.0525
Hauagge et al. [18]	0.0155	-
Hauagge et al. [17]	0.0115	0.0240
Laffont et al. [29]	0.0138	-
Our method	**0.0097**	**0.0049**

5.3 Single Image Intrinsic Decomposition

Baselines. We compare our approach against three state-of-the-art methods: Barron et al. [3], Shi et al. [48], and Janner et al. [21]. While Barron et al. hand-craft priors for shape, shading, albedo and pose the task as an optimization problem. Shi et al. [48], and Janner et al. [21] exploit deep neural network to

Table 3. Comparison against single image-based methods on ShapeNet: Our unsupervised intrinsic model is comparable to [3]. After fine-tuning, it achieves state-of-the-art performances.

Methods	Supervision	MSE			LMSE		
	Amount	Albedo	Shading	Average	Albedo	Shading	Average
Barron et al. [3]	100%	0.0203	0.0232	0.0217	0.0066	0.0043	0.0055
Janner et al. [21]	100%	0.0119	0.0145	0.0132	0.0028	0.0037	0.0032
Shi et al. [48]	100%	0.0076	0.0122	0.0099	0.0018	0.0032	0.0024
Our method (U)	0%	0.0174	0.0310	0.0242	0.0050	0.0070	0.0060
Our method (F)	100%	**0.0064**	**0.0100**	**0.0082**	**0.0016**	**0.0025**	**0.0020**

learn natural image statistics from data and predict the decomposition. All three methods require ground truth for learning.

Results. As shown in Tables 3 and 4, our unsupervised intrinsic network f^{sng}, denoted as Ours-U, achieves comparable performance to other deep learning based approaches on MIT Dataset, and is on par with Barron et al. on ShapeNet. To further evaluate the learned unsupervised representation, we use it as initialization and fine-tune the network with ground truth data. The fine-tuned representation, denoted as Ours-F, significantly outperforms all baselines on ShapeNet and is comparable with Barron et al. on MIT Dataset. We note that MIT Dataset is extremely hard for deep learning based approaches due to its scale. Furthermore, Barron et al. employ several priors specifically designed for the dataset. Yet with our unsupervised training scheme, we are able to overcome the data issue and close the gap from Barron et al. Some qualitative results are shown in Fig. 3. Our unsupervised intrinsic network, in general, produces reasonable decompositions. With further fine-tuning, it achieves the best results. For instance, our full model better recovers the albedo of the wheel cover of the car. For the motorcycle, it is capable of predicting the correct albedo of the wheel and the shading of the seat.

Table 4. Comparison against single image-based methods on MIT Dataset: Our unsupervised intrinsic model achieves comparable performance to fully supervised deep models. After fine-tuning, it is on par with the best performing method that exploits specialized priors.

Methods	Supervision	MSE			LMSE		
	Amounts	Albedo	Shading	Average	Albedo	Shading	Average
Barron et al. [3]	100%	**0.0147**	**0.0083**	**0.0115**	**0.0061**	**0.0039**	**0.0050**
Janner et al. [39]	100%	0.0336	0.0195	0.0265	0.0210	0.0103	0.0156
Shi et al. [48]	100%	0.0323	0.0156	0.0239	0.0132	0.0064	0.0098
Our method (U)	0%	0.0313	0.0207	0.0260	0.0116	0.0095	0.0105
Our method (F)	100%	0.0168	0.0093	0.0130	0.0074	0.0052	0.0063

(Semi-)supervised Intrinsic Learning. As mentioned in Sect. 4.3, our network can be easily extended to (semi-)supervised settings by exploiting ground truth images to directly supervise the intrinsic representations. To better understand how well our unsupervised representation is and exactly how much ground truth data we need in order to achieve comparable performance to previous methods, we gradually increase the degree of supervision during training and study the performance variation. The results on ShapeNet are plotted in Fig. 4. Our model is able to achieve state-of-the-art performance with only 50% of ground truth data. This suggests that our aggregation function is able to effectively constrain the solution space and capture the features that are not directly encoded in single images. In addition, we observe that our model has a larger performance gain with less ground truth data. The relative improvement gradually converges as the amount of supervision increases, showing our utility in low-data regimes.

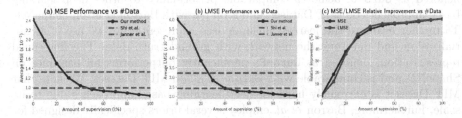

Fig. 4. Performance vs Supervision on ShapeNet: The performance of our model improves with the amount of supervision. (a) (b) Our results suggest that, with just 50% of ground truth, we can surpass the performance of other fully supervised models that used all of the labeled data. (c) The relative improvement is larger in cases with less labeled data, showing the effectiveness of our unsupervised objectives in low-data regimes.

5.4 Analysis

Ablation Study. To better understand the contribution of each component in our model, we visualize the output of the intrinsic network (*i.e.* $\hat{A}$ and $\hat{S}$) under different network configurations in Fig. 5. We start from the simple auto-encoder structure (*i.e.* using only $\mathcal{L}^{rec}$) and sequentially add other components back. At first, the model splits the image into arbitrary two components. This is expected since the representations are fully unconstrained as long as they satisfy $\mathcal{I} = \hat{A} \odot \hat{S}$. After adding the disentangle learning objective $\mathcal{L}^{dis}$, the albedo images becomes more "flat", suggesting that the model starts to learn that albedo components should be invariant of illumination. Finally, with the help of the Retinex loss $\mathcal{L}^{retinex}$, the network self-supervises the gradient images, and produces reasonable intrinsic representations without any supervision. The color is significantly improved due to the information lying in the gradient domain. The quantitative evaluations are shown in Table 5.

Table 5. Ablation studies: The performance of our model when employing different objectives.

Employed objectives			MSE		LMSE	
$\mathcal{L}_{rec}$	$\mathcal{L}_{dis}$	$\mathcal{L}_{retinex}$	Albedo	Shading	Albedo	Shading
✓			0.0362	0.0240	0.0158	0.0108
✓	✓		0.0346	0.0224	0.0141	0.0098
✓	✓	✓	**0.0313**	**0.0207**	**0.0116**	**0.0095**

Table 6. Degree of illumination invariance of the albedo image. Lower is better.

Methods	MPRE ($\times 10^{-4}$)
Barron *et al.* [3]	2.6233
Janner *et al.* [39]	4.8372
Shi *et al.* [48]	5.1589
Our method (U)	3.2341
Our method (F)	**2.4151**

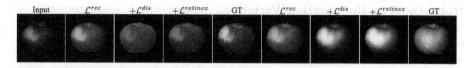

Fig. 5. Contributions of each objectives: Initially the model separates the image into two arbitrary components. After adding the disentangled loss $\mathcal{L}^{dis}$, the network learns to exclude illumination variation from albedo. Finally, with the help of the Retinex loss $\mathcal{L}^{retinex}$, the albedo color becomes more saturated.

Natural Image Disentangling. To demonstrate the generalizability of our model, we also evaluate on natural images in the wild. Specifically, we use our full model on MIT Dataset and the images provided by Barron *et al.* [3]. The images are taken by a iPhone and span a variety of categories. Despite our model is trained purely on laboratory images and have never seen other objects/scenes before, it still produces good quality results (see Fig. 6). For instance, our model successfully infers the intrinsic properties of the banana and the plants. One limitation of our model is that it cannot handle the specularity in the image. As we ignore the specular component when formulating the task, the specular parts got treated as sharp material changes and are classified as albedo. We plan to incorporate the idea of [48] to address this issue in the future.

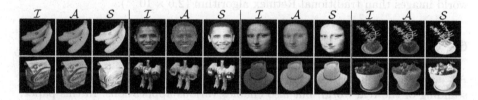

Fig. 6. Decomposing unseen natural images: Despite being trained on laboratory images, our model generalizes well to real images that it has never seen before.

Fig. 7. Network interpretation: To understand how our model sees an edge in the input image, we visualize the soft assignment mask $\mathcal{M}$ predicted by the intrinsic network. An edge has a higher probability to be assigned to albedo when there is a drastic color change. (Color figure online)

Robustness to Illumination Variation. Another way to evaluate the effectiveness of our approach is to measure the degree of illumination invariance of our albedo model. Following Zhou *et al.* [61], we compute the MSE between the input image $\mathcal{I}_1$ and the disentangled reconstruction $\hat{\mathcal{I}}_1^{dis}$ to evaluate the illumination invariance. Since our model explicitly takes into account the disentangled objective $\mathcal{L}^{dis}$, we achieve the best performance. Results on MIT Dataset are shown in Table 6.

Interpreting the Soft Assignment Mask. The soft assignment mask predicts the probability that a certain edge belongs to albedo. It not only enables the self-supervised Retinex loss, but can also serve as a probe to our model, helping us interpret the results. By visualizing the predicted soft assignment mask $\mathcal{M}$, we can understand how the network *sees* an edge—an edge caused by albedo change or variation of shading. Some visualization results of our unsupervised intrinsic network are shown in Fig. 7. The network believes that drastic color changes are most of the time due to albedo edges. Sometimes it mistakenly classify the edges, *e.g.* the variation of the blue paint on the sun should be due to shading. This mistake is consistent with the sun albedo result in Fig. 3, yet it provides another intuition of why it happens. As there is no ground truth to directly evaluate the performance of the predicted assignment map, we instead measure the pixel-wise difference between the ground truth gradient images $\nabla\mathcal{A}, \nabla\mathcal{S}$ and the "pseudo" ground truths $\nabla\mathcal{I} \odot \mathcal{M}, \nabla\mathcal{I} \odot (1-\mathcal{M})$ that we used for self-supervision. Results show that our data-driven assignment mask (1.7×10^{-4}) better explains the real world images than traditional Retinex algorithm (2.6×10^{-4}).

6   Conclusion

An accurate estimate of intrinsic properties not only provides better understanding of the real world, but also enables various applications. In this paper, we present a novel method to disentangle the factors of variations in the image. With the carefully designed architecture and objectives, our model automatically learns reasonable intrinsic representations without any supervision. We believe it is an interesting direction for intrinsic learning and we hope our model can facilitate further research in this path.

References

1. Adelson, E.H., Pentland, A.P.: The perception of shading and reflectance. In: Perception as Bayesian Inference. Cambridge University Press, New York (1996)
2. Barron, J.T., Malik, J.: Intrinsic scene properties from a single RGB-D image. In: CVPR (2013)
3. Barron, J.T., Malik, J.: Shape, illumination, and reflectance from shading. In: PAMI (2015)
4. Barrow, H., Tenenbaum, J.: Recovering intrinsic scene characteristics from images. Comput. Vis. Syst. **2**, 3–26 (1978)

5. Bell, M., Freeman, E.: Learning local evidence for shading and reflectance. In: ICCV (2001)
6. Bell, S., Bala, K., Snavely, N.: Intrinsic images in the wild. TOG **33**(4), 159 (2014)
7. Bonneel, N., Sunkavalli, K., Tompkin, J., Sun, D., Paris, S., Pfister, H.: Interactive intrinsic video editing. TOG **33**(6), 197 (2014)
8. Bousseau, A., Paris, S., Durand, F.: User-assisted intrinsic images. TOG **28**(5), 130 (2009)
9. Butler, D.J., Wulff, J., Stanley, G.B., Black, M.J.: A naturalistic open source movie for optical flow evaluation. In: Fitzgibbon, A., Lazebnik, S., Perona, P., Sato, Y., Schmid, C. (eds.) ECCV 2012. LNCS, vol. 7577, pp. 611–625. Springer, Heidelberg (2012). https://doi.org/10.1007/978-3-642-33783-3_44
10. Chang, A.X., et al.: ShapeNet: an information-rich 3D model repository. arXiv (2015)
11. Chen, Q., Koltun, V.: A simple model for intrinsic image decomposition with depth cues. In: ICCV (2013)
12. Chen, W., Fu, Z., Yang, D., Deng, J.: Single-image depth perception in the wild. In: NIPS (2016)
13. Eigen, D., Puhrsch, C., Fergus, R.: Depth map prediction from a single image using a multi-scale deep network. In: NIPS (2014)
14. Finlayson, G.D., Hordley, S.D., Drew, M.S.: Removing shadows from images using retinex. In: Color and Imaging Conference (2002)
15. Godard, C., Mac Aodha, O., Brostow, G.J.: Unsupervised monocular depth estimation with left-right consistency. In: CVPR (2016)
16. Grosse, R., Johnson, M.K., Adelson, E.H., Freeman, W.T.: Ground truth dataset and baseline evaluations for intrinsic image algorithms. In: ICCV (2009)
17. Hauagge, D., Wehrwein, S., Bala, K., Snavely, N.: Photometric ambient occlusion. In: CVPR (2013)
18. Hauagge, D.C., Wehrwein, S., Upchurch, P., Bala, K., Snavely, N.: Reasoning about photo collections using models of outdoor illumination. In: BMVC (2014)
19. Horn, B.: Robot Vision. Springer, Heidelberg (1986). https://doi.org/10.1007/978-3-662-09771-7
20. Hui, Z., Sankaranarayanan, A.C., Sunkavalli, K., Hadap, S.: White balance under mixed illumination using flash photography. In: ICCP (2016)
21. Janner, M., Wu, J., Kulkarni, T.D., Yildirim, I., Tenenbaum, J.: Self-supervised intrinsic image decomposition. In: NIPS (2017)
22. Jayaraman, D., Grauman, K.: Learning image representations tied to ego-motion. In: ICCV (2015)
23. Jeon, J., Cho, S., Tong, X., Lee, S.: Intrinsic image decomposition using structure-texture separation and surface normals. In: Fleet, D., Pajdla, T., Schiele, B., Tuytelaars, T. (eds.) ECCV 2014. LNCS, vol. 8695, pp. 218–233. Springer, Cham (2014). https://doi.org/10.1007/978-3-319-10584-0_15
24. Karsch, K., Hedau, V., Forsyth, D., Hoiem, D.: Rendering synthetic objects into legacy photographs. TOG **30**(6), 157 (2011)
25. Kim, S., Park, K., Sohn, K., Lin, S.: Unified depth prediction and intrinsic image decomposition from a single image via joint convolutional neural fields. In: Leibe, B., Matas, J., Sebe, N., Welling, M. (eds.) ECCV 2016. LNCS, vol. 9912, pp. 143–159. Springer, Cham (2016). https://doi.org/10.1007/978-3-319-46484-8_9
26. Kingma, D., Ba, J.: Adam: a method for stochastic optimization. arXiv (2014)
27. Kong, N., Black, M.J.: Intrinsic depth: improving depth transfer with intrinsic images. In: ICCV (2015)

28. Kong, N., Gehler, P.V., Black, M.J.: Intrinsic video. In: Fleet, D., Pajdla, T., Schiele, B., Tuytelaars, T. (eds.) ECCV 2014. LNCS, vol. 8690, pp. 360–375. Springer, Cham (2014). https://doi.org/10.1007/978-3-319-10605-2_24

29. Laffont, P.Y., Bazin, J.C.: Intrinsic decomposition of image sequences from local temporal variations. In: ICCV (2015)

30. Laffont, P.Y., Bousseau, A., Drettakis, G.: Rich intrinsic image decomposition of outdoor scenes from multiple views. In: TVCG (2013)

31. Land, E.H., McCann, J.J.: Lightness and retinex theory. J. Opt. Soc. Am. **61**(1), 1–11 (1971)

32. Larsson, G., Maire, M., Shakhnarovich, G.: Learning representations for automatic colorization. In: Leibe, B., Matas, J., Sebe, N., Welling, M. (eds.) ECCV 2016. LNCS, vol. 9908, pp. 577–593. Springer, Cham (2016). https://doi.org/10.1007/978-3-319-46493-0_35

33. Li, Z., Snavely, N.: Learning intrinsic image decomposition from watching the world. In: CVPR (2018)

34. Liu, X., Jiang, L., Wong, T.T., Fu, C.W.: Statistical invariance for texture synthesis. In: TVCG (2012)

35. Long, J., Shelhamer, E., Darrell, T.: Fully convolutional networks for semantic segmentation. In: CVPR (2015)

36. Matsushita, Y., Nishino, K., Ikeuchi, K., Sakauchi, M.: Illumination normalization with time-dependent intrinsic images for video surveillance. In: PAMI (2004)

37. Meka, A., Maximov, M., Zollhöfer, M., Chatterjee, A., Richardt, C., Theobalt, C.: Live intrinsic material estimation. arXiv (2018)

38. Meka, A., Zollhöfer, M., Richardt, C., Theobalt, C.: Live intrinsic video. TOG **35**(4), 109 (2016)

39. Narihira, T., Maire, M., Yu, S.X.: Direct intrinsics: learning Albedo-shading decomposition by convolutional regression. In: ICCV (2015)

40. Newell, A., Yang, K., Deng, J.: Stacked hourglass networks for human pose estimation. In: Leibe, B., Matas, J., Sebe, N., Welling, M. (eds.) ECCV 2016. LNCS, vol. 9912, pp. 483–499. Springer, Cham (2016). https://doi.org/10.1007/978-3-319-46484-8_29

41. Oh, B.M., Chen, M., Dorsey, J., Durand, F.: Image-based modeling and photo editing. In: Computer Graphics and Interactive Techniques (2001)

42. Omer, I., Werman, M.: Color lines: image specific color representation. In: CVPR (2004)

43. Pathak, D., Krahenbuhl, P., Donahue, J., Darrell, T., Efros, A.A.: Context encoders: feature learning by inpainting. In: CVPR (2016)

44. Rezende, D.J., Eslami, S.A., Mohamed, S., Battaglia, P., Jaderberg, M., Heess, N.: Unsupervised learning of 3D structure from images. In: NIPS (2016)

45. Ronneberger, O., Fischer, P., Brox, T.: U-net: convolutional networks for biomedical image segmentation. In: MIC-CAI (2015)

46. Rother, C., Kiefel, M., Zhang, L., Schölkopf, B., Gehler, P.V.: Recovering intrinsic images with a global sparsity prior on reflectance. In: NIPS (2011)

47. Shen, J., Yang, X., Jia, Y., Li, X.: Intrinsic images using optimization. In: CVPR (2011)

48. Shi, J., Dong, Y., Su, H., Yu, S.X.: Learning non-lambertian object intrinsics across shapenet categories (2017)

49. Shu, Z., Yumer, E., Hadap, S., Sunkavalli, K., Shechtman, E., Samaras, D.: Neural face editing with intrinsic image disentangling. In: CVPR (2017)

50. Tappen, M.F., Freeman, W.T., Adelson, E.H.: Recovering intrinsic images from a single image. In: NIPS (2003)

51. Tung, H.Y., Tung, H.W., Yumer, E., Fragkiadaki, K.: Self-supervised learning of motion capture. In: NIPS (2017)
52. Tung, H.Y.F., Harley, A.W., Seto, W., Fragkiadaki, K.: Adversarial inverse graphics networks: learning 2D-to-3D lifting and image-to-image translation from unpaired supervision. In: ICCV (2017)
53. Vijayanarasimhan, S., Ricco, S., Schmid, C., Sukthankar, R., Fragkiadaki, K.: SFM-Net: learning of structure and motion from video. arXiv (2017)
54. Wang, X., Gupta, A.: Unsupervised learning of visual representations using videos. In: ICCV (2015)
55. Weiss, Y.: Deriving intrinsic images from image sequences. In: ICCV (2001)
56. Yan, X., Yang, J., Yumer, E., Guo, Y., Lee, H.: Perspective transformer nets: learning single-view 3D object reconstruction without 3D supervision. In: NIPS (2016)
57. Yang, J., Reed, S.E., Yang, M.H., Lee, H.: Weakly-supervised disentangling with recurrent transformations for 3D view synthesis. In: NIPS (2015)
58. Zhang, R., Isola, P., Efros, A.A.: Colorful image colorization. In: Leibe, B., Matas, J., Sebe, N., Welling, M. (eds.) ECCV 2016. LNCS, vol. 9907, pp. 649–666. Springer, Cham (2016). https://doi.org/10.1007/978-3-319-46487-9_40
59. Zhao, H., Gan, C., Rouditchenko, A., Vondrick, C., McDermott, J., Torralba, A.: The sound of pixels. arXiv (2018)
60. Zhou, T., Brown, M., Snavely, N., Lowe, D.G.: Unsupervised learning of depth and ego-motion from video. In: CVPR (2017)
61. Zhou, T., Krahenbuhl, P., Efros, A.A.: Learning data-driven reflectance priors for intrinsic image decomposition. In: ICCV (2015)
62. Zoran, D., Isola, P., Krishnan, D., Freeman, W.T.: Learning ordinal relationships for mid-level vision. In: ICCV (2015)

Learning to Dodge A Bullet: Concyclic View Morphing via Deep Learning

Shi Jin[1,3]([envelope]), Ruiynag Liu[1,3], Yu Ji[2], Jinwei Ye[3], and Jingyi Yu[1,2]

[1] ShanghaiTech University, Shanghai, China
jinshi@shanghaitech.edu.cn
[2] Plex-VR, Baton Rouge, LA, USA
[3] Louisiana State University, Baton Rouge, LA, USA

Abstract. The bullet-time effect, presented in feature film "The Matrix", has been widely adopted in feature films and TV commercials to create an amazing stopping-time illusion. Producing such visual effects, however, typically requires using a large number of cameras/images surrounding the subject. In this paper, we present a learning-based solution that is capable of producing the bullet-time effect from only a small set of images. Specifically, we present a view morphing framework that can synthesize smooth and realistic transitions along *a circular view path* using as few as three reference images. We apply a novel cyclic rectification technique to align the reference images onto a common circle and then feed the rectified results into a deep network to predict its motion field and per-pixel visibility for new view interpolation. Comprehensive experiments on synthetic and real data show that our new framework outperforms the state-of-the-art and provides an inexpensive and practical solution for producing the bullet-time effects.

Keywords: Bullet-time effect · Image-based rendering
View morphing · Convolutional neural network (CNN)

1 Introduction

Visual effects have now become an integral part of film and television productions as they provide unique viewing experiences. One of the most famous examples is the "bullet-time" effect presented in feature film The Matrix. It creates the stopping-time illusion with smooth transitions of viewpoints surrounding the actor. To produce this effect, over 160 cameras were synchronized and precisely

---

This work was performed when Shi and Ruiyang were visiting students at LSU.

Electronic supplementary material The online version of this chapter (https://doi.org/10.1007/978-3-030-01264-9_14) contains supplementary material, which is available to authorized users.

© Springer Nature Switzerland AG 2018
V. Ferrari et al. (Eds.): ECCV 2018, LNCS 11218, pp. 230–246, 2018.
https://doi.org/10.1007/978-3-030-01264-9_14

arranged: they are aligned on a track through a laser targeting system, forming a complex curve through space. Such specialized acquisition systems, however, are expensive and require tremendous efforts to construct.

Creating the bullet-time effects has been made more flexible by using image-based rendering techniques. Classic methods rely on geometric information (e.g., visual hulls [1], depth maps [2], and optical flow [3,4]) to interpolate novel perspectives from sampled views. Latest approaches can handle fewer number of images but still generally require large overlap between the neighboring views to ensure reliable 3D reconstruction and then view interpolation. In image-based modeling, view morphing has been adopted for synthesizing smooth transitions under strong viewpoint variations. The seminal work of Seitz and Dyer [5] shows that shape-preserving morphing can be achieved by linearly interpolating corresponding pixels in two rectified images. Most recently, deep learning based techniques such as deep view morphing (DVM) [6] provides a more generic scheme by exploiting redundant patterns in the training data. By far, state-of-the-art methods unanimously assume linear camera paths and have not shown success in creating the 360° effects such as the bullet-time.

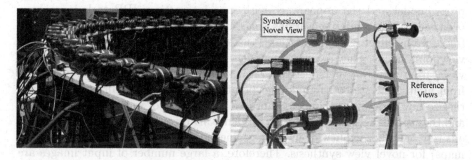

Fig. 1. Left: Specialized acquisition system with numerous cameras is often needed for producing the bullet-time effect; Right: We propose to morph transition images on a circular path from a sparse set of view samples for rendering such effect.

In this paper, we present a novel learning-based solution that is capable of producing the bullet-time effect from only a small set of images. Specifically, we design a view morphing framework that can synthesize smooth and realistic transitions along *a circular view path* using as few as three reference images (as shown in Fig. 1). We apply a novel cyclic rectification technique to align the reference images onto a common circle. Cyclic rectification allows us to rectify groups of three images with minimal projective distortions. We then feed the rectified results into a novel deep network for novel view synthesis. Our network consists of an encoder-decoder network for predicting the motion fields and visibility masks as well as a blending network for image interpolation. By using a third intermediate image, our network can reliably handle occlusions and large view angle changes (up to 120°).

We perform comprehensive experiments on synthetic and real data to validate our approach. We show that our framework outperforms the state-of-the-arts [6–8] in both visual quality and errors. For synthetic experiments, we test on the SURREAL [9] and ShapeNet datasets [10] and demonstrate the benefits of our technique on producing 360° rendering of dynamic human models and complex 3D objects. As shown in Fig. 1, we set up a three-camera system to capture real 3D human motions and demonstrate high quality novel view reconstruction. Our morphed view sequence can be used for generating the bullet-time effect.

2   Related Work

Image-based Rendering. Our work belongs to image-based rendering (IBR) that generates novel views directly from input images. The most notable techniques are light field rendering [11] and Lumigraph [12]. Light field rendering synthesizes novel views by filtering and interpolating view samples while lumigraph applies coarse geometry to compensate for non-uniform sampling. More recently, Penner *et al.* [13] utilizes a soft 3D reconstruction to improve the quality of view synthesis from a light field input. Rematas *et al.* [14] aligns the proxy model and the appearance with user interaction. IBR techniques have been widely for rendering various space-time visual effects [4,15], such as the freeze-frame effect. Carranza *et al.* [1] uses a multi-view system to produce free-viewpoint videos. They recover 3D models from silhouettes for synthesizing novel views from arbitrary perspectives. Zitnick *et al.* [2] use depth maps estimated from multi-view stereo to guide viewpoint interpolation. Ballan *et al.* [16] synthesize novel views from images captured by a group of un-structured cameras and they use structure-from-motion for dense 3D reconstruction. All these methods rely on either explicit or implicit geometric proxy (*e.g.*, 3D models or depth maps) for novel view synthesis. Therefore, a large number of input images are needed to infer reliable geometry of the scene/object. Our approach aims at synthesizing high-quality novel views using only three images without estimating the geometry. This is enabled by using a deep convolutional network that encodes the geometric information from input images into feature tensors.

Image Morphing. The class of IBR technique that is most close to our work is image morphing, which reconstructs smooth transitions between two input images. The key idea is to establish dense correspondences for interpolating colors from the source images. Earlier works study morphing between arbitrary objects using feature correspondences [3,17–19]. While our work focuses on generating realistic natural transitions between different views of the same object. The seminal work of Seitz and Dyer [5] shows that such shape-preserving morphing can be achieved by linear interpolation of corresponding pixels in two rectified images. The morphing follows the linear path between the two original optical centers. To obtain dense correspondences, either stereo matching [4,20] or optical flow [15] can be used, depending on whether the cameras are pre-calibrated. Drastic viewpoint change and occlusions often downgrade the morphing quality by introducing ghosting artifacts. Some methods adopt auxiliary geometry such as silhouettes [21] and triangulated surfaces [22] to alleviate this problem. Mahajan *et al.* [23] propose a path-based image interpolation framework that operates in the gradient domain to reduce blurry and ghosting artifacts. Our approach morphs intermediate views along a circular path and by using a third intermediate image in the middle, we can handle occlusions well without using geometry.

CNN-based Image Synthesis. In recent years, convolutional neural networks (CNNs) have been successfully applied on various image synthesis tasks. Doso-vitskiy *et al.* [24] propose a generative CNN to synthesize models given exist-ing instances. Tatarchenko *et al.* [25] use CNN to generate arbitrary perspectives of an object from one image and recover the object's 3D model using the syn-thesized views. Niklause *et al.* [26,27] apply CNN to interpolate video frames. These methods use CNN to directly predict pixel colors from scratch and often suffer from blurriness and distortions. Jaderberg *et al.* [28] propose to insert dif-ferentiable layers to CNN in order to explicitly perform geometric transforma-tions on images. This design allows CNN to exploit geometric cues (*e.g.*, depths, optical flow, epipolar geometry, *etc.*) for view synthesis. Flynn *et al.* [29] blend CNN-predicted images at different depth layers to generate new views. Kalantari *et al.* [30] apply CNN on light field view synthesis. Zhou *et al.* [8] estimate appear-ance flow by CNN and use it to synthesize new perspectives of the input image. Park *et al.* [7] propose to estimate the flow only in visible areas and then complete the rest by an adversarial image completion network. Most recently, Ji *et al.* [6] propose the deep view morphing (DVM) network that generalizes the classic view morphing scheme [5] to a learning model. This work is closely related to ours since we apply CNN on similar morphing task. However, there are a few key differences: (1) instead of synthesizing one middle view, our approach generates a sequence of morphed images using the motion field; (2) by using a third intermediate image, we can better handle occlusions and large view angle changes (up to 120°); and (3) our morphed view sequence can be considered as taken along a circular camera path that is suitable for rendering freeze-frame effect.

3   Cyclic Rectification

Stereo rectification reduces the search space for correspondence matching to 1D horizontal scan lines and the rectified images can be viewed as taken by two parallel-viewing cameras. It is usually the first step in view morphing algo-rithms since establishing correspondences is important for interpolating interme-diate views. However, such rectification scheme is not optimal for our three-view circular-path morphing: (1) the three images need to be rectified in pairs instead of as a whole group and (2) large projective distortion may appear in boundaries of the rectified images if the three cameras are configured on a circular path. We therefore propose a novel *cyclic rectification* scheme that warps three images to face towards the center of a common circle. Since three non-colinear points are cyclic, we can always fit a circumscribed circle given the center-of-projection (CoP) of the three images. By applying our cyclic rectification, correspondence matching is also constrained to 1D lines in the rectified images. Although the scan lines are not horizontal, they can be easily determined by pixel locations. In Sect. 4.3, we impose the scan line constraints onto the network training to improve matching accuracy.

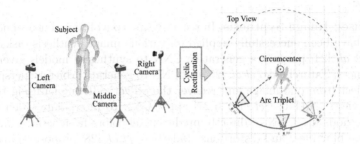

Fig. 2. Cyclic rectification. We configure three cameras along a circular path for capturing the reference images. After cyclic rectification, the reference images are aligned on a common circle (*i.e.*, their optical principal axes all pass through the circumcenter) and we call them the *arc triplet*.

Given three reference images $\{\mathcal{I}_l, \mathcal{I}_m, \mathcal{I}_r\}$ and their camera calibration parameters $\{K_i, R_i, t_i | i = l, m, r\}$ (where K_i is intrinsic matrix, R_i and t_i are extrinsic rotation and translation, subscripts l, m, and r stands for "left", "middle", and "right"), to perform cyclic rectification, we first fit the center of circumscribed circle (i.e., the circumcenter) using the cameras' CoPs and then construct homographies for warping the three images. Figure 2 illustrates this scheme.

Circumcenter Fitting. Let's consider the triangle formed by the three CoPs. The circumcenter of the triangle can be constructed as the intersection point of the edges' perpendicular bisectors. Since the three cameras are calibrated in a common world coordinate, the extrinsic translation vectors $\{t_i | i = l, m, r\}$ are essentially the CoP coordinates. Thus $\{t_i - t_j | i, j = l, r, m; i \neq j\}$ are the edges of the triangle. We first solve the normal $\mathbf{n}$ of the circle plane from

$$\mathbf{n} \cdot (t_i - t_j) = 0 \tag{1}$$

Then the normalized perpendicular bisectors of the edges can be computed as

$$\mathbf{d}_{ij} = \frac{\mathbf{n} \times (t_i - t_j)}{\|t_i - t_j\|} \tag{2}$$

We determine the circumcenter O by triangulating the three perpendicular bisectors $\{\mathbf{d}_{ij} | i, j = l, r, m; i \neq j\}$

$$O = \frac{1}{2}(t_i + t_j) + \alpha_{ij}\mathbf{d}_{ij} \tag{3}$$

where $\{\alpha_{ij} | i, j = l, r, m; i \neq j\}$ are propagation factors along $\mathbf{d}_{ij}$. Since Eq. 3 is an over-determined linear system, O can be easily solved by SVD.

Homographic Warping. Next, we derive the homographies $\{H_i|i = l, r, m\}$ for warping the three reference images $\{\mathcal{I}_l, \mathcal{I}_m, \mathcal{I}_r\}$ such that the rectified images all face towards the circumcenter O. In particular, we transform the camera coordinate in a two-step rotation: we first rotate the y axis to align with the circle plane normal $\mathbf{n}$ and then rotate the z axis to point to the circumcenter O. Given the original camera coordinates $\{\mathbf{x}_i, \mathbf{y}_i, \mathbf{z}_i|i = l, r, m\}$ as calibrated in the extrinsic rotation matrix $R_i = [\mathbf{x}_i, \mathbf{y}_i, \mathbf{z}_i]$, the camera coordinates after cyclic rectification can be calculated as

$$\begin{cases} \mathbf{x}'_i = \mathbf{y}'_i \times \mathbf{z}'_i \\ \mathbf{y}'_i = \mathrm{sgn}(\mathbf{n} \cdot \mathbf{y}_i) \cdot \mathbf{n} \\ \mathbf{z}'_i = \mathrm{sgn}(\mathbf{z}_i \cdot (O - t_i)) \cdot \pi(O - t_i) \end{cases} \tag{4}$$

where $i = r, m, l$; $\mathrm{sgn}(\cdot)$ is the sign function and $\pi(\cdot)$ is the normalization operator. We then formulate the new extrinsic rotation matrix as $R'_i = [\mathbf{x}'_i, \mathbf{y}'_i, \mathbf{z}'_i]$. As a result, the homographies for cyclic rectification can be constructed as $H_i = K_i R'^{\top}_i R_i K_i^{-1}$, $i = r, m, l$.

Finally, we use $\{H_i|i = l, r, m\}$ to warp $\{\mathcal{I}_l, \mathcal{I}_m, \mathcal{I}_r\}$ and the resulting cyclic rectified images $\{\mathcal{C}_l, \mathcal{C}_m, \mathcal{C}_r\}$ are called *arc triplet*.

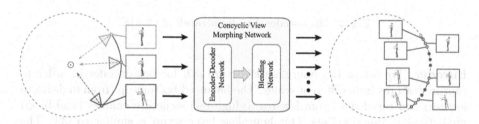

Fig. 3. The overall structure of our *Concyclic View Morphing Network* (CVMN). It takes the arc triplet as input and synthesize sequence of concyclic views.

4   Concyclic View Morphing Network

We design a novel convolutional network that takes the arc triplet as input to synthesize a sequence of evenly distributed concyclic morphing views. We call this network the *Concyclic View Morphing Network* (CVMN). The synthesized images can be viewed as taken along a circular camera path since their CoPs are concyclic. The overall structure of our CVMN is shown in Fig. 3. It consists of two sub-networks: an encoder-decoder network for estimating the motion fields $\{\mathcal{F}_i|i = 1, ..., N\}$ and visibility masks $\{\mathcal{M}_i|i = 1, ..., N\}$ of the morphing views given $\{\mathcal{C}_l, \mathcal{C}_m, \mathcal{C}_r\}$ and a blending network for synthesizing the concyclic view sequence $\{\mathcal{C}_i|i = 1, ..., N\}$ from $\{\mathcal{F}_i|i = 1, ..., N\}$ and $\{\mathcal{M}_i|i = 1, ..., N\}$. Here N represents the total number of images in the output morphing sequence.

4.1   Encoder-Decoder Network

The encoder-decoder network has proved to be effective in establishing pixel correspondences in various applications [31,32]. We therefore adopt this structure for predicting pixel-based motion vectors for morphing intermediate views. In our network, we first use an encoder to extract correlating features among the arc triplet. We then use a two-branch decoder to estimate (1) motion vectors and (2) visibility masks with respect to the left and right reference views. Our encoder-decoder network architecture is illustrated in Fig. 4.

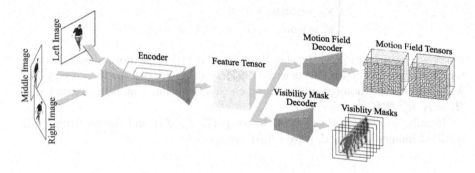

Fig. 4. The encoder-decoder network of CVMN.

Encoder. We adopt the hourglass structure [32] for our encoder in order to capture features from different scales. The balanced bottom-up (from high-res to low-res) and top-down (from low-res to high-res) structure enables pixel-based predictions in our decoders. Our hourglass layer setup is similar to [32]. The encoder outputs a full-resolution feature tensor.

Since our input has three images from the arc triplet, we apply the hourglass encoder in three separate passes (one per image) and then concatenate the output feature tensors. Although it is also possible to first concatenate the three input images and then run the encoder in one pass, such scheme results in high-dimensional input and is computationally impractical for the training process.

Motion Field Decoder. The motion field decoder takes the output feature tensor from the encoder and predicts motion fields for each image in the morphing sequence. Specifically, two motion fields are considered: one w.r.t the left reference image C_l and the other w.r.t. the right reference image C_r. We use the displacement vector between corresponding pixels to represent the motion field and we use backward mapping (from source C_i to target C_l or C_r) for computing the displacement vectors in order to reduce artifacts caused by irregular sampling.

Take $\mathcal{C}_l$ for example and let's consider an intermediate image $\mathcal{C}_i$. Given a pair of corresponding pixels $p_l = (x_l, y_l)$ in $\mathcal{C}_l$ and $p_i = (x_i, y_i)$ in $\mathcal{C}_i$, the displacement vector $\Delta_i^l(p) = (u_i^l(p), v_i^l(p))$ from p_i to p_l can be computed by

$$p_l = p_i + \Delta_i^l(p) \tag{5}$$

The right image based displacement vectors $\{\Delta_i^r(p) = (u_i^r(p), v_i^r(p)) | p = 1, ..., M\}$ (where M is the image resolution) can be computed similarly. By concatenating $\Delta_i^l(p)$ and $\Delta_i^r(p)$, we obtain a 4D motion vector $(u_i^l(p), v_i^l(p), u_i^r(p), v_i^r(p))$ for each pixel p. As a result, the motion field for the entire morphing sequence is composed of four scalar fields: $\mathcal{F} = (U^l, V^l, U^r, V^r)$, where $U^l = \{u_i^l | i = 1, ..., N\}$; V^l, U^r, and V^r follow similar construction.

Structure-wise, we arrange deconvolution and convolution layers alternately to extract motion vectors from the encoded correspondence features. The reason for this intervening layer design is because we found by experiments that appending proper convolution layer after deconvolution can reduce blocky artifacts in our output images. Since our motion field $\mathcal{F}$ has four components (U^l, V^l, U^r, and V^r), we run four instances of the decoder to predict each component in a separate pass. It is worth noting that by encoding features from the middle reference image $\mathcal{C}_m$, the accuracy of motion field estimation is greatly improved.

Visibility Mask Decoder. Large viewpoint change and occlusions cause the visibility issue in view morphing problems: pixels in an intermediate view are partially visible in both left and right reference images. Direct combining the resampled reference images results in severe ghosting artifacts. Similar to [6,8], we use visibility masks to mitigate this problem.

Given an intermediate image $\mathcal{C}_i$, we define two visibility masks $\mathcal{M}_i^l$ and $\mathcal{M}_i^r$ to indicate the per-pixel visibility levels w.r.t. to $\mathcal{C}_l$ and $\mathcal{C}_r$. The larger the value in the mask, the higher the possibility for a pixel to be seen in the reference images. However, instead following a probability model to restrict the mask values within $[0, 1]$, we relax this constraint and allow the masks to take any real numbers greater than zero. We empirically find out that this relaxation help our network converge faster in the training process.

Similar to the motion field decoder, our visibility mask decoder is composed of intervening deconvolution/convolution layers and takes the feature tensor from the encoder as input. At the end of the decoder, we use a ReLU layer to constraint the output values to be greater than zero. Since our visibility masks $\mathcal{M}$ has two components ($\mathcal{M}^l$ and $\mathcal{M}^r$), we run two instances of the decoder to estimate each component in a separate pass.

4.2 Blending Network

Finally, we use a blending network to synthesize a sequence of concyclic views $\{\mathcal{C}_i | i = 1, ..., N\}$ from the left and right reference images $\mathcal{C}_l, \mathcal{C}_r$ and the decoder outputs $\{\mathcal{F}_i | i = 1, ..., N\}, \{\mathcal{M}_i | i = 1, ..., N\}$, where N is the total number of morphed images. Our network architecture is shown in Fig. 5.

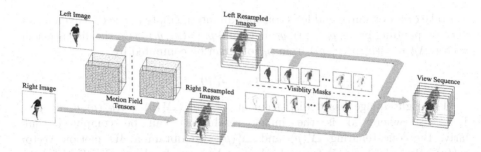

Fig. 5. The blending network of CVMN.

We first adopt two sampling layers to resample pixels in C_l and C_r using the motion field $\mathcal{F} = (U^l, V^l, U^r, V^r)$. The resampled images can be computed by $\mathcal{R}(C_{\{l,r\}}; U^{\{l,r\}}, V^{\{l,r\}})$, where $\mathcal{R}(\cdot)$ is an operator that shifts corresponding pixels in the source images according to a motion vector (see Eq. (5)). Then we blend the resampled left and right images weighted by the visibility masks $\mathcal{M} = (\mathcal{M}^l, \mathcal{M}^r)$. Notice that our decode relaxes the range constraint of the output masks, we therefore need to normalize the visibility masks: $\bar{\mathcal{M}}_i^l = \frac{\mathcal{M}_i^l}{(\mathcal{M}_i^l + \mathcal{M}_i^r)}$, $\bar{\mathcal{M}}_i^r = \frac{\mathcal{M}_i^r}{(\mathcal{M}_i^l + \mathcal{M}_i^r)}$, where $i = 1, ... N$. The final output image sequence $\{C_i | i = 1, ..., N\}$ can be computed by

$$C_i = \mathcal{R}(C_l; U_i^l, V_i^l) \otimes \bar{\mathcal{M}}_i^l + \mathcal{R}(C_r; U_i^r, V_i^r) \otimes \bar{\mathcal{M}}_i^r \qquad (6)$$

where $i = 1, ..., N$ and $\otimes$ is the pixel-wise multiplication operator.

Although all components in the blending network are fixed operations and do not have learnable weights, they are all differentiable layers [28] that can be chained into backpropagation.

4.3 Network Training

To guide the training process of our CVMN, we design a loss function that considers the following three metrics: (1) resemblance between the estimated novel views and the desired ground truth; (2) consistency between left-warped and right-warped images (since we consider motion fields in both directions); and (3) the epipolar line constraints in source images for motion field estimation. Assume Y is the underlying ground-truth view sequence and $\mathcal{R}^{\{l,r\}} = \mathcal{R}(C_{\{l,r\}}; U^{\{l,r\}}, V^{\{l,r\}})$, our loss function can be written as

$$\mathcal{L} = \sum_{i=1}^{N} \|Y_i - C_i\|_1 + \lambda \|(\mathcal{R}_i^l - \mathcal{R}_i^r) \otimes \bar{\mathcal{M}}_i^l \otimes \bar{\mathcal{M}}_i^r\|_2 + \gamma \Phi(\rho_i, p_i) \qquad (7)$$

where λ, γ are hyper parameters for balancing the error terms; $\Phi(\cdot)$ is a function calculating the distance between a line and a point; p_i is a pixel in C_i warped by the motion field $\mathcal{F}_i$; and ρ is an epipolar line in source images. The detailed derivation of ρ from p_i can be found in the supplemental material.

5 Experiments

We perform comprehensive experiments on synthetic and real data to validate our approach. For synthetic experiments, we test on the SURREAL [9] and ShapeNet datasets [10] and compare with the state-of-the-art methods DVM [6], TVSN [7] and VSAF [8]. Our approach outperforms these methods in both visual quality and quantitative errors. For real experiments, we set up a three-camera system to capture real 3D human motions and demonstrate high quality novel view reconstruction. Finally, we show a bullet-time rendering result using our morphed view sequence.

For training our CVMN, we use the Adam solver with $\beta_1 = 0.9$ and $\beta_2 = 0.999$. The initial learning rate is 0.0001. We use the same settings for training the DVM. We run our network on a single Nvidia Titan X and choose a batch size of 8. We evaluate our approach on different images resolutions (up to 256). The architecture details of our CVMN, such as number of layers, kernel sizes, etc., can be found in the supplemental material.

Fig. 6. Morphing sequences synthesized by CVMN. Due to space limit, we only pick seven samples from the whole sequence (24 images in total). The boxed images are the input reference views. More results can be found in the supplemental material.

5.1 Experiments on SURREAL

Data Preparation. The SURREAL dataset [9] includes a large number of human motion sequences parametrized by SMPL [33]. Continuous motion frames are provided in each sequence. To generate the training and testing data for human motion, we first gather a set of 3D human models and textures. We export 30439 3D human models from 312 sequences. We select 929 texture images and randomly assign them to the 3D models. We then use the textured 3D models to render image sequences for training and testing. Specifically, we move our camera on a circular path and set it to look at the center of the circle for rendering concyclic views. For a motion sequence, we render images from 30 different elevation planes and on each plane we render a sequence of 24 images where the viewing angle change varies from $30°$ to $120°$ from the left-most image to the right-most image. In total, we generate around 1M motion sequences. We randomly pick one tenth of the data for testing and the rest are used for training.

Fig. 7. Comparison with DVM. We pick the middle view in our synthesized sequence to compare with DVM. In these examples, we avoid using the middle view as our reference image.

In each training epoch, we shuffle and iterate over all the sequences and thus every sequence is labeled. We generate arc triplets from the motion sequences. Given a sequence $S = \{C_1, C_2, \cdots, C_{24}\}$, we always pick C_1 as C_l and C_{24} as C_r. The third intermediate reference image C_m is picked from S following a Gaussian distribution, since we expect our CVMN to tolerate variations in camera position.

Table 1. Quantitative evaluation on the SURREAL dataset.

Architecture	CVMN	CVMN-I2	CVMN-O3	DVM [6]
MAE	**1.453**	2.039	2.175	3.315
SSIM	**0.983**	0.966	0.967	0.945

Ablation Studies. In order to show our network design is optimal, we first compare our CVMN with its two variants: (1) CVMN-I2, which only uses two images (C_l and C_r) as input to the encoder; and (2) CVMN-O3, which uses all three images from the arc triplet as input to our decoders for estimating $\mathcal{F}$ and $\mathcal{M}$ of the whole triplet including C_m (in this case, $\mathcal{F}$ and $\mathcal{M}$ have an extra dimension for C_m), and the blending network also blends C_m. All the other settings remain the same for the three network variations. The hyper-parameter λ, γ in Eq. (7) are set to 10 and 1 for all training sessions. We use the mean absolute error (MAE) and structural similarity index (SSIM) as error metric when comparing the predicted sequence with the ground-truth sequence.

Quantitative evaluations (as shown in Table 1) demonstrate that our proposed network outperforms its two variants. This is because the third intermediate view $\mathcal{C}_m$ help us better handle occlusion and the encode sufficiently extracts the additional information. Figure 6 shows two motion sequences synthesized by our CVMN. The three reference views are marked in boxes. We can see that shapes and textures are well preserved in our synthesized images. Qualitative comparisons can be found in the supplemental material.

Comparison with Deep View Morphing (DVM). We also compare our approach with the state-of-the-art DVM [6]. We implement DVM following the description in the paper. To train the DVM, we randomly pick a pair of images from a sequence $\mathcal{S} = \{\mathcal{C}_1, \mathcal{C}_2, \cdots, \mathcal{C}_{24}\}$ and use $\mathcal{C}_{\lfloor (i+j)/2 \rfloor}$ as label. We perform quantitative and qualitative comparisons with DVM as shown in Table 1 and Fig. 7. In both evaluations, we achieve better results. As shown in Fig. 7, images synthesized by DVM suffer from ghosting artifacts this is because DVM cannot handle cases with complex occlusions (e.g., moving arms in some sequences).

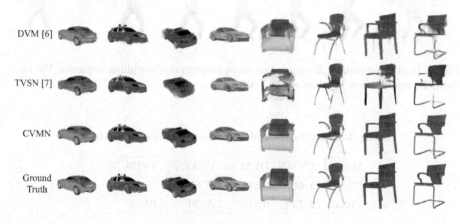

Fig. 8. Quanlitative comparisons with DVM [6] and TVSN [7] on ShapeNet.

5.2 Experiments on ShapeNet

To demonstrate that our approach is generic and also works well on arbitrary 3D objects, we perform experiments on the ShapeNet dataset [10]. Specifically, we test on the car and chair models. The data preparation process is similar to the SURREAL dataset. Except that the viewing angle variation is between 30° to 90°. We use 20% of the models for testing and the rest for training. In total, the number of training sequences for "car" and "chair" are around 100K and 200K. The training process is also similar to SURREAL.

We perform both quantitative and qualitative comparisons with DVM [6], VSAF [8] and TVSN [7]. For VSAF and TVSN, we use the pre-trained model provided by the authors. When rendering their testing data, the viewing angle variations are picked from $\{40°, 60°, 80°\}$ in order to have fair comparisons. For quantitative comparisons, we use MAE as the error metric and the results are shown in Table 2. The visual quality comparison is shown in Fig. 8. TVSN does not work well on chair models and again DVM suffers from the ghosting artifacts. Our approach works well on both categories and the synthesized images are highly close to the ground truth.

Our Method   DVM [6]

Fig. 9. Real scene results. We show four samples from our morphing sequence. We also show the middle view synthesized by DVM.

Table 2. Quantitative evaluation on the ShapeNet dataset.

Method	CVMN	DVM [6]	VSAF [8]	TVSN [7]
Car	**1.608**	3.441	7.828	5.380
Chair	**2.777**	5.579	20.54	10.02

5.3   Experiments on Real Scenes

We also test our approach on real captured motion sequences. We build a three-camera system to capture real 3D human motions for testing. This setup is shown in Fig. 1. The three cameras are well synchronized and calibrated using structure-from-motion (SfM). We moved the camera positions when capturing different sequences in order to test on inputs with different viewing angle variations. Overall, the viewing angle variations between the left and right cameras are between $30°$ to $60°$. We first pre-process the captured images to correct the radial distortion and remove the background. Then we apply the cyclic rectification to obtain the arc triplets. Finally, we feed the arc triplets into our CVMN to synthesize the morphing sequences. Here we use the CVMN model trained on SURREAL dataset. Figure 9 shows samples from the resulting morphing sequences. Although the real data is more challenging due to noise, dynamic range, and lighting variations, our approach can still generate high quality results. This shows that our approach is both accurate and robust. We also compare with the results produced by DVM. However, there exists severe ghosting due to large viewpoint variations.

Fig. 10. Bullet-time effect rendering result. We show 21 samples out of the 144 views in our bullet-time rendering sequence. We also show a visual hull reconstruction from the view sequence.

5.4   Bullet-Time Effect Rendering

Finally, we demonstrate rendering the bullet-time effect using our synthesized view sequence. Since our synthesized views are aligned on a circular path, they are suitable for creating the bullet-time effect. To render the effect in 360°, we use 6 arc triplets composed to 12 images (neighboring triplets are sharing one image) to sample the full circle. We then generate morphing sequencing for each triplet using our approach. The motion sequences are picked from the SURREAL dataset. Figure 10 shows sample images in our bullet-time rendering sequence. Complete videos and more results are available in the supplemental material. We also perform visual hull reconstruction using the image sequence. The accurate reconstruction indicates that our synthesized views are not only visually pleasant but also geometrically correct.

6   Conclusion and Discussion

In this paper, we have presented a CNN-based view morphing framework for synthesizing intermediate views along a circular view path from three reference images. We proposed a novel cyclic rectification method for aligning the three images in one pass. Further, we developed a concyclic view morphing network for synthesizing smooth transitions from motion field and per-pixel visibility. Our approach has been validated on both synthetic and real data. We also demonstrated high quality bullet time effect rendering using our framework.

However, there are several limitations in our approach. First, our approach cannot properly handle objects with specular highlights since our network assumes Lambertian surfaces when establishing correspondences. A possible solution is to consider realistic reflectance models (*e.g.*, [34]) in our network. Second, backgrounds are not considered in our current network. Therefore, accurate background subtraction is required for our network to work well. In the future, we plan to apply semantic learning in our reference images to achieve accurate and consistent background segmentation.

References

1. Carranza, J., Theobalt, C., Magnor, M.A., Seidel, H.P.: Free-viewpoint video of human actors. ACM Trans. Graph. **22**(3), 569–577 (2003)
2. Zitnick, C.L., Kang, S.B., Uyttendaele, M., Winder, S., Szeliski, R.: High-quality video view interpolation using a layered representation. ACM Trans. Graph. **23**(3), 600–608 (2004)
3. Liao, J., Lima, R.S., Nehab, D., Hoppe, H., Sander, P.V., Yu, J.: Automating image morphing using structural similarity on a halfway domain. ACM Trans. Graph. **33**(5), 168:1–168:12 (2014)
4. Linz, C., Lipski, C., Rogge, L., Theobalt, C., Magnor, M.: Space-time visual effects as a post-production process. In: Proceedings of the 1st International Workshop on 3D Video Processing. ACM (2010)
5. Seitz, S.M., Dyer, C.R.: View morphing. In: Proceedings of the 23rd Annual Conference on Computer Graphics and Interactive Techniques. In: SIGGRAPH 1996, pp. 21–30. ACM (1996)
6. Ji, D., Kwon, J., McFarland, M., Savarese, S.: Deep view morphing. In: IEEE Conference on Computer Vision and Pattern Recognition (2017)
7. Park, E., Yang, J., Yumer, E., Ceylan, D., Berg, A.C.: Transformation-grounded image generation network for novel 3D view synthesis. In: IEEE Conference on Computer Vision and Pattern Recognition (2017)
8. Zhou, T., Tulsiani, S., Sun, W., Malik, J., Efros, A.A.: View synthesis by appearance flow. In: Leibe, B., Matas, J., Sebe, N., Welling, M. (eds.) ECCV 2016. LNCS, vol. 9908, pp. 286–301. Springer, Cham (2016). https://doi.org/10.1007/978-3-319-46493-0_18
9. Varol, G., et al.: Learning from Synthetic Humans. In: The IEEE Conference on Computer Vision and Pattern Recognition (2017)
10. Chang, A.X., et al.: ShapeNet: an Information-Rich 3D Model Repository. Technical report arXiv:1512.03012 (2015)
11. Levoy, M., Hanrahan, P.: Light field rendering. In: Proceedings of the 23rd Annual Conference on Computer Graphics and Interactive Techniques, SIGGRAPH 1996, pp. 31–42. ACM (1996)
12. Gortler, S.J., Grzeszczuk, R., Szeliski, R., Cohen, M.F.: The lumigraph. In: Proceedings of the 23rd Annual Conference on Computer Graphics and Interactive Techniques. In: SIGGRAPH 1996, pp. 43–54. ACM (1996)
13. Penner, E., Zhang, L.: Soft 3D reconstruction for view synthesis. ACM Trans. Graph. **36**(6), 235:1–235:11 (2017)
14. Rematas, K., Nguyen, C.H., Ritschel, T., Fritz, M., Tuytelaars, T.: Novel views of objects from a single image. IEEE Trans. Pattern Anal. Mach. Intell. **39**(8), 1576–1590 (2017)

15. Lipski, C., Linz, C., Berger, K., Sellent, A., Magnor, M.: Virtual video camera: image-based viewpoint navigation through space and time. In: Computer Graphics Forum, pp. 2555–2568. Blackwell Publishing Ltd., Oxford (2010)
16. Ballan, L., Brostow, G.J., Puwein, J., Pollefeys, M.: Unstructured video-based rendering: Interactive exploration of casually captured videos. ACM Trans. Graph. **29**(4), 87:1–87:11 (2010)
17. Zhang, Z., Wang, L., Guo, B., Shum, H.Y.: Feature-based light field morphing. ACM Trans. Graph. **21**(3), 457–464 (2002)
18. Beier, T., Neely, S.: Feature-based image metamorphosis. In: Proceedings of the 19th Annual Conference on Computer Graphics and Interactive Techniques. In: SIGGRAPH 1992, pp. 35–42 (1992)
19. Lee, S., Wolberg, G., Shin, S.Y.: Polymorph: morphing among multiple images. IEEE Comput. Graph. Appl. **18**(1), 58–71 (1998)
20. Quenot, G.M.: Image matching using dynamic programming: application to stereovision and image interpolation. In: Image Communication (1996)
21. Chaurasia, G., Sorkine-Hornung, O., Drettakis, G.: Silhouette-aware warping for image-based rendering. In: Computer Graphics Forum (Proceedings of the Eurographics Symposium on Rendering), vol. 30, no. 4. Blackwell Publishing Ltd., Oxford (2011)
22. Germann, M., Popa, T., Keiser, R., Ziegler, R., Gross, M.: Novel-view synthesis of outdoor sport events using an adaptive view-dependent geometry. Comput. Graph. Forum **31**, 325–333 (2012)
23. Mahajan, D., Huang, F.C., Matusik, W., Ramamoorthi, R., Belhumeur, P.: Moving gradients: a path-based method for plausible image interpolation. ACM Trans. Graph. **28**(3), 42:1–42:11 (2009)
24. Dosovitskiy, A., Springenberg, J.T., Brox, T.: Learning to generate chairs with convolutional neural networks. In: IEEE Conference on Computer Vision and Pattern Recognition (2015)
25. Tatarchenko, M., Dosovitskiy, A., Brox, T.: Multi-view 3D models from single images with a convolutional network. In: European Conference on Computer Vision (2016)
26. Niklaus, S., Mai, L., Liu, F.: Video frame interpolation via adaptive convolution. In: IEEE Conference on Computer Vision and Pattern Recognition (2017)
27. Niklaus, S., Mai, L., Liu, F.: Video frame interpolation via adaptive separable convolution. In: IEEE International Conference on Computer Vision (2017)
28. Jaderberg, M., Simonyan, K., Zisserman, A., Kavukcuoglu, K.: Spatial transformer networks. In: Proceedings of the 28th International Conference on Neural Information Processing Systems, pp. 2017–2025 (2015)
29. Flynn, J., Neulander, I., Philbin, J., Snavely, N.: Deep stereo: learning to predict new views from the world's imagery. In: IEEE Conference on Computer Vision and Pattern Recognition (2016)
30. Kalantari, N.K., Wang, T.C., Ramamoorthi, R.: Learning-based view synthesis for light field cameras. ACM Trans. Graph. **35**(6), 193:1–193:10 (2016)
31. Ilg, E., Mayer, N., Saikia, T., Keuper, M., Dosovitskiy, A., Brox, T.: FlowNet 2.0: evolution of optical flow estimation with deep networks. In: IEEE Conference on Computer Vision and Pattern Recognition (2017)
32. Newell, A., Yang, K., Deng, J.: Stacked hourglass networks for human pose estimation. In: Leibe, B., Matas, J., Sebe, N., Welling, M. (eds.) ECCV 2016. LNCS, vol. 9912, pp. 483–499. Springer, Cham (2016). https://doi.org/10.1007/978-3-319-46484-8_29

33. Loper, M., Mahmood, N., Romero, J., Pons-Moll, G., Black, M.J.: SMPL: a skinned multi-person linear model. ACM Trans. Graph. **34**(6), 248:1–248:16 (2015). (Proc. SIGGRAPH Asia)
34. Rematas, K., Ritschel, T., Fritz, M., Gavves, E., Tuytelaars, T.: Deep reflectance maps. In: IEEE Conference on Computer Vision and Pattern Recognition (2016)

Compositional Learning for Human Object Interaction

Keizo Kato[1]([✉]), Yin Li[2], and Abhinav Gupta[2]

[1] Fujitsu Laboratories Ltd., Kawasaki, Japan
kato.keizo@jp.fujitsu.com
[2] Carnegie Mellon University, Pittsburgh, USA
yinl2@andrew.cmu.edu, abhinavg@cs.cmu.edu

Abstract. The world of human-object interactions is rich. While generally we sit on chairs and sofas, if need be we can even sit on TVs or top of shelves. In recent years, there has been progress in modeling actions and human-object interactions. However, most of these approaches require lots of data. It is not clear if the learned representations of actions are generalizable to new categories. In this paper, we explore the problem of zero-shot learning of human-object interactions. Given limited verb-noun interactions in training data, we want to learn a model than can work even on unseen combinations. To deal with this problem, In this paper, we propose a novel method using external knowledge graph and graph convolutional networks which learns how to compose classifiers for verb-noun pairs. We also provide benchmarks on several dataset for zero-shot learning including both image and video. We hope our method, dataset and baselines will facilitate future research in this direction.

1 Introduction

Our daily actions and activities are rich and complex. Consider the examples in Fig. 1(a). The same verb "sit" is combined with different nouns (chair, bed, floor) to describe visually distinctive actions ("sit on chair" vs. "sit on floor"). Similarly, we can interact with the same object (TV) in many different ways (turn on, clean, watch). Even small sets of common verbs and nouns will create a huge combination of action labels. It is highly unlikely that we can capture action samples covering all these combinations. What if we want to recognize an action category that we had never seen before, e.g., the one in Fig. 1(b)?

This problem is known as zero shot learning, where categories at testing time are not presented during training. It has been widely explored for object recognition [1, 11, 12, 15, 31, 37, 60]. And there is an emerging interest for zero-shot action recognition [18, 21, 24, 35, 51, 55]. How are actions different from objects in zero shot learning? What we know is that human actions are naturally compositional and humans have amazing ability to achieve similar goals with different objects and tools. For example, while one can use hammer for the hitting the nail, we can

---

Work was done when K. Kato was at CMU.

© Springer Nature Switzerland AG 2018
V. Ferrari et al. (Eds.): ECCV 2018, LNCS 11218, pp. 247–264, 2018.
https://doi.org/10.1007/978-3-030-01264-9_15

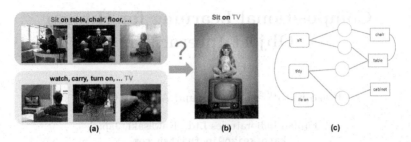

Fig. 1. (a–b) many of our daily actions are compositional. These actions can be described by motion (verbs) and the objects (nouns). We build on this composition for zero shot recognition of human-object interactions. Our method encodes motion and object cues as visual embeddings of verbs (e.g., sit) and nouns (e.g., TV), uses external knowledge for learning to assemble these embeddings into actions. We demonstrate that our method can generalize to unseen action categories (e.g., sit on a TV). (c) a graph representation of interactions: pairs of verb-noun nodes are linked via action nodes (circle), and verb-verb/noun-noun pairs can be connected.

also use a hard-cover book for the same. We can thus leverage this unique composition to help recognizing novel actions. To this end, we address the problem of zero shot action recognition. And we specifically focus on the compositional learning of daily human object interactions, which can be described by a pair of verb and noun (e.g., "wash a mirror" or "hold a laptop").

This compositional learning faces a major question: How can a model learn to compose a novel action within the context? For example, "Sitting on a TV" looks very different from "Sitting on a chair" since the underlying body motion and body poses are quite different. Even if the model has learned to recognize individual concepts like "TV" and "Sitting", it will still fail to generalize. Indeed, many of our seemly effortless interactions with novel objects build on our prior knowledge. If the model knows that people also sit on floor, vase are put on floor, and vase can be put on TV. It might be able to assemble the visual concepts of "Sitting" and "TV" to recognize the rare action of "Sitting on a TV". Moreover, what if model knows "sitting" is similar to "lean" and "TV" is similar to "Jukebox", can model also recognize "lean into Jukebox"? Thus, we propose to explore using external knowledge to bridge the gap of contextuality, and to help the modeling of compositionality for human object interactions.

Specifically, we extract Subject, Verb and Object (SVO) triplets from knowledge bases [8,30] to build an external knowledge graph. These triplets capture a large range of human object interactions, and encode our knowledge about actions. Each verb (motion) or noun (object) is a node in the graph with its word embedding as the node's feature. Each SVO-triplet defines an action node and a path between the corresponding verb and noun nodes via the action node (See Fig. 1(c)). These action nodes start with all zero features, and must learn its representation by propagating information along the graph during training. This information passing is achieved by using a multi-layer graph convolutional network [29]. Our method jointly trains a projection of visual features and the graph convolutional network, and thus learns to transform both visual features and action nodes into a shared embedding space. Our zero shot recognition of actions is thus reduced to nearest neighbor search in this space.

We present a comprehensive evaluation of our method on image datasets (HICO [7] and a subset of Visual Genome [30]), as well as a more challenging *video* dataset (Charades [48]). We define proper benchmarks for zero shot learning of human-object interactions, and compare our results to a set of baselines. Our method demonstrates strong results for unseen combinations of known concepts. Our results outperforms the state-of-the-art methods on HICO and Visual Genome, and performs comparably to previous methods on Charades. We also show that our method can generalize to unseen concepts, with a performance level that is much better than chance. We hope our method and benchmark will facilitate future research in this direction.

2 Related Work

Zero Shot Learning. Our work follows the zero-shot learning setting [53]. Early works focused on attribute based learning [26,31,41,58]. These methods follow a two-stage approach by first predicting the attributes, and then inferring the class labels. Recent works make use of semantic embeddings to model relationships between different categories. These methods learn to map either visual features [15,55], or labels [1,11,12,37], or both of them [52,52,56] into a common semantic space. Recognition is then achieved by measuring the distance between the visual inputs and the labels in this space. Similar to attribute based approaches, our method considers interactions as verb-noun pairs. However, we do not explicit predict individual verbs or nouns. Similar to embedding based approaches, we learn semantic embeddings of interactions. Yet we focus on the compositional learning [40] by leveraging external knowledge.

Our work is also related to previous works that combine side information for zero shot recognition. For example, Rohrbach et al. [43] transferred part attributes from linguistic data to recognize unseen objects. Fu et al. [16] used hyper-graph label propagation to fuse information from multiple semantic representations. Li et al. [33] explored semi-supervised learning in a zero shot setting. Inspired by these methods, our method connects actions and objects using information from external knowledge base. Yet we use graph convolution to propagate the semantic representations of verbs and nouns, and learns to assemble them into actions. Moreover, previous works considered the recognition of objects in images. Our work thus stands out by addressing the recognition of human object interactions in both images and videos. We believe our problem is an ideal benchmark for compositional learning of how to build generalizable representations.

Modeling Human Object Interactions. Modeling human object interactions has a rich history in both computer vision and psychology. It starts from the idea of "affordances" introduced by Gibson [17]. There have been lots of work in using semantics for functional understanding of objects [49]. However, none of these early attempts scaled up due to lack of data and brittle inference under noisy perception. Recently, the idea of modeling human object interactions has made a comeback [19]. Several approaches have looked at modeling semantic relationships [10,20,57], action-3D relationships [14] or completely data-driven approach [13]. However, none of them considered the use of external knowledge.

Moreover, recent works focused on creating large scale image datasets for human object interactions [7,30,36]. However, even the current largest dataset—Visual Genome [30] only contains a small subset of our daily interactions (hundreds), and did not capture the full dynamics of interactions that exist in video. Our work takes a step forward by using external knowledge for recognizing unseen interactions, and exploring the recognition of interactions for a challenging video dataset [48]. We believe an important test of intelligence and reasoning is the ability to compose primitives into novel concepts. Therefore, we hope our work can provide a step for visual reasoning based approaches to come in future.

Zero Shot Action Recognition. Our paper is inspired by compositional representations for human object interactions. There has been a lot of work in psychology and early computer vision on compositions, starting from original work by Biederman [4] and Hoffman et al. [23]. More recently, several works started to address the zero shot recognition of actions. Similar to attribute based object recognition, Liu et al. [35] learned to recognize novel actions using attributes. Going beyond recognition, Habibian et al. [21] proposed to model concepts in videos for event detection. Inspired by zero shot object recognition, Xu et al. presented a embedding based method for actions [55]. Other efforts include the exploration of text descriptions [18,51], joint segmentation of actors and actions [54], and model domain shift of actions [56]. However, these methods simply treat actions as labels and did not consider their compositionality.

Perhaps the most relevant work is from [24,25,28]. Jain et al. [24,25] noticed a strong relation between objects and actions, and thus proposed to use object classifier for zero shot action recognition. As a step forward, Kalogeition et al. [28] proposed to jointly detect objects and actions in videos. Instead of using objects alone, our method models both body motion (verb) and objects (noun). More importantly, we explore using external knowledge for assembling these concepts into novel actions. Our method thus provides a revisit to the problem of human object interactions from the perspective of compositionality.

Compositional Learning for Vision and Language. Compositional learning has been explored in Visual Question Answering (VQA). Andreas et al. [2,3] decomposed VQA task into sequence of modular sub-problems—each modeled by a neural network. Their method assembles a network from individual modules based on the syntax of a question, and predicts the answer using the instance-specific network. This idea was further extended by Johnson et al. [27], where deep models are learned to generate programs from a question and to execute the programs on the image to predict the answer. Our method shares the core idea of compositional learning, yet focuses on human object interactions. Moreover, modeling SVO pairs using graph representations has been discussed in [45,50,59]. Sadeghi et al. [45] constructed a knowledge graph of SVO nodes similar to our graph representation. However, their method aimed at verifying SVO relationships using visual data. A factor graph model with SVO nodes was presented in for video captioning [50], yet without using deep models. More recently, Zellers et al. [59] proposed a deep model for generating scene graphs of objects and their relations from an image. However, their method can not handle unseen concepts.

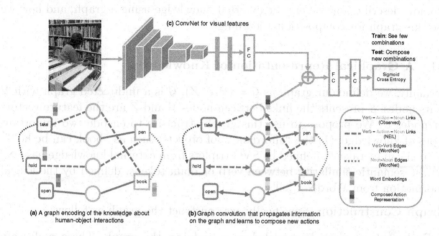

Fig. 2. Overview of our approach. (a) our graph that encodes external SVO pairs. Each verb or noun is represented as a node and comes with its word embeddings as the node's features. Every interaction defined by a SVO pair creates a new action node (orange ones) on the graph, which is linked to the corresponding noun and verb nodes. We can also add links between verbs and nouns, e.g., using WordNet [39]. (b) the graph convolution operation. Our learning will propagate features on the graph, and fill in new representations for the action nodes. These action features are further merged with visual features from a convolutional network (c) to learn a similarity metric between the action concepts and the visual inputs. (Color figure online)

3   Method

Given an input image or video, we denote its visual features as x_i and its action label as y_i. We focus on human object interactions, where y_i can be further decomposed into a verb y_i^v (e.g., "take"/"open") and a noun y_i^n (e.g., "phone"/"table"). For clarity, we drop the subscript i when it is clear that we refer to a single image or video. In our work, we use visual features from convolutional networks for x, and represent verbs y^v and nouns y^n by their word embeddings as z^v and z^n.

Our goal is to explore the use of knowledge for zero shot action recognition. Specifically, we propose to learn a score function ϕ such that

$$p(y|x) = \phi(x, y^v, y^n; \mathcal{K}) \tag{1}$$

where $\mathcal{K}$ is the prior knowledge about actions. Our key idea is to represent $\mathcal{K}$ via a graph structure and use this graph for learning to compose representations of novel actions. An overview of our method is shown in Fig. 2. The core component of our model is a graph convolutional network $g(y^v, y^n; \mathcal{K})$ (See Fig. 2(a–b)). g learns to compose action representation z_a based on embeddings of verbs and nouns, as well as the knowledge of SVO triplets and lexical information. The output z_a is further compared to the visual feature x for zero shot recognition. We now describe how we encode external knowledge using a graph, and how we use this graph for compositional learning.

3.1   A Graphical Representation of Knowledge

Formally, we define our graph as $\mathcal{G} = (\mathcal{V}, \mathcal{E}, Z)$. $\mathcal{G}$ is a undirected graph with $\mathcal{V}$ as its nodes. $\mathcal{E}$ presents the links between nodes $\mathcal{V}$ and Z are the feature vectors for nodes $\mathcal{E}$. We propose to use this graph structure to encode two important types of knowledge: (1) the "affordance" of objects, such as "book can be hold" or "pen can be taken", defined by SVO triplets from external knowledge base [8]; (2) the semantic similarity between verb or noun tokens, defined by the lexical information from WordNet [39].

Graph Construction. Specifically, we construct the graph as follows.

- Each verb or noun is modeled as a node on the graph. These nodes are denoted as $\mathcal{V}_v$ and $\mathcal{V}_n$. And they comes with their word embeddings [38,42] as the nodes features Z_v and Z_n
- Each verb-object pair in a SVO defines a human object interaction. These interactions are modeled by a separate set of action nodes $\mathcal{V}_a$ on the graph. Each interaction will have its own node, even if it share the same verb or noun with other interactions. For example, "take a book" and "hold a book" will be two different nodes. These nodes are initialized with all zero feature vectors, and must obtain their representation Z_a via learning.
- A verb node can only connect to a noun node via a valid action node. Namely, each interaction will add a new path on the graph.
- We also add links within noun or verb nodes by WordNet [39].

This graph is thus captured by its adjacency matrix $A \in R^{|\mathcal{V}| \times |\mathcal{V}|}$ and a feature matrix $Z \in R^{d \times |\mathcal{V}|}$. Based on the construction, our graph structure can be naturally decomposed into blocks, given by

$$A = \begin{bmatrix} \mathcal{A}_{vv} & 0 & \mathcal{A}_{va} \\ 0 & \mathcal{A}_{nn} & \mathcal{A}_{an}^T \\ \mathcal{A}_{va}^T & \mathcal{A}_{an} & 0 \end{bmatrix}, \quad Z = [Z_v, Z_n, 0] \tag{2}$$

where $\mathcal{A}_{vv}, \mathcal{A}_{va}, \mathcal{A}_{an}, \mathcal{A}_{nn}$ are adjacency matrix for verb-verb pairs, verb-action pairs, action-noun pairs and noun-noun pairs, respectively. Z_v and Z_n are word embedding for verbs and nouns. Moreover, we have $Z_a = 0$ and thus the action nodes need to learn new representations for recognition.

Graph Normalization. To better capture the graph structure, it is usually desirable to normalize the adjacency matrix [29]. Due to the block structure in our adjacency matrix, we add an identity matrix to the diagonal of $\mathcal{A}$, and normalize each block separately. More precisely, we have

$$\hat{A} = \begin{bmatrix} \hat{A}_{vv} & 0 & \hat{A}_{va} \\ 0 & \hat{A}_{nn} & \hat{A}_{an}^T \\ \hat{A}_{an} & \hat{A}_{va}^T & I \end{bmatrix}, \tag{3}$$

where $\hat{A}_{vv} = D_{vv}^{-\frac{1}{2}}(A_{vv}+I)D_{vv}^{\frac{1}{2}}$, $\hat{A}_{nn} = D_{nn}^{-\frac{1}{2}}(A_{nn}+I)D_{nn}^{\frac{1}{2}}$, $\hat{A}_{va} = D_{va}^{-\frac{1}{2}}A_{vv}D_{va}^{\frac{1}{2}}$ and $\hat{A}_{vn} = D_{vn}^{-\frac{1}{2}}(A_{vn}+I)D_{vn}^{\frac{1}{2}}$. D is the diagonal node degree matrix for each block. Thus, these are symmetric normalized adjacency blocks.

3.2 Graph Convolutional Network for Compositional Learning

Given the knowledge graph $\mathcal{G}$, we want to learn to compose representation of actions Z_a. Z_a can thus be further used as "action template" for zero shot recognition. The question is how can we leverage the graph structure for learning Z_a. Our key insight is that word embedding of verbs and nouns encode important semantic information, and we can use the graph to distill theses semantics, and construct meaningful action representation. To this end, we adopt the Graph Convolution Network (GCN) from [29]. The core idea of GCN is to transform the node features based on its neighbors on the graph. Formally, given normalized graph adjacency matrix $\hat{A}$ and node features Z, a single layer GCN is given by

$$\tilde{Z} = GCN(Z, A) = \hat{A}Z^T W \tag{4}$$

where W is a $d \times \tilde{d}$ weight learned from data. d is the dimension of input feature vector for each node and $\tilde{d}$ is the output feature dimension. Intuitively, GCN first transforms each feature on each node independently, then averages the features of connected nodes. This operation is usually stacked multiple times, with nonlinear activation functions (ReLU) in-between.

Note that $\hat{A}$ is a block matrix. It is thus possible to further decompose GCU operations to each block. This decomposition provides better insights to our model, and can significantly reduce the computational cost. Specially, we have

$$\tilde{Z}_v = \hat{A}_{vv}Z_v^T W_{vv} \quad \tilde{Z}_n = \hat{A}_{nn}Z_n^T W_{nn} \quad \tilde{Z}_a = \hat{A}_{an}Z_v^T W_{an} + A_{va}^T Z_n^T W_{va} \tag{5}$$

where $W_{vv} = W_{nn} = W_{an} = W_{va} = W$. We also experimented with using different parameters for each block, which is similar to [46]. Note the last line of $\tilde{Z}_a$ in Eq. 5. In a single layer GCN, this model learns linear functions W_{an} and W_{va} that transform the neighboring word embeddings into an action template. With nonlinear activations and K GCN layers, the model will construct a nonlinear transform that considers more nodes for building the action representation (from 1-neighborhood to K-neighborhood).

3.3 From Graph to Zero Shot Recognition

The outputs of our graph convolutional networks are the transformed node features $\tilde{Z} = [\tilde{Z}_v, \tilde{Z}_n, \tilde{Z}_a]$. We use the output action representations $\tilde{Z}_a$ for the zero shot recognition. This is done by learning to match action features $\tilde{Z}_a$ and visual features x. More precisely, we learn a score function h that takes the inputs of $\tilde{Z}_a$ and x, and outputs a similarity score between $[0, 1]$.

$$h(x, a) = h(f(x) \oplus \tilde{Z}_a) \tag{6}$$

where f is a nonlinear transform that maps x into the same dimension as $\tilde{Z}_a$. $\oplus$ denotes concatenation. h is realized by a two-layer network with sigmoid function at the end. h can be considered as a variant of a Siamese network [9].

3.4 Network Architecture and Training

We present the details about our network architecture and our training.

Architecture. Our network architecture is illustrated in Fig. 2. Specifically, our model includes 2 graph convolutional layers for learning action representations. Their output channels are 512 and 200, with ReLU units after each layer. The output of GCN is concatenated with image features from a convolutional network. The image feature has a reduced dimension of 512 by a learned linear transform. The concatenated feature vector as sent to two Fully Connected (FC) layer with the size of 512 and 200, and finally outputs a scalar score. For all FC layers except the last one, we attach ReLU and Dropout (ratio = 0.5).

Training the Network. Our model is trained with a logistic loss attached to g. We fix the image features, yet update all parameters in GCN. We use mini-batch SGD for the optimization. Note that there are way more negative samples (unmatched actions) than positive samples in a mini-batch. We re-sample the positives and negatives to keep the their ratio fixed (1:3). This re-sampling strategy prevents the gradients to be dominated by the negative samples, and thus is helpful for learning. We also experimented with hard-negative sampling, yet found that it leads to severe overfitting on smaller datasets.

4 Experiments

We now present our experiments and results. We first introduce our experiment setup, followed by a description of the datasets and baselines. Finally, we report our results and compare them to state-of-the-art methods.

4.1 Experiment Setup

Benchmark. Our goal is to evaluate if methods can generalize to unseen actions. Given the compositional structure of human-object interactions, these unseen actions can be characterized into two settings: (a) a novel combination of known noun and verb; and (b) a new action with unknown verbs or nouns or both of them. We design two tasks to capture both settings. Specifically, we split both noun and verb tokens into two even parts. We denote the splits of nouns as 1/2 and verbs as A/B. Thus, 1B refers to actions from the first split of nouns and the second split of verbs. We select combinations of the splits for training and testing as our two benchmark tasks.

- **Task 1.** Our first setting allows a method to access the full set of verbs and nouns during training, yet requires the method to recognize either a seen or an unseen combination of known concepts for testing. For example, a method is given the action of "hold apple" and "wash motorcycle", and is asked to recognize novel combinations of "hold motorcycle" and "wash apple". Our training set is a subset of 1A and 2B (1A + 2B). This set captures all concepts of nouns and verbs, yet misses many combination of them (1B/2A). Our testing set consists of samples from 1A and 2B and unseen combination of 1B and 2A.
- **Task 2.** Our second setting exposes only a partial set of verbs and nouns (1A) to a method during training. But the method is tasked to recognize all possible combinations of actions (1A, 1B, 2A, 2B), including those with unknown concepts. For example, a method is asked to jump from "hold apple" to "hold motorcycle" and "wash apple", as well as the complete novel combination of "wash motorcycle". This task is extremely challenging. It requires the method to generalize to completely new categories of nouns and verbs, and assemble them into new actions. We believe the prior knowledge such as word-embeddings or SVO pairs will allow the jumps from 1 to 2 and A to B. Finally, we believe this setting provides a good testbed for knowledge representation and transfer.

Generalized Zero Shot Learning. We want to highlight that our benchmark follows the setting of generalized zero shot learning [53]. Namely, during test, we did no constrain the recognition to the categories on the test set but all possible categories. For example, if we train on 1A, during testing the output class can be any of $\{1A, 2B, 2A, 2B\}$. We do also report numbers separately for each subset to understand where what approach works. More importantly, as pointed out by [53], a ImageNet pre-trained model may bias the results if the categories are already seen during pre-training. We force nouns that appears in ImageNet [44] stay in training sets for all our experiments except for Charades.

Mining from Knowledge Bases. We describe how we construct the knowledge graph for all our experiments. Specifically, we make use of WordNet to create noun-noun and verb-verb links. We consider two nodes are connected if (1) they are the immediate hypernym or hyponym to each other (denoted as 1 HOP); (2) their LCH similarity score [32] is larger than 2.0. Furthermore, we extracted SVO from NELL [5] and further verified them using COCO dataset [34]. Specifically, we parse all image captions on COCO, only keep the verb-noun pairs that appeared on COCO, and add the remaining pairs to our graph.

Implementation Details. We extracted the last FC features from ResNet 152 [22] pre-trained with ImageNet for HICO and Visual Genome HOI datasets, and I3D Network pre-trained with kinetics [6] for Charades dataset. All images are re-sized to 224×224 and the convolutional network is fixed. For all our experiments, we used GloVe [42] for embedding verb and noun tokens, leading to a 200D vector for each token. GloVe is pretrained with Wikipedia and Gigaword5 text corpus. We adapt hard negative mining for HICO and Visual Genome HOI datasets, yet disable it for Charades dataset to prevent overfitting.

Table 1. Ablation study of our methods. We report mAP for both tasks and compare different variant of our methods. These results suggest that adding more links to the graph (and thus inject more prior knowledge) helps to improve the results.

Methods	mAP on test set					
	Train 1A + 2B			Train 1A		
	All	2A + 1B	Unseen	All	1B + 2A + 2B	Unseen
Chance	0.55	0.49		0.55	0.51	
GCNCL-I	20.96	16.05		11.93	7.22	
GCNCL-I + A	21.39	16.82		11.57	6.73	
GCNCL-I + NV + A	**21.40**	**16.99**		11.51	6.92	
GCNCL	19.91	14.07		11.46	7.18	
GCNCL + A	20.43	15.65		11.72	7.19	
GCNCL + NV + A	21.04	16.35		**11.94**	**7.50**	

4.2   Dataset and Benchmark

We evaluate our method on HICO [7], Visual Genome [30] and Charades [48] datasets. We use mean Average Precision (mAP) scores averaged across all categories as our evaluation metric. We report results for both tasks (unseen combination and unseen concepts). We use 80/20 training/testing splits for all experiments unless otherwise noticed. Details of these datasets are described below.

HICO Dataset [7] is developed for Humans Interacting with Common Objects. It is thus particularly suitable for our task. We follow the classification task. The goal is to recognize the interaction in an image, with each interaction consists of a verb-noun pair. HICO has 47,774 images with 80 nouns, 117 verbs and 600 interactions. We remove the verb of "no interaction" and all its associated categories. Thus our benchmark of HICO includes 116 verbs and 520 actions.

Visual Genome HOI Dataset is derived from Visual Genome [30]—the largest dataset for structured image understanding. Based on the annotations, we carve out a sub set from Visual Genome that focuses on human object interactions. We call this dataset Visual Genome HOI in our experiments. Specifically, from all annotations, we extracted relations in the form of "human-verb-object" and their associated images. Note that we did not include relations with "be", "wear" or "have", as most of these relations did not demonstrate human object interactions. The Visual Genome HOI dataset includes 21256 images with 1422 nouns, 520 verbs and 6643 unique actions. We notice that a large amount of actions only have 1 or 2 instances. Thus, for testing, we constrain our actions to 532 categories, which include more than 10 instances.

Charades Dataset [48] contains 9848 videos clips of daily human-object interactions that can be described by a verb-noun pair. We remove actions with "no-interaction" from the original 157 category. Thus, our benchmark on Charades includes interactions with 37 objects and 34 verbs, leading to a total of 149 valid action categories. We note that Charades is a more challenging dataset as the videos are captured in naturalistic environments.

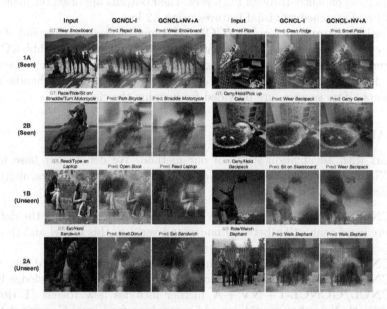

Fig. 3. Results of GCNCL-I and GCNCL + NV + A on HICO dataset. All methods are trained on 1A + 2B and tested on both seen (1A, 2B) and unseen (2A, 1B) actions. Each row shows results on a subset. Each sample includes the input image and its label, top-1 predictions from GCNCL-I and GCNCL + NV + A. We plot the attention map using the top-1 predicted labels. Red regions correspond to high prediction scores. (Color figure online)

4.3   Baseline Methods

We consider a set of baselines for our experiments. These methods include

- **Visual Product** [31] **(VP):** VP composes outputs of a verb and a noun classifier by computing their product $(p(a, b) = p(a)p(b))$. VP does not model contextuality between verbs and nouns, and thus can be considered as late fusion. VP can deal with unseen combination of known concepts but is not feasible for novel actions with unknown verb or noun.

- **Triplet Siamese Network (Triplet Siamese):** Triplet Siamese is inspired by [12,15]. We first concatenate verb and noun embedding and pass them through two FC layers (512, 200). The output is further concatenated with visual features, followed by another FC layers to output a similarity score. The network is trained with sigmoid cross entropy loss.
- **Semantic Embedding Space (SES)** [55]: SES is originally designed for zero shot action recognition. We take the average of verb and noun as the action embedding. The model learns to minimize the distance between the action embeddings and their corresponding visual features using L2 loss.
- **Deep Embedding Model** [60] **(DEM):** DEM passes verb and noun embeddings independently through FC layers. Their outputs are fused (element-wise sum) and matched to visual features using L2 loss.
- **Classifier Composition** [40] **(CC):** CC composes classifiers instead of word embeddings. Each token is represented by its SVM classifier weights. CC thus learns to transform the combination of two weights into the new classifier. The model is trained with sigmoid cross entropy loss. It can not handle novel concepts if no samples are provided for learning the classifier.

4.4   Ablation Study

We start with an ablation study of our method. We denote our base model as GCNCL (Graph Convolutional Network for Compositional Learning) and consider the following variants

- **GCNCL-I** is our base model that only includes action links on the dataset. There is no connection between nouns and verbs in this model and thus the adjacency matrix of $\mathcal{A}_{vv}$ and $\mathcal{A}_{nn}$ are identity matrix.
- **GCNCL** further adds edges within noun/verb nodes using WordNet.
- **GCNCL/GCNCL-I + A** adds action links from external knowledge base.
- **GCNCL/GCNCL-I + NV + A** further includes new tokens (1 Hop on WordNet). Note that we did not add new tokens for Visual Genome dataset.

We evaluate these methods on HICO dataset and summarize the results in Table 1. For recognizing novel combination of seen concepts, GCNCL-I works better than GCNCL versions. We postulate that removing these links will force the network to pass information through action nodes, and thus help better compose action representations from seen concepts. However, when tested with a more challenging case of recognizing novel concepts, the results are in favor of GCNCL model, especially on the unseen categories. In this case, the model has to use the extra links (verb-verb or noun-noun) for learning the represent ions for new verbs and nouns. Moreover, for both settings, adding more links generally helps to improve the performance, independent of the design of the model. This result provides a strong support to our core argument—external knowledge can be used to improve zero shot recognition of human object interactions.

Moreover, we provide qualitative results in Fig. 3. Specifically, we compare the results of GCNCL-I and GCNCL + NV + A and visualize their attention maps using Grad-Cam [47]. Figure 3 helps to understand the benefit of external knowledge. First, adding external knowledge seems to improve the recognition of nouns but not verbs. For example, GCNCL + NV + A successfully corrected the wrongly recognized objects by GCNCL-I (e.g., "bicycle" to "motorcycle", "skateboard" to "backpack"). Second, both methods are better at recognizing nouns—objects in the interactions. And their attention maps highlight the corresponding object regions. Finally, mis-matching of verbs is the main failure mode of our methods. For the rest of our experiments, we only include the best performing methods of GCNCL-I + NV + A and GCNCL + NV + A.

4.5   Results

We present the full results of our methods and compare them to our baselines.

HICO. Our methods outperformed all previous methods when tasked to recognize novel combination of actions. Especially, our results for the unseen categories achieved a relative gap of 6% when compared to the best result from previous work. When tested on more challenging task 2, our results are better overall, yet slightly worse than Triplet Siamese. We further break down the results on different test splits. It turns out that our result is only worse on the split of 1B (-2.8%), where the objects have been seen before. And our results are better in all other cases ($+2.0\%$ on 2A and $+0.9\%$ on 2B). We argue that Triplet Siamese might have over-fitted to the seen object categories, and thus will fail to transfer knowledge to unseen concepts. Moreover, we also run significance analysis to explore if the results are statistically significant. We did t-test by comparing results of our GCNCL-I + NV + A to CC (training on 1A + 2B) and GCNCL + NV + A to Triplet Siamese (training on 1A) for all classes. Our results are significantly better than CC ($P = 0.04$) and Triplet Siamese ($P = 0.05$) (Tables 2 and 3).

Table 2. Recognition results (mAP) on HICO. We benchmark both tasks of recognizing unseen combinations of known concepts and of recognizing novel concepts.

Methods	mAP on test set			
	Train 1A + 2B		Train 1A	
	All	2A + 1B Unseen	All	1B + 2A + 2B Unseen
Chance	0.55	0.49	0.55	0.51
Triplet Siamese	17.61	16.40	10.38	**7.76**
SES	18.39	13.00	11.69	7.19
DEM	12.26	11.33	8.32	6.06
VP	13.96	10.83	-	-
CC	20.92	15.98	-	-
GCNCL-I + NV + A	**21.40**	**16.99**	11.51	6.92
GCNCL + NV + A	21.04	16.35	**11.94**	7.50

Table 3. Results (mAP) on Visual Genome HOI. This is a very challenging dataset with many action classes and few samples per class.

Methods	mAP on test set				
	Train 1A + 2B			Train 1A	
	All	2A + 1B Unseen		All	1B + 2A + 2B Unseen
Chance	0.28	0.25		0.28	0.32
Triplet Siamese	5.68	4.61		2.55	1.67
SES	2.74	1.91		2.07	0.96
DEM	3.82	3.73		2.26	1.5
VP	3.84	2.34		-	-
CC	6.35	**5.74**		-	-
GCNCL-I + A	6.48	5.10		4.00	**2.63**
GCNCL + A	**6.63**	5.42		**4.07**	2.44

Visual Genome. Our model worked the best except for unseen categories on our first task. We note that this dataset is very challenging as there are more action classes than HICO and many of them have only a few instances. We want to highlight our results on task 2, where our results show a relative gap of more than 50% when compared to the best of previous method. These results show that our method has the ability to generalize to completely novel concepts (Table 4).

Table 4. Results (mAP) on Charades dataset. This is our attempt to recognize novel interactions in videos. While the gap is small, our method still works the best.

Methods	mAP on test set				
	Train 1A + 2B			Train 1A	
	ALL	2A + 1B Unseen		ALL	1B + 2A + 2B Unseen
Chance	1.37	1.45		1.37	1.00
Triplet Siamese	14.23	10.1		10.41	7.82
SES	13.12	9.56		10.14	7.81
DEM	11.78	8.97		9.57	7.74
VP	13.66	9.15		-	-
CC	14.31	10.13		-	-
GCNCL-I + A	**14.32**	10.34		10.48	7.95
GCNCL + A	**14.32**	**10.48**		**10.53**	**8.09**

Charades. Finally, we report results on Charades—a video action dataset. This experiment provides our first step towards recognizing realistic interactions in videos. Again, our method worked the best among all baselines. However, the gap is smaller on this dataset. Comparing to image datasets, Charades has less number of samples and thus less diversity. Methods can easily over-fit on this dataset. Moreover, building video representations is still an open challenge. It might be that our performance is limited by the video features.

5   Conclusion

We address the challenging problem of compositional learning of human object interactions. Specifically, we explored using external knowledge for learning to compose novel actions. We proposed a novel graph based model that incorporates knowledge representation into a deep model. To test our method, we designed careful evaluation protocols for zero shot compositional learning. We tested our method on three public benchmarks, including both image and video datasets. Our results suggested that using external knowledge can help to better recognize novel interactions and even novel concepts of verbs and nouns. As a consequence, our model outperformed state-of-the-art methods on recognizing novel combination of seen concepts on all datasets. Moreover, our model demonstrated promising ability to recognize novel concepts. We believe that our model brings a new perspective to zero shot learning, and our exploration of using knowledge provides an important step for understanding human actions.

Acknowledgments. This work was supported by ONR MURI N000141612007, Sloan Fellowship, Okawa Fellowship to AG. The authors would like to thank Xiaolong Wang and Gunnar Sigurdsson for many helpful discussions.

References

1. Akata, Z., Perronnin, F., Harchaoui, Z., Schmid, C.: Label-embedding for attribute-based classification. In: CVPR (2013)
2. Andreas, J., Rohrbach, M., Darrell, T., Klein, D.: Learning to compose neural networks for question answering. In: NAACL (2016)
3. Andreas, J., Rohrbach, M., Darrell, T., Klein, D.: Neural module networks. In: CVPR (2016)
4. Biederman, I.: Recognition-by-components: a theory of human image understanding. Psychol. Rev. **94**(2), 115 (1987)
5. Carlson, A., Betteridge, J., Kisiel, B., Settles, B., Hruschka Jr., E.R., Mitchell, T.M.: Toward an architecture for never-ending language learning. In: AAAI, pp. 1306–1313. AAAI Press (2010)
6. Carreira, J., Zisserman, A.: Quo vadis, action recognition? A new model and the kinetics dataset. In: CVPR (2017)
7. Chao, Y.W., Wang, Z., He, Y., Wang, J., Deng, J.: HICO: a benchmark for recognizing human-object interactions in images. In: ICCV (2015)
8. Chen, X., Shrivastava, A., Gupta, A.: NEIL: extracting visual knowledge from web data. In: ICCV (2013)

9. Chopra, S., Hadsell, R., LeCun, Y.: Learning a similarity metric discriminatively, with application to face verification. In: CVPR (2005)
10. Delaitre, V., Fouhey, D.F., Laptev, I., Sivic, J., Gupta, A., Efros, A.A.: Scene semantics from long-term observation of people. In: Fitzgibbon, A., Lazebnik, S., Perona, P., Sato, Y., Schmid, C. (eds.) ECCV 2012. LNCS, vol. 7577, pp. 284–298. Springer, Heidelberg (2012). https://doi.org/10.1007/978-3-642-33783-3_21
11. Deng, J., et al.: Large-scale object classification using label relation graphs. In: Fleet, D., Pajdla, T., Schiele, B., Tuytelaars, T. (eds.) ECCV 2014. LNCS, vol. 8689, pp. 48–64. Springer, Cham (2014). https://doi.org/10.1007/978-3-319-10590-1_4
12. Elhoseiny, M., Saleh, B., Elgammal, A.: Write a classifier: zero-shot learning using purely textual descriptions. In: ICCV (2013)
13. Fouhey, D., Wang, X., Gupta, A.: In defense of direct perception of affordances. In: arXiv (2015)
14. Fouhey, D.F., Delaitre, V., Gupta, A., Efros, A.A., Laptev, I., Sivic, J.: People watching: human actions as a cue for single-view geometry. Int. J. Comput. Vis. **110**(3), 259–274 (2014)
15. Frome, A., Corrado, G.S., Shlens, J., Bengio, S., Dean, J., Mikolov, T.: Devise: a deep visual-semantic embedding model. In: Burges, C.J.C., Bottou, L., Welling, M., Ghahramani, Z., Weinberger, K.Q. (eds.) NIPS, pp. 2121–2129. Curran Associates, Inc. (2013)
16. Fu, Y., Hospedales, T.M., Xiang, T., Gong, S.: Transductive multi-view zero-shot learning. IEEE Trans. Pattern Anal. Mach. Intell. **37**(11), 2332–2345 (2015)
17. Gibson, J.: The Ecological Approach to Visual Perception. Houghton Mifflin, Boston (1979)
18. Guadarrama, S., et al.: YouTube2Text: recognizing and describing arbitrary activities using semantic hierarchies and zero-shot recognition. In: ICCV (2013)
19. Gupta, A., Davis, L.S.: Objects in action: an approach for combining action understanding and object perception. In: CVPR (2007)
20. Gupta, A., Kembhavi, A., Davis, L.S.: Observing human-object interactions: using spatial and functional compatibility for recognition. IEEE Trans. Pattern Anal. Mach. Intell. **31**(10), 1775–1789 (2009)
21. Habibian, A., Mensink, T., Snoek, C.G.: Composite concept discovery for zero-shot video event detection. In: International Conference on Multimedia Retrieval (2014)
22. He, K., Zhang, X., Ren, S., Sun, J.: Deep residual learning for image recognition. In: CVPR (2016)
23. Hoffman, D.D., Richards, W.A.: Parts of recognition. Cognition **18**(1–3), 65–96 (1984)
24. Jain, M., van Gemert, J.C., Mensink, T.E.J., Snoek, C.G.M.: Objects2Action: classifying and localizing actions without any video example. In: ICCV (2015)
25. Jain, M., van Gemert, J.C., Snoek, C.G.: What do 15,000 object categories tell us about classifying and localizing actions? In: CVPR (2015)
26. Jayaraman, D., Grauman, K.: Zero-shot recognition with unreliable attributes. In: Ghahramani, Z., Welling, M., Cortes, C., Lawrence, N.D., Weinberger, K.Q. (eds.) Advances in Neural Information Processing Systems, pp. 3464–3472. Curran Associates, Inc. (2014)
27. Johnson, J., et al.: Inferring and executing programs for visual reasoning. In: ICCV (2017)
28. Kalogeiton, V., Weinzaepfel, P., Ferrari, V., Schmid, C.: Joint learning of object and action detectors. In: ICCV (2017)

29. Kipf, T.N., Welling, M.: Semi-supervised classification with graph convolutional networks (2017)
30. Krishna, R., et al.: Visual genome: connecting language and vision using crowdsourced dense image annotations. Int. J. Comput. Vis. **123**(1), 32–73 (2017)
31. Lampert, C.H., Nickisch, H., Harmeling, S.: Learning to detect unseen object classes by between-class attribute transfer. In: CVPR (2009)
32. Leacock, C., Miller, G.A., Chodorow, M.: Using corpus statistics and wordnet relations for sense identification. Comput. Linguist. **24**(1), 147–165 (1998)
33. Li, X., Guo, Y., Schuurmans, D.: Semi-supervised zero-shot classification with label representation learning. In: CVPR (2015)
34. Lin, T.-Y., et al.: Microsoft COCO: common objects in context. In: Fleet, D., Pajdla, T., Schiele, B., Tuytelaars, T. (eds.) ECCV 2014. LNCS, vol. 8693, pp. 740–755. Springer, Cham (2014). https://doi.org/10.1007/978-3-319-10602-1_48
35. Liu, J., Kuipers, B., Savarese, S.: Recognizing human actions by attributes. In: CVPR (2011)
36. Lu, C., Krishna, R., Bernstein, M., Fei-Fei, L.: Visual relationship detection with language priors. In: Leibe, B., Matas, J., Sebe, N., Welling, M. (eds.) ECCV 2016. LNCS, vol. 9905, pp. 852–869. Springer, Cham (2016). https://doi.org/10.1007/978-3-319-46448-0_51
37. Mao, J., Wei, X., Yang, Y., Wang, J., Huang, Z., Yuille, A.L.: Learning like a child: fast novel visual concept learning from sentence descriptions of images. In: ICCV (2015)
38. Mikolov, T., Sutskever, I., Chen, K., Corrado, G.S., Dean, J.: Distributed representations of words and phrases and their compositionality. In: Burges, C.J.C., Bottou, L., Welling, M., Ghahramani, Z., Weinberger, K.Q. (eds.) NIPS, pp. 3111–3119. Curran Associates, Inc. (2013)
39. Miller, G.A.: WordNet: a lexical database for English. Commun. ACM **38**(11), 39–41 (1995)
40. Misra, I., Gupta, A., Hebert, M.: From red wine to red tomato: composition with context. In: CVPR (2017)
41. Norouzi, M., et al.: Zero-shot learning by convex combination of semantic embeddings (2014)
42. Pennington, J., Socher, R., Manning, C.D.: Glove: global vectors for word representation. In: EMNLP (2014)
43. Rohrbach, M., Ebert, S., Schiele, B.: Transfer learning in a transductive setting. In: Burges, C.J.C., Bottou, L., Welling, M., Ghahramani, Z., Weinberger, K.Q. (eds.) NIPS, pp. 46–54. Curran Associates, Inc. (2013)
44. Russakovsky, O., et al.: Imagenet large scale visual recognition challenge. Int. J. Comput. Vis. **115**(3), 211–252 (2015)
45. Sadeghi, F., Kumar Divvala, S.K., Farhadi, A.: VisKE: visual knowledge extraction and question answering by visual verification of relation phrases. In: CVPR (2015)
46. Schlichtkrull, M., Kipf, T.N., Bloem, P., Berg, R.v.d., Titov, I., Welling, M.: Modeling relational data with graph convolutional networks. arXiv preprint arXiv:1703.06103 (2017)
47. Selvaraju, R.R., Cogswell, M., Das, A., Vedantam, R., Parikh, D., Batra, D.: Grad-CAM: visual explanations from deep networks via gradient-based localization. In: ICCV (2017)
48. Sigurdsson, G.A., Varol, G., Wang, X., Farhadi, A., Laptev, I., Gupta, A.: Hollywood in homes: crowdsourcing data collection for activity understanding. In: Leibe, B., Matas, J., Sebe, N., Welling, M. (eds.) ECCV 2016. LNCS, vol. 9905, pp. 842–856. Springer, Cham (2016). https://doi.org/10.1007/978-3-319-46448-0_31

49. Stark, L., Bowyer, K.: Achieving generalized object recognition through reasoning about association of function to structure. IEEE Trans. Pattern Anal. Mach. Intell. **13**, 1097–1104 (1991)
50. Thomason, J., Venugopalan, S., Guadarrama, S., Saenko, K., Mooney, R.: Integrating language and vision to generate natural language descriptions of videos in the wild. In: COLING (2014)
51. Wang, Q., Chen, K.: Alternative semantic representations for zero-shot human action recognition. In: Ceci, M., Hollmén, J., Todorovski, L., Vens, C., Džeroski, S. (eds.) ECML PKDD 2017. LNCS (LNAI), vol. 10534, pp. 87–102. Springer, Cham (2017). https://doi.org/10.1007/978-3-319-71249-9_6
52. Wang, Q., Chen, K.: Zero-shot visual recognition via bidirectional latent embedding. Int. J. Comput. Vis. **124**(3), 356–383 (2017)
53. Xian, Y., Schiele, B., Akata, Z.: Zero-shot learning-the good, the bad and the ugly. In: CVPR (2017)
54. Xu, C., Hsieh, S.H., Xiong, C., Corso, J.J.: Can humans fly? Action understanding with multiple classes of actors. In: CVPR (2015)
55. Xu, X., Hospedales, T., Gong, S.: Semantic embedding space for zero-shot action recognition. In: ICIP (2015)
56. Xu, X., Hospedales, T.M., Gong, S.: Multi-task zero-shot action recognition with prioritised data augmentation. In: Leibe, B., Matas, J., Sebe, N., Welling, M. (eds.) ECCV 2016. LNCS, vol. 9906, pp. 343–359. Springer, Cham (2016). https://doi.org/10.1007/978-3-319-46475-6
57. Yao, B., Fei-Fei, L.: Modeling mutual context of object and human pose in human-object interaction activities. In: CVPR (2010)
58. Yu, X., Aloimonos, Y.: Attribute-based transfer learning for object categorization with zero/one training example. In: Daniilidis, K., Maragos, P., Paragios, N. (eds.) ECCV 2010. LNCS, vol. 6315, pp. 127–140. Springer, Heidelberg (2010). https://doi.org/10.1007/978-3-642-15555-0_10
59. Zellers, R., Yatskar, M., Thomson, S., Choi, Y.: Neural motifs: scene graph parsing with global context. In: CVPR (2018)
60. Zhang, L., Xiang, T., Gong, S.: Learning a deep embedding model for zero-shot learning. In: CVPR (2017)

Viewpoint Estimation—Insights and Model

Gilad Divon and Ayellet Tal[(⊠)]

Technion – Israel Institute of Technology, Haifa, Israel
ayellet@ee.technion.ac.il

Abstract. This paper addresses the problem of viewpoint estimation of an object in a given image. It presents five key insights and a CNN that is based on them. The network's major properties are as follows. (i) The architecture jointly solves detection, classification, and viewpoint estimation. (ii) New types of data are added and trained on. (iii) A novel loss function, which takes into account both the geometry of the problem and the new types of data, is propose. Our network allows a substantial boost in performance: from 36.1% gained by SOTA algorithms to 45.9%.

1 Introduction

Object category viewpoint estimation refers to the task of determining the viewpoints of objects in a given image, where the objects belong to known categories, as illustrated in Fig. 1. This problem is an important component in our attempt to understand the 3D world around us and is therefore a long-term challenge in computer vision [1–4], having numerous application [5,6]. The difficulty in solving the problem stems from the fact that a single image, which is a projection from 3D, does not yield sufficient information to determine the viewpoint. Moreover, this problem suffers from scarcity of images with accurate viewpoint annotation, due not only to the high cost of manual annotation, but mostly to the imprecision of humans when estimating viewpoints.

Convolutional Neural Networks were recently applied to viewpoint estimation [7–9], leading to large improvements of state-of-the-art results on PASCAL3D+. Two major approaches were pursued. The first is a regression approach, which handles the continuous values of viewpoints naturally [8,10,11]. This approach manages to represent the periodic characteristic of the viewpoint and is invertible. However, as discussed in [7], the limitation of regression for viewpoint estimation is that it cannot represent well the ambiguities that exist between different viewpoints of objects that have symmetries or near symmetries.

The second approach is to treat viewpoint estimation as a classification problem [7,9]. In this case, viewpoints are transformed into a discrete space, where

---

Electronic supplementary material The online version of this chapter (https://doi.org/10.1007/978-3-030-01264-9_16) contains supplementary material, which is available to authorized users.

© Springer Nature Switzerland AG 2018
V. Ferrari et al. (Eds.): ECCV 2018, LNCS 11218, pp. 265–281, 2018.
https://doi.org/10.1007/978-3-030-01264-9_16

each viewpoint (angle) is represented as a single class (bin). The network predicts the probability of an object to be in each of these classes. This approach is shown to outperform regression, to be more robust, and to handle ambiguities better. Nevertheless, its downside is that similar viewpoints are located in different bins and therefore, the bin order becomes insignificant. This means that when the network errs, there is no advantage to small errors (nearby viewpoints) over large errors, as should be the case.

Fig. 1. Viewpoint estimation. Given an image containing objects from known categories, our model estimates the viewpoints (azimuth) of the objects. See supplementary material

We follow the second approach. We present five key insights, some of which were discussed before: (i) Rather than separating the tasks of object detection, object classification, and viewpoint estimation, these should be integrated into a unified framework. (ii) As one of the major issues of this problem is the lack of labeled real images, novel ways to augment the data should be developed. (iii) The loss should reflect the geometry of the problem. (iv) Since viewpoints, unlike object classes, are related to one another, integrating over viewpoint predictions should outperform the selection of the strongest activation. (v) CNNs for viewpoint estimation improve as CNNs for object classification/detection do.

Based on these observations, we propose a network that improves the state-of-the-art results by 9.8%, from 36.1% to 45.9%, on PASCAL3D+ [12]. We touch each of the three components of any learning system: architecture, data, and loss. In particular, our architecture unifies object detection, object classification, and viewpoint estimation and is built on top of Faster R-CNN. Furthermore, in addition to real and synthetic images, we also use flipped images and videos, in a semi-supervised manner. This not only augments the data for training, but also lets us refine our loss. Finally, we define a new loss function that reflects both the geometry of the problem and the new types of training data.

Thus, this paper makes two major contributions. First, it presents insights that should be the basis of viewpoint estimation algorithms (Sect. 2). Second, it introduces a network (Sect. 3) that achieves SOTA results (Sect. 4). Our network is based on three additional contributions: a loss function that uniquely suits pose estimation, a novel integration concept, which takes into account the surroundings of the object, and new ways of data augmentation.

2   Our Insights in a Nutshell

We start our study with short descriptions of five insights we make on viewpoint estimation. In the next section, we introduce an algorithm that is based on these insights and generates state-of-the-art results.

1. *Rather than separating the tasks of object detection, object classification, and viewpoint estimation, these should be integrated into a unified network.* In [7], an off-the-shelf R-CNN [13] was used. Given the detection results, a network was designed to estimate the viewpoint. In [8] classification and viewpoint estimation were solved jointly, while relying on bounding box suggestions from Deep Mask [14]/Fast R-CNN [15]. We propose a different architecture that combines the three tasks and show that training the network jointly is beneficial. This insight is in accordance with similar observations made in other domains [16–18].

2. *As one of the major issues of viewpoint estimation is the lack of labeled real images, novel ways to augment the data are necessary.* In [7,8] it was proposed to use both real data and images of CAD models, for which backgrounds were randomly synthesized. We propose to add two new types of training data, which not only increase the volume of data, but also benefit learning. First, we horizontally flip the real images. Since the orientation of these images is known, yet no new information regarding detection and classification is added, they are used within a new loss function to focus on viewpoint estimation. Second, we use unlabeled videos of objects for which, though we do not know the exact orientation, we do know that subsequent frames should be associated with nearby viewpoints. This constraint is utilized to gain better viewpoint predictions. Finally, as a minor modification, rather than randomly choosing backgrounds for the synthetic images, we choose backgrounds that suit the objects, e.g. backgrounds of the ocean should be added to boats, but not to airplanes.

3. *The loss should reflect the geometry of the problem, since viewpoint estimation is essentially a geometric problem, having geometric constraints.* In [7], the loss considers the geometry by giving larger weights to bins of close viewpoints. In [8], it was found that this was not really helpful and viewpoint estimation was solved purely as a classification problem. We show that geometric constraints are very helpful. Indeed, our loss function considers (1) the relations between the geometries of triplets of images, (2) the constraints posed by the flipped images, and (3) the constraints posed by subsequent frames within videos

4. *Integration of the results is helpful.* Previous works chose as the final result the bin that contains the viewpoint having the strongest activation. Instead, we integrate over all the viewpoints within a bin and choose as the final result the bin that maximizes this integral. Interestingly, this idea has an effect that is similar to that of denoising and it is responsible for a major improvement in performance.

5. *As object classification/detection CNNs improve, so do CNNs for viewpoint estimation.* In [7] AlexNet [19] was used as the base network, whereas in [8,9] VGG [20] was used. We use ResNet [21], not only because of its better performance in classification, but also due to its skip-connections concept. These connections enable the flow of information between non-adjacent layers and by doing so, preserve spatial information from different scales. This idea is similar to the multi-scale approach of [9], which was shown to benefit viewpoint estimation.

A Concise View on the Contribution of the Insights: Table 1 summarizes the influence of each insight on the performance of viewpoint estimation. Our results are compared to those of [7–9]. The total gain of our algorithm is 9.8% compared to [8]. Section 4 will analyze these results in depth.

Table 1. Contribution of the insights. This table summarizes the influence of our insights on the performance. The total gain is 9.8% compared to [8].

Method	Score (mAVP24)
[7]:AlexNet/R-CNN-**Geometry**-synthetic+real	19.8
[9]: VGG/R-CNN-**classification**-real	31.1
[8]: VGG/Fast R-CNN-**classification**-synthetic+real	36.1
Ours: Insights 1,5 - **Architecture**	40.6
Ours: Insights: 1,4,5 - **Integration**	43.2
Ours: Insights: 1,3,4,5 - **Loss**	44.4
Ours: Insights: 1,2,3,4,5 - **Data**	**45.9**

3   Model

Recall that we treat viewpoint estimation as a classification problem. Though a viewpoint is defined as a 3D vector, representing the camera orientation relative to the object (Fig. 2), we focus on the azimuth; finding the other angles is equivalent. The set of possible viewpoints is discretized into 360 classes, where each class represents 1°. This section presents the different components of our suggested network, which realizes the insights described in the previous section.

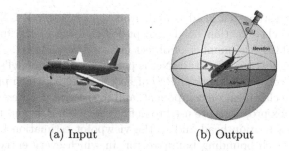

(a) Input   (b) Output

Fig. 2. Problem definition. Given an image containing an object (a), the goal is to estimate the camera orientation (Euler angles) relative to the object (b).

3.1 Architecture

Hereafter, we describe the implementation of Insights 1, 4 & 5, focusing on the integration of classification, object detection and viewpoint estimation. Figure 3 sketches our general architecture. It is based on Faster R-CNN [16], which both detects and classifies. As a base network within Faster R-CNN, we use ResNet [21], which is shown to achieve better results for classification than VGG. Another advantage of ResNet is its skip connections. To understand their importance, recall that in contrast to our goal, classification networks are trained to ignore viewpoints. Skip connection allow the data to flow directly, without being distorted by pooling, which is known to disregard the inner order of activations.

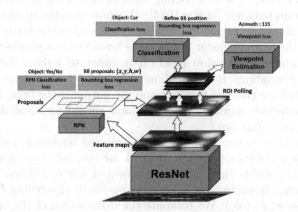

Fig. 3. Network architecture. Deep features are extracted by ResNet and passed to RPN to predict bounding boxes. After ROI pooling, they are passed both to the classification head and to the viewpoint estimation head. The output consists of a set of bounding boxes (x, y, h, w), and for each of them—the class of the object within the bounding box and its estimated viewpoint.

A viewpoint estimation head is added on top of Faster R-CNN. It is built similarly to the classification head, except for the size of the fully-connected layer, which is 4320 (the number of object classes * 360 angles).

The resulting feature map of ResNet is passed to all the model's components: to the *Region Proposal Network (RPN)* of Faster R-CNN, which predict bounding boxes, to the classification component, and to the viewpoint estimation head. The bounding box proposals are used to define the pooling regions that are input both to the classification head and to the viewpoint estimation head. The latter outputs for each bounding box a vector, in which every entry represents a viewpoint prediction, assuming that the object in the bounding box belongs to a certain class, e.g. entries 0–359 are the predictions for boats, 360–719 for bicycles etc. The relevant section of this vector is chosen as the output once the object class is predicted by the classification head. The final output of the system is a set of bounding boxes (x, y, h, w), and for each of them—the class of the object in the bounding box and object's viewpoint for this class—integrating the results of the classification head and the viewpoint estimation head.

Implementation Details: Within this general framework, three issues should be addressed. First, though viewpoint estimation is defined as a classification problem, we cannot simply use the classification head of Faster R-CNN as is for the viewpoint estimation task. This is so since the periodical pooling layers within the network are invariant to the location of the activation in the feature map. This is undesirable when evaluating an object's viewpoint, since different viewpoints have the same representation after pooling that uses Max or Average. To solve this problem, while still accounting for the importance of the pooling layers, we replace only the last pooling layer of the viewpoint estimation head with a fully connected layer (of size 1024). This preserves the spatial information, as different weights are assigned to different locations in the feature map.

Second, in the original Faster R-CNN, the bounding box proposals are passed to a non-maximum suppression function in order to reduce the overlapping bounding box suggestions. Bounding boxes whose *Intersection over Union (IoU)* is larger than 0.5 are grouped together and the output is the bounding box with the highest prediction score. Which viewpoint should be associated with this representative bounding box?

One option is to choose the angle of the selected bounding box (BB). This, however, did not yield good results. Instead, we compute the viewpoint vector (in which every possible viewpoint has a score) of BB as follows. Our network computes for each bounding box bb_i a distribution of viewpoints $P_A(bb_i)$ and a classification score $P_C(bb_i)$. We compute the distribution of the viewpoints for BB by summing over the contributions of all the overlapping bounding boxes, weighted by their classification scores:

$$viewpoint\_Score(BB) = \Sigma_i P_A(bb_i) P_C(bb_i). \tag{1}$$

This score vector, of length 360, is associated with BB. Hence, our approach considers the predictions for all the bounding boxes when selecting the viewpoint.

Given this score vector, the viewpoint should be estimated. The score is computed by summing Eq. (1) over all the viewpoints within a bin. Following [7,8], this is done for $K = 24$ bins, each representing $15°$ angles. Then, the bin selected is the one for which this sum is maximized.

Third, we noticed that small objects are consistently mis-detected by Faster R-CNN, whereas such object do exist in our dataset. To solve it, a minor modification was applied to the network. We added a set of anchors of size 64 pixels, in addition to the existing sizes of $\{128, 256, 512\}$ (anchors are the initial suggestions for the sizes of the bounding boxes). This led to a small increase of training time, but significantly improved the detection results (from 74.3% to 77.8% using mAP) and consequently improved the viewpoint estimation.

3.2 Data

In our problem, we need not only to classify objects, but also to sub-classify each object into viewpoints. This means that a huge number of parameters must be learned, and this in turn requires a large amount of labeled data. Yet, labeled real images are scarce, since viewpoint labeling is extremely difficult.

In [12], a creative procedure was proposed: Given a detected and classified object in an image, the user selects the most similar 3D CAD model (from Google 3D Warehouse [22]) and marks some corresponding key points. The 3D viewpoint is then computed for this object. Since this procedure is expensive, the resulting dataset contains only 30 K annotated images that belong to 12 categories. This is the largest dataset with ground truth available today for this task.

To overcome the challenges of training data scarcity, Su *et al.* [7] proposed to augment the dataset with synthetic rendered CAD models from ShapeNet [23]. This allows the creation of as many images as needed for a single model. Random backgrounds from images of SUN397 [24] were added to the rendered images. The images were then cropped to resemble real images taken "in the wild", where the cropping statistics maintained that of VOC2012 [25], creating 2M images. The use of this synthetic data increased the performance by ~2%.

We further augmented the training dataset, in accordance with Insight 2, in three manners. First, rather than randomly selecting backgrounds, we chose for each category backgrounds that are realistic for the objects. For instance, boats should not float in living-rooms, but rather be synthesized with backgrounds of oceans or harbors. This change increased the performance only slightly.

More importantly, we augmented the training dataset by horizontally flipping the existing real images. Since the orientation of these images is known, they are used within a new loss function to enforce correct viewpoints (Sect. 3.3).

Finally, we used unlabeled videos of objects, for which we could exploit the coherency of the motion, to further increase the volume of data and improve the results. We will show in Sect. 3.3 how to modify the loss function to use these clips for semi-supervised learning.

3.3   Loss

As shown in Fig. 3, there are five loss functions in our model, four of which are set by Faster R-CNN. This section focuses on the *viewpoint loss* function, in line of Insights 3 & 4, and shows how to combine it with the other loss functions.

Treating viewpoint estimation as a classification problem, the network predicts the probability of an object to belong to a viewpoint bin (bin = 1°). One problem with this approach is that close viewpoints are located in different bins and bin order is disregarded. In the evaluation, however, the common practice is to divide the space of viewpoints into larger bins (of 15°) [12]. This means that, in contrast to classical classification, if the network errs when estimating a viewpoint, it is better to err by outputting close viewpoints than by outputting faraway ones. Therefore, our loss should address a geometric constraint—the network should produce similar representations for close viewpoints.

To address this, Su *et al.* [7] proposed to use a geometric-aware loss function instead of a regular cross-entropy loss with one-hot label:

$$L_{geom}(q) = -\frac{1}{C} \sum_{k=1}^{360} exp(-\frac{|k_{gt} - k|}{\sigma})log(q(k)). \tag{2}$$

In this equation, q is the viewpoint probability vector of some bounding box, k is a bin index, k_{gt} is the ground truth bin index, $q(k)$ is the probability of bin k, and $\sigma = 3$. Thus, in Eq. (2) the commonly used one-hot label is replaced by an exponential decay weight w.r.t the distance between the viewpoints. By doing so, the correlation between predictions of nearby views is "encouraged". Interestingly, while this loss function was shown to improve the results of [7], it did not improve the results of a later work of [8].

We propose a different loss function, which realizes the geometric constraint. Our loss is based on the fundamental idea of the Siamese architecture [26–28], which has the property of bringing similar classes closer together, while increasing the distances between unrelated classes.

Our first attempt was to utilize the contrastive Siamese loss [27], which is applied to the embedded representation of the viewpoint estimation head (before the viewpoint classification layer). Given representations of two images $F(X_1), F(X_2)$ and the L_2 distance between them $D(X_1, X_2) = ||F(X_1) - F(X_2)||_2$, the loss is defined as:

$$L_{contrastive}(D) = (Y)\frac{1}{2}D^2 + (1 - Y)\frac{1}{2}\{max(0, m - D)\}^2. \tag{3}$$

Here, Y is the similarity label, i.e. 1 if the images have close viewpoints (in practice, up to 10°) and 0 otherwise and m is the margin. Thus, pairs whose distance is larger than m will not contribute to the loss. There are two issues that should be addressed when adopting this loss: the choice of the hyper-parameter m and the correct balance between the positive training examples and the negative ones, as this loss is sensitive to their number and to their order. This approach yielded sub-optimal results for a variety of choices of m and numbers/orders.

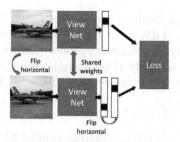

Fig. 4. Flipped images within a Siamese network. The loss attempts to minimize the distance between the representations of an image and its flip.

Therefore, we propose a different & novel Siamese loss, as illustrated in Fig. 4. The key idea is to use pairs of an image and its horizontally-flipped image. Since the only difference between these images is the viewpoint and the relation between the viewpoints is known, we define the following loss function:

$$L_{flip}(X, X_{flip}) = L_{geom}(X) + L_{geom}(X_{flip}) + \lambda ||F(X) - flip(F(X_{flip}))||_2^2, \quad (4)$$

where L_{geom} is from Eq. (2). We expect the L_2 distance term, between the embeddings of an image and the flip of its flipped image, to be close to 0. Note that while previously flipped images were used for data augmentation, we use them within the loss function, in a manner that is unique for pose estimation.

To improve the results further, we adopt the triplet network concept [29,30] and modify its loss to suit our problem. The basic idea is to "encourage" the network to output similarity-induced embeddings. Three images are provided during training: X^{ref}, X^+, X^-, where X^{ref}, X^+ are from similar classes and X^{ref}, X^- are from dissimilar classes. In [29], the distance between image representations $D(F(X_1), F(X_2))$ is the L_2 distance between them. Let $D^+ = D(X^{ref}, X^+)$, $D^- = D(X^{ref}, X^-)$, and d^+, d^- be the results of applying softmax to D^+, D^- respectively. The larger the difference between the viewpoints, the more dissimilar the classes should be, i.e. $D^+ < D^-$.

A common loss, which encourages embeddings of related classes to have small distances and embeddings of unrelated classes to have large distances, is:

$$L_{triplet}(X^{ref}, X^+, X^+) = ||(d^+, 1 - d^-)||_2^2. \quad (5)$$

We found, however, that the distances D get very large values and therefore, applying softmax to them results in d^+, d^- that are very far from each other, even for similar labels. Therefore, we replace D by the *cosine* distance:

$$D(F(x_1), F(x_2)) = \frac{F(x_1) \cdot F(x_2)}{||F(x_1)||_2 ||F(x_2)||_2}. \quad (6)$$

The distances are now in the range $[-1, 1]$, which allows faster training and convergence, since the network does not need to account for changes in the scale of the weights. For *cosine* distance we require $D^+ > D^-$ (instead of $<$), and consequentially the roles of d^+, d^- in Eq. (5) should switch.

A minor trick we apply for softmax to produce the range $[0, 1]$, while resolving convergence issues, is to multiply D by a single trainable scalar, as in [31].

Finally, the viewpoint loss is defined as (with $\lambda = 5$):

$$L_{viewpoint}(X^{ref}, X^+, X^-) = L_{triplet}(X^{ref}, X^+, X^+) + \lambda L_{flip}(X^{ref}). \quad (7)$$

Table 2 shows the gains yielded by different combinations of the loss functions discussed above. The combination of the triplet loss and the flip loss (Eq. (7)) results in the best performance.

Table 2. Results gained by different loss functions. Equation (7) gives the best performance compared to a variety of loss functions.

Loss function (real data)	Score (mAVP24)
Geometric loss, Eq. (2)	43.2
Contrastive loss, Eq. (3)	42.5
Flip loss, Eq. (4)	43.6
Triplet + Geometric loss, Eq. (5) + (2)	44.1
Viewpoint loss, Eq. (7)	44.4

Putting it all together: Finally, the whole network is trained on the sum of all the loss functions from Fig. 3:

$$L_{total} = L_{classification}^{RPN} + L_{regression}^{RPN} + L_{classification}^{Classifier} + L_{regression}^{Classifier} + L_{viewpoint}. \quad (8)$$

The first four terms are from [16] and the last term is from Eq. (7).

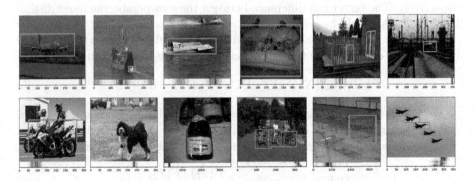

Fig. 5. Correct viewpoint estimation predictions. The bar below each image ($0°-360°$) indicates in blue our highest viewpoint prediction, in red the ground truth, and in black predictions with high confidence. Our prediction and the ground truth fall in the same bin, i.e., within $15°$ from each other.

4   Results

Our evaluation is performed on PASCAL3D+ [12], which contains manually-annotated images from VOC2012 [25] & from ImageNet [32]. All the experiments were conducted using the Keras [33] framework with TensorFlow [34] backend. Figure 5 shows examples of correct predictions made by our model, as well as the detected bounding boxes. The bar below each image indicates in blue our highest viewpoint prediction, in red the ground truth, and in black predictions with high confidence. It can be seen that in most cases our prediction falls in the same bin as the ground truth. Moreover, in most cases the predictions with high confidence (in black) are nicely clustered. The exception is the image of the boats, for which two clusters of 180°-difference are evident. This can be explained by the horizontal near-symmetry of the object.

The common evaluation metric for this problem is the *mean Average View Precision (mAVP)* [12]. Briefly, in AVP, the output from the detector is considered to be correct if the bounding boxes' overlap is larger than 50% **AND** the viewpoint is correct. The AVP is defined as the area under the Viewpoint Precision-Recall (VPR) curve. It is therefore a joint metric both for detection and for viewpoint estimation. Following previous work, we compare our results based on the discrete AVP with $K = 24$ viewpoint bins.

4.1   Training

Our model was initialized with weights from Faster R-CNN, trained on VOC2012 & VOC2007 datasets. The weights of the viewpoint estimation head were initialized with Xavier initialization [35]. Adam optimizer [36] was used with the learning rate set to $lr = 10^{-4}, \beta_1 = 0.9, \beta_2 = 0.999$, unless otherwise specified.

Each training step was performed using a single image, from which we took a mini-batch of 32 region proposals, out of the proposals the network had made. By default, half of the regions included the objects and half did not; however if the network did not provide enough regions of objects, we padded the mini-batch with more background regions.

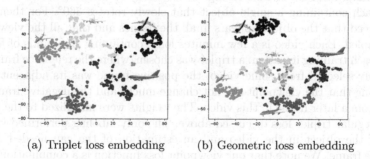

(a) Triplet loss embedding   (b) Geometric loss embedding

Fig. 6. Embeddings. Each point represents an image embedding in the feature space (using t-SNE), where color corresponds to the ground-truth viewpoint bin. The triplet loss manages not only to separate the viewpoint bins better than the geometric loss, but also to better reflect the circular nature of the problem.

We started the training with the synthetic data, followed by the real data. For the synthetic data, we created ∼100 K synthetic images per category. We fixed the weights of the detection & classification network, since we noticed that synthetic data decreased the detection results significantly. We fine-tuned only the viewpoint estimation head, training for 200 K iterations.

As real data, we used the 22 K training images from the annotated data of PASCAL3D+. We augmented the data by horizontally-flipped images. We started the training with the weights gained from the synthetic training and fine-tuned the whole network. Our model was trained for 200 K iterations. Then, we reduced the learning rate by a factor of 10 and continued the training only for the viewpoint estimation head, for 150 K iterations.

Training with Our Triplet Loss. At every iteration, we randomly selected a class and a reference image from this class. As a positive example, an image from the same class, whose viewpoint is within 5° from the reference, was chosen. As a negative example, we started from "easy" images (from the same class, but faraway viewpoints) and worked our way to more difficult ones. Specifically, for the first 100 K triplets, we sampled the distance to the reference from a Gaussian centered at 100° with std of 20° and selected a suitable image. After the loss has stabilized, we sampled from a Gaussian centered at 15° with std of 2°.

Figure 6 shows the 2D embedding of the airplane class, using t-SNE [37], as resulted from the triplet network. Similar viewpoints are better clustered when using our loss than when using the geometric loss of [7]. Moreover, the points are structured in a more "circular" shape, which reflects the circular nature of our problem, as explained in [7]. Thus, the triplet loss not only better separates the embeddings, but also manages to push the features outward.

Training with Videos. The key idea behind the use of videos is that though the viewpoint is unknown, we do know that viewpoints of subsequent frames should be similar. To realize this idea, we use the triplet architecture, this time within a semi-supervised learning scheme. We downloaded 100 unannotated YouTube videos that contain objects from our categories, for which it is unknown whether the object appears in a frame or not. All these videos have large motions, such as a landing airplane or bike racing. In addition, 10 videos per class were utilized, each containing a single object that slowly rotates 360°. For them, it is guaranteed that the object appears in all the frames and that all the viewpoints are sampled. Each video is a few minutes long, containing thousands of frames.

At each training iteration, a triplet was chosen, where the reference frame was randomly selected from some video, the positive frame was its adjacent frame (assuming that the viewpoint did not change much) and the negative frame was taken from a later frame in this video. The weights were initialized to the results of the regular triplet loss discussed above. The only labeling performed was the class of the object in the video and an estimation of the gap needed for the negative frame. We note that our viewpoint loss function is a combination of the flip loss and the triplet loss (Eq. (7)), yet videos are not associated with labels that allow us to compute the flip loss. Therefore, when using videos, the flip loss term used a random real image, rather than a video frame.

4.2   Comparison with State-of-the-Art Results

Table 3 "zooms into" the findings of Table 1, showing the gains for the different classes, attributed to the different components of our model. The upper part of the table shows the results of previous works. The middle part shows the results of applying Insights 1,4,5. In particular, when replacing VGG by ResNet and maintaining the same loss and data as [8], the results improve from 36.1 of [8] to 39.5, using both real and synthetic data (and to 37.6 using only real data). By using the geometric loss from Eq. (2), the performance is improved to 40.6. When choosing the bin that integrates on the distribution of the viewpoints within it (Eq. (1)), instead of choosing the maximum activation bin, the result is further improved to 43.2. This nice improvement can be explained by noting that the bin integral method can be considered as noise reduction, which is beneficial especially for noisy classes, such as bicycles and motorbikes.

The lower part of the table shows the influence of Insights 2,3, assuming that our model uses ResNet/Faster R-CNN, was trained on synthetic & real data and chooses the bin using an integral on the distribution. Our viewpoint loss improves the results by 1.2%; the video data further improves by 1.5%. Overall we achieved improvement of 9.8% compared to the current state-of-the-art results.

Table 3. The number of correctly-estimated viewpoints is 25% higher than SOTA results, improving from 36.1 of [8] to 45.9, on PASCAL3D+.

Method	aero	bicycle	boat	bus	car	chair	table	mbike	sofa	train	TV	mAVP24
[7]:AlexNet/R-CNN-Geometry-synthetic+real	21.5	22.0	4.1	38.6	25.5	7.4	11.0	24.4	15.0	28.0	19.8	19.8
[9]: VGG/R-CNN-Classification-real	37.0	33.4	10.0	54.1	40.0	17.5	19.9	34.3	28.9	43.9	22.7	31.1
[8]: VGG/Fast R-CNN-Classification-synthetic+real	43.2	39.4	16.8	61.0	44.2	13.5	29.4	37.5	33.5	46.6	32.5	36.1
Ours: ResNet/Faster-Classification-real	41.6	33.7	20.6	65.3	45.4	17.9	33.8	36	34.5	48.6	36.6	37.6
Ours: ResNet/Faster-Classification-synthetic+real	43.6	37.1	19.9	68.5	48.6	19.8	37.1	34.2	38.2	48.3	39.6	39.5
Ours: ResNet/Faster-Geometry-synthetic+real	43.9	35.4	20.9	70.3	51.5	20.0	38.6	34.0	41.6	50.4	40.0	40.6
Ours: ResNet/Faster-Geometry-synthetic+real-integral	43.5	41.2	23.9	68.4	52.7	22.4	41.9	42.0	44.1	50.3	45.0	43.2
Ours: all the above +Viewpoint loss	46.6	41.1	**23.9**	72.6	53.5	22.5	42.6	42.0	44.2	**54.6**	44.8	44.4
Ours: all the above +Viewpoint loss-video data	**47.7**	**42.5**	23.8	**74.8**	**54.7**	**25.9**	**42.8**	**43.5**	**46.3**	54.6	**47.9**	**45.9**

Fig. 7. Typical false viewpoint estimation cases. Our predictions for the bus and the motorbike is 180°-opposite; for the bicycle our prediction matches the viewpoint of the handlebar rather than that of the main frame; the table should have two correct viewpoints, of which our viewpoint estimator chose one.

We note that different methods improve different categories. For instance, the integration method vastly improves the motorbike and the bicycle classes. In these classes there are many images that contain more than one object from the class, which are very close to one another. Their detected bounding boxes overlap and objects produce "noisy viewpoints" for others. When integrating over all the bounding boxes, some of which do contain a single object, this noise is reduced. Moreover, the viewpoint distribution in PASCAL3D+ for these classes is more uniform than in most other classes. Hence, our network has no bias and tends to assign probabilities to all the object's symmetries. This is beneficial for the bin integral method, since collecting more information improves prediction.

The flip loss shows improvements mainly for the "rectangular" objects, such as buses, trains and tables. We infer that flipping indeed helps the network in resolving some of the symmetry ambiguities, as desired.

The viewpoint (triplet/flip) loss is mostly beneficial for classes for which the geometric loss errs by 180° (object facing backward/forward), such as airplanes, buses and trains. A possible explanation is that unlike the geometric loss, which relates between close viewpoints through its use of Gaussian weights, the viewpoint loss relates also between faraway viewpoints.

The use of video clips improves the classes for which we had videos that contain almost all viewpoints.

Limitations: Figure 7 illustrates some typical failures. For the bus and the motorbike, the failures are due to backward/forward symmetry—our model predicted the 180°-opposite viewpoint. The false prediction for the bicycle is due to the handlebar position, which is not aligned with the main frame. The table illustrates a case where two viewpoints are equally correct (i.e. there is no front & back to a rectangular table), but our algorithm chose one viewpoint whereas the ground truth is the other.

Estimating All Euler Angles: Following [8], throughout this paper only the azimuth is predicted. This is so because of two reasons: (i) Our method is general and can be applied to the other Euler angles, by simply adding a fully-connected layer for each angle; (ii) Unlike the azimuth distribution, the elevation & tilt distributions have little variation (about 85% of the images are within 20°).

Nevertheless, we achieve state-of-the-art results also when all 3 angles are considered. In [7,9], all Euler angles are predicted and the accuracy is measured on the three angles jointly, as follows. (1) *MedErr* calculates the median error between the predicted rotation matrix to the ground truth one (the lower the better) and (2) $Acc_{\frac{\pi}{6}}$ computes the fraction of instances whose predicted viewpoint is within a fixed threshold of the target viewpoint (the higher the better).

On these metrics we gain 23% improvement with *MedErr* (15.6 [9], 11.7 [7], 8.9 ours) and 8.5% improvement with $Acc_{\frac{\pi}{6}}$ (0.76 [9], 0.82 [7], 0.89 ours).

5   Conclusions

This paper has addressed the task of viewpoint estimation of an object in an image. It provides five insights, which regard all the components of the network: the architecture, the training data, the loss function, and the integration of the results.

Based on these insights, a network was designed such that: (i) The architecture jointly solves detection, classification, and pose estimation, using the most advanced CNN for performing the two former tasks. (ii) To handle the shortage in labeled data, the paper proposes to add both videos and flipped images to the training stage. (iii) A novel loss function that takes into account both the geometric nature of the problem, as well as the constraints posed by videos and flipped images, is introduced. (iv) While previous works predicted the viewpoint using the maximum activation, we propose an integration scheme for prediction.

Our network improves the state-of-the-art results for this problem on PAS-CAL3D+ by 9.8%. The paper carefully analyzes the influence of each component on the overall performance.

Future Directions: Our viewpoint estimation is based only on the information within the bounding box. However, information from the full image can be helpful. For instance, the wave direction may assist in determining the boat's viewpoint, or passengers on the platform may indicate the train's direction.

Second, the available dataset should be enhanced. As the improved performance due to our additional data may imply, larger datasets are likely to benefit viewpoint estimation. Moreover, better annotation methods are necessary, as currently some images are falsely annotated, which biases both training and testing. Finally, for certain types of objects (e.g. circular tables or the table in Fig. 7), any attempt to define a single ground-truth viewpoint is doomed to fail. Such special cases should be given proper attention.

Acknowledgements. We gratefully acknowledge the support of NVIDIA Corporation with the donation of the GPU, as well as the Ollendorff Foundation.

References

1. Huttenlocher, D.P.: Object recognition using alignment. In: Proceedings of the IEEE International Conference on Computer Vision (ICCV), pp. 102–111 (1987)
2. Lowe, D.G.: The viewpoint consistency constraint. Int. J. Comput. Vis. (IJCV) **1**(1), 57–72 (1987)
3. Lowe, D.G., et al.: Fitting parameterized three-dimensional models to images. IEEE Trans. Pattern Anal. Mach. Intell. (PAMI) **13**(5), 441–450 (1991)
4. Huttenlocher, D.P., Ullman, S.: Recognizing solid objects by alignment with an image. Int. J. Comput. Vis. (IJCV) **5**(2), 195–212 (1990)
5. Choi, C., Taguchi, Y., Tuzel, O., Liu, M.Y., Ramalingam, S.: Voting-based pose estimation for robotic assembly using a 3D sensor. In: IEEE International Conference on Robotics and Automation (ICRA), pp. 1724–1731 (2012)

6. Marchand, E., Uchiyama, H., Spindler, F.: Pose estimation for augmented reality: a hands-on survey. IEEE Trans. Vis. Comput. Graph. **22**(12), 2633–2651 (2016)
7. Su, H., Qi, C.R., Li, Y., Guibas, L.J.: Render for CNN: viewpoint estimation in images using CNNs trained with rendered 3d model views. In: Proceedings of the IEEE International Conference on Computer Vision (ICCV), pp. 2686–2694 (2015)
8. Massa, F., Marlet, R., Aubry, M.: Crafting a multi-task CNN for viewpoint estimation. arXiv:1609.03894 (2016)
9. Tulsiani, S., Malik, J.: Viewpoints and keypoints. In: Proceedings of the IEEE Conference on Computer Vision and Pattern Recognition (CVPR), pp. 1510–1519 (2015)
10. Penedones, H., Collobert, R., Fleuret, F., Grangier, D.: Improving object classification using pose information. Technical report, Idiap (2012)
11. Osadchy, M., Cun, Y.L., Miller, M.L.: Synergistic face detection and pose estimation with energy-based models. J. Mach. Learn. Res., 1197–1215 (2007)
12. Xiang, Y., Mottaghi, R., Savarese, S.: Beyond PASCAL: a benchmark for 3D object detection in the wild. In: IEEE Winter Conference on Applications of Computer Vision (WACV) (2014)
13. Girshick, R., Donahue, J., Darrell, T., Malik, J.: Rich feature hierarchies for accurate object detection and semantic segmentation. In: Proceedings of the IEEE Conference on Computer Vision and Pattern Recognition (CVPR), pp. 580–587 (2014)
14. Pinheiro, P.O., Collobert, R., Dollár, P.: Learning to segment object candidates. In: Advances in Neural Information Processing Systems (NIPS), pp. 1990–1998 (2015)
15. Girshick, R.: Fast R-CNN. arXiv:1504.08083 (2015)
16. Ren, S., He, K., Girshick, R., Sun, J.: Faster R-CNN: towards real-time object detection with region proposal networks. In: Advances in Neural Information Processing Systems (NIPS), pp. 91–99 (2015)
17. Eigen, D., Fergus, R.: Predicting depth, surface normals and semantic labels with a common multi-scale convolutional architecture. In: Proceedings of the IEEE International Conference on Computer Vision (ICCV), pp. 2650–2658 (2015)
18. Gkioxari, G., Girshick, R., Malik, J.: Contextual action recognition with R* CNN. In: Proceedings of the IEEE International Conference on Computer Vision (ICCV), pp. 1080–1088 (2015)
19. Krizhevsky, A., Sutskever, I., Hinton, G.E.: Imagenet classification with deep convolutional neural networks. In: Advances in Neural Information Processing Systems (NIPS) (2012)
20. Simonyan, K., Zisserman, A.: Very deep convolutional networks for large-scale image recognition. arXiv:1409.1556 (2014)
21. He, K., Zhang, X., Ren, S., Sun, J.: Deep residual learning for image recognition. In: Proceedings of the IEEE Conference on Computer Vision and Pattern Recognition (CVPR), pp. 770–778 (2016)
22. Google 3D warehouse. http://sketchup.google.com/3dwarehouse
23. Chang, A.X., et al.: ShapeNet: an information-rich 3D model repository. Technical Report arXiv:1512.03012 (2015)
24. Xiao, J., Hays, J., Ehinger, K.A., Oliva, A., Torralba, A.: Sun database: large-scale scene recognition from abbey to zoo. In: Proceedings of the IEEE Conference on Computer Vision and Pattern Recognition (CVPR), pp. 3485–3492 (2010)
25. Everingham, M., Van Gool, L., Williams, C.K., Winn, J., Zisserman, A.: The pascal visual object classes (VOC) challenge. Int. J. Comput. Vis. (IJCV) **88**(2), 303–338 (2010)

26. Bromley, J., Guyon, I., LeCun, Y., Säckinger, E., Shah, R.: Signature verification using a " siamese" time delay neural network. In: Advances in Neural Information Processing Systems (NIPS), pp. 737–744 (1994)

27. Chopra, S., Hadsell, R., LeCun, Y.: Learning a similarity metric discriminatively, with application to face verification. In: Proceedings of the IEEE Conference on Computer Vision and Pattern Recognition (CVPR), pp. 539–546 (2005)

28. Hadsell, R., Chopra, S., LeCun, Y.: Dimensionality reduction by learning an invariant mapping. In: Proceedings of the IEEE Conference on Computer Vision and Pattern Recognition (CVPR), pp. 1735–1742 (2006)

29. Hoffer, E., Ailon, N.: Deep metric learning using triplet network. In: Feragen, A., Pelillo, M., Loog, M. (eds.) SIMBAD 2015. LNCS, vol. 9370, pp. 84–92. Springer, Cham (2015). https://doi.org/10.1007/978-3-319-24261-3_7

30. Wang, J., et al.: Learning fine-grained image similarity with deep ranking. In: Proceedings of the IEEE Conference on Computer Vision and Pattern Recognition (CVPR), pp. 1386–1393 (2014)

31. Hoffer, E., Hubara, I., Soudry, D.: Fix your classifier: the marginal value of training the last weight layer. arXiv:1801.04540 (2018)

32. Deng, J., Dong, W., Socher, R., Li, L.J., Li, K., Fei-Fei, L.: Imagenet: A large-scale hierarchical image database. In: Proceedings of the IEEE Conference on Computer Vision and Pattern Recognition (CVPR), pp. 248–255. IEEE (2009)

33. Chollet, F., et al.: Keras (2015). https://github.com/keras-team/keras

34. Abadi, M., et al.: TensorFlow: Large-scale machine learning on heterogeneous systems (2015). https://www.tensorflow.org

35. Glorot, X., Bengio, Y.: Understanding the difficulty of training deep feedforward neural networks. In: Proceedings of the Thirteenth International Conference on Artificial Intelligence and Statistics, pp. 249–256 (2010)

36. Kingma, D., Ba, J.: Adam: A method for stochastic optimization. arXiv:1412.6980 (2014)

37. Maaten, L.V.D., Hinton, G., Visualizing data using t-SNE: Visualizing data using t-SNE. J. Mach. Learn. Res. **9**, 2579–2605 (2008)

PersonLab: Person Pose Estimation and Instance Segmentation with a Bottom-Up, Part-Based, Geometric Embedding Model

George Papandreou[✉], Tyler Zhu, Liang-Chieh Chen, Spyros Gidaris,
Jonathan Tompson, and Kevin Murphy

Google Research, Los Angeles, USA
gpapan@google.com, tylerzhu@google.com, lcchen@google.com,
spyrosg@google.com, tompson@google.com, kpmurphy@google.com

Abstract. We present a box-free bottom-up approach for the tasks of pose estimation and instance segmentation of people in multi-person images using an efficient single-shot model. The proposed PersonLab model tackles both semantic-level reasoning and object-part associations using part-based modeling. Our model employs a convolutional network which learns to detect individual keypoints and predict their relative displacements, allowing us to group keypoints into person pose instances. Further, we propose a part-induced geometric embedding descriptor which allows us to associate semantic person pixels with their corresponding person instance, delivering instance-level person segmentations. Our system is based on a fully-convolutional architecture and allows for efficient inference, with runtime essentially independent of the number of people present in the scene. Trained on COCO data alone, our system achieves COCO test-dev keypoint average precision of 0.665 using single-scale inference and 0.687 using multi-scale inference, significantly outperforming all previous bottom-up pose estimation systems. We are also the first bottom-up method to report competitive results for the person class in the COCO instance segmentation task, achieving a person category average precision of 0.417.

Keywords: Person detection and pose estimation
Segmentation and grouping

1 Introduction

The rapid recent progress in computer vision has allowed the community to move beyond classic tasks such as bounding box-level face and body detection towards

Electronic supplementary material The online version of this chapter (https://doi.org/10.1007/978-3-030-01264-9_17) contains supplementary material, which is available to authorized users.

© Springer Nature Switzerland AG 2018
V. Ferrari et al. (Eds.): ECCV 2018, LNCS 11218, pp. 282–299, 2018.
https://doi.org/10.1007/978-3-030-01264-9_17

more detailed visual understanding of people in unconstrained environments. In this work we tackle in a unified manner the tasks of multi-person detection, 2-D pose estimation, and instance segmentation. Given a potentially cluttered and crowded 'in-the-wild' image, our goal is to identify every person instance, localize its facial and body keypoints, and estimate its instance segmentation mask. A host of computer vision applications such as smart photo editing, person and activity recognition, virtual or augmented reality, and robotics can benefit from progress in these challenging tasks.

There are two main approaches for tackling multi-person detection, pose estimation and segmentation. The *top-down* approach starts by identifying and roughly localizing individual person instances by means of a bounding box object detector, followed by single-person pose estimation or binary foreground/ background segmentation in the region inside the bounding box. By contrast, the *bottom-up* approach starts by localizing identity-free semantic entities (individual keypoint proposals or semantic person segmentation labels, respectively), followed by grouping them into person instances. In this paper, we adopt the latter approach. We develop a box-free fully convolutional system whose computational cost is essentially independent of the number of people present in the scene and only depends on the cost of the CNN feature extraction backbone.

In particular, our approach first predicts all keypoints for every person in the image in a fully convolutional way. We also learn to predict the relative displacement between each pair of keypoints, also proposing a novel recurrent scheme which greatly improves the accuracy of long-range predictions. Once we have localized the keypoints, we use a greedy decoding process to group them into instances. Our approach starts from the most confident detection, as opposed to always starting from a distinguished landmark such as the nose, so it works well even in clutter.

In addition to predicting the sparse keypoints, our system also predicts dense instance segmentation masks for each person. For this purpose, we train our network to predict instance-agnostic semantic person segmentation maps. For every person pixel we also predict offset vectors to each of the K keypoints of the corresponding person instance. The corresponding vector fields can be thought as a geometric embedding representation and induce basins of attraction around each person instance, leading to an efficient association algorithm: For each pixel x_i, we predict the locations of all K keypoints for the corresponding person that x_i belongs to; we then compare this to all candidate detected people j (in terms of average keypoint distance), weighted by the keypoint detection probability; if this distance is low enough, we assign pixel i to person j.

We train our model on the standard COCO keypoint dataset [1], which annotates multiple people with 12 body and 5 facial keypoints. We significantly outperform the best previous bottom-up approach to keypoint localization [2], improving the keypoint AP from 0.655 to 0.687. In addition, we are the first bottom-up method to report competitive results on the person class for the COCO instance segmentation task. We get a mask AP of 0.417, which outperforms the strong top-down FCIS method of [3], which gets 0.386. Furthermore our method is very simple and hence fast, since it does not require any second stage box-based refinement, or clustering algorithm. We believe it will therefore be quite useful for a variety of applications, especially since it lends itself to deployment in mobile phones.

2   Related Work

2.1   Pose Estimation

Proir to the recent trend towards deep convolutional networks [4,5], early successful models for human pose estimation centered around inference mechanisms on part-based graphical models [6,7], representing a person by a collection of configurable parts. Following this work, many methods have been proposed to develop tractable inference algorithms for solving the energy minimization that captures rich dependencies among body parts [8–16]. While the forward inference mechanism of this work differs to these early DPM-based models, we similarly propose a bottom-up approach for grouping part detections to person instances.

Recently, models based on modern large scale convolutional networks have achieved state-of-art performance on both single-person pose estimation [17–26] and multi-person pose estimation [27–34]. Broadly speaking, there are two main approaches to pose-estimation in the literature: top-down (person first) and bottom-up (parts first). Examples of the former include G-RMI [33], CFN [35], RMPE [36], Mask R-CNN [34], and CPN [37]. These methods all predict key point locations within person bounding boxes obtained by a person detector (*e.g.*, Fast-RCNN [38], Faster-RCNN [39] or R-FCN [40]).

In the bottom-up approach, we first detect body parts and then group these parts to human instances. Pishchulin *et al.* [27], Insafutdinov *et al.* [28,29], and Iqbal *et al.* [30] formulate the problem of multi-person pose estimation as part grouping and labeling via a Linear Program. Cao *et al.* [32] incorporate the unary joint detector modified from [31] with a part affinity field and greedily generate person instance proposals. Newell *et al.* [2] propose associative embedding to identify key point detections from the same person.

2.2   Instance Segmentation

The approaches for instance segmentation can also be categorized into the two top-down and bottom-up paradigms.

Top-down methods exploit state-of-art detection models to either classify mask proposals [41–47] or to obtain mask segmentation results by refining the bounding box proposals [3,34,48–51].

Ours is a bottom-up approach, in which we associate pixel-level predictions to each object instance. Many recent models propose similar forms of instance-level bottom-up clustering. For instance, Liang *et al.* use a proposal-free network [52] to cluster semantic segmentation results to obtain instance segmentation. Uhrig *et al.* [53] first predict each pixel's direction towards its instance center and then employ template matching to decode and cluster the instance segmentation result. Zhang *et al.* [54,55] predict instance ID by encoding the object depth ordering within a patch and use this depth ordering to cluster instances. Wu *et al.* [56] use a prediction network followed by a Hough transform-like approach to perform prediction instance clustering. In this work, we similarly perform a Hough voting of multiple predictions. In a slightly different formulation, Liu *et al.* [57] segment and aggregate segmentation results from dense multiscale patches, and aggregate localized patches into complete object instances. Levinkov *et al.* [58] formulate the instance segmentation problem as a combinatorial optimization problem that consists of graph decomposition and node labeling and propose efficient local search algorithms to iteratively refine an initial solution. InstanceCut [59] and the work of [60] propose to predict object boundaries to separate instances. [2,61,62] group pixel predictions that have similar values in the learned embedding space to obtain instance segmentation results. Bai and Urtasun [63] propose a Watershed Transform Network which produces an energy map where object instances are represented as basin. Liu *et al.* [64] propose the Sequential Grouping Network which decomposes the instance segmentation problem into several sub-grouping problems.

3   Methods

Figure 1 gives an overview of our system, which we describe in detail next.

3.1   Person Detection and Pose Estimation

We develop a box-free bottom-up approach for person detection and pose estimation. It consists of two sequential steps, detection of K keypoints, followed by grouping them into person instances. We train our network in a supervised fashion, using the ground truth annotations of the $K = 17$ face and body parts in the COCO dataset.

Keypoint Detection. The goal of this stage is to detect, in an instance-agnostic fashion, all visible keypoints belonging to any person in the image.

For this purpose, we follow the hybrid classification and regression approach of [33], adapting it to our multi-person setting. We produce heatmaps (one channel per keypoint) and offsets (two channels per keypoint for displacements in the horizontal and vertical directions). Let x_i be the 2-D position in the image, where $i = 1, \ldots N$ is indexing the position in the image and N is the number of pixels. Let $\mathcal{D}_R(y) = \{x : \|x - y\| \leq R\}$ be a disk of radius R centered around y. Also let $y_{j,k}$ be the 2-D position of the k-th keypoint of the j-th person instance, with $j = 1, \ldots, M$, where M is the number of person instances in the image.

For every keypoint type $k = 1, \ldots, K$, we set up a binary classification task as follows. We predict a heatmap $p_k(x)$ such that $p_k(x) = 1$ if $x \in \mathcal{D}_R(y_{j,k})$ for any person instance j, otherwise $p_k(x) = 0$. We thus have K independent dense binary classification tasks, one for each keypoint type. Each amounts to predicting a disk of radius R around a specific keypoint type of any person in

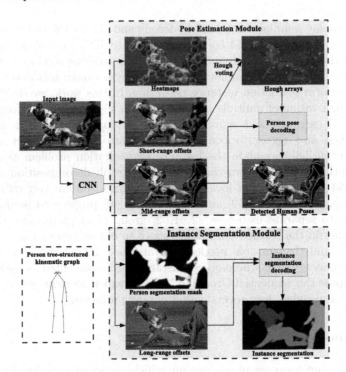

Fig. 1. Our PersonLab system consists of a CNN model that predicts: (1) keypoint heatmaps, (2) short-range offsets, (3) mid-range pairwise offsets, (4) person segmentation maps, and (5) long-range offsets. The first three predictions are used by the *Pose Estimation Module* in order to detect human poses while the latter two, along with the human pose detections, are used by the *Instance Segmentation Module* in order to predict person instance segmentation masks.

the image. The disk radius value is set to $R = 32$ pixels for all experiments reported in this paper and is independent of the person instance scale. We have deliberately opted for a disk radius which does not scale with the instance size in order to equally weigh all person instances in the classification loss. During training, we compute the heatmap loss as the average logistic loss along image positions and we back-propagate across the full image, only excluding areas that contain people that have not been fully annotated with keypoints (person crowd areas and small scale person segments in the COCO dataset).

In addition to the heatmaps, we also predict *short-range* offset vectors $S_k(x)$ whose purpose is to improve the keypoint localization accuracy. At each position x within the keypoint disks and for each keypoint type k, the short-range 2-D offset vector $S_k(x) = y_{j,k} - x$ points from the image position x to the k-th keypoint of the closest person instance j, as illustrated in Fig. 1. We generate K such vector fields, solving a 2-D regression problem at each image position and keypoint independently. During training, we penalize the short-range offset prediction errors with the L_1 loss, averaging and back-propagating the errors only at the positions $x \in \mathcal{D}_R(y_{j,k})$ in the keypoint disks. We divide the errors in the short-range offsets (and all other regression tasks described in the paper) by the radius $R = 32$ pixels in order to normalize them and make their dynamic range commensurate with the heatmap classification loss.

We aggregate the heatmap and short-range offsets via Hough voting into 2-D Hough score maps $h_k(x), k = 1, \ldots, K$, using independent Hough accumulators for each keypoint type. Each image position casts a vote to each keypoint channel k with weight equal to its activation probability,

$$h_k(x) = \frac{1}{\pi R^2} \sum_{i=1:N} p_k(x_i) B(x_i + S_k(x_i) - x), \tag{1}$$

where $B(\cdot)$ denotes the bilinear interpolation kernel. The resulting highly localized Hough score maps $h_k(x)$ are illustrated in Fig. 1.

Grouping Keypoints into Person Detection Instances.

Mid-Range Pairwise Offsets. The local maxima in the score maps $h_k(x)$ serve as candidate positions for person keypoints, yet they carry no information about instance association. When multiple person instances are present in the image, we need a mechanism to "connect the dots" and group together the keypoints belonging to each individual instance. For this purpose, we add to our network a separate pairwise *mid-range* 2-D offset field output $M_{k,l}(x)$ designed to connect pairs of keypoints. We compute $2(K-1)$ such offset fields, one for each directed edge connecting pairs (k, l) of keypoints which are adjacent to each other in a tree-structured kinematic graph of the person, see Figs. 1 and 2. Specifically, the supervised training target for the pairwise offset field from the k-th to the l-th keypoint is given by $M_{k,l}(x) = (y_{j,l} - x)I(x \in \mathcal{D}_R(y_{j,k}))$, since its purpose is to allow us to move from the k-th to the l-th keypoint of the same person instance j. During training, this target regression vector is only defined if both keypoints are present in the training example. We compute the average L_1 loss of the regression prediction errors over the source keypoint disks $x \in \mathcal{D}_R(y_{j,k})$ and back-propagate through the network.

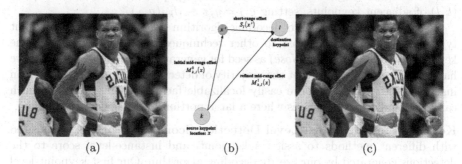

Fig. 2. Mid-range offsets. (a) Initial mid-range offsets that starting around the *RightElbow* keypoint, they point towards the *RightShoulder* keypoint. (b) Mid-range offset refinement using the short-range offsets. (c) Mid-range offsets after refinements.

Recurrent Offset Refinement. Particularly for large person instances, the edges of the kinematic graph connect pairs of keypoints such as *RightElbow* and *Right-Shoulder* which may be several hundred pixels away in the image, making it hard to generate accurate regressions. We have successfully addressed this important issue by recurrently refining the mid-range pairwise offsets using the more accurate short-range offsets, specifically:

$$M_{k,l}(x) \leftarrow x' + S_l(x'), \text{where } x' = M_{k,l}(x), \tag{2}$$

as illustrated in Fig. 2. We repeat this refinement step twice in our experiments. We employ bilinear interpolation to sample the short-range offset field at the intermediate position x' and back-propagate the errors through it along both the mid-range and short-range input offset branches. We perform offset refinement at the resolution of CNN output activations (before upsamling to the original image resolution), making the process very fast. The offset refinement process drastically decreases the mid-range regression errors, as illustrated in Fig. 2. This is a key novelty in our method, which greatly facilitates grouping and significantly improves results compared to previous papers [28,32] which also employ pairwise displacements to associate keypoints.

Fast Greedy Decoding. We have developed an extremely fast greedy decoding algorithm to group keypoints into detected person instances. We first create a priority queue, shared across all K keypoint types, in which we insert the position x_i and keypoint type k of all local maxima in the Hough score maps $h_k(x)$ which have score above a threshold value (set to 0.01 in all reported experiments). These points serve as candidate seeds for starting a detection instance. We then pop elements out of the queue in descending score order. At each iteration, if the position x_i of the current candidate detection seed of type k is within a disk $\mathcal{D}_r(y_{j',k})$ of the corresponding keypoint of previously detected person instances j', then we reject it; for this we use a non-maximum suppression radius of $r = 10$ pixels. Otherwise, we start a new detection instance j with the k-th keypoint at position $y_{j,k} = x_i$ serving as seed. We then follow the mid-range displacement vectors along the edges of the kinematic person graph to greedily connect pairs (k, l) of adjacent keypoints, setting $y_{j,l} = y_{j,k} + M_{k,l}(y_{j,k})$.

It is worth noting that our decoding algorithm does not treat any keypoint type preferentially, in contrast to other techniques that always use the same keypoint type (*e.g. Torso* or *Nose*) as seed for generating detections. Although we have empirically observed that the majority of detections in frontal facing person instances start from the more easily localizable facial keypoints, our approach can also handle robustly cases where a large portion of the person is occluded.

Keypoint- and Instance-Level Detection Scoring. We have experimented with different methods to assign a keypoint- and instance-level score to the detections generated by our greedy decoding algorithm. Our first keypoint-level scoring method follows [33] and assigns to each keypoint a confidence score $s_{j,k} = h_k(y_{j,k})$. A drawback of this approach is that the well-localizable facial keypoints typically receive much higher scores than poorly localizable keypoints like the hip or knee. Our second approach attempts to calibrate the scores of the different keypoint types. It is motivated by the object keypoint similarity (OKS) evaluation metric used in the COCO keypoints task [1], which uses different accuracy thresholds κ_k to penalize localization errors for different keypoint types.

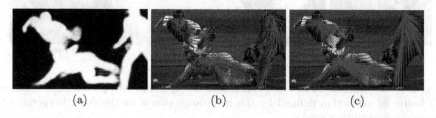

(a)   (b)   (c)

Fig. 3. Long-range offsets defined in the person segmentation mask. (a) Estimated person segmentation map. (b) Initial long range offsets for the *Nose* destination keypoint: each pixel in the foreground of the person segmentation mask points towards the *Nose* keypoint of the instance that it belongs to. (c) Long-range offsets after their refinements with the short-range offsets.

Specifically, consider a detected person instance j with keypoint coordinates $y_{j,k}$. Let λ_j be the square root of the area of the bounding box tightly containing all detected keypoints of the j-th person instance. We define the *Expected-OKS* score for the k-th keypoint by

$$s_{j,k} = E\{OKS_{j,k}\} = p_k(y_{j,k}) \int_{x \in \mathcal{D}_R(y_{j,k})} \hat{h}_k(x) \exp\left(-\frac{(x - y_{j,k})^2}{2\lambda_j^2 \kappa_k^2}\right) dx, \quad (3)$$

where $\hat{h}_k(x)$ is the Hough score normalized in $\mathcal{D}_R(y_{j,k})$. The expected OKS keypoint-level score is the product of our confidence that the keypoint is present, times the OKS localization accuracy confidence, given the keypoint's presence.

We use the average of the keypoint scores as instance-level score $s_j^h = (1/K)\sum_k s_{j,k}$, followed by non-maximum suppression (NMS). We have experimented both with hard OKS-based NMS [33] as well as a soft-NMS scheme adapted for the keypoints tasks from [65], where we use as final instance-level score the sum of the scores of the keypoints that have not already been claimed by higher scoring instances, normalized by the total number of keypoints:

$$s_j = (1/K) \sum_{k=1:K} s_{j,k}[\|y_{j,k} - y_{j',k}\| > r, \text{for every } j' < j], \quad (4)$$

where $r = 10$ is the NMS-radius. In our experiments in the main paper we report results with the best performing Expected-OKS scoring and soft-NMS but we include ablation experiments in the supplementary material.

3.2 Instance-Level Person Segmentation

Given the set of keypoint-level person instance detections, the task of our method's segmentation stage is to identify pixels that belong to people (recognition) and associate them with the detected person instances (grouping).

We describe next the respective semantic segmentation and association modules, illustrated in Fig. 4.

(a)   (b)   (c)   (d)

Fig. 4. From semantic to instance segmentation: (a) Image; (b) person segmentation; (c) basins of attraction defined by the long-range offsets to the *Nose* keypoint; (d) instance segmentation masks.

Semantic Person Segmentation. We treat semantic person segmentation in the standard fully-convolutional fashion [66,67]. We use a simple semantic segmentation head consisting of a single 1×1 convolutional layer that performs dense logistic regression and compute at each image pixel x_i the probability $p_S(x_i)$ that it belongs to at least one person. During training, we compute and backpropagate the average of the logistic loss over all image regions that have been annotated with person segmentation maps (in the case of COCO we exclude the crowd person areas).

Associating Segments with Instances Via Geometric Embeddings. The task of this module is to associate each person pixel identified by the semantic segmentation module with the keypoint-level detections produced by the person detection and pose estimation module.

Similar to [2,61,62], we follow the embedding-based approach for this task. In this framework, one computes an embedding vector $G(x)$ at each pixel location, followed by clustering to obtain the final object instances. In previous works, the representation is typically learned by computing pairs of embedding vectors at different image positions and using a loss function designed to attract the two embedding vectors if they both come from the same object instance and repel them if they come from different person instances. This typically leads to embedding representations which are difficult to interpret and involves solving a hard learning problem which requires careful selection of the loss function and tuning several hyper-parameters such as the pair sampling protocol.

Here, we opt instead for a considerably simpler, geometric approach. At each image position x inside the segmentation mask of an annotated person instance j with 2-D keypoint positions $y_{j,k}, k = 1, \ldots, K$, we define the *long-range offset* vector $L_k(x) = y_{j,k} - x$ which points from the image position x to the position of the k-th keypoint of the corresponding instance j. (This is very similar to the short-range prediction task, except the dynamic range is different, since we require the network to predict from any pixel inside the person, not just from inside a disk near the keypoint. Thus these are like two "specialist" networks. Performance is worse when we use the same network for both kinds of tasks.) We compute K such 2-D vector fields, one for each keypoint type. During training, we penalize the long-range offset regression errors using the L_1 loss, averaging and back-propagating the errors only at image positions x which belong to a single person object instance. We ignore background areas, crowd regions, and pixels which are covered by two or more person masks.

The long-range prediction task is challenging, especially for large object instances that may cover the whole image. As in Sect. 3.1, we recurrently refine the long-range offsets, twice by themselves and then twice by the short-range offsets

$$L_k(x) \leftarrow x' + L_k(x'), x' = L_k(x) \text{ and } L_k(x) \leftarrow x' + S_k(x'), x' = L_k(x), \quad (5)$$

back-propagating through the bilinear warping function during training. Similarly with the mid-range offset refinement in Eq. 2, recurrent long-range offset refinement dramatically improves the long-range offset prediction accuracy.

In Fig. 3 we illustrate the long-range offsets corresponding to the *Nose* keypoint as computed by our trained CNN for an example image. We see that the long-range vector field effectively partitions the image plane into basins of attraction for each person instance. This motivates us to define as embedding representation for our instance association task the $2 \cdot K$ dimensional vector $G(x) = (G_k(x))_{k=1,...,K}$ with components $G_k(x) = x + L_k(x)$.

Our proposed embedding vector has a very simple geometric interpretation: At each image position x_i semantically recognized as a person instance, the embedding $G(x_i)$ represents our local estimate for the absolute position of every keypoint of the person instance it belongs to, i.e., it represents the predicted shape of the person. This naturally suggests shape metric as candidates for computing distances in our proposed embedding space. In particular, in order to decide if the person pixel x_i belongs to the j-th person instance, we compute the embedding distance metric

$$D_{i,j} = \frac{1}{\sum_k p_k(y_{j,k})} \sum_{k=1}^{K} p_k(y_{j,k}) \frac{1}{\lambda_j} \|G_k(x_i) - y_{j,k}\|, \quad (6)$$

where $y_{j,k}$ is the position of the k-th detected keypoint in the j-th instance and $p_k(y_{j,k})$ is the probability that it is present. Weighing the errors by the keypoint presence probability allows us to discount discrepancies in the two shapes due to missing keypoints. Normalizing the errors by the detected instance scale λ_j allows us to compute a scale invariant metric. We set λ_j equal to the square root of the area of the bounding box tightly containing all detected keypoints of the j-th person instance. We emphasize that because we only need to compute the distance metric between the N_S pixels and the M person instances, our algorithm is very fast in practice, having complexity $\mathcal{O}(N_S * M)$ instead of $\mathcal{O}(N_S * N_S)$ of standard embedding-based segmentation techniques which, at least in principle, require computation of embedding vector distances for all pixel pairs.

To produce the final instance segmentation result: (1) We find all positions x_i marked as person in the semantic segmentation map, i.e. those pixels that have semantic segmentation probability $p_S(x_i) \geq 0.5$. (2) We associate each person pixel x_i with every detected person instance j for which the embedding distance metric satisfies $D_{i,j} \leq t$; we set the relative distance threshold $t = 0.25$ for all reported experiments. It is important to note that the pixel-instance assignment is non-exclusive: Each person pixel may be associated with more than one detected person instance (which is particularly important when doing soft-NMS in the detection stage) or it may remain an orphan (*e.g.*, a small false positive region produced by the segmentation module). We use the same instance-level score produced by the previous person detection and pose estimation stage to also evaluate on the COCO segmentation task and obtain average precision performance numbers.

3.3 Imputing Missing Keypoint Annotations

The standard COCO dataset does not contain keypoint annotations in the training set for the small person instances, and ignores them during model evaluation. However, it contains segmentation annotations and evaluates mask predictions for those small instances. Since training our geometric embeddings requires keypoint annotations for training, we have run the single-person pose estimator of [33] (trained on COCO data alone) in the COCO training set on image crops around the ground truth box annotations of those small person instances to impute those missing keypoint annotations. We treat those imputed keypoints as regular training annotations during our PersonLab model training. Naturally, this missing keypoint imputation step is particularly important for our COCO instance segmentation performance on small person instances. We emphasize that, unlike [68], we do not use any data beyond the COCO *train* split images and annotations in this process. Data distillation on additional images as described in [68] may yield further improvements.

4   Experimental Evaluation

4.1   Experimental Setup

Dataset and Tasks. We evaluate the proposed PersonLab system on the standard COCO keypoints task [1] and on COCO instance segmentation [69] for the person class alone. For all reported results we only use COCO data for model training (in addition to Imagenet pretraining). Our *train* set is the subset of the 2017 COCO training set images that contain people (64115 images). Our *val* set coincides with the 2017 COCO validation set (5000 images). We only use *train* for training and evaluate on either *val* or the *test-dev* split (20288 images).

Model Training Details. We report experimental results with models that use either ResNet-101 or ResNet-152 CNN backbones [70] pretrained on the Imagenet classification task [71]. We discard the last Imagenet classification layer and add 1×1 convolutional layers for each of our model-specific layers. During model training, we randomly resize a square box tightly containing the full

Table 1. Performance on the COCO keypoints **test-dev** split.

	AP	$AP^{.50}$	$AP^{.75}$	AP^M	AP^L	AR	$AR^{.50}$	$AR^{.75}$	AR^M	AR^L
Bottom-up methods:										
CMU-Pose [32] (+refine)	0.618	0.849	0.675	0.571	0.682	0.665	0.872	0.718	0.606	0.746
Assoc. Embed. [2] (multi-scale)	0.630	0.857	0.689	0.580	0.704	-	-	-	-	-
Assoc. Embed. [2] (mscale, refine)	0.655	0.879	0.777	0.690	0.752	0.758	0.912	0.819	0.714	0.820
Top-down methods:										
Mask-RCNN [34]	0.631	0.873	0.687	0.578	0.714	0.697	0.916	0.749	0.637	0.778
G-RMI *COCO-only* [33]	0.649	0.855	0.713	0.623	0.700	0.697	0.887	0.755	0.644	0.771
PersonLab (ours):										
ResNet101 (single-scale)	0.655	0.871	0.714	0.613	0.715	0.701	0.897	0.757	0.650	0.771
ResNet152 (single-scale)	**0.665**	0.880	0.726	0.624	0.723	0.710	0.903	0.766	0.661	0.777
ResNet101 (multi-scale)	0.678	0.886	0.744	0.630	0.748	0.745	0.922	0.804	0.686	0.825
ResNet152 (multi-scale)	**0.687**	0.890	0.754	0.641	0.755	0.754	0.927	0.812	0.697	0.830

image by a uniform random scale factor between 0.5 and 1.5, randomly translate it along the horizontal and vertical directions, and left-right flip it with probability 0.5. We sample and resize the image crop contained under the resulting perturbed box to an 801 × 801 image that we feed into the network. We use a batch size of 8 images distributed across 8 Nvidia Tesla P100 GPUs in a single machine and perform synchronous training for 1M steps with stochastic gradient descent with constant learning rate equal to 1e-3, momentum value set to 0.9, and Polyak-Ruppert model parameter averaging. We employ batch normalization [72] but fix the statistics of the ResNet activations to their Imagenet values. Our ResNet CNN network backbones have nominal output stride (*i.e.*, ratio of the input image to output activations size) equal to 32 but we reduce it to 16 during training and 8 during evaluation using atrous convolution [67]. During training we also make model predictions using as features activations from a layer in the middle of the network, which we have empirically observed to accelerate training. To balance the different loss terms we use weights equal to $(4, 2, 1, 1/4, 1/8)$ for the heatmap, segmentation, short-range, mid-range, and long-range offset losses in our model. For evaluation we report both single-scale results (image resized to have larger side 1401 pixels) and multi-scale results (pyramid with images having larger side 601, 1201, 1801, 2401 pixels). We have implemented our system in Tensorflow [73]. All reported numbers have been obtained with a single model without ensembling.

4.2 COCO Person Keypoints Evaluation

Table 1 shows our system's person keypoints performance on COCO *test-dev*. Our single-scale inference result is already better than the results of the CMU-Pose [32] and Associative Embedding [2] bottom-up methods, even when they perform multi-scale inference and refine their results with a single-person pose estimation system applied on top of their bottom-up detection proposals. Our results also outperform top-down methods like Mask-RCNN [34] and G-RMI [33]. Our best result with 0.687 AP is attained with a ResNet-152 based model and multi-scale inference. Our result is still behind the winners of the 2017 keypoints challenge (Megvii) [37] with 0.730 AP, but they used a carefully tuned two-stage, top-down model that also builds on a significantly more powerful CNN backbone.

Table 2. Performance on COCO segmentation (Person category) **test-dev** split. Our person-only results have been obtained with 20 proposals per image. The person category FCIS eval results have been communicated by the authors of [3].

	AP	AP^{50}	AP^{75}	AP^S	AP^M	AP^L	AR^1	AR^{10}	AR^{100}	AR^S	AR^M	AR^L
FCIS (baseline) [3]	0.334	0.641	0.318	0.090	0.411	0.618	0.153	0.372	0.393	0.139	0.492	0.688
FCIS (multi-scale) [3]	0.386	0.693	0.410	0.164	0.481	0.621	0.161	0.421	0.451	0.221	0.562	0.690
PersonLab (ours):												
ResNet101 (1-scale, 20 prop)	0.377	0.659	0.394	0.166	0.480	0.595	0.162	0.415	0.437	0.207	0.536	0.690
ResNet152 (1-scale, 20 prop)	**0.385**	0.668	0.404	0.172	0.488	0.602	0.164	0.422	0.444	0.215	0.544	0.698
ResNet101 (mscale, 20 prop)	0.411	0.686	0.445	0.215	0.496	0.626	0.169	0.453	0.489	0.278	0.571	0.735
ResNet152 (mscale, 20 prop)	**0.417**	0.691	0.453	0.223	0.502	0.630	0.171	0.461	0.497	0.287	0.578	0.742

Table 3. Performance on COCO Segmentation (Person category) **val** split. The Mask-RCNN [34] person results have been produced by the ResNet-101-FPN version of their publicly shared model (which achieves 0.359 AP across all COCO classes).

	AP	AP^{50}	AP^{75}	AP^S	AP^M	AP^L	AR^1	AR^{10}	AR^{100}	AR^S	AR^M	AR^L
Mask-RCNN [34]	0.455	0.798	0.472	0.239	0.511	0.611	0.169	0.477	0.530	0.350	0.596	0.721
PersonLab (ours):												
ResNet101 (1-scale, 20 prop)	0.382	0.661	0.397	0.164	0.476	0.592	0.162	0.416	0.439	0.204	0.532	0.681
ResNet152 (1-scale, 20 prop)	0.387	0.667	0.406	0.169	0.483	0.595	0.163	0.423	0.446	0.213	0.539	0.686
ResNet101 (mscale, 20 prop)	0.414	0.684	0.447	0.213	0.492	0.621	0.170	0.454	0.492	0.278	0.566	0.728
ResNet152 (mscale, 20 prop)	0.418	0.688	0.455	0.219	0.497	0.621	0.170	0.460	0.497	0.284	0.573	0.730
ResNet152 (mscale, 100 prop)	0.429	0.711	0.467	0.235	0.511	0.623	0.170	0.460	0.539	0.346	0.612	0.741

4.3   COCO Person Instance Segmentation Evaluation

Tables 2 and 3 show our person instance segmentation results on COCO *test-dev* and *val*, respectively. We use the small-instance missing keypoint imputation technique of Sect. 3.3 for the reported instance segmentation experiments, which significantly increases our performance for small objects. Our results without missing keypoint imputation are shown in the supplementary material.

Our method only produces segmentation results for the person class, since our system is keypoint-based and thus cannot be applied to the other COCO classes. The standard COCO instance segmentation evaluation allows for a maximum of 100 proposals per image for all 80 COCO classes. For a fair comparison when comparing with previous works, we report *test-dev* results of our method with a maximum of 20 person proposals per image, which is the convention also adopted in the standard COCO person keypoints evaluation protocol. For reference, we also report the *val* results of our best model when allowed to produce 100 proposals.

We compare our system with the person category results of top-down instance segmentation methods. As shown in Table 2, our method on the test split outperforms FCIS [3] in both single-scale and multi-scale inference settings. As shown in Table 3, our performance on the val split is similar to that of Mask-RCNN [34] on medium and large person instances, but worse on small person instances. However, we emphasize that our method is the first box-free, bottom-up instance segmentation method to report experiments on the COCO instance segmentation task.

4.4   Qualitative Results

In Fig. 5 we show representative person pose and instance segmentation results on COCO *val* images produced by our model with single-scale inference.

Fig. 5. Visualization on COCO *val* images. The last row shows some failure cases: missed key point detection, false positive key point detection, and missed segmentation.

5 Conclusions

We have developed a bottom-up model which jointly addresses the problems of person detection, pose estimation, and instance segmentation using a unified part-based modeling approach. We have demonstrated the effectiveness of the proposed method on the challenging COCO person keypoint and instance segmentation tasks. A key limitation of the proposed method is its reliance on keypoint-level annotations for training on the instance segmentation task. In the future, we plan to explore ways to overcome this limitation, via weakly supervised part discovery.

References

1. Lin, T.Y., et al.: Coco 2016 keypoint challenge (2016)
2. Newell, A., Deng, J.: Associative embedding: end-to-end learning for joint detection and grouping. In: NIPS (2017)
3. Li, Y., Qi, H., Dai, J., Ji, X., Wei, Y.: Fully convolutional instance-aware semantic segmentation. In: CVPR (2017)
4. LeCun, Y., Bottou, L., Bengio, Y., Haffner, P.: Gradient-based learning applied to document recognition. In: Proceedings IEEE (1998)
5. Krizhevsky, A., Sutskever, I., Hinton, G.E.: Imagenet classification with deep convolutional neural networks. In: NIPS (2012)
6. Fischler, M.A., Elschlager, R.: The representation and matching of pictorial structures. In: IEEE TOC (1973)
7. Felzenszwalb, P., McAllester, D., Ramanan, D.: A discriminatively trained, multiscale, deformable part model. In: CVPR (2008)
8. Andriluka, M., Roth, S., Schiele, B.: Pictorial structures revisited: people detection and articulated pose estimation. In: CVPR (2009)
9. Eichner, M., Ferrari, V.: Better appearance models for pictorial structures. In: BMVC (2009)
10. Sapp, B., Jordan, C., Taskar, B.: Adaptive pose priors for pictorial structures. In: CVPR (2010)
11. Yang, Y., Ramanan, D.: Articulated pose estimation with flexible mixtures of parts. In: CVPR (2011)
12. Dantone, M., Gall, J., Leistner, C., Gool., L.V.: Human pose estimation using body parts dependent joint regressors. In: CVPR (2013)
13. Johnson, S., Everingham, M.: Learning effective human pose estimation from inaccurate annotation. In: CVPR (2011)
14. Pishchulin, L., Andriluka, M., Gehler, P., Schiele, B.: Poselet conditioned pictorial structures. In: CVPR (2013)
15. Sapp, B., Taskar, B.: Modec: Multimodal decomposable models for human pose estimation. In: CVPR (2013)
16. Gkioxari, G., Arbelaez, P., Bourdev, L., Malik, J.: Articulated pose estimation using discriminative armlet classifiers. In: CVPR (2013)
17. Toshev, A., Szegedy, C.: DeepPose: human pose estimation via deep neural networks. In: CVPR (2014)
18. Jain, A., Tompson, J., Andriluka, M., Taylor, G., Bregler, C.: Learning human pose estimation features with convolutional networks. In: ICLR (2014)

19. Tompson, J., Jain, A., LeCun, Y., Bregler, C.: Join training of a convolutional network and a graphical model for human pose estimation. In: NIPS (2014)

20. Chen, X., Yuille, A.: Articulated pose estimation by a graphical model with image dependent pairwise relations. In: NIPS (2014)

21. Tompson, J., Goroshin, R., Jain, A., LeCun, Y., Bregler, C.: Efficient object localization using convolutional networks. In: Proceedings of the IEEE Conference on Computer Vision and Pattern Recognition, pp. 648–656 (2015)

22. Newell, A., Yang, K., Deng, J.: Stacked hourglass networks for human pose estimation. In: Leibe, B., Matas, J., Sebe, N., Welling, M. (eds.) ECCV 2016. LNCS, vol. 9912, pp. 483–499. Springer, Cham (2016). https://doi.org/10.1007/978-3-319-46484-8_29

23. Andriluka, M., Pishchulin, L., Gehler, P., Schiele, B.: 2D human pose estimation: new benchmark and state of the art analysis. In: CVPR (2014)

24. Bulat, A., Tzimiropoulos, G.: Human pose estimation via convolutional part heatmap regression. In: Leibe, B., Matas, J., Sebe, N., Welling, M. (eds.) ECCV 2016. LNCS, vol. 9911, pp. 717–732. Springer, Cham (2016). https://doi.org/10.1007/978-3-319-46478-7_44

25. Belagiannis, V., Zisserman, A.: Recurrent human pose estimation. arxiv (2016)

26. Gkioxari, G., Toshev, A., Jaitly, N.: Chained predictions using convolutional neural networks. In: Leibe, B., Matas, J., Sebe, N., Welling, M. (eds.) ECCV 2016. LNCS, vol. 9908, pp. 728–743. Springer, Cham (2016). https://doi.org/10.1007/978-3-319-46493-0_44

27. Pishchulin, L., et al.: DeepCut: joint subset partition and labeling for multi person pose estimation. In: CVPR (2016)

28. Insafutdinov, E., Pishchulin, L., Andres, B., Andriluka, M., Schiele, B.: DeeperCut: a deeper, stronger, and faster multi-person pose estimation model. In: Leibe, B., Matas, J., Sebe, N., Welling, M. (eds.) ECCV 2016. LNCS, vol. 9910, pp. 34–50. Springer, Cham (2016). https://doi.org/10.1007/978-3-319-46466-4_3

29. Insafutdinov, E., Andriluka, M., Pishchulin, L., Tang, S., Andres, B., Schiele, B.: Articulated multi-person tracking in the wild. arXiv:1612.01465 (2016)

30. Iqbal, U., Gall, J.: Multi-person pose estimation with local joint-to-person associations. In: Hua, G., Jégou, H. (eds.) ECCV 2016. LNCS, vol. 9914, pp. 627–642. Springer, Cham (2016). https://doi.org/10.1007/978-3-319-48881-3_44

31. Wei, S.E., Ramakrishna, V., Kanade, T., Sheikh, Y.: Convolutional pose machines. arXiv (2016)

32. Cao, Z., Simon, T., Wei, S.E., Sheikh, Y.: Realtime multi-person 2D pose estimation using part affinity fields. In: CVPR (2017)

33. Papandreou, G., et al.: Towards accurate multi-person pose estimation in the wild. In: CVPR (2017)

34. He, K., Gkioxari, G., Dollár, P., Girshick, R.: Mask R-CNN. arXiv:1703.06870v2 (2017)

35. Huang, S., Gong, M., Tao, D.: A coarse-fine network for keypoint localization. In: ICCV (2017)

36. Fang, H.S., Xie, S., Tai, Y.W., Lu, C.: RMPE: regional multi-person pose estimation. In: ICCV (2017)

37. Chen, Y., Wang, Z., Peng, Y., Zhang, Z., Yu, G., Sun, J.: Cascaded pyramid network for multi-person pose estimation. arXiv:1711.07319 (2017)

38. Girshick, R.: Fast R-CNN. In: ICCV, pp. 1440–1448 (2015)

39. Ren, S., He, K., Girshick, R., Sun, J.: Faster R-CNN: towards real-time object detection with region proposal networks. In: NIPS (2015)

40. Dai, J., Li, Y., He, K., Sun, J.: R-FCN: Object detection via region-based fully convolutional networks. In: NIPS (2016)
41. Carreira, J., Sminchisescu, C.: CPMC: automatic object segmentation using constrained parametric min-cuts. PAMI **34**(7), 1312–1328 (2012)
42. Arbeláez, P., Pont-Tuset, J., Barron, J.T., Marques, F., Malik, J.: Multiscale combinatorial grouping. In: CVPR (2014)
43. Hariharan, B., Arbeláez, P., Girshick, R., Malik, J.: Simultaneous detection and segmentation. In: Fleet, D., Pajdla, T., Schiele, B., Tuytelaars, T. (eds.) ECCV 2014. LNCS, vol. 8695, pp. 297–312. Springer, Cham (2014). https://doi.org/10.1007/978-3-319-10584-0_20
44. Pinheiro, P.O., Collobert, R., Dollár, P.: Learning to segment object candidates. In: NIPS (2015)
45. Dai, J., He, K., Sun, J.: Convolutional feature masking for joint object and stuff segmentation. In: CVPR (2015)
46. Pinheiro, P.O., Lin, T.-Y., Collobert, R., Dollár, P.: Learning to refine object segments. In: Leibe, B., Matas, J., Sebe, N., Welling, M. (eds.) ECCV 2016. LNCS, vol. 9905, pp. 75–91. Springer, Cham (2016). https://doi.org/10.1007/978-3-319-46448-0_5
47. Dai, J., He, K., Li, Y., Ren, S., Sun, J.: Instance-sensitive fully convolutional networks. In: Leibe, B., Matas, J., Sebe, N., Welling, M. (eds.) ECCV 2016. LNCS, vol. 9910, pp. 534–549. Springer, Cham (2016). https://doi.org/10.1007/978-3-319-46466-4_32
48. Dai, J., He, K., Sun, J.: Instance-aware semantic segmentation via multi-task network cascades. In: CVPR (2016)
49. Peng, C., et al.: MegDet: a large mini-batch object detector (2018)
50. Chen, L.C., Hermans, A., Papandreou, G., Schroff, F., Wang, P., Adam, H.: MaskLab: instance segmentation by refining object detection with semantic and direction features. In: CVPR (2018)
51. Liu, S., Qi, L., Qin, H., Shi, J., Jia, J.: Path aggregation network for instance segmentation. In: CVPR (2018)
52. Liang, X., Wei, Y., Shen, X., Yang, J., Lin, L., Yan, S.: Proposal-free network for instance-level object segmentation. arXiv preprint arXiv:1509.02636 (2015)
53. Uhrig, J., Cordts, M., Franke, U., Brox, T.: Pixel-level encoding and depth layering for instance-level semantic labeling. arXiv:1604.05096 (2016)
54. Zhang, Z., Schwing, A.G., Fidler, S., Urtasun, R.: Monocular object instance segmentation and depth ordering with CNNs. In: ICCV (2015)
55. Zhang, Z., Fidler, S., Urtasun, R.: Instance-level segmentation for autonomous driving with deep densely connected MRFs. In: CVPR (2016)
56. Wu, Z., Shen, C., van den Hengel, A.: Bridging category-level and instance-level semantic image segmentation. arXiv:1605.06885 (2016)
57. Liu, S., Qi, X., Shi, J., Zhang, H., Jia, J.: Multi-scale patch aggregation (MPA) for simultaneous detection and segmentation. In: CVPR (2016)
58. Levinkov, E., et al.: Joint graph decomposition & node labeling: problem, algorithms, applications. In: CVPR (2017)
59. Kirillov, A., Levinkov, E., Andres, B., Savchynskyy, B., Rother, C.: InstanceCut: from edges to instances with multicut. In: CVPR (2017)
60. Jin, L., Chen, Z., Tu, Z.: Object detection free instance segmentation with labeling transformations. arXiv:1611.08991 (2016)
61. Fathi, A., et al.: Semantic instance segmentation via deep metric learning. arXiv:1703.10277 (2017)

62. De Brabandere, B., Neven, D., Van Gool, L.: Semantic instance segmentation with a discriminative loss function. arXiv:1708.02551 (2017)
63. Bai, M., Urtasun, R.: Deep watershed transform for instance segmentation. In: CVPR (2017)
64. Liu, S., Jia, J., Fidler, S., Urtasun, R.: SGN: sequential grouping networks for instance segmentation. In: ICCV (2017)
65. Bodla, N., Singh, B., Chellappa, R., Davis, L.S.: Soft-NMS: improving object detection with one line of code. In: ICCV (2017)
66. Long, J., Shelhamer, E., Darrell, T.: Fully convolutional networks for semantic segmentation. In: CVPR (2015)
67. Chen, L.C., Papandreou, G., Kokkinos, I., Murphy, K., Yuille, A.L.: DeepLab: semantic image segmentation with deep convolutional nets, atrous convolution, and fully connected CRFs. TPAMI (2017)
68. Radosavovic, I., Dollár, P., Girshick, R., Gkioxari, G., He, K.: Data distillation: towards omni-supervised learning. arXiv:1712.04440 (2017)
69. Lin, T.-Y., et al.: Microsoft COCO: common objects in context. In: Fleet, D., Pajdla, T., Schiele, B., Tuytelaars, T. (eds.) ECCV 2014. LNCS, vol. 8693, pp. 740–755. Springer, Cham (2014). https://doi.org/10.1007/978-3-319-10602-1_48
70. He, K., Zhang, X., Ren, S., Sun, J.: Deep residual learning for image recognition. In: CVPR (2016)
71. Russakovsky, O., et al.: ImageNet large scale visual recognition challenge. IJCV 115(3), 211–252 (2015)
72. Ioffe, S., Szegedy, C.: Batch normalization: accelerating deep network training by reducing internal covariate shift. arXiv:1502.03167 (2015)
73. Abadi, M., Agarwal, A., Barham, P., Brevdo, E., et al.: TensorFlow: large-scale machine learning on heterogeneous systems (2015). tensorflow.org

Task-Driven Webpage Saliency

Quanlong Zheng[1], Jianbo Jiao[1,2], Ying Cao[1(✉)],
and Rynson W. H. Lau[1]

[1] Department of Computer Science, City University of Hong Kong,
Hong Kong, Hong Kong
{qlzheng2-c,jianbjiao2-c}@my.cityu.edu.hk, caoying59@gmail.com,
rynson.lau@cityu.edu.hk
[2] University of Illinois at Urbana-Champaign, Urbana, USA

Abstract. In this paper, we present an end-to-end learning framework
for predicting task-driven visual saliency on webpages. Given a webpage,
we propose a convolutional neural network to predict where people look
at it under different task conditions. Inspired by the observation that
given a specific task, human attention is strongly correlated with certain
semantic components on a webpage (*e.g.,* images, buttons and input
boxes), our network explicitly disentangles saliency prediction into two
independent sub-tasks: task-specific attention shift prediction and task-
free saliency prediction. The task-specific branch estimates task-driven
attention shift over a webpage from its semantic components, while the
task-free branch infers visual saliency induced by visual features of the
webpage. The outputs of the two branches are combined to produce
the final prediction. Such a task decomposition framework allows us to
efficiently learn our model from a small-scale task-driven saliency dataset
with sparse labels (captured under a single task condition). Experimental
results show that our method outperforms the baselines and prior works,
achieving state-of-the-art performance on a newly collected benchmark
dataset for task-driven webpage saliency detection.

Keywords: Webpage analysis · Saliency detection
Task-specific saliency

1 Introduction

Webpages are a ubiquitous and important medium for information communication on the Internet. Webpages are essentially task-driven, created by web design-
ers with particular purposes in mind (*e.g.,* higher click through and conversion
rates). When browsing a website, visitors often have tasks to complete, such as
finding the information that they need quickly or signing up to an online service.
Hence, being able to predict where people will look at a webpage under different

Electronic supplementary material The online version of this chapter (https://
doi.org/10.1007/978-3-030-01264-9_18) contains supplementary material, which is
available to authorized users.

© Springer Nature Switzerland AG 2018
V. Ferrari et al. (Eds.): ECCV 2018, LNCS 11218, pp. 300–316, 2018.
https://doi.org/10.1007/978-3-030-01264-9_18

task-driven conditions can be practically useful for optimizing web design [5] and informing algorithms for webpage generation [24]. Although some recent works attempt to model human attention on webpages [27,28], or graphic designs [4], they only consider the free-viewing condition.

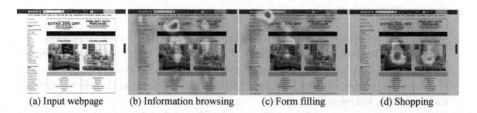

| (a) Input webpage | (b) Information browsing | (c) Form filling | (d) Shopping |

Fig. 1. Given an input webpage (a), our model can predict a different saliency map under a different task, *e.g.*, information browsing (b), form filling (c) and shopping (d).

In this paper, we are interested in predicting task-driven webpage saliency. When visiting a webpage, people often gravitate their attention to different places in different tasks. Hence, given a webpage, we aim to predict the visual saliency under multiple tasks (Fig. 1). There are two main obstacles for this problem: (1) Lack of powerful features for webpage saliency prediction: while existing works have investigated various features for natural images, effective features for graphic designs are ill-studied; (2) Scarcity of data: to our knowledge, the state-of-the art task-driven webpage saliency dataset [24] only contains hundreds of examples, and collecting task-driven saliency data is expensive.

To tackle these challenges, we propose a novel convolutional network architecture, which takes as input a webpage and a task label, and predicts the saliency under the task. Our key observation is that human attention behaviors on webpages under a particular task are mainly driven by the configurations and arrangement of semantic components (*e.g.*, buttons, images and text). For example, in order to register an email account, people tend to first recognize the key components on a webpage and then move their attention towards the sign-up form region composed of several input boxes and a button. Likewise, for online shopping, people are more likely to look at product images accompanied by text descriptions. Inspired by this, we propose to disentangle task-driven saliency prediction into two sub-tasks: task-specific attention shift prediction and task-free saliency prediction. The task-specific branch estimates task-driven global attention shift over the webpage from its semantic components, while the task-free branch predicts visual saliency independent of the task. Our network models the two sub-tasks in an unified architecture and fuses the outputs to make final prediction. We argue that such a task decomposition framework allows efficient network training using only a small-scale task-driven saliency dataset captured under the *single* task condition, *i.e.*, each webpage in the dataset contains the saliency captured on a single task.

To train our model effectively, we first pre-train the task-free subnet on a large-scale natural image saliency dataset and task-specific subnet on synthetic data generated by our proposed data synthesis approach. We then train our network end-to-end on a small-scale task-driven webpage saliency dataset. To evaluate our model, we create a benchmark dataset of 200 webpages, each with visual saliency maps captured under one or more tasks. Our results on this dataset show that our model outperforms the baselines and prior works. Our main contributions are:

- We address webpage saliency prediction under the multi-task condition.
- We propose a learning framework that disentangles the task-driven webpage saliency problem into the task-specific and task-free sub-tasks, which enables the network to be efficiently trained from a small-scale task-driven saliency dataset with sparse annotations.
- We construct a new benchmark dataset for the evaluation of webpage saliency prediction under the multi-task condition.

2   Related Work

2.1   Saliency Detection on Natural Images

Saliency detection on natural images is an active research topic in computer vision. The early works mainly explore various hand-crafted features and feature fusing strategies [1]. Recent works have made significant performance improvements, due to the strong representation power of CNN features. Some works [17,18,40] produce high-quality saliency maps using different CNNs to extract multi-scale features. Pan *et al.* [23] propose shallow and deep CNNs for saliency prediction. Wang *et al.* [32] use a multi-stage structure to handle local and global saliency. More recent works [10,16,19,31] apply fully convolutional networks for saliency detection, in order to reduce the number of parameters of the networks and preserve spatial information of internal representations throughout the networks. To get more accurate results, more complex architectures, such as recurrent neural networks [15,20,22,33], hybrid upsampling [38], multi-scale refinement [6], and skip connection [7,9,34]. However, all these works focus on natural images. In contrast, our work focuses on predicting saliency on webpages, which are very different from natural images in visual, structural and semantic characteristics [27].

2.2   Saliency Detection on Webpages

Webpages have well-designed configurations and layouts of semantic components, aiming to direct viewer attention effectively. To address webpage saliency, Shen *et al.* [28] propose a saliency model based on hand-crafted features (face, positional bias, *etc.*) to predict eye fixations on webpages. They later extend [28] to leverage the high-level features from CNNs [27], in addition to the low-level features. However, all these methods assume a free-viewing condition, without considering the effect of tasks upon saliency prediction. Recently, Bylinskii *et al.* [4] propose deep learning based models to predict saliency for data visualization and graphics. They train two separate networks for two types of designs. However, our problem setting is quite different from theirs. Each of their models is specific to a single task associated with their training data, without the ability to control the task condition. In contrast, we aim for a unified, task-conditional framework, where our model will output different saliency maps depending on the given task label.

2.3 Task-Driven Visual Saliency

There are several works on analyzing or predicting visual saliency under task-driven conditions. Some previous works [2,12,36] have shown that eye movements are influenced by the given tasks. To predict human attention under a particular task condition (*e.g.,* searching an object in an image), an early work [21] proposes a cognitive model. Recent works attempt to drive saliency prediction using various high-level signals, such as example images [8] and image captions [35]. There is also a line of research on visualizing object-level saliency using image-level supervision [25,29,37,39,41].All of the above learning based models are trained on large-scale datasets with dense labels, *i.e.,* each image in the dataset has the ground-truth for all the high-level signals. In contrast, as it is expensive to collect the task-driven webpage saliency data, we especially design our network architecture so that it can be trained efficiently on a small-scale dataset with sparse annotations. Sparse annotations in our context means that each image in our dataset only has ground-truth saliency for a single task, but our goal is to predict saliency under the multiple tasks.

3   Approach

In this section, we describe the proposed approach for task-driven webpage saliency prediction in details. First, we perform a data analysis to understand the relationship between task-specific saliency and semantic components on webpages, which motivates the design of our network and inspires our data synthesis approach. Second, we describe our proposed network that addresses the task-specific and task-free sub-problems in a unified framework. Finally, we introduce a task-driven data synthetic strategy for pre-training our task-specific subnet.

3.1   Task-Driven Webpage Saliency Dataset

To train our model, we use a publicly available, state-of-the-art task-driven webpage saliency dataset presented in [24]. This dataset contains 254 webpages, covering 6 common categories: email, file sharing, job searching, product promotion, shopping and social networking. It was collected from an eye tracking experiment, where for each webpage, the eye fixation data of multiple viewers under both a *single* task condition and a free-viewing condition were recorded. Four types of semantic components, **input field**, **text**, **button** and **image** for all the webpages were annotated. To compute a saliency map for a webpage, they aggregated the data gaze data from all the viewers and convolved the result with a Gaussian filter, as in [13]. Note that the size of the dataset is small and we only have saliency data of the webpages captured under the single task condition.

Task definition. In their data collection [24], two general tasks are defined: (1) Comparison: viewers compared a pair of webpages and decided on which one to take for a given purpose (*e.g.,* which website to sign-up for a email service); (2) Shopping: viewers were given a certain amount of cash and decided which products to buy in a given shopping website. In our paper, we define 5 common and more specific tasks according to the 6 webpage categories in their dataset: **Signing-up** (email), **Information browsing** (product promotion), **Form filling** (file sharing, job searching), **Shopping** (shopping) and **Community joining** (social networking). We use this task definition throughout the paper.

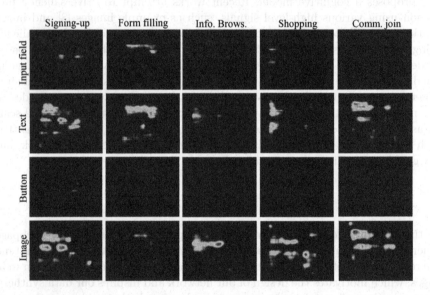

Fig. 2. Accumulative saliency of each semantic component (row) under a specific task (column). From left to right, each column represents the saliency distribution under the Signing-up, Form filling, Information browsing, Shopping or Community joining task. Warm colors represent high saliency. Better view in color.

3.2   Data Analysis

Our hypothesis is that human attention on webpages under the task-driven condition is related to the semantic components of webpages. In other words, with different tasks, human attention may be biased towards different subsets of semantic components, in order to complete their goals efficiently. Here, we explore the relationship between task-driven saliency and semantic components by analyzing the task-driven webpage saliency dataset in Sect. 3.1. Fig. 2 shows

Table 1. Component saliency ratio for each semantic component (column) under each task (row). The larger the value for a semantic component under a task is, the more likely people look at the semantic component under the task, and vice versa. For each task, we shade two salient semantic components as key components, which are used in our task-driven data synthetic approach.

Task	Input field	Text	Button	Image
Signing-up	0.953	0.971	1.040	1.124
Form filling	1.681	0.979	1.254	0.572
Information browsing	1.725	0.946	0.804	1.033
Shopping	1.444	1.022	0.816	0.770
Community joining	0.895	0.898	1.156	1.186

the accumulative saliency on each semantic component under different tasks. We can visually inspect some connections between tasks and semantic components. For example, for "Information browsing", the image component receives higher saliency, while other semantic components have relatively lower saliency. Both the input field and button components have higher saliency under "Form filling", relative to other tasks. For "Shopping", both image and text components have higher saliency, while the other two semantic components have quite low saliency. To understand such a relationship quantitatively, for each semantic component c under a task t, we define a within-task *component saliency ratio*, which measures the average saliency of c under t compared with the average saliency of all the semantic components under t:

$$SR(c,t) = \frac{S_{c,t}}{SA_t}, \tag{1}$$

In particular, $S_{c,t}$ is formulated as: $S_{c,t} = \frac{\sum_{i=1}^{n_{c,t}} s_{c,t,i}}{n_{c,t}}$, where $s_{c,t,i}$ denotes the saliency of the i-th instance of semantic component c (computed as the average saliency value of the pixels within the instance) under task t. $n_{c,t}$ denotes the total number of instances of semantic component c under task t. SA_t is formulated as: $SA_t = \frac{\sum_{c=1}^{n} \sum_{i=1}^{n_{c,t}} s_{c,t,i}}{\sum_{c=1}^{n} n_{c,t}}$, where n denotes the number of semantic components. Our component saliency ratio tells whether a semantic component under a particular task is more salient (>1), equally salient ($=1$) or less salient (<1), as compared with the average saliency. We report the component saliency ratios for all tasks and semantic components in Table 1. We find that, under each task, some semantic components apparently have higher scores than others. This means that people are more likely to look at the high-score semantic components than the low-score ones under the task. For example, for "Form filling", the scores for input and button components are high (1.681, 1.254), while the scores for other semantic components are low (≤ 1), which is consistent with our observation from the accumulative saliency maps above. Based on these component saliency scores, for each task, we identify two semantic components with higher scores as the *key components* (the shaded components in Table 1) that people tend to focus on under the task. These key components are used to synthesize task-driven saliency data for pre-training the task-specific subnet of our network, as introduced in Sect. 3.5. It is worth noting that when selecting the key components, we also avoid two tasks having exactly the same set of key components, which may confuse the learning of our model. Hence, for "Signing-up", we select "Text" instead of "Button" to prevent "Signing-up" to have the same set of key components as "Community joining". The above analysis confirms our assumption that human attention shift under a particular task is correlated with and can thus be predicted from a subset of semantic components.

3.3 Network Architecture

Figure 3 shows the architecture of our proposed network. A webpage image is first fed into a shared encoder to extract high-level feature representation. The shared encoder uses all the layers of the FCN [26] before the output layer. After that, the network splits into two branches: the task-specific branch and task-free branch. For the task-specific branch, we use a segmentation subnet (using the output layer of the FCN [26]) to generate a semantic segmentation map from the extracted feature representation. We then send a task label (*e.g.,* "Signing-up") along with the semantic segmentation map to a task-specific subnet, which outputs a task-specific attention shift map. For the task-free branch, we use a task-free subnet to map the extracted feature representation to a task-free saliency map. The task-specifc attention shift map and the task-free saliency map are added to produce the final output. We also tried other fusion operations *e.g.,* multiplication, but found addition performs better.

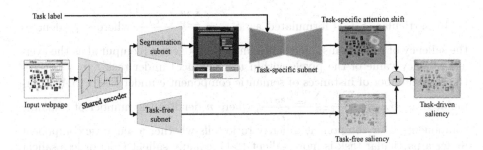

Fig. 3. Network architecture. Inputs to our model are a webpage image and a task label (*e.g.,* "Signing-up"). The webpage image is first fed to a shared encoder to extract high-level features, which are used by two subnets for predicting task-specific human attention bias and task-free visual saliency. The task-specific subnet takes as input the task label along with a semantic segmentation map from a segmentation subnet, and predicts the task-dependent attention shift (upper), while the task-free subnet predicts the task-independent saliency (lower). The task-specific attention shift and task-free saliency are combined to obtain the final saliency map under the input task.

Task-Specific Subnet: The task-specific subnet is used to model human attention shift towards particular semantic components under the task-driven condition (as validated in Sect. 3.2). To do this, we first obtain a semantic segmentation map through a segmentation subnet. To account for segmentation uncertainty, we directly take the output of the segmentation layer (probability distributions over different semantic components) as the segmentation map, and then feed it to the task-specific subnet to predict the attention shift among the semantic components. Figure 4 shows the detailed structure. The semantic segmentation map is passed through a series of convolutional layers to get a lower-dimensional segmentation representation. To encode the task label, we represent it using one-of-K representation (K = 5) and transform it into a semantic vector via a task encoder with a stack of fully connected layers. The semantic vector is then reshaped and duplicated multiple times, and concatenated with the segmentation representation. The concatenated features are finally transformed by a stack of deconvolutional layers to output a task-specific attention shift map.

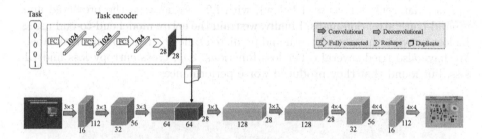

Fig. 4. Task-specific subnet. The filter sizes of the convolutional and deconvolutional layers are labeled above the corresponding layers. The channel numbers and sizes of the feature maps are also labeled nearby the feature maps.

Task-Free Subnet: The task-free subnet is used to model visual saliency, which is task-independent and driven by visual contents of the input webpage. To simplify our network, this subnet uses the output layer of the FCN [26] to directly output a saliency map, which works well in our experiments. More complex layers can be added, but at the cost of extra parameters.

Discussion: Our network architecture can be efficiently trained, even with small amounts of training data, to produce reasonable saliency predictions given different tasks. This is because our framework has the task-specific branch to model the task-related saliency shift from task-free saliency. In addition, the task-specific subnet receives a semantic segmentation map, instead of the webpage, as input. The complexity of the input space is greatly reduced, as only several semantic classes need to be encoded. This makes it easier for the model to discover consistent patterns and learn the mapping from a task label to the corresponding attention shift.

3.4   Training

Due to the deep network architecture, directly training it end-to-end on our small dataset is difficult. Thus, we propose a two-stage training strategy, where we first pre-train each part separately and then fine-tune the entire network jointly. In particular, we first pre-train the task-free subnet on a large-scale natural image saliency dataset, SALICON [11], and then fine-tune it on the webpage saliency dataset [24]. It is trained by minimizing a L2 loss between the predicted and ground-truth saliency, L_{sal}. For the segmentation subnet, we enforce a cross-entry loss between the predicted and ground-truth semantic segmentation maps, L_{seg}, and train it on the webpage saliency dataset with ground-truth semantic annotations. Since the segmentation subnet and task-free subnet share the same encoder, we thus jointly train them with a multi-task loss L_{multi},

$$L_{multi} = L_{sal} + L_{seg}, \qquad (2)$$

The task-specific subnet is pre-trained from scratch on a synthetic task-driven saliency dataset (as discussed below), with L2 loss between the predicted and ground-truth attention maps. Finally, we train the entire model end-to-end using L2 loss between the ground-truth and predicted saliency maps given a task label. We have also tried several other loss functions, $e.g.$, cross entropy loss and L1 loss, but found that they produced worse performances.

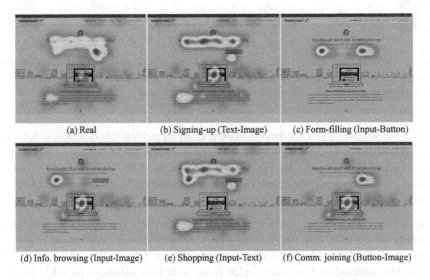

(a) Real   (b) Signing-up (Text-Image)   (c) Form-filling (Input-Button)

(d) Info. browsing (Input-Image)   (e) Shopping (Input-Text)   (f) Comm. joining (Button-Image)

Fig. 5. Synthetic saliency data. (a) Saliency map from the webpage dataset [24]. (b)–(f) Synthesized saliency maps from (a) for 5 different tasks. The corresponding key components of each task are shown in braces.

3.5 Task-Driven Data Synthesis

Pre-training the task-specific subnet requires a lot of saliency data on webpages under the multi-task condition, which is not available and expensive to collect. To address this limitation, we propose a data synthesis approach to generate our training dataset by leveraging the key semantic components for each task that we have identified in Sect. 3.2. Our data synthesis method works as follows. Given a webpage in our dataset, we take its existing task-driven saliency map. For each task of the five tasks, we only preserve the saliency of the saliency map on the corresponding key components of the task, by zeroing out the saliency in other regions. In this way, we generate 5 task-specific saliency maps for each webpage. Figure 5 shows an example of the synthesized saliency maps under different tasks. With our data synthesis approach, we generate a dataset with dense annotations (*i.e.*, the saliency data under all tasks are available for all webpages), which is sufficient for pre-training our task-specific subnet.

4 Implementation Details

The segmentation subnet and task-free subnet are based on the FCN [26], and we adopt VGG-16 [30] for the shared encoder of the FCN. The parameters are optimized by Adam optimizer [30], with a batch size of 20. During training, we use different learning rates for different parts. For the task-specific and task-free subnets, we set the initial learning rate to be 10^{-7}, and divide it by 10 every 20 epochs. For the shared encoder, we start with a small initial learning rate (10^{-10}) and set it to be the same as that of the task-free subnet after 20 epochs. We train our network for 100 epochs. The webpage images and their saliency maps are resized to 224×224.

5 Experiments

In this section, we first introduce the evaluation dataset and evaluation metrics. We then analyze our network architecture and training strategy in an ablation study. Finally, we compare our method with prior methods.

5.1 Evaluation Dataset and Metrics

To evaluate our method, a task-driven webpage saliency dataset is required, where each webpage has ground-truth saliency under different tasks. Unfortunately, such dataset is not available. Thus, we construct a new evaluation dataset, which includes 200 webpages collected from the Internet by us. The newly collected webpages cover various categories (shopping, traveling, games and email). Please refer to the supplemental for the statistics of the dataset. We assign each webpage with one or more tasks selected from the 5 tasks, depending on the type of webpage. In particular, 71 webpages are assigned 1 task,

120 webpages are assigned 2 tasks and 9 webpages are assigned 3 tasks. To collect ground-truth saliency on the webpages under different tasks, we performed an eye-tracking experiment, following the experiment setup and methodologies in [24]. We recruited 24 participants for our experiment. In each viewing session, the participants are first informed of the task, followed by one or two webpages to perform the given task. For each webpage under each task, we collect eye-tracking data from 10 different participants, which are aggregated to produce the corresponding saliency map. To the best of our knowledge, the newly collected dataset, containing 200 webpages, is the largest task-driven webpage saliency evaluation dataset (vs. 30 webpages in [24,28]). Similar to previous works [3,12,14], we use the following metrics for evaluation: Kullback-Leibler divergence (KL), shuffled Area Under Curve (sAUC) and Normalized Scanpath Saliency (NSS).

5.2 Ablation Study

To evaluate the design of our network architecture and training strategy, we compare against the following baselines:

No task-specific subnet: We remove the task-specific subnet and concatenate the semantic vector of the input task label with the output of the shared encoder (before the task-free subnet) to predict task-driven saliency.

No task-free subnet: We convert our network to a one-branch architecture by removing the task-free subnet.

Separate encoders: Rather than using a shared encoder for the segmentation and task-free subnets, we use two separate encoders (VGG-16) for the two subnets.

Separate CNNs: We train 5 separate CNNs for each of the 5 tasks, and select the corresponding CNN for a given task, to predict the saliency.

No pre-train on synthetic data: We directly train our model on the real-world dataset, without pre-training the task-specific subnet on the synthetic data.

Train only on synthetic data: Instead of training on our real-world dataset, our model is only trained end-to-end on our synthetic data in Sect. 3.5.

Table 2 shows the results on our evaluation dataset. The results are obtained by averaging the metrics across all the tasks. (Please refer to the supplemental for the results on individual tasks.) Without the task-specific subnet, the performance is the worst. This shows that having a one-branch network to directly predict saliency from a webpage is not a promising solution and our task-decomposition framework is essential for the task-driven saliency prediction problem. The network without the task-free branch is slightly worse than our proposed network. This implies that while task-driven human attention mainly focuses on the semantic components of webpages that are important to the task, it can still be attracted by other visual contents (e.g., color and contrast) as in the free-viewing condition. Training task-specific models separately does not perform well, as compared with our unified model. With only the task-specific

Table 2. Results for the ablation study. The best results are highlighted in red, while the second best are highlighted in blue.

Methods	KL ↓	sAUC ↑	NSS ↑
No task-specific subnet	1.330	0.576	0.412
No task-free subnet	0.810	0.628	0.559
Separate encoders	1.013	0.629	0.566
Separate CNNs	1.235	0.605	0.498
No pre-train on synthetic data	10.428	0.553	0.337
Train only on synthetic data	2.722	0.614	0.552
Ours	0.883	0.645	0.622

subnet (i.e., no task-free subnet), the model tends to put saliency mainly on task-relevant semantic components, but ignores the regions that people do look at (although with lower probabilities). This will result in a better KL score, which is more sensitive to the matching between high-saliency (probability) regions than between the low-saliency regions. In contrast, our full model learns to optimally allocate saliency between high-saliency task-relevant semantic components and other low-saliency regions. Therefore, although with a slightly worse KL score, it can better cover both high- and low-saliency regions, as reflected by other metrics. Finally, the results also suggest that our network can benefit from having a shared encoder for the segmentation and task-free subnets. This happens since the multi-task architecture can help our encoder learn better hidden representation to boost the performance of both tasks.

Without pre-training on the synthetic data, the performance of our model drops greatly. This confirms the importance of our task-driven data synthesis. In addition, learning with only synthetic saliency data does not perform well, due to the gap between the statistics of real and synthetic saliency data.

5.3 Comparison with Prior Works

We compare our method with several state-of-the-art works for free-viewing saliency detection, including one method for graphic design saliency, VIMGD [4], two recent methods for natural images, SalNet [23] and SALICON [10]. We also make comparison with a recent classification-driven concept localization model that is adapted to predict task-driven saliency by treating our task labels as class labels. For fair comparison, we finetune these models on the webpage saliency dataset [24] using the same training setting as ours. Unfortunately, we did not get the code for the free-viewing webpage saliency prediction method [28] for comparison. Thus, we make visual comparison with the results included in their paper (see the supplemental). For each webpage under each task, we run each method to get a saliency map. Since the free-viewing saliency detection methods do not take a task label as input, thus always producing the same results under different task conditions.

Table 3. Performances of different saliency detection approaches on our evaluation dataset. The best results are in red, and the second best are in blue.

	KL ↓							sAUC ↑					
Method	Sign-up	Form fill	Info. brows.	Shopp-ing	Comm. joining	Average	Method	Sign-up	Form fill	Info. brows.	Shopp-ing	Comm. joining	Average
Human	0	0	0	0	0	0	Human	0.750	0.734	0.727	0.745	0.736	0.738
Grad-CAM [25]	5.527	5.253	4.126	4.094	5.843	4.973	Grad-CAM [25]	0.519	0.533	0.503	0.507	0.512	0.515
VIMGD [4]	2.513	2.726	2.987	5.462	3.127	3.363	VIMGD [4]	0.596	0.576	0.577	0.540	0.583	0.576
SALICON [10]	0.651	1.116	0.569	0.771	0.595	0.739	SALICON [10]	0.612	0.598	0.604	0.601	0.607	0.605
SalNet [23]	1.129	1.893	1.041	0.941	1.028	1.207	SalNet [23]	0.638	0.603	0.629	0.631	0.636	0.627
Ours	0.867	1.152	0.731	0.861	0.812	0.883	Ours	0.654	0.633	0.644	0.642	0.652	0.645

	NSS ↑					
Method	Sign-up	Form fill	Info. brows.	Shopp-ing	Comm. joining	Average
Human	0.804	0.823	0.699	0.739	0.773	0.768
Grad-CAM [25]	0.144	0.214	0.008	0.085	0.112	0.126
VIMGD [4]	0.534	0.449	0.465	0.293	0.488	0.447
SALICON [10]	0.605	0.526	0.550	0.497	0.573	0.550
SalNet [23]	0.609	0.480	0.550	0.585	0.604	0.5652
Ours	0.646	0.594	0.624	0.607	0.638	0.622

The results are shown in Table 3. Our model outperforms all the prior methods in sAUC and NSS, and achieves the second best performance in KL. The saliency detection models (SalNet, SALICON) generally perform better than other prior methods and SALICON even has a better performance than ours in KL. This is perhaps because that those free-viewing saliency models tend to fire at almost all the salient regions in a webpage, thereby generating a more uniform saliency distribution that is more likely to cover the ground truth salient regions. This leads to a higher KL score. However, such uniform saliency predictions certainly result in more false positives, making the performance of these models worse than ours in sAUC and NSS. The task-driven saliency method, Grad-CAM [25] performs worst in our evaluation dataset. This is likely because the complex and highly variable appearance of webpages make it difficult for classification-based models to find consistent patterns and identify discriminative features for different tasks, given our small dataset. Our model generally perform well in all metrics, which demonstrates the effectiveness of our model for predicting task-driven saliency. Human performance (Human) is also provided [12], which serves as upper bound performance.

Figure 6 shows some qualitative results. Grad-CAM fails to locate salient regions for each task. The free viewing saliency models (i.e., SalNet, SALICON, VIMGD) simply highlight all the salient regions, oblivious to task conditions. Hence, we only show one result from each of the prior methods regardless of the input task label. In contrast, given different tasks, our model can predict different saliency maps that are close to the ground truth. Please refer to the supplemental for more results.

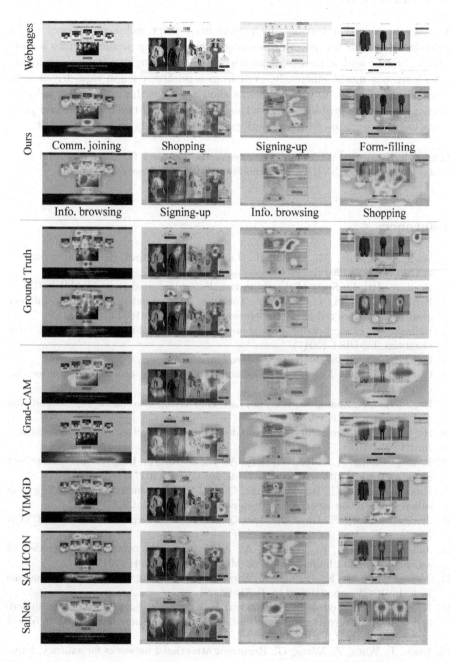

Fig. 6. Saliency prediction results of our method and prior methods under different task conditions.

6   Conclusion

We have presented a learning framework to predict webpage saliency under multiple tasks. Our framework disentangles the saliency prediction into a task-specific branch and a task-free branch. Such disentangling framework allows us to learn our model efficiently, even from a relatively small task-driven webpage saliency dataset. Our experiments show that, for the task-driven webpage saliency prediction problem, our method is superior to the baselines and prior works, achieving state-of-the-art performance on a newly collected dataset.

Acknowledgement. We thank the anonymous reviewers for their insightful comments. We also thank NVIDIA for donation of a Titan X Pascal GPU card.

References

1. Borji, A., Cheng, M., Jiang, H., Li, J.: Salient object detection: a survey. arXiv:1411.5878 (2014)
2. Borji, A., Itti, L.: State-of-the-art in visual attention modeling. TPAMI (2013)
3. Bylinskii, Z., Judd, T., Oliva, A., Torralba, A., Durand, F.: What do different evaluation metrics tell us about saliency models? arXiv:1604.03605 (2016)
4. Bylinskii, Z., et al.: Learning visual importance for graphic designs and data visualizations. In: UIST (2017)
5. EYEQUANT (2018). http://www.eyequant.com/
6. Guanbin Li, Yuan Xie, L., Yu, Y.: Instance-level salient object segmentation. In: CVPR (2017)
7. He, S., Jiao, J., Zhang, X., Han, G., Lau, R.: Delving into salient object subitizing and detection. In: ICCV (2017)
8. He, S., Lau, R.: Exemplar-driven top-down saliency detection via deep association. In: CVPR (2016)
9. Hou, Q., Cheng, M., Hu, X.W., Borji, A., Tu, Z., Torr, P.: Deeply supervised salient object detection with short connections. In: CVPR (2017)
10. Huang, X., Shen, C., Boix, X., Zhao, Q.: SALICON: reducing the semantic gap in saliency prediction by adapting deep neural networks. In: ICCV (2015)
11. Jiang, M., Huang, S., Duan, J., Zhao, Q.: SALICON: saliency in context. In: CVPR (2015)
12. Judd, T., Durand, F., Torralba, A.: A benchmark of computational models of saliency to predict human fixations. MIT Technical report (2012)
13. Judd, T., Ehinger, K., Durand, F., Torralba, A.: Learning to predict where humans look. In: ICCV, pp. 2106–2113. IEEE (2009)
14. Kruthiventi, S., Gudisa, V., Dholakiya, J., Venkatesh Babu, R.: Saliency unified: a deep architecture for simultaneous eye fixation prediction and salient object segmentation. In: CVPR (2016)
15. Kuen, J., Wang, Z., Wang, G.: Recurrent attentional networks for saliency detection. In: CVPR (2016)
16. Kümmerer, M., Theis, L., Bethge, M.: Deep gaze I: Boosting saliency prediction with feature maps trained on imagenet. In: ICLR (2015)

17. Lee, G., Tai, Y., Kim, J.: Deep saliency with encoded low level distance map and high level features. In: CVPR (2016)
18. Li, G., Yu, Y.: Visual saliency based on multiscale deep features. In: CVPR (2015)
19. Li, G., Yu, Y.: Deep contrast learning for salient object detection. In: CVPR (2016)
20. Liu, N., Han, J.: DHSNet: deep hierarchical saliency network for salient object detection. In: CVPR (2016)
21. Navalpakkam, V., Itti, L.: Modeling the influence of task on attention. Vis. Res. (2005)
22. Liu, N., Han, J.: A deep spatial contextual long-term recurrent convolutional network for saliency detection. IEEE TIP (2018)
23. Pan, J., Sayrol, E., Giro-i Nieto, X., McGuinness, K., O'Connor, N.: Shallow and deep convolutional networks for saliency prediction. In: CVPR (2016)
24. Pang, X., Cao, Y., Lau, R., Chan, A.: Directing user attention via visual flow on web designs. In: SIGGRAPH Asia (2016)
25. Selvaraju, et al.: Grad-CAM: visual explanations from deep networks via gradient-based localization. In: ICCV (2017)
26. Shelhamer, E., Long, J., Darrell, T.: Fully convolutional networks for semantic segmentation. TPAMI (2017)
27. Shen, C., Huang, X., Zhao, Q.: Predicting eye fixations on webpage with an ensemble of early features and high-level representations from deep network. IEEE Trans. Multimed. (2015)
28. Shen, C., Zhao, Q.: Webpage saliency. In: Fleet, D., Pajdla, T., Schiele, B., Tuytelaars, T. (eds.) ECCV 2014. LNCS, vol. 8695, pp. 33–46. Springer, Cham (2014). https://doi.org/10.1007/978-3-319-10584-0_3
29. Simonyan, et al.: Deep inside convolutional networks: visualising image classification models and saliency maps. In: ICLR Workshop (2014)
30. Simonyan, K., Zisserman, A.: Very deep convolutional networks for large-scale image recognition. arXiv:1409.1556 (2014)
31. Tang, Y., Wu, X.: Saliency detection via combining region-level and pixel-level predictions with CNNs. In: Leibe, B., Matas, J., Sebe, N., Welling, M. (eds.) ECCV 2016. LNCS, vol. 9912, pp. 809–825. Springer, Cham (2016). https://doi.org/10.1007/978-3-319-46484-8_49
32. Wang, L., Lu, H., Ruan, X., Yang, M.: Deep networks for saliency detection via local estimation and global search. In: CVPR (2015)
33. Wang, L., Wang, L., Lu, H., Zhang, P., Ruan, X.: Saliency detection with recurrent fully convolutional networks. In: Leibe, B., Matas, J., Sebe, N., Welling, M. (eds.) ECCV 2016. LNCS, vol. 9908, pp. 825–841. Springer, Cham (2016). https://doi.org/10.1007/978-3-319-46493-0_50
34. Xiao, H., Feng, J., Wei, Y., Zhang, M., Yan, S.: Deep salient object detection with dense connections and distraction diagnosis. IEEE Trans. Multimed. (2018)
35. Xu, Y., Wu, J., Li, N., Gao, S., Yu, J.: Personalized saliency and its prediction. IJCAI (2017)
36. Yarbus, A.: Eye movements during perception of complex objects. In: Eye Movements and Vision. Springer, Boston (1967). https://doi.org/10.1007/978-1-4899-5379-7_8
37. Zhang, J., Lin, Z., Brandt, J., Shen, X., Sclaroff, S.: Top-down neural attention by excitation backprop. In: Leibe, B., Matas, J., Sebe, N., Welling, M. (eds.) ECCV 2016. LNCS, vol. 9908, pp. 543–559. Springer, Cham (2016). https://doi.org/10.1007/978-3-319-46493-0_33
38. Zhang, P., Wang, D., Lu, H., Wang, H., Yin, B.: Learning uncertain convolutional features for accurate saliency detection. In: ICCV (2017)

39. Zhang, X., Wei, Y., Feng, J., Yang, Y., Huang, T.: Adversarial complementary learning for weakly supervised object localization. In: CVPR (2018)
40. Zhao, R., Ouyang, W., Li, H., Wang, X.: Saliency detection by multi-context deep learning. In: CVPR (2015)
41. Zhou, et al.: Learning deep features for discriminative localization. In: CVPR (2016)

Deep Image Demosaicking
Using a Cascade of Convolutional
Residual Denoising Networks

Filippos Kokkinos[✉] and Stamatios Lefkimmiatis

Skolkovo Institute of Science and Technology (Skoltech), Moscow, Russia
{filippos.kokkinos,s.lefkimmiatis}@skoltech.ru

Abstract. Demosaicking and denoising are among the most crucial
steps of modern digital camera pipelines and their joint treatment is
a highly ill-posed inverse problem where at-least two-thirds of the information are missing and the rest are corrupted by noise. This poses a great
challenge in obtaining meaningful reconstructions and a special care for
the efficient treatment of the problem is required. While there are several machine learning approaches that have been recently introduced to
deal with joint image demosaicking-denoising, in this work we propose a
novel deep learning architecture which is inspired by powerful classical
image regularization methods and large-scale convex optimization techniques. Consequently, our derived network is more transparent and has
a clear interpretation compared to alternative competitive deep learning
approaches. Our extensive experiments demonstrate that our network
outperforms any previous approaches on both noisy and noise-free data.
This improvement in reconstruction quality is attributed to the principled way we design our network architecture, which also requires fewer
trainable parameters than the current state-of-the-art deep network solution. Finally, we show that our network has the ability to generalize well
even when it is trained on small datasets, while keeping the overall number of trainable parameters low.

Keywords: Deep learning · Denoising · Demosaicking
Proximal method · Residual denoising

1   Introduction

Modern digital cameras perform a certain number of processing steps in order to
create high quality images from raw sensor data. The sequence of the required
processing steps is known as the imaging pipeline and the first two and most
crucial steps involve image denoising and demosaicking. Both of these problems
belong to the category of ill-posed problems while their joint treatment is very
challenging since two-thirds of the underlying data are missing and the rest
are perturbed by noise. It is clear that reconstruction errors during this early
stage of the camera pipeline will eventually lead to unsatisfying final results.

© Springer Nature Switzerland AG 2018
V. Ferrari et al. (Eds.): ECCV 2018, LNCS 11218, pp. 317–333, 2018.
https://doi.org/10.1007/978-3-030-01264-9_19

Furthermore, due to the modular nature of the camera processing pipelines, demosaicking and denoising were traditionally dealt in the past in a sequential manner. In detail, demosaicking algorithms reconstruct the image from unreliable spatially-shifted sensor data which introduce non-linear pixel noise, casting denoising an even harder problem. Since, demosaicking is an essential step of the camera pipeline, it has been extensively studied. For a complete survey of recent approaches, we refer to [1]. One of the main drawbacks of several of the currently introduced methods that deal with the demosaicking problem, is that they assume a specific Bayer pattern [1–6]. This is a rather strong assumption and limits their applicability since there are many cameras available in the market that employ different Color filter Array (CFA) patterns. Therefore, demosaicking methods that are able to generalize to different CFA patterns are preferred.

One simple method that works for any CFA pattern is bilinear interpolation on the neighboring values for a given pixel for each channel. The problem with this approach is the produced zippering artifacts which occur along high frequency signal changes, e.g., edges. Therefore, many approaches involve edge-adaptive interpolation schemes which follow the direction of the gradient of strong edges [1]. However, the real challenges of demosaicking extend in the exploitation of both intra and inter-channel dependencies. The most common assumption is that color differences between color channels are constant, so that the end result leads to smooth images. Other approaches make use of the self-similarity and redundancy properties of natural images [2–4,6]. Moreover, in some cases a post-processing step is applied to remove certain type of artifacts [7]. Another successful class consists of methods that act upon the frequency domain. Any Bayer CFA can be represented as the combination of a luminance component at baseband and two modulated components [8]. Upon this interpretation, Dubois [9–11] created a successful set of filter-banks using a least-squares method that was able to generalize to arbitrary sensor patterns.

From the perspective of learning based approaches, the bibliography is short. A common problem with the design of learning based demosaicking algorithms is the lack of ground-truth images. In many approaches such as those in [12,13] the authors used already processed images as references that are simulated mosaicked again, i.e. they apply a mosaick mask on the already demosaicked images, therefore obtaining non-realistic pairs for tuning trainable methods. In a recent work Khasabi et. al. [14] provided a way to produce a dataset with realistic reference images allowing for the design of machine learning demosaicking algorithms. We use the produced Microsoft Demosaicking dataset (MSR) [14] in order to train, evaluate and compare our system. The contained images have to be demosaicked in the linear RGB (linRGB) color space before being transformed via color transformation and gamma correction into standard RGB (sRGB) space. Furthermore, two common CFA patterns are contained into the dataset, namely Bayer and Fuji X Trans which enables the development and evaluation of methods that are able to deal with different CFA patterns.

Apart from the demosaicking problem, another problem that requires special attention is the elimination of noise arising from the sensor and which distorts the acquired raw data. Firstly, the sensor readings are corrupted with *shot* noise [15] which is the result of random variation of the detected photons. Second, electronic inefficiencies during reading and converting electrical charge into a digital count exhibit another type of noise, namely *read* noise. Under certain circumstances both noises can be approximated by noise following a heteroscedastic Gaussian pdf [15]. Prior work from Kalevo and Rantanen [16], analyzed whether denoising should occur before or after the demosaicking step. It was experimentally confirmed that denoising is preferably done before demosaicking. However, the case of joint denoising and demosaicking was not analyzed. In later work, many researchers [17–19] showed that joint denoising and demosaicking yields better results. Motivated by these works, we also pursue a joint approach for denoising and demosaicking of raw sensor data.

In a very recent work Gharbi et. al. [20] exploit the advantages in the field of deep learning to create a Convolutional Neural Network (CNN) that is able to jointly denoise and demosaick images. Apart from the design of the aforementioned network, a lot of effort was put by the authors to create a new large demosaicking dataset, namely the MIT Demosaicking Dataset which consists of 2.6 million patches of images. These patches were mined from a large collection of data following specific visual distortion metrics.

Our main contribution is a novel deep neural network for solving the joint image demosaicking-denoising problem[1]. The network architecture is inspired by classical image regularization approaches and a powerful optimization strategy that has been successfully used in the past for dealing with general inverse imaging problems. We demonstrate through extensive experimentation that our approach leads to higher-quality reconstruction than other competing methods in both linear RGB (linRGB) and standard RGB (sRGB) color spaces. Moreover, we further show that our derived network not only outperforms the current CNN-based state-of-the art network [20], but it achieves this by using less trainable parameters and by being trained only on a small fraction of the training data.

2   Problem Formulation

To solve the joint demosaicking-denoising problem, one of the most frequently used approaches in the literature relies on the following linear observation model

$$y = Mx + n, \tag{1}$$

which relates the observed sensor raw data, $y \in \mathbb{R}^N$, and the underlying image $x \in \mathbb{R}^N$ that we aim to restore. Both x and y correspond to the vectorized forms of the images assuming that they have been raster scanned using a lexicographical order. Under this notation, $M \in \mathbb{R}^{N \times N}$ is the degradation matrix that

---

[1] The code for both training and inference will be made available from the authors' website.

models the spatial response of the imaging device, and in particular the CFA pattern. According to this, $\mathbf{M}$ corresponds to a square diagonal binary matrix where the zero elements in its diagonal indicate the spatial and channel locations in the image where color information is missing. Apart from the missing color values, the image measurements are also perturbed by noise which hereafter, we will assume that is an i.i.d Gaussian noise $\mathbf{n} \sim \mathcal{N}(0, \sigma^2)$. Note, that this is a rather simplified assumption about the noise statistics distorting the measurements. However, this model only serves as our starting point based on which we will design our network architecture. In the sequel, our derived network will be trained and evaluated on images that are distorted by noise which follows statistics that better approximate real noisy conditions.

Recovering $\mathbf{x}$ from the measurements $\mathbf{y}$ belongs to the broad class of linear inverse problems. For the problem under study, the operator $\mathbf{M}$ is clearly singular. This fact combined with the presence of noise perturbing the measurements leads to an ill-posed problem where a unique solution does not exist. One popular way to deal with this, is to adopt a Bayesian approach and seek for the Maximum A Posteriori (MAP) estimator

$$\mathbf{x}^* = \arg\max_{\mathbf{x}} \log(p(\mathbf{x}|\mathbf{y})) = \arg\max_{\mathbf{x}} \log(p(\mathbf{y}|\mathbf{x})) + \log(p(\mathbf{x})), \tag{2}$$

where $\log(p(\mathbf{y}|\mathbf{x}))$ represents the log-likelihood of the observation $\mathbf{y}$ and $\log(p(\mathbf{x}))$ represents the log-prior of $\mathbf{x}$. Problem (2) can be equivalently re-casted as the minimization problem

$$\mathbf{x}^* = \arg\min_{\mathbf{x}} \frac{1}{2\sigma^2} \|\mathbf{y} - \mathbf{Mx}\|_2^2 + \phi(\mathbf{x}) \tag{3}$$

where the first term corresponds to the negative log-likelihood (assuming i.i.d Gaussian noise of variance σ^2) and the second term corresponds to the negative log-prior. According to the above, the restoration of the underlying image $\mathbf{x}$, boils down to computing the minimizer of the objective function in Eq. (3), which consists of two terms. This problem formulation has also direct links to variational methods where the first term can be interpreted as the data-fidelity that quantifies the proximity of the solution to the observation and the second term can be seen as the regularizer, whose role is to promotes solutions that satisfy certain favorable image properties.

In general, the minimization of the objective function

$$Q(\mathbf{x}) = \frac{1}{2\sigma^2} \|\mathbf{y} - \mathbf{Mx}\|_2^2 + \phi(\mathbf{x}) \tag{4}$$

is far from a trivial task, especially when the function $\phi(\mathbf{x})$ is not of a quadratic form, which implies that the solution cannot simply be obtained by solving a set of linear equations. From the above, it is clear that there are two important challenges that need to be dealt with before we are in position of deriving a satisfactory solution for our problem. The first one is to come up with an algorithm that can efficiently minimize $Q(\mathbf{x})$, while the second one is to select an appropriate form for $\phi(\mathbf{x})$, which will constrain the set of admissible solutions by promoting only those that exhibit the desired properties.

In Sect. 3, we will focus on the first challenge, while in Sect. 4 we will discuss how it is possible to avoid making any explicit decisions for the regularizer (or equivalently the negative log-prior) by following a machine learning approach. Such an approach will allow us to infer the form of $\phi(\mathbf{x})$, in an indirect way, from training data.

3   Majorization-Minimization Framework

One of the main difficulties in the minimization of the objective function in Eq. (4) is the coupling that exists between the singular degradation operator, $\mathbf{M}$, and the latent image $\mathbf{x}$. To circumvent this difficulty there are several optimization strategies available that we could rely on, with potential candidates being splitting variables techniques such as the Alternating Direction Method of Multipliers [21] and the Split Bregman approach [22]. However, one difficulty that arises by using such methods is that they involve additional parameters that need to be tuned so that a satisfactory convergence speed to the solution is achieved. Unfortunately, there is not a simple and straightforward way to choose these parameters. For this reason, in this work we will instead pursue a majorization-minimization (MM) approach [23,24], which does not pose such a requirement. Under this framework, as we will describe in detail, instead of obtaining the solution by minimizing (4), we compute it iteratively via the successive minimization of surrogate functions. The surrogate functions provide an upper bound of the initial objective function [23] and they are simpler to deal with than the original objective function.

Specifically, in the majorization-minimization (MM) framework, an iterative algorithm for solving the minimization problem

$$\mathbf{x}^* = \arg\min_f Q(\mathbf{x}) \tag{5}$$

takes the form

$$\mathbf{x}^{(t+1)} = \arg\min_x \tilde{Q}(\mathbf{x}; \mathbf{x}^{(t)}), \tag{6}$$

where $\tilde{Q}(\mathbf{x}; \mathbf{x}^{(t)})$ is the majorizer of the function $Q(\mathbf{x})$ at a fixed point $\mathbf{x}^{(t)}$, satisfying the two conditions

$$\tilde{Q}(\mathbf{x}; \mathbf{x}^{(t)}) > Q(\mathbf{x}), \forall \mathbf{x} \neq \mathbf{x}^{(t)} \quad \text{and} \quad \tilde{Q}(\mathbf{x}^{(t)}; \mathbf{x}^{(t)}) = Q(\mathbf{x}^{(t)}). \tag{7}$$

Here, the underlying idea is that instead of minimizing the actual objective function $Q(\mathbf{x})$, we fist upper-bound it by a suitable majorizer $\tilde{Q}(\mathbf{x}; \mathbf{x}^{(t)})$, and then minimize this majorizing function to produce the next iterate $\mathbf{x}^{(t+1)}$. Given the properties of the majorizer, iteratively minimizing $\tilde{Q}(\cdot; \mathbf{x}^{(t)})$ also decreases the objective function $Q(\cdot)$. In fact, it is not even required that the surrogate function in each iteration is minimized, but it is sufficient to only find a $\mathbf{x}^{(t+1)}$ that decreases it.

To derive a majorizer for $Q(\mathbf{x})$ we opt for a majorizer of the data-fidelity term (negative log-likelihood). In particular, we consider the following majorizer

$$\tilde{d}(\mathbf{x}, \mathbf{x}_0) = \frac{1}{2\sigma^2}\|\mathbf{y} - \mathbf{M}\mathbf{x}\|_2^2 + d(\mathbf{x}, \mathbf{x}_0), \tag{8}$$

where $d(\mathbf{x}, \mathbf{x}_0) = \frac{1}{2\sigma^2}(\mathbf{x} - \mathbf{x}_0)^T[\alpha\mathbf{I} - \mathbf{M}^T\mathbf{M}](\mathbf{x} - \mathbf{x}_0)$ is a function that measures the distance between $\mathbf{x}$ and $\mathbf{x}_0$. Since $\mathbf{M}$ is a binary diagonal matrix, it is an idempotent matrix, that is $\mathbf{M}^T\mathbf{M} = \mathbf{M}$, and thus $d(\mathbf{x}, \mathbf{x}_0) = \frac{1}{2\sigma^2}(\mathbf{x} - \mathbf{x}_0)^T[\alpha\mathbf{I} - \mathbf{M}](\mathbf{x} - \mathbf{x}_0)$. According to the conditions in (7), in order $\tilde{d}(\mathbf{x}, \mathbf{x}_0)$ to be a valid majorizer, we need to ensure that $d(\mathbf{x}, \mathbf{x}_0) \geq 0, \forall\mathbf{x}$ with equality iff $\mathbf{x} = \mathbf{x}_0$. This suggests that $a\mathbf{I} - \mathbf{M}$ must be a positive definite matrix, which only holds when $\alpha > \|\mathbf{M}\|_2 = 1$, i.e. α is bigger than the maximum eigenvalue of $\mathbf{M}$. Based on the above, the upper-bounded version of (4) is finally written as

$$\tilde{Q}(\mathbf{x}, \mathbf{x}_0) = \frac{1}{2(\sigma/\sqrt{a})^2}\|\mathbf{x} - \mathbf{z}\|_2^2 + \phi(\mathbf{x}) + c, \tag{9}$$

where c is a constant and $\mathbf{z} = \mathbf{y} + (\mathbf{I} - \mathbf{M})\mathbf{x}_0$.

Notice that following this approach, we have managed to completely decouple the degradation operator $\mathbf{M}$ from $\mathbf{x}$ and we now need to deal with a simpler problem. In fact, the resulting surrogate function in Eq. (9) can be interpreted as the objective function of a denoising problem, with $\mathbf{z}$ being the noisy measurements that are corrupted by noise whose variance is equal to σ^2/a. This is a key observation that we will heavily rely on in order to design our deep network architecture. In particular, it is now possible instead of selecting the form of $\phi(\mathbf{x})$ and minimizing the surrogate function, to employ a denoising neural network that will compute the solution of the current iteration. Our idea is similar in nature to other recent image restoration approaches that have employed denoising networks as part of alternative iterative optimization strategies, such as RED [25] and P^3 [26]. This direction for solving the joint denoising-demosaicking problem is very appealing since by using training data we can implicitly learn the function $\phi(\mathbf{x})$ and also minimize the corresponding surrogate function using a feed-forward network. This way we can completely avoid making any explicit decision for the regularizer or relying on an iterative optimization strategy to minimize the function in Eq. (9).

4   Residual Denoising Network (ResDNet)

Based on the discussion above, the most important part of our approach is the design of a denoising network that will play the role of the solver for the surrogate function in Eq. (9). The architecture of the proposed network is depicted in Fig. 1. This is a residual network similar to DnCNN [27], where the output of the network is subtracted from its input. Therefore, the network itself acts as a noise estimator and its task is to estimate the noise realization that distorts the input. Such network architectures have been shown to lead to better restoration

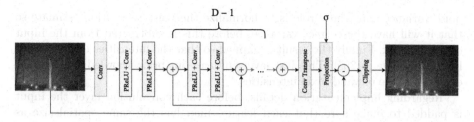

Fig. 1. The architecture of the proposed ResDNet denoising network, which serves as the back-bone of our overall system.

results than alternative approaches [27,28]. One distinctive difference between our network and DnCNN, which also makes our network suitable to be used as a part of the MM-approach, is that it accepts two inputs, namely the distorted input and the variance of the noise. This way, as we will demonstrate in the sequel, we are able to learn a single set of parameters for our network and to employ the same network to inputs that are distorted by a wide range of noise levels. While the blind version of DnCNN can also work for different noise levels, as opposed to our network it features an internal mechanism to estimate the noise variance. However, when the noise statistics deviate significantly from the training conditions such a mechanism can fail and thus DnCNN can lead to poor denoising results [28]. In fact, due to this reason in [29], where more general restoration problems than denoising are studied, the authors of DnCNN use a non-blind variant of their network as a part of their proposed restoration approach. Nevertheless, the drawback of this approach is that it requires the training of a deep network for each noise level. This can be rather impractical, especially in cases where one would like to employ such networks on devices with limited storage capacities. In our case, inspired by the recent work in [28] we circumvent this limitation by explicitly providing as input to our network the noise variance, which is then used to assist the network so as to provide an accurate estimate of the noise distorting the input. Note that there are several techniques available in the literature that can provide an estimate of the noise variance, such as those described in [30,31], and thus this requirement does not pose any significant challenges in our approach.

A ResDNet with depth D, consists of five fundamental blocks. The first block is a convolutional layer with 64 filters whose kernel size is 5×5. The second one is a non-linear block that consists of a parametrized rectified linear unit activation function (PReLU), followed by a convolution with 64 filters of 3×3 kernels. The PReLU function is defined as $\mathrm{PReLU}(\mathbf{x}) = \max(0, \mathbf{x}) + \boldsymbol{\kappa} * \min(0, \mathbf{x})$ where $\boldsymbol{\kappa}$ is a vector whose size is equal to the number of input channels. In our network we use $D * 2$ distinct non-linear blocks which we connect via a shortcut connection every second block in a similar manner to [32] as shown in Fig. 1. Next, the output of the non-linear stage is processed by a transposed convolution layer which reduces the number of channels from 64 to 3 and has a kernel size of 5×5. Then, it follows a projection layer [28] which accepts as an additional input the

noise variance and whose role is to normalize the noise realization estimate so
that it will have the correct variance, before this is subtracted from the input
of the network. Finally the result is clipped so that the intensities of the output
lie in the range $[0, 255]$. This last layer enforces our prior knowledge about the
expected range of valid pixel intensities.

Regarding implementation details, before each convolution layer the input
is padded to make sure that each feature map has the same spatial size as
the input image. However, unlike the common approach followed in most of
the deep learning systems for computer vision applications, we use reflexive
padding than zero padding. Another important difference to other networks
used for image restoration tasks [27,29] is that we don't use batch normalization
after convolutions. Instead, we use the parametric convolution representation
that has been proposed in [28] and which is motivated by image regularization
related arguments. In particular, if $\mathbf{v} \in \mathbb{R}^L$ represents the weights of a filter in a
convolutional layer, these are parametrized as

$$\mathbf{v} = \frac{s\left(\mathbf{u} - \bar{\mathbf{u}}\right)}{\|\mathbf{u} - \bar{\mathbf{u}}\|_2}, \tag{10}$$

where s is a scalar trainable parameter, $\mathbf{u} \in \mathbb{R}^L$ and $\bar{\mathbf{u}}$ denotes the mean value
of $\mathbf{u}$. In other words, we are learning zero-mean valued filters whose ℓ_2-norm is
equal to s.

Furthermore, the projection layer, which is used just before the subtraction
operation with the network input, corresponds to the following ℓ_2 orthogonal
projection

$$\mathcal{P}_C\left(\mathbf{y}\right) = \varepsilon \frac{\mathbf{y}}{max(\|\mathbf{y}\|_2, \varepsilon)}, \tag{11}$$

where $\varepsilon = e^\gamma \theta$, $\theta = \sigma\sqrt{N-1}$, N is the total number of pixels in the image
(including the color channels), σ is the standard deviation of the noise distorting
the input, and γ is a scalar trainable parameter. As we mentioned earlier, the
goal of this layer is to normalize the noise realization estimate so that it has the
desired variance before it is subtracted from the network input.

5   Demosaicking Network Architecture

The overall architecture of our approach is based upon the MM framework, presented in Sect. 3, and the proposed denoising network. As discussed, the MM is
an iterative algorithm Eq. (6) where the minimization of the majorizer in Eq. (9)
can be interpreted as a denoising problem. One way to design the demosaicking
network would be to unroll the MM algorithm as K discrete steps and then for
each step use a different denoising network to retrieve the solution of Eq. (9).
However, this approach can have two distinct drawbacks which will hinder its
performance. The first one, is that the usage of a different denoising neural network for each step like in [29], demands a high overall number of parameters,
which is equal to K times the parameters of the employed denoiser, making

Algorithm 1. The proposed demosaicking network described as an iterative process. The ResDnet parameters remain the same in every iteration.

Input: M : CFA, **y** : input, K : iterations, $\boldsymbol{w} \in \mathbb{R}^K$: extrapolation weights,
    $\boldsymbol{\sigma} \in \mathbb{R}^K$: noise vector
$\mathbf{x}^0 = \mathbf{0}, \mathbf{x}^1 = \mathbf{y}$;
for $i \leftarrow 1$ **to** K **do**
    $\mathbf{u} = \mathbf{x}^{(i)} + w_i(\mathbf{x}^{(i)} - \mathbf{x}^{(i-1)})$;
    $\mathbf{x}^{(i+1)} = \text{ResDNet}((\mathbf{I} - \mathbf{M})\mathbf{u} + \mathbf{y}, \boldsymbol{\sigma}_i)$;
end

---

the demosaicking network impractical for any real applications. To override this drawback, we opt to use our ResDNet denoiser, which can be applied to a wide range of noise levels, for all K steps of our demosaick network, using the same set of parameters. By sharing the parameters of our denoiser across all the K steps, the overall demosaicking approach maintains a low number of required parameters.

The second drawback of the MM framework as described in Sect. 3 is the slow convergence [33] that it can exhibit. Beck and Teboulle [33] introduced an accelerated version of this MM approach which combines the solutions of two consecutive steps with a certain extrapolation weight that is different for every step. In this work, we adopt a similar strategy which we describe in Algorithm 1. Furthermore, in our approach we go one step further and instead of using the values originally suggested in [33] for the weights $\boldsymbol{w} \in \mathbb{R}^K$, we treat them as trainable parameters and learn them directly from the data. These weights are initialized with $w_i = \frac{i-1}{i+2}, \forall 1 \leq i \leq K$.

The convergence of our framework can be further sped up by employing a continuation strategy [34] where the main idea is to solve the problem in Eq. (9) with a large value of σ and then gradually decrease it until the target value is reached. Our approach is able to make use of the continuation strategy due to the design of our ResDNet denoiser, which accepts as an additional argument the noise variance. In detail, we initialize the trainable vector $\boldsymbol{\sigma} \in \mathbb{R}^K$ with values spaced evenly on a log scale from σ_{max} to σ_{min} and later on the vector $\boldsymbol{\sigma}$ is further finetuned on the training dataset by back-propagation training.

In summary, our overall demosaicking network is described in Algorithm 1 where the set of trainable parameters θ consists of the parameters of the ResDNet denoiser, the extrapolation weights $\boldsymbol{w}$ and the noise level $\boldsymbol{\sigma}$. All of the aforementioned parameters are initialized as described in the current section and Sect. 4 and are trained on specific demosaick datasets. In order to speed up the learning process, the employed ResDNet denoiser is pre-trained for a denoising task where multiple noise levels are considered.

Finally, while our demosaick network shares a similar philosophy with methods such as RED [25], P^3 [26] and IRCNN [29], it exhibits some important and distinct differences. In particular, the aforementioned strategies make use of certain optimization schemes to decompose their original problem into subproblems that are solvable by a denoiser. For example, the authors of P^3 [26] decompose the original problem Eq. (1) via ADMM [21] optimization algorithm and solve instead a linear system of equations and a denoising problem, where the authors of RED [25] go one step further and make use of the Lagrangian on par with a denoiser. Both approaches are similar to ours, however their formulation involves a tunable variable λ that weights the participation of the regularizer on the overall optimization procedure. Thus, in order to obtain an accurate reconstruction in reasonable time, the user must manually tune the variable λ which is not a trivial task. On the other hand, our method does not involve any tunable variables by the user. Furthermore, the approaches P^3, RED and IRCNN are based upon static denoisers like Non Local Means [35], BM3D [36] and DCNN [27], meanwhile we opt to use a universal denoiser, like ResDnet, that can be further trained on any available training data. Finally, our approach goes one step further and we use a trainable version of an iterative optimization strategy for the task of the joint denoising-demosaicking in the form of a feed-forward neural network (Fig. 2).

6   Network Training

6.1   Image Denoising

The denoising network ResDnet that we use as part of our overall network is pre-trained on the Berkeley segmentation dataset (BSDS) [37], which consists of 500 color images. These images were split in two sets, 400 were used to form a train set and the rest 100 formed a validation set. All the images were randomly cropped into patches of size 180×180 pixels. The patches were perturbed with noise $\sigma \in [0, 15]$ and the network was optimized to minimize the Mean Square Error. We set the network depth $D = 5$, all weights are initialized as in He et al. [38] and the optimization is carried out using ADAM [39] which is a stochastic gradient descent algorithm which adapts the learning rate per parameter. The training procedure starts with an initial learning rate equal to 10^{-2}.

6.2   Joint Denoising and Demosaicking

Using the pre-trained denoiser Sect. 6.1, our novel framework is further trained in an end-to-end fashion to minimize the averaged L_1 loss over a minibatch of size d,

$$L(\theta) = \frac{1}{N} \sum_{i=1}^{d} \|\mathbf{y}_i - f(\mathbf{x}_i)\|_1, \tag{12}$$

where $\mathbf{y}_i \in \mathbb{R}^N$ and $\mathbf{x}_i \in \mathbb{R}^N$ are the rasterized groundtruth and input images, while $f(\cdot)$ is the output of our network. The minimization of the loss function is carried via the Backpropagation Through Time (BPTT) [40] algorithm since the weights of the network remain the same for all iterations.

During all our experiments, we used a small batch size of $d = 4$ images, the total steps of the network were fixed to $K = 10$ and we set for the initialization of vector σ the values $\sigma_{max} = 15$ and $\sigma_{min} = 1$. The small batch size is mandatory during training because all intermediate results have to be stored for the BPTT, thus the memory consumption increases linearly to iteration steps and batch size. Furthermore, the optimization is carried again via Adam optimizer and the training starts from a learning rate of 10^{-2} which we decrease by a factor of 10 every 30 epochs. Finally, for all trainable parameters we apply ℓ_2 weight decay of 10^{-8}. The full training procedure takes 3 hours for MSR Demosaicking Dataset and 5 days for a small subset of the MIT Demosaicking Dataset on a modern NVIDIA GTX 1080Ti GPU.

Table 1. Comparison of our system to state-of-the-art techniques on the demosaick-only scenario in terms of PSNR performance. The Kodak dataset is resized to 512×768 following the methodology of evaluation in [1]. *Our system for the MIT dataset was trained on a small subset of 40,000 out of 2.6 million images.

	Kodak	McM	Vdp	Moire
Non-ML Methods:				
Bilinear	32.9	32.5	25.2	27.6
Adobe Camera Raw 9	33.9	32.2	27.8	29.8
Buades [4]	37.3	35.5	29.7	31.7
Zhang (NLM) [2]	37.9	36.3	30.1	31.9
Getreuer [41]	38.1	36.1	30.8	32.5
Heide [5]	40.0	38.6	27.1	34.9
Trained on MSR Dataset:				
Klatzer [19]	35.3	30.8	28.0	30.3
Ours	39.2	34.1	29.2	29.7
Trained on MIT Dataset:				
Gharbi [20]	41.2	39.5	34.3	**37.0**
Ours*	**41.5**	**39.7**	**34.5**	**37.0**

7 Experiments

Initially, we compare our system to other alternative techniques on the demosaick-only scenario. Our network is trained on the MSR Demosaick dataset [14] and it is evaluated on the McMaster [2], Kodak, Moire and VDP dataset [20], where all the results are reported in Table 1. The MSR Demosaick dataset consists of 200 train images which contain both the linearized 16-bit mosaicked input images and the corresponding linRGB groundtruths that we also augment with horizontal and vertical flipping. For all experiments, in order to quantify the quality of the reconstructions we report the Peak signal-to-noise-ratio (PSNR) metric.

Apart from the MSR dataset, we also train our system on a small subset of 40,000 images from MIT dataset due to the small batch size constraint. Clearly our system is capable of achieving equal and in many cases better performance than the current the state-of-the art network [20] which was trained on the full MIT dataset, i.e. 2.6 million images. We believe that training our network on the complete MIT dataset, it will produce even better results for the noise-free scenario. Furthermore, the aforementioned dataset contains only noise-free samples, therefore we don't report any results in Table 2 and we mark the respective results by using N/A instead. We also note that in [20], the authors in order to use the MIT dataset to train their network for the joint demosaicking denoising scenario, pertubed the data by i.i.d Gaussian noise. As a result, their system's performance under the presence of more realistic noise was significantly reduced, which can be clearly seen from Table 2. The main reason for this is that their noise assumption does not account for the *shot* noise of the camera but only for the *read* noise.

Table 2. PSNR performance by different methods in both linear and sRGB spaces. The results of methods that cannot perform denoising are not included for the noisy scenario. Our system for the MIT dataset case was trained on a small subset of 40,000 out of 2.6 million images. The color space in the parentheses indicates the particular color space of the employed training dataset.

	Noise-free		Noisy	
	linRGB	sRGB	linRGB	sRGB
Non-ML Methods:				
Bilinear	30.9	24.9	-	-
Zhang(NLM) [2]	38.4	32.1	-	-
Getreuer [41]	39.4	32.9	-	-
Heide [5]	40.0	33.8	-	-
Trained on MSR Dataset:				
Khasabi [14]	39.4	32.6	37.8	31.5
Klatzer [19]	40.9	34.6	38.8	32.6
Bigdeli [42]	-	-	38.7	-
Ours	**41.0**	**34.6**	**39.2**	**33.3**
Trained on MIT Dataset:				
Gharbi (sRGB)[20]	41.6	35.3	38.4	32.5
Gharbi (linRGB)	**42.7**	**35.9**	38.6	32.6
Ours* (linRGB)	42.6	**35.9**	N/A	N/A

Similarly with the noise free case, we train our system on 200 training images from the MSR dataset which are contaminated with simulated sensor noise [15]. The model was optimized in the linRGB space and the performance was evaluated on both linRGB and sRGB space, as proposed in [14]. It is clear that in the noise free scenario, training on million of images corresponds to improved performance, however this doesn't seem to be the case on the noisy scenario as presented in Table 2. Our approach, even though it is based on deep learning techniques, is capable of generalizing better than the state-of-the-art system while being trained on a small dataset of 200 images (Fig. 3). In detail, the proposed system has a total 380,356 trainable parameters which is considerably smaller than the current state-of-the art [20] with 559,776 trainable parameters.

Our demosaicking network is also capable of handling non-Bayer patterns equally well, as shown in Table 3. In particular, we considered demosaicking using the Fuji X-Trans CFA pattern, which is a 6 × 6 grid with the green being the dominant sampled color. We trained from scratch our network on the same trainset of MSR Demosaick Dataset but now we applied the Fuji X-Trans mosaick. In

Table 3. Evaluation on noise-free linear data with the non-Bayer mosaick pattern Fuji XTrans.

	Noise-free	
	linear	sRGB
Trained on MSR Dataset:		
Khashabi [14]	36.9	30.6
Klatzer [19]	39.6	33.1
Ours	**39.9**	**33.7**
Trained on MIT Dataset:		
Gharbi [20]	39.7	33.2

Fig. 2. Progression along the steps of our demosaick network. The first image which corresponds to Step 1 represents a rough approximation of the end result while the second (Step 3) and third image (Step 10) are more refined. This plot depicts the continuation scheme of our approach.

comparison to other systems, we manage to surpass state of the art performance on both linRGB and sRGB space even when comparing with systems trained on million of images.

On a modern GPU (Nvidia GTX 1080Ti), the whole demosaicking network requires 0.05 sec for a color image of size 220×132 and it scales linearly to images of different sizes. Since our model solely consists of matrix operations, it could also be easily transfered to application specific integrated circuit (ASIC) in order to achieve a substantial execution time speedup and be integrated to cameras.

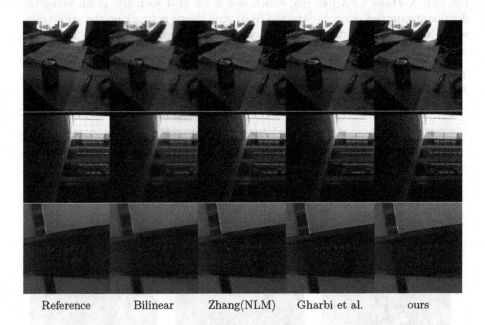

Reference   Bilinear   Zhang(NLM)   Gharbi et al.   ours

Fig. 3. Comparison of our network with other competing techniques on images from the noisy MSR Dataset. From these results is clear that our method is capable of removing the noise while keeping fine details.On the contrary, the rest of the methods either fail to denoise or they oversmooth the images.

8   Conclusion

In this work, we presented a novel deep learning system that produces high-quality images for the joint denoising and demosaicking problem. Our demosaick network yields superior results both quantitative and qualitative compared to the current state-of-the-art network. Meanwhile, our approach is able to generalize well even when trained on small datasets, while the number of parameters is kept low in comparison to other competing solutions. As an interesting future research direction, we plan to explore the applicability of our method on other image restoration problems like image deblurring, inpainting and super-resolution where the degradation operator is unknown or varies from image to image.

References

1. Li, X., Gunturk, B., Zhang, L.: Image demosaicing: a systematic survey (2008)
2. Zhang, L., Wu, X., Buades, A., Li, X.: Color demosaicking by local directional interpolation and nonlocal adaptive thresholding. J. Electron. Imaging 20(2), 023016 (2011)
3. Duran, J., Buades, A.: Self-similarity and spectral correlation adaptive algorithm for color demosaicking. IEEE Trans. Image Process. 23(9), 4031–4040 (2014)
4. Buades, A., Coll, B., Morel, J.M., Sbert, C.: Self-similarity driven color demosaicking. IEEE Trans. Image Process. 18(6), 1192–1202 (2009)
5. Heide, F., et al.: Flexisp: a flexible camera image processing framework. ACM Trans. Graph. (TOG) 33(6), 231 (2014)
6. Chang, K., Ding, P.L.K., Li, B.: Color image demosaicking using inter-channel correlation and nonlocal self-similarity. Signal Process. Image Commun. 39, 264–279 (2015)
7. Hirakawa, K., Parks, T.W.: Adaptive homogeneity-directed demosaicing algorithm. IEEE Trans. Image Process. 14(3), 360–369 (2005)
8. Alleysson, D., Susstrunk, S., Herault, J.: Linear demosaicing inspired by the human visual system. IEEE Trans. Image Process. 14(4), 439–449 (2005)
9. Dubois, E.: Frequency-domain methods for demosaicking of bayer-sampled color images. IEEE Signal Process. Lett. 12(12), 847–850 (2005)
10. Dubois, E.: Filter design for adaptive frequency-domain bayer demosaicking. In: 2006 International Conference on Image Processing, pp. 2705–2708, October 2006
11. Dubois, E.: Color filter array sampling of color images: Frequency-domain analysis and associated demosaicking algorithms, pp. 183–212, January 2009
12. Sun, J., Tappen, M.F.: Separable markov random field model and its applications in low level vision. IEEE Trans. Image Process. 22(1), 402–407 (2013)
13. He, F.L., Wang, Y.C.F., Hua, K.L.: Self-learning approach to color demosaicking via support vector regression. In: 19th IEEE International Conference on Image Processing (ICIP), pp. 2765–2768. IEEE (2012)
14. Khashabi, D., Nowozin, S., Jancsary, J., Fitzgibbon, A.W.: Joint demosaicing and denoising via learned nonparametric random fields. IEEE Trans. Image Process. 23(12), 4968–4981 (2014)
15. Foi, A., Trimeche, M., Katkovnik, V., Egiazarian, K.: Practical poissonian-gaussian noise modeling and fitting for single-image raw-data. IEEE Trans. Image Process. 17(10), 1737–1754 (2008)
16. Ossi Kalevo, H.R.: Noise reduction techniques for bayer-matrix images (2002)
17. Menon, D., Calvagno, G.: Joint demosaicking and denoisingwith space-varying filters. In: 2009 16th IEEE International Conference on Image Processing (ICIP), pp. 477–480, November 2009
18. Zhang, L., Lukac, R., Wu, X., Zhang, D.: PCA-based spatially adaptive denoising of CFA images for single-sensor digital cameras. IEEE Trans. Image Process. 18(4), 797–812 (2009)
19. Klatzer, T., Hammernik, K., Knobelreiter, P., Pock, T.: Learning joint demosaicing and denoising based on sequential energy minimization. In: 2016 IEEE International Conference on Computational Photography (ICCP), pp. 1–11, May 2016

20. Gharbi, M., Chaurasia, G., Paris, S., Durand, F.: Deep joint demosaicking and denoising. ACM Trans. Graph. **35**(6), 191:1–191:12 (2016)
21. Boyd, S., Parikh, N., Chu, E., Peleato, B., Eckstein, J., et al.: Distributed optimization and statistical learning via the alternating direction method of multipliers. Found. Trends® Mach. Learn. **3**(1), 1–122 (2011)
22. Goldstein, T., Osher, S.: The split bregman method for l1-regularized problems. SIAM J. Imaging Sci. **2**(2), 323–343 (2009)
23. Hunter, D.R., Lange, K.: A tutorial on MM algorithms. Am. Stat. **58**(1), 30–37 (2004)
24. Figueiredo, M.A., Bioucas-Dias, J.M., Nowak, R.D.: Majorization-minimization algorithms for wavelet-based image restoration. IEEE Trans. Image Process. **16**(12), 2980–2991 (2007)
25. Romano, Y., Elad, M., Milanfar, P.: The little engine that could: Regularization by denoising (red). SIAM J. Imaging Sci. **10**(4), 1804–1844 (2017)
26. Venkatakrishnan, S.V., Bouman, C.A., Wohlberg, B.: Plug-and-play priors for model based reconstruction. In: 2013 IEEE Global Conference on Signal and Information Processing, pp. 945–948, December 2013
27. Zhang, K., Zuo, W., Chen, Y., Meng, D., Zhang, L.: Beyond a gaussian denoiser: residual learning of deep cnn for image denoising. IEEE Trans. Image Process. **26**(7), 3142–3155 (2017)
28. Lefkimmiatis, S.: Universal denoising networks: a novel CNN architecture for image denoising. In: Proceedings of the IEEE Conference on Computer Vision and Pattern Recognition, pp. 3204–3213 (2018)
29. Zhang, K., Zuo, W., Gu, S., Zhang, L.: Learning deep CNN denoiser prior for image restoration. arXiv preprint (2017)
30. Foi, A.: Clipped noisy images: Heteroskedastic modeling and practical denoising. Signal Process. **89**(12), 2609–2629 (2009)
31. Liu, X., Tanaka, M., Okutomi, M.: Single-image noise level estimation for blind denoising. IEEE Trans. Image Process. **22**(12), 5226–5237 (2013)
32. He, K., Zhang, X., Ren, S., Sun, J.: Deep residual learning for image recognition. In: Proceedings of the IEEE Conference on Computer Vision and Pattern Recognition, pp. 770–778 (2016)
33. Beck, A., Teboulle, M.: A fast iterative shrinkage-thresholding algorithm for linear inverse problems. SIAM J. Imaging Sci. **2**(1), 183–202 (2009)
34. Lin, Q., Xiao, L.: An adaptive accelerated proximal gradient method and its homotopy continuation for sparse optimization. Comput. Optim. Appl. **60**(3), 633–674 (2015)
35. Buades, A., Coll, B., Morel, J.M.: A non-local algorithm for image denoising. In: IEEE Computer Society Conference on Computer Vision and Pattern Recognition, CVPR 2005, vol. 2, pp. 60–65. IEEE (2005)
36. Dabov, K., Foi, A., Katkovnik, V., Egiazarian, K.: Image denoising by sparse 3-d transform-domain collaborative filtering. IEEE Trans. Image Process. **16**(8), 2080–2095 (2007)
37. Martin, D., Fowlkes, C., Tal, D., Malik, J.: A database of human segmented natural images and its application to evaluating segmentation algorithms and measuring ecological statistics. In: Proceedings Eighth IEEE International Conference on Computer Vision, ICCV 2001, vol. 2, pp. 416–423 (2001)
38. He, K., Zhang, X., Ren, S., Sun, J.: Delving deep into rectifiers: surpassing human-level performance on imagenet classification. In: Proceedings of the IEEE International Conference on Computer Vision, pp. 1026–1034 (2015)

39. Kingma, D.P., Ba, J.: Adam: a method for stochastic optimization. arXiv preprint arXiv:1412.6980 (2014)
40. Robinson, A.J., Fallside, F.: The utility driven dynamic error propagation network. Technical report CUED/F-INFENG/TR.1, Engineering Department, Cambridge University, Cambridge, UK (1987)
41. Getreuer, P.: Color demosaicing with contour stencils. In: 2011 17th International Conference on Digital Signal Processing (DSP), pp. 1–6, July 2011
42. Bigdeli, S.A., Zwicker, M., Favaro, P., Jin, M.: Deep mean-shift priors for image restoration. In: Advances in Neural Information Processing Systems, pp. 763–772 (2017)

A New Large Scale Dynamic Texture Dataset with Application to ConvNet Understanding

Isma Hadji[(✉)] and Richard P. Wildes

York University, Toronto, ON, Canada
{hadjisma,wildes}@cse.yorku.ca

Abstract. We introduce a new large scale dynamic texture dataset. With over 10,000 videos, our Dynamic Texture DataBase (DTDB) is two orders of magnitude larger than any previously available dynamic texture dataset. DTDB comes with two complementary organizations, one based on dynamics independent of spatial appearance and one based on spatial appearance independent of dynamics. The complementary organizations allow for uniquely insightful experiments regarding the abilities of major classes of spatiotemporal ConvNet architectures to exploit appearance vs. dynamic information. We also present a new two-stream ConvNet that provides an alternative to the standard optical-flow-based motion stream to broaden the range of dynamic patterns that can be encompassed. The resulting motion stream is shown to outperform the traditional optical flow stream by considerable margins. Finally, the utility of DTDB as a pretraining substrate is demonstrated via transfer learning on a different dynamic texture dataset as well as the companion task of dynamic scene recognition resulting in a new state-of-the-art.

1 Introduction

Visual texture, be it static or dynamic, is an important scene characteristic that provides vital information for segmentation into coherent regions and identification of material properties. Moreover, it can support subsequent operations involving background modeling, change detection and indexing. Correspondingly, much research has addressed static texture analysis for single images (*e.g.* [5,6,21,35,36]). In comparison, research concerned with dynamic texture analysis from temporal image streams (*e.g.* video) has been limited (*e.g.* [15,26,27,38]).

The relative state of dynamic vs. static texture research is unsatisfying because the former is as prevalent in the real world as the latter and it provides similar descriptive power. Many commonly encountered patterns are better described by global dynamics of the signal rather than individual constituent

Electronic supplementary material The online version of this chapter (https://doi.org/10.1007/978-3-030-01264-9_20) contains supplementary material, which is available to authorized users.

V. Ferrari et al. (Eds.): ECCV 2018, LNCS 11218, pp. 334–351, 2018.
https://doi.org/10.1007/978-3-030-01264-9_20

elements. For example, it is more perspicuous to describe the global motion of the leaves on a tree as windblown foliage rather than in terms of individual leaf motion. Further, given the onslaught of video available via on-line and other sources, applications of dynamic texture analysis may eclipse those of static texture.

Dynamic texture research is hindered by a number of factors. A major issue is lack of clarity on what constitutes a dynamic texture. Typically, dynamic textures are defined as temporal sequences exhibiting certain temporal statistics or stationary properties in time [30]. In practice, however, the term dynamic texture is usually used to describe the case of image sequences exhibiting stochastic dynamics (e.g. turbulent water and windblown vegetation). This observation is evidenced by the dominance of such textures in the UCLA [30] and DynTex [24] datasets. A more compelling definition describes dynamic texture as any temporal sequence that can be characterized by the same aggregate dynamic properties across its support region [8]. Hence, the dominant dynamic textures in UCLA and DynTex are the subclass of textures that exhibit stochastic motion. Another concern with definitions applied in extant datasets is that the classes are usually determined by appearance, which defeats the purpose of studying the *dynamics* of these textures. The only dataset that stands out in this regard is YUVL [8], wherein classes were defined explicitly in terms of pattern dynamics.

The other major limiting factors in the study of dynamic textures are lack of size and diversity in extant datasets. Table 1 documents the benchmarks used in dynamic texture recognition. It is apparent that these datasets are small compared to what is available for static texture (e.g. [5,7,23]). Further, limited diversity is apparent, e.g. in cases where the number of sequences is greater than the number videos, multiple sequences were generated as clips from single videos. Diversity also is limited by different classes sometimes being derived from slightly different views of the same physical phenomenon. Moreover, diversity is limited in variations that have a small number of classes. Finally, it is notable that all current dynamic texture datasets are performance saturated [15].

Table 1. Comparison of the new DTDB dataset with other dynamic texture datasets

Dataset	DynTex [24]					UCLA [30]					YUVL [8]			DTDB (Ours)	
Dataset Variations	Alpha [11]	Beta [11]	Gamma [11]	35 [40]	++ [14]	50 [30]	9 [14]	8 [28]	7 [9]	SIR [9]	1 [8]	2 [8]	3 [15]	Appearance	Dynamics
#Videos	60	162	264	35	345	50	50	50	50	50	610	509	610	>9K	>10K
#Sequences	60	162	264	350	3600	200	200	92	400	400	610	509	610	>9K	>10K
#Frames	>140K	>397K	>553K	>8K	>17K	15K	15K	>6K	15K	15K	>65K	>55K	>65K	>3.1 million	>3.4 million
#Classes	3	10	10	35	36	50	9	8	7	50	5	6	8	45	18

Over the past few years, increasingly larger sized datasets (e.g. [18,29,41]) have driven progress in computer vision, especially as they support training of powerful ConvNets (e.g. [16,19,32]). For video based recognition, action recognition is the most heavily researched task and the availability of large scale datasets (e.g. UCF-101 [33] and the more recent Kinetics [3]) play a significant role in the progress being made. Therefore, large scale dynamic texture datasets are of particular interest to support use of ConvNets in this domain.

In response to the above noted state of affairs, we make the following contributions. (1) We present a new large scale dynamic texture dataset that is two orders of magnitude larger than any available. At over 10,000 videos, it is comparable in size to UCF-101 that has played a major role in advances to action recognition. (2) We provide two complementary organizations of the dataset. The first groups videos based on their dynamics irrespective of their static (single frame) appearance. The second groups videos purely based on their visual appearance. For example, in addition to describing a sequence as containing car traffic, we complement the description with dynamic information that allows making the distinction between smooth and chaotic car traffic. Figure 1 shows frames from the large spectrum of videos present in the dataset and illustrates how videos are assigned to different classes depending on the grouping criterion (*i.e.* dynamics vs. appearance). (3) We use the new dataset to explore the representational power of different spatiotemporal ConvNet architectures. In particular, we examine the relative abilities of architectures that directly apply 3D filtering to input videos [15,34] vs. two-stream architectures that explicitly separate appearance and motion information [12,31]. The two complementary organizations of the same dataset allow for uniquely insightful experiments regarding the capabilities of the algorithms to exploit appearance vs. dynamic information. (4) We propose a novel two-stream architecture that yields superior performance to more standard two-stream approaches on the dynamic texture recognition task. (5) We demonstrate that our new dataset is rich enough to support transfer learning to a different dynamic texture dataset, YUVL [8], and to a different task, dynamic scene recognition [13], where we establish a new state-of-the-art. Our novel Dynamic Texture DataBase (DTDB) is available at http://vision.eecs. yorku.ca/research/dtdb/.

Fig. 1. (Left) Sample frames from the proposed Dynamic Texture DataBase (DTDB) and their assigned categories in both the dynamics and appearance based organizations. (Right) Thumbnail examples of the different appearance based dynamic textures present in the new DTDB dataset. See supplemental material for videos.

2   Dynamic Texture DataBase (DTDB)

The new dataset, Dynamic Texture DataBase (DTDB), constitutes the largest dynamic texture dataset available with $> 10,000$ *videos* and ≈ 3.5 *million frames*. As noted above, the dataset is organized in two different ways with 18 dynamics based categories and 45 appearance based categories. Table 1 compares our dataset with previous dynamic texture benchmarks showing the significant improvements compared to alternatives. The videos are collected from various sources, including the web and various handheld cameras that we employed, which helps ensure diversity and large intra-class variations. Figure 1 provides thumbnail examples from the entire dataset. Corresponding videos and descriptions are provided in the supplemental material.

Dynamic Category Specification. The dataset was created with the main goal of building a true *dynamic* texture dataset where sequences exhibiting similar dynamic behaviors are grouped together irrespective of their appearance. Previous work provided a principled approach to defining five coarse dynamic texture categories based on the number of spatiotemporal orientations present in a sequence [8], as given in the left column of Table 2. We use that enumeration as a point departure, but subdivide the original categories to yield a much larger set of 18 categories, as given in the middle column of Table 2. Note that the original categories are subdivided in a way that accounts for increased variance about the prescribed orientation distributions in the original classes. For example, patterns falling under *dominant orientation* (*i.e.* sequences dominated by a single space-time orientation) were split into five sub-categories: (1) Single Rigid Objects, (2) Multiple Rigid Objects, (3) Smooth Non-Rigid Objects, (4) Turbulent Non-Rigid Objects and (5) Pluming Non-Rigid Objects, all exhibiting motion along a dominant direction, albeit with increasing variance (*c.f.* [20]); see Fig. 2. At an extreme, the original category *Isotropic* does not permit further subdivision based on increased variance about its defining orientations, because although it may have significant spatiotemporal contrast, it lacks in discernible orientation(s), *i.e.* it exhibits isotropic pattern structure. See supplemental material for video examples of all categories, with accompanying discussion.

Fig. 2. (Left) Example of the finer distinctions we make within dynamic textures falling under the broad dominant motion category. Note the increased level of complexity in the dynamics from left to right. (**Right**) Keywords wordle. Bigger font size of a word indicates higher frequency of the keyword resulting in videos in the dataset.

Table 2. Dynamics based categories in the DTDB dataset. A total of 18 different categories are defined by making finer distinctions in the spectrum of dynamic textures proposed originally in [8]. Subdivisions of the original categories occur according to increased variance (indicated by arrow directions) about the orientations specified to define the original categories; see text for details. The supplement provides videos.

Original YUVL categories	DTDB categories		
Name/Description	Name/Description		Example sources
Underconstrained spacetime orientation	↓	Aperture Problem	Conveyor belt, barber pole
		Blinking	Blinking lights, lightning
		Flicker	Fire, shimmering steam
Dominant spacetime orientation	↓	Single Rigid Object	Train, plane
		Multiple Rigid Objects	Smooth traffic, smooth crowd
		Smooth Non-Rigid Objects	Faucet water, shower water
		Turbulent Non-Rigid Objects	Geyser, fountain
		Pluming Non-Rigid Objects	Avalanche, landslide
Multi-dominant spacetime orientation	↓	Rotary Top-View	fan, whirlpool from top
		Rotary Side-View	Tornado, whirlpool from side
		Transparency	Translucent surfaces, chain link fence vs. background
		Pluming	Smoke, clouds
		Explosion	Fireworks, bombs
		Chaotic	Swarming insects, chaotic traffic
Heterogeneous spacetime orientation	↓	Waves	Wavy water, waving flags
		Turbulence	Boiling liquid, bubbles
		Stochastic	Windblown leaves, flowers
Isotropic	↓	Scintillation	TV noise, scintillating water

Keywords and Appearance Categories. For each category, we brainstormed a list of scenes, objects and natural phenomena that could contain or exhibit the desired dynamic behavior and used their names as keywords for subsequent web search. To obtain a large scale dataset, an extensive list of English keywords were generated and augmented with their translations to various languages: Russian, French, German and Mandarin. A visualization of the generated keywords and their frequency of occurrence across all categories is represented as a wordle [2] in Fig. 2. To specify appearance catergories, we selected 45 of the keywords, which taken together covered all the dynamics categories. This approach was possible, since on-line tags for videos are largely based on appearance. The resulting appearance categories are given as sub-captions in Fig. 1.

Video Collection. The generated keywords were used to crawl videos from YouTube [39], Pond5 [25] and VideoHive [37]. In doing so, it was useful to specifically crawl playlists. Since playlists are created by human users or generated by machine learning algorithms, their videos share similar tags and topics; therefore, the videos crawled from playlists were typically highly correlated and had a high probability of containing the dynamic texture of interest. Finally, the links (URLs) gathered using the keywords were cleaned to remove duplicates.

Annotation. Annotation served to verify via human inspection the categories present in each crawled video link. This task was the main bottleneck of the collection process and required multiple annotators for good results. Since the annotation required labeling the videos according to dynamics while ignoring appearance and vice versa, it demanded specialist background and did not lend itself well to tools such as Mechanical Turk [1]. Therefore, two annotators with computer vision background were hired and trained for this task.

Annotation employed a custom web-based tool allowing the user to view each video according to its web link and assign it the following attributes: a dynamics-based label (according to the 18 categories defined in Table 2), an appearance-based label (according to the 45 categories defined in Fig. 1) and start/end times of the pattern in the video. Each video was separately reviewed by both annotators. When the two main annotators disagreed, a third annotator (also with computer vision background) attempted to resolve matters with consensus and if that was not possible the link was deleted. Following the annotations, the specified portions of all videos were downloaded with their labels.

Dataset Cleaning. For a clean dynamic texture dataset, we chose that the target texture should occupy at least 90% of the spatial support of the video and all of the temporal support. Since such requirements are hard to meet with videos acquired in the wild and posted on the web, annotators were instructed to accept videos even if they did not strictly meet this requirement. In a subsequent step, the downloaded videos were visually inspected again and spatially cropped so that the resulting sequences had at least 90% of their spatial support occupied by the target dynamic texture. To ensure the cropping did not severely compromise the overall size of the texture sample, any video whose cropped spatial dimensions were less than 224×224 was deleted from the dataset. The individuals who did the initial annotations also did the cleaning.

This final cleaning process resulted in slightly over 9000 clean sequences. To obtain an even larger dataset, it was augmented in two ways. First, relevant videos from the earlier DynTex [24] and UCLA [30] datasets were selected (but none from YUVL [8]), while avoiding duplicates; second, several volunteers contributed videos that they recorded (*e.g.* with handheld cameras). These additions resulted in the final dataset containing 10,020 sequences with various spatial supports and temporal durations (5–10 s).

Dynamics and Appearance Based Organization. All the 10,020 sequences were used in the dynamics based organization with an average number of videos per category of 556 ± 153. However, because the main focus during data collection was dynamics, it was noticed that not all appearance based video tags generated enough appearance based sequences. Therefore, to keep the dataset balanced in the appearance organization as well, any category containing less than 100 sequences was ignored in the appearance based organization. This process led to an appearance based dataset containing a total 9206 videos divided into 45 different classes with an average number of videos per category of 205 ± 95.

3   Spatiotemporal ConvNets

There are largely two complementary approaches to realizing spatiotemporal ConvNets. The first works directly with input temporal image streams (*i.e.* video), *e.g.* [17,18,34]. The second takes a two-stream approach, wherein the image information is processed in parallel pathways, one for appearance (RGB images) and one for motion (optical flow), *e.g.* [12,22,31]. For the sake of our comparisons, we consider a straightforward exemplar of each class that previously has shown strong performance in spatiotemporal image understanding. In particular, we use C3D [34] as an example of working directly with input video and Simonyan and Zisserman Two-Stream [31] as an example of splitting appearance and motion at the input. We also consider two additional networks: A novel two-stream architecture that is designed to overcome limitations of optical flow in capturing dynamic textures and a learning-free architecture that works directly on video input and recently has shown state-of-the-art performance on dynamic texture recognition with previously available datasets [15]. Importantly, in selecting this set of four ConvNet architectures to compare, we are not seeking to compare details of the wide variety of instantiations of the two broad classes considered, but more fundamentally to understand the relative power of the single and two-stream approaches. In the remainder of this section we briefly outline each algorithm compared; additional details are in the supplemental material.

C3D. C3D [34] works with temporal streams of RGB images. It operates on these images via multilayer application of learned 3D, (x, y, t), convolutional filters. It thereby provides a fairly straightforward generalization of standard 2D ConvNet processing to image spacetime. This generalization entails a great increase in the number of parameters to be learned, which is compensated for by using very limited spacetime support at all layers ($3 \times 3 \times 3$ convolutions). Consideration of this type of ConvNet allows for evaluation of the ability of integrated spacetime filtering to capture both appearance and dynamics information.

Two-Stream. The standard Two-Stream architecture [31] operates in two parallel pathways, one for processing appearance and the other for motion. Input to the appearance pathway are RGB images; input to the motion path are stacks of optical flow fields. Essentially, each stream is processed separately with fairly standard 2D ConvNet architectures. Separate classification is performed by each pathway, with late fusion used to achieve the final result. Consideration of this type of ConvNet allows evaluation of the two streams to separate appearance and dynamics information for understanding spatiotemporal content.

MSOE-Two-Stream. Optical flow is known to be a poor representation for many dynamic textures, especially those exhibiting decidedly non-smooth and/or stochastic characteristics [8,10]. Such textures are hard for optical flow to capture as they violate the assumptions of brightness constancy and local smoothness that are inherent in most flow estimators. Examples include common real-world patterns shown by wind blown foliage, turbulent flow and complex lighting effects (*e.g.* specularities on water). Thus, various alternative approaches have been used for dynamic texture analysis in lieu of optical flow [4].

A particularly interesting alternative to optical flow in the present context is appearance Marginalized Spatiotemporal Oriented Energy (MSOE) filtering [8]. This approach applies 3D, (x, y, t), oriented filters to a video stream and thereby fits naturally in a convolutional architecture. Also, its appearance marginalization abstracts from purely spatial appearance to dynamic information in its output and thereby provides a natural input to a motion-based pathway. Correspondingly, as a novel two-stream architecture, we replace input optical flow stacks in the motion stream with stacks of MSOE filtering results. Otherwise, the two-stream architecture is the same, including use of RGB frames to capture appearance. Our hypothesis is that the resulting architecture, MSOE-two-stream, will be able to capture a wider range of dynamics in comparison to what can be captured by optical flow, while maintaining the ability to capture appearance.

SOE-Net. SOE-Net [15] is a learning-free spatiotemporal ConvNet that operates by applying 3D oriented filtering directly to input temporal image sequences. It relies on a vocabulary of theoretically motivated, analytically defined filtering operations that are cascaded across the network layers via a recurrent connection to yield a hierarchical representation of input data. Previously, this network was applied to dynamic texture recognition with success. This network allows for consideration of a complimentary approach to that of C3D in the study of how direct 3D spatiotemporal filtering can serve to jointly capture appearance and dynamics. Also, it serves to judge the level of challenge given by the new DTDB dataset in the face of a known strong approach to dynamic texture.

4 Empirical Evaluation

The goals of the proposed dataset in its two organizations are two fold. First, it can be used to help better understand strengths and weaknesses of learning based spatiotemporal ConvNets and thereby guide decisions in the choice of architecture depending on the task at hand. Second, it can serve as a training substrate to advance research on dynamic texture recognition, in particular, and an initialization for other related tasks, in general. Correspondingly, from an algorithmic perspective, our empirical evaluation aims at answering the following questions: **(1)** Are spatiotemporal ConvNets able to disentangle appearance and dynamics information? (**2**) What are the relative strengths and weaknesses of popular architectures in doing so? (**3**) What representations of the input data are best suited for learning strong representations of image dynamics? In complement, we also address questions from the dataset's perspective. (**1**) Does the new dataset provide sufficient challenges to drive future developments in spatiotemporal image analysis? (**2**) Can the dataset be beneficial for transfer learning to related tasks? And if so: (**3**) What organization of the dataset is more suitable in transfer learning? (**4**) Can finetuning on our dataset boost the state-of-the-art on related tasks even while using standard spatiotemporal ConvNet architectures?

4.1 What Are Spatiotemporal ConvNets Better at Learning? Appearance Vs. Dynamics

Experimental Protocol. For training purposes each organization of the dataset is split randomly into training and test sets with 70% of the videos from each category used for training and the rest for testing. The C3D [34] and standard two-stream [31] architectures are trained following the protocols given in their original papers. The novel MSOE-two-stream is trained analogously to the standard two-stream, taking into account the changes in the motion stream input (*i.e.* MSOE rather than optical flow). For a fair comparison of the relative capabilities of spatiotemporal ConvNets in capitalizing on both motion and appearance, all networks are trained from scratch on DTDB to avoid any counfounding variables (*e.g.* as would arise from using the available models of C3D and two-stream as pretrained on different datasets). Training details can be found in the supplemental material. No training is associated with SOE-Net, as all its parameters are specified by design. At test time, the held out test set is used and the reported results are obtained from the softmax scores of each network. Note that we compare recognition performance for each organization separately; it does not make sense in the present context to train on one organization and test on the other since the categories are different. (We do however report related transfer learning experiments in Sects. 4.2 and 4.3. The experiments of Sect. 4.3 also consider pretrained versions of the C3D and two-stream architectures.)

Results. Table 3 provides a detailed comparison of all the evaluated Networks. To begin, we consider the relative performance of the various architectures on the dynamics-based organization. Of the learning-based approaches (*i.e.* all but SOE-Net), it is striking that RGB stream outperforms the Flow stream as well as C3D, even though the latter two are designed to capitalize on motion information. A close inspection of the confusion matrices (Fig. 3) sheds light on this situation. It is seen that the networks are particularly hampered when similar appearances are present across different dynamics categories as evidenced by the two most confused classes (*i.e.* Chaotic motion and Dominant Multiple Rigid Objects). These two categories were specifically constructed to have this potential source of appearance-based confusion to investigate an algorithm's

Table 3. Recognition accuracy of all the evaluated networks using both organizations of the new Dynamic Texture DataBase

	DTDB-Dynamics	DTDB-Appearance
C3D [34]	74.9	75.5
RGB Stream [31]	76.4	**76.1**
Flow Stream [31]	72.6	64.8
MSOE Stream	**80.1**	72.2
MSOE-two-stream	84.0	<u>**80.0**</u>
SOE-Net [15]	<u>**86.8**</u>	<u>**79.0**</u>

ability to abstract from appearance to model dynamics; see Fig. 1 and accompanying videos in the supplemental material. Also of note is performance on the categories that are most strongly defined in terms of their dynamics and show little distinctive structure in single frames (*e.g.* Scintillation and motion Transparency). The confusions experienced by C3D and the Flow stream indicate that those approaches have poor ability to learn the appropriate abstractions. Indeed, the performance of the Flow stream is seen to be the weakest of all. The likely reason for the poor Flow stream performance is that its input, optical flow, is not able to capture the underlying dynamics in the videos because they violate standard optical flow assumptions of brightness constancy and local smoothness.

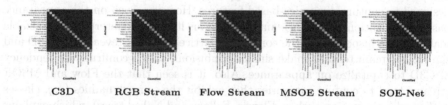

        C3D   RGB Stream   Flow Stream   MSOE Stream   SOE-Net

Fig. 3. Confusion matrices of all the compared ConvNet architectures on the *dynamics* based organization of the new DTDB

These points are underlined by noting that MSOE stream has the best performance compared to the other individual streams, with increased performance margin ranging from ≈4–8%. Based on this result, to judge the two-stream benefit we fuse the appearance (RGB) stream with MSOE stream to yield MSOE-two-stream as the overall top performer among the learning-based approaches. Importantly, recall that the MSOE input representation was defined to overcome the limitations of optical flow as a general purpose input representation for learning dynamics. These results speak decisively in favour of MSOE filtering as a powerful input to dynamics-based learning: It leads to performance that is as good as optical flow for categories that adhere to optical flow assumptions, but

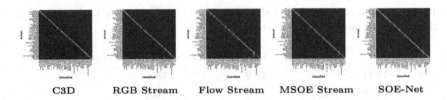

C3D   RGB Stream   Flow Stream   MSOE Stream   SOE-Net

Fig. 4. Confusion matrices of all compared ConvNet architectures on the *appearance* based organization of the new DTDB

extends performance to cases where optical flow fails. Finally, it is interesting to note that the previous top dynamic texture recognition algorithm, hand-crafted SOE-Net, is the best overall performer on the dynamics organization, showing that there remains discriminatory information to be learned from this dataset.

Turning attention to the appearance based results reveals the complementarity between the proposed dynamics and appearance based organizations. In this case, since the dataset is dominated by appearance, the best performer is the RGB stream that is designed to learn appearance information. Interestingly, C3D's performance, similar to the RGB stream, is on par for the two organizations although C3D performs slightly better on the appearance organization. This result suggests that C3D's recognition is mainly driven by similarities in appearance in both organizations and it appears relatively weak at capturing dynamics. This limitation may be attributed to the extremely small support of C3D's kernels (*i.e.* $3 \times 3 \times 3$). Also, as expected, the performance of the Flow and MSOE streams degrade on the appearance based organization, as they are designed to capture dynamics-based features. However, even on the appearance based organization, MSOE stream outperforms its Flow counterpart by a sizable margin. Here inspection of the confusion matrices (Fig. 4), reveals that C3D and the RGB stream tend to make similar confusions, which confirms the tendency of C3D to capitalize on appearance. Also, it is seen that the Flow and MSOE streams tend to confuse categories that exhibit the same dynamics (*e.g.* classes with stochastic motion such as Flower, Foliage and Naked trees), which explains the degraded performance of these two streams. Notably, MSOE streams incurs less confusions, which demonstrates the ability of MSOE filters to better capture fine grained differences. Also, once again MSOE-two-stream is the best performer among the learning based approaches and in this case it is better than SOE-Net.

Conclusions. Overall, the results on both organizations of the dataset lead to two main conclusions. First, comparison of the different architectures reveal that two-stream networks are better able to disentangle motion from appearance information for the learning-based architectures. This fact is particularly clear from the inversion of performance between the RGB and MSOE streams depending on whether the networks are trained to recognize dynamics or appearance, as well as the degraded performance of both the Flow and MSOE streams when asked to recognize sequences based on their appearance. Second, closer inspection of the confusion matrices show that optical flow fails on most categories where the sequences break the fundamental optical flow assumptions of brightness constancy and local smoothness (*e.g.* Turbulent motion, Transparency and Scintillation). In contrast, the MSOE stream performs well on such categories as well as others that are relatively easy for the Flow stream. The overall superiority of MSOE reflects in its higher performance, compared to flow, on both organizations of the dataset. These results challenge the common practice of using flow as the default representation of input data for motion stream training and should be taken into account in design of future spatiotemporal ConvNets.

Additionally, it is significant to note that a ConvNet that does not rely on learning, SOE-Net, has the best performance on the dynamics organization and is approximately tied for best on the appearance organization. These results suggests the continued value of DTDB, as there is more for future learning-based approaches to glean from its data.

4.2   Which Organization of DTDB Is Suitable in Transfer Learning?

Experimental Protocol. Transfer learning is considered with respect to a different dynamic texture dataset and a different task, dynamic scene recognition. The YUVL dataset [8] is used for the dynamic texture experiment. Before the new DTDB, YUVL was the largest dynamic texture dataset with a total of 610 sequences and it is chosen as a representative of a dataset with categories mostly dominated by the dynamics of its sequences. It provides 3 different dynamics based organizations, YUVL-1, YUVL-2 and YUVL-3 with 5, 6 and 8 classes (resp.) that make various dynamics based distinctions; see [8,15]. For the dynamic scene experiment, we use the YUP++ dataset [13]. YUP++ is the largest dynamic scenes dataset with 1200 sequences in total divided into 20 classes; however, in this case the categories are mostly dominated by differences in appearance. Notably, YUP++ provides a balanced distribution of sequences with and without camera motion, which allows for an evaluation of the various trained networks in terms of their ability to abstract scene dynamics from camera motion. Once again, for fair comparison, the various architectures trained from scratch on DTDB are used in this experiment because the goal is not to establish new state-of-the-art on either YUVL or YUP++. Instead, the goal is to show the value of the two organizations of the dataset and highlight the importance of adapting the training data to the application. The conclusions of this experiment are used next, in Sect. 4.3, as a basis to finetune the architectures under considerations using the appropriate version of DTDB.

For both the dynamic texture and dynamic scenes cases, we consider the relative benefits of training on the appearance vs. dynamics organizations of DTDB. We also compare to training using UCF-101 as a representative of a similar scale dataset but that is designed for the rather different task of action recognition. Since the evaluation datasets (*i.e.* YUVL and YUP++) are too small to support finetuning, we instead extract features from the last layers of the networks as trained under DTDB or UCF-101 and use those features for recognition (as done previously under similar constraints of small target datasets, *e.g.* [34]). A preliminary evaluation comparing the features extracted from the last pooling layer, fc6 and fc7, of the various networks used, showed that there is always a decrement in performance going from fc6 to fc7 on both datasets and out of 48 comparison points the performance of features extracted from the last pooling layer was better 75% of the time. Hence, results reported in the following rely on features extracted from the last pool layer of all used networks.

For recognition, extracted features are used with a linear SVM classifier using the standard leave-one-out protocol usually used with these datasets [8,15,27].

Results. We begin by considering results of transfer learning applied to the YUVL dataset, summarized in Table 4 (Left). Here, it is important to emphasize that YUVL categories are defined in terms of texture dynamics, rather than appearance. Correspondingly, we find that for every architecture the best performance is attained via pretraining on the DTDB dynamics-based organization as opposed to the appearance-based organization or UCF-101 pretraining. These results clearly support the importance of training for a dynamics-based task on dynamics-based data. Notably, MSOE stream, and its complementary MSOE-two-stream approach, with dynamics training show the strongest performance on this task, which provides further support for MSOE filtering as the basis for input to the motion stream of a two-stream architecture.

Table 4. Performance of spatiotemporal ConvNets, *trained* using both organizations of DTDB, **(Left)** on the various breakdowns of the YUVL dataset [8] and **(Right)** on the Static and Moving camera portions of YUP++ and the entire YUP++ [13]

		YUVL-1	YUVL-2	YUVL-3			YUP++(S)	YUP++(M)	YUP++
	C3D	61.4	65.4	55.7		C3D	62.5	55.8	58.3
UCF-101	RGB Stream	63.6	72.8	60.0	UCF-101	RGB Stream	64.9	54.4	63.5
based	Flow Stream	84.8	87.3	81.7	based	Flow Stream	83.6	51.9	68.9
training	MSOE Stream	80.0	80.2	74.4	training	MSOE Stream	74.3	52.7	62.0
	MSOE-two-stream	80.8	84.5	78.8		MSOE-two-stream	80.1	66.6	74.6
	C3D	83.3	86.4	83.4		C3D	84.3	71.8	76.5
Dynamics	RGB Stream	68.1	75.4	65.0	Dynamics	RGB Stream	81.8	73.7	78.3
based	Flow Stream	87.7	86.9	83.1	based	Flow Stream	89.3	64.7	76.8
training	MSOE Stream	89.2	89.3	84.8	training	MSOE Stream	90.0	67.5	78.4
	MSOE-two-stream	**90.7**	**91.4**	**87.6**		MSOE-two-stream	93.3	81.5	87.7
	C3D	82.2	85.4	80.9		C3D	85.0	73.7	78.1
Appearance	RGB Stream	67.6	72.8	64.3	Appearance	RGB Stream	82.0	**76.2**	**79.9**
based	Flow Stream	86.7	85.7	81.3	based	Flow Stream	90.6	65.8	77.0
training	MSOE Stream	87.7	87.3	83.6	training	MSOE Stream	91.0	69.5	79.1
	MSOE-two-stream	89.8	90.2	86.7		MSOE-two-stream	**94.7**	**83.2**	**89.6**

Comparison is now made on the closely related task of dynamic scene recognition. As previously mentioned, although YUP++ is a dynamic scenes datasets its various classes are still largely dominated by differences in appearance. This dominance of appearance is well reflected in the results shown in Table 4 (Right). As opposed to the observations made on the previous task, here networks benefited more from an appearance-based training to various extents with the advantage over UCF-101 pretraining being particularly striking. In agreement with findings on the YUVL dataset and in Sect. 4.1, the RGB stream trained on appearance is the overall best performing individual stream on this appearance dominated dataset. Comparatively, MSOE stream performed surprisingly well on the static camera portion of the dataset, where it even outperformed RGB stream. This result suggests that the MSOE stream is able to capitalize on both dynamics and appearance information in absence of distracting camera motion. In complement, MSOE-two-stream trained on appearance gives the overall best performance and even outperforms previous state-of-the-art on YUP++ [13].

Notably, all networks incur a non-negligible performance decrement in the presence of camera motion, with RGB being strongest in the presence of camera motion and Flow suffering the most. Apparently, the image dynamics resulting from camera motion dominate those from the scene intrinsics and in such cases it is best to concentrate the representation on the appearance.

Conclusions. The evaluation in this section proved the expected benefits of the proposed dataset over reliance on other available large scale datasets that are not necessarily related to the end application (*e.g.* use of action recognition datasets, *i.e.* UCF-101 [33] for pretraining, when the target task is dynamic scene recognition, as done in [13]). More importantly, the benefits and complementarity of the proposed two organizations were clearly demonstrated. Reflecting back on the question posed in the beginning of this section, the results shown here suggest that none of the organizations is better than another in considerations of transfer learning. Instead, they are complementary and can be used judiciously depending on the specifics of the end application.

4.3   Finetuning on DTDB to Establish New State-of-the-Art

Experimental Protocol. In this experiment we evaluate the ability of the architectures considered in this study to compete with the state-of-the-art on YUVL for dynamic textures and YUP++ for dynamic scenes when finetuned on DTDB. The the goal is to further emphasize the benefits of DTDB when used to improve on pretrained models. In particular, we use the C3D and two-stream models that were previously pretrained on Sports-1M [18] and ImageNet [29], respectively, then finetune those models using both versions of DTDB. Finetuning details are provided in the supplemental material.

Results. We first consider the results on the YUVL dataset, shown in Table 5 (Left). Here, it is seen that finetuning the pretrained models using either the dynamics or appearance organizations of DTDB improves the results of both C3D and MSOE-two-stream compared to the results in Table 4 (Left). Notably, the boost in performance is especially significant for C3D. This can be largely attributed to the fact that C3D is pretrained on a large video dataset (*i.e.* Sports-1M), while in the original two-stream architecture only the RGB stream is pretrained on ImageNet and the motion stream is trained from scratch. Notably, MSOE-two-stream finetuned on DTDB-dynamics still outperforms C3D and either exceeds or is on-par with previous results on YUVL using SOE-Net.

Turning attention to results obtained on YUP++, summarized in Table 5 (Right), further emphasizes the benefits of finetuning on the proper data. Similar to observations made on YUVL, the boost in performance is once again especially notable on C3D. Importantly, finetuning MSOE-two-stream on

DTDB-appearance yields the overall best results and considerably outperforms previous state-of-the-art, which relied on a more complex architecture [13].

Table 5. Performance of spatiotemporal ConvNets, *finetuned* using both organizations of DTDB, **(Left)** on the various breakdowns of the YUVL dataset [8] and **(Right)** on the Static and Moving camera portions of YUP++ and the entire YUP++ [13]

		YUVL-1	YUVL-2	YUVL-3			YUP++(S)	YUP++(M)	YUP++
State-of-the-art	SOE-Net [15]	95.6	91.7	91.0	State-of-the-art	T-ResNet [13]	92.4	81.5	89.0
Dynamics based fine-tuning	C3D	89.1	90.0	89.5	Dynamics based fine-tuning	C3D	89.4	80.8	85.5
	MSOE-two-stream	91.1	92.7	90.0		MSOE-two-stream	95.9	84.5	90.4
Appearance based fine-tuning	C3D	88.8	87.4	85.4	Appearance based fine-tuning	C3D	90.0	82.7	86.3
	MSOE-two-stream	90.2	91.2	87.8		MSOE-two-stream	97.0	87.0	91.8

Interestingly, results of finetuning using either version of DTDB also outperform previously reported results using C3D or two-stream architectures, on both YUVL and YUP++, with sizable margins [13,15]. Additional one-to-one comparisons are provided in the supplemental material.

Conclusions. The experiments in this section further highlighted the added value of the proposed dual organization of DTDB in two ways. First, on YUVL, finetuning standard architectures led to a notable boost in performance, competitive with or exceeding previous state-of-the-art that relied on SOE-Net, which was specifically hand-crafted for dynamic texture recognition. Hence, an interesting way forward, would be to finetune SOE-Net on DTDB to further benefit this network from the availability of a large scale dynamic texture dataset. Second, on YUP++, it was shown that standard spatiotemporal architectures, trained on the right data, could yield new state-of-the-art results, even while compared to more complex architectures (*e.g.* T-ResNet [13]). Once again, the availability of a dataset like DTDB could allow for even greater improvements using more complex architectures provided with data adapted to the target application.

5   Summary and Discussion

The new DTDB dataset has allowed for a systematic comparison of the learning abilities of broad classes of spatiotemporal ConvNets. In particular, it allowed for an exploration of the abilities of such networks to represent dynamics vs. appearance information. Such a systematic and direct comparison was not possible with previous datasets, as they lacked the necessary complementary organizations. The results especially show the power of two-stream networks that separate appearance and motion at their input for corresponding recognition. Moreover, the introduction of a novel MSOE-based motion stream was shown to improve performance over the traditional optical flow stream. This result has potential for important impact on the field, given the success and popularity of two-stream architectures. Also, it opens up new avenues to explore, *e.g.* using

MSOE filtering to design better performing motion streams (and spatiotemporal ConvNets in general) for additional video analysis tasks, *e.g.* action recognition. Still, a learning free ConvNet, SOE-Net, yielded best overall performance on DTDB, which further underlines the room for further development with learning based approaches. An interesting way forward is to train the analytically defined SOE-Net on DTDB and evaluate the potential benefit it can gain from the availability of suitable training data.

From the dataset perspective, DTDB not only has supported experiments that tease apart appearance vs. dynamics, but also shown adequate size and diversity to support transfer learning to related tasks, thereby reaching or exceeding state-of-the-art even while using standard spatiotemporal ConvNets. Moving forward, DTDB can be a valuable tool to further research on spacetime image analysis. For example, training additional state-of-the-art spatiotemporal ConvNets using DTDB can be used to further boost performance on both dynamic texture and scene recognition. Also, the complementarity between the two organizations can be further exploited for attribute-based dynamic scene and texture description. For example, the various categories proposed here can be used as attributes to provide more complete dynamic texture and scene descriptions beyond traditional categorical labels (*e.g.* pluming vs. boiling volcano or turbulent vs. wavy water flow). Finally, DTDB can be used to explore other related areas, including dynamic texture synthesis, dynamic scene segmentation as well as development of video-based recognition algorithms beyond ConvNets.

References

1. Amazon Mechanical Turk. www.mturk.com
2. Beautiful word clouds. www.wordle.net
3. Carreira, J., Zisserman, A.: Quo vadis, action recognition? A new model and the kinetics dataset. In: CVPR (2017)
4. Chetverikov, D., Peteri, R.: A brief survey of dynamic texture description and recognition. In: CORES (2005)
5. Cimpoi, M., Maji, S., Kokkinos, I., Mohamed, S., Vedaldi, A.: Describing textures in the wild. In: CVPR (2014)
6. Cimpoi, M., Maji, S., Vedaldi, A.: Deep filter banks for texture recognition and segmentation. In: CVPR (2015)
7. Dai, D., Riemenschneider, H., Gool, L.: The synthesizability of texture examples. In: CVPR (2014)
8. Derpanis, K., Wildes, R.P.: Spacetime texture representation and recognition based on spatiotemporal orientation analysis. PAMI **34**, 1193–1205 (2012)
9. Derpanis, K.G., Wildes, R.P.: Dynamic texture recognition based on distributions of spacetime oriented structure. In: IEEE Conference on Computer Vision and Pattern Recognition (CVPR), pp. 191–198, June 2010
10. Doretto, G., Chiuso, A., Wu, Y., Soatto, S.: Dynamic textures. IJCV **51**, 91–109 (2003)
11. Dubois, S., Peteri, R., Michel, M.: Characterization and recognition of dynamic textures based on the 2D+T curvelet. Sig. Im. Vid. Proc. **9**, 819–830 (2013)
12. Feichtenhofer, C., Pinz, A., Wildes., R.P.: Spatiotemporal residual networks for video action recognition. In: NIPS (2016)

13. Feichtenhofer, C., Pinz, A., Wildes., R.P.: Temporal residual networks for dynamic scene recognition. In: CVPR (2017)
14. Ghanem, B., Ahuja, N.: Maximum margin distance learning for dynamic texture recognition. In: Daniilidis, K., Maragos, P., Paragios, N. (eds.) ECCV 2010. LNCS, vol. 6312, pp. 223–236. Springer, Heidelberg (2010). https://doi.org/10.1007/978-3-642-15552-9_17
15. Hadji, I., Wildes, R.P.: A spatiotemporal oriented energy network for dynamic texture recognition. In: ICCV (2017)
16. He, K., Zhang, X., Ren, S., Sun., J.: Deep residual learning for image recognition. In: CVPR (2016)
17. Ji, S., Xu, W., Yang, M., Yu, K.: 3D convolutional neural networks for human action recognition. PAMI 35, 1915–1929 (2013)
18. Karpathy, A., Toderici, G., Shetty, S., Leung, T., Sukthankar, R., Fei-Fei, L.: Large-scale video classification with convolutional neural networks. In: CVPR (2014)
19. Krizhevsky, A., Sutskever, I., Hinton, G.E.: ImageNet classification with deep convolutional neural networks. In: NIPS (2012)
20. Langer, M., Mann, R.: Optical snow. IJCV 55, 55–71 (2003)
21. Lin, T.Y., Maji, S.: Visualizing and understanding deep texture representations. In: CVPR (2016)
22. Ng, J., Hausknecht, M., Vijayanarasimhan, S., Vinyals, O., Monga, R., Toderici., G.: Beyond short snippets: deep networks for video classification. In: CVPR (2015)
23. Oxholm, G., Bariya, P., Nishino, K.: The scale of geometric texture. In: Fitzgibbon, A., Lazebnik, S., Perona, P., Sato, Y., Schmid, C. (eds.) ECCV 2012. LNCS, vol. 7572, pp. 58–71. Springer, Heidelberg (2012). https://doi.org/10.1007/978-3-642-33718-5_5
24. Peteri, R., Sandor, F., Huiskes, M.: DynTex: a comprehensive database of dynamic textures. PRL 31, 1627–1632 (2010)
25. Pond5. www.pond5.com
26. Quan, Y., Bao, C., Ji, H.: Equiangular kernel dicitionary learning with applications to dynamic textures analysis. In: CVPR (2016)
27. Quan, Y., Huang, Y., Ji, H.: Dynamic texture recognition via orthogonal tensor dictionary learning. In: ICCV (2015)
28. Ravichandran, A., Chaudhry, R., R. Vidal, R.: View-invariant dynamic texture recognition using a bag of dynamical systems. In: CVPR (2009)
29. Russakovsky, O., et al.: Imagenet large scale visual recognition challenge. IJCV 115(3), 211–252 (2015)
30. Saisan, P., Doretto, G., Wu, Y., Soatto, S.: Dynamic texture recognition. In: CVPR (2001)
31. Simonyan, K., Zisserman, A.: Two-stream convolutional networks for action recognition in videos. In: NIPS (2014)
32. Simonyan, K., Zisserman, A.: Very deep convolutional networks for large-scale image recognition. In: ICLR (2015)
33. Soomro, K., Zamir, A.R., Shah, M.: UCF101: A dataset of 101 human actions classes from videos in the wild. Technical report. CRCV-TR-12-01, University of Central Florida (2012)
34. Tran, D., Bourdev, L., Fergus, R., Torresani, L., Paluri, M.: Learning spatiotemporal features with 3D convolutional networks. In: ICCV (2015)
35. Varma, M., Zisserman, A.: Texture classification: are filter banks necessary? In: CVPR (2003)
36. Varma, M., Zisserman, A.: A statistical approach to texture classification from single images. IJCV 62, 61–81 (2005)

37. VideoHive. www.videohive.net
38. Yang, F., Xia, G., Liu, G., Zhang, L., Huang, X.: Dynamic texture recognition by aggregating spatial and temporal features via SVMs. Neurocomp. **173**, 1310–1321 (2016)
39. YouTube. www.youtube.com
40. Zhao, G., Pietikäinen, M.: Dynamic texture recognition using volume local binary patterns. In: Vidal, R., Heyden, A., Ma, Y. (eds.) WDV 2005-2006. LNCS, vol. 4358, pp. 165–177. Springer, Heidelberg (2007). https://doi.org/10.1007/978-3-540-70932-9_13
41. Zhou, B., Lapedriza, A., Xiao, J., Torralba, A., Oliva, A.: Learning deep features for scene recognition using places database. In: NIPS (2014)

Deep Feature Factorization for Concept Discovery

Edo Collins[1(✉)], Radhakrishna Achanta[2], and Sabine Süsstrunk[1]

[1] School of Computer and Communication Sciences, EPFL, Lausanne, Switzerland
[2] Swiss Data Science Center, EPFL and ETHZ, Zurich, Switzerland
{edo.collins,radhakrishna.achanta,sabine.susstrunk}@epfl.ch

Abstract. We propose Deep Feature Factorization (DFF), a method capable of localizing similar semantic concepts within an image or a set of images. We use DFF to gain insight into a deep convolutional neural network's learned features, where we detect hierarchical cluster structures in feature space. This is visualized as heat maps, which highlight semantically matching regions across a set of images, revealing what the network 'perceives' as similar. DFF can also be used to perform co-segmentation and co-localization, and we report state-of-the-art results on these tasks.

Keywords: Neural network interpretability · Part co-segmentation
Co-segmentation · Co-localization · Non-negative matrix factorization

1 Introduction

As neural networks become ubiquitous, there is an increasing need to understand and interpret their learned representations [25,27]. In the context of convolutional neural networks (CNNs), methods have been developed to explain predictions and latent activations in terms of heat maps highlighting the image regions which caused them [31,37].

In this paper, we present Deep Feature Factorization (DFF), which exploits non-negative matrix factorization (NMF) [22] applied to activations of a deep CNN layer to find semantic correspondences across images. These correspondences reflect semantic similarity as indicated by clusters in a deep CNN layer feature space. In this way, we allow the CNN to show us which image regions it 'thinks' are similar or related across a set of images as well as within a single image. Given a CNN, our approach to semantic *concept discovery* is unsupervised, requiring only a set of input images to produce correspondences. Unlike previous approaches [2,11], we do not require annotated data to detect semantic features. We use annotated data for evaluation only.

We show that when using a deep CNN trained to perform ImageNet classification [30], applying DFF allows us to obtain heat maps that correspond to semantic concepts. Specifically, here we use DFF to localize objects or object

© Springer Nature Switzerland AG 2018
V. Ferrari et al. (Eds.): ECCV 2018, LNCS 11218, pp. 352–368, 2018.
https://doi.org/10.1007/978-3-030-01264-9_21

parts, such as the *head* or *torso* of an animal. We also find that parts form a hierarchy in feature space, e.g., the activations cluster for the concept *body* contains a sub-cluster for *limbs*, which in turn can be broken down to *arms* and *legs*. Interestingly, such meaningful decompositions are also found for object classes never seen before by the CNN.

In addition to giving an insight into the knowledge stored in neural activations, the heat maps produced by DFF can be used to perform co-localization or co-segmentation of objects and object parts. Unlike approaches that delineate the common object across an image set, our method is also able to retrieve distinct parts *within* the common object. Since we use a pre-trained CNN to accomplish this, we refer to our method as performing weakly-supervised co-segmentation.

Our main contribution is introducing Deep Feature Factorization as a method for semantic concept discovery, which can be used both to gain insight into the representations learned by a CNN, as well as to localize objects and object parts within images. We report results on several datasets and CNN architectures, showing the usefulness of our method across a variety of settings.

(a) Pyramids, $k = 4$ (b) Taj Mahal, $k = 3$

Fig. 1. *What in this picture is the same as in the other pictures?* Our method, Deep Feature Factorization (DFF), allows us to see how a deep CNN trained for image classification would answer this question. (a) Pyramids, animals and people correspond across images. (b) Monument parts match with each other.

2   Related Work

2.1   Localization with CNN Activations

Methods for the interpretation of hidden activations of deep neural networks, and in particular of CNNs, have recently gained significant interest [25]. Similar to DFF, methods have been proposed to localize objects within an image by means of heat maps [31,37].

In these works [31,37], localization is achieved by computing the importance of convolutional feature maps with respect to a particular output unit. These methods can therefore be seen as supervised, since the resulting heat maps are associated with a designated output unit, which corresponds to an object class from a predefined set. With DFF, however, heat maps are *not* associated with an output unit or object class. Instead, DFF heat maps capture common activation patterns in the input, which additionally allows us to localize objects never seen before by the CNN, and for which there is no relevant output unit.

2.2 CNN Features as Part Detectors

The ability of DFF to localize parts stems from the CNN's ability to distinguish parts in the first place. In Gonzales et al. [11] and Bau et al. [2] the authors attempt to detect learned part-detectors in CNN features, to see if such detectors emerge, even when the CNN is trained with object-level labels. They do this by measuring the overlap between feature map activations and ground truth labels from a part-level segmentation dataset. The availability of ground truth is essential to their analysis, yielding a catalog of CNN units that sufficiently correspond to labels in the dataset.

We confirm their observations that part detectors do indeed emerge in CNNs. However, as opposed to these previous methods, our NMF-based approach does not rely on ground truth labels to find the parts in the input. We use labeled data for evaluation only.

2.3 Non-negative Matrix Factorization

Non-negative matrix factorization (NMF) has been used to analyze data from various domains, such as audio source separation [12], document clustering [36], and face recognition [13].

There has been work extending NMF to multiple layers [6], implementing NMF using neural networks [9] and using NMF approximations as input to a neural network [34]. However, to the best of our knowledge, the application of NMF to the activations of a pre-trained neural network, as is done in DFF, has not been previously proposed.

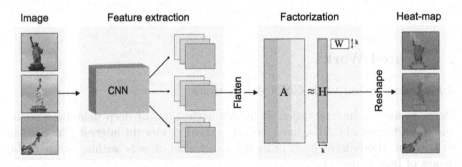

Fig. 2. An illustration of Deep Feature Factorization. We extract features from a deep CNN and view them as a matrix. We apply NMF to the feature matrix and reshape the resulting k factors into k heat maps. See Sect. 3 for a detailed explanation. Shown: Statute of Liberty subset from iCoseg with $k = 3$.

3   Method

3.1   CNN Feature Space

In the context of CNNs, an input image $\mathcal{I}$ is seen as a tensor of dimension $h_{\mathcal{I}} \times w_{\mathcal{I}} \times c_{\mathcal{I}}$, where the first two dimensions are the height and the width of the image, respectively, and the third dimension is the number of color channels, e.g., 3 for RGB. Viewed this way, the first two dimensions of $\mathcal{I}$ can be seen as a spatial grid, with the last dimension being a $c_{\mathcal{I}}$-dimensional feature representation of a particular spatial position. For an RGB image, this feature corresponds to color.

As the image gets processed layer by layer, the hidden activation at the ℓth layer of the CNN is a tensor we denote $\mathcal{A}_{\mathcal{I}}^{\ell}$ of dimension $h_{\ell} \times w_{\ell} \times c_{\ell}$. Notice that generally $h_{\ell} < h_{\mathcal{I}}$, $w_{\ell} < w_{\mathcal{I}}$ due to pooling operations commonly used in CNN pipelines. The number of channels c_{ℓ} is user-defined as part of the network architecture, and in deep layers is often on the order of 256 or 512.

The tensor $\mathcal{A}_{\mathcal{I}}^{\ell}$ is also called a *feature map* since it has a spatial interpretation similar to that of the original image $\mathcal{I}$: the first two dimensions represent a spatial grid, where each position corresponds to a *patch* of pixels in $\mathcal{I}$, and the last dimension forms a c_{ℓ}-dimensional representation of the patch. The intuition behind deep learning suggests that the deeper layer ℓ is, the more abstract and semantically meaningful are the c_{ℓ}-dimensional features [3].

Since a feature map represents multiple patches (depending on the size of image $\mathcal{I}$), we view them as points inhabiting the same c_{ℓ}-dimensional space, which we refer to as the CNN *feature space*. Having potentially many points in that space, we can apply various methods to find directions that are 'interesting'.

3.2   Matrix Factorization

Matrix factorization algorithms have been used for data interpretation for decades. For a data matrix A, these methods retrieve an approximation of the form:

$$A \approx \hat{A} = HW \tag{1}$$
$$\text{s.t. } A,\ \hat{A} \in \mathcal{R}^{n \times m},\ H \in \mathcal{R}^{n \times k},\ W \in \mathcal{R}^{k \times m}$$

where $\hat{A}$ is a low-rank matrix of a user-defined rank k. A data point, i.e., a row of A, is explained as a weighted combination of the factors which form the rows of W.

A classical method for dimensionality reduction is principal component analysis (PCA) [18]. PCA finds an optimal k-rank approximation (in the ℓ^2 sense) by solving the following objective:

$$\text{PCA}(A, k) = \underset{\hat{A}_k}{\text{argmin}} \quad \|A - \hat{A}_k\|_F^2,$$
$$\text{subject to } \hat{A}_k = AV_kV_k^{\top},\ V_k^{\top}V_k = I_k, \tag{2}$$

where $\|.\|_F$ denotes the Frobenius norm and $V_k \in \mathcal{R}^{m \times k}$. For the form of Eq. (1), we set $H = AV_k$, $W = V_k^\top$. Note that the PCA solution generally contains negative values, which means the combination of PCA factors (i.e., principal components) leads to the canceling out of positive and negative entries. This cancellation makes intuitive interpretation of individual factors difficult.

On the other hand, when the data A is non-negative, one can perform non-negative matrix factorization (NMF):

$$\mathrm{NMF}(A, k) = \underset{\hat{A}_k}{\operatorname{argmin}} \quad \|A - \hat{A}_k\|_F^2,$$
$$\text{subject to} \quad \hat{A}_k = HW, \ \forall ij, H_{ij}, W_{ij} \geq 0, \tag{3}$$

where $H \in \mathcal{R}^{n \times k}$ and $W \in \mathcal{R}^{k \times m}$ enforce the dimensionality reduction to rank k. Capturing the structure in A while forcing combinations of factors to be additive results in factors that lend themselves to interpretation [22].

3.3   Non-negative Matrix Factorization on CNN Activations

Many modern CNNs make use of the rectified linear activation function, $\max(x, 0)$, due to its desirable gradient properties. An obvious property of this function is that it results in non-negative activations. NMF is thus naturally applicable in this case.

Recall the activation tensor for image $\mathcal{I}$ and layer ℓ:

$$\mathcal{A}_\mathcal{I}^\ell \in \mathbb{R}^{h \times w \times c} \tag{4}$$

where $\mathbb{R}$ refers to the set of non-negative real numbers. To apply matrix factorization, we partially flatten $\mathcal{A}$ into a matrix whose first dimension is the product of h and w:

$$A_\mathcal{I}^\ell \in \mathbb{R}^{(h \cdot w) \times c} \tag{5}$$

Note that the matrix $A_\mathcal{I}^\ell$ is effectively a 'bag of features' in the sense that the spatial arrangement has been lost, i.e., the rows of $A_\mathcal{I}^\ell$ can be permuted without affecting the result of factorization. We can naturally extend factorization to a set of n images, by vertically concatenating their features together:

$$A = \begin{bmatrix} A_1^\ell \\ \vdots \\ A_n^\ell \end{bmatrix} \in \mathbb{R}^{(n \cdot h \cdot w) \times c} \tag{6}$$

For ease of notation we assumed all images are of equal size, however, there is no such limitation as images in the set may be of any size. By applying NMF to A we obtain the two matrices from Eq. 1, $H \in \mathbb{R}^{(n \cdot h \cdot w) \times k}$ and $W \in \mathbb{R}^{k \times c}$.

3.4   Interpreting NMF Factors

The result returned by the NMF consists of k *factors*, which we will call DFF factors, where k is the predefined rank of the approximation.

The W Matrix. Each row W_j ($1 \leq j \leq k$) forms a c-dimensional vector in the CNN feature space. Since NMF can be seen as performing clustering [8], we view a factor W_j as a centroid of an activation cluster, which we show corresponds to coherent object or object-part.

The H Matrix. The matrix H has as many rows as the activation matrix A, one corresponding to every spatial position in every image. Each row H_i holds coefficients for the weighted sum of the k factors in W, to best approximate the c-dimensional A_i.

Each column H_j ($1 \leq j \leq k$) can be reshaped into n **heat maps** of dimension $h \times w$, which highlight regions in each image that correspond to the factor W_j. These heat maps have the same spatial dimensions as the CNN layer which produced the activations, often low. To match the size of the heat map with the input image, we upsample it with bilinear interpolation.

4 Experiments

In this section we first show that DFF can produce a hierarchical decomposition into semantic parts, even for sets of very few images (Sect. 4.3). We then move on to larger-scale, realistic datasets where we show that DFF can perform state-of-the-art weakly-supervised object co-localization and co-segmentation, in addition to part co-segmentation (Sects. 4.4 and 4.5).

4.1 Implementation Details

NMF. NMF optimization with multiplicative updates [23] relies on dense matrix multiplications, and can thus benefit from fast GPU operations. Using an NVIDIA Titan X, our implementation of NMF can process over 6 K images of size 224×224 at once with $k = 5$, and requires less than a millisecond per image. Our code is available online.

Neural Network Models. We consider five network architectures in our experiments, namely VGG-16 and VGG-19 [32], with and without batch-normalization [17], as well as ResNet-101 [16]. We use the publicly available models from [26].

4.2 Segmentation and Localization Methods

In addition to gaining insights into CNN feature space, DFF has utility for various tasks with subtle but important differences in naming:

- **Segmentation vs. Localization** is the difference between predicting pixel-wise binary masks and predicting bounding boxes, respectively.
- **Segmentation vs. co-segmentation** is the distinction between segmenting a single image into regions and jointly segmenting multiple images, thereby producing a correspondence between regions in different images (e.g., *cats* in all images belong to the same segment).

– **Object co-segmentation vs. Part co-segmentation.** Given a set of images representing a common object, the former performs binary background-foreground separation where the foreground segment encompasses the entirety of the common object (e.g., *cat*). The latter, however, produces k segments, each corresponding to a *part* of the common object (e.g., *cat head, cat legs,* etc.).

When applying DFF with $k = 1$ can we compare our results against object co-segmentation (background-foreground separation) methods and object co-localization methods.

In Sect. 4.3 we compare DFF against three state-of-the-art co-segmentation methods. The supervised method of Vicente et al. [33] chooses among multiple segmentation proposals per image by learning a regressor to predict, for pairs of images, the overlap between their proposals and the ground truth. Input to the regressor included per-image features, as well as pairwise features. The methods Rubio et al. [29] and Rubinstein et al. [28] are unsupervised and rely on a Markov random field formulation, where the unary features are based on surface image features and various saliency heuristics. For pairwise terms, the former method uses a per-image segmentation into regions, followed by region-matching across images. The latter approach uses a dense pairwise correspondence term between images based on local image gradients.

In Sect. 4.4 we compare against several state-of-the-art object co-localization methods. Most of these methods operate by selecting the best of a set of object proposals, produced by a pre-trained CNN [24] or an object-saliency heuristic [5,19]. The authors of [21] present a method for unsupervised object co-localization that, like ours, also makes use of CNN activations. Their approach is to apply k-means clustering to globally max-pooled activations, with the intent of clustering all highly active CNN filters together. Their method therefore produces a *single* heat map, which is appropriate for object co-segmentation, but *cannot* be extended to part co-segmentation.

When $k > 1$, we use DFF to perform part co-segmentation. Since we have not come across examples of part co-segmentation in the literature, we compare against a method for supervised part segmentation, namely Wang et al. [35] (Table 3 in Sect. 4.5). Their method relies on a compositional model with strong explicit priors w.r.t to part size, hierarchy and symmetry. We also show results for two baseline methods described in [35]: PartBB+ObjSeg where segmentation masks are produced by intersecting part-bounding-boxes [4] with whole-object segmentation masks [14]. The method PartMask+ObjSeg is similar, but here bounding-boxes are replaced with the best of 10 pre-learned part masks.

4.3 Experiments on iCoseg

Dataset. The iCoseg dataset [1] is a popular benchmark for co-segmentation methods. As such, it consists of 38 sets of images, where each image is annotated with a pixel-wise mask encompassing the main object common to the set. Images within a set are uniform in that they were all taken on a single occasion, depicting the same objects. The challenging aspect of this datasets lies in the significant variability with respect to viewpoint, illumination, and object deformation.

We chose five sets and further labeled them with pixel-wise object-part masks (see Table 1). This process involved partitioning the given ground truth mask into sub-parts. We also annotated common background objects, e.g., *camel* in the *Pyramids* set (see Fig. 1). Our part-annotation for iCoseg is available online. The number of images in these sets ranges from as few as 5 up to 41. When comparing against [33] and [29] in Table 1, we used the subset of iCoseg used in those papers.

Part Co-segmentation. For each set in iCoseg, we obtained activations from the deepest convolutional layer of VGG19 (conv5_4), and applied NMF to these activations with increasing values of k. The resulting heat maps can be seen in Figs. 1 and 3.

Qualitatively, we see a clear correspondence between DFF factors and coherent object-parts, however, the heat maps are coarse. Due to the low resolution of deep CNN activations, and hence of the heat map, we get blobs that do not perfectly align with the underlying region of interest. We therefore also report additional results with a post-processing step to refine the heat maps, described below.

We notice that when $k = 1$, the single DFF factor corresponds to a whole object, encompassing multiple object-parts. This, however, is not guaranteed, since it is possible that for a set of images, setting $k = 1$ will highlight the *background* rather than the foreground. Nonetheless, as we increase k, we get a decomposition of the object or scene into individual parts. This behavior reveals a hierarchical structure in the clusters formed in CNN feature space.

For instance, in Fig. 3(a), we can see that $k = 1$ encompasses most of gymnast's body, $k = 2$ distinguished her midsection from her limbs, $k = 3$ adds a finer distinctions between arms and legs, and finally $k = 4$ adds a new component that localizes the beam. This observation also indicates the CNN has learned representation that 'explains' these concepts with invariance to pose, e.g., leg positions in the 2nd, 3rd, and 4th columns.

A similar decomposition into legs, torso, back, and head can be seen for the elephants in Fig. 3(b). This shows that we can localize different objects and parts even when they are all common across the image set. Interestingly, the decompositions shown in Fig. 1 exhibit similar high semantic quality in spite of their dissimilarity to the ImageNet training data, as neither pyramids nor the Taj Mahal are included as class labels in that dataset. We also note that as some of the given sets contain as few as 5 images (Fig. 1(b) comprises the whole set), our method does not require many images to find meaningful structure.

Object and Part Co-segmentation. We operationalize DFF to perform co-segmentation. To do so we have to first annotate the factors as corresponding to specific ground-truth parts. This can be done manually (as in Table 3) or

(a) Gymnastics1   (b) Elephants

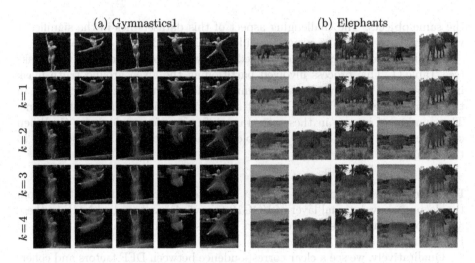

Fig. 3. Example DFF heat maps for images of two sets from iCoseg. Each row shows a separate factorization where the number of DFF factors k is incremented. Different colors correspond to the heat maps of the k different factors. DFF factors correspond well to distinct object parts. This Figure visualizes the data in Table 1, where heat map color corresponds with row color. (Best viewed electronically with a color display) Color figure online

automatically given ground truth, as described below. We report the intersection-over-union (IoU) score of each factor with its associated parts in Table 1.

Since the heat maps are of low-resolution, we refine them with post processing. We define a dense conditional random field (CRF) over the heat maps. We use the filter-based mean field approximate inference [20], where we employ guided filtering [15] for the pairwise term, and use the biliniearly upsampled DFF heat maps as unary terms. We refer to DFF with post-processing 'DFF-CRF.

Each heat map is converted to a binary mask using a thresholding procedure. For a specific DFF factor f ($1 \leq f \leq k$), let $\{H(f, 1), \cdots, H(f, n)\}$ be the set of n heat maps associated with n input images, The value of a pixel in the binary map $B(f, i)$ of factor f and image i is 0 if its intensity is lower than the 75th percentile of entries in the set of heat maps $\{H(f, j) | 1 \leq j \leq n\}$.

We associate parts with factors by considering how well a part is covered by a factor's binary masks. We define the *coverage* of part p by factor f as:

$$Cov_{f,p} = \frac{|\sum_i B(f, i) \bigcap P(p, i)|}{|\sum_i P(p, i)|} \tag{7}$$

The coverage is the percentage of pixels belonging to p that are set to 1 in the binary maps $\{B(f, i) | 1 \leq i \leq n\}$. We associate the part p with factor f when $Cov_{f,p} > Cov_{\text{th}}$. We experimentally set the threshold $Cov_{\text{th}} = 0.5$.

Finally, we measure the IoU between a DFF factor f and its m associated ground-truth parts $\{p_1^{(f)}, \cdots, p_m^{(f)}\}$ similarly to [2], specifically by considering

Table 1. Object and part discovery and segmentation on five iCoseg image sets. Part-labels are automatically assigned to DFF factors, and are shown with their corresponding IoU-scores. Our results show that clusters in CNN feature space correspond to coherent parts. More so, they indicate the presence of a cluster hierarchy in CNN feature space, where part-clusters can be seen as sub-clusters within object-clusters (See Figs. 1, 2 and 3 for visual comparison. Row color corresponds with heat map color). With $k = 1$, DFF can be used to perform object co-segmentation, which we compare against state-of-the-art methods. With $k > 1$ DFF can be used to perform part co-segmentation, which current co-segmentation methods are not able to do.

Method	Elephants		Taj Mahal		Pyramids		Gymnastics1		Statue of Liberty	
Object co-segmentation										
Vicente [33]	whole	43	whole	91	-		-		whole	94
Rubio [29]	whole	75	whole	89	-		-		whole	92
Rubinstein [28]	whole	63	whole	48	whole	57	whole	94	whole	70
DFF, k=1	whole	65	whole	41	whole	57	whole	43	whole	49
DFF-CRF, k=1	whole	**76**	whole	51	whole	70	whole	52	whole	62
Part co-segmentation										
DFF, k=2	torso/back/head	59	dome	33	animal	36	torso/waist	35	torso	36
	torso/leg	35	tower/building	46	pyramid	56	arm/leg/head	20	torch/base/head	28
DFF, k=3	back/head	46	building	45	background	27	torso/waist	38	base	14
	torso	25	dome	40	pyramid	55	arm/head	22	torso	39
	leg	21	tower	13	animal	36	leg	33	torch/head	23
DFF, k=4	torso/back/head	58	building	72	background	27	torso/waist	40	torso	39
	head	36	dome	43	pyramid	52	torso/arm/head	33	background	44
	torso	20	background	08	animal	37	leg	37	torch/head	26
	leg	16	tower	16	person	12	background	14	base	40

the dataset-wide IoU :

$$P_f(i) = \bigcup_j^m P(p_j^{(f)}) \tag{8}$$

$$IoU_{f,p} = \frac{|\sum_i B_i \bigcap P_f(i)|}{|\sum_i B_i \bigcup P_f(i)|} \tag{9}$$

In the top of Table 1 we report results for object co-segmentation ($k = 1$) and show that our method is comparable with the supervised approach of [33] and domain-specific methods of [28,29].

The bottom of Table 1 shows the labels and IoU-scores for part co-segmentation on the five image sets of iCoseg that we have annotated. These scores correspond to the visualizations of Figs. 1 and 3 and confirm what we observe qualitatively.

We can characterize the quality of a factorization as the average IoU of each factor with its single best matching part (which is not the background). In Fig. 4(a) we show the average IoU for different layer of VGG-19 on iCoseg as the value of k increases. The variance shown is due to repeated trials with different NMF initializations. There is a clear gap between convolutional blocks. Performance with in a block does not strictly follow the linear order of layers.

We also see that the optimal value for k is between 3 and 5. While this naturally varies for different networks, layers, and data batches, another deciding factor is the resolution of the part ground truth. As k increases, DFF heat maps become more localized, highlighting regions that are beyond the granularity of the ground truth annotation, e.g., a pair of factors that separates *leg* into *ankle* and *thigh*. In Fig. 4(b) we show that DFF performs similarly within the VGG family of models. For ResNet-101 however, the average IoU is distinctly lower.

4.4 Object Co-Localization on PASCAL VOC 2007

Dataset. PASCAL VOC 2007 has been commonly used to evaluate whole object co-localization methods. Images in this dataset often comprise several objects of multiple classes from various viewpoints, making it a challenging benchmark. As in previous work [5,19,21], we use the *trainval* set for evaluation and filter out images that only contain objects which are marked as *difficult* or *truncated*. The final set has 20 image sets (one per class), with 69 to 2008 images each.

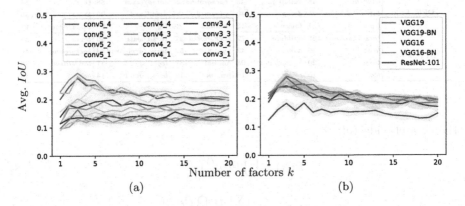

Fig. 4. (a) Average IoU score for DFF on iCoseg. for (a) different VGG19 layers and (b) the deepest convolutional layer for other CNN architectures. Expectedly, different convolutional blocks show a clear difference in matching up with semantic parts, as CNN features capture more semantic concepts. The optimal value for k is data dependent but is usually below 5. We see also that DFF performance is relatively uniform for the VGG family of models.

Evaluation. The task of co-localization involves fitting a bounding box around the common object in a set of image. With $k = 1$, we expect DFF to retrieve a heat map which localizes that object.

As described in the previous section, after optionally filtering DFF heat maps using a CRF, we convert the heat maps to binary segmentation masks. We follow [31] and extract a single bounding box per heat map by fitting a box around the largest connected component in the binary map.

Table 2. Co-localization results for PASCAL VOC 2007 with DFF $k = 1$. Numbers indicate CorLoc scores. Overall, we exceed the state-of-the-art approaches using a much simpler method.

Method	aero	bicy	bird	boa	bot	bus	car	cat	cha	cow	dtab	dog	hors	mbik	pers	plnt	she	sofa	trai	tv	mean
Joulin [19]	33	17	21	18	5	27	33	41	6	29	**35**	32	26	40	18	12	25	28	36	12	25.60
Cho [5]	50	43	30	19	4	62	**65**	43	9	49	12	44	64	57	15	9	31	34	62	**32**	36.60
Li [24]	**73**	45	43	28	7	53	58	45	6	48	14	47	**69**	67	**24**	13	**52**	26	65	17	40.00
Le (A) [21]	70	52	44	**30**	5	56	60	59	6	49	16	51	59	67	23	12	47	27	59	16	40.36
Le(V) [21]	72	**62**	48	28	12	**64**	59	72	6	37	12	45	67	72	19	11	37	29	**67**	23	41.97
DFF	61	49	**54**	20	10	60	46	**79**	4	51	32	**67**	66	70	19	**15**	40	32	66	20	42.87
DFF-CRF	64	47	50	16	10	62	52	75	8	**53**	**35**	65	65	**72**	16	14	41	**36**	63	30	**43.51**

Table 3. Avg. IoU(%) for three fully supervised methods reported in [35] (see Sect. 4.2 for details) and for our weakly-supervised DFF approach. As opposed to DFF, previous approaches shown are fully supervised. Despite not using hand-crafted features, DFF compares favorably to these approaches, and is not specific to these two image classes. We semi-automatically mapped DFF factors ($k = 3$) to their appropriate part labels by examining the heat maps of *only five* images, out of approximately 140 images. This illustrates the usefulness of DFF co-segmentation for fast semi-automatic labeling. See visualization for *cow* heat maps in Figure 5.

Method	cow			horse		
	head	neck+torso	leg	head	neck+torso	leg
PartBB+ObjSeg	26.77	53.79	11.18	37.32	60.35	27.47
PartMask+ObjSeg	33.19	56.69	11.31	41.84	63.31	21.38
Compositional model [35]	41.55	60.98	30.98	47.21	66.74	38.18
DFF	40.53	59.48	21.57	28.85	54.77	28.94
DFF-CRF	45.20	58.87	24.60	31.05	53.18	28.81

We report the standard CorLoc score [7] of our localization. The CorLoc score is defined as the percentage of predicted bounding boxes for which there exists a matching ground truth bounding box. Two bounding boxes are deemed matching if their *IoU* score exceeds 0.5.

The results of our method are shown in Table 2, along with previous methods (described in Sect. 4.2). Our method compares favorably against previous approaches. For instance, we improve co-localization for the class *dog* by 16% higher CorLoc and achieve better co-localization on average, in spite of our approach being simpler and more general.

4.5 Part Co-segmentation in PASCAL-Parts

Dataset. The PASCAL-Part dataset [4] is an extension of PASCAL VOC 2010 [10] which has been further annotated with part-level segmentation masks and bounding boxes. The dataset decomposes 16 object classes into fine grained parts, such as *bird-beak* and *bird-tail* etc. After filtering out images containing objects marked as *difficult* and *truncated*, the final set consists of 16 image sets with 104 to 675 images each.

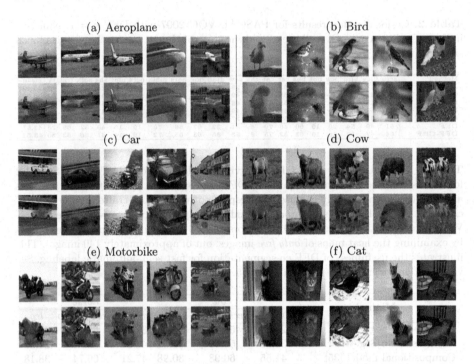

(a) Aeroplane   (b) Bird

(c) Car   (d) Cow

(e) Motorbike   (f) Cat

Fig. 5. Example DFF heat maps for images of six classes from PASCAL-Parts with $k = 3$. For each class we show four images that were successfully decomposed into parts, and a failure case on the right. DFF manages to retrieve interpretable decompositions in spite of the great variation in the data. In addition to the DFF factors for *cow* from Table 3, here visualized are the factors which appear in Table 4, where heat map colors correspond to row colors.

Table 4. IoU of DFF heat maps with PASCAL-Parts segmentation masks. Each DFF factor is autmatically labeled with part labels as in Sect. 4.3. Higher values of k allow DFF to localize finer regions across the image set, some of which go beyond the resolution of the ground truth part annotation. Figure 5 visualizes the results for $k = 3$ (row color corresponds to heat map color).

k	aeroplane		bird		car		motorbike		cat	
1	aeroplane	42	bird	40	car	29	wheel	30	eye/head/neck/nose	31
2	wheel	2	beak/eye/head/neck	13	wheel	10	wheel	38	torso	24
	body/stern/tail/wing	49	neck/torso/wing	39	door/roof/window	22	person	9	eye/head/neck/nose	36
3	wheel	2	leg	2	wheel	10	wheel	30	eye/head/neck/nose	32
	body/stern/wing	47	neck/torso/wing	43	door/headlight/licenseplate	24	headlight	1	torso	30
	body/tail	35	beak/eye/head/neck/torso	30	mirror/roof/window	20	wheel	29	ear/eye/head/neck/nose	38
4	wheel	1	foot/leg	3	wheel	9	wheel	33	eye/head/nose	31
	body/wheel/wing	44	neck/torso/wing	44	headlight/licenseplate	31	person	10	eye/neck/nose	5
	stern/tail/wing	21	beak/eye/head/neck/torso	30	front	8	wheel	17	ear/eye/head/nose	35
	body/tail	32	neck	2	mirror/roof/window	22	background	13	torso	27

Evaluation. In Table 3 we report results for the two classes, *cow* and *horse*, which are also part-segmented by Want et al. as described in Sect. 4.2. Since their method relies on strong explicit priors w.r.t to part size, hierarchy, and symmetry, and its explicit objective is to perform part-segmentation, their results serve as an upper bound to ours. Nonetheless we compare favorably to their results and even surpass them in one case, despite our method not using any hand-crafted features or supervised training.

For this experiment, our strategy for mapping DFF factors ($k = 3$) to their appropriate part labels was with semi-automatic labeling, i.e., we qualitatively examined the heat maps of *only five images*, out of approximately 140 images, and labeled factors as corresponding to the labels shown in Table 3.

In Table 4 we give *IoU* results for five additional classes from PASCAL-Parts, which have been automatically mapped to parts as in Sect. 4.3. In Fig. 5 we visualize these DFF heat maps for $k = 3$, as well as for *cow* from Table 3. When comparing the heat maps against their corresponding *IoU*-scores, several interesting conclusions can be made. For instance, in the case of *motorbike*, the first and third factors for $k = 3$ in Table 4 both seems to correspond with wheel. The visualization in Fig. 5(e) reveals that these factors in fact sub-segment the wheel into top and bottom, which is beyond the resolution of the ground truth data.

We can see also that while the first factor of the class *aeroplane* (Fig. 5(a)) consistently localizes airplane wheels, it does not to achieve high *IoU* due to the coarseness of the heat map.

Returning to Table 4, when $k = 4$, a factor emerges that localizes instances of the class *person*, which occur in 60% of motorbike images. This again shows that while most co-localization methods only describe objects that are common across the image set, our DFF approach is able to find distinctions *within* the set of common objects.

5   Conclusions

In this paper, we have presented Deep Feature Factorization (DFF), a method that is able to locate semantic concepts in individual images and across image sets. We have shown that DFF can reveal interesting structures in CNN feature space, such as hierarchical clusters which correspond to a part-based decomposition at various levels of granularity.

We have also shown that DFF is useful for co-segmentation and co-localization, achieving results on challenging benchmarks which are on par with state-of-the-art methods, and can be used to perform semi-automatic image labeling. Unlike previous approaches, DFF can also perform *part* co-segmentation as well, making fine distinction *within* the common object, e.g. matching *head* to *head* and *torso* to *torso*.

References

1. Batra, D., Kowdle, A., Parikh, D., Luo, J., Chen, T.: Icoseg: interactive co-segmentation with intelligent scribble guidance. In: Computer Vision and Pattern Recognition (CVPR), pp. 3169–3176. IEEE (2010)
2. Bau, D., Zhou, B., Khosla, A., Oliva, A., Torralba, A.: Network dissection: quantifying interpretability of deep visual representations. In: Computer Vision and Pattern Recognition (CVPR), pp. 3319–3327. IEEE (2017)
3. Bengio, Y., Courville, A., Vincent, P.: Representation learning: a review and new perspectives. IEEE Trans. Pattern Anal. Mach. Intell. (TPAMI) **35**(8), 1798–1828 (2013)
4. Chen, X., Mottaghi, R., Liu, X., Fidler, S., Urtasun, R., Yuille, A.: Detect what you can: detecting and representing objects using holistic models and body parts. In: Computer Vision and Pattern Recognition (CVPR), pp. 1971–1978 (2014)
5. Cho, M., Kwak, S., Schmid, C., Ponce, J.: Unsupervised object discovery and localization in the wild: part-based matching with bottom-up region proposals. In: Computer Vision and Pattern Recognition (CVPR) (2015)
6. Cichocki, A., Zdunek, R.: Multilayer nonnegative matrix factorisation. Electron. Lett. **42**(16), 1 (2006)
7. Deselaers, T., Alexe, B., Ferrari, V.: Weakly supervised localization and learning with generic knowledge. Int. J. Comput. Vis. (IJCV) **100**(3), 275–293 (2012)
8. Ding, C., He, X., Simon, H.D.: On the equivalence of nonnegative matrix factorization and spectral clustering. In: Proceedings of the 2005 SIAM International Conference on Data Mining, pp. 606–610. SIAM (2005)
9. Dziugaite, G.K., Roy, D.M.: Neural network matrix factorization. arXiv preprint arXiv:1511.06443 (2015)
10. Everingham, M., Van Gool, L., Williams, C.K.I., Winn, J., Zisserman, A.: The PASCAL Visual Object Classes Challenge 2010 (VOC2010) Results. http://www.pascal-network.org/challenges/VOC/voc2010/workshop/index.html
11. Gonzalez-Garcia, A., Modolo, D., Ferrari, V.: Do semantic parts emerge in convolutional neural networks? Int. J. Comput. Vis. (IJCV) **126**(5), 1–19 (2017). https://link.springer.com/article/10.1007/s11263-017-1048-0
12. Grais, E.M., Erdogan, H.: Single channel speech music separation using nonnegative matrix factorization and spectral masks. In: Digital Signal Processing (DSP), pp. 1–6. IEEE (2011)
13. Guillamet, D., Vitrià, J.: Non-negative matrix factorization for face recognition. In: Escrig, M.T., Toledo, F., Golobardes, E. (eds.) CCIA 2002. LNCS (LNAI), vol. 2504, pp. 336–344. Springer, Heidelberg (2002). https://doi.org/10.1007/3-540-36079-4_29
14. Hariharan, B., Arbeláez, P., Girshick, R., Malik, J.: Simultaneous detection and segmentation. In: Fleet, D., Pajdla, T., Schiele, B., Tuytelaars, T. (eds.) ECCV 2014. LNCS, vol. 8695, pp. 297–312. Springer, Cham (2014). https://doi.org/10.1007/978-3-319-10584-0_20
15. He, K., Sun, J., Tang, X.: Guided image filtering. IEEE Trans. Pattern Anal. Mach. Intell. (TPAMI) **35**(6), 1397–1409 (2013)
16. He, K., Zhang, X., Ren, S., Sun, J.: Deep residual learning for image recognition. In: Computer Vision and Pattern Recognition (CVPR), pp. 770–778 (2016)

17. Ioffe, S., Szegedy, C.: Batch normalization: accelerating deep network training by reducing internal covariate shift. In: International Conference on Machine Learning (ICML), pp. 448–456 (2015)

18. Jolliffe, I.T.: Principal component analysis and factor analysis. In: Principal Component Analysis, pp. 115–128. Springer, NewYork (1986). https://doi.org/10.1007/0-387-22440-8_7

19. Joulin, A., Tang, K., Fei-Fei, L.: Efficient image and video co-localization with frank-wolfe algorithm. In: Fleet, D., Pajdla, T., Schiele, B., Tuytelaars, T. (eds.) ECCV 2014. LNCS, vol. 8694, pp. 253–268. Springer, Cham (2014). https://doi.org/10.1007/978-3-319-10599-4_17

20. Krähenbühl, P., Koltun, V.: Efficient inference in fully connected CRFS with gaussian edge potentials. In: Advances in Neural Information Processing Systems (NIPS), pp. 109–117 (2011)

21. Le, H., Yu, C.P., Zelinsky, G., Samaras, D.: Co-localization with category-consistent features and geodesic distance propagation. In: Computer Vision and Pattern Recognition (CVPR), pp. 1103–1112 (2017)

22. Lee, D.D., Seung, H.S.: Learning the parts of objects by non-negative matrix factorization. Nature 401(6755), 788 (1999)

23. Lee, D.D., Seung, H.S.: Algorithms for non-negative matrix factorization. In: Advances in Neural Information Processing Systems, pp. 556–562 (2001)

24. Li, Y., Liu, L., Shen, C., van den Hengel, A.: Image co-localization by mimicking a good detector's confidence score distribution. In: Leibe, B., Matas, J., Sebe, N., Welling, M. (eds.) ECCV 2016. LNCS, vol. 9906, pp. 19–34. Springer, Cham (2016). https://doi.org/10.1007/978-3-319-46475-6_2

25. Montavon, G., Samek, W., Müller, K.: Methods for interpreting and understanding deep neural networks. Digit. Signal Process. 73, 1–15 (2018) https://doi.org/10.1016/j.dsp.2017.10.011

26. Paszke, A., et al.: Automatic differentiation in pytorch (2017)

27. Ribeiro, M.T., Singh, S., Guestrin, C.: Why should I trust you?: explaining the predictions of any classifier. In: Proceedings of the 22nd ACM SIGKDD International Conference on Knowledge Discovery and Data Mining, pp. 1135–1144 (2016)

28. Rubinstein, M., Joulin, A., Kopf, J., Liu, C.: Unsupervised joint object discovery and segmentation in internet images. In: Computer Vision and Pattern Recognition (CVPR), June 2013

29. Rubio, J.C., Serrat, J., López, A., Paragios, N.: Unsupervised co-segmentation through region matching. In: Computer Vision and Pattern Recognition (CVPR), pp. 749–756. IEEE (2012)

30. Russakovsky, O., et al.: Imagenet large scale visual recognition challenge. Int. J. Comput. Vis. (IJCV) 115(3), 211–252 (2015). https://doi.org/10.1007/s11263-015-0816-y

31. Selvaraju, R.R., Cogswell, M., Das, A., Vedantam, R., Parikh, D., Batra, D.: Grad-cam: Visual explanations from deep networks via gradient-based localization, vol. 37(8) (2016). See arxiv:1610.02391

32. Simonyan, K., Zisserman, A.: Very deep convolutional networks for large-scale image recognition. arXiv preprint arXiv:1409.1556 (2014)

33. Vicente, S., Rother, C., Kolmogorov, V.: Object cosegmentation. In: Computer Vision and Pattern Recognition (CVPR), pp. 2217–2224. IEEE (2011)

34. Vu, T.T., Bigot, B., Chng, E.S.: Combining non-negative matrix factorization and deep neural networks for speech enhancement and automatic speech recognition. In: Acoustics, Speech and Signal Processing (ICASSP), pp. 499–503. IEEE (2016)
35. Wang, J., Yuille, A.L.: Semantic part segmentation using compositional model combining shape and appearance. In: CVPR (2015)
36. Xu, W., Liu, X., Gong, Y.: Document clustering based on non-negative matrix factorization. In: Proceedings of the 26th Annual International ACM SIGIR Conference on Research and Development in Information Retrieval, pp. 267–273. ACM (2003)
37. Zhou, B., Khosla, A., Lapedriza, A., Oliva, A., Torralba, A.: Learning deep features for discriminative localization. In: Computer Vision and Pattern Recognition (CVPR), pp. 2921–2929. IEEE (2016)

Deep Regression Tracking with Shrinkage Loss

Xiankai Lu[1,3], Chao Ma[2(✉)], Bingbing Ni[1,4], Xiaokang Yang[1,4], Ian Reid[2],
and Ming-Hsuan Yang[5,6]

[1] Shanghai Jiao Tong University, Shanghai, China
[2] The University of Adelaide, Adelaide, Australia
c.ma@adelaide.edu.au
[3] Inception Institute of Artificial Intelligence, Abu Dhabi, UAE
[4] SJTU-UCLA Joint Center for Machine Perception and Inference, Shanghai, China
[5] University of California at Merced, Merced, USA
[6] Google Inc., Menlo Park, USA

Abstract. Regression trackers directly learn a mapping from regularly dense samples of target objects to soft labels, which are usually generated by a Gaussian function, to estimate target positions. Due to the potential for fast-tracking and easy implementation, regression trackers have recently received increasing attention. However, state-of-the-art deep regression trackers do not perform as well as discriminative correlation filters (DCFs) trackers. We identify the main bottleneck of training regression networks as extreme foreground-background data imbalance. To balance training data, we propose a novel shrinkage loss to penalize the importance of easy training data. Additionally, we apply residual connections to fuse multiple convolutional layers as well as their output response maps. Without bells and whistles, the proposed deep regression tracking method performs favorably against state-of-the-art trackers, especially in comparison with DCFs trackers, on five benchmark datasets including OTB-2013, OTB-2015, Temple-128, UAV-123 and VOT-2016.

Keywords: Regression networks · Shrinkage loss · Object tracking

1 Introduction

The recent years have witnessed growing interest in developing visual object tracking algorithms for various vision applications. Existing tracking-by-detection approaches mainly consist of two stages to perform tracking. The first stage draws a large number of samples around target objects in the previous

---

X. Lu and C. Ma—The First two authors contribute equally to this work.

Electronic supplementary material The online version of this chapter (https://doi.org/10.1007/978-3-030-01264-9_22) contains supplementary material, which is available to authorized users.

© Springer Nature Switzerland AG 2018
V. Ferrari et al. (Eds.): ECCV 2018, LNCS 11218, pp. 369–386, 2018.
https://doi.org/10.1007/978-3-030-01264-9_22

frame and the second stage classifies each sample as the target object or as the background. In contrast, one-stage regression trackers [1–8] directly learn a mapping from a regularly dense sampling of target objects to soft labels generated by a Gaussian function to estimate target positions. One-stage regression trackers have recently received increasing attention due to their potential to be much faster and simpler than two-stage trackers. State-of-the-art one-stage trackers [1–5] are predominantly on the basis of discriminative correlation filters (DCFs) rather than deep regression networks. Despite the top performance on recent benchmarks [9,10], DCFs trackers take few advantages of end-to-end training as learning and updating DCFs are independent of deep feature extraction. In this paper, we investigate the performance bottleneck of deep regression trackers [6–8], where regression networks are fully differentiable and can be trained end-to-end. As regression networks have greater potential to take advantage of large-scale training data than DCFs, we believe that deep regression trackers can perform at least as well as DCFs trackers.

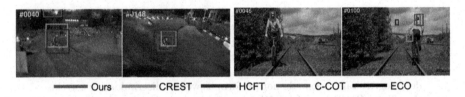

Fig. 1. Tracking results in comparison with state-of-the-art trackers. The proposed algorithm surpasses existing deep regression based trackers (CREST [8]), and performs well against the DCFs trackers (ECO [5], C-COT [4] and HCFT [3]).

We identify the main bottleneck impeding deep regression trackers from achieving state-of-the-art accuracy as the data imbalance [11] issue in regression learning. For the two-stage trackers built upon binary classifiers, data imbalance has been extensively studied. That is, positive samples are far less than negative samples and the majority of negative samples belong to easy training data, which contribute little to classifier learning. Despite the pertinence of data imbalance in regression learning as well, we note that current one-stage regression trackers [6–8] pay little attention to this issue. As the evidence of the effectiveness, state-of-the-art DCFs trackers improve tracking accuracy by re-weighting sample locations using Gaussian-like maps [12], spatial reliability maps [13] or binary maps [14]. In this work, to break the bottleneck, we revisit the shrinkage estimator [15] in regression learning. We propose a novel shrinkage loss to handle data imbalance during learning regression networks. Specifically, we use a Sigmoid-like function to penalize the importance of easy samples coming from the background (e.g., samples close to the boundary). This not only improves tracking accuracy but also accelerates network convergence. The proposed shrinkage loss differs from the recently proposed focal loss [16] in that our method penalizes the importance of easy samples only, whereas focal loss partially decreases the loss from valuable hard samples (see Sect. 3.2).

We observe that deep regression networks can be further improved by best exploiting multi-level semantic abstraction across multiple convolutional layers. For instance, the FCNT [6] fuses two regression networks independently learned on the *conv4-3* and *con5-3* layers of VGG-16 [17] to improve tracking accuracy. However, independently learning regression networks on multiple convolutional layers cannot make full use of multi-level semantics across convolutional layers. In this work, we propose to apply residual connections to respectively fuse multiple convolutional layers as well as their output response maps. All the connections are fully differentiable, allowing our regression network to be trained end-to-end. For fair comparison, we evaluate the proposed deep regression tracker using the standard benchmark setting, where only the ground-truth in the first frame is available for training. The proposed algorithm performs well against state-of-the-art methods especially in comparison with DCFs trackers. Figure 1 shows such examples on two challenging sequences.

The main contributions of this work are summarized below:

- We propose the novel shrinkage loss to handle the data imbalance issue in learning deep regression networks. The shrinkage loss helps accelerate network convergence as well.
- We apply residual connections to respectively fuse multiple convolutional layers as well as their output response maps. Our scheme fully exploits multi-level semantic abstraction across multiple convolutional layers.
- We extensively evaluate the proposed method on five benchmark datasets. Our method performs well against state-of-the-art trackers. We succeed in narrowing the gap between deep regression trackers and DCFs trackers.

2 Related Work

Visual tracking has been an active research topic with comprehensive surveys [18, 19]. In this section, we first discuss the representative tracking frameworks using the two-stage classification model and the one-stage regression model. We then briefly review the data imbalance issue in classification and regression learning.

Two-Stage Tracking. This framework mainly consists of two stages to perform tracking. The first stage generates a set of candidate target samples around the previously estimated location using random sampling, regularly dense sampling [20], or region proposal [21,22]. The second stage classifies each candidate sample as the target object or as the background. Numerous efforts have been made to learn a discriminative boundary between positive and negative samples. Examples include the multiple instance learning (MIL) [23] and Struck [24,25] methods. Recent deep trackers, such as MDNet [26], DeepTrack [27] and CNN-SVM [28], all belong to the two-stage classification framework. Despite the favorable performance on the challenging object tracking benchmarks [9,10], we note that two-stage deep trackers suffer from heavy computational load as they directly feed samples in the image level into classification neural networks. Different from object detection, visual tracking put more emphasis on slight displacement between samples for precise localization. Two-stage deep trackers benefit little from the recent advance of ROI pooling [29], which cannot highlight the difference between highly spatially correlated samples.

One-Stage Tracking. The one-stage tracking framework takes the whole search area as input and directly outputs a response map through a learned regressor, which learns a mapping between input features and soft labels generated by a Gaussian function. One representative category of one-stage trackers are based on discriminative correlation filters [30], which regress all the circularly shifted versions of input image into soft labels. By computing the correlation as an element-wise product in the Fourier domain, DCFs trackers achieve the fastest speed thus far. Numerous extensions include KCF [31], LCT [32,33], MCF [34], MCPF [35] and BACF [14]. With the use of deep features, DCFs trackers, such as DeepSRDCF [1], HDT [2], HCFT [3], C-COT [4] and ECO [5], have shown superior performance on benchmark datasets. In [3], Ma et al. propose to learn multiple DCFs over different convolutional layers and empirically fuse output correlation maps to locate target objects. A similar idea is exploited in [4] to combine multiple response maps. In [5], Danelljan et al. reduce feature channels to accelerate learning correlation filters. Despite the top performance, DCFs trackers independently extract deep features to learn and update correlation filters. In the deep learning era, DCFs trackers can hardly benefit from end-to-end training. The other representative category of one-stage trackers are based on convolutional regression networks. The recent FCNT [6], STCT [7], and CREST [8] trackers belong to this category. The FCNT makes the first effort to learn regression networks over two CNN layers. The output response maps from different layers are switched according to their confidence to locate target objects. Ensemble learning is exploited in the STCT to select CNN feature channels. CREST [8] learns a base network as well as a residual network on a single convolutional layer. The output maps of the base and residual networks are fused to infer target positions. We note that current deep regression trackers do not perform as well as DCFs trackers. We identify the main bottleneck as the data imbalance issue in regression learning. By balancing the importance of training data, the performance of one-stage deep regression trackers can be significantly improved over state-of-the-art DCFs trackers.

Data Imbalance. The data imbalance issue has been extensively studied in the learning community [11,36,37]. Helpful solutions involve data re-sampling [38–40], and cost-sensitive loss [16,41–43]. For visual tracking, Li et al. [44] use a temporal sampling scheme to balance positive and negative samples to facilitate CNN training. Bertinetto et al. [45] balance the loss of positive and negative examples in the score map for pre-training the Siamese fully convolution network. The MDNet [26] tracker shows that it is crucial to mine the hard negative samples during training classification networks. The recent work [16] on dense object detection proposes focal loss to decrease the loss from imbalance samples. Despite the importance, current deep regression trackers [6–8] pay little attention to data imbalance. In this work, we propose to utilize shrinkage loss to penalize easy samples which have little contribution to learning regression networks. The proposed shrinkage loss significantly differs from focal loss [16] in that we penalize the loss only from easy samples while keeping the loss of hard samples unchanged, whereas focal loss partially decreases the loss of hard samples as well.

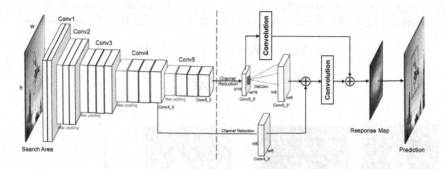

Fig. 2. Overview of the proposed deep regression network for tracking. Left: Fixed feature extractor (VGG-16). Right: Regression network trained in the first frame and updated frame-by-frame. We apply residual connections to both convolution layers and output response maps. The proposed network effectively exploits multi-level semantic abstraction across convolutional layers. With the use of shrinkage loss, our network breaks the bottleneck of data imbalance in regression learning and converges fast.

3   Proposed Algorithm

We develop our tracker within the one-stage regression framework. Figure 2 shows an overview of the proposed regression network. To facilitate regression learning, we propose a novel shrinkage loss to handle data imbalance. We further apply residual connections to respectively fuse convolutional layers and their output response maps for fully exploiting multi-level semantics across convolutional layers. In the following, we first revisit learning deep regression networks briefly. We then present the proposed shrinkage loss in detail. Last, we discuss the residual connection scheme.

3.1   Convolutional Regression

Convolutional regression networks regress a dense sampling of inputs to soft labels which are usually generated by a Gaussian function. Here, we formulate the regression network as one convolutional layer. Formally, learning the weights of the regression network is to solve the following minimization problem:

$$\arg\min_{\mathbf{W}} \|\mathbf{W} * \mathbf{X} - \mathbf{Y}\|^2 + \lambda\|\mathbf{W}\|^2, \tag{1}$$

where $*$ denotes the convolution operation and $\mathbf{W}$ denotes the kernel weight of the convolutional layer. Note that there is no bias term in Eq. (1) as we set the bias parameters to 0. $\mathbf{X}$ means the input features. $\mathbf{Y}$ is the matrix of soft labels, and each label $y \in \mathbf{Y}$ ranges from 0 to 1. λ is the regularization term. We estimate the target translation by searching for the location of the maximum value of the output response map. The size of the convolution kernel $\mathbf{W}$ is either fixed (e.g., 5×5) or proportional to the size of the input features $\mathbf{X}$. Let η be the learning rate. We iteratively optimize $\mathbf{W}$ by minimizing the square loss:

$$L(\mathbf{W}) = \|\mathbf{W} * \mathbf{X} - \mathbf{Y}\|^2 + \lambda\|\mathbf{W}\|^2$$
$$\mathbf{W}_t = \mathbf{W}_{t-1} - \eta\frac{\partial L}{\partial \mathbf{W}}, \tag{2}$$

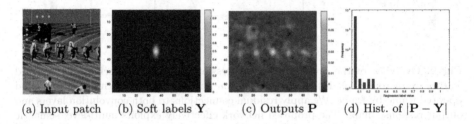

(a) Input patch   (b) Soft labels $\mathbf{Y}$ (c) Outputs $\mathbf{P}$ (d) Hist. of $|\mathbf{P} - \mathbf{Y}|$

Fig. 3. (a) Input patch. (b) The corresponding soft labels $\mathbf{Y}$ generated by Gaussian function for training. (c) The output regression map $\mathbf{P}$. (d) The histogram of the absolute difference $|\mathbf{P} - \mathbf{Y}|$. Note that easy samples with small absolute difference scores dominate the training data.

3.2   Shrinkage Loss

For learning convolutional regression networks, the input search area has to contain a large body of background surrounding target objects (Fig. 3(a)). As the surrounding background contains valuable context information, a large area of the background helps strengthen the discriminative power of target objects from the background. However, this increases the number of easy samples from the background as well. These easy samples produce a large loss in total to make the learning process unaware of the valuable samples close to targets. Formally, we denote the response map in every iteration by $\mathbf{P}$, which is a matrix of size $m \times n$. $p_{i,j} \in \mathbf{P}$ indicates the probability of the position $i \in [1, m], j \in [1, n]$ to be the target object. Let l be the absolute difference between the estimated possibility p and its corresponding soft label y, i.e., $l = |p - y|$. Note that, when the absolute difference l is larger, the sample at the location (i, j) is more likely to be the hard sample and vice versa. Figure 3(d) shows the histogram of the absolute differences. Note that easy samples with small absolute difference scores dominate the training data.

In terms of the absolute difference l, the square loss in regression learning can be formulated as:

$$L_2 = |p - y|^2 = l^2. \tag{3}$$

The recent work [16] on dense object detection shows that adding a modulating factor to the entropy loss helps alleviate the data imbalance issue. The modulating factor is a function of the output possibility with the goal to decrease the loss from easy samples. In regression learning, this amounts to re-weighting the square loss using an exponential form of the absolute difference term l as follows:

$$L_F = l^\gamma \cdot L_2 = l^{2+\gamma}. \tag{4}$$

For simplicity, we set the parameter γ to 1 as we observe that the performance is not sensitive to this parameter. Hence, the focal loss for regression learning is equal to the L_3 loss, i.e., $L_F = l^3$. Note that, as a weight, the absolute difference l, $l \in [0, 1]$, not only penalizes an easy sample (i.e., $l < 0.5$) but also penalizes a hard sample (i.e., $l > 0.5$). By revisiting the shrinkage estimator [15] and the cost-sensitive weighting strategy [37] in learning regression networks, instead of using the absolute difference l as weight, we propose a modulating factor with respect to l to re-weight the square loss to penalize easy samples only. The modulating function is with the shape of a Sigmoid-like function as:

$$f(l) = \frac{1}{1 + \exp(a \cdot (c - l))}, \tag{5}$$

where a and c are hyper-parameters controlling the shrinkage speed and the localization respectively. Figure 4(a) shows the shapes of the modulating function with different hyper-parameters. When applying the modulating factor to weight the square loss, we have the proposed shrinkage loss as:

$$L_S = \frac{l^2}{1 + \exp(a \cdot (c - l))}. \tag{6}$$

As shown in Fig. 4(b), the proposed shrinkage loss only penalizes the importance of easy samples (when $l < 0.5$) and keeps the loss of hard samples unchanged (when $l > 0.5$) when compared to the square loss (L_2). The focal loss (L_3) penalizes both the easy and hard samples.

When applying the shrinkage loss to Eq. (1), we take the cost-sensitive weighting strategy [37] and utilize the values of soft labels as an importance factor, e.g., $\exp(\mathbf{Y})$, to highlight the valuable rare samples. In summary, we rewrite Eq. (1) with the shrinkage loss for learning regression networks as:

$$L_S(\mathbf{W}) = \frac{\exp(\mathbf{Y}) \cdot \|\mathbf{W} * \mathbf{X} - \mathbf{Y}\|^2}{1 + \exp(a \cdot (c - (\mathbf{W} * \mathbf{X} - \mathbf{Y})))} + \lambda\|\mathbf{W}\|^2. \tag{7}$$

We set the value of a to be 10 to shrink the weight function quickly and the value of c to be 0.2 to suit for the distribution of l, which ranges from 0 to 1. Extensive comparison with the other losses shows that the proposed shrinkage loss not only improves the tracking accuracy but also accelerates the training speed (see Sect. 5.3) (Fig. 11).

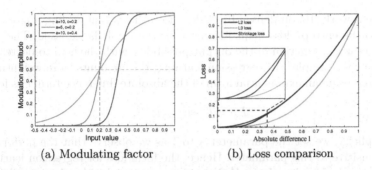

(a) Modulating factor   (b) Loss comparison

Fig. 4. (a) Modulating factors in (5) with different hyper-parameters. (b) Comparison between the square loss (L_2), focal loss (L_3) and the proposed shrinkage loss for regression learning. The proposed shrinkage loss only decreases the loss from easy samples ($l < 0.5$) and keeps the loss from hard samples ($l > 0.5$) unchanged.

3.3 Convolutional Layer Connection

It has been known that CNN models consist of multiple convolutional layers emphasizing different levels of semantic abstraction. For visual tracking, early layers with fine-grained spatial details are helpful in precisely locating target objects; while the later layers maintain semantic abstraction that are robust to significant appearance changes. To exploit both merits, existing deep trackers [3,5,6] develop independent models over multiple convolutional layers and integrate the corresponding output response maps with empirical weights. For learning regression networks, we observe that semantic abstraction plays a more important role than spatial detail in dealing with appearance changes. The FCNT exploit both the *conv4* and *conv5* layers and the CREST [8] merely uses the *conv4* layer. Our studies in Sect. 5.3 also suggest that regression trackers perform well when using the *conv4* and *conv5* layers as the feature backbone. For integrating the response maps generated over convolutional layers, we use a residual connection block to make full use of multiple-level semantic abstraction of target objects. In Fig. 3, we compare our scheme with the ECO [5] and CREST [8] methods. The DCFs tracker ECO [5] independently learns *correlation filters* over the *conv1* and *conv5* layers. The CREST [8] learns a base and a residual regression network over the *conv4* layer. The proposed method in Fig. 3(c) fuses the *conv4* and *conv5* layers before learning the regression networks. Here we use the deconvolution operation to upsample the *conv5* layer before connection. We reduce feature channels to ease the computational load as in [46,47]. Our connection scheme resembles the Option C of constructing the residual network [46]. Ablation studies affirm the effectiveness of this scheme to facilitate regression learning (see Sect. 5.3).

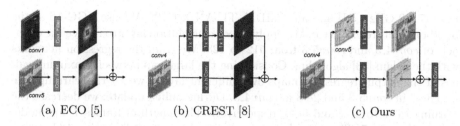

(a) ECO [5]   (b) CREST [8]   (c) Ours

Fig. 5. Different schemes to fuse convolutional layers. ECO [5] independently learns *correlation filters* over multiple convolutional layers. CREST [8] learns a base and a residual regression network over a single convolutional layer. We first fuse multiple convolutional layers using residual connection and then perform regression learning. Our regression network makes full use of multi-level semantics across multiple convolutional layers rather than merely integrating response maps as ECO and CREST.

4   Tracking Framework

We detail the pipeline of the proposed regression tracker. In Fig. 2, we show an overview of the proposed deep regression network, which consists of model initialization, target object localization, scale estimation and model update. For training, we crop a patch centered at the estimated location in the previous frame. We use the VGG-16 [17] model as the backbone feature extractor. Specifically, we take the output response of the *conv4_3* and *conv5_3* layers as features to represent each patch. The fused features via residual connection are fed into the proposed regression network. During tracking, given a new frame, we crop a search patch centered at the estimated position in the last frame. The regression networks take this search patch as input and output a response map, where the location of the maximum value indicates the position of target objects. Once obtaining the estimated position, we carry out scale estimation using the scale pyramid strategy as in [48]. To make the model adaptive to appearance variations, we incrementally update our regression network frame-by-frame. To alleviate noisy updates, the tracked results and soft labels in the last T frames are used for the model update.

5   Experiments

In this section, we first introduce the implementation details. Then, we evaluate the proposed method on five benchmark datasets including OTB-2013 [49], OTB-2015 [9], Temple128 [50], UAV123 [51] and VOT-2016 [10] in comparison with state-of-the-art trackers. Last, we present extensive ablation studies on different types of losses as well as their effect on the convergence speed.

5.1   Implementation Details

We implement the proposed Deep Shrinkage Loss Tracker (DSLT) in Matlab using the Caffe toolbox [52]. All experiments are performed on a PC with an

Intel i7 4.0 GHz CPU and an NVIDIA TITAN X GPU. We use VGG-16 as the backbone feature extractor. We apply a 1×1 convolution layer to reduce the channels of $conv4\_3$ and $conv5\_3$ from 512 to 128. We train the regression networks with the Adam [53] algorithm. Considering the large gap between maximum values of the output regression maps over different layers, we set the learning rate η to $8e\text{-}7$ in $conv5\_3$ and $2e\text{-}8$ in $conv4\_3$. During online update, we decrease the learning rates to $2e\text{-}7$ and $5e\text{-}9$, respectively. The length of frames T for model update is set to 7. The soft labels are generated by a two-dimensional Gaussian function with a kernel width proportional (0.1) to the target size. For scale estimation, we set the ratio of scale changes to 1.03 and the levels of scale pyramid to 3. The average tracking speed including all training process is 5.7 frames per second. The source code is available at https://github.com/chaoma99/DSLT.

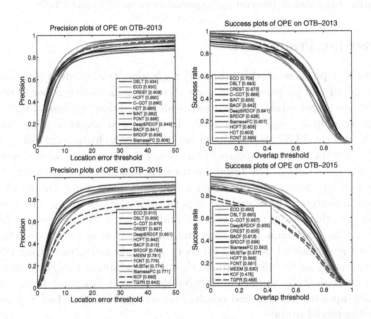

Fig. 6. Overall performance on the OTB-2013 [49] and OTB-2015 [9] datasets using one-pass evaluation (OPE). Our tracker performs well against state-of-the-art methods.

5.2   Overall Performance

We extensively evaluate our approach on five challenging tracking benchmarks. We follow the protocol of the benchmarks for fair comparison with state-of-the-art trackers. For the OTB [9,49] and Temple128 [50] datasets, we report the results of one-pass evaluation (OPE) with distance precision (DP) and overlap success (OS) plots. The legend of distance precision plots contains the thresholded scores at 20 pixels, while the legend of overlap success plots contains area-under-the-curve (AUC) scores for each tracker. See the complete results on all benchmark datasets in the supplementary document.

OTB Dataset. There are two versions of this dataset. The OTB-2013 [49] dataset contains 50 challenging sequences and the OTB-2015 [9] dataset extends the OTB-2013 dataset with additional 50 video sequences. All the sequences cover a wide range of challenges including occlusion, illumination variation, rotation, motion blur, fast motion, in-plane rotation, out-of-plane rotation, out-of-view, background clutter and low resolution. We fairly compare the proposed DSLT with state-of-the-art trackers, which mainly fall into three categories: (i) one-stage regression trackers including CREST [8], FCNT [6], GOTURN [54], SiameseFC [45]; (ii) one-stage DCFs trackers including ECO [5], C-COT [4], BACF [14], DeepSRDCF [1], HCFT [3], HDT [2], SRDCF [12], KCF [31], and MUSTer [55]; and (iii) two-stage trackers including MEEM [56], TGPR [57], SINT [58], and CNN-SVM [28]. As shown in Fig. 6, the proposed DSLT achieves the best distance precision (93.4%) and the second best overlap success (68.3%) on OTB-2013. Our DSLT outperforms the state-of-the-art deep regression trackers (CREST [8] and FCNT [6]) by a large margin. We attribute the favorable performance of our DSLT to two reasons. First, the proposed shrinkage loss effectively alleviate the data imbalance issue in regression learning. As a result, the proposed DSLT can automatically mine the most discriminative samples and eliminate the distraction caused by easy samples. Second, we exploit the residual connection scheme to fuse multiple convolutional layers to further facilitate regression learning as multi-level semantics across convolutional layers are fully exploited. As well, our DSLT performs favorably against all DCFs trackers such as C-COT, HCFT and DeepSRDCF. Note that ECO achieves the best results by exploring both deep features and hand-crafted features. On OTB-2015, our DSLT ranks second in both distance precision and overlap success.

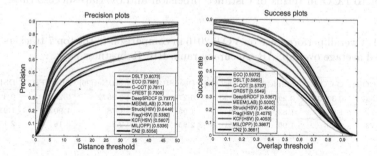

Fig. 7. Overall performance on the Temple Color 128 [50] dataset using one-pass evaluation. Our method ranks first in distance precision and second in overlap success.

Temple Color 128 Dataset. This dataset [50] consists of 128 colorful video sequences. The evaluation setting of Temple 128 is same to the OTB dataset. In

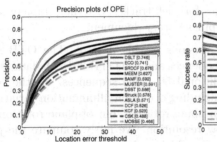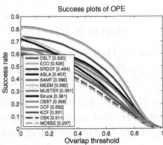

Fig. 8. Overall performance on the UAV-123 [51] dataset using one-pass evaluation (OPE). The proposed DSLT method ranks first.

addition to the aforementioned baseline methods, we fairly compare with all the trackers including Struck [24], Frag [59], KCF [31], MEEM [56], MIL [23] and CN2 [47] evaluated by the authors of Temple 128. Figure 7 shows that the proposed method achieves the best distance precision by a large margin compared to the ECO, C-COT and CREST trackers. Our method ranks second in terms of overlap success. It is worth mentioning that our regression tracker performs well in tracking small targets. Temple-128 contains a large number of small target objects. Our method achieves the best precision of 80.73%, far better than the state-of-the-art.

UAV123 Dataset. This dataset [51] contains 123 video sequences obtained by unmanned aerial vehicles (UAVs). We evaluate the proposed DSLT with several representative methods including ECO [5], SRDCF [12], KCF [31], MUSTer [55], MEEM [56], TGPR [57], SAMF [60], DSST [58], CSK [61], Struck [24], and TLD [62]. Figure 8 shows that the performance of the proposed DSLT is slightly superior to ECO in terms of distance precision and overlap success rate.

Table 1. Overall performance on VOT-2016 in comparison to the top 7 trackers. EAO: Expected average overlap. AR: Accuracy rank. RR: Robustness rank.

	ECO[5]	C-COT[4]	Staple[63]	CREST[8]	DeepSRDCF[1]	MDNet[26]	SRDCF[12]	DSLT(ours)
EAO	0.3675	0.3310	0.2952	0.2990	0.2763	0.2572	0.2471	0.3321
AR	1.72	1.63	1.82	2.09	1.95	1.78	1.90	1.91
RR	1.73	1.90	1.95	1.95	2.85	2.88	3.18	2.15

VOT-2016 Dataset. The VOT-2016 [10] dataset contains 60 challenging videos, which are annotated by the following attributes: occlusion, illumination change, motion change, size change, and camera motion. The overall performance is measured by the expected average overlap (EAO), accuracy rank (AR) and robustness rank (RR). The main criteria, EAO, takes into account both the per-frame accuracy and the number of failures. We compare our method with state-of-the-art trackers including ECO [5], C-COT [4], CREST [8], Staple [63], SRDCF [12], DeepSRDCF [1], MDNet [26]. Table 1 shows that our method performs slightly worse than the top performing ECO tracker but significantly better than the others such as the recent C-COT and CREST trackers. The VOT-2016 report [10] suggests a strict state-of-the-art bound as 0.251 with the EAO metric. The proposed DSLT achieves a much higher EAO of 0.3321.

5.3   Ablation Studies

We first analyze the contributions of the loss function and the effectiveness of the residual connection scheme. We then discuss the convergence speed of different losses in regression learning.

Loss Function Analysis. First, we replace the proposed shrinkage loss with square loss (L_2) or focal loss (L_3). We evaluate the alternative implementations on the OTB-2015 [9] dataset. Overall, the proposed DSLT with shrinkage loss significantly advances the square loss (L_2) and focal loss (L_3) by a large margin. We present the qualitative results on two sequences in Fig. 9 where the trackers with L_2 loss or L_3 loss both fail to track the targets undergoing large appearance changes, whereas the proposed DSLT can locate the targets robustly. Figure 10 presents the quantitative results on the OTB-2015 dataset. Note that the baseline tracker with L_2 loss performs much better than CREST [8] in both distance precision (87.0% vs. 83.8%) and overlap success (64.2% vs. 63.2%). This clearly proves the effectiveness of the convolutional layer connection scheme, which applies residual connection to both convolutional layers and output regression maps rather than only to the output regression maps as CREST does. In addition, we implement an alternative approach using online hard negative mining (OHNM) [26] to completely exclude the loss from easy samples. We empirically set the mining threshold to 0.01. Our DSLT outperforms the OHNM method significantly. Our observation is thus well aligned to [16] that easy samples still contribute to regression learning but they should not dominate the whole gradient. In addition, the OHNM method manually sets a threshold, which is hardly applicable to all videos.

Feature Analysis. We further evaluate the effectiveness of convolutional layers. We first remove the connections between convolutional layers. The resulted DSLT_m algorithm resembles the CREST. Figure 10 shows that DSLT_m has performance drops of around 0.3% (DP) and 0.1% (OS) when compared to the DSLT. This affirms the importance of fusing features before regression learning. In addition, we fuse conv3_3 with conv4_3 or conv5_3. The inferior performance of DSLT_34 and DSLT_35 shows that semantic abstraction is more important than spatial detail for learning regression networks. As the kernel size of the convolutional regression layer is proportional to the input feature size, we do not evaluate earlier layers for computational efficiency.

Convergence Speed. Figure 11 compares the convergence speed and the required training iterations using different losses on the OTB-2015 dataset [9]. Overall, the training loss using the shrinkage loss descends quickly and stably. The shrinkage loss thus requires the least iterations to converge during tracking.

Fig. 9. Quantitative results on the *Biker* and *Skating1* sequences. The proposed DSLT with shrinkage loss can locate the targets more robustly than L_2 loss and L_3 loss.

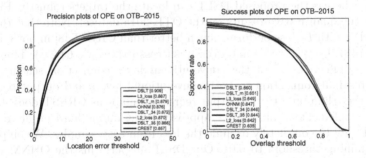

Fig. 10. Ablation studies with different losses and different layer connections on the OTB-2015 [9] dataset.

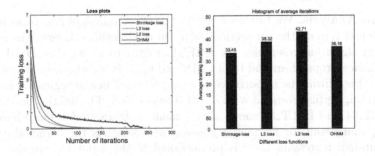

Fig. 11. Training loss plot (left) and average training iterations per sequence on the OTB-2015 dataset (right). The shrinkage loss converges the fastest and requires the least number of iterations to converge.

6   Conclusion

We revisit one-stage trackers based on deep regression networks and identify the bottleneck that impedes one-stage regression trackers from achieving state-of-the-art results, especially when compared to DCFs trackers. The main bottleneck lies in the data imbalance in learning regression networks. We propose the novel shrinkage loss to facilitate learning regression networks with better accuracy and faster convergence speed. To further improve regression learning, we exploit multi-level semantic abstraction of target objects across multiple convolutional layers as features. We apply the residual connections to both convolutional layers and their output response maps. Our network is fully differentiable and can be trained end-to-end. We succeed in narrowing the performance gap between one-stage deep regression trackers and DCFs trackers. Extensive experiments on five benchmark datasets demonstrate the effectiveness and efficiency of the proposed tracker when compared to state-of-the-art algorithms.

Acknowledgments. This work is supported in part by the National Key Research and Development Program of China (2016YFB1001003), NSFC (61527804, 61521062, U1611461, 61502301, and 61671298), the 111 Program (B07022), and STCSM (17511105401 and 18DZ2270700). C. Ma and I. Reid acknowledge the support of the Australian Research Council through the Centre of Excellence for Robotic Vision (CE140100016) and Laureate Fellowship (FL130100102). B. Ni is supported by China's Thousand Youth Talents Plan. M.-H. Yang is supported by NSF CAREER (1149783).

References

1. Danelljan, M., Häger, G., Khan, F.S., Felsberg, M.: Convolutional features for correlation filter based visual tracking. In: ICCV Workshops (2015)
2. Qi, Y., et al.: Hedged deep tracking. In: CVPR (2016)
3. Ma, C., Huang, J.B., Yang, X., Yang, M.H.: Hierarchical convolutional features for visual tracking. In: ICCV (2015)
4. Danelljan, M., Robinson, A., Shahbaz Khan, F., Felsberg, M.: Beyond correlation filters: learning continuous convolution operators for visual tracking. In: Leibe, B., Matas, J., Sebe, N., Welling, M. (eds.) ECCV 2016. LNCS, vol. 9909, pp. 472–488. Springer, Cham (2016). https://doi.org/10.1007/978-3-319-46454-1_29
5. Danelljan, M., Bhat, G., Shahbaz Khan, F., Felsberg, M.: Eco: efficient convolution operators for tracking. In: CVPR (2017)
6. Wang, L., Ouyang, W., Wang, X., Lu, H.: Visual tracking with fully convolutional networks. In: ICCV (2015)
7. Wang, L., Ouyang, W., Wang, X., Lu, H.: STCT: sequentially training convolutional networks for visual tracking. In: CVPR (2016)
8. Song, Y., Ma, C., Gong, L., Zhang, J., Lau, R.W.H., Yang, M.H.: Crest: convolutional residual learning for visual tracking. In: ICCV (2017)
9. Wu, Y., Lim, J., Yang, M.: Object tracking benchmark. TPAMI **37**(9), 585–595 (2015)
10. Kristan, M., et al.: The visual object tracking VOT2016 challenge results. In: Hua, G., Jégou, H. (eds.) ECCV 2016. LNCS, vol. 9914, pp. 777–823. Springer, Cham (2016). https://doi.org/10.1007/978-3-319-48881-3_54

11. He, H., Garcia, E.A.: Learning from imbalanced data. TKDE **21**(9), 1263–1284 (2009)
12. Danelljan, M., Häger, G., Khan, F.S., Felsberg, M.: Learning spatially regularized correlation filters for visual tracking. In: ICCV (2015)
13. Lukezic, A., Vojir, T., Zajc, L.C., Matas, J., Kristan, M.: Discriminative correlation filter with channel and spatial reliability. In: CVPR (2017)
14. Kiani Galoogahi, H., Fagg, A., Lucey, S.: Learning background-aware correlation filters for visual tracking. In: ICCV (2017)
15. Copas, J.B.: Regression, prediction and shrinkage. J. Roy. Stat. Soc. **45**, 311–354 (1983)
16. Lin, T.Y., Goyal, P., Girshick, R., He, K., Dollr, P.: Focal loss for dense object detection. In: ICCV (2017)
17. Simonyan, K., Zisserman, A.: Very deep convolutional networks for large-scale image recognition. In: ICLR (2015)
18. Salti, S., Cavallaro, A., di Stefano, L.: Adaptive appearance modeling for video tracking: survey and evaluation. TIP **21**(10), 4334–4348 (2012)
19. Smeulders, A.W.M., Chu, D.M., Cucchiara, R., Calderara, S., Dehghan, A., Shah, M.: Visual tracking: an experimental survey. TPAMI **36**(7), 1442–1468 (2014)
20. Wang, N., Shi, J., Yeung, D.Y., Jia, J.: Understanding and diagnosing visual tracking systems. In: ICCV (2015)
21. Hua, Y., Alahari, K., Schmid, C.: Online object tracking with proposal selection. In: ICCV (2015)
22. Zhu, G., Porikli, F., Li, H.: Beyond local search: tracking objects everywhere with instance-specific proposals. In: CVPR (2016)
23. Babenko, B., Yang, M., Belongie, S.J.: Robust object tracking with online multiple instance learning. TPAMI **33**(8), 1619–1632 (2011)
24. Hare, S., Saffari, A., Torr, P.H.: Struck: structured output tracking with kernels. In: ICCV (2011)
25. Ning, J., Yang, J., Jiang, S., Zhang, L., Yang, M.: Object tracking via dual linear structured SVM and explicit feature map. In: CVPR (2016)
26. Nam, H., Han, B.: Learning multi-domain convolutional neural networks for visual tracking. In: CVPR (2016)
27. Li, H., Li, Y., Porikli, F.: Deeptrack: learning discriminative feature representations by convolutional neural networks for visual tracking. In: BMVC (2014)
28. Hong, S., You, T., Kwak, S., Han, B.: Online tracking by learning discriminative saliency map with convolutional neural network. In: ICML (2015)
29. Girshick, R.B.: Fast R-CNN. In: ICCV (2015)
30. Bolme, D.S., Beveridge, J.R., Draper, B.A., Lui, Y.M.: Visual object tracking using adaptive correlation filters. In: CVPR (2010)
31. Henriques, J.F., Caseiro, R., Martins, P., Batista, J.: High-speed tracking with kernelized correlation filters. TPAMI **37**(3), 583–596 (2015)
32. Ma, C., Yang, X., Zhang, C., Yang, M.H.: Long-term correlation tracking. In: CVPR (2015)
33. Ma, C., Huang, J.B., Yang, X., Yang, M.H.: Adaptive correlation filters with long-term and short-term memory for object tracking. IJCV **10**, 1–26 (2018)
34. Wang, M., Liu, Y., Huang, Z.: Large margin object tracking with circulant feature maps. In: CVPR (2017)
35. Zhang, T., Xu, C., Yang, M.H.: Multi-task correlation particle filter for robust object tracking. In: CVPR (2017)
36. Zadrozny, B., Langford, J., Abe, N.: Cost-sensitive learning by cost-proportionate example weighting. In: ICDM (2003)

37. Kukar, M., Kononenko, I.: Cost-sensitive learning with neural networks. In: ECAI (1998)
38. Huang, C., Li, Y., Loy, C.C., Tang, X.: Learning deep representation for imbalanced classification. In: CVPR (2016)
39. Dong, Q., Gong, S., Zhu, X.: Class rectification hard mining for imbalanced deep learning. In: ICCV (2017)
40. Maciejewski, T., Stefanowski, J.: Local neighbourhood extension of SMOTE for mining imbalanced data. In: CIDM (2011)
41. Khan, S.H., Hayat, M., Bennamoun, M., Sohel, F.A., Togneri, R.: Cost-sensitive learning of deep feature representations from imbalanced data. TNNLS **99**, 1–17 (2017)
42. Tang, Y., Zhang, Y., Chawla, N.V., Krasser, S.: SVMS modeling for highly imbalanced classification. IEEE Trans. Cybern **39**(1), 281–288 (2009)
43. Ting, K.M.: A comparative study of cost-sensitive boosting algorithms. In: ICML (2000)
44. Li, H., Li, Y., Porikli, F.M.: Robust online visual tracking with a single convolutional neural network. In: ACCV (2014)
45. Bertinetto, L., Valmadre, J., Henriques, J.F., Vedaldi, A., Torr, P.H.S.: Fully-convolutional siamese networks for object tracking. In: Hua, G., Jégou, H. (eds.) ECCV 2016. LNCS, vol. 9914, pp. 850–865. Springer, Cham (2016). https://doi.org/10.1007/978-3-319-48881-3_56
46. He, K., Zhang, X., Ren, S., Sun, J.: Deep residual learning for image recognition. In: CVPR (2016)
47. Danelljan, M., Khan, F.S., Felsberg, M., van de Weijer, J.: Adaptive color attributes for real-time visual tracking. In: CVPR (2014)
48. Danelljan, M., Häger, G., Khan, F.S., Felsberg, M.: Accurate scale estimation for robust visual tracking. In: BMVC (2014)
49. Wu, Y., Lim, J., Yang, M.H.: Online object tracking: a benchmark. In: CVPR (2013)
50. Liang, P., Blasch, E., Ling, H.: Encoding color information for visual tracking: algorithms and benchmark. TIP **24**(12), 5630–5644 (2015)
51. Mueller, M., Smith, N., Ghanem, B.: A benchmark and simulator for UAV tracking. In: Leibe, B., Matas, J., Sebe, N., Welling, M. (eds.) ECCV 2016. LNCS, vol. 9905, pp. 445–461. Springer, Cham (2016). https://doi.org/10.1007/978-3-319-46448-0_27
52. Jia, Y., et al.: Caffe: convolutional architecture for fast feature embedding. In: ACMMM (2014)
53. Kingma, D.P., Ba, J.: Adam: a method for stochastic optimization. CoRR (2014)
54. Held, D., Thrun, S., Savarese, S.: Learning to track at 100 FPS with deep regression networks. In: Leibe, B., Matas, J., Sebe, N., Welling, M. (eds.) ECCV 2016. LNCS, vol. 9905, pp. 749–765. Springer, Cham (2016). https://doi.org/10.1007/978-3-319-46448-0_45
55. Hong, Z., Chen, Z., Wang, C., Mei, X., Prokhorov, D.V., Tao, D.: Multi-store tracker (muster): a cognitive psychology inspired approach to object tracking. In: CVPR (2015)
56. Zhang, J., Ma, S., Sclaroff, S.: MEEM: robust tracking via multiple experts using entropy minimization. In: Fleet, D., Pajdla, T., Schiele, B., Tuytelaars, T. (eds.) ECCV 2014. LNCS, vol. 8694, pp. 188–203. Springer, Cham (2014). https://doi.org/10.1007/978-3-319-10599-4_13

57. Gao, J., Ling, H., Hu, W., Xing, J.: Transfer learning based visual tracking with gaussian processes regression. In: Fleet, D., Pajdla, T., Schiele, B., Tuytelaars, T. (eds.) ECCV 2014. LNCS, vol. 8691, pp. 188–203. Springer, Cham (2014). https://doi.org/10.1007/978-3-319-10578-9_13
58. Tao, R., Gavves, E., Smeulders, A.W.M.: Siamese instance search for tracking. In: CVPR (2016)
59. Adam, A., Rivlin, E., Shimshoni, I.: Robust fragments-based tracking using the integral histogram. In: CVPR (2006)
60. Li, Y., Zhu, J.: A scale adaptive kernel correlation filter tracker with feature integration. In: Agapito, L., Bronstein, M.M., Rother, C. (eds.) ECCV 2014. LNCS, vol. 8926, pp. 254–265. Springer, Cham (2015). https://doi.org/10.1007/978-3-319-16181-5_18
61. Henriques, J.F., Caseiro, R., Martins, P., Batista, J.: Exploiting the circulant structure of tracking-by-detection with kernels. In: Fitzgibbon, A., Lazebnik, S., Perona, P., Sato, Y., Schmid, C. (eds.) ECCV 2012. LNCS, vol. 7575, pp. 702–715. Springer, Heidelberg (2012). https://doi.org/10.1007/978-3-642-33765-9_50
62. Kalal, Z., Mikolajczyk, K., Matas, J.: Tracking-learning-detection. IEEE Trans. Pattern Anal. Mach. Intell. 34(7), 1409–1422 (2012)
63. Bertinetto, L., Valmadre, J., Golodetz, S., Miksik, O., Torr, P.H.S.: Staple: complementary learners for real-time tracking. In: CVPR (2016)

Dist-GAN: An Improved GAN Using Distance Constraints

Ngoc-Trung Tran[✉][iD], Tuan-Anh Bui[iD], and Ngai-Man Cheung[iD]

ST Electronics - SUTD Cyber Security Laboratory, Singapore University
of Technology and Design, Singapore, Singapore
{ngoctrung_tran,tuananh_bui,ngaiman_cheung}@sutd.edu.sg

Abstract. We introduce effective training algorithms for Generative Adversarial Networks (GAN) to alleviate mode collapse and gradient vanishing. In our system, we constrain the generator by an Autoencoder (AE). We propose a formulation to consider the reconstructed samples from AE as "real" samples for the discriminator. This couples the convergence of the AE with that of the discriminator, effectively slowing down the convergence of discriminator and reducing gradient vanishing. Importantly, we propose two novel distance constraints to improve the generator. First, we propose a *latent-data distance constraint* to enforce compatibility between the latent sample distances and the corresponding data sample distances. We use this constraint to explicitly prevent the generator from mode collapse. Second, we propose a *discriminator-score distance constraint* to align the distribution of the generated samples with that of the real samples through the discriminator score. We use this constraint to guide the generator to synthesize samples that resemble the real ones. Our proposed GAN using these distance constraints, namely **Dist**-GAN, can achieve better results than state-of-the-art methods across benchmark datasets: synthetic, MNIST, MNIST-1K, CelebA, CIFAR-10 and STL-10 datasets. Our code is published here (https://github.com/tntrung/gan) for research.

Keywords: Generative Adversarial Networks · Image generation Distance constraints · Autoencoders

1 Introduction

Generative Adversarial Network [12] (GAN) has become a dominant approach for learning generative models. It can produce very visually appealing samples with few assumptions about the model. GAN can produce samples *without* explicitly estimating data distribution, e.g. in analytical forms. GAN has two main components which compete against each other, and they improve

Electronic supplementary material The online version of this chapter (https://doi.org/10.1007/978-3-030-01264-9_23) contains supplementary material, which is available to authorized users.

© Springer Nature Switzerland AG 2018
V. Ferrari et al. (Eds.): ECCV 2018, LNCS 11218, pp. 387–401, 2018.
https://doi.org/10.1007/978-3-030-01264-9_23

through the competition. The first component is the generator G, which takes low-dimensional random noise $z \sim P_z$ as an input and maps them into high-dimensional data samples, $x \sim P_x$. The prior distribution P_z is often uniform or normal. Simultaneously, GAN uses the second component, a discriminator D, to distinguish whether samples are drawn from the generator distribution P_G or data distribution P_x. Training GAN is an adversarial process: while the discriminator D learns to better distinguish the real or fake samples, the generator G learns to confuse the discriminator D into accepting its outputs as being real. The generator G uses discriminator's scores as feedback to improve itself over time, and eventually can approximate the data distribution.

Despite the encouraging results, GAN is known to be hard to train and requires careful designs of model architectures [11,24]. For example, the imbalance between discriminator and generator capacities often leads to convergence issues, such as gradient vanishing and mode collapse. Gradient vanishing occurs when the gradient of discriminator is saturated, and the generator has no informative gradient to learn. It occurs when the discriminator can distinguish very well between "real" and "fake" samples, before the generator can approximate the data distribution. Mode collapse is another crucial issue. In mode collapse, the generator is collapsed into a typical parameter setting that it always generates small diversity of samples.

Several GAN variants have been proposed [4,22,24,26,29] to solve these problems. Some of them are Autoencoders (AE) based GAN. AE explicitly encodes data samples into latent space and this allows representing data samples with lower dimensionality. It not only has the potential for stabilizing GAN but is also applicable for other applications, such as dimensionality reduction. AE was also used as part of a prominent class of generative models, Variational Autoencoders (VAE) [6,17,25], which are attractive for learning inference/generative models that lead to better log-likelihoods [28]. These encouraged many recent works following this direction. They applied either encoders/decoders as an inference model to improve GAN training [9,10,19], or used AE to define the discriminator objectives [5,30] or generator objectives [7,27]. Others have proposed to combine AE and GAN [18,21].

In this work, we propose a new design to unify AE and GAN. Our design can stabilize GAN training, alleviate the gradient vanishing and mode collapse issues, and better approximate data distribution. Our main contributions are two novel distance constraints to improve the generator. First, we propose a *latent-data distance constraint*. This enforces compatibility between latent sample distances and the corresponding data sample distances, and as a result, prevents the generator from producing many data samples that are close to each other, i.e. mode collapse. Second, we propose a *discriminator-score distance constraint*. This aligns the distribution of the fake samples with that of the real samples and guides the generator to synthesize samples that resemble the real ones. We propose a novel formulation to align the distributions through the discriminator score. Comparing to state of the art methods using synthetic and benchmark datasets, our method achieves better stability, balance, and competitive standard scores.

2   Related Works

The issue of non-convergence remains an important problem for GAN research, and gradient vanishing and mode collapse are the most important problems [3,11]. Many important variants of GAN have been proposed to tackle these issues. Improved GAN [26] introduced several techniques, such as feature matching, mini-batch discrimination, and historical averaging, which drastically reduced the mode collapse. Unrolled GAN [22] tried to change optimization process to address the convergence and mode collapse. [4] analyzed the convergence properties for GAN. Their proposed GAN variant, WGAN, leveraged the Wasserstein distance and demonstrated its better convergence than Jensen Shannon (JS) divergence, which was used previously in vanilla GAN [12]. However, WGAN required that the discriminator must lie on the space of 1-Lipschitz functions, therefore, it had to enforce norm critics to the discriminator by weight-clipping tricks. WGAN-GP [13] stabilized WGAN by alternating the weight-clipping by penalizing the gradient norm of the interpolated samples. Recent work SN-GAN [23] proposed a weight normalization technique, named as spectral normalization, to slow down the convergence of the discriminator. This method controls the Lipschitz constant by normalizing the spectral norm of the weight matrices of network layers.

Other work has integrated AE into the GAN. AAE [21] learned the inference by AE and matched the encoded latent distribution to given prior distribution by the minimax game between encoder and discriminator. Regularizing the generator with AE loss may cause the blurry issue. This regularization can not assure that the generator is able to approximate well data distribution and overcome the mode missing. VAE/GAN [18] combined VAE and GAN into one single model and used feature-wise distance for the reconstruction. Due to depending on VAE [17], VAEGAN also required re-parameterization tricks for back-propagation or required access to an exact functional form of prior distribution. InfoGAN [8] learned the disentangled representation by maximizing the mutual information for inducing latent codes. EBGAN [30] introduced the energy-based model, in which the discriminator is considered as energy function minimized via reconstruction errors. BEGAN [5] extended EBGAN by optimizing Wasserstein distance between AE loss distributions. ALI [10] and BiGAN [9] encoded the data into latent and trained jointly the data/latent samples in GAN framework. This model can learn implicitly encoder/decoder models after training. MDGAN [7] required two discriminators for two separate steps: manifold and diffusion. The manifold step tended to learn a good AE, and the diffusion objective is similar to the original GAN objective, except that the constructed samples are used instead of real samples.

In the literature, VAEGAN and MDGAN are most related to our work in term of using AE to improve the generator. However, our design is remarkably different: (1) VAEGAN combined KL divergence and reconstruction loss to train the inference model. With this design, it required an exact form of prior distribution and re-parameterization tricks for solving the optimization via back-propagation. In contrast, our method constrains AE by the data and latent sample distances. Our method is applicable to any prior distribution. (2) Unlike MDGAN, our design does not require two discriminators. (3) VAEGAN considered the reconstructed samples as "fake", and MDGAN adopts this similarly in its manifold step. In contrast, we use them as "real" samples, which is important to restrain the discriminator in order to avoid gradient vanishing, therefore, reduce mode collapse. (4) Two of these methods regularize G simply by reconstruction loss. This is inadequate to solve the mode collapse. We conduct an analysis and explain why additional regularization is needed for AE. Experiment results demonstrate that our model outperforms MDGAN and VAEGAN.

3   Proposed Method

Mode collapse is an important issue for GAN. In this section, we first propose a new way to visualize the mode collapse. Based on the visualization results, we propose a new model, namely Dist-GAN, to solve this problem.

3.1   Visualize Mode Collapse in Latent Space

Mode collapse occurs when "the generator collapses to a parameter setting where it always emits the same point. When collapse to a single mode is imminent, the gradient of the discriminator may point in similar directions for many similar points." [26]. Previous work usually examines mode collapse by visualizing a few collapsed samples (generated from random latent samples of a prior distribution). Figure 1a is an example. However, the data space is high-dimensional, therefore it is difficult to visualize points in the data space. On the other hand, the latent space is lower-dimensional and controllable, and it is possible to visualize the entire 2D/3D spaces. Thus, it could be advantageous to examine mode collapse in the latent space. However, the problem is that GAN is not invertible to map the data samples back to the latent space. Therefore, we propose the following method to visualize the samples and examine mode collapse in the latent space. We apply an off-the-shelf classifier. This classifier predicts labels of the generated samples. We visualize these class labels according to the latent samples, see Fig. 1b. This is possible because, for many datasets such as MNIST, pre-trained classifiers can achieve high accuracy, e.g. 0.04% error rate.

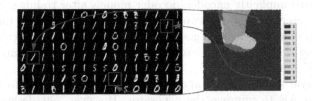

Fig. 1. (a) Mode collapse observed by data samples of the MNIST dataset, and (b) their corresponding latent samples of an uniform distribution. Mode collapse occurs frequently when the capacity of networks is small or the design of generator/discriminator networks is unbalance.

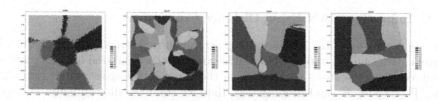

Fig. 2. Latent space visualization: The labels of 55 K 2D latent variables obtained by (a) DCGAN, (b) WGANGP, (c) our Dist-GAN$_2$ (without latent-data distance) and (d) our Dist-GAN$_3$ (with our proposed latent-data distance). The Dist-GAN settings are defined in the section of Experimental Results.

3.2   Distance Constraint: Motivation

Fig. 1b is the latent sample visualization using this technique, and the latent samples are uniformly distributed in a 2D latent space of $[-1, 1]$. Figure 1b clearly suggests the extent of mode collapse: many latent samples from large regions of latent space are collapsed into the same digit, e.g. '1'. Even some latent samples reside very far apart from each other, they map to the same digit. This suggests that a generator G_θ with parameter θ has mode collapse when there are many latent samples mapped to small regions of the data space:

$$x_i = G_\theta(z_i), x_j = G_\theta(z_j) : f(x_i, x_j) < \delta_x \qquad (1)$$

Here $\{z_i\}$ are latent samples, and $\{x_i\}$ are corresponding synthesized samples by G_θ. f is some distance metric in the data space, and δ_x is a small threshold in the data space. Therefore, we propose to address mode collapse using a distance metric g in latent space, and a small threshold δ_z of this metric, to restrain G_θ as follows:

$$g(z_i, z_j) > \delta_z \rightarrow f(x_i, x_j) > \delta_x \qquad (2)$$

However, determining good functions f, g for two spaces of different dimensionality and their thresholds δ_x, δ_z is not straightforward. Moreover, applying these constraints to GAN is not simple, because GAN has only one-way mapping from latent to data samples. In the next section, we will propose novel formulation to represent this constraint in latent-data distance and apply this to GAN.

We have also tried to apply this visualization for two state-of-the-art methods: DCGAN [24], WGANGP [13] on the MNIST dataset (using the code of [13]). Note that all of our experiments were conducted in the unsupervised setting. The off-the-shelf classifier is used here to determine the labels of generated samples solely for visualization purpose. Figure 2a and b represent the labels of the 55 K latent variables of DCGAN and WGANGP respectively at iteration of 70K. Figure 2a reveals that DCGAN is partially collapsed, as it generates very few digits '5' and '9' according to their latent variables near the bottom-right top-left corners of the prior distribution. In contrast, WGANGP does not have mode collapse, as shown in Fig. 2b. However, for WGANGP, the latent variables corresponding to each digit are fragmented in many sub-regions. It is an interesting observation for WGANGP. We will investigate this as our future work.

3.3   Improving GAN Using Distance Constraints

We apply the idea of Eq. 2 to improve generator through an AE. We apply AE to encode data samples into latent variables and use these encoded latent variables to direct the generator's mapping from the entire latent space. First, we train an AE (encoder E_ω and decoder G_θ), then we train the discriminator D_γ and the generator G_θ. Here, the generator is the decoder of AE and ω, θ, γ are the parameters of the encoder, generator, and discriminator respectively. Two main reasons for training an AE are: (i) to regularize the parameter θ at each training iteration, and (ii) to direct the generator to synthesize samples similar to real training samples. We include an additional *latent-data distance constraint* to train the AE:

$$\min_{\omega,\theta} L_R(\omega, \theta) + \lambda_r L_W(\omega, \theta) \qquad (3)$$

where $L_R(\omega, \theta) = ||x - G_\theta(E_\omega(x))||_2^2$ is the conventional AE objective. The latent-data distance constraint $L_W(\omega, \theta)$ is to regularize the generator and prevent it from being collapsed. This term will be discussed later. Here, λ_r is the constant. The reconstructed samples $G_\theta(E_\omega(x))$ can be approximated by $G_\theta(E_\omega(x)) = x + \varepsilon$, where ε is the reconstruction error. Usually the capacity of E and G are large enough so that ϵ is small (like noise). Therefore, it is reasonable to consider those reconstructed samples as "real" samples (plus noise ε). The pixel-wise reconstruction may cause blurry. To circumvent this, we instead use feature-wise distance [18] or similarly feature matching [26]: $L_R(\omega, \theta) = ||\Phi(x) - \Phi(G_\theta(E_\omega(x)))||_2^2$. Here $\Phi(x)$ is the high-level feature obtained from some middle layers of deep networks. In our implementation, $\Phi(x)$ is the feature output from the last convolution layer of discriminator D_γ. Note that in the first iteration, the parameters of discriminator are randomly initialized, and features produced from this discriminator is used to train the AE.

Our framework is shown in Fig. 3. We propose to train encoder E_ω, generator G_θ and discriminator D_γ following the order: (i) fix D_γ and train E_ω and G_θ to minimize the reconstruction loss Eq. 3 (ii) fix E_ω, G_θ, and train D_γ to minimize (Eq. 5), and (iii) fix E_ω, D_γ and train G_θ to minimize (Eq. 4).

Generator and Discriminator Objectives. When training the generator, maximizing the conventional generator objective $\mathbb{E}_z \sigma(D_\gamma(G_\theta(z)))$ [12] tends to produce samples at high-density modes, and this leads to mode collapse easily. Here, σ denotes the sigmoid function and $\mathbb{E}$ denotes the expectation. Instead, we train the generator with our proposed "discriminator-score distance". We align the synthesized sample distribution to real sample distribution with the ℓ_1 distance. The alignment is through the discriminator score, see Eq. 4. Ideally, the generator synthesizes samples similar to the samples drawn from the real distribution, and this also helps reduce missing mode issue.

$$\min_\theta \mathcal{L}_G(\theta) = |\mathbb{E}_x \sigma(D_\gamma(x)) - \mathbb{E}_z \sigma(D_\gamma(G_\theta(z)))| \qquad (4)$$

The objective function of the discriminator is shown in Eq. 5. It is different from original discriminator of GAN in two aspects. First, we indicate the reconstructed samples as "real", represented by the term $L_C = \mathbb{E}_x \log \sigma(D_\gamma(G_\theta(E_\omega(x))))$. Considering the reconstructed samples as "real" can systematically slow down the convergence of discriminator, so that the gradient from discriminator is not saturated too quickly. *In particular, the convergence of the discriminator is coupled with the convergence of AE.* This is an important constraint. In contrast, if we consider the reconstruction as "fake" in our model, this speeds up the discriminator convergence, and the discriminator converges faster than both generator and encoder. This leads to gradient saturation of D_γ. Second, we apply the gradient penalty $L_P = (||\nabla_{\hat{x}} D_\gamma(\hat{x})||_2^2 - 1)^2$ for the discriminator objective (Eq. 5), where λ_p is penalty coefficient, and $\hat{x} = \epsilon x + (1 - \epsilon)G(z)$, ϵ is a uniform random number $\epsilon \in U[0, 1]$. This penalty was used to enforce Lipschitz constraint of Wasserstein-1 distance [13]. In this work, we also find this useful for JS divergence and stabilizing our model. It should be noted that using this gradient penalty alone cannot solve the convergence issue, similar to WGANGP. The problem is partially solved when combining this with our proposed generator objective in Eq. 4, i.e., discriminator-score distance. However, the problem cannot be completely solved, e.g. mode collapse on MNIST dataset with 2D latent inputs as shown in Fig. 2c. Therefore, we apply the proposed latent-data distance constraints as additional regularization term for AE: $L_W(\omega, \theta)$, to be discussed in the next section.

$$\min_\gamma \mathcal{L}_D(\omega, \theta, \gamma) = -(\mathbb{E}_x \log \sigma(D_\gamma(x)) + \mathbb{E}_z \log(1 - \sigma(D_\gamma(G_\theta(z)))))$$
$$+ \mathbb{E}_x \log \sigma(D_\gamma(G_\theta(E_\omega(x)))) - \lambda_p \mathbb{E}_{\hat{x}}(||\nabla_{\hat{x}} D_\gamma(\hat{x})||_2^2 - 1)^2) \quad (5)$$

Regularizing Autoencoders by Latent-Data Distance Constraint. In this section, we discuss the latent-data distance constraint $L_W(\omega, \theta)$ to regularize AE in order to reduce mode collapse in the generator (the decoder in the AE). In particular, we use noise input to constrain encoder's outputs, and simultaneously reconstructed samples to constrain the generator's outputs. Mode collapse occurs when the generator synthesizes low diversity of samples in the data space given different latent inputs. Therefore, to reduce mode collapse, we aim to achieve: if the distance of any two latent variables $g(z_i, z_j)$ is small (large) in the latent space, the corresponding distance $f(x_i, x_j)$ in data space should be small (large), and vice versa. We propose a latent-data distance regularization $L_W(\omega, \theta)$:

$$L_W(\omega, \theta) = ||f(x, G_\theta(z)) - \lambda_w g(E_\omega(x), z)||_2^2 \quad (6)$$

where f and g are distance functions computed in data and latent space. λ_w is the scale factor due to the difference in dimensionality. It is not straight forward to compare distances in spaces of different dimensionality. Therefore, instead of using the direct distance functions, e.g. Euclidean, ℓ_1-norm, etc., we propose to compare the matching score $f(x, G_\theta(z))$ of real and fake distributions, and

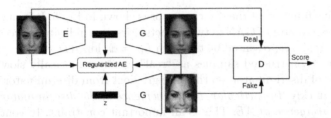

Fig. 3. The architecture of Dist-GAN includes Encoder (E), Generator (G) and Discriminator (D). Reconstructed samples are considered as "real". The input, reconstructed, and generated samples as well as the input noise and encoded latent are all used to form the latent-data distance constraint for AE (regularized AE).

the matching score $g(E_\omega(x), z)$ of two latent distributions. We use means as the matching scores. Specifically:

$$f(x, G_\theta(z)) = M_d(\mathbb{E}_x G_\theta(E_\omega(x)) - \mathbb{E}_z G_\theta(z)) \tag{7}$$

$$g(E_\omega(x), z) = M_d(\mathbb{E}_x E_\omega(x) - \mathbb{E}_z z) \tag{8}$$

where M_d computes the average of all dimensions of the input. Figure 4a illustrates 1D frequency density of 10000 random samples mapped by M_d from $[-1, 1]$ uniform distribution of different dimensionality. We can see that outputs of M_d from high dimensional spaces have small values. Thus, we require λ_w in (6) to account for the difference in dimensionality. Empirically, we found $\lambda_w = \sqrt{\frac{d_z}{d_x}}$ suitable, where d_z and d_x are dimensions of latent and data samples respectively. Figure 4b shows the frequency density of a collapse mode case. We can observe that the 1D density of generated samples is clearly different from that of the real data. Figure 4c compares 1D frequency densities of 55K MNIST samples generated by different methods. Our Dist-GAN method can estimate better 1D density than DCGAN and WGANGP measured by KL divergence (kldiv) between the densities of generated samples and real samples.

The entire algorithm is presented in Algorithm 1.

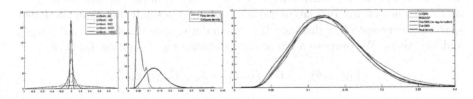

Fig. 4. (a) The 1D frequency density of outputs using M_d from uniform distribution of different dimensionality. (b) One example of the density when mode collapse occurs. (c) The 1D density of real data and generated data obtained by different methods: DCGAN (kldiv: 0.00979), WGANGP (kldiv: 0.00412), Dist-GAN$_2$ (without data-latent distance constraint of AE, kldiv: 0.01027), and Dist-GAN (kldiv: 0.00073).

Algorithm 1. Dist-GAN

1: Initialize discriminators, encoder and generator $D_\gamma, E_\omega, G_\theta$
2: **repeat**
3:     $\mathbf{x}^m \leftarrow$ Random minibatch of m data points from dataset.
4:     $\mathbf{z}^m \leftarrow$ Random m samples from noise distribution P_z
5:     // *Training encoder and generator using $\mathbf{x}^m$ and $\mathbf{z}^m$ by Eqn. 3*
6:     $\omega, \theta \leftarrow \min_{\omega,\theta} L_R(\omega, \theta) + \lambda_r L_W(\omega, \theta)$
7:     // *Training discriminators according to Eqn. 5 on $\mathbf{x}^m, \mathbf{z}^m$*
8:     $\gamma \leftarrow \min_\gamma \mathcal{L}_D(\omega, \theta, \gamma)$
9:     // *Training the generator on $\mathbf{x}^m, \mathbf{z}^m$ according to Eqn. 4.*
10:     $\theta \leftarrow \min_\theta \mathcal{L}_G(\theta)$
11: **until**
12: **return** $E_\omega, G_\theta, D_\gamma$

---

4 Experimental Results

4.1 Synthetic Data

All our experiments are conducted using the unsupervised setting. First, we use synthetic data to evaluate how well our Dist-GAN can approximate the data distribution. We use a synthetic dataset of 25 Gaussian modes in grid layout similar to [10]. Our dataset contains 50 K training points in 2D, and we draw 2 K generated samples for testing. For fair comparisons, we use equivalent architectures and setup for all methods in the same experimental condition if possible. The architecture and network size are similar to [22] on the 8-Gaussian dataset, except that we use one more hidden layer. We use fully-connected layers and Rectifier Linear Unit (ReLU) activation for input and hidden layers, sigmoid for output layers. The network size of encoder, generator and discriminator are presented in Table 1 of Supplementary Material, where $d_{in} = 2$, $d_{out} = 2$, $d_h = 128$ are dimensions of input, output and hidden layers respectively. $N_h = 3$ is the number of hidden layers. The output dimension of the encoder is the dimension of the latent variable. Our prior distribution is uniform $[-1, 1]$. We use Adam optimizer with learning rate lr $= 0.001$, and the exponent decay rate of first moment $\beta_1 = 0.8$. The learning rate is decayed every $10K$ steps with a base of 0.9. The mini-batch size is 128. The training stops after 500 epochs. To have fair comparison, we carefully fine-tune other methods (and use weight decay during training if this achieves better results) to ensure they achieve their best results on the synthetic data. For evaluation, a mode is missed if there are less than 20 generated samples registered into this mode, which is measured by its mean and variance of 0.01 [19,22]. A method has mode collapse if there are missing modes. In this experiment, we fix the parameters $\lambda_r = 0.1$ (Eq. 3), $\lambda_p = 0.1$ (Eq. 5), $\lambda_w = 1.0$ (Eq. 6). For each method, we repeat eight runs and report the average.

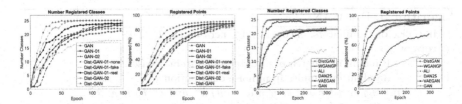

Fig. 5. From left to right figures: (a), (b), (c), (d). The number of registered modes (a) and points (b) of our method with two different settings on the synthetic dataset. We compare our Dist-GAN to the baseline GAN [12] and other methods on the same dataset measured by the number of registered modes (classes) (c) and points (d).

First, we highlight the capability of our model to approximate the distribution P_x of synthetic data. We carry out the ablation experiment to understand the influence of each proposed component with different settings:

- Dist-GAN$_1$: uses the "discriminator-score distance" for generator objective ($\mathcal{L}_G$) and the AE loss L_R but does not use data-latent distance constraint term (L_W) and gradient penalty (L_P). This setting has three different versions as using reconstructed samples (L_C) as "real", "fake" or "none" (not use it) in the discriminator objective.
- Dist-GAN$_2$: improves from Dist-GAN$_1$ (regarding reconstructed samples as "real") by adding the gradient penalty L_P.
- Dist-GAN: improves the Dist-GAN$_2$ by adding the data-latent distance constraint L_W. (See Table 3 in Supplementary Material for details).

The quantitative results are shown in Fig. 5. Figure 5a is the number of registered modes changing over the training. Dist-GAN$_1$ misses a few modes while Dist-GAN$_2$ and Dist-GAN generates all 25 modes after about 50 epochs. Since they almost do not miss any modes, it is reasonable to compare the number of registered points as in Fig. 5b. Regarding reconstructed samples as "real" achieves better results than regarding them as "fake" or "none". It is reasonable that Dist-GAN$_1$ obtains similar results as the baseline GAN when not using the reconstructed samples in discriminator objective ("none" option). Other results show the improvement when adding the gradient penalty into the discriminator (Dist-GAN$_2$). Dist-GAN demonstrates the effectiveness of using the proposed latent-data constraints, when comparing with Dist-GAN$_2$.

To highlight the effectiveness of our proposed "discriminator-score distance" for the generator, we use it to improve the baseline GAN [12], denoted by GAN$_1$. Then, we propose GAN$_2$ to improve GAN$_1$ by adding the gradient penalty. We can observe that combination of our proposed generator objective and gradient penalty can improve stability of GAN. We compare our best setting (Dist-GAN) to previous work. ALI [10] and DAN-2S [19] are recent works using encoder/decoder in their model. VAE-GAN [18] introduces a similar model. WGAN-GP [13] is one of the current state of the art. The numbers of covered modes and registered points are presented in Fig. 5c and Fig. 5d respectively.

The quantitative numbers of last epochs are shown in Table 2 of Supplementary Material. In this table, we report also Total Variation scores to measure the mode balance. The result for each method is the average of eight runs. Our method outperforms GAN [12], DAN-2S [19], ALI [10], and VAE/GAN [18] on the number of covered modes. While WGAN-GP sometimes misses one mode and diverges, our method (Dist-GAN) does not suffer from mode collapse in all eight runs. Furthermore, we achieve a higher number of registered samples than WGAN-GP and all others. Our method is also better than the rest with Total Variation (TV) [19]. Figure 6 depicts the detail proportion of generated samples of 25 modes. (More visualization of generated samples in Section 2 of Supplementary Material).

4.2 MNIST-1K

For image datasets, we use $\Phi(x)$ instead x for the reconstruction loss and the latent-data distance constraint in order to avoid the blur. We fix the parameters $\lambda_p = 1.0$, and $\lambda_r = 1.0$ for all image datasets that work consistently well. The λ_w is automatically computed from dimensions of features $\Phi(x)$ and latent samples. Our model implementation for MNIST uses the published code of WGAN-GP [13]. Figure 7 from left to right are the real samples, the generated samples and the frequency of each digit generated by our method for standard MNIST. It demonstrates that our method can approximate well the MNIST digit distribution. Moreover, our generated samples look realistic with different styles and strokes that resemble the real ones. In addition, we follow the procedure in [22] to construct a more challenging 1000-class MNIST (MNIST-1K) dataset. It has 1000 modes from 000 to 999. We create a total of 25,600 images. We compare methods by counting the number of covered modes (having at least one sample [22]) and computing KL divergence. To be fair, we adopt the equivalent network architecture (low-capacity generator and two crippled discriminators K/4 and K/2) as proposed by [22]. Table 1 presents the number of modes and KL divergence of compared methods. Results show that our method outperforms

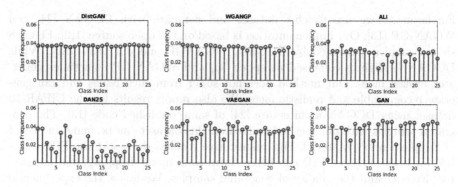

Fig. 6. The mode balance obtained by different methods.

all others in the number of covered modes, especially with the low-capacity dis-criminator (K/4 architecture), where our method has 150 modes more than the second best. Our method reduces the gap between the two architectures (e.g. about 60 modes), which is smaller than other methods. For both architectures, we obtain better results for both KL divergence and the number of recovered modes. All results support that our proposed Dist-GAN handles better mode collapse, and is robust even in case of imbalance in generator and discriminator.

Fig. 7. The real and our generated samples in one mini-batch. And the number of gen-erated samples per class obtained by our method on the MNIST dataset. We compare our frequency of generated samples to the ground-truth via KL divergence: KL = 0.01.

Table 1. The comparison on MNIST-1K of methods. We follow the setup and network architectures from Unrolled GAN.

Architecture	GAN	Unrolled GAN	WGAN-GP	Dist-GAN
K/4, #	30.6 ± 20.7	372.2 ± 20.7	640.1 ± 136.3	859.5 ± 68.7
K/4, KL	5.99 ± 0.04	4.66 ± 0.46	1.97 ± 0.70	1.04 ± 0.29
K/2, #	628.0 ± 140.9	817.4 ± 39.9	772.4 ± 146.5	917.9 ± 69.6
K/2, KL	2.58 ± 0.75	1.43 ± 0.12	1.35 ± 0.55	1.06 ± 0.23

5   CelebA, CIFAR-10 and STL-10 Datasets

Furthermore, we use CelebA dataset and compare with DCGAN [24] and WGAN-GP [13]. Our implementation is based on the open source [1,2]. Figure 8 shows samples generated by DCGAN, WGANGP and our Dist-GAN. While DCGAN is slightly collapsed at epoch 50, and WGAN-GP sometimes gener-ates broken faces. Our method does not suffer from such issues and can gen-erate recognizable and realistic faces. We also report results for the CIFAR-10 dataset using DCGAN architecture [24] of same published code [13]. The gen-erated samples with our method trained on this dataset can be found in Sect. 4 of Supplementary Material. For quantitative results, we report the FID scores [15] for both datasets. FID can detect intra-class mode dropping, and measure the diversity and the quality of generated samples. We follow the experimental procedure and model architecture in [20]. Our method outperforms others for both CelebA and CIFAR-10, as shown in the first and second rows of Table 2.

Fig. 8. Generated samples of DCGAN (50 epochs, results from [1]), WGAN-GP (50 epochs, results from [1]) and our Dist-GAN (50 epochs).

Here, the results of other GAN methods are from [20]. We also report FID score of VAEGAN on these datasets. Our method is better than VAEGAN. Note that we have also tried MDGAN, but it has serious mode collapsed for both these datasets. Therefore, we do not report its result in our paper.

Lastly, we compare our model with recent SN-GAN [23] on CIFAR-10 and STL-10 datasets with standard CNN architecture. Experimental setup is the same as [23], and FID is the score for the comparison. Results are presented in the third to fifth rows of Table 2. In addition to settings reported using synthetic dataset, we have additional settings and ablation study for image datasets, which are reported in Section 5 of Supplementary Material. The results confirm the stability of our model, and our method outperforms SN-GAN on the CIFAR-10 dataset. Interestingly, when we replace "log" by "hinge loss" functions in the discriminator as in [23], our "hinge loss" version performs even better with FID = 22.95, compared to FID = 25.5 of SN-GAN. It is worth noting that our model is trained with the default parameters $\lambda_p = 1.0$ and $\lambda_r = 1.0$. Our generator requires about 200 K iterations with the mini-batch size of 64. When we apply our "hinge loss" version on STL-10 dataset similar to [23], our model can achieve the FID score 36.19 for this dataset, which is also better than SN-GAN (FID = 43.2).

Table 2. Comparing FID score to other methods. First two rows (CelebA, CIFAR-10) follow the experimental setup of [20], and the remaining rows follow the experimental setup of [23] using standard CNN architectures.

	NS GAN	LSGAN	WGANGP	BEGAN	VAEGAN	SN-GAN	Dist-GAN
CelebA	58.0 ± 2.7	53.6 ± 4.2	26.8 ± 1.2	38.1 ± 1.1	27.5 ± 1.9	-	23.7 ± 0.3
CIFAR-10	58.6 ± 2.1	67.1 ± 2.9	52.9 ± 1.3	71.4 ± 1.1	58.1 ± 3.2	-	45.6 ± 1.2
CIFAR-10	-	-	-	-	-	29.3	28.23
CIFAR-10 (hinge)	-	-	-	-	-	25.5	22.95
STL-10 (hinge)	-	-	-	-	-	43.2	36.19

6   Conclusion

We propose a robust AE-based GAN model with novel distance constraints, called Dist-GAN, that can address the mode collapse and gradient vanishing effectively. Our model is different from previous work: (i) We propose a new generator objective using "discriminator-score distance". (ii) We propose to couple the convergence of the discriminator with that of the AE by considering reconstructed samples as "real" samples. (iii) We propose to regularize AE by "latent-data distance constraint" in order to prevent the generator from falling into mode collapse settings. Extensive experiments demonstrate that our method can approximate multi-modal distributions. Our method reduces drastically the mode collapse for MNIST-1K. Our model is stable and does not suffer from mode collapse for MNIST, CelebA, CIFAR-10 and STL-10 datasets. Furthermore, we achieve better FID scores than previous works. These demonstrate the effectiveness of the proposed Dist-GAN. Future work applies our proposed Dist-GAN to different computer vision tasks [14,16].

Acknowledgement. This work was supported by both ST Electronics and the National Research Foundation(NRF), Prime Minister's Office, Singapore under Corporate Laboratory @ University Scheme (Programme Title: STEE Infosec - SUTD Corporate Laboratory).

References

1. https://github.com/LynnHo/DCGAN-LSGAN-WGAN-WGAN-GP-Tensorflow
2. https://github.com/carpedm20/DCGAN-tensorflow
3. Arjovsky, M., Bottou, L.: Towards principled methods for training generative adversarial networks. arXiv preprint arXiv:1701.04862 (2017)
4. Arjovsky, M., Chintala, S., Bottou, L.: Wasserstein generative adversarial networks. In: ICML (2017)
5. Berthelot, D., Schumm, T., Metz, L.: Began: boundary equilibrium generative adversarial networks. arXiv preprint arXiv:1703.10717 (2017)
6. Burda, Y., Grosse, R., Salakhutdinov, R.: Importance weighted autoencoders. arXiv preprint arXiv:1509.00519 (2015)
7. Che, T., Li, Y., Jacob, A.P., Bengio, Y., Li, W.: Mode regularized generative adversarial networks. CoRR (2016)
8. Chen, X., Duan, Y., Houthooft, R., Schulman, J., Sutskever, I., Abbeel, P.: Infogan: interpretable representation learning by information maximizing generative adversarial nets. In: Advances in Neural Information Processing Systems, pp. 2172–2180 (2016)
9. Donahue, J., Krähenbühl, P., Darrell, T.: Adversarial feature learning. arXiv preprint arXiv:1605.09782 (2016)
10. Dumoulin, V., et al.: Adversarially learned inference. arXiv preprint arXiv:1606.00704 (2016)
11. Goodfellow, I.: Nips 2016 tutorial: generative adversarial networks. arXiv preprint arXiv:1701.00160 (2016)
12. Goodfellow, I., et al.: Generative adversarial nets. In: NIPS, pp. 2672–2680 (2014)

13. Gulrajani, I., Ahmed, F., Arjovsky, M., Dumoulin, V., Courville, A.C.: Improved training of wasserstein gans. In: Advances in Neural Information Processing Systems, pp. 5767–5777 (2017)
14. Guo, Y., Cheung, N.M.: Efficient and deep person re-identification using multi-level similarity. In: CVPR (2012)
15. Heusel, M., Ramsauer, H., Unterthiner, T., Nessler, B., Hochreiter, S.: GANS trained by a two time-scale update rule converge to a local nash equilibrium. In: Advances in Neural Information Processing Systems, pp. 6626–6637 (2017)
16. Hoang, T., Do, T.T., Le Tan, D.K., Cheung, N.M.: Selective deep convolutional features for image retrieval. In: Proceedings of the 2017 ACM on Multimedia Conference, pp. 1600–1608. ACM (2017)
17. Kingma, D.P., Welling, M.: Auto-encoding variational bayes. arXiv preprint arXiv:1312.6114 (2013)
18. Larsen, A.B.L., Sønderby, S.K., Larochelle, H., Winther, O.: Autoencoding beyond pixels using a learned similarity metric. arXiv preprint arXiv:1512.09300 (2015)
19. Li, C., Alvarez-Melis, D., Xu, K., Jegelka, S., Sra, S.: Distributional adversarial networks. arXiv preprint arXiv:1706.09549 (2017)
20. Lucic, M., Kurach, K., Michalski, M., Gelly, S., Bousquet, O.: Are gans created equal? a large-scale study. CoRR (2017)
21. Makhzani, A., Shlens, J., Jaitly, N., Goodfellow, I.: Adversarial autoencoders. In: International Conference on Learning Representations (2016)
22. Metz, L., Poole, B., Pfau, D., Sohl-Dickstein, J.: Unrolled generative adversarial networks. In: ICLR (2017)
23. Miyato, T., Kataoka, T., Koyama, M., Yoshida, Y.: Spectral normalization for generative adversarial networks. In: ICLR (2018)
24. Radford, A., Metz, L., Chintala, S.: Unsupervised representation learning with deep convolutional generative adversarial networks. arXiv preprint arXiv:1511.06434 (2015)
25. Rezende, D.J., Mohamed, S., Wierstra, D.: Stochastic backpropagation and approximate inference in deep generative models. In: ICML, pp. 1278–1286 (2014)
26. Salimans, T., Goodfellow, I., Zaremba, W., Cheung, V., Radford, A., Chen, X.: Improved techniques for training gans. In: NIPS, pp. 2234–2242 (2016)
27. Warde-Farley, D., Bengio, Y.: Improving generative adversarial networks with denoising feature matching. In: ICLR (2017)
28. Wu, Y., Burda, Y., Salakhutdinov, R., Grosse, R.: On the quantitative analysis of decoder-based generative models. In: ICLR (2017)
29. Yazıcı, Y., Foo, C.S., Winkler, S., Yap, K.H., Piliouras, G., Chandrasekhar, V.: The unusual effectiveness of averaging in gan training. arXiv preprint arXiv:1806.04498 (2018)
30. Zhao, J., Mathieu, M., LeCun, Y.: Energy-based generative adversarial network. In: ICLR (2017)

Pivot Correlational Neural Network for Multimodal Video Categorization

Sunghun Kang[1], Junyeong Kim[1], Hyunsoo Choi[2], Sungjin Kim[2],
and Chang D. Yoo[1]([⊠])

[1] KAIST, Daejeon, South Korea
{sunghun.kang,junyeong.kim,cd_yoo}@kaist.ac.kr
[2] Samsung Electronics Co., Ltd., Seoul, South Korea
{hsu.choi,sj9373.kim}@samsung.com

Abstract. This paper considers an architecture for multimodal video categorization referred to as Pivot Correlational Neural Network (Pivot CorrNN). The architecture consists of modal-specific streams dedicated exclusively to one specific modal input as well as modal-agnostic pivot stream that considers all modal inputs without distinction, and the architecture tries to refine the pivot prediction based on modal-specific predictions. The Pivot CorrNN consists of three modules: (1) maximizing pivot-correlation module that maximizes the correlation between the hidden states as well as the predictions of the modal-agnostic pivot stream and modal-specific streams in the network, (2) contextual Gated Recurrent Unit (cGRU) module which extends the capability of a generic GRU to take multimodal inputs in updating the pivot hidden-state, and (3) adaptive aggregation module that aggregates all modal-specific predictions as well as the modal-agnostic pivot predictions into one final prediction. We evaluate the Pivot CorrNN on two publicly available large-scale multimodal video categorization datasets, FCVID and YouTube-8M. From the experimental results, Pivot CorrNN achieves the best performance on the FCVID database and performance comparable to the state-of-the-art on YouTube-8M database.

Keywords: Video categorization · Multimodal representation
Sequential modeling · Deep learning

1 Introduction

Multimodal video categorization is a task for predicting the categories of a given video based on different modal inputs which may have been captured using diverse mixture of sensors and softwares in securing different modalities of the video. Figure 1 shows four video examples from the FCVID dataset with groundtruth and top 3 scores obtained from the proposed algorithm referred to as Pivot CorrNN. Fortifying and supplementing among different modalities for more accurate overall prediction is a key technology that can drive future innovation in better understanding and recognizing the contents in a video. Emerging applications includes video surveillance, video recommendation, autonomous

© Springer Nature Switzerland AG 2018
V. Ferrari et al. (Eds.): ECCV 2018, LNCS 11218, pp. 402–417, 2018.
https://doi.org/10.1007/978-3-030-01264-9_24

driving and sports video analysis system. The use of deep Convolutional Neural Networks (CNNs) has lead to many dramatic progress across different tasks but generally confined to a single modality- often in the form of an image, speech or text- with an optional association with an auxiliary modality such as a text query. Indeed, studies leveraging on synergistic relationship across multiple modalities have been scarce so far.

Considerable studies have been dedicated to the topic of video categorization, but these have mainly been visual. Auditory modality has very often been ignored. Some notable past studies have focused on spatio-temporal visual representation. Karpathy *et al.* [19] trained a deep CNN on large video dataset while investigating the effectiveness of various temporal fusion. Tran *et al.* [29] extended conventional two dimensional convolution operation to three dimensional for considering spatio-temporal information in a video.

Other studies have focused on utilizing motion modality alongside with visual appearance modality. Donahue *et al.* [9] studied and compared the behaviors of various configurations of CNN-LSTM combination. Here, the outputs of two CNN-LSTM combination- one taking RGB image as input while the other taking flow image- are merged in making the final prediction. In the two stream networks [10,11,25], two separate CNN streams- one taking static image as input while the other taking optical flow- are considered, and intermediate features of the two streams leading up to the final prediction are fused either by the summation [10] or multiplicative operations [11].

Auditory modality has also been considered in a minor way. Jiang *et al.* [18] proposed regularized DNN (rDNN) which jointly exploits the feature (including audio features) and class relationship to model video semantics. Miech *et al.* [23] considered an architecture with two learnable pooling layers- one taking visual input while the other taking audio input- that are merged by a fully connected layer and gated for final prediction.

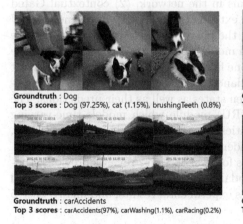

Groundtruth : Dog
Top 3 scores : Dog (97.25%), cat (1.15%), brushingTeeth (0.8%)

Groundtruth : carAccidents
Top 3 scores : carAccidents(97%), carWashing(1.1%), carRacing(0.2%)

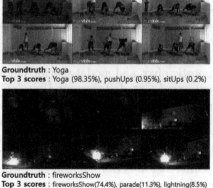

Groundtruth : Yoga
Top 3 scores : Yoga (98.35%), pushUps (0.95%), sitUps (0.2%)

Groundtruth : fireworksShow
Top 3 scores : fireworksShow(74.4%), parade(11.3%), lightning(8.5%)

Fig. 1. Four video examples from the FCVID dataset with groundtruth and top3 scores obtained from the proposed algorithm referred to as Pivot CorrNN.

Although considerable advances have been made in video categorization, there are still many unresolved issues to be investigated. First, it is often difficult to determine the relationship among heterogeneous modalities especially when the modalities involved in different entities such that it is difficult to determine the relationship between the modalities. For example, static image and its optical flow which involve a common entity- in this case, the pixels- can be easily be fused in the same spatial domain, while it is non-trvial to learn the relationship between static images and audio signals of the video. Second, multimodal sequential modeling should consider the complementary relationship between modalities with their contextual information. Information relevant for categorization vary across time due to various reasons such as occlusion and noise. It maybe more appropriate to emphasize one modality over the other. Third, depending on the category, one modality will provide far more significant information about the category than the other, and this needs to be taken into account. Most categories are defined well in the visual domain while there are categories better defined in the auditory domain. As depicted by Wang et al. [31], in most of the misclassification cases, there exists one modality that is failing while the other is correct. In this case, it is necessary to develop a model considering the level of confidence for each modality prediction.

To overcome the above issues, this paper considers an architecture for multimodal video categorization referred to as Pivot Correlational Neural Network (Pivot CorrNN). It is trained to maximize the correlation between the hidden states as well as the predictions of the modal-agnostic pivot stream and modal-specific streams in the network, and to refine the pivot prediction based on modal-specific predictions. Here, the modal-agnostic pivot hidden state considers all modal inputs without distinction while the modal-specific hidden state is dedicated exclusively to one specific modal input. The Pivot CorrNN consists of three modules: (1) maximizing pivot-correlation module that attempts to maximally correlate the hidden states as well as the predictions of the modal-agnostic pivot stream and modal-specific streams in the network, (2) contextual Gated Recurrent Unit (cGRU) module which extends the capability of a generic GRU to take multimodal inputs in updating the pivot hidden-state, and (3) adaptive aggregation module that aggregates all modal-specific predictions as well as the modal-agnostic pivot predictions into one final prediction. The maximizing pivot correlation module that provides guidance for co-occurrence between modal-agnostic pivot and modal-specific hidden states as well as their predictions. The contextual Gated Recurrent Unit (cGRU) module which models time-varying contextual information among modalities. When making the final prediction, the adaptive aggregation module considers the confidence of each modality.

The rest of the paper is organized as follows. Section 2 reviews previous studies on video categorization and multimodal learning. Section 3 discusses proposed architecture in detail. Section 4 presents experimental results, and finally, Sect. 5 concludes the paper.

2   Multimodal Learning

In this section, multimodal learning is briefly reviewed. Some related works on multimodal representation learning are introduced.

Deep learning has been shown to have the capability to model multiple modalities for useful representations [3,24,27]. Generally speaking, the mainstream of multimodal representation learning falls into two methods: joint representation learning and coordinated representation learning. In joint representation learning, the input modalities are concatenated, element-wise summed or element-wise multiplied to produce synergy in improving final performance. While in coordinated representation learning, each of the modalities is transformed separately noting the similarity among the different modalities.

Research focus on the first method aims to make joint representation using various first and second order interactions between features. Ngiam et al. [24] propose a deep autoencoder based architecture for joint representation learning of video and audio modality. Self-reconstruction and cross-reconstruction are utilized to learn joint representation for audio-visual speech recognition. Srivastava et al. [27] propose a Deep Boltzmann Machine (DBM) based architecture to learn a joint density model over the space of multimodal inputs. Joint representation can be obtained even though there exist some missing modalities through Gibbs sampling. Antol et al. [4] propose deep neural network based architecture for VQA. The element-wise multiplication is performed to fuse image features and text features and obtain joint representation. Outer product is also used to fuse input modalities [6,13,20]. Since the fully parameterized bilinear model (using the outer product) becomes intractable due to the number of parameters, simplification or approximation of model complexity is needed. Fukui et al. [13] project outer product to lower dimensional space using count-sketch projection, Kim et al. [20] constrain the rank of resulting tensor and Ben-Younes et al. [6] utilize tucker decomposition to reduce the number of parameters while preserving the model complexity.

Research focus on the second method aims to make separate representation, and a loss function is incorporated to reduce the distance between the representations. Similarity measure such as inner product or cosine similarity can be used for coordinated representation. Weston et al. [32] propose WSABIE which uses inner product to measure similarity. The inner product between image feature and textual feature is calculated and maximized so that corresponding image and annotation would have a high similarity between them. Frome et al. [12] propose DeViSE for visual-semantic embedding. DeViSE uses a hinge ranking loss function and an inner product similar to WSABIE but utilizes deep architecture to extract the image and textual feature. Huang et al. [16] utilize cosine similarity to measure the similarity between query and document. The similarity is directly used to predict posterior probability among documents. Research focus on coordinated representation is based on canonical correlation analysis (CCA) [15]. The CCA is the methods that aim to learn separate representation for each modality while the correlation between them is maximized simultaneously. Andrew et al. [3] propose Deep CCA (DCCA) which is a DNN extension of CCA. The DCCA learns a nonlinear projection using deep networks such

that the resulting representations are highly linearly correlated with different
view images. Wang *et al.* [30] propose deep canonically correlated autoencoders
(DCCAE) which is a DNN-based model combining CCA and autoencoder-based
terms. The DCCAE jointly optimizes autoencoder (AE) objective (reconstruction error) and canonical correlation objective. Chandar *et al.* [7] propose correlational neural networks (CorrNet) which is similar to the DCCAE in terms
of jointly using reconstruction objective and correlation maximization objective.
However, CorrNet only maximizes the empirical correlation within a mini-batch
instead of CCA constraints maximizing canonical correlation.

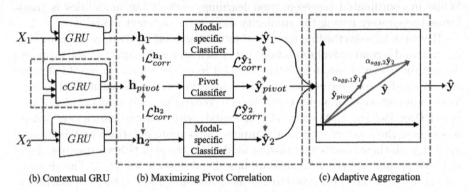

(b) Contextual GRU   (b) Maximizing Pivot Correlation   (c) Adaptive Aggregation

Fig. 2. Block diagram of the proposed Pivot CorrNN in a bi-modal scenario. The
Pivot CorrNN is composed of three modules: (a) Contextual Gated Recurrent Unit,
(b) Maximizing Pivot Correlations, and (c) Adaptive Aggregation

3   Pivot Correlational Neural Network

In this section, the Pivot CorrNN and its modules are described. The proposed
Pivot CorrNN is composed of three modules: contextual GRU (cGRU) module,
maximizing pivot correlation module and adaptive aggregation module. The proposed Pivot CorrNN can be generalized for M modalities using M modal-specific
GRUs and one modal-agnostic cGRU with its classifie.

Figure 2 shows the overall block diagram of the Pivot CorrNN illustrating the
connections between modules for sequential bi-modal scenario. In the sequential
bi-modal case which involves two sequential modal inputs $X_1 = \{\mathbf{x_1^t}\}_{t=1}^T$ and
$X_2 = \{\mathbf{x_2^t}\}_{t=1}^T$, the Pivot CorrNN fuses the two inputs and then predicts a label
$\hat{\mathbf{y}}$ corresponding to the two inputs. Two GRUs and one cGRU are utilized for
obtaining two separate modal-specific hidden states ($\mathbf{h}_1$ and $\mathbf{h}_2$) and one pivot
hidden state $\mathbf{h}_{pivot}$. Each hidden state is fed to its classifier for predicting cor-
responding labels ($\hat{\mathbf{y}}_1$, $\hat{\mathbf{y}}_2$, and $\hat{\mathbf{y}}_{pivot}$). During training proposed Pivot CorrNN,

maximizing pivot correlation module measures the correlations on both hidden state and label prediction between modal-specific and modal-agnostic pivot, and maximizes them. To produce final prediction $\hat{y}$, adaptive aggregation module is involved.

The details of proposed the cGRU, maximizing pivot correlation, and adaptive aggregation modules are introduced in Sects. 3.1, 3.2, and 3.3, respectively.

3.1 Contextual Gated Recurrent Units (cGRU)

The proposed contextual GRU (cGRU) is an extension of the GRU [8] that combines many modal inputs into one by concatenating the weighted inputs before the usual process of GRU takes over. The weight place on a particular modal input is determined by considering the hidden state of the cGRU and other modal inputs excluding itse.

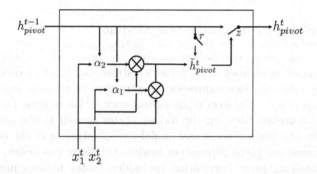

Fig. 3. Illustration of the cGRU. Gating masks α_1, and α_2 are introduced to control contextual flow of each modality input based on previous hidden pivot state and other modality input.

Figure 3 illustrates a particular cGRU taking two modal inputs $\mathbf{x}_1^t$ and $\mathbf{x}_2^t$ at time step t and updating its hidden state $\mathbf{h}_{pivot}^{t-1}$ to $\mathbf{h}_{pivot}^t$. After going through all the input sequence from $t = 1$ through $t = T$, the final modal-agnostic pivot hidden-state $\mathbf{h}_{pivot}$ is presented to the pivot classifier.

To model time-varying contextual information of each modality, two learnable sub-neural networks within cGRU are introduced. Each input modality is gated by considering the input of the other modality in the context of previous hidden pivot state $\mathbf{h}_{pivot}^{t-1}$. The gated inputs are concatenated in constructing the update gate masks as well as reset gate and the hidden pivot state. The hidden pivot state are updated in the usual GRU manner.

$$\alpha_1 = \sigma(W_{\alpha_1 h} \mathbf{h}^{t-1}_{pivot} + W_{\alpha_1 x} \mathbf{x}^t_2 + b_{\alpha_1}),$$
$$\alpha_2 = \sigma(W_{\alpha_2 h} \mathbf{h}^{t-1}_{pivot} + W_{\alpha_2 x} \mathbf{x}^t_1 + b_{\alpha_2}),$$
$$\mathbf{x}^t = [\alpha_1 \odot \mathbf{x}^t_1; \alpha_2 \odot \mathbf{x}^t_2],$$
$$\mathbf{z}^t = \sigma(W_{zh} \mathbf{h}^{t-1}_{pivot} + W_{zx} \mathbf{x}^t + b_z),$$
$$\mathbf{r}^t = \sigma(W_{rh} \mathbf{h}^{t-1}_{pivot} + W_{rx} \mathbf{x}^t + b_r),$$
$$\tilde{\mathbf{h}}^t_{pivot} = \varphi(W_{hx} \mathbf{x}^t + W_{hh}(\mathbf{r}^t \odot \mathbf{h}^{t-1}_{pivot}) + b_h),$$
$$\mathbf{h}^t_{pivot} = (1 - \mathbf{z}^t) \odot \mathbf{h}^{t-1}_{pivot} + \mathbf{z}^t \odot \tilde{\mathbf{h}}^t_{pivot},$$

where σ, φ are logistic sigmoid and hyperbolic tangent function respectively. Here, $\odot$ denotes the Hadamard product. $\mathbf{x}^t$ is the modulated input using gating masks. $\mathbf{z}^t, \mathbf{r}^t$ are the update and reset gates at time t, which are the same as original GRU. $\mathbf{h}_{pivot}$ and $\tilde{\mathbf{h}}_{pivot}$ are modal-agnostic pivot hidden state and its internal candidate hidden pivot state.

3.2   Maximizing Pivot Correlation Module

The maximizing pivot correlation module is proposed for capturing co-occurrence among modalities in both hidden states and label predictions during training. The co-occurrence expresses co-activation of neurons among modal-specific hidden states. The maximizing pivot-correlation module that attempts to maximally correlate between the hidden states as well as the predictions of the modal-agnostic pivot stream and modal-specific streams in the network The details of maximizing pivot correlation module is followed as below.

The maximizing pivot correlation in hidden states utilizes modal-specific states $\mathbf{h}_1$, and $\mathbf{h}_2$ and modal-agnostic pivot hidden state $\mathbf{h}^T_{pivot}$. The pivot correlation objective on the m-th modality hidden state $\mathcal{L}^{\mathbf{h}_m}_{corr}$ is defined as follows:

$$\mathcal{L}^{\mathbf{h}_m}_{corr} = \frac{\sum_{i=1}^N (\mathbf{h}_{m,i} - \bar{\mathbf{h}}_m)(\mathbf{h}_{pivot,i} - \bar{\mathbf{h}}_{pivot})}{\sqrt{\sum_{i=1}^N (\mathbf{h}_{m,i} - \bar{\mathbf{h}}_m)^2 \sum_{i=1}^N (\mathbf{h}_{pivot,i} - \bar{\mathbf{h}}_{pivot})^2}},$$

where the subscript i denotes the sample index. Here, $\bar{\mathbf{h}}_m = \frac{1}{N} \sum_{i=1}^N \mathbf{h}_{m,i}$ and $\bar{\mathbf{h}}_{pivot} = \frac{1}{N} \sum_{i=1}^N \mathbf{h}_{pivot,i}$ are the averages of the modal-specific and modal-agnostic hidden states, respectively. Here, $\mathbf{h}_{m,i}$ denotes the hidden state of the m-th modality of the i-th samples.

For maximizing pivot correlation objective in label predictions $\mathcal{L}^{\hat{\mathbf{y}}_m}_{corr}$ is defined as follows:

$$\mathcal{L}^{\hat{\mathbf{y}}_m}_{corr} = \frac{\sum_{i=1}^N (\hat{\mathbf{y}}_{m,i} - \bar{\mathbf{y}}_m)(\hat{\mathbf{y}}_{pivot,i} - \bar{\mathbf{y}}_{pivot})}{\sqrt{\sum_{i=1}^N (\hat{\mathbf{y}}_{m,i} - \bar{\mathbf{y}}_m)^2 \sum_{i=1}^N (\hat{\mathbf{y}}_{pivot,m} - \bar{\mathbf{y}}_{pivot})^2}},$$

where $\bar{\mathbf{y}}_m = \frac{1}{N} \sum_{i=1}^N \hat{\mathbf{y}}_{m,i}$ and $\bar{\mathbf{y}}_{pivot} = \frac{1}{N} \sum_{i=1}^N \hat{\mathbf{y}}_{pivot,i}$ denote respectively the average of the modal-specific and modal-agnostic prediction.

3.3   Adaptive Aggregation

We propose a soft-attention based late fusion algorithm referred as adaptive aggregation. The adaptive aggregation is an extension of the attention mechanism in the late fusion framework based on the confidence between modal-specific predictions and modal-agnostic pivot prediction. For M multimodal case, all the modal-specific predictions $\{\hat{\mathbf{y}}_m\}_{m=1}^{M}$ and the modal-agnostic pivot prediction $\hat{\mathbf{y}}_{pivot}$ are considered in making the final prediction $\hat{\mathbf{y}}_{agg}$ as follows:

$$\hat{\mathbf{y}}_{agg} = \sigma \left(\hat{\mathbf{y}}_{pivot} + \sum_{m=1}^{M} \alpha_{agg,m} \cdot \hat{\mathbf{y}}_m \right),$$

where $\alpha_{agg,m}$ is the scalar multimodal attention weight corresponding to the m-th modality. The multimodal attention weights are obtained using a neural network analogous to the soft-attention mechanism:

$$\alpha_{agg,m} = \frac{\exp(s_m)}{\sum_{i=1}^{M} \exp(s_i)}, \quad m = 1, \cdots, M,$$

where

$$s_m = W_s \left[\mathbf{h}_m; \mathbf{h}_{pivot} \right] + b_s, \quad m = 1, \cdots, M.$$

Unlike widely used late fusion algorithm such as mean aggregation, the adaptive aggregation can regulate the ratio of each modality on final prediction. The learned multimodal attention weights can be viewed as the reliability of each modality. Consider a video with "surfing" label. Surfing board can be visually observed but insteads of hearing the waves we hear some music. In this case, the attention weight corresponds to visual modality label should be higher than that corresponding to audio such that final prediction is made based on visual modality rather than auditory modality.

3.4   Training

The objective loss function to train the proposed Pivot CorrNN is composed of three terms. First, $(M + 2)$ cross-entropy losses are included where M denotes the number of input modalities. Additional two cross-entropy is dedicated to the pivot prediction and the prediction after the adaptive aggregation module which is responsible for the supervision in learning the confidence level of each modality prediction.

Second, M number of correlations between the hidden states as well as the predictions of each of the modal-specific and modal-agnostic subnetwork. Third, for achieving better generalization performance, ℓ^2-regularization is additionally applied. Minimizing the overall objective loss function leads to minimizing the $M + 2$ classification errors, and at the same time, maximizes the pivot correlation objectives. To handle this opposite direction, the final loss function $\mathcal{L}$ is designed to minimize cross-entropy, regularization and negative of correlations losses as below:

$$\mathcal{L} = \sum_{m=1}^{M} \left(\sum_{c=1}^{C} \mathbf{y}_c \log(\hat{\mathbf{y}}_{m,c}) + (1 - \mathbf{y}_c) \log(1 - \hat{\mathbf{y}}_{m,c}) \right)$$

$$+ \sum_{c=1}^{C} (\mathbf{y}_c \log(\hat{\mathbf{y}}_{pivot,c}) + (1 - \mathbf{y}_c) \log(1 - \hat{\mathbf{y}}_{pivot,c}))$$

$$+ \sum_{c=1}^{C} (\mathbf{y}_c \log(\hat{\mathbf{y}}_{agg,c}) + (1 - \mathbf{y}_c) \log(1 - \hat{\mathbf{y}}_{agg,c}))$$

$$- \lambda_1 \left(\sum_{m=1}^{M} \mathcal{L}_{corr}^{\mathbf{h}_m} + \mathcal{L}_{corr}^{\mathbf{y}_m} \right) + \lambda_2 \ell^2,$$

where, c and C indicate c-th category and the total number of categories, respectively. $\mathbf{y}_c$ is the groundtruth label for c-th category. λ_1 and λ_2 is the balancing term for controlling effectiveness of Pivot correlation and ℓ^2 regularization term.

To evaluate the pivot correlations, the entire N samples at the same time, but in practice, the empirical correlation is calculated within a single mini-batch as the same as Deep CCA [3]. Thus, the proposed maximizing pivot correlation module can be optimized using any types of gradient descent based methods including Adam [21].

4   Experiments

This section provides the experimental details of Pivot CorrNN. Initially, we describe the datasets used to train and evaluate the proposed architecture in Sect. 4.1. The experimental details are described in Sect. 4.2 and investigations of each proposed module are shown in Sect. 4.3 as ablation study. Finally, Sects. 4.4, and 4.5 show the experimental results of Pivot CorrNN for two datasets: FCVID, and YouTube-8M.

4.1   Datasets

FCVID [18] is a multi-label video categorization dataset containing 91,223 web videos manually annotated with 239 categories. The dataset represents over 4,232 hours of video with an average video duration of 167 seconds. The categories in FCVID cover a wide range of topics including objects (e.g., "car"), scenes (e.g., "beach"), social events (e.g., "tailgate party") and procedural events ("making cake"). There exist some broken videos which cannot be played, we filtered out broken videos that cannot be used for extracting features. After filtering, the remaining number of videos are 44,544 for training and 44,511 for testing. The partition of the training and testing are the same of previous paper [18]. FCVID distributes raw video and 8 different precomputed video level features:

SpectrogramSIFT, SIFT, IDT-Traj, CNN, IDT-HOG, IDT-HOF, IDT-MBH and MFCC. In this paper, 7 types of pre-extracted features (except Spectrogram-SIFT) are used for evaluating proposed Pivot CorrNN. For evaluation, mean Average Precision (mAP) metric is used.

YouTube-8M [2] is the largest video categorization dataset composed of about 7 million YouTube videos. Each videos are annotated one or multiple positive labels. The number of categories are 4,716, and the averaged positive labels per videos is 3.4. The training, validation and testing split are pre-defined with 70%, 20%, and 10%, respectively. Also the dataset is released to hold competition purpose, the groundtruth labels for test split is not provided. Due to its huge size, YouTube-8M provides two types of pre-extracted feature which cover visual and auditory modalities. The visual and auditory features are extracted using pre-trained Inception-V3 [28] and VGGish [14], respectively. For measuring the quality of predictions, Global Average Precision (GAP) at top 20 is used in Kaggle competition thus the performance of test split is measured in GAP solely.

4.2   Experimental Details

The entire proposed model is implemented using Tensorflow [1] framework. All the results reported in this paper were performed with Adam optimizer [21] with a mini-batch size of 128. The hyper parameters that we used are as follows. The learning rate is set to 0.001, and exponential decay rate for the 1st and 2nd moments are set to 0.9 and 0.999, respectively. For stable gradient descent procedure in cGRU and GRU, gradient clipping is adopted with clipping norm of 1.0. For the loss functions, balancing term λ_1 for maximizing pivot correlation objective, and λ_2 for ℓ^2 regularization are set to 0.001 and 3×10^{-7}. All the experiments performed under CUDA acceleration with single NVIDIA Titan Xp (12 GB of memory) GPU.

4.3   Ablation Study on FCVID

To verify the effectiveness of each module of Pivot CorrNN, we conducted ablation study on FCVID. Table 1 presents the ablation study on FCVID. In this ablation study, two modality inputs are used: C3D [29] visual and VGGish [14] auditory features.

The performance of baseline model (without proposed module) is shown on the first row of Table 1. For the baseline model, C3D and VGGish features are concatenated and fed into a standard GRU instead of cGRU to produce modal-agnostic pivot hidden state. The baseline model shows 66.86% in mAP measure. Then we applied proposed modules one by one. Replacing original GRU to cGRU for modal-agnostic pivot hidden state boosts the performance about 0.7%, and achieves 67.57% in mAP measure. With maximizing pivot correlations on hidden state and prediction, the model achieves the performance of 66.68% and 68.02%, respectively. Synergistic effect is observed when maximizing correlation on both pivot hidden state and prediction. Finally, with all of the proposed modules, the Pivot CorrNN shows the performance of 69.54%. The entire gain of proposed modules is about 2.7% and each of the proposed modules gracefully increases the performance.

Table 1. Ablation study for Pivot CorrNN on FCVID. As can be seen, each module of Pivot CorrNN gracefully increases the performance with activating each module. In this study, C3D visual and VGGish auditory features are used.

cGRU	Max. Pivot Correlation		Adaptive Aggregation	mAP(%)
	Pivot Hidden State	Pivot Prediction		
				66.86
✓				67.57
✓	✓			67.68
✓		✓		68.02
✓	✓	✓		68.45
✓	✓	✓	✓	69.54

4.4 Experimental Results on FCVID

The performances of Pivot CorrNN are shown in Table 2 for FCVID test partition. In Table 2a the performances of proposed Pivot CorrNN with previous state-of-the-art algorithms are listed. The performances of previous algorithms on FCVID were not reported their original papers except for rDNN, we referred the performance from [18]. The proposed Pivot CorrNN achieved 77.6% in mAP metric on test partition of FCVID and shows absolute mAP gain of 1.6% compared to the previous state-of-the-art results.

For details of performance gains, ablation experiments on the number of modalities are conducted and shown in Table 2b. With frame level features only, the Pivot CorrNN recorded 69.54 % mAP, and adding different types of features the performance is gracefully increased. Adding appearance, motion, and audio, 6%, 1.2%, 0.7% and 0.3% mAP gains are observed, respectively. The gains explain that there is complementary information in each feature, but there is also some redundant information.

In Table 3, the comparison for multimodal attention weights in the adaptive aggregation module is shown. In the tables, thirteen categories which are selected by descending order for visual attention weight $\alpha_{agg,1}$, and auditory attention weight $\alpha_{agg,2}$. In Table 3a, all the categories are related to actions or objects. In videos belong to those categories, there is limited information in auditory modalities to describe its context from auditory information that most of the predictions are based on the visual modalities. On the other hands, all the categories listed in Table 3b are related musical activities. Visual modality does not provide much information related to its categories, but auditory modality does.

Table 2. Experimental Results on test partition of FCVID. (a) shows performance comparison on Pivot CorrNN and previous algorithms, and (b) shows feature ablation results

Model	mAP (%)
DMF [26]	72.5
DASD [17]	72.8
M-DBM [27]	74.4
SVM-MKL [22]	75.2
rDNN-F [18]	75.4
rDNN [18]	76.0
Pivot CorrNN	**77.6**

(a) Performance comparison

Feature Names	Feature Type	mAP(%)
C3D, VGGish	Frame level features	69.54
+CNN, SIFT	Appearance feature	75.33
+IDT-HOF, IDT-HOG	Motion feature	76.58
+IDT-MBH, IDT-Traj	Motion feature	77.23
+MFCC	Audio features	**77.60**

(b) Feature ablation experiments on Pivot CorrNN

Table 3. Averaged attention weights of top thirteen categories in descending order for each modality

Category	$\alpha_{agg,1}$	$\alpha_{agg,2}$
taekwondo	0.981	0.019
rafting	0.958	0.042
surfing	0.94	0.06
kiteSurfing	0.937	0.063
swimmingProfessional	0.915	0.085
egyptianPyramids	0.901	0.099
horseRiding	0.895	0.105
bikeTricks	0.88	0.12
rhythmicGymnastics	0.867	0.133
mountain	0.863	0.137
VolcanoEruption	0.858	0.142
walkingWithDog	0.852	0.148
playingFrisbeeWithDog	0.846	0.154

(a) Ordered by visual modality

Category	$\alpha_{agg,1}$	$\alpha_{agg,2}$
flutePerformance	0.091	0.909
pianoPerformance	0.126	0.874
trumpetPerformance	0.179	0.821
harmonicaPerformance	0.186	0.814
singingInKtv	0.205	0.795
celloPerformance	0.216	0.784
accordionPerformance	0.239	0.761
chorus	0.309	0.691
saxophonePerformance	0.315	0.685
beatbox	0.377	0.623
publicSpeech	0.413	0.587
violinPerformance	0.415	0.585
guitarPerformance	0.42	0.58

(b) Ordered by auditory modality

Figure 4 shows the qualitative results of Pivot CorrNN. For each video sample, four still frames are extracted. The corresponding groundtruth category and the top three predictions of both pivot stream and adaptive aggregation are presented. The first two videos are sampled from the categories from Table 3a, and the remaining two videos are sampled from the categories from Table 3b. The correct predictions are colored red with its probabilistic scores. The rightmost bar graphs denote the multimodal attention weights of adaptive aggregation module. In this experiments $\alpha_{agg,1}$, and $\alpha_{agg,2}$ are dedicated to visual and auditory feature, respectively.

Experimental results in Fig. 4 shows that the module reduces false positive errors effectively for above examples. The predictions of sampled videos are finetuned by increasing the probability of the correct predictions, and decreasing false positive predictions. Visual modality is considered more informative than auditory modality in "surfing" and "horseRiding" categories relatively two and ten times, while auditory modality is considered more informative in "celloPerformance" and "violinPerformance" categories. For sampled video which groundtruth category is "celloPerformance", the pivot prediction was 37.8% on "celloPerformance", on the other hands "symphonyOrchestraFrom" has more confidence. However, adaptive aggregation module finetuned the probability of correct category "celloPerformance" to 95.21%. From these results, adaptive aggregation module measures which modality prediction is more reliable, then it refines the final prediction with both pivot and modal-specific predictions.

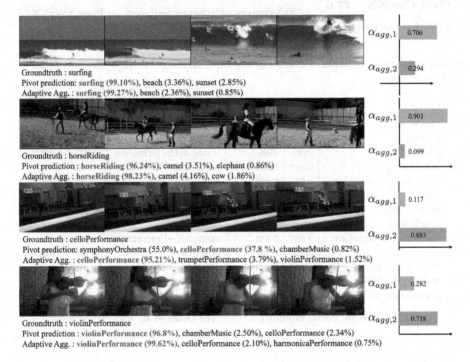

Fig. 4. Qualitative results of Pivot CorrNN. We show the groundtruth category of each video sample with top three pivot and final predictions of proposed Pivot CorrNN. The multimodal attention weights in adaptive aggregation are illustrated on the rightmost side.

4.5   Experimental Results on YouTube-8M

For evaluating proposed Pivot CorrNN on YouTube-8M dataset, two types of experiments are conducted from both video and frame level features. For the video level features, all the frame level features from each video are averaged into a single feature vector. There is no sequential information in the video level features that cGRU is not applied for experiments of video level features. For the frame level features, all the three modules are applied for Pivot CorrNN.

Table 4. Multimodal video categorization performance of two baseline models and Pivot CorrNNs on YouTube-8M dataset

Feature Level	Model	GAP (%)
Video	Logistic Regression (Concat)	76.79
Video	Pivot CorrNN (without cGRU)	77.40
Frame	Two-layer LSTM (Concat)	80.11
Frame	Pivot CorrNN (with cGRU)	81.61

The performance comparision of Pivot CorrNN with baseline models are presented in Table 4. Logistic regressions are used for all the classifiers within the models. The performance gains are observed for the proposed Pivot CorrNN 0.7% and 1.5% in GAP metric, respectively. In these experiments, pre-extracted Inception-V3 and VGGish features are used without any additional feature encoding algorithms, such as learnable pooling methods [23], NetVLAD [5], etc. With advanced feature encoding algorithms as an additional feature, we believe proposed Pivot CorrNN will achieve better performance on YouTube-8M.

5   Conclusion

This paper considers a Pivot Correlational Neural Network (Pivot CorrNN) for multimodal video categorization by maximizing the correlation between the hidden states as well as the predictions of the modal-agnostic pivot stream and modal-specific streams in the network. The Pivot CorrNN consists of three modules: (1) maximizing pivot-correlation module that maximizes the correlation between the hidden states as well as the predictions of the modal-agnostic pivot stream and modal-specific streams in the network, (2) contextual Gated Recurrent Unit (cGRU) module that models time-varying contextual information among modalities, and (3) adaptive aggregation module that considers the confidence of each modality before making one final prediction. We evaluate the Pivot CorrNN on two publicly available large-scale multimodal video categorization dataset: FCVID, and YouTube-8M. From the experimental results, Pivot CorrNN achieves best performance on the FCVID database and the performance comparable to the state-of-the-art on YouTube-8M database.

Acknowledgments. This research was supported by Samsung Research.

References

1. Abadi, M., et al.: Tensorflow: a system for large-scale machine learning. In: OSDI, vol. 16, pp. 265–283 (2016)
2. Abu-El-Haija, S., et al.: Youtube-8m: a large-scale video classification benchmark. arXiv preprint arXiv:1609.08675 (2016)

3. Andrew, G., Arora, R., Bilmes, J., Livescu, K.: Deep canonical correlation analysis. In: International Conference on Machine Learning, pp. 1247–1255 (2013)

4. Antol, S., et al.: VQA: visual question answering. In: Proceedings of the IEEE International Conference on Computer Vision, pp. 2425–2433 (2015)

5. Arandjelovic, R., Gronat, P., Torii, A., Pajdla, T., Sivic, J.: NetVLAD: CNN architecture for weakly supervised place recognition. In: Proceedings of the IEEE Conference on Computer Vision and Pattern Recognition, pp. 5297–5307 (2016)

6. Ben-Younes, H., Cadene, R., Cord, M., Thome, N.: Mutan: multimodal tucker fusion for visual question answering. In: Proceedings of IEEE International Conference on Computer Vision, vol. 3 (2017)

7. Chandar, S., Khapra, M.M., Larochelle, H., Ravindran, B.: Correlational neural networks. Neural Comput. $28(2)$, 257–285 (2016)

8. Chung, J., Gulcehre, C., Cho, K., Bengio, Y.: Empirical evaluation of gated recurrent neural networks on sequence modeling. arXiv preprint arXiv:1412.3555 (2014)

9. Donahue, J., et al.: Long-term recurrent convolutional networks for visual recognition and description. In: Proceedings of the IEEE Conference on Computer Vision and Pattern Recognition, pp. 2625–2634 (2015)

10. Feichtenhofer, C., Pinz, A., Wildes, R.: Spatiotemporal residual networks for video action recognition. In: Advances in Neural Information Processing Systems, pp. 3468–3476 (2016)

11. Feichtenhofer, C., Pinz, A., Wildes, R.P.: Spatiotemporal multiplier networks for video action recognition. In: 2017 IEEE Conference on Computer Vision and Pattern Recognition (CVPR), pp. 7445–7454. IEEE (2017)

12. Frome, A., Corrado, G.S., Shlens, J., Bengio, S., Dean, J., Mikolov, T., et al.: Devise: a deep visual-semantic embedding model. In: Advances in Neural Information Processing Systems, pp. 2121–2129 (2013)

13. Fukui, A., Park, D.H., Yang, D., Rohrbach, A., Darrell, T., Rohrbach, M.: Multimodal compact bilinear pooling for visual question answering and visual grounding. arXiv preprint arXiv:1606.01847 (2016)

14. Hershey, S., et al.: CNN architectures for large-scale audio classification. In: 2017 IEEE International Conference on Acoustics, Speech and Signal Processing (ICASSP), pp. 131–135. IEEE (2017)

15. Hotelling, H.: Relations between two sets of variates. Biometrika $28(3/4)$, 321–377 (1936)

16. Huang, P.S., He, X., Gao, J., Deng, L., Acero, A., Heck, L.: Learning deep structured semantic models for web search using clickthrough data. In: Proceedings of the 22nd ACM International Conference on Information & Knowledge Management, pp. 2333–2338. ACM (2013)

17. Jiang, Y.G., Dai, Q., Wang, J., Ngo, C.W., Xue, X., Chang, S.F.: Fast semantic diffusion for large-scale context-based image and video annotation. IEEE Trans. Image Process, $21(6)$, 3080–3091 (2012)

18. Jiang, Y.G., Wu, Z., Wang, J., Xue, X., Chang, S.F.: Exploiting feature and class relationships in video categorization with regularized deep neural networks. IEEE Trans. Pattern Anal. Mach. Intell, $40(2)$, 352–364 (2018)

19. Karpathy, A., Toderici, G., Shetty, S., Leung, T., Sukthankar, R., Fei-Fei, L.: Large-scale video classification with convolutional neural networks. In: Proceedings of the IEEE Conference on Computer Vision and Pattern Recognition, pp. 1725–1732 (2014)

20. Kim, J.H., On, K.W., Lim, W., Kim, J., Ha, J.W., Zhang, B.T.: Hadamard product for low-rank bilinear pooling. arXiv preprint arXiv:1610.04325 (2016)

21. Kingma, D.P., Ba, J.: Adam: a method for stochastic optimization. arXiv preprint arXiv:1412.6980 (2014)
22. Kloft, M., Brefeld, U., Sonnenburg, S., Zien, A.: Lp-norm multiple kernel learning. J. Mach. Learn. Res. **12**, 953–997 (2011)
23. Miech, A., Laptev, I., Sivic, J.: Learnable pooling with context gating for video classification. arXiv preprint arXiv:1706.06905 (2017)
24. Ngiam, J., Khosla, A., Kim, M., Nam, J., Lee, H., Ng, A.Y.: Multimodal deep learning. In: Proceedings of the 28th International Conference on Machine Learning (ICML 2011), pp. 689–696 (2011)
25. Simonyan, K., Zisserman, A.: Two-stream convolutional networks for action recognition in videos. In: Advances in Neural Information Processing Systems, pp. 568–576 (2014)
26. Smith, J.R., Naphade, M., Natsev, A.: Multimedia semantic indexing using model vectors. In: Proceedings of 2003 International Conference on Multimedia and Expo ICME 2003, vol. 2, p. II-445. IEEE (2003)
27. Srivastava, N., Salakhutdinov, R.R.: Multimodal learning with deep boltzmann machines. In: Advances in Neural Information Processing Systems, pp. 2222–2230 (2012)
28. Szegedy, C., Vanhoucke, V., Ioffe, S., Shlens, J., Wojna, Z.: Rethinking the inception architecture for computer vision. In: Proceedings of the IEEE Conference on Computer Vision and Pattern Recognition, pp. 2818–2826 (2016)
29. Tran, D., Bourdev, L., Fergus, R., Torresani, L., Paluri, M.: Learning spatiotemporal features with 3D convolutional networks. In: Proceedings of the IEEE International Conference on Computer Vision, pp. 4489–4497 (2015)
30. Wang, W., Arora, R., Livescu, K., Bilmes, J.: On deep multi-view representation learning. In: International Conference on Machine Learning, pp. 1083–1092 (2015)
31. Wang, Y., Long, M., Wang, J., Philip, S.Y.: Spatiotemporal pyramid network for video action recognition. In: CVPR, vol. 6, p. 7 (2017)
32. Weston, J., Bengio, S., Usunier, N.: Wsabie: scaling up to large vocabulary image annotation. In: IJCAI, vol. 11, pp. 2764–2770 (2011)

Part-Aligned Bilinear Representations
for Person Re-identification

Yumin Suh[1], Jingdong Wang[2], Siyu Tang[3,4], Tao Mei[5],
and Kyoung Mu Lee[1(✉)]

[1] ASRI, Seoul National University, Seoul, Korea
{n12345,kyoungmu}@snu.ac.kr
[2] Microsoft Research Asia, Beijing, China
jingdw@microsoft.com
[3] Max Planck Institute for Intelligent Systems, Tübingen, Germany
stang@tuebingen.mpg.de
[4] University of Tübingen, Tübingen, Germany
[5] JD AI Research, Beijing, China
tmei@jd.com

Abstract. Comparing the appearance of corresponding body parts is essential for person re-identification. As body parts are frequently misaligned between the detected human boxes, an image representation that can handle this misalignment is required. In this paper, we propose a network that learns a part-aligned representation for person re-identification. Our model consists of a two-stream network, which generates appearance and body part feature maps respectively, and a bilinear-pooling layer that fuses two feature maps to an image descriptor. We show that it results in a compact descriptor, where the image matching similarity is equivalent to an aggregation of the local appearance similarities of the corresponding body parts. Since the image similarity does not depend on the relative positions of parts, our approach significantly reduces the part misalignment problem. Training the network does not require any part annotation on the person re-identification dataset. Instead, we simply initialize the part sub-stream using a pre-trained sub-network of an existing pose estimation network and train the whole network to minimize the re-identification loss. We validate the effectiveness of our approach by demonstrating its superiority over the state-of-the-art methods on the standard benchmark datasets including Market-1501, CUHK03, CUHK01 and DukeMTMC, and standard video dataset MARS.

Keywords: Person re-identification · Part alignment · Bilinear pooling

Electronic supplementary material The online version of this chapter (https://doi.org/10.1007/978-3-030-01264-9_25) contains supplementary material, which is available to authorized users.

© Springer Nature Switzerland AG 2018
V. Ferrari et al. (Eds.): ECCV 2018, LNCS 11218, pp. 418–437, 2018.
https://doi.org/10.1007/978-3-030-01264-9_25

1   Introduction

The goal of person re-identification is to identify the same person across videos captured from different cameras. It is a fundamental visual recognition problem in video surveillance with various applications [55]. It is challenging because the camera views are usually disjoint, the temporal transition time between cameras varies considerably, and the lighting conditions/person poses differ across cameras in real-world scenarios.

Body part misalignment (i.e., the problem that body parts are spatially misaligned across person images) is one of the key challenges in person re-identification. Figure 1 shows some examples. This problem causes conventional strip/grid-based representations [1,10,25,58,69,71] to be unreliable as they implicitly assume that every person appears in a similar pose within a tightly surrounded bounding box. Thus, a body part-aligned representation, which can ease the representation comparison and avoid the need for complex comparison techniques, should be designed.

To resolve this problem, recent approaches have attempted to localize body parts explicitly and combine the representations over them [23,50,74,75,78]. For example, the body parts are represented by the pre-defined (or refined [50]) bounding boxes estimated from the state-of-the-art pose estimators [4,50,74,78]. This scheme requires highly-accurate pose estimation. Unfortunately, state-of-the-art pose estimation solutions are still not perfect. Also, these schemes are bounding box-based and lack fine-grained part localization within the boxes. To mitigate the problems, we propose to encode human poses by feature maps rather than by bounding boxes. Recently, Zhao et al. [75] represented body parts through confidence maps, which are estimated using attention techniques. The method has a lack of guidance on body part locations during the training, thereby failing to attend to certain body regions consistently.

In this paper, we propose a part-aligned representation for person re-identification. Our approach learns to represent the human poses as part maps and combine them directly with the appearance maps to compute part-aligned representations. More precisely, our model consists of a two-stream network and an aggregation module. (1) Each stream separately generates appearance and body part maps. (2) The aggregation module first generates the part-aligned

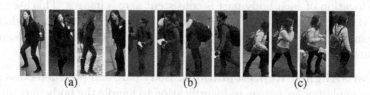

(a)   (b)   (c)

Fig. 1. (a, b) As a person appears in different poses/viewpoints in different cameras, and (c) human detections are imperfect, the corresponding body parts are usually not spatially aligned across the human detections, causing person re-identification to be challenging.

feature maps by computing the bilinear mapping of the appearance and part descriptors at each location, and then spatially averages the local part-aligned descriptors. The resulting image matching similarity is equivalent to an aggregation of the local appearance similarities of the corresponding body parts. Since it does not depend on the relative positions of parts, the misalignment problem is reduced.

Training the network does not require any body part annotations on the person re-identification dataset. Instead, we simply initialize the part map generation stream using the pre-trained weights, which are trained from a standard pose estimation dataset. Surprisingly, although our approach only optimizes the re-identification loss function, the resulting two-stream network successfully separates appearance and part information into each stream, thereby generating the appearance and part maps from each of them, respectively. In particular, the part maps adapt from the original form to further differentiate informative body parts for person re-identification. Through extensive experiments, we verify that our approach consistently improves the accuracy of the baseline and achieves competitive/superior performance over standard image datasets, Market-1501, CUHK03, CUHK01 and DukeMTMC, and one standard video dataset, MARS.

2   Related Work

The early solutions of person re-identification mainly relied on hand-crafted features [18,27,36,39], metric learning techniques [20,22,26,28,42,70, 72], and probabilistic patch matching algorithms [5,6,48] to handle resolution/light/view/pose changes. Recently, attributes [51,52,76], transfer learning [43,49], re-ranking [15,80], partial person matching [82], and human-in-the-loop learning [38,60], have also been studied. More can be found in the survey [81]. In the following, we review recent spatial-partition-based and part-aligned representations, matching techniques, and some works using bilinear pooling.

Regular Spatial-Partition Based Representations. The approaches in this stream of research represent an image as a combination of local descriptors, where each local descriptor represents a spatial partition such as grid cell [1,25, 71] and horizontal stripe [10,58,69]. They work well under a strict assumption that the location of each body part is consistent across images. This assumption is often violated under realistic conditions, thereby causing the methods to fail. An extreme case is that no spatial partition is used and a global representation is computed over the whole image [7,42,63–65,77].

Body Part-Aligned Representations. Body part and pose detection results have been exploited for person re-identification to handle the body part misalignment problem [3,11–13,62,68]. Recently, these ideas have been re-studied using deep learning techniques. Most approaches [50,74,78] represent an image as a combination of body part descriptors, where a dozen of pre-defined body parts are detected using the off-the-shelf pose estimator (possibly an additional RoI refinement step). They usually crop bounding boxes around the detected body parts and compute the representations over the cropped boxes. In contrast, we propose part-map-based representations, which is different from the previously used box-based representations [50,74,78].

Tang et al. [55] also introduced part maps for person re-identification to solve the multi-people tracking problem. They used part maps to augment appearances as another feature, rather than to generate part-aligned representations, which is different from our method. Some works [34,75] proposed the use of attention maps, which are expected to attend to informative body parts. They often fail to produce reliable attentions as the attention maps are estimated from the appearance maps; guidance from body part locations is lacking, resulting in a limited performance.

Matching. The simple similarity functions [10,58,69], e.g., cosine similarity or Euclidean distance, have been adapted, for part-aligned representations, such as our approach, or under an assumption that the representations are body part/pose aligned. Various schemes [1,25,59,71] were designed to eliminate the influence from body part misalignment for spatial partition-based representations. For instance, a matching sub-network was proposed to conduct convolution and max-pooling operations, over the differences [1] or the concatenation [25,71] of grid-based representation of a pair of person images. Varior et al. [57] proposed the use of matching maps in the intermediate features to guide feature extraction in the later layers through a gated CNN.

Bilinear Pooling. Bilinear pooling is a scheme to aggregate two different types of feature maps by using the outer product at each location and spatial pooling them to obtain a global descriptor. This strategy has been widely adopted in fine-grained recognition [14,21,30] and showed promising performance. For person re-identification, Ustinova et al. [56] adopted a bilinear pooling to aggregate two different appearance maps; this method does not generate part-aligned representations and leads to poor performance. Our approach uses a bilinear pooling to aggregate appearance and part maps to compute part-aligned representations.

3   Our Approach

The proposed model consists of a two-stream network and an aggregation module. It receives an image $\mathbf{I}$ as an input and outputs a part-aligned feature representation $\tilde{\mathbf{f}}$ as illustrated in Fig. 2. The two-stream network contains two separate sub-networks, the appearance map extractor $\mathcal{A}$ and the part map extractor $\mathcal{P}$, which extract the appearance map $\mathbf{A}$ and part map $\mathbf{P}$, respectively. The two types of maps are aggregated through bilinear pooling to generate the part-aligned feature $\mathbf{f}$, which is subsequently normalized to generate the final feature vector $\tilde{\mathbf{f}}$.

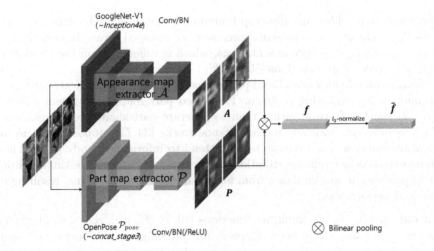

Fig. 2. Overview of the proposed model. The model consists of a two-stream network and an aggregator (bilinear pooling). For a given image **I**, the appearance and part map extractors, $\mathcal{A}$ and $\mathcal{P}$, generate the appearance and part maps, **A** and **P**, respectively. The aggregator performs bilinear pooling over **A** and **P** and generates a feature vector **f**. Finally, the feature vector is l_2-normalized, resulting in a final part-aligned representation $\tilde{\mathbf{f}}$. Conv and BN denote the convolution and batch normalization layers, respectively.

3.1   Two-Stream Network

Appearance Map Extractor. We feed an input image **I** into the appearance map extractor $\mathcal{A}$, thereby outputting the appearance map **A**:

$$\mathbf{A} = \mathcal{A}(\mathbf{I}). \tag{1}$$

$\mathbf{A} \in \mathbb{R}^{h \times w \times c_A}$ is a feature map of size $h \times w$, where each location is described by c_A-dimensional local appearance descriptor. We use the sub-network of GoogLeNet [54] to form and initialize $\mathcal{A}$.

Part Map Extractor. The part map extractor $\mathcal{P}$ receives an input image **I** and outputs the part map **P**:

$$\mathbf{P} = \mathcal{P}(\mathbf{I}). \tag{2}$$

$\mathbf{P} \in \mathbb{R}^{h \times w \times c_P}$ is a feature map of size $h \times w$, where each location is described by a c_P-dimensional local part descriptor. Considering the rapid progress in pose estimation, we use the sub-network of the pose estimation network, OpenPose [4], to form and initialize $\mathcal{P}$. We denote the sub-network of the OpenPose as $\mathcal{P}_{pose}$.

3.2   Bilinear Pooling

Let $\mathbf{a}_{xy}$ be the appearance descriptor at the position (x, y) from the appearance map **A**, and $\mathbf{p}_{xy}$ be the part descriptor at the position (x, y) from the part map $\mathbf{P}$. We perform bilinear pooling over $\mathbf{A}$ and $\mathbf{P}$ to compute the part-aligned representation $\mathbf{f}$. There are two steps, bilinear transformation and spatial global pooling, which are mathematically given as follows:

$$\mathbf{f} = \text{pooling}_{xy}\{\mathbf{f}_{xy}\} = \frac{1}{S}\sum_{xy}\mathbf{f}_{xy}, \qquad \mathbf{f}_{xy} = \text{vec}(\mathbf{a}_{xy} \otimes \mathbf{p}_{xy}), \qquad (3)$$

where S is the spatial size. The pooling operation we use here is average-pooling. vec(.) transforms a matrix to a vector, and $\otimes$ represents the outer product of two vectors, with the output being a matrix. The part-aligned feature $\mathbf{f}$ is then normalized to generate the final feature vector $\tilde{\mathbf{f}}$ as follows:

$$\tilde{\mathbf{f}} = \frac{\mathbf{f}}{\|\mathbf{f}\|_2}. \qquad (4)$$

Considering the normalization, we denote the normalized part-aligned representation as $\tilde{\mathbf{f}}_{xy} = \text{vec}(\tilde{\mathbf{a}}_{xy} \otimes \tilde{\mathbf{p}}_{xy})$, where $\tilde{\mathbf{a}}_{xy} = \frac{\mathbf{a}_{xy}}{\sqrt{\|\mathbf{f}\|_2}}$ and $\tilde{\mathbf{p}}_{xy} = \frac{\mathbf{p}_{xy}}{\sqrt{\|\mathbf{f}\|_2}}$. Therefore, $\tilde{\mathbf{f}} = \frac{1}{S}\sum_{xy}\tilde{\mathbf{f}}_{xy}$.

Part-Aligned Interpretation. We can decompose $\mathbf{a}\otimes\mathbf{p}^1$ into c_P components:

$$\text{vec}(\mathbf{a} \otimes \mathbf{p}) = [(p_1\mathbf{a})^\top \ (p_2\mathbf{a})^\top \ \dots (p_{c_P}\mathbf{a})^\top]^\top, \qquad (5)$$

where each sub-vector $p_i\mathbf{a}$ corresponds to a i-th part channel. For example, if $p_{knee} = 1$ on knee and 0 otherwise, then $p_{knee}\mathbf{a}$ becomes $\mathbf{a}$ only on the knee and $\mathbf{0}$ otherwise. Thus, we call vec($\mathbf{a} \otimes \mathbf{p}$) as part-aligned representation. In general, each channel c does not necessarily correspond to a certain body part. However, the part-aligned representation remains valid as $\mathbf{p}$ encodes the body part information. Section 4 describes this interpretation in detail.

3.3 Loss

To train the network, we utilize the widely-used triplet loss function. Let $\mathbf{I}_q$, $\mathbf{I}_p$ and $\mathbf{I}_n$ denote the query, positive and negative images, respectively. Then, $(\mathbf{I}_q, \mathbf{I}_p)$ is a pair of images of the same person, and $(\mathbf{I}_q, \mathbf{I}_n)$ is that of different persons. Let $\tilde{\mathbf{f}}_q$, $\tilde{\mathbf{f}}_p$, and $\tilde{\mathbf{f}}_n$ indicate their representations. The triplet loss function is formulated as

$$\ell_{\text{triplet}}(\tilde{\mathbf{f}}_q, \tilde{\mathbf{f}}_p, \tilde{\mathbf{f}}_n) = \max(m + \text{sim}(\tilde{\mathbf{f}}_q, \tilde{\mathbf{f}}_n) - \text{sim}(\tilde{\mathbf{f}}_q, \tilde{\mathbf{f}}_p), 0), \qquad (6)$$

where m denotes a margin and $\text{sim}(\mathbf{x}, \mathbf{y}) = <\mathbf{x}, \mathbf{y}>$. The margin is empirically set as $m = 0.2$. The overall loss function is written as follows.

$$\mathcal{L} = \frac{1}{|\mathcal{T}|}\sum_{(\mathbf{I}_q, \mathbf{I}_p, \mathbf{I}_n)\in\mathcal{T}} \ell_{\text{triplet}}(\tilde{\mathbf{f}}_q, \tilde{\mathbf{f}}_p, \tilde{\mathbf{f}}_n), \qquad (7)$$

where $\mathcal{T}$ is the set of all triplets, $\{(\mathbf{I}_q, \mathbf{I}_p, \mathbf{I}_n)\}$.

---

[1] We drop the subscript xy for presentation clarification.

4 Analysis

Part-Aware Image Similarity. We show that under the proposed part-aligned representation in Eqs. (3) and (4), the similarity between two images is equivalent to the aggregation of local appearance similarities between the corresponding body parts. The similarity between two images can be represented as the sum of local similarities between every pair of locations as follows.

$$
\begin{aligned}
\mathrm{sim}_I(\mathbf{I}, \mathbf{I}') = <\tilde{\mathbf{f}}, \tilde{\mathbf{f}}'> &= \frac{1}{S^2} < \sum_{xy} \tilde{\mathbf{f}}_{xy}, \sum_{x'y'} \tilde{\mathbf{f}}'_{x'y'} > \\
&= \frac{1}{S^2} \sum_{xy} \sum_{x'y'} < \tilde{\mathbf{f}}_{xy}, \tilde{\mathbf{f}}'_{x'y'} > \\
&= \frac{1}{S^2} \sum_{xy} \sum_{x'y'} \mathrm{sim}(\tilde{\mathbf{f}}_{xy}, \tilde{\mathbf{f}}'_{x'y'}),
\end{aligned} \tag{8}
$$

where $\mathrm{sim}_I(,)$ measures the similarity between images. Here, the local similarity is computed by an inner product:

$$
\begin{aligned}
\mathrm{sim}(\tilde{\mathbf{f}}_{xy}, \tilde{\mathbf{f}}'_{x'y'}) &= < \mathrm{vec}(\tilde{\mathbf{a}}_{xy} \otimes \tilde{\mathbf{p}}_{xy}), \mathrm{vec}(\tilde{\mathbf{a}}'_{x'y'} \otimes \tilde{\mathbf{p}}'_{x'y'}) > \\
&= < \tilde{\mathbf{a}}_{xy}, \tilde{\mathbf{a}}'_{x'y'} > < \tilde{\mathbf{p}}_{xy}, \tilde{\mathbf{p}}'_{x'y'} > \\
&= \mathrm{sim}(\tilde{\mathbf{a}}_{xy}, \tilde{\mathbf{a}}'_{x'y'}) \, \mathrm{sim}(\tilde{\mathbf{p}}_{xy}, \tilde{\mathbf{p}}'_{x'y'}).
\end{aligned} \tag{9}
$$

This local similarity can be interpreted as the appearance similarity weighted by the body part similarity or vice versa. Thus, from Eqs. (8) and (9), the similarity between two images is computed as the average of local appearance similarities weighted by the body part similarities at the corresponding positions:

$$
\mathrm{sim}_I(\mathbf{I}, \mathbf{I}') = \frac{1}{S^2} \sum_{xyx'y'} \mathrm{sim}(\tilde{\mathbf{a}}_{xy}, \tilde{\mathbf{a}}'_{x'y'}) \, \mathrm{sim}(\tilde{\mathbf{p}}_{xy}, \tilde{\mathbf{p}}'_{x'y'}).
$$

As a result, the image similarity does not depend on the relative positions of parts in images, and therefore the misalignment problem is reduced. To make the local part similarity to be always non-negative and therefore the sign of the local similarity depends only on the sign of the local appearance similarity, we can also restrict the part descriptors $\mathbf{p}_{xy}$ to be element-wise non-negative by adding a ReLU layer after the part map extractor $\mathcal{P}$ as shown in Fig. 2. As this variant results in similar accuracy to the original one, we used the model without the ReLU layer for all the experiments. See supplementary material for more details.

Relationship to the Baseline Models. Consider a baseline approach that only uses the appearance maps and spatial global pooling for image representation. Then, the image similarity is computed as $\mathrm{sim}_I(\mathbf{I}, \mathbf{I}') = \frac{1}{S^2} \sum_{xyx'y'} \mathrm{sim}(\tilde{\mathbf{a}}_{xy}, \tilde{\mathbf{a}}'_{x'y'})$. Unlike our model, this approach cannot reflect part similarity. Consider another model based on the box-based representation, which represents an image as a concatenation of K body part descriptors, where k-th body part is represented as the average-pooled appearance feature within the corresponding bounding box. This model is equivalent to our model when $\mathbf{p}_{xy}$ is defined as $\mathbf{p}_{xy} = [\delta[(x, y) \in R_1], \cdots, \delta[(x, y) \in R_K]]$, where R_k is the region within the k-th part bounding box and $\delta[\cdot]$ is an indicator function, i.e., $\delta[x] = 1$ if x is true otherwise 0. Because our model contains these baselines as special cases and is trained to optimize the re-identification loss, it is guaranteed to perform better than them.

The Two-Stream Network Yields a Decomposed Appearance and Part Maps. At the beginning of the training, the two streams of the network mainly represent the appearance and part maps because the appearance map extractor $\mathcal{A}$ and the part map extractor $\mathcal{P}$ are initialized using GoogleNet [54] pretrained on ImageNet [46] and OpenPose [4] model pre-trained on COCO [29], respectively. During training, we do not set any constraints on the two streams, i.e., no annotations for the body parts, but only optimize the re-identification loss. Surprisingly, the trained two-stream network maintains to decompose the appearance and part information into two streams: one stream corresponds to the appearance maps and the other corresponds to the body part maps.

We visualize the distribution of the learned local appearance and part descriptors using t-SNE [37] as shown in Figs. 3(a) and (b). Figure 3(a) shows that the appearance descriptors are clustered depending on the appearance while being independent on the parts that they come from. For example, the red/yellow box shows that the red/black-colored patches are closely embedded, respectively. By contrast, Fig. 3(b) illustrates that the local part embedding maps the similar

(a) Appearance features   (b) Part features

Fig. 3. The t-SNE visualization of the normalized local appearance and part descriptors on the Market-1501 dataset. It illustrates that our two-stream network decomposes the appearance and part information into two streams successfully. (a) Appearance descriptors are clustered roughly by colors, independently from the body parts where they came from. (b) Part descriptors are clustered by body parts where they came from, regardless of the colors. (Best viewed on a monitor when zoomed in) (Color figure online)

426   Y. Suh et al.

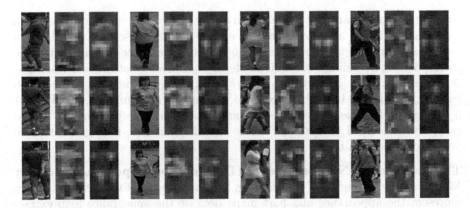

Fig. 4. Visualization of the appearance maps **A** and part maps **P** obtained from the proposed method. For a given input image (left), appearance (center) and part (right) maps encode the appearance and body parts, respectively. For both appearance and part maps, the same color implies that the descriptors are similar, whereas different colors indicate that the descriptors are different. The appearance maps share similar color patterns among the images from the same person, which means that the patterns of appearance descriptors are similar as well. In the part maps, the color differs depending on the location of the body parts where the descriptors came from. (Best viewed in color)

Fig. 5. Comparing the body part descriptors. For a given image (left), the conventional joint-based (center) and the proposed (right) descriptors are visualized. (Best viewed in color) (Color figure online)

body parts into close regions regardless of color. For example, the green/blue box shows that the features from the head/lower leg are clustered, respectively. In addition, physically adjacent body parts, such as head–shoulder and shoulder–torso, are also closely embedded.

To understand how the learned appearance/part descriptors are used in person re-identification, we visualize the appearance maps **A** and the part maps **P** following the visualization used in SIFTFlow [32], as shown in Fig. 4. For a given input image (left), the appearance (center) and part (right) maps encode the appearance and body parts, respectively. The figure shows how the appearance maps differentiate different persons while being invariant for each person. By contrast, the part maps encode the body parts independently from their appearance. In particular, a certain body part is represented by a similar color across images, which confirms our observation in Fig. 3 that the part features from physically adjacent regions are closely embedded.

Our approach learns the optimal part descriptor for person re-identification, rather than relying on the pre-defined body parts. Figure 5 qualitatively compares the conventional body part descriptor and the one learned by our approach.[2] In the previous works on human pose estimation [4,41,61], human poses are represented as a collection of pre-defined key body joint locations. It corresponds to a part descriptor which one-hot encodes the key body joints depending on the existence of a certain body joint at the location, e.g., $p_{knee} = 1$ on knee and 0 otherwise. Compared to the baseline, ours smoothly maps the body parts. In other words, the colors are continuous over the whole body in ours, which implies that the adjacent body parts are mapped closely. By contrast, the baseline not always maps adjacent body parts maps closely. For example, the upper leg between the hip and knee is more close to the background descriptors than to ankle or knee descriptors. This smooth mapping makes our method to work robustly against the pose estimation error because the descriptors do not change rapidly along the body parts and therefore are insensitive to the error in estimation. In addition, the part descriptors adopt to distinguish the informative parts more finely. For example, the mapped color varies sharply from elbow to shoulder and differentiates the detailed regions. Based on these properties, the learned part descriptors better support the person re-identification task and improve the accuracy.

5   Implementation Details

Network Architecture. We use a sub-network of the first version of GoogLeNet [54] as the appearance map extractor $\mathcal{A}$, from the image input of size 160×80 to the output of *inception4e*, which is followed by a 1×1 convolution layer and a batch normalization layer to reduce the dimension to 512 (Fig. 2). Moreover, we optionally adopt dilation filters in the layers from the *inception4a* to the final layer, resulting in 20×10 response maps. Figure 2 illustrates the architecture of the part map extractor $\mathcal{P}$. We use a sub-network of the OpenPose network [4], from the image input to the output of stage2 (i.e., *concat_stage3*) to extract 185 pose heat maps, which is followed by a 3×3 convolution layer and a batch normalization layer, thereby outputting 128 part maps. We adopt the compact bilinear pooling [14] to aggregate the two feature maps into a 512-dimensional vector **f**.

Compact Bilinear Pooling. The bilinear transformation over the 512-dimensional appearance vector and the 128-dimensional part vector results in an extremely high dimensional vector, which consumes large computational cost and memory. To resolve this issue, we use the tensor sketch approach [44] to compute a compact representation as in [14]. The key idea of the tensor sketch approach is that the original inner product, on which the Euclidean distance is based, between two high-dimensional vectors can be approximated as an inner

---

[2] We used the visualization method proposed in SIFTFlow [32].

product of the dimension-reduced vectors, which are random projections of the original vectors. Details can be found in [44].

Network Training. The appearance map extractor $\mathcal{A}$ and part map extractor $\mathcal{P}$ are fine-tuned from the network pre-trained on ImageNet [46] and COCO [29], respectively. The added layers are initialized following [17]. We use the stochastic gradient descent algorithm. The initial learning rate, weight decay, and the momentum are set to 0.01, 2×10^{-4}, and 0.9, respectively. The learning rate is decreased by a factor of 5 after every 20,000 iterations. All the networks are trained for 75,000 iterations.

We follow [75] to sample a mini-batch of samples at each iteration and use all the possible triplets within each mini-batch. The gradients are computed using the acceleration trick presented in [75]. In each iteration, we sample a mini-batch of 180 images, e.g., there are on average 18 identities with each containing 10 images. In total, there are approximately $10^2 \cdot (180 - 10) \cdot 18 \approx 3 \times 10^5$ triplets in each iteration.

6   Experiments

6.1   Datasets

Market-1501 [79]. This dataset is one of the largest benchmark datasets for person re-identification. Six cameras are used: five high-resolution cameras and one low-resolution camera. There are 32,668 DPM-detected pedestrian image boxes of 1,501 identities: 750 identities are utilized for training and the remaining 751 identities are used for testing. There are 3,368 query images and 19,732 gallery images with 2,793 distractors.

CUHK03 [25]. This dataset consists of 13,164 images of 1,360 people captured by six cameras. Each identity appears in two disjoint camera views (i.e., 4.8 images in each view on average). We divided the train/test set following the previous work [25]. For each test identity, two images are randomly sampled as the probe and gallery images and the average accuracy over 20 trials is reported as the final result.

CUHK01 [24]. This dataset comprises 3884 images of 971 people captured in two disjoint camera views. Two images are captured for each person from each of the two cameras (i.e., a total of four images). Experiments are performed under two evaluation settings [1], using 100 and 486 test IDs. Following the previous works [1,7,10,75], we fine-tuned the model from the one learned from the CUHK03 training set for the experiments with 486 test IDs.

DukeMTMC [45]. This dataset is originally proposed for video-based person tracking and re-identification. We use the fixed train/test split and evaluation setting following [31][3]. It includes 16,522 training images of 702 identities, 2,228 query images of 702 identities and 17,661 galley images.

---

[3] https://github.com/layumi/DukeMTMC-reID_evaluation.

MARS [77]. This dataset is proposed for video-based person re-identification. It consists of 1261 different pedestrians captured by at least two cameras. There are $509,914$ bounding boxes and $8,298$ tracklets from 625 identities for training and $681,089$ bounding boxes and $12,180$ tracklets from 636 identities for testing.

6.2 Evaluation Metrics

We use both the cumulative matching characteristics (CMC) and mean average precision (mAP) to evaluate the accuracy. The CMC score measures the quality of identifying the correct match at each rank. For multiple ground truth matches, CMC cannot measure how well all the images are ranked. Therefore, we report the mAP scores for Market-1501, DukeMTMC, and MARS where more than one ground truth images are in the gallery.

6.3 Comparison with the Baselines

We compare the proposed method with the baselines in three aspects. In this section, when not specified, all the experiments are performed on the Market-1501 dataset, all the models do not use dilation, and $\mathcal{P}_{pose}$ is trained together with the other parameters.

Effect of Part Maps. We compare our method with a baseline that does not explicitly use body parts. As a baseline network, we use the appearance map extractor of Eq. (1), which is followed by a global spatial average pooling and a fully connected layer, thereby outputting the 512-dimensional image descriptor. Figures 6(a) and (b) compare the proposed method with the baseline, while varying the training strategy: *fixing* and *training* $\mathcal{P}_{pose}$. *Fixing* $\mathcal{P}_{pose}$ initializes $\mathcal{P}_{pose}$ using the pre-trained weights [4,29] and fixes the weight through the training. *Training* $\mathcal{P}_{pose}$ also initializes $\mathcal{P}_{pose}$ in the same way, but fine-tunes the network using the loss of Eq. (7) during training. Figure 6(a) illustrates the accuracy comparison on three datasets, Market-1501, MARS, and Duke. It shows that using

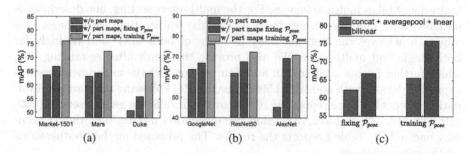

Fig. 6. (a) Comparison of different pooling methods on the appearance maps. (c) Comparing models, with and without part maps, on different datasets. (d) Comparing models, with and without part maps, on different architectures of the appearance map extractor. If not specified, the results are reported on Market-1501. (b) Comparison of different methods to aggregate the appearance and part maps.

part maps consistently improves the accuracy on all the three datasets from the baseline. In addition, training $\mathcal{P}_{pose}$ largely improves the accuracy than fixing $\mathcal{P}_{pose}$. It implies that the part descriptors are adopted to better serve the person re-identification task. Figure 6(b) shows the accuracy comparison while varying the appearance sub-network architecture. Similarly, the baseline accuracy is improved when part maps are introduced and further improved when $\mathcal{P}_{pose}$ is fine-tuned during training.

Effect of Bilinear Pooling. Figure 6(c) compares the proposed method (*bilinear*) to the baseline with a different aggregator. For the given appearance and part maps, *concat+averagepool+linear* generates a feature vector by concatenating two feature maps, spatially average pooling, and feeding through a fully connected layer, resulting in a 512-dimensional vector. The result shows that bilinear pooling consistently achieves higher accuracy than the baseline, for both cases when $\mathcal{P}_{pose}$ is fixed/trained.

Comparison with Previous Pose-Based Methods. Finally, we compare our method with three previous works [50,74,78], which use human pose estimation, on Market-1501. For a fair comparison, we use the reduced CPM(R-CPM [~3M param]) utilized in [50][4] as $\mathcal{P}_{pose}$. The complexity of the R-CPM is lower than the standard FCN (~6M param) used in [74] and CPM (30M param) used in [78]. As the appearance network, [74] used GoogLeNet and [78] used ResNet50. [50] used 13 inception modules, whereas we use 7. Table 1 shows the comparison. In comparison with the method adopted by [50,74,78], the proposed method (Inception V1, R-CPM) achieves an increase of 4% and 9% for rank@1 accuracy and mAP, respectively. It shows that our method effectively uses the part information compared with the previous approaches.

6.4 Comparison with State-of-the-Art Methods

Market-1501. Table 1 shows the comparison over two query schemes, single query and multi-query. Single query takes one image from each person whereas multi-query takes multiple images. For the multi-query setting, one descriptor is obtained from multiple images by averaging the feature from each image. Our approach achieves the best accuracy in terms of both mAP and rank@K for both single and multi-query. We also provide the result after re-ranking [85], which further boosts accuracy. In addition, we conduct the experiment over an expanded dataset with additional $500K$ images [79]. Following the standard evaluation protocol [19], we report the results over four different gallery sets, $19,732$, $119,732$, $219,732$, and $519,732$, using two evaluation metrics (i.e., rank-1 accuracy and mAP). Table 2 reports the results. The proposed method outperforms all the other methods.

CUHK03. We report the results with two person boxes: manually labeled and detected. Table 3 presents the comparison with existing solutions. In the case of

---

[4] https://github.com/yokattame/SpindleNet.

Table 1. Accuracy comparison on Market-1501

Rank	Single query					Multi query				
	1	5	10	20	mAP	1	5	10	20	mAP
Varior et al. 2016 [57]	61.6	-	-	-	35.3	-	-	-	-	-
Zhong et al. 2017 [85]	77.1	-	-	-	63.6	-	-	-	-	-
Zhao et al. 2017 [75]	80.9	91.7	94.7	96.6	63.4	-	-	-	-	-
Sun et al. 2017 [53]	82.3	92.3	95.2	-	62.1	-	-	-	-	-
Geng et al. 2016 [16]	83.7	-	-	-	65.5	89.6	-	-	-	73.8
Lin et al. 2017 [31]	84.3	93.2	95.2	97.0	64.7	-	-	-	-	-
Bai et al. 2017 [2]	82.2	-	-	-	68.8	88.2	-	-	-	76.2
Chen et al. 2017 [9]	72.3	88.2	91.9	95.0	-	-	-	-	-	-
Hermans et al. 2017 [19]	84.9	94.2	-	-	69.1	90.5	96.3	-	-	76.4
+ re − ranking	86.7	93.4	—	—	81.1	91.8	95.8	-	-	87.2
Zhang et al. 2017 [73]	87.7	-	-	-	68.8	91.7	-	-	-	77.1
Zhong et al. 2017 [86]	87.1	-	-	-	71.3	-	-	-	-	-
+ re − ranking	89.1	-	-	-	83.9	-	-	-	-	-
Chen et al. 2017 [8] (MobileNet)	90.0	-	-	-	70.6	-	-	-	-	-
Chen et al. 2017 [8] (Inception-V3)	88.6	-	-	-	72.6	-	-	-	-	-
Ustinova et al. 2017 [56] (Bilinear)	66.4	85.0	90.2	-	41.2	-	-	-	-	-
Zheng et al. 2017 [78] (Pose)	79.3	90.8	94.4	96.5	56.0	-	-	-	-	-
Zhao et al. 2017 [74] (Pose)	76.9	91.5	94.6	96.7	-	-	-	-	-	-
Su et al. 2017 [50] (Pose)	84.1	92.7	94.9	96.8	65.4	-	-	-	-	-
Proposed (Inception-V1, R-CPM)	88.8	95.6	97.3	98.6	74.5	92.9	97.3	98.4	99.1	81.7
Proposed (Inception-V1, OpenPose)	90.2	96.1	97.4	98.4	76.0	93.2	97.5	98.4	99.1	82.7
+ dilation	91.7	96.9	98.1	98.9	79.6	94.0	98.0	98.8	99.3	85.2
+ re − ranking	93.4	96.4	97.4	98.2	89.9	95.4	97.5	98.2	98.9	93.1

Table 2. Accuracy comparison on Market-1501+500k.

		Gallery size			
	Metric	19732	119732	219732	519732
Zheng et al. 2017 [83]	rank-1	79.5	73.8	71.5	68.3
	mAP	59.9	52.3	49.1	45.2
Linet al. 2017 [31]	rank-1	84.0	79.9	78.2	75.4
	mAP	62.8	56.5	53.6	49.8
Hermans et al. 2017 [19]	rank-1	84.9	79.7	77.9	74.7
	mAP	69.1	61.9	58.7	53.6
Proposed (Inception V1, OpenPose)	rank-1	**91.7**	**88.3**	**86.6**	**84.1**
	mAP	**79.6**	**74.2**	**71.5**	**67.2**

detected boxes, the state-of-the-art accuracy is achieved. With manual bounding boxes, our method also achieves the best accuracy.

CUHK01. We compare the results with two evaluation settings (i.e., 100 and 486 test IDs) in Table 3. For 486 test IDs, the proposed method shows the best result. For 100 test IDs, our method achieves the second best result, following [16]. Note that [16] fine-tuned the model which is learned from the CUHK03+Market1501,

Table 3. Accuracy comparison on CUHK03 and CUHK01

| | CUHK03 | | | | | | | | CUHK01 | | | | | | | |
| | Detected | | | | Manual | | | | 100 test IDs | | | | 486 test IDs | | | |
Rank	1	5	10	20	1	5	10	20	1	5	10	20	1	5	10	20
Shi et al. [70]	52.1	84.0	92.0	96.8	61.3	88.5	96.0	99.0	69.4	90.8	96.0	-	-	-	-	-
SIR-CIR [60]	52.2	-	-	-	-	-	-	-	71.8	91.6	96.0	98.0	-	-	-	-
Varior et al. [58]	68.1	88.1	94.6	98.8	-	-	-	-	-	-	-	-	-	-	-	-
Bai et al. [2]	72.7	92.4	96.1	-	76.6	94.6	98.0	-	-	-	-	-	-	-	-	-
Zhang et al. [72]	-	-	-	-	80.2	97.7	99.2	99.8	89.6	97.8	98.9	99.7	76.5	94.2	97.5	-
Sun et al. [53]	81.8	95.2	97.2	-	-	-	-	-	-	-	-	-	-	-	-	-
Zhao et al. [76]	81.6	97.3	98.4	99.5	85.4	97.6	99.4	99.9	88.5	98.4	99.6	99.9	74.7	92.6	96.2	98.4
Geng et al. [16]	84.1	-	-	-	85.4	-	-	-	93.2	-	-	-	77.0	-	-	-
Chen et al. [9]	87.5	97.4	98.7	99.5	-	-	-	-	-	-	-	-	74.5	91.2	94.8	97.1
Ustinova et al. [57] (Bilinear)	63.7	89.2	94.7	97.5	69.7	93.4	98.9	99.4	-	-	-	-	52.9	78.1	86.3	92.6
Zheng et al. [79] (Pose)	67.1	92.2	96.6	98.1	-	-	-	-	-	-	-	-	-	-	-	-
Zhao et al. [75] (Pose)	-	-	-	-	88.5	97.8	98.6	99.2	-	-	-	-	79.9	94.4	97.1	98.6
Su et al. [50] (Pose)	78.3	94.8	97.2	98.4	88.7	98.6	99.2	99.7	-	-	-	-	-	-	-	-
Proposed	**88.0**	**97.6**	**98.6**	**99.0**	**91.5**	**99.0**	**99.5**	**99.9**	**90.4**	**97.1**	**98.1**	**98.9**	**80.7**	**94.4**	**97.3**	**98.6**

Table 4. Accuracy comparison on DukeMTMC

Rank	1	5	10	20	mAP
Zheng et al. [84]	67.7	-	-	-	47.1
Tong et al. [66]	68.1	-	-	-	-
Lin et al. [31]	70.7	-	-	-	51.9
Schumann et al. [47]	72.6	-	-	-	52.0
Sun et al. [53]	76.7	86.4	89.9	-	56.8
Chen et al. [8] (MobileNet)	77.6	-	-	-	58.6
Chen et al. [8] (Inception-V3)	79.2	-	-	-	60.6
Zhun et al. [86]	79.3	-	-	-	62.4
+ re − ranking	84.0	—	—	—	78.3
Proposed (Inception V1, OpenPose)	82.1	90.2	92.7	95.0	64.2
+ dilation	**84.4**	**92.2**	**93.8**	**95.7**	**69.3**
+ re − ranking	**88.3**	**93.1**	**95.0**	**96.1**	**83.9**

whereas we trained the model using 871 training IDs of the CUHK01 dataset, following the settings in previous works [1,7,10,75].

DukeMTMC. We follow the setting in [31] to conduct the experiments. Table 4 reports the results. The proposed method achieves the best result for both with and without re-ranking.

MARS. We also evaluate our method on one video-based person re-identification dataset [77]. We use our approach to extract the representation for each frame and aggregate the representations of all the frames using temporal average pooling, which shows similar accuracy to other aggregation schemes (RNN and LSTM). Table 5 presents the comparison with the competing methods. Our method shows the highest accuracy over both image-based and video-based approaches.

Table 5. Accuracy comparison on MARS

Rank	1	5	10	20	mAP
Xu et al. [67] (Video)	44	70	74	81	-
McLaughlin et al. [40] (Video)	45	65	71	78	27.9
Zheng et al. [77] (Video)	68.3	82.6	-	89.4	49.3
Liu et al. [33] (Video)	68.3	81.4	-	90.6	52.9
Zhou et al. [87]	70.6	90.0	-	97.6	50.7
Li et al. [23]	71.8	86.6	-	93.1	56.1
+ re − ranking	83.0	93.7	−	97.6	66.4
Liu et al. [35]	73.7	84.9	-	91.6	51.7
Hermans et al. [19]	79.8	91.4	-	-	67.7
+ re − ranking	81.2	90.8	−	−	77.4
Proposed (Inception V1, OpenPose)	83.0	92.8	95	96.8	72.2
+ dilation	**84.7**	**94.4**	**96.3**	**97.5**	**75.9**
+ re − ranking	**85.1**	**94.2**	**96.1**	**97.4**	**83.9**

7 Conclusions

We propose a new method for person re-identification. The key factors that contribute to the superior performance of our approach are as follows. (1) We adopt part maps where parts are not pre-defined but learned specially for person re-identification. They are learned to minimize the re-identification loss with the guidance of the pre-trained pose estimation model. (2) The part map representation provides a fine-grained/robust differentiation of the body part depending on their usefulness for re-identification. (3) We use part-aligned representations to handle the body part misalignment problem. The resulting approach achieves superior/competitive person re-identification performances on the standard image and video benchmark datasets.

Acknowledgement. This work was partially supported by Microsoft Research Asia and the Visual Turing Test project (IITP-2017-0-01780) from the Ministry of Science and ICT of Korea.

References

1. Ahmed, E., Jones, M., Marks, T.K.: An improved deep learning architecture for person re-identification. In: CVPR (2015)
2. Bai, S., Bai, X., Tian, Q.: Scalable person re-identification on supervised smoothed manifold. In: CVPR (2017)
3. Bak, S., Corvée, E., Brémond, F., Thonnat, M.: Person re-identification using spatial covariance regions of human body parts. In: AVSS (2010)
4. Cao, Z., Simon, T., Wei, S.E., Sheikh, Y.: Realtime multi-person 2D pose estimation using part affinity fields. In: CVPR (2017)

5. Chen, D., Yuan, Z., Chen, B., Zheng, N.: Similarity learning with spatial constraints for person re-identification. In: CVPR (2016)
6. Chen, D., Yuan, Z., Hua, G., Zheng, N., Wang, J.: Similarity learning on an explicit polynomial kernel feature map for person re-identification. In: CVPR (2015)
7. Chen, S.Z., Guo, C.C., Lai, J.H.: Deep ranking for person re-identification via joint representation learning. IEEE TIP **25**(5), 2353–2367 (2016)
8. Chen, Y., Zhu, X., Gong, S.: Person re-identification by deep learning multi-scale representations. In: CVPR Workshop (2017)
9. Chen, Y.C., Zhu, X., Zheng, W.S., Lai, J.H.: Person re-identification by camera correlation aware feature augmentation. IEEE TPAMI **40**(2), 392–408 (2017)
10. Cheng, D., Gong, Y., Zhou, S., Wang, J., Zheng, N.: Person re-identification by multi-channel parts-based CNN with improved triplet loss function. In: CVPR (2016)
11. Cheng, D.S., Cristani, M.: Person re-identification by articulated appearance matching. In: Gong, S., Cristani, M., Yan, S., Loy, C.C. (eds.) Person Re-Identification. ACVPR, pp. 139–160. Springer, London (2014). https://doi.org/10.1007/978-1-4471-6296-4_7
12. Cheng, D.S., Cristani, M., Stoppa, M., Bazzani, L., Murino, V.: Custom pictorial structures for re-identification. In: BMVC (2011)
13. Farenzena, M., Bazzani, L., Perina, A., Murino, V., Cristani, M.: Person re-identification by symmetry-driven accumulation of local features. In: CVPR (2010)
14. Gao, Y., Beijbom, O., Zhang, N., Darrell, T.: Compact bilinear pooling. In: CVPR (2016)
15. Garcia, J., Martinel, N., Micheloni, C., Gardel, A.: Person re-identification ranking optimisation by discriminant context information analysis. In: ICCV (2015)
16. Geng, M., Wang, Y., Xiang, T., Tian, Y.: Deep transfer learning for person re-identification. arXiv:1611.05244 (2016)
17. Glorot, X., Bengio, Y.: Understanding the difficulty of training deep feedforward neural networks. In: AISTATS (2010)
18. Gray, D., Tao, H.: Viewpoint invariant pedestrian recognition with an ensemble of localized features. In: Forsyth, D., Torr, P., Zisserman, A. (eds.) ECCV 2008. LNCS, vol. 5302, pp. 262–275. Springer, Heidelberg (2008). https://doi.org/10.1007/978-3-540-88682-2_21
19. Hermans, A., Beyer, L., Leibe, B.: In defense of the triplet loss for person re-identification. arXiv:1703.07737 (2017)
20. Jing, X.Y., et al.: Super-resolution person re-identification with semi-coupled low-rank discriminant dictionary learning. In: CVPR (2015)
21. Kim, J.H., On, K.W., Kim, J., Ha, J.W., Zhang, B.T.: Hadamard product for low-rank bilinear pooling. In: ICLR (2017)
22. Kodirov, E., Xiang, T., Fu, Z., Gong, S.: Person re-identification by unsupervised ℓ_1 graph learning. In: Leibe, B., Matas, J., Sebe, N., Welling, M. (eds.) ECCV 2016. LNCS, vol. 9905, pp. 178–195. Springer, Cham (2016). https://doi.org/10.1007/978-3-319-46448-0_11
23. Li, D., Chen, X., Zhang, Z., Huang, K.: Learning deep context-aware features over body and latent parts for person re-identification. In: CVPR (2017)
24. Li, W., Zhao, R., Wang, X.: Human reidentification with transferred metric learning. In: Lee, K.M., Matsushita, Y., Rehg, J.M., Hu, Z. (eds.) ACCV 2012. LNCS, vol. 7724, pp. 31–44. Springer, Heidelberg (2013). https://doi.org/10.1007/978-3-642-37331-2_3
25. Li, W., Zhao, R., Xiao, T., Wang, X.: DeepREiD: deep filter pairing neural network for person re-identification. In: CVPR (2014)

26. Li, X., Zheng, W.S., Wang, X., Xiang, T., Gong, S.: Multi-scale learning for low-resolution person re-identification. In: ICCV (2015)
27. Liao, S., Hu, Y., Zhu, X., Li, S.Z.: Person re-identification by local maximal occurrence representation and metric learning. In: CVPR (2015)
28. Liao, S., Li, S.Z.: Efficient PSD constrained asymmetric metric learning for person re-identification. In: ICCV (2015)
29. Lin, T.-Y., et al.: Microsoft COCO: common objects in context. In: Fleet, D., Pajdla, T., Schiele, B., Tuytelaars, T. (eds.) ECCV 2014. LNCS, vol. 8693, pp. 740–755. Springer, Cham (2014). https://doi.org/10.1007/978-3-319-10602-1_48
30. Lin, T.Y., RoyChowdhury, A., Maji, S.: Bilinear CNN models for fine-grained visual recognition. In: ICCV (2015)
31. Lin, Y., Zheng, L., Zheng, Z., Wu, Y., Yang, Y.: Improving person re-identification by attribute and identity learning. arXiv:1703.07220 (2017)
32. Liu, C., Yuen, J., Torralba, A.: SIFT flow: dense correspondence across scenes and its applications. IEEE TPAMI 5(33), 978–994 (2011)
33. Liu, H., Jie, Z., Jayashree, K., Qi, M., Jiang, J., Yan, S.: Video-based person re-identification with accumulative motion context. arXiv:1701.00193 (2017)
34. Liu, X., et al.: HydraPlus-Net: attentive deep features for pedestrian analysis. In: ICCV (2017)
35. Liu, Y., Yan, J., Ouyang, W.: Quality aware network for set to set recognition. In: CVPR (2017)
36. Ma, B., Su, Y., Jurie, F.: Local descriptors encoded by fisher vectors for person re-identification. In: Fusiello, A., Murino, V., Cucchiara, R. (eds.) ECCV 2012. LNCS, vol. 7583, pp. 413–422. Springer, Heidelberg (2012). https://doi.org/10.1007/978-3-642-33863-2_41
37. van der Maaten, L., Hinton, G.: Visualizing data using t-SNE. JMLR 9, 2579–2605 (2008)
38. Martinel, N., Das, A., Micheloni, C., Roy-Chowdhury, A.K.: Temporal model adaptation for person re-identification. In: Leibe, B., Matas, J., Sebe, N., Welling, M. (eds.) ECCV 2016. LNCS, vol. 9908, pp. 858–877. Springer, Cham (2016). https://doi.org/10.1007/978-3-319-46493-0_52
39. Matsukawa, T., Okabe, T., Suzuki, E., Sato, Y.: Hierarchical Gaussian descriptor for person re-identification. In: CVPR (2016)
40. McLaughlin, N., Martinez del Rincon, J., Miller, P.: Recurrent convolutional network for video-based person re-identification. In: CVPR (2016)
41. Newell, A., Yang, K., Deng, J.: Stacked hourglass networks for human pose estimation. In: Leibe, B., Matas, J., Sebe, N., Welling, M. (eds.) ECCV 2016. LNCS, vol. 9912, pp. 483–499. Springer, Cham (2016). https://doi.org/10.1007/978-3-319-46484-8_29
42. Paisitkriangkrai, S., Shen, C., van den Hengel, A.: Learning to rank in person re-identification with metric ensembles. In: CVPR (2015)
43. Peng, P., et al.: Unsupervised cross-dataset transfer learning for person re-identification. In: CVPR (2016)
44. Pham, N., Pagh, R.: Fast and scalable polynomial kernels via explicit feature maps. In: SIGKDD (2013)
45. Ristani, E., Solera, F., Zou, R., Cucchiara, R., Tomasi, C.: Performance measures and a data set for multi-target, multi-camera tracking. In: Hua, G., Jégou, H. (eds.) ECCV 2016. LNCS, vol. 9914, pp. 17–35. Springer, Cham (2016). https://doi.org/10.1007/978-3-319-48881-3_2
46. Russakovsky, O., et al.: ImageNet large scale visual recognition challenge. Int. J. Comput. Vis. (IJCV) 115(3), 211–252 (2015)

47. Schumann, A., Stiefelhagen, R.: Person re-identification by deep learning attribute-complementary information. In: CVPR Workshops (2017)
48. Shen, Y., Lin, W., Yan, J., Xu, M., Wu, J., Wang, J.: Person re-identification with correspondence structure learning. In: ICCV (2015)
49. Shi, Z., Hospedales, T.M., Xiang, T.: Transferring a semantic representation for person re-identification and search. In: CVPR (2015)
50. Su, C., Li, J., Zhang, S., Xing, J., Gao, W., Tian, Q.: Pose-driven deep convolutional model for person re-identification. In: ICCV (2017)
51. Su, C., Yang, F., Zhang, S., Tian, Q., Davis, L.S., Gao, W.: Multi-task learning with low rank attribute embedding for person re-identification. In: ICCV (2015)
52. Su, C., Zhang, S., Xing, J., Gao, W., Tian, Q.: Deep attributes driven multi-camera person re-identification. In: Leibe, B., Matas, J., Sebe, N., Welling, M. (eds.) ECCV 2016. LNCS, vol. 9906, pp. 475–491. Springer, Cham (2016). https://doi.org/10.1007/978-3-319-46475-6_30
53. Sun, Y., Zheng, L., Deng, W., Wang, S.: SVDNet for pedestrian retrieval. In: ICCV (2017)
54. Szegedy, C., et al.: Going deeper with convolutions. In: CVPR (2015)
55. Tang, S., Andriluka, M., Andres, B., Schiele, B.: Multi people tracking with lifted multicut and person re-identification. In: CVPR (2017)
56. Ustinova, E., Ganin, Y., Lempitsky, V.: Multiregion bilinear convolutional neural networks for person re-identification. In: AVSS (2017)
57. Varior, R.R., Haloi, M., Wang, G.: Gated siamese convolutional neural network architecture for human re-identification. In: Leibe, B., Matas, J., Sebe, N., Welling, M. (eds.) ECCV 2016. LNCS, vol. 9912, pp. 791–808. Springer, Cham (2016). https://doi.org/10.1007/978-3-319-46484-8_48
58. Varior, R.R., Shuai, B., Lu, J., Xu, D., Wang, G.: A Siamese long short-term memory architecture for human re-identification. In: Leibe, B., Matas, J., Sebe, N., Welling, M. (eds.) ECCV 2016. LNCS, vol. 9911, pp. 135–153. Springer, Cham (2016). https://doi.org/10.1007/978-3-319-46478-7_9
59. Wang, F., Zuo, W., Lin, L., Zhang, D., Zhang, L.: Joint learning of single-image and cross-image representations for person re-identification. In: CVPR (2016)
60. Wang, H., Gong, S., Zhu, X., Xiang, T.: Human-in-the-loop person re-identification. In: Leibe, B., Matas, J., Sebe, N., Welling, M. (eds.) ECCV 2016. LNCS, vol. 9908, pp. 405–422. Springer, Cham (2016). https://doi.org/10.1007/978-3-319-46493-0_25
61. Wei, S.E., Ramakrishna, V., Kanade, T., Sheikh, Y.: Convolutional pose machines. In: CVPR (2016)
62. Weinrich, C., Gross, M.V.H.M.: Appearance-based 3D upper-body pose estimation and person re-identification on mobile robots. In: ICSMC. IEEE (2013)
63. Wu, L., Shen, C., van den Hengel, A.: PersonNet: person re-identification with deep convolutional neural networks. arXiv:1601.07255 (2016)
64. Xiao, T., Li, H., Ouyang, W., Wang, X.: Learning deep feature representations with domain guided dropout for person re-identification. In: CVPR (2016)
65. Xiao, T., Li, S., Wang, B., Lin, L., Wang, X.: End-to-end deep learning for person search. arXiv:1604.01850 (2016)
66. Xiao, T., Li, S., Wang, B., Lin, L., Wang, X.: Joint detection and identification feature learning for person search. In: CVPR (2017)
67. Xu, S., Cheng, Y., Gu, K., Yang, Y., Chang, S., Zhou, P.: Jointly attentive spatial-temporal pooling networks for video-based person re-identification. In: ICCV (2017)

68. Xu, Y., Lin, L., Zheng, W., Liu, X.: Human re-identification by matching compositional template with cluster sampling. In: ICCV (2013)
69. Yi, D., Lei, Z., Liao, S., Li, S.Z.: Deep metric learning for person re-identification. In: ICLR (2014)
70. Zhang, L., Xiang, T., Gong, S.: Learning a discriminative null space for person re-identification. In: CVPR (2016)
71. Zhang, Y., Li, X., Zhao, L., Zhang, Z.: Semantics-aware deep correspondence structure learning for robust person re-identification. In: IJCAI (2016)
72. Zhang, Y., Li, B., Lu, H., Irie, A., Ruan, X.: Sample-specific SVM learning for person re-identification. In: CVPR (2016)
73. Zhang, Y., Xiang, T., Hospedales, T.M., Lu, H.: Dual mutual learning. In: CVPR (2018)
74. Zhao, H., et al.: Spindle net: person re-identification with human body region guided feature decomposition and fusion. In: CVPR (2017)
75. Zhao, L., Li, X., Zhuang, Y., Wang, J.: Deeply-learned part-aligned representations for person re-identification. In: ICCV (2017)
76. Zhao, R., Ouyang, W., Wang, X.: Learning mid-level filters for person re-identification. In: CVPR (2014)
77. Zheng, L., et al.: MARS: a video benchmark for large-scale person re-identification. In: Leibe, B., Matas, J., Sebe, N., Welling, M. (eds.) ECCV 2016. LNCS, vol. 9910, pp. 868–884. Springer, Cham (2016). https://doi.org/10.1007/978-3-319-46466-4_52
78. Zheng, L., Huang, Y., Lu, H., Yang, Y.: Pose invariant embedding for deep person re-identification. arXiv:1701.07732 (2017)
79. Zheng, L., Shen, L., Tian, L., Wang, S., Wang, J., Tian, Q.: Scalable person re-identification: a benchmark. In: ICCV (2015)
80. Zheng, L., Wang, S., Tian, L., He, F., Liu, Z., Tian, Q.: Query-adaptive late fusion for image search and person re-identification. In: CVPR (2015)
81. Zheng, L., Yang, Y., Hauptmann, A.G.: Person re-identification: past, present and future. arXiv:1610.02984 (2016)
82. Zheng, W.S., Li, X., Xiang, T., Liao, S., Lai, J., Gong, S.: Partial person re-identification. In: ICCV (2015)
83. Zheng, Z., Zheng, L., Yang, Y.: A discriminatively learned CNN embedding for person re-identification. arXiv:1611.05666 (2016)
84. Zheng, Z., Zheng, L., Yang, Y.: Unlabeled samples generated by GAN improve the person re-identification baseline in vitro. In: ICCV (2017)
85. Zhong, Z., Zheng, L., Cao, D., Li, S.: Re-ranking person re-identification with k-reciprocal encoding. In: CVPR (2017)
86. Zhong, Z., Zheng, L., Kang, G., Shaozi, L., Yi, Y.: Random erasing data augmentation. arXiv:1708.04896 (2017)
87. Zhou, Z., Huang, Y., Wang, W., Wang, L., Tan, T.: See the forest for the trees: joint spatial and temporal recurrent neural networks for video-based person re-identification. In: CVPR (2017)

Learning to Navigate for Fine-Grained Classification

Ze Yang[1], Tiange Luo[1], Dong Wang[1], Zhiqiang Hu[1], Jun Gao[1],
and Liwei Wang[1,2]

[1] Key Laboratory of Machine Perception, MOE, School of EECS,
Peking University, Beijing, China
{yangze,luotg,wangdongcis,huzq,jun.gao}@pku.edu.cn
[2] Center for Data Science, Beijing Institute of Big Data Research,
Peking University, Beijing, China
wanglw@cis.pku.edu.cn

Abstract. Fine-grained classification is challenging due to the difficulty of finding discriminative features. Finding those subtle traits that fully characterize the object is not straightforward. To handle this circumstance, we propose a novel self-supervision mechanism to effectively localize informative regions without the need of bounding-box/part annotations. Our model, termed NTS-Net for Navigator-Teacher-Scrutinizer Network, consists of a Navigator agent, a Teacher agent and a Scrutinizer agent. In consideration of intrinsic consistency between informativeness of the regions and their probability being ground-truth class, we design a novel training paradigm, which enables Navigator to detect most informative regions under the guidance from Teacher. After that, the Scrutinizer scrutinizes the proposed regions from Navigator and makes predictions. Our model can be viewed as a multi-agent cooperation, wherein agents benefit from each other, and make progress together. NTS-Net can be trained end-to-end, while provides accurate fine-grained classification predictions as well as highly informative regions during inference. We achieve state-of-the-art performance in extensive benchmark datasets.

1 Introduction

Fine-grained classification aims at differentiating subordinate classes of a common superior class, *e.g.* distinguishing wild bird species, automobile models, *etc.* Those subordinate classes are usually defined by domain experts with complicated rules, which typically focus on subtle differences in particular regions. While deep learning has promoted the research in many computer vision [24,33,38] tasks, its application in fine-grained classification is more or less unsatisfactory, due in large part to the difficulty of finding informative regions and extracting discriminative features therein. The situation is even worse for subordinate classes with varied poses like birds.

As a result, the key to fine-grained classification lies in developing automatic methods to accurately identify informative regions in an image. Some previous

© Springer Nature Switzerland AG 2018
V. Ferrari et al. (Eds.): ECCV 2018, LNCS 11218, pp. 438–454, 2018.
https://doi.org/10.1007/978-3-030-01264-9_26

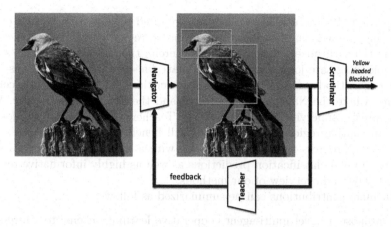

Fig. 1. The overview of our model. The Navigator navigates the model to focus on the most informative regions (denoted by yellow rectangles), while Teacher evaluates the regions proposed by Navigator and provides feedback. After that, the Scrutinizer scrutinizes those regions to make predictions. (Color figure online)

works [2,3,8,13,29,45,46] take advantage of fine-grained human annotations, like annotations for bird parts in bird classification. While achieving decent results, the fine-grained human annotations they require are expensive, making those methods less applicable in practice. Other methods [43,47–49] employ an unsupervised learning scheme to localize informative regions. They eliminate the need for the expensive annotations, but lack a mechanism to guarantee that the model focuses on the right regions, which usually results in degraded accuracy.

In this paper, we propose a novel self-supervised mechanism to effectively localize informative regions without the need of fine-grained bounding-box/part annotations. The model we develop, which we term NTS-Net for Navigator-Teacher-Scrutinizer Network, employs a multi-agent cooperative learning scheme to address the problem of accurately identifying informative regions in an image. Intuitively, the regions assigned higher probability to be ground-truth class should contain more object-characteristic semantics enhancing the classification performance of the whole image. Thus we design a novel loss function to optimize the informativeness of each selected region to have the same order as its probability being ground-truth class, and we take the ground-truth class of full image as the ground-truth class of regions.

Specifically, our NTS-Net consists of a Navigator agent, a Teacher agent and a Scrutinizer agent. The Navigator navigates the model to focus on the most informative regions: for each region in the image, Navigator predicts how informative the region is, and the predictions are used to propose the most informative regions. The Teacher evaluates the regions proposed by Navigator and provides feedbacks: for each proposed region, the Teacher evaluates its probability belonging to ground-truth class; the confidence evaluations guide the Navigator to propose more informative regions with our novel ordering-consistent loss function. The Scrutinizer scrutinizes proposed regions from Navigator and makes fine-grained classifications: each proposed region is enlarged to the same size and the Scrutinizer extracts features therein; the features of regions and of the whole image are jointly processed to make fine-grained classifications. As a whole, our method can be viewed as an actor-critic [21] scheme in reinforcement learning, where the Navigator is the actor and the Teacher is the critic. With a more precise supervision provided by the Teacher, the Navigator will localize more informative regions, which in turn will benefit the Teacher. As a result, agents make progress together and end up with a model which provides accurate fine-grained classification predictions as well as highly informative regions. Figure 1 shows an overview of our methods.

Our main contributions can be summarized as follows:

- We propose a novel multi-agent cooperative learning scheme to address the problem of accurately identifying informative regions in the fine-grained classification task without bounding-box/part annotations.
- We design a novel loss function, which enables Teacher to guide Navigator to localize the most informative regions in an image by enforcing the consistency between regions' informativeness and their probability being ground-truth class.
- Our model can be trained end-to-end, while provides accurate fine-grained classification predictions as well as highly informative regions during inference. We achieve state-of-the-art performance in extensive benchmark datasets.

The remainder of this paper is organized as follows: We will review the related work in Sect. 2. In Sect. 3 we will elaborate our methods. Experimental results are presented and analyzed in Sect. 4 and finally, Sect. 5 concludes.

2 Related Work

2.1 Fine-Grained Classification

There have been a variety of methods designed to distinguish fine-grained categories. Since some fine-grained classification datasets provide bounding-box/part annotations, early works [2,8,45] take advantage of those annotations at both training and inference phase. However in practice when the model is deployed, no human annotations will be available. Later on, some works [3,46] use bounding-box/part annotations only at training phase. Under this setting, the framework is quite similar to detection: selecting regions and then classifying the pose-normalized objects. Besides, Jonathan *et al.* [22] use co-segmentation and alignment to generate parts without part annotations but the bounding-box annotations are used during training. Recently, a more general setting has emerged that does not require bounding box/part annotations either at training or inference time. This setting makes fine-grained classification more useful in practice. This paper will mainly consider the last setting, where bounding-box/part annotations are not needed either at training or inference phase.

In order to learn without fine-grained annotations, Jaderberg *et al.* [19] propose Spatial Transformer Network to explicitly manipulate data representation within the network and predict the location of informative regions. Lin *et al.* [28] use a bilinear model to build discriminative features of the whole image; the model is able to capture subtle differences between different subordinate classes. Zhang *et al.* [47] propose a two-step approach to learn a bunch of part detectors and part saliency maps. Fu *et al.* [12] use an alternate optimization scheme to train attention proposal network and region-based classifier; they show that two tasks are correlated and can benefit each other. Zhao *et al.* [48] propose Diversified Visual Attention Network (DVAN) to explicitly pursues the diversity of attention and better gather discriminative information. Lam *et al.* [25] propose a Heuristic-Successor Network (HSNet) to formulate the fine-grained classification problem as a sequential search for informative regions in an image.

2.2 Object Detection

Early object detection methods employ SIFT [34] or HOG [10] features. Recent works are mainly focusing on convolutional neural networks. Approaches like R-CNN [14], OverFeat [40] and SPPnet [16] adopt traditional image-processing methods to generate object proposals and perform category classification and bounding box regression. Later works like Faster R-CNN [38] propose Region Proposal Network (RPN) for proposal generation. YOLO [37] and SSD [31] improve detection speed over Faster R-CNN [38] by employing a single-shot architecture. On the other hand, Feature Pyramid Networks (FPN) [27] focuses on better addressing multi-scale problem and generates anchors from multiple feature maps. Our method requires selecting informative regions, which can also be viewed as object detection. To the best of our knowledge, we are the first one to introduce FPN into fine-grained classification while eliminates the need of human annotations.

2.3 Learning to Rank

Learning to rank is drawing attention in the field of machine learning and information retrieval [30]. The training data consist of lists of items with assigned orders, while the objective is to learn the order for item lists. The ranking loss function is designed to penalize pairs with wrong order. Let $X = \{X_1, X_2, \cdots, X_n\}$ denote the objects to rank, and $Y = \{Y_1, Y_2, \cdots, Y_n\}$ the indexing of the objects, where $Y_i \geq Y_j$ means X_i should be ranked before X_j. Let $\mathbb{F}$ be the hypothesis set of ranking function. The goal is to find a ranking function $\mathcal{F} \in \mathbb{F}$ that minimize a certain loss function defined on $\{X_1, X_2 \cdots X_n\}$, $\{Y_1, Y_2, \cdots, Y_n\}$ and $\mathcal{F}$. There are many ranking methods. Generally speaking, these methods can be divided into three categories: the point-wise approach [9], pair-wise approach [4,18] and list-wise approach [6,44].

Point-wise approach assign each data with a numerical score, and the learning-to-rank problem can be formulated as a regression problem, for example with $L2$ loss function:

$$L_{point}(\mathcal{F}, X, Y) = \sum_{i=1}^{n} (\mathcal{F}(X_i) - Y_i)^2 \qquad (1)$$

In the pair-wise ranking approach, the learning-to-rank problem is formulated as a classification problem. *i.e.* to learn a binary classifier that chooses the superiority in a pair. Suppose $\mathcal{F}(X_i, X_j)$ only takes a value from $\{1, 0\}$, where $\mathcal{F}(X_i, X_j) = 0$ means X_i is ranked before X_j. Then the loss is defined on all pairs as in Eq. 2, and the goal is to find an optimal $\mathcal{F}$ to minimize the average number of pairs with wrong order.

$$L_{pair}(\mathcal{F}, X, Y) = \sum_{(i,j): Y_i < Y_j} \mathcal{F}(X_i, X_j) \qquad (2)$$

List-wise approach directly optimizes the whole list, and it can be formalized as a classification problem on permutations. Let $\mathcal{F}(X, Y)$ be the ranking function, the loss is defined as:

$$L_{list}(\mathcal{F}, X, Y) = \begin{cases} 1, & \text{if } \mathcal{F}(X) \neq Y \\ 0, & \text{if } \mathcal{F}(X) = Y \end{cases} \qquad (3)$$

In our approach, our navigator loss function adopts from the multi-rating pair-wise ranking loss, which enforces the consistency between region's informativeness and probability being ground-truth class.

3 Methods

3.1 Approach Overview

Our approach rests on the assumption that informative regions are helpful to better characterize the object, so fusing features from informative regions and the full image will achieve better performance. Therefore the goal is to localize the most informative regions of the objects. We assume all regions[1] are rectangle, and we denote $\mathbb{A}$ as the set of all regions in the given image[2]. We define information function $\mathcal{I} : \mathbb{A} \to (-\infty, \infty)$ evaluating how informative the region $R \in \mathbb{A}$ is, and we define the confidence function $\mathcal{C} : \mathbb{A} \to [0, 1]$ as a classifier to evaluate the confidence that the region belongs to ground-truth class. As mentioned in Sect. 1, more informative regions should have higher confidence, so the following condition should hold:

---

[1] Without loss of generality, we also treat full image as a region.

[2] Notation: we use $\mathcal{C}$alligraphy font to denote mapping, $\mathbb{B}$lackboard bold font to denote special sets, And we use **B**old font to denote parameters in network.

- Condition 1: for any $R_1, R_2 \in \mathbb{A}$, if $\mathcal{C}(R_1) > \mathcal{C}(R_2)$, $\mathcal{I}(R_1) > \mathcal{I}(R_2)$

We use Navigator network to approximate information function $\mathcal{I}$ and Teacher network to approximate confidence function $\mathcal{C}$. For the sake of simplicity, we choose M regions $\mathbb{A}_M$ in the region space $\mathbb{A}$. For each region $R_i \in \mathbb{A}_M$, the Navigator network evaluates its informativeness $\mathcal{I}(R_i)$, and the Teacher network evaluates its confidence $\mathcal{C}(R_i)$. In order to satisfy Condition. 1, we optimize Navigator network to make $\{\mathcal{I}(R_1), \mathcal{I}(R_2), \cdots, \mathcal{I}(R_M)\}$ and $\{\mathcal{C}(R_1), \mathcal{C}(R_2), \cdots, \mathcal{C}(R_M)\}$ having the same order.

As the Navigator network improves in accordance with the Teacher network, it will produce more informative regions to help Scrutinizer network make better fine-grained classification result.

In Sect. 3.2, we will describe how informative regions are proposed by Navigator under Teacher's supervision. In Sect. 3.3, we will present how to get fine-grained classification result from Scrutinizer. In Sects. 3.4 and 3.5, we will introduce the network architecture and optimization in detail, respectively.

3.2   Navigator and Teacher

Navigating to possible informative regions can be viewed as a region proposal problem, which has been widely studied in [1,7,11,20,41]. Most of them are based on a sliding-windows search mechanism. Ren *et al.* [38] introduce a novel region proposal network (RPN) that shares convolutional layers with the classifier and mitigates the marginal cost for computing proposals. They use anchors to simultaneously predict multiple region proposals. Each anchor is associated with a sliding window position, aspect ratio, and box scale. Inspired by the idea of anchors, our Navigator network takes an image as input, and produce a bunch of rectangle regions $\{R_1', R_2', \ldots R_A'\}$, each with a score denoting the informativeness of the region (Fig. 2 shows the design of our anchors). For an input image X of size 448, we choose anchors to have scales of $\{48, 96, 192\}$ and ratios $\{1:1, 3:2, 2:3\}$, then Navigator network will produce a list denoting the informativeness of all anchors. We sort the information list as in Eq. 4, where A is the number of anchors, $\mathcal{I}(R_i)$ is the i-th element in sorted information list.

$$\mathcal{I}(R_1) \geq \mathcal{I}(R_2) \geq \cdots \geq \mathcal{I}(R_A) \tag{4}$$

To reduce region redundancy, we adopt non-maximum suppression (NMS) on the regions based on their informativeness. Then we take the top-M informative regions $\{R_1, R_2, \ldots, R_M\}$ and feed them into the Teacher network to get the confidence as $\{\mathcal{C}(R_1), \mathcal{C}(R_2), \ldots \mathcal{C}(R_M)\}$. Figure 3 shows the overview with $M = 3$, where M is a hyper-parameters denoting how many regions are used to train Navigator network. We optimize Navigator network to make $\{\mathcal{I}(R_1), \mathcal{I}(R_2), \ldots \mathcal{I}(R_M)\}$ and $\{\mathcal{C}(R_1), \mathcal{C}(R_2), \ldots \mathcal{C}(R_M)\}$ having the same order. Every proposed region is used to optimize Teacher by minimizing the cross-entropy loss between ground-truth class and the predicted confidence.

Fig. 2. The design of anchors. We use three scales and three ratios. For an image of size 448, we construct anchors to have scales of {48, 96, 192} and ratios {1:1, 2:3, 3:2}.

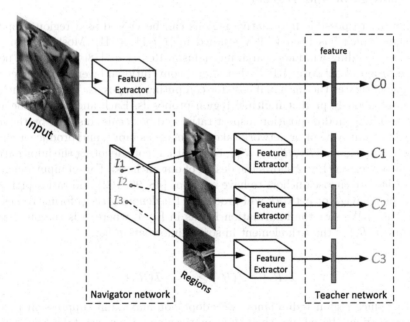

Fig. 3. Training method of Navigator network. For an input image, the feature extractor extracts its deep feature map, then the feature map is fed into Navigator network to compute the informativeness of all regions. We choose top-M (here $M = 3$ for explanation) informative regions after NMS and denote their informativeness as $\{I_1, I_2, I_3\}$. Then we crop the regions from the full image, resize them to the pre-defined size and feed them into Teacher network, then we get the confidences $\{C_1, C_2, C_3\}$. We optimize Navigator network to make $\{I_1, I_2, I_3\}$ and $\{C_1, C_2, C_3\}$ having the same order.

3.3   Scrutinizer

As Navigator network gradually converges, it will produce informative object-characteristic regions to help Scrutinizer network make decisions. We use the top-K informative regions combined with the full image as input to train the Scrutinizer network. In other words, those K regions are used to facilitate fine-grained recognition. Figure 4 demonstrates this process with $K = 3$. Lam *et al.* [25] show that using informative regions can reduce intra-class variance and are likely to generate higher confidence scores on the correct label. Our comparative experiments show that adding informative regions substantially improve fine-grained classification results in a wide range of datasets including CUB-200-2001, FGVC Aircraft, and Stanford Cars, which are shown in Tables 2 and 3.

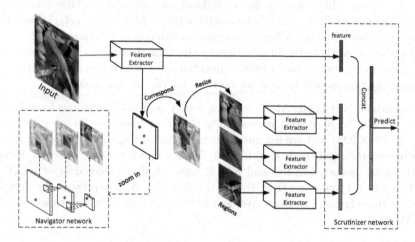

Fig. 4. Inference process of our model (here $K = 3$ for explanation). The input image is first fed into feature extractor, then the Navigator network proposes the most informative regions of the input. We crop these regions from the input image and resize them to the pre-defined size, then we use feature extractor to compute the features of these regions and fuse them with the feature of the input image. Finally, the Scrutinizer network processes the fused feature to predict labels.

3.4   Network Architecture

In order to obtain correspondence between region proposals and feature vectors in feature map, we use fully-convolutional network as the feature extractor, without fully-connected layers. Specifically, we choose ResNet-50 [17] pre-trained on ILSVRC2012 [39] as the CNN feature extractor, and Navigator, Scrutinizer, Teacher network all share parameters in feature extractor. We denote parameters in feature extractor as $\mathbf{W}$. For input image X, the extracted deep representations are denoted as $X \otimes \mathbf{W}$, where $\otimes$ denotes the combinations of convolution, pooling, and activation operations.

Navigator Network. Inspired by the design of Feature Pyramid Networks (FPN) [27], we use a top-down architecture with lateral connections to detect multi-scale regions. We use convolutional layers to compute feature hierarchy layer by layer, followed by ReLU activation and max-pooling. Then we get a series of feature maps of different spatial resolutions. The anchors in larger feature maps correspond to smaller regions. Navigator network in Figure. 4 shows the sketch of our design. Using multi-scale feature maps from different layers we can generate informativeness of regions among different scales and ratios. In our setting, we use feature maps of size $\{14 \times 14, 7 \times 7, 4 \times 4\}$ corresponding to regions of scale $\{48 \times 48, 96 \times 96, 192 \times 192\}$. We denote the parameters in Navigator network as $\mathbf{W}_\mathcal{I}$ (including shared parameters in feature extractor).

Teacher Network. The Teacher network (Fig. 3) approximates the mapping $\mathcal{C} : \mathbb{A} \rightarrow [0, 1]$ which denotes the confidence of each region. After receiving M scale-normalized (224×224) informative regions $\{R_1, R_2, \dots, R_M\}$ from Navigator network, Teacher network outputs confidence as teaching signals to help Navigator network learn. In addition to the shared layers in feature extractor, the Teaching network has a fully connected layer which has 2048 neurons. We denote the parameters in Teacher network as $\mathbf{W}_\mathcal{C}$ for convenience.

Scrutinizer Network. After receiving top-K informative regions from Navigator network, the K regions are resized to the pre-defined size (in our experiments we use 224×224) and are fed into feature extractor to generate those K regions' feature vector, each with length 2048. Then we concatenate those K features with input image's feature, and feed it into a fully-connected layer which has $2048 \times (K + 1)$ neurons (Fig. 4). We use function $\mathcal{S}$ to represent the composition of these transformations. We denote the parameters in Scrutinizer network as $\mathbf{W}_\mathcal{S}$.

3.5   Loss Function and Optimization

Navigation loss. We denote the M most informative regions predicted by Navigator network as $R = \{R_1, R_2, \dots, R_M\}$, their informativeness as $I = \{I_1, I_2, \dots, I_M\}$, and their confidence predicted by Teacher network as $C = \{C_1, C_2, \dots, C_M\}$. Then the navigation loss is defined as follow:

$$L_\mathcal{I}(I, C) = \sum_{(i,s):C_i < C_s} f(I_s - I_i) \tag{5}$$

where the function f is a non-increasing function that encourages $I_s > I_i$ if $C_s > C_i$, and we use hinge loss function $f(x) = \max\{1 - x, 0\}$ in our experiment. The loss function penalize reversed pairs[3] between I and C, and encourage that I and C is in the same order. Navigation loss function is differentiable, and

---

[3] Given a list $x = \{x_1, x_2, \cdots, x_n\}$ be the data and a permutation $\pi = \{\pi_1, \pi_2, \cdots, \pi_n\}$ be the order of the data. Reverse pairs are pairs of elements in x with reverse order. *i.e.* if $x_i < x_j$ and $\pi_i > \pi_j$ holds at same time, then x_i and x_j is an reverse pair.

calculating the derivative *w.r.t.* $\mathbf{W}_{\mathcal{I}}$ by the chain rule in back-propagation we get:

$$\frac{\partial L_{\mathcal{I}}(I, C)}{\partial \mathbf{W}_{\mathcal{I}}} \tag{6}$$

$$= \sum_{(i,s):C_i < C_s} f'(I_s - I_i) \cdot \left(\frac{\partial \mathcal{I}(x)}{\partial \mathbf{W}_{\mathcal{I}}} \Big|_{x=R_s} - \frac{\partial \mathcal{I}(x)}{\partial \mathbf{W}_{\mathcal{I}}} \Big|_{x=R_i} \right)$$

The equation follows directly by the definition of $I_i = \mathcal{I}(R_i)$.

Teaching Loss. We define the Teacher loss $L_{\mathcal{C}}$ as follows:

$$L_{\mathcal{C}} = - \sum_{i=1}^{M} \log \mathcal{C}(R_i) - \log \mathcal{C}(X) \tag{7}$$

where $\mathcal{C}$ is the confidence function which maps the region to its probability being ground-truth class. The first term in Eq. 7 is the sum of cross entropy loss of all regions, the second term is the cross entropy loss of full image.[4]

Scrutinizing Loss. When the Navigator network navigates to the most informative regions $\{R_1, R_2, \cdots, R_K\}$, the Scrutinizer network makes the fine-grained recognition result $P = \mathcal{S}(X, R_1, R_2, \cdots, R_K)$. We employ cross entropy loss as classification loss:

$$L_{\mathcal{S}} = - \log \mathcal{S}(X, R_1, R_2, \cdots, R_K) \tag{8}$$

Algorithm 1. NTS-Net algorithm

Input: full image X, hyper-parameters K, M, λ, μ, assume $K \leq M$
Output: predict probability P

1 **for** $t = 1, T$ **do**
2   Take full image $= X$
3   Generate anchors $\{R'_1, R'_2, \ldots, R'_A\}$
4     $\{I'_1, \ldots, I'_A\} := \mathcal{I}(\{R'_1, \ldots, R'_A\})$
5     $\{I_i\}_{i=1}^{A}, \{R_i\}_{i=1}^{A} := \text{NMS}(\{I'_i\}_{i=1}^{A}, \{R'_i\}_{i=1}^{A})$
6   Select top M: $\{I_i\}_{i=1}^{M}, \{R_i\}_{i=1}^{M}$
7     $\{C_1, \ldots, C_K\} := \mathcal{C}(\{R_1, \ldots, R_K\})$
8     $P = \mathcal{S}(X, R_1, R_2, \cdots, R_K)$
9   Calculate L_{total} from Eq. 9
10   BP(L_{total}) get gradient *w.r.t.* $\mathbf{W}_{\mathcal{I}}$, $\mathbf{W}_{\mathcal{C}}$, $\mathbf{W}_{\mathcal{S}}$
11   Update $\mathbf{W}_{\mathcal{I}}$, $\mathbf{W}_{\mathcal{C}}$, $\mathbf{W}_{\mathcal{S}}$ using SGD
12 **end**

---

[4] The second term helps training. For simplicity, we also denote the confidence function of full image as $\mathcal{C}$.

Joint Training Algorithm. The total loss is defined as:

$$L_{total} = L_{\mathcal{I}} + \lambda \cdot L_{\mathcal{S}} + \mu \cdot L_{\mathcal{C}} \tag{9}$$

where λ and μ are hyper-parameters. In our setting, $\lambda = \mu = 1$. The overall algorithm is summarized in Algorithm 1. We use stochastic gradient method to optimize L_{total}.

4 Experiments

4.1 Dataset

We comprehensively evaluate our algorithm on Caltech-UCSD Birds (CUB-200-2011) [42], Stanford Cars [23] and FGVC Aircraft [35] datasets, which are widely used benchmark for fine-grained image classification. We do not use any bounding box/part annotations in all our experiments. Statistics of all 3 datasets are shown in Table 1, and we follow the same train/test splits as in the table.

Caltech-UCSD Birds. CUB-200-2011 is a bird classification task with 11,788 images from 200 wild bird species. The ratio of train data and test data is roughly 1 : 1. It is generally considered one of the most competitive datasets since each species has only 30 images for training.

Stanford Cars. Stanford Cars dataset contains 16,185 images over 196 classes, and each class has a roughly 50-50 split. The cars in the images are taken from many angles, and the classes are typically at the level of production year and model (*e.g.* 2012 Tesla Model S).

FGVC Aircraft. FGVC Aircraft dataset contains 10,000 images over 100 classes, and the train/test set split ratio is around 2 : 1. Most images in this dataset are airplanes. And the dataset is organized in a four-level hierarchy, from finer to coarser: Model, Variant, Family, Manufacturer.

Table 1. Statistics of benchmark datasets.

Dataset	#Class	#Train	#Test
CUB-200-2011	200	5,994	5,794
Stanford cars	196	8,144	8,041
FGVC aircraft	100	6,667	3,333

4.2 Implementation Details

In all our experiments, we preprocess images to size 448×448, and we fix $M = 6$ which means 6 regions are used to train Navigator network for each image (there is no restriction on hyper-parameters K and M). We use fully-convolutional network ResNet-50 [17] as feature extractor and use Batch Normalization as regularizer. We use Momentum SGD with initial learning rate 0.001 and multiplied by 0.1 after 60 epochs, and we use weight decay 1e−4. The NMS threshold is set to 0.25, no pre-trained detection model is used. Our model is robust to the selection of hyper-parameters. We use Pytorch to implement our algorithm and the code will be available at https://github.com/yangze0930/NTS-Net.

4.3   Quantitative Results

Overall, our proposed system outperforms all previous methods. Since we do not use any bounding box/part annotations, we do not compare with methods which depend on those annotations. Table 2 shows the comparison between our results and previous best results in CUB-200-2011. ResNet-50 is a strong baseline, which by itself achieves 84.5% accuracy, while our proposed NTS-Net outperforms it by a clear margin 3.0%. Compared to [26] which also use ResNet-50 as feature extractor, we achieve a 1.5% improvement. It is worth noting that when we use only full image ($K = 0$) as input to the Scrutinizer, we achieve 85.3% accuracy, which is also higher than ResNet-50. This phenomenon demonstrates that, in navigating to informative regions, Navigator network also facilitates Scrutinizer by sharing feature extractor, which learns better feature representation.

Table 2. Experimental results in CUB-200-2011.

Method	top-1 accuracy
MG-CNN [43]	81.7%
Bilinear-CNN [28]	84.1%
ST-CNN [19]	84.1%
FCAN [32]	84.3%
ResNet-50 (implemented in [26])	84.5%
PDFR [47]	84.5%
RA-CNN [12]	85.3%
HIHCA [5]	85.3%
Boost-CNN [36]	85.6%
DT-RAM [26]	86.0%
MA-CNN [49]	86.5%
Our NTS-Net ($K = 2$)	87.3%
Our NTS-Net ($K = 4$)	**87.5%**

Table 3 shows our result in FGVC Aircraft and Stanford Cars, respectively. Our model achieves new state-of-the-art results with 91.4% top-1 accuracy in FGVC Aircraft and 93.9% top-1 accuracy in Stanford Cars.

4.4   Ablation Study

In order to analyze the influence of different components in our framework, we design different runs in CUB-200-2011 and report the results in Table 4. We

Table 3. Experimental results in FGVC Aircraft and Stanford Cars.

Method	Top-1 on FGVC aircraft	Top-1 on stanford cars
FV-CNN [15]	81.5%	-
FCAN [32]	-	89.1%
Bilinear-CNN [28]	84.1%	91.3%
RA-CNN [12]	88.2%	92.5%
HIHCA [5]	88.3%	91.7%
Boost-CNN [36]	88.5%	92.1%
MA-CNN [49]	89.9%	92.8%
DT-RAM [26]	-	93.1%
Our NTS-Net (K = 2)	90.8%	93.7%
Our NTS-Net (K = 4)	**91.4%**	**93.9%**

use NS-Net to denote the model without Teacher's guidance, NS-Net let the Navigator network alone to propose regions and the accuracy drops from 87.5% to 83.3%, we hypothesize it is because the navigator receives no supervision from teacher and will propose random regions, which we believe cannot benefit classification. We also study the role of hyper-parameter K, *i.e.* how many part regions have been used for classification. Referring to Table 4, accuracy only increases 0.2% when K increases from 2 to 4, the accuracy improvement is minor while feature dimensionality nearly doubles. On the other hand, accuracy increases 2.0% when K increases from 0 to 2, which demonstrate simply increasing feature dimensionality will only get minor improvement, but our multi-agent framework will achieve considerable improvements (0.2% vs 2%).

Table 4. Study of influence factor in CUB-200-2011.

Method	Top-1 accuracy
ResNet-50 baseline	84.5%
NS-Net (K = 4)	83.3%
Our NTS-Net (K = 0)	85.3%
Our NTS-Net (K = 2)	87.3%
Our NTS-Net (K = 4)	**87.5%**

4.5   Qualitative Results

To analyze where Navigator network navigates the model, we draw the navigation regions predicted by Navigator network in Fig. 5. We use red, orange, yellow, green rectangles to denote the top four informative regions proposed by Navigator network, with red rectangle denoting most informative one. It can be seen that the localized regions are indeed informative for fine-grained classification. The first row shows $K = 2$ in CUB-200-2011 dataset: we can find that using two regions are able to cover informative parts of birds, especially in the second picture where the color of the bird and the background is quite similar. The second row shows $K = 4$ in CUB-200-2011: we can see that the most informative regions of birds are head, wings and main body, which is consistent with the human perception. The third row shows $K = 4$ in Stanford Cars: we can find that the headlamps and grilles are considered the most informative regions of cars. The fourth row shows $K = 4$ in FGVC Airplane: the Navigator network locates the airplane wings and head, which are very helpful for classification.

Fig. 5. The most informative regions proposed by Navigator network. The first row shows $K = 2$ in CUB-200-2011 dataset. The second to fourth rows show $K = 4$ in CUB-200-2011, Stanford Cars and FGVC Aircraft, respectively.

5 Conclusions

In this paper, we propose a novel method for fine-grained classification without the need of bounding box/part annotations. The three networks, Navigator, Teacher and Scrutinizer cooperate and reinforce each other. We design a novel loss function considering the ordering consistency between regions' informativeness and probability being ground-truth class. Our algorithm is end-to-end trainable and achieves state-of-the-art results in CUB-200-2001, FGVC Aircraft and Stanford Cars datasets.

Acknowledgments. This work is supported by National Basic Research Program of China (973 Program) (grant no. 2015CB352502), NSFC (61573026) and BJNSF (L172037).

References

1. Arbelaez, P., Ponttuset, J., Barron, J., Marques, F., Malik, J.: Multiscale combinatorial grouping. In: CVPR, pp. 328–335 (2014)
2. Berg, T., Belhumeur, P.N.: POOF: part-based one-vs.-one features for fine-grained categorization, face verification, and attribute estimation. In: CVPR (2013)
3. Branson, S., Horn, G.V., Belongie, S., Perona, P.: Bird species categorization using pose normalized deep convolutional nets. In: BMVC (2014)
4. Burges, C., et al.: Learning to rank using gradient descent. In: ICML, pp. 89–96 (2005)
5. Cai, S., Zuo, W., Zhang, L.: Higher-order integration of hierarchical convolutional activations for fine-grained visual categorization. In: ICCV, October 2017
6. Cao, Z., Qin, T., Liu, T.Y., Tsai, M.F., Li, H.: Learning to rank: from pairwise approach to listwise approach. In: ICML, pp. 129–136 (2007)
7. Carreira, J., Sminchisescu, C.: CPMC: Automatic Object Segmentation Using Constrained Parametric Min-Cuts. IEEE Computer Society (2012)
8. Chai, Y., Lempitsky, V., Zisserman, A.: Symbiotic segmentation and part localization for fine-grained categorization. In: ICCV, pp. 321–328 (2013)
9. Cossock, D., Zhang, T.: Statistical analysis of bayes optimal subset ranking. IEEE Trans. Inf. Theory **54**(11), 5140–5154 (2008)
10. Dalal, N., Triggs, B.: Histograms of oriented gradients for human detection. In: CVPR, pp. 886–893 (2005)
11. Endres, I., Hoiem, D.: Category independent object proposals. In: Daniilidis, K., Maragos, P., Paragios, N. (eds.) ECCV 2010. LNCS, vol. 6315, pp. 575–588. Springer, Heidelberg (2010). https://doi.org/10.1007/978-3-642-15555-0_42
12. Fu, J., Zheng, H., Mei, T.: Look closer to see better: recurrent attention convolutional neural network for fine-grained image recognition. In: CVPR
13. Gavves, E., Fernando, B., Snoek, C.G.M., Smeulders, A.W.M., Tuytelaars, T.: Fine-grained categorization by alignments. In: ICCV, pp. 1713–1720 (2014)
14. Girshick, R., Donahue, J., Darrell, T., Malik, J.: Rich feature hierarchies for accurate object detection and semantic segmentation. In: CVPR, pp. 580–587 (2014)
15. Gosselin, P.H., Murray, N., Jgou, H., Perronnin, F.: Revisiting the fisher vector for fine-grained classification. Patt. Recogn. Lett. **49**, 92–98 (2014)
16. He, K., Zhang, X., Ren, S., Sun, J.: Spatial pyramid pooling in deep convolutional networks for visual recognition. TPAMI **37**(9), 1904–1916 (2015)
17. He, K., Zhang, X., Ren, S., Sun, J.: Deep residual learning for image recognition. In: CVPR, pp. 770–778 (2016)
18. Herbrich, R.: Large margin rank boundaries for ordinal regression. In: Advances in Large Margin Classifiers, vol. 88 (2000)
19. Jaderberg, M., Simonyan, K., Zisserman, A., kavukcuoglu, k.: Spatial transformer networks. In: NIPS, pp. 2017–2025 (2015)
20. Jie, Z., Liang, X., Feng, J., Jin, X., Lu, W., Yan, S.: Tree-structured reinforcement learning for sequential object localization. In: NIPS, pp. 127–135 (2016)
21. Konda, V.R.: Actor-critic algorithms. SIAM J. Control Optim. **42**(4), 1143–1166 (2002)

22. Krause, J., Jin, H., Yang, J., Fei-Fei, L.: Fine-grained recognition without part annotations. In: CVPR, June 2015
23. Krause, J., Stark, M., Jia, D., Li, F.F.: 3D object representations for fine-grained categorization. In: ICCV Workshops, pp. 554–561 (2013)
24. Krizhevsky, A., Sutskever, I., Hinton, G.E.: ImageNet classification with deep convolutional neural networks. In: NIPS, pp. 1097–1105 (2012)
25. Lam, M., Mahasseni, B., Todorovic, S.: Fine-grained recognition as HSnet search for informative image parts. In: CVPR, July 2017
26. Li, Z., Yang, Y., Liu, X., Zhou, F., Wen, S., Xu, W.: Dynamic computational time for visual attention. In: ICCV, October 2017
27. Lin, T.Y., Dollar, P., Girshick, R., He, K., Hariharan, B., Belongie, S.: Feature pyramid networks for object detection. In: CVPR, July 2017
28. Lin, T.Y., RoyChowdhury, A., Maji, S.: Bilinear CNN models for fine-grained visual recognition. In: ICCV (2015)
29. Liu, J., Kanazawa, A., Jacobs, D., Belhumeur, P.: Dog breed classification using part localization. In: Fitzgibbon, A., Lazebnik, S., Perona, P., Sato, Y., Schmid, C. (eds.) ECCV 2012. LNCS, vol. 7572, pp. 172–185. Springer, Heidelberg (2012). https://doi.org/10.1007/978-3-642-33718-5_13
30. Liu, T.Y.: Learning to rank for information retrieval. Found. Trends Inf. Retr. **3**(3), 225–331 (2009)
31. Liu, W., et al.: SSD: single shot multibox detector. In: Leibe, B., Matas, J., Sebe, N., Welling, M. (eds.) ECCV 2016. LNCS, vol. 9905, pp. 21–37. Springer, Cham (2016). https://doi.org/10.1007/978-3-319-46448-0_2
32. Liu, X., Xia, T., Wang, J., Lin, Y.: Fully convolutional attention localization networks: efficient attention localization for fine-grained recognition. CoRR (2016)
33. Long, J., Shelhamer, E., Darrell, T.: Fully convolutional networks for semantic segmentation. In: CVPR, November 2015
34. Lowe, D.G.: Distinctive image features from scale-invariant keypoints. IJCV (2004)
35. Maji, S., Kannala, J., Rahtu, E., Blaschko, M., Vedaldi, A.: Fine-grained visual classification of aircraft. Technical report (2013)
36. Moghimi, M., Belongie, S., Saberian, M., Yang, J., Vasconcelos, N., Li, L.J.: Boosted convolutional neural networks. In: BMVC, pp. 24.1–24.13 (2016)
37. Redmon, J., Divvala, S., Girshick, R., Farhadi, A.: You only look once: unified, real-time object detection. In: CVPR, pp. 779–788 (2016)
38. Ren, S., He, K., Girshick, R., Sun, J.: Faster R-CNN: towards real-time object detection with region proposal networks. In: NIPS, pp. 91–99 (2015)
39. Russakovsky, O., et al.: ImageNet large scale visual recognition challenge. IJCV **115**(3), 211–252 (2015)
40. Sermanet, P., Eigen, D., Zhang, X., Mathieu, M., Fergus, R., Lecun, Y.: OverFeat: integrated recognition, localization and detection using convolutional networks. Arxiv (2013)
41. Uijlings, J.R., Sande, K.E., Gevers, T., Smeulders, A.W.: Selective search for object recognition. IJCV **104**(2), 154–171 (2013)
42. Wah, C., Branson, S., Welinder, P., Perona, P., Belongie, S.: The Caltech-UCSD Birds-200-2011 Dataset. Technical report (2011)
43. Wang, D., Shen, Z., Shao, J., Zhang, W., Xue, X., Zhang, Z.: Multiple granularity descriptors for fine-grained categorization. In: ICCV, pp. 2399–2406 (2015)
44. Xia, F., Liu, T.Y., Wang, J., Li, H., Li, H.: Listwise approach to learning to rank: theory and algorithm. In: ICML, pp. 1192–1199 (2008)
45. Xie, L., Tian, Q., Hong, R., Yan, S.: Hierarchical part matching for fine-grained visual categorization. In: ICCV, pp. 1641–1648 (2013)

46. Zhang, N., Donahue, J., Girshick, R., Darrell, T.: Part-based R-CNNs for fine-grained category detection. In: Fleet, D., Pajdla, T., Schiele, B., Tuytelaars, T. (eds.) ECCV 2014. LNCS, vol. 8689, pp. 834–849. Springer, Cham (2014). https://doi.org/10.1007/978-3-319-10590-1_54

47. Zhang, X., Xiong, H., Zhou, W., Lin, W., Tian, Q.: Picking deep filter responses for fine-grained image recognition. In: CVPR, June 2016

48. Zhao, B., Wu, X., Feng, J., Peng, Q., Yan, S.: Diversified visual attention networks for fine-grained object classification. Trans. Multi. **19**(6), 1245–1256 (2017)

49. Zheng, H., Fu, J., Mei, T., Luo, J.: Learning multi-attention convolutional neural network for fine-grained image recognition. In: ICCV, October 2017

NAM: Non-Adversarial Unsupervised Domain Mapping

Yedid Hoshen[1](✉) and Lior Wolf[1,2]

[1] Facebook AI Research, Tel Aviv, Israel
yedidh@fb.com
[2] Tel Aviv University, Tel Aviv, Israel

Abstract. Several methods were recently proposed for the task of translating images between domains without prior knowledge in the form of correspondences. The existing methods apply adversarial learning to ensure that the distribution of the mapped source domain is indistinguishable from the target domain, which suffers from known stability issues. In addition, most methods rely heavily on "cycle" relationships between the domains, which enforce a one-to-one mapping. In this work, we introduce an alternative method: Non-Adversarial Mapping (NAM), which separates the task of target domain generative modeling from the cross-domain mapping task. NAM relies on a pre-trained generative model of the target domain, and aligns each source image with an image synthesized from the target domain, while jointly optimizing the domain mapping function. It has several key advantages: higher quality and resolution image translations, simpler and more stable training and reusable target models. Extensive experiments are presented validating the advantages of our method.

1 Introduction

The human ability to think in spontaneous analogies motivates the field of unsupervised domain alignment, in which image to image translation is achieved without correspondences between samples in the training set. Unsupervised domain alignment methods typically operate by finding a function for mapping images between the domains so that after mapping, the distribution of mapped source images is identical to that of the target images.

Successful recent approaches, e.g. DTN [28], CycleGANs [37] and Disco-GAN [14], utilize Generative Adversarial Networks (GANs) [9] to model the distributions of the two domains, $\mathcal{X}$ and $\mathcal{Y}$. GANs are very effective tools for generative modeling of images, however they suffer from instability in training, making their use challenging. The instability typically requires careful choice of hyper-parameters and often multiple initializations due to mode collapse. Current methods also make additional assumptions that can be restrictive, e.g., DTN assumes that a pre-trained high-quality domain specific feature extractor exists which is effective for both domains. This assumption is good for the domain

V. Ferrari et al. (Eds.): ECCV 2018, LNCS 11218, pp. 455–470, 2018.
https://doi.org/10.1007/978-3-030-01264-9_27

of faces (which is the main application of DTN) but may not be valid for all cases. CycleGAN and DiscoGAN make the assumption that a transformation T_{XY} can be found for every $\mathcal{X}$-domain image x to a unique $\mathcal{Y}$-domain image y, and another transformation T_{YX} exists between the $\mathcal{Y}$ domain and the original X-domain image $y = T_{XY}(x)$, $x = T_{YX}(y)$. This is problematic if the actual mapping is many-to-one or one-to-many, as in super-resolution or coloring.

We propose a novel approach motivated by cross-domain matching. We separate the problem of modeling the distribution of the target domain from the source to target mapping problem. We assume that the target image domain distribution is parametrized using a generative model. This model can be trained using any state-of-the-art unconditional generation method such as GAN [25], GLO [2], VAE [15] or an existing graphical or simulation engine. Given the generative model, we solve an unsupervised matching problem between the input $\mathcal{Y}$ domain images and the $\mathcal{X}$ domain. For each source input image y, we synthesize an $\mathcal{X}$ domain image $G(z_y)$, and jointly learn the mapping function $T()$, which maps images from the X domain to the $\mathcal{Y}$ domain. The synthetic images and mapping function are trained using a reconstruction loss on the input $\mathcal{Y}$ domain images.

Our method is radically different from previous approaches and it presents the following advantages:

1. A generative model needs to be trained only once per target dataset, and can be used to map to this dataset from all source datasets without adversarial generative training.
2. Our method is one-way and does not assume a one-to-one relationship between the two domains, e.g., it does not use cycle-constraints.
3. Our work directly connects between the vast literature of unconditional image generation and the task of cross-domain translation. Any progress in unconditional generation architectures can be simply plugged in with minimal changes. Specifically, we can utilize recent very high-resolution generators to obtain high quality results.

2   Previous Work

Unsupervised Domain Alignment: Mapping across similar domains without supervision has been successfully achieved by classical methods such as Congealing [22]. Unsupervised translation across very different domains has only very recently began to generate strong result, due to the advent of generative adversarial networks (GANs), and all state-of-the-art unsupervised translation methods we are aware of employ GAN technology. As this constraint is insufficient for generating good translations, current methods are differentiated by additional constraints that they impose.

The most popular constraint is cycle-consistency: enforcing that a sample that is mapped from $\mathcal{X}$ to $\mathcal{Y}$ and back to $\mathcal{X}$, reconstructs the original sample. This is the approach taken by DiscoGAN [14], CycleGAN [37] and DualGAN [30]. Recently, StarGAN [5] created multiple cycles for mapping in any direction between multiple (two or more) domains. The generator receives as input the source image as well as the specification of the target domain.

For the case of linear mappings, orthogonality has a similar effect to circularity. Very recently, it was used outside computer vision by several methods [6,12,33,34] for solving the task of mapping words between two languages without using parallel corpora.

Another type of constraint is provided by employing a shared latent space. Given samples from two domains $\mathcal{X}$ and $\mathcal{Y}$, CoGAN [21], learns a mapping from a random input vector z to matching samples, one in each domain. The domains $\mathcal{X}$ and $\mathcal{Y}$ are assumed to be similar and their generators (and GAN discriminators) share many of the layers' weights, similar to [27]. Specifically, the earlier generator layers are shared while the top layer are domain specific. CoGAN can be modified to perform domain translation in the following way: given a sample $x \in \mathcal{X}$, a latent vector z_x is fitted to minimize the distance between the image generated by the first generator $G_{\mathcal{X}}(z_x)$ and the input image x. Then, the analogous image in $\mathcal{Y}$ is given by $G_{\mathcal{Y}}(z_x)$. This method was shown in [37] to be less effective than cycle-consistency based methods.

UNIT [20] employs an encoder-decoder pair per each domain. The latent spaces of the two are assumed to be shared, and similarly to CoGAN, the layers that are distant from the image (the top layers of the encoder and the bottom layers of the encoder) are shared between the two domains. Cycle-consistency is added as well, and structure is added to the latent space using variational autoencoder [16] loss terms.

As mentioned above our method does not use adversarial or cycle-consistency constraints.

Mapping Using Domain Specific Features. Using domain specific features has been found by DTN [28] to be important for some tasks. It assumed that a feature extractor can be found, for which the source and target would give the same activation values. Specifically it uses face specific features to map faces to emojis. While for some of the tasks, our work does use a "perceptual loss" that employs a pretrained imagenet-trained network, this is a generic feature extraction method that is not domain specific. We claim therefore that our method still qualifies as unsupervised. For most of the tasks presented, the VGG loss alone, would not be sufficient to recover good mappings between the two domains, as shown in ANGAN [11].

Unconditional Generative Modeling. Many methods were proposed for generative models of image distributions. Currently the most popular approaches rely on GANs and VAEs [15]. GAN-based methods are plagued by instability during training. Many methods were proposed to address this issue for unconditional generation, e.g., [1,10,23]. The modifications are typically not employed in cross-domain mapping works. Our method trains a generative model (typically a GAN), in the $\mathcal{X}$ domain separately from any $\mathcal{Y}$ domain considerations, and can directly benefit from the latest advancements in the unconditional image generation literature. GLO [3] is an alternative to GAN, which iteratively fits per-image latent vectors (starting from random "noise") and learns a mapping $G()$ between the noise vectors and the training images. GLO is trained using a reconstruction loss, minimizing the difference between the training images and those generated from the noise vectors. Differently from our approach is tackles unconditional generation rather than domain mapping.

3   Unsupervised Image Mapping Without GANs

In this section, we present our method - NAM - for unsupervised domain mapping. The task we aim to solve, is finding analogous images across domains. Let $\mathcal{X}$ and $\mathcal{Y}$ be two image domains, each with some unique characteristics. For each domain we are given a set of example images. The objective is to find for every image y in the $\mathcal{Y}$ domain, an analogous image x which appears to come from the $\mathcal{X}$ domain but preserves the unique content of the original y image.

3.1   Non-Adversarial Exact Matching

To motivate our approach, we first consider the simpler case, where we have two image domains $\mathcal{X}$ and $\mathcal{Y}$, consisting of sets of images $\{x_i\}$ and $\{y_i\}$ respectively. We assume that the two sets are approximately related by a transformation T, and that a matching paired image x exists for every image y in domain $\mathcal{Y}$ such that $T(x) = y$. The task of matching becomes a combination of two tasks: (i) inferring the transformation between the two domains (ii) finding matching pairs across the two domains. Formally this becomes:

$$L = \sum_i \|T(\sum_j M_{ij}x_j), y_i\| \tag{1}$$

Where M_{ij} is the matching matrix containing $M_{i,j} = 1$ if x_j and y_i are matching and 0 otherwise. The optimization is over both the transformation $T()$ as well as binary match matrix M.

Since the optimization of this problem is hard, a relaxation method - *ANGAN* - was recently proposed [11]. The binary constraint on the matrix was replaced by the requirement that $M_{ij} \geq 0$ and $\sum_j M_{ij} = 1$. As optimization progresses, a barrier constraint on M, pushes the values of M to 0 or 1.

ANGAN was shown to be successful in cases where exact matches exist and $T()$ is initialized with a reasonably good solution obtained by CycleGAN.

3.2   Non-Adversarial Inexact Matching

In Sect. 3.1, we described the scenario in which exact matches exist between the images in domains $\mathcal{X}$ and $\mathcal{Y}$. In most situations, exact matches do not exist between the two domains. In such situations it is not sufficient to merely find an image x in the domain $\mathcal{X}$ training set such that for a target $\mathcal{Y}$ domain image y, we have $y = T(x)$ as we cannot hope that such a match will exist. Instead,

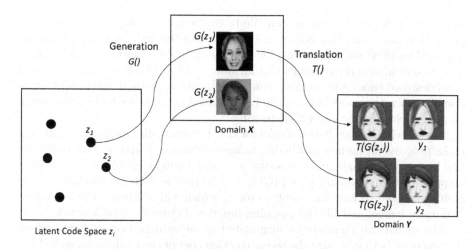

Fig. 1. Given a generator G for domain $\mathcal{X}$ and training samples $\{y_i\}$ in domain $\mathcal{Y}$, NAM jointly learns the transformation $T : \mathcal{X} \to \mathcal{Y}$ and the latent vectors $\{z_i\}$ that give rise to samples $\{T(G(z_i))\}$ that resemble the training images in $\mathcal{Y}$

we need to synthesize an image $\tilde{x}$ that comes from the $\mathcal{X}$ domain distribution, and satisfies $y = T(\tilde{x})$. This can be achieved by removing the stochasticity requirement in Eq. 1. Effectively, this models the images in the $\mathcal{X}$ domain as:

$$\tilde{x} = \sum_j \alpha_i x_i \qquad (2)$$

This solution is unsatisfactory on several counts: (i) the simplex model for the $\mathcal{X}$ domain cannot hope to achieve high quality image synthesis for general images (ii) The complexity scales quadratically with the number of training images making both training and evaluation very slow.

3.3   Non-Adversarial Mapping (NAM)

In this section we generalize the ideas presented in the previous sections into an effective method for mapping between domains without supervision or the use of adversarial methods.

In Sect. 3.2, we showed that to find analogies between domains $\mathcal{X}$ and $\mathcal{Y}$, the method requires two components: (i) a model for the distribution of the $\mathcal{X}$ domain, and (ii) a mapping function $T()$ between domains $\mathcal{X}$ and $\mathcal{Y}$.

Instead of the linear simplex model of Sect. 3.2, we propose to model the $\mathcal{X}$ domain distribution by a neural generative model $G(z)$, where z is a latent vector. The requirements on the generative model $G()$ are such that for every image x in the $\mathcal{X}$ domain distribution we can find z such $x = G(z)$ and that $G()$ is compact, that is, for no z, will $G(z)$ lie outside the $\mathcal{X}$ domain. The task of learning such generative models, is the research focus of several communities.

In this work we do not aim to contribute to the methodology of unsupervised generative modeling, but rather use the state-of-the-art modeling techniques obtained by previous approaches, for our generator $G()$. Methods which can be used to obtain generative model $G()$ include: GLO [2], VAE [15], GAN [9] or a hand designed simulator (see for example [29]). In our method, the task of single domain generative modeling is entirely decoupled from the task of cross-domain mapping, which is the one we set to solve.

Armed with a much better model for the $\mathcal{X}$ domain distribution, we can now make progress on finding synthetic analogies between $\mathcal{X}$ and $\mathcal{Y}$. Our task is to find for every $\mathcal{Y}$ domain image y, a synthetic $\mathcal{X}$ domain image $G(z_y)$ so that when mapped to the $\mathcal{Y}$ domain $y = T(G(z_y))$. The task is therefore twofold: (i) for each y, we need to find the latent vector z_y which will synthesize the analogous $\mathcal{X}$ domain image, and (ii) the mapping function $T()$ needs to be learned.

The model can therefore be formulated as an optimization problem, where the objective is to minimize the reconstruction cost of the training images of the $\mathcal{Y}$ domain. The optimization is over the latent codes, a unique latent code z_y vector for every input $\mathcal{Y}$ domain image y, as well as the mapping function $T()$. It is formally written as below:

$$argmin_{T,z_y} \sum_{y \in B} \|T(G(z_y)), y\| \tag{3}$$

The model is fully differentiable, as both the generative model $G()$ and the mapping function $T()$ are parameterized by neural networks. The above objective is jointly optimized for z_y and $T()$, but not for $G()$ which is kept fixed. The method is illustrated in Fig. 1.

3.4   Perceptual Loss

Although the optimization described in Sect. 3.3 can achieve good solutions, we found that introducing a perceptual loss, can significantly help further improve the quality of analogies. Let $\phi_i()$ be the features extracted from a deep-network at the end of the i'th block (we use VGG [26]). The perceptual loss is given by:

$$\|.,.\|_{VGG} = \sum_i \|\phi_i(T(G(z_y))), \phi_i(y)\|_1 + \|T(G(z_y)), y\|_1 \tag{4}$$

The final optimization problem becomes:

$$argmin_{T,z_y} \sum_{y \in B} \|T(G(z_y)), y\|_{VGG} \tag{5}$$

The VGG perceptual loss was found by several recent papers [4,35] to give perceptually pleasing results. There have been informal claims in the past that methods using perceptual loss functions should count as supervised. We claim that the perceptual loss does not make our method supervised, as the VGG network does not come from our domains and does not require any new labeling effort. Our view is that taking advantage of modern feature extractors will benefit the field of unsupervised learning in general and unsupervised analogies in particular.

3.5   Inference and Multiple Solutions

Once training has completed, we are now in possession of the mapping function $T()$ which is now fixed (the pre-trained $G()$ was never modified as a part of training).

To infer the analogy of a new $\mathcal{Y}$ domain image y, we need to recover the latent code z_y which would yield the optimal reconstruction. The mapping function $T()$ is now fixed, and is not modified after training. Inference is therefore performed via the following optimization:

$$argmin_{z_y} \|T(G(z_y)), y\| \tag{6}$$

The synthetic $\mathcal{X}$ domain image $G(z_y)$ is our proposed solution to $\mathcal{Y}$ domain image y.

This inference procedure is a non-convex optimization problem. Different initializations, yield different final analogies. Let us denote initialization z_0^t where t is the ID of the solution. At the end of the optimization procedure for each initialization, the synthetic images $G(z^t)$ yield multiple proposed analogies for the task. We find $G(z^0)...G(z^T)$ are very diverse when in fact many analogies are available. For example, when the $\mathcal{X}$ domain is Shoes and the $\mathcal{Y}$ domain is Edges, there are many shoes that can result in the same edge image.

3.6   Implementation Details

In this section we give a detailed description of the procedure used to generate the experiments presented in this paper.

$\mathcal{X}$ *Domain Generative Model* $G(.)$: Our method takes as input a pre-trained generative model for the $\mathcal{X}$ domain. In our MNIST, SVHN and cars, Edges2 (Shoes,Handbags) experiments, we used DCGAN [25] with (32,32,32,100,100) latent dimensions. The low resolution face image generator was trained on celebA and used the training method of [23]. The high resolution face generator is provided by [13] and the Dog generator by [32]. The hyperparameters of all trained generators were set to their default value. In our experiments GAN unconditional generators provided more compelling results than competing SOTA methods such as GLO and VAE.

Mapping Function $T(.)$: The mapping function was designed so that it is powerful enough but not too large as to overfit. Additionally, it needs to preserve image locality, in the case of spatially aligned domains. We elected to use a network with an architecture based on [4]. We found that as we only rely on the networks to find correspondences rather than generate high-fidelity visual outputs, small networks were the preferred choice. We used a similar architecture to [4], with a single layer per scale, and linearly decaying number of filters per layer starting with $4F$, and decreasing by F with every layer. $F = 8$ for SVHN and MNIST and $F = 32$ for the other experiments.

Optimization: We optimized using SGD with ADAM [17]. For all datasets we used a learning rate of 0.03 for the latent codes z_y and 0.001 for the mapping function $T(.)$ (due to the uneven update rates of each z_y and $T()$). On all datasets training was performed on 2000 randomly selected examples (a subset) from the $\mathcal{Y}$ domain. Larger training sets were not more helpful as each z_y is updated less frequently.

Generating Results: The $\mathcal{X}$ domain translation of $\mathcal{Y}$ domain image y is given by $G(z_y)$, where z_y is the latent code found in optimization. The $\mathcal{X} \to \mathcal{Y}$ mapping $T(x)$, typically resulted in weaker results due to the relatively shallow architecture selected for $T(.)$. A strong $T(.)$ can be trained by calculating a set of $G(z_y)$ and y (obtained using NAM), and training a fully-supervised network $T(.)$, e.g. as described by [4]. A similar procedure was carried out in [11].

4   Experiments

To evaluate the merits of our method, we carried out an extensive set of qualitative and quantitative experiments.

SVHN-MNIST Translation: We evaluated our method on the SVHN-MNIST translation task. Although SVHN [24] and MNIST [18] are simple datasets, the mapping task is not trivial. The MNIST dataset consists of simple handwritten single digits written on black background. In contrast, SVHN images are taken from house numbers and typically contain not only the digit of interest but also parts of the adjacent digits, which are nuisance information. We translate in both directions SVHN→MNIST and MNIST→SVHN. The results are presented in Fig. 2. We can observe that in the easier direction of SVHN→MNIST, in which there is information loss, NAM resulted in more accurate translations than CycleGAN. In the reverse direction of MNIST→SVHN, which is harder due to information gain, CycleGAN did much worse, whereas NAM was often successful. Note that perceptual loss was not used in the MNIST→SVHN translation task.

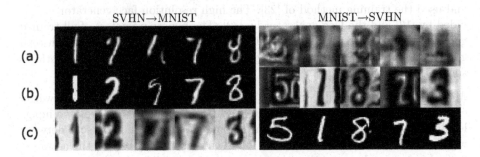

Fig. 2. Converting digits between SVHN and MNIST (both directions). (a) CycleGAN results (b) NAM results (c) the input images.

Table 1. Translation quality measured by translated digit classification accuracy (%)

	SVHN→MNIST	MNIST→SVHN
CycleGAN	26.8	17.7
NAM	33.3	31.9

We performed a quantitative evaluation of the quality of SVHN↔MNIST translation. This was achieved by mapping an image from the one dataset to appear like the other dataset, and classifying it using a pre-trained classifier trained on the clean target data (the classifier followed a NIN architecture [19], and achieved test accuracies of around 99.5% on MNIST and 95.0% on SVHN). The results are presented in Table 1. We can see that the superior translations of NAM are manifested in higher classification accuracies.

Edges2Shoes: The task of mapping edges to shoes is commonly used to qualitatively evaluate unsupervised domain mapping methods. The two domains are a set of Shoe images first collected by [31], and their edge maps. The transformation between an edge map and the original photo-realistic shoe image is non-trivial, as much information needs to be hallucinated.

Examples of NAM and DiscoGAN results can be seen in Fig. 3(a). The higher quality of the analogies generated by NAM is apparent. This stems from using a pre-learned generative model rather than learning jointly with mapping, which is hard and results in worse performance. We also see the translations result in more faithful analogies. Another advantage of our method is the ability to map

Fig. 3. (a) Comparison of NAM and DiscoGAN for Edges2Shoes. Each triplet shows NAM (center row) vs. DiscoGAN (top row) for a given input (bottom row). (b) A similar visualization for Edges2Handbags. (c, d) NAM mapping from a single source edge image (shown first) for different random initializations.

Fig. 4. Comparison of NAM results for different generators

one input into many proposed solutions. Two examples are shown in Fig. 3(c) and (d). It is apparent that the solutions all give correct analogies, however they give different possibilities for the correct analogy. This captures the one-to-many property of the edge to shoes transformation.

As mentioned in the method description, NAM requires high-quality generators, and performs better for better pre-trained generators. In Fig. 4 we show NAM results for generators trained with: VAE [15] with high (VAE-h) and low (VAE-l) regularization, GLO [2], DCGAN [25] and Spectral-Normalization GAN [23]. We can see from the results that NAM works is all cases. however results are much better for the best generators (DCGAN, Spectral-Norm GAN).

Edges2Handbags: The Edges2Handbags [36] dataset is constructed similarly to Edges2Shoes. Sample results on this dataset can be seen in Fig. 3(b). The conclusions are similar to Edges2Shoes: NAM generates analogies that are both more appealing and more precise than DiscoGAN.

Shoes2Handbags: One of the major capabilities displayed by DiscoGAN is being able to relate domains that are very different. The example shown in [14], of mapping images of handbags to images of shoes that are semantically related, illustrates the ability of making distant analogies.

In this experiment we show that NAM is able to make analogies between handbags and shoes, resulting in higher quality solutions than those obtained by DiscoGAN. In order to achieve this, we replace the reconstruction VGG loss by a Gram matrix VGG loss, as used in Style Transfer [8]. DiscoGAN also uses a Gram matrix loss (with feature extracted from its discriminator). For this task, we also add a skip connection from $G(z)$, as the domains are already similar under a style loss.

Example images can be seen in Fig. 5. The superior quality of the NAM generated mapped images is apparent. The better quality is a result of using an interpretable and well understood non-adversarial loss which is quite straight forward to optimize. Another advantage comes from being able to "plug-in" a high-quality generative model.

Car2Car: The Car2Car dataset is a standard numerical baseline for cross-domain image mapping. Each domain consists of a set of different cars, presented in angles varying from -75 to $75°$. The objective is to align the two domains such that a simple relationship exists between orientation of car image y and mapped image x (typically, either the orientation of x and y should be equal or

Fig. 5. Example results for mapping from bags (original images - top) to shoes. NAM mapped images (center) are clearly better than DiscoGAN mapped images (bottom).

Table 2. Car2Car root median residual deviation from linear alignment (lower is better).

DiscoGAN	NAM
13.81	1.47

reversed). A few cars mapped by NAM and DiscoGAN can be seen in Fig. 6. Our method results in a much cleaner mapping. We also quantitatively evaluate the mapping, by training a simple regressor on the car orientation in the $\mathcal{X}$ domain, and comparing the ground-truth orientation of y with the predicted orientation of the mapped image x. We evaluate using the root median residuals (as the regressor sometimes flips orientations of -75 to 75 resulting in anomalies). For car2car, we used a skip connection from $G(z)$ to the output. Results are seen in Table 2. Our method significantly outperforms DiscoGAN. Interestingly, on this task, on this task, it was not necessary to use a perceptual loss, a simple Euclidean pixel loss was sufficient for a very high-quality solution on this task. As a negative result, on the car2head task i.e. mapping between car images and images of heads of different people at different azimuth angles; NAM did not generate a simple relation between the orientations of the cars and heads but a more complex relationship. Our interpretation from looking at results is that black cars were inversely correlated with the head orientation, whereas white cars were positively correlated.

Avatar2Face: One of the first applications of cross-domain translation was face to avatar generation by DTN [28]. This was achieved by using state-of-the-art face features, and ensured the features are preserved in the original face and the output avatar (f-constancy). Famously however, DTN does not generate good results on avatar2face generation, which involves adding rather than taking away information. Due to the many-to-one nature of our approach, NAM is better

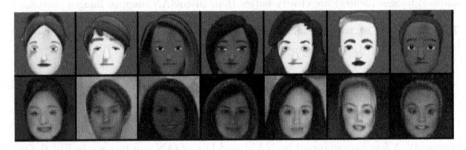

Fig. 6. Example results for mapping across two sets of car models at different orientations. Although DiscoGAN (bottom) does indeed preserve orientation of the original images (top) to some extent, NAM (center) preserves both orientation and general car properties very accurately - despite the target domain containing few sports cars.

Fig. 7. Example results for mapping Avatars (top) to Faces (bottom) using NAM.

suited for this task. In Fig. 7 we present example images of our avatar2face conversions. This was generated by a small generative model with a DCGAN [25] architecture, trained using Spectral Normalization GAN [23] using celebA face images. The avatar dataset was obtained from the authors of [29].

Plugging in State-of-the-Art Generative Models: One of the advantages of our method is the independence between mapping and generative modeling. The practical consequence is that any generative model, even very large models that take weeks to train, can be effortlessly plugged into our framework. We can then map any suitable source domain to it, very quickly and efficiently.

Amazing recent progress has been recently carried out on generative modeling. One of the most striking examples of it is Progressive Growing of GANs (PGGAN) [13], which has yielded generative models of faces with unprecedented resolutions of 1024×1024. The generative model training took 4 days of 8 GPUs, and the architecture selection is highly non-trivial. Including the training of such generative models in unsupervised domain mapping networks is therefore very hard.

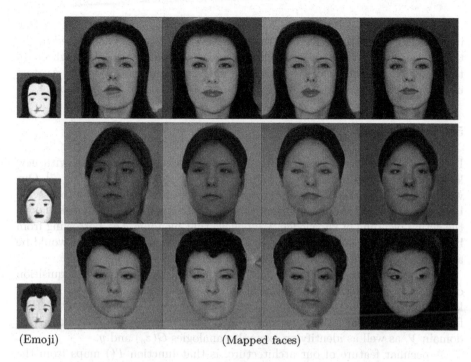

(Emoji)   (Mapped faces)

Fig. 8. One-to-many high-resolution mapping from Avatars to Faces using the pretrained generator from [13]

(Emoji1)   (Mapped1)   (Emoji2)   (Mapped2)   (Emoji3)   (Mapped3)

Fig. 9. High-resolution mapping from Avatars to Dogs, using the pre-trained generator from [32].

For NAM, however, we simply set $G()$ as the trained generative model from the authors' code release. A spatial transformer layer, with parameters optimized by SGD per-image, reduced the model outputs to the Avatar scale (which we chose to be 64X64). We present visual results in Fig. 9. Our method is able to find very compelling analogous high-resolution faces. Scaling up to such high resolution would be highly-nontrivial with state-of-the-art domain translation methods. We mention that DTN [28], the state-of-the-art approach for unsupervised face-to-emoji mapping, has not been successful at this task, even though it uses domain specific facial features.

To show the generality of our approach, we also mapped Avatars to Dog images. The generator was trained using StackGAN-v2 [32]. We plugged in the trained generators from the publicly released code into NAM. Although emoji to dogs is significantly more distant than emoji to human face (all the Avatars used, were human faces), NAM was still able to find compelling analogies.

5 Discussion

Human knowledge acquisition typically combines existing knowledge with new knowledge obtained from novel domains. This process is called blending [7]. Our work (as most of the existing literature) focuses on the mapping process i.e. being able to relate the information from both domains, but does not deal with the actual blending of knowledge. We believe that blending, i.e., borrowing from both domains to create a unified view that is richer than both sources would be an extremely potent direction for future research.

An attractive property of our model, is the separation between the acquisition of the existing knowledge and the fitting of a new domain. The preexisting knowledge is modeled as the generative model of domain $\mathcal{X}$, given by G; The fitting process includes the optimization of a learned mapper from domain $\mathcal{X}$ to domain $\mathcal{Y}$, as well as identifying exemplar analogies $G(z_y)$ and y.

A peculiar feature of our architecture, is that function $T()$ maps from the target ($\mathcal{X}$ domain) to the source ($\mathcal{Y}$ domain) and not the other way around. Mapping in the other direction would fail, since it can lead to a form of mode-collapse, in which all $\mathcal{Y}$ samples are mapped to the same generated $G(z)$ for a fixed z. While additional loss terms and other techniques can be added in order to avoid this, mode collapse is a challenge in generative systems and it is better to avoid the possibility of it altogether. Mapping as we do avoids this issue.

6 Conclusions

Unsupervised mapping between domains is an exciting technology with many applications. While existing work is currently dominated by adversarial training, and relies on cycle constraints, we present results that support other forms of training.

Since our method is very different from the existing methods in the literature, we have been able to achieve success on tasks that do not fit well into other models. Particularly, we have been able to map low resolution face avatar images into very high resolution images. On lower resolution benchmarks, we have been able to achieve more visually appealing and quantitatively accurate analogies.

Our method relies on having a high quality pre-trained unsupervised generative model for the $\mathcal{X}$ domain. We have shown that we can take advantage of very high resolution generative models, e.g., [13,32]. As the field of unconditional generative modeling progresses, so will the quality and scope of NAM.

References

1. Arjovsky, M., Chintala, S., Bottou, L.: Wasserstein GAN. arXiv preprint arXiv:1701.07875 (2017)
2. Bojanowski, P., Joulin, A., Lopez-Paz, D., Szlam, A.: Optimizing the latent space of generative networks. arXiv preprint arXiv:1707.05776 (2017)
3. Bojanowski, P., Joulin, A., Lopez-Paz, D., Szlam, A.: Optimizing the latentspace of generative networks. arXiv preprint arXiv:1707.05776 (2017)
4. Chen, Q., Koltun, V.: Photographic image synthesis with cascaded refinement networks. In: ICCV (2017)
5. Choi, Y., Choi, M., Kim, M., Ha, J.W., Kim, S., Choo, J.: StarGAN: unified generative adversarial networks for multi-domain image-to-image translation. arXiv preprint arXiv:1711.09020 (2017)
6. Conneau, A., Lample, G., Ranzato, M., Denoyer, L., Jégou, H.: Word translation without parallel data. arXiv preprint arXiv:1710.04087 (2017)
7. Fauconnier, G., Turner, M.: The Way We Think: Conceptual Blending and the Mind's Hidden Complexities. Basic Books, New York (2002)
8. Gatys, L.A., Ecker, A.S., Bethge, M.: Image style transfer using convolutional neural networks. In: CVPR (2016)
9. Goodfellow, I., et al.: Generative adversarial nets. In: NIPS, pp. 2672–2680 (2014)
10. Gulrajani, I., Ahmed, F., Arjovsky, M., Dumoulin, V., Courville, A.C.: Improved training of wasserstein GANs. In: Advances in Neural Information Processing Systems, pp. 5769–5779 (2017)
11. Hoshen, Y., Wolf, L.: Identifying analogies across domains. In: International Conference on Learning Representations (2018)
12. Hoshen, Y., Wolf, L.: An iterative closest point method for unsupervised word translation. arXiv preprint arXiv:1801.06126 (2018)
13. Karras, T., Aila, T., Laine, S., Lehtinen, J.: Progressive growing of GANs for improved quality, stability, and variation. arXiv preprint arXiv:1710.10196 (2017)
14. Kim, T., Cha, M., Kim, H., Lee, J., Kim, J.: Learning to discover cross-domain relations with generative adversarial networks. arXiv preprint arXiv:1703.05192 (2017)
15. Kingma, D.P., Welling, M.: Auto-encoding variational Bayes. arXiv preprint arXiv:1312.6114 (2013)
16. Kingma, D.P., Welling, M.: Auto-encoding variational Bayes. Stat **1050**, 10 (2014)
17. Kingma, D., Ba, J.: Adam: a method for stochastic optimization. In: The International Conference on Learning Representations (ICLR) (2016)
18. LeCun, Y., Cortes, C.: MNIST handwritten digit database (2010)
19. Lin, M., Chen, Q., Yan, S.: Network in network. In: ICLR (2014)
20. Liu, M.Y., Breuel, T., Kautz, J.: Unsupervised image-to-image translation networks. In: Advances in Neural Information Processing Systems, pp. 700–708 (2017)
21. Liu, M.Y., Tuzel, O.: Coupled generative adversarial networks. In: NIPS, pp. 469–477 (2016)
22. Miller, E.G., Matsakis, N.E., Viola, P.A.: Learning from one example through shared densities on transforms. In: 2000 IEEE Conference on Computer Vision and Pattern Recognition, Proceedings, vol. 1, pp. 464–471. IEEE (2000)
23. Miyato, T., Kataoka, T., Koyama, M., Yoshida, Y.: Spectral normalization for generative adversarial networks. In: International Conference on Learning Representations (2018)

24. Netzer, Y., Wang, T., Coates, A., Bissacco, A., Wu, B., Ng, A.Y.: Reading digits in natural images with unsupervised feature learning. In: NIPS Workshop on Deep Learning and Unsupervised Feature Learning (2011)
25. Radford, A., Metz, L., Chintala, S.: Unsupervised representation learning with deep convolutional generative adversarial networks. arXiv preprint arXiv:1511.06434 (2015)
26. Simonyan, K., Zisserman, A.: Very deep convolutional networks for large-scale image recognition. In: ICLR (2015)
27. Sutskever, I., Jozefowicz, R., Gregor, K., Rezende, D., Lillicrap, T., Vinyals, O.: Towards principled unsupervised learning. In: ICLR Workshop (2016)
28. Taigman, Y., Polyak, A., Wolf, L.: Unsupervised cross-domain image generation. In: International Conference on Learning Representations (ICLR) (2017)
29. Wolf, L., Taigman, Y., Polyak, A.: Unsupervised creation of parameterized avatars. In: Proceedings of the IEEE Conference on Computer Vision and Pattern Recognition, pp. 1530–1538 (2017)
30. Yi, Z., Zhang, H., Tan, P., Gong, M.: DualGAN: unsupervised dual learning for image-to-image translation. arXiv preprint arXiv:1704.02510 (2017)
31. Yu, A., Grauman, K.: Fine-grained visual comparisons with local learning. In: CVPR (2014)
32. Zhang, H., et al.: StackGAN++: realistic image synthesis with stacked generative adversarial networks. arXiv: 1710.10916 (2017)
33. Zhang, M., Liu, Y., Luan, H., Sun, M.: Adversarial training for unsupervised bilingual lexicon induction. In: Proceedings of the 55th Annual Meeting of the Association for Computational Linguistics, (volume 1: Long Papers), vol. 1, pp. 1959–1970 (2017)
34. Zhang, M., Liu, Y., Luan, H., Sun, M.: Earth mover's distance minimization for unsupervised bilingual lexicon induction. In: Proceedings of the 2017 Conference on Empirical Methods in Natural Language Processing, pp. 1934–1945 (2017)
35. Zhang, R., Isola, P., Efros, A.A., Shechtman, E., Wang, O.: The unreasonable effectiveness of deep features as a perceptual metric. arXiv preprint arXiv:1801.03924 (2018)
36. Zhu, J.-Y., Krähenbühl, P., Shechtman, E., Efros, A.A.: Generative visual manipulation on the natural image manifold. In: Leibe, B., Matas, J., Sebe, N., Welling, M. (eds.) ECCV 2016. LNCS, vol. 9909, pp. 597–613. Springer, Cham (2016). https://doi.org/10.1007/978-3-319-46454-1_36
37. Zhu, J.Y., Park, T., Isola, P., Efros, A.A.: Unpaired image-to-image translation using cycle-consistent adversarial networkss. arXiv preprint arXiv:1703.10593 (2017)

Transferable Adversarial Perturbations

Wen Zhou[✉][iD], Xin Hou[iD], Yongjun Chen[iD], Mengyun Tang[iD],
Xiangqi Huang[iD], Xiang Gan[iD], and Yong Yang[iD]

Basic Research Group, Security Platform Department, Tencent, Beijing, China
wen8.zhou@gmail.com, hx173149@gmail.com,
{yongjunchen,mengyuntang,angelahuang,xenosgan,coolcyang}@tencent.com

Abstract. State-of-the-art deep neural network classifiers are highly
vulnerable to adversarial examples which are designed to mislead classifiers with a very small perturbation. However, the performance of
black-box attacks (without knowledge of the model parameters) against
deployed models always degrades significantly. In this paper, We propose a novel way of perturbations for adversarial examples to enable
black-box transfer. We first show that maximizing distance between natural images and their adversarial examples in the intermediate feature
maps can improve both white-box attacks (with knowledge of the model
parameters) and black-box attacks. We also show that smooth regularization on adversarial perturbations enables transferring across models. Extensive experimental results show that our approach outperforms
state-of-the-art methods both in white-box and black-box attacks.

Keywords: Adversarial perturbations · Transferability
Black-box attacks

1 Introduction

Recently, deep neural networks achieve state-of-the-art performance in many
fields such as computer vision [1,2], speech recognition [3], and machine translation [4]. However, recent works [5–9] show that deep neural networks are highly
vulnerable to adversarial perturbations of the data. Adversarial examples are
modified very slightly in a way that is intended to cause a classifier to misclassify
them. Several methods have been proposed to generated adversarial examples
using the gradient information of neural networks. Fast Gradient Sign Method
(FGSM) [7] and Basic Iterative Method (BIM) [8] serve as two baseline methods
to generate adversarial examples with different transfer abilities. FGSM generates adversarial examples by linearizing the cost function around the current
parameters of models. It can be computed efficiently using back-propagation.

W. Zhou and X. Hou—Equal contribution.

Electronic supplementary material The online version of this chapter (https://
doi.org/10.1007/978-3-030-01264-9_28) contains supplementary material, which is
available to authorized users.

However, it usually has a low success rate with white-box attacks since it does not increase the cost function sufficiently with a single step. BIM extends FGSM by taking multiple steps of FGSM. It usually induces higher error rates than the FGSM for white-box attacks since it can produce more harmful adversarial examples without any approximation for the white-box model. However, BIM transfers across models at lower rates and it produces weaker black-box attacks than FGSM, which indicates that BIM tends to *overfit* on the white-box model. Because of the huge search space, both one-step and iterative methods can not search the transferrable perturbations efficiently, where the transferrable perturbations are insensitive to diverse parameters and architectures of models.

We propose a novel adversarial perturbations generation method which enables black-box transfer. We introduce two terms into cost function to guide the search directions of perturbations.

First, we maximize the distances between natural images and their adversarial examples in the intermediate feature maps which can address vanishing gradients for adversarial perturbations generation. Thus, it can search perturbations efficiently with back-propagation. Besides, since large distances in the intermediate feature maps correlate with the large distances in the predictions of neural networks, it will cause error predictions with high probability. We show that it also can increase the probability of successful black-box transfer.

Second, we introduce a regularization term into cost function to remove the high-frequency perturbations, which enables black-box transfer with high error rates. Because of the continuity of the neighboring pixels emerged in data, the convolutional kernels learned by deep neural networks also capture this property. Thus, the high-frequency perturbations are smoothed by these kernels layer by layer without effort, which makes no changes in the final predictions of neural networks. The regularization term reduces the variations of adversarial perturbations and makes them difficult to be smoothed by layer-by-layer convolutions, which enables black-box transfer. Figure 1 gives several adversarial examples generated by FGSM, BIM and the proposed method using Inception-V3 model.

Fig. 1. Different adversarial examples for Inception V3 model using FGSM, BIM and our method respectively.

We evaluate the proposed method on two public datasets with various models including state-of-the-art classifiers [10] and defense models [11]. Experimental results show that our method outperforms state-of-the-art methods both in white-box and black-box attacks.

2 Related Work

In this section, we review some of the relevant work. Szegedy et al. [12] first introduce adversarial examples generation by analyzing the instability of deep neural networks. They show that the adversarial perturbations are more effective than random perturbations for deep neural networks despite of the larger magnitude of random perturbations, which indicates that adversarial examples expose fundamental blind spots of learning algorithms. Goodfellow et al. [7] further explain the phenomenon of adversarial examples by analyzing the linear behavior of deep neural network and propose a simple and efficient adversarial examples generating method: FGSM. It can generalize across models by taking advantage of the linear behavior of neural networks.

Kurakin et al. [8] investigate adversarial examples for large-scale dataset: ImageNet and they compare FGSM and BIM in terms of the robustness of black-box adversarial attacks. They show that BIM with multi-step of FGSM is less transferable than a single-step FGSM despite of the higher error rates for white-box attacks. Kurakin et al. [13] further explore the adversarial examples in the physical world and demonstrate BIM is also not robust to transformations caused by the camera. Both of these two works show multi-step optimization is less transferable than single-step optimization. However, we show that with properly guided gradients, multi-step optimization can achieve higher error rates for both white-box and black-box attacks.

It is natural to use ensemble methods for both inputs and architectures to enable transferring across models. Moosavi-Dezfooli et al. [6] use an ensemble of inputs to seek universal perturbations which generalize across both deep neural networks and inputs. Unlike prior works which compute perturbations for each example independently, they aggregate atomic perturbations to reduce the variations of perturbations. They show that such perturbations generalize well across different classification models. Another type of work uses an ensemble of different architectures to enable transferring across models which is widely used in the competitions. From the defensive point of view, Florian et al. [11] incorporate adversarial examples transferred from other pre-trained models to take the advantage of ensemble of different architectures, which improves the robustness of deep neural networks against black-box attacks. Both of these ensemble methods encourage algorithms to search a *shared* space to reduce the variations of perturbations with high computational complexity. We show that a smooth regularization on perturbations can reduce the variations of perturbations efficiently.

3 Transferable Perturbations

Let $f(x)$ denote an arbitrary deep neural network which takes x ($x \in R^n$) as input and outputs the probability of classes y ($y \in R^m$), we first define an adversarial example fooling the model $f(x)$ for a chosen p-norm and noise parameter ϵ as follows:

$$\tilde{x} = \underset{\|\tilde{x}-x\|^p \leq \epsilon}{\mathrm{argmax}}\ l(\tilde{x}, t) \tag{1}$$

where t and $l(\cdot, \cdot)$ denote the label of x and the loss function used to train the model respectively. In all our experiments, we use the cross entropy as the loss function. FGSM [7,8] and BIM [13] can be used to optimize above function and generate adversarial examples $\tilde{x}$. FGSM finds adversarial perturbations which increase the value of the loss function with one step. BIM extends FGSM which applies it multiple times with a small step size to increase the loss function further. It usually achieves higher success rate than FGSM for white-box attacks. However, it is less transferable than FGSM. To address this, we first maximize the distances between natural images and adversarial examples in feature space to increase transfer rates. Besides, we introduce the smooth regularization on perturbations which punishes the discontinuity of the neighboring pixels.

3.1 Maximizing Distance

Standard neural network architectures are deep hierarchy of convolutions and max-pooling with large capacity. Previous adversarial examples generation methods aim to increase the loss function as defined in (1) using gradient ascent. However, due to the deep hierarchy of architectures, the gradients of loss with respect to input x become extremely small (vanishing gradient problem). Thus, it is insufficient to maximize loss with few steps. To address this issue, we add an intermediate loss which measures the distance of intermediate feature maps between input x and adversarial examples $\tilde{x}$. The gradient of intermediate loss with respect to input x is sufficient to maximize intermediate loss in few steps. Besides, these gradients also provide good guides to maximize the loss function (1). Large distance of intermediate feature maps between x and $\tilde{x}$ will eventually result in large distance in final outputs of neural networks between x and $\tilde{x}$ with high probability, which will increase the loss function (1) and make error predictions.

Let $L(x, d)$ denote the intermediate feature map in layer $d \in D$, we maximize the $l2$-norm distance between $T(L(x, d))$ and $T(L(\tilde{x}, d))$ for all layers, where $T(L(\tilde{x}, d))$ denotes the power normalization [14] of $L(\tilde{x}, d)$. The power normalization is used to down-weight the contribution of large value in $L(x, d)$, which is defined as follows:

$$T(L(\tilde{x}, d)) = \mathrm{sign}(L(\tilde{x}, d)) \odot \mathrm{abs}\, L(\tilde{x}, d)^\alpha \tag{2}$$

where $0 \leq \alpha \leq 1$ is a parameter of the normalization and $\odot$ denotes element-wise production. In our experiments, we find above transformation is quite effective for black-box transfer.

By maximizing the distance of intermediate feature maps between input x and adversarial examples $\tilde{x}$, we generate adversarial examples as follows:

$$\tilde{x} = \underset{\|\tilde{x}-x\|^p \leq \epsilon}{\operatorname{argmax}} \ (l(\tilde{x},t) + \lambda \sum_{d \in D} \|T(L(x,d)) - T(L(\tilde{x},d))\|^2), \tag{3}$$

where λ denotes the trade-off between the loss (1) and the intermediate loss. To make the feature in each layer contribute equally, we normalize $L(x,d)$ to $[0,1]$ using min-max scaling.

3.2 Regularization

Due to the diverse inputs and architectures of deep neural networks, the maximization of loss function used in one architecture does not guarantee the maximization of loss function used in other architectures. Thus, the transfer rate always degrades, especially when transferring to complex architectures such as Inception-Resnet-V2 and ResNet. An ensemble of diverse inputs [6] or architectures can partially solve this problem with high computational complexity. Both of these methods want to remove high-frequency perturbations and reduce the variations of adversarial perturbations to make adversarial examples more transferable. We introduce regularization on perturbations to reduce variations with much more efficiency:

$$\tilde{x} = \underset{\|\tilde{x}-x\|^p}{\operatorname{argmax}} J(\tilde{x}, x, t, w_s) = \underset{\|\tilde{x}-x\|^p \leq \epsilon}{\operatorname{argmax}} \ (l(\tilde{x},t)$$
$$+ \lambda \sum_{d \in D} \|T(L(x,d)) - T(L(\tilde{x},d))\|^2 \tag{4}$$
$$+ \eta \sum_i \operatorname{abs} R_i(\tilde{x} - x, w_s))$$

where η controls the balance between regularization and loss function. $R_i(\tilde{x} - x, w_s)$ denotes the i-th element in the response map which is calculated by doing a convolution between the kernel w_s (with size s) and the perturbation $\tilde{x} - x$. w_s is designed to be a box linear filter which is a spatial domain linear filter in which each pixel in the resulting image has a value equal to the average value of its neighboring pixels in the input. It is a form of low-pass filter which enforces the continuity of the neighboring pixels and reduces the variations of adversarial perturbations.

3.3 Optimization

To optimize (4), we use Iterative FGSM (I-FGSM) [11] which iteratively applies FGSM k times with budget $\epsilon' = \epsilon/k$. First, we scale the input x into $[-1,1]$ and initialize $\tilde{x}_0 = x$. And then, we compute the gradients of loss (4) with respect to input x. After that, the adversarial examples are updated by multiple steps. In each step, we take the sign function of the gradients and clip the adversarial examples into $[-1,1]$ to make valid images. Finally, adversarial examples are calculated by adding the pixel differences between the last updated adversarial examples and the input x with ϵ. Algorithm 1 gives the details of perturbations generation.

Algorithm 1. Computation of transferable perturbations

---

initialize: $\tilde{x}_0 = x$, $\epsilon' = \epsilon/k$, $i = 0$,
while $i < k$ **do**
　　$\tilde{x}_{i+1} = \mathrm{clip}(\tilde{x}_i + \epsilon' \mathrm{sign}(\nabla_x J(\tilde{x}_i, x, t, w_s)), -1, 1)$
end while
return $\tilde{x} = \mathrm{clip}(x + \epsilon \mathrm{sign}(x - \tilde{x}_k), -1, 1)$

4　Experiments

In this section, we describe the implementation details and experimental results on two public datasets. We first analyze the transferability of our method, FGSM, BIM, C&W [23], MI-FGSM [22] and Universal Adversarial Perturbations (**UAP**) on a ImageNet-compatible dataset[1]. This dataset contains 1000 images which are not used in the original ImageNet dataset. To avoid overfitting on above dataset, we perform hyper-parameter selection on a subset of ImageNet dataset [15] which contains 1000 images randomly selected from ILSVRC 2012 validation set [16].

We use diverse architectures including VGG16 [17], Inception V3 [18], Inception V4 [10], Inception-ResNet-v2 [10], ResNet V2 [2,19][2] as defense models. Besides, we average the predicted probabilities of above models as the ensemble model (**Ensemble**). We also use adversarially trained Inception v3 model [8] (**adv-v3**), adversarially trained Inception-ResNet-V2 model (**adv-res-v2**), and adversarially trained Inception v3 with an ensemble of 3 models (**ens3-inc-v3**) and 4 models (**ens4-inc-v3**) [11][3] respectively as defense models. In all our experiments, we report the **recognition accuracy** for comparison. Besides, to address "label leaking" problem [8], we use the prediction of the current model as the ground truth t (4). We use **TAP** to represent the proposed method for short (Table 1).

---

[1] This dataset can be download at https://github.com/tensorflow/cleverhans/tree/master/examples/nips17_adversarial_competition/dataset.
[2] https://github.com/tensorflow/models/tree/master/research/slim.
[3] https://github.com/tensorflow/models/tree/master/research/adv_imagenet_models.

Table 1. The comparisons of transferability in terms of recognition accuracies. Perturbations are generated using VGG16 and Inception-V3 respectively.

	VGG16	InceptionV3	InceptionV4	Inception ResNet-V2	ResNet-V2	Ensemble
No perturbation	86.8%	96.4%	97.6%	100%	89.6%	99.8%
Random noise	81.3%	91.7%	94.6%	97.8%	84.5%	98.1%
VGG16-TAP	**3.2%**	**23.9%**	28.1%	32.3%	**23.9%**	26.7%
VGG16-FGSM	3.7%	34.9%	44.0%	50.0%	34.7%	46.4%
VGG16-BIM	4.0%	24.2%	**24.5%**	**28.5%**	**23.9%**	**22.7%**
VGG16-UAP	12.4%	31.2 %	32.8%	46.9 %	33.2%	43.7%
Inc-V3-TAP	**29.4%**	**0.0%**	**22.1%**	**24.7%**	**46.9%**	**30.8%**
Inc-V3-FGSM	57.7%	26.9%	70.2%	72.9%	65.7%	75.4%
Inc-V3-BIM	66.0%	0.01%	67.7%	70.2%	76.8%	73.6%
Inc-V3-UAP	39.8%	52.2%	56.4%	63.1%	50.5%	64.6%
Inc-V3-MI-FGSM	45.9%	0.1%	47.3%	50.7%	61.8%	62.5%
Inc-V3-CW	84.9%	24.5%	93.5%	98.6%	86.9%	96.9%

We use FGSM and BIM as our two baseline methods for comparison which are defined as follows:

$$FGSM : \tilde{x} = x + \epsilon \, \text{sign} \nabla_x l(\tilde{x}, t)$$
$$BIM : \tilde{x}_0 = x, \tilde{x}_k = \text{clip}(\tilde{x}_{k-1} + \epsilon \, \text{sign} \nabla_x l(\tilde{x}_{k-1}, t)). \tag{5}$$

We use implementations of FGSM, BIM and C&W with default parameters from CleverHans [20,21] in our experiments. We also modify CleverHans to implement our approach. We also use the implementation of MI-FGSM [22][4] for comparison. To fairly compared with these methods, the perturbation size is set to 16. We linearly normalize the perturbation size of C&W method [23] to 16 for fair comparison and use simple gradient descent to optimize the objective function defined in [23].

In our experiments, the perturbation size ϵ is set to 16 for all experiments. λ and η are set to 0.05 and 10^3 respectively to make each loss contribute equally. The parameter of the normalization α is set to 0.5 for best performance. The size of kernel w_s in (4) is set to 3 for balancing the smooth term and loss. The number of iterations k is empirically set to 5. We will analyze the effects of these parameters on transferability using the subset of ImageNet dataset as described above.

We first use above models to evaluate the clean images and those images added with random noise perturbations ($\epsilon = 16$). The results are listed in Table 2. Inception-Resnet-V2 (100%) achieves significantly better performance than VGG16 (86.8%) for clean images because of the higher capacity. Both of these models can resist random noise attacks and the models with higher capacity also perform better.

---

[4] https://github.com/dongyp13/Non-Targeted-Adversarial-Attacks.

Table 2. The comparisons of transferability in terms of recognition accuracies. Perturbations are generated using Inception-ResNet-V2, ResNet-V2 and ResNet-V1 respectively.

	VGG16	InceptionV3	InceptionV4	Inception ResNet-V2	ResNet-V2	Ensemble
Inc-ResV2-TAP	**37.0%**	25.9%	**33.2%**	4.8%	53.3%	48.2%
Inc-ResV2-FGSM	59.4%	69.0%	76.5%	57.2%	71.7%	78.7%
Inc-ResV2-BIM	48.9%	41.5%	51.5%	1.2%	60.4%	54.5%
Inc-ResV2-MI-FGSM	38.8%	**25.3%**	**33.2%**	**0.1%**	**51.6%**	**46.3%**
Inc-ResV2-CW	83.4%	91.7%	92.4%	49.0%	85.6%	93.5%
ResNet-V2-TAP	**31.8%**	48.2%	55.7%	55.5%	7.6%	**47.4%**
ResNet-V2-FGSM	37.3%	56.3%	64.8%	66.8%	14.6%	63.3%
ResNet-V2-BIM	44.8%	53.2%	62.0%	63.8%	**4.4%**	54.3%
ResNet-V2-MI-FGSM	46.3%	**45.2%**	**51.6%**	**55.2%**	24.1%	56.2%
ResNet-V2-CW	84.0%	94.5%	96.4%	99.5%	37.7%	98.5%
ResNet-V1-TAP	**20.2%**	**38.1%**	**48.7%**	**49.1%**	**25.3%**	**44.4%**
ResNet-V1-UAP	35.3%	41.6%	50.2%	57.8%	40.3%	56.8%
ResNet-V1-MI-FGSM	65.3%	74.3%	78.7%	82.0%	71.3%	86.8%
ResNet-V1-CW	86.9%	96.0%	97.5%	99.9%	89.4 %	99.6%

The Transferability Across Models. We first use VGG16, Inception-V3, Inception-V4, Inception-ResNet-V2, ResNet-V2 and an ensemble of these models as defense models. We iteratively generate perturbations using one model and report the recognition accuracy on all these models. For each iteration, we use all feature maps for the selected model except ResNet-V1 and ResNet-V2 because of the large number of layers. We use the feature maps: "block3/uint_23" ∼ "block3/uint_36" and "block4/uint_3" in ResNet-V2 and "block1" and "block2" in ResNet-V1 for adversarial examples generation. To demonstrate the superiority of the proposed method, we also compare our method with FGSM, BIM and UAP respectively. From Table 2 we can see that, our method achieves 3.2%, 0.0%, 4.8% and 7.6% accuracy for VGG16, Inception-V3, Inception-ResNet-V2 and ResNet-V2 respectively for white-box attacks, which are significantly better than FGSM, BIM, UAP, MI-FGSM and C&W except ResNet-V2-BIM, Inc-ResV2-MI-FGSM and Inc-ResV2-BIM. As for black-box transfer, our method achieves lowest recognition accuracy using Inception-V3 and ResNet-V1 to generate adversarial perturbations. Our method also get comparable or better results using Inception-ResNet-V2 and ResNet-V2 with MI-FGSM. Notably, using VGG16 model to generate perturbations has the highest transfer rate for all methods. We find the gradients of loss with respect to inputs for VGG model are several orders of magnitude larger than those gradients for more complex architectures because of the relatively small number of layers. Our method is unable to gain more benefits for VGG model.

Table 3. The robustness of TAP, FGSM, BIM and UAP to adversarially trained models.

	adv-v3	adv-res-v2	ens3-inc-v3	ens4-inc-v3
VGG16-TAP	**38.8%**	63.8%	**41.9%**	47.3%
VGG16-FGSM	50.9%	71.1%	56.1%	58.5%
VGG16-BIM	57.3%	73.6%	53.5%	55.4%
VGG16-UAP	39.4%	**57.3%**	47.4%	**43.9%**
Inc-V3-TAP	**52.8%**	**68.8%**	**60.9%**	**59.8%**
Inc-V3-FGSM	72.1%	93.6%	85.1%	86.4%
Inc-V3-BIM	82.4%	93.9%	88.2%	88.5%
Inc-V3-UAP	65.5%	82.4%	77.0%	76.9%
Inc-V3-MI-FGSM	74.3%	90.6%	80.7%	82.0%
Inc-V3-CW	93.0%	96.4%	92.3%	90.0%
Inc-ResV2-TAP	**60.5%**	**87.8%**	**79.1%**	**82.1%**
Inc-ResV2-FGSM	73.9%	92.7%	86.9%	87.3%
Inc-ResV2-BIM	70.8%	92.9%	84.8%	86.9%
Inc-ResV2-MI-FGSM	66.9%	83.6%	71.8%	73.4%
Inc-ResV2-CW	91.8%	94.9%	91.9%	89.3%
ResNet-V2-TAP	**49.2%**	**64.1%**	**57.8%**	**56.0%**
ResNet-V2-FGSM	62.1%	85.7%	77.4%	77.8%
ResNet-V2-BIM	64.7%	82.6%	72.3%	74.7%
ResNet-V2-MI-FGSM	71.1%	86.6%	76.9%	77.9%
ResNet-V2-CW	94.0%	96.3%	92.8%	90.5%
ResNet-V1-TAP	**50.2%**	**64.4%**	**55.5%**	**57.7%**
ResNet-V1-UAP	60.4%	77.9%	68.8%	66.1%
ResNet-V1-MI-FGSM	84.5%	93.4%	90.3%	90.2%
ResNet-V1-CW	95.0%	97.5%	94.2%	91.8%

We also evaluate the robustness of TAP to adversarially trained models as shown in Table 3. We show that VGG16 model still gives the highest transfer rate for black-box transfer. Kurakin et al. [8] show that adversarial training provides robustness to adversarial examples generated using one-step methods such as FGSM, but it can not help much against iterative methods such as BIM. They also show that adversarial examples generated by iterative methods are less likely to be transferred across models. However, we show that our method, which generates adversarial examples using iterative methods, still enables adversarial examples transferring across models because of the guided gradients.

We calculate the regularization term of (4): $\sum_i$ abs $R_i(\tilde{x} - x, w_s)$ to inspect the low-frequency information captured by FGSM, BIM and TAP respectively. The values of regularization term in Fig. 1 are 3.72×10^5, 2.71×10^5 and 5.35×10^5

respectively. Since we use low-pass filter w_s for convolution, larger value of the regularization term means that the neighbor pixels vary more smoothly.

The Influence of Loss Functions. We remove two terms in the loss function (4) for each time to inspect the influence of these terms on performance. We remove the second and third terms by setting λ and η to 0 respectively. Figure 2 shows the performance of the proposed method which generates adversarial examples using Inception-V3 with different conditions. From Fig. 2 we can see that, adversarial training can resist adversarial examples. For example, adversarially trained Inception-ResNet-V2 (adv-res-v2) gets much higher recognition accuracy than original Inception-ResNet-V2.

With $\lambda = 0$ and $\eta = 0$, the proposed method degrades to BIM which has the highest recognition accuracy for all defense models, which indicates these defense models are robust to adversarial examples generated using BIM.

By adding the regularization term in (4) ($\lambda = 0$ and $\eta = 10^3$), we show that such operation reduces the recognition accuracy for all adversarially trained models (ens3-inc-v3, ens4-inc-v3, adv-res-v2, adv-v3) consistently. Such operation can also reduce the recognition accuracy for ResNet-V2 and the ensemble model, and it performs slightly worse on Inception-V4 and Inception-ResNet-V2 than BIM. Since it imposes restrictions on perturbations with smooth regularization, it removes the subtle and optimal perturbations for white-box attack (Inception-V3). Thus, it has higher recognition accuracy than BIM.

With $\lambda = 0.05$ and $\eta = 0$, the proposed method takes feature distances into consideration. We show that the proposed method achieves slightly lower accuracy on adversarially trained models than BIM. It reduces the recognition accuracy significantly on Inception-V3, Inception-V4 and Inception-ResNet-V2, ResNet-V2 and the ensemble model. Notably, for white-box attacks, it achieves extremely low recognition rate on Inception-V3.

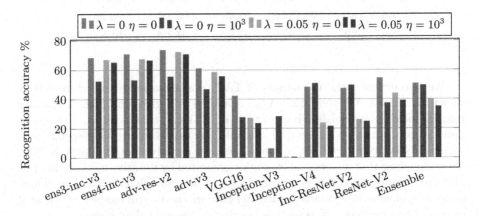

Fig. 2. Recognition accuracies of the proposed method with different configurations of λ and η. Inception-V3 is used to generate adversarial examples.

From above experiments we can see that, adversarially trained models (ens3-inc-v3, ens4-inc-v3, adv-res-v2 and adv-v3) and original models (Inception-V3, VGG16, Inception-V4, Inception-ResNet-V2, ResNet-V2 and Ensemble) are very complementary. Adversarial training injects adversarial examples from other models into the training set and it tends to solve the weaknesses of original models. Two terms in (4) behave differently on these two types of models. We set $\lambda = 0.05$ and $\eta = 10^3$ to balance the performance on these two types of models.

The Sensibility of Parameters on Transferability. To analyze the sensibility of parameters on transferability, we vary one parameter and fix other parameters to report recognition accuracies on defense models. λ varies from 5×10^{-4} to 100 ($\lambda \in \{5 \times 10^{-4}, 10^{-3}, 5 \times 10^{-3}, 0.01, 0.02, 0.05, 0.1, 0.5, 1, 2, 5, 10, 50, 100\}$) and α and η are set to 0.5 and 10^3 respectively. The recognition accuracies on defense models are reported in Fig. 3. With increasing value of λ, the adversarial examples generated by our method perform differently on two groups of models (with and without adversarial training). Adversarial examples are more difficult to be transferred to adversarially trained models with larger λ while it is easier for those models without adversarial training.

Figure 4 shows the recognition accuracies with varied α ($\alpha \in \{0, 0.5, 1, 1.5, 2\}$). We observe that there is an optimal value $\alpha = .5$ of α yielding best robustness. Figure 5 presents the performance of the proposed methods with different size of w_s as in (4). With large s, the transfer rates of the proposed method degrades for all models slightly and consistently. Thus, we choose $s = 3$ for best performance.

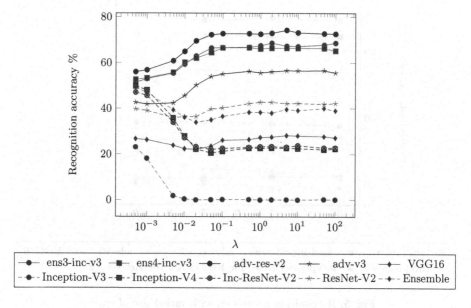

Fig. 3. Recognition accuracies with varied λ.

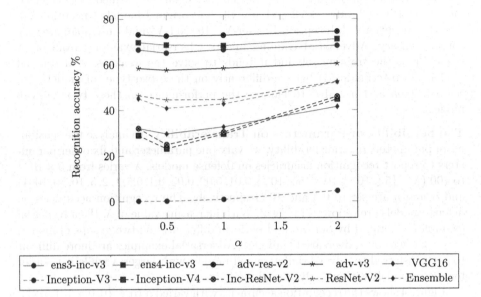

Fig. 4. Recognition accuracies with varied α.

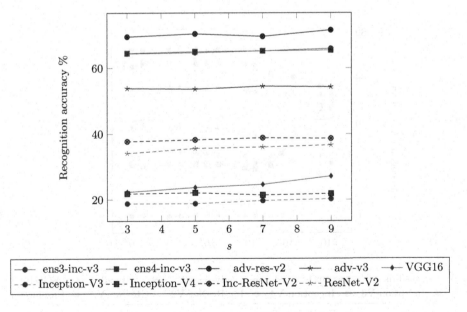

Fig. 5. Recognition accuracies with varied size of w_s.

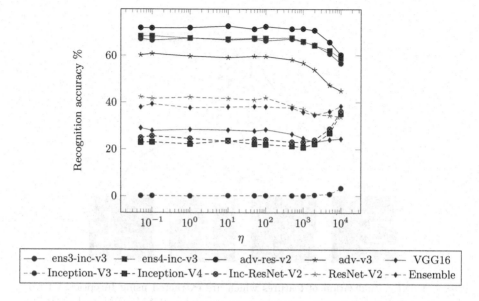

Fig. 6. Recognition accuracies with varied η.

We vary η from 0.05 to 10^4 ($\eta \in \{0.05, 0.1, 1, 10, 50, 100, 500, 10^3, 2 \times 10^3, 5 \times 10^3, 10^4\}$) and observe two distinct patterns for two types of models in Fig. 6. With increasing value of η, the recognition accuracies of adversarial examples on adversarially trained models decrease, which means that adversarially trained models are less robust to adversarial examples with larger value of η. However, with larger value of η, the proposed method performs better on those models without adversarial training.

t-SNE Visualization of Adversarial Examples. To demonstrate the influence of adversarial examples intuitively, we visualize the extracted features of black-box model as shown in Fig. 7. Specifically, we generate adversarial examples using Inception-V3 and extract 1536-dimensional features using Inception-V4 in the penultimate layer. We use t-SNE to compute a 3-dimensional embedding that respects the high-dimensional (L2) distances. Adversarial examples of our method and other two baseline methods are connected to the clean image by straight lines with red and blue color respectively.

By adding perturbations into clean images, it causes the perturbations in the penultimate feature space which will result in error predictions. For white-box attacks, it is clear that we optimize the objective function to find the perturbations in pixels to maximize the perturbations in the penultimate feature space directly. It will cause the extreme low accuracies on white-box models. For black-box attacks, such perturbations in pixels generated using one model can not transfer to the perturbations in the penultimate feature spaces of another model effectively because of different architectures.

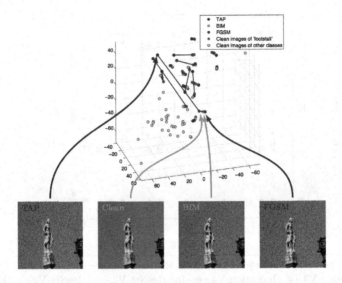

Fig. 7. t-SNE visualization of features which are extracted using Inception-V4 from clean images and adversarial examples (generated by FGSM, BIM and TAP (our method) on Inception-V3 respectively). The distances between adversarial examples generated by TAP and clean images in the embedding space are much larger than those distances corresponding to FGSM and BIM, which means the perturbations generated by TAP are more transferrable than FGSM and BIM.

Both FGSM and BIM can perturb adversarial examples in the penultimate feature space to make error predictions for Inception-V4 as shown in Fig. 7. However, Table 2 shows that Inception-V4 model can still achieve 70.2% and 67.7% on those adversarial examples generated using FGSM and BIM respectively. It means that most of the perturbations in pixels can not cause large enough perturbations in the penultimate feature space to make error predictions for Inception-V4.

As shown in Fig. 7, the distances between adversarial examples generated by our method and clean images are larger than those corresponding distances of FGSM and BIM. It will cause error predictions in Inception-V4 with high probability, which is validated by Table 2. We show that our method can generate the perturbations in pixels using Inception-V3 which can transfer to the perturbations in the penultimate feature space of Inception-V4 with high probability.

5   Conclusion

In this paper, we propose a novel transferable adversarial perturbations generating method to fool deep neural networks. We use two extra penalty terms to guide the search directions efficiently. We show that maximizing the distance of intermediate feature maps between inputs and adversarial examples makes adversarial examples transfer across models. In addition, we observe that a smooth regularization can enable black-box transfer by reducing the variations of adversarial perturbations. We further use t-SNE to visualize the correlations between transferable ability and the distance in the penultimate feature space which also provides a insight for future research.

Acknowledgments. We thank Zhifei Yue and Shuisheng Liu for helpful discussions and suggestions.

References

1. Krizhevsky, A., Sutskever, I., Hinton, G.E.: ImageNet classification with deep convolutional neural networks. In: Advances in Neural Information Processing Systems, pp. 1097–1105 (2012)
2. He, K., Zhang, X., Ren, S., Sun, J.: Deep residual learning for image recognition. In: Proceedings of the IEEE Conference on Computer Vision and Pattern Recognition, pp. 770–778 (2016)
3. Hinton, G., et al.: Deep neural networks for acoustic modeling in speech recognition: the shared views of four research groups. IEEE Sig. Process. Mag. **29**(6), 82–97 (2012)
4. Sutskever, I., Vinyals, O., Le, Q.V.: Sequence to sequence learning with neural networks. In: Advances in Neural Information Processing Systems, pp. 3104–3112 (2014)
5. Nguyen, A., Yosinski, J., Clune, J.: Deep neural networks are easily fooled: high confidence predictions for unrecognizable images. In: Proceedings of the IEEE Conference on Computer Vision and Pattern Recognition, pp. 427–436 (2015)
6. Moosavi-Dezfooli, S.M., Fawzi, A., Fawzi, O., Frossard, P.: Universal adversarial perturbations. arXiv preprint arXiv:1610.08401 (2016)
7. Goodfellow, I.J., Shlens, J., Szegedy, C.: Explaining and harnessing adversarial examples. In: International Conference on Learning Representations (2015)
8. Kurakin, A., Goodfellow, I.J., Bengio, S.: Adversarial machine learning at scale. arXiv: Computer Vision and Pattern Recognition (2016)
9. Moosavi-Dezfooli, S.M., Fawzi, A., Frossard, P.: DeepFool: a simple and accurate method to fool deep neural networks. In: Proceedings of the IEEE Conference on Computer Vision and Pattern Recognition, pp. 2574–2582 (2016)
10. Szegedy, C., Ioffe, S., Vanhoucke, V., Alemi, A.A.: Inception-v4, inception-ResNet and the impact of residual connections on learning. In: AAA, pp. 4278–4284 (2017)
11. Tramèr, F., Kurakin, A., Papernot, N., Boneh, D., McDaniel, P.: Ensemble adversarial training: attacks and defenses. arXiv preprint arXiv:1705.07204 (2017)
12. Szegedy, C., et al.: Intriguing properties of neural networks. arXiv preprint arXiv:1312.6199 (2013)
13. Kurakin, A., Goodfellow, I.J., Bengio, S.: Adversarial examples in the physical world. arXiv: Computer Vision and Pattern Recognition (2016)
14. Perronnin, F., Sánchez, J., Mensink, T.: Improving the fisher kernel for large-scale image classification. In: Daniilidis, K., Maragos, P., Paragios, N. (eds.) ECCV 2010. LNCS, vol. 6314, pp. 143–156. Springer, Heidelberg (2010). https://doi.org/10.1007/978-3-642-15561-1_11
15. Deng, J., Dong, W., Socher, R., Li, L.J., Li, K., Fei-Fei, L.: ImageNet: a large-scale hierarchical image database. In: Proceedings of the IEEE Conference on Computer Vision and Pattern Recognition, pp. 248–255. IEEE (2009)

16. Russakovsky, O., et al.: ImageNet large scale visual recognition challenge. Int. J. Comput. Vis. (IJCV) **115**(3), 211–252 (2015)
17. Simonyan, K., Zisserman, A.: Very deep convolutional networks for large-scale image recognition. arXiv preprint arXiv:1409.1556 (2014)
18. Szegedy, C., Vanhoucke, V., Ioffe, S., Shlens, J., Wojna, Z.: Rethinking the inception architecture for computer vision. In: Proceedings of the IEEE Conference on Computer Vision and Pattern Recognition, pp. 2818–2826 (2016)
19. He, K., Zhang, X., Ren, S., Sun, J.: Identity mappings in deep residual networks. In: Leibe, B., Matas, J., Sebe, N., Welling, M. (eds.) ECCV 2016. LNCS, vol. 9908, pp. 630–645. Springer, Cham (2016). https://doi.org/10.1007/978-3-319-46493-0_38
20. Nicolas, P., et al.: cleverhans v2.0.0: an adversarial machine learning library. arXiv preprint arXiv:1610.00768 (2017)
21. Abadi, M., et al.: TensorFlow: large-scale machine learning on heterogeneous distributed systems. arXiv preprint arXiv:1603.04467 (2016)
22. Dong, Y., et al.: Boosting adversarial attacks with momentum. In: The IEEE Conference on Computer Vision and Pattern Recognition (CVPR), June 2018
23. Carlini, N., Wagner, D.: Towards evaluating the robustness of neural networks. arXiv preprint arXiv:1608.04644 (2016)

Semantically Aware Urban 3D Reconstruction with Plane-Based Regularization

Thomas Holzmann[(✉)], Michael Maurer, Friedrich Fraundorfer,
and Horst Bischof

Institute of Computer Graphics and Vision,
Graz University of Technology, Graz, Austria
{holzmann,maurer,fraundorfer,bischof}@icg.tugraz.at

Abstract. We propose a method for urban 3D reconstruction, which incorporates semantic information and plane priors within the reconstruction process in order to generate visually appealing 3D models. We introduce a plane detection algorithm using 3D lines, which detects a more complete and less spurious plane set compared to point-based methods in urban environments. Further, the proposed normalized visibility-based energy formulation eases the combination of several energy terms within a tetrahedra occupancy labeling algorithm and, hence, is well suited for combining it with class specific smoothness terms. As a result, we produce visually appealing and detailed building models (i.e., straight edges and planar surfaces) and a smooth reconstruction of the surroundings.

1 Introduction

Nowadays 3D reconstruction software is available, with which it is possible to easily create accurate 3D models from image data (commercial products as well as research community-based approaches). However, for certain applications like visualization of urban environments for construction industry, real estate companies and mapping services like Google Maps, a compact and visually appealing reconstruction consisting of planar surfaces and straight outlines is desired. Such a reconstruction should contain little noise and not necessarily all details from every scene part. We define the following criteria for a visually appealing urban 3D model, which are usually not tackled by current 3D reconstruction approaches:

- *Planar shape prior:* When planar and nearly planar surfaces exist in the scene (e.g., facades, roofs), they should also be reconstructed as planar surfaces.

Electronic supplementary material The online version of this chapter (https://doi.org/10.1007/978-3-030-01264-9_29) contains supplementary material, which is available to authorized users.

© Springer Nature Switzerland AG 2018
V. Ferrari et al. (Eds.): ECCV 2018, LNCS 11218, pp. 487–503, 2018.
https://doi.org/10.1007/978-3-030-01264-9_29

- *Straight building outlines:* Edges of buildings should be straight and represented by a straight line (i.e., no noisy edges).
- *Detailed buildings and smoothed surroundings:* As for several applications (e.g., real estate companies) detailed building reconstructions are required, details should be kept while regularizing with a plane prior. Simultaneously, the surrounding of buildings does not necessarily be reconstructed with high details but with a smoothed, visually appealing surface.

These criteria do not only define a visually appealing reconstruction, but make it also easier to reduce the amount of data in a post-processing step (i.e., points lying on a planar surface can be diminished without changing the surface).

To apply these criteria, we use semantic priors in the reconstruction process to treat building and surrounding scene parts differently. For building parts, we incorporate plane priors in order to achieve planar surfaces and straight outlines while still keeping important details. For non-building parts, we impose a smooth surface by reestimating a smoother 3D representation of the scene, setting class specific sparsification parameters and smoothness terms. We partition the scene into volumetric cells using a Delaunay triangulation and perform Graph Cut-based inside/outside labeling. As a result, we compute a watertight polygonal mesh resulting from the interface of inside and outside labeled cells of the triangulation. In order to reduce the amount of data needed, mesh simplification can be applied in a post-processing step without loosing accuracy.

Our main contributions are threefold: First, a plane detection algorithm using 3D lines for detecting planes. Compared to point-based RANSAC methods like [29] we are able to detect more planes especially in urban environments which often contain poorly textured and, hence, sparsely reconstructed scene parts (e.g., white building facades). Second, we introduce an improved visibility-based energy term. In order to intuitively combine visibility-based terms with additional energy terms, a normalized energy is necessary. Currently used formulations (e.g., proposed by Labatut et al. [16]) lack in the possibility of normalizing the resulting energy. Third, we incorporate semantic priors into the reconstruction process. Depending on the semantic classes, we process the 3D data differently and set class-specific shape priors in order to get planar surfaces

Fig. 1. *Results of the proposed approach textured with* [33]. One can observe that planar parts in the scene (facades, windows, roof) are represented by planar surfaces and building edges where two facades intersect each other are represented by straight lines. Note that holes in the model are due to missing visibility information during texturing.

and straight edges for buildings and a smooth reconstruction for the surrounding. Figure 1 visualizes textured results of our approach.

2   Related Work

In the past years, several works were presented focusing on creating visually appealing results for urban 3D reconstruction. Generally, most of them follow the idea that urban scenes can be largely approximated by geometric primitives and, hence, detected primitives are used to approximate the scene or to denoise and smooth the 3D reconstruction. Others use semantic information in order to simultaneously optimize the reconstruction and the semantic labeling.

Primitive Fitting. Several approaches try to fit primitives and then create a 3D scene reconstruction by directly using the fitted primitives (e.g., [20,21,24,35]) or incorporating them into an optimization framework (e.g., [11,17,18,25]) in order to create compact and visually appealing 3D models. Often, a RANSAC-based primitive detection approach (e.g., as described by Schnabel et al. [29]) is used, but there exist also other methods, especially for plane detection (e.g., [4]). However, all these methods use point clouds for fitting primitives and, hence, the extracted primitive set is likely to be incomplete if primitives are represented with too few points (frequently happens at poorly textured facades reconstructed with image-based methods). Hence, we are using a different scene information (3D lines) which is more likely to be present at poorly textured urban scenes.

Reconstruction Using a Scene Hypothesis. Different works focus on reconstructing scenes with a very specific scene prior and, hence, work well for these specific scenes but do not generalize to others. Li et al. [20] use detected planes to create a set of axis-aligned boxes that approximate the geometry of a building. Following the idea of slicing of the scene (as proposed for indoor scenes in [26,34]), Holzmann et al. [10] presented an approach to create visually appealing building models. Even though these approaches produce well regularized models, they are restricted to a specific scene arrangement (Manhattan world assumption or scene dividable into slices). Assuming a mainly planar scene, Monszpart et al. [24] aim to extract a regular arrangement of planes. Nan and Wonka [25] proposed an approach where they fit planes and intersect all the detected planes with each other to generate a possible set of faces for the final reconstruction. The final surface is generated by solving an optimization problem using all these face candidates. Even though these methods are not constrained to a Manhattan world assumption, they are designed for scenes containing mainly planar surfaces. In contrast, our approach has a special regularization prior for planar surfaces but can handle arbitrary scene structure.

Shape Priors Incorporated in Global Optimization. In the works of Labatut et al. [17] and Lafarge et al. [18,19] primitives are incorporated within a tetrahedral representation of the scene and can be selected within the Graph Cut optimization. Following their idea, [11] added an improved plane augmentation which does not require a dense oversampling of the scene and added additional regularization terms. All these methods can reconstruct arbitrary scenes and regularize scene parts depending on detected shapes. However, wrongly regularized scene parts may result in artifacts, which we tackle by using semantic information and regularizing differently depending on semantic label.

Semantic Reconstruction. Recently, several methods incorporated semantic information in the 3D reconstruction process [1,7,32]: They incorporate semantic information into an optimization framework to solve a multi-label 3D reconstruction problem using a voxel grid or tetrahedral representation. By using class-specific shape priors, they simultaneously optimize the 3D reconstruction and the semantic labeling. Compared to them, we do not simultaneously optimize semantics and the 3D reconstruction but use the semantic information in order to create visually appealing 3D models following our defined criteria.

3   Urban 3D Reconstruction with Semantic Priors

In this section, we give an overview of our processing pipeline and subsequently describe each part in detail. As a result, we deliver beautiful, visually appealing 3D models from urban scenes where buildings have planar surfaces and straight edges while still containing relevant details embedded in a smoothed surrounding.

Taking images from a scene as input, we first compute the camera poses using Structure-from-Motion, a dense point cloud using a Multi-View Stereo algorithm and a line-based 3D reconstruction. As further preprocessing steps, we compute dense depth maps for every camera and semantically label every image. In order to generate a very smooth reconstruction of the surrounding and a detailed but prior-based smoothing of the buildings, we semantically label all 3D information and incorporate the building and non-building classes differently into a Delaunay triangulation-based reconstruction framework. For buildings, we use all the available 3D information (i.e., 3D lines and points). We detect planes in the scene by using the reconstructed 3D lines from buildings and enforce the triangulation to include all planes. For non-building parts, we compute a smooth Poisson surface reconstruction and use a sampled representation of this surface. Our final 3D reconstruction results from a 3D Delaunay triangulation, where every cell is labeled inside or outside by solving an energy minimization problem using Graph Cuts including energy terms depending on the semantic label.

3.1   Semantic Segmentation

The goal of the semantic segmentation is to get the 3D reconstruction semantically enhanced to be able to perform automated decisions throughout our processing pipeline. To achieve this goal we follow the work of [23] to perform pixel-wise semantical segmentation of the input images. To transfer the labels from 2D to 3D, each 3D point is back projected according to its visibility to 2D and a final majority voting determines the label of the 3D point.

For the semantic segmentation of the input images we use a Fully Convolutional Neural Network (FCN) [22] to get pixel-wise segmentations. The network presented in [22] is adjusted to represent the number of output classes required for our task. We define five output classes, namely: street/pavement, building, vegetation, sky and clutter. As our intermediate aim is to semantically enhance the 3D reconstruction we need a pixel accurate segmentation of the input images where the segmentation boundaries are aligned with the objects present. Thus, the receptive field of the FCN of 32 px and the final up sampling by a factor of eight are too coarse to achieve this goal. We extend the 2D segmentation network by adding a Conditional Random Field represented as Recurrent Neural Network (CRFasRNN) as presented in [36]. The Conditional Random Field exploits the probabilities of the FCN and refines them by taking binary constraints into account. This enforces label changes being aligned with edges.

Having the pixel-wise semantic segmentation of the input images, we propagate this information to 3D: Assuming 3D points with visibility information, we back project every point into every image in which it is visible in and compute a point label by majority voting. For getting labels of the 3D lines, we sample every line with points and compute a label for every point as explained above. The most frequent label within the sampled points defines the line label.

3.2 Plane Detection Using Lines

A very common approach to detect planes in 3D is to use a RANSAC-based algorithm with a point cloud as input (e.g., [29]). However, especially in urban environments where scene parts like facades might be poorly textured, these approaches fail due to missing reconstructed 3D points. In comparison, 3D lines are more likely to be detected at building facades, as some high-gradient elements like windows or building outlines usually exist. Hence, we are using this 3D line information to improve plane detection in urban environments. As our goal is to reconstruct a well smoothed surrounding of the building, we just use lines labeled as building and ignore all the others.

Assuming to have a 3D reconstruction consisting of line segments, we first detect line triples which already describe a plane hypothesis. Then we cluster the triples which are coplanar and in vicinity. Finally, we detect all inlier lines from the plane hypothesis.

Line Triple Detection. As we explicitly want to model man-made scenes frequently having rectangular outlines, we search for perpendicular coplanar line pairs which can be used to describe a plane. Additionally, we only accept line pairs which have a small distance between each other. For the coplanarity and perpendicularity tests we accept errors up to $\alpha_{error} = 5$ deg, and the normal distance from start/end point of the line segment to the computed plane hypothesis must not be bigger than $d_{inlier} = 0.15$ m. The distance between start/end point of the two line segments must not be bigger than 1.5 m and we ignore line segments shorter than 0.8 m. In order to perform an early removal of spurious planes, we search for a third supporting line which has to be coplanar with the line pair and with small distance to the pair. We just accept the line pair if a third line exists. Note that line segments can also be part of several line triples, which is beneficial for lines which are exactly, e.g., at corners of a house.

Line Triple Clustering. After having estimated plane hypotheses by detecting line triples, several hypotheses can be nearly identical. Therefore, we cluster line triples which represent the same planar surface. We cluster line triples by first checking if the triples are nearly coplanar (i.e., normals of plane hypotheses with enclosing angle smaller α_{error}, normal distance from line triple (i.e., start/end point of its segments) to the current plane hypothesis lower than d_{inlier}). From these coplanar line triples, we greedily add all line triples to a cluster which have a maximum distance of the line projections on the plane of 12 m to the previous line triple. After having clustered the triples, the lines are sampled and the sampled points are used to reestimate the plane using SVD.

Inlier Detection and Outline Estimation. Finally, we detect all inlier (i.e., lines segments being nearly coplanar in terms of angle α_{error} and distance d_{inlier}) which have a distance of the line projections on the plane smaller than 1.2 m. We estimate an outline of the plane by computing a bounding box around all inlier segments and reestimate the plane parameters with all inliers using SVD.

Plane Filtering and Plane-Based Denoising. Having estimated the planes, we filter out plane segments which are included in another plane hypothesis (i.e., having the same plane parameters and the outline is included). Additionally, we filter out planes which don't have sufficient supporting 3D data (i.e., points and sampled line segments, see Sect. 3.3) within d_{inlier} normal distance. These planes are usually erroneous detections due to a specific line segment arrangement. Finally, the input data is denoised: We move all points and line segments which are in d_{inlier} normal distance to a plane onto the plane by normal projection.

3.3   Input Data Subdivision and Processing

Depending on the semantic label, we subdivide the scene into two parts which will be processed differently: For the building part we keep all available 3D information. For the non-building part we sparsify the input data, compute a Poisson surface and use the sampled Poisson surface which results in a smoother, visually appealing reconstruction (e.g., less spurious peaks at vegetation). In the final optimization the subdivided parts are combined again in order to create a reconstruction of the whole scene.

As we want to have a point cloud representation of the building part which covers all important details, we add all input points and additionally add points from sampled building line segments to the scene (line sampling distance 0.05 m). Adding the sampled line points especially helps at poorly textured scene parts where few reconstructed points are available.

In contrast to the building part, we want a very smooth representation of the surroundings of the building. Hence, we first sparsify these classes: For the clutter class we just keep every fifth point, for street/pavement and vegetation we keep every third point. Then, we compute a Poisson surface [14] using these selected points. For the subsequent reconstruction steps, we don't use the original street/pavement, vegetation and clutter points but a sampled point representation of the computed Poisson surface. This results in a much smoother surface of this part of the scene in the final reconstruction.

3.4 3D Reconstruction Using Tetrahedral Occupancy Labeling

In this section, we describe the final reconstruction process. We explain the tetrahedra subdivision using the detected planes and the visibility prediction using depth maps, we propose a normalized visibility-based energy term and define class-dependent energy terms. As our approach is using a tetrahedral representation of the whole scene, we compute a Delaunay Triangulation of all the scene points (i.e., all available points of building parts and the sampled Poisson surface for the surroundings). Then, we subdivide the tetrahedra using the detected planes and solve an energy minimization problem by minimizing the following energy using Graph Cuts [2]:

$$\underset{\ell}{\text{minimize}} \quad E_{\text{Vis}}(\ell) + E_{\text{Class}}(\ell) \ , \tag{1}$$

where $E_{\text{Vis}}(\ell)$ is the visibility-based energy and $E_{\text{Class}}(\ell)$ are class-specific energy terms, which will be explained in more detail in this section. Finally, we get an inside/outside labeling for every cell from which a surface mesh can be extracted.

Tetrahedra Subdivision. Even though many points lying on the detected planes are included in the triangulation, it is not guaranteed that the whole planar surfaces are included as faces. Hence, following the method described in [11], we compute intersections of planes and tetrahedra and add the resulting facets and vertices to the triangulation. After this subdivision step, the triangulation is not necessarily Delaunay any more but contains all detected planar surfaces which consequently can be selected by the final optimization.

Visibility Prediction Using Depth Maps. To compute visibility-based energy terms, the knowledge of the visibility information of every 3D point (i.e., camera-point correspondences) is necessary. Hence, most of the methods following visibility-based cost computations similar to Labatut et al. [16] assume that the visibility information is known. However, when tetrahedra are subdivided, new points without visibility information are created. Additionally, input 3D information without visibility information cannot be used. Hence, we propose to compute this information for all 3D points using depth maps.

Assuming to have dense depth maps for every camera, we project every 3D point into all cameras. If the point is within the image boundaries and in front of the camera, we compare the actual distance of the point to the camera with the depth value in the depth map (using nearest neighbor). If the depth difference is small enough (i.e., smaller than 0.03 m), we assume that the current point is actually visible in this camera and store this camera-point correspondence.

Improved Visibility-Based Energy. Visibility-based energy terms as proposed by Labatut et al. [16] tend to be very hard to normalize, as the magnitude of the energy depends on the density of the point cloud, the number of cameras the current tetrahedron is visible in and the visibility information of the surrounding. Hence, combining it with other energy terms tends to be hard.

Therefore, we propose an improved energy formulation, which is slightly better in terms of accuracy and, more importantly, has a normalized magnitude with which a more intuitive combination with additional energy terms is possible.

Inspired by [12,16], the energy terms are based on ray casting from every vertex to every camera the vertex is visible in. Unary costs are assigned to cells intersected by a ray adjacent to the visible vertex (i.e., before and behind the vertex) and pairwise costs are assigned to facets intersected by rays (see Fig. 2). Opposing to [16], we do not only assign pairwise terms in one direction but in both, and we additionally add unary costs in front of a visible vertex. This has shown to significantly improve the result when using normalization afterwards. In order to generate normalized cost terms, our general idea is the following: The visibility-based energies should change significantly when the terms are still low and additional information is added, but the influence of additional visibility information when already sufficient information is available should be decreased. Hence, it should have a significant effect if a point is visible by 1 or 5 cameras, but the effect should be reduced if the visibility is changed from 21 to 25 cameras.

The normalized unary terms for cells directly in front of and behind visible vertices are defined as follows:

$$E_{unary}(t) = (1 - e^{-\frac{\#rays}{limit_u}})limit_u, \tag{2}$$

where t defines the current tetrahedron, $\#rays$ define the number of rays intersecting the tetrahedron and $limit_u$ is the energy limit approached asymptotically.

Additionally, cells including a camera and infinite cells are labeled as outside. The normalized pairwise terms for every facet are defined as follows:

$$E_{pairwise}(f) = (1 - e^{-\frac{\#rays}{limit_p}})limit_p, \tag{3}$$

where f defines the current facet, $\#rays$ define the facet's number of ray intersections and $limit_p$ defines the energy limit. The limits of the unary and pairwise energies need to be set so that additional energy information is not ignored too early. Additionally, the pairwise terms need to be allowed to become stronger, as otherwise at large facets at holes or below roofs the unary term might spuriously dominate and, hence, artifacts might arise. We found out empirically that a setting for $limit_u = 8$ and $limit_p = 24$ is a good choice for most scenes.

These improved visibility-based energy terms are non-negative and submodular. The output is a normalized energy having maximum unary and pairwise terms, which is crucial for combining it with additional energy terms and, hence, makes it possible to easier find scene-independent parameter settings.

Class-Dependent Energy Terms. Depending on the semantic class facets and cells in the triangulation are assigned to, additional energy terms are added. First, we compute the class dependence for every facet and cell by computing a majority vote using all their corresponding vertices. Then, scene parts get assigned different energy terms depending on their semantic labels.

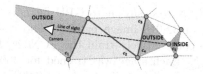

Fig. 2. *Visibility-based energy computation.* We use ray casting to compute the visibility terms: The cell where the camera is located in (c_1) is labeled as outside by adding infinite weights. Then, every facet (green) which is intersected by the line of sight (red) gets pairwise costs assigned in both directions. Finally, the cell in front of the visible vertex (c_4) is labeled as outside by adding finite weights and the cell behind the vertex (c_5) is labeled as inside by adding finite weights. (Color figure online)

The energy terms assigned to building parts favor Manhattan-like structures but simultaneously aim to keep important details and are defined in [11]: They consist of a Manhattan regularity term E_{Man}, which favors label transitions with Manhattan-like surface structures (i.e., neighboring faces with enclosing angles similar to 0 or multiples of 90°), and a level of detail term E_{LoD}, which punishes volumetric errors with respect to the unregularized model. Hence, E_{LoD} is the counterpart to E_{Man} and brings back smoothed out details which are not supported by planes. Using these energy terms, we strongly favor planar and Manhattan-like structure while still keeping sufficiently big details.

For non-building parts, our goal is to get a reconstruction which is as smooth as possible. Therefore, we just add an area smoothness term E_{area} as defined in [16]. This term should remove spurious artifacts.

Hence, the class-specific energies are defined as follows:

$$E_{\mathrm{Class}}(\ell) = \begin{cases} \alpha_{\mathrm{Man}} E_{\mathrm{Man}}(\ell) + \alpha_{\mathrm{LoD}} E_{\mathrm{LoD}}(\ell) & \text{if building} \\ \alpha_{\mathrm{area}} E_{\mathrm{area}}(\ell) & \text{else} \end{cases}, \qquad (4)$$

where α_{Man}, α_{LoD} and α_{area} define the amount of smoothing.

4 Experiments

In this section, we first describe implementation details and the input data. Then, we evaluate the plane detection algorithm, the improved visibility-based energy and the effect of semantic priors. Finally, we compare results from our approach with others and show the effect of mesh simplification as post-processing step.

Implementation Details. Our pipeline is mainly implemented in C++ using CGAL [3] for the Delaunay triangulation and the Poisson meshing (used for the surroundings of the building). The semantic segmentation network is realized in the Caffe framework [13]. For initialization we exploited the weights of the PASCAL-Context network [27] and performed a transfer learning of the network based on 27 labeled training images (16 manually labeled, 11 taken from eTRIMS dataset [15]) that were augmented in scale (0.8, 1.0, 1.2), rotation [deg] (0, 90, 180, 270) and mirroring. Additionally the augmented images were cropped to patches of 256 × 256 px to easily fit to GPU memory. In total we resulted in a training database of 32,016 image patches. The training itself has been performed in stages to consecutively train the FCN32s, FCN16s, FCN8s and FCN8s with CRFasRNN. Each stage was trained for 400,000 iterations using Stochastic Gradient Descent with a momentum of 0.99, weight-decay of 0.0005 and a learning rate of $1e^{-9}, 1e^{-10}, 1e^{-12}$ and $1e^{-12}$ for each stage respectively.

The parameters for the final reconstruction were set as follows: For datasets *House* and *Residential Area* the parameter set was $\alpha_{Man} = 1000$, $\alpha_{Lod} = 500$. For the dataset *Block Building*, the parameters were set differently to impose a stronger plane prior as this dataset contains more noise near to planar surfaces ($\alpha_{Man} = 2500$, $\alpha_{Lod} = 1250$). α_{area} was set to 0.5 for all datasets.

Input Data. We evaluated on three datasets, from which example images are depicted in Fig. 3. Each of them consists of images acquired with a Micro Aerial Vehicle (MAV) and captured with a Sony Alpha 6000 camera with 24.3 MPixel. The first dataset, to which we refer to as *House*, contains 233 images and shows a scene with a family house and surroundings consisting of mostly grass and trees. The second dataset, *Residential Area*, contains 446 images and consists of two family houses (the others are not covered sufficiently by the images). For these two datasets, also ground truth captured with a total station is available and ground control points were measured to align the ground truth with the image based reconstruction. The third dataset is named *Block Building*, contains 232 images and includes a Manhattan-like building consisting mainly of poorly textured facades and windows. As this dataset has no metric scale, we manually scaled it to be approximately metric.

To compute the camera poses, we used our own Structure-from-Motion implementation. The dense point cloud for *House* was computed using Sure [28] and consists of approx. 900K points. The dense point clouds for *Residential Area* and *Block Building* were computed with PMVS2 [5] and contain 3.6M points and 1.4M points, respectively. The 3D line reconstructions were computed with Line3D++ [9] and the input depth maps with PlaneSweepLib [8].

Plane Detection Using Lines. In this experiment, we compare our proposed plane detection algorithm using lines with a state-of-the-art RANSAC-based plane detection algorithm proposed by Schnabel et al. [29]. Figure 4 shows an

House   Residential Area   Block Building

Fig. 3. *Example input images from the evaluation datasets.* The *House* dataset consists of a family house surrounded mainly by vegetation. The *Residential Area* dataset consists of several family houses and the *Block Building* dataset consists of a office building with mainly Manhattan-like structure.

Fig. 4. *Comparison to point-based plane detection.* In the left column, one can see 3D input data (top: 3D points, bottom: 3D line segments): Especially at the front facade the point cloud has very few points while the line representation still contains some lines (e.g., at windows and at building edges). In the middle column, points and lines corresponding to extracted planes are illustrated (randomly colored). One can observe that the point-based approach detects planes at densely sampled surfaces well while missing sparsely reconstructed surfaces. The proposed line-based approach also detects planes which are just represented with few line segments. In the right column, one can see plane segments created by fitting bounding boxes around the inlier data on the plane surfaces. In the result of the point-based approach, spurious plane segments become visible while the line-based approach mainly contains the planes of the building. (Color figure online)

overview of the detection process for both approaches. For comparison, we used the implementation of [29] in CGAL [3]. We changed the default parameters to make the results comparable to our approach: We set the inlier distance to 0.15 m as in the line-based approach and reduced the minimum supporting points per plane to 0.5% to generate more plane hypotheses. As can be seen in the results in Fig. 4, [29] misses out important facade planes due to missing 3D points and detects several spurious planes whereas our approach detects a more complete plane set due to the availability of line structure on the facades. For additional comparisons we refer to the supplementary material.

Normalized Visibility-Based Energy Term. In this experiment, we show that the proposed normalized visibility-based energy formulation slightly improves the reconstruction accuracy while simultaneously being easier to handle in combination with other energy terms. We evaluated the proposed energy term on the *Residential Area* dataset and, additionally, on the *Fountain-P11* [30] dataset. In Fig. 5, one can see the results and error metrics with just using visibility-based energies (i.e., without additional energy terms). One can observe that the visual results are similar. For both datasets, the error metrics are very similar but slightly better for the proposed, normalized visibility-based energy formulation. For a more detailed evaluation of the individual steps changed in the energy formulation we refer the reader to the supplementary material.

When looking at the result of *Residential Area* using just visibility-based energy, it can be seen that some surfaces are very noisy. Hence, regularizing

| Energy from [16] | Proposed | Energy from [16] | Proposed |
| $\mu = 0.035$, $\sigma = 0.071$ | $\mu = 0.034$, $\sigma = 0.069$ | $\mu = 0.037$, $\sigma = 0.146$ | $\mu = 0.034$, $\sigma = 0.135$ |

Fig. 5. *Errors of proposed visibility-based energy terms compared to the visibility-based energy in* [16] *(in m). Left:* Evaluation on the *Residential Area* dataset. Visually, the result of the proposed energy is very similar while having a slightly lower error (error definition see Sect. 4) and being normalized, which is crucial for combining it with other energies. *Right:* Error visualization of the Fountain-P11 [30] dataset. Blue means low error, red high error. Also on this dataset, the errors of the proposed formulation are slightly lower (error definition see [30]). (Color figure online)

some parts with plane priors and using a smooth surface approximation for others like vegetation is very beneficial for creating visually appealing models.

Semantic Priors. In Fig. 6 it can be observed that when using no semantics (same as treating everything as building), the surroundings of buildings are noisy and less visually appealing. Also, more data needs to be used to describe the noisy mesh, while with semantics a sparser Poisson reconstruction describes the surroundings. Further, artifacts may arise as the Manhattan regularity term is applied everywhere even though it might not be suited to smooth e.g. vegetation.

Results. Below we compare reconstruction results from the proposed algorithm with generic 3D reconstruction algorithms and with specialized urban reconstruction approaches. For a comparison with commercial reconstruction pipelines we refer the reader to the supplementary material.

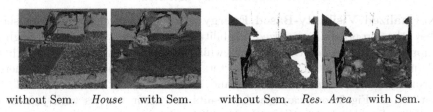

without Sem.   *House*   with Sem.   without Sem.   *Res. Area*   with Sem.

Fig. 6. *Comparison of results computed with/without semantic information.* As can be seen in the detail examples of two datasets, the reconstructed surface of the surroundings of buildings is more noisy without semantics. Due to the Poisson reconstruction and the different smoothness terms, the surroundings get reconstructed much smoother and with less points (i.e. less data) when using semantics. Also, detected planes are removed in the surroundings, as just building lines are used for plane detection. These changes due to semantics contribute to a more visually appealing final reconstruction.

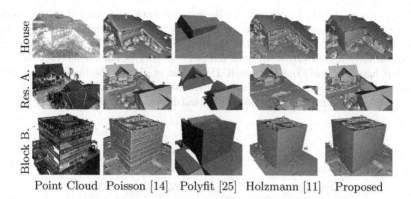

Point Cloud Poisson [14] Polyfit [25] Holzmann [11] Proposed

Fig. 7. *Results and comparison with state-of-the-art methods.* From left to right: Input point clouds, Poisson meshes [14] computed from the input point clouds, results of Polyfit [25], Holzmann et al. [11] and the proposed approach. The Poisson mesh looks visually appealing, but often produces rounded edges and spurious surfaces like bubbles where data is missing. Polyfit is not able to reconstruct all buildings sufficiently well. As it depends on planes detected from point clouds, undetected surfaces were just not included in the possible solution set and spurious planes lead to erroneous reconstruction results. Holzmann et al. regularizes some parts of the scene well with its included plane prior. However, at some parts of the scene not all planes were detected and, hence, planar surfaces remain noisy. Further, due to an unpredictable visibility-based energy term it is difficult to set correct weights for smoothness terms. Hence, some parts of the scene can be smoothed out very quickly. The proposed approach creates 3D models with planar surfaces at facades/roofs while still keeping the building details like chimneys and reconstructs the surroundings with a smooth surface.

In Figs. 1 and 7, results from the proposed approach and state-of-the-art reconstruction algorithms are depicted, where some of them also try to follow the same idea of a visually appealing 3D reconstruction. The Poisson surface reconstruction produces smooth surfaces, which results in rounded edges. Additionally, it cannot handle missing data very well and creates spurious artifacts. Polyfit [25] heavily depends on the (point-based) plane detection result and reconstructs non-planar parts not very well, as it just relies on detected planes and uses only the plane surfaces to create an optimized surface model. The method of Holzmann et al. [11] incorporates plane priors into the reconstruction and, hence, aims to follow a similar idea of a visually appealing 3D model. However, some planar surfaces are not detected correctly and due to the unpredictability of the visibility-based energy it is hard to set the smoothness energy weights correctly. This might lead to artifacts like smoothed out wall parts or whole buildings. As this approach has no semantic class specific smoothing, also the surroundings of buildings are smoothed heavily according to a plane prior and, hence, some parts (like, e.g., vegetation) are smoothed too aggressively and artifacts looking like slices might arise. In comparison, the proposed approach uses a more complete plane set as shape prior and imposes planar surfaces just

Table 1. *Error statistics compared to the ground truth.* We computed the minimal distances of the ground truth points to the surface reconstructions with a maximum distance of 1 m. On both datasets, the proposed approach has the lowest error. Polyfit has significantly higher errors on both datasets, as it does not reconstruct the whole scene but just (parts of) buildings well. Holzmann et al. has the highest error on the *Residential Area* dataset due to a wrongly smoothed out building. Poisson produces over-smoothed (i.e., no sharp edges) results, but has comparable errors.

	House		Residential area	
	μ [m]	σ [m]	μ [m]	σ [m]
Poisson [14]	0.165	0.237	0.101	0.157
Polyfit [25]	0.515	0.352	0.304	0.375
Holzmann et al. [11]	0.137	0.237	0.415	0.385
Proposed	**0.126**	**0.233**	**0.055**	**0.086**

on buildings. Due to the improved visibility-based energy formulation it is easier to set correct smoothness term weights and, hence, to avoid over-smoothing. The representation of the surroundings is smooth while still not over-smoothed.

In Table 1 error metrics for two datasets with respect to the ground truth are depicted. It can be observed that the error metrics for the proposed approach are the best for both the *House* and *Residential Area* data set. Apparently, the plane prior incorporated within the reconstruction process handles noise and clutter better than, for example, a smooth Poisson surface. For more information about the ground truth, we refer to the supplementary material.

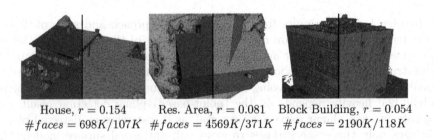

House, $r = 0.154$ Res. Area, $r = 0.081$ Block Building, $r = 0.054$
$\#faces = 698K/107K$ $\#faces = 4569K/371K$ $\#faces = 2190K/118K$

Fig. 8. *Simplification as post-processing.* Every subfigure consists of the resulting mesh of the proposed approach (*left*) and the mesh simplified by Quadric Edge Collapse [6] in a lossless way (*right*) (i.e., restricting the edge collapse to a quadric error of 10^{-13}). Below, reduction factors and $\#faces$ before/after simplification are depicted. Due to the perfect planarity of the building parts, faces can be merged without changing the surface of the mesh. Though, non-building parts stay untouched as they are not perfectly planar. Very low reduction factors $r = \frac{\#faces_{simpl}}{\#faces_{orig}}$ (i.e., high compression) can be reached for all models. In comparison, when applying Quadric Edge Collapse on Poisson meshes in Fig. 7, the best reduction factor was 0.929 ($\#faces = 393k/365K$) at House. Quadric Edge Collapse was performed with VCGlib [31].

For this comparisons, we used the following parameter settings: For Poisson surface reconstruction we set octree depth to 9. For Polyfit we used default parameters. We also tried to vary the parameters, but the results did not improve significantly. For Holzmann et al. [11] we used the parameter settings as described in the paper for *House* and *Block B*. For *Residential Area* we set α_{LoD} to 250K.

Due to the planarity of big parts of the resulting mesh of the proposed method, the amount of faces in the mesh can be significantly reduced without changing the surface. In Fig. 8, results of applying Quadric Edge Collapse [6] as post-processing step are depicted. As the maximum error of Quadric Edge Collapse was set to 10^{-13} (i.e., nearly zero), only edges on planar surfaces were removed. It can be observed that even though the mesh surface did not change, the amount of data was extremely reduced.

Assuming to have a precomputed dense point cloud, 3D line model, depth maps and semantically labeled images, our approach needs 13 min for the *House* dataset, 60 min for the *Block Building* and 153 min for the *Residential Area* (on an Intel Xeon E5-2680 running at 2.8 GHz with 40 cores and 264 GB RAM). Most of the time is needed for cell cutting and visibility term computations.

5   Conclusion

We presented a 3D reconstruction approach for urban scenes, with which it is possible to get planar surfaces and straight outlines for buildings, while the surroundings of buildings are represented by a smooth surface. Our introduced line-based plane detection algorithm detects a more complete plane set compared to point-based approaches and by using semantic information we can regularize individual scene parts differently. We have shown that we can produce visually appealing and compact 3D reconstructions while still reaching slightly better accuracies compared to state-of-the-art methods.

Acknowledgements. This research was funded by the Austrian Science Fund (FWF) in the project V-MAV (I-1537). We thank Prof. Werner Lienhart and Slaven Kalenjuk from IGMS, TU Graz, Jesus Pestana and Christian Mostegel for providing datasets and Martin R. Oswald for discussion.

References

1. Blaha, M., Vogel, C., Richard, A., Wegner, J., Schindler, K., Pock, T.: Large-scale semantic 3D reconstruction: an adaptive multi-resolution model for multi-class volumetric labeling. In: Proceedings IEEE Conference Computer Vision and Pattern Recognition (2016). https://doi.org/10.1109/CVPR.2016.346
2. Boykov, Y., Veksler, O., Zabih, R.: Fast approximate energy minimization via graph cuts. IEEE Trans. Patt. Anal. Mach. Intell. **20**(12), 1222–1239 (2001)
3. CGAL. Computational Geometry Algorithms Library. http://www.cgal.org
4. Dzitsiuk, M., Sturm, J., Maier, R., Ma, L., Cremers, D.: De-noising, stabilizing and completing 3D reconstructions on-the-go using plane priors. In: International Conference on Robotics and Automation, May 2017

5. Furukawa, Y., Ponce, J.: Accurate, dense, and robust multi-view stereopsis. IEEE Trans. Patt. Anal. Mach. Intell. **32**(8), 1362–1376 (2010)
6. Garland, M., Heckbert, P.S.: Surface simplification using quadric error metrics. In: ACM Transactions on Graphics (SIGGRAPH), pp. 209–216. ACM Press/Addison-Wesley Publishing Co., New York (1997)
7. Häne, C., Zach, C., Cohen, A., Angst, R., Pollefeys, M.: Joint 3D scene reconstruction and class segmentation. In: Proceedings IEEE Conference Computer Vision and Pattern Recognition (2013)
8. Häne, C., Heng, L., Lee, G.H., Sizov, A., Pollefeys, M.: Real-time direct dense matching on fisheye images using plane-sweeping stereo. In: International Conference on 3D Vision (3DV) (2014)
9. Hofer, M., Maurer, M., Bischof, H.: Efficient 3D scene abstraction using line segments. Comput. Vis. Image Underst. **157**, 167–178 (2016). https://doi.org/10.1016/j.cviu.2016.03.017
10. Holzmann, T., Fraundorfer, F., Bischof, H.: Regularized 3D modeling from noisy building reconstructions. In: Fourth International Conference on 3D Vision, 3DV 2016, Stanford, CA, USA, 25–28 October 2016, pp. 528–536 (2016)
11. Holzmann, T., Oswald, M.R., Pollefeys, M., Fraundorfer, F., Bischof, H.: Plane-based surface regularization for urban 3D reconstruction. In: 28th British Machine Vision Conference, vol. 28 (2017)
12. Hoppe, C., Klopschitz, M., Donoser, M., Bischof, H.: Incremental surface extraction from sparse structure-from-motion point clouds. In: Proceedings British Machine Vision Conference (2013)
13. Jia, Y., et al.: Caffe: Convolutional architecture for fast feature embedding. arXiv preprint arXiv:1408.5093 (2014)
14. Kazhdan, M., Bolitho, M., Hoppe, H.: Poisson surface reconstruction. In: Eurographics Symposium on Geometry Processing (2006)
15. Korč, F., Förstner, W.: eTRIMS Image Database for interpreting images of man-made scenes. Technical report, TR-IGG-P-2009-01, April 2009. http://www.ipb.uni-bonn.de/projects/etrims_db/
16. Labatut, P., Pons, J.P., Keriven, R.: Efficient multi-view reconstruction of large-scale scenes using interest points, delaunay triangulation and graph cuts. In: Proceedings International Conference on Computer Vision (2007)
17. Labatut, P., Pons, J.P., Keriven, R.: Hierarchical shape-based surface reconstruction for dense multi-view stereo. In: International Workshop on 3-D Digital Imaging and Modeling (3DIM), ICCV Workshops, Kyoto, Japan, pp. 1598–1605, October 2009
18. Lafarge, F., Alliez, P.: Surface reconstruction through point set structuring. Comput. Graph. Forum **32**(2), 225–234 (2013)
19. Lafarge, F., Keriven, R., Brédif, M., Vu, H.: A hybrid multiview stereo algorithm for modeling urban scenes. IEEE Trans. Patt. Anal. Mach. Intell. **35**(1), 5–17 (2013)
20. Li, M., Wonka, P., Nan, L.: Manhattan-world urban reconstruction from point clouds. In: Leibe, B., Matas, J., Sebe, N., Welling, M. (eds.) ECCV 2016. LNCS, vol. 9908, pp. 54–69. Springer, Cham (2016). https://doi.org/10.1007/978-3-319-46493-0_4
21. Li, Y., Wu, X., Chrysanthou, Y., Sharf, A., Cohen-Or, D., Mitra, N.J.: GlobFit: consistently fitting primitives by discovering global relations. ACM Trans. Graph. **30**(4), 52:1–52:12 (2011)

22. Long, J., Shelhamer, E., Darrell, T.: Fully convolutional networks for semantic segmentation. In: Proceedings of the IEEE Conference on Computer Vision and Pattern Recognition, pp. 3431–3440 (2015)
23. Maurer, M., Hofer, M., Fraundorfer, F., Bischof, H.: Automated inspection of power line corridors to measure vegetation undercut using UAV-based images. In: ISPRS Annals of the Photogrammetry, Remote Sensing and Spatial Information Sciences (2017)
24. Monszpart, A., Mellado, N., Brostow, G., Mitra, N.: RAPter: rebuilding man-made scenes with regular arrangements of planes. In: ACM SIGGRAPH 2015 (2015)
25. Nan, L., Wonka, P.: PolyFit: polygonal surface reconstruction from point clouds. In: Proceedings International Conference on Computer Vision (2017)
26. Oesau, S., Lafarge, F., Alliez, P.: Planar shape detection and regularization in tandem. Comput. Graph. Forum **35**(1), 203–215 (2016)
27. PASCAL-Context network. http://dl.caffe.berkeleyvision.org/pascalcontext-fcn32s-heavy.caffemodel
28. Rothermel, M., Wenzel, K., Fritsch, D., Haala, N.: Sure: photogrammetric surface reconstruction from imagery. In: Proceedings LC3D Workshop, Berlin (2012)
29. Schnabel, R., Wahl, R., Klein, R.: Efficient ransac for point-cloud shape detection. Comput. Graph. Forum **26**(2), 214–226 (2007)
30. Strecha, C., von Hansen, W., Gool, L.V., Fua, P., Thoennessen, U.: On benchmarking camera calibration and multi-view stereo for high resolution imagery. In: Proceedings IEEE Conference Computer Vision and Pattern Recognition (2008)
31. The VCG Library. http://vcg.isti.cnr.it/vcglib/
32. Vogel, C., Richard, A., Pock, T., Schindler, K.: Semantic 3D reconstruction with finite element bases. In: 28th British Machine Vision Conference, vol. 28 (2017)
33. Waechter, M., Moehrle, N., Goesele, M.: Let there be color! Large-scale texturing of 3D reconstructions. In: Fleet, D., Pajdla, T., Schiele, B., Tuytelaars, T. (eds.) ECCV 2014. LNCS, vol. 8693, pp. 836–850. Springer, Cham (2014). https://doi.org/10.1007/978-3-319-10602-1_54
34. Xiao, J., Furukawa, Y.: Reconstructing the world's museums. Int. J. Comput. Vis. **110**(3), 243–258 (2014)
35. Zebedin, L., Bauer, J., Karner, K., Bischof, H.: Fusion of feature- and area-based information for urban buildings modeling from aerial imagery. In: Forsyth, D., Torr, P., Zisserman, A. (eds.) ECCV 2008. LNCS, vol. 5305, pp. 873–886. Springer, Heidelberg (2008). https://doi.org/10.1007/978-3-540-88693-8_64
36. Zheng, S., et al.: Conditional random fields as recurrent neural networks. In: IEEE Computer Vision and Pattern Recognition (CVPR), pp. 1529–1537 (2015). https://doi.org/10.1109/ICCV.2015.179, arXiv: 1502.03240

Joint 3D Tracking of a Deformable Object in Interaction with a Hand

Aggeliki Tsoli[✉] and Antonis A. Argyros

Institute of Computer Science, FORTH, Heraklion, Greece
{aggeliki,argyros}@ics.forth.gr

Abstract. We present a novel method that is able to track a complex deformable object in interaction with a hand. This is achieved by formulating and solving an optimization problem that jointly considers the hand, the deformable object and the hand/object contact points. The optimization evaluates several hand/object contact configuration hypotheses and adopts the one that results in the best fit of the object's model to the available RGBD observations in the vicinity of the hand. Thus, the hand is not treated as a distractor that occludes parts of the deformable object, but as a source of valuable information. Experimental results on a dataset that has been developed specifically for this new problem illustrate the superior performance of the proposed approach against relevant, state of the art solutions.

1 Introduction

Deformable objects are nearly everywhere and humans interact with them continuously. Thus, tracking the interaction of human hands with such objects based on visual input can support a number of applications in domains that include but are not limited to augmented/virtual reality and robotics.

Although there has been a lot of previous work on capturing the interaction of hands with rigid objects [2,8,10,11,20,34], there has been very limited work on capturing the interaction of hands with complex deformable objects under arbitrary contact configurations. The most related work so far is the one by Tzionas et al. [42] on hands and articulated object tracking based on depth input. To capture deformations, this approach models non-rigid objects as articulated objects with a tree-structured skeleton and a large number of bones. When the fingers of a hand come close to the object, the tracking of the hand and the object is aided by physics-based modeling and simulation (Bullet). This works fine, unless the object exhibits complex deformations that cannot be modeled effectively by the assumed tree-structured, skeleton-based representation (e.g., general

---

Electronic supplementary material The online version of this chapter (https://doi.org/10.1007/978-3-030-01264-9_30) contains supplementary material, which is available to authorized users.

V. Ferrari et al. (Eds.): ECCV 2018, LNCS 11218, pp. 504–520, 2018.
https://doi.org/10.1007/978-3-030-01264-9_30

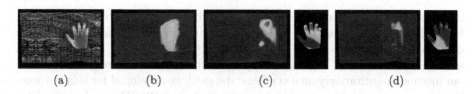

(a)   (b)   (c)   (d)

Fig. 1. Contrary to previous work on tracking hands in interaction with non-rigid objects, we capture complex object deformations by modeling the object with a textured 3D mesh. (a) A result of joint optimization for a frame. Colors on the hand show points that are closer (red) or further away (blue). (b) Heatmap-based visualization of object tracking error with [41]. (c) Heatmap-based visualization of the error in object tracking (left) and hand tracking (right) when performed independently. (d) Same as (c), but for the proposed joint optimization method. (Color figure online)

deformation of a planar sheet of paper or of a piece of cloth). Furthermore, tracking relies solely on depth information, so fitting the template mesh of the object to the observed point cloud becomes susceptible to sliding.

To deal with these problems, we propose an approach where the deformable object is modeled as a 3D triangular textured mesh. The method reasons explicitly and in every frame about the contact configuration of all fingertips with the object. The proposed joint tracking framework (see Fig. 1) relies on concepts from the Shape from Template community to model and track the object, and on a hybrid approach for tracking the hand. An initial estimate of the pose of the hand is computed as in [24], i.e., by fitting a 3D hand model to the 2D joint locations estimated by the discriminative method in [32]. Given this initial estimate, we can compute the area of the object that is occluded by the hand. Then, we refine the 3D hand pose and estimate the 3D deformation of the object jointly. This is formulated as an optimization problem that minimizes an error function that considers a variety of image features between consecutive frames as well as between the reference and the current frame, while keeping the mesh of the object close to the observed data. We, additionally, preserve the overall structure of the mesh using inextensibility constraints and a Laplacian-based smoothness prior [36]. Still, these constraints are not sufficient to represent the typically non-smooth deformations of the occluded part of the object occurring due to contact with the hand. To deal with this problem, our method reasons about contacts explicitly. More specifically, in our joint optimization framework, we examine all $2^5 = 32$ possible contact/no-contact configurations of the 5 fingertips with the object and we select the one that yields the best fit of the object's model to the observed data in the area around the hand. Essentially, the best contact configuration is the one that maximizes the fit of the deformable object model to the available observations, after tracking jointly the hand and the object.

The proposed approach is the first to achieve detailed tracking of complex deformable objects that are represented as 3D meshes and which interact with a human hand in a complex way. We show that the tracking of the deformable object is performed with an accuracy that has not been achieved before. At the same time, by plugging it in our joint optimization framework, the performance of a state of the art hand tracker is considerably improved. Our approach can be used in grasping scenarios with various contact configurations and relative distances between the object and hand and it is particularly effective in fine manipulation scenarios, i.e., finger tapping on the object of interest. We evaluate our method quantitatively on a synthetic dataset[1] we developed for this purpose. We also compare our approach to a state of the art RGBD-based method for deformable surfaces tracking [41] and we provide results obtained from a state of the art RGB-based method [17] as a reference baseline. Additionally, we showcase our method on real data and on a variety of object deformations produced by the interaction of an actual hand with materials such as cloth, paper and carton.

2   Previous Work

We present previous work on tracking deformable objects, hands as well as hand and object interactions from monocular input.

Monocular Tracking of Deformable Objects: Recovering the shape of deformable surfaces from single images is inherently ambiguous [29], given that many different shape/camera configurations can produce the same images. Shape-from-Template methods reconstruct a deformable surface assuming that a reference 2D template and the corresponding 3D shape of the object are known. For instance, Ostlund et al. [22] track control points of a surface in 2D and infer its 3D shape using the control points and a Laplacian deformation model. Bartoli et al. [3] perform template-based deformable 3D reconstruction from a single input image and provide analytical solutions to the problem accounting for both isometric and conformal surface deformations. The works in [6,9] present optical flow-based surface tracking. Parashar et al. [25] present volumetric Shape-from-Template to reconstruct the surface and interior deformation of a 3D object using constraints of local rigidity. Ngo et al. [17] address the problem of 3D reconstruction of poorly textured, occluded surfaces, proposing a framework based on a template-matching approach that ranks dense robust features by a relevancy score. Their method is capable of considering an externally provided occlusion mask. This makes it possible to test this method in sequences with hand object interaction, i.e., by providing the hand mask that is computed automatically based on hand tracking. A direct comparison of this method to ours would be unffair (RGB vs RGBD input). However, we test this method on our datasets and provide the obtained results as a reference baseline.

With respect to tracking from single view point cloud data, Schulman et al. [30] propose an algorithm based on a probabilistic generative model that incorporates point cloud observations and the physical properties of the tracked object and its environment. Wuhrer et al. [47] combine a tracking-based approach with fitting a volumetric elastic model. Petit et al. [26] track a 3D object which undergoes large elastic deformations and fast rigid motions. They perform non-rigid fitting of a mesh to the 3D point cloud of the object based on

---

[1] Available online at: https://www.ics.forth.gr/cvrl/deformable_interaction/.

the Finite Element Method to model elasticity and on geometrical point-to-point correspondences to compute external forces exerted on the mesh. Tsoli and Argyros [41] present a method for tracking isometric deformable surfaces that undergo topological changes such as a paper that is getting torn. We provide a comparison of our approach to this method.

Tracking of Hands: A common categorization of hand motion/pose estimation methods is into generative, discriminative, and hybrid methods. Generative methods use a kinematics and potentially an appearance model of the hand to synthesize visual features that are comparable to the observed ones. Given that, a top-down search identifies the pose that maximizes the agreement between the synthesized and the observed visual features [10,11,19,27,37]. Generative methods result in accurate and physically plausible hand poses. On the other hand, their execution time and their inability to perform single-shot pose estimation are among their weak points. Discriminative methods for monocular hand tracking search in a large database of poses [28] or learn a mapping from depth and/or color input to pose space, typically in a large offline step [7,18,32,33,38,40,45,46]. Contrary to generative methods, discriminative ones are faster and do not suffer from drift, but may exhibit limited accuracy or the resulting estimation can be physically implausible. Hybrid approaches [16,24,31,35,44,48] combine the strengths of generative and discriminative ones. In our framework, we incorporate an extension of the RGB-based method in [24] that exploits RGBD data.

Tracking of Hand-Object Interactions: Several previous works consider tracking hands in interaction with one or more known rigid objects [2,8,10, 11,20,34]. In a few cases the models of rigid [23] or articulated [43] objects are reconstructed on the fly. With the exception of methods tracking two interacting hands (e.g., [11,21]) which therefore constitute special cases, Tzionas et al. [42] presented the single existing method for tracking a hand in interaction with an articulated object, from monocular RGBD. The hand and the object are represented as articulated meshes and their pose is inferred by fitting the meshes to the point cloud data while ensuring physical plausibility through a physics-based simulation of the scene. A problem with purely depth-based methods for tracking is that it is very hard to prevent the surface of interest (object or even the hand) from "sliding" along the surface of the observed point cloud. Moreover, the assumption of a tree-structured skeletal representation of the object limits the complexity of the deformations that can be handled effectively. On the contrary, we leverage on representing the non-rigid object as a 3D mesh and on using appearance features (SIFT, GBDF texture features) and inextensibility constraints to capture detailed mesh deformations. Deformable object tracking is also aided by considering it together with 3D hand pose estimation and by reasoning about hand-object contact points in a joint optimization framework.

Our Contribution: We present the first method for tracking in 3D, the interaction of a human hand and a non-rigid object undergoing complex deformations from RGBD input. Our approach reasons about the contacts of a hand

and the object during object manipulation. This is achieved through the joint optimization of the hand pose, the deformable object shape and their contact configuration that results in the best fitting of the deformable object model to the available visual observations in the vicinity of the detected and tracked hand. Our approach outperforms relevant existing methods on the first dataset that is suitable for the problem and which we will make publicly available.

3   The Proposed Method

Input: The input is a monocular RGBD sequence $\{I_f, D_f\}_{f=1}^K$ consisting of K frames where I_f and D_f are the RGB image and the corresponding depth map at frame f. To eliminate high-frequency noise on the depth values, we perform bilateral filtering. We assume knowledge of the camera's projection matrix P and, based on this, we derive a point cloud P_f out of each D_f.

Deformable Object Model: We denote with $M_f = (V_f, \mathcal{E})$ the template mesh at a frame f. M_f consists of N_o vertices stored in $V_f = [\mathbf{v}_1^f \dots \mathbf{v}_{N_o}^f] \in \mathbb{R}^{3 \times N_o}$ where each column represents a vertex and V_0 denotes the 3D vertex locations at the reference frame. Thus, $\mathbf{v}_i^j$ represents the i-th vertex of the mesh at frame j. The connectivity of the template mesh is expressed through a set of edges $\mathcal{E} \subset V_0 \times V_0$. We assume that for the first (reference) frame of the sequence the template is manually registered to the visual data, that is $M_0 = (V_0, \mathcal{E})$ is known and that the mesh topology $\mathcal{E}$ does not change over time.

Hand Model: We use a hand model comprising of $B = 16$ bones and a detailed 3D triangular mesh with $N_h = 1597$ vertices. It has 26 degrees of freedom (DoFs) represented using 27 parameters. 7 are used to model the global translation and rotation (as quaternion) of the hand. The joint at the base of each finger is modeled using two DoFs and the rest of the finger joints require one DoF, each. The finger joints are bound by the joint limits that apply to a real hand [1]. Let $H(\theta_0) = (W_0, \theta_0)$ denote the 3D model of the hand at the reference pose θ_0 where $W_0 = [\mathbf{w}_1^0 \dots \mathbf{w}_N^0] \in \mathbb{R}^{3 \times N}$ are the 3D locations of the surface vertices of the hand at the reference pose. Let also θ_f be the hand pose at frame f. The posed hand for the new pose θ_f is given by $H(\theta_f) = (W_f, \theta_f; W_0, \theta_0)$ where $W_f = [\mathbf{w}_1^f \dots \mathbf{w}_{N_h}^f] \in \mathbb{R}^{3 \times N_h}$ denotes the vertices $\mathbf{w}_i^f$ on the surface of the hand that were transformed using linear blend skinning as:

$$\mathbf{w}_i^f = \sum_{b=1}^B a_{ib} T_b(\theta_f) T_b(\theta_0)^{-1} \mathbf{w}_i^0. \tag{1}$$

In Eq. (1), a_{ib} is the skinning weight of vertex i with respect to bone b and $T_b(\theta)$ denotes the global translation and/or rotation transformation of bone b due to pose θ. We define joints at the heads of all bones as well as at the tails of the bones closest to the fingertips and we end up with 21 joints in total. Let l_i^0 be the 3D location of each joint at the reference 3D model of the hand. The location of the joints at the posed hand model at frame f is given by

$$\mathbf{l}_i^f(\theta_f) = T_{b(i)}(\theta_f) T_{b(i)}(\theta_0)^{-1} \mathbf{l}_i^0, \tag{2}$$

where $b(i)$ is the bone that is associated with joint i. Our hand model was rigged in Blender [39]. The skinning weights are fixed for all frames and at most three skinning weights per vertex are nonzero.

Output: Our goal is to infer $\{M_f = (V_f, \mathcal{E})\}_{f=1}^K$, that is, the 3D coordinates of the template vertices $\{V_f\}_{f=1}^K$, as well as the pose of the hand $\{\theta_f\}_{f=1}^K$ at all frames f. This is performed in four steps. First, we estimate only the 3D pose of the hand from the input RGB image (Sect. 3.1). This gives us a rough estimate of the area where the hand lies, thus the area on the image where we expect the deformable object to be occluded. In turn, this provides an initialization for the second step in which we optimize jointly for the 3D location of the deformable object vertices and the pose of the hand (Sect. 3.2). Third, we select the optimal contact configuration of the fingers with respect to the deformable object (Sect. 3.3). Fourth, we fine-tune the joint fitting of the hand and the deformable object to our data considering the optimal contact configuration and coarse-to-fine texture features (Sect. 3.4).

3.1   Initial Hand Pose Estimation

Given an RGB frame I_f and a bounding box around the hand, we estimate the 2D joint locations of the hand using the work in [32]. Let $J_i^f = (u_i^f, v_i^f, p_i^f)$, $i \in [1, 2]$, represent the 21 detected 2D hand joints at frame f. (u_i^f, v_i^f) are the 2D coordinates of the i-th joint on the input image I_f and p_i^f is the method's confidence for the joint i, $(p_i^f \in [0, 1])$. Let also $Q_i(\theta, P) = (x_i, y_i)$ be the projection of joints $l_i(\theta)$ on the image plane, given (a) a pose θ and (b) the camera's projection matrix P. To avoid using false detections, we do not consider joints with confidence p_i below an experimentally identified value $p^{th} = 0.1$.

For a given pose θ, we quantify the discrepancy $d(Q_i(\theta, P), J_i)$ between the observed joint J_i and the computed one Q_i as in [24]:

$$d(Q_i(\theta, P), J_i) = (p_i^3 \cdot (x_i - u_i))^2 + (p_i^3 \cdot (y_i - v_i))^2. \tag{3}$$

Similarly, the total discrepancy between the observed and model joints is:

$$E_J(\theta) = \sum_{i=0}^{21} d(Q_i(\theta, P), J_i). \tag{4}$$

The 3D hand pose θ'_f that is most compatible to the observed 2D joints can be estimated by minimizing the objective function of Eq. (4):

$$\theta'_f = \arg\min_\theta \{E_J(\theta)\}. \tag{5}$$

This is achieved by the Levenberg-Marquardt optimizer [12,14] that minimizes this objective function after the automatic differentiation of the residuals. The bounding box around the hand is defined manually for the first frame and around the previous solution for the following frames.

The initial fitting of the hand provides a coarse occlusion mask $\mathcal{M}_f$ around the hand that we use both for fitting the deformable object (Sect. 3.2) and for assessing the quality of hypotheses about the contact configuration, i.e. which fingers touch the object (Sect. 3.3). The occlusion mask is calculated as the convex hull of the hand rendered at pose θ'_f dilated by a 50×50 kernel.

3.2 Joint Estimation of Hand Pose and Object Deformation

We jointly estimate the pose θ_f of the hand and perform non-rigid registration of V_f on the point cloud P_f. This is performed by the minimization

$$V_f*, \theta_f* = \text{argmin}_{V_f, \theta_f} E(V_f, \theta_f, W_f, P_f, S_f, S_0, \mathcal{M}_f, V_0, \mathcal{E}, A, \mathbf{f}, Y), \quad (6)$$

of the following energy function:

$$\begin{aligned}E(V_f, \theta_f, W_f, P_f, S_f, S_0, \mathcal{M}_f, V_0, \mathcal{E}, A, \mathbf{f}, Y) &= \lambda_J E_J(\theta_f) + \lambda_{G\_h} E_G^h(W_f, P_f) \\ &+ \lambda_{G\_o} E_G^o(V_f, P_f) + \lambda_F E_F(V_f, S_f, S_{f-1}, S_0, \mathcal{M}_f) + \lambda_T E_T(V_f, V_0, \mathcal{M}_f) \\ &+ \lambda_S E_S(V_f, \mathcal{E}, V_0) + \lambda_L E_L(V_f, A) + \lambda_C E_C(V_f, \theta_f, W_f, \mathbf{f}, Y).\end{aligned} \quad (7)$$

In addition to the hand pose estimation error term E_J (see Sect. 3.1), the defined energy function consists of several error terms presented in detail below.

Registration of the Geometry of the Hand to the Point Cloud: The second term in Eq. (7) aims at bringing the visible geometry of the hand as close as possible to that of the point cloud. So, $E_G^h(W_f, P_f)$ is defined as:

$$E_G^h(W_f, P_f) = \sum_{\mathbf{w}_i^f \in W_f} ||\mathbf{w}_i^f - \mathbf{g}_i^f||_2^2, \quad (8)$$

where W_f is the set of visible hand vertices $\mathbf{w}_i^f$ based on pose θ'_f and $\mathbf{g}_i^f$ is the closest point of $\mathbf{w}_i^f$ to the point cloud P_f.

Registration of the Geometry of the Template to the Point Cloud: In a similar way, the third term of Eq. (7) is designed to register the geometry of the deformable template to the point cloud. So, $E_G^o(V_f, P_f)$ is defined as the sum of distances of the template vertices $\mathbf{v}_i^f$ to their closest points $\mathbf{g}_i^f$ on the point cloud:

$$E_G^o(V_f, P_f) = \sum_{i=1}^{N_o} ||\mathbf{v}_i^f - \mathbf{g}_i^f||_2^2. \quad (9)$$

Account for Feature Correspondences: For each RGB frame I_f, we extract a set S_f of N_f SIFT features [13], $S_f = \{s_i^f\}_{i=1}^{N_f}$. To make sure that we take into account SIFT features solely on the deformable object, we consider only features that are outside the hand mask $\mathcal{M}_f$ estimated in Sect. 3.1. Given the registration of I_f with D_f and P_f, we assume that all SIFT features s_i^f are represented as 3D points in the camera centered coordinate system. Finally, we denote with $c_k(s_i^f)$ the corresponding of feature s_i^f at frame k. For each SIFT feature s_i^f, we compute its projection $b_f(s_i^f)$ on the surface of M_f. Essentially, this entails (a) finding the triangular patch of M_f on which s_i^f projects and (b) expressing s_i^f in barycentric coordinates. This way, a SIFT feature is expressed as a function of the coordinates of the vertices of the template which permits the deformation of the template. Given the above, $E_F(V_f, S_f, S_{f-1}, S_0, \mathcal{M}_f)$ is defined as:

$$E_F(V_f, S_f, S_{f-1}, S_0, \mathcal{M}_f) = t_1 \sum_{j=1}^{r_f^{f-1}} \left\| b_{f-1}(s_j^{f-1}) - c_f(s_j^{f-1}) \right\|_2^2$$

$$+ t_2 \sum_{i=1}^{r_f^0} \left\| b_1(s_i^0) - c_f(s_i^0) \right\|_2^2, \tag{10}$$

for all r_f^0 features from the reference frame and r_f^{f-1} features from frame $f - 1$ whose correspondences at frame f fall outside the hand mask $\mathcal{M}_f$. The scalars t_1, t_2 determine the relative importance of the features from the previous and reference frames and are set empirically to $t_1 = 1$, $t_2 = 5$.

Account for Texture Compatibility: Let $\{t_i^0\}_{i=1}^{s_t}$ be a set of dense color samples on the template mesh of the deformable object expressed in barycentric coordinates with respect to vertices V_0 and projected to the reference image I_0. We optimize for the 3D vertex locations V_f so that the texture of each projected sample t_i^0 at the reference frame matches the texture at its corresponding projected location t_i^f at frame f. As texture features $\phi(\cdot)$ we use the Gradient Based Descriptor Fields (GBDF) [5] that are robust under light changes.

$$E_T(V_f, V_0, \mathcal{M}_f) = \sum_{i=1}^{s_t} \left\| \phi(t_i^0) - \phi(t_i^f) \right\|_2^2. \tag{11}$$

We consider only dense samples that given the last solution V_{f-1} for the deformable object project outside the hand mask $\mathcal{M}_f$ estimated in Sect. 3.1.

Preserve Structure: The fifth term in Eq. (7) aims at preserving the template edge lengths, as those were defined in M_0. Thus, $E_S(V_f, \mathcal{E}_f, V_0)$ is defined as:

$$E_S(V_f, \mathcal{E}, V_0) = \sum_{(v_i^f, v_j^f) \in \mathcal{E}} \left(\|v_i^f - v_j^f\|_2 - \|v_i^0 - v_j^0\|_2 \right)^2. \tag{12}$$

Smoothness Prior: To favor physically plausible deformations, especially in the occluded areas of the deformable object, we use a Laplacian-based regularizer as in [17,36]. We penalize non-rigid deformations away from the reference shape of the deformable object using the following error term where A is the Laplacian smoothing matrix defined based on the reference mesh M_0.

$$E_L(V_f, A) = ||AV_f||_2. \tag{13}$$

Hand-Object Contact Constraint: We assume that a hand may interact with/touch the deformable object by any of its fingertips represented by vertex indices $\mathbf{f} = \{f_i\}_{i=1}^5$. Thus, we define a contact configuration as a vector $Y = [y_1, y_2, y_3, y_4, y_5]$ where $y_i = 1$ if contact is assumed for the i-th fingertip and zero otherwise. For a hypothesized contact configuration Y, we want to minimize the distance of the fingertips assumed to be in contact from the surface of the deformable mesh. That leads to the following energy term

$$E_C(V_f, \theta_f, W_f, \mathbf{f}, Y) = \sum_{i=1}^{5} y_i ||\mathbf{w}_{f_i}^f - \mathbf{z}_i||_2, \tag{14}$$

where $\mathbf{z}_i$ is the closest point of the deformable mesh M_f to the i-th fingertip.

Optimization: At each frame f, the minimization problem of Eq. (6) is solved based on the Levenberg-Marquardt method as implemented in the Ceres solver [4] initialized with the inferred coordinates of the template vertices V_{f-1} at the previous frame $f - 1$ and the hand pose estimate θ'_f from Sect. 3.1. The weights quantifying the relative importance of the corresponding error terms were empirically set to $\lambda_J = 800$, $\lambda_{G\_h} = 10^3$, $\lambda_{G\_o} = 10^3$, $\lambda_F = 400$, $\lambda_T = 0.05$, $\lambda_S = 220 \times 10^3$, $\lambda_L = 0.3$ and $\lambda_C = 100$ for real data and were subsequently normalized by the number of subterms in the corresponding error term. The weights were kept constant throughout all quantitative experiments. The optimization runs for a maximum number of 100 iterations.

3.3   Optimal Contact Configuration Selection

We minimize the energy function of Eq. (6) for all 32 possible contact configurations of the fingertips and end up with a solution M_f^i and θ_f^i, $i = 1, \dots, 32$ for each contact configuration. We select the optimal contact configuration to be the one that results in the best fit of the object template mesh to the point cloud in the area around the hand. This is motivated by the fact that the correctness of a contact configuration can be judged by the consequences that it has on the estimation of the shape of the deformable object close to the contacting fingers. As an example, consider that a hand is at a certain distance from the object. The configuration $Y = [1, 1, 1, 1, 1]$ of full contact will result in "magnetizing" the deformable object towards the fingers and in a bad fit of the estimated object model to the point cloud. At the same time, the consequences of contacts are attenuated as we move away from the hand, especially for large surfaces.

More specifically, let $\{\mathbf{m}_f^{ij}\}_{j=1}^{N_{if}}$ be a set of 3D samples on the surface of M_f^i that project on the image I_f at least 10 and at most 30 pixels away from the contour of the hand rendered at pose θ_f^i. Let also $\{\mathbf{n}_f^{ij}\}_{j=1}^{N_{if}}$ be the closest points of $\{\mathbf{m}_f^{ij}\}_{j=1}^{N_{if}}$ on the point cloud P_f. The optimal contact configuration is the one that minimizes the Euclidean distance of the samples from the point cloud

$$i^* = \operatorname{argmin}_i \sum_{j=1}^{N_{if}} ||\mathbf{m}_f^{ij} - \mathbf{n}_f^{ij}||_2. \tag{15}$$

Intuitively, that means that in the optimal contact configuration the fingers neither "magnetize"/attract nor penetrate the deformable object. The solution that we end up with at this point is $V_f'' = M_f^{i^*}$ for the shape of the deformable object and $\theta_f'' = \theta_f^{i^*}$ for the pose of the hand.

3.4 Solution Refinement Based on Multiresolution Texture Features

We calculate the GBDF descriptors per pixel and we subsequently smooth out the descriptors using three Gaussian kernels with standard deviation $\sigma = 8, 4$ and 1 pixels respectively and kernel size 3σ, thus forming a feature pyramid. We minimize the energy function in Eq. (7) for each hypothesized contact configuration using the coarse descriptors ($\sigma = 8$). After we decide on the optimal contact configuration, we further refine the solution for the pose of the hand and the shape of the deformable object by minimizing Eq. (7) using the optimal contact configuration and the descriptors first for $\sigma = 4$ and then for $\sigma = 1$. Ideally, this step should have been part of the optimization loop. Practically, bringing it to the end of the optimization process reduces the computational requirements without significant degradation of tracking accuracy.

The resulting solutions V_f, θ_f will be used as initializations for fitting the hand and deformable objects to the data of the following frame $f + 1$.

4 Experimental Results

Evaluation Datasets: So far, the Shape-from-Template community has treated human hands as occluders [17] and previous work on tracking hand-object interactions has focused mainly on objects with simple deformations. As a result, there are no compelling datasets containing complex deformable objects interacting with hands of varying articulation. We evaluate our method quantitatively using a set of synthetic sequences involving interaction between hands and deformable objects that we have generated with the Blender modeling software. We have also captured sequences using a Microsoft Kinect 2 [15] to show the applicability of our approach in real-world data[2].

---

[2] Available online at https://www.ics.forth.gr/cvrl/deformable_interaction/.

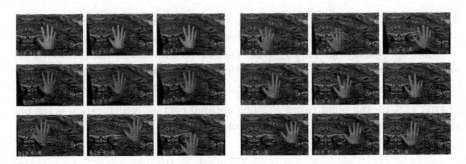

Fig. 2. Triplets of indicative frames for the synthetic sequences S1 to S6 (left to right, top to bottom). Each sequence consists of 23–51 frames and the template mesh consists of 529 vertices.

Figure 2 shows sample frames from the synthetic sequences that we used for quantitative evaluation. We consider sequences where the hand pushes the object causing significant deformations (S1–S3) as well as sequences where the hand moves mainly along the surface of the object (S4–S6). We differentiate the sequences further by considering various scenarios such as rigid motion of the hand (S1), coarse hand articulation (powergrasp - S2), fine articulation (finger tapping - S3, S6), static hand and fine articulation (finger tapping - S4) and minimal variation in articulation (S5).

Evaluated Methods: To showcase the importance of inferring the optimal contact configuration for tracking, we compare our "joint" optimization approach against two variations. In the first that we term "independent", tracking involves no contact constraints and corresponds to tracking the hand and deformable object independently, utilizing only the mask around the hand to determine the occluded area of the object. In the second that we term "fullcontact", tracking corresponds to assuming contact of all fingers with the deformable object.

Despite the fact that the work presented in [42] is the closest to ours in spirit, a comparison with it is not meaningful as it would require to represent deformable 3D meshes as tree-structured articulated objects. Instead, we compare with an implementation[3] of the RGBD method described in [41], by providing to this method the part of the deformable object that is occluded by the hand as an occlusion mask. We also provide results obtained from the state-of-the-art Shape-from-Template method by Ngo et al. [17] that fits the deformable object given the same occlusion mask. As mentioned in Sect. 2, this is an RGB-based method that does not consider depth information. Therefore, its results are not provided for direct comparison but rather for serving as a reference baseline.

Evaluation Metrics: The quantitative evaluation of all methods in this study is performed using two error metrics. The first one, E_1, denotes the percentage of template vertices over all frames in a sequence whose inferred 3D locations

---

[3] Original implementation provided by the authors of [41] and modified to consider an occlusion mask.

are within distance T from their ground truth locations. We consider only the vertices $\mathbf{v}_i^f$, $i \in N_m^*$ that fall within the hand mask at each frame f. Because the methods in [17,41] do not track the human hand, in that case we use the mask coming from our joint tracking method. Thus,

$$E_1(T) = \frac{1}{|N_m^*| \cdot K} \sum_{i \in N_m^*} \sum_{f=1}^{K} g\left(||\mathbf{v}_i^f - \mathbf{x}_i^f||_2 < T \right), \qquad (16)$$

where $g(x < T) = 1$ if $x < T$ and 0 otherwise. In Eq. (16), $\mathbf{x}_i^f$ is the ground truth location of vertex $\mathbf{v}_i^f$.

In a similar way, we calculate the percentage of hand joints over all frames in a sequence whose estimated 3D locations $\mathbf{l}_i^f$ are within distance T from their ground truth 3D locations $\mathbf{h}_i^f$. Thus,

$$E_2(T) = \frac{1}{21 \cdot K} \sum_{i=1}^{21} \sum_{f=1}^{K} g\left(||\mathbf{l}_i^f - \mathbf{h}_i^f||_2 < T \right). \qquad (17)$$

Evaluation of Object Deformation Tracking: Figure 3 shows the error metric E_1 for the synthetic sequences S1–S6. Distance T is expressed as a multiple of the length of a horizontal edge of the template. In S1–S6 this is equal to the width of the index finger of the hand model ($T = 2$ cm).

In sequences S1 to S3, where the hand interacts strongly with the object, we observe that tracking assuming full contact predicts more accurately the

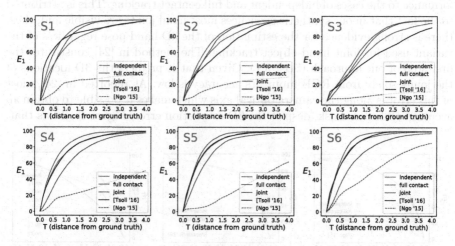

Fig. 3. Quantitative evaluation on synthetic data. For each sequence, we show the percentage of vertices inside the hand mask over all frames within Euclidean distance T from their ground truth location. Distance is expressed as a multiple of the length of a horizontal edge of the template. Each sequence consists of 23–51 frames, the template mesh consists of 529 vertices and the mask occupies on average around 20% of the surface of the deformable object.

object's deformation in the occluded area than tracking the object and hand with no contact constraints (independent tracking). That holds true no matter how coarse or fine the articulation of the hand is. This is also the case that is most challenging for Ngo et al. [17]. Apart from the fact that the method proposed in [17] relies on RGB input and, thus, on less information about the observed geometry, the smoothness prior is not able to capture effectively the deformations of the object due to contact with the hand. The method in [41] is effective in the case of object deformations caused by a hand moving rigidly (S1), but underperforms when the articulation of the hand varies (S2–S3).

In sequences where the hand does not cause significant deformations of the object or contact points vary a lot in time due to the fine manipulation actions (S4–S6), making no contact assumptions is preferable than assuming full contact. The finer the articulation of the hand, the worst the full contact assumption performs (S5 vs S6). The method in [41] exhibits similar performance to tracking the deformable object with the variant of the proposed method that imposes no contact constraints. We also observe improved performance of the method in [17] relative to S1–S3. The global motion of the hand (static hand in S4 vs. hand moving along the object's surface in sequences S5, S6) does not influence the relative performance of the methods. However, joint tracking outperforms tracking assuming full contact, tracking with no contact and tracking based on [41] or based on [17]. The overall superior performance of our method is also highlighted in Fig. 4a that shows the aggregate error over all sequences.

Tracking of the Human Hand: Figure 4b shows the E_2 metric for joint, independent and full contact tracking. Joint tracking exhibits very similar performance to the cases of independent and full contact tracking. This is attributed to the fact that in our synthetic sequences most hand joints are visible and, thus, there is strong evidence for the estimation of the 3D hand pose regardless of the variant used for joint hand-object tracking. The method in [24] constitutes the first step of our approach (Sect. 3.1). Given that it predicts the 3D locations of the joints solely from RGB input, its accuracy is low. As reported in [24], most of this error is along the camera optical axis which makes it possible to obtain an accurate occlusion mask, despite the 3D estimation error. Figure 4b shows that,

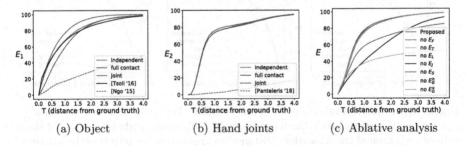

(a) Object   (b) Hand joints   (c) Ablative analysis

Fig. 4. (a, b) Aggregate results and (c) ablative analysis on synthetic sequences.

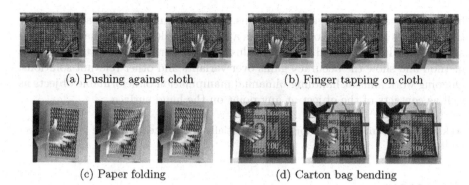

(a) Pushing against cloth   (b) Finger tapping on cloth

(c) Paper folding   (d) Carton bag bending

Fig. 5. Qualitative results on sequences obtained with MS Kinect 2.

when combined with depth and contact information in our joint optimization framework, the overall accuracy of 3D hand tracking is dramatically increased.

Ablative Analysis: Figure 4c shows a combined error metric E denoting the percentage of vertices for both the object and the hand within distance T from their ground truth location for the objective function of Eq. (7) ('proposed') as well as when a certain term X is excluded ('no X'). Feature correspondences, texture and smoothness play a solution-refining role, while hand joints estimation, 3D structure-matching for the hand and mesh edges length preservation are critical. Note that some terms are correlated, i.e., E_F and E_T leverage color information and E_F and E_G^o take into account the observed geometry. Omitting only one term in these pairs has little impact on the overall performance, but omitting both of them will decrease tracking accuracy significantly. In any case, the best performance is obtained when all terms are employed.

Qualitative Evaluation: Figure 5 shows indicative results on real data obtained with a Microsoft Kinect 2. Examples include motion of an open hand against a cloth, finger tapping on cloth, folding a paper with a single hand and bending a carton bag. The color coding on the hand denotes the relative depth of its vertices. The results are better viewed in the supplementary video[4].

5   Conclusions

Most of the deformable object tracking works either deal with such objects in isolation or consider a hand interacting with an object that can be effectively represented by a tree-structured articulated model. In this work, we presented the first method that tracks a complex deformable object represented as a 3D mesh, interacting with a hand. We formulated a joint optimization problem involving the minimization of an energy function whose terms depend on the appearance and the kinematics of the hand, the object and their interaction in the form of

---

[4] Youtube video: https://youtu.be/JSOIy3D_5I0.

hand-object contact configurations. Thus, the hand is not treated as a distractor that occludes parts of the object, but as a source of valuable information. Evaluation on synthetic and real sequences illustrate the performance of the proposed method and show the accuracy gains over variants and other relevant solutions. Ongoing work aims at handling bimanual manipulation of deformable objects as well as contacts of the object at any point on the hand surface.

Acknowledgments. This work was partially supported by the EU project Co4Robots.

References

1. Albrecht, I., Haber, J., Seidel, H.P.: Construction and animation of anatomically based human hand models. In: Eurographics Symposium on Computer Animation, p. 109. Eurographics Association (2003)
2. Ballan, L., Taneja, A., Gall, J., Van Gool, L., Pollefeys, M.: Motion capture of hands in action using discriminative salient points. In: Fitzgibbon, A., Lazebnik, S., Perona, P., Sato, Y., Schmid, C. (eds.) ECCV 2012. LNCS, vol. 7577, pp. 640–653. Springer, Heidelberg (2012). https://doi.org/10.1007/978-3-642-33783-3_46
3. Bartoli, A., Gerard, Y., Chadebecq, F., Collins, T., Pizarro, D.: Shape-from-template. IEEE Trans. Patt. Anal. Mach. Intell. **37**(10), 2099–2118 (2015)
4. Ceres Solver. http://ceres-solver.org/
5. Crivellaro, A., Lepetit, V.: Robust 3D tracking with descriptor fields. In: Conference on Computer Vision and Pattern Recognition (CVPR), No. EPFL-CONF-198219 (2014)
6. Garg, R., Roussos, A., Agapito, L.: A variational approach to video registration with subspace constraints. Int. J. Comput. Vis. **104**(3), 286–314 (2013)
7. Ge, L., Liang, H., Yuan, J., Thalmann, D.: Robust 3D hand pose estimation in single depth images: from single-view CNN to multi-view CNNs. In: Proceedings of the IEEE Conference on Computer Vision and Pattern Recognition, pp. 3593–3601 (2016)
8. Hamer, H., Schindler, K., Koller-Meier, E., Van Gool, L.: Tracking a hand manipulating an object. In: IEEE International Conference on Computer Vision (ICCV), pp. 1475–1482. IEEE (2009)
9. Hilsmann, A., Eisert, P.: Tracking deformable surfaces with optical flow in the presence of self occlusion in monocular image sequences. In: 2008 IEEE Computer Society Conference on Computer Vision and Pattern Recognition Workshops, VPRW 2008, pp. 6, 1 (2008). https://doi.org/10.1109/CVPRW.2008.4563081
10. Kyriazis, N., Argyros, A.: Physically plausible 3D scene tracking: the single actor hypothesis. In: IEEE Conference on Computer Vision and Pattern Recognition (CVPR), pp. 9–16. IEEE (2013)
11. Kyriazis, N., Argyros, A.: Scalable 3D tracking of multiple interacting objects. In: IEEE Conference on Computer Vision and Pattern Recognition (CVPR), pp. 3430–3437. IEEE (2014)
12. Levenberg, K.: A method for the solution of certain non-linear problems in least squares. Q. Appl. Math. **2**(2), 164–168 (1944)
13. Lowe, D.G.: Distinctive image features from scale-invariant keypoints. Int. J. Comput. Vis. **60**(2), 91–110 (2004)

14. Marquardt, D.W.: An algorithm for least-squares estimation of nonlinear parameters. J. Soc. Ind. Appl. Math. **11**(2), 431–441 (1963)
15. Microsoft Kinect 2. https://developer.microsoft.com/en-us/windows/kinect
16. Mueller, F., Mehta, D., Sotnychenko, O., Sridhar, S., Casas, D., Theobalt, C.: Real-time hand tracking under occlusion from an egocentric RGB-D sensor. In: Proceedings of International Conference on Computer Vision (ICCV), vol. 10 (2017)
17. Ngo, D.T., Park, S., Jorstad, A., Crivellaro, A., Yoo, C., Fua, P.: Dense image registration and deformable surface reconstruction in presence of occlusions and minimal texture. In: International Conference on Computer Vision (ICCV) (2015)
18. Oberweger, M., Wohlhart, P., Lepetit, V.: Training a feedback loop for hand pose estimation. In: Proceedings of the IEEE International Conference on Computer Vision, pp. 3316–3324 (2015)
19. Oikonomidis, I., Kyriazis, N., Argyros, A.A.: Efficient model-based 3D tracking of hand articulations using kinect. In: BMVC, Dundee, UK, August 2011
20. Oikonomidis, I., Kyriazis, N., Argyros, A.A.: Full DOF tracking of a hand interacting with an object by modeling occlusions and physical constraints. In: International Conference on Computer Vision (ICCV), pp. 2088–2095. IEEE (2011)
21. Oikonomidis, I., Kyriazis, N., Argyros, A.A.: Tracking the articulated motion of two strongly interacting hands. In: IEEE Computer Vision and Pattern Recognition (CVPR 2012), pp. 1862–1869. IEEE, Providence, June 2012
22. Östlund, J., Varol, A., Ngo, D.T., Fua, P.: Laplacian meshes for monocular 3D shape recovery. In: Fitzgibbon, A., Lazebnik, S., Perona, P., Sato, Y., Schmid, C. (eds.) ECCV 2012. LNCS, vol. 7574, pp. 412–425. Springer, Heidelberg (2012). https://doi.org/10.1007/978-3-642-33712-3_30
23. Panteleris, P., Kyriazis, N., Argyros, A.A.: 3D tracking of human hands in interaction with unknown objects. In: British Machine Vision Conference (BMVC 2015), pp. 123–1. BMVA, Swansea, September 2015
24. Panteleris, P., Oikonomidis, I., Argyros, A.: Using a single RGB frame for real time 3D hand pose estimation in the wild (2018)
25. Parashar, S., Pizarro, D., Bartoli, A., Collins, T.: As-rigid-as-possible volumetric shape-from-template. In: Proceedings of the IEEE International Conference on Computer Vision, pp. 891–899 (2015)
26. Petit, A., Lippiello, V., Siciliano, B.: Tracking an elastic object with an RGB-D sensor for a pizza chef robot
27. Qian, C., Sun, X., Wei, Y., Tang, X., Sun, J.: Realtime and robust hand tracking from depth. In: Proceedings of the IEEE Conference on Computer Vision and Pattern Recognition, pp. 1106–1113 (2014)
28. Romero, J., Kjellstrom, H., Kragic, D.: Monocular real-time 3D articulated hand pose estimation. In: IEEE-RAS International Conference on Humanoid Robots, December 2009. https://doi.org/10.1109/ICHR.2009.5379596, http://ieeexplore.ieee.org/lpdocs/epic03/wrapper.htm?arnumber=5379596
29. Salzmann, M., Lepetit, V., Fua, P.: Deformable surface tracking ambiguities. In: 2007 IEEE Conference on Computer Vision and Pattern Recognition, CVPR 2007, pp. 1–8. IEEE (2007)
30. Schulman, J., Lee, A., Ho, J., Abbeel, P.: Tracking deformable objects with point clouds. In: Proceedings of the International Conference on Robotics and Automation (ICRA) (2013)
31. Sharp, T., et al.: Accurate, robust, and flexible real-time hand tracking. In: Proceedings of the 33rd Annual ACM Conference on Human Factors in Computing Systems, pp. 3633–3642. ACM (2015)

32. Simon, T., Joo, H., Matthews, I., Sheikh, Y.: Hand keypoint detection in single images using multiview bootstrapping. In: IEEE Conference on Computer Vision and Pattern Recognition (CVPR), vol. 2 (2017)
33. Sinha, A., Choi, C., Ramani, K.: DeepHand: robust hand pose estimation by completing a matrix imputed with deep features. In: Proceedings of the IEEE Conference on Computer Vision and Pattern Recognition, pp. 4150–4158 (2016)
34. Sridhar, S., Mueller, F., Zollhöfer, M., Casas, D., Oulasvirta, A., Theobalt, C.: Real-time joint tracking of a hand manipulating an object from RGB-D input. In: Leibe, B., Matas, J., Sebe, N., Welling, M. (eds.) ECCV 2016. LNCS, vol. 9906, pp. 294–310. Springer, Cham (2016). https://doi.org/10.1007/978-3-319-46475-6_19
35. Sridhar, S., Oulasvirta, A., Theobalt, C.: Interactive markerless articulated hand motion tracking using RGB and depth data. In: IEEE International Conference on Computer Vision (ICCV), pp. 2456–2463. IEEE (2013)
36. Sumner, R.W., Popović, J.: Deformation transfer for triangle meshes. In: ACM Transactions on Graphics (TOG), vol. 23, pp. 399–405. ACM (2004)
37. Tagliasacchi, A., Schröder, M., Tkach, A., Bouaziz, S., Botsch, M., Pauly, M.: Robust articulated-ICP for real-time hand tracking. In: Computer Graphics Forum, vol. 34, pp. 101–114. Wiley Online Library (2015)
38. Tang, D., Jin Chang, H., Tejani, A., Kim, T.K.: Latent regression forest: structured estimation of 3D articulated hand posture. In: Proceedings of the IEEE Conference on Computer Vision and Pattern Recognition, pp. 3786–3793 (2014)
39. The Blender open source 3D creation suite. https://docs.blender.org/
40. Tompson, J., Stein, M., Lecun, Y., Perlin, K.: Real-time continuous pose recovery of human hands using convolutional networks. ACM Trans. Graph. (ToG) 33(5), 169 (2014)
41. Tsoli, A., Argyros, A.: Tracking deformable surfaces that undergo topological changes using an RGB-D camera. In: Proceedings of International Conference on 3D Vision (3DV), Stanford University, CA, USA, October 2016
42. Tzionas, D., Ballan, L., Srikantha, A., Aponte, P., Pollefeys, M., Gall, J.: Capturing hands in action using discriminative salient points and physics simulation. Int. J. Comput. Vis. 118(2), 172–193 (2016)
43. Tzionas, D., Gall, J.: 3D object reconstruction from hand-object interactions. In: International Conference on Computer Vision (ICCV), pp. 729–737, December 2015
44. Tzionas, D., Srikantha, A., Aponte, P., Gall, J.: Capturing hand motion with an RGB-D sensor, fusing a generative model with salient points. In: Jiang, X., Hornegger, J., Koch, R. (eds.) GCPR 2014. LNCS, vol. 8753, pp. 277–289. Springer, Cham (2014). https://doi.org/10.1007/978-3-319-11752-2_22
45. Wan, C., Probst, T., Van Gool, L., Yao, A.: Crossing nets: combining GANs and VAEs with a shared latent space for hand pose estimation. In: IEEE Conference on Computer Vision and Pattern Recognition (CVPR). IEEE (2017)
46. Wan, C., Yao, A., Van Gool, L.: Hand pose estimation from local surface normals. In: Leibe, B., Matas, J., Sebe, N., Welling, M. (eds.) ECCV 2016. LNCS, vol. 9907, pp. 554–569. Springer, Cham (2016). https://doi.org/10.1007/978-3-319-46487-9_34
47. Wuhrer, S., Lang, J., Shu, C.: Tracking complete deformable objects with finite elements. In: 3DIMPVT, pp. 1–8. IEEE Computer Society (2012). http://dblp.uni-trier.de/db/conf/3dim/3dimpvt2012.html#WuhrerLS12
48. Ye, Q., Yuan, S., Kim, T.-K.: Spatial attention deep net with partial PSO for hierarchical hybrid hand pose estimation. In: Leibe, B., Matas, J., Sebe, N., Welling, M. (eds.) ECCV 2016. LNCS, vol. 9912, pp. 346–361. Springer, Cham (2016). https://doi.org/10.1007/978-3-319-46484-8_21

HBE: Hand Branch Ensemble Network for Real-Time 3D Hand Pose Estimation

Yidan Zhou[1], Jian Lu[2], Kuo Du[1], Xiangbo Lin[1(✉)], Yi Sun[1], and Xiaohong Ma[1]

[1] Dalian University of Technology, Dalian, China
{shine0910,dumyy2728}@mail.dlut.edu.cn
{linxbo,lslwf,maxh}@dlut.edu.cn
[2] Dalian University, Dalian, China
lujian@dlu.edu.cn

Abstract. The goal of this paper is to estimate the 3D coordinates of the hand joints from a single depth image. To give consideration to both the accuracy and the real time performance, we design a novel three-branch Convolutional Neural Networks named Hand Branch Ensemble network (HBE), where the three branches correspond to the three parts of a hand: the thumb, the index finger and the other fingers. The structural design inspiration of the HBE network comes from the understanding of the differences in the functional importance of different fingers. In addition, a feature ensemble layer along with a low-dimensional embedding layer ensures the overall hand shape constraints. The experimental results on three public datasets demonstrate that our approach achieves comparable or better performance to state-of-the-art methods with less training data, shorter training time and faster frame rate.

Keywords: Hand pose estimation · Depth image
Convolutional Neural Networks

1 Introduction

The research of 3D hand pose estimation is a hotspot in the field of computer vision, virtual reality and robotics [5,18]. With the advent of depth cameras, studies based on depth image have made significant progress [28]. Nevertheless, there is still a challenge for the recovery of 3D hand poses due to the poor quality of depth images, high joint flexibility, local self-similarity and severe self-occlusions.

In general, depth based hand pose estimation can be categorized into two main approaches as either generative model-based or discriminative learning-based methods. Model based approaches assume a pre-defined hand model and then fit it to the input depth image by minimizing specific objective functions [13,21,22,24,26,31,32]. However, the accuracy of these methods is highly dependent on the objective function and sensitive to initialization. Additionally,

© Springer Nature Switzerland AG 2018
V. Ferrari et al. (Eds.): ECCV 2018, LNCS 11218, pp. 521–536, 2018.
https://doi.org/10.1007/978-3-030-01264-9_31

such tracking-based model approaches are awkward to deal with large changes between two adjacent frames, which are common as the hand tends to move fast. Alternatively, learning based approaches train a model with a large amount of data, and the hand pose parameters can be regressed directly. In this way, detecting hand pose frame by frame is easy to handle with fast hand movements.

Recently, learning based approaches have achieved remarkable performance in hand estimation from a single depth image. Although traditional machine learning methods have made significant progress, their performances are too dependent on the hand-craft features [12,27,28,30,35]. In recent years, Deep Learning methods have been paid more attention due to their abilities of learning effective features automatically. Early studies regressed joint locations from a depth image with a simple 2D Convolutional Neural Network [16,20,33,39], which had high frame rate but low precision. To improve the accuracy, different strategies were proposed. One way was to improve the data quality. [19] used data augmentation to reduce the prediction error. [8,17] converted the 2.5D depth image to 3D voxel representation to make use of the 3D spatial structure. [23] learned the feature mapping from a synthetic image with high quality to a real image. The other way was to design more complex network to extract more features. [9,10,17,19] added residual module in their network. [17,34] used encoder and decoder to learn features in the latent space. [8,17] applied a 3D CNN instead of 2D CNN to estimate per-voxel likelihood of 3D locations for each hand joint. By combining the effective strategies mentioned above, [17] achieved the best results in the Hands In the Million (HIM2017) Challenge Competition so far [36]. However, their methods were too complex both in data preprocessing procedure and in network structure to get the efficient training and testing.

In order to improve the efficiency while ensuring accuracy, in this paper, we design a highly efficient and relatively simple Convolutional Neural Network structure named Hand Branch Ensemble network (HBE). The proposed network can achieve comparable accuracy with state-of-the-art studies even better than them using fewer training data and shorter training time but faster frame rates. Figure 1 gives an overview of our proposed network structure. The core idea is to take advantage of the prior knowledge of the motion and the functional importance of different fingers [2,4,15,29]. Since the thumb and the index finger play an even more important role in the grasping, manipulation and communication, while the middle finger, ring finger and little finger play an auxiliary role in most cases, we simplify the five-finger structure into three parts: thumb, index fingers and the other fingers. Correspondingly, the proposed HBE network learns the features of each part by each branch respectively. It makes full use of the shallow low-level image features that are more sensitive to the size, orientation and location information, which can greatly reduce the computational complexity and the training time. Moreover, we propose a branch ensemble strategy by concatenating features from the last fully connected layers of each branch and then the integrated features are used to infer the joint coordinates with the extra regression layers. Different from REN [10] training individual fully-connected layers on multiple feature regions and combining them as ensembles, our ensemble strategy directly exploits the features of different hand parts, which is more intuitive for the hand pose estimation. Motivated by Deep Prior [20], we add a bottleneck layer as a low dimensional embedding to learn the hand pose physical prior before the output layer.

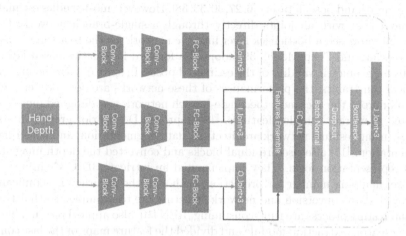

Fig. 1. The Hand Branch Ensemble (HBE) network: based on the activity space and functional importance of five fingers. The top branch handles the thumb, the median branch handles the index finger and the bottom branch handles the other fingers. The features are ensemble along with an additional fully connected layer and a bottleneck layer

The proposed HBE network is evaluated on three challenging benchmarks: the HIM2017 Challenge Dataset [37], the ICVL hand pose dataset [30] and the MSRA dataset [27]. The experiments show that our method achieves results comparable or better than state-of-the-art methods.

In summary, our contributions are:

1. We propose a new three-branch Convolutional Neural Network estimating full 3D hand joint locations from a single depth image. The structural design inspiration comes from the understanding of the differences in the functional importance of different fingers. In addition, a branch feature ensemble strategy is introduced to merge features of each branch along with a fully connected layer and a low-dimensional embedding layer, which emphasizes the correlation of different hand parts and ensures the overall hand shape constraints.

2. We design a relatively lightweight architecture and achieve comparable or better performance to state-of-the-art methods on publicly available datasets with less training data, shorter training time and faster frame rate.

The paper is organized as follows. After reviewing the related work in Sect. 2, we describe our proposed method in Sect. 3. Experimental results and discussions are reported in Sect. 4, and the conclusions are drawn in Sect. 5.

2 Related Work

In this section, we briefly discuss the Deep Learning based works on hand pose estimation, especially those closely related to our method. These approaches have achieved good performance due to the success of Deep Learning as well as the public large hand pose datasets [6,27,30,33,38]. However, most studies estimated the hand pose with all joints directly through a single-branch network. Deep Prior [20] proposed a bottleneck layer into the network for the first time to learn a pose prior, and Deep Model [39] adopted a forward kinematics based layer to ensure the geometric validity of the estimated poses. In spite of introducing hand physical constraints, the performances of these networks are not good enough.

To improve the accuracy, the single-branch network was designed more complicated to extract complex features. [19] improved Deep Prior greatly in accuracy by using residual network architecture, data augmentation, and better hand segmentation. [17] also used residual blocks and converted the depth image into a 3D representation form. They implemented an intricate 3D CNN in a voxel-to-voxel mapping manner for prediction. Although the accuracy is significantly improved, data conversion and network structure are too complex so that training and testing process are time-consuming. REN [10] also applied residual blocks in their feature extraction module and divided the feature maps of the last convolutional layer into several regions which were integrated in the subsequent fully connected layers. However, REN used uniform grid to extract region features without considering the spatial information of the hand feature maps.

Hierarchical branch structure can better model the hand topology. Based on REN, Pose-REN [3] boosted the accuracy by iterative refinement. Similar to our approach, they fused features of different joints and different fingers according to the topology of the hand. But they used posterior branch strategy focusing on the iterative refinement. In contrast, we use anterior branch to extract features of different hand parts. The network designed in this way can estimate simpler local poses, and let the training process converge faster. By a posterior branch structure [16] uses 6 branches to represent the wrist and each finger based on the hand geometric structure. Different from their work, we consider it both from the hand functional and kinematic features according to the biological viewpoint, designing an anterior branch structure with learning specific features of each functional part first and then merging them to learn the global features by a bottleneck layer. In addition, we group the last three fingers in one branch rather than one branch for each finger, which guarantees the muscle-association among them and speeds up the network convergence.

3 Methodology

In this section, we will elaborate on our proposed method, network structure and implementation details. Our goal is to estimate the 3D coordinates of J joints: $C = \{c_i\}_{i=1}^{J}$ with $c_i = [x_i; y_i; z_i]$ in the hand from a single depth image. We design a novel three-branch Convolutional Neural Network based on the functional importance and activity space of different fingers, and then ensemble features to regress all 3D joint locations. The overview of our proposed HBE network is shown in Fig. 1.

3.1 Network Architecture

Hands are frequently used to deal with different tasks, and each finger has different importance and occupies different activity space [2,15]. The thumb has a unique structure as the opposable characteristic, which plays an important role in in communication or dexterous manipulation. Therefore, the thumb is the most important due to the highest DOF and the largest activity space, so we use a separate branch to learn its features. Although each of the other four fingers have the same DOF, the index finger is closest to thumb and the two fingers alone can generate some gestures, thus the index finger is the second most important and is assigned to a separate branch. Considering the muscle-associated movement among the last three fingers and high correlation in activity, we group them in a single branch.

We design the hand pose estimation network based on above mentioned fingers functional importance. The five-finger structure of the hand is simplified into three parts, corresponding to the three branches of the network respectively. As shown in Fig. 1, three convolutional branches in this network are used to extract the features of each hand part. Since the function of the middle, the ring and the little finger is less important and similar in movements, we merge them into one part and abstractly understand the 5-finger structure of the hand as a 3-part structure. Each part is of equal importance. Therefore, the feature extraction network structure of each branch is the same.

The features from each branch are fused to predict the hand pose. Here we introduce the branch ensemble strategy: features from the last fully connected layers in all branches are concatenated and used to infer 3D joint coordinates with an extra regression layer. It should be pointed out that before the output layer, inspired by the idea of Deep Prior [20], we add a linear bottleneck layer. The bottleneck embedding forces the network to learn a low dimensional representation of the hand pose as a global physical constraint of the hand shape in the network. The label dimensions ($J \times 3$) of the training data are reduced by Principal Component Analysis (PCA) and used as the ground truth of the bottleneck embedding layer. The principal component and the mean value of the low-dimensional data are used as the weights and the biases of the output layer respectively. Finally, the output layer recovers the low-dimensional predictions of the bottleneck layer to the original $J \times 3$-dimensional joint positions.

3.2 Branch Details

When designing the feature extraction layers, we believe that the regression problem of predicting joint positions is rather different from the classification problem of object recognition, because semantic features are crucial to the latter one. Since shallow network learns low-level spatial features that are more sus-ceptible to the size, direction, and position of an object. Common convolutional layers and max pooling layers for the feature extraction module in each branch are shown in Fig. 2. The estimation of the complex global pose is reduced to the estimations of simpler local poses, enabling the network to be more lightweight and easier to train. A larger convolution kernel that can obtain more spatial information and lager receptive fields, is very useful for location regression and effective to infer the occluded joints. At each branch, we use a stack of two 5×5 convolutional layers instead of a single larger one, which gains the same size of effective receptive field to a single 9×9 convolutional layer as well as decreases the number of parameters, as calculated in [25]. In the feature mapping mod-ule, we add Batch Normalization (BN) layer after each fully connected layer. The distribution change of the training data is accumulated after processed by the middle hidden layers, which will affect the network training. The BN layer has the ability to solve this data distribution change problem, which makes the gradient transfer more fluent and improves the robustness and generalization ability of the training model [11]. All layers use Rectified Linear Unit (ReLU) activation functions.

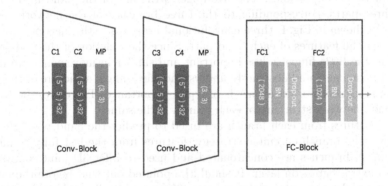

Fig. 2. The structure details of the feature extraction branch. Ci represents the con-volutional layer, MP represents the maxpooling layer, and FC represents the fully connected layer

3.3 Loss Function

The loss function of our network is defined as:

$$Loss = L + \lambda R(w) \tag{1}$$

where $\lambda R(w)$ is the L2-norm regularization term and the regularization coeffi-cient λ is set to 0.001 in our experiments. L is the mean square error between the predicted value and the ground truth. Specifically, we define the loss term L in the form:

$$L = \alpha \times L_{thumb} + \beta \times L_{index} + \gamma \times L_{others} + \sigma \times L_d \tag{2}$$

where L_{thumb} is the loss of the thumb branch, L_{index} is the loss of the index finger branch, L_{others} is the loss of the other fingers branch, L_d is the loss of low-dimensional embedding layer, and $\{\alpha, \beta, \gamma, \sigma\}$ are factors to balance these losses. In our experiment we set them to be 1 for simplification.

Let c_i be the outputs of the branch predicting joint positions in 3D form and C_i be the ground-truth, both c_i and C_i have the form of $[x_i; y_i; z_i]$. We define the loss of each branch as:

$$L_b = \sum_{i=1}^{J_b} \|c_i - C_i\|_2^2, \quad b \in \{thumb, index, others\} \tag{3}$$

where J_b is the number of joints in each branch.

As for the bottleneck embedding, let D be the number of reduced dimension which is much less than $J \times 3$, p_i be the output of the bottleneck layer, P_i be the dimension reduced training label as the ground truth. We define the loss of the low-dimensional embedding as:

$$L_d = \sum_{i=1}^{D} \|p_i - P_i\|_2^2 \tag{4}$$

3.4 Implementation Details

The input of our network is a hand-only depth image, which is generated after a series of preprocessing steps on the dataset. First of all, we cut out the hand area according to the ground truth labels provided by the dataset, then fill the cropped image up into a square, at last resize it to 128×128, and in the meanwhile, we normalize the hand depth value in $[-1,1]$. Pixel values that are larger than the maximum hand depth or unavailable because of noise are set to 1. This depth normalization step is important for the network to adapt to different distances from the hand to the camera.

Our model is trained and tested on a computer with Intel Core i7 CPU, 32 GB of RAM and an NVIDIA GTX1080 GPU. Our network is implemented in Python using the Tensorflow [1] framework. Except for the output layer, all weights are initialized from the zero-mean Normal distribution with 0.01 standard deviation. The network is trained with back propagation using Adam [14] optimizer with a batch size of 128 for 100 epochs. We use a dynamic learning rate with an initial value of 0.001 and reduce it by a factor 0.95 for every epoch. And the dropout rate is set to be 0.85 (keep probability).

4 Experiments

In this section we evaluate our Hand Branch Ensemble(HBE) network on several challenging public hand pose datasets. First of all, we introduce these datasets and the parameters of our methods. Then we describe the evaluation metrics, and finally we present and discuss our quantitative as well as qualitative results.

4.1   Datasets

We evaluate our network on three recent public hand pose datasets: the latest high-quality HIM2017 Challenge dataset [37], the traditional widely used ICVL dataset [30] and MSRA dataset [27].

ICVL Dataset [30] includes a training set of 330K hand pose depth frames with additional in-plane rotations augmented frames and 1.5K testing depth images. In our experiments, we only use 110K training data by random sampling. The dataset provides 16 annotated 3D joints.

MSRA Dataset [27] contains 76K depth frames from 9 subjects with 21 annotated joints. Following [27], we use the leave-one-subject-out cross-validation strategy and average the results over the 9 subjects.

Hands In the Million (HIM2017) Challenge Dataset contains the frame based hand pose estimation dataset and the continuous action tracking dataset [36]. We focus on the frame based estimation dataset, which samples poses from BigHand2.2M dataset [38] and FHAD datasets [6] consisting 957K training and 295K testing depth images. The training data is randomly shuffled instead of continuous action sequence. Including both the first-person view and the third-person view hand pose depth images, this dataset is more challenging for its abundant perspectives and hand poses. Moreover, this dataset provides accurate 21-joint 3D location annotations.

In our experiment, we randomly sample 72K training data from the original HIM2017 Challenge dataset as our training set. Since the original test set provided by the Challenge does not contain the ground truth, we have difficulties to measure the accuracy of our method by ourselves. In order to evaluate more fairly, considering that the original test set contains a total of 295,510 frames of SEEN and UNSEEN subjects, we randomly sample 295,510 frames from the original training set to form a new test set (not included in our training set). Since our test set only contains the SEEN subject, we only compare the results of SEEN in the Challenge leaderboard.

4.2   Evaluation Metrics

We follow the common evaluation metrics on hand pose estimation:

1. Mean joint error: The mean 3D distance error for all joints for each frame and average across all testing frames.

2. Correct frame proportion: The proportion of frames that have all joints within a certain distance to ground truth annotation.

4.3   Self-comparisons

Firstly, we compare the effect of the number of branches on the results, as shown in the left figure of Fig. 3. *Single-branch* means that we do not decompose the hand by part but predict all the joints of the hand directly through a single branch CNN. With regard to the *Two-branch*, we train a two-branch network with one branch handles the thumb and the other branch manages the other fingers. Obviously, the *Three-branch* stands for the original three-branch network. As for the *Four-branch*, the last branch handles the ring and the little finger together, the other branches handle the other fingers one by one. The *Five-branch* means that each branch corresponds to one finger. By adjusting the number of convolution channels, the parameters of each network remain roughly constant. These networks are trained and tested on the HIM2017 Challenge dataset.

As shown in the left figure of Fig. 3, the original three-branch structure achieves the best accuracy. The horizontal ordinate of Fig. 3 represents each joint. C means the wrist, and $Ti(i = \{1, 2, 3, 4\})$, Ii, Mi, Ri and Li represent the joint in the thumb, index, middle, ring, and little finger, respectively. And Avg means the mean joint error. For each finger, take the thumb for example, $T1$, $T2$, $T3$ and $T4$ represent the MCP joint, PIP joint, DIP joint and the fingertip respectively. The following graphs are represented in the same way.

There is a linkage between the middle finger and the ring finger, which is forcibly destroyed by the structure of the Four-branch and the Five-branch. Further more, in most cases, the last three fingers are in the same activity range, and the Three-branch networks can extract their associated features and reduce the redundancy in the feature combining and mapping. Therefore, the performance of the Three-branch outperforms the others.

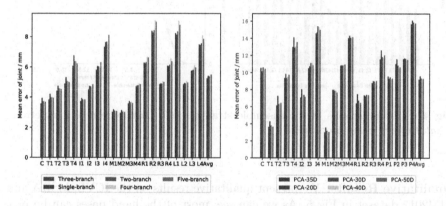

Fig. 3. Self-comparisons. *Left:* Distribution of joint errors in different branch-structures. *Right:* Distribution of joint errors in different bottleneck dimensions

The effect of the bottleneck layer with low-dimensional embedding has been proved in the paper of Deep Prior [20]. In our experiments, we also use this method to introduce the physical prior of the overall hand pose shape. As for the ICVL dataset, we follow [20] using a 30-dimensional embedding bottleneck layer. And on the MSRA and HIM2017 dataset, we use a 35-dimensional embedding layer according to our experimental results as shown in the right at Fig. 3, which is evaluated on the MSRA P0 test set. The distribution of joint errors shows that the 35 dimensions out of the original 63-dimensional pose spaces performs best. The evaluation shows that enforcing a pose prior is beneficial compared to direct regression in the full pose space, which is in line with the conclusion of [20], but it is not significant in the improvement of accuracy according to our experiments.

Then we evaluate the importance of our ensemble strategy on the HIM2017 dataset. When we directly concatenating the joint predictions of three branches instead of fusing features of each branch as our ensemble strategy, the mean joint error reaches 5.71 mm, while the mean joint error of our original network with feature ensemble achieves 5.26 mm, and the distribution of joint errors and the correct frame proportion are shown in Fig. 4, which shows that the ensemble strategy in fully connected layer achieves the best performance and further confirms the effectiveness of the ensemble method used in our network.

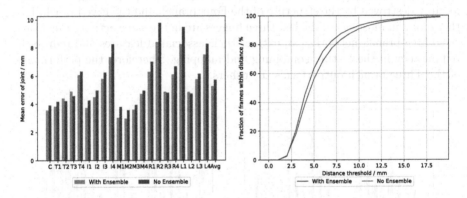

Fig. 4. Self-comparisons of the ensemble strategy. *Left:* Distribution of joint errors. *Right:* Correct frame proportion

Qualitative Results: We present qualitative results on the ICVL, MSRA and HIM2017 dataset in Fig. 5. As we can see, most of the hand poses can be predicted correctly on the three datasets.

4.4   Comparison with State-of-the-Art Methods

We compare the performance of the Hand Branch Ensemble(HBE) network on three public challenging 3D hand pose datasets (HIM2017, ICVL and MSRA) with some of the state-of-the-art methods, including Deep Prior [20], Deep Model [39], latent random forest (LRF) [30], Crossing Nets [34], V2V-PoseNet [17], Cascade [27], MultiView [7], Pose-REN [3] and Global2Local [16]. Some reported results of previous works [17,20,30,39] are calculated by their prediction available online. Other results [3,7,16,27,34] are calculated from the figures and tables of their papers.

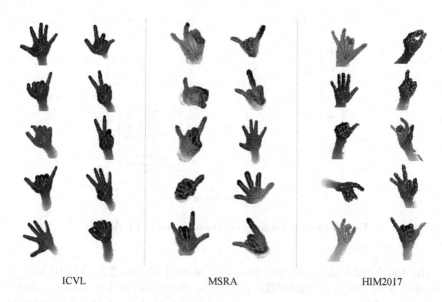

ICVL   MSRA   HIM2017

Fig. 5. The qualitative results on the MSRA, ICVL and HIM2017 Challenge dataset. The ground truth is marked in blue lines and the prediction is marked in red lines. (Color figure online)

Table 1. The mean Joint Error on the ICVL Dataset

Methods	Mean Joint Error (mm)
LRF	12.58
Deep Prior	11.56
Deep Model	10.4
Crossing Net	10.2
Cascade	9.9
Ours	**8.62**
V2V-PoseNet	6.28

Our network is evaluated on the ICVL dataset and compared with the state-of-the-art methods. As shown in Table 1, we get better results than Cascade but inferior to V2V-PoseNet. However, we use less data than them to train our method and the parameters complexity is much less than them. Figure 6 shows the correct frame proportion on the ICVL dataset compared with Deep Prior [20], Deep Model [39], latent random forest (LRF) [30], Crossing Nets [34] and Cascade [27], where the horizontal axis represents the maximum allowed distance to ground truth. In general, we achieve comparable performance with state-of-the-art methods on the ICVL dataset in standard evaluation metrics.

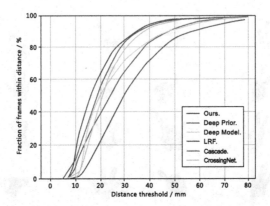

Fig. 6. Correct frame proportion on the ICVL dataset

On the MSRA dataset, we compared with Cascade [27], MultiView [7], Crossing Nets [34] and Global2Local [16] as shown in the left figure in Fig. 7. Global2Local [16] also uses a branch-like structure, but our method is quite different from them as described in Sect. 2. The result also proves that our three-branch anterior branch structure achieves a better performance.

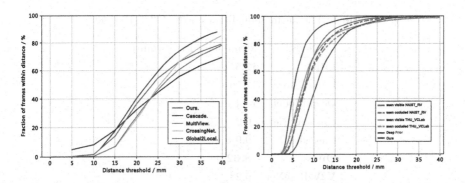

Fig. 7. Comparison with state-of-the-art methods. *Left:* Correct frame proportion on the MSRA dataset. *Right:* Correct frame proportion of SEEN subjects on the HIM2017 dataset. The curves of THU VCLab and NAIST RVLab are from [36]

We also implement our HBE network and Deep Prior network on HIM2017 Challenge dataset, and get the prediction results of all the joints on our test set. Since our test set has the same size of the original test set, but only contains the SEEN subjects, we only compare the results of SEEN in the Challenge leaderboard. Table 2 shows the Challenge leaderboard and our comparison of mean joint error in millimeter. The right figure in Fig. 7 shows the correct frame proportion of SEEN subjects whose mean joint error within a certain value. The result of Pose-REN from the THU VCLab and the result of NAIST RVLab are from [36]. What we need to emphasize is that the comparison of the above is only an approximate comparison. In spite of this, it can be seen from the results that our method has a superior performance.

Table 2. The approximate comparison on the HIM2017 Challenge Dataset

Teams	Methods	AVG	**SEEN**	UNSEEN
mks0601	V2V-PoseNet	9.95	**6.97**	12.43
NVResearch & UMontreal	RCN+	9.97	**7.55**	12.00
NTU	3D CNN	11.30	**8.86**	13.33
THU VCLab	Pose-REN	11.70	**9.15**	13.83
NAIST RVLab	5-branch 3D CNN	11.90	**9.34**	14.04
Deep Prior	Deep Prior	–	**9.63**	–
Ours	**HBE**	–	**5.26**	–

4.5 Computational Complexity

We take the HIM2017 Challenge dataset as an example to compare the computational complexity of the proposed HBE network and V2V-PoseNet. We train our network on a single GPU for 100 epochs taking 26250.24 s (7.2 h). The input generation and data pretreatment take 435 s, and loading the input data takes 7.04 s. In the testing stage, it takes 1.5 ms for processing a frame.

Table 3 compares the computational complexity of our HBE network with V2V-PoseNet. We only use part of the original training set for training, while V2V-PoseNet uses the entire training set spending 6 days training including time-consuming I/O operations. With regard to the testing stage, we can achieve 673 fps on a single GPU, while V2V-PoseNet reaches 3.5 fps on a single GPU and 35 fps in a multi-GPU environment. Unlike them, we don't need to do voxel data conversion and epoch models ensemble for testing, and our network has a fast forwarding due to its simplicity. Besides, the number of parameters in our proposed method is much less than V2V-PoseNet regressing 3D coordinates. In summary, we use a much less training set and simpler network structure but reach the same level as their result even better than them. Our method is faster, more efficient and suitable for real-time applications.

Table 3. The comparison of computational complexity on the HIM2017 Challenge dataset

Items	Parameter quantity	Testing on single GPU	Testing on muti-GPU
V2V-PoseNet	457.5M	3.5 fps	35 fps
Ours	**67.27M**	**673 fps**	–

5 Conclusions

We propose a novel three-branch network called the Hand Branch Ensemble (HBE) network for 3D hand pose estimation from a single depth image. According to fingers activity space and functional importance we decompose the hand to three parts: the thumb, the index and the other fingers. Each branch corresponds to one part. The features of three branches are ensemble to predict all 3D joint locations. Our network is trained with a small amount of training data and evaluated on three challenging datasets. Both the training and testing time are quite short, and the experimental results demonstrate that our method outperforms the state-of-the-art methods on the HIM2017 Challenge dataset and achieves comparable performance on the ICVL and MSRA dataset. Our method has less complexity and can adapt to a large range of view-points and varied hand poses. Our proposed method provides a technical approach for tracking and analyzing the complex interaction between humans and environment.

References

1. Abadi, M., et al.: Tensorflow: a system for large-scale machine learning. OSDI **16**, 265–283 (2016)
2. Braido, P., Zhang, X.: Quantitative analysis of finger motion coordination in hand manipulative and gestic acts. Hum. Mov. Sci. **22**(6), 661–678 (2004)
3. Chen, X., Wang, G., Guo, H., Zhang, C.: Pose guided structured region ensemble network for cascaded hand pose estimation. arXiv preprint arXiv:1708.03416 (2017)
4. Cotugno, G., Althoefer, K., Nanayakkara, T.: The role of the thumb: study of finger motion in grasping and reachability space in human and robotic hands. IEEE Trans. Syst. Man Cybern. Syst. **47**(7), 1061–1070 (2017)
5. Erol, A., Bebis, G., Nicolescu, M., Boyle, R.D., Twombly, X.: Vision-based hand pose estimation: a review. Comput. Vis. Image Underst. **108**(1–2), 52–73 (2007)
6. Garcia-Hernando, G., Yuan, S., Baek, S., Kim, T.K.: First-person hand action benchmark with RGB-D videos and 3D hand pose annotations. In: CVPR, vol. 1 (2018)
7. Ge, L., Liang, H., Yuan, J., Thalmann, D.: Robust 3d hand pose estimation in single depth images: from single-view CNN to multi-view CNNs. In: Proceedings of the IEEE Conference on Computer Vision and Pattern Recognition, pp. 3593–3601 (2016)
8. Ge, L., Liang, H., Yuan, J., Thalmann, D.: 3d convolutional neural networks for efficient and robust hand pose estimation from single depth images. In: Proceedings of the IEEE Conference on Computer Vision and Pattern Recognition, vol. 1, p. 5 (2017)
9. Guo, H., Wang, G., Chen, X., Zhang, C.: Towards good practices for deep 3d hand pose estimation. arXiv preprint arXiv:1707.07248 (2017)
10. Guo, H., Wang, G., Chen, X., Zhang, C., Qiao, F., Yang, H.: Region ensemble network: improving convolutional network for hand pose estimation. In: 2017 IEEE International Conference on Image Processing (ICIP), pp. 4512–4516. IEEE (2017)
11. Ioffe, S., Szegedy, C.: Batch normalization: accelerating deep network training by reducing internal covariate shift. In: International Conference on Machine Learning, pp. 448–456 (2015)

12. Keskin, C., Kıraç, F., Kara, Y.E., Akarun, L.: Hand pose estimation and hand shape classification using multi-layered randomized decision forests. In: Fitzgibbon, A., Lazebnik, S., Perona, P., Sato, Y., Schmid, C. (eds.) ECCV 2012. LNCS, vol. 7577, pp. 852–863. Springer, Heidelberg (2012). https://doi.org/10.1007/978-3-642-33783-3_61

13. Khamis, S., Taylor, J., Shotton, J., Keskin, C., Izadi, S., Fitzgibbon, A.: Learning an efficient model of hand shape variation from depth images. In: Proceedings of the IEEE Conference on Computer Vision and Pattern Recognition, pp. 2540–2548 (2015)

14. Kingma, D.P., Ba, J.: Adam: a method for stochastic optimization. arXiv preprint arXiv:1412.6980 (2014)

15. Lin, Y., Sun, Y.: Robot grasp planning based on demonstrated grasp strategies. Int. J. Robot. Res. **34**(1), 26–42 (2015)

16. Madadi, M., Escalera, S., Baró, X., Gonzalez, J.: End-to-end global to local CNN learning for hand pose recovery in depth data. arXiv preprint arXiv:1705.09606 (2017)

17. Moon, G., Chang, J.Y., Lee, K.M.: V2V-PoseNet: voxel-to-voxel prediction network for accurate 3d hand and human pose estimation from a single depth map. In: CVPR, vol. 2 (2018)

18. Mueller, F., Mehta, D., Sotnychenko, O., Sridhar, S., Casas, D., Theobalt, C.: Real-time hand tracking under occlusion from an egocentric RGB-D sensor. In: Proceedings of International Conference on Computer Vision (ICCV) (2017). https://handtracker.mpi-inf.mpg.de/projects/OccludedHands/

19. Oberweger, M., Lepetit, V.: Deepprior++: improving fast and accurate 3d hand pose estimation. In: ICCV Workshop, vol. 840, p. 2 (2017)

20. Oberweger, M., Wohlhart, P., Lepetit, V.: Hands deep in deep learning for hand pose estimation. In: Computer Vision Winter Workshop (2015)

21. Oikonomidis, I., Kyriazis, N., Argyros, A.: Efficient model-based 3d tracking of hand articulations using kinect. In: BMVC (2011)

22. Qian, C., Sun, X., Wei, Y., Tang, X., Sun, J.: Realtime and robust hand tracking from depth. In: Proceedings of the IEEE Conference on Computer Vision and Pattern Recognition, pp. 1106–1113 (2014)

23. Rad, M., Oberweger, M., Lepetit, V.: Feature mapping for learning fast and accurate 3d pose inference from synthetic images. In: Proceedings of the IEEE Conference on Computer Vision and Pattern Recognition, pp. 4663–4672 (2018)

24. Sharp, T., et al.: Accurate, robust, and flexible real-time hand tracking. In: Proceedings of the 33rd Annual ACM Conference on Human Factors in Computing Systems, pp. 3633–3642. ACM (2015)

25. Simonyan, K., Zisserman, A.: Very deep convolutional networks for large-scale image recognition. arXiv preprint arXiv:1409.1556 (2014)

26. Sridhar, S., Mueller, F., Oulasvirta, A., Theobalt, C.: Fast and robust hand tracking using detection-guided optimization. In: Proceedings of the IEEE Conference on Computer Vision and Pattern Recognition, pp. 3213–3221 (2015)

27. Sun, X., Wei, Y., Liang, S., Tang, X., Sun, J.: Cascaded hand pose regression. In: Proceedings of the IEEE Conference on Computer Vision and Pattern Recognition, pp. 824–832 (2015)

28. Supancic, J.S., Rogez, G., Yang, Y., Shotton, J., Ramanan, D.: Depth-based hand pose estimation: data, methods, and challenges. In: Proceedings of the IEEE International Conference on Computer Vision, pp. 1868–1876 (2015)

29. Susman, R.L.: Hand function and tool behavior in early hominids. J. Hum. Evol. **35**(1), 23–46 (1998)

30. Tang, D., Jin Chang, H., Tejani, A., Kim, T.K.: Latent regression forest: Structured estimation of 3d articulated hand posture. In: Proceedings of the IEEE Conference on Computer Vision and Pattern Recognition, pp. 3786–3793 (2014)

31. Taylor, J., et al.: Articulated distance fields for ultra-fast tracking of hands interacting. ACM Trans. Graph. **36**(6), 1–12 (2017)

32. Tkach, A., Pauly, M., Tagliasacchi, A.: Sphere-meshes for real-time hand modeling and tracking. ACM Trans. Graph. (TOG) **35**(6), 222 (2016)

33. Tompson, J., Stein, M., Lecun, Y., Perlin, K.: Real-time continuous pose recovery of human hands using convolutional networks. ACM Trans. Graph. (ToG) **33**(5), 169 (2014)

34. Wan, C., Probst, T., Van Gool, L., Yao, A.: Crossing nets: combining GANs and VAEs with a shared latent space for hand pose estimation. In: 2017 IEEE Conference on Computer Vision and Pattern Recognition (CVPR). IEEE (2017)

35. Xu, C., Cheng, L.: Efficient hand pose estimation from a single depth image. In: Proceedings of the IEEE International Conference on Computer Vision, pp. 3456–3462 (2013)

36. Yuan, S., et al.: Depth-based 3d hand pose estimation: from current achievements to future goals. In: IEEE CVPR (2018)

37. Yuan, S., Ye, Q., Garcia-Hernando, G., Kim, T.K.: The 2017 hands in the million challenge on 3d hand pose estimation. arXiv preprint arXiv:1707.02237 (2017)

38. Yuan, S., Ye, Q., Stenger, B., Jain, S., Kim, T.K.: BigHand2. 2M benchmark: Hand pose dataset and state of the art analysis. In: 2017 IEEE Conference on Computer Vision and Pattern Recognition (CVPR), pp. 2605–2613. IEEE (2017)

39. Zhou, X., Wan, Q., Zhang, W., Xue, X., Wei, Y.: Model-based deep hand pose estimation. In: Proceedings of the Twenty-Fifth International Joint Conference on Artificial Intelligence, pp. 2421–2427. AAAI Press (2016)

Sequential Clique Optimization for Video Object Segmentation

Yeong Jun Koh[1(✉)], Young-Yoon Lee[2], and Chang-Su Kim[1]

[1] School of Electrical Engineering, Korea University, Seoul, Korea
yjkoh@mcl.korea.ac.kr,changsukim@korea.ac.kr
[2] Samsung Electronics Co., Ltd., Seoul, Korea
yy77lee@gmail.com

Abstract. A novel algorithm to segment out objects in a video sequence is proposed in this work. First, we extract object instances in each frame. Then, we select a visually important object instance in each frame to construct the salient object track through the sequence. This can be formulated as finding the maximal weight clique in a complete k-partite graph, which is NP hard. Therefore, we develop the sequential clique optimization (SCO) technique to efficiently determine the cliques corresponding to salient object tracks. We convert these tracks into video object segmentation results. Experimental results show that the proposed algorithm significantly outperforms the state-of-the-art video object segmentation and video salient object detection algorithms on recent benchmark datasets.

Keywords: Video object segmentation
Primary object segmentation · Salient object detection
Sequential clique optimization

1 Introduction

Video object segmentation (VOS) [1–4] is the task to segment out primary objects from the background in a video sequence, where a 'primary' object refers to the most salient one in the sequence [5,6]. In this regard, VOS is closely related to video salient object detection (SOD) [7–10], in which the objective is to detect salient objects in a video. Note that the 'salient' objects mean that they appear frequently in the video and have dominant color and motion features. VOS can be used in many vision applications, including object recognition, action recognition, and video summarization. However, it is challenging to delineate salient objects in videos without any user annotations. Also, various factors, such as background clutter, fast motion, and object occlusion, make VOS even more difficult.

Recent object instance segmentation techniques for still images achieve remarkable performances, by employing convolutional neural networks (CNNs) [11–14]. On the other hand, many VOS techniques [15,16] and video

© Springer Nature Switzerland AG 2018
V. Ferrari et al. (Eds.): ECCV 2018, LNCS 11218, pp. 537–556, 2018.
https://doi.org/10.1007/978-3-030-01264-9_32

SOD techniques   [9,10,17] focus on the combination of spatial and temporal results. However, the fusion processes often cause temporal inconsistency and may fail to segment out primary objects properly when either spatial or temporal results are inaccurate. Also, although these techniques can effectively extract objects with dominant color and motion features, they do not consider the appearance frequency of an object in a video sequence. In other words, they may fail to detect primary objects, which have less dominant features in each frame but appear frequently in the sequence.

In this work, we propose a novel approach to segment out foreground objects in a video sequence. First, we generate object instances in each frame. Then, we perform instance matching, by selecting one object instance from each frame, in order to construct the most salient object track. This is formulated as finding a clique in a complete k-partite graph [18] of object instances. Note that the clique should contain the instances over frames, corresponding to an identical object. Thus, the instances should be similar to one another. However, finding the optimal clique with the maximal similarity weights is NP hard. We hence develop the sequential clique optimization (SCO) process, which considers both the node energy and the edge energy. By repeating the SCO process, we can extract multiple salient object tracks. Finally, we convert these salient object tracks into VOS results in unsupervised and semi-supervised settings. Experimental results demonstrate that the proposed algorithm significantly outperforms the state-of-the-art VOS and video SOD algorithms on the DAVIS [19] and FBMS [20] datasets.

This work has the following major contributions:

- We develop the SCO process that determines a suboptimal clique efficiently with time complexity $O(NT^2)$, where T is the number of frames in a video and N is the number of instances in each frame.
- The proposed algorithm can extract multiple primary objects effectively, whereas most conventional algorithms assume a single primary object.
- The proposed algorithm provides remarkable performances on the DAVIS 2016, DAVIS 2017, and FBMS benchmark datasets.

2   Related Work

Video Object Segmentation: VOS attempts to separate foreground objects from the background in a video. Many VOS algorithms extract a single primary object. Papazoglou and Ferrari [1] generate motion boundaries using optical flows, construct a foreground model for the regions within the motion boundaries, and then use it to extract moving objects. Lee *et al.* [21] extract object proposals with the objectness scores from all frames. The proposals are clustered, and each cluster is ranked according to the objectness score. In [3,22], object proposals are used to construct a locally connected graph, and the optimal path in the graph is determined to describe a primary object. Koh *et al.* [23] consider the recurrence property of a primary object to choose proposals. Also, saliency detection techniques are widely employed to estimate initial regions of a primary object [2,4,24,25]. Wang et al. [24] adopt geodesic distances for saliency estimation and design an energy function to enforce the temporal smoothness of a primary object. Jang et al. [4] obtain foreground and background distributions by adopting the boundary prior, and dichotomize each region into the primary object or background class by minimizing a hybrid energy function. Yang et al. [25] use saliency maps to build an appearance model. Faktor and Irani [2] employ saliency maps as the initial distribution of random walk simulation.

Another approach to VOS is motion segmentation [20,26–30], which clusters point trajectories. Shi and Malik [26] divide a video into motion segments using the normalized cuts. Brox and Malik [27] construct sparse long-term trajectories and cluster them. Ochs and Brox [28] convert sparse motion clusters into dense segmentation via the sparse-to-dense interpolation scheme. They also adopt the spectral clustering based on a higher-order motion model [29]. Fragkiadaki et al. [30] analyze trajectory discontinuities at object boundaries to improve the segmentation accuracy.

Recently, deep learning techniques have been developed for VOS [15,16,31–35]. Jain et al. [15] propose an end-to-end learning framework, which combines appearance and motion information to provide pixel-wise segmentation results for salient objects. Tokmakov et al. [16,31] learn motion patterns with a fully convolutional network by employing synthetic video sequences. Deep learning models are also used in semi-supervised VOS, which requires manually annotated masks at the first frame to segment out target objects in subsequent frames [33–35]. Caelles et al. [33] fine-tune a CNN using user annotations to extract a target object. In [34,35], propagation errors of segmentation masks are recovered by deep learning models.

Salient Object Detection: Early SOD algorithms [36–42] for still images are based on bottom-up models, which use global or local contrast of image features. Some algorithms [40–42] adopt a priori knowledge, such as the boundary prior that boundary regions tend to belong to the background and thus be less salient than center regions. Recently, deep learning techniques have been adopted prevalently for SOD. Many deep fully convolutional networks are trained in an end-to-end manner to yield pixel-wise saliency maps [43–45]. Also, an instance-level segmentation algorithm for salient objects was proposed in [14], which uses both saliency maps and object proposals.

Image SOD has been extended to video SOD [7,9,17,46,47]. Kim et al. [7] produce a spatiotemporal saliency map via the pixel-wise multiplication of spatial and temporal saliency maps. In the multiplication, adaptive weights can be used to yield more robust results. For instance, Fang et al. [46] fuse spatial and temporal maps using entropy-based uncertainty weights. Also, Yang et al. [17] generate six kinds of saliency maps and superpose them adaptively. Chen et al. [9] combine color and motion saliency maps based on the salient foreground model and the non-salient background model.

Some algorithms [8,10,48] exploit spatial and temporal features jointly to detect spatiotemporally salient regions. Wang *et al.* [48] propose the gradient flow field to merge intra-frame boundaries and inter-frame features. Kim *et al.* [8] exploit spatial and temporal features in the random walk with restart framework. Wang *et al.* [10] design two networks for static saliency and dynamic saliency, respectively. They feed the output of the static network into the dynamic network to obtain a saliency map.

3   Proposed Algorithm

We segment primary objects in a sequence of video frames $\mathcal{I} = \{I_1, \ldots, I_T\}$. The output is the corresponding sequence of pixel-wise maps, which locate the primary objects in the frames. Figure 1 shows an overview of the proposed algorithm. First, we generate object instances in each frame. Second, we construct a complete k-partite graph using the set of object instances. Third, we extract salient object tracks by finding cliques in the graph and convert the tracks into VOS results.

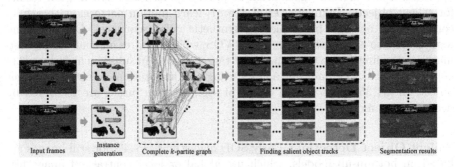

Fig. 1. An overview of the proposed algorithm.

3.1   Generating Object Instances

To detect object instances without manual annotations, we employ the instance-aware semantic segmentation method FCIS [11]. FCIS measures the category-wise detection scores of region proposals, generated by the network in [49], and segments out foreground regions from the proposals. We choose only the proposals whose detection scores are higher than 0.5 and declare the corresponding foreground regions as object instances. For each proposal, we use the maximum of the category-wise scores, since the purpose of the proposed algorithm is to segment out salient objects in videos regardless of their categories. Figure 2(b) shows object instances in a frame. The set of detected object instances in frame I_t is denoted by $\mathcal{O}_t = \{o_{t,\theta} \mid \theta \in \mathbb{N}_{N_t}\}$, where $\mathbb{N}_m = \{1, 2, \ldots, m\}$ is the finite index set and N_t is the number of object instances in frame I_t. The θth object instance $o_{t,\theta}$ in frame I_t has two attributes: saliency score $s_{t,\theta}$ and feature vector $\mathbf{f}_{t,\theta}$.

To determine the saliency score $s_{t,\theta}$, we simply estimate a foreground distribution based on the boundary prior. We over-segment a frame into superpixels using [50], and construct a 4-ring graph of superpixels. We compute edge weights by summing up the average LAB color difference and the average optical flow difference between two superpixels. We then obtain the background distribution using the random walk with restart (RWR) simulation [51], where only superpixels at the frame boundary are assigned nonzero restart probabilities. Finally, we invert the background distribution to yield the foreground distribution, as illustrated in Fig. 2(c). We then compute $s_{t,\theta}$ by averaging the foreground probabilities within the instance $o_{t,\theta}$.

Also, we construct the feature vector $\mathbf{f}_{t,\theta}$ using the bag-of-visual-words (BoW) approach [52]. We quantize the LAB colors, extracted from the 40 training sequences in the VSB100 dataset [53], into 300 codewords using the K-means algorithm. We then construct the histogram of the codewords for the pixels within $o_{t,\theta}$, and normalize it into the feature vector $\mathbf{f}_{t,\theta}$.

(a)   (b)   (c)

Fig. 2. Object instance generation in the "Boxing-fisheye" sequence: (a) input frame, (b) object instances, and (c) foreground distribution.

3.2 Finding Salient Object Tracks

Problem: The set of all object instances, $\mathcal{V} = \mathcal{O}_1 \cup \mathcal{O}_2 \cup \cdots \cup \mathcal{O}_T$, includes non-salient objects, as well as salient ones. From $\mathcal{V}$, we extract as many salient objects as possible, while excluding non-salient ones, assuming that a salient object should have dominant features in each frame and appear frequently through the sequence. To this end, we construct the most salient object track, by selecting an object instance in each frame, which corresponds to one identical salient object. Then, after removing all instances in the track from $\mathcal{V}$, we repeat the process to extract the next salient track, and so on.

Sequential Clique Optimization: Using the set of object instances $\mathcal{V} = \mathcal{O}_1 \cup \mathcal{O}_2 \cup \cdots \cup \mathcal{O}_T$, we construct a complete k-partite graph $\mathcal{G} = (\mathcal{V}, \mathcal{E})$. Thus,

$\mathcal{V}$ becomes the node set, and each object instance becomes a node in the graph $\mathcal{G}$. Since $\mathcal{O}_t \cap \mathcal{O}_\tau = \emptyset$ for $t \neq \tau$, $\mathcal{O}_1, \mathcal{O}_2, \cdots, \mathcal{O}_T$ form a partition of $\mathcal{V}$. Also, we define the edge set as $\mathcal{E} = \{(o_{t,i}, o_{\tau,j}) \mid t \neq \tau\}$. In other words, every pair of object instances in different frames are connected by an edge in $\mathcal{E}$, whereas two instances in the same frame are not adjacent in the graph $\mathcal{G}$. As a result, $\mathcal{G}$ is complete k-partite [18], where $k = T$. For example, Fig. 3(a) illustrates the complete k-partite graph for four frames, $i.e.$ $k = 4$. We assign a weight to edge $(o_{t,i}, o_{\tau,j})$ by

$$w(o_{t,i}, o_{\tau,j}) = \exp\left(-\frac{d_{\chi^2}(\mathbf{f}_{t,i}, \mathbf{f}_{\tau,j})}{\sigma^2}\right) \tag{1}$$

where $\sigma^2 = 0.01$ is a scaling parameter and d_{χ^2} denotes the chi-square distance.

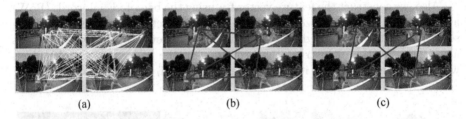

Fig. 3. Illustration of finding salient object tracks over four frames in "Boxing-fisheye": (a) complete 4-partite graph, (b) 1st salient object track Θ_1, and (c) 2nd salient object track Θ_2.

To extract the most salient object, we perform the instance matching by selecting one object instance (one node) from each frame (each node subset) $\mathcal{O}_t$. This process of finding an object track is equivalent to finding a clique in the graph $\mathcal{G}$. Notice that selecting one node from each frame satisfies the condition of a clique [18]: every pair of nodes within the clique are adjacent. In the clique, which represents the track of an identical object in the video sequence, the features of the member nodes should be similar to one another. Therefore, we determine the clique to maximize the sum of the edge weights. Let $\Theta = \{\theta_t\}_{t=1}^T$ denote a clique, which is represented by the sequence of the node indices in the clique. Here, $\theta_t \in \mathbb{N}_{N_t}$ is the index of the selected node from the tth frame $\mathcal{O}_t$. Then, we define the similarity $E_{\text{similarity}}(\Theta)$ of clique Θ as

$$E_{\text{similarity}}(\Theta) = \sum_{t=1}^T \sum_{\tau=1, \tau \neq t}^T w(o_{t,\theta_t}, o_{\tau,\theta_\tau}), \tag{2}$$

which is the sum of all edge weights in Θ. We attempt to maximize the similarity, assuming that the features of an identical object do not change drastically over frames.

Also, object instances in a clique, representing a salient object track, should have high saliency scores. We hence define the saliency $E_{\text{saliency}}(\Theta)$ of clique Θ as

$$E_{\text{saliency}}(\Theta) = \sum_{t=1}^{T} s_{t,\theta_t}. \tag{3}$$

We attempt to find the maximal weight clique Θ^* that maximizes the similarity energy:

$$\Theta^* = \arg\max_{\Theta} E_{\text{similarity}}(\Theta) \tag{4}$$

subject to the constraint that the saliency $E_{\text{saliency}}(\Theta)$ is also high. However, even the unconstrained problem in (4) is NP hard [54,55]. There are $N_1 \times N_2 \times \cdots \times N_T$ possible cliques, which make the exhaustive search infeasible. Some approximation methods, *e.g.* multi-greedy heuristics [56], local search [55], and binary integer program [57], have been developed to obtain suboptimal cliques in complete k-partite graphs. But, these methods are still computationally expensive and do not consider the node energy (*i.e.* the saliency E_{saliency} in this work). Instead, we develop an efficient optimization technique, called SCO, to find the clique that considers both the node energy E_{saliency} and the edge energy $E_{\text{similarity}}$.

In SCO, we first initialize the clique $\Theta^{(0)}$ to maximize the saliency E_{saliency} in (3). Specifically, the tth element in $\Theta^{(0)}$ is determined by

$$\theta_t^{(0)} = \arg\max_{\theta \in \mathbb{N}_{N_t}} s_{t,\theta}. \tag{5}$$

Then, at iteration κ, we update $\theta_t^{(\kappa)}$, by selecting the node that is the most similar to the nodes in the other frames,

$$\theta_t^{(\kappa)} = \arg\max_{\theta \in \mathbb{N}_{N_t}} \sum_{\tau=1,\tau \neq t}^{T} w(o_{t,\theta}, o_{\tau,\theta_\tau}), \tag{6}$$

and then set θ_t to be $\theta_t^{(\kappa)}$ for each t sequentially from 1 to T. We repeat this sequential update of the nodes in all frames, until $\Theta^{(\kappa)} = \{\theta_t^{(\kappa)}\}_{t=1}^{T}$ is unaltered from $\Theta^{(\kappa-1)} = \{\theta_t^{(\kappa-1)}\}_{t=1}^{T}$. This process is theoretically guaranteed to converge, since $E_{\text{similarity}}(\Theta^{(\kappa)})$ is a monotonically increasing function of κ. To summarize, SCO initializes the clique to maximize the saliency E_{saliency} and then refines it iteratively to achieve a local maximum of $E_{\text{similarity}}$. Thus, at the initialization, the clique consists of salient object instances over frames, which may not represent an identical object. However, as the iteration goes on, the clique converges to a salient object track, in which the nodes represent an identical object and thus exhibit high similarity weights in general. Algorithm 1 summarizes the proposed SCO technique. In most cases, less than 10 iterations are required for the convergence.

Let Θ_1 denote the most salient object track, obtained by this SCO process. To extract the next track Θ_2, we exclude the nodes in Θ_1 from $\mathcal{G}$ and perform SCO again. This is repeated to yield the set of tracks, $\{\Theta_1, \Theta_2, \ldots, \Theta_M\}$, until no node remains in $\mathcal{G}$. In general, if $p < q$, Θ_p is more salient than Θ_q. Thus, the subscript p in Θ_p is the saliency rank of the track. Figures 3(b) and (c) illustrate the first two tracks Θ_1 and Θ_2.

Algorithm 1. (SCO) Sequential Clique Optimization

Input: Sets of object instances $\mathcal{V} = \mathcal{O}_1 \cup \mathcal{O}_2 \cup \cdots \cup \mathcal{O}_T$

1: Construct a complete k-partite graph $\mathcal{G} = (\mathcal{V}, \mathcal{E})$
2: **for** each frame I_t **do**
3:     Initialize the node index in clique Θ via
4:         $\theta_t \leftarrow \arg\max_{\theta \in \mathbb{N}_{N_t}} s_{t,\theta}$
5: **end for**
6: **repeat**
7:     **for** each frame I_t **do**
8:         Update the node index via
9:             $\theta_t \leftarrow \arg\max_{\theta \in \mathbb{N}_{N_t}} \sum_{\tau=1, \tau \neq t}^{T} w(o_{t,\theta}, o_{\tau,\theta_\tau})$
10:    **end for**
11: **until** node indices are unaltered

Output: Optimized clique $\Theta = \{\theta_1, \theta_2, \ldots, \theta_T\}$

Postprocessing. The track selection is greedy in the sense that, if an object instance is mistakenly included in a track Θ_p, it cannot be included in a later track Θ_q even though it indeed belongs to Θ_q. To alleviate this problem, we perform postprocessing to maximize the sum of the similarities

$$\sum_{m=1}^{M} E_{\text{similarity}}(\Theta_m) \tag{7}$$

as follows. At each frame I_t, we match object instances in $\mathcal{O}_t$ to the tracks in $\{\Theta_p\}_{p=1}^{M}$. The matching cost $C(o_{t,i}, \Theta_p)$ between an instance $o_{t,i}$ and a track Θ_p is defined as the sum of the feature distances from $o_{t,i}$ to all object instances in Θ_p, except for the instance at the same frame t. After computing the matching costs, we find the optimal matching pairs using the Hungarian algorithm [58], and update the tracks to include the matched instances. This is performed for all frames. As a result, we obtain the set of the refined salient object tracks $\{\tilde{\Theta}_1, \tilde{\Theta}_2, \ldots, \tilde{\Theta}_M\}$.

Disappearance Detection. Also, we detect disappearing events for each refined salient object track. When an object disappears or is fully occluded at some frames, noisy objects are selected at those frames. Given a refined salient object track $\tilde{\Theta} = \{\tilde{\theta}_t\}_{t=1}^{T}$, we determine whether to discard $o_{t,\tilde{\theta}_t}$ at frame t from $\tilde{\Theta}$. To this end, for each $\tau \neq t$, we compare the weight $w(o_{\tau,\tilde{\theta}_\tau}, o_{t,\tilde{\theta}_t})$ against the average weight. Specifically, we count the number of object instances $o_{\tau,\tilde{\theta}_\tau}$ for $\tau \neq t$, which satisfy $w(o_{\tau,\tilde{\theta}_\tau}, o_{t,\tilde{\theta}_t}) < \frac{1}{N-2} \sum_{k=1, k \neq t}^{T} w(o_{\tau,\tilde{\theta}_\tau}, o_{k,\tilde{\theta}_k})$. If the number is larger than $0.7T$, we declare $o_{t,\tilde{\theta}_t}$ to be noisy and discard it.

3.3   Segmentation Results

Using the object tracks in $\{\tilde{\Theta}_1, \tilde{\Theta}_2, \ldots, \tilde{\Theta}_M\}$, we generate a pixel-wise segmentation map for each frame, which delineates primary objects in the frame. We propose four schemes to yield final segmentation results: Proposed-F, Proposed-O, and Proposed-M for unsupervised VOS and Proposed-S for semi-supervised VOS.

- **Proposed-F:** The first track $\tilde{\Theta}_1$ extracts the primary object in a video in general. Thus, Proposed-F selects $\tilde{\Theta}_1$. However, it may fail to extract spatially connected objects. For example, given a motorbike and its rider, it may detect only one of them. Therefore, Proposed-F additionally picks another salient object track $\tilde{\Theta}_p$, only when $\tilde{\Theta}_1$ and $\tilde{\Theta}_p$ are spatially adjacent in most frames in a video.
- **Proposed-O:** The aforementioned Proposed-F is an offline approach, which constructs the global T-partite graph for an entire video. In contrast, Proposed-O is an online approach, which uses the t-partite graph for frames $1, \ldots, t$ to obtain the segmentation result for the current frame t. In other words, Proposed-O uses the information in the current and past frames only to yield the segmentation result.
- **Proposed-M:** To handle multiple primary objects, which are not spatially connected, we choose multiple tracks from $\{\tilde{\Theta}_1, \tilde{\Theta}_2, \ldots, \tilde{\Theta}_M\}$. We compute the mean saliency score of object instances in each track, and discard the tracks whose mean scores are lower than a pre-specified threshold δ. We fix $\delta = 0.1$ in all experiments.
- **Proposed-S:** Proposed-S is for semi-supervised VOS, which chooses the ground-truth segment in the first frame and fixes it in SCO. Proposed-S is based on the online approach, Proposed-O. Moreover, we warp a segment result to the next frame using optical flow, and then add the warped segment to the set of object instances.

Finally, we improve the segmentation qualities of object instances in the selected tracks using a two-class Markov random field (MRF) optimizer in [59].

3.4 Complexity Analysis

Let us analyze the computational complexity of the proposed SCO process. For the convenience of analysis, we fix the number of object instances in each frame to N. Note that SCO has two steps: initialization and update. In the initialization, $N - 1$ comparisons are made to find the maximum saliency in each frame, requiring $O(NT)$ comparisons in total. In the update step, $N(T - 2)$ additions and $(N-1)$ comparisons are performed for each frame in one iteration. Thus, the update step demands $O(KNT^2)$ complexity, where K is the number of iterations and is restricted to be less than 10 in this work.

We repeat the SCO process N times to extract N object tracks. Thus, the complexity is $O(KN^2T^2)$. Finally, in the postprocessing, the Hungarian matching of $O(N^3)$ complexity is performed for each frame. Hence the complexity of the postprocessing is $O(N^3T)$. The overall complexity of the proposed algorithm can be approximated to $O(KN^2T^2)$, since T is larger than N in general. This complexity is significantly lower than the binary integer program in [57], which requires $O(2^{T^2 N^2})$ complexity in the worst case because of the depth-first node selection [60]. Moreover, the proposed SCO yields better segmentation performance than [57], as will be shown in Sect. 4.

Table 1. Comparison with the conventional VOS algorithms on the DAVIS 2016 dataset. The best results are boldfaced, and the second best ones are underlined.

Algorithm	Region similarity $\mathcal{J}$		Contour accuracy $\mathcal{F}$	
	Mean	Recall	Mean	Recall
NLC [2]	0.641	0.731	0.593	0.658
CVOS [61]	0.514	0.581	0.490	0.578
TRC [30]	0.501	0.560	0.478	0.519
MSG [28]	0.543	0.636	0.525	0.613
KEY [21]	0.569	0.671	0.503	0.534
SAL [24]	0.426	0.386	0.383	0.264
FST [1]	0.575	0.652	0.536	0.579
ACO [4]	0.531	0.611	0.504	0.558
LMP [16]	0.697	0.829	0.663	0.783
FSEG [15]	0.716	0.877	0.658	0.790
ARP [23]	0.763	0.892	0.711	0.828
Proposed-F	**0.796**	**0.947**	**0.770**	**0.912**
Proposed-O	0.783	<u>0.932</u>	0.758	<u>0.896</u>
Proposed-M	<u>0.787</u>	0.928	<u>0.764</u>	0.895

4   Experimental Results

Given a video sequence, the proposed algorithm can yield a segmentation mask for each frame, which delineates primary objects at the pixel level. Hence, we compare the proposed algorithm with the conventional VOS algorithms in [1,2, 4,15,16,21,23,24,28,30,33,35,61,62] and the conventional SOD algorithms in [8, 10,24,48,63–65], which also extract primary or salient objects from each frame at the pixel level. For the comparison, we use the DAVIS dataset [19] and the FBMS dataset [20].

DAVIS Dataset [19]: It has two versions, DAVIS 2016 and DAVIS 2017. DAVIS 2016 is a benchmark to evaluate VOS algorithms. It consists of 50 video sequences, which are divided into training and test sequences. We assess the proposed algorithm using both the training and test sequences. Each sequence contains a single object or spatially connected objects, *e.g.* a motorbike and its rider, which appear repeatedly in the sequence. The spatially connected objects are also regarded as a primary object.

DAVIS 2016 was extended to DAVIS 2017, which is for semi-supervised VOS. It is composed of the train-validation, test-develop, and test-challenge subsets, which contain 90, 30, and 30 videos, respectively. We evaluate the proposed algorithm on the train-validation set. Note that DAVIS 2017 is more challenging than DAVIS 2016, since multiple objects, which are not connected to one another, correspond to different targets. The union region of those multiple instances is regarded as the ground for the evaluation of the unsupervised algorithms, while multiple instance annotations are used for that of the semi-supervised algorithms.

FBMS Dataset: The FBMS dataset [20] is for segmenting out moving objects in videos, where multiple objects are labeled as the ground-truth. It consists of 59 video sequences, which are split into 29 training and 30 test sequences. We assess the proposed algorithm using the test sequences.

Table 2. Comparison with the conventional VOS algorithms on the DAVIS 2017 dataset. The best results are boldfaced, and the second best ones are underlined.

Algorithm	Region similarity $\mathcal{J}$		Contour accuracy $\mathcal{F}$	
	Mean	Recall	Mean	Recall
A. Unsupervised VOS				
NLC [2]	0.514	0.555	0.486	0.494
FST [1]	0.496	0.529	0.480	0.468
ACO [4]	0.450	0.464	0.448	0.430
ARP [23]	0.633	0.729	0.612	0.678
Proposed-F	<u>0.685</u>	<u>0.792</u>	<u>0.677</u>	<u>0.773</u>
Proposed-O	0.674	0.785	0.663	0.759
Proposed-M	**0.714**	**0.839**	**0.705**	**0.813**
B. Semi-supervised VOS				
OSVOS [33]	0.566	0.638	0.639	0.738
OnAVOS [62]	0.616	0.674	0.691	0.754
Proposed-S	**0.665**	**0.797**	**0.688**	**0.821**

4.1 Comparison with Video Object Segmentation Techniques

We compare the proposed algorithm with the conventional VOS algorithms, by employing the metrics of the region similarity $\mathcal{J}$ and the contour accuracy $\mathcal{F}$ [19]. The region similarity $\mathcal{J}$ is defined as the intersection over union (IoU) ratio $\mathcal{J} = \frac{|\mathcal{S}_p \cap \mathcal{S}_{gt}|}{|\mathcal{S}_p \cup \mathcal{S}_{gt}|}$, where $\mathcal{S}_p$ and $\mathcal{S}_{gt}$ are an estimated segment and the ground-truth. Also, the contour accuracy $\mathcal{F}$ is the F-measure, which is the harmonic mean

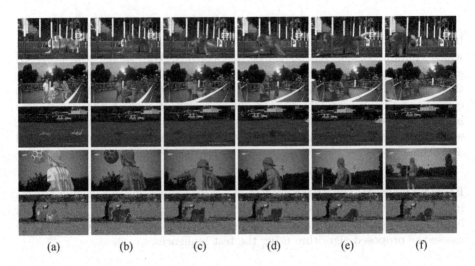

(a)   (b)   (c)   (d)   (e)   (f)

Fig. 4. VOS results of Proposed-M on the DAVIS 2017 dataset: (a) the ground-truth of primary objects in 1st frames, (b) the detection results in 1st frames, and (c)~(f) the detection results in the subsequent frames. From top to bottom, "Dog-agility," "Boxing-fisheye," "Dog-gooses," "Kid-football," and "Sheep." Detected regions are depicted in red.

of contour precision and recall rates. In these metrics, there are two statistics: 'Mean' measures the average score and 'Recall' denotes the proportion of the frames whose scores are higher than 0.5.

Evaluation on DAVIS 2016 Dataset: Table 1 compares the results on DAVIS 2016 dataset. The scores of the conventional algorithms are from the DAVIS dataset website [19]. All three versions of the proposed algorithm (Proposed-F, Proposed-O, and Proposed-M) outperform all conventional algorithms. Note that even the online version Proposed-O performs better than the state-of-the-art algorithm ARP [23], even though ARP is an offline approach. Also, Proposed-F surpasses all conventional algorithms significantly, *e.g.* by convincing margins of 3.3% and 5.9% against ARP in terms of Mean $\mathcal{J}$ and Mean $\mathcal{F}$. Especially, Proposed-F yields a very high recall score of the region similarity $\mathcal{J}$, which is almost as high as 95%. As compared with Proposed-F, Proposed-M provides lower performances, since it selects non-primary objects, as well as primary ones, in some videos.

Evaluation on DAVIS 2017 Dataset: Table 2 compares the proposed algorithm with the conventional unsupervised algorithms [1,2,4,23] and semi-supervised ones [33,62] on DAVIS 2017. The train-validation set and validation set are used for evaluating unsupervised and semi-supervised algorithms, respectively. We compute the results of [1,2,4,23] using the source codes, provided by the respective authors, and take the scores of [33,62] from the DAVIS website [19]. All unsupervised algorithms yield lower scores on DAVIS 2017 than on DAVIS 2016, since DAVIS 2017 is more challenging due to multiple primary objects. Nevertheless, the three versions of the proposed algorithm provide the best results in all metrics. Especially, Proposed-M undergoes the least degradation in the performance. This indicates that the proposed algorithm extracts multiple primary objects more reliably than the conventional ones. Figure 4 presents examples of segmentation results.

Also, notice that Proposed-S outperforms the conventional semi-supervised algorithms [33,62], even though [33,62] involve the fine-tuning, which requires the high computational complexity.

Table 3. Comparison of the Mean $\mathcal{J}$ scores on the FBMS dataset. The best result is boldfaced, and the second best one is underlined.

Video	[1]	[3]	[2]	[4]	[23]	Proposed-F	Proposed-M
Average	0.555	0.473	0.445	0.542	0.598	<u>0.625</u>	**0.686**

Table 4. Comparison of the proposed SCO with the conventional matching techniques [3,57] on the DAVIS 2016 and DAVIS 2017 datasets.

Algorithm	DAVIS 2016		DAVIS 2017	
	Mean $\mathcal{J}$	Recall $\mathcal{J}$	Mean $\mathcal{J}$	Recall $\mathcal{J}$
FCIS+[3]	0.737	0.869	0.635	0.734
FCIS+[57]	0.710	0.829	0.623	0.725
FCIS + SCO + Proposed-M w/o PPMRF	0.769	0.921	0.694	0.827
FCIS + SCO + Proposed-M	0.787	0.928	0.714	0.839
FCIS + SCO + Oracle	0.799	0.959	0.769	0.923
FCIS + SCO + Proposed-M + DF	0.755	0.878	0.666	0.775

Evaluation on FMBS Dataset: Table 3 compares the Mean $\mathcal{J}$ scores on the FBMS dataset. The scores of the conventional algorithms are from [23]. Compared with the state-of-the-art algorithm [23], Proposed-M improves the performance by 8.8%.

Efficacy of SCO: We analyze the efficacy of the proposed SCO. Note that SCO yields multiple salient object tracks, which are used to produce VOS results. We compare SCO with the conventional matching techniques for primary object segmentation [3] and multiple object tracking [57]. More specifically, given object instances from FCIS [11], we obtain multiple object tracks by employing the conventional techniques [3,57]. Since [3] is designed to yield a single object track, we repeatedly perform [3] to obtain multiple object tracks. On the other hand, [57] solves the binary integer problem to produce multiple suboptimal cliques directly. Table 4 compares the proposed SCO with these conventional techniques. For all three methods, we produce segmentation results from the multiple object tracks using the method of Proposed-M.

We see that the proposed SCO outperforms the conventional methods [3,57] significantly, even when the postprocessing and MRF (PPMRF) are not applied. Also, we perform oracle experiments for the performance upper bounds: we obtain segmentation results by matching object instances with the ground-truth segments. The proposed algorithm yields scores close to these oracle results. Finally, we use deep features (DF) instead of color-based bag-of-visual-words to compute edge weights in the graph. To this end, we extract feature maps by concatenating outputs of conv1, conv3, and conv5 in VGG-16 [66]. To generate a feature of an object instance, we average the values of pixels within the object for each channel of the feature maps. DF degrades the performance in this application, since deep semantic features undesirably yield high similarity weights between different objects in the same class.

4.2   Comparison with Salient Object Detection Techniques

To assess SOD results, we adopt three performance metrics: precision-recall (PR) curves, F-measure, and mean absolute error (MAE). The precision is the ratio $\frac{|S_p \cap S_{gt}|}{|S_p|}$ and the recall is $\frac{|S_p \cap S_{gt}|}{|S_{gt}|}$, where S_p and S_{gt} are an estimated result and the ground-truth, respectively. F-measure is defined as the harmonic mean of the precision and the recall, $i.e.$ F-measure $= \frac{(1+\beta^2) \cdot \text{precision} \cdot \text{recall}}{\beta^2 \cdot \text{precision} + \text{recall}}$ where β^2 is set to 0.3 as in [10]. Also, MAE is defined as the average of pixel-wise differences between S_p and S_{gt}.

Figure 5 compares the proposed algorithm with the conventional SOD algorithms for still images [63,64] and video sequences [8,10,24,48,65]. The scores of the conventional algorithms are from [10]. The conventional algorithms use thresholds to binarize continuous saliency maps to compute precision and recall rates. Thus, in Fig. 5, the PR curves are obtained by varying the thresholds from 0 to 255. In contrast, the proposed algorithm provides a single binary map for primary objects, without requiring a threshold. Therefore, the performance of Proposed-F or Proposed-M is given by a single dot for the pair of the average precision and recall. Both Proposed-F and Proposed-M significantly surpass all conventional algorithms on both DAVIS and FBMS datasets.

Table 5 compares the F-measure and MAE performances. The proposed algorithm yields only one F-measure score, corresponding to the dot in Fig. 5. In contrast, each conventional algorithm yields 256 F-measure scores by varying the binarization threshold. Its maximum F-score is reported in Table 5 for impartial comparison. The proposed algorithm outperforms the conventional algo-

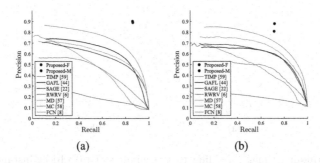

(a)   (b)

Fig. 5. Comparison of the precision-recall performances of the proposed algorithm with those of the conventional algorithms: (a) DAVIS 2016 and (b) FBMS datasets.

Table 5. Comparison with the conventional SOD algorithms. The best results are boldfaced.

Algorithm	DAVIS 2016		FBMS	
	F-measure	MAE	F-measure	MAE
MD [63]	0.561	0.129	0.646	0.105
MC [64]	0.440	0.176	0.479	0.195
TIMP [65]	0.454	0.185	0.444	0.177
GAFL [48]	0.624	0.098	0.596	0.133
SAGE [24]	0.559	0.101	0.589	0.131
RWRV [8]	0.231	0.246	0.227	0.260
FCN [10]	0.699	0.064	0.696	0.077
Proposed-F	**0.896**	**0.017**	0.801	0.112
Proposed-M	0.888	0.020	**0.816**	**0.072**

rithms significantly. For example, Proposed-M yields about 0.19 and 0.12 higher F-measure scores than the state-of-the-art algorithm [10] on the DAVIS and FBMS datasets, respectively.

4.3 Running Time Analysis

We measure the running times of the SCO algorithm for finding cliques in a complete k-partite graph. In this test, we use the "Boxing-fisheye" sequence in the DAVIS 2017 dataset. Also, we use a computer with a 2.6GHz CPU. The running time of the proposed SCO algorithm is affected by two factors: (1) the number N of object instances in a frame and (2) the number T of frames in a sequence. Figure 6(a) shows the running times according to N, when T is fixed to 50. Figure 6(b) plots the running times according to T, when N is limited to 10. We see that the proposed algorithm is faster than the binary integer program in [57], which consumes about 1 second when $N = 10$ and $T = 50$.

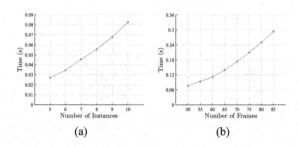

(a)   (b)

Fig. 6. The running times according to the number of (a) object instances and (b) frames.

Table 6 lists the average running times per frame on DAVIS 2016. The proposed algorithm performs FCIS [11] for generating object instances and also the optical flow estimation, saliency estimation, feature extraction at each frame. Then, it does SCO for the global optimization. SCO takes 0.304 s for the entire sequence, which is negligible. Then, the proposed algorithm also performs the MRF optimization at each frame. In total, the proposed algorithm takes 3.44 seconds per frame (SPF). It is much faster than the conventional deep-learning-based VOS algorithms [15, 16], which take about 18 SPF and 7 SPF, respectively.

Table 6. Running times in seconds per frame (SPF).

	FCIS	Optical flow	Saliency estimation	Feature extraction	MRF	Total
Time (SPF)	0.24	0.93	1.16	0.15	0.96	3.44

5   Conclusions

We proposed a novel algorithm to segment out primary objects in a video sequence, by solving the problem of finding cliques in a complete k-partite graph. We first generated object instances in each frame. Then, we chose a salient instance from each frame to construct the salient object track. For this purpose, we developed the SCO technique to consider both the saliency and similarity energies. By applying SCO repeatedly, we obtained multiple salient object tracks. Experimental results showed that the proposed algorithm significantly outperforms the state-of-the-art VOS and video SOD algorithms.

Acknowledgement. This work was supported partly by the Ministry of Science and ICT (MSIT), Korea, under the Information Technology Research Center (ITRC) support program (IITP-2018-2016-0-00464) supervised by the Institute for Information & communications Technology Promotion, and the National Research Foundations of Korea (NRF) grant funded by the Korea government (MSIP) (No. NRF-2015R1A2A1A10055037 and No. NRF-2018R1A2B3003896).

References

1. Papazoglou, A., Ferrari, V.: Fast object segmentation in unconstrained video. In: ICCV, pp. 1777–1784 (2013)
2. Faktor, A., Irani, M.: Video segmentation by non-local consensus voting. In: BMVC (2014)
3. Zhang, D., Javed, O., Shah, M.: Video object segmentation through spatially accurate and temporally dense extraction of primary object regions. In: CVPR, pp. 628–635 (2013)
4. Jang, W.D., Lee, C., Kim, C.S.: Primary object segmentation in videos via alternate convex optimization of foreground and background distributions. In: CVPR, pp. 696–704 (2016)
5. Koh, Y.J., Jang, W.D., Kim, C.S.: POD: discovering primary objects in videos based on evolutionary refinement of object recurrence, background, and primary object models. In: CVPR, pp. 1068–1076 (2016)
6. Koh, Y.J., Kim, C.S.: Unsupervised primary object discovery in videos based on evolutionary primary object modeling with reliable object proposals. IEEE Trans. Image Process. 26(11), 5203–5216 (2017)
7. Kim, W., Jung, C., Kim, C.: Spatiotemporal saliency detection and its applications in static and dynamic scenes. IEEE Trans. Circuits Syst. Video Technol. 21(4), 446–456 (2011)
8. Kim, H., Kim, Y., Sim, J.Y., Kim, C.S.: Spatiotemporal saliency detection for video sequences based on random walk with restart. IEEE Trans. Image Process. 24(8), 2552–2564 (2015)
9. Chen, C., Li, S., Wang, Y., Qin, H., Hao, A.: Video saliency detection via spatial-temporal fusion and low-rank coherency diffusion. IEEE Trans. Image Process. 26(7), 3156–3170 (2017)
10. Wang, W., Shen, J., Shao, L.: Video salient object detection via fully convolutional networks. IEEE Trans. Image Process. 27(1), 38–49 (2018)
11. Li, Y., Qi, H., Dai, J., Ji, X., Wei, Y.: Fully convolutional instance-aware semantic segmentation. In: CVPR (2017) 2359–2367
12. Arnab, A., Torr, P.H.: Pixelwise instance segmentation with a dynamically instantiated network. In: CVPR, pp. 44–450 (2017)
13. He, K., Gkioxari, G., Dollár, P., Girshick, R.: Mask R-CNN. In: ICCV, pp. 2980–2988 (2017)
14. Li, G., Xie, Y., Lin, L., Yu, Y.: Instance-level salient object segmentation. In: CVPR, pp. 2386–2395 (2017)
15. Jain, S.D., Xiong, B., Grauman, K.: FusionSeg: learning to combine motion and appearance for fully automatic segmentation of generic objects in videos. In: CVPR, pp. 3664–3673 (2017)
16. Tokmakov, P., Alahari, K., Schmid, C.: Learning motion patterns in videos. In: CVPR, pp. 3386–3394 (2017)
17. Yang, J., et al.: Discovering primary objects in videos by saliency fusion and iterative appearance estimation. IEEE Trans. Circuits Syst. Video Technol. 26(6), 1070–1083 (2016)
18. Chartrand, G., Zhang, P.: Chromatic Graph Theory. CRC Press, New York (2008)
19. Perazzi, F., Pont-Tuset, J., McWilliams, B., Van Gool, L., Gross, M., Sorkine-Hornung, A.: A benchmark dataset and evaluation methodology for video object segmentation. In: CVPR, pp. 724–732 (2016)

20. Ochs, P., Malik, J., Brox, T.: Segmentation of moving objects by long term video analysis. IEEE Trans. Pattern Anal. Mach. Intell. **36**(6), 1187–1200 (2014)
21. Lee, Y.J., Kim, J., Grauman, K.: Key-segments for video object segmentation. In: ICCV, pp. 1995–2002 (2011)
22. Ma, T., Latecki, L.J.: Maximum weight cliques with mutex constraints for video object segmentation. In: CVPR, pp. 670–677 (2012)
23. Koh, Y.J., Kim, C.S.: Primary object segmentation in videos based on region augmentation and reduction. In: CVPR, pp. 3442–3450 (2017)
24. Wang, W., Shen, J., Porikli, F.: Saliency-aware geodesic video object segmentation. In: CVPR, pp. 3395–3402 (2015)
25. Yang, J., Price, B., Shen, X., Lin, Z., Yuan, J.: Fast appearance modeling for automatic primary video object segmentation. IEEE Trans. Image Process. **25**(2), 503–515 (2016)
26. Shi, J., Malik, J.: Motion segmentation and tracking using normalized cuts. In: ICCV, pp. 1154–1160 (1998)
27. Brox, T., Malik, J.: Object segmentation by long term analysis of point trajectories. In: Daniilidis, K., Maragos, P., Paragios, N. (eds.) ECCV 2010. LNCS, vol. 6315, pp. 282–295. Springer, Heidelberg (2010). https://doi.org/10.1007/978-3-642-15555-0_21
28. Ochs, P., Brox, T.: Object segmentation in video: a hierarchical variational approach for turning point trajectories into dense regions. In: ICCV, pp. 1583–1590 (2011)
29. Ochs, P., Brox, T.: Higher order motion models and spectral clustering. In: CVPR, pp. 614–621 (2012)
30. Fragkiadaki, K., Zhang, G., Shi, J.: Video segmentation by tracing discontinuities in a trajectory embedding. In: CVPR, pp. 1846–1853 (2012)
31. Tokmakov, P., Alahari, K., Schmid, C.: Learning video object segmentation with visual memory. In: ICCV, pp. 4491–4500 (2017)
32. Cheng, J., Tsai, Y.H., Wang, S., Yang, M.H.: SegFlow: joint learning for video object segmentation and optical flow. In: ICCV, pp. 686–695 (2017)
33. Caelles, S., Maninis, K.K., Pont-Tuset, J., Leal-Taixe, L., Cremers, D., Van Gool, L.: One-shot video object segmentation. In: CVPR, pp. 221–230 (2017)
34. Perazzi, F., Khoreva, A., Benenson, R., Schiele, B., Sorkine-Hornung, A.: Learning video object segmentation from static images. In: CVPR, pp. 2663–2672 (2017)
35. Jang, W.D., Kim, C.S.: Online video object segmentation via convolutional trident network. In: CVPR, pp. 5849–5858 (2017)
36. Yan, Q., Xu, L., Shi, J., Jia, J.: Hierarchical saliency detection. In: CVPR, pp. 1155–1162 (2013)
37. Goferman, S., Zelnik-Manor, L., Tal, A.: Context-aware saliency detection. IEEE Trans. Pattern Anal. Mach. Intell. **34**(10), 1915–1926 (2012)
38. Cheng, M.M., Mitra, N.J., Huang, X., Torr, P.H., Hu, S.M.: Global contrast based salient region detection. IEEE Trans. Pattern Anal. Mach. Intell. **37**(3), 569–582 (2015)
39. Perazzi, F., Krähenbühl, P., Pritch, Y., Hornung, A.: Saliency filters: contrast based filtering for salient region detection. In: CVPR, pp. 733–740 (2012)
40. Wei, Y., Wen, F., Zhu, W., Sun, J.: Geodesic saliency using background priors. In: Fitzgibbon, A., Lazebnik, S., Perona, P., Sato, Y., Schmid, C. (eds.) ECCV 2012. LNCS, vol. 7574, pp. 29–42. Springer, Heidelberg (2012). https://doi.org/10.1007/978-3-642-33712-3_3
41. Zhu, W., Liang, S., Wei, Y., Sun, J.: Saliency optimization from robust background detection. In: CVPR, pp. 2814–2821 (2014)

42. Yang, C., Zhang, L., Lu, H., Ruan, X., Yang, M.H.: Saliency detection via graph-based manifold ranking. In: CVPR, pp. 3166–3173 (2013)
43. Li, G., Yu, Y.: Deep contrast learning for salient object detection. In: CVPR, pp. 478–487 (2016)
44. Luo, Z., Mishra, A., Achkar, A., Eichel, J., Li, S., Jodoin, P.M.: Non-local deep features for salient object detection. In: CVPR, pp. 6609–6617 (2017)
45. Hu, P., Shuai, B., Liu, J., Wang, G.: Deep level sets for salient object detection. In: CVPR, pp. 2300–2309 (2017)
46. Fang, Y., Wang, Z., Lin, W., Fang, Z.: Video saliency incorporating spatiotemporal cues and uncertainty weighting. IEEE Trans. Image Process. **23**(9), 3910–3921 (2014)
47. Liu, Z., Zhang, X., Luo, S., Le Meur, O.: Superpixel-based spatiotemporal saliency detection. IEEE Trans. Circuits Syst. Video Technol. **24**(9), 1522–1540 (2014)
48. Wang, W., Shen, J., Shao, L.: Consistent video saliency using local gradient flow optimization and global refinement. IEEE Trans. Image Process. **24**(11), 4185–4196 (2015)
49. Ren, S., He, K., Girshick, R., Sun, J.: Faster R-CNN: towards real-time object detection with region proposal networks. In: Advances in Neural Information Processing Systems, pp. 91–99 (2015)
50. Achanta, R., Shaji, A., Smith, K., Lucchi, A., Fua, P., Susstrunk, S.: SLIC superpixels compared to state-of-the-art superpixel methods. IEEE Trans. Pattern Anal. Mach. Intell. **34**(11), 2274–2282 (2012)
51. Pan, J.Y., Yang, H.J., Faloutsos, C., Duygulu, P.: Automatic multimedia cross-modal correlation discovery. In: Proceedings of the ACM SIGKDD, pp. 653–658 (2004)
52. Fei-Fei, L., Perona, P.: A Bayesian hierarchical model for learning natural scene categories. In: CVPR, pp. 524–531 (2005)
53. Galasso, F., Nagaraja, N.S., Cardenas, T.J., Brox, T., Schiele, B.: A unified video segmentation benchmark: Annotation, metrics and analysis. In: ICCV, pp. 3527–3534 (2013)
54. Feremans, C., Labbé, M., Laporte, G.: Generalized network design problems. Eur. J. Oper. Res. **148**(1), 1–13 (2003)
55. Roshan Zamir, A., Dehghan, A., Shah, M.: GMCP-tracker: global multi-object tracking using generalized minimum clique graphs. In: Fitzgibbon, A., Lazebnik, S., Perona, P., Sato, Y., Schmid, C. (eds.) ECCV 2012. LNCS, pp. 343–356. Springer, Heidelberg (2012). https://doi.org/10.1007/978-3-642-33709-3_25
56. Althaus, E., Kohlbacher, O., Lenhof, H.P., Müller, P.: A combinatorial approach to protein docking with flexible side chains. J. Comput. Biol. **9**(4), 597–612 (2002)
57. Dehghan, A., Modiri Assari, S., Shah, M.: GMMCP tracker: globally optimal generalized maximum multi clique problem for multiple object tracking. In: CVPR, pp. 4091–4099 (2015)
58. Kuhn, H.W.: The Hungarian method for the assignment problem. Nav. Res. Logist. Q. **2**(1–2), 83–97 (1955)
59. Rother, C., Kolmogorov, V., Blake, A.: GrabCut: interactive foreground extraction using iterated graph cuts. ACM Trans. Graph. **23**, 309–314 (2004)
60. Chinneck, J.W.: Practical Optimization: A Gentle Introduction. Systems and Computer Engineering (2006)
61. Taylor, B., Karasev, V., Soatto, S.: Causal video object segmentation from persistence of occlusions. In: CVPR, pp. 4268–4276 (2015)
62. Voigtlaender, P., Leibe, B.: Online adaptation of convolutional neural networks for video object segmentation. In: BMVC (2017)

63. Li, G., Yu, Y.: Visual saliency based on multiscale deep features. In: CVPR, pp. 5455–5463 (2015)
64. Jiang, B., Zhang, L., Lu, H., Yang, C., Yang, M.H.: Saliency detection via absorbing Markov chain. In: ICCV, pp. 1665–1672 (2013)
65. Zhou, F., Kang, S.B., Cohen, M.F.: Time-mapping using space-time saliency. In: CVPR, pp. 3358–3365 (2014)
66. Simonyan, K., Zisserman, A.: Very deep convolutional networks for large-scale image recognition. In: ICLR (2015)

Joint 3D Face Reconstruction and Dense Alignment with Position Map Regression Network

Yao Feng[1](✉)(iD), Fan Wu[2](iD), Xiaohu Shao[3,4](iD), Yanfeng Wang[1](iD), and Xi Zhou[1,2](iD)

[1] Cooperative Medianet Innovation Center, Shanghai Jiao Tong University, Shanghai, China
fengyao@sjtu.edu.cn
[2] CloudWalk Technology, Guangzhou, China
[3] CIGIT, Chinese Academy of Sciences, Chongqing, China
[4] University of Chinese Academy of Sciences, Beijing, China

Abstract. We propose a straightforward method that simultaneously reconstructs the 3D facial structure and provides dense alignment. To achieve this, we design a 2D representation called UV position map which records the 3D shape of a complete face in UV space, then train a simple Convolutional Neural Network to regress it from a single 2D image. We also integrate a weight mask into the loss function during training to improve the performance of the network. Our method does not rely on any prior face model, and can reconstruct full facial geometry along with semantic meaning. Meanwhile, our network is very light-weighted and spends only 9.8 ms to process an image, which is extremely faster than previous works. Experiments on multiple challenging datasets show that our method surpasses other state-of-the-art methods on both reconstruction and alignment tasks by a large margin. Code is available at https://github.com/YadiraF/PRNet.

Keywords: 3D face reconstruction · Dense face alignment

1 Introduction

3D face reconstruction and face alignment are two fundamental and highly related topics in computer vision. In the last decades, researches in these two fields benefit each other. In the beginning, face alignment that aims at detecting a special 2D fiducial points [38,46,64,66] is commonly used as a prerequisite for other facial tasks such as face recognition [59] and assists 3D face reconstruction [27,68] to a great extent. However, researchers find that 2D alignment has difficulties [30,65] in dealing with problems of large poses or occlusions. With the

Electronic supplementary material The online version of this chapter (https://doi.org/10.1007/978-3-030-01264-9_33) contains supplementary material, which is available to authorized users.

© Springer Nature Switzerland AG 2018
V. Ferrari et al. (Eds.): ECCV 2018, LNCS 11218, pp. 557–574, 2018.
https://doi.org/10.1007/978-3-030-01264-9_33

development of deep learning, many computer vision problems have been well solved by utilizing Convolution Neural Networks (CNNs). Thus, some works start to use CNNs to estimate the 3D Morphable Model (3DMM) coefficients [32,39,40,47,48,67] or 3D model warping functions [4,53] to restore the corresponding 3D information from a single 2D facial image, which provides both dense face alignment and 3D face reconstruction results. However, the performance of these methods is restricted due to the limitation of the 3D space defined by face model basis or templates. The required operations including perspective projection or 3D Thin Plate Spline (TPS) transformation also add complexity to the overall process.

Recently, two end-to-end works [9,28], which bypass the limitation of model space, achieve the state-of-the-art performances on their respective tasks. [9] trains a complex network to regress 68 facial landmarks with 2D coordinates from a single image, but needs an extra network to estimate the depth value. Besides, dense alignment is not provided by this method. [28] develops a volumetric representation of 3D face and uses a network to regress it from a 2D image. However, this representation discards the semantic meaning of points, thus the network needs to regress the whole volume in order to restore the facial shape, which is only part of the volume. So this representation limits the resolution of the recovered shape, and need a complex network to regress it. To sum up, model-based methods keep semantic meaning of points well but are restricted in model space, recent model-free methods are unrestricted and achieve state-of-the-art performance but discard the semantic meaning, which motivate us to find a new approach to reconstruct 3D face with alignment information in a model-free manner.

In this paper, we propose an end-to-end method called Position map Regression Network (PRN) to jointly predict dense alignment and reconstruct 3D face shape. Our method surpasses all other previous works on both 3D face alignment and reconstruction on multiple datasets. Meanwhile, our method is straightforward with a very light-weighted model which provides the result in one pass with 9.8 ms. All of these are achieved by the elaborate design of the 2D representation of 3D facial structure and the corresponding loss function. Specifically, we design a UV position map, which is a 2D image recording the 3D coordinates of a complete facial point cloud, and at the same time keeping the semantic meaning at each UV place. We then train a simple encoder-decoder network with a weighted loss that focuses more on discriminative region to regress the UV position map from a single 2D facial image. Figure 1 shows our method is robust to poses, illuminations and occlusions.

In summary, our main contributions are:

- For the first time, we solve the problems of face alignment and 3D face reconstruction together in an end-to-end fashion without the restriction of low-dimensional solution space.
- To directly regress the 3D facial structure and dense alignment, we develop a novel representation called UV position map, which records the position

Fig. 1. The qualitative results of our method. Odd row: alignment results (only 68 key points are plotted for display). Even row: 3D reconstruction results (reconstructed shapes are rendered with head light for better view).

information of 3D face and provides dense correspondence to the semantic meaning of each point on UV space.

- For training, we proposed a weight mask which assigns different weight to each point on position map and compute a weighted loss. We show that this design helps improving the performance of our network.
- We finally provide a light-weighted framework that runs at over 100FPS to directly obtain 3D face reconstruction and alignment result from a single 2D facial image.
- Comparison on the AFLW2000-3D and Florence datasets shows that our method achieves more than 25% relative improvements over other state-of-the-art methods on both tasks of 3D face reconstruction and dense face alignment.

2   Related Works

2.1   3D Face Reconstruction

Since Blanz and Vetter proposed 3D Morphable Model(3DMM) in 1999 [6], methods based on 3DMM are popular in completing the task of monocular 3D face reconstruction. Most of earlier methods are to establish the correspondences of the special points between input images and the 3D template including landmarks [10,19,27,29,37,56,68] and local features [19,26,49], then solve the non-linear optimization function to regress the 3DMM coefficients. However, these methods heavily rely on the accuracy of landmarks or other feature points detector. Thus, some methods [22,63] firstly use CNNs to learn the dense correspondence between input image and 3D template, then calculate the 3DMM parameters with predicted dense constrains. Recent works also explore the usage of

CNN to predict 3DMM parameters directly. [32,39,47,48,67] use cascaded CNN structure to regress the accurate 3DMM coefficients, which take a lot of time due to iterations. [15,31,36,57] propose end-to-end CNN architectures to directly estimate the 3DMM shape parameters. Unsupervised methods have been also researched recently, [3,55] can regress the 3DMM coefficients without the help of training data, which performs badly in faces with large poses and strong occlusions. However, the main defect of those methods is model-based, resulting in a limited geometry which is constrained in model space. Some other methods can reconstruct 3D faces without 3D shape basis, [20,24,33,51,53] can produce a 3D structure by warping the shape of a reference 3D model. [4] also reconstruct the 3D shape of faces by learning a 3D Thin Plate Spline(TPS) warping function via a deep network which warps a generic 3D model to a subject specific 3D shape. Obviously, the reconstructed face geometry from these methods are also restricted by the reference model, which means the structure differs when the template changes. Recently, [28] propose to straightforwardly map the image pixels to full 3D facial structure via volumetric CNN regression. This method is not restricted in the model space any more, while needs a complex network structure and a lot of time to predict the voxel data. Different from above methods, Our framework is model-free and light-weighted, can run at real time and directly obtain the full 3D facial geometry along with its correspondence information.

2.2   Face Alignment

In the field of computer vision, face alignment is a long-standing problem which attracts lots of attention. In the beginning, there are a number of 2D facial alignment approaches which aim at locating a set of fiducial 2D facial landmarks, such as classic Active Appearance Model (AMM) [43,52,58] and Constrained Local Models (CLM) [1,34]. Then cascaded regression [14,60] and CNN-based methods [9,38,46] are largely used to achieve state-of-the-art performance in 2D landmarks location. However, 2D landmarks location only regresses visible points on faces, which is limited to describe face shape when the pose is large. Recent works then research the 3D facial alignment, which begins with fitting a 3DMM [18,44,67] or registering a 3D facial template [5,51] with a 2D facial image. Obviously, 3D reconstruction methods based on model can easily complete the task of 3D face alignment. Actually, [31,63,67] are specially designated methods to achieve 3D face alignment by means of 3DMM fitting. Recently [8,9] use a deep network to directly predict the heat map to obtain the 3D facial landmarks and achieves state-of-the-art performance. Thus, as sparse face alignment tasks are highly completed by aforementioned methods, the task of dense face alignment begins to develop. Notice that, the dense face alignment means the methods should offer the correspondence between two face images as well as between a 2D facial image and a 3D facial reference geometry. [40] use multi-constraints to train a CNN which estimates the 3DMM parameters and then provides a very dense 3D alignment. [22,63] directly learn the correspondence between 2D input image and 3D template via a deep network, while those correspondence is not complete, only visible face region is considered. Compared to prior works, our method can directly establish the dense correspondence of all regions once the position map is regressed. No intermediate parameters such as 3DMM coefficients and TPS warping parameters are needed in our method, which means our network can run very fast.

3   Proposed Method

This section describes the framework and the details of our proposed method. Firstly, we introduce the characteristics of the position map for our representation. Then we elaborate the CNN architecture and the loss function designed specially for learning the mapping from unconstrained RGB image to its 3D structure. The implementation details of our method are shown in the last subsection.

3.1   3D Face Representation

Our goal is to regress the 3D facial geometry and its dense correspondence information from a single 2D image. Thus we need a proper representation which can be directly predicted via a deep network. One simple and commonly used idea is to concatenate the coordinates of all points in 3D face as a vector and use a network to predict it. However, this projection from 3D space into 1D vector which discards the spatial adjacency information among points increases the difficulties in training deep neural networks. Spatially adjacent points could share weights in predicting their positions, which can be easily achieved by using convolutional layers, while the coordinates as a 1D vector needs a fully connected layer to predict each point with much more parameters that increases the network size and is hard to train. [16] proposed a point set generation network to directly predict the point cloud of 3D object as a vector from a single image. However, the max number of points is only 1024, far from enough to represent an accurate 3D face. So model-based methods [15,40,67] regress a few model parameters rather than the coordinates of points, which usually needs special care in training such as using Mahalanobis distance and inevitably limits the estimated face geometry to the their model space. [28] proposed 3D binary volume as the representation of 3D structure and uses Volumetric Regression Network (VRN) to output a $192 \times 192 \times 200$ volume as the discretized version of point cloud. By using this representation, VRN can be built with full convolutional layers. However, discretization limits the resolution of point cloud, and most part of the network output correspond to non-surface points which are of less usage.

To address the problems in previous works, we propose UV position map as the presentation of full 3D facial structure with alignment information. UV position map or position map for short, is a 2D image recording 3D positions of all points in UV space. In the past years, UV space or UV coordinates, which is a 2D image plane parameterized from the 3D surface, has been utilized as a way to express information including the texture of faces (texture map) [3, 13,45,61], 2.5D geometry (height map) [41,42], 3D geometry (geometry image)

[21,54] and the correspondences between 3D facial meshes [7]. Different from previous works, we use UV space to store the 3D position of points from 3D face model aligned with corresponding 2D facial image. As shown in Fig. 2, we assume the projection from 3D model to 2D image is weak perspective projection and define the 3D facial position in Left-handed Cartesian Coordinate system. The origin of the 3D space overlaps with the upper-left of the input image, with the positive x-axis pointing to the right of the image and minimum z at origin. The ground truth 3D facial shape exactly matches the face in the 2D image when projected to the x-y plane. Thus the position map can be expressed as $Pos(u_i, v_i) = (x_i, y_i, z_i)$, where (u_i, v_i) represents the UV coordinate of ith point in face surface and (x_i, y_i, z_i) represents the corresponding 3D position of facial structure with (x_i, y_i) representing corresponding 2D position of face in the input RGB images and z_i representing the depth of this point. Note that, (u_i, v_i) and (x_i, y_i) represent the same position of face so alignment information can be reserved. Our position map can be easily comprehended as replacing the r, g, b value in texture map by x, y, z coordinates.

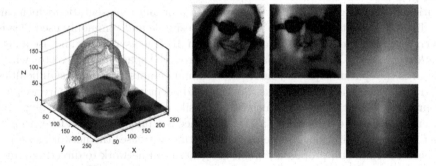

Fig. 2. The illustration of UV position map. Left: 3D plot of input image and its corresponding aligned 3D point cloud (as ground truth). Right: The first row is the input 2D image, extracted UV texture map and corresponding UV position map. The second row is the x, y, z channel of the UV position map.

Thus our position map records a dense set of points from 3D face with its semantic meaning, we are able to simultaneously obtain the 3D facial structure and dense alignment result by using a CNN to regress the position map directly from unconstrained 2D images. The network architecture in our method could be greatly simplified due to this convenience. Notice that the position map contains the information of the whole face, which makes it different from other 2D representations such as Projected Normalized Coordinate Code (PNCC) [48,67], an ordinary depth image [53] or quantized UV coordinates [22], which only reserve the information of visible face region in the input image. Our proposed position map also infers the invisible parts of face, thus our method can predict a complete 3D face.

Since we want to regress the 3D full structure from 2D image directly, the unconstrained 2D facial images and their corresponding 3D shapes are needed for end-to-end training. 300W-LP [67] is a large dataset that contains more than 60K unconstrained images with fitted 3DMM parameters, which is suitable to form our training pairs. Besides, the 3DMM parameters of this dataset are based on the Basel Face Model(BFM) [6]. Thus, in order to make full use of this dataset, we conduct the UV coordinates corresponding to BFM. To be specific, we use the parameterized UV coordinates from [3] which computes a Tutte embedding [17] with conformal Laplacian weight and then maps the mesh boundary to a square. Since the number of vertices in BFM is more than 50K, we choose 256 as the position map size, which get a high precision point cloud with negligible re-sample error.

3.2 Network Architecture and Loss Function

Since our network transfers the input RGB image into position map image, we employ an encoder-decoder structure to learn the transfer function. The encoder part of our network begins with one convolution layer followed by 10 residual blocks [25] which reduce the $256 \times 256 \times 3$ input image into $8 \times 8 \times 512$ feature maps, the decoder part contains 17 transposed convolution layers to generate the predicted $256 \times 256 \times 3$ position map. We use kernel size of 4 for all convolution or transposed convolution layers, and use ReLU layer for activation. Given that the position map contains both the full 3D information and dense alignment result, we don't need extra network module for multi-task during training or inferring. The architecture of our network is shown in Fig. 3.

In order to learn the parameters of the network, we build a loss function to measure the difference between ground truth position map and the network output. Mean square error (MSE) is a commonly used loss for such learning task, such as in [12,63]. However, MSE treats all points equally, so it is not entirely appropriate for learning the position map. Since central region of face has more discriminative features than other regions, we employ a weight mask to form our loss function. As shown in Fig. 4, the weight mask is a gray image recording the weight of each point on position map. It has the same size and pixel-to-pixel correspondence to position map. According to our objective, we separate points into four categories, each has its own weights in the loss function. The position of 68 facial keypoints has the highest weight, so that to ensure the network to

Fig. 3. The architecture of PRN. The Green rectangles represent the residual blocks, and the blue ones represent the transposed convolutional layers. (Color figure online)

learn accurate locations of these points. The neck region usually attracts less attention, and is often occluded by hairs or clothes in unconstrained images. Since learning the 3D shape of neck or clothes is beyond our interests, we assign 0 weight to points in neck region to reduce disturbance in the training process.

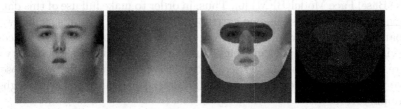

Fig. 4. The illustration of weight mask. From left to right: UV texture map, UV position map, colored texture map with segmentation information (blue for eye region, red for nose region, green for mouth region and purple for neck region), the final weight mask. (Color figure online)

Thus, we denote the predicted position map as $Pos(u, v)$ for u, v representing each pixel coordinate. Given the ground truth position map $\tilde{Pos}(u, v)$ and weight mask $W(u, v)$, our loss function is defined as:

$$Loss = \sum \|Pos(u, v) - \tilde{Pos}(u, v)\| \cdot W(u, v) \tag{1}$$

Specifically, We use following weight ratio in our experiments, subregion1 (68 facial landmarks): subregion2 (eye, nose, mouth): subregion3 (other face area): subregion4 (neck) = 16:4:3:0. The final weight mask is shown in Fig. 4.

3.3   Training Details

As described above, we choose **300W-LP** [67] to form our training sets, since it contains face images across different angles with the annotation of estimated 3DMM coefficients, from which the 3D point cloud could be easily generated. Specifically, we crop the images according the ground truth bounding box and rescale them to size 256×256. Then utilize their annotated 3DMM parameters to generate the corresponding 3D position, and render them into UV space to obtain the ground truth position map, the map size in our training is also 256×256, which means a precision of more than 45K point cloud to regress. Notice that, although our training data is generated from 3DMM, our network's output, the position map is not restricted to any face template or linear space of 3DMM.

We perturb the training set by randomly rotating and translating the target face in 2D image plane. To be specific, the rotation is from -45 to $45°$ angles, translation changes is random from 10% of input size, and scale is from 0.9 to 1.2. Like [28], we also augment our training data by scaling color channels with scale range from 0.6 to 1.4. In order to handle images with occlusions, we synthesize occlusions by adding noise texture into raw images, which is similar to the work of [50,63]. With all above augmentation operations, our training data covers all the difficult cases. We use the network described in Sect. 3 to train our model. For optimization, we use Adam optimizer with a learning rate begins at 0.0001 and decays half after each 5 epochs. The batch size is set as 16.

4   Experimental Results

In this part, we evaluate the performance of our proposed method on the tasks of 3D face alignment and 3D face reconstruction. We first introduce the test datasets used in our experiments in Sect. 4.1. Then in Sects. 4.2 and 4.3 we compare our results with other methods in both quantitative and qualitative way. We then compare our method's runtime with other methods in Sect. 4.4. In the end, the ablation study is conducted in Sect. 4.5 to evaluate the effect of weight mask in our method.

4.1   Test Dataset

To evaluate our performance on the task of dense alignment and 3D face reconstruction, multiple test datasets listed below are used in our experiments:

AFLW2000-3D is constructed by [67] to evaluate 3D face alignment on challenging unconstrained images. This database contains the first 2000 images from AFLW [35] and expands its annotations with fitted 3DMM parameters and 68 3D landmarks. We use this database to evaluate the performance of our method on both face reconstruction and face alignment tasks.

AFLW-LFPA is another extension of AFLW dataset constructed by [32]. By picking images from AFLW according to the poses, the authors construct this dataset which contains 1299 test images with a balanced distribution of yaw angle. Besides, each image is annotated with 13 additional landmarks as a expansion to only 21 visible landmarks in AFLW. This database is evaluated on the task of 3D face alignment. We use 34 visible landmarks as the ground truth to measure the accuracy of our results.

Florence is a 3D face dataset that contains 53 subjects with its ground truth 3D mesh acquired from a structured-light scanning system [2]. On experiments, each subject generates renderings with different poses as the same with [28]: a pitch of −15, 20 and 25° and spaced rotations between −80 and 80. We compare the performance of our method on face reconstruction against other very recent state-of-the-art methods VRN-Guided [28] and 3DDFA [67] on this dataset.

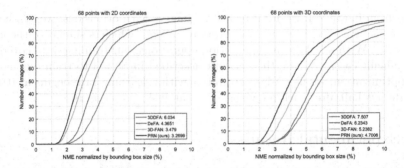

Fig. 5. Cumulative Errors Distribution (CED) curves on AFLW2000-3D. Evaluation is performed on 68 landmarks with both the 2D (left) and 3D (right) coordinates. Overall 2000 images from AFLW2000-3D dataset are used here. The mean NME% of each method is also showed in the legend.

4.2 3D Face Alignment

To evaluate the face alignment performance. We employ the Normalized Mean Error(NME) to be the evaluation metric, bounding box size is used as the normalization factor. Firstly, we evaluate our method on a sparse set of 68 facial landmarks, and compare our result with 3DDFA [67], DeFA [40] and 3D-FAN [9] on dataset AFLW2000-3D. As shown in Fig. 5, our result slightly outperforms state-of-the-art method 3D-FAN when calculating per distance with 2D coordinates. When considering the depth value, the performance discrepancy between our method and 3D-FAN increases. Notice that, the 3D-FAN needs another network to predict the z coordinate of landmarks, while the depth value can be obtained directly in our method.

To further investigate the performance of our method across poses and datasets, we also report the NME with small, medium and large yaw angles on AFLW2000-3D dataset and the mean NME on both AFLW2000-3D and AFLW-LPFA datasets. Table 1 shows the results, note that the numerical values are recorded from their published papers. Follow the work [67], we also randomly select 696 faces from AFLW2000 to balance the distribution. The result shows that our method is robust to changes of pose and datasets. Although all the state-of-the-art methods of 3D face alignment conduct evaluation on AFLW2000-3D dataset, the ground truth is still controversial [9,63] due to its annotation pipeline which is based on Landmarks Marching method [68]. Thus, we visualize some results in Fig. 6 that have NME larger than 6.5% and we find our results are more accurate than the ground truth in some cases. We also compare our dense alignment results against other methods including 3DDFA [67] and DeFA [40] on the only test dataset AFLW2000-3D. In order to compare different methods with the same set of points, we select the points from the largest common face region provided by all methods, and finally around 45K points were used for the evaluation. As shown in Fig. 7, our method outperforms the best methods with a large margin of more than **27%** on both 2D and 3D coordinates.

Table 1. Performance comparison on AFLW2000-3D (68 landmarks) and AFLW-LFPA (34 visible landmarks). The NME (%) for faces with different yaw angles are reported. The first best result in each category is highlighted in bold, the lower is the better.

| Method | AFLW2000-3D | | | | AFLW-LFPA |
	0 to 30	30 to 60	60 to 90	Mean	Mean
SDM [60]	3.67	4.94	9.67	6.12	-
3DDFA [67]	3.78	4.54	7.93	5.42	-
3DDFA + SDM [67]	3.43	4.24	7.17	4.94	-
PAWF [32]	-	-	-	-	4.72
Yu et al. [63]	3.62	6.06	9.56	-	-
3DSTN [4]	3.15	4.33	5.98	4.49	-
DeFA [40]	-	-	-	4.50	3.86
PRN (ours)	**2.75**	**3.51**	**4.61**	**3.62**	**2.93**

Fig. 6. Examples from AFLW2000-3D dataset show that our predictions are more accurate than ground truth in some cases. Green: predicted landmarks by our method. Red: ground truth from [67]. (Color figure online)

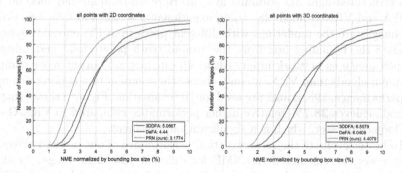

Fig. 7. CED curves on AFLW2000-3D. Evaluation is performed on all points with both the 2D (left) and 3D (right) coordinates. Overall 2000 images from AFLW2000-3D dataset are used here. The mean NME% is showed in the legend.

4.3   3D Face Reconstruction

In this part, we evaluate our method on 3D face reconstruction task and compare
with 3DDFA [67], DeFA [40] and VRN-Guided [28] on AFLW2000-3D and Florence datasets. We use the same set of points as in evaluating dense alignment
and changes the metric so as to keep consistency with other 3D face reconstruction evaluation methods. We first use Iterative Closest Points (ICP) algorithm to
find the corresponding nearest points between the network output and ground
truth point cloud, then calculate Mean Squared Error (MSE) normalized by
outer interocular distance of 3D coordinates.

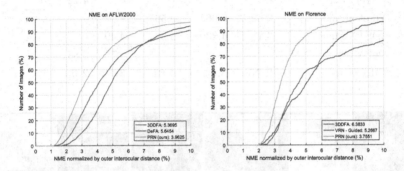

Fig. 8. 3D reconstruction performance (CED curves) on in-the-wild AFLW2000-3D
dataset and Florence dataset. The mean NME% of each method is showed in the legend.
On AFLW2000-3D, more than 45K points are used for evaluation. On Florence, about
19K points are used.

The result is shown in Fig. 8 our method greatly exceeds the performance
of other two state-of-the-art methods. Since AFLW2000-3D dataset is labeled
with results from 3DMM fitting, we further evaluate the performance of our
method on Florence dataset, where ground truth 3D point cloud is obtained
from structured-light 3D scanning system. Here we compare our method with
3DDFA and VRN-Guided [28], using experimental settings in [28]. The evaluation images are the renderings with different poses from Florence database, we
calculate the bounding box from the ground truth point cloud and using the
cropped image as network input. Although our method output more complete
face point clouds than VRN, we only choose the common face region to compare
the performance, 19K points are used for the evaluation. Figure 8 shows that our
method achieves **28.7%** relative higher performance compared to VRN-Guided
on Florence dataset, which is a significant improvement.

To better evaluate the reconstruction performance of our method across different poses, we calculated the NME for different yaw angle range. As shown
in Fig. 9, all the methods perform well in near frontal view, however, 3DDFA
and VRN-Guided fail to keep low error as pose becomes large, while our method
keeps relatively stable performance in all pose ranges. We also illustrate the qualitative comparison in Fig. 9, our restored point cloud covers a larger region than

in VRN-Guided, which ignores the lateral facial parts. Besides, due to the limitation on resolution of VRN, our method provides finer details of face, especially on the nose and mouth region.

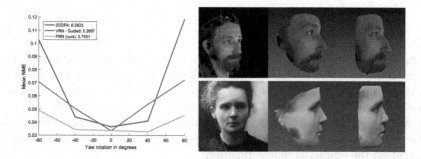

Fig. 9. Left: CED curves on Florence dataset with different yaw angles. Right: the qualitative comparison with VRN-Guided. The first column is the input images from Florence dataset and the Internet, the second column is the reconstructed face from our method, the third column is the results from VRN.

We also provide additional quantitative results on BU-3DFE [62] and qualitative results on 300VW [11] and Multi-PIE [23] datasets, please refer to supplementary material for full details.

4.4   Runtime

Surpassing the performance of all other state-of-the-art methods on 3D face alignment and reconstruction, our method is surprisingly more light-weighted and faster. Since our network uses basic encoder-decoder structure, our model size is only 160 MB compared to 1.5 GB in VRN [28]. We also compare the runtime, Table 2 shows the result. The results of 3DDFA and 3DSTN are directly recorded from their published papers and others are recorded by running their publicly available source codes. Notice that, We measure the run time of the process which is defined from inputing the cropped face image until recovering the 3D geometry (point cloud, mesh or voxel data) for 3D reconstruction methods or obtaining the 3D landmarks for alignment methods. The harware used for evaluation is an NVIDIA GeForce GTX 1080 GPU and an Intel(R) Xeon(R) CPU E5-2640 v4 @ 2.40 GHz. Specifically, DeFA needs 11.8 ms (GPU) to predict 3DMM parameters and another 23.6 ms (CPU) to generate mesh data from predicted parameters, 3DFAN needs 29.1 ms (GPU) to estimate 2D coordinates first and 25.6 ms (GPU) to obtain depth value, VRN-Guided detects 68 2D landmarks with 28.4 ms (GPU), then regress the voxel data with 40.6 ms (GPU), our method provides both 3D reconstruction and dense alignment result from cropped image in one pass in 9.8 ms (GPU).

Table 2. Run time in Milliseconds per Image

3DDFA [67]	DeFA [40]	3D-FAN [9]	3DSTN [4]	VRN-Guided [28]	PRN (ours)
75.7	35.4	54.7	19.0	69.0	9.8

4.5   Ablation Study

In this section, we conduct several experiments to evaluate the influence of our weight mask on training and provide both sparse and dense alignment CED on AFLW2000 to evaluate different settings. Specifically, we experimented with three different weight ratios: (1) weight ratio 1 = 1:1:1:1, (2) weight ratio 2 = 1:1:1:0, (3) weight ratio 3 = 16:4:3:0. We could see that weight ratio 1 corresponds to the situation when no weight mask is used, weight ratio 2 and 3 are slightly different on the emphasis in loss function.

The results are shown in Fig. 10. Network trained without using weight mask has worst performance compared with other two settings. By adding weights to specific regions such as 68 facial landmarks or central face region, weight ratio 3 shows considerable improvement on 68 points datasets over weight ratio 2.

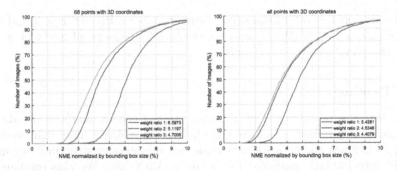

Fig. 10. The effect of weight mask evaluated on AFLW2000-3D dataset with 68 landmarks (left) and all points (right).

5   Conclusion

In this paper, we propose an end-to-end method, which well solves the problems of 3D face alignment and 3D face reconstruction simultaneously. By learning the position map, we directly regress the complete 3D structure along with semantic meaning from a single image. Quantitative and qualitative results demonstrate our method is robust to poses, illuminations and occlusions. Experiments on three test datasets show that our method achieves significant improvements over others. We further show that our method runs faster than other methods and is suitable for real time usage.

References

1. Asthana, A., Zafeiriou, S., Cheng, S., Pantic, M.: Robust discriminative response map fitting with constrained local models. In: 2013 IEEE Conference on Computer Vision and Pattern Recognition (CVPR), pp. 3444–3451. IEEE (2013)
2. Bagdanov, A.D., Del Bimbo, A., Masi, I.: The florence 2D/3D hybrid face dataset. In: Proceedings of the 2011 Joint ACM Workshop on Human Gesture and Behavior Understanding, pp. 79–80. ACM (2011)
3. Bas, A., Huber, P., Smith, W.A.P., Awais, M., Kittler, J.: 3D morphable models as spatial transformer networks. In: ICCV 2017 Workshop on Geometry Meets Deep Learning (2017)
4. Bhagavatula, C., Zhu, C., Luu, K., Savvides, M.: Faster than real-time facial alignment: a 3D spatial transformer network approach in unconstrained poses. In: The IEEE International Conference on Computer Vision (ICCV), vol. 2, p. 7 (2017)
5. de Bittencourt Zavan, F.H., Nascimento, A.C.P., e Silva, L.P., Bellon, O.R.P., Silva, L.: 3D face alignment in the wild: a landmark-free, nose-based approach. In: Hua, G., Jégou, H. (eds.) ECCV 2016. LNCS, vol. 9914, pp. 581–589. Springer, Cham (2016). https://doi.org/10.1007/978-3-319-48881-3_40
6. Blanz, V., Vetter, T.: A morphable model for the synthesis of 3D faces. In: International Conference on Computer Graphics and Interactive Techniques, pp. 187–194 (1999)
7. Booth, J., Zafeiriou, S.: Optimal UV spaces for facial morphable model construction. In: 2014 IEEE International Conference on Image Processing (ICIP), pp. 4672–4676. IEEE (2014)
8. Bulat, A., Tzimiropoulos, G.: Two-stage convolutional part heatmap regression for the 1st 3D face alignment in the wild (3DFAW) challenge. In: Hua, G., Jégou, H. (eds.) ECCV 2016. LNCS, vol. 9914, pp. 616–624. Springer, Cham (2016). https://doi.org/10.1007/978-3-319-48881-3_43
9. Bulat, A., Tzimiropoulos, G.: How far are we from solving the 2D and 3D face alignment problem? (and a dataset of 230,000 3D facial landmarks) (2017)
10. Cao, C., Hou, Q., Zhou, K.: Displaced dynamic expression regression for real-time facial tracking and animation. ACM (2014)
11. Chrysos, G.G., Antonakos, E., Zafeiriou, S., Snape, P.: Offline deformable face tracking in arbitrary videos. In: Proceedings of the IEEE International Conference on Computer Vision Workshops, pp. 1–9 (2015)
12. Crispell, D., Bazik, M.: Pix2face: direct 3D face model estimation (2017)
13. Deng, J., Cheng, S., Xue, N., Zhou, Y., Zafeiriou, S.: UV-GAN: adversarial facial uv map completion for pose-invariant face recognition. arXiv preprint arXiv:1712.04695 (2017)
14. Dollár, P., Welinder, P., Perona, P.: Cascaded pose regression. In: 2010 IEEE Conference on Computer Vision and Pattern Recognition (CVPR), pp. 1078–1085. IEEE (2010)
15. Dou, P., Shah, S.K., Kakadiaris, I.A.: End-to-end 3D face reconstruction with deep neural networks (2017)
16. Fan, H., Su, H., Guibas, L.: A point set generation network for 3D object reconstruction from a single image, pp. 2463–2471 (2016)
17. Floater, M.S.: Parametrization and smooth approximation of surface triangulations. Comput. Aided Geom. Des. **14**(3), 231–250 (1997)
18. Gou, C., Wu, Y., Wang, F.-Y., Ji, Q.: Shape augmented regression for 3D face alignment. In: Hua, G., Jégou, H. (eds.) ECCV 2016. LNCS, vol. 9914, pp. 604–615. Springer, Cham (2016). https://doi.org/10.1007/978-3-319-48881-3_42

19. Grewe, C.M., Zachow, S.: Fully automated and highly accurate dense correspondence for facial surfaces. In: Hua, G., Jégou, H. (eds.) ECCV 2016. LNCS, vol. 9914, pp. 552–568. Springer, Cham (2016). https://doi.org/10.1007/978-3-319-48881-3_38

20. Gu, L., Kanade, T.: 3D alignment of face in a single image. In: 2006 IEEE Computer Society Conference on Computer Vision and Pattern Recognition, vol. 1, pp. 1305–1312. IEEE (2006)

21. Gu, X., Gortler, S.J., Hoppe, H.: Geometry images. ACM Trans. Graph. (TOG) **21**(3), 355–361 (2002)

22. Güler, R.A., Trigeorgis, G., Antonakos, E., Snape, P., Zafeiriou, S., Kokkinos, I.: DenseReg: fully convolutional dense shape regression in-the-wild. In: Proceedings of the CVPR, vol. 2 (2017)

23. Hartley, R., Zisserman, A.: Multiple view geometry in computer vision. Kybernetes **30**(9/10), 1865–1872 (2003)

24. Hassner, T.: Viewing real-world faces in 3D. In: IEEE International Conference on Computer Vision, pp. 3607–3614 (2013)

25. He, K., Zhang, X., Ren, S., Sun, J.: Deep residual learning for image recognition. In: Computer Vision and Pattern Recognition, pp. 770–778 (2016)

26. Huber, P., Feng, Z.H., Christmas, W., Kittler, J., Ratsch, M.: Fitting 3D morphable face models using local features. In: IEEE International Conference on Image Processing, pp. 1195–1199 (2015)

27. Huber, P., et al.: A multiresolution 3D morphable face model and fitting framework, pp. 79–86 (2016)

28. Jackson, A.S., Bulat, A., Argyriou, V., Tzimiropoulos, G.: Large pose 3D face reconstruction from a single image via direct volumetric CNN regression. In: 2017 IEEE International Conference on Computer Vision (ICCV), pp. 1031–1039. IEEE (2017)

29. Jeni, L.A., Cohn, J.F., Kanade, T.: Dense 3D face alignment from 2D videos in real-time. In: 2015 11th IEEE International Conference and Workshops on Automatic Face and Gesture Recognition (FG), vol. 1, pp. 1–8. IEEE (2015)

30. Jeni, L.A., Tulyakov, S., Yin, L., Sebe, N., Cohn, J.F.: The first 3D face alignment in the wild (3DFAW) challenge. In: Hua, G., Jégou, H. (eds.) ECCV 2016. LNCS, vol. 9914, pp. 511–520. Springer, Cham (2016). https://doi.org/10.1007/978-3-319-48881-3_35

31. Jourabloo, A., Liu, X.: Pose-invariant 3D face alignment. In: Proceedings of the IEEE International Conference on Computer Vision, pp. 3694–3702 (2015)

32. Jourabloo, A., Liu, X.: Large-pose face alignment via CNN-based dense 3D model fitting. In: Computer Vision and Pattern Recognition (2016)

33. Kemelmacher-Shlizerman, I., Basri, R.: 3D face reconstruction from a single image using a single reference face shape. IEEE Trans. Pattern Anal. Mach. Intell. **33**(2), 394 (2011)

34. Kim, J., Liu, C., Sha, F., Grauman, K.: Deformable spatial pyramid matching for fast dense correspondences. In: Computer Vision and Pattern Recognition, pp. 2307–2314 (2013)

35. Koestinger, M., Wohlhart, P., Roth, P.M., Bischof, H.: Annotated facial landmarks in the wild: a large-scale, real-world database for facial landmark localization. In: 2011 IEEE International Conference on Computer Vision Workshops (ICCV Workshops), pp. 2144–2151. IEEE (2011)

36. Laine, S., Karras, T., Aila, T., Herva, A., Lehtinen, J.: Facial performance capture with deep neural networks. arXiv preprint arXiv:1609.06536 (2016)

37. Lee, Y.J., Lee, S.J., Kang, R.P., Jo, J., Kim, J.: Single view-based 3D face reconstruction robust to self-occlusion. EURASIP J. Adv. Signal Process. **2012**(1), 1–20 (2012)

38. Liang, Z., Ding, S., Lin, L.: Unconstrained facial landmark localization with backbone-branches fully-convolutional networks. arXiv preprint arXiv:1507.03409 (2015)

39. Liu, F., Zeng, D., Zhao, Q., Liu, X.: Joint face alignment and 3D face reconstruction. In: Leibe, B., Matas, J., Sebe, N., Welling, M. (eds.) ECCV 2016. LNCS, vol. 9909, pp. 545–560. Springer, Cham (2016). https://doi.org/10.1007/978-3-319-46454-1_33

40. Liu, Y., Jourabloo, A., Ren, W., Liu, X.: Dense face alignment. arXiv preprint arXiv:1709.01442 (2017)

41. Maninchedda, F., Häne, C., Oswald, M.R., Pollefeys, M.: Face reconstruction on mobile devices using a height map shape model and fast regularization. In: 2016 Fourth International Conference on 3D Vision (3DV), pp. 489–498. IEEE (2016)

42. Maninchedda, F., Oswald, M.R., Pollefeys, M.: Fast 3D reconstruction of faces with glasses. In: 2017 IEEE Conference on Computer Vision and Pattern Recognition (CVPR), pp. 4608–4617. IEEE (2017)

43. Matthews, I., Baker, S.: Active appearance models revisited. Int. J. Comput. Vis. **60**(2), 135–164 (2004)

44. McDonagh, J., Tzimiropoulos, G.: Joint face detection and alignment with a deformable hough transform model. In: Hua, G., Jégou, H. (eds.) ECCV 2016. LNCS, vol. 9914, pp. 569–580. Springer, Cham (2016). https://doi.org/10.1007/978-3-319-48881-3_39

45. Moschoglou, S., Ververas, E., Panagakis, Y., Nicolaou, M., Zafeiriou, S.: Multi-attribute robust component analysis for facial UV maps. arXiv preprint arXiv:1712.05799 (2017)

46. Peng, X., Feris, R.S., Wang, X., Metaxas, D.N.: A recurrent encoder-decoder network for sequential face alignment. In: Leibe, B., Matas, J., Sebe, N., Welling, M. (eds.) ECCV 2016. LNCS, vol. 9905, pp. 38–56. Springer, Cham (2016). https://doi.org/10.1007/978-3-319-46448-0_3

47. Richardson, E., Sela, M., Kimmel, R.: 3D face reconstruction by learning from synthetic data. In: Fourth International Conference on 3D Vision, pp. 460–469 (2016)

48. Richardson, E., Sela, M., Or-El, R., Kimmel, R.: Learning detailed face reconstruction from a single image (2016)

49. Romdhani, S., Vetter, T.: Estimating 3D shape and texture using pixel intensity, edges, specular highlights, texture constraints and a prior. In: IEEE Computer Society Conference on Computer Vision and Pattern Recognition, pp. 986–993 (2005)

50. Saito, S., Li, T., Li, H.: Real-time facial segmentation and performance capture from RGB input. In: Leibe, B., Matas, J., Sebe, N., Welling, M. (eds.) ECCV 2016. LNCS, vol. 9912, pp. 244–261. Springer, Cham (2016). https://doi.org/10.1007/978-3-319-46484-8_15

51. Sánta, Z., Kato, Z.: 3D face alignment without correspondences. In: Hua, G., Jégou, H. (eds.) ECCV 2016. LNCS, vol. 9914, pp. 521–535. Springer, Cham (2016). https://doi.org/10.1007/978-3-319-48881-3_36

52. Saragih, J., Goecke, R.: A nonlinear discriminative approach to AAM fitting. In: IEEE 11th International Conference on Computer Vision, ICCV 2007, pp. 1–8. IEEE (2007)

53. Sela, M., Richardson, E., Kimmel, R.: Unrestricted facial geometry reconstruction using image-to-image translation (2017)
54. Sinha, A., Unmesh, A., Huang, Q., Ramani, K.: SurfNet: generating 3D shape surfaces using deep residual networks. In: IEEE CVPR, vol. 1 (2017)
55. Tewari, A., et al.: MoFA: model-based deep convolutional face autoencoder for unsupervised monocular reconstruction (2017)
56. Thies, J., Zollhöfer, M., Stamminger, M., Theobalt, C., Nießner, M.: Face2Face: real-time face capture and reenactment of RGB videos. In: Computer Vision and Pattern Recognition, p. 5 (2016)
57. Tran, A.T., Hassner, T., Masi, I., Medioni, G.: Regressing robust and discriminative 3D morphable models with a very deep neural network (2016)
58. Tzimiropoulos, G., Pantic, M.: Optimization problems for fast AAM fitting in-the-wild. In: 2013 IEEE International Conference on Computer Vision (ICCV), pp. 593–600. IEEE (2013)
59. Wagner, A., Wright, J., Ganesh, A., Zhou, Z., Mobahi, H., Ma, Y.: Toward a practical face recognition system: robust alignment and illumination by sparse representation. IEEE Trans. Pattern Anal. Mach. Intell. **34**(2), 372–386 (2012)
60. Xiong, X., Torre, F.D.L.: Global supervised descent method. In: IEEE Conference on Computer Vision and Pattern Recognition, pp. 2664–2673 (2015)
61. Xue, N., Deng, J., Cheng, S., Panagakis, Y., Zafeiriou, S.: Side information for face completion: a robust PCA approach. arXiv preprint arXiv:1801.07580 (2018)
62. Yin, L., Wei, X., Sun, Y., Wang, J., Rosato, M.J.: A 3D facial expression database for facial behavior research. In: 7th international conference on Automatic face and gesture recognition, FGR 2006, pp. 211–216. IEEE (2006)
63. Yu, R., Saito, S., Li, H., Ceylan, D., Li, H.: Learning dense facial correspondences in unconstrained images (2017)
64. Zhang, Z., Luo, P., Loy, C.C., Tang, X.: Facial landmark detection by deep multi-task learning. In: Fleet, D., Pajdla, T., Schiele, B., Tuytelaars, T. (eds.) ECCV 2014. LNCS, vol. 8694, pp. 94–108. Springer, Cham (2014). https://doi.org/10.1007/978-3-319-10599-4_7
65. Zhao, R., Wang, Y., Benitez-Quiroz, C.F., Liu, Y., Martinez, A.M.: Fast and precise face alignment and 3D shape reconstruction from a single 2D image. In: Hua, G., Jégou, H. (eds.) ECCV 2016. LNCS, vol. 9914, pp. 590–603. Springer, Cham (2016). https://doi.org/10.1007/978-3-319-48881-3_41
66. Zhou, E., Fan, H., Cao, Z., Jiang, Y., Yin, Q.: Extensive facial landmark localization with coarse-to-fine convolutional network cascade. In: 2013 IEEE International Conference on Computer Vision Workshops (ICCVW), pp. 386–391. IEEE (2013)
67. Zhu, X., Lei, Z., Liu, X., Shi, H., Li, S.Z.: Face alignment across large poses: a 3D solution. In: Computer Vision and Pattern Recognition, pp. 146–155 (2016)
68. Zhu, X., Lei, Z., Yan, J., Yi, D., Li, S.Z.: High-fidelity pose and expression normalization for face recognition in the wild, pp. 787–796 (2015)

Efficient Relative Attribute Learning Using Graph Neural Networks

Zihang Meng[1(✉)], Nagesh Adluru[1], Hyunwoo J. Kim[1], Glenn Fung[2], and Vikas Singh[1]

[1] University of Wisconsin – Madison, Madison, USA
{zihangm,hwkim}@cs.wisc.edu,adluru@wisc.edu,vsingh@biostat.wisc.edu
[2] American Family Insurance, Madison, USA
gfung@amfam.com

Abstract. A sizable body of work on relative attributes provides evidence that relating pairs of images along a continuum of strength pertaining to a visual attribute yields improvements in a variety of vision tasks. In this paper, we show how emerging ideas in graph neural networks can yield a solution to various problems that broadly fall under relative attribute learning. Our main idea is the observation that relative attribute learning naturally benefits from exploiting the graph of dependencies among the different relative attributes of images, especially when only partial ordering is provided at training time. We use message passing to perform end to end learning of the image representations, their relationships as well as the interplay between different attributes. Our experiments show that this simple framework is effective in achieving competitive accuracy with specialized methods for both relative attribute learning and binary attribute prediction, while relaxing the requirements on the training data and/or the number of parameters, or both.

Keywords: Relative attribute learning · Graph neural networks
Multi-task learning · Message passing

1 Introduction

Visual attributes [6] correspond to mid-level semantic and even non-semantic concepts or properties of the image or objects contained in the image that are interpretable by humans. For instance, an image can be "natural", "smiling" or "furry" depending on the properties of the key entities contained in it. The ability to associate such attributes with images has enabled systems to perform better in traditional categorization tasks, and even go beyond basic level naming [18]. The insight in this line of work is to first select features that can predict attributes for the object class of interest – the subsequent classifier must then leverage only

---

H. J. Kim—Work performed during studies at UW-Madison in 2017, before joining Amazon.

V. Ferrari et al. (Eds.): ECCV 2018, LNCS 11218, pp. 575–590, 2018.
https://doi.org/10.1007/978-3-030-01264-9_34

those "relevant" features since material properties or shape may be differentially important for different categories. The concept of "relative attributes" takes this idea further [18] by arguing that the strength of an attribute in an image is best judged in the context of its strength with respect to all other images in the training data rather than as a binary concept. For example, while it is difficult to characterize how "man-made" an image is, one could setup a comparison where humans compare the images in terms of *this* attribute. This strategy of describing images in relative terms works well in challenging cases [13] – for instance, calculating how "open" an image is versus another.

Since the early works on relative attributes [20,21,23], several papers have proposed more task-specific models for ranking based on specialized features. But given the success of convolutional neural networks (CNN) architectures, most recent proposals utilize CNNs for feature learning in the context of learning the overall ranking. For instance, given a set of annotated image-pairs with respect to one/more attributes, the network learns weights that are maximally consistent with the attribute-specific ranking of the images. Related ideas have also explored designing image-part specific detectors, that are aligned to an attribute. For instance, what is the spatial support for an attribute such as "smiling". Clearly, this will involve localizing the visual concept to a part of the image, say the mouth or lips region. In [20], the authors transitively connect the visual chains across the attribute continuum and make the case that feature extraction and ranking should not be performed separately.

The starting point of our work is the observation that the space of attributes which induce a ranking over the images share a great deal of correlational structure. For instance, the attribute "furry" may be associated with the attribute "four-legged" and the attribute "congested" may have some information to provide to the attribute "man-made". This induces a natural graph of attributes and images, where the input data provides either pair-wise relationships between images for one/more attributes or a partial (or full) ranking of the images for the attribute. We do not assume that the annotation is exhaustive – many edges (or relationships) between the images may, in fact, be unavailable. Extending recent work on graph neural networks (GNNs) which extends the notion of convolution and other basic deep learning operations to non-Euclidean grids [3,9,11,16,19], we show how these ideas yield a natural model for learning on this graph involving image↔attribute and image↔image edges. Not only are the image features (relevant for each attribute) extracted automatically but we also concurrently learn the similarity function that is most consistent with the given pair-wise annotations as well as the latent relationships between the attributes (similar to multi-task learning). This machinery is simple, yet performs competitively with more specialized proposals on several different problems.

Our **contributions** are: (1) we formulate and solve relative attribute learning via a message passing scheme on a graph, where the convolutional layers, ranking as well as imputation of unseen relationships is performed concurrently. (2) our framework yields results similar to the best reported for each task with minimal change, often providing sizable reduction in the number of parameters to be estimated or with far less stringent requirements on the training data annotations. We note that GNNs were independently used in a classification task very recently in a paper made available on arXiv [8].

2   Related Work

Visual Attributes. Visual attributes are semantic properties in images which can be understood by humans and are shared among all images of similar categories (e.g. all images of human faces share the attribute "smiling", whose strength can vary from weak to strong as we will show with examples shortly. Most existing work in visual attributes focuses on binary attribute prediction (BAP) where each attribute is predicted from a given image and cast as a binary classification problem. "Relative attributes" were proposed in [18] and have been explored in a number of settings [20,21,23]. Several current techniques use deep neural networks to learn relative attributes (e.g. [21]), and also borrow ideas from attention mechanism research (e.g. [20]) to help the networks focus only on the most informative areas in the images. Most of these works deal with a pair of images at a time. Our work shows that dealing with groups of images on a fully connected graph instead of just pairwise comparisons improves performance.

Multi-task Learning. Multi-task learning is intended to achieve knowledge sharing by learning several correlated tasks at the same time. This technique has recently been used in binary attribute prediction. Learning several correlated attributes together can improve performance, and this has been demonstrated by some recent works [1,12,22]. Abdulnabi et al. [1] propose a multi-task CNN framework which improves accuracy compared with learning one attribute at a time. Wang et al. [22] designed a simpler deep multi-task network for prediction of face attributes. In contrast to most strategies related to multi-task learning, our multi-task formulation learns attributes simultaneously and is shown to benefit relative attribute learning.

Graph Neural Networks (GNN). Graph neural networks were proposed by [11,19], where the authors describe GNN as a parameterized message passing scheme which can be trained. Later, Li et al. [16] proposed using gated recurrent units (GRUs) within GNNs, which much improves the representation capacity of the network and makes it suitable for graph structured data. Gilmer et al. [9] generalized the GNN using message passing neural network and demonstrated state-of-the-art results on molecular prediction benchmarks. More recently, concurrent to and independent of our work, [8] applied GNNs for classification and achieved good results on several different datasets.

3   Approach

Our approach is based on the observation that in a relative attribute learning task, different images are correlated and the attributes may or may not be correlated. The learning procedure can benefit from exploring the similarity among multiple images on a graph, where each node represents an image and the edges are formed based on the relationship between the to-be-learned representations of the nodes. Furthermore, such a graphical structure can benefit multi-task learning where we can add different *types* of nodes to the graph for representing different attributes that are being learned. In this way, we explicitly learn the properties of certain attributes, the interplay between the attributes when necessary, the representations of the images and their relationships on the graph in a way that best informs the task at hand.

We first explain how the input images are mapped into the graph representation, and give the details of our network architecture for relative attribute learning in the context of *one attribute*. Then, we show how the construction can be used to perform multi-task attribute learning with minimal modifications. Finally, we also show how our model can be used for a binary attribute prediction (BAP) task efficiently. The overview of our framework is shown in Fig. 1.

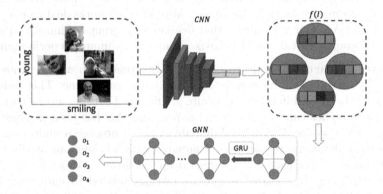

Fig. 1. Overview of our framework for RAL and BAP tasks. Since many natural attributes of images are interrelated, discovering their common latent representations would be beneficial to the attribute learning tasks. This can be efficiently achieved by mapping these images to a graphical structure. Every image has a corresponding node on the graph and a corresponding output node. The initial features $f(\cdot)$ for the nodes are generated using a CNN on the images and the edge features and following updates are performed using GNNs (details in Fig. 2). The weights in the entire framework including those in the CNN and GNN are trained end-to-end.

3.1 Network Architecture

Let $\mathcal{I} = \{I_1, I_2, \cdots, I_n\}$ be the set of input images, and for a certain attribute t (e.g., smile), we assume that a set of pairwise relationship labels $\mathcal{P}_l^t = \{\phi(I_i, I_j)\}_{i,j=1;i\neq j}^n$, where $\phi(I_i, I_j)$ indicates the relative strength of the attribute t between the two images I_i and I_j. This relationship may be logical (e.g.,"stronger than" or "weaker than"). With this data, a generalized GNN is trained where both the node features (representations of the images) and edge weights are learned. The core architecture of our GNN is shown in Fig. 2.

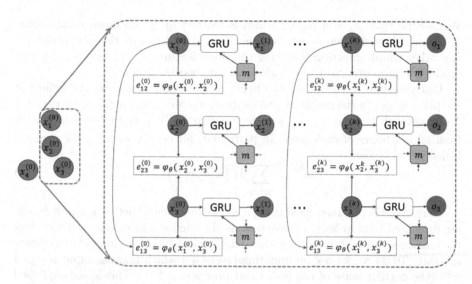

Fig. 2. The architectural details of our GNN which remains the same for both RAL and BAP. The edges on the graph are learned from adjacent nodes using a parameterized function (φ_ϑ, see (3)), which is shared among all edges. The "m" in this figure refers to the message for a node passed from its connected nodes and edges, which is defined in (4). Then, a GRU cell takes as input a node and its corresponding message, and outputs the updated node. The parameters in GRU are also shared across all nodes.

Assume that we operate on groups (or mini-batches) of a certain size (which is allowed to vary) sampled with or without replacement from the underlying training dataset. The relationships among all the images in each mini-batch (S) in the training set are represented using a fully-connected graph $G_S = (V, E)$, where each node v_i in V corresponds to an image I_i in the mini-batch S. Each time, the network takes in a group of images and passes them through a convolutional neural network. This may also be thought of as a set of $|S|$ convolutional networks that share weights. The representations derived from this network yield the initial representations of the node features as

$$x_i^{(0)} = f(I_i),\tag{1}$$

where $f(\cdot)$ refers to a CNN which operates on the images. Here, I_i is the input image and $x_i^{(0)}$ is the initial node feature for the image at time $k = 0$. Next, the network learns edge features as,

$$e_{i,j}^{(k)} = \varphi_\vartheta\left(x_i^{(k)}, x_j^{(k)}\right),\tag{2}$$

where φ is a symmetric function parameterized with a single layer Neural Network:

$$\varphi_\vartheta(x_i^{(k)}, x_j^{(k)}) = \mathfrak{N}_\vartheta^{\text{edges}}\left(||x_i^{(k)} - x_j^{(k)}||_1\right). \tag{3}$$

We assume that φ_ϑ is a metric which is learned by a non-linear combination of the absolute difference between the learned features of the two nodes (or any other simple function involving the node features). This ensures that the symmetric property $\varphi_\vartheta(a, b) = \varphi_\vartheta(b, a)$ is satisfied by design.

Our goal now is to update the belief at each node based on the beliefs at the other nodes in the graph as well as its own state at the previous time point. To accomplish this, we use a message function $M(\cdot)$ to aggregate information from all neighbors of each node. In particular, for each node $x_i^{(k)}$, the message is defined as below,

$$m_i^{(k)} = \sum_{j, j \neq i} M\left(x_j^{(k)}, e_{i,j}^{(k)}\right). \tag{4}$$

Here, $M(\cdot)$ is parameterized using a single layer neural network whose details are presented later in Sect. 3.2. We now need to define a mechanism that utilizes the messages received from the node's neighbors and its previous state to update its state. To do so, we use an updating layer $G(\cdot)$ which takes as input a signal $x^{(k)}$ (the current state of the node) and produces $x^{(k+1)}$. This is accomplished using a Gated Recurrent Unit (GRU) as the updating function.

$$x_i^{(k+1)} = G\left(x_i^{(k)}, m_i^{(k)}\right). \tag{5}$$

With this setup in hand, we simply use a readout function $o_i = R(x_i)$ to get the output from each node and finally define our loss function based on these outputs from all relevant nodes on the graph as

$$\text{Loss} = \mathcal{R}\left(\{o_i\}_{i=1}^n\right), \tag{6}$$

where n is the number of graph nodes. Note that $\mathcal{R}(\cdot)$ can also be parameterized with a simple (or more complicated) neural network depending on the needs of the application. The specific form of $\mathcal{R}(\cdot)$ depends on the concrete task, which will be specified in the following Sects. 3.2 and 3.3.

3.2   Learning Relative Attributes, One at a Time

The Relative Attribute Learning (RAL) task seeks to learn a network that, given input images, outputs pairwise labels according to the relative strength of certain attributes between each pair of images. In this section, we consider training a network for one attribute at a time.

Recall that our network is designed to better explore the correlated information among different images. So unlike other approaches in RAL [20,21] which take two images at a time as an input, we sample a group of images from the training set as input at every draw. The size of the group need not be fixed and can vary for learning different attributes in a single dataset or different datasets, because our network has the benefit of weight sharing on the graphical structure of the samples. We use the five convolutional layers and the first two fully-connected layers in `AlexNet` [15] (`conv1` through `fc7`) although other architectures can be substituted in. The dimension of the output feature vector of the node is fixed to be 4096.

Messages. We impose a fully-connected graphical structure on the images in each group. After mapping these images on the graph, we perform message passing, which is effective in information propagation among the nodes. We adopt the strategy to *learn* edge features from the current node hidden representation formulated by Gilmer et al. [9], as suggested in (2). The parameters of the edge learning function φ_ϑ are shared among all nodes on the graph. Then for every node $x_i^{(k)}$ on the graph, a message signal will be extracted from all the in-coming nodes through the edges, see (4). Here, we specify the message function $M(\cdot)$ as,

$$M(x_j^{(k)}, e_{i,j}^{(k)}) = \mathrm{ReLU}\left(W\left(x_j^{(k)}\|e_{i,j}^{(k)}\right) + b\right), \tag{7}$$

where $\|$ denotes the concatenation operator of two vectors, W and b are the weight matrix and the bias respectively, and $\mathrm{ReLU}(\cdot)$ is the rectified linear unit (ReLU) function. We would also like to note that the parameters (W and b) of the message function $M(\cdot)$ are also shared by all nodes and edges in our graph, thus providing an explicit control on the number of parameters.

Updating. Let us now discuss the updating function for nodes. At each iteration, each GRU takes the previous state of the node and an incoming message as input, and produces a new hidden state as the output (see Fig. 2). Let $x_i^{(k-1)}$ be the node's hidden representation at the previous time step, $m_i^{(k)}$ be the message received via (4), and $x_i^{(k)}$ be the updated node. With these notations, the basic operations of GRU are simply given as,

$$z_i^k = \sigma\left(W^z m_i^{(k)} + U^z x_i^{(k-1)}\right),$$
$$r_i^k = \sigma\left(W^r m_i^{(k)} + U^r x_i^{(k-1)}\right),$$
$$\tilde{x}_i^{(k)} = \tanh\left(W m_i^{(k)} + U\left(r_i^k \odot x_i^{(k-1)}\right)\right),$$
$$x_i^{(k)} = (1 - z_i^k) \odot x_i^{(k-1)} + z_i^k \odot \tilde{x}_i^{(k)}, \tag{8}$$

where z and r are the intermediate variables in the GRU cells, $\sigma(x) = 1/(1+e^{-x})$ is the sigmoid function and $\odot$ is element-wise multiplication.

Each node in our graph maintains its internal state in the corresponding GRU, and all nodes share the same weights of the GRU, which makes our model efficient while can also seamlessly deal with differently sized groups as input. In this work, we use one time step of GRU updating. During testing time, any number of images are allowed, and the network will output a pairwise label for every two images based on the obtained value of output nodes on the graph.

After constructing our graph using (1)–(6), the loss defined on the output of graph takes the form

$$\text{RALLoss} = \sum_{i,j,i\neq j} -\mathcal{L}\log(P_{ij}) - (1-\mathcal{L})\log(1-P_{ij}), \text{where} \qquad (9)$$

$$\mathcal{L} = \begin{cases} 1 & \text{if } I_i \succ I_j, \\ 0 & \text{if } I_i \prec I_j, \\ 0.5 & \text{otherwise,} \end{cases}$$

and $P_{i,j} = o_i - o_j$ (outputs of nodes i and j). This formulation has a nice property that it is robust to noise as described in [4], and symmetric by construction so that we can easily utilize training data where some pairs of images appear with "equal" label for one/more attributes.

3.3   Learning Relative Attributes, All at Once

In this section, we show that our graphical structure can be efficiently applied to learn multiple relative attributes all at the same time i.e., perform multi-task attribute learning. We consider two aspects of multi-task learning, (1) the performance of RAL can be improved by utilizing several attributes which have common latent representations. Although this has been demonstrated in binary attribute prediction (BAP) setting, we present experimental results showing that RAL can benefit from multi-task learning. (2) The second aspect is the efficiency of the construction. While multi-task learning can improve the performance when attributes are correlated, in the previous methods [1,22], the number of parameters of the network grows *much faster* as a function of the number of attributes learned together, which increases the cost of training a multi-task network. As an example, if the number of parameters trained in RAL one at a time is $O(K^2)$ then our version only increases the number to $O(K^2 + nK)$, where n is the number of different relative attributes learned simultaneously. This is much smaller than $O(nK^2)$ which may be needed within other multi-task approaches [1,22].

We note that a näive way to adapt our network (Fig. 2) to the multi-task setting proceeds as follows. We simply change the dimension of the output o_i from 1 to m where m is the number of attributes. But the only change this induces is in the size of the weight matrix in the readout function. We find that in this case, the graphical structure may slightly lose its expressive capacity. To address this issue, unlike Sect. 3.2, which treats all nodes in the graph in the same way, here, we define two different *types* of nodes x_i, $i = 1, 2, \cdots, n$, and r_i, $i = n+1, n+2, \cdots, n+m$, where n is the number of input images in each group (to be consistent, we choose $n = 5$ throughout our experiments) and m equals the number of attributes the network is learning at the same time. Here, x_i has the same meaning as in Sect. 3.2, which corresponds to one image and each r_j corresponds to a certain attribute. It is important to note that while the representation at x_i is learned by the convolutional network, the attribute node r_j is randomly initialized at the beginning of the training phase and keeps getting updated in a global manner, similar to the other parameters in the GNN.

This scheme allows us to explicitly learn a hidden representation for each attribute in a way that the latent variables of the graphical model are influencing all attribute nodes—this is similar to multi-task learning where we expect that learning related tasks can benefit each other when carried out concurrently. The feature extraction process using the convolutional network and the GNN procedure remain identical as in Sect. 4.1. The only change needed is to redefine how we use the readout function $R(\cdot)$ to get the output. Here, $o_{i,j} = R(\|x_i - r_j\|_1)$, where for $o_{i,j}$, i gives the index of nodes for the images (from 1 to n) and j gives the index of different attributes (from 1 to m). The loss function is then defined as the sum of the loss for each single attribute (see (9)) as,

$$\text{RALLoss}_{\text{multi}} = \sum_{i=1}^{m} \text{RALLoss}_i. \tag{10}$$

3.4 Binary Attribute Prediction

In this section, we present details of how our graphical model can also be used to predict binary attributes with comparable accuracy as the multi-task CNN model [1], but using much fewer number of parameters.

Binary attribute prediction (BAP) task seeks to predict whether an image has a certain attribute (e.g. whether a person is wearing a necktie), which can be thought of as a binary classification task. As suggested in papers for multi-task learning [1,22], simultaneously learning several attributes which are correlated can improve the performance of BAP. In this setting, the labels no longer provide pairwise information. So, it is not simple to easily extend other RAL methods and adapt them for BAP. For example, the construction using Siamese network [20] cannot be easily modified for BAP since the subnetworks are no longer linked – this is because it is the pairwise annotations that link the networks. But our network can still benefit from a fully-connected graph structure on the training samples because despite the unavailability of pairwise annotations, the images themselves are still related. So, we can use the *same* basic architecture. The framework before loss layer remains the same as the network in Sect. 3.3. The loss function for BAP is simply defined as

$$\text{BAPLoss}_i = -\mathcal{L}\log(P_i) - (1 - \mathcal{L})\log(1 - P_i), \tag{11}$$

where $\mathcal{L}$ is the binary label of image I_i, and $P_i = o_i$. The total loss is defined as,

$$\text{BAPLoss}_{\text{multi}} = \sum_{i=1}^{m} \text{BAPLoss}_i. \tag{12}$$

4 Experimental Results

In this section, we analyze the performance of our model on several different settings described in Sect. 3. First, we present some key **implementation details**.

Our network takes in a group of images and outputs the pairwise relationships for this group (in a relative attribute task) or a binary label for each image (in a attribute prediction task). We split the train/test set randomly. Then, we randomly split the train/test set into groups (we choose 5 images per group, but the number can vary) and use this as the input to our network. We report the pairwise accuracy measured on the groups of images. In a preprocessing step, we subtract the mean of training set and crop images to size 227×227.

For training, we initialize the `conv1` to `fc7` layers using `AlexNet` pre-trained on the ILSVRC 2012 [15] dataset and randomly initialize other parts using the Xavier initializer [10]. We use mini-batches of size 10 and Adam optimizer [14] with $\beta_1 = 0.9$, $\beta_2 = 0.999$. The learning rate of relative attribute learning task is 0.0001, and for attribute prediction task, we set the learning rate to 0.00001.

4.1 Relative Attribute Learning, One at a Time

In this experiment, we evaluate the network described in Sect. 3.2. The goal is to compare pairs or sets of images according to the strength of a given attribute. We used the OSR scene dataset [17] and a subset of the Public Figure Face Dataset (PubFig) [18]. The OSR scene dataset consists of 2,688 images with outdoor scene attributes (`natural`, `open`, `perspective`, `large-objects`, `diagonal-plane` and `close-depth`). The subset of the PubFig contains nearly 800 images from 8 random identities. We split the train/test set randomly and then split the train/test set into groups and use this as the input of network. We report the results in terms of pairwise accuracy on the groups of images.

Our scheme makes it possible to make use of the information in the group of images as a whole, which is more informative than just a pair of images (common to Siamese Networks construction). For a fair comparison with other methods, we measure the performance of our model by computing the pairwise accuracy for all pairs in each group.

We choose two methods for baseline comparisons. The first one is the work of Souri et al. [21], which trains a deep convolutional network to learn relative attributes for pairs of images. The second one is the DeepPermNet [2], which learns relative attributes by learning permutations. Note that this method needs fully ranked sequences of images as input, which is a more stringent requirement compared to our network and the work of Souri et al. [21], which only needs pairwise labels during training. The accuracy results are shown in Tables 1 and 2. Qualitative results are shown in Fig. 3.

Compared to the work of Souri et al. [21], we outperform that method by a margin of 4% on the Public Figure Face Dataset, and by 1% on the OSR scene dataset. Since the accuracy on the OSR dataset is already high, a 1% improvement is meaningful. Compared with the DeepPermNet [2] algorithm, we outperform that algorithm on both datasets on average. Note that DeepPermNet requires *ranked sequences* of data with the same length as training data, which may not be possible in some applications. Also note that both Souri et al. [21] and DeepPermNet [2] use `VGG CNN` model in their experiments, while we choose the simpler `Alexnet` [15] in all experiments, which has far fewer parameters. As a result, our model can be trained faster than the baseline models.

Table 1. Relative attribute learning accuracy evaluated on **OSR** dataset. On average, we outperform all previous methods. The penultimate row presents the results of our network in Sect. 4.1 and the last row presents the results of our multi-task network in Sect. 4.2, which learns all of the six attributes at once.

Method	natural	open	perspective	large-objects	diagonal-plane	close-depth	Mean
Souri et al. [21]	99.4	97.44	96.88	96.79	98.43	97.65	97.77
Cruz et al.(AlexNet) [2]	97.21	96.65	96.46	98.77	94.53	96.09	96.62
Cruz et al.(VGG) [2]	96.87	99.79	99.82	99.55	97.99	96.87	98.48
Ours	99.56	99.19	99.30	98.08	**99.63**	97.98	98.96
Ours (multi-task)	**99.89**	99.42	98.71	98.80	99.46	**98.93**	**99.20**

Table 2. Relative attribute learning accuracy evaluated on the **PubFig** dataset. Our results outperform the work of Souri et al. [21], which is the state-of-art for the traditional setting where only pairwise labels are used. Our results are also competitive and get slightly better results than those in Cruz et al. [2], which uses ranked input data. The last row shows the results of our network with multi-task loss function, which learns all of the 11 attributes at once.

Method	lips	eyebrows	chubby	male	eyes	nose	face	smiling	forehead	white	young	Mean
Souri et al. [21]	93.62	94.53	92.32	95.59	93.19	94.24	94.76	95.36	97.28	94.60	94.33	94.52
Cruz et al. [2]	99.55	97.21	97.66	99.44	96.54	96.21	99.11	97.88	99.00	97.99	99.00	98.14
Ours	98.28	97.11	98.67	98.05	**98.62**	**99.24**	97.32	**99.26**	98.37	**99.36**	**99.31**	98.51
Ours (multi-task)	**99.67**	**99.33**	**99.00**	98.33	97.32	98.46	99.00	97.51	**99.12**	97.66	98.66	**98.55**

4.2   Relative Attribute Learning, All at once

In this experiment, we evaluate our multi-task network described in Sect. 3.3. We learn all the attributes in each dataset and report the prediction accuracy results for each of the attributes on two different datasets in Tables 1 and 2. Qualitative results are shown in Fig. 4.

As the data presented show, our multi-task model slightly outperforms our single attribute learning model (Sect. 3.2) and this indicates that some of the attributes are interrelated thus helping the learning process when we learn them all at once. Note that in our framework, with every additional attribute to learn, the increase in the number of parameters of the network is equal to the dimension of the two vectors, one in the readout function and one in the attribute node (in our work, the dimension of these two vectors is 4096×1). The reader may contrast this with most multi-task learning networks, such as [1,12,22], many of which use an additional CNN or several more fully connected layers for each additional attribute, which contribute to more parameters compared to our model.

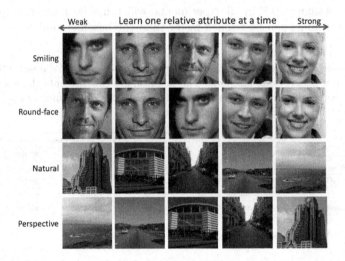

Fig. 3. Qualitative results on RAL (**one at a time**) from our network. We randomly choose five different images from four different attributes from the PubFig and OSR datasets and show the results by ordering them for those attributes. The images are ranked by the corresponding output value of our network. The first two rows are from the PubFig dataset and the last two rows are images from the OSR dataset.

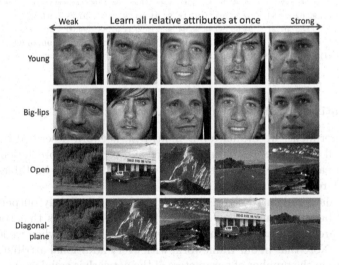

Fig. 4. Qualitative results on RAL (**all at once**) using our network. The images are arranged again by ordering them according to the output of our network as Fig. 3 but these are learnt from our multi-task loss function (Eq. (10)). We can see that the images are quite nicely ordered even without learning the order explicitly as is done in DeepPermNet. We also note that the performance on almost all the images and the attributes is consistent and any randomly chosen subset gives us good quality results.

4.3   Binary Attribute Prediction

Here we evaluate our network for attribute prediction task described in Sect. 3.4.
The multi-task CNN model [1] is a natural choice for the baseline. This model
proposes to pre-train a convolutional neural network on each attribute to get the
feature vectors, and then performs multi-task learning for multiple attributes.
That model has a large number of parameters and a rich representation capacity.
Similar to [1], we also evaluate our model on Clothing Attributes Dataset [5].
It contains 1,856 images and 26 attributes. The ground truth is provided at the
image-level, and each image is annotated for every attribute. For comparison,
we ignore the multi-class value attributes as in [1] and use this information in
the same way to divide the 23 binary attributes into groups. We then use our
multi-task network to train each group of attributes together. We report our
results in Table 3 and the group information is provided in Table 4. M-CNN
is the multi-task framework without group information in [1] and MG-CNN is
their multi-task framework with group encoding. The performance of our model
is comparable to the results presented in MG-CNN framework, but is far more
efficient both in the number of parameters and convergence time. For the number
of parameters, [1] needs one CNN for each attribute, while we only add 4096×1
parameters twice. In terms of training time, MG-CNN [1] takes 1.5 days for
training on the Clothing dataset with two NVIDIA TK40 16 GB GPU, while our
training takes less than 4 hours for all 4 groups of attributes on two NVIDIA
Geforce GTX 1080Ti 12 GB GPU.

Table 3. Attribute prediction accuracy on the Clothing Dataset [5]. Similar to [1]
we partition the 23 binary attributes into 4 groups (shown in Table 4). We achieve
comparable results as those from MG-CNN [1], but with significantly fewer parameters
(see Sect. 3.3) and faster training speed.

Method	Colors	Patterns	Cloth-parts	Appearance	Total
M-CNN [1]	91.72	94.26	87.96	91.51	91.70
MG-CNN [1]	93.12	95.37	88.65	91.93	92.82
Ours	91.64	96.81	89.25	89.53	92.39

4.4   Limitations

For our network to get a sizable performance benefit, we want that the graph
formed by each random sample, i.e., group or mini-batch of n (e.g., $n = 5$)
images should be "connected" or at least a subgraph with more than 2 nodes
is connected. This allows learning from more than one image pair at a time to
be meaningful – which is the main strength of our proposal. But if most pair
labels do not have any node overlap, then the graph formed by a group or mini-
batch of images will not have a connected component of size larger than two.
We refer the reader to [7] (Chap. 4) to see the technical aspects of connectivity.

Table 4. Grouping information used in Clothing Dataset [5]

Group	Attributes
Colors	black, blue, brown, cyan, gray, green, many, red, purple, white,yellow
Patterns	floral, graphics, plaid, solid, stripe, spot
Cloth-parts	necktie, scarf, placket, collar
Appearance	skin-exposure, gender

The UT-Zappos50K dataset [24, 25] manifests this behavior (and is not ideal for our model to deliver performance gains). Under this condition, our model actually performs similar to (although not exactly the same) a Siamese network used in the literature. The results in Table 5 indeed support this intuition: our performance is only slightly better than [21], rather than stronger improvements we see elsewhere.

Table 5. Relative attribute learning evaluated on UT-Zappos50K-lexicon dataset. It contains 50025 images of shoes with annotations on 4000 ordered pairs for each of 10 fine-grained attributes. The method in [2] does not directly work on this dataset because of its "ordered sequence" requirement on the input data.

Method	comfort	casual	simple	sporty	colorful	durable	supportive	bold	sleek	open	Mean
Souri et al. [3]	88.93	89.20	88.27	91.33	91.67	89.27	91.00	88.40	88.27	86.80	89.31
Ours	88.80	**89.82**	**90.13**	**92.60**	91.87	**90.07**	**92.73**	88.00	87.53	**89.13**	**90.07**

5   Conclusions

We presented a simple framework that can perform both relative attribute learning and attribute prediction. To exploit the underlying relationships between latent representations of a variety of attributes among a collection of images in a dataset, we proposed a simple framework based on natural instantiation of graph neural network. This formulation of a graph neural network can effectively encode the correlational information among multiple images and the multiple attributes as demonstrated in our experiments on three different datasets. Our framework can be used to learn the relative attributes either one at a time or all at once with only a modest increase in the number of parameters compared to other multi-task based methods. Because our framework learns mainly from pairs of images and does not require a full ranking it concurrently is less stringent on the annotation requirements of the training dataset. To the best of our knowledge, this proposal is among the first to explore the efficacy of multi-task GNN formulations for relative attribute learning. Our experiments also demonstrate the effectiveness of this architecture in achieving or surpassing the state-of-the-art results even for binary attributes prediction, where each attribute is predicted in a binary classification setup. The project webpage includes results on other applications, including predicting body mass index (BMI) that were not covered in detail in the main paper.

Acknowledgment. This work was partially supported by funding from American Family Insurance and UW CPCP AI117924. Partial support from NSF CAREER award 1252725, NIH grants R01 AG040396, BRAIN Initiative R01-EB022883, and Waisman IDDRC U54-HD090256 is also acknowledged. The authors are grateful to Haoliang Sun for help with illustrations and other suggestions/advice on this project. The code will appear in https://github.com/zihangm/RAL_GNN.

References

1. Abdulnabi, A.H., Wang, G., Lu, J., Jia, K.: Multi-task CNN model for attribute prediction. IEEE Trans. Multimed. **17**(11), 1949–1959 (2015)
2. Cruz, R.S., Fernando, B., Cherian, A., Gould, S.: DeepPermNet: visual permutation learning. Learning **33**, 25 (2017)
3. Bronstein, M.M., Bruna, J., LeCun, Y., Szlam, A., Vandergheynst, P.: Geometric deep learning: going beyond euclidean data. IEEE Signal Process. Mag. **34**(4), 18–42 (2017)
4. Burges, C., et al.: Learning to rank using gradient descent. In: Proceedings of the 22nd International Conference on Machine Learning, pp. 89–96. ACM (2005)
5. Chen, H., Gallagher, A., Girod, B.: Describing clothing by semantic attributes. In: Fitzgibbon, A., Lazebnik, S., Perona, P., Sato, Y., Schmid, C. (eds.) ECCV 2012. LNCS, vol. 7574, pp. 609–623. Springer, Heidelberg (2012). https://doi.org/10.1007/978-3-642-33712-3_44
6. Farhadi, A., Endres, I., Hoiem, D., Forsyth, D.: Describing objects by their attributes. In: IEEE Conference on Computer Vision and Pattern Recognition, CVPR 2009, pp. 1778–1785. IEEE (2009)
7. Frieze, A., Karoński, M.: Introduction to Random Graphs. Cambridge University Press, New York (2015)
8. Garcia, V., Bruna, J.: Few-shot learning with graph neural networks. arXiv preprint arXiv:1711.04043 (2017)
9. Gilmer, J., Schoenholz, S.S., Riley, P.F., Vinyals, O., Dahl, G.E.: Neural message passing for quantum chemistry. arXiv preprint arXiv:1704.01212 (2017)
10. Glorot, X., Bengio, Y.: Understanding the difficulty of training deep feedforward neural networks. In: Proceedings of the Thirteenth International Conference on Artificial Intelligence and Statistics, pp. 249–256 (2010)
11. Gori, M., Monfardini, G., Scarselli, F.: A new model for learning in graph domains. In: Proceedings of the IEEE International Joint Conference on Neural Networks, IJCNN 2005, vol. 2, pp. 729–734. IEEE (2005)
12. Han, H., Jain, A.K., Shan, S., Chen, X.: Heterogeneous face attribute estimation: A deep multi-task learning approach. IEEE Trans. Pattern Anal. Mach. Intell. **PP**(99), 1 (2017)
13. Jamieson, K.G., Jain, L., Fernandez, C., Glattard, N.J., Nowak, R.: Next: a system for real-world development, evaluation, and application of active learning. In: Advances in Neural Information Processing Systems, pp. 2656–2664 (2015)
14. Kingma, D.P., Ba, J.: Adam: a method for stochastic optimization. arXiv preprint arXiv:1412.6980 (2014)

15. Krizhevsky, A., Sutskever, I., Hinton, G.E.: ImageNet classification with deep convolutional neural networks. In: Advances in Neural Information Processing Systems, pp. 1097–1105 (2012)
16. Li, Y., Tarlow, D., Brockschmidt, M., Zemel, R.: Gated graph sequence neural networks. arXiv preprint arXiv:1511.05493 (2015)
17. Oliva, A., Torralba, A.: Modeling the shape of the scene: a holistic representation of the spatial envelope. Int. J. Comput. Vis. **42**(3), 145–175 (2001)
18. Parikh, D., Grauman, K.: Relative attributes. In: 2011 IEEE International Conference on Computer Vision (ICCV), pp. 503–510. IEEE (2011)
19. Scarselli, F., Gori, M., Tsoi, A.C., Hagenbuchner, M., Monfardini, G.: The graph neural network model. IEEE Trans. Neural Netw. **20**(1), 61–80 (2009)
20. Singh, K.K., Lee, Y.J.: End-to-end localization and ranking for relative attributes. In: Leibe, B., Matas, J., Sebe, N., Welling, M. (eds.) ECCV 2016. LNCS, vol. 9910, pp. 753–769. Springer, Cham (2016). https://doi.org/10.1007/978-3-319-46466-4_45
21. Souri, Y., Noury, E., Adeli, E.: Deep relative attributes. In: Lai, S.-H., Lepetit, V., Nishino, K., Sato, Y. (eds.) ACCV 2016. LNCS, vol. 10115, pp. 118–133. Springer, Cham (2017). https://doi.org/10.1007/978-3-319-54193-8_8
22. Wang, F., Han, H., Shan, S., Chen, X.: Deep multi-task learning for joint prediction of heterogeneous face attributes. In: 2017 12th IEEE International Conference on Automatic Face & Gesture Recognition (FG 2017), pp. 173–179. IEEE (2017)
23. Xiao, F., Jae Lee, Y.: Discovering the spatial extent of relative attributes. In: Proceedings of the IEEE International Conference on Computer Vision, pp. 1458–1466 (2015)
24. Yu, A., Grauman, K.: Fine-grained visual comparisons with local learning. In: Computer Vision and Pattern Recognition (CVPR), June 2014
25. Yu, A., Grauman, K.: Semantic jitter: dense supervision for visual comparisons via synthetic images. In: International Conference on Computer Vision (ICCV), October 2017

Deep Kalman Filtering Network for Video Compression Artifact Reduction

Guo Lu[1], Wanli Ouyang[2,3], Dong Xu[2(✉)], Xiaoyun Zhang[1], Zhiyong Gao[1], and Ming-Ting Sun[4]

[1] Shanghai Jiao Tong University, Shanghai, China
{luguo2014,xiaoyun.zhang,zhiyong.gao}@sjtu.edu.cn
[2] The University of Sydney, Sydney, Australia
{wanli.ouyang,dong.xu}@sydney.edu.au
[3] SenseTime Computer Vision Research Group, The University of Sydney, Sydney, Australia
[4] University of Washington, Seattle, USA
mts@uw.edu

Abstract. When lossy video compression algorithms are applied, compression artifacts often appear in videos, making decoded videos unpleasant for human visual systems. In this paper, we model the video artifact reduction task as a Kalman filtering procedure and restore decoded frames through a deep Kalman filtering network. Different from the existing works using the noisy previous *decoded* frames as temporal information in the restoration problem, we utilize the less noisy previous *restored* frame and build a recursive filtering scheme based on the Kalman model. This strategy can provide more accurate and consistent temporal information, which produces higher quality restoration results. In addition, the strong prior information of prediction residual is also exploited for restoration through a well designed neural network. These two components are combined under the Kalman framework and optimized through the deep Kalman filtering network. Our approach can well bridge the gap between the model-based methods and learning-based methods by integrating the recursive nature of the Kalman model and highly non-linear transformation ability of deep neural network. Experimental results on the benchmark dataset demonstrate the effectiveness of our proposed method.

Keywords: Compression artifact reduction · Deep neural network
Kalman model · Recursive filtering · Video restoration

1 Introduction

Compression artifact reduction methods aim at generating artifact-free images from lossy decoded images. To store and transfer a large amount of images and videos on the Internet, image and video compression algorithms (e.g., JPEG,

© Springer Nature Switzerland AG 2018
V. Ferrari et al. (Eds.): ECCV 2018, LNCS 11218, pp. 591–608, 2018.
https://doi.org/10.1007/978-3-030-01264-9_35

H.264) are widely used [1–3]. However, these algorithms often introduce unde-
sired compression artifacts, such as blocking, blurring and ringing artifacts. Thus,
compression artifact reduction has attracted increasing attention and many
methods have been developed in the past few decades.

Early works use manually designed filters [4,5] and sparse coding methods
[6–9] to remove compression artifacts. Recently, convolutional neural network
(CNN) based approaches have been successfully applied for a lot of computer
vision tasks [10–20], such as super-resolution [15,16], denoising [17] and artifact
reduction [18–20]. In particular, Dong et al. [18] firstly proposed a four-layer
neural network to eliminate the JPEG compression artifacts.

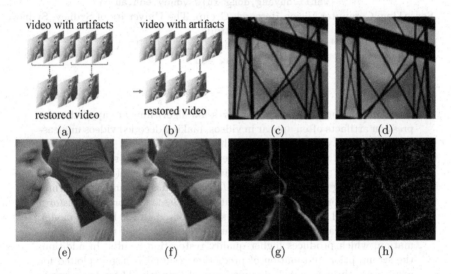

Fig. 1. Different methodologies for video artifact reduction (a) the traditional pipeline
without considering previous restored frames. (b) our Kalman filtering pipeline. Artifact reduction results between (c) Xue *et al.* [21] and (d) our proposed deep Kalman
filtering network. (e) original frame (f) decoded frame (g) quantized prediction residual
(h) distortion between the original frame and the decoded frame.

For the video artifact reduction task, our motivations are two-fold. First,
the restoration process for the current frame could benefit from the previous
restored frames. A reason is that when compared to the decoded frame, the previous restored frame can provide more accurate information. Therefore temporal
information (such as motion clues) from neighbouring frames is more precise and
robust, and can provide the potential to further improve the performance. In
addition, the dependence of previous restored frames naturally leads to a recursive pipeline for video artifact reduction. Therefore it recursively restores the current frame by potentially utilizing all past restored frames, which means we can
leverage effective information propagated from previous estimations. Currently,
most of the state-of-the-art deep learning approaches for compression artifact

reduction are limited to remove artifacts in a single image [16–19]. Although the video artifact reduction method [21] or video super-resolution methods [22–24] try to combine temporal information for the restoration tasks, their methods ignore the previous restored frame and restore each frame separately as shown in Fig. 1(a). Therefore, the video artifact reduction performance can be further improved by using an appropriate dynamic filtering scheme.

Second, modern video compression algorithms may contain powerful prior information that can be utilized to restore the decoded frame. It has been observed that practical video compression standards are not optimal according to the information theory [9], therefore the resulting compression code streams still have redundancies. It is possible, at least theoretically, to improve the restoration results by exploiting the knowledge hidden in the code streams. For video compression algorithms, *inter prediction* is a fundamental technique used to reduce temporal redundancy. Therefore, the decoded frame consists of two components: prediction frame and quantized prediction residual. As shown in Fig. 1(g)–(h), the distortion between the original frame and the decoded frame has a strong relationship with quantized prediction residual, i.e., the region which has high distortion often corresponds to high quantized prediction residual values. Therefore, it is possible to enhance the restoration by employing this task-specific prior information.

In this paper, we propose a deep Kalman filtering network (DKFN) for video artifact reduction. The proposed approach can be used as a post-processing technique, and thus can be applied to different compression algorithms. Specifically, we model the video artifact reduction problem as a Kalman filtering procedure, which can recursively restore the decoded frame and capture information that propagated from previous restored frames. To perform Kalman filtering for decoded frames, we build two deep convolutional neural networks: prediction network and measurement network. The prediction network aims to obtain *prior estimation* based on the previous restored frame. At the same time, we investigate the quantized prediction residual in the coding algorithms and a novel measurement net incorporating this strong prior information is proposed for robust *measurement*. After that, the restored frame can be obtained by fusing the *prior estimation* and the *measurement* under the Kalman framework. Our proposed approach bridges the gap between model-based methods and learning-based methods by integrating the recursive nature of the Kalman model and highly non-linear transform ability of neural network. Therefore, our approach can restore high quality frames from a series of decoded video frames. To the best of our knowledge, we are the first to develop a new deep convolutional neural network under the Kalman filtering framework for video artifact reduction.

In summary, the main contributions of this work are two-fold. First, we formulate the video artifact reduction problem as a Kalman filtering procedure, which can recursively restore the decoded frames. In this procedure, we utilize the CNN to predict and update the state of Kalman filtering. Second, we employ the quantized prediction residual as the strong prior information for video artifact reduction through deep neural network. Experimental results show that our proposed approach outperforms the state-of-the-art methods for reducing video compression artifacts.

2   Related Work

2.1   Single Image Compression Artifact Reduction

A lot of methods have been proposed to remove the compression artifacts. Early methods [25,26] designed new filters to reduce blocking and ringing artifacts. One of the disadvantages for these methods is that such manually designed filters cannot sufficiently handle the compression degradation and may over-smooth the decoded images. Learning methods based on sparse coding were also proposed for image artifact reduction [8,9,27]. Chang et al. [8] proposed to learn a sparse representation from a training image set, which is used to reduce artifacts introduced by compression. Liu et al. [9] exploited the DCT information and built a sparsity-based dual domain approach.

Recently, deep convolutional neural network based methods have been successfully utilized for the low-level computer vision tasks. Dong et al. [18] proposed artifact reduction CNN (ARCNN) to remove the artifacts from JPEG compression. Inspired by ARCNN, several methods have been proposed to reduce compression artifact by using various techniques, such as residual learning [28], skip connection [28,29], batch normalization [17], perceptual loss [30], residual block [20] and generative adversarial network [20]. For example, Zhang et al. [17] proposed a 20-layer neural network based on batch normalization and residual learning to eliminate Gaussian noise with unknown noise level. Tai et al. [16] proposed a memory block, consisting of a recursive unit and a gate unit, to explicitly mine persistent memory through an adaptive learning process. In addition, a lot of methods [31–33] were proposed to learn the image prior by using CNN and achieved competitive results for the image restoration tasks.

As mentioned in [9], compression code streams still have redundancies. Therefore, it is possible to obtain a more robust estimation by exploiting the prior knowledge hidden in the encoder. However, most of the previous works do not exploit this important prior information. Although the works in [9,19,27] proposed to combine DCT information, it is not sufficient especially for the video artifact reduction task. In our work, we further exploit the prior information in the code streams and incorporate prediction residual into our framework for robust compression artifact reduction.

2.2   Deep Learning for Video Restoration

Due to the popularity of neural networks for image restoration, several CNN based methods [21,22,34–36] were also proposed for the video restoration tasks. For video super-resolution, Liao et al. [34] first generated an ensemble of SR draft via motion compensation, and then used a CNN model to restore the high resolution frame from all drafts. Kappeler et al. [35] estimated optical flow and selected the corresponding patches across frames to train a CNN model for video super-resolution. Based on the spatial transformation network (STN) [36], the works in [21–24] aligned the neighboring frames according to the estimated optical flow or transform parameters and increased the temporal coherence for the video SR task. Tao *et al.* [22] achieved sub-pixel motion compensation and resolution enhancement with high performance. Xue *et al.* [21] utilized a joint training strategy to optimize the motion estimation and video restoration tasks and achieved the state-of-the-art results for video artifact reduction.

Compared to the methods for single image compression artifact reduction (see Sect. 2.1), the video restoration methods exploit temporal information. However, these methods process noisy/low-resolution videos separately without considering the previous restored frames. Therefore, they cannot improve video restoration performance by utilizing more accurate temporal information. In our work, we recursively restore each frame in the videos by leveraging the previous restored frame for video artifact reduction. Although the work [37, 38] try to combine deep neural network and Kalman filter, they are not designed for the image/video enhancement tasks.

3 Methodology

We first give a brief introduction about the basic Kalman filter and then describe our formulation for video artifact reduction and the corresponding network design.

Introduction of Denotations. Let $\mathcal{V} = \{X | X_1, X_2, ..., X_{t-1}, X_t, ...\}$ denote an uncompressed video sequence, where $X_t \in \mathcal{R}^{mn \times 1}$ is a video frame at time step t and mn represents the spatial resolution. In order to simplify the description, we only analyze video frame with a single channel, although we consider RGB/YUV channels in our implementation. After compression, X_t^c is the decoded frame of X_t. $\hat{X}_t^-$ denotes the prior estimation and $\hat{X}_t$ denotes the posterior estimation for restoring X_t from the decoded frame X_t^c. R_t^c is the quantized prediction residual in video coding standards, such as H.264. R_t is the corresponding unquantized prediction residual.

3.1 Brief Introduction of Kalman Filter

Kalman filter [39] is an efficient recursive filter that estimates the internal state from a series of noisy measurements. In artifact reduction task, the internal state is the original image to be restored, and the noisy measurements can be considered as the images with compression artifacts.

Preliminary Formulation. The Kalman filter model assumes that the state X_t at time t is changed from the state X_{t-1} at time $t-1$ according to

$$X_t = A_t X_{t-1} + w_{t-1}, \tag{1}$$

where A_t is the transition matrix at time t and w_{t-1} is the process noise. The measurement Z_t of the true state X_t is defined as follows,

$$Z_t = HX_t + v_t, \tag{2}$$

where H is the measurement matrix and v_t represents the measurement noise. However, the system may be non-linear in some complex scenarios. Therefore, a non-linear model for the transition process in Eq. (1) can be formulated as follows,

$$X_t = f(X_{t-1}, w_{t-1}), \tag{3}$$

where $f(\cdot)$ is the non-linear transition model. Linear Kalman filter corresponds to Eqs. (1) and (2). Non-linear Kalman filter corresponds to Eq. (3) and Eq. (2).

Kalman Filtering. As shown in Fig. 2(a), Kalman filtering consists of two steps, prediction and update.

In the *prediction step*, it calculates the prior estimation from the posterior estimation of the previous time step. For non-linear model Eqs. (3) and (2), the prediction step is accomplished by two sub-steps as follows,

$$\text{Prior state estimation: } \hat{X}_t^- = f(\hat{X}_{t-1}, 0), \tag{4}$$

$$\text{Covariance estimation: } P_t^- = A_t P_{t-1} A_t^{\mathrm{T}} + Q_{t-1}, \tag{5}$$

where Q_{t-1} is the covariance of the process noise w_{t-1} at time $t-1$, P_t^- is a covariance matrix used for the update step. A_t in Eq. (5) is defined as the Jacobian matrix of $f(\cdot)$, i.e., $A_t = \frac{\partial f(\hat{X}_{t-1}, 0)}{\partial X}$ [40]. Prediction procedure for the linear model can be considered as a special case by setting $f(\hat{X}_{t-1}, 0) = A_t \hat{X}_{t-1}$.

In the *update step*, Kalman filter will calculate the posterior estimate by fusing the prior estimate from the prediction step and the measurement. Details about the update step can be found in Sect. 3.6.

An overview of Kalman filtering is shown in Fig. 2(a). First, the prediction step uses the estimated state $\hat{X}_{t-1}$ at time $t-1$ to obtain a prior state estimation $\hat{X}_t^-$ at time t. Then the prior state estimation $\hat{X}_t^-$ and the measurement Z_t are used by the update step to obtain the posterior estimation of the state, denoted by $\hat{X}_t$. These two steps are performed recursively.

3.2   Overview of Our Deep Kalman Filtering Network

Figure 2(b) shows an overview of the proposed deep Kalman filtering network. In this framework, the previous restored frame $\hat{X}_{t-1}$ and the decoded frame X_t^c are used for obtaining a prior estimate $\hat{X}_t^-$. Then the measurement Z_t obtained from the measurement network and the prior estimate $\hat{X}_t^-$ are used by the update step for obtaining the posterior estimation $\hat{X}_t$.

The proposed DKFN framework follows the Kalman filtering procedure by using the prediction and update steps for obtaining the predicted state $\hat{X}_t$. The main differences to the original Kalman filtering are as follows.

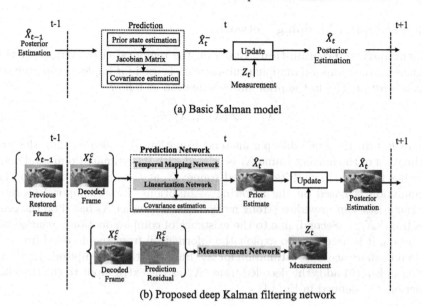

(a) Basic Kalman model

(b) Proposed deep Kalman filtering network

Fig. 2. (a) Basic Kalman model. (b) Overview of the proposed deep Kalman filtering network for video artifact reduction. X_t^c is the decoded frame at time t. $\hat{X}_{t-1}$ represents the restored frame from $t-1$. The prediction network generates prior estimate $\hat{X}_t^-$ for original frame based on X_t^c and $\hat{X}_{t-1}$. The measurement network uses the decoded frame X_t^c and the quantized prediction residual R_t^c to obtain an initial measurement Z_t. After that, we can build the posterior estimate by fusing the prior estimate $\hat{X}_t^-$ and the measurement Z_t.

First, in the prior estimation sub-step of the prediction step, we use the temporal mapping sub-network as the non-linear function $f(\cdot)$ in Eq. (3) to obtain the prior state estimation. Specifically, the temporal mapping sub-network takes the previous restored frame $\hat{X}_{t-1}$ and the decoded frame X_t^c as the input and generates the prior estimate $\hat{X}_t^-$ for the current frame. Details are given in Sect. 3.3.

Second, in the covariance estimation sub-step, the transition matrix A_t in Eq. (5) is approximated by a linearization sub-network. In conventional non-linear Kalman filter, the Jacobian matrix of the non-linear function $f(\cdot)$ is used to obtain A_t. For our CNN implementation of $f(\cdot)$, however, it is too complex to compute, especially when we need to compute the Jacobian matrix for each pixel location. Therefore, we approximate the calculation of Jacobian matrix by using a linearization sub-network. Details are given in Sect. 3.4.

Third, in the update procedure, we use a measurement network to generate the measurement. In comparison, the conventional Kalman filter might directly use the decoded frame with compression artifacts as the measurement. Details are given in Sect. 3.5.

3.3 Temporal Mapping Network

Mathematical Formulation. Based on the temporal characteristic of video sequences, the temporal mapping sub-network is used for implementing the non-linear function $f(\cdot)$ in the prior state estimation as follows:

$$\hat{X}_t^- = \mathcal{F}(\hat{X}_{t-1}, X_t^c; \theta_f), \tag{6}$$

where θ_f are the trainable parameters. Equation(6) indicates that the prior estimation of the current frame X_t is related with its estimated temporal neighbouring frame $\hat{X}_{t-1}$ and its decoded frame X_t^c at the current time step. This formulation is based on the following assumptions. First, temporal evolution characteristic can provide a strong motion clue to predict X_t based on the previous frame $\hat{X}_{t-1}$. Second, due to the existence of complex motion scenarios with occlusion, it is necessary to exploit the information from the decoded frame X_t^c to build a more accurate estimation for X_t. Based on this assumption, our formulation in Eq. (6) adds the decoded frame X_t^c as the extra input to the transition function $f(\cdot)$ defined in Eq. (4).

Network Implementation. The temporal mapping sub-network architecture is shown in Fig. 3(a). Specifically, each residual block contains two convolutional layers with the pre-activation structure [41]. We use convolutional layers with 3×3 kernels and 64 output channels in the whole network except the last layer. The last layer is a simple convolutional neural network with one feature map without non-linear transform. Generalized divisive normalization (GDN) and inverse GDN (IGDN) [42] are used because they are well-suited for Gaussianizing data from natural images. More training details are discussed in Sect. 3.7.

3.4 Linearization Network

Linearization network aims to learn a linear transition matrix A_t for the covariance estimation in Eq. (5) adaptively for different image regions. It is non-trivial to calculate the Jacobian matrix of transition function $\mathcal{F}(\cdot)$ and linearize it through Taylor series. Therefore, we use a simple neural network to learn a transition matrix. Specifically, given the prior estimation $\hat{X}_t^-$, previous restored frame $\hat{X}_{t-1}$ and decoded frame X_t^c, the problem is expressed by the following way,

$$\hat{X}_t^- = \mathcal{F}(\hat{X}_{t-1}, X_t^c; \theta_f) \approx \tilde{A}_t \hat{X}_{t-1}, \text{ where } \tilde{A}_t = \mathcal{G}(\hat{X}_{t-1}, X_t^c; \theta_m), \tag{7}$$

$\mathcal{G}(\hat{X}_{t-1}, X_t^c; \theta_m)$ is the linearization network with the parameters θ_m. $\tilde{A}_t$ is the output of this network. The network architecture is shown in Fig. 3(b). Given $\hat{X}_{t-1}, X_t^c \in \mathcal{R}^{mn \times 1}$, the network will generate a transition matrix $\tilde{A}_t \in \mathcal{R}^{mn \times mn}$ as an approximation to A_t in Eq. (5).

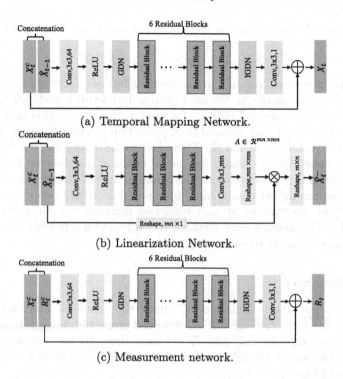

(a) Temporal Mapping Network.

(b) Linearization Network.

(c) Measurement network.

Fig. 3. Network architecture of the proposed (a) Temporal Mapping Network (b) Linearization network. (c) Measurement Network. For better illustration, we omit the matrix conversion process of X_t, $\hat{X}_t^c$ and R_t^c from $\mathcal{R}^{mn \times 1}$ to $\mathcal{R}^{m \times n}$. Here 'Conv,3 × 3,64' represents the convolution operation with the 3×3 kernel and 64 feature maps. 'Reshape, $m \times n$' is the operation that reshapes one matrix to $m \times n$. $\oplus$ and $\otimes$ represent element-wise addition and matrix multiplication.

3.5   Measurement Network

Since prediction based coding is one of the most important techniques for video coding standards (such as MPEG2, H.264 or H.265), we take this coding approach into consideration when designing the measurement network. In prediction based coding, the decoded frame X_t^c can be decoupled into two components, i.e., $X_t^c = X_t^p + R_t^c$, where X_t^p and R_t^c represent the prediction frame and the quantized prediction residual, respectively. Note that quantization is only used for the prediction residual and the distortion in compression only comes from R_t^c. In addition, for non-predictive video codecs, such as JPEG2000, we use an existing warp operation [23,36] from the previous decoded frame to the current decoded frame, and the difference between them is considered as the prediction residual R_t^c. For most of video codecs (e.g.,H.264 and H.265), we can directly utilize the quantized prediction residual in the code streams.

We obtain the measurement using the quantized prediction residual R_t^c as follows,

$$Z_t = X_t^p + \hat{R}_t, \text{ where } \hat{R}_t = \mathcal{M}(X_t^c, R_t^c; \theta_z), \tag{8}$$

where $\hat{R}_t$ is the restored residual to remove the effect of quantization so that Z_t is close to the original image X_t. We use a deep neural network as shown in Fig. 3(c) (with same architecture as Fig. 3(a)) for the function $\mathcal{M}(\cdot)$. This network takes the decoded frame X_t^c and the quantized prediction residual R_t^c as the input and estimates the restored residual $\hat{R}_t$. There are two advantages of our formulation for measurement. On one hand, instead of utilizing the decoded frame X_t^c as the measurement, our measurement formulation avoids explicitly modeling the complex relationship between original frames and decoded frames. On the other hand, most of the existing artifact reduction methods can be embedded into our model as the measurement method, which provides a flexible framework to obtain a more accurate measurement value.

3.6   Update Step

Given the prior state estimation $\hat{X}_t^-$ from the temporal mapping network (Sect. 3.3), the transition matrix $\tilde{A}_t$ obtained from the linearization network (Sect. 3.4), and the measurement Z_t obtained from the measurement network (Sect. 3.5), we can use the following steps[1] to obtain the posterior estimation of the restored image:

$$P_t^- = \tilde{A}_t P_{t-1} \tilde{A}_t^T + Q_{t-1}, \tag{9}$$

$$K_t = P_t^- H^T (H P_t^- H^T + U_t)^{-1}, \tag{10}$$

$$\hat{X}_t = \hat{X}_t^- + K_t(Z_t - H\hat{X}_t^-), \tag{11}$$

$$P_t = (I - K_t H)P_t^-, \tag{12}$$

where $\hat{X}_t$ represents the posterior estimation for the image X_t. P_t^- and P_t are the estimated state covariance matrixs for the prior estimation and the posterior estimation respectively. K_t is the Kalman gain at time t. H is the measurement matrix defined in Eq. (2) and is assumed to be an identity matrix in this work. Q_{t-1} and U_t are the process noise covariance matrix and the measurement noise covariance matrix respectively. We assume Q_{t-1} and U_t to be constant over time. For more details about the update procedure of Kalman filtering, please refer to [40].

Discussion. Our approach can solve the error accumulation problem of the recursive pipeline through the adaptive Kalman gain. For example, when the errors accumulate in the previous restored frames, the degree of reliability for prior estimation (i.e., information from the previous frame) will be decreased and the final result will depend more on the measurement (i.e., the current frame).

---

[1] Eq. (9) corresponds to the covariance estimation and listed here for better presentation.

3.7   Training Strategy

There are three sets of trainable parameters θ_f, θ_m and θ_z in our approach. First, the parameters θ_f in the temporal mapping network are optimized as follows,

$$\mathcal{L}_f(\theta_f) = ||X_t - \mathcal{F}(\hat{X}_{t-1}, X_t^c; \theta_f)||_2^2, \tag{13}$$

Note that in the minimization procedure for Eq. (13), the restored frame of the previous one $\hat{X}_{t-1}$ is required. This leads to the chicken-and-egg problem. A straightforward method is to feed several frames of a clip into the network and train all the input frames in the iteration. However, this strategy increases GPU memory consumption significantly and simultaneous training multi-frames for a video clip is non-trivial. Alternatively, we adopt an on-line update strategy. Specifically, the estimation results $\hat{X}_t$ in each iteration will be saved in a buffer. In the following iterations, $\hat{X}_t$ in the buffer will be used to provide more accurate temporal information when estimating X_{t+1}. Therefore, each training sample in the buffer will be updated in an epoch. We only need to optimize one frame for a video clip in each iteration, which is more efficient.

After that, the parameters θ_f are fixed and we can optimize the linearization network $\mathcal{G}(\theta_m)$ by using the following loss function:

$$\mathcal{L}_m(\theta_m) = ||\hat{X}_t^- - \mathcal{G}(\hat{X}_{t-1}, X_t^c; \theta_m)\hat{X}_{t-1}||_2^2, \tag{14}$$

Note that we use a small patch size (4×4) to reduce the computational cost when optimizing θ_m.

Then, we will train the measurement net and optimize θ_z based on the following loss function,

$$\mathcal{L}_z(\theta_z) = ||X_t - (\mathcal{M}(X_t^c, R_t^c; \theta_z) + X_t^p)||_2^2, \tag{15}$$

Finally, we fine-tune the whole deep Kalman filtering network based on the loss $\mathcal{L}$ defined as follows,

$$\mathcal{L}(\theta) = ||X_t - \hat{X}_t||_2^2, \tag{16}$$

θ are the trainable parameters in the deep Kalman filtering network.

4   Experiments

To demonstrate the effectiveness of the proposed model for video artifact reduction, we perform the experiments on the benchmark dataset Vimeo-90K [21]. Our approach is implemented by using the Tensorflow [43] platform. It takes 22 h to train the whole model by using two Titan X GPUs.

4.1   Experimental Setup

Dataset. The Vimeo-90K dataset [21] is recently built for evaluating different video processing tasks, such as video denoising, video super-resolution (SR) and

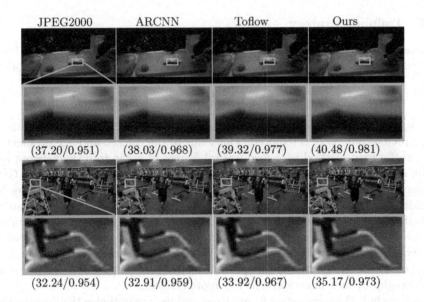

Fig. 4. Quantitative (PSNR/SSIM) and visual comparison of JPEG2000 artifact reduction on the Vimeo dataset for q = 20.

video artifact reduction. It consists of 4,278 videos with 89,800 independent clips that are different from each other in content. All frames have the resolutio of 448×256. For video compression artifact reduction, we follow [21] to use 64,612 clips for training and 7,824 clips for performance evaluation. In this section, PSNR and SSIM [44] are utilized as the evaluation metrics.

To demonstrate the effectiveness of the proposed method, we generate compressed/decoded frames through two coding settings, i.e., codec HEVC (x265) with quantization parameter $qp = 32$ and $qp = 37$ and codec JPEG2000 with quality $q = 20$ and $q = 40$.

Implementation Details. For model training, we use the Adam solver [45] with the initial learning rate of 0.001, $\beta_1 = 0.9$ and $\beta_2 = 0.999$. The learning rate is divided by 10 after every 20 epochs. We apply gradient clip with global norm 0.001 to stabilize the training process. The mini-batch size is set to 32. We use the method in [46] for weight initialization. Our approach takes 0.15 s to restore a color image with the size of 448×256.

We first train the temporal mapping network using the loss $\mathcal{L}_f$ in Eq. (13). After 40 epochs, we fix the parameters θ_f and train the linearization network by using the loss $\mathcal{L}_m$. Then we train the measurement network using the loss $\mathcal{L}_z$ in Eq. (15). After 40 epochs, the training loss will become stable. Finally, we fine-tune the whole model. In the following experiments, we train different models for different codecs or quality levels.

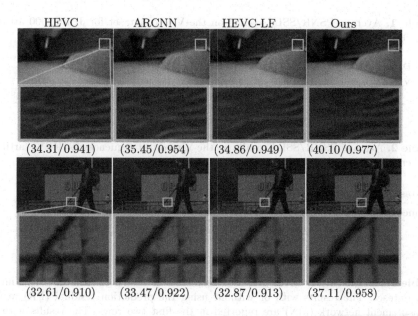

HEVC	ARCNN	HEVC-LF	Ours
(34.31/0.941)	(35.45/0.954)	(34.86/0.949)	(40.10/0.977)
(32.61/0.910)	(33.47/0.922)	(32.87/0.913)	(37.11/0.958)

Fig. 5. Quantitative (PSNR/SSIM) and visual comparison of different methods for HEVC artifact reduction on the Vimeo dataset at qp = 37.

4.2 Experimental Results

Comparison with the State-of-the-Art Methods. To demonstrate the effectiveness of our approach, we compare it with several recent image and video artifact reduction methods: ARCNN [18], DnCNN [17], V-BM4D [47] and Toflow [21]. In addition, modern video codecs already have a default artifact reduction scheme. For example, HEVC utilizes loop filter [1] (HEVC-LF) to reduce the blocking artifacts. This technique is also included for comparison.

For ARCNN [18] and DnCNN [17], we use the code provided by the authors and train their models on the Vimeo training dataset. For V-BM4D and Toflow, we directly cited their results in [21]. The results of HEVC-LF are generated by enabling loop filter and SAO [1] in HEVC codec (x265). For fair comparison with the existing approaches, we follow [21] and only evaluate the 4th frame of each clip in the Vimeo dataset. The quantitative results are reported in Tables 1 and 2. As we can see, our proposed approach outperforms the state-of-the-art methods by more than 0.6db in term of PSNR.

Qualitative comparisons of ARCNN [18], Toflow [21], HEVC-LF [1] and ours are shown in Figs. 4 and 5. In these figures, the blocking artifacts exist in JPEG2000/HEVC decoded frame, our proposed method successfully removes these artifacts while other methods still have observable artifacts. For example, the equipment (the fourth row in Fig. 4) and the railing (the fourth row in Fig. 5) both have complex texture and structure, our method can well recover these complex regions while other baseline methods may fail.

Table 1. Average PSNR/SSIM results on the Vimeo dataset for JPEG2000 artifact reduction (q = 20,40).

Dataset	Setting	ARCNN [18]	DnCNN [17]	V-BM4D [47]	Toflow [21]	Ours
Vimeo	q = 20	36.11/0.960	37.26/0.967	35.75/0.959	36.92/0.966	**37.93/0.971**
	q = 40	34.21/0.944	35.22/0.953	33.99/0.940	34.97/0.953	**35.88/0.958**

Table 2. Average PSNR/SSIM results on the Vimeo test sequences for HEVC artifact reduction (qp = 32,37).

Dataset	Setting	ARCNN [18]	DnCNN [17]	HEVC-LF [1]	Ours
Vimeo	qp = 32	34.87/0.954	35.58/0.961	34.19/0.950	**35.81/0.962**
	qp = 37	32.54/0.930	33.01/0.936	31.98/0.923	**33.23/0.939**

Table 3. Ablation study of the proposed deep Kalman filtering method on the Vimeo-90k dataset. The results with or without using the prediction residual (PR) in the measurement network (MN) are reported in the first two rows. The results with or without using the recursive filtering (RF) scheme in the temporal network (TM) are reported in the 3rd and 4th rows. Our full model is MN+PR+TM+RF (the 5th row).

MN	PR	TM	RF	PSNR/SSIM
✓				37.15/0.967
✓	✓			37.49/0.968
		✓		37.35/0.967
		✓	✓	37.76/0.970
✓	✓	✓	✓	37.93/0.971

Ablation Study of Measurement Network (MN).In this subsection, we investigate the effectiveness of the proposed measurement network. Note that the output of our measurement network itself can be readily used as the artifact reduction result. So the results in this subsection are obtained without using the temporal mapping network. In order to validate that prediction residual can serve as important prior information for improving the performance, we train another model with the same architecture but without using prediction residual (PR) as the input. Therefore, it generates restored frames by only using the decoded frames as the input. Quantitative results on the Vimeo-90k dataset are listed in Table 3. When compared with our simplified model without prediction residual(see the 1st row), our simplified model with prediction residual (MN+PR, see the 2nd row) can boost the performance by 0.34 dB in term of PSNR. It demonstrates that incorporating strong prior information can improve the restoration performance.

Ablation Study on the Temporal Mapping Network (TM). We further evaluate the effectiveness of the temporal mapping network. Note that the output of our temporal mapping network itself can be also readily used for the video artifact reduction. So the results in this subsection are obtained without using the measurement network. For comparison, we train another model, which utilizes the same network architecture as our temporal mapping network but the input is the concatenation of X_t^c and X_{t-1}^c. Namely, it restores the current frame without considering previous restored frames. The quantitative results are reported in Table 3. When compared with our simplified model without using recursive filtering (RF) (see the 3rd row), our simplified model with recursive filtering (TM+RF, see the 4th row) can significantly improve the quality of restored frame by 0.41dB in term of PSNR. A possiable explanation is our recursive filtering scheme can effectively leverage information from previous restored frames, which provides more accurate pixel information.

It is worth mentioning that the result in the 5th row is the best as we combine the outputs from both the measurement network and the temporal mapping network through the Kalman update process.

Table 4. Average PSNR/SSIM results evaluated on two new datasets for video artifact reduction (JPEG2000, q = 20) for cross dataset validation.

Test dataset	Toflow [21]	DnCNN [17]	Ours
HEVC dequneces	32.37/0.948	33.19/0.953	**33.83/0.958**
MPI Sintel datast	34.78/0.959	36.40/0.969	**37.01/0.973**

Cross Dataset Validation. The results on the HEVC standard sequences (Class D) and the MPI Sintel Flow dataset in Table 4 show that our approach performs better than the state-of-the-art methods.

Comparison with the RNN Based Approach. We use the recurrent network to completely replace the Kalman filter in Fig. 2. Specifically, the same CNN architecture is used to extract the features from the distorted frames at each time step and a convolutional gated recurrent unit (GRU) module is used to restore the original image based on these features. The result of our work is 37.93 dB, which outperforms the recurrent network based method (37.10 dB). One possible explanation is that it is difficult to train the recurrent network, while our pipeline makes it easier to learn the network by using the domain knowledge of prediction residual and combining both measurement and prior estimation.

5   Conclusions

In this paper, we have proposed a deep Kalman filtering network for video artifact reduction. We model the video compression artifact reduction task as a

Kalman filtering procedure and update the state function by learning deep neural networks. Our framework can take advantage of both the recursive nature of Kalman filtering and representation learning ability of neural network. Experimental results have demonstrated the superiority of our deep Kalman filtering network over the state-of-the-art methods. Our methodology can also be extended to solve other low-level computer vision tasks, such as video super-resolution or denoising, which will be studied in the future.

Acknowledgement. This work was supported by s research project from Sense-Time. This work was also supported in part by National Natural Science Foundation of China (61771306, 61521062), Natural Science Foundation of Shanghai(18ZR1418100)Chinese National Key S&T Special Program(2013ZX01033001-002-002), STCSM Grant 17DZ1205602, Shanghai Key Laboratory of Digital Media Processing and Transmissions (STCSM 18DZ2270700).

References

1. Sullivan, G.J., Ohm, J., Han, W.J., Wiegand, T.: Overview of the high efficiency video coding (HEVC) standard. TCSVT **22**(12), 1649–1668 (2012)
2. Schwarz, H., Marpe, D., Wiegand, T.: Overview of the scalable video coding extension of the H. 264/AVC standard. TCSVT **17**(9), 1103–1120 (2007)
3. Lu, G., Zhang, X., Chen, L., Gao, Z.: Novel integration of frame rate up conversion and HEVC coding based on rate-distortion optimization. TIP **27**(2), 678–691 (2018)
4. Shen, M.Y., Kuo, C.C.J.: Review of postprocessing techniques for compression artifact removal. J. Vis. Commun. Image Represent. **9**(1), 2–14 (1998)
5. Reeve, H.C., Lim, J.S.: Reduction of blocking effects in image coding. Opt. Eng. **23**(1) (1984)
6. Jung, C., Jiao, L., Qi, H., Sun, T.: Image deblocking via sparse representation. Signal Process. Image Commun. **27**(6), 663–677 (2012)
7. Choi, I., Kim, S., Brown, M.S., Tai, Y.W.: A learning-based approach to reduce JPEG artifacts in image matting. In: ICCV (2013)
8. Chang, H., Ng, M.K., Zeng, T.: Reducing artifacts in JPEG decompression via a learned dictionary. IEEE Trans. Signal Process. **62**(3), 718–728 (2014)
9. Liu, X., Wu, X., Zhou, J., Zhao, D.: Data-driven sparsity-based restoration of JPEG-compressed images in dual transform-pixel domain. In: CVPR, vol. 1. p. 5 (2015)
10. Ouyang, W., Wang, X.: Joint deep learning for pedestrian detection. In: ICCV (2013)
11. Ouyang, W., et al.: Deepid-net: deformable deep convolutional neural networks for object detection. In: CVPR (2015)
12. Wang, L., Ouyang, W., Wang, X., Lu, H.: Visual tracking with fully convolutional networks. In: ICCV (2015)
13. Zhao, R., Ouyang, W., Wang, X.: Unsupervised salience learning for person re-identification. In: CVPR (2013)
14. Dong, C., Loy, C.C., He, K., Tang, X.: Learning a deep convolutional network for image super-resolution. In: Fleet, D., Pajdla, T., Schiele, B., Tuytelaars, T. (eds.) ECCV 2014. LNCS, vol. 8692, pp. 184–199. Springer, Cham (2014). https://doi.org/10.1007/978-3-319-10593-2_13

15. Dong, C., Loy, C.C., He, K., Tang, X.: Image super-resolution using deep convolutional networks. IEEE Trans. Pattern Anal. Mach. Intell. **38**(2), 295–307 (2016)
16. Tai, Y., Yang, J., Liu, X., Xu, C.: Memnet: a persistent memory network for image restoration. In: CVPR (2017)
17. Zhang, K., Zuo, W., Chen, Y., Meng, D., Zhang, L.: Beyond a Gaussian denoiser: residual learning of deep CNN for image denoising. TIP **26**(7), 3142–3155 (2017)
18. Dong, C., Deng, Y., Change Loy, C., Tang, X.: Compression artifacts reduction by a deep convolutional network. In: ICCV (2015)
19. Guo, J., Chao, H.: Building dual-domain representations for compression artifacts reduction. In: Leibe, B., Matas, J., Sebe, N., Welling, M. (eds.) ECCV 2016. LNCS, vol. 9905, pp. 628–644. Springer, Cham (2016). https://doi.org/10.1007/978-3-319-46448-0_38
20. Galteri, L., Seidenari, L., Bertini, M., Del Bimbo, A.: Deep generative adversarial compression artifact removal. arXiv preprint arXiv:1704.02518 (2017)
21. Xue, T., Chen, B., Wu, J., Wei, D., Freeman, W.T.: Video enhancement with task-oriented flow. arXiv preprint arXiv:1711.09078 (2017)
22. Tao, X., Gao, H., Liao, R., Wang, J., Jia, J.: Detail-revealing deep video super-resolution. In: ICCV (2017)
23. Liu, D., et al.: Robust video super-resolution with learned temporal dynamics. In: CVPR (2017)
24. Caballero, J., et al.: Real-time video super-resolution with spatio-temporal networks and motion compensation. In: CVPR (2017)
25. Foi, A., Katkovnik, V., Egiazarian, K.: Pointwise shape-adaptive DCT for high-quality denoising and deblocking of grayscale and color images. TIP **16**(5), 1395–1411 (2007)
26. Zhang, X., Xiong, R., Fan, X., Ma, S., Gao, W.: Compression artifact reduction by overlapped-block transform coefficient estimation with block similarity. TIP **22**(12), 4613–4626 (2013)
27. Wang, Z., Liu, D., Chang, S., Ling, Q., Yang, Y., Huang, T.S.: D3: dep dual-domain based fast restoration of JPEG-compressed images. In: CVPR (2016)
28. Svoboda, P., Hradis, M., Barina, D., Zemcik, P.: Compression artifacts removal using convolutional neural networks. arXiv preprint arXiv:1605.00366 (2016)
29. Mao, X.J., Shen, C., Yang, Y.B.: Image denoising using very deep fully convolutional encoder-decoder networks with symmetric skip connections. arXiv preprint (2016)
30. Guo, J., Chao, H.: One-to-many network for visually pleasing compression artifacts reduction. In: CVPR (2017)
31. Zhang, K., Zuo, W., Gu, S., Zhang, L.: Learning deep CNN denoiser prior for image restoration. arXiv preprint (2017)
32. Chang, J.R., Li, C.L., Poczos, B., Kumar, B.V., Sankaranarayanan, A.C.: One network to solve them allsolving linear inverse problems using deep projection models. arXiv preprint (2017)
33. Bigdeli, S.A., Zwicker, M., Favaro, P., Jin, M.: Deep mean-shift priors for image restoration. In: NIPS (2017)
34. Liao, R., Tao, X., Li, R., Ma, Z., Jia, J.: Video super-resolution via deep draft-ensemble learning. In: ICCV (2015)
35. Kappeler, A., Yoo, S., Dai, Q., Katsaggelos, A.K.: Video super-resolution with convolutional neural networks. IEEE Trans. Comput. Imaging **2**(2), 109–122 (2016)
36. Jaderberg, M., Simonyan, K., Zisserman, A., et al.: Spatial transformer networks. In: NIPS (2015)

37. Shashua, S.D.C., Mannor, S.: Deep robust kalman filter. arXiv preprint arXiv:1703.02310 (2017)
38. Krishnan, R.G., Shalit, U., Sontag, D.: Deep Kalman filters. arXiv preprint arXiv:1511.05121 (2015)
39. Kalman, R.E.: A new approach to linear filtering and prediction problems. J. Basic Eng. **82**(1), 35–45 (1960)
40. Haykin, S.S.: Kalman Filtering and Neural Networks. Wiley Online Library, New York (2001)
41. He, K., Zhang, X., Ren, S., Sun, J.: Identity mappings in deep residual networks. In: Leibe, B., Matas, J., Sebe, N., Welling, M. (eds.) ECCV 2016. LNCS, vol. 9908, pp. 630–645. Springer, Cham (2016). https://doi.org/10.1007/978-3-319-46493-0_38
42. Ballé, J., Laparra, V., Simoncelli, E.P.: Density modeling of images using a generalized normalization transformation. arXiv preprint arXiv:1511.06281 (2015)
43. Abadi, M., et al.: Tensorflow: Large-scale machine learning on heterogeneous distributed systems. arXiv preprint arXiv:1603.04467 (2016)
44. Wang, Z., Bovik, A.C., Sheikh, H.R., Simoncelli, E.P.: Image quality assessment: from error visibility to structural similarity. TIP **13**(4), 600–612 (2004)
45. Kingma, D.P., Ba, J.: Adam: a method for stochastic optimization. arXiv preprint arXiv:1412.6980 (2014)
46. Glorot, X., Bengio, Y.: Understanding the difficulty of training deep feedforward neural networks. In: International Conference on Artificial Intelligence and Statistics (2010)
47. Maggioni, M., Boracchi, G., Foi, A., Egiazarian, K.: Video denoising, deblocking, and enhancement through separable 4-d nonlocal spatiotemporal transforms. TIP **21**(9), 3952–3966 (2012)

A Deeply-Initialized Coarse-to-fine Ensemble of Regression Trees for Face Alignment

Roberto Valle[1]([✉])(iD), José M. Buenaposada[2](iD), Antonio Valdés[3], and Luis Baumela[1]

[1] Univ. Politécnica de Madrid, Madrid, Spain
{rvalle,lbaumela}@fi.upm.es
[2] Univ. Rey Juan Carlos, Móstoles, Spain
josemiguel.buenaposada@urjc.es
[3] Univ. Complutense de Madrid, Madrid, Spain
avaldes@ucm.es

Abstract. In this paper we present DCFE, a real-time facial landmark regression method based on a coarse-to-fine Ensemble of Regression Trees (ERT). We use a simple Convolutional Neural Network (CNN) to generate probability maps of landmarks location. These are further refined with the ERT regressor, which is initialized by fitting a 3D face model to the landmark maps. The coarse-to-fine structure of the ERT lets us address the combinatorial explosion of parts deformation. With the 3D model we also tackle other key problems such as robust regressor initialization, self occlusions, and simultaneous frontal and profile face analysis. In the experiments DCFE achieves the best reported result in AFLW, COFW, and 300 W private and common public data sets.

Keywords: Face alignment · Cascaded shape regression Convolutional neural networks · Coarse-to-Fine · Occlusions Real-time

1 Introduction

Facial landmarks detection is a preliminary step for many face image analysis problems such as verification and recognition [25], attributes estimation [2], etc. The availability of large annotated data sets has recently encouraged research in this area with important performance improvements. However, it is still a challenging task especially when the faces suffer from large pose variations and partial occlusions.

The top performers in the recent 300 W benchmark are all based in deep regression models [20,23,30,33] (see Table 1). The most prominent feature of these approaches is their robustness, due to the large receptive fields of deep nets. However, in these models it is not easy to enforce facial shape consistency or estimate self occlusions.

© Springer Nature Switzerland AG 2018
V. Ferrari et al. (Eds.): ECCV 2018, LNCS 11218, pp. 609–624, 2018.
https://doi.org/10.1007/978-3-030-01264-9_36

ERT-based models [6,7,18,24], on the other hand, are easy to parallelize and implicitly impose shape consistency in their estimations. They are much more efficient than deep models and, as we demonstrate in our experiments (see Fig. 4), with a good initialization, they are also very accurate.

In this paper we present a hybrid method, termed Deeply-initialized Coarse-to-Fine Ensemble (DCFE). It uses a simple CNN to generate probability maps of landmarks location. Hence, obtaining information about the position of individual landmarks without a globally imposed shape. Then we fit a 3D face model, thus enforcing a global face shape prior. This is the starting point of the coarse-to-fine ERT regressor. The fitted 3D face model provides the regressor with a valid initial shape and information about landmarks visibility. The coarse-to-fine approach lets the ERT easily address the combinatorial explosion of all possible deformations of non-rigid parts and at the same time impose a part shape prior. The proposed method runs in real-time (32 FPS) and provides the best reported results in AFLW, COFW, and 300 W private and common public data sets.

2   Related Work

Face alignment has been a topic of intense research for more than twenty years. Initial successful results were based on 2D and 3D generative approaches such as the Active Appearance Models (AAM) [8] or the 3D Morphable Models [4]. More recent discriminative methods are based on two key ideas: indexing image description relative to the current shape estimate [12] and the use of a regressor whose predictions lie on the subspace spanned by the training face shapes [7], this is the so-called Cascade Shape Regressor (CSR) framework. Kazemi et al. [18] improved the original cascade framework by proposing a real-time ensemble of regression trees. Ren et al. [24] used locally binary features to boost the performance up to 3000 FPS. Burgos-Artizzu et al. [6] included occlusion information. Xiong et al. [31,32] use SIFT features and learn a linear regressor dividing the search space into individual regions with similar gradient directions. Overall, the CSR approach is very sensitive to the starting point of the regression process. An important part of recent work revolves around how to find good initialisations [37,38]. In this paper we use the landmark probability maps produced by a CNN to find a robust starting point for the CSR.

Current state-of-the-art methods in face alignment are based on CNNs. Sun et al. [26] were pioneers to apply a three-level CNN to obtain accurate landmark estimation. Zhang et al. [36] proposed a multi-task solution to deal with face alignment and attributes classification. Lv et al.'s [23] uses global and local face parts regressors for fine-grained facial deformation estimation. Yu et al. [34] transforms the landmarks rather than the input image for the refinement cascade. Trigeorgis et al. [27] and Xiao et al. [30] are the first approaches that fuse the feature extraction and regression steps of CSR into a recurrent neural network trained end-to-end. Kowalski et al. [20] and Yang et al. [33] are among the top performers in the Menpo competition [35]. Both use a global similarity transform to normalize landmark locations followed by a VGG-based and a Stacked Hourglass network respectively to regress the final shape. The large receptive fields of deep neural nets convey these approaches with a high degree of robustness to face rotation, scale and deformation. However, it is not clear how to impose facial shape consistency on the estimated set of landmarks. Moreover, to achieve accuracy they resort to a cascade of deep models that progressively refine the estimation, thus incrementing the computational requirements.

There is also an increasing number of works based on 3D face models. In the simplest case they fit a mean model to the estimated image landmarks position [19] or jointly regress the pose and shape of the face [17,29]. These approaches provide 3D pose information that may be used to estimate landmark self-occlusions or to train simpler regressors specialized in a given head orientation. However, building and fitting a 3D face model is a difficult task and the results of the full 3D approaches in current benchmarks are not as good as those described above.

Our proposal tries to leverage the best features of the previous approaches. Using a CCN-based initialization we inherit the robustness of deep models. Like the simple 3D approaches we fit a rigid 3D face model to initialize the ERT and estimate global face orientation to address self occlusions. Finally, we use an ERT within a coarse-to-fine framework to achieve accuracy and efficiency.

3   Deeply Initialized Coarse-to-Fine Ensemble

In this section, we present the Deeply-initialized Coarse-to-fine Ensemble method (DCFE). It consists of two main steps: CNN-based rigid face pose computation and ERT-based non-rigid face deformation estimation, both shown in Fig. 1.

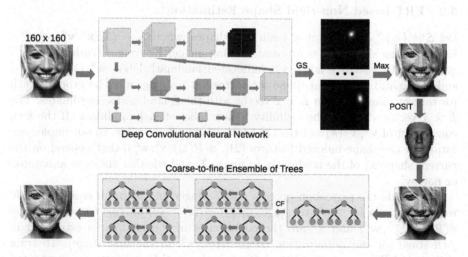

Fig. 1. DCFE framework diagram. GS, Max and POSIT represent the Gaussian smoothing filter, the maximum of each probability map and the 3D pose estimation respectively.

3.1   Rigid Pose Computation

ERT-based regressors require an acceptable initialization to converge to a good solution. We propose the use of face landmark location probability maps like [3, 9, 30] to generate plausible shape initialization candidates. We have modified Honari *et al.*'s [16] RCN introducing a loss function to handle missing landmarks, thus enabling semi-supervised training. We train this CNN to obtain a set of probability maps, $\mathcal{P}(\mathtt{I})$, indicating the position of each landmark in the input image (see Fig. 1). The maximum of each smoothed probability map determines our initial landmark positions. Note in Fig. 1 that these predictions are sensitive to occlusions and may not be a valid face shape. Compared to typical CNN-based approaches, *e.g.*, [33], our CNN is simpler, since we only require a rough estimation of landmark locations.

To start the ERT with a plausible face, we compute the initial shape by fitting a rigid 3D head model to the estimated 2D landmarks locations. To this end we use the softPOSIT algorithm proposed by David *et al.* [10]. As a result, we project the 3D model onto the image using the estimated rigid transformation. This provides the ERT with a rough estimation of the scale, translation and 3D pose of the target face (see Fig. 1).

Let $\mathbf{x}^0 = g_0(\mathcal{P}(\mathtt{I}))$ be the *initial shape*, the output of the initialization function g_0 after processing the input image $\mathtt{I}$. In this case $\mathbf{x}^0$ is a $L \times 2$ vector with L 2D landmarks coordinates. With our initialization we ensure that $\mathbf{x}^0$ is a valid face shape. This guarantees that the predictions in the next step of the algorithm will also be valid face shapes [7].

3.2   ERT-based Non-rigid Shape Estimation

Let $\mathcal{S} = \{s_i\}_{i=1}^N$ be the set of train face shapes, where $s_i = (\mathtt{I}_i, \mathbf{x}_i^g, \mathbf{v}_i^g, \mathbf{w}_i^g, \mathbf{x}_i^0)$. Each training shape s_i has its own: training image, $\mathtt{I}_i$; ground truth shape, $\mathbf{x}_i^g$; ground truth visibility label, $\mathbf{v}_i^g$; annotated landmark label, $\mathbf{w}_i^g$ (1 annotated and 0 missing) and initial shape for regression training, $\mathbf{x}_i^0$. The ground truth (or target) shape, $\mathbf{x}_i^g$, is a $L \times 2$ vector with the L landmarks coordinates. The $L \times 1$ vector $\mathbf{v}_i^g$ holds the visibility binary label of each landmark. If the k-th component of $\mathbf{v}^g$, $\mathbf{v}^g(k) = 1$ then the k-th landmark is visible. In our implementation we use shape-indexed features [21], $\phi(\mathcal{P}(\mathtt{I}_i), \mathbf{x}_i^t, \mathbf{w}_i^g)$, that depend on the current shape $\mathbf{x}_i^t$ of the landmarks in image $\mathtt{I}_i$ and whether they are annotated or not, $\mathbf{w}_i^t$.

We divide the regression process into T stages and learn an ensemble of K regression trees for the t-th stage, $\mathcal{C}_t(f_i) = \mathbf{x}^{t-1} + \sum_{k=1}^K g_k(f_i)$, where $f_i = \phi(\mathcal{P}(\mathtt{I}), \mathbf{x}^{t-1}, \mathbf{w}_i^g)$ and $\mathbf{x}^j$ are the coordinates of the landmarks estimated in j-th stage (or the initialization coordinates, $\mathbf{x}^0$, in the first stage). To train the whole ERT we use the N training samples in $\mathcal{S}$ to generate an augmented training set, $\mathcal{S}_A$ with cardinality $N_A = |\mathcal{S}_A|$. From each training shape s_i we generate additional training samples by changing their initial shape. To this end we randomly sample new candidate landmark positions from the smoothed probability maps to generate the new initial shapes (see Sect. 3.1).

We incorporate the visibility label $\mathbf{v}$ with the shape to better handle occlusions (see Fig. 5c) in a way similar to Burgos-Artizzu et al. [6] and naturally handling partially labelled training data like Kazemi et al. [18] using ground-truth annotation labels $\mathbf{w} \in \{0, 1\}$. Each initial shape is progressively refined by estimating a shape and visibility increments $C_t^{\mathbf{v}}(\phi(\mathcal{P}(\mathbf{I}_i), \mathbf{x}_i^{t-1}, \mathbf{w}_i^g))$ where $\mathbf{x}_i^{t-1}$ represents the current shape of the i-th sample (see Algorithm 1). $C_t^{\mathbf{v}}$ is trained to minimize only the landmark position errors but on each tree leaf, in addition to the mean shape, we also output the mean of all training shapes visibilities, $\mathbf{v}_i^g$, that belong to that node. We define $\mathcal{U}_{t-1} = \{(\mathbf{x}_i^{t-1}, \mathbf{v}_i^{t-1})\}_{i=1}^{N_A}$ as the set of all current shapes and corresponding visibility vectors for all training data.

Algorithm 1. Training an Ensemble of Regression Trees

Input: Training data $\mathcal{S}$, T

   Generate augmented training samples set, $\mathcal{S}_A$

   for t=1 to T **do**

      Extract features for all samples, $\mathcal{F}_A = \{f_i\}_{i=1}^{N_A} = \{\phi(\mathcal{P}(\mathbf{I}_i), \mathbf{x}_i^{t-1}, \mathbf{w}_i^g)\}_{i=1}^{N_A}$

      Learn coarse-to-fine regressor, $C_t^{\mathbf{v}}$, from $\mathcal{S}_A$, $\mathcal{F}_A$ and $\mathcal{U}_{t-1} = \{(\mathbf{x}_i^{t-1}, \mathbf{v}_i^{t-1})\}_{i=1}^{N_A}$

      Update current shapes and visibilities, $\{(\mathbf{x}_i^t, \mathbf{v}_i^t) = (\mathbf{x}_i^{t-1}, \mathbf{v}_i^{t-1}) + C_t^{\mathbf{v}}(f_i)\}_{i=1}^{N_A}$

   end for

Output: $\{C_t^{\mathbf{v}}\}_{t=1}^T$

Compared with conventional ERT approaches, our ensemble is simpler. It will require fewer trees because we only have to estimate the non-rigid face shape deformation, since the 3D rigid component has been estimated in the previous step. In the following, we describe the details of our ERT.

Initial Shapes for Regression. The selection of the starting point in the ERT is fundamental to reach a good solution. The simplest choice is the mean of the ground truth training shapes, $\bar{x}^0 = \sum_{i=1}^N \mathbf{x}_i^g/N$. However, such a poor initialization leads to wrong alignment results in test images with large pose variations. Alternative strategies are running the ERT several times with different initializations and taking the median [6], initializing with other ground truth shapes $x_i^0 \leftarrow x_j^g$ where $i \neq j$ [18] or randomly deforming the initial shape [20].

In our approach we initialize the ERT using the algorithm described in Sect. 3.1, that provides a robust and approximate shape for initialization (see Fig. 2). Hence, the ERT only needs to estimate the non-rigid component of face pose.

Feature Extraction. ERT efficiency depends on the feature extraction step. In general, descriptor features such as SIFT used by [31,38] improve face alignment results, but have higher computational cost compared to simpler features such as plain pixel value differences [6,7,18,24]. In our case, a simple feature suffices, since shape landmarks are close to their ground truth location.

Fig. 2. Worst initial shapes for the 300 W training subset.

In DCFE we use the probability maps $\mathcal{P}(\mathtt{I})$ to extract features for the cascade. To this end, we select a landmark l and its associated probability map $\mathcal{P}^l(\mathtt{I})$. The feature is computed as the difference between two pixels values in $\mathcal{P}^l(\mathtt{I})$ from a FREAK descriptor pattern [1] around l. Our features are similar to those in Lee *et al.* [21]. However, ours are defined on the probability maps, $\mathcal{P}(\mathtt{I})$, instead of the image, $\mathtt{I}$. We let the training algorithm select the most informative landmark and pair of pixels in each iteration.

Learn a Coarse-to-fine Regressor. To train the t-th stage regressor, $\mathcal{C}_t^{\mathbf{v}}$, we fit an ERT. Thus, the goal is to sequentially learn a series of weak learners to greedily minimize the regression loss function:

$$\mathcal{L}_t(\mathcal{S}_A, \mathcal{F}_A, \mathcal{U}_{t-1}) = \sum_{i=1}^{N_A} ||\mathbf{w}_i^g \odot (\mathbf{x}_i^g - \mathbf{x}_i^{t-1} - \sum_{k=1}^{K} g_k(f_i))||^2, \qquad (1)$$

where $\odot$ is the Hadamard product. There are different ways of minimizing Eq. 1. Kazemi *et al.* [18] present a general framework based on Gradient Boosting for learning an ensemble of regression trees. Lee *et al.* [21] establish an optimization method based on Gaussian Processes also learning an ensemble of regression trees but outperforming previous literature by reducing the overfitting.

A crucial problem when training a global face landmark regressor is the lack of examples showing all possible combinations of face parts deformations. Hence, these regressors quickly overfit and generalize poorly to combinations of part deformations not present in the training set. To address this problem we introduce the coarse-to-fine ERT architecture.

The goal is to be able to cope with combinations of face part deformations not seen during training. A single monolithic regressor is not able to estimate these local deformations (see difference between Figs. 3b and c). Our algorithm is agnostic in the number of parts or levels of the coarse-to-fine estimation. Algorithm 2 details the training of P face parts regressors (each one with a subset of the landmarks) to build a coarse-to-fine regressor. Note that $\mathbf{x}_i^0$ and $\mathbf{v}_i^0$ in this context are the shape and visibility vectors from the last regressor output (*e.g.*, the previous part regressor or a previous full stage regressor). In our implementation we use $P = 1$ (all landmarks) with the first K_1 regressors and in the last K_2 regressors the number of parts is increased to $P = 10$ (left/right eyebrow, left/right eye, nose, top/bottom mouth, left/right ear and chin), see all the parts connected by lines in Fig. 3c.

Algorithm 2. Training P parts regressors

Input: $\mathcal{S}_A, \mathcal{F}_A, \{(\mathbf{x}_i^0, \mathbf{v}_i^0)\}_{i=1}^{N_A}, \nu, K, P$

  for k=1 to K **do**

    for p=1 to P **do**

      // $\odot$ is the Hadamard product, (p) selects elements of a vector in that part

      Compute shape residuals $\{\mathbf{r}_i^k(p) = \mathbf{w}_i^g(p) \odot (\mathbf{x}_i^g(p) - \mathbf{x}_i^{k-1}(p))\}_{i=1}^{N_A}$

      Fit a regression tree g_k^p using the residuals $\{\mathbf{r}_i^k(p)\}$ and $\mathcal{F}_A(p)$

      // ν is the shrinkage factor to scale the contribution of each tree

      Update samples $\{(\mathbf{x}_i^k(p), \mathbf{v}_i^k(p)) = (\mathbf{x}_i^{k-1}(p), \mathbf{v}_i^{k-1}(p)) + \nu \cdot g_k^p(f_i(p))\}_{i=1}^{N_A}$

    end for

  end for

Output: P part regressors $\{\mathcal{C}^p\}_{p=1}^P$, with K weak learners each $\mathcal{C}^p = \{g_k^p\}_{k=1}^K$

Fit a Regression Tree. The training objective for the k-th regression tree is to minimize the sum of squared residuals, taking into account the annotated landmark labels:

$$\mathcal{E}_k = \sum_{i=1}^{N_A} ||\mathbf{r}_i^k||^2 = \sum_{i=1}^{N_A} ||\mathbf{w}_i^g \odot (\mathbf{x}_i^g - \mathbf{x}_i^{k-1})||^2 \tag{2}$$

We learn each regression binary tree by recursively splitting the training set into the left (l) and right (r) child nodes. The tree node split function is designed to minimize $\mathcal{E}_k$ from Eq. 2 in the selected landmark. To train a regression tree node we randomly generate a set of candidate split functions, each of them involving four parameters $\theta = (\tau, \mathbf{p}_1, \mathbf{p}_2, l)$, where $\mathbf{p}_1$ and $\mathbf{p}_2$ are pixels coordinates on a fixed FREAK structure around the l-th landmark coordinates in $\mathbf{x}_i^{k-1}$. The feature value corresponding to θ for the i-th training sample is $f_i(\theta) = \mathcal{P}^l(\mathbf{I}_i)[\mathbf{p}_1] - \mathcal{P}^l(\mathbf{I}_i)[\mathbf{p}_2]$, the difference of probability values in the maps for the given landmark. Finally, we compute the split function thresholding the feature value, $f_i(\theta) > \tau$.

Given $\mathcal{N} \subset \mathcal{S}_A$ the set of training samples at a node, fitting a tree node for the k-th tree, consists of finding the parameter θ that minimizes $E_k(\mathcal{N}, \theta)$

$$\arg\min_\theta E_k(\mathcal{N}, \theta) = \arg\min_\theta \sum_{b \in \{l, r\}} \sum_{s \in \mathcal{N}_{\theta,b}} ||\mathbf{r}_s^k - \boldsymbol{\mu}_{\theta,b}||^2 \tag{3}$$

where $\mathcal{N}_{\theta,l}$ and $\mathcal{N}_{\theta,r}$ are, respectively, the samples sent to the left and right child nodes due to the decision induced by θ. The mean residual $\boldsymbol{\mu}_{\theta,b}$ for a candidate split function and a subset of training data is given by

$$\boldsymbol{\mu}_{\theta,b} = \frac{1}{|\mathcal{N}_{\theta,b}|} \sum_{s \in \mathcal{N}_{\theta,b}} \mathbf{r}_s^k \tag{4}$$

Once we know the optimal split each leaf node stores the mean residual, $\boldsymbol{\mu}_{\theta,b}$, as the output of the regression for any example reaching that leaf.

4   Experiments

To train and evaluate our proposal, we perform experiments with 300W, COFW
and AFLW that are considered the most challenging public data sets. In addition,
we also show qualitative face alignment results with the Menpo competition
images.

- **300W**. It provides bounding boxes and 68 manually annotated landmarks.
  We follow the most established approach and divide the 300 W annotations
  into 3148 training and 689 testing images (public competition). Evaluation is
  also performed on the newly updated 300 W private competition.
- **Menpo**. Consist of 8979 training and 16259 testing faces containing 12006
  semi-frontal and 4253 profile images. The images were annotated with the
  previous set of 68 landmarks but without facial bounding boxes.
- **COFW**. It focuses on occlusion. Commonly, there are 1345 training faces
  in total. The testing set is made of 507 images. The annotations include the
  landmark positions and the binary occlusion labels for 29 points.
- **AFLW**. Provides an extensive collection of 25993 in-the-wild faces, with
  21 facial landmarks annotated depending on their visibility. We have found
  several annotations errors and, consequently, removed these faces from our
  experiments. From the remaining faces we randomly choose 19312 images for
  training/validation and 4828 instances for testing.

4.1   Evaluation

We use the Normalized Mean Error (NME) as a metric to measure the shape
estimation error

$$NME = \frac{100}{N} \sum_{i=1}^{N} \left(\frac{1}{\|\mathbf{w}_i^g\|_1} \sum_{l=1}^{L} \left(\frac{\mathbf{w}_i^g(l) \cdot \|\mathbf{x}_i(l) - \mathbf{x}_i^g(l)\|}{d_i} \right) \right). \tag{5}$$

It computes the euclidean distance between the ground-truth and estimated
landmark positions normalized by d_i. We report our results using different values
of d_i: the distance between the eye centres (*pupils*), the distance between the
outer eye corners (*corners*) and the bounding box size (*height*).

In addition, we also compare our results using Cumulative Error Distribution (CED) curves. We calculate AUC_ε as the area under the CED curve for
images with an NME smaller than ε and FR_ε as the failure rate representing
the percentage of testing faces with NME greater than ε. We use precision/recall
percentages to compare occlusion prediction.

To train our algorithm we shuffle the training set and split it into 90% trainset and 10% validation-set.

4.2   Implementation

All experiments have been carried out with the settings described in this section. We train from scratch the CNN selecting the model parameters with lowest validation error. We crop faces using the original bounding boxes annotations enlarged by 30%. We generate different training samples in each epoch by applying random in plane rotations between $\pm 30°$, scale changes by $\pm 15\%$ and translations by $\pm 5\%$ of bounding box size, randomly mirroring images horizontally and generating random rectangular occlusions. We use Adam stochastic optimization with $\beta_1 = 0.9$, $\beta_2 = 0.999$ and $\epsilon = 1e^{-8}$ parameters. We train during 400 epochs with an initial learning rate $\alpha = 0.001$, without decay and a batch size of 35 images. In the CNN the cropped input face is reduced from 160×160 to 1×1 pixels gradually dividing by half their size across $B = 8$ branches applying a 2×2 pooling[1]. All layers contain 64 channels to describe the required landmark features.

We train the coarse-to-fine ERT with the Gradient Boosting algorithm [15]. It requires $T = 20$ stages of $K = 50$ regression trees per stage. The depth of trees is set to 5. The number of tests to choose the best split parameters, θ, is set to 200. We resize each image to set the face size to 160 pixels. For feature extraction, the FREAK pattern diameter is reduced gradually in each stage (*i.e.*, in the last stages the pixel pairs for each feature are closer). We generate several initializations for each face training image to create a set of at least $N_A = 60000$ samples to train the cascade. To avoid overfitting we use a shrinkage factor $\nu = 0.1$ in the ERT. Our regressor triggers the coarse-to-fine strategy once the cascade has gone through 40% of the stages (see Fig. 3a).

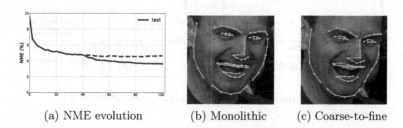

(a) NME evolution   (b) Monolithic   (c) Coarse-to-fine

Fig. 3. Example of a monolithic ERT regressor vs our coarse-to-fine approach. (a) Evolution of the error through the different stages in the cascade (dashed line represents the algorithm without the coarse-to-fine improvement); (b) predicted shape with a monolithic regressor; (c) predicted shape with our coarse-to-fine approach.

For the Mempo data set training the CNN and the coarse-to-fine ensemble of trees takes 48 h using a NVidia GeForce GTX 1080 (8 GB) GPU and an Intel Xeon E5-1650 at 3.50 GHz (6 cores/12 threads, 32 GB of RAM). At runtime our method process test images on average at a rate of 32 FPS, where the CNN takes 25 ms and the ERT 6.25 ms per face image using C++, Tensorflow and OpenCV libraries.

---

[1] Except when the 5×5 images are reduced to 2×2 where we apply a 3×3 pooling.

4.3   Results

Here we compare our algorithm, DCFE, with the best reported results for each data set. To this end we have trained our model and those in DAN [20], RCN [16], cGPRT [21], RCPR [6] and ERT [18] with the code provided by the authors and the same settings including same training, validation and bounding boxes. In Fig. 4 we plot the CED curves and we provide AUC_8 and FR_8 values for each algorithm. Also, for comparison with other methods in Tables 1, 2, 3, 4 we show the original results published in the literature.

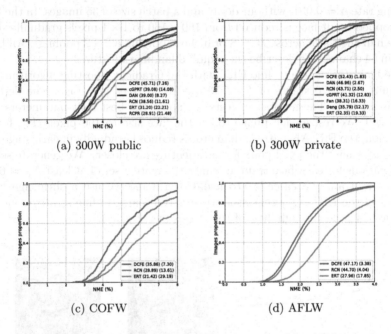

(a) 300W public   (b) 300W private

(c) COFW   (d) AFLW

Fig. 4. Cumulative error distributions sorted by AUC.

In Tables 1 and 2 we provide the results of the state-of-the-art methods in the 300 W public and private data sets. Our approach obtains the best performance in the private (see Table 2) and in the common and full subsets of the 300 W competition public test set (see Table 1). This is due to the excellent accuracy achieved by the coarse-to-fine ERT scheme enforcing valid face shapes. In the challenging subset of the 300 W competition public test set SHN [33] achieves better results. This is caused by errors in initializing the ERT in a few images with very large scale and pose variations, that are not present in the training set. Our method exhibits superior capability in handling cases with low error since we achieve the best NME results in the 300 W common subset by the largest margin. The CED curves in Figs. 4a and b show that DCFE is better than all its competitors that provide code in all types of images in both data sets.

In the 300 W private challenge we obtain the best results outperforming Deng *et al.* [11] and Fan *et al.* [13] that were the academia and industry winners of the competition (see Fig. 4b).

Table 1. Error of face alignment methods on the 300 W public test set.

Method	Common		Challenging		Full			
	Pupils	Corners	Pupils	Corners	Pupils	Corners		
	NME	*NME*	*NME*	*NME*	*NME*	*NME*	AUC_8	FR_8
RCPR [6]	6.18	-	17.26	-	8.35	-	-	-
ESR [7]	5.28	-	17.00	-	7.58	-	43.12	10.45
SDM [31]	5.60	-	15.40	-	7.52	-	42.94	10.89
ERT [18]	-	-	-	-	6.40	-	-	-
LBF [24]	4.95	-	11.98	-	6.32	-	-	-
cGPRT [21]	-	-	-	-	5.71	-	-	-
CFSS [38]	4.73	-	9.98	-	5.76	-	49.87	5.08
DDN [34]	-	-	-	-	5.65	-	-	-
TCDCN [36]	4.80	-	8.60	-	5.54	-	-	-
MDM [27]	-	-	-	-	-	-	52.12	4.21
RCN [16]	4.67	-	8.44	-	5.41	-	-	-
DAN [20]	4.42	3.19	7.57	5.24	5.03	3.59	55.33	1.16
TSR [23]	4.36	-	7.56	-	4.99	-	-	-
RAR [30]	4.12	-	8.35	-	4.94	-	-	-
SHN [33]	4.12	-	7.00	4.90	-	-	-	-
DCFE	3.83	2.76	7.54	5.22	4.55	3.24	60.13	1.59

We may appreciate the improvement achieved by the ERT by comparing the results of DCFE in the full subset of 300W, 4.55, with Honari's baseline RCN [16], 5.41. It represents an 16% improvement. The coarse-to-fine strategy in our ERT only affects difficult cases, with rare facial part combinations. Zooming-in Figs. 3b and c you may appreciate how it improves the adjustment of the cheek and mouth. Although it is a crucial step to align local parts properly, the global NME is only marginally affected.

Table 3 and Fig. 4c compare the performance of our model and baselines using the COFW data set. We obtain the best results (*i.e.*, NME 5.27) establishing a new state-of-the-art without requiring a sophisticated network, which demonstrates the importance of preserving the facial shape and the robustness of our framework to severe occlusions. In terms of landmark visibility, we have obtained comparable performance with previous methods.

Table 2. Error of face alignment methods on the 300 W private test set.

Method	Indoor Corners			Outdoor Corners			Full Corners		
	NME	AUC_8	FR_8	NME	AUC_8	FR_8	NME	AUC_8	FR_8
ESR [7]	-	-	-	-	-	-	-	32.35	17.00
cGPRT [21]	-	-	-	-	-	-	-	41.32	12.83
CFSS [38]	-	-	-	-	-	-	-	39.81	12.30
MDM [27]	-	-	-	-	-	-	5.05	45.32	6.80
DAN [20]	-	-	-	-	-	-	4.30	47.00	2.67
SHN [33]	4.10	-	-	4.00	-	-	4.05	-	-
DCFE	3.96	52.28	2.33	3.81	52.56	1.33	3.88	52.42	1.83

Table 3. COFW results.

Method	Pupils			Occlusion
	NME	AUC_8	FR_8	Precision/Recall
ESR [7]	11.20	-	-	-
RCPR [6]	8.50	-	-	80/40
TCDCN [36]	8.05	-	-	-
RAR [30]	6.03	-	-	-
DAC-CSR [14]	6.03	-	-	-
Wu *et al.* [28]	5.93	-	-	80/49.11
SHN [33]	5.6	-	-	-
DCFE	5.27	35.86	7.29	81.59/49.57

Table 4. AFLW results.

Method	Height
	NME
ESR [7]	4.35
CFSS [38]	3.92
RCPR [6]	3.73
Bulat *et al.* [5]	2.85
CCL [37]	2.72
DAC-CSR [14]	2.27
TSR [23]	2.17
DCFE	2.17

In Table 4 and Fig. 4d we show the results with AFLW. This is a challenging data set not only because of its size, but also because of the number of samples with self-occluded landmarks that are not annotated. This is the reason for the small number of competitors in Fig. 4d, very few approaches allow training with missing data. Although the results in Table 4 are not strictly comparable because each paper uses its own train and test subsets, we get a NME of 2.17 that again establishes a new state-of-the-art, considering that [14,23,37] do not use the two most difficult landmarks, the ones in the ears.

Menpo test annotations have not been released, but we have processed their testing images to visually perform an analysis of the errors. In comparison with many other approaches our algorithm evaluates in both subsets training a unique semi-supervised model through the 68 (semi-frontal) and 39 (profile) landmark annotations all together. We detect test faces using the public Single Shot Detector [22] from OpenCV. We manually filter the detected face bounding boxes to reduce false positives and improve the accuracy.

In Fig. 5 we present some qualitative results for all data sets, including Menpo.

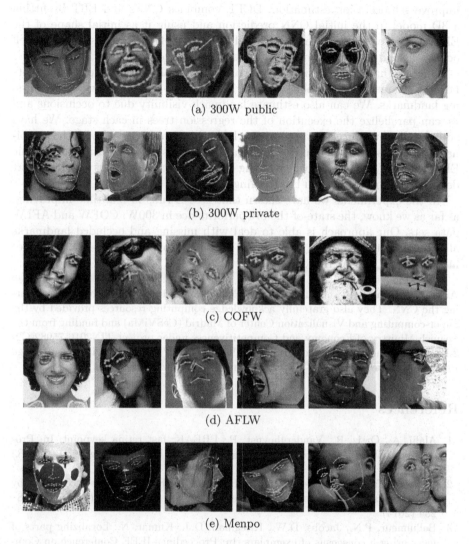

(a) 300W public

(b) 300W private

(c) COFW

(d) AFLW

(e) Menpo

Fig. 5. Representative results using DCFE in 300W, COFW, AFLW and Menpo testing subsets. Blue colour represents ground truth, green and red colours point out visible and non-visible shape predictions respectively. (Color figure online)

5   Conclusions

In this paper we have introduced DCFE, a robust face alignment method that leverages on the best features of the three main approaches in the literature: 3D face models, CNNs and ERT. The CNN provides robust landmark estimations with no face shape enforcement. The ERT is able to enforce face shape and achieve better accuracy in landmark detection, but it only converges when properly initialized. Finally, 3D models exploit face orientation information to improve self-occlusion estimation. DCFE combines CNNs and ERT by fitting a 3D model to the initial CNN prediction and using it as initial shape of the ERT. Moreover, the 3D reasoning capability allows DCFE to easily handle self occlusions and deal with both frontal and profile faces.

Once we have solved the problem of ERT initialization, we can exploit its benefits. Namely, we are able to train it in a semi-supervised way with missing landmarks. We can also estimate landmark visibility due to occlusions and we can parallelize the execution of the regression trees in each stage. We have additionally introduced a coarse-to-fine ERT that is able to deal with the combinatorial explosion of local parts deformation. In this case, the usual monolithic ERT will perform poorly when fitting faces with combinations of facial part deformations not present in the training set.

In the experiments we have shown that DCFE runs in real-time improving, as far as we know, the state-of-the-art performance in 300W, COFW and AFLW data sets. Our approach is able to deal with missing and occluded landmarks allowing us to train a single regressor for both full profile and semi-frontal images in the Mempo and AFLW data sets.

Acknowledgments. The authors thank Pedro López Maroto for his help implementing the CNN. They also gratefully acknowledge computing resources provided by the Super-computing and Visualization Center of Madrid (CeSViMa) and funding from the Spanish Ministry of Economy and Competitiveness under project TIN2016-75982-C2-2-R. José M. Buenaposada acknowledges the support of Computer Vision and Image Processing research group (CVIP) from Universidad Rey Juan Carlos.

References

1. Alahi, A., Ortiz, R., Vandergheynst, P.: FREAK: fast retina keypoint. In: Proceedings IEEE Conference on Computer Vision and Pattern Recognition (CVPR) (2012)
2. Bekios-Calfa, J., Buenaposada, J.M., Baumela, L.: Robust gender recognition by exploiting facial attributes dependencies. Pattern Recognit. Lett. (PRL) **36**, 228–234 (2014)
3. Belhumeur, P.N., Jacobs, D.W., Kriegman, D.J., Kumar, N.: Localizing parts of faces using a consensus of exemplars. In: Proceedings IEEE Conference on Computer Vision and Pattern Recognition (CVPR) (2011)
4. Blanz, V., Vetter, T.: Face recognition based on fitting a 3D morphable model. IEEE Trans. Pattern Anal. Mach. Intell. (TPAMI) (2003)
5. Bulat, A., Tzimiropoulos, G.: Binarized convolutional landmark localizers for human pose estimation and face alignment with limited resources. In: Proceedings International Conference on Computer Vision (ICCV) (2017)
6. Burgos-Artizzu, X.P., Perona, P., Dollar, P.: Robust face landmark estimation under occlusion. In: Proceedings International Conference on Computer Vision (ICCV) (2013)

7. Cao, X., Wei, Y., Wen, F., Sun, J.: Face alignment by explicit shape regression. In: Proceedings IEEE Conference on Computer Vision and Pattern Recognition (CVPR) (2012)

8. Cootes, T.F., Edwards, G.J., Taylor, C.J.: Active appearance models. In: Burkhardt, H., Neumann, B. (eds.) ECCV 1998. LNCS, vol. 1407, pp. 484–498. Springer, Heidelberg (1998). https://doi.org/10.1007/BFb0054760

9. Dantone, M., Gall, J., Fanelli, G., Gool, L.V.: Real-time facial feature detection using conditional regression forests. In: Proceedings IEEE Conference on Computer Vision and Pattern Recognition (CVPR) (2012)

10. David, P., DeMenthon, D., Duraiswami, R., Samet, H.: SoftPOSIT: simultaneous pose and correspondence determination. Int. J. Comput. Vis. (IJCV) **59**(3), 259–284 (2004)

11. Deng, J., Liu, Q., Yang, J., Tao, D.: CSR: multi-view, multi-scale and multi-component cascade shape regression. Image Vis. Comput. (IVC) **47**, 19–26 (2016)

12. Dollar, P., Welinder, P., Perona, P.: Cascaded pose regression. In: Proceedings IEEE Conference on Computer Vision and Pattern Recognition (CVPR) (2010)

13. Fan, H., Zhou, E.: Approaching human level facial landmark localization by deep learning. Image Vis. Comput. (IVC) **47**, 27–35 (2016)

14. Feng, Z., Kittler, J., Christmas, W.J., Huber, P., Wu, X.: Dynamic attention-controlled cascaded shape regression exploiting training data augmentation and fuzzy-set sample weighting. In: Proceedings IEEE Conference on Computer Vision and Pattern Recognition (CVPR) (2017)

15. Hastie, T., Tibshirani, R., Friedman, J.H.: The Elements of Statistical Learning. Springer, New York (2009). https://doi.org/10.1007/978-0-387-84858-7

16. Honari, S., Yosinski, J., Vincent, P., Pal, C.J.: Recombinator networks: Learning coarse-to-fine feature aggregation. In: Proceedings IEEE Conference on Computer Vision and Pattern Recognition (CVPR) (2016)

17. Jourabloo, A., Ye, M., Liu, X., Ren, L.: Pose-invariant face alignment with a single CNN. In: Proceedings International Conference on Computer Vision (ICCV) (2017)

18. Kazemi, V., Sullivan, J.: One millisecond face alignment with an ensemble of regression trees. In: Proceedings IEEE Conference on Computer Vision and Pattern Recognition (CVPR) (2014)

19. Kowalski, M., Naruniec, J.: Face alignment using K-Cluster regression forests with weighted splitting. IEEE Signal Process. Lett. **23**(11), 1567–1571 (2016)

20. Kowalski, M., Naruniec, J., Trzcinski, T.: Deep alignment network: a convolutional neural network for robust face alignment. In: Proceedings IEEE Conference on Computer Vision and Pattern Recognition Workshops (CVPRW) (2017)

21. Lee, D., Park, H., Yoo, C.D.: Face alignment using cascade gaussian process regression trees. In: Proceedings IEEE Conference on Computer Vision and Pattern Recognition (CVPR) (2015)

22. Liu, W., et al.: SSD: single shot multibox detector. In: Leibe, B., Matas, J., Sebe, N., Welling, M. (eds.) ECCV 2016. LNCS, vol. 9905, pp. 21–37. Springer, Cham (2016). https://doi.org/10.1007/978-3-319-46448-0_2

23. Lv, J., Shao, X., Xing, J., Cheng, C., Zhou, X.: A deep regression architecture with two-stage re-initialization for high performance facial landmark detection. In: Proceedings IEEE Conference on Computer Vision and Pattern Recognition (CVPR) (2017)

24. Ren, S., Cao, X., Wei, Y., Sun, J.: Face alignment at 3000 fps via regressing local binary features. In: Proceedings IEEE Conference on Computer Vision and Pattern Recognition (CVPR) (2014)

25. Soltanpour, S., Boufama, B., Wu, Q.M.J.: A survey of local feature methods for 3D face recognition. Pattern Recogn. (PR) **72**, 391–406 (2017)

26. Sun, Y., Wang, X., Tang, X.: Deep convolutional network cascade for facial point detection. In: Proceedings IEEE Conference on Computer Vision and Pattern Recognition (CVPR) (2013)

27. Trigeorgis, G., Snape, P., Nicolaou, M.A., Antonakos, E., Zafeiriou, S.: Mnemonic descent method: A recurrent process applied for end-to-end face alignment. In: Proceedings IEEE Conference on Computer Vision and Pattern Recognition (CVPR) (2016)

28. Wu, Y., Ji, Q.: Robust facial landmark detection under significant head poses and occlusion. In: Proceedings International Conference on Computer Vision (ICCV) (2015)

29. Xiao, S., et al.: Recurrent 3D–2D dual learning for large-pose facial landmark detection. In: Proceedings International Conference on Computer Vision (ICCV) (2017)

30. Xiao, S., Feng, J., Xing, J., Lai, H., Yan, S., Kassim, A.: Robust facial landmark detection via recurrent attentive-refinement networks. In: Leibe, B., Matas, J., Sebe, N., Welling, M. (eds.) ECCV 2016. LNCS, vol. 9905, pp. 57–72. Springer, Cham (2016). https://doi.org/10.1007/978-3-319-46448-0_4

31. Xiong, X., la Torre, F.D.: Supervised descent method and its applications to face alignment. In: Proceedings IEEE Conference on Computer Vision and Pattern Recognition (CVPR) (2013)

32. Xiong, X., la Torre, F.D.: Global supervised descent method. In: Proceedings IEEE Conference on Computer Vision and Pattern Recognition (CVPR) (2015)

33. Yang, J., Liu, Q., Zhang, K.: Stacked hourglass network for robust facial landmark localisation. In: Proceedings IEEE Conference on Computer Vision and Pattern Recognition Workshops (CVPRW) (2017)

34. Yu, X., Zhou, F., Chandraker, M.: Deep deformation network for object landmark localization. In: Leibe, B., Matas, J., Sebe, N., Welling, M. (eds.) ECCV 2016. LNCS, vol. 9909, pp. 52–70. Springer, Cham (2016). https://doi.org/10.1007/978-3-319-46454-1_4

35. Zafeiriou, S., Trigeorgis, G., Chrysos, G., Deng, J., Shen, J.: The menpo facial landmark localisation challenge: a step towards the solution. In: Proceedings IEEE Conference on Computer Vision and Pattern Recognition Workshops (CVPRW) (2017)

36. Zhang, Z., Luo, P., Loy, C.C., Tang, X.: Facial landmark detection by deep multi-task learning. In: Fleet, D., Pajdla, T., Schiele, B., Tuytelaars, T. (eds.) ECCV 2014. LNCS, vol. 8694, pp. 94–108. Springer, Cham (2014). https://doi.org/10.1007/978-3-319-10599-4_7

37. Zhu, S., Li, C., Change, C., Tang, X.: Unconstrained face alignment via cascaded compositional learning. In: Proceedings IEEE Conference on Computer Vision and Pattern Recognition (CVPR) (2016)

38. Zhu, S., Li, C., Loy, C.C., Tang, X.: Face alignment by coarse-to-fine shape searching. In: Proceedings IEEE Conference on Computer Vision and Pattern Recognition (CVPR) (2015)

DeepVS: A Deep Learning Based Video Saliency Prediction Approach

Lai Jiang⑩, Mai Xu$^{(\boxtimes)}$⑩, Tie Liu, Minglang Qiao, and Zulin Wang

Beihang University, Beijing, China
{jianglai.china,maixu,liutie,minglangqiao,wzulin}@buaa.edu.cn

Abstract. In this paper, we propose a novel deep learning based video saliency prediction method, named DeepVS. Specifically, we establish a large-scale eye-tracking database of videos (LEDOV), which includes 32 subjects' fixations on 538 videos. We find from LEDOV that human attention is more likely to be attracted by objects, particularly the moving objects or the moving parts of objects. Hence, an object-to-motion convolutional neural network (OM-CNN) is developed to predict the intra-frame saliency for DeepVS, which is composed of the objectness and motion subnets. In OM-CNN, cross-net mask and hierarchical feature normalization are proposed to combine the spatial features of the objectness subnet and the temporal features of the motion subnet. We further find from our database that there exists a temporal correlation of human attention with a smooth saliency transition across video frames. We thus propose saliency-structured convolutional long short-term memory (SS-ConvLSTM) network, using the extracted features from OM-CNN as the input. Consequently, the inter-frame saliency maps of a video can be generated, which consider both structured output with center-bias and cross-frame transitions of human attention maps. Finally, the experimental results show that DeepVS advances the state-of-the-art in video saliency prediction.

Keywords: Saliency prediction · Convolutional LSTM
Eye-tracking database

1 Introduction

The foveation mechanism in the human visual system (HVS) indicates that only a small fovea region captures most visual attention at high resolution, while other peripheral regions receive little attention at low resolution. To predict human attention, saliency prediction has been widely studied in recent years, with multiple applications [5,21,22,38] in object recognition, object segmentation, action recognition, image caption, and image/video compression, among others. In this

Electronic supplementary material The online version of this chapter (https://doi.org/10.1007/978-3-030-01264-9_37) contains supplementary material, which is available to authorized users.

paper, we focus on predicting video saliency at the pixel level, which models attention on each video frame.

The traditional video saliency prediction methods mainly focus on the feature integration theory [16,19,20,26], in which some spatial and temporal features were developed for video saliency prediction. Differing from the integration theory, the deep learning (DL) based methods [13,18,28,29,32] have been recently proposed to learn human attention in an end-to-end manner, significantly improving the accuracy of image saliency prediction. However, only a few works have managed to apply DL in video saliency prediction [1,2,23,27]. Specifically, Cagdas *et al.* [1] applied a two-stream CNN structure taking both RGB frames and motion maps as the inputs for video saliency prediction. Bazzani *et al.* [2] leveraged a deep convolutional 3D (C3D) network to learn the representations of human attention on 16 consecutive frames, and then a long short-term memory (LSTM) network connected to a mixture density network was learned to generate saliency maps in a Gaussian mixture distribution.

For training the DL networks, we establish a large-scale eye-tracking database of videos (LEDOV) that contains the free-view fixation data of 32 subjects viewing 538 diverse-content videos. We validate that 32 subjects are enough through consistency analysis among subjects, when establishing our LEDOV database. The previous databases [24,33] do not investigate the sufficient number of subjects in the eye-tracking experiments. For example, although Hollywood [24] contains 1857 videos, it only has 19 subjects and does not show whether the subjects are sufficient. More importantly, Hollywood focuses on task-driven attention, rather than free-view saliency prediction.

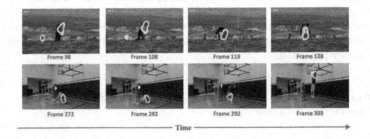

Fig. 1. Attention heat maps of some frames selected from two videos. The heat maps show that: (1) the regions with object can draw a majority of human attention, (2) the moving objects or the moving parts of objects attract more human attention, and (3) a dynamic pixel-wise transition of human attention occurs across video frames.

In this paper, we propose a new DL based video saliency prediction (DeepVS) method. We find from Fig. 1 that people tend to be attracted by the moving objects or the moving parts of objects, and this finding is also verified in the analysis of our LEDOV database. However, all above DL based methods do not explore the motion of objects in predicting video saliency. In DeepVS, a novel object-to-motion convolutional neural network (OM-CNN) is constructed to learn the features of object motion, in which the cross-net mask and hierarchical feature normalization (FN) are proposed to combine the subnets of objectness and motion. As such, the moving objects at different scales can be located as salient regions.

Both Fig. 1 and the analysis of our database show that the saliency maps are smoothly transited across video frames. Accordingly, a saliency-structured convolutional long short-term memory (SS-ConvLSTM) network is developed to predict the pixel-wise transition of video saliency across frames, with the output features of OM-CNN as the input. The traditional LSTM networks for video saliency prediction [2, 23] assume that human attention follows the Gaussian mixture distribution, since these LSTM networks cannot generate structured output. In contrast, our SS-ConvLSTM network is capable of retaining spatial information of attention distribution with structured output through the convolutional connections. Furthermore, since the center-bias (CB) exists in the saliency maps as shown in Fig. 1, a CB dropout is proposed in the SS-ConvLSTM network. As such, the structured output of saliency considers the CB prior. Consequently, the dense saliency prediction of each video frame can be obtained in DeepVS in an end-to-end manner. The experimental results show that our DeepVS method advances the state-of-the-art of video saliency prediction in our database and other 2 eye-tracking databases. Both the DeepVS code and the LEDOV database are available online.

2   Related Work

Feature Integration Methods. Most early saliency prediction methods [16, 20, 26, 34] relied on the feature integration theory, which is composed of two main steps: feature extraction and feature fusion. In the image saliency prediction task, many effective spatial features were extracted to predict human attention with either a top-down [17] or bottom-up [4] strategy. Compared to image, video saliency prediction is more challenging because temporal features also play an important role in drawing human attention. To achieve this, a countable amount of motion-based features [11, 42] were designed as additional temporal information for video saliency prediction. Besides, some methods [16, 40] focused on calculating a variety of temporal differences across video frames, which are effective in video saliency prediction. Taking advantage of sophisticated video coding standards, the methods of [7, 37] explored the spatio-temporal features in compressed domain for predicting video saliency. In addition to feature extraction, many works have focused on the fusion strategy to generate video saliency maps. Specifically, a set of probability models [15, 31, 40] were constructed to integrate different kinds of features in predicting video saliency. Moreover, other machine learning algorithms, such as support vector machine and neutral network, were also applied to linearly [26] or non-linearly [20] combine the saliency-related features. Other advanced methods [9, 19, 41] applied phase spectrum analysis in the fusion model to bridge the gap between features and video saliency. For instance,

Guo *et al.* [9] exploited phase spectrum of quaternion Fourier transform (PQFT) on four feature channels to predict video saliency.

DL Based Methods. Most recently, DL has been successfully incorporated to automatically learn spatial features for predicting the saliency of images [13, 18, 28, 29, 32]. However, only a few works have managed to apply DL in video saliency prediction [1–3, 23, 27, 33, 35]. In these works, the dynamic characteristics were explored in two ways: adding temporal information to CNN structures [1, 3, 27, 35] or developing a dynamic structure with LSTM [2, 23]. For adding temporal information, a four-layer CNN in [3] and a two-stream CNN in [1] were trained with both RGB frames and motion maps as the inputs. Similarly, in [35], the pair of consecutive frames concatenated with a static saliency map (generated by the static CNN) are fed into the dynamic CNN for video saliency prediction, allowing the CNN to generalize more temporal features. In our work, the OM-CNN structure of DeepVS includes the subnets of objectness and motion, since human attention is more likely to be attracted by the moving objects or the moving parts of objects. For developing the dynamic structure, Bazzani *et al.* [2] and Liu *et al.* [23] applied LSTM networks to predict video saliency maps, relying on both short- and long-term memory of attention distribution. However, the fully connected layers in LSTM limit the dimensions of both the input and output; thus, it is unable to obtain the end-to-end saliency map and the strong prior knowledge needs to be assumed for the distribution of saliency in [2, 23]. In our work, DeepVS explores SS-ConvLSTM to directly predict saliency maps in an end-to-end manner. This allows learning the more complex distribution of human attention, rather than a pre-assumed distribution of saliency.

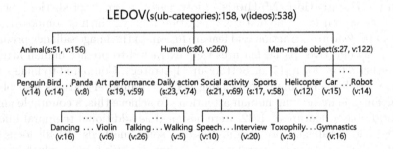

Fig. 2. Category tree of videos in LEDOV according to the content. The numbers of categories/sub-categories are shown in the brackets. Besides, the number of videos for each category/sub-category is also shown in the brackets.

3   LEDOV Database

For training the DNN models of DeepVS, we establish the LEDOV database. Some details of establishing LEDOV database are as follows.

Stimuli. In order to make the content of LEDOV diverse, we constructed a hierarchical tree of key words for video categories as shown in Fig. 2. There were three main categories, i.e., animal, human and man-made object. Note that the natural scene videos were not included, as they are scarce in comparison with other categories. The category of animal had 51 sub-categories. Similarly, the category of man-made objects was composed of 27 sub-categories. The category of human had the sub-categories of daily action, sports, social activity and art performance. These sub-categories of human were further classified as can be seen in Fig. 2. Consequently, we obtained 158 sub-categories in total, and then collected 538 videos belonging to these 158 sub-categories from YouTube. The number of videos for each category/sub-category can be found in Fig. 2. Some examples of the collected videos are provided in the supplementary material. It is worth mentioning that LEDOV contains the videos with a total of 179,336 frames and 6,431 seconds, and that all videos are at least 720p resolution and 24 Hz frame rate.

Procedure. For monitoring the binocular eye movements, a Tobii TX300 eye tracker [14] was used in our experiment. During the experiment, the distance between subjects and the monitor was fixed at 65 cm. Before viewing videos, each subject was required to perform a 9-point calibration for the eye tracker. Afterwards, the subjects were asked to free-view videos displayed at a random order. Meanwhile, the fixations of the subjects were recorded by the eye tracker.

Subjects. A new scheme was introduced for determining the sufficient number of participants. We stopped recruiting subjects for eye-tracking experiments once recorded fixations converged. Specifically, the subjects (with even numbers), who finished the eye-tracking experiment, were randomly divided into 2 equal groups by 5 times. Then, we measured the linear correlation coefficient (CC) of the fixation maps from two groups, and the CC values are averaged over the 5-time division. Figure 3 shows the averaged CC values of two groups, when the number of subjects increases. As seen in this figure, the CC value converges when the subject number reaches 32. Thus, we stopped recruiting subjects, when we collected the fixations of 32 subjects. Finally, 5,058,178 fixations of all 32 subjects on 538 videos were collected for our eye-tracking database.

Findings. We mine our database to analyze human attention on videos. Specifically, we have the following 3 findings, the analysis of which is presented in the supplemental material. *Finding 1*: High correlation exists between objectness and human attention. *Finding 2*: Human attention is more likely to be attracted by the moving objects or the moving parts of objects. *Finding 3*: There exists a temporal correlation of human attention with a smooth saliency transition across video frames.

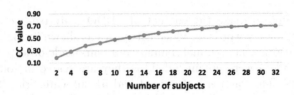

Fig. 3. The consistency (CC value) for different numbers of subjects over all videos in LEDOV.

4   Proposed Method

4.1   Framework

For video saliency prediction, we develop a new DNN architecture that combines OM-CNN and SS-ConvLSTM. According to *Findings 1 and 2*, human attention is highly correlated to objectness and object motion. As such, OM-CNN integrates both regions and motion of objects to predict video saliency through two subnets, i.e., the subnets of objectness and motion. In OM-CNN, the objectness subnet yields a cross-net mask on the features of the *convolutional layers* in the motion subnet. Then, the spatial features from the objectness subnet and the temporal features from the motion subnet are concatenated by the proposed hierarchical feature normalization to generate the spatio-temporal features of OM-CNN. The architecture of OM-CNN is shown in Fig. 4. Besides, SS-ConvLSTM with the CB dropout is developed to learn the dynamic saliency of video clips, in which the spatio-temporal features of OM-CNN serve as the input. Finally, the saliency map of each frame is generated from 2 *deconvolutional layers* of SS-ConvLSTM. The architecture of SS-ConvLSTM is shown in Fig. 5.

4.2   Objectness and Motion Subnets in OM-CNN

In OM-CNN, an objectness subnet is designed for extracting multi-scale spatial features related to objectness information, which is based on a pre-trained YOLO [30]. To avoid over-fitting, a pruned structure of YOLO is applied as the objectness subnet, including 9 *convolutional layers*, 5 *pooling layers* and 2 *fully connected layers* (*FC*). To further avoid over-fitting, an additional *batch-normalization layer* is added to each *convolutional layer*. Assuming that $BN(\cdot)$, $P(\cdot)$ and $*$ are the batch-normalization, max pooling and convolution operations, the output of the k-th *convolutional layer* $\mathbf{C}_o^k$ in the objectness subnet can be computed as

$$\mathbf{C}_o^k = L_{0.1}(BN(P(\mathbf{C}_o^{k-1}) * \mathbf{W}_o^{k-1} + \mathbf{B}_o^{k-1})), \tag{1}$$

where $\mathbf{W}_o^{k-1}$ and $\mathbf{B}_o^{k-1}$ indicate the kernel parameters of weight and bias at the $(k-1)$-th *convolutional layer*, respectively. Additionally, $L_{0.1}(\cdot)$ is a leaky ReLU activation with leakage coefficient of 0.1. In addition to the objectness subnet, a motion subnet is also incorporated in OM-CNN to extract multi-scale temporal

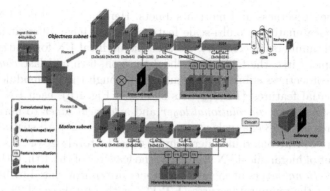

(a) The overall architecture of OM-CNN

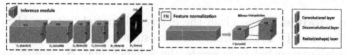

(b) The details for sub-modules of inference module and feature normalization

Fig. 4. Overall architecture of our OM-CNN for predicting video saliency of intra-frame. The sizes of convolutional kernels are shown in the figure. For instance, $3 \times 3 \times 16$ means 16 convolutional kernels with size of 3×3. Note that the $7 - $9th *convolutional layers* (C_o^7, C_o^8 & C_o^9) in the objectness subnet have the same size of convolutional kernels, thus sharing the same cube in (a) but not sharing the parameters. Similarly, each of the last four cubes in the motion subnet represents 2 *convolutional layers* with same kernel size. The details of the inference and feature normalization modules are shown in (b). Note that the proposed cross-net mask, hierarchical feature normalization and saliency inference module are highlighted with gray background.

features from the pair of neighboring frames. Similar to the objectness subnet, a pruned structure of FlowNet [6] with 10 *convolutional layers* is applied as the motion subnet. For details about objectness and motion subnets, please refer to Fig. 4(a). In the following, we propose combining the subnets of objectness and motion.

4.3 Combination of Objectness and Motion Subnets

In OM-CNN, we propose the hierarchical FN and cross-net mask to combine the multi-scale features of both objectness and motion subnets for predicting saliency. In particular, the cross-net mask can be used to encode objectness information when generating temporal features. Moreover, the inference module is developed to generate the cross-net mask or saliency map, based on the learned features.

Hierarchical FN. For leveraging the multi-scale information with various receptive fields, the output features are extracted from different *convolutional*

layers of the objectness and motion subnets. Here, a hierarchical FN is introduced to concatenate the multi-scale features, which have different resolutions
and channel numbers. Specifically, we take hierarchical FN for spatial features
as an example. First, the features of the 4-th, 5-th, 6-th and last *convolutional
layer* in the objectness subnet are normalized through the FN module to obtain
4 sets of spatial features $\{\mathbf{FS}_i\}_{i=1}^4$. As shown in Fig. 4(b), each FN module is
composed of a 1×1 *convolutional layer* and a *bilinear layer* to normalize the
input features into 128 channels at a resolution of 28×28. All spatial features[1]
$\{\mathbf{FS}_i\}_{i=1}^5$ are concatenated in a hierarchy to obtain a total size of $28 \times 28 \times 542$,
as the output of hierarchical FN. Similarly, the features of the 4-th, 6-th, 8-th and
10-th *convolutional layers* of the motion subnet are concatenated by hierarchical
FN, such that the temporal features $\{\mathbf{FT}_i\}_{i=1}^4$ with a total size of $28 \times 28 \times 512$
are obtained.

Inference Module. Then, given the extracted spatial features $\{\mathbf{FS}_i\}_{i=1}^5$ and
temporal features $\{\mathbf{FT}_i\}_{i=1}^4$ from the two subnets of OM-CNN, an inference
module I_f is constructed to generate the saliency map $\mathbf{S}_f$, which models the
intra-frame saliency of a video frame. Mathematically, $\mathbf{S}_f$ can be computed as

$$\mathbf{S}_f = I_f(\{\mathbf{FS}_i\}_{i=1}^5, \{\mathbf{FT}_i\}_{i=1}^4). \tag{2}$$

The inference module I_f is a CNN structure that consists of 4 *convolutional
layers* and 2 *deconvolutional layers* with a stride of 2. The detailed architecture
of I_f is shown in Fig. 4(b). Consequently, $\mathbf{S}_f$ is used to train the OM-CNN model,
as discussed in Sect. 4.5. Additionally, the output of *convolutional layer* C_4 with
a size of $28 \times 28 \times 128$ is viewed as the final spatio-temporal features, denoted
as **FO**. Afterwards, **FO** is fed into SS-ConvLSTM for predicting intra-frame
saliency.

Cross-Net Mask. *Finding 2* shows that attention is more likely to be attracted
by the moving objects or the moving parts of objects. However, the motion
subnet can only locate the moving parts of a whole video frame without any
object information. Therefore, the cross-net mask is proposed to impose a mask
on the *convolutional layers* of the motion subnet, for locating the moving objects
and the moving parts of objects. The cross-net mask $\mathbf{S}_c$ can be obtained upon the
multi-scale features of the objectness subnet. Specifically, given spatial features
$\{\mathbf{FS}_i\}_{i=1}^5$ of the objectness subnet, $\mathbf{S}_c$ can be generated by another inference
module I_c as follows,

$$\mathbf{S}_c = I_c(\{\mathbf{FS}_i\}_{i=1}^5). \tag{3}$$

Note that the architecture of I_c is same as that of I_f as shown in Fig. 4(b), but
not sharing the parameters. Consequently, the cross-net mask $\mathbf{S}_c$ can be obtained
to encode the objectness information, roughly related to salient regions. Then,
the cross-net mask $\mathbf{S}_c$ is used to mask the outputs of the first 6 *convolutional*

---

[1] $\mathbf{FS}_5$ is generated by the output of the last *FC layer* in the objectness subnet, encoding the high level information of the sizes, class and confidence probabilities of candidate objects in each grid.

layers of the motion subnet. Accordingly, the output of the k-th *convolutional layer* $\mathbf{C}_m^k$ in the motion subnet can be computed as

$$\mathbf{C}_m^k = L_{0.1}(M(\mathbf{C}_m^{k-1}, \mathbf{S}_c) * \mathbf{W}_m^{k-1} + \mathbf{B}_m^{k-1}),$$
$$\text{where} \quad M(\mathbf{C}_m^{k-1}, \mathbf{S}_c) = \mathbf{C}_m^{k-1} \cdot (\mathbf{S}_c \cdot (1 - \gamma) + \mathbf{1} \cdot \gamma). \tag{4}$$

In (4), $\mathbf{W}_m^{k-1}$ and $\mathbf{B}_m^{k-1}$ indicate the kernel parameters of weight and bias at the $(k-1)$-th *convolutional layer* in the motion subnet, respectively; γ $(0 \leq \gamma \leq 1)$ is an adjustable hyper-parameter for controlling the mask degree, mapping the range of $\mathbf{S}_c$ from $[0, 1]$ to $[\gamma, 1]$. Note that the last 4 *convolutional layers* are not masked with the cross-net mask for considering the motion of the non-object region in saliency prediction.

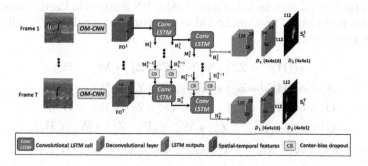

Fig. 5. Architecture of our SS-ConvLSTM for predicting saliency transition across inter-frame, following the OM-CNN. Note that the training process is not annotated in the figure.

4.4 SS-ConvLSTM

According to *Finding 3*, we develop the SS-ConvLSTM network for learning to predict the dynamic saliency of a video clip. At frame t, taking the OM-CNN features $\mathbf{FO}$ as the input (denoted as $\mathbf{FO}^t$), SS-ConvLSTM leverages both long- and short-term correlations of the input features through the memory cells $(\mathbf{M}_1^{t-1}, \mathbf{M}_2^{t-1})$ and hidden states $(\mathbf{H}_1^{t-1}, \mathbf{H}_2^{t-1})$ of the 1-st and 2-nd LSTM layers at last frame. Then, the hidden states of the 2-nd LSTM layer $\mathbf{H}_2^t$ are fed into 2 *deconvolutional layers* to generate final saliency map $\mathbf{S}_l^t$ at frame t. The architecture of SS-ConvLSTM is shown in Fig. 5.

We propose a CB dropout for SS-ConvLSTM, which improves the generalization capability of saliency prediction via incorporating the prior of CB. It is because the effectiveness of the CB prior in saliency prediction has been verified [37]. Specifically, the CB dropout is inspired by the Bayesian dropout [8]. Given an input dropout rate p_b, the CB dropout operator $\mathbf{Z}(p_b)$ is defined based on an

L-time Monte Carlo integration:

$$\mathbf{Z}(p_b) = \text{Bino}(L, p_b \cdot \mathbf{S}_{\text{CB}})/(L \cdot \text{Mean}(\mathbf{S}_{\text{CB}})),$$
$$\text{where } \mathbf{S}_{\text{CB}}(i,j) = 1 - \frac{\sqrt{(i - W/2)^2 + (j - H/2)^2}}{\sqrt{(W/2)^2 + (H/2)^2}}. \tag{5}$$

$\text{Bino}(L, \mathbf{P})$ is a randomly generated mask, in which each pixel (i, j) is subject to a L-trial Binomial distribution according to probability $\mathbf{P}(i, j)$. Here, the probability matrix $\mathbf{P}$ is modeled by CB map $\mathbf{S}_{\text{CB}}$, which is obtained upon the distance from pixel (i, j) to the center $(W/2, H/2)$. Consequently, the dropout operator takes the CB prior into account, the dropout rate of which is based on p_b.

Next, similar to [36], we extend the traditional LSTM by replacing the Hadamard product (denoted as $\circ$) by the convolutional operator (denoted as $*$), to consider the spatial correlation of input OM-CNN features in the dynamic model. Taking the first layer of SS-ConvLSTM as an example, a single LSTM cell at frame t can be written as

$$\mathbf{I}_1^t = \sigma((\mathbf{H}_1^{t-1} \circ \mathbf{Z}_i^h) * \mathbf{W}_i^h + (\mathbf{F}^t \circ \mathbf{Z}_i^f) * \mathbf{W}_i^f + \mathbf{B}_i),$$
$$\mathbf{A}_1^t = \sigma((\mathbf{H}_1^{t-1} \circ \mathbf{Z}_a^h) * \mathbf{W}_a^h + (\mathbf{F}^t \circ \mathbf{Z}_a^f) * \mathbf{W}_a^f + \mathbf{B}_a),$$
$$\mathbf{O}_1^t = \sigma((\mathbf{H}_1^{t-1} \circ \mathbf{Z}_o^h) * \mathbf{W}_o^h + (\mathbf{F}^t \circ \mathbf{Z}_o^f) * \mathbf{W}_o^f + \mathbf{B}_o),$$
$$\mathbf{G}_1^t = \tanh((\mathbf{H}_1^{t-1} \circ \mathbf{Z}_g^h) * \mathbf{W}_g^h + (\mathbf{F}^t \circ \mathbf{Z}_g^f) * \mathbf{W}_g^f + \mathbf{B}_g),$$
$$\mathbf{M}_1^t = \mathbf{A}_1^t \circ \mathbf{M}_1^{t-1} + \mathbf{I}_1^t \circ \mathbf{G}_1^t, \quad \mathbf{H}_1^t = \mathbf{O}_1^t \circ \tanh(\mathbf{M}_1^t), \tag{6}$$

where σ and $\tanh$ are the activation functions of sigmoid and hyperbolic tangent, respectively. In (6), $\{\mathbf{W}_i^h, \mathbf{W}_a^h, \mathbf{W}_o^h, \mathbf{W}_g^h, \mathbf{W}_i^f, \mathbf{W}_a^f, \mathbf{W}_o^f, \mathbf{W}_g^f\}$ and $\{\mathbf{B}_i, \mathbf{B}_a, \mathbf{B}_o, \mathbf{B}_g\}$ denote the kernel parameters of weight and bias at each *convolutional layer*; $\mathbf{I}_1^t$, $\mathbf{A}_1^t$ and $\mathbf{O}_1^t$ are the gates of input (i), forget (a) and output (o) for frame t; $\mathbf{G}_1^t$, $\mathbf{M}_1^t$ and $\mathbf{H}_1^t$ are the input modulation (g), memory cells and hidden states (h). They are all represented by 3-D tensors with a size of $28 \times 28 \times 128$. Besides, $\{\mathbf{Z}_i^h, \mathbf{Z}_a^h, \mathbf{Z}_o^h, \mathbf{Z}_g^h\}$ are four sets of randomly generated CB dropout masks ($28 \times 28 \times 128$) through $\mathbf{Z}(p_h)$ in (5) with a hidden dropout rate of p_h. They are used to mask on the hidden states $\mathbf{H}_1^t$, when computing different gates or modulation $\{\mathbf{I}_1^t, \mathbf{A}_1^t, \mathbf{O}_1^t, \mathbf{G}_1^t\}$. Similarly, given feature dropout rate p_f, $\{\mathbf{Z}_i^f, \mathbf{Z}_a^f, \mathbf{Z}_o^f, \mathbf{Z}_g^f\}$ are four randomly generated CB dropout masks from $\mathbf{Z}(p_f)$ for the input features $\mathbf{F}^t$. Finally, saliency map $\mathbf{S}_l^t$ is obtained upon the hidden states of the 2-nd LSTM layer $\mathbf{H}_2^t$ for each frame t.

4.5   Training Process

For training OM-CNN, we utilize the Kullback-Leibler (KL) divergence-based loss function to update the parameters. This function is chosen because [13] has proven that the KL divergence is more effective than other metrics in training DNNs to predict saliency. Regarding the saliency map as a probability distribution of attention, we can measure the KL divergence D_{KL} between the saliency map $\mathbf{S}_f$ of OM-CNN and the ground-truth distribution $\mathbf{G}$ of human fixations as follows:

$$D_{\mathrm{KL}}(\mathbf{G}, \mathbf{S}_f) = (1/WH) \sum_{i=1}^{W} \sum_{j=1}^{H} G_{ij} \log(G_{ij}/S_f^{ij}), \qquad (7)$$

where G_{ij} and S_f^{ij} refer to the values of location (i, j) in $\mathbf{G}$ and $\mathbf{S}_f$ (resolution: $W \times H$). In (7), a smaller KL divergence indicates higher accuracy in saliency prediction. Furthermore, the KL divergence between the cross-net mask $\mathbf{S}_c$ of OM-CNN and the ground-truth $\mathbf{G}$ is also used as an auxiliary function to train OM-CNN. This is based on the assumption that the object regions are also correlated with salient regions. Then, the OM-CNN model is trained by minimizing the following loss function:

$$L_{\mathrm{OM-CNN}} = \frac{1}{1+\lambda} D_{\mathrm{KL}}(\mathbf{G}, \mathbf{S}_f) + \frac{\lambda}{1+\lambda} D_{\mathrm{KL}}(\mathbf{G}, \mathbf{S}_c). \qquad (8)$$

In (8), λ is a hyper-parameter for controlling the weights of two KL divergences. Note that OM-CNN is pre-trained on YOLO and FlowNet, and the remaining parameters of OM-CNN are initialized by the Xavier initializer. We found from our experimental results that the auxiliary function can decrease KL divergence by 0.24.

To train SS-ConvLSTM, the training videos are cut into clips with the same length T. In addition, when training SS-ConvLSTM, the parameters of OM-CNN are fixed to extract the spatio-temporal features of each T-frame video clip. Then, the loss function of SS-ConvLSTM is defined as the average KL divergence over T frames:

$$L_{\mathrm{SS-ConvLSTM}} = \frac{1}{T} \sum_{i=1}^{T} D_{\mathrm{KL}}(\mathbf{S}_l^i, \mathbf{G}_i). \qquad (9)$$

In (9), $\{\mathbf{S}_l^i\}_{i=1}^{T}$ are the final saliency maps of T frames generated by SS-ConvLSTM, and $\{\mathbf{G}_i\}_{i=1}^{T}$ are their ground-truth attention maps. For each LSTM cell, the kernel parameters are initialized by the Xavier initializer, while the memory cells and hidden states are initialized by zeros.

5   Experimental Results

5.1   Settings

In our experiment, the 538 videos in our eye-tracking database are randomly divided into training (456 videos), validation (41 videos) and test (41 videos) sets. Specifically, to learn SS-ConvLSTM of DeepVS, we temporally segment 456 training videos into 24,685 clips, all of which contain T (=16) frames. An overlap of 10 frames is allowed in cutting the video clips, for the purpose of data augmentation. Before inputting to OM-CNN of DeepVS, the RGB channels of each frame are resized to 448×448, with their mean values being removed. In training

OM-CNN and SS-ConvLSTM, we learn the parameters using the stochastic gradient descent algorithm with the Adam optimizer. Here, the hyper-parameters of OM-CNN and SS-ConvLSTM are tuned to minimize the KL divergence of saliency prediction over the validation set. The tuned values of some key hyper-parameters are listed in Table 1. Given the trained models of OM-CNN and SS-ConvLSTM, all 41 test videos in our eye-tracking database are used to evaluate the performance of our method, in comparison with 8 other state-of-the-art methods. All experiments are conducted on a single Nvidia GTX 1080 GPU. Benefiting from that, our method is able to make real-time prediction for video saliency at a speed of 30 Hz.

Table 1. The values of hyper-parameters in OM-CNN and SS-ConvLSTM.

OM-CNN	Objectness mask parameter γ in (4)	0.5
	KL divergences weight λ in (8)	0.5
	Stride k between input frames in motion subnet	5
	Initial learning rate	1×10^{-5}
	Training epochs (iterations)	$12(\sim 1.5 \times 10^5)$
	Batch size	12
	Weight decay	5×10^{-6}
SS-ConvLSTM	Bayesian dropout rates p_h and p_f	0.75 & 0.75
	Times of Monte Carlo integration L	100
	Initial learning rate	1×10^{-4}
	Training epochs (iterations)	$15(\sim 2 \times 10^5)$
	Weight decay	5×10^{-6}

5.2   Evaluation on Our Database

In this section, we compare the video saliency prediction accuracy of our DeepVS method and to other state-of-the-art methods, including GBVS [11], PQFT [9], Rudoy [31], OBDL [12], SALICON [13], Xu [37], BMS [39] and SalGAN [28]. Among these methods, [9,11,12,31] and [37] are 5 state-of-the-art saliency prediction methods for videos. Moreover, we compare two latest DNN-based methods: [13,28]. Note that other DNN-based methods on video saliency prediction [1,2,23] are not compared in our experiments, since their codes are not public. In our experiments, we apply four metrics to measure the accuracy of saliency prediction: the area under the receiver operating characteristic curve (AUC), normalized scanpath saliency (NSS), CC, and KL divergence. Note that larger values of AUC, NSS or CC indicate more accurate prediction of saliency, while a smaller KL divergence means better saliency prediction. Table 2 tabulates the results of AUC, NSS, CC and KL divergence for our method and 8 other methods, which are averaged over the 41 test videos of our eye-tracking database. As shown in this table, our DeepVS method performs considerably better than all other methods in terms of all 4 metrics. Specifically, our method achieves at least 0.01, 0.51, 0.12 and 0.33 improvements in AUC, NSS, CC and KL, respectively. Moreover, the two DNN-based methods, SALICON [13] and SalGAN [28], outperform other conventional methods. This verifies the effectiveness of saliency-related features automatically learned by DNN. Meanwhile, our method is significantly superior to [13,28]. The main reasons for this result are as follows. (1) Our method embeds the objectness subnet to utilize objectness information in saliency prediction. (2) The object motion is explored in the motion subnet to predict video saliency. (3) The network of SS-ConvLSTM is leveraged to model saliency transition across video frames. Section 5.4 analyzes the above three reasons in more detail.

Table 2. Mean (standard deviation) of saliency prediction accuracy for our and 8 other methods over all test videos in our database.

	Ours	GBVS [11]	PQFT [9]	Rudoy [31]	OBDL [12]	SALICON* [13]	Xu [37]	BMS [39]	SalGAN* [28]
AUC	**0.90**(0.04)	0.84(0.06)	0.70(0.08)	0.80(0.08)	0.80(0.09)	0.89(0.06)	0.83(0.06)	0.76(0.09)	0.87(0.06)
NSS	**2.94**(0.85)	1.54(0.74)	0.69(0.46)	1.45(0.64)	1.54(0.84)	2.43(0.87)	1.47(0.47)	0.98(0.48)	2.39(0.59)
CC	**0.57**(0.12)	0.32(0.13)	0.14(0.08)	0.32(0.14)	0.32(0.16)	0.43(0.13)	0.38(0.11)	0.21(0.09)	0.45(0.09)
KL	**1.24**(0.39)	1.82(0.39)	2.46(0.39)	2.42(1.53)	2.05(0.74)	1.57(0.42)	1.65(0.30)	2.23(0.39)	1.62(0.33)

* DNN-based methods have been fine-tuned by our database with their default settings.

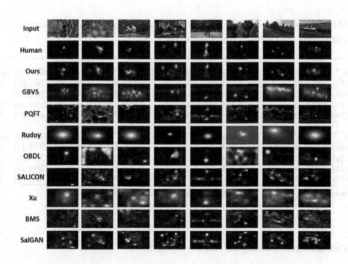

Fig. 6. Saliency maps of 8 videos randomly selected from the test set of our eye-tracking database. The maps were yielded by our and 8 other methods as well the ground-truth human fixations. Note that the results of only one frame are shown for each selected video.

Next, we compare the subjective results in video saliency prediction. Figure 6 demonstrates the saliency maps of 8 randomly selected videos in the test set, detected by our DeepVS method and 8 other methods. In this figure, one frame is selected for each video. As shown in Fig. 6, our method is capable of well locating the salient regions, which are close to the ground-truth maps of human fixations. In contrast, most of the other methods fail to accurately predict the regions that attract human attention.

5.3   Evaluation on Other Databases

To evaluate the generalization capability of our method, we further evaluate the performance of our method and 8 other methods on two widely used databases, SFU [10] and DIEM [25]. In our experiments, the models of OM-CNN and SS-ConvLSTM, learned from the training set of our eye-tracking database, are directly used to predict the saliency of test videos from the DIEM and SFU databases. Table 3 presents the average results of AUC, NSS, CC and KL for our method and 8 other methods over SFU and DIEM. As shown in this table, our method again outperforms all compared methods, especially in the DIEM database. In particular, there are at least 0.05, 0.57, 0.11 and 0.34 improvements in AUC, NSS, CC and KL, respectively. Such improvements are comparable to those in our database. This demonstrates the generalization capability of our method in video saliency prediction.

Table 3. Mean (standard deviation) values for saliency prediction accuracy of our and other methods over SFU and DIEM databases.

	SFU								
	Ours	GBVS [11]	PQFT [9]	Rudoy [31]	OBDL [12]	SALICON* [13]	Xu [37]	BMS [39]	SalGAN* [28]
AUC	**0.81**(0.07)	0.76(0.07)	0.61(0.09)	0.73(0.08)	0.74(0.10)	0.78(0.08)	0.80(0.07)	0.66(0.08)	0.79(0.07)
NSS	**1.46**(0.65)	0.91(0.47)	0.31(0.34)	0.83(0.45)	1.03(0.64)	1.24(0.60)	1.24(0.39)	0.50(0.31)	1.25(0.47)
CC	**0.55**(0.15)	0.44(0.15)	0.12(0.15)	0.34(0.15)	0.42(0.21)	0.58(0.22)	0.43(0.12)	0.25(0.11)	0.51(0.13)
KL	0.67(0.24)	**0.61**(0.19)	0.98(0.27)	0.93(0.36)	0.80(0.33)	1.12(1.76)	1.35(0.25)	0.83(0.20)	0.70(0.25)
	DIEM								
	Our	GBVS [11]	PQFT [9]	Rudoy [31]	OBDL [12]	SALICON* [13]	Xu [37]	BMS [39]	SalGAN* [28]
AUC	**0.86**(0.08)	0.81(0.09)	0.71(0.11)	0.80(0.11)	0.75(0.14)	0.79(0.11)	0.80(0.11)	0.77(0.11)	0.81(0.08)
NSS	**2.25**(1.16)	1.21(0.82)	0.86(0.71)	1.40(0.83)	1.26(1.03)	1.68(1.04)	1.34(0.74)	1.20(0.80)	1.60(0.71)
CC	**0.49**(0.21)	0.30(0.18)	0.19(0.14)	0.38(0.20)	0.29(0.22)	0.36(0.19)	0.35(0.17)	0.28(0.17)	0.35(0.13)
KL	**1.30**(0.55)	1.64(0.48)	1.73(0.44)	2.33(2.05)	2.77(1.58)	1.66(0.58)	1.67(0.39)	1.96(1.13)	1.64(0.41)

* DNN-based methods have been fine-tuned by our database with their default settings.

5.4   Performance Analysis of DeepVS

Performance Analysis of Components. Depending on the independently trained models of the objectness subnet, motion subnet and OM-CNN, we further analyze the contribution of each component for saliency prediction accuracy in DeepVS, i.e., the combination of OM-CNN and SS-ConvLSTM. The comparison results are shown in Fig. 7. We can see from this figure that OM-CNN performs better than the objectness subnet with a 0.05 reduction in KL divergence, and it outperforms the motion subnet with a 0.09 KL divergence reduction. Similar results hold for the other metrics of AUC, CC and NSS. These results indicate the effectiveness of integrating the subnets of objectness and motion. Moreover, the combination of OM-CNN and SS-ConvLSTM reduces the KL divergence by 0.09 over the single OM-CNN architecture. Similar results can be found for the other metrics. Hence, we can conclude that SS-ConvLSTM can further improve the performance of OM-CNN due to exploring the temporal correlation of saliency across video frames.

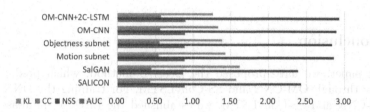

Fig. 7. Saliency prediction accuracy of objectness subnet, motion subnet, OM-CNN and the combination of OM-CNN and SS-ConvLSTM (i.e., DeepVS), compared with SALICON [13] and SalGAN [28]. Note that the smaller KL divergence indicates higher accuracy in saliency prediction.

Performance Analysis of SS-ConvLSTM. We evaluate the performance of the proposed CB dropout of SS-ConvLSTM. To this end, we train the SS-ConvLSTM models at different values of hidden dropout rate p_h and feature dropout rate p_f, and then test the trained SS-ConvLSTM models over the validation set. The averaged KL divergences are shown in Fig. 8(a). We can see that the CB dropout can reduce KL divergence by 0.03 when both p_h and p_f are set to 0.75, compared to the model without CB dropout ($p_h = p_f = 1$). Meanwhile, the KL divergence sharply rises by 0.08, when both p_h and p_f decrease from 0.75 to 0.2. This is caused by the under-fitting issue, as most connections in SS-ConvLSTM are dropped. Thus, p_h and p_f are set to 0.75 in our model. The SS-ConvLSTM model is trained for a fixed video length ($T = 16$). We further evaluate the saliency prediction performance of the trained SS-ConvLSTM model over variable-length videos. Here, we test the trained SS-ConvLST model over the validation set, the videos of which are clipped at different lengths. Figure 8(b) shows the averaged KL divergences for video clips at various lengths. We can see that the performance of SS-ConvLSTM is even a bit better, when the video length is 24 or 32. This is probably because the well-trained LSTM cell is able to utilize more inputs to achieve a better performance for video saliency prediction.

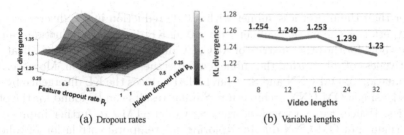

(a) Dropout rates   (b) Variable lengths

Fig. 8. (a): KL divergences of our models with different dropout rates. (b): KL divergences over test videos with variable lengths.

6 Conclusion

In this paper, we have proposed the DeepVS method, which predicts video saliency through OM-CNN and SS-ConvLSTM. For training the DNN models of OM-CNN and SS-ConvLSTM, we established the LEDOV database, which has the fixations of 32 subjects on 538 videos. Then, the OM-CNN architecture was proposed to explore the spatio-temporal features of the objectness and object motion to predict the intra-frame saliency of videos. The SS-ConvLSTM architecture was developed to model the inter-frame saliency of videos. Finally, the experimental results verified that DeepVS significantly outperforms 8 other state-of-the-art methods over both our and other two public eye-tracking databases, in terms of AUC, CC, NSS, and KL metrics. Thus, the prediction accuracy and generalization capability of DeepVS can be validated.

Acknowledgment. This work was supported by the National Nature Science Foundation of China under Grant 61573037 and by the Fok Ying Tung Education Foundation under Grant 151061.

References

1. Bak, C., Kocak, A., Erdem, E., Erdem, A.: Spatio-temporal saliency networks for dynamic saliency prediction. IEEE Trans. Multimed. (2017)
2. Bazzani, L., Larochelle, H., Torresani, L.: Recurrent mixture density network for spatiotemporal visual attention (2017)
3. Chaabouni, S., Benois-Pineau, J., Amar, C.B.: Transfer learning with deep networks for saliency prediction in natural video. In: ICIP, pp. 1604–1608. IEEE (2016)
4. Cheng, M.M., Mitra, N.J., Huang, X., Torr, P.H., Hu, S.M.: Global contrast based salient region detection. IEEE PAMI **37**(3), 569–582 (2015)
5. Deng, X., Xu, M., Jiang, L., Sun, X., Wang, Z.: Subjective-driven complexity control approach for HEVC. IEEE Trans. Circuits Syst. Video Technol. **26**(1), 91–106 (2016)
6. Dosovitskiy, A., et al.: FlowNet: learning optical flow with convolutional networks. In: ICCV, pp. 2758–2766 (2015)

7. Fang, Y., Lin, W., Chen, Z., Tsai, C.M., Lin, C.W.: A video saliency detection model in compressed domain. IEEE TCSVT **24**(1), 27–38 (2014)
8. Gal, Y., Ghahramani, Z.: A theoretically grounded application of dropout in recurrent neural networks. In: NIPS, pp. 1019–1027 (2016)
9. Guo, C., Zhang, L.: A novel multiresolution spatiotemporal saliency detection model and its applications in image and video compression. IEEE TIP **19**(1), 185–198 (2010)
10. Hadizadeh, H., Enriquez, M.J., Bajic, I.V.: Eye-tracking database for a set of standard video sequences. IEEE TIP **21**(2), 898–903 (2012)
11. Harel, J., Koch, C., Perona, P.: Graph-based visual saliency. In: NIPS, pp. 545–552 (2006)
12. Hossein Khatoonabadi, S., Vasconcelos, N., Bajic, I.V., Shan, Y.: How many bits does it take for a stimulus to be salient? In: CVPR, pp. 5501–5510 (2015)
13. Huang, X., Shen, C., Boix, X., Zhao, Q.: SALICON: reducing the semantic gap in saliency prediction by adapting deep neural networks. In: ICCV, pp. 262–270 (2015)
14. T. T. INC.: Tobii TX300 eye tracker. http://www.tobiipro.com/product-listing/tobii-pro-tx300/
15. Itti, L., Baldi, P.: Bayesian surprise attracts human attention. Vis. Res. **49**(10), 1295–1306 (2009)
16. Itti, L., Dhavale, N., Pighin, F.: Realistic avatar eye and head animation using a neurobiological model of visual attention. Opt. Sci. Technol. **64**, 64–78 (2004)
17. Judd, T., Ehinger, K., Durand, F., Torralba, A.: Learning to predict where humans look. In: ICCV, pp. 2106–2113 (2009)
18. Kruthiventi, S.S., Ayush, K., Babu, R.V.: DeepFix: a fully convolutional neural network for predicting human eye fixations. IEEE TIP (2017)
19. Leboran, V., Garcia-Diaz, A., Fdez-Vidal, X.R., Pardo, X.M.: Dynamic whitening saliency. IEEE PAMI **39**(5), 893–907 (2017)
20. Lee, S.H., Kim, J.H., Choi, K.P., Sim, J.Y., Kim, C.S.: Video saliency detection based on spatiotemporal feature learning. In: ICIP, pp. 1120–1124 (2014)
21. Li, S., Xu, M., Ren, Y., Wang, Z.: Closed-form optimization on saliency-guided image compression for HEVC-MSP. IEEE Trans. Multimed. (2017)
22. Li, S., Xu, M., Wang, Z., Sun, X.: Optimal bit allocation for CTU level rate control in HEVC. IEEE Trans. Circuits Syst. Video Technol. **27**(11), 2409–2424 (2017)
23. Liu, Y., Zhang, S., Xu, M., He, X.: Predicting salient face in multiple-face videos. In: CVPR, July 2017
24. Mathe, S., Sminchisescu, C.: Actions in the eye: dynamic gaze datasets and learnt saliency models for visual recognition. IEEE PAMI **37**(7), 1408–1424 (2015)
25. Mital, P.K., Smith, T.J., Hill, R.L., Henderson, J.M.: Clustering of gaze during dynamic scene viewing is predicted by motion. Cogn. Comput. **3**(1), 5–24 (2011)
26. Nguyen, T.V., Xu, M., Gao, G., Kankanhalli, M., Tian, Q., Yan, S.: Static saliency vs. dynamic saliency: a comparative study. In: ACMM, pp. 987–996. ACM (2013)
27. Palazzi, A., Solera, F., Calderara, S., Alletto, S., Cucchiara, R.: Learning where to attend like a human driver. In: Intelligent Vehicles Symposium (IV), 2017 IEEE, pp. 920–925. IEEE (2017)
28. Pan, J., et al.: SalGAN: visual saliency prediction with generative adversarial networks. In: CVPR workshop, January 2017
29. Pan, J., Sayrol, E., Giro-i Nieto, X., McGuinness, K., O'Connor, N.E.: Shallow and deep convolutional networks for saliency prediction. In: CVPR, pp. 598–606 (2016)

30. Redmon, J., Divvala, S., Girshick, R., Farhadi, A.: You only look once: unified, real-time object detection. In: CVPR, pp. 779–788 (2016)
31. Rudoy, D., Goldman, D.B., Shechtman, E., Zelnik-Manor, L.: Learning video saliency from human gaze using candidate selection. In: CVPR, pp. 1147–1154 (2013)
32. Wang, L., Wang, L., Lu, H., Zhang, P., Ruan, X.: Saliency detection with recurrent fully convolutional networks. In: Leibe, B., Matas, J., Sebe, N., Welling, M. (eds.) ECCV 2016. LNCS, vol. 9908, pp. 825–841. Springer, Cham (2016). https://doi.org/10.1007/978-3-319-46493-0_50
33. Wang, W., Shen, J., Guo, F., Cheng, M.M., Borji, A.: Revisiting video saliency: a large-scale benchmark and a new model (2018)
34. Wang, W., Shen, J., Shao, L.: Consistent video saliency using local gradient flow optimization and global refinement. IEEE Trans. Image Process. 24(11), 4185–4196 (2015)
35. Wang, W., Shen, J., Shao, L.: Video salient object detection via fully convolutional networks. IEEE TIP (2017)
36. Xingjian, S., Chen, Z., Wang, H., Yeung, D.Y., Wong, W.K., Woo, W.C.: Convolutional lstm network: a machine learning approach for precipitation nowcasting. In: NIPS, pp. 802–810 (2015)
37. Xu, M., Jiang, L., Sun, X., Ye, Z., Wang, Z.: Learning to detect video saliency with HEVC features. IEEE TIP 26(1), 369–385 (2017)
38. Xu, M., Liu, Y., Hu, R., He, F.: Find who to look at: turning from action to saliency. IEEE Transactions on Image Processing 27(9), 4529–4544 (2018)
39. Zhang, J., Sclaroff, S.: Exploiting surroundedness for saliency detection: a boolean map approach. IEEE PAMI 38(5), 889–902 (2016)
40. Zhang, L., Tong, M.H., Cottrell, G.W.: SUNDAy: saliency using natural statistics for dynamic analysis of scenes. In: Annual Cognitive Science Conference, pp. 2944–2949 (2009)
41. Zhang, Q., Wang, Y., Li, B.: Unsupervised video analysis based on a spatiotemporal saliency detector. arXiv preprint (2015)
42. Zhou, F., Bing Kang, S., Cohen, M.F.: Time-mapping using space-time saliency. In: CVPR, pp. 3358–3365 (2014)

Learning Efficient Single-Stage Pedestrian Detectors by Asymptotic Localization Fitting

Wei Liu[1,3], Shengcai Liao[1,2($\boxtimes$)], Weidong Hu[3], Xuezhi Liang[1,2],
and Xiao Chen[3]

[1] Center for Biometrics and Security Research and National Laboratory of Pattern
Recognition, Institute of Automation, Chinese Academy of Sciences, Beijing, China
{liuwei16,wdhu,chenxiao15}@nudt.edu.cn, scliao@nlpr.ia.ac.cn,
xzliang@cbsr.ia.ac.cn
[2] University of Chinese Academy of Sciences, Beijing, China
[3] National University of Defense Technology, Changsha, China

Abstract. Though Faster R-CNN based two-stage detectors have witnessed significant boost in pedestrian detection accuracy, it is still slow for practical applications. One solution is to simplify this working flow as a single-stage detector. However, current single-stage detectors (e.g. SSD) have not presented competitive accuracy on common pedestrian detection benchmarks. This paper is towards a successful pedestrian detector enjoying the speed of SSD while maintaining the accuracy of Faster R-CNN. Specifically, a structurally simple but effective module called *Asymptotic Localization Fitting* (ALF) is proposed, which stacks a series of predictors to directly evolve the default anchor boxes of SSD step by step into improving detection results. As a result, during training the latter predictors enjoy more and better-quality positive samples, meanwhile harder negatives could be mined with increasing IoU thresholds. On top of this, an efficient single-stage pedestrian detection architecture (denoted as ALFNet) is designed, achieving state-of-the-art performance on CityPersons and Caltech, two of the largest pedestrian detection benchmarks, and hence resulting in an attractive pedestrian detector in both accuracy and speed. Code is available at https://github.com/VideoObjectSearch/ALFNet.

Keywords: Pedestrian detection · Convolutional neural networks
Asymptotic localization fitting

1 Introduction

Pedestrian detection is a key problem in a number of real-world applications including auto-driving systems and surveillance systems, and is required to have

W. Liu—Finished his part of work during his visit in CASIA.

© Springer Nature Switzerland AG 2018
V. Ferrari et al. (Eds.): ECCV 2018, LNCS 11218, pp. 643–659, 2018.
https://doi.org/10.1007/978-3-030-01264-9_38

both high accuracy and real-time speed. Traditionally, scanning an image in a sliding-window paradigm is a common practice for object detection. In this paradigm, designing hand-crafted features [2,10,11,29] is of critical importance for state-of-the-art performance, which still remains as a difficult task.

Beyond early studies focusing on hand-craft features, RCNN [17] firstly introduced CNN into object detection. Following RCNN, Faster-RCNN [32] proposed Region Proposal Network (RPN) to generate proposals in a unified framework. Beyond its success on generic object detection, numerous adapted Faster-RCNN detectors were proposed and demonstrated better accuracy for pedestrian detection [42,44]. However, when the processing speed is considered, Faster-RCNN is still unsatisfactory because it requires two-stage processing, namely proposal generation and classification of ROIpooling features. Alternatively, as a representative one-stage detector, Single Shot MultiBox Detector (SSD) [27] discards the second stage of Faster-RCNN [32] and directly regresses the default anchors into detection boxes. Though faster, SSD [27] has not presented competitive results on common pedestrian detection benchmarks (e.g. CityPersons [44] and Caltech [12]). It motivates us to think what the key is in Faster R-CNN and whether this key could be transfered to SSD. Since both SSD and Faster R-CNN have default anchor boxes, we guess that the key is the two-step prediction of the *default anchor boxes*, with RPN one step, and prediction of ROIs another step, but not the ROI-pooling module. Recently, Cascade R-CNN [6] has proved that Faster R-CNN can be further improved by applying multi-step ROI-pooling and prediction after RPN. Besides, another recent work called RefineDet [45] suggests that ROI-pooling can be replaced by a convolutional transfer connection block after RPN. Therefore, it seems possible that the default anchors in SSD could be directly processed in multi-steps for an even simpler solution, with neither RPN nor ROI-pooling.

Another problem for SSD based pedestrian detection is caused by using a single IoU threshold for training. On one hand, a lower IoU threshold (e.g. 0.5) is helpful to define adequate number of positive samples, especially when there are limited pedestrian instances in the training data. For example, as depicted in Fig. 1(a), the augmented training data [42] on Caltech has 42782 images, among which about 80% images have no pedestrian instances, while the remains have only 1.4 pedestrian instances per image. However, a single lower IoU threshold during training will result in many "close but not correct" false positives during inference, as demonstrated in Cascade R-CNN [6]. On the other hand, a higher IoU threshold (e.g. 0.7) during training is helpful to reject close false positives during inference, but there are much less matched positives under a higher IoU threshold, as pointed out by Cascade R-CNN and also depicted in Fig. 1(b). This positive-negative definition dilemma makes it hard to train a high-quality SSD, yet this problem is alleviated by the two-step prediction in Faster R-CNN.

The above analyses motivate us to train the SSD in multi-steps with improving localization and increasing IoU thresholds. Consequently, in this paper a simple but effective module called Asymptotic Localization Fitting (ALF) is proposed. It directly starts from the default anchors in SSD, and convolution-

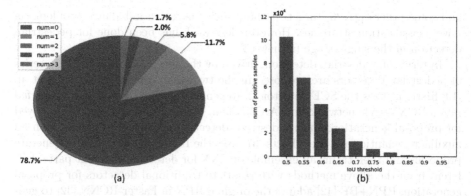

(a)   (b)

Fig. 1. (a) Percentage of images with different number of pedestrian instances on the Caltech training dataset newly annotated by [43]. (b) Number of positive anchors w.r.t. different IoU threshold. Each bar represents the number of default anchors matched with any ground truth higher than the corresponding IoU threshold.

ally evolves all anchor boxes step by step, pushing more anchor boxes closer to groundtruth boxes. On top of this, a novel pedestrian detection architecture is constructed, denoted as Asymptotic Localization Fitting Network (ALFNet). ALFNet significantly improves the pedestrian detection accuracy while maintaining the efficiency of single-stage detectors. Extensive experiments and analysis on two large-scale pedestrian detection datasets demonstrate the effectiveness of the proposed method independent of the backbone network.

To sum up, the main contributions of this work lie in: (1) a module called ALF is proposed, using multi-step prediction for asymptotic localization to overcome the limitations of single-stage detectors in pedestrian detection; (2) the proposed method achieves new state-of-the-art results on two of the largest pedestrian benchmarks (i.e., CityPerson [44], Caltech [12]).

2   Related Work

Generally, CNN-based generic object detection can be roughly classified into two categories. The first type is named as two-stage methods [8,16,17,32], which first generates plausible region proposals, then refines them by another sub-network. However, its speed is limited by repeated CNN feature extraction and evaluation. Recently, in the two-stage framework, numerous methods have tried to improve the detection performance by focusing on network architecture [8,22,23,25], training strategy [34,39], auxiliary context mining [1,15,35], and so on, while the heavy computational burden is still an unavoidable problem. The second type [27,30,31], which is called single-stage methods, aims at speeding up detection by removing the region proposal generation stage. These single-stage detector directly regress pre-defined anchors and thus are more computationally efficient, but yield less satisfactory results than two-stage methods. Recently, some of these methods [14,33] pay attention to enhancing the feature representation of CNN, and some others [21, 26] target at the positive-negative imbalance problem via novel classification strategies. However, less work has been done for pedestrian detection in the single-stage framework.

In terms of pedestrian detection, driven by the success of RCNN [17], a series of pedestrian detectors are proposed in the two-stage framework. Hosang et al. [19] firstly utilizes the SCF detector [2] to generate proposals which are then fed into a RCNN-style network. In TA-CNN [38], the ACF detector [10] is employed for proposal generation, then pedestrian detection is jointly optimized with an auxiliary semantic task. DeepParts [37] uses the LDCF detector [29] to generate proposals and then trains an ensemble of CNN for detecting different parts. Different from the above methods with resort to traditional detectors for proposal generation, RPN+BF [42] adapts the original RPN in Faster-RCNN [32] to generate proposals, then learns boosted forest classifiers on top of these proposals. Towards the multi-scale detection problem, MS-CNN [4] exploits multi-layers of a base network to generate proposals, followed by a detection network aided by context reasoning. SA-FastRCNN [24] jointly trains two networks to detect pedestrians of large scales and small scales respectively, based on the proposals generated from ACF detector [10]. Brazil et al. [3], Du et al. [13] and Mao et al. [28] further improve the detection performance by combining semantic information. Recently, Wang et al. [40] designs a novel regression loss for crowded pedestrian detection based on Faster-RCNN [32], achieving state-of-the-art results on CityPersons [44] and Caltech [12] benchmark. However, less attention is paid to the speed than the accuracy.

Most recently, Cascade R-CNN [6] proposes to train a sequence of detectors step-by-step via the proposals generated by RPN. The proposed method shares the similar idea of multi-step refinement to Cascade R-CNN. However, the differences lie in two aspects. Firstly, Cascade R-CNN is towards a better detector based on the Faster R-CNN framework, but we try to answer what the key in Faster R-CNN is and whether this key could be used to enhance SSD for speed and accuracy. The key we get is the multi-step prediction, with RPN one step, and prediction of ROIs another step. Given this finding, the default anchors in SSD could be processed in multi-steps, in fully convolutional way without ROI pooling. Secondly, in the proposed method, all default anchors are convolutionally processed in multi-steps, without re-sampling or iterative ROI pooling. In contrast, the Cascade R-CNN converts the detector part of the Faster R-CNN into multi-steps, which unavoidably requires RPN, and iteratively applying anchor selection and individual ROI pooling within that framework.

Another close related work to ours is the RefineDet [45] proposed for generic object detection. It contains two inter-connected modules, with the former one filtering out negative anchors by objectness scores and the latter one refining the anchors from the first module. A transfer connection block is further designed to transfer the features between these two modules. The proposed method differs from RefineDet [45] mainly in two folds. Firstly, we stack the detection module on the backbone feature maps without the transfer connection block, thus is simpler and faster. Secondly, all default anchors are equally processed in multi-steps without filtering. We consider that scores from the first step are not confident enough for decisions, and the filtered "negative" anchor boxes may contain hard positives that may still have chances to be corrected in latter steps.

3 Approach

3.1 Preliminary

Our method is built on top of the single-stage detection framework, here we give a brief review of this type of methods.

In single-stage detectors, multiple feature maps with different resolutions are extracted from a backbone network (e.g. VGG [36], ResNet [18]), these multi-scale feature maps can be defined as follows:

$$\Phi_n = f_n(\Phi_{n-1}) = f_n(f_{n-1}(...f_1(I))), \tag{1}$$

where I represents the input image, $f_n(.)$ is an existing layer from a base network or an added feature extraction layer, and Φ_n is the generated feature maps from the nth layer. These feature maps decrease in size progressively thus multi-scale object detection is feasible of different resolutions. On top of these multi-scale feature maps, detection can be formulated as:

$$Dets = F(p_n(\Phi_n, \mathcal{B}_n), p_{n-1}(\Phi_{n-1}, \mathcal{B}_{n-1}), ..., p_{n-k}(\Phi_{n-k}, \mathcal{B}_{n-k})), n > k > 0, \tag{2}$$

$$p_n(\Phi_n, \mathcal{B}_n) = \{cls_n(\Phi_n, \mathcal{B}_n), regr_n(\Phi_n, \mathcal{B}_n)\}, \tag{3}$$

where $\mathcal{B}_n$ is the anchor boxes pre-defined in the nth layer's feature map cells, $p_n(.)$ is typically a convolutional predictor that translates the nth feature maps Φ_n into detection results. Generally, $p_n(.)$ contains two elements, $cls_n(.)$ which predicts the classification scores, and $regr_n(.)$ which predicts the scaling and offsets of the default anchor boxes associated with the nth layer and finally gets the regressed boxes. $F(.)$ is the function to gather all regressed boxes from all layers and output final detection results. For more details please refer to [27].

We can find that Eq. (2) plays the same role as RPN in Faster-RCNN, except that RPN applies the convolutional predictor $p_n(.)$ on the feature maps of the last layer for anchors of all scales (denoted as $\mathcal{B}$), which can be formulated as:

$$Proposals = p_n(\Phi_n, \mathcal{B}), n > 0 \tag{4}$$

In two-stage methods, the region proposals from Eq. (4) is further processed by the ROI-pooling and then fed into another detection sub-network for classification and regression, thus is more accurate but less computationally efficient than single-stage methods.

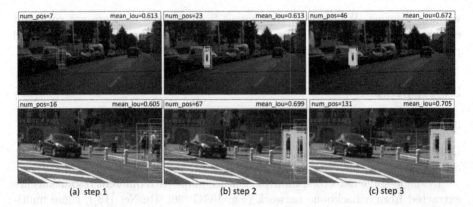

Fig. 2. Two examples from the CityPersons [44] training data. Green and red rectangles are anchor boxes and groundtruth boxes, respectively. Values on the upper left of the image represent the number of anchor boxes matched with the groundtruth under the IoU threshold of 0.5, and values on the upper right of the image denote the mean value of overlaps with the groundtruth from all matched anchor boxes.

3.2 Asymptotic Localization Fitting

From the above analysis, it can be seen that the single-stage methods are sub-optimal primarily because it is difficult to ask a single predictor $p_n(.)$ to perform perfectly on the default anchor boxes uniformly paved on the feature maps. We argue that a reasonable solution is to stack a series of predictors $p_n^t(.)$ applied on coarse-to-fine anchor boxes $\mathcal{B}_n^t$, where t indicates the t_{th} step. In this case, Eq. 3 can be re-formulated as:

$$p_n(\Phi_n, \mathcal{B}_n^0) = p_n^T(p_n^{T-1}(...(p_n^1(\Phi_n, \mathcal{B}_n^0)))), \qquad (5)$$

$$\mathcal{B}_n^t = regr_n^t(\Phi_n, \mathcal{B}_n^{t-1}), \qquad (6)$$

where T is the number of total steps and $\mathcal{B}_n^0$ denotes the default anchor boxes paved on the nth layer. In each step, the predictor $p_n^t(.)$ is optimized using the regressed anchor boxes $\mathcal{B}_n^{t-1}$ instead of the default anchor boxes. In other words, with the progressively refined anchor boxes, which means more positive samples could be available, the predictors in latter steps can be trained with a higher IoU threshold, which is helpful to produce more precise localization during inference [6]. Another advantage of this strategy is that multiple classifiers trained with different IoU thresholds in all steps will score each anchor box in a 'multi-expert' manner, and thus if properly fused the score will be more confident than a single classifier. Given this design, the limitations of current single-stage detectors could be alleviated, resulting in a potential of surpassing the two-stage detectors in both accuracy and efficiency.

Figure 2 gives two example images to demonstrate the effectiveness of the proposed ALF module. As can be seen from Fig. 2(a), there are only 7 and 16 default anchor boxes respectively assigned as positive samples under the IoU threshold of 0.5, this number increases progressively with more ALF steps, and the value of mean overlaps with the groundtruth is also going up. It indicates that the former predictor can hand over more anchor boxes with higher IoU to the latter one.

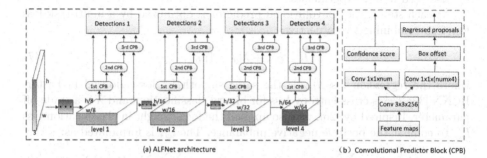

(a) ALFNet architecture   (b) Convolutional Predictor Block (CPB)

Fig. 3. (a) ALFNet architecture, which is constructed by four levels of feature maps for detecting objects with different sizes, where the first three blocks in yellow are from the backbone network, and the green one is an added convolutional layer to the end of the truncated backbone network. (b) Convolutional Predictor Block (CPB), which is attached to each level of feature maps to translate default anchor boxes to corresponding detection results.

3.3   Overall Framework

In this section we will present details of the proposed ALFNet pedestrian detection pipeline.

The details of our detection network architecture is pictorially illustrated in Fig. 3. Our method is based on a fully-convolutional network that produces a set of bounding boxes and confidence scores indicating whether there is a pedestrian instance or not. The base network layers are truncated from a standard network used for image classification (e.g. ResNet-50 [18] or MobileNet [20]). Taking ResNet-50 as an example, we firstly emanate branches from feature maps of the last layers of *stage 3, 4 and 5* (denoted as Φ_3, Φ_4 and Φ_5, the yellow blocks in Fig. 3(a)) and attach an additional convolutional layer at the end to produce Φ_6, generating an auxiliary branch (the green block in Fig. 3(a)). Detection is performed on $\{\Phi_3, \Phi_4, \Phi_5, \Phi_6\}$, with sizes downsampled by 8, 16, 32, 64 w.r.t. the input image, respectively. For proposal generation, anchor boxes with width of $\{(16, 24), (32, 48), (64, 80), (128, 160)\}$ pixels and a single aspect ratio of 0.41, are assigned to each level of feature maps, respectively. Then, we append the Convolutional Predictor Block (CPB) illustrated in Fig. 3(b) with several stacked steps for bounding box classification and regression.

3.4 Training and Inference

Training. Anchor boxes are assigned as positives S_+ if the IoUs with any ground truth are above a threshold u_h, and negatives S_- if the IoUs lower than a threshold u_l. Those anchors with IoU in $[u_l, u_h)$ are ignored during training. We assign different IoU threshold sets $\{u_l, u_h\}$ for progressive steps which will be discussed in our experiments.

At each step t, the convolutional predictor is optimized by a multi-task loss function combining two objectives:

$$L = l_{cls} + \lambda[y = 1]l_{loc}, \tag{7}$$

where the regression loss l_{loc} is the same smooth L1 loss adopted in Faster-RCNN [32], l_{cls} is cross-entropy loss for binary classification, and λ is a trade-off parameter. Inspired by [26], we also append the focal weight in classification loss l_{cls} to combat the positive-negative imbalance. The l_{cls} is formulated as:

$$l_{cls} = -\alpha \sum_{i \in S_+} (1 - p_i)^\gamma \log(p_i) - (1 - \alpha) \sum_{i \in S_-} p_i^\gamma \log(1 - p_i), \tag{8}$$

where p_i is the positive probability of sample i, α and γ are the focusing parameters, experimentally set as $\alpha = 0.25$ and $\gamma = 2$ suggested in [26]. In this way, the loss contribution of easy samples are down-weighted.

To increase the diversity of the training data, each image is augmented by the following options: after random color distortion and horizontal image flip with a probability of 0.5, we firstly crop a patch with the size of [0.3, 1] of the original image, then the patch is resized such that the shorter side has N pixels ($N = 640$ for CityPersons, and $N = 336$ for Caltech), while keeping the aspect ratio of the image.

Inference. ALFNet simply involves feeding forward an image through the network. For each level, we get the regressed anchor boxes from the final predictor and hybrid confidence scores from all predictors. We firstly filter out boxes with scores lower than 0.01, then all remaining boxes are merged with the Non-Maximum Suppression (NMS) with a threshold of 0.5.

4 Experiments and Analysis

4.1 Experiment Settings

Datasets. The performance of ALFNet is evaluated on the CityPersons [44] and Caltech [12] benchmarks. The CityPersons dataset is a newly published large-scale pedestrian detection dataset, which has 2975 images and approximately 20000 annotated pedestrian instances in the training subset. The proposed model is trained on this training subset and evaluated on the validation subset. For Caltech, our model is trained and test with the new annotations provided by [43]. We use the 10x set (42782 images) for training and the standard test subset (4024 images) for evaluation.

The evaluation metric follows the standard Caltech evaluation [12]: log-average Miss Rate over False Positive Per Image (FPPI) range of $[10^{-2}, 10^0]$ (denoted as MR^{-2}). Tests are only applied on the original image size without enlarging for speed consideration.

Training Details. Our method is implemented in the Keras [7], with 2 GTX 1080Ti GPUs for training. A mini-batch contains 10 images per GPU. The Adam solver is applied. For CityPersons, the backbone network is pretrained on ImageNet [9] and all added layers are randomly initialized with the 'xavier' method. The network is totally trained for $240k$ iterations, with the initial learning rate of 0.0001 and decreased by a factor of 10 after $160k$ iterations. For Caltech, we also include experiments with the model initialized from CityPersons as done in [40,44] and totally trained for $140k$ iterations with the learning rate of 0.00001. The backbone network is ResNet-50 [18] unless otherwise stated.

4.2   Ablation Experiments

In this section, we conduct the ablation studies on the CityPersons validation dataset to demonstrate the effectiveness of the proposed method.

ALF Improvement. For clarity, we trained a detector with two steps. Table 1 summarizes the performance, where $C_i B_j$ represents the detection results obtained by the confidence scores on step i and bounding box locations on step j. As can be seen from Table 1, when evaluated with different IoU thresholds (e.g. 0.5, 0.75), the second convolutional predictor consistently performs better than the first one. With the same confidence scores C_1, the improvement from $C_1 B_2$ to $C_1 B_1$ indicates the second regressor is better than the first one. On the other hand, with the same bounding box locations B_2, the improvement from $C_2 B_2$ to $C_1 B_2$ indicates the second classifier is better than the first one.

We also combine the two confidence scores by summation or multiplication, which is denoted as $(C_1 + C_2)$ and $(C_1 * C_2)$. For the IoU threshold of 0.5, this kind of score fusion is considerably better than both C_1 and C_2. Yet interestingly, under a stricter IoU threshold of 0.75, both the two hybrid confidence scores underperform the second confidence score C_2, which reasonably indicates that the second classifier is more discriminative between groundtruth and many "close but not accurate" false positives. It is worth noting that when we increase the IoU threshold from 0.5 to a stricter 0.75, the largest improvement increases by a large margin (from 1.45 to 11.93), demonstrating the high-quality localization performance of the proposed ALFNet.

To further demonstrate the effectiveness of the proposed method, Fig. 4 depicts the distribution of anchor boxes over the IoU range of $[0.5, 1]$. The total number of matched anchor boxes increases by a large margin (from 16351 up to 100571). Meanwhile, the percentage of matched anchor boxes in higher IoU intervals is increasing stably. In other words, anchor boxes with different IoU values are relatively well-distributed with the progressive steps.

IoU Threshold for Training. As shown in Fig. 4, the number of matched anchor boxes increases drastically in latter steps, and the gap among different

Table 1. The ALF improvement evaluated under IoU threshold of 0.5 and 0.75. C_i represents the confidence scores from step i and B_j means the bounding box locations from step j. MR^{-2} on the reasonable subset is reported.

IoU	C_1B_1	C_1B_2	C_2B_2	$(C_1+C_2)B_2$	$(C_1*C_2)B_2$	Improvement
0.5	13.46	13.17	12.64	12.03	**12.01**	+1.45 (10.8%)
0.75	46.83	45.00	**34.90**	36.49	36.49	+11.93 (25.5%)

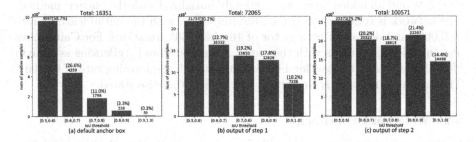

Fig. 4. It depicts the number of anchor boxes matched with the ground-truth boxes w.r.t. different IoU thresholds ranging from 0.5 to 1. (a), (b) and (c) represent the distribution of default anchor boxes, refined anchor boxes after the first and second step, respectively. The total number of boxes with IoU above 0.5 is presented in the heads of the three sub-figures. The numbers and percentages of each IoU threshold range are annotated on the head of the corresponding bar.

IoU thresholds is narrowing down. A similar finding is also observed in the Cascade R-CNN [6] with a single threshold, instead of dual thresholds here. This inspires us to study how the IoU threshold for training affects the final detection performance. Experimentally, the $\{u_l, u_h\}$ for the first step should not be higher than that for the second step, because more anchors with higher quality are assigned as positives after the first step (shown in Fig. 4). Results in Table 2 shows that training predictors of two steps with the increasing IoU thresholds is better than that with the same IoU thresholds, which indicates that optimizing the later predictor more strictly with higher-quality positive anchors is vitally important for better performance. We choose $\{0.3, 0.5\}$ and $\{0.5, 0.7\}$ for two steps in the following experiments, which achieves the lowest MR^{-2} in both of the two evaluated settings (IoU = 0.5, 0.75).

Number of Stacked Steps. The proposed ALF module is helpful to achieve better detection performance, but we have not yet studied how many stacked steps are enough to obtain a speed-accuracy trade-off. We train our ALFNet up to three steps when the accuracy is saturated. Table 3 compares the three variants of our ALFNet with 1, 2 and 3 steps, denoted as ALFNet-1s, ALFNet-2s and ALFNet-3s. Experimentally, the ALFNet-3s is trained with IoU thresholds $\{0.3, 0.5\}$, $\{0.4, 0.65\}$ and $\{0.5, 0.75\}$). By adding a second step, ALFNet-2s significantly surpasses ALFNet-1s by a large margin (12.01 VS. 16.01). It is worth noting that the results from the first step of ALFNet-2s and ALFNet-3s are

Table 2. Comparison of training the two-step ALFNet with different IoU threshold sets. $\{u_l, u_h\}$ represents the IoU threshold to assign positives and negatives defined in Sect. 3.3. Bold and italic indicate the best and second best results.

Training IoU thresholds		MR^{-2}	
Step 1	Step 2	IoU = 0.5	IoU = 0.75
{0.3, 0.5}	{0.3, 0.5}	13.75	44.27
	{0.4, 0.6}	13.31	39.30
	{0.5, 0.7}	**12.01**	*36.49*
{0.4, 0.6}	{0.4, 0.6}	13.60	42.31
	{0.5, 0.7}	*12.80*	**36.43**
{0.5, 0.7}	{0.5, 0.7}	13.72	38.20

substantially better than ALFNet-1s with the same computational burden, which indicates that multi-step training is also beneficial for optimizing the former step. Similar findings can also be seen in Cascade R-CNN [6], in which the three-stage cascade achieves the best trade-off.

Table 3. Comparison of ALFNet with various steps evaluated in terms of MR^{-2}. Test time is evaluated on the original image size (1024 × 2048 on CityPersons).

Method	# Steps	Test step	Test time	MR^{-2}	
				IoU = 0.5	IoU = 0.75
ALFNet-1s	1	1	0.26s/img	16.01	48.95
ALFNet-2s	2	1	0.26s/img	13.17	45.00
	2	2	0.27s/img	**12.01**	**36.49**
ALFNet-3s	3	1	0.26s/img	14.53	46.70
	3	2	0.27s/img	12.67	37.75
	3	3	0.28s/img	12.88	39.31

From the results shown in Table 3, it appears that the addition of the 3rd step can not provide performance gain in terms of MR^{-2}. Yet when taking a deep look at the detection results of this three variants of ALFNet, the detection performance based on the metric of F-measure is further evaluated, as shown in Table 4. In this case, ALFNet-3s tested on the 3rd step performs the best under the IoU threshold of both 0.5 and 0.75. It substantially outperforms ALFNet-1s and achieves a 6.3% performance gain from ALFNet-2s under the IoU of 0.5, and 6.5% with IoU = 0.75. It can also be observed that the number of false positives decreases progressively with increasing steps, which is pictorially illustrated in Fig. 5. Besides, as shown in Table 4, the average mean IoU of the detection results matched with the groundtruth is increasing, further demonstrating the improved

Table 4. Comparison of ALFNet with various steps evaluated with F-measure. # TP and # FP denote the number of True Positives and False Positives.

Method	Test step	Ave. mIoU	IoU = 0.5			IoU = 0.75		
			# TP	# FP	F-mea.	# TP	# FP	F-mea.
ALFNet-1s	1	0.49	**2404**	13396	0.263	1786	14014	0.195
ALFNet-2s	1	0.55	2393	9638	0.330	**1816**	10215	0.250
	2	0.76	2198	1447	0.717	1747	1898	0.570
ALFNet-3s	1	0.57	2361	7760	0.375	1791	8330	0.284
	2	0.76	2180	1352	0.725	1734	1798	0.576
	3	0.80	2079	**768**	**0.780**	1694	**1153**	**0.635**

(a) step 1   (b) step 2   (c) step 3

Fig. 5. Examples of detection results of ALFNet-3s. Red and green rectangles represent groundtruth and detection bounding boxes, respectively. It can be seen that the number of false positives decreases progressively with increasing steps, which indicates that more steps are beneficial for higher detection accuracy.

detection quality. However, the improvement of step 3 over step 2 is saturating, compared to the large gap of step 2 over step 1. Therefore, considering the speed-accuracy trade-off, we choose ALFNet-2s in the following experiments.

Different Backbone Network. Large backbone network like ResNet-50 is *strong* in feature representation. To further demonstrate the improvement from the ALF module, a light-weight network like MobileNet [20] is chosen as the backbone and the results are shown in Table 5. Notably, the *weaker* MobileNet equipped with the proposed ALF module is able to beat the *strong* ResNet-50 without ALF (15.45 VS. 16.01).

4.3   Comparison with State-of-the-Art

CityPersons. Table 6 shows the comparison to previous state-of-the art on CityPersons. Detection results test on the original image size are compared. Note that it is a common practice to upsample the image to achieve a better

Table 5. Comparison of different backbone network with our ALF design.

Backbone	Asymptotic localization fitting	# Parameters	MR^{-2}	
			IoU = 0.5	IoU = 0.75
ResNet-50		39.5M	16.01	48.94
	✓	48.4M	12.01	36.49
MobileNet		12.1M	18.88	56.26
	✓	17.4M	15.45	47.42

Table 6. Comparison with the state-of-the-art on the CityPersons [44]. Detection results test on the original image size (1024 × 2048 on CityPersons) is reported.

Method	+RepGT	+RepBox	+Seg	Reasonable	Heavy	Partial	Bare
Faster-RCNN [44] (VGG16)				15.4	-	-	-
			✓	14.8	-	-	-
RepLoss [40] (ResNet-50)				14.6	60.6	18.6	7.9
	✓			13.7	57.5	17.3	**7.2**
			✓	13.7	59.1	17.2	7.8
	✓	✓		13.2	56.9	16.8	7.6
ALFNet [ours]				**12.0**	**51.9**	**11.4**	8.4

Table 7. Comparisons of running time on Caltech. The time of LDCF, CCF, CompACT-Deep and RPN+BF are reported in [42], and that of SA-FastRCNN and F-DNN are reported in [13]. MR^{-2} is based on the new annotations [43]. The original image size on Caltech is 480 × 640.

Method	Hardware	Scale	Test time	MR^{-2}	
				IoU = 0.5	IoU = 0.75
LDCF [29]	CPU	x1	0.6 s/img	23.6	72.2
CCF [41]	Titan Z GPU	x1	13 s/img	23.8	97.4
CompACT-Deep [5]	Tesla K40 GPU	x1	0.5 s/img	9.2	59.0
RPN+BF [42]	Tesla K40 GPU	x1.5	0.5 s/img	7.3	57.8
SA-FastRCNN [24]	Titan X GPU	x1.7	0.59 s/img	7.4	55.5
F-DNN [13]	Titan X GPU	x1	0.16 s/img	6.9	59.8
ALFNet [ours]	GTX 1080Ti GPU	x1	**0.05 s/img**	6.1	22.5
ALFNet+City [ours]	GTX 1080Ti GPU	x1	**0.05 s/img**	**4.5**	**18.6**

detection accuracy, but with the cost of more computational expense. We only test on the original image size as pedestrian detection is more critical on both accuracy and efficiency. Besides the reasonable subset, following [40], we also test our method on three subsets with different occlusion levels. On the Reasonable subset, without any additional supervision like semantic labels (as done in [44]) or auxiliary regression loss (as done in [40]), our method achieves the best performance, with an improvement of 1.2 MR^{-2} from the closest competitor RepLoss

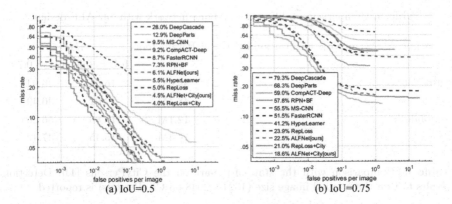

Fig. 6. Comparisons of state-of-the-arts on Caltech (reasonable subset).

[40]. Note that RepLoss [40] is specifically designed for the occlusion problem, however, without bells and whistles, the proposed method with the same backbone network (ResNet-50) achieves comparable or even better performance in terms of different levels of occlusions, demonstrating the self-contained ability of our method to handle occlusion issues in crowded scenes. This is probably because in the latter ALF steps, more positive samples are recalled for training, including occluded samples. On the other hand, harder negatives are mined in the latter steps, resulting in a more discriminant predictor.

Caltech. We also test our method on Caltech and the comparison with state-of-the-arts on this benchmark is shown in Fig. 6. Our method achieves MR^{-2} of 4.5 under the IoU threshold of 0.5, which is comparable to the best competitor (4.0 of RepLoss [40]). However, in the case of a stricter IoU threshold of 0.75, our method is the first one to achieve the MR^{-2} below 20.0%, outperforming all previous state-of-the-arts with an improvement of 2.4 MR^{-2} over RepLoss [40]. It indicates that our method has a substantially better localization accuracy.

Table 7 reports the running time on Caletch, our method significantly outperforms the competitors on both speed and accuracy. The speed of the proposed method is 20 FPS with the original 480 × 640 images. Thanks to the ALF module, our method avoids the time-consuming proposal-wise feature extraction (ROIpooling), instead, it refines the default anchors step by step, thus achieves a better speed-accuracy trade-off.

5 Conclusions

In this paper, we present a simple but effective single-stage pedestrian detector, achieving competitive accuracy while performing faster than the state-of-the-art methods. On top of a backbone network, an asymptotic localization fitting module is proposed to refine anchor boxes step by step into final detection results. This novel design is flexible and independent of any backbone network, without being limited by the single-stage detection framework. Therefore, it is also interesting to incorporate the proposed ALF module with other single-stage detectors like YOLO [30,31] and FPN [25,26], which will be studied in future.

References

1. Bell, S., Lawrence Zitnick, C., Bala, K., Girshick, R.: Inside-outside net: Detecting objects in context with skip pooling and recurrent neural networks. In: Proceedings of the IEEE Conference on Computer Vision and Pattern Recognition, pp. 2874–2883 (2016)
2. Benenson, R., Omran, M., Hosang, J., Schiele, B.: Ten years of pedestrian detection, what have we learned? In: Agapito, L., Bronstein, M.M., Rother, C. (eds.) ECCV 2014. LNCS, vol. 8926, pp. 613–627. Springer, Cham (2015). https://doi.org/10.1007/978-3-319-16181-5_47
3. Brazil, G., Yin, X., Liu, X.: Illuminating pedestrians via simultaneous detection & segmentation. arXiv preprint arXiv:1706.08564 (2017)
4. Cai, Z., Fan, Q., Feris, R.S., Vasconcelos, N.: A unified multi-scale deep convolutional neural network for fast object detection. In: Leibe, B., Matas, J., Sebe, N., Welling, M. (eds.) ECCV 2016. LNCS, vol. 9908, pp. 354–370. Springer, Cham (2016). https://doi.org/10.1007/978-3-319-46493-0_22
5. Cai, Z., Saberian, M., Vasconcelos, N.: Learning complexity-aware cascades for deep pedestrian detection. In: International Conference on Computer Vision, pp. 3361–3369 (2015)
6. Cai, Z., Vasconcelos, N.: Cascade R-CNN: delving into high quality object detection. arXiv preprint arXiv:1712.00726 (2017)
7. Chollet, F.: Keras. published on github (2015). https://github.com/fchollet/keras
8. Dai, J., Li, Y., He, K., Sun, J.: R-FCN: object detection via region-based fully convolutional networks. In: Advances in Neural Information Processing Systems, pp. 379–387 (2016)
9. Deng, J., Dong, W., Socher, R., Li, L.J., Li, K., Li, F.F.: ImageNet: a large-scale hierarchical image database. In: IEEE Conference on Computer Vision and Pattern Recognition, CVPR 2009, pp. 248–255. IEEE (2009)
10. Dollár, P., Appel, R., Belongie, S., Perona, P.: Fast feature pyramids for object detection. IEEE Trans. Pattern Anal. Mach. Intell. **36**(8), 1532–1545 (2014)
11. Dollár, P., Tu, Z., Perona, P., Belongie, S.: Integral channel features (2009)
12. Dollar, P., Wojek, C., Schiele, B., Perona, P.: Pedestrian detection: an evaluation of the state of the art. IEEE Trans. Pattern Anal. Mach. Intell. **34**(4), 743–761 (2012)
13. Du, X., El-Khamy, M., Lee, J., Davis, L.: Fused DNN: a deep neural network fusion approach to fast and robust pedestrian detection. In: 2017 IEEE Winter Conference on Applications of Computer Vision (WACV), pp. 953–961. IEEE (2017)
14. Fu, C.Y., Liu, W., Ranga, A., Tyagi, A., Berg, A.C.: DSSD: deconvolutional single shot detector. arXiv preprint arXiv:1701.06659 (2017)
15. Gidaris, S., Komodakis, N.: Object detection via a multi-region and semantic segmentation-aware CNN model. In: Proceedings of the IEEE International Conference on Computer Vision, pp. 1134–1142 (2015)
16. Girshick, R.: Fast R-CNN. In: Proceedings of the IEEE International Conference on Computer Vision, pp. 1440–1448 (2015)

17. Girshick, R., Donahue, J., Darrell, T., Malik, J.: Rich feature hierarchies for accurate object detection and semantic segmentation. In: Proceedings of the IEEE Conference on Computer Vision and Pattern Recognition, pp. 580–587 (2014)
18. He, K., Zhang, X., Ren, S., Sun, J.: Deep residual learning for image recognition. In: Proceedings of the IEEE Conference on Computer Vision and Pattern Recognition, pp. 770–778 (2016)
19. Hosang, J., Omran, M., Benenson, R., Schiele, B.: Taking a deeper look at pedestrians. In: Proceedings of the IEEE Conference on Computer Vision and Pattern Recognition, pp. 4073–4082 (2015)
20. Howard, A.G., et al.: MobileNets: efficient convolutional neural networks for mobile vision applications. arXiv preprint arXiv:1704.04861 (2017)
21. Kong, T., Sun, F., Yao, A., Liu, H., Lu, M., Chen, Y.: RON: reverse connection with objectness prior networks for object detection. arXiv preprint arXiv:1707.01691 (2017)
22. Kong, T., Yao, A., Chen, Y., Sun, F.: HyperNet: towards accurate region proposal generation and joint object detection. In: Proceedings of the IEEE Conference on Computer Vision and Pattern Recognition, pp. 845–853 (2016)
23. Lee, H., Eum, S., Kwon, H.: ME R-CNN: multi-expert region-based CNN for object detection. arXiv preprint arXiv:1704.01069 (2017)
24. Li, J., Liang, X., Shen, S., Xu, T., Feng, J., Yan, S.: Scale-aware fast R-CNN for pedestrian detection. IEEE Trans. Multimed. (2017)
25. Lin, Y.T., Dollár, P., Girshick, R., He, K., Hariharan, B., Belongie, S.: Feature pyramid networks for object detection. arXiv preprint arXiv:1612.03144 (2016)
26. Lin, Y.T., Goyal, P., Girshick, R., He, K., Dollár, P.: Focal loss for dense object detection. arXiv preprint arXiv:1708.02002 (2017)
27. Liu, W., Anguelov, D., Erhan, D., Szegedy, C., Reed, S., Fu, C.-Y., Berg, A.C.: SSD: single shot multibox detector. In: Leibe, B., Matas, J., Sebe, N., Welling, M. (eds.) ECCV 2016. LNCS, vol. 9905, pp. 21–37. Springer, Cham (2016). https://doi.org/10.1007/978-3-319-46448-0_2
28. Mao, J., Xiao, T., Jiang, Y., Cao, Z.: What can help pedestrian detection? In: The IEEE Conference on Computer Vision and Pattern Recognition (CVPR), vol. 1, p. 3 (2017)
29. Nam, W., Dollár, P., Han, J.H.: Local decorrelation for improved pedestrian detection. In: Advances in Neural Information Processing Systems, pp. 424–432 (2014)
30. Redmon, J., Divvala, S., Girshick, R., Farhadi, A.: You only look once: unified, real-time object detection. In: Proceedings of the IEEE Conference on Computer Vision and Pattern Recognition, pp. 779–788 (2016)
31. Redmon, J., Farhadi, A.: Yolo9000: better, faster, stronger. arXiv preprint 1612 (2016)
32. Ren, S., He, K., Girshick, R., Sun, J.: Faster R-CNN: towards real-time object detection with region proposal networks. In: Advances in Neural Information Processing Systems, pp. 91–99 (2015)
33. Shen, Z., Liu, Z., Li, J., Jiang, Y.G., Chen, Y., Xue, X.: DSOD: learning deeply supervised object detectors from scratch. In: The IEEE International Conference on Computer Vision (ICCV), vol. 3, p. 7 (2017)
34. Shrivastava, A., Gupta, A., Girshick, R.: Training region-based object detectors with online hard example mining. In: Proceedings of the IEEE Conference on Computer Vision and Pattern Recognition, pp. 761–769 (2016)
35. Shrivastava, A., Gupta, A.: Contextual priming and feedback for faster R-CNN. In: Leibe, B., Matas, J., Sebe, N., Welling, M. (eds.) ECCV 2016. LNCS, vol. 9905, pp. 330–348. Springer, Cham (2016). https://doi.org/10.1007/978-3-319-46448-0_20

36. Simonyan, K., Zisserman, A.: Very deep convolutional networks for large-scale image recognition. arXiv preprint arXiv:1409.1556 (2014)
37. Tian, Y., Luo, P., Wang, X., Tang, X.: Deep learning strong parts for pedestrian detection. In: Proceedings of the IEEE International Conference on Computer Vision, pp. 1904–1912 (2015)
38. Tian, Y., Luo, P., Wang, X., Tang, X.: Pedestrian detection aided by deep learning semantic tasks. In: Proceedings of the IEEE Conference on Computer Vision and Pattern Recognition, pp. 5079–5087 (2015)
39. Wang, X., Shrivastava, A., Gupta, A.: A-fast-RCNN: hard positive generation via adversary for object detection. arXiv preprint arXiv:1704.03414 2 (2017)
40. Wang, X., Xiao, T., Jiang, Y., Shao, S., Sun, J., Shen, C.: Repulsion loss: detecting pedestrians in a crowd. arXiv preprint arXiv:1711.07752 (2017)
41. Yang, B., Yan, J., Lei, Z., Li, S.Z.: Convolutional channel features. In: 2015 IEEE International Conference on Computer Vision (ICCV), pp. 82–90. IEEE (2015)
42. Zhang, L., Lin, L., Liang, X., He, K.: Is faster R-CNN doing well for pedestrian detection? In: Leibe, B., Matas, J., Sebe, N., Welling, M. (eds.) ECCV 2016. LNCS, vol. 9906, pp. 443–457. Springer, Cham (2016). https://doi.org/10.1007/978-3-319-46475-6_28
43. Zhang, S., Benenson, R., Omran, M., Hosang, J., Schiele, B.: How far are we from solving pedestrian detection? In: Proceedings of the IEEE Conference on Computer Vision and Pattern Recognition, pp. 1259–1267 (2016)
44. Zhang, S., Benenson, R., Schiele, B.: Citypersons: A diverse dataset for pedestrian detection. arXiv preprint arXiv:1702.05693 (2017)
45. Zhang, S., Wen, L., Bian, X., Lei, Z., Li, S.Z.: Single-shot refinement neural network for object detection. arXiv preprint arXiv:1711.06897 (2017)

Scenes-Objects-Actions: A Multi-task, Multi-label Video Dataset

Jamie Ray[1], Heng Wang[1(✉)], Du Tran[1], Yufei Wang[1], Matt Feiszli[1],
Lorenzo Torresani[1,2], and Manohar Paluri[1]

[1] Facebook AI, Menlo Park, USA
[2] Dartmouth College, Hanover, USA
{jamieray,hengwang,trandu,yufei22,mdf,torresani,mano}@fb.com

Abstract. This paper introduces a large-scale, multi-label and multi-task video dataset named **S**cenes-**O**bjects-**A**ctions (**SOA**). Most prior video datasets are based on a predefined taxonomy, which is used to define the keyword queries issued to search engines. The videos retrieved by the search engines are then verified for correctness by human annotators. Datasets collected in this manner tend to generate high classification accuracy as search engines typically rank "easy" videos first. The SOA dataset adopts a different approach. We rely on uniform sampling to get a better representation of videos on the Web. Trained annotators are asked to provide free-form text labels describing each video in three different aspects: scene, object and action. These raw labels are then merged, split and renamed to generate a taxonomy for SOA. All the annotations are verified again based on the taxonomy. The final dataset includes 562K videos with 3.64M annotations spanning 49 categories for scenes, 356 for objects, 148 for actions, and naturally captures the long tail distribution of visual concepts in the real world. We show that datasets collected in this way are quite challenging by evaluating existing popular video models on SOA. We provide in-depth analysis about the performance of different models on SOA, and highlight potential new directions in video classification. We compare SOA with existing datasets and discuss various factors that impact the performance of transfer learning. A key-feature of SOA is that it enables the empirical study of correlation among scene, object and action recognition in video. We present results of this study and further analyze the potential of using the information learned from one task to improve the others. We also demonstrate different ways of scaling up SOA to learn better features. We believe that the challenges presented by SOA offer the opportunity for further advancement in video analysis as we progress from single-label classification towards a more comprehensive understanding of video data.

Keywords: Video dataset · Multi-task · Scene · Object · Action

© Springer Nature Switzerland AG 2018
V. Ferrari et al. (Eds.): ECCV 2018, LNCS 11218, pp. 660–676, 2018.
https://doi.org/10.1007/978-3-030-01264-9_39

1 Introduction

In this work we introduce a new video dataset aimed at advancing research on video understanding. We name the dataset **S**cenes-**O**bjects-**A**ctions (SOA), as each video is annotated with respect to three different aspects: scenes, objects, and actions. Our objective is to introduce a benchmark that will spur research in video understanding as a comprehensive, multi-faceted problem. We argue that in order to achieve this goal a video dataset should fulfill several fundamental requirements, as discussed below.

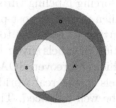

Table 1. Statistics of the SOA dataset for different tasks.

Task	Scene	Object	Action	SOA
# videos	173K	560K	308K	562K
# classes	49	356	148	553
# annotations	223K	2.93M	484K	3.64M

Fig. 1. Coverage of Scene, Object and Action labels on SOA videos. 105K videos (18.7%) have all three types of labels.

1. **Large-scale.** While KTH [29], HMDB51 [22] and UCF101 [34] have played a fundamental role in the past by inspiring the design of effective hand-engineered features for action recognition [23,40], larger video datasets are necessary to support modern end-to-end training of deep models. Datasets such as Sports1M [18], Kinetics [19] and AVA [27] were recently introduced to fill this gap and they have already led to the development of a new generation of more effective models based on deep learning [2,4,6,18,35,38,43]. SOA belongs to this new genre of large-scale video datasets. Despite being only in its first version, SOA already includes as many videos as Kinetics while containing ten times more annotations. Compared to crowdsourced datasets such as Charades [31] and Something-Something [9], SOA is both larger and more densely labeled. Table 1 summarizes the statistics of SOA.
2. **Unbiased Videos.** It is useful to fairly represent in the dataset the distribution of videos on the Internet. By doing so, models trained on the dataset can be directly applied to understand and recognize popular concepts in every-day Internet videos. For this purpose we build SOA by uniformly sampling videos from Web platforms. This procedure avoids biases on video length, content, metadata, and style. It provides a diverse collection of samples matching the actual distribution of Internet videos. On the contrary, prior datasets [1,18,19,34] have used keyword-based searches to find Web videos matching predefined concepts. The tags used for the searches skew the distribution of the dataset. Furthermore, search engines typically returns in the

top positions videos that match unambiguously the query. This yields prototypical examples that tend to be easy to classify. As evidence, the top-5
accuracy on Kinetics is already over 93% [24] less than one year from its
public release. In our experiments we demonstrate that SOA is a much more
challenging benchmark than prior datasets, with even the best video classification models hovering only around 45% top-5 accuracy[1].

3. **Unbiased Labels.** Rather than constraining annotators to adopt a predefined ontology to label the videos, as done in most prior video datasets, we
allow annotators to enter free-from textual tags describing the video. We
argue that this yields a more fitting set of annotations than those obtained
by forcing labeling through a fixed ontology. The collection of free-form tags
is then manually post-processed via concept renaming, deleting, merging and
splitting to give rise to a final taxonomy, which directly reflects the distribution of labels given by annotators labeling the data in an unconstrained
fashion. Moreover, SOA naturally captures the long tail distribution of visual
labels in the real world, whereas existing datasets are often hand designed
to be well balanced. This opens the door of studying few shot learning and
knowledge transfer to model the long tail [41] on a large scale video dataset.

4. **Multi-task.** A video is much more than the depiction of a human action.
It often portrays a scene or an environment (an office, a basketball court, a
beach), and includes background objects (a picture, a door, a bus) as well as
objects manipulated or utilized by a person (e.g., lipstick, a tennis racquet, a
wrench). An action label provides a human-centric description of the video but
ignores this relevant contextual information. Yet, today most existing video
classification datasets contain only human action tags. While a few object-
centric video datasets have been proposed [14,28], there is no established
video benchmark integrating joint recognition of scenes, objects and actions.
To the best of our knowledge the only exceptions are perhaps YouTube-8M [1]
and Charades [31], where some of the classes are pure actions (e.g., wrestling),
some represent objects (e.g., bicycle), and some denote "objects in action"
(e.g., drinking from a cup). Unlike in these prior datasets, where contextual
information (scenes and objects) is coupled with action categorization in the
form of flat classification, we propose a dataset that integrates scene, object,
and action categorization in the form of multi-task classification, where labels
are available for each of these three aspects in a video. This makes it possible
to quantitatively assess synergy among the three tasks and leverage it during
modeling. For example, using SOA annotations it is possible to determine
how object recognition contributes to disambiguating the action performed
in the video. Furthermore, this multi-task formulation recasts video understanding as a comprehensive problem that encompasses the recognition of
multiple semantic aspects in the dynamic scene. Figure 1 shows the coverage
of annotations from different tasks on SOA videos.

---

[1] Top-5 accuracy on SOA is computed by considering each label from a given video
independently, i.e., matching each label against top-5 predictions from the model.

5. **Multi-label.** Finally, we argue that a single class label per task is often not sufficient to describe the content of a video. Even a single frame may contain multiple prominent objects; the addition of a temporal dimension makes multi-label even more important for video than for images. As discussed above, datasets that use search queries to perform biased sampling can sidestep this issue, as they mostly contain prototypical examples for which a single-label assumption is reasonable. With closer fidelity to the true distribution and all of the hard positives it contains, the content of a given video is no longer dominated by a given label. In SOA we ask the annotator to provide as many labels as needed to describe each of the three individual aspects of recognition (Scenes, Objects and Actions) and we adopt mAP (mean Average Precision) as the metric accordingly.

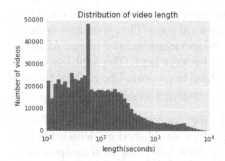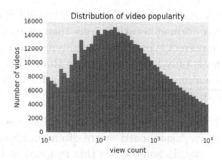

Fig. 2. Histograms of length and view count for sampled videos. These distributions contain heavy tails that will be lost by biased sampling.

2   Scenes-Objects-Actions

This section describes the creation of SOA in four steps: sampling videos, open-world annotation, generating the taxonomy and closed-world verification.

2.1   Sampling Videos

We sample publicly available videos shared on Facebook. The sampling is not biased by length or view count. The resulting videos are diverse and approximate the true distribution of Internet videos, as demonstrated by Fig. 2. From each video, we sample only one clip of about 10 s with the start time selected uniformly across the whole video. It is important to note that unbiased sampling yields an unbalanced long-tail class distribution, with many more videos containing mundane labels like "speaking to camera" compared to the kinds of actions popular in existing action recognition datasets, e.g., "ice skating".

After collecting the videos, we follow the protocol used for Kinetics [19] to de-duplicate videos within the SOA dataset. Our only modification is to use a ResNet-50 [11] image model as the feature extractor. We use the same protocol to remove SOA videos that match the testing and validation sets of the following action recognition datasets: Kinetics [19], UCF101 [33], and HMDB51 [21].

2.2 Open-World Annotation

The first stage of annotation provides an interface with a video player and three text-entry fields, one for each of the three SOA aspects (Scenes, Objects, and Actions). The annotator watches a clip (often multiple times) and types in any applicable textual tags corresponding to these three aspects. Note that the set of tags are not predefined. Each field includes an auto-complete mechanism so that the annotator does not need to type the whole tag. Each annotator is required to enter at least one label per aspect per clip. To improve recall, we send each clip to at least two annotators. The process takes on average 80 seconds per clip for a trained annotator.

2.3 Generating the Taxonomy

As described above, the initial round of labeling was unconstrained. The resulting free-form annotations were then cleaned in several ways. They were first sanitized to correct typos, unify synonyms and plurals, and merge similar terms. After this pass, only labels with more than 1500 samples were kept. The kept labels were then manually inspected and refined into a final taxonomy. The goals of the final taxonomy included:

1. Reduce label noise. Labels like "headphone" vs "headset", or "snowboard" vs "skateboard" were often confused, and we established guidelines for their use. In some cases this resulted in labels with less than 1500 samples being reintroduced.
2. Visual coherence. Certain free-form labels like "jumping" or "weight lifting" lacked visual coherence, and were replaced with more fine-grained labels. If there were not enough samples to split a label into multiple labels, we eliminated the incoherent label.
3. Sharing terminology. In structuring the final taxonomy we appealed to existing datasets and ontologies (e.g., MIT Places dataset [45], WordNet [26]) for guidance when possible, but there is no strict mapping to any existing taxonomy.

In particular, this process was aimed to preserve the true distribution of labels. The taxonomy was refined in certain areas and coarsened in others, so the granularity was changed, but additional videos were not retrieved to support new labels. Instead, all the videos were re-annotated with the new list of labels, as described below.

2.4 Closed-World Verification

When placing these labels into a visual taxonomy, we produced a set of mappings from free-form labels to curated labels. Many free-form labels were unchanged and mapped to a single curated label. Others were split or merged with other labels. These created mappings from free-form labels to groups of multiple curated labels.

Fig. 3. Different labels tend to co-occur in SOA. Here we visualize their relationship with t-SNE [25]. This embedding is purely based on label co-occurrence, without using video content. The superscript indicates the number of samples for each class. Scenes, Objects and Actions are in red, green and blue respectively. (Color figure online)

These mappings define a set of verification tasks for the second stage of annotation. Each label from the first stage may correspond to n labels in the new taxonomy (where n is zero if the label was discarded) for each aspect (Scenes, Objects, and Actions). These are provided to a second annotation tool which plays the video and displays these n choices as options (selected via hotkeys), with a default "NONE OF THE ABOVE" option included. Trained annotators watch a video and then select all labels that apply. This verification step takes about 30 seconds per clip on average. In practice, n is often equal to 1, making the task binary. This process can filter out erroneous labels, improving precision, but may yield low recall if the original labels or the mapping were too sparse. We noticed low recall for a small subset of labels and densified the mapping to correct for it. We measured the rate of "NONE OF THE ABOVE" to be about 30%. This indicates that our defined mapping provided a true label for 70% of the verification tasks.

Finally, we remove all the labels with less than 200 samples, and summarize the statistics of SOA in Table 1. Semantically related labels tend to co-occur on SOA, which we visualize using t-SNE in Fig. 3.

3 Comparing Video Models on SOA

This section compares different video models on SOA. We outline the experimental setup and three models used, then present and discuss the results.

3.1 Experimental Setup

SOA includes a total of 562K videos, which are randomly split into training, validation and testing with a percentage of 70, 10 and 20, respectively. For all the experiments, we only use the training set for training and report metrics on the validation set. The performance on SOA is measured by computing the average precision (AP) for each class since it is a multi-label dataset. For each individual task (e.g., Scenes), we report the mean AP over all its classes (mAP). To measure the overall multi-task performance on SOA, we use a weighted average over the three tasks, by weighting each task differently to reflect the perceived importance of the three tasks to video understanding: $mAP_{SOA} = 1/6 * mAP_{Scene} + 1/3 * mAP_{Object} + 1/2 * mAP_{Action}$.

3.2   Video Models

We briefly describe the three popular video models used for evaluation on SOA.

Res2D. ResNet [11] is among the most successful CNN models for image classification. Res2D [39] applies a ResNet to a group of video frames instead of a single image. The input to Res2D is $3L \times H \times W$ instead of $3 \times H \times W$, where L is the number of frames and $H \times W$ is the spatial resolution. As the channel and temporal dimension are combined into a single dimension, convolution in Res2D is only on the two spatial dimensions. Note that 2D CNNs for video [32] ignore the temporal ordering in the video and are in general considered to be inferior for learning motion information from video.

Res3D. 3D CNNs [16,38] are designed to model the temporal dynamics of video data by performing convolution in 3D instead of 2D. Res3D [39] applies 3D convolutions to ResNet. Unlike Res2D, the channel and temporal dimensions are treated separately. As a result, each filter is 4-dimensional (channel, temporal and two spatial dimensions), and is convolved in 3D, i.e., over both temporal and spatial dimensions. Both Res2D and Res3D used in this paper have 18 layers.

I3D. The inflated 3D ConvNet (I3D) [4] is another example of 3D CNN for video data. It is based on the Inception-v1 [36] model with Batch Normalization [15]. I3D was originally proposed as a way to leverage the ImageNet dataset [5] for pre-training in video classification via the method of 2D-to-3D inflation. Here we only adopt this model architecture without pre-training on ImageNet as we are interested in comparing different model architectures on SOA trained under the same setup (no pre-training).

For a fair comparison, we use the same input to all three models, which is a clip of 32 consecutive frames containing RGB or optical flow. We choose the Farneback [7] algorithm to compute optical flow due to its efficiency. For data augmentation, we apply temporal jittering when sampling a clip from a given video. A clip of size 112×112 is randomly cropped from the video after resizing it to a resolution of 171×128. Training is done with synchronous distributed SGD on GPU clusters using Caffe2 [3]. Cross entropy loss is used for multi-label classification on SOA. For testing, we uniformly sample 10 clips from each video and do average pooling over the 10 clips to generate the video level predictions. We train all models from scratch with these settings unless stated otherwise.

Table 2. Three models trained with different inputs on SOA. For each task, we only use the videos and labels from that task for training and testing as listed in Table 1. Parameters and FLOPs are computed for RGB input. For optical flow, they are about the same as RGB.

Model	# params	FLOPs	Input	Scenes	Objects	Actions	SOA
Res2D	11.5M	2.6G	RGB	44.1	22.8	26.8	23.0
			Optical flow	29.7	14.6	21.5	16.7
			Late fusion	48.7	24.7	32.2	27.6
Res3D	33.2M	81.4G	RGB	48.0	25.9	33.6	27.3
			Optical flow	39.4	20.2	32.1	23.6
			Late fusion	**51.5**	**27.4**	**37.7**	**30.9**
I3D	12.3M	13.0G	RGB	45.4	22.6	30.3	24.5
			Optical flow	34.0	16.3	29.2	20.5
			Late fusion	49.4	24.4	35.4	28.5

3.3 Classification Results on SOA

Table 2 presents the mAP of each model, input, and task. For late fusion of RGB and optical flow streams, we uniformly sample 10 clips from a given video, and extract a 512-dimensional feature vector from each clip using the global average pooling layer of the trained model. Features are aggregated with average pooling over the 10 clips. We normalize and concatenate the features from RGB and optical flow. A linear SVM is trained to classify the extracted features.

Model vs. Task. Comparing the performance of different models in Table 2, we find that 3D models (i.e., Res3D and I3D) are consistently better than 2D models (i.e., Res2D) across different tasks. This indicates that 3D CNNs are generally advantageous for video classification problems. The gap between 2D and 3D models becomes wider when we move from Scene and Object tasks to Action task. This is presumably due to the fact that Scenes and Objects can often be recognized from a single frame, whereas Actions require more temporal information to be disambiguated and thus can benefit more from 3D CNNs.

Input vs. Model. We observe an interaction between the input modality and the model type. Optical flow yields much better accuracy when using 3D models, while in the case of RGB the performances of 2D and 3D CNNs are closer. For example, optical flow yields about the same mAP as RGB for Actions when using Res3D and I3D, but the accuracy with optical flow drops by about 5% when switching to Res2D. A similar observation applies to Scenes and Objects. This again suggests that 3D models are superior for leveraging motion information.

Task vs. Input. Choosing the right input for a target task is critical, as the input encapsulates all the information that a model can learn. RGB shows a great advantage over optical flow for Scenes and Objects. As expected, optical flow is more useful for Actions. Late fusion has been shown to be very effective for combining RGB and optical flow in the two-stream network [32]. The mAP of late fusion is about $2 - 4\%$ higher than each individual input in Table 2.

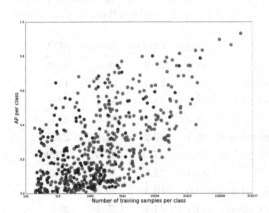

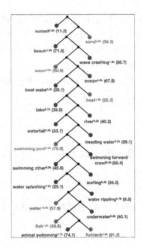

Fig. 4. The relationship between the Average Precision of each class and the number of training samples from that class. Scene, Object and Action classes are plotted in red, green and blue respectively. (Color figure online)

Fig. 5. Tree structure recovered from confusion matrix. We mark the number of training samples and testing AP for each class.

Overall, Res3D performs the best but is also the most computationally expensive, with the highest FLOPs and the most parameters, as shown in Table 2. Due to its strong performance, we use Res3D for the remaining experiments.

3.4 Discussion

In this section, we analyze the results from SOA in detail and highlight our findings. We choose the Res3D model with RGB as the input, which gives an mAP of 27.3 in Table 2. Figure 4 shows a strong correlation between AP and the number of positive samples in each class. The best two recognized classes for each task are man, overlaid text, grass field, gymnasium indoor, exercising other, speaking to camera, which are all very common categories in SOA.

To further understand the performance of the model, we construct a confusion matrix. As SOA is a multi-label dataset, we take the top-5 predictions of each sample, and consider all the pair combinations for each prediction and each ground truth annotation. All these combinations are accumulated to compute the final confusion matrix. To find meaningful structures from the confusion matrix, we recursively merge the two classes with the biggest confusion. This results in different tree structures where many classes are progressively merged together. Figure 5 shows such an example. We can clearly see that concepts appearing in the tree are semantically related with an increasing level of abstraction. There is also a gradual shift of concepts from fish to water, then water related scenery and activities, and drifting away to beach, sand and sunset.

Table 3. Comparison of SOA with Kinetics and Sports-1M for transfer learning. We consider four target datasets for fine-tuning including UCF101, HMDB51, Kinetics and Charades. Note that all these experiments are based on the Res3D model with RGB as the input. We report mAP on Charades and accuracy on the other three datasets.

Fine-tuning Pre-training	UCF101	HMDB51	Kinetics	Charades
From scratch	67.6	33.1	63.9	9.8
Kinetics	92.6	69.6	N/A	16.8
Sports-1M	90.2	63.7	64.6	13.7
SOA	84.7	57.2	63.9	15.3

We also found other trees that centered around concepts that are related to animals, cosmetics, vehicles, gym activities, etc. As in Fig. 5, these trees typically include multiple labels covering Scene, Object and Action. This is another evidence that Scene, Object and Action tasks should be solved jointly for video understanding and SOA provides an opportunity for driving computer vision research along this direction.

4   Transfer Learning

Strong transfer learning performance was not a design goal for SOA, however it is quite natural to ask what the strengths and weaknesses are with respect to this objective. The section discusses the results of using SOA for transfer learning, i.e., pre-training on SOA and fine-tuning on smaller datasets. We briefly describe the datasets used, and compare SOA with existing large-scale video datasets. We then discuss features of SOA that may influence its transfer learning ability and conclude by comparing with the state of the art.

4.1   Datasets

We compare SOA with Sports-1M [18] and Kinetics [19] for pre-training, and evaluate the performance of fine-tuning on four target datasets, i.e., UCF101 [34], HMDB51 [21], Kinetics and Charades [31].

Sports-1M is a large-scale benchmark for fine-grained classification of sport videos. It has 1.1M videos of 487 fine-grained sport categories. We only use the training set of Sports-1M for pre-training. **Kinetics** has about 300K videos covering 400 action categories. The annotations on the testing set are not public available. Here we use the training set for pre-training and report the accuracy on the validation set. **UCF101** and **HMDB51** are among the most popular datasets for action recognition. UCF101 has 13k videos and 101 classes, whereas HMDB51 is slightly smaller with 7k videos and 51 classes. Both datasets provide three splits for training and testing. We only use the first split in our experiments.

Unlike the other datasets, **Charades** is collected by crowdsourcing. It consists of 10k videos across 157 action classes of common household activities. We report mAP on the validation set of Charades.

Table 4. Compare the effectiveness of pre-training on SOA with the state of the art. For late fusion, we follow the same procedure described in Sect. 3.3 by combining the RGB results from Table 3 with the optical flow results listed in this table.

Methods	UCF101	HMDB51	Kinetics	Charades
ActionVLAD+iDT [8]	93.6	69.8	-	21.0
I3D (two-stream) [4]	98.0	80.7	75.7	-
MultiScale TRN [44]	-	-	-	25.2
S3D-G [42]	96.8	75.9	77.2	-
ResNeXt-101 (64f) [10]	94.5	70.2	65.1	-
SOA (optical flow)	86.5	65.6	59.1	16.1
SOA (late fusion)	90.7	67.0	67.9	16.9

4.2 Transfer Learning Results

We compare SOA with two popular large-scale datasets: Sports-1M and Kinetics. Fine-tuning performance is evaluated on UCF101, HMDB51, Kinetics, and Charades. The results are presented in Table 3. First, the improvement from pre-training is inversely related to the size of the fine-tuning dataset. For large datasets (e.g., Kinetics), the gain by pre-training is much smaller than datasets with less samples (e.g., UCF101, HMDB51, Charades). Pre-training is often used to mitigate scarcity of training data on the target domain. If the fine-tuning dataset is large enough, pre-training may not be needed.

Our second observation is that the improvements are also related to the source of the videos used for creating the datasets. UCF101, HMDB51, Kinetics and Sports-1M are all created with YouTube videos, whereas SOA uses publicly available videos shared on Facebook. Charades is built by crowdsourcing. Typically, improvements are largest when the pre-training and fine-tuning datasets use the same video source (e.g. YouTube) and sampling method (e.g., querying search engines). This is connected to the issue of dataset bias, which has already been observed on several datasets [37]. In Table 3, Kinetics performs remarkably well on UCF101 and HMDB51, but the gain becomes less pronounced on Charades. For SOA, its transfer learning ability is on par with Sports-1M and Kinetics on Charades, but is worse on UCF101 and HMDB51.

In Table 4 we compare against the state of the art in video classification by using SOA as a pre-training dataset for Res3D. State-of-the-art models tend to use more sophisticated architectures [42,44], more advanced pooling mechanisms [8], deeper models [10], and heavyweight inputs [4,10] (long clips with higher resolution). Pre-training on SOA with a simple Res3D model gives competitive results in general. As shown in Sect. 5.3, the improvement from pre-training on SOA can be more significant as we scale up the dataset by either adding more videos or increasing the number of categories.

Table 5. Rows correspond to the target task, columns to the type of features extracted. Res3D with RGB input was used for all experiments.

Feature / Task	Scene	Object	Action
Scene	49.7	53.9	45.6
Object	14.2	26.5	18.2
Action	18.3	29.9	34.8

	S+O	S+A	SOA
Scene	52.4	50.9	53.2
	O+S	O+A	SOA
Object	26.5	27.3	27.0
	A+S	A+O	SOA
Action	34.7	36.0	35.9

(a) Correlation among the three tasks   (b) How much one task can help another

5   Multi-task Investigations

SOA is uniquely designed for innovation in the large-scale multi-task arena. In this section we establish what we hope will be some compelling baselines about the interaction between features learned across tasks as an example of these kinds of questions. To our knowledge, SOA is the only dataset currently available on which such experimentation can be done. Previously, Jiang et al. [17] proposed to use context knowledge extracted from scene and object recognition to improve action retrieval in movie data. Ikizler-Cinbis et al. [13] extracted different types of features that can capture object and scene information, and combined them with multiple-instance learning for action recognition. More recently, Sigurdsson et al. [30] studied the effectiveness of perfect object oracles for action recognition.

5.1   Correlations Among the Three Tasks

For this experiment, we take the Res3D models (with RGB as the input) trained on the three individual tasks. We use each model in turn as a feature extractor for Scenes, Objects and Actions separately. The feature extraction process is the same as Sect. 3.3, i.e., average pooling the 512-dimensional Res3D feature vector over 10 clips for a given video. We then train a linear SVM on each of these three features for each of the three tasks (9 training runs in total).

The results are summarized in Table 5(a). It is interesting to compare the performance of the three task-specific Res3D models using RGB from Table 2 with the numbers on the diagonal axis of Table 5(a). The differences are explained by the usage of the SVM classifier on top of the Res3D features. In terms of overall performance considering all three tasks, Object features are the strongest while Scene features are the weakest. Note that this ranking is also consistent with the number of annotations we have for each task (listed in Table 1).

Overall there are strong correlations among different tasks from our preliminary results in Table 5(a). For example, even when applying the weakest Scene feature on the hardest Object task, we achieve an mAP of 14.2, which is a decent result considering the difficulty of the Object task. This highlights the potentials of leveraging different information for each task and the usefulness of SOA as a test bed to inspire new research ideas.

At first glance, Table 5(a) appears to suggest that Object features are inherently richer than Scene features: Object features gives better accuracy (53.9 mAP) than Scene features (49.7 mAP) on Scene classification. However, SOA has over 13 times more annotations for Objects than Scenes. When we control the label count by reducing the number of feature-learning samples for Objects to be the same as Scenes, the mAP drops from 53.9 to 46.5, demonstrating that there is likely inherent value in the Scene features, despite the much smaller label space for Scene.

5.2   How Multiple Tasks Can Help Another

Here we study the effectiveness of leveraging several tasks to solve another. We follow the same procedure described in Sect. 5.1 with the difference that we combine multiple features by concatenating them together for each task. The results are presented in Table 5(b).

At a glance, simply concatenating different features does not seem to boost the performance of each individual task significantly. For the Scene task, combining all three features does improve the mAP from 49.7 to 53.2. However, the improvement becomes marginal for both the Object and the Action task. As Scene is the weakest descriptor, combining it with stronger features (such as Object) can make the Scene task easier, but not the other way around.

Moreover, fusing different features by concatenating them implies that each feature has the same weight in the final classifier. This is not ideal as the strength of each feature is different. It is, thus, appealing to design more sophisticated mechanisms to adaptively fuse different features together. There are many creative ways of exploiting the correlation among different tasks, such as transfer learning and graphical models [20] that we hope to see in future research.

5.3   Number of Videos vs. Number of Categories

The comparison of the Scene features with Object features in Sect. 5.1 suggests a more careful investigation of the tradeoffs between label diversity and number of labeled samples. Given a limited budget, and assuming the resource required for each annotation is the same, how should we spend our budget to improve the representational ability of SOA? As a proxy for richness of representation, we choose to use transfer learning ability. Huh et al. [12] investigated different factors that make ImageNet [5] good for transfer learning. Here we consider the effects of varying the number of samples and the number of categories for

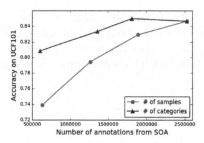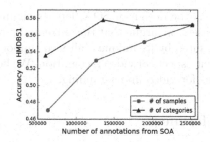

Fig. 6. How to scale up the transfer learning ability of SOA effectively: number of videos vs number of categories.

SOA. We then consider transfer performance as a function of the total number of annotations (as opposed to the total number of videos).

We randomly sample a subset (i.e., 25%, 50%, 75%, 100%) of either samples or categories to build a smaller version of SOA. In the first case, we randomly choose a given fraction of videos. In the second case, we randomly choose a given fraction of labels, remove all other labels from the dataset, and discard videos with no labels remaining. The second case generally yields more videos than the first case. A Res3D model is pre-trained with the smaller versions of SOA, and then fine-tuned on UCF101 and HMDB51.

The results in Fig. 6 are unequivocal: for a fixed number of annotations, a smaller label set applied to more videos produces better results. Fine-tuning accuracy on UCF101 and HMDB51 increases rapidly with respect to the number of videos used from SOA for pre-training, while performance seems to saturate as the number of categories is increased. This suggests that we can further boost the accuracy on UCF101 and HMDB51 by annotating more videos for SOA. This gives us a relevant guideline on how to extend SOA in the future.

6 Conclusions

In this work we introduced a new large-scale, multi-task, multi-label video dataset aimed at casting video understanding as a multi-faceted problem encompassing scene, object and action categorization. Unlike existing video datasets, videos from SOA are uniformly sampled to avoid the bias introduced by querying search engines, and labels originate from free-form annotations that sidestep the bias of fixed ontologies. This gives rise to a benchmark that appears more challenging than most existing datasets for video classification. We also present a comprehensive experimental study that provide insightful analyses on several factors of SOA, including performance achieved by popular 2D and 3D models, the role of RGB vs optical flow, transfer learning effectiveness, synergies and correlations among the three SOA tasks, as well as some observations that will guide future extensions and improvements to SOA.

As the design of SOA departs significantly from those adopted in previous datasets, we argue that the current and future value of our benchmark should be measured by its unique ability to support a new genre of experiments across different aspects of video recognition. We believe that this will inspire new research ideas for video understanding.

References

1. Abu-El-Haija, S., et al.: Youtube-8m: a large-scale video classification benchmark. arXiv preprint arXiv:1609.08675 (2016)
2. Ballas, N., Yao, L., Pal, C., Courville, A.: Delving deeper into convolutional networks for learning video representations. arXiv preprint arXiv:1511.06432 (2015)
3. Caffe2-Team: Caffe2: A New Lightweight, Modular, and Scalable Deep Learning Framework. https://caffe2.ai/
4. Carreira, J., Zisserman, A.: Quo vadis, action recognition? A new model and the kinetics dataset. In: CVPR (2017)
5. Deng, J., Dong, W., Socher, R., Li, L.J., Li, K., Fei-Fei, L.: ImageNet: a large-scale hierarchical image database. In: IEEE Conference on Computer Vision and Pattern Recognition, CVPR 2009, pp. 248–255. IEEE (2009)
6. Donahue, J., et al.: Long-term recurrent convolutional networks for visual recognition and description. In: Proceedings of the IEEE Conference on Computer Vision and Pattern Recognition, pp. 2625–2634 (2015)
7. Farnebäck, G.: Two-frame motion estimation based on polynomial expansion. In: Bigun, J., Gustavsson, T. (eds.) SCIA 2003. LNCS, vol. 2749, pp. 363–370. Springer, Heidelberg (2003). https://doi.org/10.1007/3-540-45103-X_50
8. Girdhar, R., Ramanan, D., Gupta, A., Sivic, J., Russell, B.C.: ActionVLAD: learning spatio-temporal aggregation for action classification. In: CVPR (2017)
9. Goyal, R., et al.: The? Something something? Video database for learning and evaluating visual common sense. In: Proceedings of ICCV (2017)
10. Hara, K., Kataoka, H., Satoh, Y.: Can spatiotemporal 3D CNNS retrace the history of 2D CNNS and ImageNet? arXiv preprint arXiv:1711.09577 (2017)
11. He, K., Zhang, X., Ren, S., Sun, J.: Deep residual learning for image recognition. In: CVPR (2016)
12. Huh, M., Agrawal, P., Efros, A.A.: What makes ImageNet good for transfer learning? arXiv preprint arXiv:1608.08614 (2016)
13. Ikizler-Cinbis, N., Sclaroff, S.: Object, scene and actions: combining multiple features for human action recognition. In: Daniilidis, K., Maragos, P., Paragios, N. (eds.) ECCV 2010. LNCS, vol. 6311, pp. 494–507. Springer, Heidelberg (2010). https://doi.org/10.1007/978-3-642-15549-9_36
14. ILSVRC-2015-VID: ImageNet Object Detection from Video Challenge. https://www.kaggle.com/c/imagenet-object-detection-from-video-challenge
15. Ioffe, S., Szegedy, C.: Batch normalization: accelerating deep network training by reducing internal covariate shift. In: ICML (2015)
16. Ji, S., Xu, W., Yang, M., Yu, K.: 3d convolutional neural networks for human action recognition. IEEE TPAMI **35**(1), 221–231 (2013)
17. Jiang, Y.G., Li, Z., Chang, S.F.: Modeling scene and object contexts for human action retrieval with few examples. IEEE Trans. Circuits Syst. Video Technol. **21**(5), 674–681 (2011)

18. Karpathy, A., Toderici, G., Shetty, S., Leung, T., Sukthankar, R., Fei-Fei, L.: Large-scale video classification with convolutional neural networks. In: CVPR (2014)
19. Kay, W., et al.: The kinetics human action video dataset. arXiv preprint arXiv:1705.06950 (2017)
20. Koller, D., Friedman, N.: Probabilistic Graphical Models: Principles and Techniques. MIT Press, Cambridge (2009)
21. Kuehne, H., Jhuang, H., Garrote, E., Poggio, T., Serre, T.: HMDB51: a large video database for human motion recognition. In: ICCV (2011)
22. Kuehne, H., Jhuang, H., Garrote, E., Poggio, T., Serre, T.: HMDB: a large video database for human motion recognition. In: 2011 IEEE International Conference on Computer Vision (ICCV), pp. 2556–2563. IEEE (2011)
23. Laptev, I.: On space-time interest points. Int. J. Comput. Vis. $64(2–3)$, 107–123 (2005)
24. Long, X., et al.: Multimodal keyless attention fusion for video classification (2018)
25. Maaten, L.V.D., Hinton, G.: Visualizing data using t-SNE. J. Mach. Learn. Res. 9(Nov), 2579–2605 (2008)
26. Miller, G.A.: Wordnet: a lexical database for English. Commun. ACM $38(11)$, 39–41 (1995)
27. Pantofaru, C., et al.: AVA: a video dataset of spatio-temporally localized atomic visual actions (2017)
28. Real, E., Shlens, J., Mazzocchi, S., Pan, X., Vanhoucke, V.: YouTube-BoundingBoxes: a large high-precision human-annotated data set for object detection in video. In: 2017 IEEE Conference on Computer Vision and Pattern Recognition (CVPR), pp. 7464–7473. IEEE (2017)
29. Schuldt, C., Laptev, I., Caputo, B.: Recognizing human actions: a local SVM approach. In: Proceedings of the 17th International Conference on Pattern Recognition, ICPR 2004, vol. 3, pp. 32–36. IEEE (2004)
30. Sigurdsson, G.A., Russakovsky, O., Gupta, A.: What actions are needed for understanding human actions in videos? In: IEEE International Conference on Computer Vision, ICCV 2017, Venice, Italy, 22–29 October 2017, pp. 2156–2165 (2017)
31. Sigurdsson, G.A., Varol, G., Wang, X., Farhadi, A., Laptev, I., Gupta, A.: Hollywood in homes: crowdsourcing data collection for activity understanding. In: Leibe, B., Matas, J., Sebe, N., Welling, M. (eds.) ECCV 2016. LNCS, vol. 9905, pp. 510–526. Springer, Cham (2016). https://doi.org/10.1007/978-3-319-46448-0_31
32. Simonyan, K., Zisserman, A.: Two-stream convolutional networks for action recognition in videos. In: NIPS (2014)
33. Soomro, K., Zamir, A.R., Shah, M.: UCF101: a dataset of 101 human action classes from videos in the wild. In: CRCV-TR-12-01 (2012)
34. Soomro, K., Zamir, A.R., Shah, M.: UCF101: a dataset of 101 human actions classes from videos in the wild. arXiv preprint arXiv:1212.0402 (2012)
35. Srivastava, N., Mansimov, E., Salakhudinov, R.: Unsupervised learning of video representations using LSTMS. In: International Conference on Machine Learning, pp. 843–852 (2015)
36. Szegedy, C., et al.: Going deeper with convolutions. In: CVPR (2015)
37. Torralba, A., Efros, A.A.: Unbiased look at dataset bias. In: 2011 IEEE Conference on Computer Vision and Pattern Recognition (CVPR), pp. 1521–1528. IEEE (2011)
38. Tran, D., Bourdev, L., Fergus, R., Torresani, L., Paluri, M.: Learning spatiotemporal features with 3D convolutional networks. In: ICCV (2015)

39. Tran, D., Wang, H., Torresani, L., Ray, J., LeCun, Y., Paluri, M.: A closer look at spatiotemporal convolutions for action recognition. arXiv preprint arXiv:1711.11248 (2017)
40. Wang, H., Kläser, A., Schmid, C., Liu, C.L.: Action recognition by dense trajectories. In: 2011 IEEE Conference on Computer Vision and Pattern Recognition (CVPR), pp. 3169–3176. IEEE (2011)
41. Wang, Y.X., Ramanan, D., Hebert, M.: Learning to model the tail. In: Advances in Neural Information Processing Systems, pp. 7029–7039 (2017)
42. Xie, S., Sun, C., Huang, J., Tu, Z., Murphy, K.: Rethinking spatiotemporal feature learning for video understanding. arXiv preprint arXiv:1712.04851 (2017)
43. Yue-Hei Ng, J., Hausknecht, M., Vijayanarasimhan, S., Vinyals, O., Monga, R., Toderici, G.: Beyond short snippets: deep networks for video classification. In: Proceedings of the IEEE Conference on Computer Vision and Pattern Recognition, pp. 4694–4702 (2015)
44. Zhou, B., Andonian, A., Torralba, A.: Temporal relational reasoning in videos. arXiv preprint arXiv:1711.08496 (2017)
45. Zhou, B., Lapedriza, A., Xiao, J., Torralba, A., Oliva, A.: Learning deep features for scene recognition using places database. In: NIPS (2014)

Accelerating Dynamic Programs via Nested Benders Decomposition with Application to Multi-Person Pose Estimation

Shaofei Wang[1]([✉]), Alexander Ihler[2], Konrad Kording[3], and Julian Yarkony[4]

[1] Baidu Inc., Beijing, China
sfwang0928@gmail.com
[2] UC Irvine, Irvine, USA
[3] University of Pennsylvania, Philadelphia, USA
[4] Experian Data Lab, San Diego, USA

Abstract. We present a novel approach to solve dynamic programs (DP), which are frequent in computer vision, on tree-structured graphs with exponential node state space. Typical DP approaches have to enumerate the joint state space of two adjacent nodes on every edge of the tree to compute the optimal messages. Here we propose an algorithm based on Nested Benders Decomposition (NBD) that iteratively lower-bounds the message on every edge and promises to be far more efficient. We apply our NBD algorithm along with a novel Minimum Weight Set Packing (MWSP) formulation to a multi-person pose estimation problem. While our algorithm is provably optimal at termination it operates in linear time for practical DP problems, gaining up to $500\times$ speed up over traditional DP algorithm which have polynomial complexity.

Keywords: Nested benders decomposition · Column generation Multi-person pose estimation

1 Introduction

Many vision tasks involve optimizing over large, combinatorial spaces, arising for example from low-level detectors generating large numbers of competing hypotheses which must be compared and combined to produce an overall prediction of the scene. A concrete example is multi-person pose estimation (MPPE), which is a foundational image processing task that can feed into many downstream vision-based applications, such as movement science, security, and rehabilitation. MPPE can be approached in a bottom-up manner, by generating

---

S. Wang—Work was done as an independent researcher before joining Baidu.

Electronic supplementary material The online version of this chapter (https://doi.org/10.1007/978-3-030-01264-9_40) contains supplementary material, which is available to authorized users.

© Springer Nature Switzerland AG 2018
V. Ferrari et al. (Eds.): ECCV 2018, LNCS 11218, pp. 677–692, 2018.
https://doi.org/10.1007/978-3-030-01264-9_40

candidate detections of body parts using, *e.g.*, a convolutional neural network (CNN), and subsequently grouping them into people.

The ensuing optimization problems, however, can be difficult for non-specialized approaches to solve efficiently. Relatively simple (tree-structured or nearly tree-structured) parts-based models can use dynamic programming (DP) to solve object detection [6], pose estimation [17] and tracking [14] tasks. However, typical dynamic programming is quadratic in the number of states that the variables take on; when this is large, it can quickly become intractable. In certain special cases, such as costs based on Euclidean distance, tricks like the generalized distance transform [7] can be used to compute solutions more efficiently, for example in deformable parts models [6,17], but are not applicable to more general cost functions.

In this paper we examine a model for MPPE that is formulated as a minimum-weight set packing problem, in which each set corresponds to an individual person in the image, and consists of the collection of all detections associated with that person (which may include multiple detections of the same part, due to noise in the low-level detectors). We solve the set packing problem as an integer linear program using implicit column generation, where each column corresponds to a pose, or collection of part detections potentially associated with a single person.

Unfortunately, while this means that the *structure* of the cost function remains tree-like, similar to single-pose parts models [6,17], the number of *states* that the variables take on in this model are extremely large – each part (head, neck, etc.) can be associated with any number of detections in the image, meaning that the variables take on values in the power set of all detections of that part. This property renders a standard dynamic program on the tree intractable.

To address this issue, we apply a *nested Benders decomposition* (NBD) [5, 13] approach, that iteratively lower bounds the desired dynamic programming messages between nodes. The process terminates with the exact messages for optimal states of each node, while typically being vastly more efficient than direct enumeration over all combinations of the two power sets.

We demonstrate the effectiveness of our approach on the MPII-Multiperson validation set [2]. Contrary to existing primal heuristic solvers (*e.g.* [10]) for the MPPE model, our formulation is provably optimal when the LP relaxation is tight, which is true for over 99% of the cases in our experiments.

Our paper is structured as follows. We review related DP algorithms and MPPE systems in Sect. 2. In Sect. 3 we formulate MPPE as a min-weight set packing problem, which we solve via Implicit Column Generation (ICG) with dynamic programming as the pricing method. In Sect. 4 we show how the pricing step of ICG can be stated as a dynamic program. In Sect. 5 we introduce our NBD message passing, which replaces traditional message passing in the DP. Finally, in Sect. 6 we conduct experiments on the MPII-Multi-Person validation set, showing that our NBD based DP achieves up to $500\times$ speed up over dynamic programming on real MPPE problems, while achieving comparable average precision results to a state-of-the-art solver based on a primal heuristic approach.

2   Related Work

In this section, we describe some of the relevant existing methodologies and applications of work which relate to our approach. Specifically, we discuss fast exact dynamic programming methodologies and combinatorial optimization based models for MPPE.

2.1   Fast Dynamic Programming

The time complexity of dynamic programming (DP) grows linearly in the number of variables in the tree and quadratically in the state space of the variables. For applications in which the quadratic growth is a key bottleneck two relevant papers should be considered. In [12] the pairwise terms between variables in the tree are known in advance of the optimization and are identical across each edge in the tree. Hence they can be pre-sorted before inference, so that for each state of a variable the pairwise terms for the remaining variable are ordered. By exploiting these sorted lists, one can compute messages by processing only the lowest cost portion of the list and still guarantee optimality.

In a separate line of work [4], a column generation approach is introduced which attacks the dual LP relaxation of the DP. Applying duality, pairwise terms in the primal become constraints in the dual. Although finding violated constraints exhaustively would require the exact same time complexity as solving the DP with a more standard approach, by lower bounding the reduced costs the exhaustive enumeration can be avoided. Similarly, the LP does not need to be solved explicitly and instead can be solved as a DP.

In contrast to these lines of work our DP has significant structure in its pairwise interactions, corresponding to a high tree width binary Ising model, which we exploit. The previously cited work was not designed with domains containing these types of structures in mind.

2.2   Multi-Person Pose Estimation in Combinatorial Context

Our experimental work is closely related to the sub-graph multi-cut integer linear programming formulation of [8, 10, 15], which we refer to as MC for shorthand. MC models the problem of MPPE as partitioning detections into body parts (or false positives) and clustering those detections into poses. The clustering process is done according to the correlation clustering [1, 3, 19] criteria, with costs parameterized by the part associated with the detection. This formulation is notable as it performs a type of non-maximum-suppression (NMS) by allowing poses to be associated with multiple detections of a given body part. However, the optimization problem of MC is often too hard to solve exactly and is thus attacked with heuristic methods. Additionally, MC has no easy way of incorporating a prior model on the number of poses in the image.

In contrast to MC, our model permits efficient inference with provable guarantees while modeling a prior using the cost of associating candidate detections with parts in advance of optimization. Optimization need not associate each such detection with a person, and can instead label it as a false positive. Associating detections with parts in advance of optimization is not problematic in practice, since the deep neural network nearly always produces highly unimodal probability distributions on the label of a given detection.

3   Multi-Person Pose Estimation as Minimum Weight Set Packing

In this section we formulate the bottom-up MPPE task as a Minimum Weight Set Packing (MWSP) problem and attack it with Implicit Column Generation. We use the body part detector of [8], which, after post-processing (thresholding, non max suppression (NMS), etc.), outputs a set of body part detections with costs that we interpret as terms in a subsequent cost function. We use the terms 'detection' and 'part detection' interchangeably in the remainder of this paper.

Each detection is associated with exactly one body part. We use fourteen body parts, consisting of the head and neck, along with right and left variants of the ankle, knee, hip, wrist and shoulder. We use the post-processing system of [8] which outputs pairwise costs that either encourage or discourage the joint assignment of two part detections to a common pose. Each pose thus consists of a selection of part detections; a pose can contain no detection of a body part (corresponding to an occlusion), or multiple detections (NMS) of that part. Each pose is associated with a cost that is a quadratic function of its members.

Given the set of poses and their associated costs we model the MPPE problem as a MWSP problem, which selects a set of poses that are pairwise disjoint (meaning that no two selected poses share a common detection) of minimum total cost.

3.1   Problem Formulation

Detections and Parts: Formally, we denote the set of part detections as $\mathcal{D}$ and index it with d. Similarly, we use $\mathcal{R}$ to denote the set of body parts and index it with r. We use $\mathcal{D}^r$ to denote the set of part detections of part r.

We use $\mathcal{S}^r$ to denote the power set of detections of part r, and index it with s. We describe mappings of detections to power set members using matrix $S^r \in \{0,1\}^{|\mathcal{D}| \times |\mathcal{S}^r|}$ where $S^r_{ds} = 1$ if and only if detection d is associated with configuration s. For convenience we explicitly define neck as part 0 and thus its power set is $\mathcal{S}^0$.

Poses: We denote the set of all possible poses over $\mathcal{D}$, i.e. the power set of $\mathcal{D}$, as $\mathcal{P}$ and index it with p. We describe mappings of detections to poses using a matrix $P \in \{0,1\}^{|\mathcal{D}| \times |\mathcal{P}|}$, and set $P_{dp} = 1$ if and only if detection d is associated with pose p. Since $\mathcal{P}$ is the power set of $\mathcal{D}$, it is too large to be considered explicitly. Thus, our algorithm works by building a subset $\hat{\mathcal{P}} \subseteq \mathcal{P}$ that captures the relevant poses to the optimization (see Sect. 3.2).

Pairwise Disjoint Constraints: We describe a selection of poses using indicator vector $\gamma \in \{0,1\}^{|\mathcal{P}|}$ where $\gamma_p = 1$ indicates that pose $p \in \mathcal{P}$ is selected, and $\gamma_p = 0$ otherwise.

A solution γ is valid if and only if the selected poses are pairwise disjoint, which is written formally as $P\gamma \leq 1$. The non-matrix version of the inequality $P\gamma \leq 1$ is $\sum_{p \in \mathcal{P}} P_{dp}\gamma_p \leq 1$ for each $d \in \mathcal{D}$.

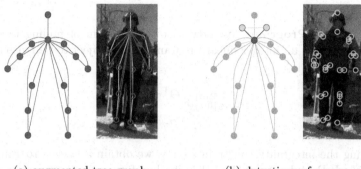

(a) augmented-tree graph   (b) detections of a pose

Fig. 1. Graphical representation of our pose model. (a) We model a pose in the image as an augmented-tree, in which each red node represents a body part, green edges are connections of traditional pictorial structure, while red edges are augmented connections from neck to all non-adjacent parts of neck. (b) Each body part can be associated with multiple part detections, a red node represents a body part while cyan nodes represent part detections of that part, blue edges indicate assignment of part detections to certain part of a person while cyan edges indicate pairwise costs among detections of the same part. The possible states of a body part thus consists of the power set of part detections of that part. (Color figure online)

Cost Function: We express the total cost of a pose in terms of unary costs $\theta \in \mathbb{R}^{|\mathcal{D}|}$, where θ_d is the cost of assigning detection d to a pose, and pairwise costs $\phi \in \mathbb{R}^{|\mathcal{D}| \times |\mathcal{D}|}$, where $\phi_{d_1 d_2}$ is the cost of assigning detections d_1 and d_2 to a common pose. We use Ω to denote the cost of instancing a pose, which serves to regularize the number of people in an image. The cost of a pose is formally defined as:

$$\Theta_p = \Omega + \sum_{d \in \mathcal{D}} \theta_d P_{dp} + \sum_{\substack{d_1 \in \mathcal{D} \\ d_2 \in \mathcal{D}}} \phi_{d_1 d_2} P_{d_1 p} P_{d_2 p} \tag{1}$$

By enforcing some structure in the pairwise costs ϕ, we ensure that this optimization problem is tractable as a dynamic program. Consider a graph $G = (V, E)$, where $V = \mathcal{R}$, i.e. each node represents a body part, and $(\hat{r}, r) \in E$ if pairwise terms between part $\hat{r}$ and part r are non-zero. A common model in computer vision is to represent the location of parts in the body using a tree-structured model, for example in the deformable part model of [6,17]; this forces the pairwise terms to be zero between non-adjacent parts in the tree[1].

In our application we augment this tree model with additional edges from the neck to all other non-adjacent body parts. This is illustrated in Fig. 1. Then, conditioned on neck configuration s from $\mathcal{S}^0$, the conditional model is tree-structured and can be optimized using dynamic programming in $O(|\mathcal{R}|k^2)$ time, where k is the maximum number of detections per part.

Integer Linear Program: We now cast the problem of finding the lowest cost set of poses as an integer linear program (ILP) subject to pairwise disjoint constraints:

$$\min_{\gamma \in \{0,1\}^{|\mathcal{P}|}} \Theta^\top \gamma$$
$$\text{s.t.} \quad P\gamma \leq 1 \tag{2}$$

By relaxing the integrality constraints on γ, we obtain a linear program relaxation of the ILP, and convert the LP to its dual form using Lagrange multiplier set $\lambda \in \mathbb{R}_{0+}^{|\mathcal{D}|}$:

$$\min_{\substack{\gamma \geq 0 \\ P\gamma \leq 1}} \Theta^\top \gamma = \max_{\substack{\lambda \geq 0 \\ \Theta + P^\top \lambda \geq 0}} -1^\top \lambda \tag{3}$$

3.2 Implicit Column Generation

In this section we describe how to optimize the LP relaxation of Eq. (3). As discussed previously, the major difficulty to optimize Eq. (3) is the intractable size of $\mathcal{P}$. Instead, we incrementally construct a sufficient subset $\hat{\mathcal{P}} \subseteq \mathcal{P}$ so as to avoid enumerating $\mathcal{P}$ while still solving Eq. (3) exactly. This algorithm is called Implicit Column Generation (ICG) in the operations research literature, and is described formally in Algorithm 1. Specifically, we alternate between finding poses with negative reduced costs (line 6) and re-optimizing Eq. (3) (line 3). Finding poses with negative reduced costs is achieved by conditioning on every neck configuration $s_0 \in \mathcal{S}^0$, and then identifying the lowest reduced cost pose among all the poses consistent with s_0 which we denote as $\mathcal{P}^{s_0}$.

---

[1] WLOG: we assume that ϕ is upper triangular and that detections are ordered by part with the parent part being lower numbered than the child.

Algorithm 1. Implicit Column Generation

1: $\hat{\mathcal{P}} \leftarrow \{\}$
2: **repeat**
3:     $\lambda \leftarrow$ Maximize dual in Eq. (3) over column set $\hat{\mathcal{P}}$
4:     $\dot{\mathcal{P}} \leftarrow \{\}$
5:     **for** $s_0 \in \mathcal{S}^0$ **do**
6:         $p_* \leftarrow \arg\min_{p \in \mathcal{P}^{s_0}} \Theta_p + \sum_{d \in \mathcal{D}} \lambda_d P_{dp}$
7:         **if** $\Theta_{p_*} + \sum_{d \in \mathcal{D}} \lambda_d P_{dp_*} < 0$ **then**
8:             $\dot{\mathcal{P}} \leftarrow [\dot{\mathcal{P}} \cup p_*]$
9:         **end if**
10:     **end for**
11:     $\hat{\mathcal{P}} \leftarrow [\hat{\mathcal{P}}, \dot{\mathcal{P}}]$
12: **until** $|\dot{\mathcal{P}}| = 0$

---

4 Pricing via Dynamic Programming

A key step of Algorithm 1 is finding the pose with lowest reduced cost given dual variables λ (line 6):

$$\min_{p \in \mathcal{P}^{s_0}} \Theta_p + \sum_{d \in \mathcal{D}} \lambda_d P_{dp} \tag{4}$$

In the operations research literature, solving Eq. (4) is often called *pricing*.

Formally, let us assume the graph depicted in Fig. 1(a) is conditioned on neck configuration, s_0, and thus becomes a tree graph. We define the set of children of part r as $\{r \rightarrow\}$. We also define $\mu_{\hat{s}}^r$ as the cost-to-go, or the *message* of part r with its parent $\hat{r}$ associated with state $\hat{s}$:

$$\mu_{\hat{s}}^r = \min_{s \in \mathcal{S}^r} \sum_{\substack{\hat{d} \in \mathcal{D}^{\hat{r}} \\ d \in \mathcal{D}^r}} S_{\hat{d}\hat{s}}^{\hat{r}} S_{ds}^r \phi_{\hat{d}d} + \nu_s^r \tag{5}$$

Where the first term computes pairwise costs between part r and its parent $\hat{r}$. ν_s^r accounts for the cost of the sub-tree rooted at part r with state s, and is defined as:

$$\nu_s^r = \psi_s^r + \sum_{\bar{r} \in \{r \rightarrow\}} \mu_s^{\bar{r}}$$

$$\psi_s^r = \sum_{d \in \mathcal{D}^r} (\theta_d + \lambda_d) S_{ds}^r + \sum_{\substack{d_1 \in \mathcal{D}^r \\ d_2 \in \mathcal{D}^r}} \phi_{d_1 d_2} S_{d_1 s}^r S_{d_2 s}^r + \sum_{\substack{d_1 \in \mathcal{D}^0 \\ d_2 \in \mathcal{D}^r}} \phi_{d_1 d_2} S_{d_1 s_0}^0 S_{d_2 s}^r \tag{6}$$

Thus solving Eq. (4) involves computing and passing messages from leaf nodes (wrists and ankles) along the (conditional) tree graph $G = (V, E)$ to root node (head); Eq. (5) for root node equals to Eq (4) minus Ω. To compute $\mu_{\hat{s}}^r$ for every $\hat{s} \in \mathcal{S}^{\hat{r}}$, a node r need to pass through its states for each state of its parent node, thus resulting in polynomial time algorithm. If we have $|\mathcal{D}^r| = |\mathcal{D}^{\hat{r}}| = 15$, then we have roughly 30k states for r and $\hat{r}$, DP would then enumerate the joint space of 9×10^8 states, which becomes prohibitively expensive for practical applications.

5   Nested Benders Decomposition

In this section we present a near linear time algorithm (w.r.t $|\mathcal{S}^r|$) in practice that computes the message terms $\mu_s^{\bar{r}}$ in Eq. (6). The key idea of this algorithm is to apply Nested Benders Decomposition (NBD), so that for every parent-child edge $(r, \bar{r}), \forall \bar{r} \in \{r \to\}$, we iteratively construct a small sufficient set of affine functions of $\mathcal{D}^r$; the maximum of these functions lower bounds messages $\mu_s^{\bar{r}}$. Essentially, each of these sets forms a lower envelope of messages, making them dependent on the maximum of the lower envelopes instead of child state $\bar{s}$; if the cardinality of the set is a small constant (relative to $|\mathcal{S}^{\bar{r}}|$), then we can compute the message on an edge for any parent state in $O(1)$ instead of $O(|\mathcal{S}^{\bar{r}}|)$, and thus computing messages for every state $s \in \mathcal{S}^r$ would take $O(|\mathcal{S}^r|)$ instead of $O(|\mathcal{S}^r| \times |\mathcal{S}^{\bar{r}}|)$.

5.1   Benders Decomposition Formulation

We now rigorously define our Benders Decomposition formulation for a specific parent-child edge pair $(r, \bar{r})$ which we denote as $e \in E$ for shorthand. We define the set of affine functions that lower bounds the message $\mu_s^{\bar{r}}$ as $\mathcal{Z}^e$ which we index by z, and parameterize the zth affine function as $(\omega_0^{ez}, \omega_1^{ez}, \ldots, \omega_{|\mathcal{D}^r|}^{ez})$. For simplicity of notation we drop the e superscript in the remaining of the paper. If $\mathcal{Z}^e$ indeed forms lower envelopes of $\mu_s^{\bar{r}}$ then we have:

$$\mu_s^{\bar{r}} = \max_{z \in \mathcal{Z}^e} \omega_0^z + \sum_{d \in \mathcal{D}^r} \omega_d^z S_{sd}^r, \quad e = (r, \bar{r}) \in E \tag{7}$$

In the context of Benders Decomposition one affine function in $\mathcal{Z}^e$ is called a *Benders row*. For an edge e, we start with nascent set $\dot{\mathcal{Z}}^e$ with a single row in which $\omega_0^0 = -\infty, \omega_d^0 = 0, d \in \mathcal{D}^r$ and iteratively add new Benders rows into $\dot{\mathcal{Z}}^e$.

We define a lower bound on the message of edge $(r, \bar{r})$ as:

$$\mu_s^{\bar{r}-} = \max_{z \in \dot{\mathcal{Z}}^e} \omega_0^z + \sum_{d \in \mathcal{D}^r} \omega_d^z S_{sd}^r, \quad e = (r, \bar{r}) \in E \tag{8}$$

which satisfies $\mu_s^{\bar{r}-} \leq \mu_s^{\bar{r}}$. The two terms become equal for $s^* = \arg\min_{s \in \mathcal{S}^r} \mu_s^{\bar{r}}$ if the lower bound is tight.

5.2   Producing New Benders Rows

Until now we define parent-child pair as $(r, \bar{r})$ in the context of Eq. (6). In this section we describe how to generate new Benders rows in the context of Eq. (5), where parent-child pair is denoted as $(\hat{r}, r)$.

Given current set $\dot{\mathcal{Z}}^e$ of an edge $(\hat{r}, r) \in E$, with $\hat{r}$ associated with state $\hat{s}$, we check if there exist a new Benders row that can increase current lower bound $\mu_{\hat{s}}^{r-}$. This is computed by:

$$\min_{s \in \mathcal{S}^r} \sum_{\substack{\hat{d} \in \mathcal{D}^{\hat{r}} \\ d \in \mathcal{D}^r}} S_{\hat{d}\hat{s}}^{\hat{r}} S_{ds}^r \phi_{\hat{d}d} + \nu_s^{r-} \tag{9}$$

where:

$$\nu_s^{r-} = \psi_s^r + \sum_{\bar{r} \in \{r \to\}} \mu_s^{\bar{r}-} \tag{10}$$

Integer Linear Program: Here we reformulate Eq. (9) as an integer linear program. We use indicator vectors $x \in \{0,1\}^{|\mathcal{D}^r|}, y \in \{0,1\}^{|\mathcal{D}^{\hat{r}}| \times |\mathcal{D}^r|}$, where $x_s = 1$ if and only if $s \in \mathcal{S}^r$ is selected and $y_{\hat{d}d} = S_{\hat{d}\hat{s}}^{\hat{r}} (\sum_{s \in \mathcal{S}^r} x_s S_{ds}^r)$:

$$\min_{\substack{x \in \{0,1\}^{|\mathcal{S}^r|} \\ y \in \{0,1\}^{|\mathcal{D}^{\hat{r}}| \times |\mathcal{D}^r|}}} \sum_{s \in \mathcal{S}^r} \nu_s^{r-} x_s + \sum_{\substack{d \in \mathcal{D}^r \\ \hat{d} \in \mathcal{D}^{\hat{r}}}} \phi_{\hat{d}d} y_{\hat{d}d}$$

$$\text{s.t.} \quad \sum_{s \in \mathcal{S}^r} x_s = 1$$

$$- y_{\hat{d}d} + S_{\hat{d}\hat{s}}^{\hat{r}} + \sum_{s \in \mathcal{S}^r} x_s S_{ds}^r \leq 1, \quad \forall \hat{d} \in \mathcal{D}^{\hat{r}}, d \in \mathcal{D}^r$$

$$y_{\hat{d}d} \leq S_{\hat{d}\hat{s}}^{\hat{r}}, \quad \forall \hat{d} \in \mathcal{D}^{\hat{r}}, d \in \mathcal{D}^r$$

$$y_{\hat{d}d} \leq \sum_{s \in \mathcal{S}^r} x_s S_{ds}^r, \quad \forall \hat{d} \in \mathcal{D}^{\hat{r}}, d \in \mathcal{D}^r \tag{11}$$

We then relax x, y to be non-negative. In the supplement we provide proof that this relaxation is always tight. We express the dual of the relaxed LP below with dual variables $\delta^0 \in \mathbb{R}$, and $\delta^1, \delta^2, \delta^3$ each lie in $R_{0+}^{|\mathcal{D}^{\hat{r}}| \times |\mathcal{D}^r|}$ which is indexed by $\hat{d}, d$:

$$\max_{\substack{\delta^0 \in \mathbb{R} \\ (\delta^1, \delta^2, \delta^3) \geq 0}} \quad \delta^0 - \sum_{\substack{\hat{d} \in \mathcal{D}^{\hat{r}} \\ d \in \mathcal{D}^r}} \delta^1_{\hat{d}d} + \sum_{\substack{\hat{d} \in \mathcal{D}^{\hat{r}} \\ d \in \mathcal{D}^r}} (\delta^1_{\hat{d}d} - \delta^2_{\hat{d}d}) S^{\hat{r}}_{\hat{d}\hat{s}}$$

$$\text{s.t.} \quad \nu^{r-}_s - \delta^0 + \sum_{\substack{\hat{d} \in \mathcal{D}^{\hat{r}} \\ d \in \mathcal{D}^r}} (\delta^1_{\hat{d}d} - \delta^3_{\hat{d}d}) S^r_{ds} \geq 0, \quad \forall s \in \mathcal{S}^r$$

$$\phi_{\hat{d}d} - \delta^1_{\hat{d}d} + \delta^2_{\hat{d}d} + \delta^3_{\hat{d}d} \geq 0, \quad \forall \hat{d} \in \mathcal{D}^{\hat{r}}, d \in \mathcal{D}^r \tag{12}$$

Observe Eq. (12) is an affine function of $\mathcal{D}^{\hat{r}}$, thus when dual variables are optimal Eq. (12) represents a new Benders row that we can add to $\dot{\mathcal{Z}}^e, e = (\hat{r}, r)$. Let us denote the new Benders row as z^*, then we construct this row from dual variables as:

$$\omega_0^{z^*} = \delta^0 - \sum_{\substack{\hat{d} \in \mathcal{D}^{\hat{r}} \\ d \in \mathcal{D}^r}} \delta^1_{\hat{d}d} \tag{13}$$

$$\omega_{\hat{d}}^{z^*} = \sum_{d \in \mathcal{D}^r} \delta^1_{\hat{d}d} - \delta^2_{\hat{d}d}, \quad \forall \hat{d} \in \mathcal{D}^{\hat{r}} \tag{14}$$

Note that if all lower bounds on child messages $\mu^{\bar{r}-}_{s^*}, \forall \bar{r} \in \{r \rightarrow\}$ are tight for $s^* \in \mathcal{S}^r$ that minimizes Eq. (9), then the new Benders row z^* forms a tight lower bound on message $\mu^r_{\hat{s}}$ for the specified parent state $\hat{s}$.

Solving Dual LP: One could directly solve (12) in closed form, or via an off-the-shelf LP solver, both of which gives maximum lower bound for one parent state $\hat{s}$. However, ideally we want this new Benders row to also give a good lower bound to other parent states $\hat{s} \in \mathcal{S}^{\hat{r}}$, so that we can use as few rows as possible to form a tight lower bound on the messages.

We achieve this by adding an L1 regularization with tiny negative magnitude weight to prefer smaller values of δ^1, δ^2. This technique is referred to as a Pareto optimal cut or a Magnanti-Wong cut [11] in the operations research literature. We give detailed derivations as for why such regularization gives better overall lower bounds in the supplement.

5.3   Nested Benders Decomposition for Exact Inference

Algorithm 2. Nested Benders Decomposition

1: $G = (\mathcal{R}, E)$, G is a tree-structured graph
2: $\dot{Z}^e \leftarrow$ single row with $\omega_0 = -\infty, \omega_{\hat{d}} = 0, \forall d \in \mathcal{D}^{\hat{r}}, \forall e = (\hat{r}, r) \in E$
3: $s_r^* \leftarrow \emptyset, \Delta^r \leftarrow 0, \forall r \in \mathcal{R}$
4: **repeat**
5:     **for** $r \in \mathcal{R}$ proceeding from leaves to root **do**
6:         **for** $z \in \dot{Z}^e, e = (\hat{r}, r), r \in \{\hat{r} \rightarrow\}$ **do**
7:             Update δ^0 via Eq. (15)
8:             Update ω_0^z via Eq. (13)
9:         **end for**
10:    **end for**
11:    $s_r^* \leftarrow \arg\min_{s \in \mathcal{S}^r} \nu_s^{r-}$, where r is root
12:    **for** $r \in \mathcal{R}$ from children of root to leaves **do**
13:        $s_r^* \leftarrow \arg\min_{s \in \mathcal{S}^r} \sum_{\substack{\hat{d} \in \mathcal{D}^{\hat{r}} \\ d \in \mathcal{D}^r}} S_{\hat{d}\hat{s}}^{\hat{r}} S_{ds}^r \phi_{\hat{d}d} + \nu_s^{r-}$, where $\hat{s} = s_{\hat{r}}^*$
14:        $\Delta^r \leftarrow \sum_{\substack{\hat{d} \in \mathcal{D}^{\hat{r}} \\ d \in \mathcal{D}^r}} S_{\hat{d}\hat{s}}^{\hat{r}} S_{ds}^r \phi_{\hat{d}d} + \nu_s^{r-} - \max_{z \in \dot{Z}^e} \omega_s^z + \sum_{\hat{d} \in \mathcal{D}^{\hat{r}}} \omega_{\hat{d}}^z S_{\hat{d}\hat{s}}^{\hat{r}}$, where $s = s_r^*, \hat{s} = s_{\hat{r}}^*, e = (\hat{r}, r), r \in \{\hat{r} \rightarrow\}$
15:    **end for**
16:    $r^* \leftarrow \arg\max_{r \in \mathcal{R}} \Delta^r$
17:    $\dot{Z}^e \leftarrow \dot{Z}^e \cup z^*$ where z^* is the new Benders row for $e = (\hat{r}, r^*), r^* \in \{\hat{r} \rightarrow\}$
18: **until** $|\Delta^r| < \epsilon, \forall r \in \mathcal{R}$
19: RETURN pose p corresponding $\{s_r^*, \forall r \in \mathcal{R}\}$

Given the basic Benders Decomposition technique described in previous sections, we now introduce the Nested Benders Decomposition algorithm which is described as Algorithm 2. The algorithm can be summarized in four steps:

Update Old Benders Rows (Line 5–10): The NBD algorithm repeatedly updates the lower bounds on the messages between nodes, which makes $\dot{Z}^e$ become less tight when messages from child nodes change. Instead of constructing $\dot{Z}^e$ from scratch every iteration, we re-use δ terms produced by previous iterations, fixing $\delta^1, \delta^2, \delta^3$ and only update δ^0 to produce valid Benders rows given new child messages in ν_s^{r-}:

$$\delta^0 \leftarrow \min_{s \in \mathcal{S}^r} \nu_s^{r-} + \sum_{\substack{\hat{d} \in \mathcal{D}^{\hat{r}} \\ d \in \mathcal{D}^r}} (\delta_{\hat{d}d}^1 - \delta_{\hat{d}d}^3) S_{ds}^r \tag{15}$$

Compute Optimal State and Gaps for Each Node (Line 11–15): Next we proceed from root to leaves and compute optimal state of each node, given current lower bounds on messages. Given current state estimates of a node r and its parent $\hat{r}$, we measure the gap between the message estimated by itself and the message estimated by its parent, and denote this gap as Δ^r (line 14). Note Δ for root is always 0 since root does not have a parent.

Find the Node that Gives Maximum Gap (Line 16): We find the node r on which the gap Δ^r is largest across all nodes, and denote this node as r^*.

Compute and Add New Benders Row (Line 17): We produce a new Benders row z^* for r^*, by solving Eqs. (12)–(14). This row z^* is then added to the corresponding set $\dot{\mathcal{Z}}^e$ where $e = (\hat{r}, r^*), r^* \in \{\hat{r} \rightarrow\}$.

We terminate when the gap Δ of every node in the graph is under a desired precision ϵ (0 in our implementation), and return the optimal state of every node. In the following we prove that Algorithm 2 terminates with optimal total cost at root part (which we denote here as part 1) as computed by DP.

Lemma 1. *At termination of Algorithm 2, $\nu_{s_1^*}^{1-}$ has cost equal to cost of the pose corresponding to configurations of nodes $\{s_r^*, \forall r \in \mathcal{R}\}$*

Proof. At termination of Algorithm 2 the following is established for each $r \in \mathcal{R}$ with states $s = s_r^*, \hat{s} = s_{\hat{r}}^*$:

$$\Delta^r = 0 = \sum_{\substack{\hat{d} \in \mathcal{D}^{\hat{r}} \\ d \in \mathcal{D}^r}} S_{\hat{d}\hat{s}}^{\hat{r}} S_{ds}^r \phi_{\hat{d}d} + \nu_s^{r-} - \max_{z \in \dot{\mathcal{Z}}^e} \omega_0^z + \sum_{\hat{d} \in \mathcal{D}^{\hat{r}}} \omega_{\hat{d}}^z S_{\hat{d}\hat{s}}^{\hat{r}} \quad (16)$$

By moving the $-\max_{z \in \dot{\mathcal{Z}}^e} \omega_0^z + \sum_{\hat{d} \in \mathcal{D}^{\hat{r}}} \omega_{\hat{d}}^z S_{\hat{d}}^{\hat{r}}$ to the other side we establish the following.

$$\sum_{\substack{\hat{d} \in \mathcal{D}^{\hat{r}} \\ d \in \mathcal{D}^r}} S_{\hat{d}\hat{s}}^{\hat{r}} S_{ds}^r \phi_{\hat{d}d} + \nu_s^{r-} = \max_{z \in \dot{\mathcal{Z}}^e} \omega_0^z + \sum_{\hat{d} \in \mathcal{D}^{\hat{r}}} \omega_{\hat{d}}^z S_{\hat{d}\hat{s}}^{\hat{r}} = \mu_{\hat{s}}^{r-} \quad (17)$$

We now substitute $\mu_s^{\hat{r}-}$ terms in Eq. (10) with Eq. (17)

$$\nu_{\hat{s}}^{\hat{r}-} = \psi_{\hat{s}}^{\hat{r}} + \sum_{\substack{\hat{d} \in \mathcal{D}^{\hat{r}} \\ d \in \mathcal{D}^r}} S_{\hat{d}\hat{s}}^{\hat{r}} S_{ds}^r \phi_{\hat{d}d} + \nu_s^{r-} \quad (18)$$

Note at the leaves $\nu_s^{r-} = \psi_s^r, \forall s \in \mathcal{S}^r$. From ν_s^{1-}, we recursively expand the ν^- terms and establish the following:

$$\nu_{s_1^*}^{1-} = \sum_{r \in \mathcal{R}} \psi_{s_r^*} + \sum_{(\hat{r}, r) \in E} \sum_{\substack{\hat{d} \in \mathcal{D}^{\hat{r}} \\ d \in \mathcal{D}^r}} S_{\hat{d}s_{\hat{r}}^*}^{\hat{r}} S_{ds_r^*}^r \phi_{\hat{d}d} \quad (19)$$

Which is the summation of all unary and pairwise terms chosen by solution $\{s_r^*, \forall r \in \mathcal{R}\}$.

Lemma 2. *At termination of Algorithm 2, $\nu_{s_1^*}^{1-}$ has cost equal to $\min_{s_1 \in \mathcal{R}^1} \nu_{s_1}^1$*

Proof. We prove this by contradiction. Suppose $\nu_{s_1^*}^{1-} \neq \min_{s_1 \in \mathcal{R}^1} \nu_{s_1}^1$, according to Lemma 1 this must mean $\nu_{s_1^*}^{1-} > \min_{s_1 \in \mathcal{R}^1} \nu_{s_1}^1$. If lower bounds on the messages from children of the root are tight, then it means $\nu_{s_1^*}^{1-}$ is not tight, Δ^1 would have been non-zero and Algorithm 2 would have not terminated, thus creating a contradiction. On the other hand, if lower bounds on certain message(s) from children is not tight, then the Δ value for that child node would have been non-zero and the algorithm would have continued running, still creating a contradiction.

Experimentally we observe that the total time consumed by steps in NBD is ordered from greatest to least as $[1, 2, 4, 3]$. Note that the step solving the LP is the second least time consuming step of NBD.

6   Experiments

We evaluate our approach against a naive dynamic programming based formulation on MPII-Multi-person validation set [2], which consists of 418 images. The terms ϕ, θ are trained using the code of [8], with the following modifications:

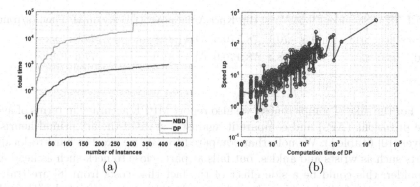

(a)   (b)

Fig. 2. Timing comparison and speed-ups achieved by NBD. (a) Accumulated running time over problem instances for NBD and DP, respectively. (b) Factor of speed-up of NBD relative to DP, as a function of computation time spent for DP pricing. Note that in general the factor of speed-up grows as the problem gets harder for DP.

1. We set $\phi_{d_1 d_2} = \infty$ for each pair of unique neck detections d_1, d_2; as a side effect this improves inference speed also since we need not explore the entire power set of neck detections.
2. We hand set Ω to a single value for the entire data set.
3. We limit the number of states of a given part/node to 50,000. We construct this set as follows: we begin with the state corresponding to zero detections included, then add in the group of states corresponding to one detection included; then add in the group of states corresponding to two detections included etc. If adding a group would have the state space exceed 50,000 states for the variable we don't add the group and terminate.

We compare solutions found by NBD and DP at each step of ICG; for all problem instances and all optimization steps, NBD obtains exactly the same solutions as DP (up to a tie in costs). Comparing total time spent doing NBD vs DP across problem instances we found that NBD is 44× faster than DP, and can be up to 500× faster on extreme problem instances. Comparison of accumulated running time used by NBD and DP over all 418 instances are shown in Fig. 2. We observe that the factor speed up provided by NBD increases as a function of the computation time of DP.

With regards to cost we observe that the integer solution produced over $\hat{\mathcal{P}}$ is identical to the LP value in over 99% of problem instances thus certifying that the optimal integer solution is produced. For those instances on which LP relaxation fails to produce integer results, the gaps between the LP objectives and the integer solutions are all within 1.5% of the LP objectives. This is achieved by solving the ILP in Eq. 2 over $\hat{\mathcal{P}}$.

Table 1. We display average precision of our approach versus [10]. Running times are measured on an Intel i7-6700k quad-core CPU.

Part	Head	Shoulder	Elbow	Wrist	Hip	Knee	Ankle	mAP (UBody)	mAP	Time (s/frame)
Ours	90.6	87.3	79.5	70.1	78.5	70.5	64.8	81.8	77.6	1.95
[10]	93.0	88.2	78.2	68.4	78.9	70.0	64.3	81.9	77.6	0.136

For the sake of completeness, we also report MPPE accuracy in terms of average precisions (APs) and compare it against a state-of-the-art primal heuristic solver [10] (Table 1). We note that compared to [10], we excel in hard-to-localize parts such as wrists and ankles, but fails at parts close to neck such as head and shoulder; this could be a side effect of the fact that costs from [8] are trained on power set of all detections including neck, thus pose associated with multiple neck detections could be a better choice for certain cases. In a more robust model, one could make a reliable head/neck detector, restricting each person to have only one head/neck. Qualitative results are shown in Fig. 3.

7   Conclusion

We have described MPPE as MWSP problem which we address using ICG with corresponding pricing problem solved by NBD. For over 99% of cases we find provably optimal solutions, which is practically important in domains where knowledge of certainty matters, such as interventions in rehabilitation. Our procedure for solving the pricing problem vastly outperforms a baseline dynamic programming approach. We expect that NBD will find many applications in machine learning and computer vision, especially for solving dynamic programs with over high tree-width graphs. For example we could formulate sub-graph multi-cut tracking [16] as a MWSP problem solved with ICG with pricing solved

Fig. 3. Example output of our system.

via NBD. Moreover, for general graphs that main contain cycles, our NBD is directly applicable with dual decomposition algorithms [9,18], which decompose the graph into a set of trees that are solvable by dynamic programs.

References

1. Andres, B., Kappes, J.H., Beier, T., Kothe, U., Hamprecht, F.A.: Probabilistic image segmentation with closedness constraints. In: Proceedings of ICCV (2011)
2. Andriluka, M., Pishchulin, L., Gehler, P., Schiele, B.: 2D human pose estimation: new benchmark and state of the art analysis. In: Proceedings of CVPR (2014)
3. Bansal, N., Blum, A., Chawla, S.: Correlation clustering. J. Mach. Learn, 238–247 (2002)
4. Belanger, D., Passos, A., Riedel, S., McCallum, A.: Map inference in chains using column generation. In: Proceedings of NIPS (2012)
5. Birge, J.R.: Decomposition and partitioning methods for multistage stochastic linear programs. Oper. Res. **33**(5), 989–1007 (1985)
6. Felzenszwalb, P.F., Girshick, R.B., McAllester, D., Ramanan, D.: Object detection with discriminatively trained part-based models. IEEE Trans. Pattern Anal. Mach. Intell. **32**(9), 1627–1645 (2010)
7. Felzenszwalb, P.F., Huttenlocher, D.P.: Distance transforms of sampled functions. Technical report, Cornell Computing and Information Science (2004)
8. Insafutdinov, E., Pishchulin, L., Andres, B., Andriluka, M., Schiele, B.: Deeper-Cut: a deeper, stronger, and faster multi-person pose estimation model. CoRR abs/1605.03170 (2016), http://arxiv.org/abs/1605.03170
9. Komodakis, N., Paragios, N., Tziritas, G.: MRF optimization via dual decomposition: message-passing revisited. In: Proceedings of ICCV (2007)
10. Levinkov, E., et al.: Joint graph decomposition and node labeling: problem, algorithms, applications. In: Proceedings of CVPR (2017)

11. Magnanti, T.L., Wong, R.T.: Accelerating benders decomposition: algorithmic enhancement and model selection criteria. Oper. Res. **29**(3), 464–484 (1981)
12. McAuley, J.J., Caetano, T.S.: Exploiting data-independence for fast belief-propagation. In: Proceedings of ICML (2010)
13. Murphy, J.: Benders, nested benders and stochastic programming: an intuitive introduction. arXiv preprint arXiv:1312.3158 (2013)
14. Pirsiavash, H., Ramanan, D., Fowlkes, C.C.: Globally-optimal greedy algorithms for tracking a variable number of objects. In: Proceedings of CVPR (2011)
15. Pishchulin, L., et al.: DeepCut: joint subset partition and labeling for multi person pose estimation. In: Proceedings of CVPR (2016)
16. Tang, S., Andres, B., Andriluka, M., Schiele, B.: Subgraph decomposition for multi-target tracking. In: Proceedings of CVPR (2015)
17. Yang, Y., Ramanan, D.: Articulated pose estimation with flexible mixtures-of-parts. In: Proceedings of CVPR (2011)
18. Yarkony, J., Fowlkes, C., Ihler, A.: Covering trees and lower-bounds on the quadratic assignment. In: Proceedings of CVPR (2010)
19. Yarkony, J., Ihler, A., Fowlkes, C.C.: Fast planar correlation clustering for image segmentation. In: Fitzgibbon, A., Lazebnik, S., Perona, P., Sato, Y., Schmid, C. (eds.) ECCV 2012. LNCS, vol. 7577, pp. 568–581. Springer, Heidelberg (2012). https://doi.org/10.1007/978-3-642-33783-3_41

Human Motion Analysis with Deep Metric Learning

Huseyin Coskun[1]([⊠]), David Joseph Tan[1,2], Sailesh Conjeti[1], Nassir Navab[1,2], and Federico Tombari[1,2]

[1] Technische Universität München, Munich, Germany
huseyin.coskun@tum.de
[2] Pointu3D GmbH, Munich, Germany

Abstract. Effectively measuring the similarity between two human motions is necessary for several computer vision tasks such as gait analysis, person identification and action retrieval. Nevertheless, we believe that traditional approaches such as L2 distance or Dynamic Time Warping based on hand-crafted local pose metrics fail to appropriately capture the semantic relationship across motions and, as such, are not suitable for being employed as metrics within these tasks. This work addresses this limitation by means of a triplet-based deep metric learning specifically tailored to deal with human motion data, in particular with the problem of varying input size and computationally expensive hard negative mining due to motion pair alignment. Specifically, we propose (1) a novel metric learning objective based on a triplet architecture and Maximum Mean Discrepancy; as well as, (2) a novel deep architecture based on attentive recurrent neural networks. One benefit of our objective function is that it enforces a better separation within the learned embedding space of the different motion categories by means of the associated distribution moments. At the same time, our attentive recurrent neural network allows processing varying input sizes to a fixed size of embedding while learning to focus on those motion parts that are semantically distinctive. Our experiments on two different datasets demonstrate significant improvements over conventional human motion metrics.

1 Introduction

In image-based human pose estimation, the similarity between two predicted poses can be precisely assessed through conventional approaches that either evaluate the distance between corresponding joint locations [8,28,43] or the average difference of corresponding joint angles [24,37]. Nevertheless, when human poses have to be compared across a temporal set of frames, the assessment of the similarity between two sequences of poses or motion becomes a non-trivial problem. Indeed, human motion typically evolves in a different manner on different sequences, which means that specific pose patterns tend to appear at different

---

H. Coskun and D.J. Tan—Equal contribution.

© Springer Nature Switzerland AG 2018
V. Ferrari et al. (Eds.): ECCV 2018, LNCS 11218, pp. 693–710, 2018.
https://doi.org/10.1007/978-3-030-01264-9_41

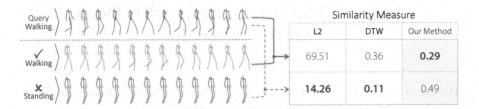

	Similarity Measure		
	L2	DTW	Our Method
✓ Walking	69.51	0.36	**0.29**
✗ Standing	**14.26**	**0.11**	0.49

Fig. 1. When asked to measure the similarity to a query sequence ("Walking", top), both the L2 and the DTW measures judge the unrelated sequence ("Standing", bottom) as notably more similar compared to a semantically correlated one ("Walking", middle). Conversely, our learned metric is able to capture the contextual information and measure the similarity correctly with respect to the given labels.

time instants on sequences representing the same human motion: see, *e.g.*, the first two sequences in Fig. 1, which depict two actions belonging to the same class. Moreover, these sequences result also in varying length (*i.e.*, a different number of frames), this making the definition of a general similarity measure more complicated. Nevertheless, albeit challenging, estimating the similarity between human poses across a sequence is a required step in human motion analysis tasks such as action retrieval and recognition, gait analysis and motion-based person identification.

Conventional approaches deployed to compare human motion sequences are based on estimating the L2 displacement error [23] or Dynamic Time Warping (DTW) [42]. Specifically, the former computes the squared distance between corresponding joints in the two sequences at a specific time t. As shown by Martinez *et al.* [23], such measure tends to disregard the specific motion characteristics, since a constant pose repeated over a sequence might turn out to be a better match to a reference sequence than a visually similar motion with a different temporal evolution. On the other hand, DTW tries to alleviate this problem by warping the two sequences via compressions or expansions so to maximize the matching between local poses. Nevertheless, DTW can easily fail in appropriately estimating the similarity when the motion dynamic in terms of peaks and plateaus exhibits small temporal variations, as shown in [18]. As an example, Fig. 1 illustrates a typical failure case of DTW when measuring the similarity among three human motions. Although the first two motions are visually similar to each other while the third one is unrelated to them, DTW estimates a smaller distance between the first and the third sequence. In general, neither the DTW nor the L2 metrics can comprehensively capture the semantic relationship between two sequences since they disregard the contextual information (in the temporal sense), this limiting their application in the aforementioned scenarios.

The goal of this work is to introduce a novel metric for estimating the similarity between two human motion sequences. Our approach relies on deep metric learning that uses a neural network to map high-dimensional data to a low-dimensional embedding [31,33,35,45]. In particular, our first contribution is to design an approach so to map semantically similar motions over nearby locations in the learned embedding space. This allows the network to express a similarity measure that strongly relies on the motion's semantic and contextual information. To this end, we employ a novel objective function based on the Maximum Mean Discrepancy (MMD) [14], which enforces motions to be embedded based on their distribution moments. The main advantage with respect to standard triplet loss learning is represented by the fact that our approach, being based on distributions and not samples, does not require hard negative mining to converge, which is computationally expensive since finding hard negatives in a human motion datasets requires the alignment of sequence pairs, which has an $O(n^2)$ complexity (n being the sequence length). As our second main contribution, we design a novel deep learning architecture based on attentive recurrent neural networks (RNNs) which exploits attention mechanisms to map an arbitrary input size to a fixed sized embedding while selectively focusing on the semantically descriptive parts of the motion.

One advantage of our approach is that, unlike DTW, we do not need any explicit synchronization or alignment of the motion patterns appearing on the two sequences, since motion patterns are implicitly and semantically matched via deep metric learning. In addition, our approach can naturally deal with varied size input thanks to the use of the recurrent model, while retaining the distinctive motion patterns by means of the attention mechanism. An example is shown in Fig. 1, comparing our similarity measure to DTW and L2. We validate the usefulness of our approach for the tasks of action retrieval and motion-based person identification on two publicly available benchmark datasets. The proposed experiments demonstrate significant improvements over conventional human motion similarity metrics.

2 Related Work

In recent literature, image-based deep metric learning has been extensively studied. However, just a few works focused on metric learning for time-series data, in particular human motion. Here, we first review metric learning approaches for human motion, then follow up with recent improvements in deep metric learning.

Metric Learning for Time Series and Human Motion. We first review metric learning approaches for time series, then focus only on works related on human motion analysis. Early works on metric learning for time series approaches measure the similarity in a two steps process [4,9,30]. First, the model determines the best alignment between two time series, then it computes the distance based on the aligned series. Usually, the model finds the best alignment by means of the DTW measure, first by considering all possible alignments, then ranking them based on hand-crafted local metric. These approaches have two main drawbacks: first, the model yields an $O(n^2)$ complexity; secondly, and most importantly, the local metric can hardly capture relationship in high dimensional data. In order to overcome these drawbacks, Mei *et al.* [25] propose to use LogDet divergence to learn a local metric that can capture the relationship in high dimensional data. Che *et al.* [5] overcome the hand crafted local metric problem by using a feed-forward network to learn local similarities. Although the proposed approaches [5,25] learn to measure the similarity between two given time series at time t, the relationship between two time steps is discarded. Moreover, finding the best alignment requires to search for all possible alignments. To address these problems, recent work focused on determining a low dimensional embedding to measure the distance between time series. To this goal, Pei et al. [29] and Zheng et al. [46] used a Siamese network which learns from pairs of inputs. While Pei et al. [29] trained their network by minimizing the binary cross entropy in order to predict whether the two given time series belong to the same cluster or not, Zheng et al. [46] propose to minimize a loss function based on the Neighbourhood Component Analysis (NCA) [32]. The main drawback of these approaches is that the siamese architecture learns the embedding by considering only the relative distances between the provided input pairs.

As for metric learning for human motion analysis, they mostly focus on directly measuring the similarity between corresponding poses along the two sequences. Lopez et al. [22] proposed a model based on [10] to learn a distance metric for two given human poses, while aligning the motions via Hidden Markov Models (HMM) [11]. Chen et al. [6] proposed a semi-supervised learning approach built on a hand-crafted geometric pose feature and aligned via DTW. By considering both the pose similarity and the pose alignment in learning, Yin et al. [44] proposed to learn pose embeddings with an auto-encoder trained with an alignment constraint. Notably, this approach requires an initial alignment based on DTW. The main drawback of these approaches is that their accuracy relies heavily on the accurate motion alignment provided by HMM or DTW, which is computationally expensive to obtain and prone to fail in many cases. Moreover, since the learning process considers only single poses, they lack at capturing the semantics of the entire motion.

Recent Improvements in Deep Metric Learning. Metric learning with deep networks started with Siamese architectures that minimize the contrastive loss [7,15]. Schroff et al. [33] suggest using a triplet loss to learn the embeddings on facial recognition and verification, showing that it performs better than contrastive loss to learn features. Since they conduct hard-negative mining, when the training set and the number of different categories increase, searching for hard-negatives become computationally inefficient. Since then, research mostly focus on carefully constructing batches and using all samples in the batch. Song et al. [36] proposed the lifted loss for training, so to use all samples in a batch. In [35], they further developed the idea and propose an n-pair loss that uses all negative samples in a batch. Other triplet-based approaches are [26,40]. In [31], the authors show that minimizing the loss function computed on individual pairs or triplets does not necessarily enforce the network to learn features that represent contextual relations between clusters. Magnet Loss [31] address some of these issues by learning features that compare the distributions rather than the samples. Each cluster distribution is represented by the cluster centroid obtained via k-means algorithm. A shortcoming of this approach is that computing cluster centers requires to interrupt training, this slowing down the process.

Proxy-NCA [27] tackle this issue by designing a network architecture that learns the cluster centroids in an end-to-end fashion, this avoiding interruptions during training. Both the Magnet Loss and the Proxy-NCA use the NCA [32] loss to compare the samples. Importantly, they both represent distributions with cluster centroids which do not convey sufficient contextual information of the actual categories, and require to set a pre-defined number of clusters. In contrast, we propose to use a loss function based on MMD [14], which relies on distribution moments that do not need to explicitly determine or learn cluster centroids.

3   Metric Learning on Human Motion

The objective is to learn an embedding for human motion sequences, such that the similarity metric between two human motion sequences $X := \{x_1, x_2, ..., x_n\}$ and $Y := \{y_1, y_2, ..., y_m\}$ (where x_t and y_t represent the poses at time t) can be expressed directly as the squared Euclidean distance in the embedding space. Mathematically, this can be written as

$$d(f(X), f(Y)) = \|f(X) - f(Y)\|^2 \tag{1}$$

where $f(\cdot)$ is the learned embedding function that maps a varied-length motion sequence to a point in a Euclidean space, and $d(\cdot, \cdot)$ is the squared Euclidean distance. The challenge of metric learning is to find a motion embedding function f such that the distance $d(f(X), f(Y))$ should be inversely proportional to the similarity of the two sequences X and Y. In this paper, we learn f by means of a deep learning model trained with a loss function (defined in Sect. 4) which is derived from the integration of MMD with a triplet learning paradigm. In addition, its architecture (described in Sect. 5) is based on an attentive recurrent neural network.

4   Loss Function

Following the standard deep metric learning approach, we model the embedding function f by minimizing the distance $d(f(X), f(Y))$ when X and Y belong to the same category, while maximizing it otherwise. A conventional way of learning f would be to train a network with the contrastive loss [7,15].

$$\mathcal{L}_{\text{contrastive}} = (r)\frac{1}{2}d + (1 - r)\frac{1}{2}[\max(0, \alpha_{\text{margin}} - d)]^2 \tag{2}$$

where $r \in \{1, 0\}$ indicates whether X and Y are from the same category or not, and α_{margin} defines the margin between different category samples. During training, the contrastive loss penalizes those cases where different category samples are closer than α_{margin} and when the same category samples have a distance greater than zero. This equation shows that the contrastive loss only takes into account pairwise relationships between samples, thus only partially exploiting relative relationships among categories. Conversely, triplet learning better exploit such relationships by taking into account three samples at the same time, where the first two are from the same category while the third is from a different one. Notably, it has been shown that exploiting relative relationships among categories play a fundamental role in terms of the quality of the learned embedding [33,45]. The triplet loss enforces embedding samples from the same category with a given margin distance with respect to samples from a different category. If we denote the three human motion samples as X, X^+ and X^-, the commonly used ranking loss [34] takes the form of

$$\mathcal{L}_{\text{triplet}} = \max(0, \ \|f(X) - f(X^+)\|^2 - \|f(X) - f(X^-)\|^2 + \alpha_{\text{margin}}) \quad (3)$$

where X and X^+ represent the motion samples from the same category and X^- represents the sample from a different category. In literature X, X^+, and X^- are often referred to as anchor, positive, and negative samples, respectively [31,33,35,45].

However, one of the main issue with the triplet loss is the parameterization of α_{margin}. We can overcome this problem by using the Neighbourhood Components Analysis (NCA) [32]. Thus, we can write the loss function using NCA as

$$\mathcal{L}_{\text{NCA}} = \frac{\exp(-\|f(X) - f(X^+)\|^2)}{\sum_{X^- \in C} \exp(-\|f(X) - f(X^-)\|^2)} \quad (4)$$

where C represents all categories except for that of the positive sample.

In the ideal scenario, when iterating over triplets of samples, we expect that the samples from the same category will be grouped in the same cluster in the embedding space. However, it has been shown that most of the formed triplets are not informative and visiting all possible triplet combinations is infeasible. Therefore, the model will be trained with only a few informative triplets [31,33,35]. An intuitive solution can be formulated by selecting those negative samples that are hard to distinguish (hard negative mining), although searching for a hard negative sample in a motion sequence dataset is computationally expensive. Another issue linked with the use of triplet loss is that, during a single update, the positive and negative samples are evaluated only in terms of their relative position in the embedding: thus, samples can end up close to other categories [35]. We address the aforementioned issue by pushing/pulling the cluster distributions instead of pushing/pulling individual samples by means of a novel loss function, dubbed MMD-NCA and described next, that is based on the distribution differences of the categories.

4.1 MMD-NCA

Assuming that given two different distributions p and q, the general formulation of MMD measures the distance between p and q while taking the differences of the mean embeddings in Hilbert spaces, written as

$$\text{MMD}[k, p, q]^2 = \|\mu_q - \mu_p\|^2 = E_{x,x'}[k(x, x')] - 2E_{x,y}[k(x, y)] + E_{y,y'}[k(y, y')] \quad (5)$$

where x and x' are drawn IID from p while y and y' are drawn IID from q, and k represents the kernel function

$$k(x, x') = \sum_{q=1}^{K} k_{\sigma_q}(x, x') \quad (6)$$

where k_{σ_q} is a Gaussian kernel with bandwidth parameter σ_q, while K (number of kernels) is a hyperparameter. If we replace the expected values from the given samples, we obtain

$$\text{MMD}[k, X, Y]^2 = \frac{1}{m^2} \sum_{i=1}^{m} \sum_{j=1}^{m} k(x_i, x'_j) - \frac{2}{mn} \sum_{i=1}^{m} \sum_{j=1}^{n} k(x_i, y_j) + \frac{1}{n^2} \sum_{i=1}^{n} \sum_{j=1}^{n} k(y_i, y'_j)$$
$$(7)$$

where $X := \{x_1, x_2, \ldots x_m\}$ is the sample set from p and $Y := \{y_1, y_2, \ldots y_n\}$ is the sample set from q. Hence, (7) allows us to measure the distance between the distribution of two sets.

We formulate our loss function in order to force the network to decrease the distance between the distribution of the anchor samples and that of the positive samples, while increasing the distance to the distribution of the negative samples.

Therefore, we can rewrite (4) for a given number N of anchor-positive sample pairs as $\{(X_1, X_1^+), (X_2, X_2^+), \ldots, (X_N, X_N^+)\}$ and $N \times M$ negative samples from the M different categories $C = \{c_1, c_2, \ldots, c_M\}$ as $\{X_{c_1,1}^-, X_{c_1,2}^-, \ldots, X_{c_1,N}^-, \ldots, X_{c_M,N}^-\}$; then,

$$\mathcal{L}_{\text{MMD-NCA}} = \frac{\exp(-\text{MMD}[k, f(X), f(X^+)])}{\sum_{j=1}^{M} \exp(-\text{MMD}[k, f(X), f(X_{c_j}^-)])} \quad (8)$$

where X and X^+ represent motion samples from the same category, while X_{c_j} represents samples from category $c_j \in C$. Our single update contains M different negative classes randomly sampled from the training data.

Since the proposed MMD-NCA loss minimizes the overlap between different category distributions in the embedding while keeping the samples from the same distribution as close as possible, we believe it is more effective for our task than the triplet loss. We demonstrate this quantitatively and qualitatively in Sect. 7.

5 Network Architecture

Our architecture is illustrated in Fig. 2. This model has two main parts: the bidirectional long short-term memory (BiLSTM) [16] and the self-attention mechanism. The reason for using the long short-term memory (LSTM) [16] is to overcome the vanishing gradient problem of the recurrent neural networks. In [12,13], they show that LSTM can capture long term dependencies. In the next sections, we briefly describe the layer normalization mechanism and attention mechanism that used in our architecture.

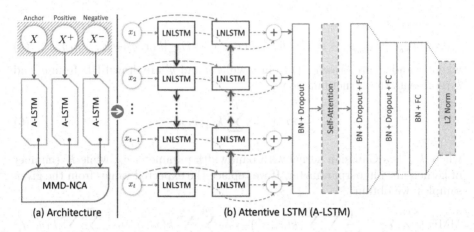

(a) Architecture | (b) Attentive LSTM (A-LSTM)

Fig. 2. (a) The proposed architecture for sequence distance learning. (b) The proposed attention-based model that uses layer normalization.

5.1 Layer Normalization

In [7,26,27,36], they have shown that batch normalization plays a fundamental role on the triplet model's accuracy. However, its straightforward application to LSTM architectures can decrease the accuracy of model [19]. Due to this, we used the layer normalized LSTM [3].

Suppose that n time steps of motion $X = (x_1, x_2, \ldots, x_n)$ are given, then the layer normalized LSTM is described by

$$\mathbf{f}_t = \sigma(\mathbf{W}_{fh}\mathbf{h}_{t-1} + \mathbf{W}_{fx}x_t + \mathbf{b}_f) \tag{9}$$

$$\mathbf{i}_t = \sigma(\mathbf{W}_{ih}\mathbf{h}_{t-1} + \mathbf{W}_{ix}x_t + \mathbf{b}_i) \tag{10}$$

$$\mathbf{o}_t = \sigma(\mathbf{W}_{oh}\mathbf{h}_{t-1} + \mathbf{W}_{ox}x_t + \mathbf{b}_o) \tag{11}$$

$$\tilde{\mathbf{c}}_t = \tanh(\mathbf{W}_{ch}\mathbf{h}_{t-1} + \mathbf{W}_{cx}x_t + \mathbf{b}_c) \tag{12}$$

$$\mathbf{c}_t = \mathbf{f}_t \odot \mathbf{c}_{t-1} + \mathbf{i}_t \odot \tilde{\mathbf{c}}_t \tag{13}$$

$$\mathbf{m}_t = \frac{1}{H}\sum_j^H \mathbf{c}_t^j, \mathbf{v}_t = \sqrt{\frac{1}{H}\sum_j^H (\mathbf{c}_t^j - m_t)^2} \tag{14}$$

$$\mathbf{h}_t = \mathbf{o}_t \odot \tanh(\frac{\gamma_t}{v_t} \odot (\mathbf{c}_t - m_t) + \beta) \tag{15}$$

where c_{t-1} and h_{t-1} denotes the cell memory and cell state which comes from the previous time steps, x_t denotes the input human pose at time t. $\sigma(\cdot)$ and $\odot$ represent the element-wise sigmoid function and multiplication respectively, and H denotes the number of hidden units in LSTM. The parameters $W_{.,.}$, γ and β are learned while γ and β has the same dimension of $\mathbf{h}_t$. Contrary to the standard LSTM, the hidden state $\mathbf{h}_t$ is computed by normalizing the cell-memory $\mathbf{c}_t$.

5.2 Self-attention Mechanism

Intuitively, in a sequence of human motion, some poses are more informative than others. Therefore, we use the recently proposed self-attention mechanism [21] to assign a score for each pose in a motion sequence. Specifically, assuming that the sequence of states $S = \{h_1, h_2, \ldots, h_n\}$ computed from a motion sequence X that consists of n time steps with (9) to (15), we can effectively compute the scores for each of them by

$$r = W_{s2} \tanh(W_{s1}S^\top) \quad \text{and} \quad a_i = -\log\left(\frac{\exp(r_i)}{\sum_j \exp(r_j)}\right) \tag{16}$$

where r_i is i-th element of the r while W_{s1} and W_{s2} are the weight matrices in $R^{k \times l}$ and $R^{l \times 1}$, respectively. a_i is the assigned score i-th pose in the sequence of motion. Thus, the final embedding E can be computed by multiplying the scores $A = [a_1, a_2, \ldots, a_n]$ and S, written as $E = AS$. Note that the final embedding size only depends on the number of hidden states in the LSTM and W_{s2}. This allows us to encode the varying size LSTM outputs to a fixed sized output. More information about the self-attention mechanism can be found in [21].

6 Implementation Details

We use the TensorFlow framework [2] for all deep metric models that are described in this paper. Our model has three branches as shown in Fig. 2. Each branch consists of an attention based bidirectional layer normalized LSTM (LNLSTM) (see Sect. 5.1). Bidirectional LNLSTM follows a forward and backward passing of the given sequence of motion. We then denote $s_t = [s_{t,f}, s_{t,b}]$ such that $s_{t,f} = \overrightarrow{\text{LNLSTM}}(w_t, x_t)$ for $t \in [0, N]$ and $s_{t,b} = \overleftarrow{\text{LNLSTM}}(w_t, x_t)$ for $t \in [N, 0]$.

Given n time steps of a motion sequence X, we compute $S = (s_1, s_2, \ldots, s_n)$ where s_t is the concatenated output of the backward and forward pass of the LNLSTM which has 128 hidden units. The bidirectional LSTM is followed by the dropout and the standard batch normalization. The output of the batch normalization layer is forwarded to the attention layer (see Sect. 5.2), which produces the fixed size of the output. The attention layer is followed by the structure: {FC(320,), dropout, BN, FC(320), BN, FC(128), BN, l_2 Norm}, where FC(m) means fully connected layer with m as the hidden units and BN means batch normalization. All the FC layers are followed by the rectified linear units except for the last FC layer. The self-attention mechanism is derived from the implementation of [21]. Here, the W_{s1} and W_{s2} parameters from (16) have the dimensionality of $R^{200 \times 10}$ and $R^{10 \times 1}$, respectively. We use the dropout rate of 0.5. The same dropout mask is used in all branches of the network in Fig. 2. In our model, all squared weight matrices are initialized with random orthogonal matrices while the others are initialized with uniform distribution with zero mean and 0.001 standard deviation. The parameters γ and β in (15) are initialized with zeros and ones, respectively.

Kernel Designs. The MMD-NCA loss function is implicitly associated with a family of characteristic kernels. Similar to the prior MMD papers [20,38], we consider a mixture of K radial basis functions in (6). We fixed $K = 5$ and σ_q to be $1, 2, 4, 8, 16$.

Training. Our single batch consists of randomly selected categories where each category has 25 samples. We selected 5 category as negative. Although the MMD [14] metric requires a high number of samples to understand the distribution moments, we found that 25 is sufficient for our tasks. Training each batch takes about 10 s on a Titan X GPU. All the networks are trained with 5000 updates and they all converged before the end of training. During training, analogous to the curriculum learning, we start training on the samples without noise and then added Gaussian noise with zero mean and increasing standard deviation. We use stochastic gradient descent with the moment as an optimizer for all models. The momentum value is set to 0.9, and the learning rate started from 0.0001 with an exponential decay of 0.96 every 50 updates. We clip the whole gradients by their global norm to the range of -25 and 25.

7   Experimental Results

We compare our MMD-NCA loss against the methods from DTW [42], MDDTW [25], CTW [47] and GDTW [48], as well as four state-of-the-art deep metric learning approaches: DCTW [41], triplet [33], triplet+GOR [45], and the N-Pairs deep metric loss [14]. Primarily, these methods are evaluated through action recognition task in Sect. 7.1. In order to look closely into the performance of this evaluation, we analyze the actions retrieved by the proposed method in the same section and the contribution of the self-attention mechanism from Sect. 5.2 into the algorithm in Sect. 7.3. Since one of the datasets [1] labeled the actions with their corresponding subjects, we also investigate the possibility of performing a person identification task wherein, instead of measuring the similarity of the pose, we intend to measure the similarity the actors themselves based on their movement. To have a fair comparison, we only used our attention based LSTM architecture for all methods and only changed the loss function except the DCTW [41]. Prosed loss function in DCTW [41] requires the two sequences, therefore we remove the attention layer and use only our LSTM model. Notably, all deep metric learning methods are evaluated and trained with the same data splits.

Performance Evaluation. We follow the same evaluation protocol as defined in [36,45]. All models are evaluated for the clustering quality and false positive rate (FPR) on the same test set which consists of unseen motion categories. We compute the FPR for 90%, 80% and 70% true positive rates. In addition, we also use the Normalized Mutual Information measure (NMI) and F_1score to measure the cluster quality where the NMI is the ratio between mutual information and sum of class and cluster labels entropies while the F_1score is the harmonic mean of precision and recall.

Datasets and Pre-processing. We tested the models on two different datasets: (1) the CMU Graphics Lab motion capture database (CMU mocap) [1]; and, (2) the Human3.6M dataset [17]. The former [1] contains 144 different subjects where each subject performs natural motions such as *walking, dancing* and *jumping.* Their data is recorded with the mocap system and the poses are represented with 38 joints in 3D space. Six joints are excluded because they have no movement. We align the poses with respect to the torso and, to avoid the gimbal lock effect, the poses are expressed in the exponential map [39]. Although the original data runs at 120 Hz with different lengths of motion sequences, we down-sampled the data to 30 Hz during training and testing.

Furthermore, the Human3.6M dataset [17] consists of 15 different actions and each action was performed by seven different professional actors. The actions are mostly selected from daily activities such as *walking, smoking, engaging in a discussion, taking pictures* and *talking on the phone.* We process the dataset in the same way as the same as CMU mocap.

7.1 Action Recognition

In this experiment, we tested our model on both the CMU mocap [1] and the Human3.6M [17] datasets for unseen motion categories. We categorize the CMU mocap dataset into 38 different motion categories where the motion sequences which contain more than one category are excluded. Among them, we selected 19 categories for training and 19 categories for testing. For the Human3.6M [17],

Table 1. False positive rate of action recognition for CMU mocap and Human3.6M datasets.

	CMU			Human3.6M		
	FPR-90	FPR-80	FPR-70	FPR-90	FPR-80	FPR-70
DTW [42]	47.98	42.92	37.62	49.64	47.96	44.38
MDDTW [25]	44.60	39.07	34.04	49.72	45.87	44.51
CTW [47]	46.02	40.96	39.11	47.63	43.10	42.18
GDTW [48]	45.61	39.95	35.24	46.06	42.72	40.04
DCTW [41]	40.56	38.83	26.95	41.39	39.18	36.71
Triplet [33]	39.72	33.82	28.77	42.78	40.15	36.01
Triplet + GOR [45]	40.32	33.97	27.78	42.03	37.61	33.95
N-Pair [35]	40.11	32.35	26.16	40.46	39.56	36.52
MMD-NCA (*Ours*)	**32.66**	**25.66**	**20.29**	**38.42**	**36.54**	**33.13**
– without Attention	41.22	35.36	30.04	45.03	42.07	41.01
– without LN	37.27	30.21	27.95	44.25	41.69	38.09
– Linear Kernel	39.80	33.92	29.00	46.35	41.68	37.69
– Polynomial Kernel	36.80	30.35	24.98	43.60	40.03	35.62

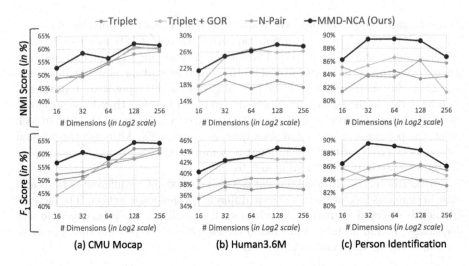

Fig. 3. NMI and F_1 score for the action recognition task using the (a) CMU Mocap and (b) Human3.6M datasets; and, (b) for person identification task.

we used all the given categories, and selected 8 categories for training and 7 categories for testing.

Although our model allows us to train with varying sizes of motion sequence, we train with a fixed size, since varying sizes slow down the training process. We divided the motion sequences into 90 consecutive frames (*i.e.* approximately 3 s) and leave a gap of 30 frames. However, at test time, we divided the motion sequences only if it is longer than 5 s by leaving a 1-s gap; otherwise, we keep the original motion sequence. We found this processing effective since we observe that, in sequence of motions longer than 5 s, the subjects usually repeat their action. We also consider training without clipping but it was not possible with available the GPU resources.

False Positive Rate. The FPR at different percentages on CMU mocap and Human3.6M are reported in Table 1. With a true positive rate of 70%, the learning approaches [33,35,41,45] including our approach achieve up to 17% improvement in FPR relative to DTW [42], MDDTW [25], CTW [47] and GDTW [48]. Moreover, our approach further improves the results up to 6% and 0.8% for CMU mocap and Human3.6m datasets, respectively, against the state-of-the-art deep learning approaches [33,35,41,45].

NMI and F_1 Score. Figure 3(a) plots the NMI and F_1 score with varying size of embedding for the CMU mocap dataset. In both the NMI and F_1 metrics, our approach produces the best clusters at all the embedding sizes. Compared to other methods, the proposed approach is less sensitive to the changes of the embedding size. Moreover, Fig. 3(b) illustrates the NMI and F_1 score on

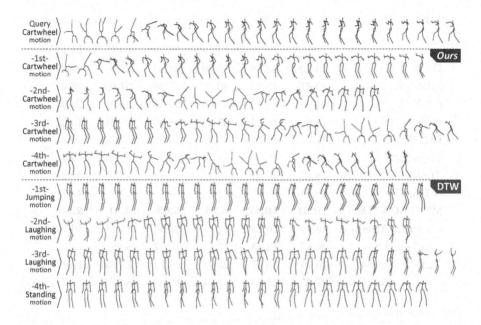

Fig. 4. Comparison of cartwheel motion query on the CMU mocap dataset between our approach and DTW [42]. The motion in the first row is query and the rest are four nearest neighbors for each method, which are sorted by the distance.

Human3.6M dataset where we observe similar performance as the CMU mocap dataset and acquire the best results.

Action Retrieval. In order to investigate further, we query a specific motion from the CMU mocap test set, and compare the closest action sequences that our approach and DTW [42] retrieve based on their respective similarity measure. In Fig. 4, we demonstrate this task as we query the challenging cartwheel motion (see first row). Our approach successfully retrieves the semantically similar motions sequences, despite the high variation on the length of sequences. On the other hand, DTW [42] fails to match the query to the dataset because the distinctive pose appears on a small portion of the sequence. This implies that the large portion, where the actor stands, dominates the similarity measure. Note that we do not have the same problem due to the self-attention mechanism from Sect. 5.2 (see Sect. 7.3 for the evaluation).

7.2 Person Identification

Since the CMU mocap dataset also includes the specific subject associated to each motion, we explore the potential application of person identification. In contrast to the action recognition and action retrieval from Sect. 7.1 where the similarity measure is calculated based on the motion category, this task tries to measure the similarity with respect the actor. In this experiment, we construct

Table 2. False positive rate of person identification for CMU mocap dataset.

	FPR-95	FPR-90	FPR-85	FPR-80	FPR-75	FPR-70
DTW [42]	46.22	43.19	38.70	32.36	27.61	22.85
MDDTW [25]	49.67	45.89	40.36	35.46	31.69	28.44
CTW [47]	45.23	40.14	35.69	29.50	25.91	20.35
GDTW [48]	44.65	40.54	35.03	28.07	24.31	19.32
DCTW [41]	32.45	20.24	18.15	15.91	13.78	10.31
Triplet [33]	22.58	18.13	11.30	9.63	8.36	6.51
Triplet + GOR [45]	28.37	16.69	10.27	8.64	7.28	4.38
N-Pair [35]	22.84	15.31	8.94	5.69	4.82	4.56
MMD-NCA (*Ours*)	**19.31**	**10.42**	**8.26**	**5.62**	**3.91**	**2.55**
− without Attention	36.10	26.15	22.48	20.94	19.21	16.78
− without LN	26.63	18.43	12.81	10.27	8.58	7.36
− Linear Kernel	35.75	30.97	25.93	15.13	11.93	10.42
− Polynomial Kernel	27.25	21.18	17.91	10.93	8.97	5.93

the training and test set in the same way as Sect. 7.1. We included the subjects which have more than three motion sequences, which resulted in 68 subjects. Among them, we selected 39 subjects for training and the rest of the 29 subjects for testing.

Table 2 shows the FPR for the person identification task for varying percentages of true positive rate with embedding size of 64. Here, all deep metric learning approaches including our work significantly improve the accuracy against the DTW, MDDTW, CTW and GDTW. Overall, our method outperforms all the approaches for all FPR with a 20% improvement against DTW [42], MDDTW [25], CTW [47] and GDTW [48], and a 2% improvement compared to the state-of-the-art deep learning approaches [33,35,41,45]. Moreover, when we evaluate the NMI and the F_1 score for the clustering quality in different embedding sizes, Fig. 3(c) demonstrates that our approach obtains the state-of-the-art results with a significant margin.

7.3 Attention Visualization

The objective of the self-attention mechanism from Sect. 5.2 is to focus on the poses which are the most informative about the semantics of the motion sequence. Thus, we expect our attention mechanism to focus on the descriptive poses in the motion, which allows the model to learn more expressive embeddings. Based on the peaks of A which is composed of a_i from (16), we illustrate this behavior in Fig. 5 where the first two rows belong to the basketball sequence while the third belong to the bending sequence. Notably, all the sequences have different lengths.

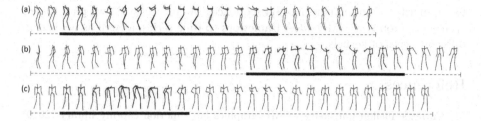

Fig. 5. Attention visualization: the poses in red show where the model mostly focused its attention. Specifically, we mark as red those frames associated with each column-wise global maximum in A, together with the previous and next 2 frames. For visualization purposes, the sequences are subsampled by a factor of 4.

Despite the variations in the length of the motion, the model focuses when the actor throws the ball which is the most informative part of the motion for Fig. 5(a–b); while, for the bending motion in Fig. 5(c), it also focuses on the distinctive regions of the motion sequence. Therefore, this figure illustrate that the self-attention mechanism successfully focuses on the most informative part of the sequence. This implies that the model discards the non-informative parts in order to embed long motion sequences to a low dimensional space without losing the semantic information.

8   Ablation Study

We evaluate our architecture with different configurations to better appreciate each of our contributions separately. All models are trained with MMD-NCA loss and with an embedding of size 128. Tables 1 and 2 show the effect of the layer normalization [3], the self-attention mechanism [21] and the kernel selection in terms of FPR. We use the same architecture for linear, polynomial, and MMD-NCA and only change the kernel function in (6). Notably, the removal of the self-attention mechanism yields the biggest drop in NMI and F_1 on all the datasets. In addition, Both the layer normalization and the self-attention improve the resulting FPR by 7% and 10%, respectively. In terms of kernel selection, the results shows that selecting the kernel which takes into account higher moments yields better results. Comparing the two tasks, the person identification is the one that benefits from our architecture the most.

9   Conclusion

In this paper, we propose a novel loss function and network architecture to measure the similarity of two motion sequences. Experimental results on the CMU mocap [1] and Human3.6M [17] datasets show that our approach obtain state-of-the-art results. We also have shown that metric learning approaches based on deep learning can improve the results up to 20% against metrics commonly used for similarity among human motion sequences. As future work, we plan to generalize the proposed MMD-NCA framework to time-series, as well as investigate different types of kernels.

References

1. Carnegie mellon university - CMU graphics lab - motion capture library (2010). http://mocap.cs.cmu.edu/. Accessed 03 Nov 2018
2. Abadi, M., et al.: TensorFlow: large-scale machine learning on heterogeneous systems (2015). https://www.tensorflow.org/. Software available from tensorflow.org
3. Ba, J.L., Kiros, J.R., Hinton, G.E.: Layer normalization. CoRR abs/1607.06450 (2016). http://arxiv.org/abs/1607.06450
4. Berndt, D.J., Clifford, J.: Using dynamic time warping to find patterns in time series. In: KDD Workshop, Seattle, WA, vol. 10, pp. 359–370 (1994)
5. Che, Z., He, X., Xu, K., Liu, Y.: DECADE: a deep metric learning model for multivariate time series (2017)
6. Chen, C., Zhuang, Y., Nie, F., Yang, Y., Wu, F., Xiao, J.: Learning a 3D human pose distance metric from geometric pose descriptor. IEEE Trans. Vis. Comput. Graph. **17**(11), 1676–1689 (2011)
7. Chopra, S., Hadsell, R., LeCun, Y.: Learning a similarity metric discriminatively, with application to face verification. In: 2005 IEEE Computer Society Conference on Computer Vision and Pattern Recognition, CVPR 2005, vol. 1, pp. 539–546. IEEE (2005)
8. Chu, X., Yang, W., Ouyang, W., Ma, C., Yuille, A.L., Wang, X.: Multi-context attention for human pose estimation. In: The IEEE Conference on Computer Vision and Pattern Recognition (CVPR), July 2017
9. Cuturi, M., Vert, J.P., Birkenes, O., Matsui, T.: A kernel for time series based on global alignments. In: 2007 IEEE International Conference on Acoustics, Speech and Signal Processing, ICASSP 2007, vol. 2, pp. II–413. IEEE (2007)
10. Davis, J.V., Kulis, B., Jain, P., Sra, S., Dhillon, I.S.: Information-theoretic metric learning. In: Proceedings of the 24th International Conference on Machine Learning, pp. 209–216. ACM (2007)
11. Eddy, S.R.: Hidden markov models. Curr. Opin. Struct. Biol. **6**(3), 361–365 (1996)
12. Graves, A., Mohamed, A.R., Hinton, G.: Speech recognition with deep recurrent neural networks. In: 2013 IEEE International Conference on Acoustics, Speech and Signal Processing (ICASSP), pp. 6645–6649. IEEE (2013)
13. Greff, K., Srivastava, R.K., Koutník, J., Steunebrink, B.R., Schmidhuber, J.: LSTM: a search space odyssey. IEEE Trans. Neural Netw. Learn. Syst. **28**(10), 2222–2232 (2017)
14. Gretton, A., Borgwardt, K.M., Rasch, M.J., Schölkopf, B., Smola, A.: A kernel two-sample test. J. Mach. Learn. Res. **13**, 723–773 (2012)
15. Hadsell, R., Chopra, S., LeCun, Y.: Dimensionality reduction by learning an invariant mapping. In: 2006 IEEE Computer Society Conference on Computer Vision and Pattern Recognition, vol. 2, pp. 1735–1742. IEEE (2006)
16. Hochreiter, S., Schmidhuber, J.: Long short-term memory. Neural Comput. **9**(8), 1735–1780 (1997)
17. Ionescu, C., Papava, D., Olaru, V., Sminchisescu, C.: Human3.6M: large scale datasets and predictive methods for 3D human sensing in natural environments. IEEE Trans. Patt. Anal. Mach. Intell. **36**(7), 1325–1339 (2014)

18. Keogh, E.J., Pazzani, M.J.: Derivative dynamic time warping. In: Proceedings of the 2001 SIAM International Conference on Data Mining, pp. 1–11. SIAM (2001)
19. Laurent, C., Pereyra, G., Brakel, P., Zhang, Y., Bengio, Y.: Batch normalized recurrent neural networks. In: 2016 IEEE International Conference on Acoustics, Speech and Signal Processing (ICASSP), pp. 2657–2661. IEEE (2016)
20. Li, Y., Swersky, K., Zemel, R.: Generative moment matching networks. In: Proceedings of the 32nd International Conference on Machine Learning (ICML 2015), pp. 1718–1727 (2015)
21. Lin, Z., et al.: A structured self-attentive sentence embedding. In: Proceedings of International Conference on Learning Representations (ICLR) (2017)
22. López-Méndez, A., Gall, J., Casas, J.R., Van Gool, L.J.: Metric learning from poses for temporal clustering of human motion. In: BMVC, pp. 1–12 (2012)
23. Martinez, J., Black, M.J., Romero, J.: On human motion prediction using recurrent neural networks. In: The IEEE Conference on Computer Vision and Pattern Recognition (CVPR), July 2017
24. Mehta, D., et al.: VNect: real-time 3D human pose estimation with a single RGB camera. ACM Trans. Graph. (TOG) **36**(4), 44 (2017)
25. Mei, J., Liu, M., Wang, Y.F., Gao, H.: Learning a mahalanobis distance-based dynamic time warping measure for multivariate time series classification. IEEE Trans. Cybern. **46**(6), 1363–1374 (2016)
26. Mishchuk, A., Mishkin, D., Radenovic, F., Matas, J.: Working hard to know your neighbor's margins: local descriptor learning loss. In: Proceedings Conference on Neural Information Processing Systems (NIPS), December 2017
27. Movshovitz-Attias, Y., Toshev, A., Leung, T.K., Ioffe, S., Singh, S.: No fuss distance metric learning using proxies. In: The IEEE International Conference on Computer Vision (ICCV), October 2017
28. Newell, A., Yang, K., Deng, J.: Stacked hourglass networks for human pose estimation. In: Leibe, B., Matas, J., Sebe, N., Welling, M. (eds.) ECCV 2016. LNCS, vol. 9912, pp. 483–499. Springer, Cham (2016). https://doi.org/10.1007/978-3-319-46484-8_29
29. Pei, W., Tax, D.M., van der Maaten, L.: Modeling time series similarity with siamese recurrent networks. CoRR abs/1603.04713 (2016)
30. Ratanamahatana, C.A., Keogh, E.: Making time-series classification more accurate using learned constraints. In: SIAM (2004)
31. Rippel, O., Paluri, M., Dollar, P., Bourdev, L.: Metric learning with adaptive density discrimination. In: International Conference on Learning Representations (2016)
32. Roweis, S., Hinton, G., Salakhutdinov, R.: Neighbourhood component analysis. Adv. Neural Inf. Process. Syst. (NIPS) **17**, 513–520 (2004)
33. Schroff, F., Kalenichenko, D., Philbin, J.: FaceNet: a unified embedding for face recognition and clustering. In: Proceedings of the IEEE Conference on Computer Vision and Pattern Recognition, pp. 815–823 (2015)
34. Schultz, M., Joachims, T.: Learning a distance metric from relative comparisons. In: Advances in Neural Information Processing Systems, pp. 41–48 (2004)
35. Sohn, K.: Improved deep metric learning with multi-class n-pair loss objective. In: Advances in Neural Information Processing Systems, pp. 1857–1865 (2016)
36. Song, H.O., Xiang, Y., Jegelka, S., Savarese, S.: Deep metric learning via lifted structured feature embedding. In: 2016 IEEE Conference on Computer Vision and Pattern Recognition (CVPR), pp. 4004–4012. IEEE (2016)
37. Sun, X., Shang, J., Liang, S., Wei, Y.: Compositional human pose regression. In: The IEEE International Conference on Computer Vision (ICCV), vol. 2 (2017)

38. Sutherland, D.J., et al.: Generative models and model criticism via optimized maximum mean discrepancy. In: Proceedings of the 32nd International Conference on Machine Learning (ICML 2017) (2017)
39. Taylor, G.W., Hinton, G.E., Roweis, S.T.: Modeling human motion using binary latent variables. In: Advances in Neural Information Processing Systems, pp. 1345–1352 (2007)
40. Tian, B.F.Y., Wu, F.: L2-Net: deep learning of discriminative patch descriptor in Euclidean space. In: Conference on Computer Vision and Pattern Recognition (CVPR), vol. 2 (2017)
41. Trigeorgis, G., Nicolaou, M.A., Schuller, B.W., Zafeiriou, S.: Deep canonical time warping for simultaneous alignment and representation learning of sequences. IEEE Trans. Patt. Anal. Mach. Intell. **5**, 1128–1138 (2018)
42. Vintsyuk, T.K.: Speech discrimination by dynamic programming. Cybernetics **4**(1), 52–57 (1968)
43. Yang, W., Li, S., Ouyang, W., Li, H., Wang, X.: Learning feature pyramids for human pose estimation. In: The IEEE International Conference on Computer Vision (ICCV), October 2017
44. Yin, X., Chen, Q.: Deep metric learning autoencoder for nonlinear temporal alignment of human motion. In: 2016 IEEE International Conference on Robotics and Automation (ICRA), pp. 2160–2166. IEEE (2016)
45. Zhang, X., Yu, F.X., Kumar, S., Chang, S.F.: Learning spread-out local feature descriptors. In: The IEEE International Conference on Computer Vision (ICCV), October 2017
46. Zheng, Y., Liu, Q., Chen, E., Zhao, J.L., He, L., Lv, G.: Convolutional nonlinear neighbourhood components analysis for time series classification. In: Cao, T., Lim, E.-P., Zhou, Z.-H., Ho, T.-B., Cheung, D., Motoda, H. (eds.) PAKDD 2015. LNCS (LNAI), vol. 9078, pp. 534–546. Springer, Cham (2015). https://doi.org/10.1007/978-3-319-18032-8_42
47. Zhou, F., Torre, F.: Canonical time warping for alignment of human behavior. In: Advances in Neural Information Processing Systems, pp. 2286–2294 (2009)
48. Zhou, F., De la Torre, F.: Generalized canonical time warping. IEEE Trans. Patt. Anal. Mach. Intell. **38**(2), 279–294 (2016)

Exploring Visual Relationship
for Image Captioning

Ting Yao[1]([✉]), Yingwei Pan[1], Yehao Li[2], and Tao Mei[1]

[1] JD AI Research, Beijing, China
tingyao.ustc@gmail.com, panyw.ustc@gmail.com, tmei@live.com
[2] Sun Yat-sen University, Guangzhou, China
yehaoli.sysu@gmail.com

Abstract. It is always well believed that modeling relationships between objects would be helpful for representing and eventually describing an image. Nevertheless, there has not been evidence in support of the idea on image description generation. In this paper, we introduce a new design to explore the connections between objects for image captioning under the umbrella of attention-based encoder-decoder framework. Specifically, we present Graph Convolutional Networks plus Long Short-Term Memory (dubbed as GCN-LSTM) architecture that novelly integrates both semantic and spatial object relationships into image encoder. Technically, we build graphs over the detected objects in an image based on their spatial and semantic connections. The representations of each region proposed on objects are then refined by leveraging graph structure through GCN. With the learnt region-level features, our GCN-LSTM capitalizes on LSTM-based captioning framework with attention mechanism for sentence generation. Extensive experiments are conducted on COCO image captioning dataset, and superior results are reported when comparing to state-of-the-art approaches. More remarkably, GCN-LSTM increases CIDEr-D performance from 120.1% to 128.7% on COCO testing set.

Keywords: Image captioning · Graph convolutional networks
Visual relationship · Long short-term memory

1 Introduction

The recent advances in deep neural networks have convincingly demonstrated high capability in learning vision models particularly for recognition. The achievements make a further step towards the ultimate goal of image understanding, which is to automatically describe image content with a complete and natural sentence or referred to as image captioning problem. The typical solutions [7,34,37,39] of image captioning are inspired by machine translation and equivalent to translating an image to a text. As illustrated in Fig. 1(a) and (b), a Convolutional Neural Network (CNN) or Region-based CNN (R-CNN) is usually

© Springer Nature Switzerland AG 2018
V. Ferrari et al. (Eds.): ECCV 2018, LNCS 11218, pp. 711–727, 2018.
https://doi.org/10.1007/978-3-030-01264-9_42

exploited to encode an image and a decoder of Recurrent Neural Network (RNN) w/ or w/o attention mechanism is utilized to generate the sentence, one word at each time step. Regardless of these different versions of CNN plus RNN image captioning framework, a common issue not fully studied is how visual relationships should be leveraged in view that the mutual correlations or interactions between objects are the natural basis for describing an image.

Visual relationships characterize the interactions or relative positions between objects detected in an image. The detection of visual relationships involves not only localizing and recognizing objects, but also classifying the interaction (predicate) between each pair of objects. In general, the relationship can be represented as ⟨subject-predicate-object⟩, e.g., ⟨man-eating-sandwich⟩ or ⟨dog-inside-car⟩. In the literature, it is well recognized that reasoning such visual relationships is crucial to a richer semantic understanding [19,23] of the visual world. Nevertheless, the fact that the objects could be with a wide range of scales, at arbitrary positions in an image and from different categories results in difficulty in determining the type of relationships. In this paper, we take the advantages of the inherent relationships between objects for interpreting the images holistically and novelly explore the use of visual connections to enhance image encoder for image captioning. Our basic design is to model the relationships on both semantic and spatial levels, and integrate the connections into image encoder to produce relation-aware region-level representations. As a result, we endow image representations with more power when feeding into sentence decoder.

By consolidating the idea of modeling visual relationship for image captioning, we present a novel Graph Convolutional Networks plus Long Short-Term Memory (GCN-LSTM) architecture, as conceptually shown in Fig. 1(c). Specifically, Faster R-CNN is firstly implemented to propose a set of salient image regions. We build semantic graph with directed edges on the detected regions, where the vertex represents each region and the edge denotes the relationship (predicate) between each pair of regions which is predicted by semantic relationship detector learnt on Visual Genome [16]. Similarly, spatial graph is also constructed on the regions and the edge between regions models relative geometrical relationship. Graph Convolutional Networks are then exploited to enrich region representations with visual relationship in the structured semantic and spatial graph respectively. After that, the learnt relation-aware region represen-

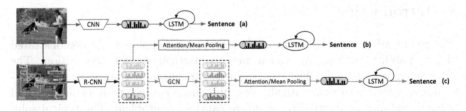

Fig. 1. Visual representations generated by image encoder in (a) CNN plus LSTM, (b) R-CNN plus LSTM, and (c) our GCN-LSTM for image captioning.

tations on each kind of relationships are feed into one individual attention LSTM decoder to generate the sentence. In the inference stage, to fuse the outputs of two decoders, we linearly average the predicted score distributions on words from two decoders at each time step and pop out the word with the highest probability as the input word to both decoders at the next step.

The main contribution of this work is the proposal of the use of visual relationship for enriching region-level representations and eventually enhancing image captioning. This also leads to the elegant views of what kind of visual relationships could be built between objects, and how to nicely leverage such visual relationships to learn more informative and relation-aware region representations for image captioning, which are problems not yet fully understood.

2   Related Work

Image Captioning. With the prevalence of deep learning [17] in computer vision, the dominant paradigm in modern image captioning is sequence learning methods [7,34,37–40] which utilize CNN plus RNN model to generate novel sentences with flexible syntactical structures. For instance, Vinyals *et al.* propose an end-to-end neural networks architecture by utilizing LSTM to generate sentence for an image in [34], which is further incorporated with soft/hard attention mechanism in [37] to automatically focus on salient objects when generating corresponding words. Instead of activating visual attention over image for every generated word, [24] develops an adaptive attention encoder-decoder model for automatically deciding when to rely on visual signals/language model. Recently, in [35,39], semantic attributes are shown to clearly boost image captioning when injected into CNN plus RNN model and such attributes can be further leveraged as semantic attention [40] to enhance image captioning. Most recently, a novel attention based encoder-decoder model [2] is proposed to detect a set of salient image regions via bottom-up attention mechanism and then attend to the salient regions with top-down attention mechanism for sentence generation.

Visual Relationship Detection. Research on visual relationship detection has attracted increasing attention. Some early works [9,10] attempt to learn four spatial relations (i.e., "above", "below", "inside" and "around") to improve segmentation. Later on, semantic relations (e.g., actions or interactions) between objects are explored in [6,32] where each possible combination of semantic relation is taken as a visual phrase class and the visual relationship detection is formulated as a classification task. Recently, quite a few works [5,19,23,29,36] design deep learning based architectures for visual relationship detection. [36] treats visual relationship as the directed edges to connect two object nodes in the scene graph and the relationships are inferred along the processing of constructing scene graph in an iterative way. [5,19] directly learn the visual features for relationship prediction based on additional union bounding boxes which cover object and subject together. In [23,29], the linguistic cues of the participating objects/captions are further considered for visual relationship detection.

Summary. In short, our approach in this paper belongs to sequence learning method for image captioning. Similar to previous approaches [2,8], GCN-LSTM explores visual attention over the detected image regions of objects for sentence generation. The novelty is on the exploitation of semantic and spatial relations between objects for image captioning, that has not been previously explored. In particular, both of the two kinds of visual relationships are seamlessly integrated into LSTM-based captioning framework via GCN, targeting for producing relation-aware region representations and thus potentially enhancing the quality of generated sentence through emphasizing the object relations.

3   Image Captioning by Exploring Visual Relationship

We devise our Graph Convolutional Networks plus Long Short-Term Memory (GCN-LSTM) architecture to generate image descriptions by additionally incorporating both semantic and spatial object relationships. GCN-LSTM firstly utilizes an object detection module (e.g., Faster R-CNN [30]) to detect objects within images, aiming for encoding and generalizing the whole image into a set of salient image regions containing objects. Semantic and spatial relation graphs are then constructed over all the detected image regions of objects based on their semantic and spatial connections, respectively. Next, the training of GCN-LSTM is performed by contextually encoding the whole image region set with semantic or spatial graph structure via GCN, resulting in relation-aware region representations. All of encoded relation-aware region representations are further injected into LSTM-based captioning framework, enabling region-level attention mechanism for sentence generation. An overview of our image captioning architecture is illustrated in Fig. 2.

3.1   Problem Formulation

Suppose we have an image I to be described by a textual sentence $\mathcal{S}$, where $\mathcal{S} = \{w_1, w_2, ..., w_{N_s}\}$ consisting of N_s words. Let $\mathbf{w}_t \in \mathbb{R}^{D_s}$ denote the D_s-dimensional textual feature of the t-th word in sentence $\mathcal{S}$. Faster R-CNN is firstly leveraged to produce the set of detected objects $\mathcal{V} = \{v_i\}_{i=1}^{K}$ with K image regions of objects in I and $\mathbf{v}_i \in \mathbb{R}^{D_v}$ denotes the D_v-dimensional feature of each image region. Furthermore, by treating each image region v_i as one vertex, we can construct semantic graph $\mathcal{G}_{sem} = (\mathcal{V}, \mathcal{E}_{sem})$ and spatial graph $\mathcal{G}_{spa} = (\mathcal{V}, \mathcal{E}_{spa})$, where $\mathcal{E}_{sem}$ and $\mathcal{E}_{spa}$ denotes the set of semantic and spatial relation edges between region vertices, respectively. More details about how we mine the visual relationships between objects and construct the semantic and spatial graphs will be elaborated in Sect. 3.2.

Inspired by the recent successes of sequence models leveraged in image/video captioning [26,27,34] and region-level attention mechanism [2,8], we aim to formulate our image captioning model in a R-CNN plus RNN scheme. Our R-CNN plus RNN method firstly interprets the given image as a set of image regions with R-CNN, then uniquely encodes them into relation-aware features conditioned on

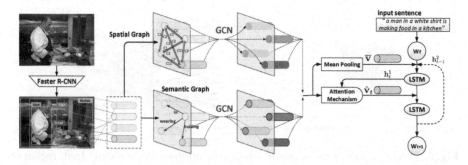

Fig. 2. An overview of our Graph Convolutional Networks plus Long Short-Term Memory (GCN-LSTM) for image captioning (better viewed in color). Faster R-CNN is first leveraged to detect a set of salient image regions. Next, semantic/spatial graph is built with directional edges on the detected regions, where the vertex represents each region and the edge denotes the semantic/spatial relationship in between. Graph Convolutional Networks (GCN) is then exploited to contextually encode regions with visual relationship in the structured semantic/spatial graph. After that, the learnt relation-aware region-level features from each kind of graph are feed into one individual attention LSTM decoder for sentence generation. In the inference stage, we adopt a late fusion scheme to linearly fuse the results from two decoders.

semantic/spatial graph, and finally decodes them to each target output word via attention LSTM decoder. Derived from the idea of Graph Convolutional Networks [15, 25], we leverage a GCN module in image encoder to contextually refine the representation of each image region, which is endowed with the inherent visual relationships between objects. Hence, the sentence generation problem we explore here can be formulated by minimizing the following energy loss function:

$$E(\mathcal{V}, \mathcal{G}, \mathcal{S}) = -\log \Pr(\mathcal{S}|\mathcal{V}, \mathcal{G}), \qquad (1)$$

which is the negative log probability of the correct textual sentence given the detected image regions of objects $\mathcal{V}$ and constructed relation graph $\mathcal{G}$. Note that we use $\mathcal{G} \in \{\mathcal{G}_{sem}, \mathcal{G}_{spa}\}$ for simplicity, i.e., $\mathcal{G}$ denotes either semantic graph $\mathcal{G}_{sem}$ or spatial graph $\mathcal{G}_{spa}$. Here the negative log probability is typically measured with cross entropy loss, which inevitably results in the discrepancy of evaluation between training and inference. Accordingly, to further boost our captioning model by amending such discrepancy, we can directly optimize the LSTM with expected sentence-level reward loss as in [18, 22, 31].

3.2 Visual Relationship Between Objects in Images

Semantic Object Relationship. We draw inspiration from recent advances in deep learning based visual relationship detection [5, 19] and simplify it as a classification task to learn semantic relation classifier on visual relationship benchmarks (e.g., Visual Genome [16]). The general expression of semantic relation is

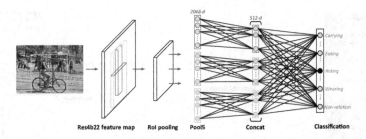

Fig. 3. Detection model for semantic relation ⟨*subject-predicate-object*⟩ (red: region of subject noun, blue: region of object noun, yellow: the union bounding box). (Color figure online)

⟨*subject-predicate-object*⟩ between pairs of objects. Note that the semantic relation is directional, i.e., it relates one object (subject noun) and another object (object noun) via a predicate which can be an action or interaction between objects. Hence, given two detected regions of objects v_i (subject noun) and v_j (object noun) within an image I, we devise a simple deep classification model to predict the semantic relation between v_i and v_j depending on the union bounding box which covers the two objects together.

Figure 3 depicts the framework of our designed semantic relation detection model. In particular, the input two region-level features $\mathbf{v}_i$ and $\mathbf{v}_j$ are first separately transformed via an embedding layer, which are further concatenated with the transferred region-level feature $\mathbf{v}_{ij}$ of the union bounding box containing both v_i and v_j. The combined features are finally injected into the classification layer that produces softmax probability over N_{sem} semantic relation classes plus a non-relation class, which is essentially a multi-class logistic regression model. Here each region-level feature is taken from the D_v-dimensional ($D_v = 2,048$) output of Pool5 layer after RoI pooling from the Res4b22 feature map of Faster R-CNN in conjunction with ResNet-101 [11].

After training the visual relation classifier on visual relationship benchmark, we directly employ the learnt visual relation classifier to construct the corresponding semantic graph $\mathcal{G}_{sem} = (\mathcal{V}, \mathcal{E}_{sem})$. Specifically, we firstly group the detected K image regions of objects within image I into $K \times (K - 1)$ object pairs (two identical regions will not be grouped). Next, we compute the probability distribution on all the ($N_{sem} + 1$) relation classes for each object pair with the learnt visual relation classifier. If the probability of non-relation class is less than 0.5, a directional edge from the region vertex of subject noun to the region vertex of object noun is established and the relation class with maximum probability is regarded as the label of this edge.

Spatial Object Relationship. The semantic graph only unfolds the inherent action/interaction between objects, while leaving the spatial relations between image regions unexploited. Therefore, we construct another graph, i.e., spatial graph, to fully explore the relative spatial relations between every two regions within one image. Here we generally express the directional spatial relation as

$\langle object_i\text{-}object_j \rangle$, which represents the relative geometrical position of $object_j$ against $object_i$. The edge and the corresponding class label for every two object vertices in spatial graph $\mathcal{G}_{spa} = (\mathcal{V}, \mathcal{E}_{spa})$ are built and assigned depending on their Intersection over Union (IoU), relative distance and angle. Detailed definition of spatial relations are shown in Fig. 4.

Concretely, given two regions v_i and v_j, the locations of them are denoted as (x_i, y_i) and (x_j, y_j), which are the normalized coordinates of the centroid of the bounding box on the image plane for v_i and v_j, respectively. We can thus achieve the IoU between v_i and v_j, relative distance d_{ij} ($d_{ij} = \sqrt{(x_j - x_i)^2 + (y_j - y_i)^2}$) and relative angle θ_{ij} (i.e., the argument of the vector from the centroid of v_i to that of v_j). Two kinds of special cases are firstly considered for classifying the spatial relation between v_i and v_j. If v_i completely includes v_j or v_i is fully covered by v_j, we establish an edge from v_i to v_j and set the label of spatial relation as "inside" (**class 1**) and "cover" (**class 2**), respectively. Except for the two special classes, if the IoU between v_i and v_j is larger than 0.5, we directly connect v_i to v_j with an edge, which is classified as "overlap" (**class 3**). Otherwise, when the ratio ϕ_{ij} between the relative distance d_{ij} and the diagonal length of the whole image is less than 0.5, we classify the edge between v_i and v_j solely relying on the size of relative angle θ_{ij} and the index of class is set as $\lceil \theta_{ij}/45° \rceil + 3$ (**class 4-11**). When the ratio $\phi_{ij} > 0.5$ and IoU < 0.5, the spatial relation between them is tend to be weak and no edge is established in this case.

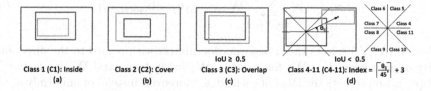

Fig. 4. Definition of eleven kinds of spatial relations $\langle object_i\text{-}object_j \rangle$ (red: region of $object_i$, blue: region of $object_j$). (Color figure online)

3.3 Image Captioning with Visual Relationship

With the constructed graphs over the detected objects based on their spatial and semantic connections, we next discuss how to integrate the learnt visual relationships into sequence learning with region-based attention mechanism for image captioning via our designed GCN-LSTM. Specifically, a GCN-based image encoder is devised to contextually encode all the image regions with semantic or spatial graph structure via GCN into relation-aware representations, which are further injected into attention LSTM for generating sentence.

GCN-based Image Encoder. Inspired from Graph Convolutional Networks for node classification [15] and semantic role labeling [25], we design a GCN-based image encoder for enriching the region-level features by capturing the semantic/spatial relations on semantic/spatial graph, as illustrated in the middle part of Fig. 2. The original GCN is commonly operated on an undirected graph, encoding information about the neighborhood of each vertex v_i as a real-valued vector, which is computed by

$$\mathbf{v}_i^{(1)} = \rho\Big(\sum_{v_j \in \mathcal{N}(v_i)} \mathbf{W} \mathbf{v}_j + \mathbf{b}\Big), \tag{2}$$

where $\mathbf{W} \in \mathbb{R}^{D_v \times D_v}$ is the transformation matrix, $\mathbf{b}$ is the bias vector and ρ denotes an activation function (e.g., ReLU). $\mathcal{N}(v_i)$ represents the set of neighbors of v_i, i.e., the region vertices have visual connections with v_i here. Note that $\mathcal{N}(v_i)$ also includes v_i itself. Although the original GCN refines each vertex by accumulating the features of its neighbors, none of the information about directionality or edge labels is included for encoding image regions. In order to enable the operation on labeled directional graph, the original GCN is upgraded by fully exploiting the directional and labeled visual connections between vertices.

Formally, consider a labeled directional graph $\mathcal{G} = (\mathcal{V}, \mathcal{E}) \in \{\mathcal{G}_{sem}, \mathcal{G}_{spa}\}$ where $\mathcal{V}$ is the set of all the detected region vertices and $\mathcal{E}$ is a set of visual relationship edges. Separate transformation matrices and bias vectors are utilized for different directions and labels of edges, respectively, targeting for making the modified GCN sensitive to both directionality and labels. Accordingly, each vertex v_i is encoded via the modified GCN as

$$\mathbf{v}_i^{(1)} = \rho\Big(\sum_{v_j \in \mathcal{N}(v_i)} \mathbf{W}_{\mathrm{dir}(v_i,v_j)} \mathbf{v}_j + \mathbf{b}_{\mathrm{lab}(v_i,v_j)}\Big), \tag{3}$$

where $\mathrm{dir}(v_i, v_j)$ selects the transformation matrix with regard to the directionality of each edge (i.e., $\mathbf{W}_1$ for v_i-to-v_j, $\mathbf{W}_2$ for v_j-to-v_i, and $\mathbf{W}_3$ for v_i-to-v_i). $\mathrm{lab}(v_i, v_j)$ represents the label of each edge. Moreover, instead of uniformly accumulating the information from all connected vertices, an edge-wise gate unit is additionally incorporated into GCN to automatically focus on potentially important edges. Hence each vertex v_i is finally encoded via the GCN in conjunction with an edge-wise gate as

$$\mathbf{v}_i^{(1)} = \rho\Big(\sum_{v_j \in \mathcal{N}(v_i)} g_{v_i,v_j} \big(\mathbf{W}_{\mathrm{dir}(v_i,v_j)} \mathbf{v}_j + \mathbf{b}_{\mathrm{lab}(v_i,v_j)}\big)\Big),$$
$$g_{v_i,v_j} = \sigma\Big(\widetilde{\mathbf{W}}_{\mathrm{dir}(v_i,v_j)} \mathbf{v}_j + \widetilde{b}_{\mathrm{lab}(v_i,v_j)}\Big), \tag{4}$$

where g_{v_i,v_j} denotes the scale factor achieved from edge-wise gate, σ is the logistic sigmoid function, $\widetilde{\mathbf{W}}_{\mathrm{dir}(v_i,v_j)} \in \mathbb{R}^{1 \times D_v}$ is the transformation matrix and $\widetilde{b}_{\mathrm{lab}(v_i,v_j)} \in \mathbb{R}$ is the bias. Consequently, after encoding all the regions $\{\mathbf{v}_i\}_{i=1}^K$ via GCN-based image encoder as in Eq. (4), the refined region-level features $\{\mathbf{v}_i^{(1)}\}_{i=1}^K$ are endowed with the inherent visual relationships between objects.

Attention LSTM Sentence Decoder. Taking the inspiration from region-level attention mechanism in [2], we devise our attention LSTM sentence decoder by injecting all of the relation-aware region-level features $\{\mathbf{v}_i^{(1)}\}_{i=1}^K$ into a two-layer LSTM with attention mechanism, as shown in the right part of Fig. 2. In particular, at each time step t, the attention LSTM decoder firstly collects the maximum contextual information by concatenating the input word w_t with the previous output of the second-layer LSTM unit $\mathbf{h}_{t-1}^2$ and the mean-pooled image feature $\overline{\mathbf{v}} = \frac{1}{K}\sum_{i=1}^K \mathbf{v}_i^{(1)}$, which will be set as the input of the first-layer LSTM unit. Hence the updating procedure for the first-layer LSTM unit is as

$$\mathbf{h}_t^1 = f_1\left(\left[\mathbf{h}_{t-1}^2, \mathbf{W}_s\mathbf{w}_t, \overline{\mathbf{v}}\right]\right), \tag{5}$$

where $\mathbf{W}_s \in \mathbb{R}^{D_s^1 \times D_s}$ is the transformation matrix for input word w_t, $\mathbf{h}_t^1 \in \mathbb{R}^{D_h}$ is the output of the first-layer LSTM unit, and f_1 is the updating function within the first-layer LSTM unit. Next, depending on the output $\mathbf{h}_t^1$ of the first-layer LSTM unit, a normalized attention distribution over all the relation-aware region-level features is generated as

$$a_{t,i} = \mathbf{W}_a\left[\tanh\left(\mathbf{W}_f\mathbf{v}_i^{(1)} + \mathbf{W}_h\mathbf{h}_t^1\right)\right], \quad \lambda_t = softmax\left(\mathbf{a}_t\right), \tag{6}$$

where $a_{t,i}$ is the i-th element of $\mathbf{a}_t$, $\mathbf{W}_a \in \mathbb{R}^{1 \times D_a}$, $\mathbf{W}_f \in \mathbb{R}^{D_a \times D_v}$ and $\mathbf{W}_h \in \mathbb{R}^{D_a \times D_h}$ are transformation matrices. $\lambda_t \in \mathbb{R}^K$ denotes the normalized attention distribution and its i-th element $\lambda_{t,i}$ is the attention probability of $\mathbf{v}_i^{(1)}$. Based on the attention distribution, we calculate the attended image feature $\hat{\mathbf{v}}_t = \sum_{i=1}^K \lambda_{t,i}\mathbf{v}_i^{(1)}$ by aggregating all the region-level features weighted with attention. We further concatenate the attended image feature $\hat{\mathbf{v}}_t$ with $\mathbf{h}_t^1$ and feed them into the second-layer LSTM unit, whose updating procedure is thus given by

$$\mathbf{h}_t^2 = f_2\left(\left[\hat{\mathbf{v}}_t, \mathbf{h}_t^1\right]\right), \tag{7}$$

where f_2 is the updating function within the second-layer LSTM unit. The output of the second-layer LSTM unit $\mathbf{h}_t^2$ is leveraged to predict the next word w_{t+1} through a softmax layer.

3.4   Training and Inference

In the training stage, we pre-construct the two kinds of visual graphs (i.e., semantic and spatial graphs) by exploiting the semantic and spatial relations among detected image regions as described in Sect. 3.2. Then, each graph is separately utilized to train one individual GCN-based encoder plus attention LSTM decoder. Note that the LSTM in decoder can be optimized with conventional cross entropy loss or the expected sentence-level reward loss as in [22,31].

At the inference time, we adopt a late fusion scheme to connect the two visual graphs in our designed GCN-LSTM architecture. Specifically, we linearly fuse the predicted word distributions from two decoders at each time step and pop out the word with the maximum probability as the input word to both decoders at the next time step. The fused probability for each word w_i is calculated as:

$$\Pr\left(w_t = w_i\right) = \alpha \Pr_{sem}\left(w_t = w_i\right) + (1 - \alpha)\Pr_{spa}\left(w_t = w_i\right), \qquad (8)$$

where α is the tradeoff parameter, $\Pr_{sem}\left(w_t = w_i\right)$ and $\Pr_{spa}\left(w_t = w_i\right)$ denotes the predicted probability for each word w_i from the decoder trained with semantic and spatial graph, respectively.

4   Experiments

We conducted the experiments and evaluated our proposed GCN-LSTM model on COCO captioning dataset (COCO) [21] for image captioning task. In addition, Visual Genome [16] is utilized to pre-train the object detector and semantic relation detector in our GCN-LSTM.

4.1   Datasets and Experimental Settings

COCO, is the most popular benchmark for image captioning, which contains 82,783 training images and 40,504 validation images. There are 5 human-annotated descriptions per image. As the annotations of the official testing set are not publicly available, we follow the widely used settings in [2,31] and take 113,287 images for training, 5K for validation and 5 K for testing. Similar to [13], we convert all the descriptions in training set to lower case and discard rare words which occur less than 5 times, resulting in the final vocabulary with 10,201 unique words in COCO dataset.

Visual Genome, is a large-scale image dataset for modeling the interactions/relationships between objects, which contains 108 K images with densely annotated objects, attributes, and relationships. To pre-train the object detector (i.e., Faster R-CNN in this work), we strictly follow the setting in [2], taking 98 K for training, 5K for validation and 5 K for testing. Note that as part of images (about 51K) in Visual Genome are also found in COCO, the split of Visual Genome is carefully selected to avoid contamination of the COCO validation and testing sets. Similar to [2], we perform extensive cleaning and filtering of training data, and train Faster R-CNN over the selected 1,600 object classes and 400 attributes classes. To pre-train the semantic relation detector, we adopt the same data split for training object detector. Moreover, we select the top-50 frequent predicates in training data and manually group them into 20 predicate/relation classes. The semantic relation detection model is thus trained over the 20 relation classes plus a non-relation class.

Features and Parameter Settings. Each word in the sentence is represented as "one-hot" vector (binary index vector in a vocabulary). For each image, we apply Faster R-CNN to detect objects within this image and select top $K = 36$ regions with highest detection confidences to represent the image. Each region is represented as the 2,048-dimensional output of pool5 layer after RoI pooling from the Res4b22 feature map of Faster R-CNN in conjunction with ResNet-101 [11]. In the attention LSTM decoder, the size of word embedding D_s^1 is set as 1,000. The dimension of the hidden layer D_h in each LSTM is set as 1,000. The dimension of the hidden layer D_a for measuring attention distribution is set as 512. The tradeoff parameter α in Eq. (8) is empirically set as 0.7.

Implementation Details. We mainly implement our GCN-LSTM based on Caffe [12], which is one of widely adopted deep learning frameworks. The whole system is trained by Adam [14] optimizer. We set the initial learning rate as 0.0005 and the mini-batch size as 1,024. The maximum training iteration is set as 30 K iterations. For sentence generation in inference stage, we adopt the beam search strategy and set the beam size as 3.

Evaluation Metrics. We adopt five types of metrics: BLEU@N [28], METEOR [3], ROUGE-L [20], CIDEr-D [33] and SPICE [1]. All the metrics are computed by using the codes[1] released by COCO Evaluation Server [4].

Compared Approaches. We compared the following state-of-the-art methods: (1) **LSTM** [34] is the standard CNN plus RNN model which only injects image into LSTM at the initial time step. We directly extract results reported in [31]. (2) **SCST** [31] employs a modified visual attention mechanism of [37] for captioning. Moreover, a self-critical sequence training strategy is devised to train LSTM with expected sentence-level reward loss. (3) **ADP-ATT** [24] develops an adaptive attention based encoder-decoder model for automatically determining when to look (sentinel gate) and where to look (spatial attention). (4) **LSTM-A** [39] integrates semantic attributes into CNN plus RNN captioning model for boosting image captioning. (5) **Up-Down** [2] designs a combined bottom-up and top-down attention mechanism that enables region-level attention to be calculated. (6) **GCN-LSTM** is the proposal in this paper. Moreover, two slightly different settings of GCN-LSTM are named as GCN-LSTM$_{sem}$ and GCN-LSTM$_{spa}$ which are trained with only semantic graph and spatial graph, respectively.

Note that for fair comparison, all the baselines and our model adopt ResNet-101 as the basic architecture of image feature extractor. Moreover, results are reported for models optimized with both cross entropy loss or expected sentence-level reward loss. The sentence-level reward is measured with CIDEr-D score.

4.2   Performance Comparison and Experimental Analysis

Quantitative Analysis. Table 1 shows the performances of different models on COCO image captioning dataset. Overall, the results across six evaluation metrics optimized with cross-entropy loss and CIDEr-D score consistently indicate that our proposed GCN-LSTM achieves superior performances against other state-of-the-art techniques including non-attention models (LSTM, LSTM-A) and attention-based approach (SCST, ADP-ATT and Up-Down). In particular, the CIDEr-D and SPICE scores of our GCN-LSTM can achieve 117.1% and 21.1% optimized with cross-entropy loss, making the relative improvement over

---

[1] https://github.com/tylin/coco-caption.

Table 1. Performance of our GCN-LSTM and other state-of-the-art methods on COCO, where B@N, M, R, C and S are short for BLEU@N, METEOR, ROUGE-L, CIDEr-D and SPICE scores. All values are reported as percentage (%).

	Cross-entropy loss						CIDEr-D score optimization					
	B@1	B@4	M	R	C	S	B@1	B@4	M	R	C	S
LSTM [34]	-	29.6	25.2	52.6	94.0	-	-	31.9	25.5	54.3	106.3	-
SCST [31]	-	30.0	25.9	53.4	99.4	-	-	34.2	26.7	55.7	114.0	-
ADP-ATT [24]	74.2	33.2	26.6	-	108.5	-	-	-	-	-	-	-
LSTM-A [39]	75.4	35.2	26.9	55.8	108.8	20.0	78.6	35.5	27.3	56.8	118.3	20.8
Up-Down [2]	77.2	36.2	27.0	56.4	113.5	20.3	79.8	36.3	27.7	56.9	120.1	21.4
GCN-LSTM$_{spa}$	77.2	36.5	27.8	56.8	115.6	20.8	80.3	37.8	28.4	58.1	127.0	21.9
GCN-LSTM$_{sem}$	77.3	36.8	27.9	57.0	116.3	20.9	80.5	38.2	28.5	58.3	127.6	22.0
GCN-LSTM	**77.4**	**37.1**	**28.1**	**57.2**	**117.1**	**21.1**	**80.9**	**38.3**	**28.6**	**58.5**	**128.7**	**22.1**

the best competitor Up-Down by 3.2% and 3.9%, respectively, which is generally considered as a significant progress on this benchmark. As expected, the CIDEr-D and SPICE scores are boosted up to 128.7% and 22.1% when optimized with CIDEr-D score. LSTM-A exhibits better performance than LSTM, by further explicitly taking the high-level semantic information into account for encoding images. Moreover, SCST, ADP-ATT and Up-Down lead to a large performance boost over LSTM, which directly encodes image as one global representation. The results basically indicate the advantage of visual attention mechanism by learning to focus on the image regions that are most indicative to infer the next word. More specifically, Up-Down by enabling attention to be calculated at the level of objects, improves SCST and ADP-ATT. The performances of Up-Down are still lower than our GCN-LSTM$_{spa}$ and GCN-LSTM$_{sem}$ which additionally exploits spatial/semantic relations between objects for enriching region-level representations and eventually enhancing image captioning, respectively. In addition, by utilizing both spatial and semantic graphs in a late fusion manner, our GCN-LSTM further boosts up the performances.

Qualitative Analysis. Figure 5 shows a few image examples with the constructed semantic and spatial graphs, human-annotated ground truth sentences and sentences generated by three approaches, i.e., LSTM, Up-Down and our GCN-LSTM. From these exemplar results, it is easy to see that the three automatic methods can generate somewhat relevant and logically correct sentences, while our model GCN-LSTM can generate more descriptive sentence by enriching semantics with visual relationships in graphs to boost image captioning. For instance, compared to the same sentence segment "with a cake" in the sentences generated by LSTM and Up-Down for the first image, "eating a cake" in our GCN-LSTM depicts the image content more comprehensive, since the detected relation "eating" in semantic graph is encoded into relation-aware region-level features for guiding sentence generation.

Performance on COCO Online Testing Server. We also submitted our GCN-LSTM optimized with CIDEr-D score to online COCO testing server and

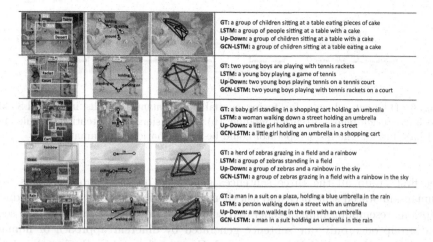

Fig. 5. Graphs and sentences generation results on COCO dataset. The semantic graph is constructed with semantic relations predicted by our semantic relation detection model. The spatial graph is constructed with spatial relations as defined in Fig. 4. The output sentences are generated by (1) Ground Truth (GT): One ground truth sentence, (2) LSTM, (3) Up-Down and (4) our GCN-LSTM.

Table 2. Leaderboard of the published state-of-the-art image captioning models on the online COCO testing server, where B@N, M, R, and C are short for BLEU@N, METEOR, ROUGE-L, and CIDEr-D scores. All values are reported as percentage (%).

Model	B@2		B@3		B@4		M		R		C	
	c5	c40	c5	c40	c5	c40	c5	c40	c5	c40	c5	c40
GCN-LSTM	**65.5**	**89.3**	**50.8**	**80.3**	**38.7**	**69.7**	**28.5**	**37.6**	**58.5**	**73.4**	**125.3**	**126.5**
Up-Down [2]	64.1	88.8	49.1	79.4	36.9	68.5	27.6	36.7	57.1	72.4	117.9	120.5
LSTM-A [39]	62.7	86.7	47.6	76.5	35.6	65.2	27.0	35.4	56.4	70.5	116.0	118.0
SCST [31]	61.9	86.0	47.0	75.9	35.2	64.5	27.0	35.5	56.3	70.7	114.7	116.7
G-RMI [22]	59.1	84.2	44.5	73.8	33.1	62.4	25.5	33.9	55.1	69.4	104.2	107.1
ADP-ATT [24]	58.4	84.5	44.4	74.4	33.6	63.7	26.4	35.9	55.0	70.5	104.2	105.9

evaluated the performance on official testing set. Table 2 summarizes the performance Leaderboard on official testing image set with 5 (c5) and 40 (c40) reference captions. The latest top-5 performing methods which have been officially published are included in the table. Compared to the top performing methods on the leaderboard, our proposed GCN-LSTM achieves the best performances across all the evaluation metrics on both c5 and c40 testing sets.

Human Evaluation. To better understand how satisfactory are the sentences generated from different methods, we also conducted a human study to compare our GCN-LSTM against two approaches, i.e., LSTM and Up-Down. All of the three methods are optimized with CIDEr-D score. 12 evaluators are invited and a subset of 1 K images is randomly selected from testing set for the subjective evaluation. All the evaluators are organized into two groups. We show

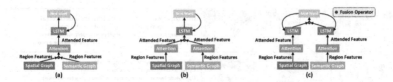

Fig. 6. Different schemes for fusing spatial and semantic graphs in GCN-LSTM: (a) Early fusion before attention module, (b) Early fusion after attention module and (c) Late fusion. The fusion operator could be concatenation or summation.

the first group all the three sentences generated by each approach plus five human-annotated sentences and ask them the question: Do the systems produce captions resembling human-generated sentences? In contrast, we show the second group once only one sentence generated by different approach or human annotation (Human) and they are asked: Can you determine whether the given sentence has been generated by a system or by a human being? From evaluators' responses, we calculate two metrics: (1) M1: percentage of captions that are evaluated as better or equal to human caption; (2) M2: percentage of captions that pass the Turing Test. The results of M1 are 74.2%, 70.3%, 50.1% for GCN-LSTM, Up-Down and LSTM. For the M2 metric, the results of Human, GCN-LSTM, Up-Down and LSTM are 92.6%, 82.1%, 78.5% and 57.8%. Overall, our GCN-LSTM is clearly the winner in terms of two criteria.

Effect of Fusion Scheme. There are generally two directions for fusing semantic and spatial graphs in GCN-LSTM. One is to perform early fusion scheme by concatenating each pair of region features from graphs before attention module or the attended features from graphs after attention module. The other is our adopted late fusion scheme to linearly fuse the predicted word distributions from two decoders. Figure 6 depicts the three fusion schemes. We compare the performances of our GCN-LSTM in the three fusion schemes (with cross-entropy loss). The results are 116.4%, 116.6% and 117.1% in CIDEr-D metric for early fusion before/after attention module and late fusion, respectively, which indicate that the adopted late fusion scheme outperforms other two early fusion schemes.

Effect of the Tradeoff Parameter α. To clarify the effect of the tradeoff parameter α in Eq. (8), we illustrate the performance curves over three evaluation metrics with a different tradeoff parameter in Fig. 7. As shown in the figure, we

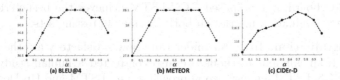

Fig. 7. The effect of the tradeoff parameter α in our GCN-LSTM with cross-entropy loss over (a) BLEU@4 (%), (b) METEOR (%) and (c) CIDEr-D (%) on COCO.

can see that all performance curves are generally like the "∧" shapes when α varies in a range from 0 to 1. The best performance is achieved when α is about 0.7. This proves that it is reasonable to exploit both semantic and spatial relations between objects for boosting image captioning.

5   Conclusions

We have presented Graph Convolutional Networks plus Long Short-Term Memory (GCN-LSTM) architecture, which explores visual relationship for boosting image captioning. Particularly, we study the problem from the viewpoint of modeling mutual interactions between objects/regions to enrich region-level representations that are feed into sentence decoder. To verify our claim, we have built two kinds of visual relationships, i.e., semantic and spatial correlations, on the detected regions, and devised Graph Convolutions on the region-level representations with visual relationships to learn more powerful representations. Such relation-aware region-level representations are then input into attention LSTM for sentence generation. Extensive experiments conducted on COCO image captioning dataset validate our proposal and analysis. More remarkably, we achieve new state-of-the-art performances on this dataset. One possible future direction would be to generalize relationship modeling and utilization to other vision tasks.

References

1. Anderson, P., Fernando, B., Johnson, M., Gould, S.: SPICE: semantic propositional image caption evaluation. In: Leibe, B., Matas, J., Sebe, N., Welling, M. (eds.) ECCV 2016. LNCS, vol. 9909, pp. 382–398. Springer, Cham (2016). https://doi.org/10.1007/978-3-319-46454-1_24
2. Anderson, P., et al.: Bottom-up and top-down attention for image captioning and visual question answering. In: CVPR (2018)
3. Banerjee, S., Lavie, A.: METEOR: an automatic metric for MT evaluation with improved correlation with human judgments. In: ACL Workshop (2005)
4. Chen, X., et al.: Microsoft COCO captions: data collection and evaluation server. arXiv preprint arXiv:1504.00325 (2015)
5. Dai, B., Zhang, Y., Lin, D.: Detecting visual relationships with deep relational networks. In: CVPR (2017)
6. Divvala, S.K., Farhadi, A., Guestrin, C.: Learning everything about anything: webly-supervised visual concept learning. In: CVPR (2014)
7. Donahue, J., et al.: Long-term recurrent convolutional networks for visual recognition and description. In: CVPR (2015)
8. Fu, K., Jin, J., Cui, R., Sha, F., Zhang, C.: Aligning where to see and what to tell: image captioning with region-based attention and scene-specific contexts. IEEE Trans. PAMI **39**, 2321–2334 (2017)
9. Galleguillos, C., Rabinovich, A., Belongie, S.: Object categorization using co-occurrence, location and appearance. In: CVPR (2008)
10. Gould, S., Rodgers, J., Cohen, D., Elidan, G., Koller, D.: Multi-class segmentation with relative location prior. IJCV **80**, 300–316 (2008)

11. He, K., Zhang, X., Ren, S., Sun, J.: Deep residual learning for image recognition. In: CVPR (2016)
12. Jia, Y., et al.: Caffe: Convolutional architecture for fast feature embedding. In: MM (2014)
13. Karpathy, A., Fei-Fei, L.: Deep visual-semantic alignments for generating image descriptions. In: CVPR (2015)
14. Kingma, D., Ba, J.: Adam: a method for stochastic optimization. In: ICLR (2015)
15. Kipf, T.N., Welling, M.: Semi-supervised classification with graph convolutional networks. In: ICLR (2017)
16. Krishna, R., et al.: Visual genome: connecting language and vision using crowd-sourced dense image annotations. IJCV (2017)
17. Krizhevsky, A., Sutskever, I., Hinton, G.E.: ImageNet classification with deep convolutional neural networks. In: NIPS (2012)
18. Li, Y., Yao, T., Pan, Y., Chao, H., Mei, T.: Jointly localizing and describing events for dense video captioning. In: CVPR (2018)
19. Li, Y., Ouyang, W., Zhou, B., Wang, K., Wang, X.: Scene graph generation from objects, phrases and region captions. In: ICCV (2017)
20. Lin, C.Y.: ROUGE: a package for automatic evaluation of summaries. In: ACL Workshop (2004)
21. Lin, T.-Y., et al.: Microsoft COCO: common objects in context. In: Fleet, D., Pajdla, T., Schiele, B., Tuytelaars, T. (eds.) ECCV 2014. LNCS, vol. 8693, pp. 740–755. Springer, Cham (2014). https://doi.org/10.1007/978-3-319-10602-1_48
22. Liu, S., Zhu, Z., Ye, N., Guadarrama, S., Murphy, K.: Optimization of image description metrics using policy gradient methods. In: ICCV (2017)
23. Lu, C., Krishna, R., Bernstein, M., Fei-Fei, L.: Visual relationship detection with language priors. In: Leibe, B., Matas, J., Sebe, N., Welling, M. (eds.) ECCV 2016. LNCS, vol. 9905, pp. 852–869. Springer, Cham (2016). https://doi.org/10.1007/978-3-319-46448-0_51
24. Lu, J., Xiong, C., Parikh, D., Socher, R.: Knowing when to look: adaptive attention via a visual sentinel for image captioning. In: CVPR (2017)
25. Marcheggiani, D., Titov, I.: Encoding sentences with graph convolutional networks for semantic role labeling. In: EMNLP (2017)
26. Pan, Y., Mei, T., Yao, T., Li, H., Rui, Y.: Jointly modeling embedding and translation to bridge video and language. In: CVPR (2016)
27. Pan, Y., Yao, T., Li, H., Mei, T.: Video captioning with transferred semantic attributes. In: CVPR (2017)
28. Papineni, K., Roukos, S., Ward, T., Zhu, W.J.: BLEU: a method for automatic evaluation of machine translation. In: ACL (2002)
29. Plummer, B.A., Mallya, A., Cervantes, C.M., Hockenmaier, J., Lazebnik, S.: Phrase localization and visual relationship detection with comprehensive image-language cues. In: ICCV (2017)
30. Ren, S., He, K., Girshick, R., Sun, J.: Faster R-CNN: towards real-time object detection with region proposal networks. In: NIPS (2015)
31. Rennie, S.J., Marcheret, E., Mroueh, Y., Ross, J., Goel, V.: Self-critical sequence training for image captioning. In: CVPR (2017)
32. Sadeghi, M.A., Farhadi, A.: Recognition using visual phrases. In: CVPR (2011)
33. Vedantam, R., Lawrence Zitnick, C., Parikh, D.: CIDEr: consensus-based image description evaluation. In: CVPR (2015)
34. Vinyals, O., Toshev, A., Bengio, S., Erhan, D.: Show and tell: a neural image caption generator. In: CVPR (2015)

35. Wu, Q., Shen, C., Liu, L., Dick, A., van den Hengel, A.: What value do explicit high level concepts have in vision to language problems? In: CVPR (2016)
36. Xu, D., Zhu, Y., Choy, C.B., Fei-Fei, L.: Scene graph generation by iterative message passing. In: CVPR (2017)
37. Xu, K., et al.: Show, attend and tell: neural image caption generation with visual attention. In: ICML (2015)
38. Yao, T., Pan, Y., Li, Y., Mei, T.: Incorporating copying mechanism in image captioning for learning novel objects. In: CVPR (2017)
39. Yao, T., Pan, Y., Li, Y., Qiu, Z., Mei, T.: Boosting image captioning with attributes. In: ICCV (2017)
40. You, Q., Jin, H., Wang, Z., Fang, C., Luo, J.: Image captioning with semantic attention. In: CVPR (2016)

Single Shot Scene Text Retrieval

Lluís Gómez[✉], Andrés Mafla, Marçal Rusiñol, and Dimosthenis Karatzas

Computer Vision Center, Universitat Autònoma de Barcelona,
Edifici O, 08193 Bellaterra (Barcelona), Spain
{lgomez,andres.mafla,marcal,dimos}@cvc.uab.es

Abstract. Textual information found in scene images provides high level semantic information about the image and its context and it can be leveraged for better scene understanding. In this paper we address the problem of scene text retrieval: given a text query, the system must return all images containing the queried text. The novelty of the proposed model consists in the usage of a single shot CNN architecture that predicts at the same time bounding boxes and a compact text representation of the words in them. In this way, the text based image retrieval task can be casted as a simple nearest neighbor search of the query text representation over the outputs of the CNN over the entire image database. Our experiments demonstrate that the proposed architecture outperforms previous state-of-the-art while it offers a significant increase in processing speed.

Keywords: Image retrieval · Scene text · Word spotting
Convolutional neural networks · Region proposals networks · PHOC

1 Introduction

The world we have created is full of written information. A large percentage of everyday scene images contain text, especially in urban scenarios [1,2]. Text detection, text recognition and word spotting are important research topics which have witnessed a rapid evolution during the past few years. Despite significant advances achieved, propelled by the emergence of deep learning techniques [3], scene text understanding in unconstrained conditions remains an open problem attracting an increasing interest from the Computer Vision research community. Apart from the scientific interest, a key motivation comes by the plethora of potential applications enabled by automated scene text understanding, such as improved scene-text based image search, image geo-localization, human-computer interaction, assisted reading for the visually-impaired, robot navigation and industrial automation to mention just a few.

The textual content of scene images carries high level semantics in the form of explicit, non-trivial data, which is typically not possible to obtain from analyzing the visual information of the image alone. For example, it is very challenging,

---

L. Gómez and A. Mafla—Contributed equally to this work.

© Springer Nature Switzerland AG 2018
V. Ferrari et al. (Eds.): ECCV 2018, LNCS 11218, pp. 728–744, 2018.
https://doi.org/10.1007/978-3-030-01264-9_43

even for humans, to automatically label images such as the ones illustrated in Fig. 1 as tea shops solely by their visual appearance, without actually reading the storefront signs. Recent research actually demonstrated that a shop classifier ends up automatically learning to interpret textual information, as this is the only way to distinguish between businesses [4]. In recent years, several attempts to take advantage of text contained in images have been proposed not only to achieve fine-grained image classification [5,6] but to facilitate image retrieval.

Mishra *et al.* [7] introduced the task of scene text retrieval, where, given a text query, the system must return all images that are likely to contain such text. Successfully tackling such a task entails fast word-spotting methods, able to generalize well to out-of-dictionary queries never seen before during training.

Fig. 1. The visual appearance of different tea shops' images can be extremely variable. It seems impossible to correctly label them without reading the text within them. Our scene text retrieval method returns all the images shown here within the top-10 ranked results among more than 10, 000 distractors for the text query "tea".

A possible approach to implement scene text retrieval is to use an end-to-end reading system and simply look for the occurrences of the query word within its outputs. It has been shown [7] that such attempts generally yield low performance for various reasons. First, it is worth noting that end-to-end reading systems are evaluated on a different task, and optimized on different metrics, opting for high precision, and more often than not making use of explicit information about each of the images (for example, short dictionaries given for each image). In contrary, in a retrieval system, a higher number of detections can be beneficial. Secondly, end-to-end systems are generally slow in processing images, which hinders their use in real-time scenarios or for indexing large-scale collections.

In this paper we propose a real-time, high-performance word spotting method that detects and recognizes text in a single shot. We demonstrate state of the art performance in most scene text retrieval benchmarks. Moreover, we show that our scene text retrieval method yields equally good results for in-dictionary and out-of-dictionary (never before seen) text queries. Finally, we show that the resulting method is significantly faster than any state of the art approach for word spotting in scene images.

The proposed architecture is based on YOLO [8,9], a well known single shot object detector which we recast as a PHOC (Pyramidal Histogram Of Characters) [10,11] predictor, thus being able to effectively perform word detection and recognition at the same time. The main contribution of this paper is the demonstration that using PHOC as a word representation instead of a direct word classification over a closed dictionary, provides an elegant mechanism to generalize to any text string, allowing the method to tackle efficiently out-of-dictionary queries. By learning to predict PHOC representations of words the proposed model is able to transfer the knowledge acquired from training data to represent words it has never seen before.

The remainder of this paper is organized as follows. Section 2 presents an overview of the state of the art in scene text understanding tasks, Sect. 3 describes the proposed architecture for single shot scene text retrieval. Section 4 reports the experiments and results obtained on different benchmarks for scene text based image retrieval. Finally, the conclusions and pointers to further research are given in Sect. 5.

2 Related Work

The first attempts at recognizing text in scene images divided the problem in two distinguished steps, text detection and text recognition. For instance, in the work of Jaderberg et al. [12] scene text segmentation was performed by a text proposals mechanism that was later refined by a CNN that regressed the correct position of bounding boxes. Afterwards, those bounding boxes were inputed to a CNN that classified them in terms of a predefined vocabulary. Gupta et al. [13] followed a similar strategy by first using a Fully Convolutional Regression Network for detection and the same classification network than Jaderberg for recognition. Liao et al. [14,15] used a modified version of the SSD [16] object detection architecture adapted to text and then a CRNN [17] for text recognition. However, breaking the problem into two separate and independent steps presented an important drawback since detection errors might significantly hinder the further recognition step. Recently, end-to-end systems that approach the problem as a whole have gained the attention of the community. Since the segmentation and recognition tasks are highly correlated from an end to end perspective, in the sense that learned features can be used to solve both problems, researchers started to jointly train their models. Buvsta et al. [18] proposed to use a Fully Convolutional Neural Network for text detection and another module that employed a CTC (Connectionist Temporal Classification) for text recognition. Both modules were first trained independently and further joined together in order to make an end-to-end trainable architecture. Li et al. [19] proposed a pipeline that included a CNN to obtain text region proposals followed by a region feature encoding module that is the input to an LSTM to detect text. The detected regions are the input to another LSTM which outputs features to be decoded by a LSTM with attention to recognize the words. In that sense, we strongly believe that single shot object detection paradigms such as YOLO [9] can bring many benefits to the field of scene text recognition by having a unique architecture that is able to locate and recognize the desired text in an unique step.

However, the scene text retrieval problem slightly differs from classical scene text recognition applications. In a retrieval scenario the user should be able to cast whatever textual query he wants to retrieve, whereas most of recognition approaches are based on using a predefined vocabulary of the words one might find within scene images. For instance, both Mishra *et al.* [7], who introduced the scene text retrieval task, and Jaderberg *et al.* [12], use a fixed vocabulary to create an inverted index which contains the presence of a word in the image. Such approach obviously limits the user that does not have the freedom to cast out of vocabulary queries. In order to tackle such problem, text string descriptors based on n-gram frequencies, like the PHOC descriptor, have been successfully used for word spotting applications [10,20,21]. By using a vectorial codification of text strings, users can cast whatever query at processing time without being restricted to specific word sets.

3   Single Shot Word Spotting Architecture

The proposed architecture, illustrated in Fig. 2, consists in a single shot CNN model that predicts at the same time bounding boxes and a compact text representation of the words within them. To accomplish this we adapt the YOLOv2 object detection model [8,9] and recast it as a PHOC [10] predictor. Although the proposed method can be implemented on top of other object detection frameworks we opted for YOLOv2 because it can be up to $10 \times$ faster than two-stage frameworks like Faster R-CNN [22], and processing time is critical for us since we aim at processing images at high resolution to correctly deal with small text.

The YOLOv2 architecture is composed of 21 convolutional layers with a leaky ReLU activation and batch normalization [7] and 5 max pooling layers. It uses 3×3 filters and double the number of channels after every pooling step as in VGG models [17], but also uses 1×1 filters interspersed between 3×3 convolutions to compress the feature maps as in [9]. The backbone includes a pass-through layer from the second convolution layer and is followed by a final 1×1 convolutional layer with a linear activation with the number of filters matching the desired output tensor size for object detection. For example, in the PASCAL VOC challenge dataset (20 object classes) it needs 125 filters to predict 5 boxes with 4 coordinates each, 1 objectness value, and 20 classes per box $((4 + 1 + 20) \times 5 = 125)$. The resulting model achieves state of the art in object detection, has a smaller number of parameters than other single shot models, and features real time object detection.

A straightforward application of the YOLOv2 architecture to the word spotting task would be to treat each possible word as an object class. This way the one hot classification vectors in the output tensor would encode the word class probability distribution among a predefined list of possible words (the dictionary) for each bounding box prediction. The downside of such an approach is that we are limited in the number of words the model can detect. For a dictionary of 20 words the model would theoretically perform as well as for the 20 object classes of the PASCAL dataset, but training for a larger dictionary (e.g.

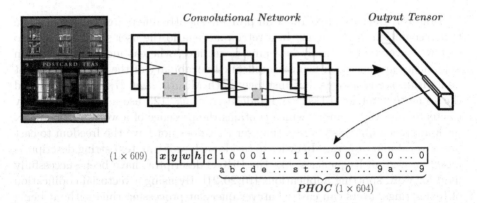

Fig. 2. Our Convolutional Neural Network predicts at the same time bounding box coordinates x, y, w, h, an objectness score c, and a pyramidal histogram of characters (PHOC) of the word in each bounding box.

the list of $100,000$ most frequent words from the English vocabulary [12]) would require a final layer with $500,000$ filters, and a tremendous amount of training data if we want to have enough samples for each of the $100,000$ classes. Even if we could manage to train such a model, it would still be limited to the dictionary size and not able to detect any word not present on it.

Instead of the fixed vocabulary approach we would like to have a model that is able to generalize to words that were not seen at training time. This is the rationale behind casting the network as a PHOC predictor. PHOC [10] is a compact representation of text strings that encodes if a specific character appears in a particular spatial region of the string (see Fig. 3). Intuitively a model that effectively learns to predict PHOC representations will implicitly learn to identify the presence of a particular character in a particular region of the bounding box by learning character attributes independently. This way the knowledge acquired from training data can be transfered at test time for words never observed during training, because the presence of a character at a particular location of the word translates to the same information in the PHOC representation independently of the other characters in the word. Moreover, the PHOC representation offers unlimited expressiveness (it can represent any word) with a fixed length low dimensional binary vector (604 dimensions in the version we use).

In order to adapt the YOLOv2 network for PHOC prediction we need to address some particularities of this descriptor. First, since the PHOC representation is not a one hot vector we need to get rid of the softmax function used by YOLOv2 in the classification output. Second, since the PHOC is a binary representation it makes sense to squash the network output corresponding to the PHOC vector to the range $0...1$. To accomplish this, a sigmoid activation function was used in the last layer. Third, we propose to modify the original YOLOv2 loss function in order to help the model through the learning process.

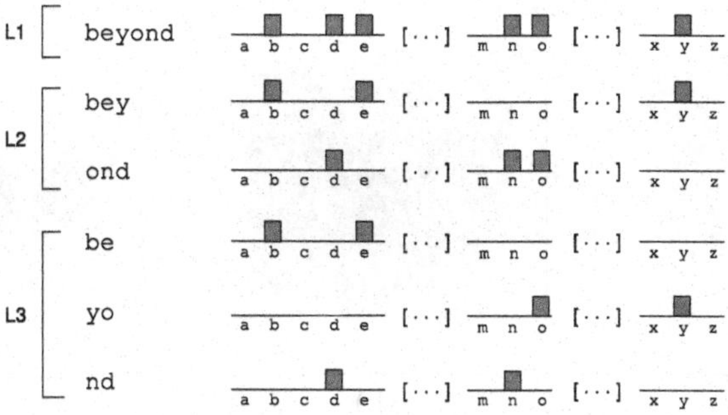

Fig. 3. Pyramidal histogram of characters (PHOC) [10] of the word "beyond" at levels 1, 2, and 3. The final PHOC representation is the concatenation of these partial histograms.

The original YOLOv2 model optimizes the following multi-part loss function:

$$L(b, C, c, \hat{b}, \hat{C}, \hat{c}) = \lambda_{box} L_{box}(b, \hat{b}) + L_{obj}(C, \hat{C}, \lambda_{obj}, \lambda_{noobj}) + \lambda_{cls} L_{cls}(c, \hat{c}) \quad (1)$$

where b is a vector with coordinates' offsets to an anchor bounding box, C is the probability of that bounding box containing an object, c is the one hot classification vector, and the three terms L_{box}, L_{obj}, and L_{cls} are respectively independent losses for bounding box regression, objectness estimation, and classification. All the aforementioned losses are essentially the sum-squared errors of ground truth (b, C, c) and predicted $(\hat{b}, \hat{C}, \hat{c})$ values. In the case of PHOC prediction, with c and $\hat{c}$ being binary vectors but with an unrestricted number of 1 values we opt for using a cross-entropy loss function in L_{cls} as in a multi-label classification task:

$$L_{cls}(c, \hat{c}) = \frac{-1}{N} \sum_{n=1}^{N} [c_n \log(\hat{c}_n) + (1 - c_n) \log(1 - \hat{c}_n)] \quad (2)$$

where N is the dimensionality of the PHOC descriptor.

Similarly as in [8] the combination of the sum-squared errors L_{box} and L_{obj} with the cross-entropy loss L_{cls} is controlled by the scaling parameters λ_{box}, λ_{obj}, λ_{noobj}, and λ_{cls}.

Apart of the modifications made so far on top of the original YOLOv2 architecture we also changed the number, the scales, and the aspect ratios of the pre-defined anchor boxes used by the network to predict bounding boxes. Similarly as in [8] we have found the ideal set of anchor boxes B for our training dataset by requiring that for each bounding box annotation there exists at least one anchor box in B with an intersection over union of at least 0.6. Figure 4 illustrates the 13 bounding boxes found to be better suited for our training data and their difference with the ones used in object detection models.

At test time, our model provides a total of $W/32 \times H/32 \times 13$ bounding box proposals, with W and H being the image input size, each one of them with an objectness score ($\hat{C}$) and a PHOC prediction ($\hat{c}$). The original YOLOv2 model

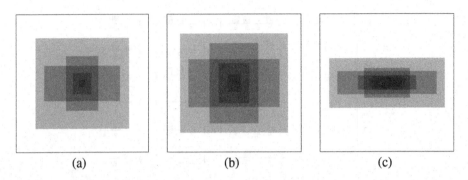

(a)   (b)   (c)

Fig. 4. Anchor boxes used in the original YOLOv2 model for object detection in COCO (a) and PASCAL (b) datasets. (c) Our set of anchor boxes for text detection.

filters the bounding box candidates with a detection threshold τ considering that a bounding box is a valid detection if $\hat{C}max(\hat{c}) \geq \tau$. If the threshold condition is met, a non-maximal suppression (NMS) strategy is applied in order to get rid of overlapping detections of the same object. In our case the threshold is applied only on the objectness score $(\hat{C})$ but with a much smaller value ($\tau = 0.0025$) than in the original model ($\tau \approx 0.2$), and we do not apply NMS. The reason is that any evidence of the presence of a word, even if it is small, it may be beneficial in terms of retrieval if its PHOC representation has a small distance to the PHOC of the queried word. With this threshold we generate an average of 60 descriptors for every image in the dataset and all of them conform our retrieval database.

In this way, the scene text retrieval of a given query word is performed with a simple nearest neighbor search of the query PHOC representation over the outputs of the CNN in the entire image database. While the distance between PHOCs is usually computed using the cosine similarity, we did not find any noticeable downside on using an Euclidean distance for the nearest neighbor search.

3.1   Implementation Details

We have trained our model in a modified version of the synthetic dataset of Gupta *et al.* [13]. First the dataset generator has been evenly modified to use a custom dictionary with the 90 K most frequent English words, as proposed by Jaderberg *et al.* [12], instead of the Newsgroup20 dataset [23] dictionary originally used by Gupta *et al.* The rationale was that in the original dataset there was no control about word occurrences, and the distribution of word instances had a large bias towards stop-words found in newsgroups' emails. Moreover, the text corpus of the Newsgroup20 dataset contains words with special characters and non ASCII strings that we do not contemplate in our PHOC representations. Finally, since the PHOC representation of a word with a strong rotation does not make sense under the pyramidal scheme employed, the dataset generator was modified to allow rotated text up to 15°. This way we generated a dataset of 1 million images for training purposes. Figure 5 shows a set of samples of our training data.

Fig. 5. Synthetic training data generated with a modified version of the method of Gupta *et al.* [13]. We make use of a custom dictionary with the 90 K most frequent English words, and restrict the range of random rotation to 15°.

The model was trained for 30 epochs of the dataset using SGD with a batch size of 64, an initial learning rate of 0.001, a momentum of 0.9, and a decay of 0.0005. We initialize the weights of our model with the YOLOv2 backbone pre-trained on Imagenet. During the firsts 10 epochs we train the model only for word detection, without backpropagating the loss of the PHOC prediction and using a fixed input size of 448 × 448. On the following 10 epochs we start learning the PHOC prediction output with the λ_{cls} parameter set to 1.0. After that, we continue learning for 10 more epochs with a learning rate of 0.0001 and setting the parameters λ_{box} and λ_{cls} to 5.0 and 0.015 respectively. At his point we also adopted a multi-resolution training, by randomly resizing the input images among 14 possible sizes in the range from 352 × 352 to 800 × 800, and we added new samples in our training data. In particular, the added samples were the 1, 233 training images of the ICDAR2013 [24] and ICDAR2015 [25] datasets. During the whole training process we used the same basic data augmentation as in [8].

4   Experiments and Results

In this section we present the experiments and results obtained on different standard benchmarks for text based image retrieval. First we describe the datasets used throughout our experiments, after that we present our results and compare them with the published state-of-the-art. Finally we discuss the scalability of the proposed retrieval method.

4.1   Datasets

The IIIT Scene Text Retrieval (STR). [7] dataset is a scene text image retrieval dataset composed of 10, 000 images collected from the Google image search engine and Flickr. The dataset has 50 predefined query words and for each of them a list of 10–50 relevant images (that contain the query word) is provided. It is a challenging dataset where relevant text appears in many different fonts and styles, and from different view points, among many distractors (images without any text).

The IIIT Sports-10k Dataset. [7] is another scene text retrieval dataset composed of 10,000 images extracted from sports video clips. It has 10 pre-defined query words with their corresponding relevant images' lists. Scene text retrieval in this dataset is specially challenging because images are low resolution and often noisy or blurred, with small text generally located on advertisements signboards.

The Street View Text (SVT) Dataset. [26] is comprised of images harvested from Google Street View where text from business signs and names appear. It contains more than 900 words annotated in 350 different images. In our exper-iments we use the official partition that splits the images in a train set of 100 images and a test set of 249 images. This dataset also provides a lexicon of 50 words per image for recognition purposes, but we do not make use of it. For the image retrieval task we consider as queries the 427 unique words annotated on the test set.

4.2   Scene Text Retrieval

In the scene text retrieval task, the goal is to retrieve all images that contain instances of the query words in a dataset partition. Given a query, the database elements are sorted with respect to the probability of containing the queried word. We use the mean average precision as the accuracy measure, which is the standard measure of performance for retrieval tasks and is essentially equivalent to the area below the precision-recall curve. Notice that, since the system always returns a ranked list with all the images in the dataset, the recall is always 100%. An alternative performance measure consist in considering only the top-n ranked images and calculating the precision at this specific cut-off point ($P@n$).

Table 1 compares the proposed method to previous state of the art for text based image retrieval on the IIIT-STR, Sports-10K, and SVT datasets. We show the mean average precision (mAP) and processing speed for the same trained model using two different input sizes (576×576 and 608×608), and a multi-resolution version that combines the outputs of the model at three resolu-tions (544, 576 and 608). Processing time has been calculated using a Titan X (Pascal) GPU with a batch size of 1. We appreciate that our method outper-forms previously published methods in two of the benchmarks while it shows a competitive performance on the SVT dataset. In order to compare with state-of-the-art end-to-end text recognition methods, we also provide a comparison with pre-trained released versions of the models of Bušta et al. [18] and He et al. [27]. For recognition-based results the look-up is performed by a direct matching between the query and the text detected by each model. Even when making use of a predefined word dictionary to filter results, our method, which is dictionary-free, yields superior results. Last, we compared against a variant of He et al. [27] but this time both queries and the model's results are first transformed to PHOC descriptors and the look-up is based on similarity on PHOC space. It can be seen that the PHOC space does not offer any advantage to end-to-end recognition methods.

Table 1. Comparison to previous state of the art for text based image retrieval: mean average precision (mAP) for IIIT-STR, and Sports-10K, and SVT datasets. (*) Results reported by Mishra et al. in [7], not by the original authors. (†) Results computed with publicly available code from the original authors.

Method	STR (mAP)	Sports (mAP)	SVT (mAP)	fps
SWT [28] + Mishra et al. [29]	-	-	19.25	
Wang et al. [26]	-	-	21.25*	
TextSpotter [30]	-	-	23.32*	1.0
Mishra et al. [7]	42.7	-	56.24	0.1
Ghosh et al. [31]	-	-	60.91	
Mishra [32]	44.5	-	62.15	0.1
Almazán et al. [10]	-	-	79.65	
TextProposals [33] + DictNet [34]	64.9†	67.5†	85.90†	0.4
Jaderberg et al. [12]	66.5	66.1	**86.30**	0.3
Bušta et al. [18]	62.94†	59.62†	69.37†	44.21
He et al. [27]	50.16†	50.74†	72.82†	1.25
He et al. [27] (with dictionary)	66.95†	74.27†	80.54†	2.35
He et al. [27] (PHOC)	46.34†	52.04†	57.61†	2.35
Proposed (576 × 576)	**68.13**	72.99	82.02	**53.0**
Proposed (608 × 608)	**69.83**	73.75	83.74	43.5
Proposed (multi-res.)	**71.37**	**74.67**	85.18	16.1

Table 2 further compares the proposed method to previous state of the art by the precisions at 10 (P@10) and 20 (P@20) on the Sports-10K dataset.

In Table 3 we show per-query mean average precision and precisions at 10 and 20 for the Sports-10K dataset. The low performance for the query "castrol" in comparison with the rest may initially be attributed to the fact that it is the only query word not seen by our model at training time. However, by visualizing the top-10 ranked images for this query, shown in Fig. 6 we can see that the dataset has many unannotated instances of "castrol". The real P@10 of our model is in fact 90% and not 50%. It appears that the annotators did not consider occluded words, while our model is able to retrieve images with partial occlusions in a consistent manner. Actually, the only retrieved image among the top-10 without the "castrol" word contains an instance of "castel". By manual inspection we have computed P@10 and P@20 to be 95.0 and 93.5 respectively.

Table 2. Comparison to previous state of the art for text based image retrieval: precision at n (P@n) for Sports-10K dataset.

Method	Sports-10K (P@10)	Sports-10K (P@20)
Mishra *et al.* [7]	44.82	43.42
Mishra [32]	47.20	46.25
Jaderberg *et al.* [12]	91.00	**92.50**
Proposed (576 × 576)	91.00	90.50
Proposed (multi-res.)	**92.00**	90.00

Table 3. Sports-10K per-query average precision (AP), P@10, and P@20 scores.

	Adidas	Castrol	Duty	Free	Hyundai	Nokia	Pakistan	Pepsi	Reliance	Sony
AP	94	16	74	61	77	75	92	70	89	89
P@10	100	50	100	90	100	80	100	90	100	90
P@20	100	55	100	85	100	85	100	95	100	90

Overall, the performance exhibited with the "castrol" query is a very important result, since it demonstrates that our model is able to generalize the PHOC prediction for words that has never seen at training time, and even to correctly retrieve them under partial occlusions. We found further support for this claim by analyzing the results for the six IIIT-STR query words that our model has not seen during training. Figure 7 shows the top-5 ranked images for the queries "apollo", "bata", "bawarchi", "maruti", "newsagency", and "vodafone". In all of them our model reaches a 100% precision at 5. In terms of mAP the results for these queries do not show a particular decrease when compared to those obtained with other words that are part of the training set, in fact in some cases they are even better. The mean average precision for the six words in question is 74.92, while for the remaining 44 queries is 69.14. To further analyze our model's ability for recognizing words it has never seen at training time, we have done an additional experiment within a multi-lingual setup. For this we manually added some images with text in different Latin script languages (French, Italian, Catalan, and Spanish) to the IIIT-STR dataset. We have observed that our model, while being trained only using English words, was always able to correctly retrieve the queried text in any of those languages.

Fig. 6. Top 10 ranked images for the query "castrol". Our model has not seen this word at training time.

In order to analyze the errors made by our model we have manually inspected the output of our model as well as the ground truth for the five queries with a lower mAP on the IIIT-STR dataset: "ibm", "indian", "institute", "sale", and "technology". In most of these queries the low accuracy of our model can be explained in terms of having only very small and blurred instances in the database. In the case of "ibm", the characteristic font type in all instances of this word tends to be ignored by our model, and the same happens for some computer generated images (*i.e.*non scene images) that contain the word "sale". Figure 8 shows some examples of those instances. All in all, the analysis indicates that while our model is able to generalize well for text strings not seen at training time it does not perform properly with text styles, fonts, sizes not seen before. Our intuition is that this problem can be easily alleviated with a richer training dataset.

4.3   Retrieval Speed Analysis

To analyze the retrieval speed of the proposed system, we have run the retrieval experiments for the IIIT-STR and Sports-10K datasets with different approximate nearest neighbor (ANN) algorithms in a standard PC with an i7 CPU and 32Gb of RAM. In Table 4 we appreciate that those ANN methods, with a search time sublinear in the number of indexed samples, reach retrieval speeds a couple of orders of magnitude faster than the exact nearest neighbor search based on ball-trees without incurring in any significant loss of retrieval accuracy.

Fig. 7. From top to bottom, top-5 ranked images for the queries "apollo", "bata", "bawarchi", "maruti", "newsagency", and "vodafone". Although our model has not seen this words at training time it is able to achieve a 100% P@5 for all of them.

Fig. 8. Error analysis: most of the errors made by our model come from text instances with a particular style, font type, size, etc. that is not well represented in our training data.

Table 4. Mean Average Precision and retrieval time performance (in seconds) of different approximate nearest neighbor algorithms on the IIIT-STR and Sports datasets.

Algorithm	IIIT-STR			Sports-10K		
	mAP	Secs	#PHOCs	mAP	Secs	#PHOCs
Baseline (Ball tree)	0.6983	0.4321	620K	0.7375	0.6826	1M
Annoy (approx NN) [35]	0.6883	0.0027	620K	0.7284	0.0372	1M
HNSW (approx NN) [36]	0.6922	0.0018	620K	0.7247	0.0223	1M
Falconn LSH (approx NN) [37]	0.6903	0.0151	620K	0.7201	0.0178	1M

5   Conclusion

In this paper we detailed a real-time word spotting method, based on a simple architecture that allows it to detect and recognise text in a single shot and real-time speeds.

The proposed method significantly improves state of the art results on scene text retrieval on the IIIT-STR and Sports-10K datasets, while yielding comparable results to state of the art in the SVT dataset. Moreover, it can do so achieving faster speed compared to other state of the art methods.

Importantly, the proposed method is fully capable to deal with out-of-dictionary (never before seen) text queries, seeing its performance unaffected compared to query words previously seen in the training set.

This is due to the use of PHOC as a word representation instead of aiming for a direct word classification. It can be seen that the network is able to learn how to extract such representations efficiently, generalizing well to unseen text strings. Synthesizing training data with different characteristics could boost performance, and is one of the directions we will be exploring in the future along with investigating the use of word embeddings other than PHOC.

The code, pre-trained models, and data used in this work are made publicly available at https://github.com/lluisgomez/single-shot-str.

Acknowledgement. This work has been partially supported by the Spanish research project TIN2014-52072-P, the CERCA Programme/Generalitat de Catalunya, the H2020 Marie Skłodowska-Curie actions of the European Union, grant agreement No 712949 (TECNIOspring PLUS), the Agency for Business Competitiveness of the Government of Catalonia (ACCIO), CEFIPRA Project 5302-1 and the project "aBSINTHE - AYUDAS FUNDACIÓN BBVA A EQUIPOS DE INVESTIGACION CIENTIFICA 2017. We gratefully acknowledge the support of the NVIDIA Corporation with the donation of the Titan X Pascal GPU used for this research.

References

1. Lin, T.-Y., et al.: Microsoft COCO: common objects in context. In: Fleet, D., Pajdla, T., Schiele, B., Tuytelaars, T. (eds.) ECCV 2014. LNCS, vol. 8693, pp. 740–755. Springer, Cham (2014). https://doi.org/10.1007/978-3-319-10602-1_48
2. Veit, A., Matera, T., Neumann, L., Matas, J., Belongie, S.: COCO-text: dataset and benchmark for text detection and recognition in natural images. arXiv preprint arXiv:1601.07140 (2016)
3. LeCun, Y., Bengio, Y., Hinton, G.: Deep learning. Nature **521**(7553) (2015)
4. Movshovitz-Attias, Y., Yu, Q., Stumpe, M.C., Shet, V., Arnoud, S., Yatziv, L.: Ontological supervision for fine grained classification of street view storefronts. In: Proceedings of the IEEE Conference on Computer Vision and Pattern Recognition, pp. 1693–1702 (2015)
5. Karaoglu, S., Tao, R., van Gemert, J.C., Gevers, T.: Con-text: text detection for fine-grained object classification. IEEE Trans. Image Process. **26**(8), 3965–3980 (2017)
6. Bai, X., Yang, M., Lyu, P., Xu, Y.: Integrating scene text and visual appearance for fine-grained image classification with convolutional neural networks. arXiv preprint arXiv:1704.04613 (2017)
7. Mishra, A., Alahari, K., Jawahar, C.: Image retrieval using textual cues. In: Proceedings of the IEEE International Conference on Computer Vision, pp. 3040–3047 (2013)
8. Redmon, J., Divvala, S., Girshick, R., Farhadi, A.: You only look once: unified, real-time object detection. In: Proceedings of the IEEE Conference on Computer Vision and Pattern Recognition, pp. 779–788 (2016)
9. Redmon, J., Farhadi, A.: YOLO9000: better, faster, stronger. arXiv preprint arXiv:1612.08242 (2016)
10. Almazán, J., Gordo, A., Fornés, A., Valveny, E.: Word spotting and recognition with embedded attributes. IEEE Trans. Pattern Anal. Mach. Intell. **36**(12), 2552–2566 (2014)
11. Sudholt, S., Fink, G.A.: PHOCNET: a deep convolutional neural network for word spotting in handwritten documents. In: Proceedings of the IEEE International Conference on Frontiers in Handwriting Recognition, pp. 277–282 (2016)
12. Jaderberg, M., Simonyan, K., Vedaldi, A., Zisserman, A.: Reading text in the wild with convolutional neural networks. Int. J. Comput. Vis. **116**(1), 1–20 (2016)
13. Gupta, A., Vedaldi, A., Zisserman, A.: Synthetic data for text localisation in natural images. In: Proceeding of the IEEE Conference on Computer Vision and Pattern Recognition, pp. 2315–2324 (2016)
14. Liao, M., Shi, B., Bai, X., Wang, X., Liu, W.: TextBoxes: a fast text detector with a single deep neural network. In: Proceedings of the AAAI Conference on Artificial Intelligence, pp. 4161–4167 (2017)

15. Liao, M., Shi, B., Bai, X.: TextBoxes++: a single-shot oriented scene text detector. arXiv preprint arXiv:1801.02765 (2018)
16. Liu, W., et al.: SSD: single shot multibox detector. In: Leibe, B., Matas, J., Sebe, N., Welling, M. (eds.) ECCV 2016. LNCS, vol. 9905, pp. 21–37. Springer, Cham (2016). https://doi.org/10.1007/978-3-319-46448-0_2
17. Shi, B., Bai, X., Yao, C.: An end-to-end trainable neural network for image-based sequence recognition and its application to scene text recognition. IEEE Trans. Pattern Anal. Mach. Intell. 39(11) (2017)
18. Buvsta, M., Neumann, L., Matas, J.: Deep TextSpotter: an end-to-end trainable scene text localization and recognition framework. In: Proceedings of the IEEE International Conference on Computer Vision, pp. 2204–2212 (2017)
19. Li, H., Wang, P., Shen, C.: Towards end-to-end text spotting with convolutional recurrent neural networks. arXiv preprint arXiv:1707.03985 (2017)
20. Aldavert, D., Rusiñol, M., Toledo, R., Lladós, J.: Integrating visual and textual cues for query-by-string word spotting. In: Proceedings of the IEEE International Conference on Document Analysis and Recognition, pp. 511–515 (2013)
21. Ghosh, S.K., Valveny, E.: Query by string word spotting based on character bi-gram indexing. In: Proceedings of the IEEE International Conference on Document Analysis and Recognition, pp. 881–885 (2015)
22. Ren, S., He, K., Girshick, R., Sun, J.: Faster R-CNN: towards real-time object detection with region proposal networks. In: Proceedings of the International Conference on Neural Information Processing Systems, pp. 91–99 (2015)
23. Lang, K., Mitchell, T.: Newsgroup 20 dataset (1999)
24. Karatzas, D., et al.: ICDAR 2013 robust reading competition. In: Proceedings of the IEEE International Conference on Document Analysis and Recognition, pp. 1484–1493 (2013)
25. Karatzas, D., et al.: ICDAR 2015 competition on robust reading. In: Proceedings of the IEEE International Conference on Document Analysis and Recognition, pp. 1156–1160 (2015)
26. Wang, K., Babenko, B., Belongie, S.: End-to-end scene text recognition. In: Proceedings of the IEEE International Conference on Computer Vision, pp. 1457–1464 (2011)
27. He, T., Tian, Z., Huang, W., Shen, C., Qiao, Y., Sun, C.: An end-to-end TextSpotter with explicit alignment and attention. In: CVPR (2018)
28. Epshtein, B., Ofek, E., Wexler, Y.: Detecting text in natural scenes with stroke width transform. In: Proceedings of the IEEE Conference on Computer Vision and Pattern Recognition, pp. 2963–2970 (2010)
29. Mishra, A., Alahari, K., Jawahar, C.: Top-down and bottom-up cues for scene text recognition. In: Proceedings of the IEEE Conference on Computer Vision and Pattern Recognition, pp. 2687–2694 (2012)
30. Neumann, L., Matas, J.: Real-time scene text localization and recognition. In: Proceedings of the IEEE Conference on Computer Vision and Pattern Recognition (2012)
31. Ghosh, S.K., Gomez, L., Karatzas, D., Valveny, E.: Efficient indexing for query by string text retrieval. In: Proceedings of the IEEE International Conference on Document Analysis and Recognition, pp. 1236–1240 (2015)
32. Mishra, A.: Understanding Text in Scene Images. Ph.D. thesis, International Institute of Information Technology Hyderabad (2016)
33. Gómez, L., Karatzas, D.: TextProposals: a text-specific selective search algorithm for word spotting in the wild. Pattern Recogn. 70, 60–74 (2017)

34. Jaderberg, M., Simonyan, K., Vedaldi, A., Zisserman, A.: Synthetic data and artificial neural networks for natural scene text recognition. arXiv preprint arXiv:1406.2227 (2014)
35. Bernhardsson, E.: ANNOY: approximate nearest neighbors in C++/Python optimized for memory usage and loading/saving to disk (2013)
36. Malkov, Y.A., Yashunin, D.: Efficient and robust approximate nearest neighbor search using hierarchical navigable small world graphs. arXiv:1603.09320 (2016)
37. Andoni, A., Indyk, P., Laarhoven, T., Razenshteyn, I., Schmidt, L.: Practical and optimal LSH for angular distance. In: NIPS (2015)

Folded Recurrent Neural Networks
for Future Video Prediction

Marc Oliu[1,3(✉)], Javier Selva[2,3], and Sergio Escalera[2,3]

[1] Universitat Oberta de Catalunya,
Rambla del Poblenou, 156, 08018
Barcelona, Spain
moliusimon@uoc.edu
[2] Universitat de Barcelona,
Gran Via de les Corts Catalanes, 585, 08007 Barcelona, Spain
jselvaca21@alumnes.ub.edu, sescalera@ub.edu
[3] Centre de Visió per Computador, Campus UAB, Edifici O,
08193 Cerdanyola del Vallès, Spain

Abstract. This work introduces double-mapping Gated Recurrent Units (dGRU), an extension of standard GRUs where the input is considered as a recurrent state. An extra set of logic gates is added to update the input given the output. Stacking multiple such layers results in a recurrent auto-encoder: the operators updating the outputs comprise the encoder, while the ones updating the inputs form the decoder. Since the states are shared between corresponding encoder and decoder layers, the representation is stratified during learning: some information is not passed to the next layers. We test our model on future video prediction. Main challenges for this task include high variability in videos, temporal propagation of errors, and non-specificity of future frames. We show how only the encoder or decoder needs to be applied for encoding or prediction. This reduces the computational cost and avoids re-encoding predictions when generating multiple frames, mitigating error propagation. Furthermore, it is possible to remove layers from a trained model, giving an insight to the role of each layer. Our approach improves state of the art results on MMNIST and UCF101, being competitive on KTH with 2 and 3 times less memory usage and computational cost than the best scored approach.

Keywords: Future video prediction · Unsupervised learning
Recurrent neural networks

1 Introduction

Future video prediction is a challenging task that recently received much attention due to its capabilities for learning in an unsupervised manner, making it

Electronic supplementary material The online version of this chapter (https://doi.org/10.1007/978-3-030-01264-9_44) contains supplementary material, which is available to authorized users.

© Springer Nature Switzerland AG 2018
V. Ferrari et al. (Eds.): ECCV 2018, LNCS 11218, pp. 745–761, 2018.
https://doi.org/10.1007/978-3-030-01264-9_44

possible to leverage large volumes of unlabelled data for video-related tasks such as action and gesture recognition [10,11,22], task planning [4,14], weather prediction [20], optical flow estimation [15] and new view synthesis [10].

One of the main problems in this task is the need of expensive models, both in terms of memory and computational power, in order to capture the variability present in video data. Another problem is the propagation of errors in recurrent models, which is tied to the inherent uncertainty of video prediction: given a series of previous frames, there are multiple feasible futures. Left unchecked, this results in blurry predictions averaging the space of possible futures. When predicting subsequent frames, the blur is propagated back into the network, accumulating errors over time.

In this work we propose a new type of recurrent auto-encoder (AE) with state sharing between encoder and decoder. We show how the exposed state in Gated Recurrent Units (GRU) can be used to create a bidirectional mapping between the input and output of each layer. To do so, the input is treated as a recurrent state, adding another set of logic gates to update it based on the output. Creating a stack of these layers allows for a bidirectional flow of information: The forward gates encode inputs and the backward ones generate predictions, obtaining a structure similar to an AE[1], but with many inherent advantages. Only the encoder or decoder is executed for input encoding or prediction, reducing memory and computational costs. Furthermore, the representation is stratified: low level information not necessary to capture higher level dynamics is not passed to the next layer. Also, it naturally provides a noisy identity mapping of the input, facilitating the initial stages of training. While the approach does not solve the problem of blur, it prevents its magnification by mitigating the propagation of errors. Moreover, a trained network can be deconstructed to analyse the role of each layer in the final predictions, making the model more explainable. Since the states are shared, the architecture can be thought of as a recurrent AE folded in half, with encoder and decoder layers overlapping. We call our method Folded Recurrent Neural Network (fRNN).

Our main contributions are: (1) A new shared-state recurrent AE with lower memory and computational costs. (2) Mitigation of error propagation through time. (3) It naturally provides an identity function during training. (4) Model explainability and optimisation through layer removal. (5) Demonstration of representation stratification.

2   Related Work

Video prediction is usually approached using deep recurrent models. While initial proposals focused on predicting small patches [13,17], it is now common to generate the whole frame based on the previous ones.

---

[1] Code available at https://github.com/moliusimon/frnn.

Building Blocks. Due to the characteristics of the problem, an AE setting has been widely used [3,5,14,22,24]: the encoder extracts information from the input and the decoder produces new frames. Usually, encoder and decoder are CNNs that tackle the spatial dimension. LSTMs are commonly used to handle the temporal dynamics and project the representations into the future. Some works compute the temporal dynamics at the deep representation bridging the encoder and decoder [2,3,14,15]. Others jointly handle space and time by using Convolutional LSTMs [5,8,9,11,15] (or GRUs, as in our case), which use convolutional kernels at their gates. For instance, Lotter *et al.* [11] use a recurrent residual network with ConvLSTMs where each layer minimises the discrepancies from previous block predictions. Common variations also include a conditional term to guide the temporal transform, such as a time differential [25] or prior knowledge of scene events, reducing the space of possible futures. Oh *et al.* [14] predict future frames on Atari games conditioning on the player action. Some works propose such action conditioned models foreseeing an application for autonomous agents learning in an unsupervised fashion [5,8]. Finn *et al.* [5] condition their predictions for a physical system on the actions taken by a robotic arm interacting with the scene. The method was recently applied to task planning [4] and adapted to stochastic future video prediction [1].

Bridge Connections. Introducing bridge connections (connections between equivalent layers of the encoder and decoder) is also common [2,5,10,24]. This allows for a stratified representation of the input sequence, reducing the capacity needs of subsequent layers. *Video Ladder Networks* (VLN) [2] use a conv. AE where pairs of convolutions are grouped into residual blocks. Bridge connections are added between corresponding blocks, both directly and by using a recurrent bridge layer. This topology was further extended with *Recurrent Ladder Networks* (RLN) [16], where the recurrent bridge connections were removed, and the residual blocks replaced by recurrent layers. We propose an alternative to bridge connections by completely sharing the state between encoder and decoder.

Prediction Atom. Most of the proposed architectures for future frame prediction work at the pixel level. However, some models have been designed to predict motion and use it to project the last frame into the future. These may generate optical flow maps [10,15] or conv. kernels [7,27]. Other methods propose mapping the input sequence onto predefined feature spaces, such as affine transforms [23] or human pose vectors [26]. These systems use sequences of such features to generate the next frame at the pixel level.

Loss and GANs. Commonly used loss functions such as L2 or MSE tend to average the space of possible futures. For this reason, some works [9,12,24,26] propose using Generative Adversarial Networks (GAN) [6] to aid in the generation of realistic looking frames and coherent sequences. Mathieu *et al.* [12] use a plain multi-scale CNN in an adversarial setting and propose the Gradient Difference Loss to sharpen the predictions.

Disentangled Motion/Content. Some authors encode content and motion separately. Villegas *et al.* [24] use an AE architecture with a two-stream encoder: for motion, a CNN + LSTM encodes difference images; for appearance, a CNN encodes the last input frame. In a similar fashion, Denton *et al.* [3] use two separate encoders and an adversarial setting to obtain a disentangled representation of content and motion. Alternatively, some works predict motion and content in parallel to benefit from the combined strengths of both tasks. While Sedaghat *et al.* [19] propose using a single representation with a dual objective (optical flow and future frame prediction), Liang *et al.* [9] use a dual GAN setting and use predicted motion to refine the future frame prediction.

Feedback Predictions. Finally, most recurrent models are based on the use of feedback predictions: they input previous predictions to generate subsequent frames. If not handled properly, this may cause errors to accumulate and magnify over time. Our model mitigates this by enabling encoder and decoder to be executed any number of times independently. This is similar to the proposal by Srivastava *et al.* [22], which uses a recurrent AE approach where an input sequence is encoded and its state copied into the decoder. The decoder is then applied to generate a given number of frames. However, it is limited to a single recurrent layer at each part.

Here, stochastic video prediction is not considered. Such models learn and sample from a space of possible futures to generate the following frames. This reduces prediction blur by preventing the averaging of possible futures. fRNN could be extended to perform stochastic sampling by adding an inference model similar to that in [1] during training. Samples drawn from the predicted distribution would be placed into the deepest state of the dGRU stack. However, this would make it difficult to analyse the contribution of dGRU layers to the mitigation and recovery from blur propagation.

3 Proposed Method

We propose an architecture based on recurrent conv. AEs to deal with the network capacity and error propagation problems for future video prediction. It is built by stacking multiple double-mapping GRU layers, which allow for a bidirectional flow of information between input and output: they consider the input as a recurrent state and update it using an extra set of gates. These are then stacked, forming an encoder and decoder using, respectively, the forward and backward gates (Fig. 1). We call this architecture Folded Recurrent Neural Network (fRNN). Because of the state sharing between encoder and decoder, the topology allows for: stratification of the representation, lower memory and computational requirements compared to regular recurrent AEs, mitigated propagation of errors, and increased explainability through layer removal.

3.1 Double-Mapping Gated Recurrent Units

GRUs have their state fully exposed as output. This allows us to define a bidirectional mapping between input and output by replicating the logic gates of the GRU layer. To do so, we consider the input as a state. Lets define the output of a GRU at layer l and time step t as $h_t^l = f_f^l(h_t^{l-1}, h_{t-1}^l)$ given an input h_t^{l-1} and its state at the previous time step h_{t-1}^l. A second set of weights can be used to define an inverse mapping $h_t^{l-1} = f_b^l(h_t^l, h_{t-1}^{l-1})$ using the output of the forward function at the current time step to update its input, which is treated as the hidden state of the inverse function. This is illustrated in Fig. 1. We will refer to this bidirectional mapping as a double-mapping GRU (dGRU).

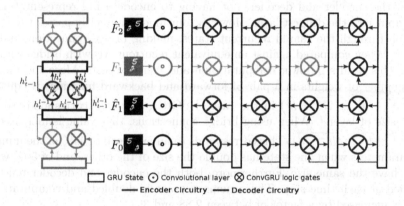

Fig. 1. Left: Scheme of a dGRU. Shadowed areas illustrate additional dGRU layers. Right: fRNN topology. State cells are shared between encoder and decoder, creating a bidirectional state mapping. Shadowed areas represent unnecessary circuitry: re-encoding of the predictions is avoided due to the decoder updating all the states.

3.2 Folded Recurrent Neural Network

By stacking multiple dGRUs, a recurrent AE is obtained. Given n dGRUs, the encoder is defined by the set of forward functions $E = \{f_f^1, \ldots, f_f^n\}$ and the decoder by the set of backward functions $D = \{f_b^n, \ldots, f_b^1\}$. This is illustrated in Fig. 1, and is equivalent to a recurrent AE, but with shared states, having 3 main advantages: (1) It is not necessary to feed the predictions back into the network in order to generate the following predictions. Because of state sharing, the decoder already updates all the states except for the bridge state between encoder and decoder, which is updated by applying the last layer of the encoder before decoding. The shadowed area in Fig. 1 shows the section of the computational graph that is not required when performing multiple sequential predictions. For the same reason, when considering multiple sequential elements before prediction, only the encoder is required. (2) Since the network updates its states from the higher level representations to the lowest ones during prediction, errors introduced at a given layer are not propagated into deeper layers, leaving higher-level dynamics unaffected. (3) The model implicitly provides a noisy identity function during training: the input state of the first dGRU layer is either the input image itself, when preceded by conv. Layers, or an over-complete representation of the same. A noise signal is then introduced to the representation by the backward function of the untrained first dGRU layer. This is exemplified in Fig. 7, when all dGRU layers are removed. As shown in Sect. 4.3, this helps the model to converge on MMNIST: when the same background is shared across instances, it prevents the model from killing the gradients by adjusting the biases to match the background and setting the weights to zero.

This approach shares some similarities with VLN [2] and RLN [16]. As with them, part of the information can be passed directly between corresponding layers of the encoder and decoder, not having to encode a full representation of the input into the deepest layer. However, our model implicitly passes the information through the shared recurrent states, making bridge connections unnecessary. When compared against an equivalent recurrent AE with bridge connections, this results in lower computational and memory costs. More specifically, the number of weights in a pair of forward and backward functions is equal to $3(\overline{h^{l-1}}^2 + \overline{h^l}^2 + 2\overline{h^{l-1}}\,\overline{h^l})$ in the case of dGRU, where $\overline{h^l}$ corresponds to the state size of layer l. When using bridge connections, that value is increased to $3(\overline{h^{l-1}}^2 + \overline{h^l}^2 + 4\overline{h^{l-1}}\,\overline{h^l})$. This corresponds to an overhead of 44% in the number of parameters when one state has double the size of the other, and of 50% when they have the same size. Furthermore, both the encoder and decoder must be applied at each time step. Thus, memory usage is doubled and computational cost is increased by a factor of between 2.88 and 3.

3.3 Training Folded RNNs

We propose a training approach for fRNNs that exploits their ability to skip the encoder or decoder at a given time step. First g ground truth frames are passed to the encoder. The decoder is then applied p times, producing p predictions. This uses up only half the memory: either encoder or decoder is applied at each step, never both. This has the same advantage as the approach by Srivastava [22], where recurrently applying the decoder without further ground truth inputs encourages the network to learn video dynamics. This also prevents the network from learning an identity model, i.e. copying the last input to the output.

4 Experiments

In this section, we first discuss the data, evaluation protocol, and methods. We then provide quantitative and qualitative evaluations. We finish with a brief analysis on the stratification of the sequence representation among dGRU layers.

4.1 Data and Evaluation Protocol

Three datasets of different complexity are considered: Moving MNIST (MMNIST) [22], KTH [18], and UCF101 [21]. MMNIST consists of 64×64 grayscale sequences of length 20 displaying pairs of digits moving around the image. We generated a million training samples by randomly sampling pairs of digits and trajectories. The test set is fixed and contains 10000 sequences. KTH consists of 600 videos of 15–20 seconds with 25 subjects performing 6 actions in 4 different settings. The videos are grayscale, at a resolution of 120×160 pixels and 25 fps. The dataset has been split into subjects 1 to 16 for training, and 17 to 25 for testing, resulting in 383 and 216 sequences, respectively. Frame size is reduced to 64×80 by removing 5 pixels from the left and right borders and using bilinear interpolation. UCF101 displays 101 actions, such as playing instruments, weight lifting or sports. It is the most challenging dataset considered, with a high intra-class variability. It contains 9950 training and 3361 test sequences. These are RGB at a resolution of 320×240 pixels and 25 fps. The frame size is reduced to 64×85 and the frame rate halved to magnify frame differences.

Table 1. Parameters of the topology used for the experiments. The decoder applies the same topology in reverse, using nearest neighbours interpolation and transposed convolutions to revert the pooling and convolutional layers.

	Conv 1	Conv 2	Pool 1	dGRU 1	dGRU 2	Pool 2	dGRU 3	dGRU 4	Pool 3	dGRU 5	dGRU 6	Pool 4	dGRU 7	dGRU 8
Num. Units	32	64	-	128	128	-	256	256	-	512	512	-	256	256
Kernel size	5 × 5	5 × 5	2 × 2	5 × 5	5 × 5	2 × 2	5 × 5	5 × 5	2 × 2	3 × 3	3 × 3	2 × 2	3 × 3	3 × 3
Stride	1	1	2	1	1	2	1	1	2	1	1	2	1	1
Activation	tanh	tanh	-	sigmoid & tanh		-	sigmoid & tanh		-	sigmoid & tanh		-	sigmoid & tanh	

All methods are tested using 10 input frames to generate the following 10 frames. We use 3 common metrics for video prediction analysis: Mean Squared Error (MSE), Peak Signal-to-Noise Ratio (PSNR), and Structural Dissimilarity (DSSIM). MSE and PSNR are objective measurements of reconstruction quality. DSSIM is a measure of the perceived quality. For DSSIM we use a Gaussian sliding window of size 11×11 and $\sigma = 1.5$.

4.2 Methods

The proposed method was trained using RMSProp with a learning rate of 0.0001 and a batch size of 12, sampling a random sub-sequence at each epoch. Weights were orthogonally initialised and biases set to 0. For testing, all sub-sequences of length 20 were considered. Our network topology consists of two convolutional layers followed by 8 convolutional dGRU layers, applying a 2×2 max pooling every 2 layers. Topology details are shown in Table 1. The convolutional and max pooling layers are reversed by using transposed convolutions and nearest neighbours interpolation, respectively. We train with an L1 loss.

For evaluation, we include a stub baseline model predicting the last input frame, and a second baseline (RLadder) to evaluate the advantages of using state sharing. RLadder has the same topology as the fRNN model, but uses bridge connections instead of state sharing. Note that to keep the same state size on ConvGRU layers, using bridge connections doubles the memory size and almost triples the computational cost (Sect. 3.2). This is similar to how RLN [16] works, but using regular ConvGRU layers in the decoder. We also compare against Srivastava [22] and Mathieu [12]. The former handles only the temporal dimension with LSTMs, while the latter uses a 3D-CNN, not providing memory management mechanisms. Next, we compare against Villegas [24], which, contrary to our proposal, uses feedback predictions. Finally, we compare against Lotter *et al.* [11] which is based on residual error reduction. All of them were adapted to train using 10 frames as input and predicting the next 10, using the topologies and parameters defined by the authors.

4.3   Quantitative Analysis

The first row of Fig. 2 displays the results for the MMNIST dataset for the considered methods. Mean scores are shown in Table 2. fRNN performs best on all time steps and metrics, followed by Srivastava *et al.* [22]. These two are the only methods to provide valid predictions on this dataset: Mathieu *et al.* [12] progressively blurs the digits, while the other methods predict a black frame. This is caused by a loss of gradient during the first training stages. On more complex datasets the methods start by learning an identity function, then refining the results. This is possible since in many sequences most of the frame remains unchanged. In the case of MMNIST, where the background is homogeneous, it is easier for the models to set the weights of the output layer to zero and set the biases to match the background colour. This truncates the gradient and prevents further learning. Srivastava *et al.* [22] use an auxiliary decoder to reconstruct the input frames, forcing the model to learn an identity function. This, as discussed at the end of Sect. 3.2, is implicitly handled in our method, giving an initial solution to improve on and preventing the models from learning a black image. In order to verify this effect, we pre-trained RLadder on the KTH dataset and then fine-tuned it on the MMNIST dataset. While KTH has different dynamics, the initial step to solve the problem remains: providing an identity function. As shown in Fig. 2 (dashed lines), this results in the model converging, with an accuracy comparable to Srivastava *et al.* [22] for the 3 evaluation metrics.

On the KTH dataset, Table 2 shows the best approach is our RLadder baseline followed by fRNN and Villegas *et al.* [24], both having similar results, but with Villegas *et al.* having slightly lower MSE and higher PSNR, and fRNN a lower DSSIM. While both approaches obtain comparable average results, the error increases faster over time in the case of Villegas *et al.* (second row in Fig. 2). Mathieu obtains good scores for MSE and PSNR, but has a much worse DSSIM.

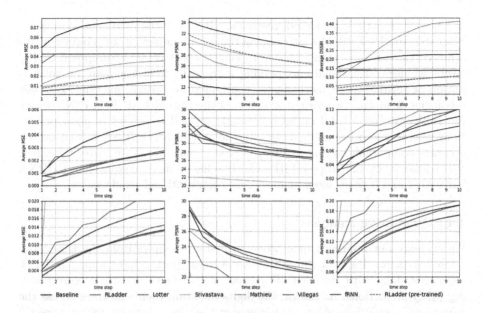

Fig. 2. Quantitative results on the considered datasets in terms of the number of time steps since the last input frame. From top to bottom: MMNIST, KTH, and UCF101. From left to right: MSE, PSNR, and DSSIM. For MMNIST, RLadder is pre-trained to learn an initial identity mapping, allowing it to converge.

For the UCF101 dataset, Table 2, our fRNN approach is the best performing for all 3 metrics. At third row of Fig. 5 one can see that Villegas *et al.* start out with results similar to fRNN on the first frame, but as in the case of KTH and MMNIST, the predictions degrade faster. Two methods display low performance in most cases. Lotter *et al.* work well for the first predicted frame in the case of KTH and UCF101, but the error rapidly increases on the following predictions. This is due to a magnification of prediction artefacts, making the method unable to predict multiple frames without supervision. In the case of Srivastava *et al.* the problem is about capacity: it uses fully connected LSTM layers, making the number of parameters explode quickly with the state cell size. This severely limits the representation capacity for complex datasets such as KTH and UCF101.

Table 2. Average results over 10 time steps.

	MMNIST			KTH			UCF101		
	MSE	PSNR	DSSIM	MSE	PSNR	DSSIM	MSE	PSNR	DSSIM
Baseline	0.06989	11.745	0.20718	0.00366	29.071	0.07900	0.01294	22.859	0.15043
RLadder	0.04254	13.857	0.13788	**0.00139**	**31.268**	**0.05945**	0.00918	23.558	0.13395
Lotter [11]	0.04161	13.968	0.13825	0.00309	28.424	0.09170	0.01550	19.869	0.21389
Srivastava [22]	0.01737	18.183	0.08164	0.00995	21.220	0.19860	0.14866	10.021	0.42555
Mathieu [12]	0.02748	15.969	0.29565	0.00180	29.341	0.10410	0.00926	22.781	0.16262
Villegas [24]	0.04254	13.857	0.13896	0.00165	30.946	0.07657	0.00940	23.457	0.14150
fRNN	**0.00947**	**21.386**	**0.04376**	0.00175	29.299	0.07251	**0.00908**	**23.872**	**0.13055**

Overall, for the considered methods, fRNN is the best performing on MMINST and UCF101, the latter being the most complex of the 3 datasets. We achieved these results with a simple topology: apart from the proposed dGRU layers, we use conventional max pooling with an L1 loss. There are no normalisation or regularisation mechanisms, specialised activation functions, complex topologies or image transform operators. In the case of MMNIST, fRNN shows the ability to find a valid initial representation and converges to good predictions where most other methods fail. In the case of KTH, fRNN has an overall accuracy comparable to that of Villegas *et al.*, being more stable over time. It is only surpassed by the proposed RLadder baseline, a method equivalent to fRNN but with 2 and 3 times more memory and computational requirements.

4.4   Qualitative Analysis

We evaluate our approach qualitatively on some samples from the three considered datasets. Figure 3 shows the last 5 input frames from some MMNIST sequences along with the next 10 ground truth frames and their corresponding fRNN predictions. As shown, the digits maintain their sharpness across the sequence of predictions. Also, the bounces at the edges of the image are correctly predicted and the digits do not distort or deform when crossing each other. This shows the network internally encodes the appearance of each digit, facilitating their reconstruction after sharing the same region in the image plane.

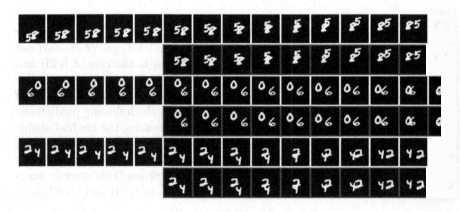

Fig. 3. fRNN predictions on MMNIST. First row for each sequence shows last 5 inputs and target frames. Yellow frames are model predictions.

Qualitative examples of fRNN predictions on the KTH dataset are shown in Fig. 4. It shows three actions: hand waving, walking, and boxing. The blur stops increasing after the first three predictions, generating plausible motions for the corresponding actions while background artefacts are not introduced. Although the movement patterns for each type of action have a wide range of variability on its trajectory, dGRU gives relatively sharp predictions for the limbs. The first and third examples also show the ability of the model to recover from blur. The blur slightly increases for the arms while the action is performed, but decreases again as these reach the final position.

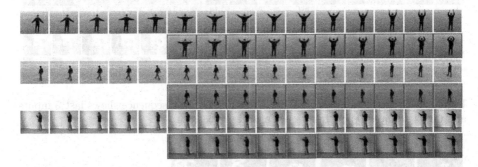

Fig. 4. fRNN predictions on KTH. First row for each sequence shows last 5 inputs and target frames. Yellow frames are model predictions.

Figure 5 shows fRNN predictions on the UCF101 dataset. These correspond to two different physical exercises and a girl playing the piano. Common to all predictions, the static parts do not lose sharpness over time, and the background is properly reconstructed after an occlusion. The network correctly predicts actions with low variability, as shown in rows 1–2, where a repetitive movement is performed, and in the last row, where the girl recovers a correct body posture. Blur is introduced to these dynamic regions due to uncertainty, averaging the possible futures. The first row also shows an interesting behaviour: while the woman is standing up the upper body becomes blurry, but the frames sharpen again as the woman finishes her motion. Since the model does not propagate errors to deeper layers nor makes use of previous predictions for the following ones, the introduction of blur does not imply it will be propagated. In this example, while the middle motion could have multiple predictions depending on the movement pace and the inclination of the body, the final body pose has lower uncertainty.

In Fig. 6 we compare predictions from the proposed approach against the RLadder baseline and other state of the art methods. For the MMNIST dataset we do not consider Villegas et al. and Lotter et al. since these methods fail to successfully converge and they predict a sequence of black frames. From the rest of approaches, fRNN obtains the best predictions, with little blur or distortion. The RLadder baseline is the second best approach. It does not introduce blur, but heavily deforms the digits after they cross. Srivastava et al. and Mathieu et al. both accumulate blur over time, but while the former does so to a smaller degree, the latter makes the digits unrecognisable after five frames.

Fig. 5. fRNN predictions on UCF101. First row for each sequence shows last 5 inputs and target frames. Yellow frames are model predictions.

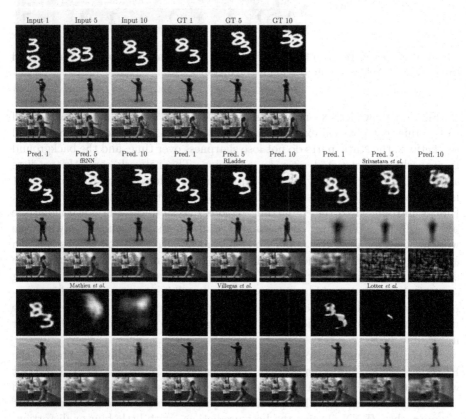

Fig. 6. Predictions at 1, 5, and 10 time steps from the last ground truth frame. RLadder predictions on MMNIST are from the model pre-trained on KTH.

For KTH, Villegas *et al.* obtains outstanding qualitative results. It predicts plausible dynamics and maintains the sharpness of both the individual and background. Both fRNN and RLadder follow closely, predicting plausible dynamics, but not being as good at maintaining the sharpness of the individual. On UCF101, our model obtains the best predictions, with little blur or distortion compared to the other methods. The second best is Villegas *et al.*, successfully capturing the movement patterns but introducing more blur and important distortions on the last frame. When looking at the background, fRNN proposes a plausible initial estimate and progressively completes it as the woman moves. On the other hand, Villegas *et al.* modifies already generated regions as more background is uncovered, producing an unrealistic sequence. Srivastava *et al.* and Lotter *et al.* fail on both KTH and UCF101. Srivastava *et al.* heavily distort the frames. As discussed in Sect. 4.3, this is due to the use of fully connected recurrent layers, which constrains the state size and prevents the model from encoding relevant information on complex scenarios. In the case of Lotter *et al.*, it makes good predictions for the first frame, but rapidly accumulates artefacts.

4.5   Representation Stratification Analysis

Here we analyse the stratification of the sequence representation among dGRU layers. Because dGRU units allow for a bidirectional mapping between states, it is possible to remove the deepest layers of a trained model in order to check how the predictions are affected, providing an insight on the dynamics captured by each layer. To our knowledge, this is the first topology allowing for a direct observation of the behaviour encoded on each layer.

In Fig. 7, the same MMNIST sequences are predicted multiple times, removing a layer each time. The analysed model consists of 2 convolutional layers and 8 dGRU layers. Firstly, removing the last 2 dGRU layers has no significant impact on prediction. This shows that, for this dataset, the network has a higher capacity than required. Further removing layers results in a progressive loss of behaviours, from more complex to simpler ones. This means information at a given level of abstraction is not encoded into higher level layers. When removing the third deepest dGRU layer, the digits stop bouncing at the edges, exiting the image. This indicates this layer encodes information on bouncing dynamics. When removing the next one, digits stop behaving consistently at the edges: parts of the digit bounce while others keep the previous trajectory. While this also has to do with bouncing dynamics, the layer seems to be in charge of recognising digits as single units following the same movement pattern. When removed, different segments of the digit are allowed to move as separate elements. Finally, with only 3–2 dGRU layers the digits are distorted in various ways. With only two layers left, the general linear dynamics are still captured by the model. By leaving a single dGRU layer, the linear dynamics are lost.

According to these results, the first two dGRU layers capture pixel-level movement dynamics. The next two aggregate the dynamics into single-trajectory components, preventing their distortion, and detect the collision of these components with image bounds. The fifth layer aggregates single-motion components into digits, forcing them to behave equally. This has the effect of preventing bounces, likely due to only one of the components reaching the edge of the image. The sixth dGRU layer provides coherent bouncing patterns for the digits.

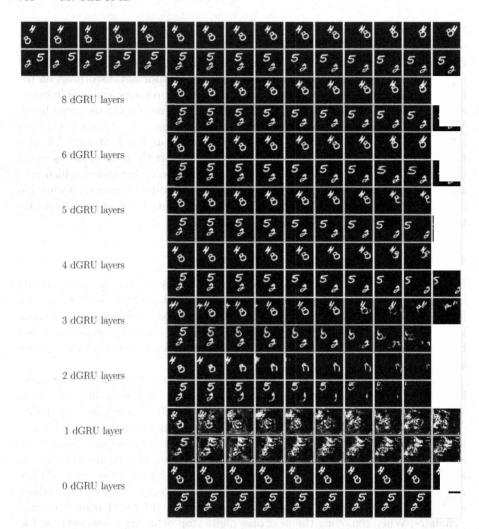

8 dGRU layers

6 dGRU layers

5 dGRU layers

4 dGRU layers

3 dGRU layers

2 dGRU layers

1 dGRU layer

0 dGRU layers

Fig. 7. Moving MNIST predictions with fRNN layer removal. Removing all dGRU layers (last row) leaves two convolutional layers and their transposed convolutions, providing an identity mapping.

5   Conclusions

We have presented Folded Recurrent Neural Networks, a new recurrent architecture for video prediction with lower computational and memory costs compared to equivalent recurrent AE models. This is achieved by using the proposed double-mapping GRUs, which horizontally pass information between the encoder and decoder. This eliminates the need for using the entire AE at any given step: only the encoder or decoder is executed for both input encoding and prediction, respectively. It also facilitates the convergence by naturally providing a noisy identity function during training. We evaluated our approach on three video datasets, outperforming state of the art techniques on MMNIST and UCF101, and obtaining competitive results on KTH with 2 and 3 times less memory usage and computational cost than the best scored approach. Qualitatively, the model can limit and recover from blur by preventing its propagation from low to high level dynamics. We also demonstrated stratification of the representation, topology optimisation, and model explainability through layer removal. Layers have been shown to successively introduce more complex behaviours: removing a layer eliminates its behaviours but leaves lower-level ones untouched.

Acknowledgements. The work of Marc Oliu is supported by the FI-DGR 2016 fellowship, granted by the Universities and Research Secretary of the Knowledge and Economy Department of the Generalitat de Catalunya. Also, the work of Javier Selva is supported by the APIF 2018 fellowship, granted by the Universitat de Barcelona. This work has been partially supported by the Spanish project TIN2016-74946-P (MINECO/FEDER, UE) and CERCA Programme/Generalitat de Catalunya. We gratefully acknowledge the support of NVIDIA Corporation with the donation of the GPU used for this research.

References

1. Babaeizadeh, M., Finn, C., Erhan, D., Campbell, R.H., Levine, S.: Stochastic variational video prediction. In: 6th International Conference on Learning Representations (2018)
2. Cricri, F., Honkala, M., Ni, X., Aksu, E., Gabbouj, M.: Video ladder networks. arXiv preprint arXiv:1612.01756 (2016)
3. Denton, E.L., Birodkar, V.: Unsupervised learning of disentangled representations from video. In: Guyon, I., et al. (eds.) Advances in Neural Information Processing Systems, vol. 30, pp. 4417–4426. Curran Associates, Inc. (2017)
4. Ebert, F., Finn, C., Lee, A.X., Levine, S.: Self-supervised visual planning with temporal skip connections. arXiv preprint arXiv:1710.05268 (2017)
5. Finn, C., Goodfellow, I., Levine, S.: Unsupervised learning for physical interaction through video prediction. In: Lee, D., Sugiyama, M., Luxburg, U., Guyon, I., Garnett, R. (eds.) Advances in Neural Information Processing Systems, vol. 29, pp. 64–72. Curran Associates, Inc. (2016)
6. Goodfellow, I., et al.: Generative adversarial nets. In: Ghahramani, Z., Welling, M., Cortes, C., Lawrence, N., Weinberger, K. (eds.) Advances in Neural Information Processing Systems, vol. 27, pp. 2672–2680. Curran Associates, Inc. (2014)
7. Jia, X., De Brabandere, B., Tuytelaars, T., Gool, L.V.: Dynamic filter networks. In: Lee, D.D., Sugiyama, M., Luxburg, U.V., Guyon, I., Garnett, R. (eds.) Advances in Neural Information Processing Systems, vol. 29, pp. 667–675. Curran Associates, Inc. (2016)
8. Kalchbrenner, N., et al.: Video pixel networks. In: Precup, D., Teh, Y.W. (eds.) Proceedings of the 34th International Conference on Machine Learning. Proceedings of Machine Learning Research, vol. 70, pp. 1771–1779. PMLR (2017)
9. Liang, X., Lee, L., Dai, W., Xing, E.P.: Dual motion gan for future-flow embedded video prediction. In: Proceedings of the International Conference on Computer Vision, pp. 1762–1770. IEEE, Curran Associates, Inc. (2017)

10. Liu, Z., Yeh, R., Tang, X., Liu, Y., Agarwala, A.: Video frame synthesis using deep voxel flow. In: Proceedings of the International Conference on Computer Vision. IEEE, Curran Associates, Inc. (2017). https://doi.org/10.1109/ICCV.2017.478
11. Lotter, W., Kreiman, G., Cox, D.: Deep predictive coding networks for video prediction and unsupervised learning. In: International Conference on Learning Representations (2016)
12. Mathieu, M., Couprie, C., LeCun, Y.: Deep multi-scale video prediction beyond mean square error. In: International Conference on Learning Representations (ICLR) (2016)
13. Michalski, V., Memisevic, R., Konda, K.: Modeling deep temporal dependencies with recurrent grammar cells. In: Ghahramani, Z., Welling, M., Cortes, C., Lawrence, N.D., Weinberger, K.Q. (eds.) Advances in Neural Information Processing Systems, vol. 27, pp. 1925–1933. Curran Associates, Inc. (2014)
14. Oh, J., Guo, X., Lee, H., Lewis, R.L., Singh, S.: Action-conditional video prediction using deep networks in atari games. In: Cortes, C., Lawrence, N., Lee, D., Sugiyama, M., Garnett, R. (eds.) Advances in Neural Information Processing Systems, vol. 28, pp. 2845–2853. Curran Associates, Inc. (2015)
15. Patraucean, V., Handa, A., Cipolla, R.: Spatio-temporal video autoencoder with differentiable memory. In: International Conference on Learning Representations Workshops (2015)
16. Prémont-Schwarz, I., Ilin, A., Hao, T., Rasmus, A., Boney, R., Valpola, H.: Recurrent ladder networks. In: Guyon, I., et al. (eds.) Advances in Neural Information Processing Systems, vol. 30, pp. 6009–6019. Curran Associates, Inc. (2017)
17. Ranzato, M., Szlam, A., Bruna, J., Mathieu, M., Collobert, R., Chopra, S.: Video (language) modeling: a baseline for generative models of natural videos. arXiv preprint arXiv:1412.6604 (2014)
18. Schuldt, C., Laptev, I., Caputo, B.: Recognizing human actions: a local SVM approach. In: Kittler, J., Petrou, M., Nixon, M.S. (eds.) Proceedings of the 17th International Conference on Pattern Recognition, vol. 3, pp. 32–36. IEEE (2004)
19. Sedaghat, N., Zolfaghari, M., Brox, T.: Hybrid learning of optical flow and next frame prediction to boost optical flow in the wild. arXiv preprint arXiv:1612.03777 (2016)
20. SHI, X., Chen, Z., Wang, H., Yeung, D.Y., Wong, W.k., WOO, W.c.: Convolutional lstm network: a machine learning approach for precipitation nowcasting. In: Cortes, C., Lawrence, N., Lee, D., Sugiyama, M., Garnett, R. (eds.) Advances in Neural Information Processing Systems, vol. 28, pp. 802–810. Curran Associates, Inc. (2015)
21. Soomro, K., Zamir, A.R., Shah, M.: Ucf101: A dataset of 101 human actions classes from videos in the wild. arXiv preprint arXiv:1212.0402 (2012)
22. Srivastava, N., Mansimov, E., Salakhudinov, R.: Unsupervised learning of video representations using lstms. In: Bach, F., Blei, D. (eds.) Proceedings of the 32nd International Conference on Machine Learning. Proceedings of Machine Learning Research, vol. 37, pp. 843–852. PMLR (2015)
23. Van Amersfoort, J., Kannan, A., Ranzato, M., Szlam, A., Tran, D., Chintala, S.: Transformation-based models of video sequences. arXiv preprint arXiv:1701.08435 (2017)
24. Villegas, R., Yang, J., Hong, S., Lin, X., Lee, H.: Decomposing motion and content for natural video sequence prediction. In: 5th International Conference on Learning Representations (2017)

25. Vukotić, V., Pintea, S.L., Raymond, C., Gravier, G., Van Gemert, J.: One-step time-dependent future video frame prediction with a convolutional encoder-decoder neural network. In: Netherlands Conference on Computer Vision (2017)
26. Walker, J., Marino, K., Gupta, A., Hebert, M.: The pose knows: video forecasting by generating pose futures. In: Proceedings of the International Conference on Computer Vision, pp. 3332–3341. IEEE, Curran Associates, Inc. (2017). https://doi.org/10.1109/ICCV.2017.361
27. Xue, T., Wu, J., Bouman, K., Freeman, B.: Visual dynamics: probabilistic future frame synthesis via cross convolutional networks. In: Lee, D.D., Sugiyama, M., Luxburg, U.V., Guyon, I., Garnett, R. (eds.) Advances in Neural Information Processing Systems, vol. 29, pp. 91–99. Curran Associates, Inc. (2016)

Matching and Recognition

CornerNet: Detecting
Objects as Paired Keypoints

Hei Law$^{(\boxtimes)}$ⓘ and Jia Dengⓘ

University of Michigan, Ann Arbor, USA
{heilaw,jiadeng}@umich.edu

Abstract. We propose CornerNet, a new approach to object detection where we detect an object bounding box as a pair of keypoints, the top-left corner and the bottom-right corner, using a single convolution neural network. By detecting objects as paired keypoints, we eliminate the need for designing a set of anchor boxes commonly used in prior single-stage detectors. In addition to our novel formulation, we introduce corner pooling, a new type of pooling layer that helps the network better localize corners. Experiments show that CornerNet achieves a 42.1% AP on MS COCO, outperforming all existing one-stage detectors.

Keyword: Object detection

1 Introduction

Object detectors based on convolutional neural networks (ConvNets) [15,20,36] have achieved state-of-the-art results on various challenging benchmarks [8,9, 24]. A common component of state-of-the-art approaches is anchor boxes [25, 32], which are boxes of various sizes and aspect ratios that serve as detection candidates. Anchor boxes are extensively used in one-stage detectors [10,23,25, 31], which can achieve results highly competitive with two-stage detectors [11–13,32] while being more efficient. One-stage detectors place anchor boxes densely over an image and generate final box predictions by scoring anchor boxes and refining their coordinates through regression.

But the use of anchor boxes has two drawbacks. First, we typically need a very large set of anchor boxes, e.g. more than 40k in DSSD [10] and more than 100k in RetinaNet [23]. This is because the detector is trained to classify whether each anchor box sufficiently overlaps with a ground truth box, and a large number of anchor boxes is needed to ensure sufficient overlap with most ground truth boxes. As a result, only a tiny fraction of anchor boxes will overlap with ground truth; this creates a huge imbalance between positive and negative anchor boxes and slows down training [23].

Second, the use of anchor boxes introduces many hyperparameters and design choices. These include how many boxes, what sizes, and what aspect ratios. Such choices have largely been made via ad-hoc heuristics, and can become even more

© Springer Nature Switzerland AG 2018
V. Ferrari et al. (Eds.): ECCV 2018, LNCS 11218, pp. 765–781, 2018.
https://doi.org/10.1007/978-3-030-01264-9_45

complicated when combined with multiscale architectures where a single network makes separate predictions at multiple resolutions, with each scale using different features and its own set of anchor boxes [10, 23, 25].

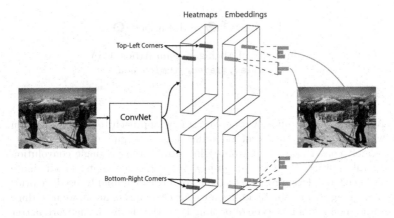

Fig. 1. We detect an object as a pair of bounding box corners grouped together. A convolutional network outputs a heatmap for all top-left corners, a heatmap for all bottom-right corners, and an embedding vector for each detected corner. The network is trained to predict similar embeddings for corners that belong to the same object.

In this paper we introduce CornerNet, a new one-stage approach to object detection that does away with anchor boxes. We detect an object as a pair of keypoints—the top-left corner and bottom-right corner of the bounding box. We use a single convolutional network to predict a heatmap for the top-left corners of all instances of the same object category, a heatmap for all bottom-right corners, and an embedding vector for each detected corner. The embeddings serve to group a pair of corners that belong to the same object—the network is trained to predict similar embeddings for them. Our approach greatly simplifies the output of the network and eliminates the need for designing anchor boxes. Our approach is inspired by the associative embedding method proposed by Newell et al. [27], who detect and group keypoints in the context of multiperson human-pose estimation. Figure 1 illustrates the overall pipeline of our approach.

Fig. 2. Often there is no local evidence to determine the location of a bounding box corner. We address this issue by proposing a new type of pooling layer.

Another novel component of CornerNet is *corner pooling*, a new type of pooling layer that helps a convolutional network better localize corners of bounding boxes. A corner of a bounding box is often outside the object—consider the case of a circle as well as the examples in Fig. 2. In such cases a corner cannot be localized based on local evidence. Instead, to determine whether there is a top-left corner at a pixel location, we need to look horizontally towards the right for the topmost boundary of the object, and look vertically towards the bottom for the leftmost boundary. This motivates our corner pooling layer: it takes in two feature maps; at each pixel location it max-pools all feature vectors to the right from the first feature map, max-pools all feature vectors directly below from the second feature map, and then adds the two pooled results together. An example is shown in Fig. 3.

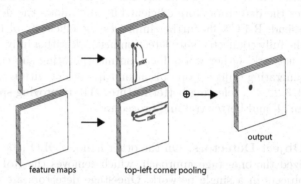

Fig. 3. Corner pooling: for each channel, we take the maximum values *(red dots)* in two directions *(red lines)*, each from a separate feature map, and add the two maximums together *(blue dot)*. (Color figure online)

We hypothesize two reasons why detecting corners would work better than bounding box centers or proposals. First, the center of a box can be harder to localize because it depends on all 4 sides of the object, whereas locating a corner depends on 2 sides and is thus easier, and even more so with corner pooling, which encodes some explicit prior knowledge about the definition of corners. Second, corners provide a more efficient way of densely discretizing the space of boxes: we just need $O(wh)$ corners to represent $O(w^2h^2)$ possible anchor boxes.

We demonstrate the effectiveness of CornerNet on MS COCO [24]. CornerNet achieves a 42.1% AP, outperforming all existing one-stage detectors. In addition, through ablation studies we show that corner pooling is critical to the superior performance of CornerNet. Code is available at https://github.com/umich-vl/CornerNet.

2   Related Works

Two-Stage Object Detectors. Two-stage approach was first introduced and popularized by R-CNN [12]. Two-stage detectors generate a sparse set of regions of interest (RoIs) and classify each of them by a network. R-CNN generates RoIs using a low level vision algorithm [41,47]. Each region is then extracted from the image and processed by a ConvNet independently, which creates lots of redundant computations. Later, SPP [14] and Fast-RCNN [11] improve R-CNN by designing a special pooling layer that pools each region from feature maps instead. However, both still rely on separate proposal algorithms and cannot be trained end-to-end. Faster-RCNN [32] does away low level proposal algorithms by introducing a region proposal network (RPN), which generates proposals from a set of pre-determined candidate boxes, usually known as anchor boxes. This not only makes the detectors more efficient but also allows the detectors to be trained end-to-end. R-FCN [6] further improves the efficiency of Faster-RCNN by replacing the fully connected sub-detection network with a fully convolutional sub-detection network. Other works focus on incorporating sub-category information [42], generating object proposals at multiple scales with more contextual information [1,3,22,35], selecting better features [44], improving speed [21], cascade procedure [4] and better training procedure [37].

One-Stage Object Detectors. On the other hand, YOLO [30] and SSD [25] have popularized the one-stage approach, which removes the RoI pooling step and detects objects in a single network. One-stage detectors are usually more computationally efficient than two-stage detectors while maintaining competitive performance on different challenging benchmarks.

SSD places anchor boxes densely over feature maps from multiple scales, directly classifies and refines each anchor box. YOLO predicts bounding box coordinates directly from an image, and is later improved in YOLO9000 [31] by switching to anchor boxes. DSSD [10] and RON [19] adopt networks similar to the hourglass network [28], enabling them to combine low-level and high-level features via skip connections to predict bounding boxes more accurately. However, these one-stage detectors are still outperformed by the two-stage detectors until the introduction of RetinaNet [23]. In [23], the authors suggest that the dense anchor boxes create a huge imbalance between positive and negative anchor boxes during training. This imbalance causes the training to be inefficient and hence the performance to be suboptimal. They propose a new loss, Focal Loss, to dynamically adjust the weights of each anchor box and show that their one-stage detector can outperform the two-stage detectors. RefineDet [45] proposes to filter the anchor boxes to reduce the number of negative boxes, and to coarsely adjust the anchor boxes.

DeNet [39] is a two-stage detector which generates RoIs without using anchor boxes. It first determines how likely each location belongs to either the top-left, top-right, bottom-left or bottom-right corner of a bounding box. It then generates RoIs by enumerating all possible corner combinations, and follows the standard two-stage approach to classify each RoI. Our approach is very different from DeNet. First, DeNet does not identify if two corners are from the same objects and relies on a sub-detection network to reject poor RoIs. In contrast, our approach is a one-stage approach which detects and groups the corners using a single ConvNet. Second, DeNet selects features at manually determined locations relative to a region for classification, while our approach does not require any feature selection step. Third, we introduce corner pooling, a novel type of layer to enhance corner detection.

Our approach is inspired by Newell et al. work [27] on Associative Embedding in the context of multi-person pose estimation. Newell et al. propose an approach that detects and groups human joints in a single network. In their approach each detected human joint has an embedding vector. The joints are grouped based on the distances between their embeddings. To the best of our knowledge, we are the first to formulate the task of object detection as a task of detecting and grouping corners simultaneously. Another novelty of ours is the corner pooling layers that help better localize the corners. We also significantly modify the hourglass architecture and add our novel variant of focal loss [23] to help better train the network.

3 CornerNet

3.1 Overview

In CornerNet, we detect an object as a pair of keypoints—the top-left corner and bottom-right corner of the bounding box. A convolutional network predicts two sets of heatmaps to represent the locations of corners of different object categories, one set for the top-left corners and the other for the bottom-right corners. The network also predicts an embedding vector for each detected corner [27] such that the distance between the embeddings of two corners from the same object is small. To produce tighter bounding boxes, the network also predicts offsets to slightly adjust the locations of the corners. With the predicted heatmaps, embeddings and offsets, we apply a simple post-processing algorithm to obtain the final bounding boxes.

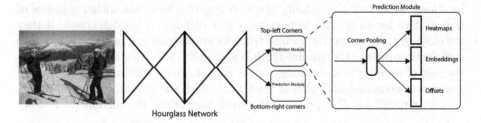

Fig. 4. Overview of CornerNet. The backbone network is followed by two prediction modules, one for the top-left corners and the other for the bottom-right corners. Using the predictions from both modules, we locate and group the corners.

Figure 4 provides an overview of CornerNet. We use the hourglass network [28] as the backbone network of CornerNet. The hourglass network is followed by two prediction modules. One module is for the top-left corners, while the other one is for the bottom-right corners. Each module has its own corner pooling module to pool features from the hourglass network before predicting the heatmaps, embeddings and offsets. Unlike many other object detectors, we do not use features from different scales to detect objects of different sizes. We only apply both modules to the output of the hourglass network.

3.2   Detecting Corners

We predict two sets of heatmaps, one for top-left corners and one for bottom-right corners. Each set of heatmaps has C channels, where C is the number of categories, and is of size $H \times W$. There is no background channel. Each channel is a binary mask indicating the locations of the corners for a class.

Fig. 5. "Ground-truth" heatmaps for training. Boxes *(green dotted rectangles)* whose corners are within the radii of the positive locations *(orange circles)* still have large overlaps with the ground-truth annotations *(red solid rectangles)*. (Color figure online)

For each corner, there is one ground-truth positive location, and all other locations are negative. During training, instead of equally penalizing negative locations, we reduce the penalty given to negative locations within a radius of the positive location. This is because a pair of false corner detections, if they are close to their respective ground truth locations, can still produce a box that sufficiently overlaps the ground-truth box (Fig. 5). We determine the radius by the size of an object by ensuring that a pair of points within the radius would generate a bounding box with at least t IoU with the ground-truth annotation (we set t to 0.7 in all experiments). Given the radius, the amount of penalty reduction is given by an unnormalized 2D Gaussian, $e^{-\frac{x^2+y^2}{2\sigma^2}}$, whose center is at the positive location and whose σ is 1/3 of the radius.

Let p_{cij} be the score at location (i, j) for class c in the predicted heatmaps, and let y_{cij} be the "ground-truth" heatmap augmented with the unnormalized Gaussians. We design a variant of focal loss [23]:

$$L_{det} = \frac{-1}{N} \sum_{c=1}^{C} \sum_{i=1}^{H} \sum_{j=1}^{W} \begin{cases} (1 - p_{cij})^{\alpha} \log(p_{cij}) & \text{if } y_{cij} = 1 \\ (1 - y_{cij})^{\beta} (p_{cij})^{\alpha} \log(1 - p_{cij}) & \text{otherwise} \end{cases} \tag{1}$$

where N is the number of objects in an image, and α and β are the hyperparameters which control the contribution of each point (we set α to 2 and β to 4 in all experiments). With the Gaussian bumps encoded in y_{cij}, the $(1 - y_{cij})$ term reduces the penalty around the ground truth locations.

Many networks [15,28] involve downsampling layers to gather global information and to reduce memory usage. When they are applied to an image fully convolutionally, the size of the output is usually smaller than the image. Hence, a location (x, y) in the image is mapped to the location $(\lfloor \frac{x}{n} \rfloor, \lfloor \frac{y}{n} \rfloor)$ in the heatmaps, where n is the downsampling factor. When we remap the locations from the heatmaps to the input image, some precision may be lost, which can greatly affect the IoU of small bounding boxes with their ground truths. To address this issue we predict location offsets to slightly adjust the corner locations before remapping them to the input resolution.

$$o_k = \left(\frac{x_k}{n} - \left\lfloor \frac{x_k}{n} \right\rfloor, \frac{y_k}{n} - \left\lfloor \frac{y_k}{n} \right\rfloor \right) \tag{2}$$

where o_k is the offset, x_k and y_k are the x and y coordinate for corner k. In particular, we predict one set of offsets shared by the top-left corners of all categories, and another set shared by the bottom-right corners. For training, we apply the smooth L1 Loss [11] at ground-truth corner locations:

$$L_{off} = \frac{1}{N} \sum_{k=1}^{N} \text{SmoothL1Loss}(o_k, \hat{o}_k) \tag{3}$$

3.3 Grouping Corners

Multiple objects may appear in an image, and thus multiple top-left and bottom-right corners may be detected. We need to determine if a pair of the top-left corner and bottom-right corner is from the same bounding box. Our approach is inspired by the Associative Embedding method proposed by Newell et al. [27] for the task of multi-person pose estimation. Newell et al. detect all human joints and generate an embedding for each detected joint. They group the joints based on the distances between the embeddings.

The idea of associative embedding is also applicable to our task. The network predicts an embedding vector for each detected corner such that if a top-left corner and a bottom-right corner belong to the same bounding box, the distance between their embeddings should be small. We can then group the corners based on the distances between the embeddings of the top-left and bottom-right corners. The actual values of the embeddings are unimportant. Only the distances between the embeddings are used to group the corners.

We follow Newell et al. [27] and use embeddings of 1 dimension. Let e_{t_k} be the embedding for the top-left corner of object k and e_{b_k} for the bottom-right corner. As in [26], we use the "pull" loss to train the network to group the corners and the "push" loss to separate the corners:

$$L_{pull} = \frac{1}{N} \sum_{k=1}^{N} \left[(e_{t_k} - e_k)^2 + (e_{b_k} - e_k)^2 \right], \tag{4}$$

$$L_{push} = \frac{1}{N(N-1)} \sum_{k=1}^{N} \sum_{\substack{j=1 \\ j \neq k}}^{N} \max \left(0, \Delta - |e_k - e_j| \right), \tag{5}$$

where e_k is the average of e_{t_k} and e_{b_k} and we set Δ to be 1 in all our experiments. Similar to the offset loss, we only apply the losses at the ground-truth corner location.

3.4   Corner Pooling

As shown in Fig. 2, there is often no local visual evidence for the presence of corners. To determine if a pixel is a top-left corner, we need to look horizontally towards the right for the topmost boundary of an object and vertically towards the bottom for the leftmost boundary. We thus propose *corner pooling* to better localize the corners by encoding explicit prior knowledge.

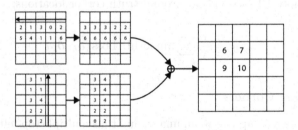

Fig. 6. The top-left corner pooling layer can be implemented very efficiently. We scan from left to right for the horizontal max-pooling and from bottom to top for the vertical max-pooling. We then add two max-pooled feature maps.

Suppose we want to determine if a pixel at location (i, j) is a top-left corner. Let f_t and f_l be the feature maps that are the inputs to the top-left corner pooling layer, and let $f_{t_{ij}}$ and $f_{l_{ij}}$ be the vectors at location (i, j) in f_t and f_l respectively. With $H \times W$ feature maps, the corner pooling layer first max-pools all feature vectors between (i, j) and (i, H) in f_t to a feature vector t_{ij}, and max-pools all feature vectors between (i, j) and (W, j) in f_l to a feature vector

l_{ij}. Finally, it adds t_{ij} and l_{ij} together. This computation can be expressed by the following equations:

$$t_{ij} = \begin{cases} \max\left(f_{t_{ij}}, t_{(i+1)j}\right) & \text{if } i < H \\ f_{t_{Hj}} & \text{otherwise} \end{cases} \tag{6}$$

$$l_{ij} = \begin{cases} \max\left(f_{l_{ij}}, l_{i(j+1)}\right) & \text{if } j < W \\ f_{l_{iW}} & \text{otherwise} \end{cases} \tag{7}$$

where we apply an elementwise max operation. Both t_{ij} and l_{ij} can be computed efficiently by dynamic programming as shown Fig. 6.

We define bottom-right corner pooling layer in a similar way. It max-pools all feature vectors between $(0, j)$ and (i, j), and all feature vectors between $(i, 0)$ and (i, j) before adding the pooled results. The corner pooling layers are used in the prediction modules to predict heatmaps, embeddings and offsets.

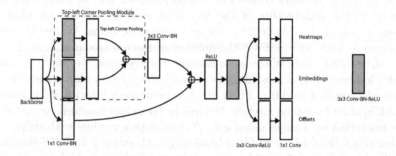

Fig. 7. The prediction module starts with a modified residual block, in which we replace the first convolution module with our corner pooling module. The modified residual block is then followed by a convolution module. We have multiple branches for predicting the heatmaps, embeddings and offsets.

The architecture of the prediction module is shown in Fig. 7. The first part of the module is a modified version of the residual block [15]. In this modified residual block, we replace the first 3×3 convolution module with a corner pooling module, which first processes the features from the backbone network by two 3×3 convolution modules[1] with 128 channels and then applies a corner pooling layer. Following the design of a residual block, we then feed the pooled features into a 3×3 Conv-BN layer with 256 channels and add back the projection shortcut. The modified residual block is followed by a 3×3 convolution module with 256 channels, and 3 Conv-ReLU-Conv layers to produce the heatmaps, embeddings and offsets.

---

[1] Unless otherwise specified, our convolution module consists of a convolution layer, a BN layer [17] and a ReLU layer.

3.5   Hourglass Network

CornerNet uses the hourglass network [28] as its backbone network. The hourglass network was first introduced for the human pose estimation task. It is a fully convolutional neural network that consists of one or more hourglass modules. An hourglass module first downsamples the input features by a series of convolution and max pooling layers. It then upsamples the features back to the original resolution by a series of upsampling and convolution layers. Since details are lost in the max pooling layers, skip layers are added to bring back the details to the upsampled features. The hourglass module captures both global and local features in a single unified structure. When multiple hourglass modules are stacked in the network, the hourglass modules can reprocess the features to capture higher-level of information. These properties make the hourglass network an ideal choice for object detection as well. In fact, many current detectors [10,19,22,35] already adopted networks similar to the hourglass network.

Our hourglass network consists of two hourglasses, and we make some modifications to the architecture of the hourglass module. Instead of using max pooling, we simply use stride 2 to reduce feature resolution. We reduce feature resolutions 5 times and increase the number of feature channels along the way $(256, 384, 384, 384, 512)$. When we upsample the features, we apply 2 residual modules followed by a nearest neighbor upsampling. Every skip connection also consists of 2 residual modules. There are 4 residual modules with 512 channels in the middle of an hourglass module. Before the hourglass modules, we reduce the image resolution by 4 times using a 7×7 convolution module with stride 2 and 128 channels followed by a residual block [15] with stride 2 and 256 channels.

Following [28], we also add intermediate supervision in training. However, we do not add back the intermediate predictions to the network as we find that this hurts the performance of the network. We apply a 3×3 Conv-BN module to both the input and output of the first hourglass module. We then merge them by element-wise addition followed by a ReLU and a residual block with 256 channels, which is then used as the input to the second hourglass module. The depth of the hourglass network is 104. Unlike many other state-of-the-art detectors, we only use the features from the last layer of the whole network to make predictions.

4   Experiments

4.1   Training Details

We implement CornerNet in PyTorch [29]. The network is randomly initialized under the default setting of PyTorch with no pretraining on any external dataset. As we apply focal loss, we follow [23] to set the biases in the convolution layers that predict the corner heatmaps. During training, we set the input resolution of the network to 511×511, which leads to an output resolution of 128×128. To reduce overfitting, we adopt standard data augmentation techniques including random horizontal flipping, random scaling, random cropping and random color jittering, which includes adjusting the brightness, saturation and contrast of an image. Finally, we apply PCA [20] to the input image.

We use Adam [18] to optimize the full training loss:

$$L = L_{det} + \alpha L_{pull} + \beta L_{push} + \gamma L_{off} \qquad (8)$$

where α, β and γ are the weights for the pull, push and offset loss respectively. We set both α and β to 0.1 and γ to 1. We find that 1 or larger values of α and β lead to poor performance. We use a batch size of 49 and train the network on 10 Titan X (PASCAL) GPUs (4 images on the master GPU, 5 images per GPU for the rest of the GPUs). To conserve GPU resources, in our ablation experiments, we train the networks for 250k iterations with a learning rate of 2.5×10^{-4}. When we compare our results with other detectors, we train the networks for an extra 250k iterations and reduce the learning rate to 2.5×10^{-5} for the last 50k iterations.

4.2 Testing Details

During testing, we use a simple post-processing algorithm to generate bounding boxes from the heatmaps, embeddings and offsets. We first apply non-maximal suppression (NMS) by using a 3×3 max pooling layer on the corner heatmaps. Then we pick the top 100 top-left and top 100 bottom-right corners from the heatmaps. The corner locations are adjusted by the corresponding offsets. We calculate the L1 distances between the embeddings of the top-left and bottom-right corners. Pairs that have distances greater than 0.5 or contain corners from different categories are rejected. The average scores of the top-left and bottom-right corners are used as the detection scores.

Instead of resizing an image to a fixed size, we maintain the original resolution of the image and pad it with zeros before feeding it to CornerNet. Both the original and flipped images are used for testing. We combine the detections from the original and flipped images, and apply soft-nms [2] to suppress redundant detections. Only the top 100 detections are reported. The average inference time is 244 ms per image on a Titan X (PASCAL) GPU.

4.3 MS COCO

We evaluate CornerNet on the very challenging MS COCO dataset [24]. MS COCO contains 80k images for training, 40k for validation and 20k for testing. All images in the training set and 35k images in the validation set are used for training. The remaining 5k images in validation set are used for hyper-parameter searching and ablation study. All results on the test set are submitted to an external server for evaluation. To provide fair comparisons with other detectors, we report our main results on the test-dev set. MS COCO uses average precisions (APs) at different IoUs and APs for different object sizes as the main evaluation metrics.

4.4   Ablation Study

Corner Pooling. Corner pooling is a key component of CornerNet. To understand its contribution to performance, we train another network without corner pooling but with the same number of parameters.

Table 1. Ablation on corner pooling on MS COCO validation.

	AP	AP^{50}	AP^{75}	AP^s	AP^m	AP^l
w/o corner pooling	36.5	52.0	38.9	17.6	38.7	48.8
w/ corner pooling	38.5	54.1	41.1	17.7	41.1	52.5
improvement	+2.0	+2.1	+2.2	+0.1	+2.4	+3.7

Table 1 shows that adding corner pooling gives significant improvement: 2.0% on AP, 2.1% on AP^{50} and 2.2% on AP^{75}. We also see that corner pooling is especially helpful for medium and large objects, improving their APs by 2.4% and 3.7% respectively. This is expected because the topmost, bottommost, leftmost, rightmost boundaries of medium and large objects are likely to be further away from the corner locations.

Reducing Penalty to Negative Locations. We reduce the penalty given to negative locations around a positive location, within a radius determined by the size of the object (Sect. 3.2). To understand how this helps train CornerNet, we train one network with no penalty reduction and another network with a fixed radius of 2.5. We compare them with CornerNet on the validation set.

Table 2. Reducing the penalty given to the negative locations near positive locations helps significantly improve the performance of the network

	AP	AP^{50}	AP^{75}	AP^s	AP^m	AP^l
w/o reducing penalty	32.9	49.1	34.8	19.0	37.0	40.7
fixed radius	35.6	52.5	37.7	18.7	38.5	46.0
object-dependent radius	38.5	54.1	41.1	17.7	41.1	52.5

Table 2 shows that a fixed radius improves AP over the baseline by 2.7%, AP^m by 1.5% and AP^l by 5.3%. Object-dependent radius further improves the AP by 2.9%, AP^m by 2.6% and AP^l by 6.5%. In addition, we see that the penalty reduction especially benefits medium and large objects.

Error Analysis. CornerNet simultaneously outputs heatmaps, offsets, and embeddings, all of which affect detection performance. An object will be missed if either corner is missed; precise offsets are needed to generate tight bounding boxes; incorrect embeddings will result in many false bounding boxes. To understand how each part contributes to the final error, we perform an error analysis by replacing the predicted heatmaps and offsets with the ground-truth values and evaluting performance on the validation set.

Table 3. Error analysis. We replace the predicted heatmaps and offsets with the ground-truth values. Using the ground-truth heatmaps alone improves the AP from 38.5% to 74.0%, suggesting that the main bottleneck of CornerNet is detecting corners.

	AP	AP^{50}	AP^{75}	AP^s	AP^m	AP^l
	38.5	54.1	41.1	17.7	41.1	52.5
w/ gt heatmaps	74.0	88.5	79.3	60.8	82.0	82.6
w/ gt heatmaps + offsets	87.1	90.0	86.7	85.0	87.9	83.1

Table 3 shows that using the ground-truth corner heatmaps alone improves the AP from 38.5% to 74.0%. AP^s, AP^m and AP^l also increase by 43.1%, 40.9% and 30.1% respectively. If we replace the predicted offsets with the ground-truth offsets, the AP further increases by 13.1% to 87.1%. This suggests that although there is still ample room for improvement in both detecting and grouping corners, the main bottleneck is detecting corners. Figure 8 shows two qualitative examples of the predicted corners.

Fig. 8. Example bounding box predictions overlaid on predicted heatmaps of corners.

4.5   Comparisons with State-of-the-Art Detectors

We compare CornerNet with other state-of-the-art detectors on MS COCO test-dev (Table 4). With multi-scale evaluation, CornerNet achieves an AP of 42.1%, the state of the art among existing one-stage methods and competitive with two-stage methods.

Table 4. CornerNet versus others on MS COCO test-dev. CornerNet outperforms all one-stage detectors and achieves results competitive to two-stage detectors

Method	Backbone	AP	AP^{50}	AP^{75}	AP^s	AP^m	AP^l	AR^1	AR^{10}	AR^{100}	AR^s	AR^m	AR^l
Two-stage detectors													
DeNet [39]	ResNet-101	33.8	53.4	36.1	12.3	36.1	50.8	29.6	42.6	43.5	19.2	46.9	64.3
CoupleNet [46]	ResNet-101	34.4	54.8	37.2	13.4	38.1	50.8	30.0	45.0	46.4	20.7	53.1	68.5
Faster R-CNN by G-RMI [16]	Inception-ResNet-v2 [38]	34.7	55.5	36.7	13.5	38.1	52.0	-	-	-	-	-	-
Faster R-CNN+++ [15]	ResNet-101	34.9	55.7	37.4	15.6	38.7	50.9	-	-	-	-	-	-
Faster R-CNN w/ FPN [22]	ResNet-101	36.2	59.1	39.0	18.2	39.0	48.2	-	-	-	-	-	-
Faster R-CNN w/ TDM [35]	Inception-ResNet-v2	36.8	57.7	39.2	16.2	39.8	52.1	31.6	49.3	51.9	28.1	56.6	71.1
D-FCN [7]	Aligned-Inception-ResNet	37.5	58.0	-	19.4	40.1	52.5	-	-	-	-	-	-
Regionlets [43]	ResNet-101	39.3	59.8	-	21.7	43.7	50.9	-	-	-	-	-	-
Mask R-CNN [13]	ResNeXt-101	39.8	62.3	43.4	22.1	43.2	51.2	-	-	-	-	-	-
Soft-NMS [2]	Aligned-Inception-ResNet	40.9	62.8	-	23.3	43.6	53.3	-	-	-	-	-	-
LH R-CNN [21]	ResNet-101	41.5	-	-	25.2	45.3	53.1	-	-	-	-	-	-
Fitness-NMS [40]	ResNet-101	41.8	60.9	44.9	21.5	45.0	57.5	-	-	-	-	-	-
Cascade R-CNN [4]	ResNet-101	42.8	62.1	46.3	23.7	45.5	55.2	-	-	-	-	-	-
D-RFCN + SNIP [37]	DPN-98 [5]	45.7	67.3	51.1	29.3	48.8	57.1	-	-	-	-	-	-
One-stage detectors													
YOLOv2 [31]	DarkNet-19	21.6	44.0	19.2	5.0	22.4	35.5	20.7	31.6	33.3	9.8	36.5	54.4
DSOD300 [33]	DS/64-192-48-1	29.3	47.3	30.6	9.4	31.5	47.0	27.3	40.7	43.0	16.7	47.1	65.0
GRP-DSOD320 [34]	DS/64-192-48-1	30.0	47.9	31.8	10.9	33.6	46.3	28.0	42.1	44.5	18.8	49.1	65.0
SSD513 [25]	ResNet-101	31.2	50.4	33.3	10.2	34.5	49.8	28.3	42.1	44.4	17.6	49.2	65.8
DSSD513 [10]	ResNet-101	33.2	53.3	35.2	13.0	35.4	51.1	28.9	43.5	46.2	21.8	49.1	66.4
RefineDet512 (single scale) [45]	ResNet-101	36.4	57.5	39.5	16.6	39.9	51.4	-	-	-	-	-	-
RetinaNet800 [23]	ResNet-101	39.1	59.1	42.3	21.8	42.7	50.2	-	-	-	-	-	-
RefineDet512 (multi scale) [45]	ResNet-101	41.8	62.9	45.7	25.6	45.1	54.1	-	-	-	-	-	-
CornerNet511 (single scale)	Hourglass-104	40.5	56.5	43.1	19.4	42.7	53.9	35.3	54.3	59.1	37.4	61.9	76.9
CornerNet511 (multi scale)	Hourglass-104	42.1	57.8	45.3	20.8	44.8	56.7	36.4	55.7	60.0	38.5	62.7	77.4

5 Conclusion

We have presented CornerNet, a new approach to object detection that detects bounding boxes as pairs of corners. We evaluate CornerNet on MS COCO and demonstrate competitive results.

Acknowledgements. Toyota Research Institute ("TRI") provided funds to assist the authors with their research but this article solely reflects the opinions and conclusions of its authors and not TRI or any other Toyota entity.

References

1. Bell, S., Lawrence Zitnick, C., Bala, K., Girshick, R.: Inside-outside net: detecting objects in context with skip pooling and recurrent neural networks. In: Proceedings of the IEEE Conference on Computer Vision and Pattern Recognition, pp. 2874–2883 (2016)
2. Bodla, N., Singh, B., Chellappa, R., Davis, L.S.: Soft-NMS improving object detection with one line of code. In: 2017 IEEE International Conference on Computer Vision (ICCV), pp. 5562–5570. IEEE (2017)
3. Cai, Z., Fan, Q., Feris, R.S., Vasconcelos, N.: A unified multi-scale deep convolutional neural network for fast object detection. In: Leibe, B., Matas, J., Sebe, N., Welling, M. (eds.) ECCV 2016. LNCS, vol. 9908, pp. 354–370. Springer, Cham (2016). https://doi.org/10.1007/978-3-319-46493-0_22
4. Cai, Z., Vasconcelos, N.: Cascade R-CNN: delving into high quality object detection. arXiv preprint arXiv:1712.00726 (2017)

5. Chen, Y., Li, J., Xiao, H., Jin, X., Yan, S., Feng, J.: Dual path networks. In: Advances in Neural Information Processing Systems, pp. 4470–4478 (2017)
6. Dai, J., Li, Y., He, K., Sun, J.: R-FCN: object detection via region-based fully convolutional networks. arXiv preprint arXiv:1605.06409 (2016)
7. Dai, J., Qi, H., Xiong, Y., Li, Y., Zhang, G., Hu, H., Wei, Y.: Deformable convolutional networks. CoRR, abs/1703.06211, vol. 1(2), p. 3 (2017)
8. Deng, J., Dong, W., Socher, R., Li, L.J., Li, K., Fei-Fei, L.: Imagenet: a large-scale hierarchical image database. In: IEEE Conference on Computer Vision and Pattern Recognition CVPR 2009, pp. 248–255. IEEE (2009)
9. Everingham, M., Eslami, S.A., Van Gool, L., Williams, C.K., Winn, J., Zisserman, A.: The pascal visual object classes challenge: a retrospective. Int. J. Comput. Vis. 111(1), 98–136 (2015)
10. Fu, C.Y., Liu, W., Ranga, A., Tyagi, A., Berg, A.C.: DSSD: Deconvolutional single shot detector. arXiv preprint arXiv:1701.06659 (2017)
11. Girshick, R.: FAST R-CNN. arXiv preprint arXiv:1504.08083 (2015)
12. Girshick, R., Donahue, J., Darrell, T., Malik, J.: Rich feature hierarchies for accurate object detection and semantic segmentation. In: Proceedings of the IEEE Conference on Computer Vision and Pattern Recognition, pp. 580–587 (2014)
13. He, K., Gkioxari, G., Dollár, P., Girshick, R.: Mask R-CNN. arxiv preprint arxiv: 170306870 (2017)
14. He, K., Zhang, X., Ren, S., Sun, J.: Spatial pyramid pooling in deep convolutional networks for visual recognition. In: Fleet, D., Pajdla, T., Schiele, B., Tuytelaars, T. (eds.) ECCV 2014. LNCS, vol. 8691, pp. 346–361. Springer, Cham (2014). https://doi.org/10.1007/978-3-319-10578-9_23
15. He, K., Zhang, X., Ren, S., Sun, J.: Deep residual learning for image recognition. In: Proceedings of the IEEE Conference on Computer Vision and Pattern Recognition, pp. 770–778 (2016)
16. Huang, J., et al.: Speed/accuracy trade-offs for modern convolutional object detectors. In: IEEE CVPR (2017)
17. Ioffe, S., Szegedy, C.: Batch normalization: accelerating deep network training by reducing internal covariate shift. In: International Conference on Machine Learning, pp. 448–456 (2015)
18. Kingma, D.P., Ba, J.: Adam: a method for stochastic optimization. arXiv preprint arXiv:1412.6980 (2014)
19. Kong, T., Sun, F., Yao, A., Liu, H., Lu, M., Chen, Y.: Ron: reverse connection with objectness prior networks for object detection. arXiv preprint arXiv:1707.01691 (2017)
20. Krizhevsky, A., Sutskever, I., Hinton, G.E.: Imagenet classification with deep convolutional neural networks. In: Advances in Neural Information Processing Systems, pp. 1097–1105 (2012)
21. Li, Z., Peng, C., Yu, G., Zhang, X., Deng, Y., Sun, J.: Light-head R-CNN: in defense of two-stage object detector. arXiv preprint arXiv:1711.07264 (2017)
22. Lin, T.Y., Dollár, P., Girshick, R., He, K., Hariharan, B., Belongie, S.: Feature pyramid networks for object detection. arXiv preprint arXiv:1612.03144 (2016)
23. Lin, T.Y., Goyal, P., Girshick, R., He, K., Dollár, P.: Focal loss for dense object detection. arXiv preprint arXiv:1708.02002 (2017)
24. Lin, T.-Y., et al.: Microsoft COCO: common objects in context. In: Fleet, D., Pajdla, T., Schiele, B., Tuytelaars, T. (eds.) ECCV 2014. LNCS, vol. 8693, pp. 740–755. Springer, Cham (2014). https://doi.org/10.1007/978-3-319-10602-1_48

25. Liu, W., et al.: SSD: single shot multibox detector. In: Leibe, B., Matas, J., Sebe, N., Welling, M. (eds.) ECCV 2016. LNCS, vol. 9905, pp. 21–37. Springer, Cham (2016). https://doi.org/10.1007/978-3-319-46448-0_2

26. Newell, A., Deng, J.: Pixels to graphs by associative embedding. In: Advances in Neural Information Processing Systems, pp. 2168–2177 (2017)

27. Newell, A., Huang, Z., Deng, J.: Associative embedding: end-to-end learning for joint detection and grouping. In: Advances in Neural Information Processing Systems, pp. 2274–2284 (2017)

28. Newell, A., Yang, K., Deng, J.: Stacked hourglass networks for human pose estimation. In: Leibe, B., Matas, J., Sebe, N., Welling, M. (eds.) ECCV 2016. LNCS, vol. 9912, pp. 483–499. Springer, Cham (2016). https://doi.org/10.1007/978-3-319-46484-8_29

29. Paszke, A., et al.: Automatic differentiation in pytorch (2017)

30. Redmon, J., Divvala, S., Girshick, R., Farhadi, A.: You only look once: unified, real-time object detection. In: Proceedings of the IEEE Conference on Computer Vision and Pattern Recognition, pp. 779–788 (2016)

31. Redmon, J., Farhadi, A.: Yolo9000: better, faster, stronger. arXiv preprint 1612 (2016)

32. Ren, S., He, K., Girshick, R., Sun, J.: Faster R-CNN: towards real-time object detection with region proposal networks. In: Advances in Neural Information Processing Systems, pp. 91–99 (2015)

33. Shen, Z., Liu, Z., Li, J., Jiang, Y.G., Chen, Y., Xue, X.: DSOD: learning deeply supervised object detectors from scratch. In: The IEEE International Conference on Computer Vision (ICCV), vol. 3, p. 7 (2017)

34. Shen, Z., et al.: Learning object detectors from scratch with gated recurrent feature pyramids. arXiv preprint arXiv:1712.00886 (2017)

35. Shrivastava, A., Sukthankar, R., Malik, J., Gupta, A.: Beyond skip connections: top-down modulation for object detection. arXiv preprint arXiv:1612.06851 (2016)

36. Simonyan, K., Zisserman, A.: Very deep convolutional networks for large-scale image recognition. arXiv preprint arXiv:1409.1556 (2014)

37. Singh, B., Davis, L.S.: An analysis of scale invariance in object detection-snip. arXiv preprint arXiv:1711.08189 (2017)

38. Szegedy, C., Ioffe, S., Vanhoucke, V., Alemi, A.A.: Inception-v4, inception-resnet and the impact of residual connections on learning. In: AAAI, vol. 4, p. 12 (2017)

39. Tychsen-Smith, L., Petersson, L.: Denet: scalable real-time object detection with directed sparse sampling. arXiv preprint arXiv:1703.10295 (2017)

40. Tychsen-Smith, L., Petersson, L.: Improving object localization with fitness nms and bounded iou loss. arXiv preprint arXiv:1711.00164 (2017)

41. Uijlings, J.R., van de Sande, K.E., Gevers, T., Smeulders, A.W.: Selective search for object recognition. Int. J. Comput. Vis. **104**(2), 154–171 (2013)

42. Xiang, Y., Choi, W., Lin, Y., Savarese, S.: Subcategory-aware convolutional neural networks for object proposals and detection. arXiv preprint arXiv:1604.04693 (2016)

43. Xu, H., Lv, X., Wang, X., Ren, Z., Chellappa, R.: Deep regionlets for object detection. arXiv preprint arXiv:1712.02408 (2017)

44. Zhai, Y., Fu, J., Lu, Y., Li, H.: Feature selective networks for object detection. arXiv preprint arXiv:1711.08879 (2017)

45. Zhang, S., Wen, L., Bian, X., Lei, Z., Li, S.Z.: Single-shot refinement neural network for object detection. arXiv preprint arXiv:1711.06897 (2017)

46. Zhu, Y., Zhao, C., Wang, J., Zhao, X., Wu, Y., Lu, H.: Couplenet: coupling global structure with local parts for object detection. In: Proceedings of International Conference on Computer Vision (ICCV) (2017)
47. Zitnick, C.L., Dollár, P.: Edge boxes: locating object proposals from edges. In: Fleet, D., Pajdla, T., Schiele, B., Tuytelaars, T. (eds.) ECCV 2014. LNCS, vol. 8693, pp. 391–405. Springer, Cham (2014). https://doi.org/10.1007/978-3-319-10602-1_26

RelocNet: Continuous Metric Learning Relocalisation Using Neural Nets

Vassileios Balntas$^{(\boxtimes)}$, Shuda Li, and Victor Prisacariu

Active Vision Lab, University of Oxford, Oxford, UK
{balntas,shuda,victor}@robots.ox.ac.uk
https://www.robots.ox.ac.uk/~lav

Abstract. We propose a method of learning suitable convolutional representations for camera pose retrieval based on nearest neighbour matching and continuous metric learning-based feature descriptors. We introduce information from camera frusta overlaps between pairs of images to optimise our feature embedding network. Thus, the final camera pose descriptor differences represent camera pose changes. In addition, we build a pose regressor that is trained with a geometric loss to infer finer relative poses between a query and nearest neighbour images. Experiments show that our method is able to generalise in a meaningful way, and outperforms related methods across several experiments.

1 Introduction

Robust 6-DoF camera relocalisation is a core component of many practical computer vision problems, such as loop closure for SLAM [4,13,37], reuse a pre-built map for augmented reality [16] or autonomous multi- agent exploration and navigation [39].

Specifically, given some type of prior knowledge base about the world, the relocalisation task aims to estimate the 6-DoF pose of a novel (unseen) frame in the coordinate system given by the prior model of the world. Traditionally, the world is captured using a sparse 3D map built from 2D point features and some visual tracking or odometry algorithm [37]. To relocalise, another set of features is extracted from the query frame and is matched with the global model, establishing 2D to 3D correspondences. The camera pose is then estimated by solving the perspective-n-point problem [29,30,32,47]. While this approach provides usable results in many scenarios, it suffers from exponentially growing computational costs, making it unsuitable for large-scale applications.

More recently, machine learning methods, such as the random forest RGB-D approach of [5] and the neural network RGB method of [25] have been shown to provide viable alternatives to the traditional geometric relocalisation pipeline, improving on both accuracy and range. However, this comes with certain downsides. The former approach produces state-of-the-art relocalisation results but requires depth imagery and has only been shown to work effectively indoors. The latter set of methods has to be retrained fully and slowly for each novel scene,

© Springer Nature Switzerland AG 2018
V. Ferrari et al. (Eds.): ECCV 2018, LNCS 11218, pp. 782–799, 2018.
https://doi.org/10.1007/978-3-030-01264-9_46

which means that the learnt internal network representations are not transferable, limiting its practical deployability.

Our method (Fig. 1) leverages the ability of neural networks to deal with large-scale environments, does not require depth and aims to be transferable i.e. produce accurate results on novel sequences and environments, even when not trained on them. Inspired by the image retrieval literature, we build a database of whole-image features, but, unlike in previous works, these are trained specifically for camera pose retrieval, and not holistic image retrieval. At relocalisation time, a nearest neighbour is identified using simple brute-forcing of L2 distances. Accuracy is further improved by feeding both the query image and the nearest neighbour features, in a Siamese manner, to a neural network, that is trained with a geometric loss and aims to regress the 6-DoF pose difference between the two images.

Briefly, our main contributions are:

- we employ a continuous metric learning-based approach, with a camera frustum overlap loss in order to learn global image features suitable for camera relocalisation;
- retrieved results are further improved by being fed to a network regressing pose differences, which is trained with exponential and logarithmic map layers directly in the pose homogeneous matrices space, without the need for separate translation and orientation terms;
- we introduce a new RGBD dataset with accurate ground truth targeting experiments in relocalisation.

The remainder of the paper is structured as follows: Sect. 2 describes related work. Section 3 discusses our main contributions, including the train and test methodologies and Sect. 4 shows our quantitative and qualitative evaluations. We conclude in Sect. 5.

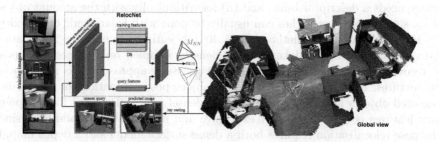

Fig. 1. Our system is able to retrieve a relevant item from a database, which presents high camera frustum overlap with an unseen query. Subsequently, we can use the pose information from the images stored in a database, to compute the pose of a previously unseen query by applying a transformation produced by a deep neural network. Note that the differential nature of our method enables the successful transfer of our learnt representation to previously unseen novel sequences (best viewed on screen).

2   Related Work

Existing relocalisation methods can be generally grouped into five major categories: appearance similarity based, geometric, Hough transform, random forest and deep learning approaches.

Appearance similarity based approaches rely on a method to measure the similarity between pairs of images, such as Normalised Cross Correlation [15], Random Ferns [16] and bag of 2D features [14]. The similarity measurement can identify one or multiple reference images that match the query frame. The pose is then be estimated e.g. by a linear combination of poses from multiple neighbours, or simply by using the pose corresponding to the best match. However, these methods are often not accurate if the query frame is captured from a viewing pose that is far from those in the reference database. For this reason, similarity-based approaches, such as DBoW [14], are usually used as an early warning system to trigger a geometric approach for pose estimation [37]. The first stage of our own work is inspired by this category of methods, with pose-specific descriptors representing the database and query images.

Geometric relocalisation approaches [6,21,30] tackle the relocalisation problem by solving either the absolute orientation problem [1,20,31,35,41] or the perspective-n-point problem [29,32,47] given a set of point correspondences between the query frame and a global reference model. The correspondences are usually provided using 2D or 3D local feature matching. Matching local features can be noisy and unreliable, so pairwise information can be utilised to reduce feature matching ambiguity [30]. Geometric approaches are simple, accurate and especially useful when the query pose has large $\mathbb{SE}(3)$ distance to the reference images. However, such methods are restricted to a relatively small working space due to the fact that matching cost, depending on the matching scheme employed, can grow exponentially with respect to the number of key points. In contrast, our approach scales (i) linearly with the amount of training data, since each image needs a descriptor built, and (ii) logarithmically with the amount of test data, since database searches can usually be done with logarithmic complexity.

Hough Transform methods [2,11,40] rely entirely on pairwise information between pairs of oriented key points, densely sampled on surfaces. The pose is recovered by voting in the Hough Space. Such approaches do not depend on textures, making them attractive in object pose estimation for minimally-textured objects [40]. However, sampling densely on a 3D model for the point pair features is computationally expensive and not scalable. In addition, since the pose relocalisation requires both a dense surface model and a depth map, it is unsuitable for vison-only sensors. In contrast, our method only requires RGB frames for both training and testing.

Random forest based methods [17,42,45] deliver state-of-the-art accuracy, by regressing the camera location for each point in an RGBD query frame. Originally, such approaches required expensive re-training for each novel scene, but [5] showed that this can be limited to the leaf nodes of the random forest, which allowed for real-time performance. However, depth information is still required for accurate relocalisation results.

Convolutional neural network methods, starting with PoseNet [25], regress camera poses from single RGB images. Subsequent works (i) examined the use of recurrent neural networks (i.e. LSTMs) to introduce temporal information to the problem [7,46], and (ii) trained the regression with geometric losses [24].

Most similar to our own approach are the methods of [28,44], with the former assuming the two frames are given, and regressing depth and camera pose jointly, and the later using ImageNet-trained ResNet feature descriptor similarity to identify the nearest neighbouring frame.

Compared to these approaches, we use a simpler geometric pose loss, and introduce a novel continuous metric learning method to train full frame descriptors specifically for camera pose-oriented retrieval.

3 Methodology

In this section, we present a complete overview of our method (Fig. 2), consisting of learning (i) robust descriptors for camera pose-related retrieval, and (ii) a shallow differential pose regressor from pairs of images.

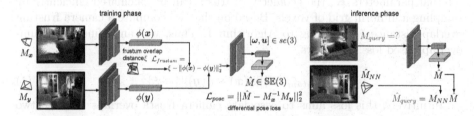

Fig. 2. (left) *Training stage.* We use a Siamese architecture to train global feature descriptors driven by a continuous metric learning loss based on camera frustum overlaps. This forces the representations that are learnt to be relevant to fine-grained camera pose retrieval. In addition, a final query pose is learnt based on a loss on a subsequent set of layers which are trained to infer the differential pose between two inputs. (right) *Inference stage.* Given an unseen image, and its nearest neighbour retrieved using our optimised frustum feature descriptors, we are able to compute a pose estimation for the unseen query based on the output of our differential pose network, and the stored nearest neighbour pose.

3.1 Learning Camera Pose Descriptors for Retrieval Using Camera Frustum Overlaps

The first part of our method deals with learning suitable feature descriptors for retrieval of nearest neighbours that are consistent with the camera movement.

Motivation. Several methods use pre-trained models for retrieval of relevant images, because such models are trained on large datasets such as ImageNet [9] or Places [48], and are able to capture relevant image features in their penultimate layers. With no significant effort, such models can be used for several other transfer learning scenarios. However, such features are trained for detection and recognition of final objectives, and might not be directly relevant to our problem, i.e. understanding the camera movement.

Recent work has shown that features that are learnt guided from object poses [3] can lead to a more successful object pose retrieval. To tackle the equivalent issue in terms of camera poses, we make use of the camera frustum overlaps as described below.

Frustum Overlap Loss. To capture relevant features in the layers of our network, our main idea is to use a geometric quantity, which is the overlap between two camera frusta. Retrieval of nearest neighbours with high overlap will improve results of high-accuracy methods that are based on appearance matching such as [31], since there is a stronger probability that a consistent set of feature points will be visible in both images.

Given a pair of images, $\{x, y\}$, with known poses $\{M_x, M_y\}$, and camera internal parameters K, the geometry of frusta can be calculated efficiently by sampling a uniform grid of voxels. Based on this, we compute a camera frustum overlap distance ξ according to Algorithm 1. Thus, we can define a frustum-overlap based loss, as follows

$$\mathcal{L}_{frustum} = \{||\phi(x) - \phi(y)||_2^2 - \xi\}^2 \tag{1}$$

Intuitively, this loss aims to associate camera frusta overlaps between two frames, with their respective distance in the learnt embedding space.

Some sample pairs of images from random sequences (e.g. taken from the ScanNet Dataset [8]), which are similar to the ones that are used in our optimisation process, are shown in Fig. 3. We can observe that the frustum intersection ratio is a very good proxy for visual image similarity. Note that the number written below each image pair is the frustum overlap ratio $(1 - \xi)$, and not the frustum overlap distance (ξ). The results in Fig. 3 are computed with D being 4 meters which is a reasonable selection for indoors scenes. The selection of D is dependent on the scale of the scene since the camera frustum clipping plane is related to the distance of the camera to the nearest object. Thus, if this method is to be applied on outside large-scale scenes, this parameter would need to be adjusted accordingly.

3.2   Pose Regression

While retrieval of nearest neighbours is the most important step in our pipeline, it is also crucial to refining the estimations that are given by the neighbours to improve the final inference stage of the unknown query pose.

Algorithm 1: *Frustum overlap distance* between a pair of camera poses

---

Input : Relative pair pose $M \in \mathbb{SE}(3)$, camera intrinsics K, maximum clipping depth D, sampling step τ

1 Use K to sample a uniform grid $\mathcal{V}$ of voxels with size τ inside the first frustum with max clipping distance D.

2 Compute the subset of voxels $\mathcal{V}_+ \subseteq \mathcal{V}$ which lie inside the second frustum.

Return: Frustum overlap distance $\xi = 1 - \frac{|\mathcal{V}_+|}{|\mathcal{V}|}$, *with* $\xi \in [0, 1]$

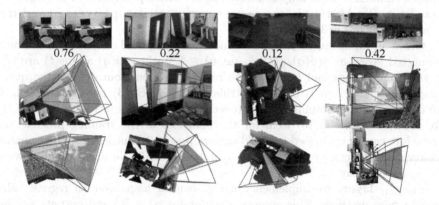

Fig. 3. Samples of our frustum overlap score that is inverted and used as a loss function for learning suitable camera pose descriptors for retrieval. We show pairs of images, together with their respective frustum overlap scores, and two views of the 3D geometry of the scene that lead to the RGB image observations. We can observe that the frustum overlap score is a good indicator of the covisibility of the scenes, and thus a meaningful objective to optimise.

To improve the estimation that is given from the retrieved nearest neighbours, we add a shallow neural network on top of the feature network, that is trained for regressing differential camera poses between two neighbouring frames.

The choice of the camera pose representation is very important, but the literature finds no ideal candidate [26]: *unit quaternions* were used in [24,25], *axis-angle* representations in [33,44] and *Euler angles* [34,36].

Below, we adopt the matrix representation of rotation with its extension to represent the $\mathbb{SE}(3)$ transformation space similarly to [18]. Specifically, $M = \begin{pmatrix} R\ t \\ 0\ 1 \end{pmatrix} \in \mathbb{SE}(3)$ with $R \in \mathbb{SO}(3)$ and $t \in \mathbb{R}^3$. We adopt the $\mathbb{SE}(3)$ matrix for both transformation amongst different coordinate systems but also for measuring the loss, which shows great convenience in training the network. In addition, since our network directly outputs a camera pose, the validity of the regressed pose is guaranteed, unlike the quaternion method used in [24,25] where a valid rotation representation for a random $q \in \mathbb{R}^4$ is enforced a-posteriori by normalising the quaternion q to have unit norm.

Our goal is to learn a differential pose regression that is able to use a pair of feature descriptors in order to regress the differential camera poses between them. To that end, we build our pose regression layers on top of the feature layers of RelocNet allowing for a joint forward operation during inference, thus significantly reducing computational time.

The D-dimensional feature descriptors that are extracted from the feature layers of RelocNet, are concatenated into a single feature vector, and are forwarded through a set of fully connected layers which performs a transformation from $\mathbb{R}^D$ to $\mathbb{R}^6$. Afterwards, we can use an exponential map layer to convert this to an element in $\mathbb{SE}(3)$ [18].

Given an input image q, we can denote the computed output from the fully connected layers as $\gamma(\phi(q), \phi(t)) = (\omega, u) \in \mathbb{R}^6$, where $\phi(q)$ and $\phi(t)$ are two feature embeddings and (ω, u) is the relative motion from $\phi(t)$ to the query image. Our next step is to convert this to a valid $\mathbb{SE}(3)$ pose matrix, which we then use in the training process together with the loss introduced in Eq. 10. By considering the $\mathbb{SE}(3)$ item for the final loss of the training process, the procedure can be optimised for valid camera poses without needing to normalise quaternions. To convert between $se(3)$ items to $\mathbb{SE}(3)$ we utilise the following two specialised layers:

$exp_{\mathbb{SE}(3)}$ **layer.** we implement an exponential map layer to regress valid camera pose matrices. This accepts a vector $(\omega, u) \in \mathbb{R}^6$ and outputs a valid $M \in \mathbb{SE}(3)$ by using the exponential map from the $se(3)$ element δ to the $\mathbb{SE}(3)$ element M and can be computed as follows [12]:

$$exp((\omega, u)) = \left[\begin{array}{c|c} R & Vu \\ \hline 0 & 1 \end{array}\right] \tag{2}$$

with

$$\theta = \sqrt{\omega^T \omega} \tag{3}$$

$$R = I + \frac{sin(\theta)}{\theta}[\omega]_\times + \frac{1 - cos(\theta)}{\theta^2}[\omega]_\times^2 \tag{4}$$

$$V = I + \frac{1 - cos(\theta)}{\theta^2}[\omega]_\times + \frac{\theta - sin(\theta)}{\theta^3}[\omega]_\times^2 \tag{5}$$

where $[\omega]_\times$ represents the skew symmetric matrix generator for the vector $\omega \in \mathbb{R}^3$ [12].

Subsequently, we are able to do a forward pass in this layer, using the output of the network $\gamma(q, t) = (\omega, u)$, and passing it through as per Eq. 2.

$log_{\mathbb{SE}(3)}$ **layer.** To return from $\mathbb{SE}(3)$ items to $se(3)$, we implement a logarithmic map layer, which is defined as follows:

$$log(\left[\begin{array}{c|c} R & Vu \\ \hline 0 & 1 \end{array}\right]) = (log(R), V^{-1}u) \tag{6}$$

$$log(R) = \frac{\theta}{2 \sin(\theta)}(R - R^T) \tag{7}$$

As suggested by [12], the Taylor expansion of $\frac{\theta}{2\sin(\theta)}$ should be used when the norm of ω is below the machine precision. However, in our training process, we did not observe elements suffering from this issue.

Joint Learning of Feature Descriptors and Poses with a Siamese Network. As previously discussed, one of the main issues with the recent work on CNN relocalisers is the need to use the global world coordinate system as a training label. This strongly restricts the learning process and thus requires re-training for each new sequence that the system encounters. To address this issue, we instead propose to focus on learning a shallow differential pose regressor, which returns the camera motion between two arbitrary frames of a sequence. In addition, by expanding the training process to pairs of frames, we expand the amount of information, since we can use exponentially more training samples than when training with individual images. We thus design our training process as a Siamese convolutional regressor [10].

For training the Siamese architecture, a pair of images (q_L, q_R) is given as input and the network outputs a single estimate $\tilde{M} \in \mathbb{SE}(3)$. Intuitively, this $\tilde{M}$ represents the differential pose between the two pose matrices. More formally, let M_{wL} represent the pose of an image q_L, and M_{wR} the pose of an image q_R, with both poses representing the transformation from the camera coordinate system to the world. The differential transformation matrix that transfers the camera from $R \to L$ is given by $M_{RL} = M_{wR}^{-1} M_{wL}$.

Assuming we have a set of K training items inside a mini-batch,

$$\{q_L^{(i)}, M_{wL}^{(i)}, q_R^{(i)}, M_{wR}^{(i)}, M_{RL}^{(i)}, \xi_{LR}\} \; i \in [1, K] \tag{8}$$

we train our network with the following loss

$$\mathcal{L} = \alpha \mathcal{L}_{\mathbb{SE}(3)} + \beta \mathcal{L}_{frustum} \tag{9}$$

with

$$\mathcal{L}_{\mathbb{SE}(3)} = \sum_{i=0}^{K} ||log_{\mathbb{SE}(3)}\{\tilde{M}^{(i)^{-1}}(M_{wR}^{(i)^{-1}} M_{wL})\}||_1 \tag{10}$$

which considers the L_1 norm of the $log_{\mathbb{SE}(3)}$ map of the composition of the inverse of the prediction $\tilde{M}$ and the ground truth $M_{wR}^{(i)^{-1}} M_{wL}$. Intuitively, this will become 0 when the $M_{wR}^{(i)^{-1}} M_{wL}$ becomes $I_{4\times 4}$ due to the fact that the logarithm of the identity element of $\mathbb{SE}(3)$ is 0. Note that we can extend the above method, to focus on single image based regression, where for each training item $\{q_i, M_i\}$ we infer a pose $\hat{M}_i$, and we instead modify the loss function to optimise $\hat{M}_i^{-1} M_i$. We provide a visual overview of the training stage on Fig. 2 (left).

3.3 Inference Stage

In this section, we discuss our inference framework, starting by using one nearest neighbour (*NN*) for pose estimation, and subsequently using multiple nearest neighbours.

Pose from a Single Nearest Neighbour. During inference, we assume that there exists a pool of images in the database $q_{db}^{(i)}$, together with their corresponding poses $M_{db}^{(i)}$ for $i \in [0, N_{db}]$. Let s_{NN1} represent the index of the nearest neighbour in the D-dimensional feature space for the query q_q, with unknown pose M_q.

After computing the estimate $\tilde{M} = \gamma(q_q, q_{db}^{(NN1)})$, we can infer a pose $\tilde{M}_{db}$ for the unknown ground-truth pose M_{db} by a simple matrix multiplication, since $\tilde{M} = M_{db}^{-1} M_q$. We provide a visual overview of the inference stage on Fig. 2 (right).

Pose from Multiple Nearest Neighbours. We also briefly discuss a method to infer a prediction from multiple candidates. As shown in Fig. 6, for each pose query we can obtain top K-NN, and use each one of them to predict a distinct pose for the query using our differential pose regressor. We aim to aggregate these matrices into a single estimate $\tilde{M}^{(e)}$.

We consider the (ω, u) representation of a pose matrix in $se(3)$ as discussed before, and compute

$$\log(\hat{M}^{(e)}) = \sum_k \beta_k \log(M^{(k)}) + k \log(M^{(e)}) \sum_K \beta_k + k \qquad (11)$$

with $\beta_k = \frac{\sqrt{2t\hat{r} - t^2}}{\hat{r}}$ and $\hat{r} = \max(\|\log(M^{(e)}) - log(\hat{M}^{(e)})\|, t)$, resulting from the robust Huber error norm, with t denoting the outlier threshold, and k the number of nearest neighbours that contribute to the estimation $M^{(e)}$. We then use iteratively reweighted least squares, to estimate $\log(M^{(e)})$ and the inliers amongst the set of the k neural network predictions [22,38]. For our implementation we use $k = 5$ and $t = 0.5$.

3.4 Training Process

We use ResNet18 [19] as a feature extractor, and we run our experiments for the training of the retrieval stage with maximum clipping depth $D = 4\,m$ and grid step $0.2\,m$. In addition, to avoid the fact that most pairs in a sequence are not covisible, we limit our selection of pairs to cases where the translation distance is below $0.3\,m$ and the rotation is below $30°$.

We append three fully connected layers of sizes $(512 \to 512)$, $(512 \to 256)$ and $(256 \to 6)$ to reduce the 512 dimensional output of the Siamese output feature layer $\phi(x) - \phi(y)$ of the network to a valid element in $\mathbb{R}^6$. This is then fed to the $exp_{SE(3)}$ layer to produce a valid 4×4 pose matrix. For training, we use Adam [27], with a learning rate of 10^{-4}. We also use weight decay that we set to 10^{-5}. We provide a general visual overview of the training process in Fig. 2 (left). For our joint training loss, we set $a = 0.1$ and $\beta = 0.9$.

4 Results

In this section, we briefly introduce the datasets that are used for evaluating our method, and we then present experiments that show that our feature descriptors are significantly better at relocalisation compared to previous work. In addition, we show that the shallow differential pose regressor is able to perform meaningfully when transferred to a novel dataset, and is able to outperform other methods when trained and tested on the same dataset.

4.1 Evaluation Datasets

We use two datasets to evaluate our methods, namely 7scenes [16], and our new RelocDB which is introduced later in this paper. Training is done primarily on the ScanNet dataset [8].

ScanNet. The ScanNet dataset [8] consists of over $1k$ sequences, with respective ground truth poses. We keep this dataset for training since there do not exist multiple sequences for each scene globally aligned such that they can be used for relocalisation purposes. In addition, the size of the dataset makes it easy to examine the generalisation capabilities of our method.

7Scenes. The 7Scenes dataset consists of 7 scenes each containing multiple sequences that are split into train and test sets. We use the train set to generate our database of stored features, and we treat the images in the test set as the set of unknown queries.

RelocDB Dataset. While 7Scenes has been widely used, is it significantly smaller than ScanNet and other datasets that are suitable for training deep networks. ScanNet aims to address this issue, however, it is not designed for relocalisation. To that end, we introduce a novel dataset, RelocDB that is aimed at being a helpful resource at evaluating retrieval methods in the context of camera relocalisation.

We collected 500 sequences with a Google Tango device, each split into train and test parts. The train and test set are built by moving two times over a similar path, and thus are very similar in terms of size. These sets are aligned to the same global coordinate framework, and thus can be used for relocalisation. In Fig. 4, we show some examples of sequences from our RelocDB dataset.

4.2 Frustum Overlap Feature Descriptors

Below we discuss several experiments demonstrating the retrieval performance of our feature learning method. For each of these cases, the frusta descriptors are trained on ScanNet and evaluated on 7Scenes sequences. In all cases, we use *relocalisation success rate* as a performance indicator, which simply counts the percentage of query items that were relocalised from the test set to the saved trained dataset by setting a frustum overlap threshold.

We compare with features extracted from ResNet18 [19], VGG [43], PoseNet [25], and a non-learning based method [16]. Fig. 5(a) indicates that the size of the training set is crucial for the good generalisation of the learnt descriptors for the heads sequence in 7Scenes. It is clear that descriptors that are learnt

Fig. 4. Sample sequences from our RelocDB dataset.

with a few sequences quickly overfit and are not suitable for retrieval. In Fig. 5(b) we plot the performance of our learnt descriptor across different frustum overlap thresholds, where we can observe that our method outperforms other methods across all precisions. It is also worth noting, that the features extracted from the penultimate PoseNet layer does not seem to be relevant for relocalisation, presumably due to the fact that they are trained for direct regression, and more importantly are over-fitted to each specific training sequence. To test the effect of the size of a training set that is used as a reference DB of descriptors in the performance of our method, we increasingly reduce the number of items in the training set, by converting the 1000 training frames to a sparser set of keyframes based on removing redundant items, according to camera motion thresholds of $0.1\,\mathrm{m}$, $10°$. Thus, the descriptor for a new frame will be added in the retrieval descriptors pool, only if it presents larger values in both threshold than all of the items already stored. In Fig. 5(c), we show results in terms of accuracy versus retrieval pool size for our method compared to a standard pre-trained ImageNet retrieval method. We can observe that our descriptor is more relevant across several different keyframes training set sizes. We can also see that our method is able to deal with smaller retrieval pools in a more efficient way.

In Table 1, we show a general comparison between several related methods. As we can observe, our descriptors are very robust and can generalise in a meaningful way between two different datasets. The low performance of the features extracted from PoseNet is also evident here. It is also worth noting that our method can be used instead of other methods in several popular relocalisers and SLAM systems, such as [38], where Ferns [16] are used.

4.3   Pose Regression Experiments

In Table 2 we show the results of the proposed pose regression method, compared to several state-of-the-art CNN based methods for relocalisation. We compare our work with the following methods: PoseNet [25] which uses a

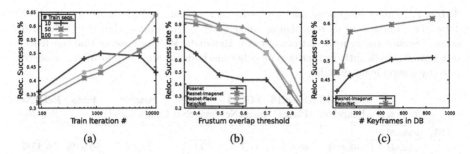

Fig. 5. (a) Relation of training dataset size and relocalisation performance. We can observe that there is a clear advantage of using more training data for training descriptors relevant to relocalisation (b) Relocalisation success rate in relation with the frustum overlap threshold. Our RelocNet is able to outperform pre-trained methods with significantly more training data, due to the fact that it is trained with a relevant geometric loss. (c) Relation of number of keyframes stored in the database with relocalisation success rate. Our retrieval descriptor shows consistent performance over datasets with different amounts of stored keyframes.

weighted quaternion and translation loss, the Bayesian and geometric extensions to PoseNet [23,24] which uses geometric re-projection error for training, and an approach that extends regression to the temporal domain using recurrent neural networks [46]. We can observe that even by using the descriptors and the pose regressors learnt on ScanNet, we are able to perform on par with methods that are trained and tested on the same sequences. This is a significant result as it shows the potential of large-scale training in relocalisation. In addition, we can observe that when we apply our relocalisation training framework by training and testing on the same sequence as the other methods do, we are able to outperform several related methods.

4.4   Fusing Multiple Nearest Neighbours

In Fig. 6 we show results comparing the single NN performance with the fusing method from Eq. 11. We can observe that in most cases, fusing from multiple NNs slightly improves the performance. The fact that the improvement is not significant and consistent is potentially attributed to the way the nearest neighbours are extracted from the dataset, which might lead to significantly similar candidates. One possible solution to this, would be to actively enforce some notion of dissimilarity between the retrieved nearest neighbours, therefore ensuring that the fusion operates on a more diverse set of proposals.

4.5   Qualitative Examples

In the top two rows of Fig. 7, we show examples of a synthetic view of the global scene model using the predicted pose from the first nearest neighbour, while the bottom row shows the query image whose pose we are aiming to infer.

Table 1. Nearest neighbour matching success rate using a brute force approach. We show the success rate of relocalising when using a frustum overlap threshold of 0.7 across 7Scenes and sequences from our new RelocDB. We can observe that our feature descriptors significantly outperform all other methods in terms of relocalisation success rate, by a significant margin.

	train set	ResNet18 ImageNet	ResNet18 Places	VGG11 ImageNet	VGG19 ImageNet	PoseNet Cambr. Land.	Ferns -	**RelocNet** ScanNet
DB	sequence							
7scenes	heads	48.6 %	46.6 %	37.7 %	39.8 %	29.1%	30.63%	**70.33%**
	fire	67.3 %	73.1 %	64.9 %	66.8%	33.70%	37.03%	**79.01%**
	redkitchen	65.0%	62.6%	64.8%	61.1%	30.9%	40.47%	**73.42%**
	chess	71.25%	69.50%	67.90%	74.90%	18.6%	51.73%	**78.95%**
	stairs	32.5%	54.6%	42.7%	41.0%	7.8%	28.16%	**62.77%**
	pumpkin	73.1%	68.8%	69.2%	69.8%	12.2 %	52.17%	**79.25%**
	office	69.0%	69.3%	64.0%	57.5%	10.3%	47.34 %	**72.41%**
RelocDB	caution	78.1%	78.1%	72.1%	70.9%	30.1%	61.8%	**83.6%**
	desk	59.6%	61.5%	59.6%	61.5%	31.3%	47.3%	**68.4%**
	lecture	66.6%	62.0%	55.1%	64.3%	29.40%	40.2%	**70.1%**
	meetingroom	57.2%	56.7%	54.3%	53.5%	12.81%	36.4%	**62.5%**
	posters	62.6%	67.3%	58.1%	62.6%	39.94%	49.3%	**74.3%**
	printer	67.0%	70.8%	63.2%	70.8%	27.69%	31.0%	**72.1%**

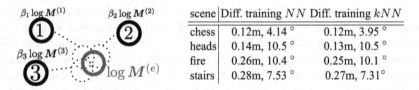

scene	Diff. training NN	Diff. training kNN
chess	0.12m, 4.14 °	0.12m, 3.95 °
heads	0.14m, 10.5 °	0.13m, 10.5 °
fire	0.26m, 10.4 °	0.25m, 10.1 °
stairs	0.28m, 7.53 °	0.27m, 7.31°

Fig. 6. Effect of fusing multiple nearest neighbours. We can observe that we are able to improve performance over single nearest neighbour, by incorporating pose information from multiple nearest neighbours.

Note that for this experiment, we use the high accuracy per-database trained variant of our network. From the figure, we can see that in most of the cases the predicted poses are well aligned with the query image (first 5 columns). We also show some failure cases for our method (last 3 columns). The failure cases might be characterised by the limited overlap between the query and training frames, something that is an inherent disadvantage of our method.

In Fig. 7 (bottom), we show typical cases of the camera poses of the nearest neighbours (red) selected by the feature network, as well as the estimated query pose for each nearest neighbour (cyan). Note that these results are sample test images when using the network that is trained on the non-overlapping train set. In addition, we show the ground truth query pose which is indicated by the blue frustum. Surprisingly, we see that the inferred poses are significantly stable

Table 2. Median localisation errors in the *7Scenes* [42] dataset. We can observe that we can outperform the original version of PoseNet even by training and testing on separate datasets. This indicates the potential of our method in terms of transferability between datasets. In addition, we can outperform other methods when we train and test our method on the same datasets. Finally, it is also worth noting that the performance boost from using temporal information (LSTM) is smaller than the one given by using our method.

Scene	PoseNet (β weight) [25]	Bayesian PoseNet [23]	PoseNet Spatial LSTM [46]	PoseNet Geometric [24]	**RelocNet** ScanNet	**RelocNet** 7scenes
Chess	0.32m, 6.60°	0.37m, 7.24°	0.24m, 5.77°	0.13m, 4.48°	0.21m, 10.9°	**0.12m, 4.14°**
Fire	0.47m, 14.0°	0.43m, 13.7°	0.34m, 11.9°	0.27m, 11.3°	0.32m, 11.8°	**0.26m, 10.4°**
Heads	0.30m, 12.2°	0.31m, 12.0°	0.21m, 13.7°	0.17m, 13.0°	0.15m, 13.4°	**0.14m, 10.5°**
Office	0.48m, 7.24°	0.48m, 8.04°	0.30m, 8.08°	0.19m, 5.55°	0.31m,10.3°	**0.18m, 5.32°**
Pumpkin	0.49m, 8.12°	0.61m, 7.08°	0.33m, 7.00°	**0.26m**, 4.75°	0.40m,10.9°	0.26m, **4.17°**
Red Kitchen	0.58m, 8.34°	0.58m, 7.54°	0.37m, 8.83°	**0.23m**, 5.35°	0.33m,10.3°	0.23m, **5.08°**
Stairs	0.48m, 13.1°	0.48m, 13.1°	0.40m, 13.7°	0.35m, 12.4°	0.33m, 11.4°	**0.28m, 7.53°**

even for cases where the nearest neighbours that are retrieved are noisy (e.g. 1st and 2nd columns). In addition, we can observe that in the majority of the cases, the predicted poses are significantly closer to the ground truth than the retrieved poses of the nearest neighbours. Lastly, we show a failure case (last column) where the system was not able to recover, due to the fact that the nearest neighbour is remarkably far from the ground truth, something that is likely due to the limited overlap between train and test poses.

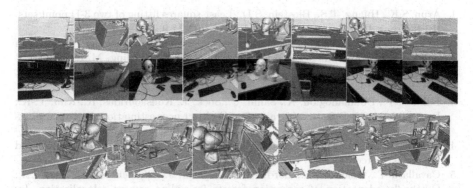

Fig. 7. (top 2 rows) Examples of the global map rendered using our predicted pose (top 1st row) compared to the actual ground truth view (top 2nd row) (bottom) Examples of how our network "corrects" the poses of the nearest neighbours (red frusta) to produce novel camera poses (cyan frusta). We can observe that in most cases, the corrected poses are significantly closer to the ground truth (blue frustum). (Color figure online)

5   Conclusions

We have presented a method to train a network using frustum overlaps that is able to retrieve nearest pose neighbours with high accuracy. We show experimental results that indicate that the proposed method is able to outperform previous works, and is able to generalise in a meaningful way to novel datasets. Finally, we illustrate that our system is able to predict reasonably accurate candidate poses, even when the retrieved nearest neighbours are noisy. Lastly, we introduce a novel dataset specifically aimed at relocalisation methods, that we make public.

For future work, we aim to investigate more advanced methods of training the retrieval network, together with novel ways of fusing multiple predicted poses. Significant progress can also be made in the differential regression stage to boost the good performance of our fine-grained camera pose descriptors. In addition, an interesting extension to our work would be to address the scene scaling issue, using some online estimation of the scene, and adjusting the learning method accordingly.

Acknowledgments. We gratefully acknowledge the Huawei Innovation Research Program (HIRP) FLAGSHIP grant and the European Commission Project Multiple-actOrs Virtual Empathic CARegiver for the Elder (MoveCare) for financially supporting the authors for this work.

References

1. Arun, S.K., Huang, T.S., Blostein, S.D.: Least-squares fitting of two 3-D point sets. IEEE Trans. Pattern Anal. Machine Intell. (PAMI) **9**, 698–700 (1987)
2. Hinterstoisser, S., Lepetit, V., Rajkumar, N., Konolige, K.: Going further with point pair features. In: Leibe, B., Matas, J., Sebe, N., Welling, M. (eds.) ECCV 2016. LNCS, vol. 9907, pp. 834–848. Springer, Cham (2016). https://doi.org/10.1007/978-3-319-46487-9_51
3. Balntas, V., Doumanoglou, A., Sahin, C., Sock, J., Kouskouridas, R., Kim, T.-K.: Pose guided RGB-D feature learning for 3D object pose estimation. In: Proceedings of International Conference on Computer Vision (ICCV) (2017)
4. Cadena, C., et al.: Simultaneous localization and mapping: present, future, and the robust-perception age. IEEE Trans. Robot. (ToR), 1–27 (2016)
5. Cavallari, T., Golodetz, S., Lord, N.A., Valentin, J., Di Stefano, L., Torr, P.H.: On-the-fly adaptation of regression forests for online camera relocalisation. In: Proceedings of IEEE International Conference on Computer Vision and Pattern Recognition (CVPR) (2017)
6. Chekhlov, D., Pupilli, M., Mayol, W., Calway, A.: Robust real-time visual SLAM using scale prediction and exemplar based feature description. In: Proceedings of IEEE International Conference on Computer Vision and Pattern Recognition (CVPR) (2007)
7. Clark, R., Wang, S., Markham, A., Trigoni, N., Wen, H.: 6-DoF video-clip relocalization. In: Proceedings of IEEE International Conference on Computer Vision and Pattern Recognition (CVPR) (2017)

8. Dai, A., Chang, A.X., Savva, M., Halber, M., Funkhouser, T., Nießner, M.: Scan-Net: richly-annotated 3D reconstructions of indoor scenes. In: Proceedings of IEEE International Conference on Computer Vision and Pattern Recognition (CVPR) (2017)

9. Deng, J., Dong, W., Socher, R., Li, L.-J., Li, K., Fei-Fei, L.: ImageNet: a large-scale hierarchical image database. In: Proceedings of IEEE International Conference on Computer Vision and Pattern Recognition (CVPR) (2009)

10. Doumanoglou, A., Balntas, V., Kouskouridas, R., Kim, T.: Siamese regression networks with efficient mid-level feature extraction for 3D object pose estimation. arXiv preprint arXiv:1607.02257 (2016)

11. Drost, B., Ulrich, M., Navab, N., Ilic, S.: Model globally, match locally: efficient and robust 3D object recognition. In: Proceedings of IEEE International Conference on Computer Vision and Pattern Recognition (CVPR), pp. 998–1005 (2010)

12. Eade, E.: Lie Groups for 2D and 3D Transformations. Technical report, University of Cambridge (2017)

13. Engel, J., Schöps, T., Cremers, D.: LSD-SLAM: large-scale direct monocular SLAM. In: Fleet, D., Pajdla, T., Schiele, B., Tuytelaars, T. (eds.) ECCV 2014. LNCS, vol. 8690, pp. 834–849. Springer, Cham (2014). https://doi.org/10.1007/978-3-319-10605-2_54

14. Galvez-Lopez, D., Tardos, J.D.: Bags of binary words for fast place recognition in image sequences. In: Proceedings of IEEE International Conference on Computer Vision and Pattern Recognition (CVPR), vol. 28, pp. 1188–1197 (2012)

15. Gee, A., Mayol-Cuevas, W.: 6D relocalisation for RGBD cameras using synthetic view regression. In: Proceedings of British Machine Vision Conference (BMVC) (2012)

16. Glocker, B., Izadi, S., Shotton, J., Criminisi, A.: Real-time RGB-D camera relocalization. In: Proceedings of IEEE/ACM International Symposium on Mixed and Augmented Reality (ISMAR), vol. 21, pp. 571–583 (2013)

17. Guzman-Rivera, A., et al.: Multi-output learning for camera relocalization. In: Proceedings of IEEE International Conference on Computer Vision and Pattern Recognition (CVPR) (2014)

18. Handa, A., Bloesch, M., Patraucean, V., Stent, S., McCormac, J., Davison, A.: GVNN: neural network library for geometric computer vision. In: Proceedings of the European Conference on Computer Vision Workshops (2016)

19. He, K., Zhang, X., Ren, S., Sun, J.: Deep residual learning for image recognition. In: Proceedings of IEEE International Conference on Computer Vision and Pattern Recognition (CVPR), pp. 770–778 (2016)

20. Horn, B.K.: Closed-form solution of absolute orientation using unit quaternions. J. Opt. Soc. Am. A 4, 629–642 (1986)

21. Huang, A.S., et al.: Visual odometry and mapping for autonomous flight using an RGB-D camera. In: Proceedings of International Symposium on Robotics Research (ISRR) (2011)

22. Kähler, O., Prisacariu, V.A., Murray, D.W.: Real-time large-scale dense 3D reconstruction with loop closure. In: Leibe, B., Matas, J., Sebe, N., Welling, M. (eds.) ECCV 2016. LNCS, vol. 9912, pp. 500–516. Springer, Cham (2016). https://doi.org/10.1007/978-3-319-46484-8_30

23. Kendall, A., Cipolla, R.: Modelling uncertainty in deep learning for camera relocalization. In: Proceedings of IEEE International Conference on Robotics and Automation (ICRA), pp. 4762–4769 (2016)

24. Kendall, A., Cipolla, R.: Geometric loss functions for camera pose regression with deep learning. In: Proceedings of IEEE International Conference on Computer Vision and Pattern Recognition (CVPR), pp. 6555–6564 (2017)

25. Kendall, A., Grimes, M., Cipolla, R.: PoseNet: a convolutional network for real-time 6-DOF camera relocalization. In: Proceedings of International Conference on Computer Vision (ICCV), pp. 2938–2946 (2015)

26. Kengo, H., Satoko, T., Toru, T., Bisser, R., Kazufumi, K., Toshiyuki, A.: Comparison of 3 DOF pose representations for pose estimations. In: Korea-Japan Joint Workshop on Frontiers of Computer Vision (FCV) (2010)

27. Kingma, D., Ba, J.: Adam: a method for stochastic optimization. In: Proceedings of International Conference on Learning Representations (ICLR) (2015)

28. Laskar, Z., Melekhov, I., Kalia, S., Kannala, J.: Camera relocalization by computing pairwise relative poses using convolutional neural network. arXiv preprint arXiv:1707.09733 (2017)

29. Lepetit, V., Moreno-Noguer, F., Fua, P.: EPnP: an accurate O(n) solution to the PnP problem. Intl. J. Comput. Vis. (IJCV) **81**, 155–166 (2009)

30. Li, S., Calway, A.: RGBD relocalisation using pairwise geometry and concise key point sets. In: Proceedings of IEEE International Conference on Robotics and Automation (ICRA) (2015)

31. Li, S., Calway, A.: Absolute pose estimation using multiple forms of correspondences from RGB-D frames. In: Proceedings of IEEE International Conference on Robotics and Automation (ICRA), pp. 4756–4761 (2016)

32. Li, S., Xu, C., Xie, M.: A robust O(n) solution to the perspective-n-point problem. IEEE Trans. Pattern Anal. Machine Intell. (PAMI) **34**, 1444–1450 (2012)

33. Mahendran, S., Ali, H., Vidal, R.: 3D pose regression using convolutional neural networks. In: Proceedings of IEEE International Conference on Computer Vision and Pattern Recognition Workshops (CVPRW), pp. 494–495 (2017)

34. Massa, F., Marlet, R., Aubry, M.: Crafting a multi-task CNN for viewpoint estimation. In: Proceedings of British Machine Vision Conference (BMVC), pp. 91.1–91.12 (2016)

35. Micheals, R.J., Boult, T.E.: On the robustness of absolute orientation. In: Proceedings of IEEE International Conference on Robotics and Automation (ICRA) (2000)

36. Moo Yi, K., Verdie, Y., Fua, P., Lepetit, V.: Learning to assign orientations to feature points. In: Proceedings of IEEE International Conference on Computer Vision and Pattern Recognition (CVPR), pp. 107–116 (2016)

37. Mur-Artal, R., Montiel, J.M.M., Tardos, J.D.: ORB-SLAM: a versatile and accurate monocular SLAM system. IEEE Trans. Robot. (ToR) **31**(5), 1147–1163 (2015)

38. Prisacariu, V.A., et al.: InfiniTAM v3: A Framework for Large-Scale 3D Reconstruction with Loop Closure. arXiv preprint arXiv:1708.00783 (2017)

39. Saeedi, S., Trentini, M., Li, H., Seto, M.: Multiple-robot simultaneous localization and mapping - a review. J. Field Robot. (2015)

40. Salas-Moreno, R.F., Newcombe, R.A., Strasdat, H., Kelly, P.H., Davison, A.J.: SLAM++: simultaneous localisation and mapping at the level of objects. In: Proceedings of IEEE International Conference on Computer Vision and Pattern Recognition (CVPR), pp. 1352–1359 (2013)

41. Shinji, U.: Least-squares estimation of transformation parameters between two point patterns. IEEE Trans. Pattern Anal. Machine Intell. (PAMI) **13**(4), 376–380 (1991)

42. Shotton, J., Glocker, B., Zach, C., Izadi, S., Criminisi, A., Fitzgibbon, A.: Scene coordinate regression forests for camera relocalization in RGB-D images. In: Proceedings of IEEE International Conference on Computer Vision and Pattern Recognition (CVPR), pp. 2930–2937 (2013)
43. Simonyan, K., Zisserman, A.: Very Deep Convolutional Networks for Large-scale Image Recognition. arXiv preprint arXiv:1409.1556 (2014)
44. Ummenhofer, B., et al.: DeMoN: depth and motion network for learning monocular stereo. In: Proceedings of IEEE International Conference on Computer Vision and Pattern Recognition (CVPR), pp. 5622–5631 (2017)
45. Valentin, J., Fitzgibbon, A., Nießner, M., Shotton, J., Torr, P.: Exploiting uncertainty in regression forests for accurate camera relocalization. In: Proceedings of IEEE International Conference on Computer Vision and Pattern Recognition (CVPR) (2015)
46. Walch, F., Hazirbas, C., Leal-Taixé, L., Sattler, T., Hilsenbeck, S., Cremers, D.: Image-based Localization with Spatial LSTMs. arXiv preprint arXiv:1611.07890 (2016)
47. Zheng, Y., Kuang, Y., Sugimoto, S., Astrom, K., Okutomi, M.: Revisiting the PnP problem: a fast, general and optimal solution. In: Proceedings of International Conference on Computer Vision (ICCV), pp. 2344–2351 (2013)
48. Zhou, B., Lapedriza, A., Khosla, A., Oliva, A., Torralba, A.: Places: a 10 million image database for scene recognition. IEEE Trans. Pattern Anal. Machine Intell. (PAMI) (2017)

The Contextual Loss for Image Transformation with Non-aligned Data

Roey Mechrez[✉], Itamar Talmi, and Lihi Zelnik-Manor

Technion - Israel Institute of Technology, Haifa, Israel
{roey,titamar}@campus.technion.ac.il, lihi@ee.technion.ac.il

Abstract. Feed-forward CNNs trained for image transformation problems rely on loss functions that measure the similarity between the generated image and a target image. Most of the common loss functions assume that these images are spatially aligned and compare pixels at corresponding locations. However, for many tasks, aligned training pairs of images will not be available. We present an alternative loss function that does not require alignment, thus providing an effective and simple solution for a new space of problems. Our loss is based on both context and semantics – it compares regions with similar semantic meaning, while considering the context of the entire image. Hence, for example, when transferring the style of one face to another, it will translate eyes-to-eyes and mouth-to-mouth. Our code can be found at https://www.github.com/roimehrez/contextualLoss.

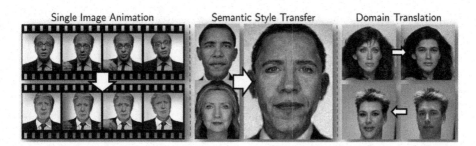

Fig. 1. Our Contextual loss is effective for many image transformation tasks: It can make a Trump cartoon imitate Ray Kurzweil, give Obama some of Hillary's features, and, turn women more masculine or men more feminine. Mutual to these tasks is the absence of ground-truth targets that can be compared pixel-to-pixel to the generated images. The Contextual loss provides a simple solution to all of these tasks.

R. Mechrez and I. Talmi—Contributed equally.

V. Ferrari et al. (Eds.): ECCV 2018, LNCS 11218, pp. 800–815, 2018.
https://doi.org/10.1007/978-3-030-01264-9_47

1   Introduction

Many classic problems can be framed as image transformation tasks, where a system receives some source image and generates a corresponding output image. Examples include image-to-image translation [1,2], super-resolution [3–5], and style-transfer [6–8]. Samples of our results for some of these applications are presented in Fig. 1.

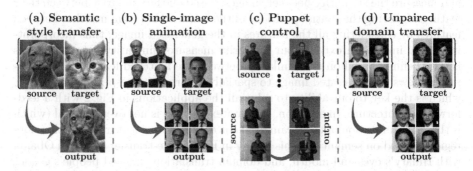

(a) Semantic style transfer

source   target

output

(b) Single-image animation

source   target

output

(c) Puppet control

source   target

source

output

(d) Unpaired domain transfer

source   target

output

Fig. 2. Non-aligned data: In many image translation tasks the desired *output* images are *not* spatially aligned with any of the available *target* images. (a) In *semantic style transfer* regions in the output image should share the style of corresponding regions in the target, e.g., the dog's fur, eyes and nose should be styled like those of the cat. (b) In *single-image animation* we animate a single target image according to input animation images. (c) In *puppet control* we animate a target "puppet" according to an input "driver" but we have available multiple training pairs of driver-puppet images. (d) In *domain transfer*, e.g., gender translation, the training images are not even paired, hence, clearly the outputs and targets are not aligned.

One approach for solving image transformation tasks is to train a feed-forward convolutional neural network. The training is based on comparing the image generated by the network with a target image via a differentiable loss function. The commonly used loss functions for comparing images can be classified into two types: (i) Pixel-to-pixel loss functions that compare pixels at the same spatial coordinates, e.g., $L2$ [3,9], $L1$ [1,2,10], and the perceptual loss of [8] (often computed at a coarse level). (ii) Global loss functions, such as the Gram loss [6], which successfully captures style [6,8] and texture [4,11] by comparing statistics collected over the entire image. Orthogonal to these are adversarial loss functions (GAN) [12], that push the generated image to be of high likelihood given examples from the target domain. This is complementary and does not compare the generated and the target image directly.

Both types of image comparison loss functions have been shown to be highly effective for many tasks, however, there are some cases they do not address. Specifically, the pixel-to-pixel loss functions explicitly assume that the generated image and target image are spatially aligned. They are not designed for problems where the training data is, by definition, not aligned. This is the case, as illustrated in Figs. 1 and 2, in tasks such as semantic style transfer, single-image animation, puppet control, and unpaired domain translation. Non-aligned images can be compared by the Gram loss, however, due to its global nature it translates global characteristics to the entire image. It cannot be used to constrain the content of the generated image, which is required in these applications.

In this paper we propose the *Contextual Loss* – a loss function targeted at non-aligned data. Our key idea is to treat an image as a collection of features, and measure the similarity between images, based on the similarity between their features, ignoring the spatial positions of the features. We form matches between features by considering all the features in the generated image, thus incorporating global image context into our similarity measure. Similarity between images is then defined based on the similarity between the matched features. This approach allows the generated image to spatially deform with respect to the target, which is the key to our ability to solve all the applications in Fig. 2 with a feed-forward architecture. In addition, the Contextual loss is not overly global (which is the main limitation of the Gram loss) since it compares features, and therefore regions, based on semantics. This is why in Fig. 1 style-transfer endowed Obama with Hillary's eyes and mouth, and domain translation changed people's gender by shaping/thickening their eyebrows and adding/removing makeup.

A nice characteristic of the Contextual loss is its tendency to maintain the appearance of the target image. This enables generation of images that look real even without using GANs, whose goal is specifically to distinguish between 'real' and 'fake', and are sometimes difficult to fine tune in training.

We show the utility and benefits of the Contextual loss through the applications presented in Fig. 2. In all four applications we show state-of-the-art or comparable results without using GANs. In style transfer, we offer an advancement by translating style in a semantic manner, without requiring segmentation. In the tasks of puppet-control and single-image-animation we show a significant improvement over previous attempts, based on pixel-to-pixel loss functions. Finally, we succeed in domain translation without paired data, outperforming CycleGAN [2], even though we use a single feed-forward network, while they train four networks (two generators, and two discriminators).

2   Related Work

Our key contribution is a new loss function that could be effective for many image transformation tasks. We review here the most relevant approaches for solving image-to-image translation and style transfer, which are the applications domains we experiment with.

Image-to-Image Translation includes tasks whose goal is to transform images from an input domain to a target domain, for example, day-to-night, horse-to-zebra, label-to-image, BW-to-color, edges-to-photo, summer-to-winter, photo-to-painting and many more. Isola *et al.* [1] (pix2pix) obtained impressive results with a feed-forward network and adversarial training (GAN) [12]. Their solution demanded pairs of aligned input-target images for training the network with a pixel-to-pixel loss function ($L2$ or $L1$). Chen and Koltun [10] proposed a Cascaded Refinement Network (CRN) for solving label-to-image, where an image is generated from an input semantic label map. Their solution as well used pixel-to-pixel losses, (Perceptual [8] and $L1$), and was later appended with GAN [13]. These approaches require paired and aligned training images.

Domain transfer has recently been applied also for problems were paired training data is not available [2,14,15]. To overcome the lack of training pairs the simple feed-forward architectures were replaced with more complex ones. The key idea being that translating from one domain to the other, and then going back, should take us to our starting point. This was modeled by complex architectures, e.g., in CycleGAN [2] four different networks are required. The circular process sometimes suffers from the mode collapse problem, a prevalent phenomenon in GANs, where data from multiple modes of a domain map to a single mode of a different domain [14].

Style Transfer aims at transferring the style of a target image to an input image [16–19]. Most relevant to our study are approaches based on CNNs. These differ mostly in the choice of architecture and loss function [6–8,20,21], a review is given in [22]. Gatys *et al.* [6] presented stunning results obtained by optimizing with a gradient based solver. They used the pixel-to-pixel Perceptual loss [8] to maintain similarity to the input image and proposed the Gram loss to capture the style of the target. Their approach allows for arbitrary style images, but this comes at a high computational cost. Methods with lower computational cost have also been proposed [8,21,23,24]. The speedup was obtained by replacing the optimization with training a feed-forward network. The main drawback of these latter methods is that they need to be re-trained for each new target style.

Another line of works aim at *semantic* style transfer, were the goal is to transfer style across regions of corresponding semantic meaning, e.g., sky-to-sky and trees-to-trees (in the methods listed above the target style is transfered globally to the entire image). One approach is to replace deep features of the input image with matching features of the target and then invert the features via efficient optimization [20] or through a pre-trained decoder [25]. Li *et al.* [7] integrate a Markov Random Field into the output synthesis process (CNNMRF). Since the matching in these approaches is between neural features semantic correspondence is obtained. A different approach to semantic style transfer is based on segmenting the image into regions according to semantic meaning [26,27]. This leads to semantic transfer, but depends on the success of the segmentation process. In [28] a histogram loss was suggested in order to synthesize textures that match the target statistically. This improves the color fatefulness but does not contribute to the semantic matching. Finally, there are also approaches tailored to a specific domain and style, such as faces or time-of-day in city-scape images [29,30].

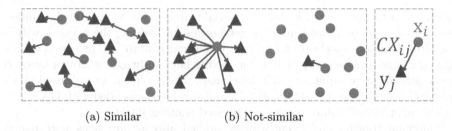

(a) Similar   (b) Not-similar

Fig. 3. Contextual similarity between images: Orange circles represent the features of an image x while the blue triangles represent the features of a target image y. The red arrows match each feature in y with its most *contextually similar* (Eq.(4)) feature in x. (a) Images x and y are similar: many features in x are matched with similar features in y. (b) Images x and y are not-similar: many features in x are not matched with any feature in y. The Contextual loss can be thought of as a weighted sum over the red arrows. It considers only the features and not their spatial location in the image. (Color figure online)

3   Method

Our goal is to design a loss function that can measure the similarity between images that are not necessarily aligned. Comparison of non-aligned images is also the core of template matching methods, that look for image-windows that are similar to a given template under occlusions and deformations. Recently, Talmi *et al.* [31] proposed a statistical approach for template matching with impressive results. Their measure of similarity, however, has no meaningful derivative, hence, we cannot adopt it as a loss function for training networks. We do, nonetheless, draw inspiration from their underlying observations.

3.1   Contextual Similarity Between Images

We start by defining a measure of similarity between a pair of images. Our key idea is to represent each image as a set of high-dimensional points (features), and consider two images as similar if their corresponding sets of points are similar. As illustrated in Fig. 3, we consider a pair of images as similar when for most features of one image there exist similar features in the other. Conversely, when the images are different from each other, many features of each image would have no similar feature in the other image. Based on this observation we formulate the contextual similarity measure between images.

Given an image x and a target image y we represent each as a collection of points (e.g., VGG19 features [32]): $X = \{x_i\}$ and $Y = \{y_j\}$. We assume $|Y| = |X| = N$ (and sample N points from the bigger set when $|Y| \neq |X|$). To calculate the similarity between the images we find for each feature y_j the feature x_i that is most similar to it, and then sum the corresponding feature similarity values over all y_j. Formally, the contextual similarity between images is defined as:

$$\mathrm{CX}(x,y) = \mathrm{CX}(X,Y) = \frac{1}{N} \sum_j \max_i \mathrm{CX}_{ij} \qquad (1)$$

where CX_{ij}, to be defined next, is the similarity between features x_i and y_j.

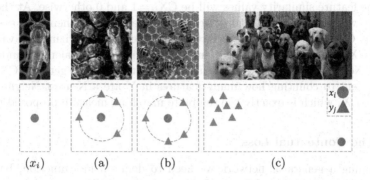

Fig. 4. Contextual similarity between features: We define the contextual similarity CX_{ij} between features x_i (queen bee) and y_j by considering the context of all the features in y. (a) x_i overlaps with a single y_j (the queen bee) while being far from all others (worker bees), hence, its contextual similarity to it is high while being low to all others. (b) x_i is far from all y_j's (worker bees), hence, its contextual similarity to all of them is low. (c) x_i is very far (different) from all y_j's (dogs), however, for scale robustness the contextual similarity values here should resemble those in (b).

We incorporate global image context via our definition of the similarity CX_{ij} between features. Specifically, we consider feature x_i as contextually similar to feature y_j if it is significantly closer to it than to all other features in Y. When this is not the case, i.e., x_i is not closer to any particular y_j, then its contextual similarity to all y_j should be low. This approach is robust to the scale of the distances, e.g., if x_i is far from all y_j then CX_{ij} will be low $\forall j$ regardless of how far apart x_i is. Figure 4 illustrates these ideas via examples.

We next formulate this mathematically. Let d_{ij} be the Cosine distance between x_i and y_j[1]. We consider features x_i and y_j as similar when $d_{ij} \ll d_{ik}, \forall k \neq j$. To capture this we start by normalizing the distances:

$$\tilde{d}_{ij} = \frac{d_{ij}}{\min_k d_{ik} + \epsilon} \tag{2}$$

for a fixed $\epsilon = 1e-5$. We shift from distances to similarities by exponentiation:

$$w_{ij} = \exp\left(\frac{1 - \tilde{d}_{ij}}{h}\right) \tag{3}$$

where $h > 0$ is a band-width parameter. Finally, we define the contextual similarity between features to be a scale invariant version of the normalized similarities:

$$CX_{ij} = w_{ij}/\sum_k w_{ik} \tag{4}$$

---

[1] $d_{ij} = (1 - \frac{(x_i - \mu_y)\cdot(y_j - \mu_y)}{\|x_i - \mu_y\|_2 \|y_j - \mu_y\|_2})$ where $\mu_y = \frac{1}{N}\sum_j y_j$.

Extreme Cases.   Since the Contextual Similarity sums over normalized values we get that $\text{CX}(X,Y) \in [0,1]$. Comparing an image to itself yields $\text{CX}(X,X)=1$, since the feature similarity values will be $\text{CX}_{ii}=1$ and 0 otherwise. At the other extreme, when the sets of features are far from each other then $\text{CX}_{ij} \approx \frac{1}{N} \forall i,j$, and thus $\text{CX}(X,Y) \approx \frac{1}{N} \to 0$. We further observe that binarizing the values by setting $\text{CX}_{ij}=1$ if $w_{ij} > w_{ik}, \forall k \neq j$ and 0 otherwise, is equivalent to finding the Nearest Neighbor in Y for every feature in X. In this case we get that $\text{CX}(X,Y)$ is equivalent to counting how many features in Y are a Nearest Neighbor of a feature in X, which is exactly the template matching measure proposed by [31].

3.2   The Contextual Loss

For training a generator network we need to define a loss function, based on the contextual similarity of Eq.(1). Let x and y be two images to be compared. We extract the corresponding set of features from the images by passing them through a perceptual network Φ, where in all of our experiments Φ is VGG19 [32]. Let $\Phi^l(x)$, $\Phi^l(y)$ denote the feature maps extracted from layer l of the perceptual network Φ of the images x and y, respectively. The contextual loss is defined as:

$$\mathcal{L}_{\text{CX}}(x,y,l) = -\log\left(\text{CX}\left(\Phi^l(x), \Phi^l(y)\right)\right) \tag{5}$$

In image transformation tasks we train a network G to map a given source image s into an output image $G(s)$. To demand similarity between the generated image and the target we use the loss $\mathcal{L}_{\text{CX}}(G(s),t,l)$. Often we demand also similarity to the source image by the loss $\mathcal{L}_{\text{CX}}(G(s),s,l)$. In Sect. 4 we describe in detail how we use such loss functions for various different applications and what values we select for l.

Other Loss Functions: In the following we compare the Contextual loss to other popular loss functions. We provide here their definitions for completeness:

- The Perceptual loss [8] $\mathcal{L}_P(x,y,l_P) = ||\Phi^{l_P}(x) - \Phi^{l_P}(y)||_1$, where Φ is VGG19 [32] and l_P represents the layer.
- The $L1$ loss $\mathcal{L}_1(x,y) = ||x-y||_1$.
- The $L2$ loss $\mathcal{L}_2(x,y) = ||x-y||_2$.
- The Gram loss [6] $\mathcal{L}_{Gram}(x,y,l_G) = ||\mathcal{G}_\Phi^{l_G}(x) - \mathcal{G}_\Phi^{l_G}(y)||_F^2$, where the Gram matrices $\mathcal{G}_\Phi^{l_G}$ of layer l_G of Φ are as defined in [6].

The first two are pixel-to-pixel loss functions that require alignment between the images x and y. The Gram loss is global and robust to pixel locations.

3.3   Analysis of the Contextual Loss

Expectation Analysis: The Contextual loss compares sets of features, thus implicitly, it can be thought of as a way for comparing distributions. To support this observation we provide empirical statistical analysis, similar to that

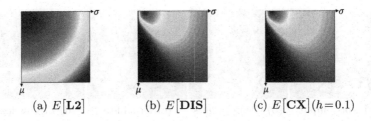

(a) $E[\mathbf{L2}]$　　　　　(b) $E[\mathbf{DIS}]$　　　　(c) $E[\mathbf{CX}]\,(h\!=\!0.1)$

Fig. 5. Expected behavior in the 1D Gaussian case: Two point sets, X and Y, are generated by sampling $N = M = 100$ points from $N(0;1)$, and $N(\mu;\sigma)$, respectively, with $[\mu,\sigma]\in[0,10]$. The approximated expectations of (a) $L2$ (from [33]), (b) DIS (from [31]), and, (c) the proposed CX, as a function of μ and σ show that CX drops much more rapidly than $L2$ as the distributions move apart.

presented in [31,33]. Our goal is to show that the expectation of $CX(X,Y)$ is maximal when the points in X and Y are drawn from the same distribution, and drops sharply as the distance between the two distributions increases. This is done via a simplified mathematical model, in which each image is modeled as a set of points drawn from a 1D Gaussian distribution. We compute the similarity between images for varying distances between the underlying Gaussians. Figure 5 presents the resulting approximated expected values. It can be seen that $CX(X,Y)$ is likely to be maximized when the distributions are the same, and falls rapidly as the distributions move apart from each other. Finally, similar to [31,33], one can show that this holds also for the multi-dimensional case.

Toy Experiment with Non-aligned Data: In order to examine the robustness of the contextual loss to non-aligned data, we designed the following toy experiment. Given a single noisy image s, and multiple clean images of the same scene (targets t^k), the goal is to reconstruct a clean image $G(s)$. The target images t^k are not aligned with the noisy source image s. In our toy experiment the source and target images were obtained by random crops of the same image, with random translations $\in[-10,10]$ pixels. We added random noise to the crop selected as source s. Reconstruction was performed by iterative optimization using gradient descent where we directly update the image values of s. That is, we minimize the objective function $\mathcal{L}(s,t^k)$, where $\mathcal{L}$ is either $\mathcal{L}_{CX}$ or $\mathcal{L}_1$, and we iterate over the targets t^k. In this specific experiment the features we use for the contextual loss are vectorized RGB patches of size 5×5 with stride 2 (and not VGG19).

The results, presented in Fig. 6, show that optimizing with $\mathcal{L}_1$ yields a drastically blurred image, because it cannot properly compare non-aligned images. The contextual loss, on the other hand, is designed to be robust to spatial deformations. Therefore, optimizing with $\mathcal{L}_{CX}$ leads to complete noise removal, without ruining the image details.

(a) Noisy input   (b) Clean targets   (c) $\mathcal{L}_1$ as loss   (d) $\mathcal{L}_{CX}$ as loss

Fig. 6. Robustness to misalignments: A noisy input image (a) is cleaned via gradient descent, where the target clean images (b) show the same scene, but are not aligned with the input. Optimizing with $\mathcal{L}_1$ leads to a highly blurred result (c) while optimizing with our contextual loss $\mathcal{L}_{CX}$ removes the noise nicely (d). This is since $\mathcal{L}_{CX}$ is robust to misalignments and spatial deformations.

We refer to reader to [34], were additional theoretical and empirical analysis of the contextual loss is presented.

4   Applications

We experiment on the tasks presented in Fig. 2. To asses the contribution of the proposed loss function we adopt for each task a state-of-the-art architecture and modify only the loss functions. In some tasks we also compare to other recent solutions. For all applications we used TensorFlow [35] and Adam optimizer [36] with the default parameters ($\beta_1 = 0.9, \beta_2 = 0.999, \epsilon = 1e-08$). Unless otherwise mentioned we set $h=0.5$ (of Eq. (3)).

Table 1. Applications settings: A summary of the settings for our four applications. We use here simplified notations: $\mathcal{L}^t$ marks which loss is used between the generated image $G(s)$ and the target t. Similarly, $\mathcal{L}^s$ stands for the loss between $G(s)$ and the source (input) s. We distinguish between paired and unpaired data and between semi-aligned (x+v) and non-aligned data. Definitions of the loss functions are in the text.

Application	Architecture	Proposed	Previous	Paired	Aligned
Style transfer	Optim. [6]	$\mathcal{L}^t_{CX}+\mathcal{L}^s_{CX}$	$\mathcal{L}^t_{Gram}+\mathcal{L}^s_P$	✓	✗
Single-image animation	CRN [10]	$\mathcal{L}^t_{CX}+\mathcal{L}^s_{CX}$	$\mathcal{L}^t_{Gram}+\mathcal{L}^s_P$	✓	✗
Puppet control	CRN [10]	$\mathcal{L}^t_{CX}+\mathcal{L}^s_P$	$\mathcal{L}^t_1+\mathcal{L}^t_P$	✓	✓✗
Domain transfer	CRN [10]	$\mathcal{L}^t_{CX}+\mathcal{L}^s_{CX}$	CycleGAN[2]	✗	✗

The tasks and the corresponding setups are summarized in Table 1. We use shorthand notation $\mathcal{L}^t_{type} = \mathcal{L}_{type}(G(s), t, l)$ to demand similarity between the generated image $G(s)$ and the target t and $\mathcal{L}^s_{type} = \mathcal{L}_{type}(G(s), s, l)$ to demand similarity to the source image s. The subscripted notation $\mathcal{L}_{type}$ stands for either the proposed $\mathcal{L}_{CX}$ or one of the common loss functions defined in Sect. 3.2.

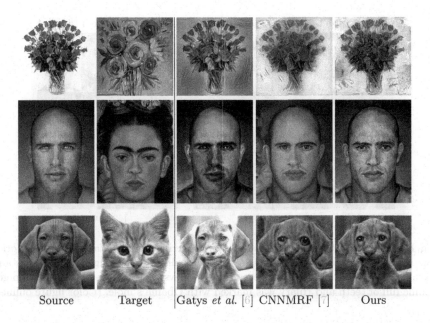

| Source | Target | Gatys *et al.* [6] | CNNMRF [7] | Ours |

Fig. 7. Semantic style transfer: The Contextual loss naturally provides semantic style transfer across regions of corresponding semantic meaning. Notice how in our results: (row1) the flowers and the stalks changed their style correctly, (row2) the man's eyebrows got connected, a little mustache showed up and his lips changed their shape and color, and (row3) the cute dog got the green eyes, white snout and yellowish head of the target cat. Our results are much different from those of [6] that transfer the style globally over the entire image. CNNMRF [7] achieves semantic matching but is very prone to artifacts. See supplementary for many more results and comparisons. (Color figure online)

4.1 Semantic Style Transfer

In style-transfer the goal is to translate the style of a target image t onto a source image s. A landmark approach, introduced by Gatys *et al.* [6], is to minimize a combination of two loss functions, the perceptual loss $\mathcal{L}_P(G(s), s, l_P)$ to maintain the content of the source image s, and the Gram loss $\mathcal{L}_{Gram}(G(s), t, l_G)$ to enforce style similarity to the target t (with $l_G = \{conv\mathbf{k}\_1\}_{\mathbf{k}=1}^{5}$ and $l_P = conv4\_2$).

We claim that the Contextual loss is a good alternative for both. By construction it makes a good choice for the style term, as it does not require alignment. Moreover, it will allow transferring style features between regions according to their semantic similarity, rather than globally over the entire image, which is what one gets with the Gram loss. The Contextual loss is also a good choice for the content term since it demands similarity to the source, but allows some positional deformations. Such deformations are advantageous, since due to the style change the stylized and source images will not be perfectly aligned.

source-1 target-1│source-2 target-2│source-3 target-3│source-4 target-4

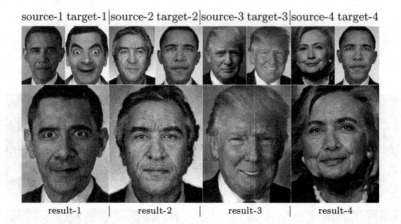

result-1   │   result-2   │   result-3   │   result-4

Fig. 8. Playing with target: Results of transferring different target targets. Notice how in each result we mapped features semantically, transferring shapes, colors and textures to the hair, mouth, nose, eyes and eyebrows. It is nice to see how Trump got a smile full of teeth and Hilary was marked with Obama's mole. (Color figure online)

To support these claims we adopt the optimization-based framework of Gatys *et al.* [6][2], that directly minimizes the loss through an iterative process, and replace their objective with:

$$\mathcal{L}(G) = \mathcal{L}_{\text{CX}}(G(s), t, l_t) + \mathcal{L}_{\text{CX}}(G(s), s, l_s) \tag{6}$$

where $l_s = conv4\_2$ (to capture content) and $l_t = \{conv\mathbf{k}\_2\}_{\mathbf{k}=2}^{4}$ (to capture style). We set h as 0.1 and 0.2 for the content term and style term respectively. In our implementation we reduced memory consumption by random sampling of layer $conv2\_2$ into 65×65 features.

Figure 8 presents a few example results. It can be seen that the style is transfered across corresponding regions, e.g., eyes-to-eyes, hair-to-hair, etc. In Fig. 7 we compare our style transfer results with two other methods: Gatys *et al.* [6] and CNNMRF [7]. The only difference between our setup and theirs is the loss function, as all three use the same optimization framework. It can be seen that our approach transfers the style semantically across regions, whereas, in Gatys' approach the style is spread all over the image, without semantics. CNN-MRF, on the other hand, does aim for semantic transfer. It is based on nearest neighbor matching of features, which indeed succeeds in replacing semantically corresponding features, however, it suffers from severe artifacts.

4.2 Single Image Animation

In single-image animation the data consists of many animation images from a source domain (e.g., person S) and only a single image t from a target domain

---

[2] We used the implementation in https://github.com/anishathalye/neural-style.

| source | baseline-1 | baseline-2 | baseline-3 |

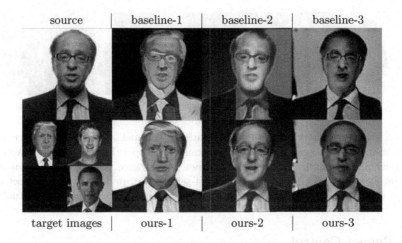

| target images | ours-1 | ours-2 | ours-3 |

Fig. 9. Single image animation: This figure is an animated gif showing every 20th frame from the test-set (video provided in project page (http://cgm.technion.ac.il/Computer-Graphics-Multimedia/Software/Contextual/), Supplementary 1). Given an input video (top-left) we animate three different target images (bottom-left). Comparing our animations (bottom) with the baseline (top) shows that we are much more faithful to the appearance of the targets and the motions of the input. Note, that our solution and the baseline differ only in the loss functions.

(e.g., person $\mathcal{T}$). The goal is to animate the target image according to the input source images. This implies that by the problem definition the generated images $G(s)$ are not aligned with the target t.

This problem setup is naturally handled by the Contextual loss. We use it both to maintain the animation (spatial layout) of the source s and to maintain the appearance of the target t:

$$\mathcal{L}(G) = \mathcal{L}_{\mathrm{CX}}(G(s), t, l_t) + \mathcal{L}_{\mathrm{CX}}(G(s), s, l_s) \qquad (7)$$

where $l_s = conv4\_2$ and $l_t = \{conv3\_2, conv4\_2\}$. We selected the CRN architecture of [10][3] and trained it for 10 epochs on 1000 input frames.

Results are shown in Fig. 9. We are not aware of previous work the solves this task with a generator network. We note, however, that our setup is somewhat related to fast style transfer [8], since effectively the network is trained to generate images with content similar to the input (source) but with style similar to the target. Hence, as baseline for comparison, we trained the same CRN architecture and replaced only the objective with a combination of the Perceptual (with $l_P = conv5\_2$) and Gram losses (with $l_G = \{convk\_1\}_{k=1}^{5}$), as proposed by [8]. It can be seen that using our Contextual loss is much more successful, leading to significantly fewer artifacts.

---

[3] We used the original implementation http://cqf.io/ImageSynthesis/.

Source   pix2pix [1]   CycleGAN [2]   CRN [10]   Ours

Fig. 10. Puppet control: Results of animating a "puppet" (Ray Kurzweil) according to the input video shown on the left. Our result is sharper, less prone to artifacts and more faithful to the input pose and the "puppet" appearance. This figure is an animated gif showing every 10th frame from the test-set (video provided in the project page (http://cgm.technion.ac.il/Computer-Graphics-Multimedia/Software/Contextual/).

4.3 Puppet Control

Our task here is somewhat similar to single-image animation. We wish to animate a target "puppet" according to provided images of a "driver" person (the source). This time, however, available to use are training pairs of source-target (driver-puppet) images, that are semi-aligned. Specifically, we repeated an experiment published online, were Brannon Dorsey (the driver) tried to control Ray Kurzweil (the puppet)[4]. For training he filmed a video ($\sim$1K frames) of himself imitating Kurzweil's motions. Then, given a new video of Brannon, the goal is to generate a corresponding animation of the puppet Kurzweil.

The generated images should look like the target puppet, hence we use the Contextual loss to compare them. In addition, since in this particular case the training data available to us consists of pairs of images that are semi-aligned, they do share a very coarse level similarity in their spatial arrangement. Hence, to further refine the optimization we add a Perceptual loss, computed at a very coarse level, that does not require alignment. Our overall objective is:

$$\mathcal{L}(G) = \mathcal{L}_{CX}(G(s), t, l_{CX}) + \lambda_P \cdot \mathcal{L}_P(G(s), t, l_P) \tag{8}$$

where $l_{CX} = \{conv\mathbf{k}\_2\}_{\mathbf{k}=2}^4$, $l_P = conv5\_2$, and $\lambda_P = 0.1$ to let the contextual loss dominate. As architecture we again selected CRN [10] and trained it for 20 epochs.

We compare our approach with three alternatives: (i) Using the exact same CRN architecture, but with the pixel-to-pixel loss function $\mathcal{L}_1$ instead of $\mathcal{L}_{CX}$. (ii) The Pix2pix architecture of [1] that uses $\mathcal{L}_1$ and adversarial training (GAN), since this was the original experiment. (iii) We also compare to CycleGAN [2] that treats the data as unpaired and compares images with $\mathcal{L}_1$ and uses adversarial training (GAN). Results are presented in Fig. 10. It can be seen that the puppet animation generated with our approach is much sharper, with significantly fewer artifacts, and captures nicely the poses of the driver, even though we don't use GAN.

---

[4] B. Dorsey, https://twitter.com/brannondorsey/status/808461108881268736.

Fig. 11. Unpaired domain transfer: Gender transformation with unpaired data (CelebA) [37], (Top) Male-to-female, (Bottom) Female-to-male. Our approach successfully modifies the facial attributes making the men more feminine (or the women more masculine) while preserving the original person identity. The changes are mostly noticeable in the eye makeup, eyebrows shaping and lips. Our gender modification is more successful than that of CycleGAN [2], even though we use a single feed-forward network, while they train a complex 4-network architecture.

4.4   Unpaired Domain Transfer

Finally, we use the Contextual loss also in the unpaired scenario of domain transfer. We experimented with gender change, i.e., making male portraits more feminine and vice versa. Since the data is unpaired (i.e., we do not have the female versions of the male images) we sample random pairs of images from the two domains. As the Contextual loss is robust to misalignments this is not a problem. We use the exact same architecture and loss as in single-image-animation.

Our results, presented in Fig. 11, are quite successful when compared with CycleGAN [2]. This is a nice outcome since our approach provides a much simpler alternative – while the CycleGAN framework trains four networks (two generators and two discriminators), our approach uses a single feed-forward generator network (without GAN). This is possible because the Contextual loss does not require aligned data, and hence, can naturally train on non-aligned random pairs.

5   Conclusions

We proposed a novel loss function for image generation that naturally handles tasks with non-aligned training data. We have applied it for four different applications and showed state-of-the-art (or comparable) results on all.

In our follow-up work, [34], we suggest to use the Contextual loss for realistic restoration, specifically for the tasks of super-resolution and surface normal estimation. We draw a theoretical connection between the Contextual loss and KL-divergence, which is supported by empirical evidence. In future work we hope to seek other loss functions, that could overcome further drawbacks of the existing ones.

In the supplementary we present limitations of our approach, ablation studies, and explore variations of the proposed loss.

Acknowledgements. This research was supported by the Israel Science Foundation under Grant 1089/16 and by the Ollendorf foundation.

References

1. Isola, P., Zhu, J.Y., Zhou, T., Efros, A.A.: Image-to-image translation with conditional adversarial networks. In: CVPR (2017)
2. Zhu, J.Y., Park, T., Isola, P., Efros, A.A.: Unpaired image-to-image translation using cycle-consistent adversarial networks. In: ICCV (2017)
3. Ledig, C., et al.: Photo-realistic single image super-resolution using a generative adversarial network. In: CVPR (2017)
4. Sajjadi, M.S., Scholkopf, B., Hirsch, M.: Enhancenet: single image super-resolution through automated texture synthesis. In: ICCV (2017)
5. Lai, W.S., Huang, J.B., Ahuja, N., Yang, M.H.: Deep Laplacian pyramid networks for fast and accurate super-resolution. In: IEEE Conference on Computer Vision and Pattern Recognition (2017)
6. Gatys, L.A., Ecker, A.S., Bethge, M.: Image style transfer using convolutional neural networks. In: CVPR (2016)
7. Li, C., Wand, M.: Combining Markov random fields and convolutional neural networks for image synthesis. In: CVPR (2016)
8. Johnson, J., Alahi, A., Fei-Fei, L.: Perceptual losses for real-time style transfer and super-resolution. In: Leibe, B., Matas, J., Sebe, N., Welling, M. (eds.) ECCV 2016. LNCS, vol. 9906, pp. 694–711. Springer, Cham (2016). https://doi.org/10.1007/978-3-319-46475-6_43
9. Xu, L., Ren, J.S., Liu, C., Jia, J.: Deep convolutional neural network for image deconvolution. In: NIPS (2014)
10. Chen, Q., Koltun, V.: Photographic image synthesis with cascaded refinement networks. In: ICCV (2017)
11. Li, Y., Fang, C., Yang, J., Wang, Z., Lu, X., Yang, M.H.: Diversified texture synthesis with feed-forward networks. In: CVPR (2017)
12. Goodfellow, I., et al.: Generative adversarial nets. In: NIPS (2014)
13. Wang, T.C., Liu, M.Y., Zhu, J.Y., Tao, A., Kautz, J., Catanzaro, B.: High-resolution image synthesis and semantic manipulation with conditional gans. arXiv preprint arXiv:1711.11585 (2017)

14. Kim, T., Cha, M., Kim, H., Lee, J., Kim, J.: Learning to discover cross-domain relations with generative adversarial networks. arXiv preprint arXiv:1703.05192 (2017)

15. Yi, Z., Zhang, H., Gong, P.T., et al.: DualGAN: unsupervised dual learning for image-to-image translation. arXiv preprint arXiv:1704.02510 (2017)

16. Hertzmann, A., Jacobs, C.E., Oliver, N., Curless, B., Salesin, D.H.: Image analogies. In: Computer Graphics and Interactive Techniques. ACM (2001)

17. Liang, L., Liu, C., Xu, Y.Q., Guo, B., Shum, H.Y.: Real-time texture synthesis by patch-based sampling. ACM ToG **20**(3), 127–150 (2001)

18. Elad, M., Milanfar, P.: Style transfer via texture synthesis. IEEE Trans. Image Process. **26**(5), 23338–2351 (2017)

19. Frigo, O., Sabater, N., Delon, J., Hellier, P.: Split and match: example-based adaptive patch sampling for unsupervised style transfer. In: CVPR (2016)

20. Chen, T.Q., Schmidt, M.: Fast patch-based style transfer of arbitrary style. arXiv preprint arXiv:1612.04337 (2016)

21. Ulyanov, D., Vedaldi, A., Lempitsky, V.: Instance normalization: the missing ingredient for fast stylization. arXiv preprint arXiv:1607.08022 (2016)

22. Jing, Y., Yang, Y., Feng, Z., Ye, J., Song, M.: Neural style transfer: a review. arXiv preprint arXiv:1705.04058 (2017)

23. Dumoulin, V., Shlens, J., Kudlur, M.: A learned representation for artistic style. In: ICLR (2017)

24. Ulyanov, D., Lebedev, V., Vedaldi, A., Lempitsky, V.S.: Texture networks: feedforward synthesis of textures and stylized images. In: ICML, pp. 1349–1357 (2016)

25. Huang, X., Belongie, S.: Arbitrary style transfer in real-time with adaptive instance normalization. In: ICCV (2017)

26. Luan, F., Paris, S., Shechtman, E., Bala, K.: Deep photo style transfer. In: CVPR (2017)

27. Zhao, H., Rosin, P.L., Lai, Y.K.: Automatic semantic style transfer using deep convolutional neural networks and soft masks. arXiv preprint arXiv:1708.09641 (2017)

28. Risser, E., Wilmot, P., Barnes, C.: Stable and controllable neural texture synthesis and style transfer using histogram losses. arXiv preprint arXiv:1701.08893 (2017)

29. Shih, Y., Paris, S., Durand, F., Freeman, W.T.: Data-driven hallucination of different times of day from a single outdoor photo. In: ACM ToG (2013)

30. Shih, Y., Paris, S., Barnes, C., Freeman, W.T., Durand, F.: Style transfer for headshot portraits. ACM ToG **33**(4), 148 (2014)

31. Talmi, I., Mechrez, R., Zelnik-Manor, L.: Template matching with deformable diversity similarity. In: CVPR (2017)

32. Simonyan, K., Zisserman, A.: Very deep convolutional networks for large-scale image recognition. arXiv preprint arXiv:1409.1556 (2014)

33. Dekel, T., Oron, S., Rubinstein, M., Avidan, S., Freeman, W.T.: Best-buddies similarity for robust template matching. In: Proceedings of the IEEE Conference on Computer Vision and Pattern Recognition, pp. 2021–2029 (2015)

34. Mechrez, R., Talmi, I., Shama, F., Zelnik-Manor, L.: Learning to maintain natural image statistics. arXiv preprint arXiv:1803.04626 (2018)

35. Abadi, M., et al.: Tensorflow: Large-scale machine learning on heterogeneous distributed systems. arXiv preprint arXiv:1603.04467 (2016)

36. Kingma, D., Ba, J.: Adam: a method for stochastic optimization. arXiv preprint arXiv:1412.6980 (2014)

37. Liu, Z., Luo, P., Wang, X., Tang, X.: Deep learning face attributes in the wild. In: ICCV (2015)

Acquisition of Localization Confidence for Accurate Object Detection

Borui Jiang[1,3], Ruixuan Luo[1,3], Jiayuan Mao[2,4(✉)], Tete Xiao[1,3], and Yuning Jiang[4]

[1] School of Electronics Engineering and Computer Science, Peking University, Beijing, China
{jbr,luoruixuan97,jasonhsiao97}@pku.edu.cn
[2] ITCS, Institute for Interdisciplinary Information Sciences, Tsinghua University, Beijing, China
mjy14@mails.tsinghua.edu.cn
[3] Megvii Inc. (Face++), Beijing, China
[4] Toutiao AI Lab, Beijing, China
jiangyuning@bytedance.com

Abstract. Modern CNN-based object detectors rely on bounding box regression and non-maximum suppression to localize objects. While the probabilities for class labels naturally reflect classification confidence, localization confidence is absent. This makes properly localized bounding boxes degenerate during iterative regression or even suppressed during NMS. In the paper we propose IoU-Net learning to predict the IoU between each detected bounding box and the matched ground-truth. The network acquires this confidence of localization, which improves the NMS procedure by preserving accurately localized bounding boxes. Furthermore, an optimization-based bounding box refinement method is proposed, where the predicted IoU is formulated as the objective. Extensive experiments on the MS-COCO dataset show the effectiveness of IoU-Net, as well as its compatibility with and adaptivity to several state-of-the-art object detectors.

Keywords: Object localization · Bounding box regression
Non-maximum suppression

1 Introduction

Object detection serves as a prerequisite for a broad set of downstream vision applications, such as instance segmentation [18,19], human skeleton [26], face recognition [25] and high-level object-based reasoning [29]. Object detection combines both object classification and object localization. A majority of modern object detectors are based on two-stage frameworks [7–9,15,21], in which object

---

B. Jiang, R. Luo and J. Mao—Equal contribution.

V. Ferrari et al. (Eds.): ECCV 2018, LNCS 11218, pp. 816–832, 2018.
https://doi.org/10.1007/978-3-030-01264-9_48

detection is formulated as a multi-task learning problem: (1) distinguish foreground object proposals from background and assign them with proper class labels; (2) regress a set of coefficients which localize the object by maximizing intersection-over-union (IoU) or other metrics between detection results and the ground-truth. Finally, redundant bounding boxes (duplicated detections on the same object) are removed by a non-maximum suppression (NMS) procedure.

Classification and localization are solved differently in such detection pipeline. Specifically, given a proposal, while the probability for each class label naturally acts as an "classification confidence" of the proposal, the bounding box regression module finds the optimal transformation for the proposal to best fit the ground-truth. However, the "localization confidence" is absent in the loop.

(a) Demonstrative cases of the misalignment between classification confidence and localization accuracy. The yellow bounding boxes denote the ground-truth, while the red and green bounding boxes are both detection results yielded by FPN [16]. Localization confidence is computed by the proposed IoU-Net. Using classification confidence as the ranking metric will cause accurately localized bounding boxes (in green) being incorrectly eliminated in the traditional NMS procedure. Quantitative analysis is provided in Section 2.1

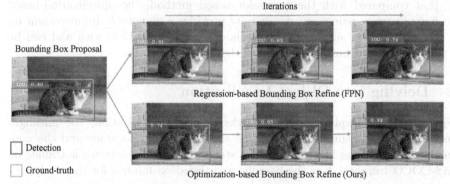

(b) Demonstrative cases of the non-monotonic localization in iterative bounding box regression. Quantitative analysis is provided in Section 2.2.

Fig. 1. Visualization on two drawbacks brought by the absence of localization confidence. Examples are selected from MS-COCO *minival* [16]. (Color figure online)

This brings about two drawbacks. (1) First, the suppression of duplicated detections is ignorant of the localization accuracy while the classification scores are typically used as the metric for ranking the proposals. In Fig. 1(a), we show a set of cases where the detected bounding boxes with higher classification confidences contrarily have smaller overlaps with the corresponding ground-truth. Analog to Gresham's saying that *bad money drives out good*, the misalignment between classification confidence and localization accuracy may lead to accurately localized bounding boxes being suppressed by less accurate ones in the NMS procedure. (2) Second, the absence of localization confidence makes the widely-adopted bounding box regression less interpretable. As an example, previous works [3] report the non-monotonicity of iterative bounding box regression. That is, bounding box regression may degenerate the localization of input bounding boxes if applied for multiple times (shown as Fig. 1(b)).

In this paper we introduce IoU-Net, which predicts the IoU between detected bounding boxes and their corresponding ground-truth boxes, making the networks aware of the localization criterion analog to the classification module. This simple coefficient provides us with new solutions to the aforementioned problems:

1. IoU is a natural criterion for localization accuracy. We can replace classification confidence with the predicted IoU as the ranking keyword in NMS. This technique, namely IoU-guided NMS, help to eliminate the suppression failure caused by the misleading classification confidences.
2. We present an optimization-based bounding box refinement procedure on par with the traditional regression-based methods. During the inference, the predicted IoU is used as the optimization objective, as well as an interpretable indicator of the localization confidence. The proposed Precise RoI Pooling layer enables us to solve the IoU optimization by gradient ascent. We show that compared with the regression-based method, the optimization-based bounding box refinement empirically provides a monotonic improvement on the localization accuracy. The method is fully compatible with and can be integrated into various CNN-based detectors [3,9,15].

2   Delving into Object Localization

First of all, we explore two drawbacks in object localization: the misalignment between classification confidence and localization accuracy and the non-monotonic bounding box regression. A standard FPN [15] detector is trained on MS-COCO *trainval35k* as the baseline and tested on *minival* for the study.

2.1   Misaligned Classification and Localization Accuracy

With the objective to remove duplicated bounding boxes, NMS has been an indispensable component in most object detectors since [4]. NMS works in an iterative manner. At each iteration, the bounding box with the maximum classification confidence is selected and its neighboring boxes are eliminated using a predefined overlapping threshold. In Soft-NMS [2] algorithm, box elimination is replaced by the decrement of confidence, leading to a higher recall. Recently, a set of learning-based algorithms have been proposed as alternatives to the parameter-free NMS

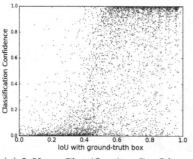

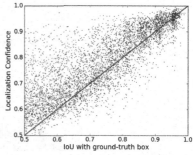

(a) IoU vs. Classification Confidence   (b) IoU vs. Localization Confidence

Fig. 2. The correlation between the IoU of bounding boxes with the matched ground-truth and the classification/localization confidence. Considering detected bounding boxes having an IoU (>0.5) with the corresponding ground-truth, the Pearson correlation coefficients are: (a) 0.217, and (b) 0.617. (a) The classification confidence indicates the category of a bounding box, but cannot be interpreted as the localization accuracy. (b) To resolve the issue, we propose IoU-Net to predict the localization confidence for each detected bounding box, *i.e.*, its IoU with corresponding ground-truth.

and Soft-NMS. [23] calculates an overlap matrix of all bounding boxes and performs affinity propagation clustering to select exemplars of clusters as the final detection results. [10] proposes the GossipNet, a post-processing network trained for NMS based on bounding boxes and the classification confidence. [11] proposes an end-to-end network learning the relation between detected bounding boxes. However, these parameter-based methods require more computational resources which limits their real-world application.

In the widely-adopted NMS approach, the classification confidence is used for ranking bounding boxes, which can be problematic. We visualize the distribution of classification confidences of all detected bounding boxes before NMS, as shown in Fig. 2(a). The x-axis is the IoU between the detected box and its matched ground-truth, while the y-axis denotes its classification confidence. The Pearson correlation coefficient indicates that the localization accuracy is not well correlated with the classification confidence.

We attribute this to the objective used by most of the CNN-based object detectors in distinguishing foreground (positive) samples from background (negative) samples. A detected bounding box box_{det} is considered positive during training if its IoU with one of the ground-truth bounding box is greater than a threshold Ω_{train}. This objective can be misaligned with the localization accuracy. Figure 1(a) shows cases where bounding boxes having higher classification confidence have poorer localization.

Recall that in traditional NMS, when there exists duplicated detections for a single object, the bounding box with maximum classification confidence will be preserved. However, due to the misalignment, the bounding box with better localization will probably get suppressed during the NMS, leading to the poor localization of objects. Figure 3 quantitatively shows the number of posi-

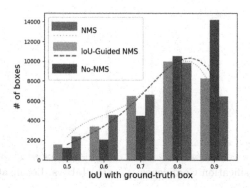

Fig. 3. The number of positive bounding boxes after the NMS, grouped by their IoU with the matched ground-truth. In traditional NMS (blue bar), a significant portion of accurately localized bounding boxes get mistakenly suppressed due to the misalignment of classification confidence and localization accuracy, while IoU-guided NMS (yellow bar) preserves more accurately localized bounding boxes. (Color figure online)

tive bounding boxes after NMS. The bounding boxes are grouped by their IoU with the matched ground-truth. For multiple detections matched with the same ground-truth, only the one with the highest score is considered positive. Therefore, No-NMS could be considered as the upper-bound for the number of positive bounding boxes. We can see that the absence of localization confidence makes more than half of detected bounding boxes with IoU >0.9 being suppressed in the traditional NMS procedure, which degrades the localization quality of the detection results.

2.2 Non-monotonic Bounding Box Regression

In general, single object localization can be classified into two categories: bounding box-based methods and segment-based methods. The segment-based methods [9,12,18,19] aim to generate a pixel-level segment for each instance but inevitably require additional segmentation annotation. This work focuses on the bounding box-based methods.

Single object localization is usually formulated as a bounding box regression task. The core idea is that a network directly learns to transform (*i.e.*, scale or shift) a bounding box to its designated target. In [7,8] linear regression or fully-connected layer is applied to refine the localization of object proposals generated by external pre-processing modules (*e.g.*, Selective Search [27] or Edge-Boxes [32]). Faster R-CNN [22] proposes region proposal network (RPN) in which only predefined anchors are used to train an end-to-end object detector. [13,31] utilize anchor-free, fully-convolutional networks to handle object scale variation. Meanwhile, Repulsion Loss is proposed in [28] to robustly detect objects with crowd occlusion. Due to its effectiveness and simplicity, bounding box regression has become an essential component in most CNN-based detectors.

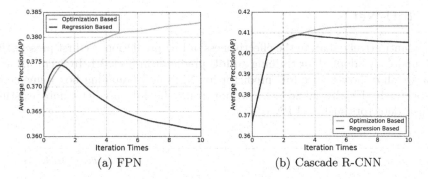

(a) FPN   (b) Cascade R-CNN

Fig. 4. Optimization-based *v.s.* Regression-based BBox refinement. **(a)** Comparison in FPN. When applying the regression iteratively, the AP of detection results firstly get improved but drops quickly in later iterations. **(b)** Comparison in Cascade R-CNN. Iteration 0, 1 and 2 represents the 1st, 2nd and 3rd regression stages in Cascade R-CNN. For iteration $i \geq 3$, we refine the bounding boxes with the regressor of the third stage. After multiple iteration, AP slightly drops, while the optimization-based method further improves the AP by 0.8%.

A broad set of downstream applications such as tracking and recognition will benefit from accurately localized bounding boxes. This raises the demand for improving localization accuracy. In a series of object detectors [5,6,20,30], refined boxes will be fed to the bounding box regressor again and go through the refinement for another time. This procedure is performed for several times, namely iterative bounding box regression. Faster R-CNN [22] first performs the bounding box regression twice to transform predefined anchors into final detected bounding boxes. [14] proposes a group recursive learning approach to iteratively refine detection results and minimize the offsets between object proposals and the ground-truth considering the global dependency among multiple proposals. G-CNN is proposed in [17] which starts with a multi-scale regular grid over the image and iteratively pushes the boxes in the grid towards the ground-truth. However, as reported in [3], applying bounding box regression more than twice brings no further improvement. [3] attribute this to the distribution mismatch in multi-step bounding box regression and address it by a resampling strategy in multi-stage bounding box regression.

We experimentally show the performance of iterative bounding box regression based on FPN and Cascade R-CNN frameworks. The Average Precision (AP) of the results after each iteration are shown as the blue curves in Fig. 4(a) and (b), respectively. The AP curves in Fig. 4 show that the improvement on localization accuracy, as the number of iterations increase, is non-monotonic for iterative bounding box regression. The non-monotonicity, together with the non-interpretability, brings difficulties in applications. Besides, without localization confidence for detected bounding boxes, we can not have fine-grained control over the refinement, such as using an adaptive number of iterations for different bounding boxes.

3   IoU-Net

To quantitatively analyze the effectiveness of IoU prediction, we first present the methodology adopted for training an IoU predictor in Sect. 3.1. In Sects. 3.2 and 3.3, we show how to use IoU predictor for NMS and bounding box refinement, respectively. Finally in Sect. 3.4 we integrate the IoU predictor into existing object detectors such as FPN [15].

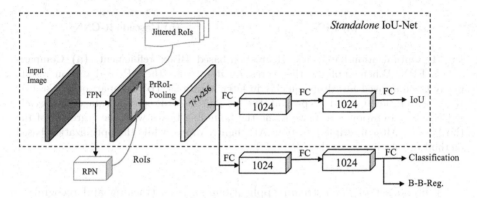

Fig. 5. Full architecture of the proposed IoU-Net described in Sect. 3.4. Input images are first fed into an FPN backbone. The IoU predictor takes the output features from the FPN backbone. We replace the RoI Pooling layer with a PrRoI Pooling layer described in Sect. 3.3. The IoU predictor shares a similar structure with the R-CNN branch. The modules marked within the dashed box form a *standalone* IoU-Net.

3.1   Learning to Predict IoU

Shown in Fig. 5, the IoU predictor takes visual features from the FPN and estimates the localization accuracy (IoU) for each bounding box. We generate bounding boxes and labels for training the IoU-Net by augmenting the ground-truth, instead of taking proposals from RPNs. Specifically, for all ground-truth bounding boxes in the training set, we manually transform them with a set of randomized parameters, resulting in a candidate bounding box set. We then remove from this candidate set the bounding boxes having an IoU less than $\Omega_{train} = 0.5$ with the matched ground-truth. We uniformly sample training data from this candidate set w.r.t. the IoU. This data generation process empirically brings better performance and robustness to the IoU-Net. For each bounding box, the features are extracted from the output of FPN with the proposed Precise RoI Pooling layer (see Sect. 3.3). The features are then fed into a two-layer feedforward network for the IoU prediction. For a better performance, we use class-aware IoU predictors.

The IoU predictor is compatible with most existing RoI-based detectors. The accuracy of a *standalone* IoU predictor can be found in Fig. 2. As the training procedure is independent of specific detectors, it is robust to the change of the

Algorithm 1. IoU-guided NMS. Classification confidence and localization confidence are disentangled in the algorithm. We use the localization confidence (the predicted IoU) to rank all detected bounding boxes, and update the classification confidence based on a clustering-like rule.

Input: $\mathcal{B} = \{b_1, ..., b_n\}$, $\mathcal{S}$, $\mathcal{I}$, Ω_{nms}
    $\mathcal{B}$ is a set of detected bounding boxes.
    $\mathcal{S}$ and $\mathcal{I}$ are functions (neural networks) mapping bounding boxes to their classification confidence and IoU estimation (localization confidence) respectively.
    Ω_{nms} is the NMS threshold.
Output: $\mathcal{D}$, the set of detected bounding boxes with classification scores.
1: $\mathcal{D} \leftarrow \varnothing$
2: **while** $\mathcal{B} \neq \varnothing$ **do**
3:     $b_m \leftarrow \arg\max \mathcal{I}(b_j)$
4:     $\mathcal{B} \leftarrow \mathcal{B} \setminus \{b_m\}$
5:     $s \leftarrow \mathcal{S}(b_m)$
6:     **for** $b_j \in \mathcal{B}$ **do**
7:         **if** $IoU(b_m, b_j) > \Omega_{nms}$ **then**
8:             $s \leftarrow max(s, \mathcal{S}(b_j))$
9:             $\mathcal{B} \leftarrow \mathcal{B} \setminus \{b_j\}$
10:        **end if**
11:     **end for**
12:     $\mathcal{D} \leftarrow \mathcal{D} \cup \{\langle b_m, s \rangle\}$
13: **end while**
14: **return** $\mathcal{D}$

input distributions (*e.g.*, when cooperates with different detectors). In later sections, we will further demonstrate how this module can be jointly optimized in a full detection pipeline (*i.e.*, jointly with RPNs and R-CNN).

3.2 IoU-Guided NMS

We resolve the misalignment between classification confidence and localization accuracy with a novel IoU-guided NMS procedure, where the classification confidence and localization confidence (an estimation of the IoU) are disentangled. In short, we use the predicted IoU instead of the classification confidence as the ranking keyword for bounding boxes. Analog to the traditional NMS, the box having the highest IoU with a ground-truth will be selected to eliminate all other boxes having an overlap greater than a given threshold Ω_{nms}. To determine the classification scores, when a box i eliminates box j, we update the classification confidence s_i of box i by $s_i = \max(s_i, s_j)$. This procedure can also be interpreted as a confidence clustering: for a group of bounding boxes matching the same ground-truth, we take the most confident prediction for the class label. A psuedo-code for this algorithm can be found in Algorithm 1.

IoU-guided NMS resolves the misalignment between classification confidence and localization accuracy. Quantitative results show that our method

---

Algorithm 2. Optimization-based bounding box refinement

Input: $\mathcal{B} = \{b_1, ..., b_n\}$, $\mathcal{F}$, T, λ, Ω_1, Ω_2

$\quad$ $\mathcal{B}$ is a set of detected bounding boxes, in the form of (x_0, y_0, x_1, y_1).

$\quad$ $\mathcal{F}$ is the feature map of the input image.

$\quad$ T is number of steps. λ is the step size, and Ω_1 is an early-stop threshold and $\Omega_2 < 0$ is an localization degeneration tolerance.

$\quad$ Function PrPool extracts the feature representation for a given bounding box and function IoU denotes the estimation of IoU by the IoU-Net.

Output: The set of final detection bounding boxes.

$\quad$ 1: $\mathcal{A} \leftarrow \varnothing$

$\quad$ 2: **for** $i = 1$ *to* T **do**

$\quad$ 3: $\quad$ **for** $b_j \in \mathcal{B}$ and $b_j \notin \mathcal{A}$ **do**

$\quad$ 4: $\quad\quad$ $\boldsymbol{grad} \leftarrow \nabla_{b_j} \text{IoU}(\text{PrPool}(\mathcal{F}, b_j))$

$\quad$ 5: $\quad\quad$ $PrevScore \leftarrow \text{IoU}(\text{PrPool}(\mathcal{F}, b_j))$

$\quad$ 6: $\quad\quad$ $b_j \leftarrow b_j + \lambda * scale(\boldsymbol{grad}, b_j)$

$\quad$ 7: $\quad\quad$ $NewScore \leftarrow \text{IoU}(\text{PrPool}(\mathcal{F}, b_j))$

$\quad$ 8: $\quad\quad$ **if** $|PrevScore - NewScore| < \Omega_1$ or $NewScore - PrevScore < \Omega_2$ **then**

$\quad$ 9: $\quad\quad\quad$ $\mathcal{A} \leftarrow \mathcal{A} \cup \{b_j\}$

$\quad$ 10: $\quad\quad$ **end if**

$\quad$ 11: $\quad$ **end for**

$\quad$ 12: **end for**

$\quad$ 13: **return** $\mathcal{B}$

---

outperforms traditional NMS and other variants such as Soft-NMS [2]. Using IoU-guided NMS as the post-processor further pushes forward the performance of several state-of-the-art object detectors.

3.3 Bounding Box Refinement as an Optimization Procedure

The problem of bounding box refinement can formulated mathematically as finding the optimal c^* *s.t.*:

$$c^* = \arg\min_c crit(\mathbf{transform}(box_{\text{det}}, c), box_{\text{gt}}), \tag{1}$$

where box_{det} is the detected bounding box, box_{gt} is a (targeting) ground-truth bounding box and **transform** is a bounding box transformation function taking c as parameter and transform the given bounding box. $crit$ is a criterion measuring the distance between two bounding boxes. In the original Fast R-CNN [5] framework, $crit$ is chosen as an smooth-L1 distance of coordinates in log-scale, while in [31], $crit$ is chosen as the $-\ln(\text{IoU})$ between two bounding boxes.

$\quad$ Regression-based algorithms directly estimate the optimal solution c^* with a feed-forward neural network. However, iterative bounding box regression methods are vulnerable to the change in the input distribution [3] and may result in non-monotonic localization improvement, as shown in Fig. 4. To tackle these issues, we propose an optimization-based bounding box refinement method utilizing IoU-Net as a robust localization accuracy (IoU) estimator. Furthermore,

IoU estimator can be used as an early-stop condition to implement iterative refinement with adaptive steps.

IoU-Net directly estimates $\text{IoU}(box_{\text{det}}, box_{\text{gt}})$. While the proposed Precise RoI Pooling layer enables the computation of the gradient of IoU w.r.t. bounding box coordinates[1], we can directly use gradient ascent method to find the optimal solution to Eq. 1. Shown in Algorithm 2, viewing the estimation of the IoU as an optimization objective, we iteratively refine the bounding box coordinates with the computed gradient and maximize the IoU between the detected bounding box and its matched ground-truth. Besides, the predicted IoU is an interpretable indicator of the localization confidence on each bounding box and helps explain the performed transformation.

In the implementation, shown in Algorithm 2 Line 6, we manually scale up the gradient w.r.t. the coordinates with the size of the bounding box on that axis (*e.g.*, we scale up ∇x_1 with $width(b_j)$). This is equivalent to perform the optimization in log-scaled coordinates $(x/w, y/h, \log w, \log h)$ as in [5]. We also employ a one-step bounding box regression for an initialization of the coordinates.

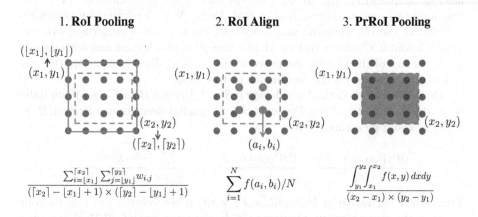

Fig. 6. Illustration of RoI Pooling, RoI Align and PrRoI Pooling.

Precise RoI Pooling. We introduce Precise RoI Pooling (PrRoI Pooling, for short) powering our bounding box refinement[2]. It avoids any quantization of coordinates and has a continuous gradient on bounding box coordinates. Given the feature map $\mathcal{F}$ before RoI/PrRoI Pooling (*e.g.* from Conv4 in ResNet-50), let $w_{i,j}$ be the feature at one discrete location (i, j) on the feature map. Using

---

[1] We prefer Precise RoI-Pooling layer to RoI-Align layer [9] as Precise RoI-Pooling layer is continuously differentiable w.r.t. the coordinates while RoI-Align is not.

[2] The code is released at: https://github.com/vacancy/PreciseRoIPooling.

bilinear interpolation, the discrete feature map can be considered continuous at any continuous coordinates (x, y):

$$f(x, y) = \sum_{i,j} IC(x, y, i, j) \times w_{i,j},\qquad(2)$$

where $IC(x, y, i, j) = max(0, 1 - |x - i|) \times max(0, 1 - |y - j|)$ is the interpolation coefficient. Then denote a bin of a RoI as $bin = \{(x_1, y_1), (x_2, y_2)\}$, where (x_1, y_1) and (x_2, y_2) are the continuous coordinates of the top-left and bottom-right points, respectively. We perform pooling (e.g., average pooling) given bin and feature map $\mathcal{F}$ by computing a two-order integral:

$$\text{PrPool}(bin, \mathcal{F}) = \frac{\int_{y1}^{y2} \int_{x1}^{x2} f(x, y) \, dx dy}{(x_2 - x_1) \times (y_2 - y_1)}.\qquad(3)$$

For a better understanding, we visualize RoI Pooling, RoI Align [9] and our PrRoI Pooing in Fig. 6: in the traditional RoI Pooling, the continuous coordinates need to be quantized first to calculate the sum of the activations in the bin; to eliminate the quantization error, in RoI Align, $N = 4$ continuous points are sampled in the bin, denoted as (a_i, b_i), and the pooling is performed over the sampled points. Contrary to RoI Align where N is pre-defined and not adaptive w.r.t. the size of the bin, the proposed PrRoI pooling directly compute the two-order integral based on the continuous feature map.

Moreover, based on the formulation in Eq. 3, $\text{PrPool}(Bin, \mathcal{F})$ is differentiable w.r.t. the coordinates of bin. For example, the partial derivative of $\text{PrPool}(B, \mathcal{F})$ w.r.t. x_1 could be computed as:

$$\frac{\partial \text{PrPool}(bin, \mathcal{F})}{\partial x_1} = \frac{\text{PrPool}(bin, \mathcal{F})}{x_2 - x_1} - \frac{\int_{y1}^{y2} f(x_1, y) \, dy}{(x_2 - x_1) \times (y_2 - y_1)}.\qquad(4)$$

The partial derivative of $\text{PrPool}(bin, \mathcal{F})$ w.r.t. other coordinates can be computed in the same manner. Since we avoids any quantization, PrPool is continuously differentiable.

3.4   Joint Training

The IoU predictor can be integrated into standard FPN pipelines for end-to-end training and inference. For clarity, we denote *backbone* as the CNN architecture for image feature extraction and *head* as the modules applied to individual RoIs.

Shown in Fig. 5, the IoU-Net uses ResNet-FPN [15] as the backbone, which has a top-down architecture to build a feature pyramid. FPN extracts features of RoIs from different levels of the feature pyramid according to their scale. The original RoI Pooling layer is replaced by the Precise RoI Pooling layer. As for the network head, the IoU predictor works in parallel with the R-CNN branch (including classification and bounding box regression) based on the same visual feature from the backbone.

We initialize weights from pre-trained ResNet models on ImageNet [24]. All new layers are initialized with a zero-mean Gaussian with standard deviation 0.01 or 0.001. We use smooth-L1 loss for training the IoU predictor. The training data for the IoU predictor is separately generated as described in Sect. 3.1 within images in a training batch. IoU labels are normalized s.t. the values are distributed over $[-1, 1]$.

Input images are resized to have 800 px along the short axis and a maximum of 1200 px along the long axis. The classification and regression branch take 512 RoIs per image from RPNs. We use a batch size 16 for the training. The network is optimized for 160k iterations, with a learning rate of 0.01 which is decreased by a factor of 10 after 120k iterations. We also warm up the training by setting the learning rate to 0.004 for the first 10k iteration. We use a weight decay of 1e-4 and a momentum of 0.9.

During inference, we first apply bounding box regression for the initial coordinates. To speed up the inference, we first apply IoU-guided NMS on all detected bounding boxes. 100 bounding boxes with highest classification confidence are further refined using the optimization-based algorithm. We set $\lambda = 0.5$ as the step size, $\Omega_1 = 0.001$ as the early-stop threshold, $\Omega_2 = -0.01$ as the localization degeneration tolerance and $T = 5$ as the number of iterations.

4   Experiments

We perform experiments on the 80-category MS-COCO detection dataset [16]. Following [1,15], the models are trained on the union of 80k training images and 35k validation images (*trainval35k*) and evaluated on a set of 5k validation images (*minival*). To validate the proposed methods, in both Sects. 4.1 and 4.2, a *standalone* IoU-Net (without R-CNN modules) is trained separately with the object detectors. IoU-guided NMS and optimization-based bounding box refinement, powered by the IoU-Net, are applied to the detection results.

4.1   IoU-Guided NMS

Table 1 summarizes the performance of different NMS methods. While Soft-NMS preserve more bounding boxes (there is no real "suppression"), IoU-guided NMS improves the results by improving the localization of the detected bounding boxes. As a result, IoU-guided NMS performs significantly better than the baselines on high IoU metrics (*e.g.*, AP$_{90}$).

We delve deeper into the behavior of different NMS algorithms by analyzing their recalls at different IoU threshold. The raw detected bounding boxes are generated by a ResNet50-FPN without any NMS. As the requirement of localization accuracy increases, the performance gap between IoU-guided NMS and other methods goes larger. In particular, the recall at matching IoU $\Omega_{test} = 0.9$ drops to 18.7% after traditional NMS, while the IoU-NMS reaches 28.9% and the No-NMS "upper bound" is 39.7%.

Table 1. Comparison of IoU-guided NMS with other NMS methods. By preserving bounding boxes with accurate localization, IoU-guided NMS shows significant improvement in AP with high matching IoU threshold (*e.g.*, AP_{90}).

Method	+Soft-NMS	+IoU-NMS	AP	AP_{50}	AP_{60}	AP_{70}	AP_{80}	AP_{90}
FPN			36.4	**58.0**	**53.1**	44.9	31.2	9.8
	✓		36.8	57.5	**53.1**	**45.7**	32.3	10.3
		✓	**37.3**	56.0	52.2	45.6	**33.9**	**13.3**
Cascade R-CNN			40.6	**59.3**	55.2	49.1	38.7	16.7
	✓		**40.9**	58.2	**54.7**	**49.4**	**39.9**	17.8
		✓	40.7	58.0	**54.7**	49.2	38.8	**18.9**
Mask-RCNN			37.5	**58.6**	**53.9**	46.3	33.2	10.9
	✓		37.9	58.2	**53.9**	**47.1**	34.4	11.5
		✓	**38.1**	56.4	52.7	46.7	**35.1**	**14.6**

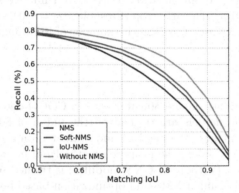

Fig. 7. Recall curves of different NMS methods at different IoU threshold for matching detected bounding boxes with the ground-truth. No-NMS (no box is suppressed) is provided as the upper bound of the recall. The proposed IoU-NMS has a higher recall and effectively narrows the gap to the upper-bound at high IoU threshold (*e.g.*, >0.8).

Table 2. The optimization-based bounding box refinement further improves the performance of several CNN-based object detectors.

Method	+Refinement	AP	AP_{50}	AP_{60}	AP_{70}	AP_{80}	AP_{90}
FPN		36.4	**58.0**	**53.1**	44.9	31.2	9.8
	✓	**38.0**	57.7	**53.1**	**46.1**	**34.3**	**14.6**
Cascade R-CNN		40.6	**59.3**	55.2	49.1	38.7	16.7
	✓	**41.4**	**59.3**	**55.3**	**49.6**	**39.4**	**19.5**
Mask-RCNN		37.5	**58.6**	**53.9**	46.3	33.2	10.9
	✓	**39.2**	57.9	53.6	**47.4**	**36.5**	**16.4**

4.2 Optimization-Based Bounding Box Refinement

The proposed optimization-based bounding box refinement is compatible with most of the CNN-based object detectors [3,9,15], as shown in Table 2. Applying the bounding box refinement after the original pipelines with the *standalone* IoU-Net further improve the performance by localizing object more accurately. The refinement further improves AP_{90} by 2.8% and the overall AP by 0.8% even for Cascade R-CNN which has a three-stage bounding box regressor.

4.3 Joint Training

IoU-Net can be end-to-end optimized in parallel with object detection frameworks. We find that adding IoU predictor to the network helps the network to learn more discriminative features which improves the overall AP by 0.6 and 0.4 percent for ResNet50-FPN and ResNet101-FPN respectively. The IoU-guided NMS and bounding box refinement further push the performance forward. We achieve 40.6% AP with ResNet101-FPN compared to the baseline 38.5% (improved by 2.1%). The inference speed is demonstrated in Table 3, showing that IoU-Net improves the detection performance with tolerable computation overhead.

We mainly attribute the inferior results on AP_{50} in Table 3 to the IoU estimation error. When the bounding boxes have a lower IoU with the ground-truth, they have a larger variance in appearance. Visualized in Fig. 2(b), the IoU estimation becomes less accurate for boxes with lower IoU. This degenerates the performance of the downstream refinement and suppression. We empirically find that this problem can be partially solved by techniques such as sampling more bounding boxes with lower IoU during the training (Table 4).

Table 3. Final experiment results on MS-COCO. IoU-Net denotes ResNet-FPN embedded with IoU predictor. We improve the FPN baseline by ≈2% in AP.

Backbone	Method	+IoU-NMS	+Refine	AP	AP_{50}	AP_{60}	AP_{70}	AP_{80}	AP_{90}
ResNet-50	FPN			36.4	58.0	53.1	44.9	31.2	9.8
	IoU-Net			37.0	**58.3**	**53.8**	45.7	31.9	10.7
		✓		37.6	56.2	52.4	46.0	34.1	14.0
		✓	✓	**38.1**	56.3	52.4	**46.3**	**35.1**	**15.5**
ResNet-101	FPN			38.5	**60.3**	**55.5**	47.6	33.8	11.3
	IoU-Net			38.9	60.2	**55.5**	47.8	34.6	12.0
		✓		40.0	59.0	55.1	48.6	37.0	15.5
		✓	✓	**40.6**	59.0	55.2	**49.0**	**38.0**	**17.1**

Table 4. Inference speed of multiple object detectors on a single TITAN X GPU. The models share the same backbone network ResNet50-FPN. The input resolution is 1200 × 800. All hyper-parameters are set to be the same.

Method	FPN	Mask-RCNN	Cascade R-CNN	IoU-Net
Speed (sec./image)	0.255	0.267	0.384	0.305

5   Conclusion

In this paper, a novel network architecture, namely IoU-Net, is proposed for accurate object localization. By learning to predict the IoU with matched ground-truth, IoU-Net acquires "localization confidence" for the detected bounding box. This empowers an IoU-guided NMS procedure where accurately localized bounding boxes are prevented from being suppressed. The proposed IoU-Net is intuitive and can be easily integrated into a broad set of detection models to improve their localization accuracy. Experimental results on MS-COCO demonstrate its effectiveness and potential in practical applications.

This paper points out the misalignment of classification and localization confidences in modern detection pipelines. We also formulate an novel optimization view on the problem of bounding box refinement, and the proposed solution surpasses the regression-based methods. We hope these novel viewpoints provide insights to future works on object detection, and beyond.

References

1. Bell, S., Lawrence Zitnick, C., Bala, K., Girshick, R.: Inside-outside net: detecting objects in context with skip pooling and recurrent neural networks. In: Proceedings of the IEEE Conference on Computer Vision and Pattern Recognition, pp. 2874–2883 (2016)
2. Bodla, N., Singh, B., Chellappa, R., Davis, L.S.: Improving object detection with one line of code. arXiv preprint arXiv:1704.04503 (2017)
3. Cai, Z., Vasconcelos, N.: Cascade R-CNN: delving into high quality object detection. arXiv preprint arXiv:1712.00726 (2017)
4. Dalal, N., Triggs, B.: Histograms of oriented gradients for human detection. In: IEEE Computer Society Conference on Computer Vision and Pattern Recognition, CVPR 2005, vol. 1, pp. 886–893. IEEE (2005)
5. Gidaris, S., Komodakis, N.: Object detection via a multi-region and semantic segmentation-aware CNN model. In: Proceedings of the IEEE International Conference on Computer Vision, pp. 1134–1142 (2015)
6. Gidaris, S., Komodakis, N.: Attend refine repeat: active box proposal generation via in-out localization. arXiv preprint arXiv:1606.04446 (2016)
7. Girshick, R.: Fast R-CNN. In: The IEEE International Conference on Computer Vision (ICCV), December 2015
8. Girshick, R., Donahue, J., Darrell, T., Malik, J.: Rich feature hierarchies for accurate object detection and semantic segmentation. In: The IEEE Conference on Computer Vision and Pattern Recognition (CVPR), June 2014

9. He, K., Gkioxari, G., Dollár, P., Girshick, R.: Mask R-CNN. In: The IEEE International Conference on Computer Vision (ICCV) (2017)
10. Hosang, J., Benenson, R., Schiele, B.: Learning non-maximum suppression. arXiv preprint (2017)
11. Hu, H., Gu, J., Zhang, Z., Dai, J., Wei, Y.: Relation networks for object detection. arXiv preprint arXiv:1711.11575 (2017)
12. Hu, H., Lan, S., Jiang, Y., Cao, Z., Sha, F.: FastMask: segment multi-scale object candidates in one shot. In: Proceedings of the IEEE Conference on Computer Vision and Pattern Recognition, pp. 991–999 (2017)
13. Huang, L., Yang, Y., Deng, Y., Yu, Y.: DenseBox: unifying landmark localization with end to end object detection. arXiv preprint arXiv:1509.04874 (2015)
14. Li, J., et al.: Multi-stage object detection with group recursive learning. IEEE Trans. Multimedia (2017)
15. Lin, T.Y., Dollár, P., Girshick, R., He, K., Hariharan, B., Belongie, S.: Feature pyramid networks for object detection. In: The IEEE Conference on Computer Vision and Pattern Recognition (CVPR) (2017)
16. Lin, T.-Y., et al.: Microsoft COCO: common objects in context. In: Fleet, D., Pajdla, T., Schiele, B., Tuytelaars, T. (eds.) ECCV 2014. LNCS, vol. 8693, pp. 740–755. Springer, Cham (2014). https://doi.org/10.1007/978-3-319-10602-1_48
17. Najibi, M., Rastegari, M., Davis, L.S.: G-CNN: an iterative grid based object detector. In: Proceedings of the IEEE Conference on Computer Vision and Pattern Recognition, pp. 2369–2377 (2016)
18. Pinheiro, P.O., Collobert, R., Dollár, P.: Learning to segment object candidates. In: Advances in Neural Information Processing Systems, pp. 1990–1998 (2015)
19. Pinheiro, P.O., Lin, T.-Y., Collobert, R., Dollár, P.: Learning to refine object segments. In: Leibe, B., Matas, J., Sebe, N., Welling, M. (eds.) ECCV 2016. LNCS, vol. 9905, pp. 75–91. Springer, Cham (2016). https://doi.org/10.1007/978-3-319-46448-0_5
20. Rajaram, R.N., Ohn-Bar, E., Trivedi, M.M.: RefineNet: iterative refinement for accurate object localization. In: 2016 IEEE 19th International Conference on Intelligent Transportation Systems (ITSC), pp. 1528–1533. IEEE (2016)
21. Ren, S., He, K., Girshick, R., Sun, J.: Faster R-CNN: towards real-time object detection with region proposal networks. In: Advances in Neural Information Processing Systems, pp. 91–99 (2015)
22. Ren, S., He, K., Girshick, R., Sun, J.: Faster R-CNN: towards real-time object detection with region proposal networks. In: Cortes, C., Lawrence, N.D., Lee, D.D., Sugiyama, M., Garnett, R. (eds.) Advances in Neural Information Processing Systems, vol. 28, pp. 91–99. Curran Associates, Inc. (2015). http://papers.nips.cc/paper/5638-faster-r-cnn-towards-real-time-object-detection-with-region-proposal-networks.pdf
23. Rothe, R., Guillaumin, M., Van Gool, L.: Non-maximum suppression for object detection by passing messages between windows. In: Cremers, D., Reid, I., Saito, H., Yang, M.-H. (eds.) ACCV 2014. LNCS, vol. 9003, pp. 290–306. Springer, Cham (2015). https://doi.org/10.1007/978-3-319-16865-4_19
24. Russakovsky, O., et al.: ImageNet large scale visual recognition challenge. Int. J. Comput. Vis. (IJCV) 115(3), 211–252 (2015). https://doi.org/10.1007/s11263-015-0816-y
25. Taigman, Y., Yang, M., Ranzato, M., Wolf, L.: DeepFace: closing the gap to human-level performance in face verification. In: Proceedings of the IEEE Conference on Computer Vision and Pattern Recognition, pp. 1701–1708 (2014)

26. Toshev, A., Szegedy, C.: DeepPose: human pose estimation via deep neural networks. In: Proceedings of the IEEE Conference on Computer Vision and Pattern Recognition, pp. 1653–1660 (2014)
27. Uijlings, J.R., Van De Sande, K.E., Gevers, T., Smeulders, A.W.: Selective search for object recognition. Int. J. Comput. Vis. **104**(2), 154–171 (2013)
28. Wang, X., Xiao, T., Jiang, Y., Shao, S., Sun, J., Shen, C.: Repulsion loss: detecting pedestrians in a crowd. arXiv preprint arXiv:1711.07752 (2017)
29. Wu, J., Lu, E., Kohli, P., Freeman, W.T., Tenenbaum, J.B.: Learning to see physics via visual de-animation. In: Advances in Neural Information Processing Systems (2017)
30. Yang, B., Yan, J., Lei, Z., Li, S.Z.: Craft objects from images. arXiv preprint arXiv:1604.03239 (2016)
31. Yu, J., Jiang, Y., Wang, Z., Cao, Z., Huang, T.: Unitbox: an advanced object detection network. In: Proceedings of the 2016 ACM on Multimedia Conference, pp. 516–520. ACM (2016)
32. Zitnick, C.L., Dollár, P.: Edge boxes: locating object proposals from edges. In: Fleet, D., Pajdla, T., Schiele, B., Tuytelaars, T. (eds.) ECCV 2014. LNCS, vol. 8693, pp. 391–405. Springer, Cham (2014). https://doi.org/10.1007/978-3-319-10602-1_26

Deep Model-Based 6D Pose Refinement in RGB

Fabian Manhardt[1]([✉]), Wadim Kehl[2], Nassir Navab[1], and Federico Tombari[1]

[1] Technical University of Munich, 85748 Garching b. Muenchen, Germany
{fabian.manhardt,nassir.navab}@tum.de, tombari@in.tum.de
[2] Toyota Research Institute, Los Altos, CA 94022, USA
wadim.kehl@tri.global

Abstract. We present a novel approach for model-based 6D pose refinement in color data. Building on the established idea of contour-based pose tracking, we teach a deep neural network to predict a translational and rotational update. At the core, we propose a new visual loss that drives the pose update by aligning object contours, thus avoiding the definition of any explicit appearance model. In contrast to previous work our method is correspondence free, segmentation-free, can handle occlusion and is agnostic to geometrical symmetry as well as visual ambiguities. Additionally, we observe a strong robustness towards rough initialization. The approach can run in real-time and produces pose accuracies that come close to 3D ICP without the need for depth data. Furthermore, our networks are trained from purely synthetic data and will be published together with the refinement code at http://campar.in.tum.de/Main/FabianManhardt to ensure reproducibility.

Keywords: Pose estimation · Pose refinement · Tracking

1 Introduction

The problem of tracking CAD models in images is frequently encountered in contexts such as robotics, augmented reality (AR) and medical procedures. Usually, tracking has to be carried out in the full 6D pose, i.e. one seeks to retrieve both the 3D metric translation as well as the 3D rotation of the object in each frame. Another typical scenario is pose refinement, where an object detector provides a rough 6D pose estimate, which has to be corrected in order to provide a better fit (Fig. 1). The usual difficulties that arise include viewpoint ambiguities, occlusions, illumination changes and differences in appearance between the model and the object in the scene. Furthermore, for tracking applications the method should also be fast enough to cover large inter-frame motions.

F. Manhardt and W. Kehl—The first two authors contributed equally to this work.

Electronic supplementary material The online version of this chapter (https://doi.org/10.1007/978-3-030-01264-9_49) contains supplementary material, which is available to authorized users.

© Springer Nature Switzerland AG 2018
V. Ferrari et al. (Eds.): ECCV 2018, LNCS 11218, pp. 833–849, 2018.
https://doi.org/10.1007/978-3-030-01264-9_49

(a) Input Image   (b) Initial pose hypotheses (c) Poses after 10 iterations

Fig. 1. Exemplary illustration of our method. While (a) depicts an input RGB frame, (b) shows our four initial 6D pose hypotheses. For each obtained frame we refine each pose for a better fit to the scene. In (c) we show the final results after convergence. Note the rough pose initializations as well as the varying amount of occlusion the objects of interest undergo. (Color figure online)

Most related work based on RGB data can be roughly divided into sparse and region-based methods. The former methods try to establish local correspondences between frames [23,40] and work well for textured objects, whereas latter ones exploit more holistic information about the object such as shape, contour or color [8,27,37,38] and are usually better suited for texture-less objects. It is worth mentioning that mixtures of the two sets of methods have been proposed as well [6,24,30,31]. Recently, methods that use only depth [34] or both modalities [10,18,21] have shown that depth can make tracking more robust by providing more clues about occlusion and scale.

This work aims to explore how RGB information alone can be sufficient to perform visual tasks such as 3D tracking and 6-Degree-of-Freedom (6DoF) pose refinement by means of a Convolutional Neural Network (CNN). While this has already been proposed for camera pose and motion estimation [19,39,41,43], it has not been well-studied for the problem at hand.

As a major contribution we provide a differentiable formulation of a new visual loss that aligns object contours and implicitly optimizes for metric translation and rotation. While our optimization is inspired by region-based approaches, we can track objects of any texture or shape since we do not need to model global [18,27,37] or local appearance [11,38]. Instead, we show that we can do away with these hand-crafted approaches by letting the network learn the object appearance implicitly. We teach the CNN to align contours between synthetic object renderings and scene images under changing illumination and occlusions and show that our approach can deal with a variety of shapes and textures. Additionally, our method allows to deal with geometrical symmetries and visual ambiguities without manual tweaking and is able to recover correct poses from very rough initializations.

Notably, our formulation is parameter-free and avoids typical pitfalls of handcrafted tracking or refinement methods (e.g. via segmentation or correspondences + RANSAC) that require tedious tuning to work well in practice. Furthermore, like with depth-based approaches such as ICP, we are robust to occlusion and produce results which come close to RGB-D methods without the need for depth data, making it thus very applicable to the domains of AR, medical and robotics.

2   Related Work

Since the field of tracking and pose refinement is vast, we will only focus here on works that deal with CAD models in RGB data. Early methods in this field used either 2D-3D correspondences [29,30] or 3D edges [9,32,35] and fit the model in an ICP fashion with iterative, projective update steps. Successive methods in this direction managed to obtain improved performance [6,31]. Additionally, other works focused on tracking the contour densely via level-sets [3,8].

Based on these works, [27] presented a new approach that follows the projected model contours to estimate the 6D pose update. In a follow-up work [26], the authors extended their method to simultaneously track and reconstruct a 3D object on a mobile phone in real-time. The authors from [37] improved the convergence behavior with a new optimization scheme and presented a real-time implementation on a GPU. Consequently, [38] showed how to improve the color segmentation by using local color histograms over time. Orthogonally, the work [18] approximates the model pose space to avoid GPU computations and enables real-time performance on a single CPU core. All these approaches share the property that they rely on hand-crafted segmentation methods that can fail in the case of sudden appearance changes or occlusion. We instead want to entirely avoid hand-crafting manual appearance descriptions.

Another set of works tries to combine learning with simultaneous detection and pose estimation in RGB. The method presented in [17] couples the SSD paradigm [22] with pose estimation to produce 6D pose pools per instance which are then refined with edge-based ICP. On the contrary, the approach from [5] uses auto-context Random Forests to regress object coordinates in the scene that are used to estimate poses. In [28] a method is presented that instead regresses the projected 3D bounding box and recovers the pose from these 2D-3D correspondences whereas the authors in [25] infer keypoint heatmaps that are then used for 6D pose computation. Similarly, the 3D Interpreter Network [42] infers heatmaps for categories and regresses projection and deformation to align synthetic with real imagery. In the work [10], a deep learning approach is used to track models in RGB-D data. Their work goes along similar grounds but we differ in multiple ways including data generation, energy formulation and their use of RGB-D data. In particular, we show that a naive formulation of pose regression does not work in the case of symmetry which is often the case for man-made objects.

We also find common ground with Spatial Transformer Networks in 2D [16] and especially 3D [2], where the employed network architecture contains a submodule to transform the 2D/3D input via a regressed affine transformation on a discrete lattice. Our network instead regresses a rigid body motion on a set of continuous 3D points to minimize the visual error.

3   Methodology

In this section we explain our approach to train a CNN to regress a 6D pose refinement from RGB information alone. We design the problem in such a way

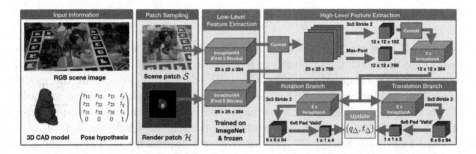

Fig. 2. Schematic overview of the full pipeline. Given input image and pose hypothesis (R, t), we render the object, compute the center of the bounding box of the hypothesis (green point) and then cut out a scene patch $\mathcal{S}$ and a render patch $\mathcal{H}$. We resize both to 224×224 and feed them separately into pre-trained InceptionV4 layers to extract low-level features. Thereafter, we concatenate and compute high-level features before diverging into separate branches. Eventually, we retrieve our pose update as 3D translation and normalized 4D quaternion. (Color figure online)

that we supply two color patches ($\mathcal{S}$ and $\mathcal{H}$) to the network in order to infer a translational and rotational update. In Fig. 2 we depict our pipeline and show a typical scenario where we have a 6D hypothesis (coming from a detector or tracker) that is not correctly aligned. We want to estimate a refinement such that eventually the updated hypothesis overlaps perfectly with the real object.

3.1   Input Patch Sampling

We first want to discuss our patch extraction strategy. Provided a CAD model and a 6D pose estimate (R, t) in camera space, we create a rendering and compute the center of the associated bounding box of the hypothesis around which we subsequently extract $\mathcal{S}$ and $\mathcal{H}$. Since different objects have varying sizes and shapes it is important to adapt the cropping size to the spatial properties of the specific object. The most straightforward method would be to simply crop $\mathcal{S}$ and $\mathcal{H}$ with respect to a tight 2D bounding box of the rendered mask. However, when employing such metric crops, the network loses the ability to robustly predict an update along the Z-axis: indeed, since each crop would almost entirely fill out the input patch, no estimate of the difference in depth can be drawn. Due to this, we explicitly calculate the spatial extent in pixels at a minimum metric distance (with some added padding) and use this as a fixed-size 'window' into our scene. In particular, prior to training, we render the object from various different viewpoints, compute their bounding boxes, and take the maximum width or height of all produced bounding boxes.

3.2   Training Stage

To create training data we randomly sample a ground truth pose (R^*, t^*) of the object in camera coordinates and render the object with that pose onto a random background to create a scene image. To learn pose refinement, we perturb the true pose to get a noisy version (R, t) and render a hypothesis image. Given those two images, we cut out patches $\mathcal{S}$ and $\mathcal{H}$ with the strategy mentioned above.

The Naive Approach. Provided these patches, we now want to infer a separate correction (R_Δ, t_Δ) of the perturbed pose (R, t) such that

$$R^* = R_\Delta \cdot R, \quad t^* = t + t_\Delta. \tag{1}$$

Due to the difficulty of optimizing in SO(3) we parametrize via unit quaternions q^*, q, q_Δ to define a regression problem, i.e. similar to what [20] proposed for camera localization or [10] for model pose tracking:

$$\min_{q_\Delta, t_\Delta} \left\| q^* - \frac{q_\Delta}{||q_\Delta||} \right\| + \gamma \cdot ||t^* - t_\Delta|| \tag{2}$$

In essence, this energy weighs the numerical error in rotation against the one in translation by means of the hyper-parameter γ and can be optimized correctly when solutions are unique (as is the case, e.g., of camera pose regression). Unfortunately, the above formulation only works for injective relations where an input image pair gets always mapped to the same transformation. In the case of one-to-many mappings, i.e. an image pair can have multiple correct solutions, the optimization does not converge since it is pulled into multiple directions and regresses the average instead. In the context of our task, visual ambiguity is common for most man-made objects because they are either symmetric or share the same appearance from multiple viewpoints. For these objects there is a large (sometimes infinite) set of refinement solutions that yield the same visual result. In order to regress q_Δ and t_Δ under ambiguity, we therefore propose an alternative formulation.

Proxy Loss for Visual Alignment. Instead of explicitly minimizing an ambiguous error in transformation, we strive to minimize an unambiguous error that measures similarity in appearance. We thus treat our search for the pose refinement parameters as a subproblem inside another proxy loss that optimizes for visual alignment. While there are multiple ways to define a similarity measure, we seek one that fulfills the following properties: (1) invariant to symmetric or indistinguishable object views, (2) robust to color deviation, illumination change and occlusion as well as (3) smooth and differentiable with respect to the pose.

To fulfill the first two properties we propose to align the object contours. Tracking the 6D pose of objects via projective contours has been presented before [18,27,37] but, to the best of our knowledge, has not so far been introduced in a deep learning framework. Contour tracking allows to reduce the difficult problem of 3D geometric alignment to a simpler task of 2D silhouette matching by moving through a distance transform, avoiding explicit correspondence search. Furthermore, a physical contour is not affected by deviations in coloring or lighting which makes it even more appealing for pure RGB methods. We refer to Fig. 3 for a training example and the visualization of the contours we align.

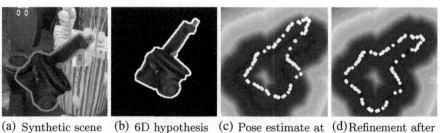

(a) Synthetic scene   (b) 6D hypothesis   (c) Pose estimate at   (d)Refinement after
    input image $\mathcal{S}$ rendering $\mathcal{H}$ initial training state   convergence

Fig. 3. Visualization of our training procedure. In (a) and (b) we show the two image patches that constitute one training sample and the input to our network. We highlight for the reader the contours for which we seek the projective alignment from white to red. In (c) we see the initial state of training with no refinement together with the distance transform of the scene $\mathcal{D}_\mathcal{S}$ and the projection of 3D sample points $V_\mathcal{H}$ from the initial 6D hypothesis. Finally, in (d) we can see the refinement after convergence. (Color figure online)

Fulfilling smoothness and differentiability is more difficult. An optimization step for this energy requires to render the object with the current pose hypothesis for contour extraction, estimate the similarity with the target contour and back-propagate the error gradient such that the refined hypothesis' projected contour is closer in the next iteration. Unfortunately, back-propagating through a rendering pipeline is non-trivial (due to, among others, z-buffering and rasterization). We therefore propose here a novel formulation to drive the network optimization successfully through the ambiguous 6D solution space. We employ an idea, introduced in [18], that allows us to use an approximate contour for optimization without iterative rendering. When creating a training sample, we use the depth map of the rendering to compute a 3D point cloud in camera space and sample a sparse point set on the contour, denoted as $V := \{v \in \mathbb{R}^3\}$. The idea is then to transform these contour points with the current refinement estimate (q_Δ, t_Δ), followed by a projection into the scene. This mimics a rendering plus contour extraction at no cost and allows for back-propagation.

For a given training sample with input patch pair $(\mathcal{S}, \mathcal{H})$, a distance transform of the scene contour $\mathcal{D}_\mathcal{S}$ and hypothesis contour points $V_\mathcal{H}$, we define the loss

$$\mathcal{L}(q_\Delta, t_\Delta, \mathcal{D}_\mathcal{S}, V_\mathcal{H}) := \sum_{v \in V_\mathcal{H}} \mathcal{D}_\mathcal{S}\left[\pi\left(q_\Delta \cdot v \cdot q_\Delta^{-1} + t_\Delta\right)\right] \tag{3}$$

with q_Δ^{-1} being the conjugate quaternion. With the formulation above we also free ourselves from any γ-balancing issue between quaternion and translation magnitudes as in a standard regression formulation.

Minimizing the above loss with a gradient descent step forces a step towards the 0-level set of the distance transform. We basically tune the network weights to rotate and translate the object in 6D to maximize the projected contour overlap. While this works well in practice, we have observed that for certain objects and stronger pose perturbations the optimization can get stuck in local minima. This occurs when our loss drives the contour points into a configuration where the distance transform allows them to settle in local valleys. To remedy this problem we introduce a bi-directional loss formulation that simultaneously aligns the contours of hypothesis as well as scene onto each other, coupled and constrained by the same pose update. We thus have an additional term that runs into the opposite direction:

$$\mathcal{L} := \mathcal{L}(q_\Delta, t_\Delta, \mathcal{D}_\mathcal{S}, V_\mathcal{H}) + \mathcal{L}(q_\Delta^{-1}, -t_\Delta, \mathcal{D}_\mathcal{H}, V_\mathcal{S}). \tag{4}$$

This final loss $\mathcal{L}$ does not only alleviate the locality problem but has also shown to lead to faster training overall. We therefore chose this energy for all experiments.

3.3   Network Design and Implementation

We give a schematic overview of our network structure in Fig. 2 and provide here more details. In order to ensure fast inference, our network follows a fully-convolutional design. The network is fed with two $224 \times 224 \times 3$ input patches representing the cropped scene image $\mathcal{S}$ and cropped render image $\mathcal{H}$. Both patches run in separate paths through the first levels of an InceptionV4 [33] instance to extract low-level features. Thereafter we concatenate the two feature tensors, down-sample by employing max-pooling as well as a strided 3×3 convolution, and concatenate the results again. After two Inception-A blocks we branch off into two separate paths for the regression of rotation and translation. In each we employ two more Inception-A blocks before down-sampling by another strided 3×3 convolution. The resulting tensors are then convolved with either a $6 \times 6 \times 4$ kernel to regress a 4D quaternion or a $6 \times 6 \times 3$ kernel to predict a 3D update translation vector.

Initial experiments showed clearly that training the network from scratch made it impossible to bridge the domain gap between synthetic and real images. Similarly to [13,17] we found that the network focused on specific appearance details of the rendered CAD models and the performance on real imagery collapsed drastically. Synthetic images usually possess very sharp edges and clear corners. Since the first layers learn low-level features they overfit quickly to this perfect rendered world during training. We therefore copied the first five convolutional blocks from a pre-trained model and froze their parameters. We show the improvements in terms of generalization to real data in the supplement.

Further, we initialize the final regression layers such that the bias equals identity quaternion and zero translation whereas the weights are given a small Gaussian noise level of $\sigma = 0.001$. This ensures that we start refinement from a neutral pose, which is crucial for the evaluation of the projective visual loss.

While our approach produces very good refinements in a single shot we decided to also implement an iterative version where we run the pose refinement multiple times until the regressed update falls under a threshold.

4   Evaluation

We ran our method with TensorFlow 1.4 [1] on a i7-5820K@3.3GHz with an NVIDIA GTX 1080. For all experiments we ran the training with 100k iterations, a batch size of 16 and ADAM with a learning rate of $3 \cdot 10^{-4}$. Furthermore, we fixed the number of 3D contour points per view to $|V_S| = |V_{\mathcal{H}}| = 100$. Additionally, our method is real-time capable since one iteration requires approximately 25 ms during testing.

To evaluate our method, we carried out experiments on three, both synthetic and real, datasets and will convey that our method can come close to RGB-D based approaches. In particular, the first dataset, referred to as 'Hinterstoisser', was introduced in [12] and consists of 15 sequences each possessing approximately 1000 images with clutter and mild occlusion. Only 13 of these provide water-tight CAD models and we therefore, like others before us, skip the other two sequences. The second one, which we refer to as 'Tejani', was proposed in [36] and consists of six mostly semi-symmetric, textured objects each undergoing different levels of occlusion. In contrast to the first two real datasets, the latter one, referred to as 'Choi' [7], consists of four synthetic tracking sequences.

In essence, we will first conduct some self-evaluation in which we illustrate our convergence properties with respect to different degrees of pose perturbation on real data. Then we show our method when applied to object tracking on 'Choi'. As a second application, we compare our approach to a variety of other state-of-the-art RGB and RGB-D methods by conducting experiments in pose refinement on 'Hinterstoisser', the 'Occlusion' dataset and 'Tejani'. Finally, we depict some failure cases and conclude with a qualitative category-level experiment.

4.1   Pose Perturbation

We study the convergence behavior of our method by taking correct poses, applying a perturbation by a certain amount and measure how well we can refine back to the original pose. To this end, we use the 'Hinterstoisser' dataset since it provides a lot of variety in terms of both colors and shapes. For each frame of a particular sequence we perturb the ground truth pose either by an angle or by a translation vector. In Fig. 4 we illustrate our results for the 'ape' and the 'bvise' objects and kindly refer the reader to the supplement for all graphs. In particular, we report our results for increasing degrees of angular perturbations from

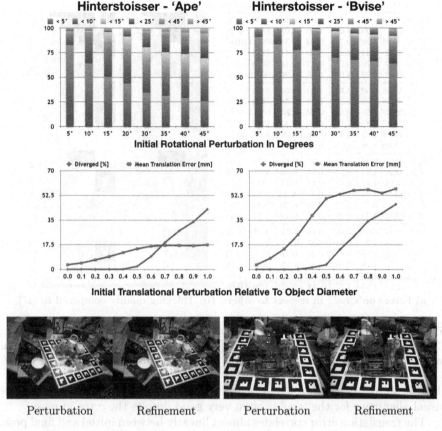

Fig. 4. Top: Perturbation results for two objects from [12] for increasing rotation and translation levels. Bottom: Qualitative results from the same experiment.

5° to 45° and for increasing translation perturbations from 0 to 1 relative to the object's diameter. We define divergence if the refined rotation is above 45° in error or the refined translation larger than half of the object's diameter and we employ 10 iterative steps to maximize our possible precision.

In general, our method can recover poses very robustly even under strong perturbations. Even for the extreme case of rotating the 'bvise' with 45° we can refine back to an error less than 5° in more than 60% of all trials, and to an error less than 10° in more than 80% of all runs. Additionally, our approach only diverged for less than 1%. However, for the more difficult 'ape' object our numbers worsen. In particular, in almost 50% of the cases we were not able to rotate back the object to an error of less than 10%. Yet, this can be easily explained by the object's appearance. The 'ape' is a rather small object with poor texture and non-distinctive shape, which does not provide enough information to hook onto whereas the 'bvise' is large and rich in appearance. It is noteworthy

		PCL	C&C	Krull	Tan	Kehl	Tjaden	Ours
(a) Kinect Box	t_x	43.99	1.84	0.8	1.54	**0.76**	55.75	1.46
	t_y	42.51	2.23	1.67	1.90	**1.09**	70.57	2.28
	t_z	55.89	1.36	0.79	**0.34**	0.38	402.14	10.61
	α	7.62	6.41	1.11	0.42	**0.17**	42.61	1.84
	β	1.87	0.76	0.55	0.22	**0.18**	27.74	2.09
	γ	8.31	6.32	1.04	0.68	**0.20**	38.979	1.23
(b) Milk	t_x	13.38	0.93	**0.51**	1.23	0.64	39.21	3.89
	t_y	31.45	1.94	1.27	0.74	**0.59**	48.13	4.25
	t_z	26.09	1.09	0.62	**0.24**	**0.24**	332.11	57.68
	α	59.37	3.83	2.19	0.50	**0.41**	45.54	38.74
	β	19.58	1.41	1.44	**0.28**	0.29	26.37	27.62
	γ	75.03	3.26	1.90	0.46	**0.42**	21.72	42.68
(c) Orange Juice	t_x	2.53	0.96	0.52	1.10	**0.50**	2.29	0.65
	t_y	2.20	1.44	0.74	0.94	**0.69**	2.85	**0.69**
	t_z	1.91	1.17	0.63	0.18	**0.17**	48.61	6.49
	α	85.81	1.32	1.28	0.35	**0.12**	8.46	1.5
	β	42.12	0.75	1.08	0.24	**0.20**	5.95	0.68
	γ	46.37	1.39	1.20	0.37	**0.19**	2.24	0.39
(d) Tide	t_x	1.46	0.853	0.69	0.73	**0.34**	1.31	1.74
	t_y	2.25	1.37	0.81	0.56	**0.49**	0.83	0.74
	t_z	0.92	1.20	0.81	0.24	**0.18**	12.49	10.71
	α	5.15	1.78	2.10	0.31	**0.15**	2.03	1.78
	β	2.13	1.09	1.38	**0.25**	0.39	1.56	1.64
	γ	2.98	1.13	1.27	**0.34**	0.37	1.39	0.80

(a) Errors on 'Choi' in respect to others. (b) Tracking quality compared to [37].

Fig. 5. Left: Translation (mm) and rotation (degrees) errors on Choi for PCL's ICP, Choi and Christensen (C&C)[7], Krull [21], Tan [34], Kehl [18], Tjaden [37] and our method. Right: Comparing [37] (left) to us (right) using only RGB.

that the actual divergence behavior in rotation is similar for both and that the visual alignment for the 'ape' is often very good despite the error in pose.

The translation error correlates almost linearly between initial and final pose. We also observe an interesting tendency starting from perturbation levels at around 0.6 after which the results can be divided up into two distinct sets: either the pose diverges or the error settles on a certain level. This implies that certain viewpoints are easy to align as long as they have a certain visual overlap to begin with, rather independent of how strong we perturb. Other views instead are more difficult with higher perturbations and diverge from some point on.

4.2   Tracking

As a first use case we evaluated our method as a tracker on the 'Choi' benchmark [7]. This RGB-D dataset consists of four synthetic sequences and we present detailed numbers in Fig. 5. Note that all other methods utilize depth information. We decided for this dataset because it is very hard for RGB-only methods: it is poor in terms of color and the objects are of (semi-)symmetric nature. To provide an interesting comparison we also qualitatively evaluated against our tracker implementation of [37]. While their method is usually robust for texture-less objects it diverges on 3 sequences which we show and for which we provide

Table 1. VSS scores for each sequence of [12] with poses initialized from SSD-6D [17]. The first three rows are provided by [17]. We evidently outperform 2D-based ICP by a large margin and are on par with 3D-based ICP.

	ape	bvise	cam	can	cat	driller	duck	box	glue	holep	iron	lamp	phone	total
No Refinement	0.64	0.65	0.71	0.72	0.63	0.62	0.65	0.64	0.64	0.69	0.71	0.63	0.69	0.66
2D Edge-based ICP	0.73	0.67	0.73	0.76	0.68	0.67	0.72	0.73	0.72	0.71	0.74	0.67	0.70	0.71
3D Cloud-based ICP	**0.86**	**0.88**	**0.91**	**0.87**	**0.87**	0.85	0.83	0.84	0.75	0.77	**0.85**	**0.84**	0.81	**0.84**
Ours	0.83	0.83	0.75	**0.87**	0.79	**0.85**	**0.87**	**0.88**	**0.85**	**0.82**	**0.85**	0.80	0.83	0.83

Table 2. Refinement scores with poses initialized from SSD-6D [17]. Left: Average ADD scores on 'Hinterstoisser' [12] (top) and 'Occlusion' [4] (bottom). Right: VSS scores on 'Tejani'. We compare our visual loss to naive pose regression as well as two state-of-the-art trackers for the case of RGB [37] and RGB-D [18].

	Rot. Error [°]	Transl. Error [mm]	ADD [%]
No Ref.	27.96	9.75, 9.33, 71.09	7.4
3D ICP	17.62	10.42, 10.56, **27.31**	**90.9**
Ours	**16.17**	**4.9, 5.87,** 42.69	34.1
[28]	–	–	43.6
[5]	–	–	50.2

	Rot. Error [°]	Transl. Error [mm]	ADD [%]
No Ref.	34.42	13.7, 13.4, 77.5	6.2
Ours	24.36	8.5, 9.0, 49.1	27.5

(a) Absolute pose errors on [12] and [4].

Sequence	Ours	MSE Loss	Kehl [18]	Tjaden [37]
Camera	**0.803**	0.562	0.493	0.385
Coffee	**0.848**	0.717	0.747	0.170
Joystick	**0.850**	0.746	0.773	0.298
Juice	**0.828**	0.613	0.523	0.205
Milk	**0.766**	0.721	0.580	0.514
Shampoo	**0.804**	0.700	0.648	0.250
Total	**0.817**	0.676	0.627	0.304

(b) VSS scores for each sequence of [36].

reasoning[1] in Fig. 5 and in the supplementary material. In essence, except for the 'Milk' sequence we can report very good results. The reason why we performed comparably bad on the 'Milk' resides in the fact that our method already treats it as a rather symmetric object. Thus, sometimes it rotates the object along its Y-axis, which has a negative impact on the overall numbers. In particular, while already being misaligned, the method still tries to completely fill the object into the scene, thus, it slightly further rotates and translates the object. Referring to the remaining objects, we can easily outperform PCL's ICP for all objects and also Choi and Christensen [7] for most of the cases. Compared to Krull [21], which is a learned RGB-D approach, we perform better for some values and worse for others. Note that our translation error along the Z-axis is quite high. Since the difference in pixels is almost nonexistent when the object is moved only a few millimeters, it is almost impossible to estimate the exact distance of the object without leveraging depth information. This has also been discussed in [15] and is especially true for CNNs due to pooling operations.

4.3   Detection Refinement

This set of experiments analyzes our performance in a detection scenario where an object detector will provide rough 6D poses and the goal is to refine them. We

---

[1] The authors acknowledged our conclusions in correspondence.

Fig. 6. Comparison on Tejani between (from left to right) our visual loss, mean squared error loss, the RGB-D tracker from [18] and the RGB tracker from [37].

decided to use the results from SSD-6D [17], an RGB-based detection method, that outputs 2D detections with a pool of 6D pose estimates each. The authors publicly provide their trained networks and we use them to detect and create 6D pose estimates which we feed into our system. Tables 1 and 2 (a) and (b) depict our results for the 'Hinterstoisser', 'Occlusion' and the 'Tejani' dataset using different metrics. We maximally ran 5 iterations of our method, yet, we also stopped if the last update was less than 1.5° and 7.5 mm. Since our method is particularly strong at recovering from bad initializations, we employ the same RGB-verification strategy as SSD-6D. However, we apply it before conducting the refinement, since in contrast to them, we can also deal with imperfect initializations, as long as they are not completely misaligned. We report our errors with the VSS metric (which is VSD from [14] with $\tau = \infty$) that calculates a visual 2D error as the pixel-wise overlap between the renderings of ground truth pose and estimated pose. Furthermore, to compare better to related work, we also use the ADD score [12] to measure a 3D metrical error as the average point cloud deviation between real pose and inferred pose when transformed into the scene. A pose is counted as correct if the deviation is less than a $\frac{1}{10}$th of the object diameter.

Referring to 'Hinterstoisser' with the VSS metric, we can strongly improve the state-of-the-art for most objects. In particular, for the case of RGB only, we can report an average VSS score of 83%, which is an improvement of impressive and can thus successfully bridge the gap between RGB and RGB-D in terms of pose accuracy.

Except for the 'cam' and the 'cat' object our results are on par with or even better than SSD-6D + 3D refinement. ICP relies on good correspondences and robust outlier removal which in turn requires very careful parameter tuning. Furthermore, ICP is often unstable for rougher initializations. In contrast, our method learns refinement end-to-end and is more robust since it adapts to the specific properties of the object during training. However, due to this, our method requires meshes of good quality. Hence, similar to SSD-6D we have especially problems for the 'cam' object since the model appearance strongly differs from the real images which exacerbates training. Also note that their 3D refinement strategy uses ICP for each pose in the pool, followed by a verification over depth normals to decide for the best pose. Our method instead uses a simple check over image gradients to pick the best.

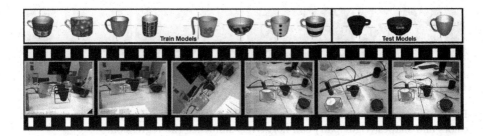

Fig. 7. Qualitative category-level experiment where we train our network on a specific set of mugs and bowls and track hitherto unseen models. The first frame depicts very rough initialization while the next frames show some intermediate refined poses throughout the sequence. The supplement shows the full video.

With respect to the ADD metric we fall slightly behind the other state-of-the-art RGB methods [5,28]. We got the 3D-ICP refined poses from the SSD-6D authors and analyzed the errors in more detail in Table 2(a). We see again that we have bigger errors along the Z-axis, but less errors along X and Y. Unfortunately, the ADD metric penalizes this deviation overly strong. Interestingly, [5,28] have better scores and we reason this to come from two facts. The datasets are annotated via ICP with 3D models against depth data. Unfortunately, inaccurate intrinsics and the sensor registration error between RGB and D leads to an inherent mismatch where the ICP 6D pose does not always align perfectly in RGB. Purely synthetic RGB methods like ours or [17] suffer from (1) a domain gap in terms of texture/shape and (2) the dilemma that better RGB performance can worsen results when comparing to that 'true' ICP pose. We suspect that [5,28] can learn this registration error implicitly since they train on real RGB cut-outs with associated ICP pose information and thus avoid both problems. We often observe that our visually-perfect alignments in RGB fail the ADD criterion and we show examples in the supplement. Since our loss actually optimizes a form of VSS to maximize contour overlap, we can expect the ADD scores to go up only when perfect alignment in color equates perfect alignment in depth.

Eventually, referring to the 'Occlusion' dataset, we can report a strong improvement compared to the original numbers from SSD-6D, despite the presence of strong occlusion. In particular, while the rotational error decreased by approximately 8°, the translational error dropped by 4 mm along 'X' and 'Y' axes and by 28 mm along 'Z'. Thus, we can increase ADD from 6.2% up to 28.5%, which demonstrates that we can deal with strong occlusion in the scene.

For 'Tejani' we decided to show the improvement over networks trained with a standard regression loss (MSE). Additionally, we re-implemented the RGB tracker from [37] and were kindly provided with numbers from the authors of the RGB-D tracker from [18] (see Fig. 6). Since the dataset mostly consists of objects with geometric symmetry, we do not measure absolute pose errors here but instead report our numbers with the VSS metric. The MSE-trained networks

Fig. 8. Two prominent failure cases: Occlusion (left pair) and objects of very similar colors and shapes (right pair) can negatively influence the regression.

constantly underperform since the dataset models are of symmetric nature which in turn leads to a large difference of 14% in comparison to our visual loss. This result stresses the importance of correct symmetry entangling during training. The RGB tracker was not able to refine well due to the fact that the color segmentation was corrupted by either occlusions or imperfect initialization. The RGB-D tracker, which builds on the same idea, performed better because it uses the additional depth channel for segmentation and optimization.

4.4   Category-Level Tracking

We were curious to find out whether our approach can generalize beyond a specific CAD model, given that many objects from the same category share similar appearance and shape properties. To this end, we conducted a final qualitative experiment (see Fig. 7) where we collected a total of eight CAD models of cups, mugs and a bowl and trained simultaneously on all. During testing we then used this network to track new, unseen models from the same category. We were surprised to see that the approach has indeed learned to metrically track previously unseen but nonetheless similar structures. While the poses are not as accurate as for the single-instance case, it seems that one can indeed learn the projective relation of structure and how it changes under 6D motion, provided that at least the projection functions (i.e. camera intrinsics) are constant. We show the full sequence in the supplementary material.

4.5   Failure Cases

Figure 8 illustrates two known failure cases where the left image of each pair represents initialization and the right image the refined result. Although we train with occlusion certain occurrences can worsen our refinement nonetheless. While two 'milk' instances were refined well despite occlusion, the left 'milk' instance could not be recovered correctly. The network assumes the object to end at the yellow pen and only maximizes the remaining pixel-wise overlap. Besides occlusion, objects of similar color and shape can in rare cases lead to confusion. As shown in the right pair, the network mistakenly assumed the stapler, instead of the cup, to be the real object of interest.

5   Conclusion

We believe to have presented a new approach towards 6D model tracking in RGB with the help of deep learning and we demonstrated the power of our approach on multiple datasets and for the scenarios of pose refinement and for instance/category tracking. Future work will include investigation towards generalization to other domains, e.g. the suitability towards visual odometry.

Acknowledgments. We would like to thank Toyota Motor Corporation for funding and supporting this work.

References

1. Abadi, M., et al.: TensorFlow: Large-scale machine learning on heterogeneous systems. In: OSDI (2016). http://download.tensorflow.org/paper/whitepaper2015.pdf
2. Bhagavatula, C., Zhu, C., Luu, K., Savvides, M.: Faster than real-time facial alignment: a 3D spatial transformer network approach in unconstrained poses. In: ICCV (2017). http://arxiv.org/abs/1707.05653
3. Bibby, C., Reid, I.: Robust real-time visual tracking using pixel-wise posteriors. In: Forsyth, D., Torr, P., Zisserman, A. (eds.) ECCV 2008. LNCS, vol. 5303, pp. 831–844. Springer, Heidelberg (2008). https://doi.org/10.1007/978-3-540-88688-4_61
4. Brachmann, E., Krull, A., Michel, F., Gumhold, S., Shotton, J., Rother, C.: Learning 6D object pose estimation using 3D object coordinates. In: Fleet, D., Pajdla, T., Schiele, B., Tuytelaars, T. (eds.) ECCV 2014. LNCS, vol. 8690, pp. 536–551. Springer, Cham (2014). https://doi.org/10.1007/978-3-319-10605-2_35
5. Brachmann, E., Michel, F., Krull, A., Yang, M.Y., Gumhold, S., Rother, C.: uncertainty-driven 6D pose estimation of objects and scenes from a single RGB image. In: CVPR (2016)
6. Brox, T., Rosenhahn, B., Gall, J., Cremers, D.: Combined region and motion-based 3D tracking of rigid and articulated objects. TPAMI **32**(3), 402–415 (2010)
7. Choi, C., Christensen, H.: RGB-D object tracking: a particle filter approach on GPU. In: IROS (2013)
8. Dambreville, S., Sandhu, R., Yezzi, A., Tannenbaum, A.: A geometric approach to joint 2D region-based segmentation and 3D pose estimation using a 3D shape prior. SIAM J. Imaging Sci. **3**, 110–132 (2010)
9. Drummond, T., Cipolla, R.: Real-time visual tracking of complex structures. TPAMI **24**, 932–946 (2002)
10. Garon, M., Lalonde, J.F.: Deep 6-DOF tracking. In: ISMAR (2017). https://doi.org/10.1109/TVCG.2017.2734599
11. Hexner, J., Hagege, R.R.: 2D–3D pose estimation of heterogeneous objects using a region based approach. IJCV **118**, 95–112 (2016)
12. Hinterstoisser, S., et al.: Model based training, detection and pose estimation of texture-less 3D objects in heavily cluttered scenes. In: Lee, K.M., Matsushita, Y., Rehg, J.M., Hu, Z. (eds.) ACCV 2012. LNCS, vol. 7724, pp. 548–562. Springer, Heidelberg (2013). https://doi.org/10.1007/978-3-642-37331-2_42

13. Hinterstoisser, S., Lepetit, V., Wohlhart, P., Konolige, K.: On pre-trained image features and synthetic images for deep learning. CoRR abs/1710.10710 (2017). http://arxiv.org/abs/1710.10710

14. Hodaň, T., Matas, J., Obdržálek, Š.: On evaluation of 6D object pose estimation. In: Hua, G., Jégou, H. (eds.) ECCV 2016. LNCS, vol. 9915, pp. 606–619. Springer, Cham (2016). https://doi.org/10.1007/978-3-319-49409-8_52

15. Holloway, R.L.: Registration error analysis for augmented reality. Presence Teleoper. Virtual Environ. **6**(4), 413–432 (1997). https://doi.org/10.1162/pres.1997.6.4.413

16. Jaderberg, M., Simonyan, K., Zisserman, A., Kavukcuoglu, K.: Spatial transformer networks. In: NIPS (2015). http://arxiv.org/abs/1509.05329

17. Kehl, W., Manhardt, F., Ilic, S., Tombari, F., Navab, N.: SSD-6D: making RGB-based 3D detection and 6D pose estimation great again. In: ICCV (2017)

18. Kehl, W., Tombari, F., Ilic, S., Navab, N.: Real-time 3D model tracking in color and depth on a single CPU core. In: CVPR (2017)

19. Kendall, A., Cipolla, R.: Geometric loss functions for camera pose regression with deep learning. In: CVPR (2017). http://arxiv.org/abs/1704.00390

20. Kendall, A., Grimes, M., Cipolla, R.: PoseNet: a convolutional network for real-time 6-DOF camera relocalization. In: ICCV (2015)

21. Krull, A., Michel, F., Brachmann, E., Gumhold, S., Ihrke, S., Rother, C.: 6-DOF model based tracking via object coordinate regression. In: Cremers, D., Reid, I., Saito, H., Yang, M.-H. (eds.) ACCV 2014. LNCS, vol. 9006, pp. 384–399. Springer, Cham (2015). https://doi.org/10.1007/978-3-319-16817-3_25

22. Liu, W., et al.: SSD: single shot multibox detector. In: Leibe, B., Matas, J., Sebe, N., Welling, M. (eds.) ECCV 2016. LNCS, vol. 9905, pp. 21–37. Springer, Cham (2016). https://doi.org/10.1007/978-3-319-46448-0_2

23. Park, Y., Lepetit, V.: Multiple 3D object tracking for augmented reality. In: ISMAR (2008)

24. Pauwels, K., Rubio, L., Diaz, J., Ros, E.: Real-time model-based rigid object pose estimation and tracking combining dense and sparse visual cues. In: CVPR (2013)

25. Pavlakos, G., Zhou, X., Chan, A., Derpanis, K.G., Daniilidis, K.: 6-DoF object pose from semantic keypoints. In: ICRA (2017). http://arxiv.org/abs/1703.04670

26. Prisacariu, V.A., Murray, D.W., Reid, I.D.: Real-time 3D tracking and reconstruction on mobile phones. TVCG **21**, 557–570 (2015)

27. Prisacariu, V.A., Reid, I.D.: PWP3D: real-time segmentation and tracking of 3D objects. IJCV **98**, 335–354 (2012)

28. Rad, M., Lepetit, V.: BB8: A scalable, accurate, robust to partial occlusion method for predicting the 3D poses of challenging objects without using depth. In: ICCV, pp. 3848–3856 (2017). https://doi.org/10.1109/ICCV.2017.413

29. Rosenhahn, B., Brox, T., Cremers, D., Seidel, H.-P.: A comparison of shape matching methods for contour based pose estimation. In: Reulke, R., Eckardt, U., Flach, B., Knauer, U., Polthier, K. (eds.) IWCIA 2006. LNCS, vol. 4040, pp. 263–276. Springer, Heidelberg (2006). https://doi.org/10.1007/11774938_21

30. Schmaltz, C., et al.: Region-based pose tracking. In: Martí, J., Benedí, J.M., Mendonça, A.M., Serrat, J. (eds.) IbPRIA 2007. LNCS, vol. 4478, pp. 56–63. Springer, Heidelberg (2007). https://doi.org/10.1007/978-3-540-72849-8_8

31. Schmaltz, C., Rosenhahn, B., Brox, T., Weickert, J.: Region-based pose tracking with occlusions using 3D models. MVA **23**, 557–577 (2012)

32. Seo, B.K., Park, H., Park, J.I., Hinterstoisser, S., Ilic, S.: Optimal local searching for fast and robust textureless 3D object tracking in highly cluttered backgrounds. In: TVCG (2014)

33. Szegedy, C., Ioffe, S., Vanhoucke, V., Alemi, A.A.: Inception-v4, inception-resnet and the impact of residual connections on learning. In: ICLR Workshop (2016). https://arxiv.org/abs/1602.07261

34. Tan, D.J., Tombari, F., Ilic, S., Navab, N.: A versatile learning-based 3D temporal tracker: scalable, robust. In: ICCV, Online (2015)

35. Tateno, K., Kotake, D., Uchiyama, S.: Model-based 3D object tracking with online texture update. In: MVA (2009)

36. Tejani, A., Tang, D., Kouskouridas, R., Kim, T.-K.: Latent-class hough forests for 3D object detection and pose estimation. In: Fleet, D., Pajdla, T., Schiele, B., Tuytelaars, T. (eds.) ECCV 2014. LNCS, vol. 8694, pp. 462–477. Springer, Cham (2014). https://doi.org/10.1007/978-3-319-10599-4_30

37. Tjaden, H., Schwanecke, U., Schömer, E.: Real-time monocular segmentation and pose tracking of multiple objects. In: Leibe, B., Matas, J., Sebe, N., Welling, M. (eds.) ECCV 2016. LNCS, vol. 9908, pp. 423–438. Springer, Cham (2016). https://doi.org/10.1007/978-3-319-46493-0_26

38. Tjaden, H., Schwanecke, U., Schömer, E.: Real-time monocular pose estimation of 3D objects using temporally consistent local color histograms. In: ICCV (2017). https://doi.org/10.1109/ICCV.2017.23

39. Ummenhofer, B., et al.: DeMoN: depth and motion network for learning monocular stereo. In: CVPR (2017)

40. Vacchetti, L., Lepetit, V., Fua, P.: Stable real-time 3D tracking using online and offline information. TPAMI **26**, 1385–1391 (2004)

41. Wang, S., Clark, R., Wen, H., Trigoni, N.: DeepVO: Towards End to End Visual Odometry with Deep Recurrent Convolutional Neural Networks. In: ICRA (2017)

42. Wu, J., et al.: Single image 3D interpreter network. In: Leibe, B., Matas, J., Sebe, N., Welling, M. (eds.) ECCV 2016. LNCS, vol. 9910, pp. 365–382. Springer, Cham (2016). https://doi.org/10.1007/978-3-319-46466-4_22. http://dblp.uni-trier.de/db/conf/eccv/eccv2016-6.html#0001XLTTTF16

43. Zhou, T., Brown, M., Snavely, N., Lowe, D.G.: Unsupervised learning of depth and ego-motion from video. In: CVPR (2017). http://arxiv.org/abs/1704.07813

Author Index